Contemporary Authors®

NEW REVISION SERIES

Explore your options!
Gale databases offered in
a variety of formats

DISKETTE/MAGNETIC TAPE

Many Gale databases are available on diskette or magnetic tape, allowing systemwide access to your most-used information sources through existing computer systems. Data can be delivered on a variety of mediums (DOS-formatted diskette, 9-track tape, 8mm data tape) and in industry-standard formats (comma-delimited, tagged, fixed-field). Retrieval software is also available with many of Gale's databases that allows you to search, display, print and download the data.

ONLINE

For your convenience, many Gale databases are available through popular online services, including DIALOG, NEXIS (Mead Data Central), Data-Star, Orbit, Questel, OCLC, I/Plus Direct, Prodigy, HOOVER and Telebase Systems.

CD-ROM

A variety of Gale titles are available on CD-ROM, offering maximum flexibility and powerful search software.

The information in this Gale publication is also available in some or all of the formats described here. Your Gale Representative will be happy to fill you in.

For information, call

GALE

Gale Research
1-800-877-GALE

ISSN 0275-7176

Contemporary Authors®

**A Bio-Bibliographical Guide to
Current Writers in Fiction, General Nonfiction,
Poetry, Journalism, Drama, Motion Pictures,
Television, and Other Fields**

PAMELA S. DEAR
Editor

NEW REVISION SERIES
volume 48

Gale Research

An ITP Information/Reference Group

I(T)P
Changing the Way the World Learns

NEW YORK • LONDON • BONN • BOSTON • DETROIT
MADRID • MELBOURNE • MEXICO CITY • PARIS
SINGAPORE • TOKYO • TORONTO • WASHINGTON
ALBANY NY • BELMONT CA • CINCINNATI OH

STAFF

Pamela S. Dear, *Editor, New Revision Series*

John D. Jorgenson, *Pre-Manuscript Coordinator*
Thomas Wiloch, *Sketchwriting Coordinator*
Deborah A. Stanley, *Post-Manuscript Coordinator*

Jeff Chapman, Matt McDonough, Brigham Narins, Polly A. Vedder, and Kathleen Wilson, *Associate Editors*

George H. Blair, *Assistant Editor*

Jennifer Brostrom, Christopher Giroux, Mary L. Onorato, Geri J. Speace,
Aarti Dhawan Stephens, Brandon Trenz, and Janet Witalec, *Contributing Editors*

Anne Blankenbaker, Stephen Desmond, Joan Goldsworthy, Lisa Harper, Elizabeth Judd,
Brett A. Lealand, Greg Mazurkiewicz, Margaret Mazurkiewicz, Julie Monahan,
Jean W. Ross, Pamela L. Shelton, Kenneth R. Shepherd, Denise Wiloch,
Michaela Swart Wilson, and Tim Winter-Damon, *Sketchwriters*

James P. Draper, *Managing Editor*

Victoria B. Cariappa, *Research Manager*

Maria E. Bryson, Donna Melnychenko, Tamara C. Nott,
Michele P. Pica, Norma Sawaya, and Amy Terese Steel, *Research Associates*

Julia C. Daniel, *Research Assistant*

♾ ™ This book is printed on acid-free paper that meets the minimum requirements
of American National Standard for Information Sciences-
Permanence Paper for Printed Library Materials, ANSI Z39.48-1984.

Library of Congress Catalog Card Number 81-640179

ISBN 0-8103-9338-7
ISSN 0275-7176

Printed in the United States of America.

I(T)P™ Gale Research Inc., an International Thomson Publishing Company.
ITP logo is a trademark under license.
10 9 8 7 6 5 4 3 2 1

Contents

Indexing note: All *Contemporary Authors New Revision Series* entries are indexed in the *Contemporary Authors* cumulative index, which is published separately and distributed with even-numbered *Contemporary Authors* original volumes and odd-numbered *Contemporary Authors New Revision Series* volumes.

As always, the most recent *Contemporary Authors* cumulative index continues to be the user's guide to the location of an individual author's listing.

Contemporary Authors
was named an
**"Outstanding
Reference Source"** *by
the American Library
Association Reference
and Adult Services
Division after its 1962
inception.
In 1985 it was listed by
the same organization
as one of the
twenty-five most
distinguished reference
titles published in the
past twenty-five years.*

Preface

The *Contemporary Authors New Revision Series* (*CANR*) provides completely updated information on authors listed in earlier volumes of *Contemporary Authors* (*CA*). Entries for individual authors from *any* volume of *CA* may be included in a volume of the *New Revision Series*. *CANR* updates only those sketches requiring significant change.

Authors are included on the basis of specific criteria that indicate the need for significant revision. These criteria include bibliographical additions, changes in addresses or career, major awards, and personal information such as name changes or death dates. All listings in this volume have been revised or augmented in various ways. Some sketches have been extensively rewritten, and many include informative new sidelights. As always, a *CANR* listing entails no charge or obligation.

How to Get the Most out of *CA*: Use the Index

The key to locating an author's most recent entry is the *CA* cumulative index, which is published separately and distributed with even-numbered original volumes and odd-numbered revision volumes. It provides access to *all* entries in *CA* and *CANR*. Always consult the latest index to find an author's most recent entry.

For the convenience of users, the *CA* cumulative index also includes references to all entries in these Gale literary series: *Authors and Artists for Young Adults, Authors in the News, Bestsellers, Black Literature Criticism, Black Writers, Children's Literature Review, Concise Dictionary of American Literary Biography, Concise Dictionary of British Literary Biography, Contemporary Authors Autobiography Series, Contemporary Authors Bibliographical Series, Contemporary Literary Criticism, Dictionary of Literary Biography, DISCovering Authors, Drama Criticism, Hispanic Literature Criticism, Hispanic Writers, Junior DISCovering Authors, Major Authors and Illustrators for Children and Young Adults, Major 20th-Century Writers, Native North American Literature, Poetry Criticism, Short Story Criticism, Something about the Author, Something about the Author Autobiography Series, Twentieth-Century Literary Criticism, World Literature Criticism,* and *Yesterday's Authors of Books for Children.*

A Sample Index Entry:

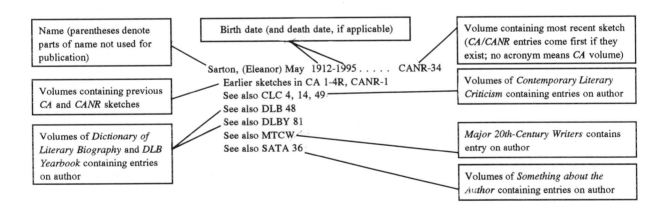

For the most recent *CA* information on Sarton, users should refer to Volume 34 of the *New Revision Series*, as designated by "CANR-34"; if that volume is unavailable, refer to CANR-1. And if CANR-1 is unavailable, refer to CA 1-4R, published in 1967, for Sarton's First Revision entry.

How Are Entries Compiled?

The editors make every effort to secure new information directly from the authors. Copies of all sketches in selected *CA* and *CANR* volumes previously published are routinely sent to listees at their last-known addresses, and returns from these authors are then assessed. For deceased writers, or those who fail to reply to requests for data, we consult other reliable biographical sources, such as those indexed in Gale's *Biography and Genealogy Master Index,* and bibliographical sources, such as *National Union Catalog, LC MARC,* and *British National Bibliography.* Further details come from published interviews, feature stories, and book reviews, and often the authors' publishers supply material.

* Indicates that a listing has been compiled from secondary sources believed to be reliable but has not been personally verified for this edition by the author sketched.

What Kinds of Information Does an Entry Provide?

Sketches in *CANR* contain the following biographical and bibliographical information:

- **Entry heading:** the most complete form of author's name, plus any pseudonyms or name variations used for writing

- **Personal information:** author's date and place of birth, family data, educational background, political and religious affiliations, and hobbies and leisure interests

- **Addresses:** author's home, office, or agent's addresses as available

- **Career summary:** name of employer, position, and dates held for each career post; resume of other vocational achievements; military service

- **Membership information:** professional, civic, and other association memberships and any official posts held

- **Awards and honors:** military and civic citations, major prizes and nominations, fellowships, grants, and honorary degrees

- **Writings:** a comprehensive, chronological list of titles, publishers, dates of original publication and revised editions, and production information for plays, television scripts, and screenplays

- **Adaptations:** a list of films, plays, and other media which have been adapted from the author's work

- **Work in progress:** current or planned projects, with dates of completion and/or publication, and expected publisher, when known

- **Sidelights:** a biographical portrait of the author's development; information about the critical reception of the author's works; revealing comments, often by the author, on personal interests, aspirations, motivations, and thoughts on writing

- **Biographical and critical sources:** a list of books and periodicals in which additional information on an author's life and/or writings appears

Related Titles in the *CA* Series

Contemporary Authors Autobiography Series complements *CA* original and revised volumes with specially commissioned autobiographical essays by important current authors, illustrated with personal photographs they provide. Common topics include their motivations for writing, the people and experiences that shaped their careers, the rewards they derive from their work, and their impressions of the current literary scene.

Contemporary Authors Bibliographical Series surveys writings by and about important American authors since World War II. Each volume concentrates on a specific genre and features approximately ten writers; entries list works written by and about the author and contain a bibliographical essay discussing the merits and deficiencies of major critical and scholarly studies in detail.

Available in Electronic Formats

CD-ROM. Full-text bio-bibliographic entries from the entire *CA* series, covering approximately 100,000 writers, are available on CD-ROM through lease and purchase plans. The disc combines entries from the *CA, CANR,* and *Contemporary Authors Permanent Series* (*CAP*) print series to provide the most recent author listing. It can be searched by name, title, subject/genre, and personal data, and by using boolean logic. The disc will be updated every six months. For more information, call 1-800-877-GALE.

Magnetic Tape. *CA* is available for licensing on magnetic tape in a fielded format. Either the complete database or a custom selection of entries may be ordered. The database is available for internal data processing and nonpublishing purposes only. For more information, call 1-800-877-GALE.

Online. The *Contemporary Authors* database is made available online to libraries and their patrons through online public access catalog (OPAC) vendors. Currently, *CA* is offered through Ameritech Library Services' Vista Online (formerly Dynix), and is expected to become available through CARL Systems and The Library Corporation. More OPAC vendor offerings will follow soon.

GaleNet. *CA* is available on a subscription basis through GaleNet, a new online information resource that features an easy-to-use end-user interface, the powerful search capabilities of the BRS/Search retrieval software, and ease of access through the World-Wide Web. For more information, call Melissa Kolehmainen at 1-800-877-GALE, ext. 1598.

Suggestions Are Welcome

The editors welcome comments and suggestions from users on any aspects of the *CA* series. If readers would like to recommend authors whose entries should appear in future volumes of the series, they are cordially invited to write: The Editors, *Contemporary Authors,* 835 Penobscot Bldg., Detroit, MI 48226-4094; call toll-free at 1-800-347-GALE; or fax to 1-313-961-6599.

CA Numbering System and Volume Update Chart

Occasionally questions arise about the *CA* numbering system and which volumes, if any, can be discarded. Despite numbers like "29-32R," "97-100" and "147," the entire *CA* series consists of only 122 physical volumes with the publication of *CA New Revision Series* Volume 48. The following charts note changes in the numbering system and cover design, and indicate which volumes are essential for the most complete, up-to-date coverage.

CA First Revision

- 1-4R through 41-44R (11 books)
  Cover: Brown with black and gold trim.
  There will be no further First Revision volumes because revised entries are now being handled exclusively through the more efficient *New Revision Series* mentioned below.

CA Original Volumes

- 45-48 through 97-100 (14 books)
  Cover: Brown with black and gold trim.
- 101 through 147 (47 books)
  Cover: Blue and black with orange bands.
  The same as previous *CA* original volumes but with a new, simplified numbering system and new cover design.

CA Permanent Series

- *CAP*-1 and *CAP*-2 (2 books)
  Cover: Brown with red and gold trim.
  There will be no further *Permanent Series* volumes because revised entries are now being handled exclusively through the more efficient *New Revision Series* mentioned below.

CA New Revision Series

- *CANR*-1 through *CANR*-48 (48 books)
  Cover: Blue and black with green bands.
  Includes only sketches requiring extensive changes; **sketches are taken from any previously published *CA*, *CAP*, or *CANR* volume.**

If You Have: You May Discard:

If You Have:	You May Discard:
CA First Revision Volumes 1-4R through 41-44R **and** *CA Permanent Series* Volumes 1 and 2	*CA* Original Volumes 1, 2, 3, 4 Volumes 5-6 through 41-44
CA Original Volumes 45-48 through 97-100 **and** 101 through 147	**NONE:** These volumes will not be superseded by corresponding revised volumes. Individual entries from these and all other volumes appearing in the left column of this chart may be revised and included in the various volumes of the *New Revision Series*.
CA New Revision Series Volumes *CANR*-1 through *CANR*-48	**NONE:** The *New Revision Series* does not replace any single volume of *CA*. Instead, volumes of *CANR* include entries from many previous *CA* series volumes. All *New Revision Series* volumes must be retained for full coverage.

A Sampling of Authors and Media People
Featured in This Volume

Ann Nolan Clark
American-born Clark's goal is to provide Native-American and Spanish-American children with a means to learn about their heritage through stories such as *In My Mother's House, Santiago,* and the Newbery Medal-winning *Secret of the Andes.*

James Clavell
Clavell is best remembered for *Shogun,* adapted for television and stage, and other epic novels of the Far East including *Tai-Pan* and *Noble House.*

Barbara Corcoran
Themes featured in Corcoran's young adult novels such as *A Dance to Still Music* and *Sasha, My Friend* include family and teen troubles, wilderness adventures, and the love of animals.

James Dickey
Dickey left a lucrative career in advertising to become a full-time author with the publication of *Into the Stone, and Other Poems* in 1960. His bestselling novel *Deliverance* was made into a feature film in 1972.

William Gaddis
An award-winning American author, Gaddis' *Recognitions, J R,* and *Carpenter's Gothic* are familiar to critics but not to the reading public. His 1994 novel, *A Frolic of His Own,* won that year's National Book Award.

James S. Haskins
Haskins is the author of over 100 nonfiction books for both children and adults. His award-winning works include *Street Gangs: Yesterday and Today,* the "Count Your Way" series, and biographies of Stevie Wonder, Martin Luther King Jr., and James Van DerZee.

Stephen W. Hawking
Physicist Hawking makes complex scientific theory accessible to the average reader in *A Brief History of Time* and *Black Holes and Baby Universes,* explorations of the origins and future of the universe.

Seamus Heaney
Heaney is recognized as one of Ireland's finest living poets for works including *Death of a Naturalist, Bog Poems,* and *Seeing Things.*

Patricia Highsmith
Mystery writer Highsmith's work has been more popular in Europe than her native United States, but American interest in her works such as *Strangers on a Train* and *The Talented Mr. Ripley* continues to grow.

Meredith Ann Pierce
Pierce's award-winning fantasy novels for young adults include *The Woman Who Loved Reindeer* and the "Darkangel" and "Firebringer" trilogies. She has also written a picture book, *Where the Wild Geese Go.*

Ishmael Reed
Reed presents provocative explorations of contemporary black American life in novels such as *The Free-Lance Pallbearers, Yellow Back Radio Broke-Down, Mumbo Jumbo, The Terrible Twos,* and *The Terrible Threes.*

Berton Roueche
A former *New Yorker* columnist, Roueche has published many nonfiction works on medical and travel topics such as *The Medical Detectives* and *The River World,* as well as novels including *Black Weather* and *Fago.*

Alvin Sargent
Academy Award-winning screenwriter Sargent is the author of popular films such as *Paper Moon, Ordinary People,* and *What about Bob?.* He is recognized for his talent in characterization, especially apparent in *The Sterile Cuckoo.*

Jack Denton Scott
Scott specializes in life histories of animals in his books for children and writes novels and books on cooking and travel for adults. Among his Junior Literary Guild Selection books are *Canada Geese, The Gulls of Smuttynose Island, The Submarine Bird,* and *Swans.*

Ntozake Shange
Shange became famous for her play *For Colored Girls Who Have Considered Suicide/When the Rainbow Is Enuf,* first produced in 1975. She is also an acclaimed poet and novelist.

Alex Shoumatoff
Naturalist and journalist Shoumatoff is best known for *The World Is Burning,* an account of the murder of Amazon rain forest defender Chico Mendes.

Joyce Carol Thomas
Thomas' childhood in rural Oklahoma and California informs her writing. She has received critical attention for her poetry collection *Brown Honey in Broomwheat Tea* and her young adult novels *Marked by Fire* and *Bright Shadow.*

Rosemary Wells
An author and illustrator of picture books and young adult novels, Wells is best known for her "Max" series of children's books, including *Max's First Word* and *Max's Toys: A Counting Book.*

Contemporary Authors®

NEW REVISION SERIES

*Indicates that a listing has been compiled from secondary sources believed to be reliable but has not been personally verified for this edition by the author sketched.

AKSYONOV, Vassily (Pavlovich) 1932-

PERSONAL: Given name transliterated as Vasily, Vasilii, Vasilli, and Vasilij, and surname transliterated as Aksenov and Aksehov in some sources; born August 20, 1932 in Kazan, U.S.S.R. (now Russia); came to United States in 1980; son of Pavel Vassilievich and Evgenia Semenovna (Ginzburg) Aksyonov; married Kira Ludvigouna Mendeleva, March 11, 1957; divorced, 1980; married Maya Afanasievna Zmeul, May 30, 1980; children: (first marriage) Alexey. *Education:* First Leningrad Medical Institute, medical degree, 1956. *Politics:* Non-party. *Religion:* Christian. *Avocational interests:* Music, traveling, running.

ADDRESSES: Home—4434 Lingan Road N.W., Washington, DC 20007. *Office*—George Mason University, Department of English, Fairfax, VA 22030-4444. *Agent*—c/o Random House Inc., 201 East 50th St. New York, NY 10022.

CAREER: Physician, Leningrad Hospital, 1956-60; writer, 1960—. Writer-in-residence, University of Southern California, 1981, George Washington University, 1982, and Goucher College, 1984; George Mason University, Fairfax, VA, Clarence Robinson Professor, 1988—.

MEMBER: French PEN, Swedish PEN, Danish PEN.

AWARDS, HONORS: Golden Prize in International Competition of Satirical Authors, Bulgaria, 1967; fellow, Woodrow Wilson International Center, 1982.

WRITINGS:

NOVELS

Kollegi, Soviet Writer Publishing House, 1961, translation by Margaret Wettlin published as *Colleagues,* Foreign Languages Publishing House (Moscow), 1961, translation by Alec Brown published under same title, Putnam (New York City), 1962.

Zvezdnyi bilet, Youth Magazine, 1961, translation by Brown published as *A Starry Ticket,* Putnam, 1962, translation by Andrew R. MacAndrew published as *A Ticket to the Stars,* New American Library (New York City), 1963.

Apel'siny iz Marokko, Youth Magazine, 1963.

Pora, moi drug, pora, Young Guard Publishing House, 1965, translation by Olive Stevens published as *It's Time, My Friend, It's Time,* Macmillan (New York City), 1969, published as *It's Time, My Love, It's Time,* Aurora Publishers (Nashville), 1970.

Zatovarennaia bochkotara, Youth Magazine, 1968.

Moy dedushka pamjatnik, Children's Literature Publishing House, 1969.

Liubov'k elektrichestvu, Youth Magazine, 1971.

Zolotaia nasha zhelezka, Ardis (Ann Arbor, MI), 1980.

Ozhog, Ardis, 1980, translation by Michael Glenny published as *The Burn,* Random House and Houghton Mifflin (Boston), 1984.

Ostrov Krym, Ardis, 1981, translation by Michael Henry Heim, published as *The Island of Crimea,* Vintage Books (New York City), 1983.

Bumazhnyi Peizazh, Ardis, 1983.

Quest for an Island, Farrar, Straus (New York), 1988.

Say Cheese!, translated by Antonina W. Bouis, Random House (New York City), 1989.

Our Golden Ironburg: A Novel with Formulas, translated by Ronald E. Peterson, Ardis, 1989.

Generations of Winter, translated by John Glad, Random House, 1994.

SHORT STORIES

Katapul'ta, Soviet Writer Publishing House, 1964.

Na polputi k lune, Soviet Russia Publishing House, 1966.

Zhal', chto vas ne bylo s nami, Soviet Writer Publishing House, 1969.

The Steel Bird, and Other Stories, translated by Rae Slonek and others, Ardis, 1979.

Surplussed Barrelware, edited and translated by Joel Wilkinson and Slava Yastremski, Ardis, 1985.

Skazhi izium: roman v moskovskikh traditsiiakh, Ardis, 1985.

Den' pervogo snegopada: romany, Sov. pisatel' (Leningrad), 1990.

PLAYS

Vsegda v prodazhe, first produced in Moscow at Sovremennik Theater, 1965.

Vash ubiytsa, published in *Performing Arts Journal,* spring, 1977.

Aristofaniana Silyagushkami: Aristophaniana and the Frogs (collection), Hermitage (Ann Arbor), 1981.

Tsaplya, produced in Paris at Theatre de Chaillot, February, 1984.

EDITOR

(With Viktor Yerofeyev, Fazil Iskander, Andrei Bitov, and Yevgeny Popov) *Metropol* (anthology), Ardis, 1979, published as *Metropol: A Literary Almanac,* Norton (New York City), 1982.

OTHER

V poiskakh grustnogo bebi: Kniga ob Amerike (biography) Liberty (New York City), 1987, published as *In Search of Melancholy Baby,* translated by Helm and Antonina W. Bouis, Random House, 1987.

Sobranie sochinenii (also known as *Works*), Ardis, 1987.

The Destruction of Pompeii (selections), Ardis, 1991.

Also author of *The Box Inside Which Something Knocks* (juvenile), 1976; *Twenty-four Hours Non-Stop,* 1976; *Four Temperaments* (comedy), 1979; and *Poiski zhanra.* Author of screenplays, including *Travelling,* 1967; *The Murmur House,* 1972; *Colleague, My Young Friend,* and *When They Raise the Bridges.* Former member of editorial board, *Yunost.*

SIDELIGHTS: In July, 1980, Russian novelist, playwright, and short story writer Vassily Aksyonov left his native land to join a growing number of his fellow countrymen in the West. A popular literary figure for nearly twenty years, especially among the so-called "Children of 1956," the first generation to come of age after Soviet dictator Joseph Stalin's death, Aksyonov was celebrated for his depiction of youth culture. In a *Washington Post Magazine* article, David Remnick sums up the ironies of Aksyonov's achievement this way: "Aksyonov was the preeminent writer of his generation, a wooly, funny figure, as much a literary cult figure in his time and place as Kerouac and Salinger were in theirs. Few serious American novelists dare dream of Aksyonov's popularity. In the

'60s, a Soviet journal with a press run of 2 million featuring one of his stories would sell out in less than a week; an edition of one of his new novels had a run of 100,000 in a couple of days."

Before he was stripped of his citizenship by a direct order from Leonid Brezhnev in 1980, Aksyonov had long been subjected to the routine harassment and censorship that many writers faced during the communist period in the Soviet Union. During the 1970s, however, the crackdowns increased to the point where he was doing most of his work "for the drawer"—that is, for himself and not for publication. "I was becoming like a kind of iceberg," he explained to Michiko Kakutani in a *New York Times* interview. "Only a small part of my work was being published; the invisible part grew more and more. I was only one-third Aksyonov, and at last I became fed up. 'For what am I writing?' I thought. What is this pile of yellow paper—you retype it and retype it and send it all over the country to publishers, and everywhere it is rejected because they think it is dangerous."

In 1979 Aksyonov clashed with the government for what would prove to be the last time. In a move intended to challenge censorship laws, he and twenty-two other writers requested that an anthology of their banned works entitled *Metropol* be published. Soviet authorities refused the request and, as punishment, expelled the two youngest contributors to the collection from the Writers' Union. An angry Aksyonov then resigned from the same union in protest and was subsequently expelled from two other professional unions, leaving him without an official way of earning a living and therefore subject to prosecution under the law of *tuneyadstvo*—parasitism. At about the same time, incidents of physical harassment against the writer became more frequent and more threatening; his phone was tapped, the tires of his car were slashed, and mysterious vehicles veered suddenly in his direction. "I had no choice but to leave," Aksyonov told Kakutani. "I was under great psychological pressure, and I was exhausted from all the years of fighting—for every publication, every book. I was just looking for a peaceful place to write. It was a retreat after fighting."

Aksyonov has been a fighter his entire life. His father died in the Gulag Archipelago and his mother spent eighteen years in Siberian exile as Stalin's political prisoner. The author himself spent part of his youth in an orphanage for "Children of Enemies of the State." At the age of sixteen, he was allowed to join his mother in Siberia. Although his mother, Evgenia Ginzburg, wrote and published her memoirs of life in Stalin's camps in *Journey into the Whirlwind* and *Within the Whirlwind,* she encouraged her son to become a doctor because the doctors in the camps stood the best chance for survival. Aksyonov did indeed become a physician, but he soon abandoned the profession in order to pursue another, more compelling interest: writing fiction.

Aksyonov first experimented with fiction in the late 1950s while he was still a medical student in Leningrad. A member of a local literary club, he specialized in writing short stories, some of which were published in the Soviet journal *Yunost.* These early stories were largely autobiographical and, for the most part, adhered to the tenets of Socialist Realism "with its obligatory jargon and hortatory themes," as *Time*'s Patricia Blake observes. Aksyonov made a dramatic break with convention in 1961, however, with his novel *Zvezdnyi bilet,* published in English as *A Ticket to the Stars* and also as *A Starry Ticket.* About the forbidden subject of modern Soviet youth, *A Ticket to the Stars* shocked readers with its frank portrayal of what *Newsweek* writers Kenneth Woodward and Eloise Salholz describe as "the inner confusions, sexual ventures and spiritual yearnings" of the post-Stalin generation.

Soon dubbed "a Slavic J. D. Salinger," Aksyonov spent the next several years writing novels and short stories featuring, as Blake notes, "teenage runaways who craved *rokmuzyka,* wore Keds and *dzhinsy* and talked a nonstop street slang larded with Americanisms, just like real-life Russians." But the author was not entirely Western in his outlook, according to *Times Literary Supplement* reviewer Geoffrey Hosking. "For all their surface irreverence," explains the critic, "the young people whom Aksyonov and his associates portrayed were not deeply disaffected from Soviet society: their personal revolt was directed to the new and creative, and it usually ended with rededication to the building of socialism, conceived in the new post-Stalin spirit—a socialism replete with beat music, sputniks, transistor radios and very possibly (since 'convergence' was also in the air) even Coca-Cola." While some Soviet critics praised the novelist for his sensitivity to the problems and concerns of youth and for his attempts to rescue Russian literature from the drabness of Socialist Realism, others deplored his penchant for racy colloquial language and his preoccupation with the activities of rebellious and alienated members of the "Beatle generation."

Despite the controversial nature of his fiction, Aksyonov did not have a great deal of difficulty getting published during the early 1960s, a period of relative freedom in Soviet literature. From the mid-1960s onwards, however, he and other non-conformist writers began to encounter more and more resistance to their work. Explains Hosking: "One reason for this—though not the only one—was that 'youth prose' itself had developed notes of individual revolt, experimentation and subjectivity were becoming stronger, the ultimate rededication to socialism fainter. In Aksyonov's own work, the hoped for goal of a warm and brotherly society took on more stylized and metaphorical

forms." By the end of the decade, Aksyonov had abandoned the youth theme entirely and was directing his efforts to avant-garde satire and stylistic methods. "We had grown disappointed with the atheism and Marxism of our youth," the author said of himself and his contemporaries in a *Newsweek* article. "We wanted the spiritual freedom to think, to pray, to probe universal human questions."

In his book *Twentieth-Century Russian Drama: From Gorky to the Present,* Harold B. Segal notes that Aksyonov's newfound interest in the grotesque and the fantastic "found a felicitous creative outlet in dramatic writing before [it] became manifest . . . in his prose fiction." According to the critic, the Russian's plays from this era—*Always on Sale* and *Your Murderer*—are "satires rooted in a darkening vision of an increasingly conformist society." Daniel C. Gerould elaborates on this description in a *Performing Arts Journal* article. "In both plays," he writes, "we find extensive use of grotesque metamorphosis, the device of accelerating demagoguery producing craven conformity, an atmosphere of deepening nightmare followed by a brief and ironically triumphant epilogue, and a mirror-image opposition between a prissy, idealistic do-gooder and a raunchy, foul-mouthed con-man. . . . In the classic tradition of savage satire Aksyonov functions as a moralist and voices his outrage at human venality and folly." Both Segal and Gerould maintain that Aksyonov's work owes much to the avant-garde writers of the 1920s through the 1950s. In fact, remarks Gerould, "with these two plays, Aksyonov performed an invaluable service: he reestablished contact between modern Soviet drama and the great line of Russian and early Soviet satirists."

By the late 1960s Aksyonov had returned to writing prose fiction, though very little of his new work appeared in print in the Soviet Union. For example, *Ozhog* (translated as *The Burn*), published for the first time in 1980 by the American firm Ardis, was actually written between 1969 and 1975. As Hosking declares in his *Times Literary Supplement* review, this novel "is nothing less than the testimony of Aksyonov and his generation, a panorama of their hopes, their illusions and disillusions, and of the spiritual reappraisal which political aesthetic reaction forced upon them."

Part autobiography and part fiction, *Ozhog* is the story of Tolya von Shteinbok, a half-Jewish, half-Russian boy who witnesses his mother's arrest and the brutal beating of his best friend by security police. Cared for by his stepfather, Tolya grows up in the Siberian town where his mother lives as an exiled prisoner. He wants desperately to be like his classmates and to believe in what they all have been taught about the benevolence of the state, but he fears that his mother's status as a political outcast may make it impossible for him to do so. Complicating matters still further is Tolya's stepfather, a deeply religious man who impresses the boy with the depth of his faith and helps him discover "a whiff of freedom, of risk, of alienation from this world." Consequently, Tolya finds himself torn between two ways of life in a spiritual struggle that Aksyonov believes mirrors the one facing his generation.

The author develops his narrative in an unconventional manner. Dividing the novel into three parts, he begins the first section with a look at the 1970s as the youth culture has what Hosking calls "its final drunken fling." The narrator for this section is a collective personality consisting of five young people (a writer, a sculptor, a jazz musician, a surgeon, and a scholar) whose lives constantly intermingle and who share the same childhood—that of Tolya von Shteinbok. On different occasions in the first part, all five catch a fleeting glimpse of a man they think is the security police agent who many years before beat up their best friend. The reappearance of this man sets the stage for a flashback to Tolya's post-war childhood, the focus of *Ozhog*'s second section. The third part then takes the reader back to the 1970s and Aksyonov's five young protagonists, all of whom, says Hosking, are left "to find their way forward in a world where [the] harbingers of both damnation and redemption now play a full part."

In the *New York Times* Walter Goodman describes Aksyonov's achievement this way: "*The Burn,* translated with considerable energy by Michael Glenny, is like one of the jazz sessions it celebrates, with riff following riff in displays of virtuosity. Political allusions keep popping up—the Soviet invasion of Czechoslovakia, the war in Vietnam, the rule of Nikita Khrushchev, here called Korneponevich, even Spiro Agnew, who makes a brief appearance as a Communist Party official." Commenting in *World Literature Today,* Vytas Dukas calls *Ozhog* an "unusual and rewarding work" that "borders on magic realism" with its blend of current events and imaginative fiction. He describes the author's prose as vibrant, and has special praise for the poems and poetic devices he makes use of throughout the novel.

Though Hosking maintains that the first part of *Ozhog* is too long and that the hesitations and contradictions of the third part underscore the author's unfamiliarity with religious tradition, the critic nevertheless hails the novel as one of "the most significant works Aksyonov has yet published." Continues Hosking: "*Ozhog* is a rich and many-sided work, the product of self-examination as well as literary experimentation. It exhibits its author's weaknesses as well as his strengths, but as a whole it is the creation of a powerful imagination seeking a way forward in the spiritual maelstrom of 1970s Moscow." With the publication of *Ozhog,* concludes the critic, Aksyonov has proven himself to be "a Western as well as a Russian writer," an artist who "will now reach, and be appreciated by, an international audience."

Other critics have identified *The Burn* as a classic that secures a place for Aksyonov in the great literary tradition of the Soviet Union. In *Publishers Weekly* Wendy Smith calls the novel "dazzling," and describes it as "a fierce, emotional chronicle of the extraordinary historical journey taken by his generation of Russian intellectuals." Dukas offers this assessment: "Aksyonov shows us [in *Ozhog*] that he is an excellent student of Gogol, Dostoevsky and Bulgakov in Russia and of Hemingway, Faulkner and Salinger in the USA. His language is rich and innovative . . . [He] writes eloquently and expressively." Bronwyn Drainie, writing in the Toronto *Globe and Mail,* is equally enthusiastic: "Reviewing a masterpiece isn't easy, especially when it is as sprawling, audacious and apocalyptic as Vassily Askyonov's *The Burn.* The book invites inevitable comparisons with the great Russian authors . . . . But in its daring use of syntax, structure and sexuality, there are also echoes of James Joyce, Henry Miller, William S. Burroughs, Thomas Pynchon and Joseph Heller. In short, a thoroughly modern masterpiece, shaped by a formidably synthetic mind."

Four months after leaving the Soviet Union, Askyonov's citizenship was revoked by the Soviet authorities. Aksyonov traveled and lectured throughout Western Europe and the United States, while Washington, DC, has became his home base. Unusually prolific, he found he was not at all like many of his fellow exiles who founnd that they are unable to write away from the sights and sounds of their native land. "I brought enough baggage with me in my head to last for the rest of my life," he assured *Time* reporter Blake. Furthermore, Aksyonov commented in the *New York Times* interview with Kakutani, he and other Soviet writers now living in the West have an obligation to continue their work. Explains the author: "Sometimes we think the new emigration is a brain drain. But sometimes I think it is not a tragedy, that it is our duty as writers now in the West to try to restore the links between Russian culture and Western culture, to prove we haven't become people without any spiritual life."

In Search of Melancholy Baby, written after Aksyonov had settled in Washington, D.C., is the tale of the author's own Americanization. In Chicago *Tribune Books* John Blades describes the book as a "full-throttle joy ride across America's sociopolitical, literary and pop-cultural landscape." In his account, Aksyonov turns a satiric eye to everything from TV newscasts and the squalor of some American cities to all-beef patties and his fellow immigrants. A jazz aficionado in the Soviet Union, Aksyonov learns that the United States is no longer listening to songs like "Melancholy Baby." Writes Donald Morrison in *Time* magazine: "The transplanted jazz fan is disappointed to learn that his beloved music has been shouldered out of the marketplace by rock. But he gains a grudging, un-Marxist respect for the market itself. 'The sad fact,' he writes, 'is that the human race has failed to invent a system of economic relations more natural than money.'" Ironically, even though most publishers in the Soviet Union refused to publish Aksyonov's work when he was a citizen, in 1988 the Russian humor magazine *Krokodil* published an excerpt from *In Search of Melancholy Baby* that Aksyonov wrote as an emigre and that was extremely critical of the Soviet Union.

Aksyonov has never believed that the future of Russian literature rests entirely in the hands of those writers who fled to the West. In his interview with Kakutani, he admitted that "for a long time I thought that we had no new wave behind us, that after our so-called literature of the post-Stalin years, there would be no more. But with the support in literary circles for *Metropol*, we found there are many new writers who don't want to be utilized by the official literature. For that reason, *Metropol* was not a complete failure." In short, concludes Aksyonov, "there are many talented people inside Russia, and despite all the restrictions, this will never be emptied—from under the pavement, there is always green grass rising. Maybe some day I will be allowed to come back to see it." In 1990, following the collapse of Soviet communism, Aksyonov's Russian citizenship was restored.

BIOGRAPHICAL/CRITICAL SOURCES:

BOOKS

Clark, Katerina, *The Soviet Novel: History as Ritual,* University of Chicago Press, 1981.
Contemporary Literary Criticism, Gale (Detroit), Volume 22, 1982, Volume 37, 1986.
Hayward, Max, and Edward L. Crowley, editors, *Soviet Literature in the Sixties: An International Symposium,* Methuen (New York City), 1964.
Segal, Harold B., *Twentieth-Century Russian Drama: From Gorky to the Present,* Columbia University Press (New York City), 1979.

PERIODICALS

Chicago Tribune Book World, February 19, 1984.
Globe and Mail (Toronto), January 26, 1985; July 25, 1987; August 26, 1989.
Los Angeles Times, January 23, 1985.
Los Angeles Times Book Review, January 23, 1983; March 12, 1989; August 13, 1989.
New Republic, November 30, 1987; September 18, 1989, p. 52; September 16, 1991.
Newsweek, December 8, 1980; November 21, 1983; May 1, 1989, p. 72.
New York Times, October 24, 1979; December 20, 1979; September 20, 1980; December 8, 1983; November 13, 1984; January 18, 1986; June 5, 1988; July 26, 1989.
New York Times Book Review, June 17, 1987; January 24, 1988; July 23, 1989, p. 18; July 30, 1989, p. 13.
Observer (London), March 25, 1990.
Performing Arts Journal, spring, 1977.
Publishers Weekly, August 31, 1984.
Soviet Literature, Number 3, 1967.
Time, June 23, 1980; November 8, 1982; August 31, 1987.
Times (London), May 23, 1985.
Times Literary Supplement, September 3, 1964; September 25, 1981; March 30, 1990.
Tribune Books (Chicago), July 3, 1987.
Virginia Quarterly Review, spring, 1990.
Washington Post, January 23, 1981; May 18, 1981; March 27, 1987; January 8, 1988; March 9, 1988.
Washington Post Book World, December 18, 1983; October 1, 1989.
Washington Post Magazine, February 15, 1987.
World Literature Today, summer, 1979; spring, 1981; summer, 1981; winter, 1982.

*   *   *

ALEXANDER, Bevin (Ray)   1928-

PERSONAL: Born February 17, 1928, in Gastonia, NC; son of John McAuley (an executive in the textile industry) and Odessa (a housewife; maiden name, Beaty) Alexander; married Peggy Tyndall (an owner of an herbal products company; marriage ended); children: Bevin Ray, Jr., Troy, David. *Education:* The Citadel, A.B. (with honors), 1949; Northwestern University, M.S. (with distinction), 1954.

ADDRESSES: Office—Arvon Grove, Bremo Bluff, VA 23022.

CAREER: Richmond Times-Dispatch, Richmond, VA, government reporter, 1954-58; *Rural Virginia,* Richmond, editor, 1958-61; University of Virginia, Charlottesville, director of information and editor of university magazine, 1961-66; Virginia Hotel and Motel Association, Richmond, executive vice president and director of relations with government, 1966-82; *Fremdenverkehrswirtschaft International,* Hamburg, West Germany, U.S. correspondent, beginning 1982; president of Alexander-Hood, Inc. (a government consulting firm), beginning 1982. *Military service:* U.S. Army, commanding officer of Fifth Historical Detachment, 1951-52; served in Korea; became first lieutenant; received three battle stars. U.S. Army Reserve, 1949-62; became captain.

MEMBER: Sigma Delta Chi, Kappa Tau Alpha, Richmond Rotary Club (president, 1985-86).

WRITINGS:

Korea: The First War We Lost, Hippocrene (New York City), 1986.

The Strange Connection: U.S. Intervention in China, 1944-1972, Greenwood (Westport, CT), 1992.

Lost Victories: The Military Genius of Stonewall Jackson, Holt (New York City), 1992.

How Great Generals Win, Norton (New York City), 1993.

The Future of Warfare, Norton, 1995.

SIDELIGHTS: Bevin Alexander told *CA:* "I am especially interested in two fields of writing: U.S. relations with East Asia and military strategy." Alexander once operated a cattle farm in the Piedmont area of Virginia. He has traveled in the Far East, Europe, Mexico, and the Caribbean.

*   *   *

ANDREWS, John F(rank) 1942-

PERSONAL: Born November 2, 1942, in Carlsbad, NM; son of Frank Randolph and Mary Lucille (Wimberley) Andrews; married Vicky Roberta Anderson, August 20, 1966 (divorced August 10, 1983); children: Eric John, Lisa Gail. *Education:* Princeton University, A.B., 1965; Harvard University, M.A., 1966; Vanderbilt University, Ph.D., 1971.

ADDRESSES: Home—2032 Belmont Rd. N.W., 605, Washington, DC 20009.

CAREER: University of Tennessee at Nashville (now Tennessee State University), instructor in English, 1969-70; Florida State University, Tallahassee, assistant professor of English, 1970-74, director of graduate studies, 1973-74; Folger Shakespeare Library, Washington, DC, director of academic programs, executive editor of Folger Books, and chairman of Folger Institute, all 1974-84, publications editor of multimedia touring exhibition "Shakespeare: The Globe and the World," 1978-82; National Endowment for the Humanities, Washington, DC, deputy director of Division of Education Programs, 1984-88; U.S. Department of Education, Washington, DC, consultant to Assistant Secretary for Postsecondary Education, 1992-93. Host of *AAUP Outlook,* a weekly program on WFSU-FM Radio, 1973-74, and *Behind the Scenes: Three Views of Shakespeare,* a lecture series on National Public Radio (NPR), 1979; chairman of national advisory panel for Public Broadcasting Service (PBS) series *The Shakespeare Plays,* 1979-85; principal adviser for PBS series *The Shakespeare Hour,* 1986. Margery Bailey Lecturer at Oregon Shakespearean Festival, 1976. Guest on television and radio programs, 1979—. Member of distinguished advisory council of Institute for Humanistic Studies at State University of New York at Albany, 1977-80; member of advisory board, Newberry Library's Center for Renaissance Studies, 1978-84, Theatre for a New Audience, 1982—, Alliance for Creative Theatre, Education, and Research (ACTER), 1982-84, Shakespeare Theatre at the Folger, 1986-90, Orlando Shakespeare Festival, Florida, 1987—, Grove Shakespeare Festival, California, 1991-92, and Center for Renaissance and Baroque Studies, University of Maryland, College Park, 1993—; consultant to Time-Life Television, PBS, and NPR, 1977-84, and numerous other Shakespeare productions and projects.

MEMBER: International Shakespeare Association, International Shakespeare Conference, Shakespeare Association of America (member of board of trustees, 1979-82), Modern Language Association of America, Milton Society of America, Renaissance Society of America, Surratt Society, South Atlantic Modern Language Association, Southeastern Renaissance Conference, Washington Book Publishers, Washington Independent Writers, Lincoln Group of the District of Columbia, Princeton Club (Washington, DC), Harvard Club (Washington, DC), Cosmos Club, Shakespeare Guild (founder and president, 1987—).

AWARDS, HONORS: Grants from Andrew W. Mellon Foundation, 1975, National Endowment for the Humanities, 1976-79, 1979-82, 1982-85, 1983-86, and 1991, Surdna Foundation, 1977, Conference for the Study of Political Thought, 1980, and Embassy of Spain, 1982.

WRITINGS:

(Author of foreword) J. G. A. Pocock, editor, *Three British Revolutions: 1641, 1688, 1776,* Princeton University Press (Princeton, NY), 1980.

(Editor-in-chief and contributor) *William Shakespeare: His World, His Work, His Influence,* three volumes, Scribner (New York City), 1985.

(Editor) *The Guild Shakespeare,* nineteen volumes, Doubleday/GuildAmerica Books (New York City), 1989-92.

(Editor and contributor) *"Romeo and Juliet": Critical Essays,* Garland (New York City), 1993.

(Editor) *The Everyman Shakespeare,* J. M. Dent/Everyman Library, 1993, Volume 1: *Romeo and Juliet,* foreword by Julie Harris, Volume 2: *A Midsummer Night's Dream,* foreword by F. Murray Abraham, Volume 3: *The Merchant of Venice,* foreword by Kelly McGillis, Volume 4: *Macbeth,* foreword by Zoe Caldwell, Volume 5: *Julius Caesar,* Volume 6: *Hamlet,* Volume 7: *King Lear,* Volume 8: *Antony and Cleopatra.*

OTHER

Also author of program notes and educational materials. Contributor to books, including *The Shakespeare Plays: A Study Guide,* 1978; *Poetry and Drama in the English Renaissance: In Honour of Professor Jiro Ozu,* 1980; and *The Shakespeare Hour: A Companion to the PBS-TV Series,* 1985. Also contributor to *Dictionary of Literary Biography,* Volume 62: *Elizabethan Dramatists,* Gale (Detroit), 1987, and *Concise Dictionary of British Literary Biography,* Volume 1: *Writers of the Middle Ages and Renaissance before 1660,* Gale, 1992. Member of editorial board of "The Folger Library Edition of the Works of Richard Hooker," Harvard University Press (Cambridge, MA), 1974-84. Contributor of articles and reviews to periodicals, including *Humanities, American Historical Review, Milton Studies, Atlantic, Washington Book Review,* and *Shakespeare Newsletter.* Editor of *Shakespeare Quarterly,* 1974-86, and *The Guild Shakespeare,* Literary Guild/Doubleday Book and Music Clubs, 1989-92; member of editorial board of *Medieval and Renaissance Drama in England,* 1982-92, and *Bibliotheca Shakespeariana,* 1983-85.

WORK IN PROGRESS: "This Our Lofty Scene": The Lincoln Assassination as a Reenactment of Shakespearean Tragedy, for Viking; revising *The Reader's Encyclopedia of Shakespeare* (Andrews was not associated with first edition published by Crowell), for HarperCollins.

SIDELIGHTS: John F. Andrews, a noted Shakespearean scholar, edited and contributed to *William Shakespeare: His World, His Work, His Influence,* a three-volume perspective on the sixteenth-century dramatist and poet. The work contains essays by scholars, historians, actors, directors, and critics, who comment on aspects of Shakespeare's life and art as well as on the writer's influence on the literature and art of succeeding generations. Richard L. Coe of the *Washington Post* describes the collection of sixty essays as "extraordinary," while Edmund Fuller writes in the *Wall Street Journal* that "a few are splendid, a few are terrible, the greater number are adequate." Although Fuller doesn't recommend the collection for the general reader, he maintains that the work contains "worthwhile things for selective reading." *Choice* reviewer C. Rees notes that while much of the information is "highly specialized and complex," the essays have "lucidity and wit" and "all are stimulating." Rees concludes that "no contemporary collection approaches the range and accessibility of this set."

Andrews once told *CA:* "My views on Shakespeare, and my reason for accepting the invitation from Charles Scribner, Jr., to undertake the project that became *William Shakespeare: His World, His Work, His Influence,* are perhaps best summarized in the introduction to that three-volume reference set: 'No other dramatist, in English or in any other language, can approach Shakespeare's primacy as poet, psychologist, and philosopher; and no one else in any humanistic endeavor has projected a vision as comprehensive or commanded an influence as all-pervasive. Shakespeare's phrases and cadences have become so familiar to us that it is sometimes with a start that we realize how many of our everyday expressions were first minted in his fertile mind. . . . His poems and plays have inspired more than eight hundred symphonic and operatic scores, and his themes have enriched the repertoires of composers as varied as [Hector] Berlioz and [Aaron] Copland and [Pyotr Ilich] Tchaikovsky and [Giuseppe] Verdi. Shakespeare's resonance can be felt in the writings of hundreds of subsequent authors. . . . [And] if we consider the dozens of Shakespearean scenes that have enriched the canvases of painters like Henry Fuseli and Eugene Delacroix and Pablo Picasso, we realize that Shakespeare has also expanded our visual horizons. No matter where we turn . . . we are continually reminded of the omnipresence of Shakespeare. In well nigh every nation that has a dramatic or literary tradition, Shakespeare is the playwright whose works are most frequently performed, the poet whose writings furnish the most accessible source of allusion. As ideological symbol or as standard of excellence, then, as literary model or as universal language, Shakespeare is part of us. And because he is so central to our lives, sooner or later we feel a desire to know and understand him better.'

"I edited the set, in other words, for the same reason that I edited *Shakespeare Quarterly* from 1974 to 1986: to celebrate Shakespeare's genius (James Joyce referred to him, aptly, as 'Shapesphere') and to do everything at my disposal to make the poet and his work available in an appealing, accessible form.

"Because Shakespeare was first and foremost a man of the theater, I've devoted a good deal of my career to efforts to bring the theater and the academy into closer communication with each other. Hence my desire, in the Scribner's set, to include articles by such figures as actor and director Sir John Gielgud, actor and playwright Peter Ustinov, director and producer Jonathan Miller, author Anthony Burgess, and critic John Simon. But if one of my goals has been to build bridges between the different kinds of 'professional Shakespeareans,' an equally important goal has been to help enlarge Shakespeare's audiences. Hence my role in helping to organize a touring exhibition, 'Shakespeare: The Globe and the World,' which took treasures from the Folger Shakespeare Library to museums in eight American cities between 1979 and 1982. Hence my involvement in educational outreach efforts connected with *The Shakespeare Plays,* and the sequel I helped to bring about, *The Shakespeare Hour,* with actor Walter Matthau as host. Hence the annotated edition, *The Guild Shake-*

speare, I produced for the Literary Guild (1989-92) and the paperback sequel, *The Everyman Shakespeare,* ... for J. M. Dent and the Everyman Library.

"And how do I interpret Shakespeare? The most succinct statement of how I read his works is to be found in my Scribner's contribution on 'Ethical and Theological Questions in Shakespeare's Dramatic Works.' Using Hamlet's advice to the visiting actors as a touchstone on 'the purpose of playing,' I argue that Shakespeare's dramaturgy depends for its success on a company faithful to all the clues in the playwright's script and a 'judicious' audience capable of apprehending the subtleties of the play's 'matter.' In most of the plays, particularly the tragedies, the audience is required to resolve what sometimes appear to be contradictions (e.g., the disparity between what Mark Antony says about Brutus in the funeral oration about the 'honorable men' who have assassinated Julius Caesar and what he says at the end of the play in his eulogy over the fallen Brutus, whom he now describes as 'the noblest Roman of them all'), and quite often the only way to do so is to follow Polonius's counsel and 'by indirections find directions out.' What this means in practice is that an attentive reader or audience member will often find himself surprised into a recognition that even the most attractive and intelligent of Shakespeare's characters (Hamlet, for instance) are frequently irrational or remiss in their thoughts and actions, with the consequence that in order to apprehend the playwright's 'matter' the reader or audience member must understand things that impulsive or unreflective characters do not themselves understand. This might seem self-evident, but to judge from what I regard as common misreadings of such plays as *Romeo and Juliet, Hamlet,* and *Antony and Cleopatra,* I can only conclude that it is not."

BIOGRAPHICAL/CRITICAL SOURCES:

PERIODICALS

Choice, March, 1986.
Chronicle of Higher Education, April 30, 1986.
Kansas City Star, February 7, 1980.
San Francisco Chronicle, October 17, 1979.
San Francisco Examiner, November 4, 1979.
Shakespeare Quarterly, spring, 1988.
Sun (Paducah), January 8, 1986.
Wall Street Journal, December 17, 1986.
Washington Post, January 19, 1986.

*   *   *

ANDREWS, William G(eorge) 1930-

PERSONAL: Born August 5, 1930, in Windsor, CO; son of Nathan Edwin (a chiropractor) and Ellen Margarethe (Wilse-Samson) Andrews; married Solange Benchetrit, September 4, 1954 (divorced, 1966); married Monika Wickert (a nurse), March 22, 1969; children: (first marriage) Donna Ellen (Rifken), William George, Jr., Jennifer Louise (Hughes), Edwin Bartilon; (second marriage) Christopher Scott, Thomas Nathan. *Education:* University of Oslo, certificate, 1951; Colorado State University, B.A., 1952; University of Bordeaux, C.E.P., 1955; Cornell University, Ph.D., 1959. *Politics:* Republican. *Religion:* Lutheran.

ADDRESSES: Home—46 College St., Brockport, NY 14420. *Office*—Department of Political Science, State University of New York, Brockport, NY 14420.

CAREER: Full-time or part-time writer for various newspapers, 1944-59; Dartmouth College, Hanover, NH, instructor, 1958-59, assistant professor of government, 1959-61; Tufts University, Medford, MA, assistant professor of government, 1961-64, associate professor of political science, 1964-67; State University of New York College at Brockport, Brockport, NY, professor of political science, 1967—, chairman of department, 1967-71, social science dean, 1970-76, liberal studies dean, 1976-79, director of social sciences program in Paris, 1983-85 and 1989-91. Chair of Monroe County Special Committee for the Constitution Bicentennial Celebration, 1987-89; member of Rochester Bicentennial Constitutional Convention Commission. Visiting professor at American College, and at Institut d'Etudes Americaines. Fulbright research scholar at Institut d'Etudes Politiques, Paris, France, 1962-63. State University of New York Faculty Exchange Scholar 1976—. Consulting editor, D. Van Nostrand Co., Inc., 1960-70. *Military service:* U.S. Air Force, 1952-54; became first lieutenant.

MEMBER: American Political Science Association.

AWARDS, HONORS: Fulbright fellow, 1954-55; National Endowment for the Humanities fellow, 1973-74, 1983; Brockport Senior Faculty Fellow, 1994-95.

WRITINGS:

PUBLISHED BY VAN NOSTRAND (NEW YORK CITY), EXCEPT AS NOTED

(Editor) *Constitutions and Constitutionalism,* 1961, 3rd edition, 1968.
(Editor) *European Political Institutions,* 1962, 2nd edition, 1966.
French Politics and Algeria: The Process of Policy Formation, 1954-62, Appleton (New York City), 1962.
(Editor) *American National Political Institutions,* 1962.
(Co-author) *The British General Elections of 1964,* Macmillan (New York City), 1965.
(Editor and co-author) *European Politics: The Restless Search,* 1966.

(Editor and co-author) *European Politics II: Plus ca change,* 1968.

(Editor) *Soviet Institutions and Policies: Inside Views,* 1966.

(Co-editor and co-author) *Le Grand Defi: USA/USSR,* two volumes, Laffont (Paris), 1967.

(Co-editor) *Politics and Civil Liberties in Europe: Four Case Studies,* 1967.

(Co-editor) *The Politics of the Coup d'Etat: Five Case Studies,* 1969.

(Editor) *Coordinate Magistrates,* 1969.

(Editor) *International Crises: Four Case Studies,* 1970.

(Editor with Stanley Hoffmann, and coauthor) *The Fifth Republic at Twenty,* State University of New York Press (Albany), 1981.

(Editor with Hoffman, and co-author) *The Impact of the Fifth Republic on France,* State University of New York Press, 1981.

(Editor and co-author) *International Handbook of Political Science,* Greenwood Press (Westport, CT), 1982.

Presidential Government in Gaullist France: A Study of Executive-Legislative Relations 1958-74, State University of New York Press, 1982.

The Land and People of the Soviet Union, HarperCollins (New York City), 1991.

OTHER

Also contributor to books, including *Modern European Governments,* edited by Roy C. Macridis, Prentice-Hall (Englewood Cliffs, NJ), 1968; *Politics in Europe,* edited by Martin O. Heisler, McKay (New York City), 1974. Contributor to periodicals, including *Boston Globe, Christian Science Monitor, Nation, New York Times, Yale Review,* and to political science journals in United States, Great Britain, and France.

WORK IN PROGRESS: A textbook of European integration; a study of presidential signing statements.

SIDELIGHTS: William G. Andrews told *CA:* "My publication efforts in political science have been directed mainly toward presenting detailed information on the operations of political systems through illustrative and documentary material, insiders' views, and case studies in order that students may form their own opinions on a well-informed basis." He added: "Although I have done some journalistic writing, all of my earlier books were for academic audiences. I wrote *The Land and People of the Soviet Union* mainly for my son Thomas, who was thirteen when it was published."*

AULETTA, Robert 1940-

PERSONAL: Born March 5, 1940, in Woodside, NY; son of Anthony Andrew (a Teamster) and Margaret (a secretary and homemaker; maiden name, Stark) Auletta; married Carol Carey, 1964 (divorced, 1980); married Jeni Breen (a dancer and choreographer), 1985; children: Colleen, Deirdre. *Education:* Queens College of the City University of New York, B.A., 1964; Yale University, M.F.A., 1969. *Politics:* "Utopian socialist." *Religion:* "Born a Catholic and still recovering."

ADDRESSES: Home—484 West 43rd St., New York, NY 10036. *Office*—School of Visual Arts, 209 East 23rd St., New York, NY 10010. *Agent*—Helen Merrill, 435 West 23 St., #1A, New York, NY 10011.

CAREER: University of Illinois, Champaign, assistant professor of theatre, 1969-74; School of Visual Arts, New York City, teacher of theatre, 1975—. Playwright in residence, Yale School of Drama, New Haven, CT, 1974-77, and teacher, 1974-77, 1993; teacher of theatre at Southern Connecticut State College, New Haven, 1974-76, and at O'Neill Theatre Center, Waterford, CT, 1978-79; conducts summer playwriting classes at Harvard University, Cambridge, MA, 1984—; taught playwriting at Columbia University, New York City, 1986; visiting lecturer in playwriting, Yale School of Drama, 1993—.

AWARDS, HONORS: Peter Pauper Press Award for Creative Writing, 1964; John Golden fellowship, Leonard Elmster fellowship, at Yale School of Drama, 1967-69; Mollie Kazan Award, 1969, for *Red Mountain High;* Rockefeller grant, 1972; Columbia Broadcasting System playwriting fellowship, 1975-76; Hazan Foundation grant, 1974; Citation from American Theatre Critics' Association for one of eight most outstanding plays produced outside of New York City during 1982-83 season, for *Rundown;* National Endowment for the Arts Foundation grant, 1982; *Village Voice* Obie Award, 1982, for *Virgins* and *Stops;* Hollywood Drama Logue award for *Sophocles' Ajax,* 1986; New York State Foundation for the Arts grant, 1987; National Endowment for the Arts Foundation grant, 1987.

WRITINGS:

PLAYS

The National Guard (one-act), first produced in New Haven, CT, at Experimental Theatre, Yale School of Drama, 1966.

Foreplay—Doorplay, first produced in New Haven at Yale School of Drama, 1967.

Red Mountain High (two-act), first produced in New Haven at the Studio Theatre, Yale School of Drama, 1968.

Coocooshay (two-act), first produced in New York at New York Shakespeare Festival, December, 1970.

Stops (one-act), first produced in New Haven at Yale Repertory Theatre, February, 1973.

Walk the Dog, Willie (two-act), first produced in New Haven at Yale Repertory Theatre, February, 1976, Broadway Play Publishing, 1986.

Wednesday Sharp (one-act), first produced in New Haven at Yale Cabaret, April, 1977.

Guess Work (one-act), first produced in New Haven at Yale Repertory Theatre, October, 1978.

Expo 99 (one-act), first produced in New Haven at Yale Cabaret, December, 1978.

Joe: A Dramatic Idiocy (one-act), first produced in New York at Theatre for the New City, April, 1980.

Hage: The Sexual History (two-act), first produced in Waterford, CT, at Eugene O'Neill Theatre Center, July, 1981.

The Tobogganists (one-act), first produced in New York at Ensemble Studio Theatre, September, 1981.

Virgins (one-act), first produced in New York at P.S. #122, January, 1982.

Rundown (two-act), first produced in Cambridge, MA, at American Repertory Theatre, April, 1982, Theatre Communications Group, 1981-82.

Days in a Can (one-act), first produced in New York at West Bank Cabaret, November, 1983.

Birth (one-act), first produced in New York at Cooper Union, December 12, 1983.

A Bull Refusing to Die in Madrid (one-act), first produced in New York at West Bank Cabaret, November, 1985.

Diesel Moon, first produced as a staged reading in Cleveland, OH, at Cleveland Play House, January, 1986.

(Adaptor) *Sophocles' Ajax,* first produced in Washington, DC, at Kennedy Center, June 7, 1986, published in *Theatre,* fall/winter, 1986.

(With Donald Byrd) *Blue Margaritas,* first produced in New York at La Mama, 1987.

Speak Easy, first performed in New York City at Symphony Space, with the Donald Byrd Dance Company, 1988.

Alimony Tales, first performed in New York City at West Bank Theatre Bar, 1989.

White Bucks, first performed in New York City at West Bank Cabaret, 1990.

Amazons and Nuclear Ear, first performed at the Harold Clurman Theatre, 1990.

Hey, Hey, LBJ (one-act), first performed in Chicago at Organic Theatre, 1992.

Lucifer Distracted, first performed as a staged reading at Vassar College, 1992.

(Adaptor) George Buchner, *Danton's Death,* first performed in Houston, TX, at Alley Theatre, 1992.

(Adaptor) Aeschylus, *The Persians,* first performed in Austria at Salzburg Festival, 1993.

(Adaptor) Aeschylus, *The Oresteia,* first performed in Cambridge, MA, at the American Repertory Theatre,

OTHER

Contributor of theatre articles to periodicals. *The National Guard, Red Mountain High, Walk the Dog, Willie,* and *Foreplay—Doorplay* were published in *Yale/Theatre; Stops* was published in *Playwrights for Tomorrow,* vol. 10, Minnesota Press; author's version of Aeschylus's *The Persians* was published by Sun and Moon Press.

WORK IN PROGRESS: A modern version of Goethe's *Faust,* parts one and two; two collections of poems, *Bedouins, and Other Poems of New York,* and *Cold City;* and *Carlsbad,* a full length, three character play.

SIDELIGHTS: Playwright Robert Auletta wrote *CA:* "When did it all begin, the words, where did they start, come from? Often writers talk about the books around them as they were growing up. That was not the case for me, though. The words that later became part of my life seemed to have had their origin somewhere else. Outside books. Later I located them in books. But it all began in play, I believe, in those endless mid-century days of light and darkness, alive with the myriad somersaults, antics and tricks that children seem able to conjure so easily, Prospero-like, out of the raw elements, and then turn to their wonder and advantage—fall and winter, shadows and movement, the early cold snapping the body to attention with its dangerous voltage, icy with living excitement, tires burning in vacant lots, potatoes blackening in the flames, geese streaking through the sky, and those mysterious elm trees brushing back the wind; and, on the other side of the equinox, the sun, with all its unending gifts, all those wonderful spring-summer mornings, in Flushing, New York.

"But what exactly is this 'play' that I am trying to speak about? No more than the imagination, really, turning, twisting, and teasing the world around you; and the world returning the favor. Later, buildings and automobiles, people and passions became involved; but in the beginning the play that I am concerned with is devoid of these things—just the basic lineaments of geography and nature, solitary and mysterious: just sunlight, a small hill, green and gold and shadows; or an animal, or the thought of an animal hiding in the high grass, with you standing and squinting into this sea of grass and sun, playing warriors and animals, and great battles beginning and ending, and creatures that cannot be described, dancing weirdly about, and the sight of fire filling the darkness, and maybe some mysterious lovely face speaking to you, giving you chills; someone who is everywhere, and all things, and nothing. Nothing at all, really. And looking back at it now, you know that it was the secret, the landscape where this happiness, the happiness of creativity lay, the secret that spoke to you. No, not so much books; we didn't have many of them in the house in those days. And there wasn't any television till later on, to interrupt things.

"Something else quite important happened during this time. At the age of seven I became an altar boy and began serving mass at St. Ann's Catholic Church, just up the street from where I lived on 59th Avenue in Flushing, Queens. This was where the theatre began for me, and the possibility of language first came alive; but the language that entered my mind at that time, that special, magical tongue, capable of so many amazing things, wasn't En-

glish; but something entirely different: it was Latin; the Latin of the Catholic mass. It was the ritual of the Mass, and the mystery of that ancient language, that, I believe, prepared me for the theatre."

BIOGRAPHICAL/CRITICAL SOURCES:

PERIODICALS

American Theatre, February, 1995, pp. 10-15, 68.
Boston Globe, December 2, 1994, pp. 43, 51.
Boston Phoenix, April 13, 1982.
New York Times, May 2, 1982; March 28, 1985.
Other Stages, January 13-26, 1986.
Theater, fall/winter, 1986.

B

BABBIE, Earl (Robert) 1938-

PERSONAL: Born January 8, 1938, in Detroit, MI; son of Herman Octave (an automobile body mechanic) and Marion (Towle) Babbie; married Sheila Trimble (a project assistant for Erhard Seminars Training), May 17, 1965; children: Aaron Robert. *Education:* Harvard University, A.B. (cum laude), 1960; University of California, Berkeley, M.A., 1966, Ph.D., 1969. *Politics:* "Active, reformist, civil libertarian." *Religion:* None. *Avocational interests:* "Saving the world."

ADDRESSES: Home—6640 Paseo Fiesta, Anaheim, Hills, CA 92807. *Office*—Department of Sociology, Chapman University, Orange, CA 92666.

CAREER: University of California, Berkeley, research sociologist at Survey Research Center, 1966-68, assistant director of center, 1967-68; University of Hawaii, Honolulu, assistant professor, 1968-70, associate professor, 1970-74, professor, 1974-80, affiliate professor of sociology, 1980-87, chairman of department, 1973-74, 1977-79, program director for survey research at Social Science Research Institute, 1968-69, director of Institutional Research Office, 1970, director of Survey Research Office, 1970-73, associate director of Social Science Research Institute, 1972-73; Babbie Enterprises, Mill Valley, CA, president, 1976—; Chapman University, Orange, CA, professor of sociology, 1987—. University of California, Berkeley, visiting scholar, 1975, visiting professor, 1980. Partner, Pacific Poll Co., 1968-70; member of Hawaii State Census Tract Committee, 1969-74; president of Save Wawamalu Association, 1971-73; member of research committee of Hawaii Visitors Bureau, 1972-74; vice-president of Hawaii Center for Environmental Education, 1973-74; Erhard Seminars Training of Hawaii, vice-president, 1975-76, member of national advisory board, 1976-80. Member of board of directors of Citizens for Ha-

waii, 1972-74, Policy Research Institute, 1976-79, and Holiday Project, 1981-83; member of planning committee of University of Hawaii Gerontology Center, 1977-78. Member of research advisory committee of Hawaii Commission on Children and Youth, 1972-74; chairman of advisory council of Hunger Project, 1978-83. *Military service:* U.S. Marine Corps, 1960-66; active duty, 1960-63; became first lieutenant.

MEMBER: American Sociological Association (council member), American Association for Public Opinion Research, American Civil Liberties Union, Zero Population Growth (member of board of directors, 1981-83).

AWARDS, HONORS: Grant from Haas Community Fund, 1973, for the writing of *The Practice of Social Research;* grant from Erhard Seminars Training of Hawaii, 1975.

WRITINGS:

(With Charles Y. Glock and Benjamin B. Ringer) *To Comfort and to Challenge,* University of California Press (Berkeley, CA), 1967.
(With William Nicholls) *Oakland in Transition: A Summary of the 701 Household Survey* (monograph), Survey Research Center, University of California, 1969.
Science and Morality in Medicine, University of California Press, 1970.
A Profile of the Honolulu Model Neighborhoods: 1969 (monograph), Honolulu Model Cities Project, 1970.
Hubris: Hawaii Uniform Bank and Remote Interactive System (monograph), Survey Research Office, University of Hawaii (Honolulu, HI), 1971.
The Maximillion Report (monograph), Citizens for Hawaii, 1972.
Survey Research Methods, with instructor's manual, Wadsworth (Belmont, CA), 1973.

(Contributor) Glock, editor, *Religion in Sociological Perspective,* Wadsworth, 1973.

The Practice of Social Research, Wadsworth, 1975, 4th edition, 1985.

(With Robert Huitt) *Practicing Social Research* (manual), Wadsworth, 1975, 2nd edition, 1979.

Society by Agreement, Wadsworth, 1977, 2nd edition published as *Sociology: An Introduction,* 1980, 3rd edition, 1983.

Understanding Sociology: A Context for Action, Wadsworth, 1981.

Social Research for Consumers, Wadsworth, 1982.

Apple LOGO for Teachers, Wadsworth, 1984.

You Can Make a Difference: The Heroic Potential within Us All, St. Martin's (New York City), 1985.

The Sociological Spirit, Wadsworth, 1987, 2nd edition, 1994.

(With Allen Rubin) *Research Methods for Social Work,* Brook/Cole, 1989, 2nd edition, 1993.

(With Fred Halley) *Adventures in Social Research: Data Analysis Using SPSS,* Pine Forge Press, 1993.

What Is Society?: Reflections on Freedom, Order, and Change, Pine Forge Press, 1993.

Also author of *Observing Ourselves,* 1986. Contributor to academic journals, including *Review of Religious Research, Journal for the Scientific Study of Religion, American Sociological Review, Social Forces, American Journal of Correction,* and *Graduate Review.* Editorial reader for *Sociology of Education,* 1967.

WORK IN PROGRESS: Doorways to Beyond.

SIDELIGHTS: Earl Babbie told *CA:* "You can make a difference. Indeed, you do and will make a difference—inevitably. A question worth asking yourself is: 'What kind of difference am I making—today, right now?' "

*   *   *

BALTZELL, E(dward) Digby 1915-

PERSONAL: Born November 14, 1915, in Philadelphia, PA; son of Edward Digby (an insurance broker) and Caroline Adelaide (Duhring) Baltzell; married Jane Piper (an artist), February 21, 1943; children: Eve, Jan. *Education:* University of Pennsylvania, Philadelphia, B.S., 1939; Columbia University, New York City, Ph.D., 1952. *Politics:* Democrat. *Religion:* Episcopalian.

ADDRESSES: Home—1724 DeLancey St., Philadelphia, PA 19103. *Office*—Department of Sociology, 113 McNeil Building, 3718 Locust Walk, University of Pennsylvania, Philadelphia, PA 19104.

CAREER: University of Pennsylvania, Philadelphia, instructor, 1947-55, assistant professor, 1955-58, associate professor, 1958-65, professor of sociology, 1965—. *Military service:* U.S. Naval Reserve, active duty, 1942-45; became lieutenant junior grade; received Air Medal.

MEMBER: American Sociological Association, American Studies Association, Eastern Sociological Society, Pennsylvania Historical Society.

AWARDS, HONORS: Danforth fellow, Society for Religion in Higher Education, Princeton Theological Seminary, NJ, 1967-68; Charles Warren research fellow, Harvard University, 1972-73; Hardy Chair lecturer, Hartwick College, 1975; Guggenheim fellow, 1978-79; LL.D., La Salle College, 1981; L.H.D., University of Pennsylvania, 1989, Kenyon College, 1992.

WRITINGS:

(Contributor) Richard Bendix and Seymour M. Lipset, editors, *Class, Status and Power,* Free Press (New York City), 1953, revised edition, 1966.

Philadelphia Gentleman: The Making of a National Upper Class, Quadrangle, 1958, revised edition with new introduction by author, Transaction, 1989.

Protestant Establishment, Random House (New York City), 1964.

Puritan Boston and Quaker Philadelphia: Two Protestant Ethics and the Spirit of Class Authority and Leadership, Free Press, 1979.

The Protestant Establishment Revisited, edited and with introduction by Howard G. Schneiderman, Transaction, 1991.

Judgment and Sensibility: Religion and Stratification, edited and with introduction by Howard G. Schneiderman, Transaction, 1994.

SIDELIGHTS: E. Digby Baltzell is a respected sociologist and author. His *Puritan Boston and Quaker Philadelphia: Two Protestant Ethics and the Spirit of Class Authority and Leadership* was favorably received by critics. Andrew Hacker remarks that "it is a vast and stunning volume, displaying sociology at its best." "To understand the problem of authority and leadership in America today," Baltzell writes, "one must study the history of Philadelphia and Pennsylvania." The *Washington Post Book World* notes that "Baltzell argues that Boston produced leaders in politics and the law, while Philadelphia fostered the development of the more anti-establishment talents of artists and musicians," while Pauline Maier concludes that "those who read Baltzell's book and reflect upon recent history might well consider it a saving grace that the United States has not just a Boston but a Philadelphia."

BIOGRAPHICAL/CRITICAL SOURCES:

BOOKS

Social Class and Democratic Leadership: Essays in Honor of E. Digby Baltzell, edited by Harold J. Bershady, University of Pennsylvania, 1989.

PERIODICALS

Nation, April 3, 1967.
New Republic, June 28, 1980, p. 36.
New York Times Book Review, March 9, 1980, p. 7; March 15, 1987, p. 28.
Times Literary Supplement, November 14, 1980, p. 1289.
Washington Post Book World, October 3, 1982, p. 12.

*   *   *

BANNISTER, Jo   1951-

PERSONAL: Born July 31, 1951, in Rochdale, England; daughter of Alan (in transport) and Marjorie (Ashworth) Bannister. *Education:* Attended grammar schools and technical secondary school in Bangor, Northern Ireland. *Politics:* Liberal. *Avocational interests:* Horseback riding, archery, astronomy, archaeology, sailing, travel (Europe, North Africa, the Middle East).

ADDRESSES: Home and office—5 Hillfoot, Groomsport, County Down BT19 6JJ, Northern Ireland.

CAREER: County Down Spectator, Bangor, Northern Ireland, reporter, 1969-74, deputy editor, 1975-83, editor, 1983-87; *Belfast Newsletter,* Belfast, Northern Ireland, feature writer, 1974-75. Editor of *Newtownards Spectator.*

MEMBER: Amnesty International, International League for the Protection of Horses, Worldwide Fund for Nature, Society of Authors.

AWARDS, HONORS: Catherine Pakenham Award, Fleet Street publishers, 1972; runner-up, British Press Award, 1974; Northern Ireland Press Award, 1981; runner-up, Ellery Queen Readers Award, 1992, and nomination for Edgar Allan Poe Award, 1993, both for short story "Howler."

WRITINGS:

SCIENCE FICTION

The Matrix, R. Hale (London), 1981.
The Winter Plain, R. Hale, 1982.
A Cactus Garden, R. Hale, 1983.

CRIME

Striving with Gods, Doubleday (New York City), 1984.
Gilgamesh, Doubleday, 1989.
The Going Down of the Sun, Doubleday, 1989.

Death and Other Lovers, Doubleday, 1991.
A Bleeding of Innocents, St. Martin's (New York City), 1993.
Charisma, St. Martin's, 1994.

THRILLERS

Mosaic, Doubleday, 1987.
The Mason Codex, Doubleday, 1988.
Shards, Doubleday, 1990.

OTHER

Also author of short stories, some published in German, Italian, and Norwegian. Manuscripts collected at the Mugar Memorial Library, Boston University, MA.

WORK IN PROGRESS: Short stories; audiotape editions of books.

SIDELIGHTS: Jo Bannister once told *CA:* "Too many 'serious' writers look down on the entertainment aspect of their own and other people's work. But entertainment is the writer's side of the contract; it is what he supplies to a reader to make him want to wade through all these words and ideas. It's the rent he pays for a space in the reader's mind. If he begrudges or stints that, he's likely to get evicted."

BIOGRAPHICAL/CRITICAL SOURCES:

PERIODICALS

Armchair Detective, spring, 1994, p. 239.
Booklist, August, 1994, p. 2025.
Drood Review of Mystery, June 21, 1981.
Kirkus Reviews, July 15, 1984; September 1, 1989, p. 1281; July 15, 1990, p. 966; March 1, 1991, p. 285; July 1, 1993, p. 818; July 1, 1994, p. 886.
New York Times Book Review, September 18, 1994, p. 34.
Publishers Weekly, September 22, 1989, p. 41; July 26, 1993, p. 60; July 25, 1994, p. 36.
Wilson Library Bulletin, December, 1984, p. 279.

*   *   *

BARBER, Patricia   1946-
(Patricia Barrie)

PERSONAL: Born April 16, 1946, in Cardiff, Wales; daughter of Sydney James (a mariner) and Anna (a hospital matron; maiden name, Crukley) Barber; married John Keith Barber (an engineer), March 30, 1968. *Education:* Newport School of Art and Design, B.A., 1969; University of Wales, University College, Cardiff, Art Teachers Diploma, 1970.

ADDRESSES: Home—17 Bloomfield Close, Timsbury Bath, Avon BA3 1LP, England. *Agent*—Julie Fallowfield,

McIntosh & Otis, Inc., 475 Fifth Ave., New York, NY 10017; and Amanda Little, Watson, Little Ltd., 12 Egbert St., London NW1 8LJ, England.

CAREER: Teacher of art and design at comprehensive school in Bristol, England, 1970-79; American Museum in Britain, Bath, England, part-time guide, 1979—.

WRITINGS:

Devotions (novel), Chatto & Windus (London), 1986, Dutton (New York City), 1987.
Rosie (novel), Hamish Hamilton (London), 1988, Hodder Coronet, 1990.

Sometimes writes under the pseudonym Patricia Barrie.

WORK IN PROGRESS: Songs of Silence, a novel set in the mountains of North Wales.

SIDELIGHTS: Patricia Barber told *CA:* "My father was half English, half Scots. My mother was half Irish, half Russian. I learned Welsh and studied Russian, but that was some time ago. I was brought up in Wales in an atmosphere of rich Celtic tradition: a lot of ghosts, devils, poetry, and passionate music. The big day of the year was St. David's Day, when there was a holiday from school for the Eisteddfod, a festival of music, art, and poetry with the added excitement of prizes.

"My five years of training as a painter is scarcely worth mentioning. I learned to paint, but I didn't learn to think as a painter. I learned to see, however; and for this single reason, I don't regret that I studied art rather than literature, to which I was infinitely better suited. I would say that an ability to 'see' makes up a very large part of the writer's art. Thanks to my training as a painter, I can see almost without looking, and I collect visual impressions rather than taking verbal notes. It makes life very much easier. (On reflection, however, I've discovered recently that I can also hear without listening, so perhaps it has nothing to do with my art training after all.)

"I taught art for nine years in a Bristol comprehensive school. It was this experience, more than any other I can think of, which best prepared me for authorship. It's hard to say why, except that when one is constantly in the honest and critical company of adolescents, one must (if not completely lacking a sense of humor) begin to shed one's most dearly loved pretensions and begin to see oneself more clearly. Teaching the impressionable young is also a good training ground for editing one's text. Try being long-winded with an impatient class of thirteen-year-olds, and see where it gets you! I could go on for hours about the things I learned from teaching, but it taught me not to be long-winded, so I won't.

"As a means of keeping in touch with humanity, I joined the American Museum in Britain as soon as I realized how lonely a life an author is bound to lead. I have specialized in Shaker history, and in pursuit of greater understanding I have visited most of the Shaker villages and museums between Kentucky and Maine, and I have met all of the surviving Shakers both at Sabbathday Lake, Maine, and at Canterbury, New Hampshire. My travels closer to home include Greece and North Africa. I have little time to pursue interests other than writing and reading, but I have a passion for gardening, and I am saved from turning it into an obsession only by the general inclemency of British weather.

"I've never attempted to analyze such things as motivation for my writing. The only thing I can think of which I deem vital to my work is peace of mind. I work a twelve-hour day in a very small room in a house in the country, coming up for air occasionally only to walk my dog. I have quite powerful views on politics, religion, life, and society, but these are subject to change. I think it is essential to keep my mind open to change and closed to any ideas of 'final judgment.' I am a decisive person and extremely positive in both my actions and my thoughts, but I think it wrong (at the moment) to set down my decisions with a view to influencing other people—except to decide the issue for themselves. I can see that a 'trend of ideas' (feminism springs to mind as an example) is an essential factor in making necessary changes to society, but such trends so often become entrenchments of thought, and this appalls me. I feel that a writer should always be aware of his power to influence others and to use that power responsibly.

"This seems to indicate that I despise the whole notion of proselytizing, which is by no means true. When I have an opinion which I think is good, I certainly want to express it and know the satisfaction of having other people agree. But I also want to give them a fair chance not to agree. The lines which divide good from bad, right from wrong, are as well defined, seen from a distance (or from a prejudice), as are the edges of a cumulus cloud. But if you claim to be able to touch those edges when you fly close to the cloud, you are a liar. There are powerful forces of goodness lurking at the periphery of every evil, and vice versa. An artist should always consider this before he draws in his cloud. Having set this down, I can now say that, for the moment at least, my chief concern as a writer is to make that precise point: that the edges are not defined and can never be so.

"Until I wrote the first draft of *Rosie* I thought I was a writer because I enjoyed writing. This has now been proved untrue. I didn't enjoy writing *Rosie.* I was driven to it by an irresistible compulsion, and I stayed with it merely because my agent liked the first few chapters! I suspect that writing has become an addiction, and that I now have to keep on taking it in order to live. I certainly begin to feel withdrawal symptoms when I stop writing for any length of time; and having no idea in mind for a new project plunges me into depths of gloom. This is scarcely the picture of a noble artist. I'm a junkie, I suppose, hooked on words, and I do not yet wish to be cured of it.

"I hesitate to make any remarks about the writings of others. I imagine that I took the customary amount of influence and inspiration from the great classics. 'Pure' writing (in the Austen mold) rings more inspirational bells for me than does the more flamboyant Dickensian tradition. Paradoxically, though, I think Dickens has more lessons for the modern writer—and that's too large a subject to begin here. I have a tendency to worry about the state of modern fiction. When I find a book by a contemporary author that excites, inspires, elevates, and enlightens me, and is in addition a darned good read, my usual response, after a sigh of satisfaction, is a feeling of sadness that such books are so rare."

*   *   *

BARRIE, Patricia
    See BARBER, Patricia

*   *   *

BASS, George F(letcher) 1932-

PERSONAL: Born December 9, 1932, in Columbia, SC; son of Robert D. (a professor of English and writer) and Virginia (a writer; maiden name, Wauchope) Bass; married Ann Singletary (a piano teacher), March 19, 1960; children: Gordon Wauchope, Alan Joseph. *Education:* Johns Hopkins University, M.A.; University of Pennsylvania, Ph.D., 1964.

ADDRESSES: Home—1600 Dominik Dr., College Station, TX 77840. *Office*—Department of Nautical Archaeology, Texas A & M University, College Station, TX 77843.

CAREER: University of Pennsylvania, Philadelphia, research assistant in classical archaeology at university museum, 1962, research associate, 1963-64, assistant professor, 1964-68, associate professor of classical archaeology, 1968-73; Texas A & M University, College Station, distinguished professor of anthropology, 1980—, George T. and Gladys H. Abell Professor of Nautical Archaeology, 1986—. Visiting scholar in archaeology at St. John's College, Cambridge, 1969-70; Geddes-Harrower Professor of Greek Art and Archaeology, University of Aberdeen, Scotland, 1984; advisory board member, Center for the Study of Architecture, Bryn Mawr College, 1987—; mem-

ber of managing committee, American School of Classical Studies at Athens, 1987—. Founder and president of Institute for Nautical Archaeology, 1973-82; advisor for World Ship Trust. *Military service:* U.S. Army Security Agency, 1957-59, became first lieutenant.

MEMBER: Archaeological Institute of America (vice president, 1989-90), American Philosophical Society, American Oriental Society, British Institute of Archaeology at Ankara, Institute of Nautical Archaeology, Society of Professional Archaeologists, Society for Historical Archaeology, Explorers Club.

AWARDS, HONORS: Gold Trident for Science, 6th International Congress of Subaquatics Activities, 1964; Outstanding Young Man in Philadelphia, Philadelphia Jaycees, 1966; named One of the Ten Outstanding Young Men in the Nation, United States Jaycees, 1967; American Council of Learned Societies Fellowship, 1969-79; First Annual Philadelphia Explorers Award, 1973; NOGI Award for Science, Underwater Society of America, 1974; John Oliver La Gorce gold medal from National Geographic Society, 1979; Keith Muckelroy Memorial Award, National Maritime Museum, 1984; gold medal from Archaeological Institute of America, 1986; Lowell Thomas Award from Explorers Club, 1986; honorary doctorate, Bogazici University, Istanbul, Turkey, 1987; Centennial Award, National Geographic Society, 1988; President's Award of Honor, Texas A & M University, 1989; honorary fellow, Institute for Advanced Studies in the Humanities, University of Edinburgh, 1989.

WRITINGS:

Cape Gelidonya: A Bronze Age Shipwreck, University Microfilms (Ann Arbor, MI), 1965.
Archaeology under Water, Praeger (New York City), 1966, revised and expanded paperback edition, Penguin (Baltimore, MD), 1970.
Smithsonian Twentieth-Century Treasury of Science, Simon & Schuster (New York City), 1966.
(Editor and contributor) *A History of Seafaring: Based on Underwater Archaeology*, Walker & Co. (New York City), 1972.
Archaeology beneath the Sea, Walker & Co., 1975.
(With Frederick H. van Doorninck, Jr.) *Yassi Ada, Volume I: A Seventh-Century Byzantine Shipwreck*, Texas A & M University Press (College Station), 1982.
(Editor) *A History of Seafaring in the Americas Based on Underwater Archaeology*, Thames & Hudson (New York City), 1986.
Ships and Shipwrecks of the Americas, Thames & Hudson, 1988.

Contributor to books, including *Smithsonian Institution: Annual Report, 1963*, (Washington, DC), 1964; *Smithsonian Treasury of 20th-Century Science*, edited by Webster

True, Simon & Schuster (New York City), 1966; *Orient and Occident* (festschrift for Cyrus Gordon), edited by Harry A. Hoffner, Kevelaer, 1973; *The Princeton Encyclopedia of Classical Sites,* Princeton University Press, 1976; (with Donald M. Rosencrantz) *Submersibles and Their Use in Oceanography and Ocean Engineering,* edited by R. A. Geyer, Elsevier Scientific Publishing Co. (Amsterdam, Oxford, New York City), 1977; *Beneath the Waters of Time: The Proceedings of the Ninth Conference on Underwater Archaeology,* edited by J. Barto Arnold III, Texas Antiquities Committee Publication (Austin, TX), 1978; *Ocean Yearbook 2,* edited by Elisabeth Mann Borgese and Norton Ginsburg, University of Chicago Press, 1980; *Archaeology under Water: An Atlas of the World's Submerged Sites,* edited by Keith Muckelroy, McGraw Hill (New York City), 1980; *Underwater Archaeology: The Challenge before Us, The Proceedings of the Twelfth Conference on Underwater Archaeology,* edited by Gordon P. Watts, Jr., Fathom Eight Special Publications (San Marino, CA), 1981; *Science Year 1982, The World Book Science Annual,* World Book-Childcraft International (Chicago, IL), 1982; *Shipwreck Anthropology,* edited by Richard A. Gould, University of New Mexico Press (Albuquerque, NM), 1983; *Introduction to Anthropology* (reprinted from *Archaeology beneath the Sea*), edited by Warren T. Morrill, Kendall/Hunt (Dubuque, IA), 1983; *The Mariner's Guide to Oceanography,* edited by Nixon Griffis, Hearst Marine Books (New York City), 1984; *Medieval Archaeology,* edited by Charles L. Redman, State University of New York at Binghamton, 1989; *Underwater Archaeology Proceedings from the Society for Historical Archaeology Conference, Baltimore, Maryland 1989,* edited by Arnold, Society for Historical Archaeology, 1989; *Underwater Archaeology: Proceedings of the 1990 Society for Historical Archaeology Conference,* edited by Toni L. Carrell, Society for Historical Archaeology, 1990; *Science and Archaeology: Bronze Age Trade in the Mediterranean,* edited by N. H. Gale and Z. A. Stos-Gale, 1991; *Underwater Archaeology Proceedings from the Society for Historical Archaeology Conference,* edited by D. H. Keith and T. L. Carrell, Society for Historical Archaeology, 1992; *McGraw-Hill Yearbook of Science & Technology 1993,* McGraw-Hill (New York City), 1993.

Editorial board member for the *American Journal of Archaeology, Archaeology, International Journal of Nautical Archaeology,* and *National Geographic Research.* Contributor of articles to journals, including *American Journal of Archaeology, American Scholar, Anatolian Studies, Antiquity, Archaeology, Biblical Archaeologist, Expedition, Explorers Journal, International Journal of Nautical Archaeology, Modern Maturity, National Geographic, Scientific American,* and *Sea History.*

WORK IN PROGRESS: The Bronze Age Shipwreck at Ulu Burun, Turkey, Texas A & M University Press, publication expected in 1995.

SIDELIGHTS: In *Archaeology under Water* George F. Bass provides a survey of his field—the excavation of sunken ships and the technology required to do it. Believing that archaeologists should not neglect the artifacts buried in the oceans, Bass has directed a number of underwater expeditions noted for technical excellence, and in his book he expresses his "convictions about how underwater excavations should be carried out," observed a reviewer in the *Times Literary Supplement.* Finding the book an "admirable new survey," the critic asserted that "Bass is always clear, both in his explanations of purely archaeological problems and while discussing such fascinating gadgets as air-lifts, mapping grids, and midget submarines; and he is never dull."

Bass once told *CA:* "Having had the good fortune to direct the first complete excavation of an ancient shipwreck on the seabed—at Cape Gelidonya, Turkey, in 1960—I have devoted the past quarter of a century to the development of nautical archaeology as a serious scholarly pursuit. I founded the Institute of Nautical Archaeology in 1973, and already it has been actively engaged in excavations of shipwrecks dating from the sixteenth century B.C. to the nineteenth century A.D. on four continents."

Since its initial English-language publication, Bass's *A History of Seafaring: Based on Underwater Archaeology* has been reprinted in Dutch, French, Swedish, Italian, and German editions.

BIOGRAPHICAL/CRITICAL SOURCES:

PERIODICALS

Times Literary Supplement, November 17, 1966; January 12, 1973.

*   *   *

BAYER, William 1939-
(Leonie St. John, a joint pseudonym)

PERSONAL: Surname is pronounced "buy-er"; born February 20, 1939, in Cleveland, OH; son of Lee G. Bayer (a lawyer) and Eleanor Perry (a writer; maiden name, Rosenfeld); married Paula Wolfert (a food writer), August 10, 1983. *Education:* Harvard University, B.A. (cum laude), 1960. *Avocational interests:* Photography.

ADDRESSES: Home and office—P.O. Box 322, Newtown, CT 06470. *Agent*—Arlene Donovan, International Creative Management, 40 West 57th St., New York, NY 10019.

CAREER: United States Information Agency, Washington, DC, Saigon, Vietnam, and New York City, foreign service officer/staff filmmaker, 1963-68; freelance writer and filmmaker, 1968—.

MEMBER: Authors Guild, Writers Guild of America (East), PEN, International Association of Crime Writers, North America (president, 1991—).

AWARDS, HONORS: American Film Institute, grant for screenplay, 1968, grant for film production, 1969; Golden Hugo Award, Chicago International Film Festival, 1970, for *Mississippi Summer;* National Endowment for the Arts research grant, 1973; Edgar Allan Poe Award for best novel, Mystery Writers of America, 1982, for *Peregrine.*

WRITINGS:

NOVELS

(With Nancy Harmon, under joint pseudonym Leonie St. John) *Love with a Harvard Accent,* Ace (New York City), 1962.
In Search of a Hero, World Publishing, 1966.
Stardust, Dell (New York City), 1974.
Visions of Isabelle, Delacorte (New York City), 1976.
Tangier, Dutton (New York City), 1978.
Punish Me with Kisses, Congdon & Lattes, 1980.
Peregrine, Congdon & Lattes, 1981.
Switch, Linden/Simon & Schuster (New York City), 1984.
Pattern Crimes, Villard/Random House (New York City), 1987.
Blind Side, with photographs by Bayer, Villard/Random House, 1989.
Wallflower, Villard/Random House, 1991.
Mirror Maze, Villard/Random House, 1994.

NONFICTION

Breaking Through, Selling Out, Dropping Dead: And Other Notes on Filmmaking, Macmillan (New York City), 1971, revised and updated, Limelight Editions (New York City), 1989.
The Great Movies, Grosset, 1973.

OTHER

Also author of film *Mississippi Summer.* Bayer's work has been translated into French, German, Italian, Dutch, Danish, Czech, Norwegian, Portuguese, and Japanese.

WORK IN PROGRESS: Tarot, a crime novel.

SIDELIGHTS: Although he began his career as a foreign service officer and a documentary filmmaker, William Bayer found his niche as a best-selling crime novelist with the publication of *Tangier* in 1978. For Bayer crime fiction is a family tradition. His father, a lawyer, and his mother, a playwright, co-authored a series of mysteries under their joint pseudonym, Oliver Weld Bayer, in the 1940s. In a 1989 *Publishers Weekly* interview, Bayer told Mark Harris: "I remember going to a publicity luncheon for something they did called *Cleveland Murders.* . . . On a table in front of my parents were a gun, a skull, a bottle that said POISON, a dagger. It was so corny. But now I'm a second-generation crime writer."

Tangier was followed by *Punish Me with Kisses* and *Peregrine,* which won the prestigious Edgar Allan Poe Award for best novel in 1982. Bayer captured an even wider audience with his next novel, *Switch,* a psychological thriller that sold more than one million copies in paperback. The crime is a bizarre one: a murderer decapitates two women, one a French teacher in a private school and the other a prostitute, and switches the heads of the two victims. Bayer's detective/hero, Frank Janek, is a sensitive and insightful investigator, who repairs and plays accordions in his spare time. In the *Washington Post Book World* Carolyn Banks described Janek as a well-rounded character, and noted, "By the time Bayer is finished with Janek, we feel we'd recognize him on the street. We'd smile fondly at him, too."

Douglas Hill, who reviewed *Switch* for the Toronto *Globe and Mail,* praised Bayer for the good, solid police work in this novel. "As for the psychology of the book," wrote Hill, "it's not memorable, but it's not excessive either . . . . *Switch* is sensational all right, but it manages to be a decently competent thriller in spite of that." Similarly, Banks concluded that *Switch* satisfied her requirements for a psychological thriller: "I believed it while I was reading it, it frightened me a sufficient number of times, and it didn't haunt me after I'd snapped the covers closed. It's a clean, fast read."

Set in Jerusalem, Bayer's next thriller, *Pattern Crimes,* was described by Peter Gorner of the *Chicago Tribune* as "sort of an Israeli *Gorky Park.*" Set in Israel, where serial murders are known as pattern crimes, the book tells the tale of a diverse group of people who are murdered and mutilated in exactly the same way. Although *Pattern Crimes* conforms to the rules of the crime/mystery genre, many critics found that Bayer makes the conventions seem fresh because he writes so convincingly. Of David Bar-Lev, the detective who ultimately solves the case, Gorner said, "He is a most likable hero, this Israeli detective; tough, intense, savvy, obsessed and tormented; the most appealing fictional cop to come along in a long time." Marcel Berlins, writing in the London *Times,* praised *Pattern Crimes* for being "exceptionally well plotted" and for its "exciting action and first-class characterization."

For his next thriller, *Blind Side,* Bayer researched the literature on photography and even included eight of his own original photographs in the published novel. *Blind Side* is the story of a war-time photographer, Geoffrey

Barnett, who finds himself unable to photograph human faces until he becomes involved with a mysterious and duplicitous model. Harris, who interviewed Bayer for *Publishers Weekly,* explained the presence of the photos this way: "Interspersed throughout the text are eight photographs, taken by the author—not clues or essential plot points, but views of the unfolding drama through Barnett's eye and lens. Flavored with the brutality and cynicism of *film noir,* the novel draws as much of its inspiration from movies as from books."

BIOGRAPHICAL/CRITICAL SOURCES:

PERIODICALS

Chicago Tribune, July 15, 1987.
Chicago Tribune Book World, August 9, 1981; July 7, 1985.
Globe and Mail (Toronto), August 10, 1985.
Los Angeles Times, October 14, 1980.
Los Angeles Times Book Review, August 23, 1987; June 4, 1989.
New Yorker, October 29, 1971.
New York Times Book Review, August 19, 1984, p. 20; July 20, 1989; August 11, 1991, p. 25.
Publishers Weekly, June 9, 1989; March 30, 1990; May 17, 1991.
Times (London), December 30, 1987.
Times Literary Supplement, November 20-26, 1987.
Washington Post, July 21, 1989.
Washington Post Book World, October 5, 1980, p. 6; August 31, 1984; May 17, 1987.

*   *   *

BEALES, Peter   1936-

PERSONAL: Born July 22, 1936, in Norfolk, England; son of Walter (a farmer) and Evelyn (a nursemaid; maiden name, May) Beales; married Joan Elizabeth Allington (a nurse), September 23, 1961; children: Amanda, Richard. *Education:* Attended technical secondary school in Norwich, England.

ADDRESSES: Home—Swangey Cottage, Hargham, Norwich, Norfolk, England. *Office*—Peter Beales Roses, London Rd., Attleborough, Norfolk NR17 1AY, England.

CAREER: E. B. Legrice Roses, North Walsham, England, horticultural apprentice, 1953-55; T. Hilling & Co. Ltd., Chobham, England, manager of nursery department, 1959-63; Peter Beales Roses, Attleborough, England, owner, 1964—. International lecturer on roses. *Military service:* British Army, bombardier in Royal Artillery, 1957-59.

MEMBER: Royal Horticultural Society, Royal National Rose Society, National Farmers Union, Rotary International, Bermuda Rose Society (honorary member), Horticultural Trades Association, Institute of Horticulture, Worshipful Company of Gardeners.

AWARDS, HONORS: Silver Medal from International Rose Trials, Genoa, Italy, 1986, for developing the rose "Anna Pavlova"; Lester E. Harrol Award, Californian Heritage Rose Society, 1986, for outstanding contribution to heritage roses; named Freeman of the City of London.

WRITINGS:

Georgian and Regency Roses, Jarrolds (London), 1977.
Early Victorian Roses, Jarrolds, 1977.
Late Victorian Roses, Jarrolds, 1978.
Edwardian Roses, Jarrolds, 1978.
Classic Roses, Collins (London), 1985.
Twentieth Century Roses, Collins, 1989.
Roses, Henry Holt (New York City), 1991.

Presenter of video, *A Celebration of Old Roses,* directed by Vivian Russell, 1993.

WORK IN PROGRESS: A book on rose gardens of the world, written in collaboration with Vivian Russell, publication by Little, Brown (Boston) expected in 1996.

SIDELIGHTS: Peter Beales is responsible for at least twenty new varieties of roses, including the award-winning "Anna Pavlova." He has lectured all over the world, most recently in America. Beales once told *CA:* "The one and only rose in my grandfather's garden was an ancient bush which, each year as I grew up, flaunted her sweetly perfumed, soft pink flowers and drew me to admire her. This subconscious, youthful flirtation surely led to my lifelong career with her kind. My first love, 'Maiden's Blush,' has to be my favorite rose; but, being fickle, I have shared her with many favorites since.

The author more recently added: "Although, in her more prickly moods, the rose has forced me to live on the bread line, my long love affair with her has taught me to respect and enjoy Mother Nature, to appreciate things beautiful, and has helped me to broaden my horizons and enlarge my circle of friends. In return, I try to ensure that the more lovely of her forebears do not perish and, when possible, are resurrected and preserved. On my travels and through my writings I try to extol her virtues and criticize her faults, but most of all I try to share my pleasure in roses with others."

*   *   *

BECERRA, Rosina M.   1939-

PERSONAL: Born March 6, 1939, in San Diego, CA; daughter of Ray and Ruth (a homemaker; maiden name,

Albanez) Becerra. *Education:* San Diego State College (now University), B.A., 1961, M.S.W., 1971; Brandeis University, Ph.D., 1975; Pepperdine University, M.B.A., 1981.

ADDRESSES: Home—611 Granada St., Glendale, CA 91205. *Office*—School of Public Policy and Social Research, Department of Social Welfare, University of California, 405 Hilgard Ave., Los Angeles, CA 90024.

CAREER: San Diego State College (now State University), San Diego, CA, lecturer in mathematics, 1969; Boston University, Boston, MA, adjunct assistant professor of social work, 1973-74; Brandeis University, Waltham, MA, lecturer in social work, 1974-75; University of California, Los Angeles, acting associate professor, beginning in 1975, became professor of social welfare, associate dean of School of Social Welfare, 1986, dean of School of Social Welfare, 1990. Member of California Committee for the Protection of Human Subjects, 1978-80; member of Review Panel on Sexual Assault and Criminal Violence, National Institute of Mental Health, 1982-85; chairperson of Regional Citizens' Advisory Committee of California Youth Authority, 1986—; member of California State Commission on Juvenile Justice, Crime, and Delinquency, 1986—. Adviser to director of International Institute of Los Angeles, 1979-81; member of advisory board of Venice Health Clinic, Venice, CA, 1986—. Worked as a child therapist, drug counselor, psychiatric social worker, and probation officer for San Diego County Probation Department; U.S. Peace Corps volunteer worker in Brazil; consultant to Abt Associates, Technical Systems Institute, and Organization for Technical Innovation.

MEMBER: Council of Social Work Education (member of board, 1983-84), National Association of Social Workers.

AWARDS, HONORS: Grants from Office of Child Development, 1977-79, Administration on Aging, 1980-81, Veterans Administration, 1980-82, California Office of Child Abuse Prevention, 1981-83, U.S. Department of Defense, 1982-83, Office of Adolescent Life, 1982-85, and Office of Adolescent Pregnancy Programs, 1985-88; Chicano Faculty Award from Ford Foundation's Hispanic Council of Higher Education, 1980; award from *Choice* for *The Hispanic Elderly: A Research Guide.*

WRITINGS:

(With Jeanne M. Giovannoni) *Defining Child Abuse,* Free Press (New York City), 1979.
(Editor with Marvin Karno and Javier I. Escobar, and contributor) *Mental Health and Hispanic Americans: Clinical Perspectives,* Grune (New York City), 1982.

(With Milton Greenblatt) *Hispanic Veterans Seek Health Care,* University Press of America (Lanham, MD), 1983.
(With David Shaw) *The Hispanic Elderly: A Research Guide,* University Press of America, 1983.
(Contributor) R. L. McNeeley and John Colon, editors, *Aging in Minority Groups,* Sage Publications (Beverly Hills, CA), 1983.
(Contributor) Richard Hough and others, editors, *Psychiatric Epidemiology and Prevention: The Possibilities,* Neuropsychiatric Institute, University of California, Los Angeles, 1985.
(With Alfreda P. Iglehart) *Social Services and Ethnic Organizations,* Allyn & Bacon (Newton, MA), 1994.

Contributor to *Encyclopedia of Social Work, Ethnicity and Aging,* and *Ethnic Families in America.* Also contributor of articles and reviews to various social work journals. Member of editorial boards of *Evaluation Review,* 1978-81, *Social Work,* 1980-82, *Urban and Social Change Review,* 1982—, *Encyclopedia of Social Work,* 1983-86, and *Administration and Social Work,* 1986—.

BIOGRAPHICAL/CRITICAL SOURCES:

PERIODICALS

Annals of the American Academy of Political and Social Science, May, 1980.
New York Times Book Review, January 27, 1980.

*   *   *

BELL, Roger 1947-

PERSONAL: Born November 19, 1947, in West Wyalong, New South Wales, Australia; son of Norman (a farmer) and Rita (Wilder) Bell; married Jan Marie Provis (a research scientist), September 17, 1978; children: Emily Catherine, Nicholas Matthew. *Education:* University of New South Wales, B.A. (with honors), 1969; University of Sydney, M.A. (with honors), 1971, Ph.D., 1974.

ADDRESSES: Home—7 Gardyne St., Bronte, Sydney, New South Wales 2024, Australia. *Office*—Department of History, University of New South Wales, Kensington, New South Wales 2033, Australia.

CAREER: Sydney Technical College, Sydney, New South Wales, history teacher, 1974; University of New South Wales, Sydney, lecturer, 1975-80, senior lecturer, 1980-85, associate professor, 1985-94, professor of history, 1994—.

MEMBER: Amnesty International (vice president of Australian section, 1981-82; president of New South Wales branch, 1984-86), Organization of American Historians, American Historical Association, Australian and New

Zealand American Studies Association (treasurer, 1980-84; president, 1994—).

AWARDS, HONORS: Rotary graduate scholarship for University of Hawaii, 1969-70; Louis Knott Koontz Award from American Historical Association west coast branch, 1982-83, for article "Testing the Open Door Thesis in Australia, 1941-1945"; USIS study tour in the United States, 1989.

WRITINGS:

Unequal Allies: Australian-American Relations and the Pacific War, Melbourne University Press, 1977.
(Editor with Ian J. Bickerton) *American Studies: New Essays from Australia and New Zealand,* Australian and New Zealand American Studies Association, 1981.
Last among Equals: Hawaiian Statehood and American Politics, University of Hawaii Press (Honolulu, HI) 1984.
Multicultural Societies: A Comparative Reader, Sable, 1987.
(With Ralph Hall) *Impacts: Contemporary Issues and Global Problems,* Jacaranda Press, 1991.
(With Philip Bell) *Implicated: The United States in Australia,* Oxford University Press (New York City), 1993.

WORK IN PROGRESS: Asia's Transformation and the Australian-American Relationship; with Bell, *Documentary Reality: History, Ethnography and Film.*

SIDELIGHTS: In *Last among Equals: Hawaiian Statehood and American Politics,* Roger Bell looks at the social, economic, and political concerns attending Hawaii's transition to statehood. While fear of communism and economic self-interest stirred some congressional antistatehood sentiments, it was Hawaii's multiracial and cultural distinctiveness, the author maintains, that provided the major impediment to full statehood support from the legislature. Deeming Bell's thesis "generally convincing" in a critique for the *American Historical Review,* Gary W. Reichard determined: "[Bell's] sources provide the basis for a well-informed and interesting discussion of the interplay of territorial or state and national politics, something rarely achieved in a state history. Although the book contains more exhaustive detail than any but a specialist on Hawaii will want, it nevertheless transcends parochialism by tying the question of Hawaiian statehood to issues of major national importance."

Bell once told *CA:* "My principal research interests are American expansion in the Pacific—with special reference to Australia—and the comparative study of multicultural or mixed societies in the Pacific region. In addition, I take a keen academic and personal interest in the related subjects of political violence and human rights in the contemporary world. This is reflected in my work for Amnesty International."

BIOGRAPHICAL/CRITICAL SOURCES:

PERIODICALS

American Historical Review, April, 1985.

*   *   *

BELL, Rudolph M(ark) 1942-

PERSONAL: Born November 5, 1942, in New York, NY; son of Rudolph Albert (in business) and Amy (Thienpont) Bell; married Laura Tomici, December 5, 1964; children: Tara. *Education:* Queens College of the City University of New York, B.A., 1963; City University of New York, Ph.D., 1969.

ADDRESSES: Office—Department of History, Rutgers University, New Brunswick, NJ 08903.

CAREER: Metropolitan Life Insurance Co., New York City, systems analyst, 1963-68; Rutgers University, New Brunswick, NJ, instructor, 1968-69, assistant professor, 1969-73, associate professor, 1973-80, professor of history, 1980—. Fulbright-Hays lecturer in American history at University of Genoa, 1971-72.

MEMBER: American Historical Association, Organization of American Historians.

WRITINGS:

Party and Faction in American Politics: The U.S. House of Representatives, 1789-1801, Greenwood Press (Westport, CT), 1973.
Fate and Honor, Family and Village: Demographic and Cultural Change in Rural Italy Since 1800, University of Chicago Press, 1979.
(With Donald Weinstein) *Saints and Society: The Two Worlds of Western Christendom, 1000-1700,* University of Chicago Press, 1982.
Holy Anorexia, University of Chicago Press, 1985.

Contributor to journals.

SIDELIGHTS: In *Party and Faction in American Politics: The U.S. House of Representatives, 1789-1801,* historian Rudolph M. Bell presents a revisionist interpretation of early congressional politics. Bell performs a quantitative analysis on the voting patterns of the first six years in the House of Representatives. He concludes that until the mid-1790s, members of Congress voted in blocs based on issues such as the proper limits of federal power, and only after that period did a tendency to vote along party lines emerge. According to R. R. Beeman in *Choice,* this "highly controversial" book is "the first full-scale quantitative analysis of the first American party system."

In his next work, Bell refutes the stereotype of the rural Italian peasantry as a passive and backward class. *Fate and Honor, Family and Village: Demographic and Cultural Change in Rural Italy Since 1800* is a sociocultural analysis of four Italian villages based on nearly two centuries of records in parish and communal archives. Drawing from these records, Bell shows that the Italian peasant family structure "displays remarkable social dynamics in its search for survival and stability," in the words of a reviewer for *Choice*. A *Library Journal* reviewer comments that although Bell's sample of data is too small to reap wide generalizations, the book provides "a useful body of data and some interesting analyses."

While cowriting *Saints and Society: The Two Worlds of Western Christendom, 1000-1700* with Donald Weinstein, an analysis of the Western definition of sainthood, Bell became interested in a possible connection between the self-starvation practiced by several Roman Catholic religious figures in the Middle Ages and the present-day eating disorder anorexia nervosa. The disorder is now considered a psychological condition which largely afflicts middle-class adolescent girls. In his study *Holy Anorexia,* Bell examines the lives of a dozen medieval Italian women whose demonstrations of piety were marked by starving themselves to death, or nearly to death.

John Boswell summarizes Bell's thesis in his review for *New Republic:* Bell argues that the practices of these medieval women and the eating disorder anorexia nervosa are "essentially the same: the phenomenon that was interpreted as a mark of exemplary holiness in late medieval and early modern Europe was simply reclassified in the 19th century as a medical condition." While Boswell finds Bell's accounts of these women's lives fascinating and well-researched, he takes issue with the equation of medieval and modern modes of starvation. "Modern definitions of anorexia are so diffuse and vague that almost any peculiarly abstemious eating pattern could be given the name. . . . But even if one applies a broad definition, the differences often outweigh the similarities. How many modern anorexics . . . flog themselves three times a day?" Boswell asks.

Mary Lassance Parthun, writing for *Globe and Mail,* praises *Holy Anorexia* as "a significant contribution to revisionist history," and calls Bell "particularly skilful in describing behavior within its time and culture, which would be bizarre by today's norms, without reducing it to the pathological." Parthun highlights Bell's point that as the "holy anorexics" broke out of the accepted role for medieval women, they paved the way for another generation of religious women to make advances in early social work, in health care and in education. In conclusions, Parthun infers that present-day anorexics may not simply be "victims of a materialist, sexist culture" but could in fact be "martyrs to a social breakthrough."

BIOGRAPHICAL/CRITICAL SOURCES:

PERIODICALS

Choice, June, 1974; July/August, 1980.
Globe and Mail, February 8, 1986, p. C8.
Library Journal, January 15, 1980.
Los Angeles Times Book Review, January 19, 1986, p. 2.
New Republic, August 24, 1987, p. 36-8.
New Statesman, March 21, 1986, p. 27.
New York Review of Books, January 30, 1986, p. 3.
Observer (London), February 9, 1986, p. 27.
Times Literary Supplement, April 25, 1986, p. 438.*

*   *   *

BELSKY, Dick 1945-

PERSONAL: Born May 9, 1945, in Cleveland, OH; son of Gilbert Louis and Florence (Levis) Belsky; married Laura Morgan (a computer systems analyst). *Education:* Ohio University, B.S., 1967. *Religion:* Protestant.

ADDRESSES: Home—150 East 18th St., Apt. 6G, New York, NY 10003. *Office*—STAR Magazine, 660 White Plains Rd., Tarrytown, NY 10591. *Agent*—Meg Ruley, Jane Rotrosen Agency, 318 East 51st St., New York, NY 10022.

CAREER: New York Post, New York City, reporter, 1970-71, rewriter, 1971-75, assistant city editor, 1975-76, city editor, 1976-88, metropolitan editor, 1988-89; *STAR Magazine,* Tarrytown, NY, news editor, 1990—. *Military service:* U.S. Army, intelligence analyst, 1968-70; served in Vietnam.

MEMBER: Mystery Writers of America.

WRITINGS:

MYSTERY NOVELS

One for the Money, Academy Chicago (Chicago), 1985.
South Street Confidential, St. Martin's (New York City), 1989, published as *Broadcast Clues,* Berkley (New York City), 1993.
Live from New York, Berkley, 1993.
The Mourning Show, Berkley, 1994.
Summertime News, Berkley, 1995.

JUVENILE NONFICTION

Tom Seaver: Baseball Superstar, McKay (New York City), 1977.
The Juice: The O.J. Simpson Story, McKay, 1977.

Also contributor of stories to *Alfred Hitchcock's Mystery Magazine* and *Gallery,* and of nonfiction to *Writer's Digest.*

SIDELIGHTS: Dick Belsky told *CA:* "I'm the author of the Jenny McKay series, published by Berkley. Jenny is a forty-year-old TV reporter who solves murders in New York City. She was described in a review as a 'streetwise version of TV's Murphy Brown.' Basically, she combines a lot of the qualities of some of the terrific female reporters I've worked with in New York journalism—bright, aggressive and dogged in her pursuit of a big story. She's also a lot of fun. I like her. I'm now working on the fifth of the series. I also have a full-time job as news editor of *STAR Magazine,* and I spent a lot of years before that as city editor of the *New York Post.* I think this helps me write about the world of journalism more realistically. It's also good for ideas—since real-life news is often even stranger than fiction."

*   *   *

BENCE-JONES, Mark   1930-

PERSONAL: Born May 29, 1930, in London, England; son of Philip (an engineer and landowner) and Victoria May (Thomas) Bence-Jones; married Gillian Enid Pretyman (a poet), 1965; children: one son, two daughters. *Education:* Attended Pembroke College, Cambridge, 1949-52; Royal Agricultural College, B.A., 1952, M.R.A.C., 1954, M.A., 1958. *Politics:* Conservative. *Religion:* Roman Catholic.

ADDRESSES: Home—Glenville Park, County Cork, Ireland. *Agent*—Anthony Sheil Associates Ltd., 2-3 Morwell St., London WC1B 3AR, England.

CAREER: Writer; also engaged in estate management in Ireland.

MEMBER: Irish Georgian Society, Latin Mass Society, Cork Preservation Society, Ulster Architectural Heritage Society, Irish Tree Society, Kildare Street Club, University Club, Brooks's Club, Royal Irish Automobile Club.

AWARDS, HONORS: Sovereign Military Order of Malta, Knight of Honour and Devotion, 1976, and Knight of Obedience, 1983; Knight of Justice, Constantinian Order of St. George, 1984; Irish Association, Chancellor, 1985-88, and Vice-President, 1988-94.

WRITINGS:

NOVELS

All a Nonsense, P. Davies (London), 1957.
Paradise Escaped, P. Davies, 1958.
Nothing in the City, Sidgwick & Jackson (London), 1965.

NONFICTION

The Remarkable Irish, McKay (New York City), 1966.
Palaces of the Raj, Allen & Unwin (London), 1973.
(Contributor) *Burke's Guide to the Royal Family,* Burke's Peerage (London), 1973.
Clive of India, Constable (London), 1974.
The Cavaliers, Constable, 1976.
(Consulting editor) *Burke's Irish Family Records,* Burke's Peerage, 1976.
(Contributor) *Burke's Royal Families of the World,* Burke's Peerage, Volume 1, 1977, Volume 2, 1980.
Burke's Guide to the Country Houses of Ireland, Burke's Peerage, 1978, revised edition, 1980.
(With Hugh Montgomery-Massingberd) *The British Aristocracy,* Constable, 1979.
The Viceroys of India, Constable, 1982.
Great English Homes: Ancestral Homes of England and Wales and the People Who Lived in Them, British Heritage Press (New York City), 1984, published in England as *Ancestral Houses,* Weidenfeld and Nicolson (London), 1984.
Twilight of the Ascendancy, Constable, 1987.
Guide to Irish Country Houses, Constable, 1988, revised edition, 1990.
The Catholic Families, Constable, 1991.

OTHER

Author of introductions for *Burke's Landed Gentry of Ireland,* 1958; *Burke's Landed Gentry of Great Britain,* Volume 1, 1965, Volume 2, 1969, Volume 3, 1972; and *Burke's Peerage,* 1970. Also contributor of satirical articles and articles on art, architecture, and travel to numerous magazines and newspapers, including *Holiday, Vogue, Country Life, Tatler, Sunday Graphic, Nottingham Observer,* and *Irish Times.*

SIDELIGHTS: Mark Bence-Jones told *CA:* "I am a strong upholder of an ordered and hierarchal society. I love the great European civilization which we have inherited from the past—particularly from Renaissance Italy—and which is now threatened from all sides. All this, I think, is reflected in my writings; not only in the content, but also in the style. I endeavour to write English as it should be written, with a proper regard [for] the sound and rhythm of words and sentences. In former times, most educated people had a natural gift for writing good English; now, in the vast majority of cases, good English can only be written by dint of extremely hard work. The amount of work entailed in writing good English is something which all too many contemporaries do not seem to realise; they appear to imagine that anyone from the English-speaking world who is well-educated and has something to write about can write passable English, which is just not true."

BIOGRAPHICAL/CRITICAL SOURCES:

PERIODICALS

Globe and Mail (Toronto), August 15, 1987.
Stet (Cork), summer, 1992.
Sunday Telegraph (London), July 19, 1992.
Times (London), February 5, 1987.
Times Literary Supplement, March 18, 1983; September 11, 1987; March 24, 1989.

*   *   *

BENDICK, Jeanne 1919-

PERSONAL: Born February 25, 1919, in New York, NY; daughter of Louis Xerxes (an inventor) and Amelia (Hess) Garfunkel; married Robert Louis Bendick (a television and film producer and director), November 24, 1940; children: Robert Louis, Jr., Karen Watson Holton. *Education:* Parsons School of Design, B.A., 1939. *Avocational interests:* Sailing, beachcombing, science mysteries, cooking, Inuit art, and "helping elementary school teachers to conquer their fear of teaching science."

ADDRESSES: Home—19 Sea View, Guilford, CT 06437.

CAREER: Author and illustrator, 1944—. Illustrator for *Jack and Jill* and fabric designer in 1930s. Volunteer in American Women's Voluntary Services (AWVS) during World War II. Trustee, Rye Free Reading Room, New York, 1960s. American Red Cross Bloodmobile aide, Guilford, CT, 1990s.

MEMBER: Authors Guild, Authors League of America, American Library Association, Writers Guild, National Science Teachers Association.

AWARDS, HONORS: Spring Book Festival award, 1946, for *Let's Find Out: A Picture Science Book,* and 1953, for *The First Book of Space Travel;* Boy's Club Junior Book Award, 1949, for *How Much and How Many: The Story of Weights and Measures;* New York Academy of Sciences Children's Science Honor Book Awards, 1974, for *Discovering Cycles;* Eva L. Gordon Award, American Nature Society, 1975.

WRITINGS:

CHILDREN'S FICTION; AUTHOR AND ILLUSTRATOR

The Good Knight Ghost, F. Watts (New York City), 1956.
The Blonk from beneath the Sea, F. Watts, 1958.

CHILDREN'S NONFICTION; AUTHOR AND ILLUSTRATOR EXCEPT WHERE NOTED

Electronics for Boys and Girls, McGraw (New York City), 1944, published as *Electronics for Young People,* 1947, 5th edition with R. J. Lefkowitz, McGraw, 1972.

(With husband, Robert Bendick) *Making the Movies,* McGraw, 1945, revised as *Filming Works Like This,* McGraw, 1970.
How Much and How Many: The Story of Weights and Measures, McGraw, 1947, revised edition, 1960, revised edition, F. Watts, 1989.
(With R. Bendick) *Television Works Like This,* McGraw, 1948, revised edition, 1965.
All Around You: A First Look at the World, McGraw, 1950.
The First Book of Space Travel, F. Watts, 1953, revised edition published as *Space Travel,* 1969.
(With Barbara Berk) *The First Book of Costume and Makeup,* F. Watts, 1953.
The First Book of Supermarkets, F. Watts, 1954.
(With Berk) *How to Have a Show,* F. Watts, 1954.
The First Book of Automobiles, F. Watts, revised edition, 1955, reprinted as *Automobiles,* 1984.
*What Could You
See?: Adventures in Looking,* McGraw, 1957.
The First Book of Ships, F. Watts, 1958.
(With children, Candy Bendick and Robert Bendick, Jr.) *Have a Happy Measle, A Merry Mumps and a Cheery Chickenpox,* McGraw, 1958.
Lightning, Rand McNally (Chicago), 1961.
(With Berk) *The First Book of How to Fix It,* F. Watts, 1961.
(With Marcia Levin) *Take a Number,* McGraw, 1961.
Archimedes and the Door of Science, F. Watts, 1962.
(With M. Levin) *Take Shapes, Lines, and Letters: New Horizons in Mathematics,* McGraw, 1962.
(With Leonard Simon) *The Day the Numbers Disappeared,* McGraw, 1963.
(With Levin) *Pushups and Pinups: Diet, Exercise, and Grooming for Young Teens,* McGraw, 1963.
Sea So Big, Ship So Small, Rand McNally, 1963.
The First Book of Time, F. Watts, 1963.
A Fresh Look at Night, F. Watts, 1963.
The First Book of Fishes, F. Watts, 1964.
The Wind, Rand McNally, 1964.
(With Levin) *Illustrated Mathematics Dictionary,* McGraw, 1965, revised edition published as *Mathematics Illustrated Dictionary: Facts, Figures, and People,* F. Watts, 1989.
The Shape of the Earth, Rand McNally, 1965.
(With Levin) *New Mathematics Practice Workbooks: Sets and Addition; Sets and Subtraction; Sets and Multiplication; Sets and Division,* Grosset, 1965.
(With Marian Warren) *What to Do: Everyday Guides for Everyone,* McGraw, 1967.
The Emergency Book, Rand McNally, 1967.
Shapes, F. Watts, 1967.
Space and Time, F. Watts, 1968.
The Human Senses, F. Watts, 1968.

Living Things, F. Watts, 1969.

What Can't I?, McGraw, 1969.

A Place to Live: A Study of Ecology, Parents Magazine Press (New York City), 1970.

How to Make a Cloud, Parents Magazine Press, 1971.

Names, Sets, and Numbers, F. Watts, 1971.

Measuring, F. Watts, 1971.

Adaptation, F. Watts, 1971.

What Made You You?, McGraw, 1971.

Motion and Gravity, F. Watts, 1971.

Observation, F. Watts, 1972.

Why Things Work: A Book about Energy, illustrated by daughter, Karen Bendick Watson, Parents Magazine Press, 1972.

The Future Explorers' Club Meets Here, illustrated by Joan Paley, Ginn (Aylesbury), 1973.

Why Things Change: The Story of Evolution, illustrated by Watson, Parents Magazine Press, 1973.

(With R. Bendick) *The Consumer's Catalog of Economy and Ecology,* illustrated by Watson, McGraw, 1974.

Heat and Temperature, F. Watts, 1974.

Solids, Liquids, and Gases, F. Watts, 1974.

Ecology, F. Watts, 1974.

Ginn Science Program, three volumes, Ginn, 1975.

How Heredity Works: Why Living Things Are as They Are, Parents Magazine Press, 1975.

The First Book of Airplanes, F. Watts, 1976, reprinted as *Airplanes,* 1982.

(With R. Bendick) *Finding Out about Jobs: TV Reporting,* Parents Magazine Press, 1976.

The Mystery of the Loch Ness Monster, McGraw, 1976.

How Animals Behave, Parents Magazine Press, 1976.

Exploring an Ocean Tide Pool, Garrard (Easton, MD), 1976, revised version published with illustrations by Todd Telander, Henry Holt (New York City).

The Big Strawberry Book of Astronomy, illustrated by Sal Murdocca, Strawberry Books/McGraw, 1979.

Putting the Sun to Work, Garrard, 1980.

The Big Strawberry Book of the Earth: Our Ever-Changing Planet, illustrated by Luppold Junkins, Strawberry Books/McGraw, 1980.

Superpeople: Who Will They Be?, McGraw, 1980.

Elementary Science, Volume 4, Ginn, 1980.

Artificial Satellites, F. Watts, 1983.

Space Travel, F. Watts, 1983.

Scare a Ghost! Tame a Monster!, Westminster (Philadelphia, PA), 1983.

Egyptian Tombs, F. Watts, 1987.

Tombs of the Ancient Americas, F. Watts, 1993.

Caves, Henry Holt, 1995.

"EARLYBIRD ASTRONOMY" SERIES

Artificial Satellites: Helpers in Space, illustrated by Mike Roffe, Millbrook (Brookfield, CT), 1991.

Comets and Meteors: Visitors from Space, illustrated by Roffe, Millbrook, 1991.

Moons and Rings: Companions to the Planets, illustrated by Roffe, Millbrook, 1991.

The Planets: Neighbors in Space, illustrated by Roffe, Millbrook, 1991.

The Stars: Lights in the Night Sky, illustrated by Chris Forsey, Millbrook, 1991.

The Sun: Our Very Own Star, illustrated by Roffe, Millbrook, 1991.

The Universe: Think Big!, illustrated by Roffe and Lynne Willey, Millbrook, 1991.

"INVENTING" SERIES; ILLUSTRATED BY SAL MURDOCCA

Eureka! It's an Airplane!, Millbrook, 1992.

Eureka! It's an Automobile!, Millbrook, 1992.

Eureka! It's a Telephone!, Millbrook, 1993.

(With R. Bendick) *Eureka! It's Television!,* Millbrook, 1993.

ILLUSTRATOR

Modeling for Money, by Carol Lynn, Greenberg (Sykesville, MD), 1937; *Let's Find Out: A Picture Science Book,* by Herman and Nina Schneider, Scott, 1946; *Everyday Machines and How They Work,* by H. Schneider, McGraw, 1950; *Our Wonderful Eyes,* by John Perry, McGraw, 1955; *The Storybook of Science,* Rand McNally, 1959; *Discovering Cycles,* by Glenn O. Blough, McGraw, 1973; *Saving Electricity,* by Sam and Beryl Epstein, Garrard, 1977; and numerous other books.

OTHER

Author of filmstrips, including *The Seasons* for the Society for Visual Education, and *You and Me and Our World, Monsters and Other Science Mysteries,* and *Dreams and Other Science Mysteries,* all for Miller-Brody. Author of multimedia educational program "Starting Points" for Ginn. Story editor and script writer of television programs for the National Broadcasting Co., Inc. (NBC-TV), *The First Look,* 1965-66, and *Giant Step,* 1968, plus a segment for *20/20* for the American Broadcasting Co., Inc. (ABC-TV) entitled "Evolution/Creation"; associate producer of documentary for public television, *Fight for Food.* Contributor to *Britannica Junior Encyclopaedia, Book of Knowledge,* and other publications.

WORK IN PROGRESS: Markets (tentative title), F. Watts, 1996.

SIDELIGHTS: Jeanne Bendick once told *CA:* "One of the most exciting things in the world to me is starting a book. The things I find out as I research new ideas and discoveries! Then, it's like putting together a complicated puzzle. . . . How can I involve readers so they will ask questions themselves, and try to answer them? And, most important to me, how can I get them to see that science—like life itself—is open-ended and exciting? Who knows what will happen next to change everything? I can hardly wait, myself, for the next episode."

In the decades following the end of World War II, the United States witnessed an ever-growing list of scientific and technological marvels, from the atomic bomb to manned space flight. Through it all, as both author and illustrator, Bendick has been prominent in documenting and explaining these developments to young readers. As one of the nation's foremost writers about science, she is the author of a long list of titles that have introduced the wonders of science to two generations of children.

Bendick told *Something About the Author Autobiography Series:* "I am not, by training, a scientist. Maybe what I am is a translator. I enjoy taking a complex science concept, breaking it down into components simple enough for *me* to understand, and then writing it that way for young people." She began her career when she was unable to find a simple book about electronics for young readers. To fill the breach, she wrote *Electronics for Boys and Girls,* which has been translated into twenty languages and gone through six editions. She went on to explain her motives in writing for young people: "Everything they learn about the world is another piece they can fit into a giant puzzle. Where does each piece fit to make the picture clearer? One part of the job I set for myself is to make those young readers see that everything is connected to everything—that science isn't something apart. . . . Science, like life, is open-ended and nobody knows all the answers." These motives have sustained Bendick through dozens of books. Many of those books, especially those written during the 1940s and 1950s, strive to explain technological marvels such as the automobile. Others focus on mathematics, trying to make the abstract, logical underpinnings of math more accessible for young readers. More recently, her books have emphasized astronomy and outer space: The "Earlybird" series she wrote for Millbrook Press is one noteworthy example. Another theme that has informed much of Bendick's recent work is ecology—again as a way of stressing the interconnectedness of the world.

Critical reaction to Bendick's books has been largely favorable with an occasional dissenting voice. In *Appraisal: Science Books for Young People,* for instance, Ethanne Smith found *Solids, Liquids, and Gases* "confusing." Likewise, in *School Library Journal,* Virginia Reese declared *How Heredity Works: Why Living Things Are as They Are* "simplistic and confusing." More typical, however, are those reviewers who praise Bendick for her ability to present complex scientific information with vigor and clarity. About *Making the Movies,* Margaret C. Scoggin in *Library Journal* noted that although the book presented information simply, it is "amazingly well-organized and informa-

tive." In the *New York Herald Tribune Weekly Book Review,* Louise S. Bechtel joins many other critics in praising Bendick's " 'easy' but never patronizing" writing style. The reviewer of *Lightning* in *Virginia Kirkus' Service* similarly expressed a widely held view in praising the author's "talent for reducing the complicated and technical to the simple and lucid." In regards to her illustrations, May Lamberton Becker in a *New York Herald Tribune Weekly Book Review* summary of *How Much and How Many: The Story of Weights and Measures,* said that "Bendick's art in lending vivacity to facts will keep [children] fascinated" and commented that her pictures are "funny without being flippant."

Bendick talked about her illustrations in *Science and Children:* "I am certainly not the best artist in the world. . . . But I get a lot of letters from children saying that they like my pictures because that's the way *they* would draw things. Children do see things in a different way from adults. Maybe that's because they look for different things. I like the way they look and what they see. I've tried to keep looking at the world their way."

BIOGRAPHICAL/CRITICAL SOURCES:

BOOKS

Books for Children, 1960-65, American Library Association, 1966.

The Children's Bookshelf, Child Study Association of America/Bantam, 1965. *Children's Literature Review,* Volume 5, Gale, 1983.

Fisher, Margery, *Matters of Fact: Aspects of Non-Fiction for Children,* Harper, 1972.

Good Books for Children, edited by Mary K. Eakin, Phoenix, 1966.

Hopkins, Lee Bennett, *Books Are by People,* Citation Press, 1969.

Illustrators of Children's Books: 1957-1966, Horn Book, 1968.

Larrick, Nancy, *A Teacher's Guide to Children's Books,* Merrill, 1966.

Larrick, Nancy, *A Parent's Guide to Children's Reading,* 3rd edition, Doubleday, 1969.

Major Authors and Illustrators for Children and Young Adults, Gale, 1991.

More Junior Authors, H. W. Wilson, 1963.

Something about the Author, Volume 68, Gale, 1992.

Something about the Author Autobiography Series, Volume 4, Gale, 1987, pp. 53-74.

Sutherland, Zena, *The Best in Children's Books,* University of Chicago Press, 1973.

Sutherland, Zena, Diane L. Monson, and May Hill Arbuthnot, *Children and Books,* 6th edition, Scott, Foresman, 1981.

PERIODICALS

Appraisal: Science Books for Young People, spring, 1972; fall, 1972; spring, 1980; winter, 1981.

Atlantic, December, 1947.

Booklist, June 15, 1979.

Children's Book Review, February, 1971.

Grade Teacher, March, 1972.

Instructor, August, 1971.

Library Journal, December 1, 1945, p. 1139.

New Statesman, November 6, 1970.

New York Herald Tribune Weekly Book Review, November 23, 1947, p. 8; May 17, 1953, p. 7.

New York Times Book Review, November 11, 1945; November 8, 1970; May 7, 1972.

Saturday Review, March 25, 1972.

School Librarian and School Library Review, July, 1964.

School Library Journal, September, 1975.

Science and Children, April, 1973, pp. 20-21.

Science Books, September, 1973; March, 1974; March, 1975; December, 1976; March, 1977; May, 1977.

Science Books and Films, March-April, 1981.

Spectator, March, 1971.

Teacher, March, 1978.

Virginia Kirkus' Service, January 1, 1961, p. 12.

*   *   *

BENTLEY, Judith (McBride) 1945-

PERSONAL: Born April 8, 1945, in Indianapolis, IN; daughter of Robert Edward (a college president) and Luella (Hart) McBride; married Allen Bentley (an attorney), June 6, 1970; children: Anne, Peter. *Education:* Oberlin College, B.A., 1967; New York University, M.A. (history of American civilization), 1969, M.A. (educational psychology), 1975. *Religion:* Protestant.

ADDRESSES: Home and office—4747 132nd Ave. S.E., Bellevue, WA 98006.

CAREER: Saturday Review, New York City, editorial assistant, 1970-71, assistant editor, 1972; Newsweek Books, New York City, copy editor, 1973-74; New York City Community College, Brooklyn, NY, adjunct instructor in reading skills, 1975-77; Dalton School, New York City, preceptor, 1977-79; writer and editor, 1979—; South Seattle Community College, instructor in English and history, 1982—.

MEMBER: Pacific Northwest Writers Conference, Hedgebrook Alumni Writers Group.

WRITINGS:

FOR YOUNG PEOPLE

State Government, F. Watts (New York City), 1978.

The National Health Care Controversy, F. Watts, 1981.

American Immigration Today: Pressures, Problems, Policies, Messner (New York City), 1981.

Busing: The Continuing Controversy, F. Watts, 1982.

Justice O'Connor, Messner, 1983.

The Nuclear Freeze Movement, F. Watts, 1984.

Refugees Search for a Haven, Messner, 1986.

Archbishop Desmond Tutu, Enslow (Hillside, NJ), 1988.

Harriet Tubman, F. Watts, 1990.

Fidel Castro of Cuba, Messner, 1991.

Speakers of the House, F. Watts, 1994.

OTHER

Contributor to magazines, including *Family Health* and *Back-Packer.*

WORK IN PROGRESS: Esteemed Friends, for Cobblehill Books; editing and writing two books in a six-book series called "Settling the West," to be published by Henry Holt: *Brides, Midwives, and Widows,* and *Explorers, Trappers, and Guides.*

SIDELIGHTS: Judith Bentley once told *CA:* "When I was growing up, I loved to read those orange, hardcover historical biographies with silhouette illustrations published by Bobbs-Merrill in my hometown of Indianapolis. I now realize that many of them were as much fiction as fact, with likely thoughts and feelings put into the heads and hearts of the heroes and heroines. Yet they were lively, and they recreated history in a way my textbooks did not.

"I also realize now that some people were missing in books for children and young adults. Daniel Boone and Clara Barton were fine subjects; their rough edges were sanded, and their radical ideas didn't sound so radical a hundred years later, but there were others—like Jeannette Rankin, Sojourner Truth, and William Still—whose lives were just as heroic.

"My goal is to write the kind of biographies that bring historical and contemporary leaders to life for young people and to tell their stories with the rough edges intact and the conflicts of history unsoftened. Fortunately, as the world has broadened, the world of subjects has expanded, too."

*   *   *

BERMAN, Larry 1951-

PERSONAL: Born April 29, 1951, in Bronx, NY; son of Irving (a judge) and Selma (a teacher; maiden name, Genzer) Berman; children: Scott, Lindsay. *Education:* American University, B.A., 1973; Princeton University, M.A., 1975, Ph.D., 1977.

ADDRESSES: Office—Department of Political Science, University of California, Davis, CA 95616.

CAREER: University of California, Davis, assistant professor, 1977-80, associate professor, 1981-85, professor of political science, 1985—, chair of department, 1988—.

MEMBER: American Political Science Association, Academy of Political Science.

AWARDS, HONORS: Award from American Council of Learned Societies, 1984; Guggenheim fellowship, 1985; Bernath Lecture Prize.

WRITINGS:

The Office of Management and Budget and the Presidency, 1921-1979, Princeton University Press (Princeton, NJ), 1979.
Planning a Tragedy: The Americanization of the War in Vietnam, Norton (New York City), 1982.
Lyndon Johnson's War: The Road to Stalemate in Vietnam, Norton, 1989.
(Co-collaborator) *How Presidents Test Reality: Decisions on Vietnam, 1954 and 1965,* Russell Sage (New York City), 1989.
(Editor) *Looking Back on the Reagan Presidency,* Johns Hopkins University Press (Baltimore), 1990.
(Editor with Ariel E. Levite and Bruce W. Jentleson) *Foreign Military Intervention: The Dynamics of Protracted Conflict,* Columbia University Press (New York City), 1992.

Contributor to political science journals.

*　　*　　*

BERTHOLD, Margot 1922-

PERSONAL: Born November 8, 1922, in Markersdorf, Germany; daughter of Curt and Lina (Klaus) Berthold. *Education:* Attended University of Berlin, 1946-49; University of Munich, Ph.D., 1951.

ADDRESSES: Home—Reitmorstrasse 26, 8 Munich 22, Germany.

CAREER: Writer, 1952—. Instructor in history of theater and film, University of Munich, 1968-84.

WRITINGS:

Weltgeschichte des Theaters, Kroener-Verlag, 1968, translation by Edith Simmons published as *A History of World Theater: From the Beginnings to the Baroque,* Ungar (New York City), 1972.
Michel Butor, Oxford University Press, 1970.
Theophile Gautier: auteur dramatique, Nizet, 1972.
Historia social del teatro, [Barcelona], 1974.

Komodiantenfibel: Gaukler, Kasperl, Harlekin, [Munich], 1979.
Historia teatru, [Warsaw], 1980.

Editor of *Cabiria: Ein Film von Giovanni Pastrone,* two volumes, 1979, and *Max Reinhardt's Theater in Film,* 1983. Also contributor to professional journals and *Schweizer Theater-Jahrbuch 20.* Author of television films, including *Nach den Traumen jagen,* 1976, about E. T. A. Hoffmann; *Von einem, der auszog, sein Fell zu riskieren,* 1978, about the *Commedia dell' arte;* and *Der Traum vom immerwaehrenden Tag,* 1982, about Edvard Grieg.

BIOGRAPHICAL/CRITICAL SOURCES:

PERIODICALS

Le Monde, October 27, 1972.*

*　　*　　*

BIALOSTOCKI, Jan 1921-

PERSONAL: Born August 14, 1921, in Saratov, Saratov Oblast, U.S.S.R. (now Russia); son of Jan (a musician) and Valentina (Vereninov) Bialostocki; married Jolanta Maurin (an art historian), August 8, 1950; children: Martha.

ADDRESSES: Home—Dluga 30/34, m. 7, 00-238 Warsaw, Poland. *Office*—Muzeum Narodowe, al. Jerozolimskie, 00-495 Warsaw, Poland.

CAREER: Polish art historian. Muzeum Narodowe, Warsaw, Poland, curator of foreign art, 1955—; University of Warsaw, Warsaw, extraordinary professor, 1962-72, professor of modern art history, 1972—.

MEMBER: International Committee for the History of Art (vice-president, 1969—), International Council of Philosophy and Human Sciences (president, 1984), Polish Academy of Sciences (chair of committee for the history of art, 1972—), Royal Academy of Letters and Sciences (Netherlands), Flemish Academy of Sciences and Letters (Belgium), Bavarian Academy of Sciences (West Germany), San Fernando Academy of Fine Arts (Madrid, Spain), Academy of Sciences and Literature (Mainz, Germany), Saxon Academy of Sciences (Leipzig, Germany), Norwegian Academy of Sciences (Oslo), Accademia Clementina (Bologna, Italy), PEN.

AWARDS, HONORS: LL.D. from University of Groningen, 1969; Herder Prize, 1970; Polish State Prize (first class), 1978; Warburg Prize (Hamburg), 1981; Reuchlin Prize (Heidelberg-Pforzheim), 1983.

WRITINGS:

IN ENGLISH

The Art of the Renaissance in Eastern Europe: Hungary, Bohemia, and Poland, Cornell University Press (Ithaca, NY), 1976.

Duerer and His Critics, 1500-1971: Chapters in the History of Ideas, including a Collection of Texts, Korner Verlag (West Germany), 1986.

IN POLISH

Krajobrazy flamandzkie epoki manieryzmu, Muzeum Narodowe w Warszawa, 1951.

Malarstwo europejski w zbiorach polskich, 1300-1800 (title means "European Paintings in Polish Collections, 1300-1800"), Panstwowy Instytut Wydawniczy, 1955.

Bruegel, pejzazysta, Panstwowe Wydawnictwo Naukowe, 1956.

W pracowniach dawnych grafikow, Arkady, 1957.

Hogarth, Arkady, 1959.

Piec wiekow mysli o sztuce: Studia i rozprawy z dziejow teorii i historii sztuki, Panstwowe Wydawnictwo Naukowe, 1959, 2nd edition, 1976.

Malarstwo Niderlandzkie w zbiorach Polskich, 1450-1550, Muzeum Narodowe w Warszawa, 1960.

Teoria i tworczosc: O tradycji i inwencji w teorii sztuki i ikonografii, Panstwowe Wydawnictwo Naukowe, 1961.

Sztuka cenniejsza niz zloto: Opowiesc o sztuce europejskiej naszej ery, Panstwowe Wydawnictwo Naukowe, 1963, 4th edition, 1974.

Sztuka czasow Michala Aniola, Muzeum Narodowe w Warszawie, 1963.

Sztuka i mysl humanistyczna: Studia z dziejow sztuki i mysli o sztuce, Panstwowy Instytut Wydawniczy, 1966.

(Editor) *Mysl o sztuce i sztuka XVII i XVIII wieku,* Panstwowe Wydawnictwo Naukowe, 1970.

O sztuce dawnej Ameryki: Meksyk i Peru, Wydawnictwa Artystyczne i Filmowe, 1972.

(With others) *Narodziny krajobrazu; katalog wystawy ze zbiorow: Ermitazu, Drezdna, Pragi, Budapesztu oraz muzeow polskich,* Muzeum Narodowe w Warszawie, 1972.

(Editor) *Pojecia, problemy, metody, wspolczesnej nauki o sztuce: Dwadziescia szesc artykulow uczonych europejskich i amerykanskich,* Panstwowe Wydawnictwo Naukowe, 1976.

Refleksje i syntezy ze swiata sztuki, Panstwowe Wydawnictwo Naukowe, 1978.

Mysliciele, kronikarze i artysci o sztuce: Od starozytnosci do 1500 r, Panstwowe Wydawnictwo Naukowe, 1978.

Historia sztuki wsrod nauk humanistycznych, Zaklad Narodowy im Ossolinskich, 1980.

Obrazy i symbole, two volumes, Panstwowe Wydawnictwo Naukowe, 1983.

Teoretycy, prisarze i artysci o sztuce: 1500-1600, Panstwowe Wydawnictwo Naukowe, 1986.

(With Iwona Danielewicz) *Felicien Rops, 1833-1898,* Muzeum Narodowe w Warszawie, 1988.

IN OTHER LANGUAGES

Les Musees de Pologne, Gdansk, Krakow, Warszawa (in French), Centre National de Recherches (Belgium), 1966.

Stil und Ikonographie: Studien zur Kunstwissenschaft (in German), VEB Verlag der Kunst, 1966, 2nd edition, DuMont, 1981.

(With Beitraegen von Fedja Anzelewsky and others) *Spaetmittelalter und beginnende Neuzeit* (in German), Propylaen Verlag, 1972, 2nd edition, 1984.

Die Eigenart der Kunst Venedigs (in German), [Mainz-Wiesbaden, West Germany], 1979.

Bucher der Weisheit und Buecher der Vergaeuglichkeit, Heidelberg Akademie der Wissenschaften, 1984.

EDITOR

Poussin i teoria klasycyzmu, Zaklad Narodowy im Ossolinskich, 1953.

Albrecht Duerer jako pisarz i teoretyk sztuki, Zaklad Narodowy im Ossolinskich, 1956.

Rembrandt w oczach wspolczesnych, Panstwowy Instytut Wydawniczy, 1957.

Dwuglos o Berninim: Baldinucci i Chantelou, Zaklad Narodowy im Ossolinskich, 1962.

Sztuka i historia: Ksiega pamiatkowa ku czci profesora Michala Walickiego, Artystyczne i Filmowe, 1966.

Sarmatia artistica, Panstwowe Wydawnictwo Naukowe, 1968.

Granice sztuki: Z badan nad teoria i historia sztuki, kultura artystyczna oraz sztuka ludowa, Panstwowe Wydawnictwo Naukowe, 1972.

(With Irena Koloszynska) *Polska i Anglia: Stosunki kulturalno-artystyczne,* Muzeum Narodowe w Warszawa, 1974.

Interpretacja dziela sztuki: Studia i dyskusje, Panstwowe Wydawnictwo Naukowe, 1976.

OTHER

Also contributor of numerous articles to scholarly journals.

WORK IN PROGRESS: *L'Arte del quattrocento nel nord di Europa,* for UTET (Italy); *Pieter Breugels Johannespredigt,* for Corvina; *The Message of Images* for IRSA.

SIDELIGHTS: In *The Art of the Renaissance in Eastern Europe: Hungary, Bohemia, and Poland,* Bialostocki discusses the diffusion of the Italian Renaissance artistic style into Eastern European countries, where, he concludes, the style ultimately became more "original" and "pure" than it had been in Western Europe. A *Book Forum* reviewer praised the book's illustrations and bibliography, recommending the work as a useful addition to art history collections.

In 1981, in honor of Bialostocki's sixtieth birthday, Panstwowe Wydawnictwo Naukowe published a book of essays dedicated to him, *Ars auro prior: Studia Ioanni Biastocki sexagenario dicta,* including a bibliography of his 478 works to that date.

BIOGRAPHICAL/CRITICAL SOURCES:

PERIODICALS

Book Forum, fall, 1976.*

*   *   *

BISHOP, Gavin 1946-

PERSONAL: Born February 13, 1946, in Invercargill, New Zealand; son of Stanley Alan (a railway employee) and Doris Hinepau (a homemaker; maiden name, McKay) Bishop; married Vivien Carol Edwards (a teacher and artist), August 27, 1966; children: Cressida, Charlotte, Alexandra. *Education:* University of Canterbury, Diploma of Fine Arts (with honors), 1967; Christchurch Teachers' College, diploma, 1968. *Politics:* Liberal.

ADDRESSES: Home and office—11 Cracroft Ter., Christchurch 2, New Zealand. *Agent*—Studio Goodwin Sturges, 154 West Newton St., Boston, MA 02118.

CAREER: Linwood High School, Christchurch, New Zealand, art teacher and department chairman, 1969-89; Christ's College, Christchurch, head of art department, 1989—.

MEMBER: International PEN.

AWARDS, HONORS: Russell Clark Medal for Illustration from New Zealand Library Association, 1982, for *Mrs. McGinty and the Bizarre Plant;* New Zealand Children's Picture Book of the Year, New Zealand Government Publishers and New Zealand Literary Fund, 1983, for *Mr. Fox;* Grand Prix, Noma Concours from UNESCO and Kodansha International, 1984, for illustrations in *Mr. Fox;* Russell Clark Medal finalist, 1991, for *Katarina;* AIM Award for Children's Picture Book of the Year, 1994, for *Hinepau.*

WRITINGS:

FOR CHILDREN; SELF-ILLUSTRATED

Mrs. McGinty and the Bizarre Plant, Oxford University Press, 1981.
Bidibidi, Oxford University Press, 1982.
Mr. Fox, Oxford University Press, 1982.
Chicken Licken, Oxford University Press, 1984.
The Horror of Hickory Bay, Oxford University Press, 1984.
Mother Hubbard, Oxford University Press, 1986.
A Apple Pie, Oxford University Press, 1987.
The Three Little Pigs, Ashton Scholastic (New York), 1989.
Katarina, Random House (New York City), 1990.
Hinepau, Ashton Scholastic, 1993.

ILLUSTRATOR

Katherine O'Brien, *The Year of the Yelvertons,* Oxford University Press, 1981.
Kathleen Leverich, *The Hungry Fox,* Houghton (Boston, MA), 1986.
Beverley Dietz, *The Lion and the Jackal,* Simon & Schuster (New York), 1991.
Jeffrey Leask, *Little Red Rocking Hood,* Ashton Scholastic, 1992.
Philip Bailey, *The Wedding of Mistress Fox,* North-South (Lanham, MD), 1994.
Kana Riley, *A Moose Is Loose,* Brown Publishing Network, 1994.

OTHER

Author of libretto for *Terrible Tom,* a ballet commissioned by Royal New Zealand Ballet Company, 1985, and *Te Maia and the Sea-Devil,* a ballet, Royal New Zealand Ballet Company, 1986; author of scripts for TVNZ television series *Bidibidi,* broadcast November and December, 1990, and *Bidibidi to the Rescue,* broadcast November and December, 1991, both based on his book, *Bidibidi.*

WORK IN PROGRESS: "Preparation for two picture books based on stories from the Maui cycle."

SIDELIGHTS: Gavin Bishop told *CA:* "Over the last few years I have turned increasingly to stories that reflect the bicultural nature of New Zealand's society and my own extended family. Two recent books of mine reflect this interest: *Katarina* and *Hinepau. Katarina* is based on the life story of a great aunt of mine, a Maori woman from the North Island who married a Scot and travelled to the far south of the South Island where eventually the branch of the family that I come from developed. *Hinepau* was my mother's maiden name, and I gave it to the Maori heroine of my story about an outcast who saves her tribe by sacrificing herself.

"In 1990 I visited the island of Sakhalin [off Southeast Russia] with a group of children. I believe that we were one of the first Western groups to ever visit the island. In 1992 I gave lectures and workshops in Beijing and Shanghai about writing and illustrating for children at the invitation of the Asian Cultural Centre for UNESCO. A major retrospective exhibition of my work was held at various public galleries throughout New Zealand from 1991 through 1993."

BIOGRAPHICAL/CRITICAL SOURCES:

BOOKS

Marantz, Sylvia and Kenneth, *Artists of the Page,* McFarland, 1992.

PERIODICALS

British Book News, March, 1985.
Child Education, June, 1985.
Fact, April 2, 1983.
New Zealand Listener, December 11-17, 1982; February 4, 1991; September 25, 1993.

*   *   *

BLADES, Ann (Sager) 1947-

PERSONAL: Born November 16, 1947, in Vancouver, British Columbia, Canada; daughter of Arthur Hazelton (an administrator) and Dorothy (a teacher; maiden name, Planche) Sager; divorced; children: two sons. *Education:* University of British Columbia, elementary teaching certificate, 1970; British Columbia Institute of Technology, R.N., 1974. *Avocational interests:* Garage sales, gardening.

ADDRESSES: Home—2701 Crescent Dr., Surrey, British Columbia, Canada V4A 3J9. *Agent*—Bella Pomer, 22 Shallmar Blvd., P.H. 2, Toronto, Ontario, Canada M5N 2Z8.

CAREER: Author and illustrator of children's books. Elementary school teacher in Peace River North School District, Mile 18, British Columbia, 1967-68, Department of Indian Affairs and Northern Development, Tache, British Columbia, 1969, and Surrey School District, Surrey, British Columbia, 1969-71; parttime registered nurse in Vancouver, British Columbia, Vancouver General Hospital, 1974-75, and Mount St. Joseph Hospital, 1975-80; artist, 1976—, with illustrations and paintings exhibited in Toronto, Vancouver, Bologna; New York City; and Bratislava, Slovakia.

MEMBER: Canadian Society for Children's Authors, Illustrators, and Performers.

AWARDS, HONORS: Book of the Year Award, Canadian Association of Children's Literature (CALC), 1972, Best Illustrated Book Award runner-up, CALC, 1972, and Honour List, Austrian and German kinderbuchpreis, 1976, all for *Mary of Mile 18;* Amelia Francis Howard-Gibbon Illustrator's Award runner-up, CALC and Canadian Library Association, 1974, Best Children's Book Award, Child Study Association, 1977, and recommendation by National Conference for Christians and Jews: Books for Brotherhood, 1977, all for *A Boy of Tache;* Children's Literature Award for Illustration (now called the Governor General's Award), Canada Council, and Amelia Francis Howard-Gibbon Illustrator's Award, both 1979, for *A Salmon for Simon;* Honourable Mention, Children's Literature Award for Illustration, Canada Council, 1981, for *Pettranella;* Amelia Francis Howard-Gibbon Illustrator's Award runner-up, 1985, and Elizabeth Mrazik-Cleaver Canadian Picture Book Award, Canadian Section of International Board on Books for Young People, 1986, both for *By the Sea: An Alphabet Book;* Canadian nominee for Hans Christian Andersen Award for Illustration, 1987.

WRITINGS:

FOR CHILDREN; SELF-ILLUSTRATED

Mary of Mile 18, Tundra Books (Montreal), 1971.
A Boy of Tache, Tundra Books, 1973.
The Cottage at Crescent Beach, Magook, 1977.
By the Sea: An Alphabet Book, Kids Can Press (Toronto), 1985.

"SEASONS" BOARD BOOK SERIES; FOR CHILDREN; SELF-ILLUSTRATED

Summer, Lothrop (New York City), 1989.
Fall, Lothrop, 1989.
Winter, Lothrop, 1989.
Spring, Lothrop, 1989.

ILLUSTRATOR

Michael Macklem, *Jacques the Woodcutter,* Oberon (Ottawa), 1977.
Betty Waterton, *A Salmon for Simon,* Douglas & McIntyre (Vancouver), 1978, Atheneum (New York City), 1980.
Margaret Laurence, *Six Darn Cows,* Lorimer (Toronto), 1979.
Margaret Atwood and Joyce Barkhouse, *Anna's Pet,* Lorimer, 1980.
Waterton, *Pettranella,* Vanguard (Chicago), 1980.
Jean Speare, *A Candle for Christmas,* Douglas & McIntyre, 1986, Macmillan, 1987.
Sue Ann Alderson, *Ida and the Wool Smugglers,* Macmillan, 1987, McElderry Books (New York City), 1988.
The Singing Basket, edited by Kit Pearson, Camden House (Columbia, SC), 1990.

Ainslie Manson, *A Dog Came, Too: A True Story,* Macmillan, 1992, McElderry Books, 1993.

Alderson, *A Ride for Martha,* Douglas & McIntyre, 1993.

Also contributor of cover illustration for *Canadian Books for Children: A Guide to Authors and Illustrators,* by Jon Stott and Raymond Jones, Harcourt (Toronto), 1988. Some of Blades's works have been published in Germany, Sweden, Finland, Denmark, and Australia.

ADAPTATIONS: Mary of Mile 18 was adapted into a filmstrip and distributed by Weston Woods Studios, Connecticut, 1978, and adapted for a Canadian film distributed by the National Film Board of Canada, 1981; *A Salmon for Simon* was adapted into a filmstrip and distributed by Weston Woods Studios, 1980.

SIDELIGHTS: Ann Blades's first teaching positions were remote—Mile 18 is a small rural community in northern British Columbia, and Tache is a Native American reservation on Stuart Lake—and she found out early that the books her students read had no relation to the world in which they lived. She decided to write her own books, and *Mary of Mile 18* and *A Boy of Tache* grew out of these early teaching experiences.

Mary of Mile 18 was well-received by reviewers, many of whom praised Blades for her unadorned story line and her colorful paintings capturing the frigid northern Canadian countryside. In the Book of the Year Award-winning story, Mary's life is changed when she finds a wolf pup and tries to convince her father to let her keep it. *A Boy of Tache,* based on a real episode, tells the story of Charlie, a Native American youth who must set out for help by himself when his grandfather falls ill on a trek to the trapping grounds.

During the late 1970s, Blades began illustrating works of other authors. Among these was Betty Waterton's *A Salmon for Simon,* which earned Blades the Canadian Children's Literature Award for Illustration.

BIOGRAPHICAL/CRITICAL SOURCES:

BOOKS

Children's Literature Review, Volume 15, Gale (Detroit), 1988.

The Republic of Childhood: A Critical Guide to Canadian Children's Literature in English, 2nd edition, Oxford University Press (Canada), 1975.

PERIODICALS

Best Sellers, March, 1977.

Books in Canada, December, 1979.

Canadian Children's Literature, spring, 1975, pp. 77-79; number 21, 1981, pp. 58-65; numbers 39-40, 1985.

Chatelaine, February, 1975.

Children's Literature: Annual of the Modern Language Association Seminar on Children's Literature and the Children's Literature Association, Volume 4, 1975.

Globe and Mail (Toronto), June 12, 1975; November 15, 1986.

Kirkus Reviews, February 15, 1977; May 1, 1980.

World of Children's Books, number 1, 1978.

*   *   *

BLAU, Judith R. 1942-

PERSONAL: Born April 27, 1942, in Lansing, MI; daughter of Harold W. Fritz (a mechanical engineer) and Theda (Struck) Fritz (a secretary); married Peter M. Blau (a sociologist), July 31, 1968; children: Reva T. *Education:* University of Chicago, B.A., 1964, M.A., 1967; Northwestern University, Ph.D., 1972. *Politics:* Socialist.

ADDRESSES: Office—Department of Sociology, CB# 3210, Hamilton Hall, University of North Carolina, Chapel Hill, NC 27599-3210.

CAREER: William Paterson College, Wayne, NJ, assistant professor, 1972-73; Bernard M. Baruch College of the City University of New York, New York City, assistant professor, 1973-76; Yeshiva University, Albert Einstein College of Medicine, Bronx, NY, postdoctoral fellow in psychiatry, 1976-78; State University of New York at Albany, assistant professor, 1978-82, associate professor of sociology, 1982-88, adjunct at Institute for Government and Policy Studies, Nelson A. Rockefeller College, 1986-88, adjunct at School of Business, 1987-88, associate director, Center for Social and Demographic Analysis, 1988; University of North Carolina at Chapel Hill, professor, 1988—, fellow, Institute for the Arts and Humanities, 1992—. Netherlands Institute for Advanced Studies, visitor, 1975-76; Columbia University Summer School and Hunter College of the City University of New York, visiting assistant professor, 1977; Nankai University, lecturer, summer, 1981; Center for the Social Sciences, Columbia University, research scholar, 1983-88; New York University, visiting associate professor, 1986-87. Member of National Science Foundation review panel for dissertation awards, 1991, General Social Survey advisory committee, Culture Module, 1991-92, and National Endowment for the Arts, Survey of Public Participation in the Arts advisory panel, 1992-93.

MEMBER: International Association for Cultural Economics, International Sociological Association, American Sociological Association (chair of papers committee, 1987-88, nominations committee, 1989-90, 1994-95, book award committee, 1993-94), Sociologists for Women in

Society, Eastern Sociological Society (co-chair of committee on professions, 1984-86).

AWARDS, HONORS: Grants from National Science Foundation, National Endowment for the Arts, and U.S. Department of Labor.

WRITINGS:

(Editor with John S. Pipkin and Mark LaGory) *Professions and Urban Form,* State University of New York Press (Albany, NY), 1983.

(Editor with Pipkin and LaGory) *Remaking the City,* State University of New York Press, 1983.

Architects and Firms: A Sociological Perspective, MIT Press (Cambridge, MA), 1984.

The Shape of Culture: A Study of Contemporary Cultural Patterns in the United States, Cambridge University Press (Cambridge, MA), 1989.

(With Gail Quets) *Cultural Life in City and Region,* International Association of Cultural Economics (Akron, OH), 1989.

(Editor with Arnold Foster) *Art and Society: Readings in the Sociology of the Arts,* State University of New York Press, 1989.

(Edited with Norman Goodman) *Social Roles and Social Institutions: Essays in Honor of Rose Laub Coser,* Westview Press (Boulder, CO), 1991.

Social Contracts and Economic Markets, Plenum (New York City), 1993.

Editor of "Sociology of Work" series, State University of New York Press. Contributor to books, including *Social Science Research,* edited by Kenneth C. Land and Kent Redding, 1992. Contributor to numerous sociology journals. Book review editor of *Work and Occupations.* Member of editorial board, *Quarterly Journal of Ideology,* 1979-91, and *Sociological Quarterly,* 1987-89. Member of advisory board, *American Sociologist,* 1990—, and *Poetics: International Journal of Empirical Research,* 1992—.

WORK IN PROGRESS: A book tentatively titled *The American Newspaper: Pluralism and Contention: 1800-1990.**

*   *   *

BLOOM, Ursula (Harvey) 1893-1984
(Sheila Burns, Mary Essex, Rachel Harvey, Deborah Mann, Sara Sloane; Lozania Prole, a joint pseudonym)

PERSONAL: Born in Chelmsford, Essex, England; died October 29, 1984, in Nether Wallop, Hampshire, England; daughter of J. Harvey (a clergyman) and Mary Bloom; married Arthur Brownlow Denham-Cookes (a British Army captain), 1916 (died in World War I, 1918); married Charles Gower Robinson (a Royal Navy commander; retired), 1925; children: (first marriage) Phillip. *Education:* "No education save reading."

ADDRESSES: Home—Chelsea, England.

CAREER: Author and journalist, 1920s-1984. Former beauty editor of *Women's Own* magazine; former staff member of *Sunday Pictorial.*

MEMBER: Royal Historical Society (fellow), Woman's Press Club (London).

WRITINGS:

FICTION

The Great Beginning, Hutchinson (London), 1924.
Vagabond Harvest, Hutchinson, 1925.
Driving of Destiny, Hutchinson, 1925.
Our Lady of Marble, Hutchinson, 1926.
The Judge of Jerusalem, Harrap (London), 1926.
Spilled Salt: The Story of a Spy, Hutchinson, 1927.
Candleshades: The Story of a Soul, Hutchinson, 1927.
Base Metal: The Story of a Man, Hutchinson, 1928, published as *Veneer,* G. H. Watt, 1929.
An April After, Hutchinson, 1928.
The Eternal Tomorrow, G. H. Watt, 1929, published in England as *Tomorrow for Apricots,* Hutchinson, 1929.
The Secret Lover, Hutchinson, 1930, Dutton (New York City), 1931.
The Passionate Heart, Hutchinson, 1930.
Gossamer Dream, Hutchinson, 1930.
Pack Mule, Hutchinson, 1931, Dutton, 1932.
Trackless Way, Hurst & Blackett, 1931.
Fruit on the Bough, Hutchinson, 1931, published as *Flood of Passion,* Dutton, 1932.
The Pilgrim Soul, Hutchinson, 1932.
Breadwinners, Hutchinson, 1932.
Cypresses Grow Dark, Hutchinson, 1932.
Love's Plaything, Hutchinson, 1932.
The Log of a Naval Officer's Wife, Hurst & Blackett, 1932.
Rose Sweetman, Hutchinson, 1933.
Spread Wings, Hutchinson, 1933.
Wonder Cruise, Hutchinson, 1933.
Crazy Quilt (story collection), Hutchinson, 1933.
Enchanted Journey, Hutchinson, 1933.
Love, Old and New, Dutton, 1933, published in England as *Love Is Everything,* Hutchinson, 1933.
Mediterranean Madness, Hutchinson, 1934.
The Questing Trout, Hutchinson, 1934.
Pastoral, Hutchinson, 1934.
Young Parent, Hutchinson, 1934.
This Is Marriage, Hutchinson, 1935.
Harvest of a House, Hutchinson, 1935.
The Gipsy Vans Come Through, Hutchinson, 1936.

The Laughing Lady, Collins, 1936.

Laughter in Cheyne Walk, Collins, 1936, Lippincott (Philadelphia, PA), 1937.

Marriage of Pierrot, Allied Newspapers, 1937.

Three Cedars, Collins, 1937.

Leaves before the Storm, Rich & Cowan (London), 1937.

Golden Venture, Rich & Cowan, 1938.

Lily-of-the-Valley, Rich & Cowan, 1938.

The Brittle Shadow, Readers Library Publishing Co., 1938.

Beloved Creditor, Cassell (London), 1939.

These Roots Go Deep, Cassell, 1939.

Trailing Orchids, R. Hale (London), 1940.

The Woman Who Was Tomorrow, Cassell, 1940.

The Flying Swans, Cassell, 1940.

Silver Orchids, R. Hale, 1941.

Spring in September, R. Hale, 1941.

The Virgin Thorn, Cassell, 1941.

Dinah's Husband, Cassell, 1941.

The Golden Flame, R. Hale, 1941.

Age Cannot Wither, Cassell, 1942.

Lonely Shadow, Cassell, 1942.

No Lady Buys a Cot, Chapman & Hall (London), 1943.

Marriage in Heaven, R. Hale, 1943.

Robin in a Cage, Cassell, 1943.

Nightshade at Morning, privately printed, 1944, R. Hale, 1952.

No Lady in Bed, Chapman & Hall, 1944.

The Fourth Cedar, Cassell, 1944.

The Painted Lady, Macdonald & Co. (London), 1945.

The Faithless Dove, Cassell, 1945.

Three Sons, Macdonald & Co., 1946.

Garden for My Child, Gifford (London), 1946.

No Lady with a Pen, Chapman & Hall, 1947.

Adam's Daughter, Macdonald & Co., 1947.

Alien Corn, Hamish Hamilton, 1947.

Caravan for Three (young adult novel), University of London Press, 1947.

Three Sisters, Macdonald & Co., 1947, reprinted, Hutchinson, 1970.

Facade, Macdonald & Co., 1948.

Next Tuesday, Macdonald & Co., 1949.

No Lady in the Cart, Convoy, 1949.

Gipsy Flower, R. Hale, 1949.

The King's Wife, Hutchinson, 1950.

Eleanor Jowitt—Antiques, Macdonald & Co., 1950.

The Song of Philomel, Macdonald & Co., 1950.

Three Girls Come to Town (young adult novel), Macdonald & Co., 1950.

Mum's Girl Was No Lady, Convoy, 1951.

Nine Lives, Macdonald & Co., 1951.

Orange Blossom for Sandra, R. Hale, 1951.

The Sentimental Family, Macdonald & Co., 1951.

Moon Song, R. Hale, 1952.

As Bends the Bough, Macdonald & Co., 1952.

Twilight of a Tudor, Hutchinson, 1952.

Sea Fret, Hutchinson, 1953.

Marriage of Leonora, R. Hale, 1953.

The First Elizabeth, Hutchinson, 1953.

Matthew, Mark, Luke, and John, Hutchinson, 1954.

Daughters of the Rectory, Hutchinson, 1955.

The Gracious Lady, Hutchinson, 1955.

The Girl Who Loved Crippen, Hutchinson, 1955.

The Silver Ring, Hutchinson, 1956.

Tides of Spring Flow Fast, Hutchinson, 1956.

Brief Springtime, Hutchinson, 1958.

The Abiding City, Hutchinson, 1958.

Monkey Tree in a Flower Pot, Hutchinson, 1958.

Undarkening Green, Hutchinson, 1959.

The Romance of Charles Dickens (biographical novel), R. Hale, 1960.

The Thieving Magpie, Hutchinson, 1960.

The Cactus Has Courage, Hutchinson, 1961.

Prelude to Yesterday, Hutchinson, 1961.

Harvest-home Come Sunday, Hutchinson, 1962.

Ship in a Bottle, Hutchinson, 1962.

The Gated Road, Hutchinson, 1963.

The Ring Tree, Hutchinson, 1964.

The House That Died Alone, Hutchinson, 1964.

The Quiet Village, Hutchinson, 1965.

The Ugly Head, Hutchinson, 1965.

The Dandelion Clock, Hutchinson, 1966.

The Mightier Sword, R. Hale, 1966.

The Old Adam, Hutchinson, 1967.

Two Pools in a Field, Hutchinson, 1967.

A Roof and Four Walls, Hutchinson, 1967.

Yesterday's Tomorrow, Hutchinson, 1968.

The Dragonfly, Hutchinson, 1968.

The Flight of the Falcon, Hutchinson, 1969.

The Hunter's Moon, Hutchinson, 1969.

The House of Kent, R. Hale, 1969.

Rosemary for Frinton, R. Hale, 1970.

The Tune of Time, Hutchinson, 1970.

The Great Tomorrow, R. Hale, 1971.

Rosemary for Chelsea, R. Hale, 1971.

Laughter in Cheyne Walk, Lythway Press, 1972.

The Duke of Windsor, R. Hale, 1972.

Edwardian Day-dream, Hutchinson, 1972.

The Cheval Glass, Hutchinson, 1973.

Requesting the Pleasure, R. Hale, 1973.

The Old Rectory, Hutchinson, 1973.

Princesses in Love, R. Hale, 1973.

Mirage on the Horizon, Hutchinson, 1974.

The Old Elm Tree, Hutchinson, 1974.

The Twisted Road, Hutchinson, 1975.

The Turn of Life's Tide, Hutchinson, 1976.

The Woman Doctor, Hutchinson, 1978.

The House on the Hill, Firecrest, 1978.

Perchance to Dream, Chivers (Bath, England), 1982.
It Happened in Spring, Severn House, 1983.
Trailing Glory, Chivers, 1983.

Also author of *Tarnish,* 1929; *The Little Fir Tree* (juvenile), 1945; *Pumpkin, the Pup* (juvenile), 1947; *Pavilion,* 1951; and *How Dark, My Lady!,* 1951.

NONFICTION

A Lamp in the Darkness (essays on religion), Hutchinson, 1930.
The ABC of Authorship, Blackie & Son (Glasgow), 1938.
A Cad's Guide to Cruising, Rich & Cowan, 1938.
Letters to My Son, Cassell, 1939.
The Housewife's Beauty Book, R. Hale, 1941.
Me—After the War (on employment for women), Gifford, 1944.
The Changed Village, Chapman & Hall, 1945.
Ursula's Cook Book for the Woman Who Has No Time to Spare, Gifford, 1946.
Questions Answered about Knitting, Jordan & Sons, 1946.
Questions Answered about Beauty, Jordan & Sons, 1946.
You and Your Holiday, Gifford, 1946.
You and Your Child, Gifford, 1946.
You and Your Dog, Gifford, 1949.
You and Your Home, Gifford, 1949.
You and Your Looks, Gifford, 1949.
Cookery, W. & G. Foyle (London), 1949.
You and Your Life, Gifford, 1950.
You and Your Fun, Gifford, 1950.
(Editor) *Woman's Annual, 1951,* Elek (London), 1950.
For the Bride, Museum Press, 1952.
Curtain Call for the Guv'nor, Hutchinson, 1954.
Hitler's Eva, Hutchinson, 1954.
(Editor) *The Girls' Book of Popular Hobbies,* Burke Publishing (London), 1954, Roy, 1956.
Victorian Vinaigrette, Hutchinson, 1956.
The Elegant Edwardian, Hutchinson, 1957.
Down to the Sea in Ships, Hutchinson, 1958.
He Lit the Lamp (biography of Archibald Montgomery Low), Burke Publishing, 1958.
Wanting to Write (guide for writers), Stanley Paul, 1958.
The Inspired Needle, Hurst & Blackett (London), 1959.
Sixty Years of Home, Hurst & Blackett, 1960.
War Isn't Wonderful!, Hutchinson, 1961.
The Rose of Norfolk, R. Hale, 1964.
Rosemary for Stratford-on-Avon, R. Hale, 1966.
The Royal Baby, R. Hale, 1975.
The Great Queen Consort, R. Hale, 1976.
Edward and Victoria, R. Hale, 1977.

AUTOBIOGRAPHY AND REMINISCENCES

Mistress of None, Hutchinson, 1933.
Holiday Mood, Hutchinson, 1934.
Without Make-up, M. Joseph (London), 1938.

The Log of No Lady, Chapman & Hall, 1940.
Time, Tide and I, Chapman & Hall, 1942.
Rude Forefathers, Macdonald & Co., 1945.
No Lady Meets No Gentleman, Low (London), 1947.
Trilogy, Hutchinson, 1954.
No Lady Has a Dog's Day, Hutchinson, 1956.
Youth at the Gate, Hutchinson, 1959.
Mrs. Bunthorpe's Respects, Hutchinson, 1963.
Parson Extraordinary (biography of father, J. Harvey Bloom), R. Hale, 1963.
Price Above Rubies (biography of mother, Mary Bloom), Hutchinson, 1965.
A Roof and Four Walls, Hutchinson, 1967.

ONE-ACT PLAYS

A Paymaster in Every Family, Samuel French (London), 1934.
One's Wedding, Two Brides, Samuel French, 1943.
What's in a Name? (nativity play), Samuel French, 1947.
Displaced Persons, Samuel French, 1948.

OTHER

Wartime Beauty, Tod Publishing, 1943.
Smugglers Cave, Riddle Books, 1947.
New World Round the Corner, British Rubber Development Board, 1951.

Author of three privately printed stories: "Tiger," circa 1903, "Winifred," 1903, and "Girlie," 1904. Also author of over fifty plays for radio.

UNDER PSEUDONYM SHEILA BURNS

The Passionate Adventure, Cassell, 1936.
Dream Awhile, Cassell, 1937.
Take a Chance, Cassell, 1937.
Honeymoon Island, Cassell, 1938.
Lady! This Is Love!, Cassell, 1938.
Weekend Bridge, Cassell, 1939.
Wonder Trip, Cassell, 1939.
Adventurous Heart, Cassell, 1940.
Meet Love on Holiday, Cassell, 1940.
Romance Is Mine, Cassell, 1941.
Stronger Passion, Cassell, 1941.
Bridal Sweet, Cassell, 1942, published as *Bride Alone,* Arcadia House, 1943.
Thy Bride Am I, Cassell, 1942.
Romantic Fugitive, Arcadia House, 1944.
The Romance of Jenny W.R.E.N., Cassell, 1944, published as *Jenny W.R.E.N.,* Arcadia House, 1945.
Vagrant Lover, Macdonald & Co., 1945.
Hold Hard, My Heart, Macdonald & Co., 1946.
Bride—Maybe, Macdonald & Co., 1946.
Desire Is Not Dead, Macdonald & Co., 1947.
Chance Romance, Eldon, 1948.
Air Liner, Eldon, 1948.

Tomorrow Is Eternal, Macdonald & Co., 1948.
Faint with Pursuit, Eldon, 1949.
No Trespasses in Love, Macdonald & Co., 1949.
Cuckoo Never Weds, Eldon, 1950.
Primula and Hyacinth, Arcadia House, 1950.
Not Free to Love, Eldon, 1950, published under pseudonym Sara Sloane as *Heaven Lies Ahead,* Arcadia House, 1951.
Hold Back the Heart, Arcadia House, 1951.
Rosebud and Stardust, Eldon, 1951.
Live Happily—Love Song, Eldon, 1952.
Love Me Tomorrow, Eldon, 1952.
Tomorrow We Marry, Hutchinson, 1954.
Romantic Intruder, Hutchinson, 1954.
Please Burn after Reading, Hutchinson, 1954.
How Dear Is My Delight!, Hutchinson, 1955.
Beloved and Unforgettable, Hutchinson, 1955.
Adventure in Romance, Hutchinson, 1956.
Romantic Summer Sea, Hutchinson, 1956.
How Rich Is Love?, Hurst & Blackett, 1957.
Beloved Man, Hurst & Blackett, 1957.
This Dragon of Desire, Hurst & Blackett, 1958.
Sweet Impulse, Hutchinson, 1958.
Storm Bird, Hurst & Blackett, 1959.
Lasting Lover, Hurst & Blackett, 1960.
Dr. Gregory's Partner, Hurst & Blackett, 1960.
The Disheartened Doctor, R. Hale, 1961.
Dr. Irresistible, M.D., R. Hale, 1962.
The Eyes of Doctor Karl, R. Hale, 1962.
Heartbreak Surgeon, R. Hale, 1963.
Theatre Sister in Love, R. Hale, 1963.
When Doctors Love, R. Hale, 1964.
Doctor Delightful, R. Hale, 1964.
Doctor Called David, R. Hale, 1966.
Doctor Divine, R. Hale, 1966.
The Surgeon's Sweetheart, R. Hale, 1966.
The Beauty Surgeon, R. Hale, 1967.
The Flying Nurse, R. Hale, 1967.
Romantic Cottage, R. Hale, 1967.
The Dark-eyed Sister, R. Hale, 1968.
Casualty Ward, R. Hale, 1968.
Acting Sister, R. Hale, 1968.
Surgeon at Sea, R. Hale, 1969.
Sister Loving Heart, Lythway, 1978.
A Cornish Rhapsody, Chivers, 1984.

UNDER PSEUDONYM MARY ESSEX

Haircut for Samson, Chapman & Hall, 1940.
Nesting Cats, Chapman & Hall, 1941.
Eve Didn't Care, Chapman & Hall, 1941.
Marry to Taste, Chapman & Hall, 1942.
Freddy for Fun, Chapman & Hall, 1943.
Amorous Bicycle, Chapman & Hall, 1944.
Divorce?—Of Course, Chapman & Hall, 1945.

Young Kangaroos Prefer Riding, Chapman & Hall, 1947.
Domestic Blister, Chapman & Hall, 1948.
Six Fools and a Fairy, Jenkins, 1948.
Full Fruit Flavour, Jenkins, 1949.
Herring's Nest, Jenkins, 1949.
Apple for the Doctor, Jenkins, 1950.
Tea Is So Intoxicating, Jenkins, 1950.
Dark Gentleman, Fair Lady, Jenkins, 1951.
Forbidden Fiance, R. Hale, 1951.
Gentleman Called James, Jenkins, 1951.
She Had What It Takes, Jenkins, 1952.
Forty Is Beginning, Jenkins, 1952.
Danielle, My Darling, Dakers, 1954.
Passionate Springtime, R. Hale, 1956.
Dark Lover, R. Hale, 1957.
The Nightingale Once Sang, R. Hale, 1958.
It's Spring, My Heart!, R. Hale, 1958.
Doctor Duty Bound, R. Hale, 1960.
This Man Is Not for Marrying, R. Hale, 1960.
Fugitive Romantic, R. Hale, 1960.
The Love Story of Dr. Duke, R. Hale, 1960.
A Sailor's Love, R. Hale, 1961.
Doctor on Call, R. Hale, 1961.
Date with a Doctor, R. Hale, 1962.
Dr. Guardian of the Gate, R. Hale, 1962.
Nurse from Killarney, R. Hale, 1963.
A Strange Patient for Sister Smith, R. Hale, 1963.
The Sangor Hospital Story, R. Hale, 1963.
The Hard-hearted Doctor, R. Hale, 1964.
Doctor and Lover, R. Hale, 1964.
Dare-devil Doctor, R. Hale, 1965.
Romantic Theatre Sister, R. Hale, 1965.
Hospital of the Heart, R. Hale, 1966.
The Adorable Doctor, R. Hale, 1966.
The Little Nurse, R. Hale, 1967.
The Romance of Dr. Dinah, R. Hale, 1967.
Assistant Matron, R. Hale, 1967.
The Ghost of Fiddler's Hill, R. Hale, 1968.
The Sympathetic Surgeon, R. Hale, 1968.
When a Woman Doctor Loves, R. Hale, 1969.
Doctor on Duty Bound, R. Hale, 1969.
I Love My Love, R. Hale, 1977.
A Doctor's Love, Chivers, 1982.
A Nurse Called Liza, Chivers, 1982.
Forbidden Fiance, Chivers, 1983.
Romance of Summer, Chivers, 1984.

UNDER PSEUDONYM RACHEL HARVEY

The Village Nurse, Hurst & Blackett, 1967.
Dearest Doctor, Hurst & Blackett, 1968.
Weep Not for Dreams, R. Hale, 1968.
The Little Matron of the Cottage Hospital, R. Hale, 1969.
The Unbelievable Doctor, R. Hale, 1969.
Darling District Nurse, R. Hale, 1969.

The Doctor Who Fell in Love, Chivers, 1981.
Doctor Called Harry, Chivers, 1982.
The Love Story of Nurse Julie, Chivers, 1982.
Love Has No Secrets, Chivers, 1984.
Nurse on Bodmin Moor, Chivers, 1984.

UNDER PSEUDONYM DEBORAH MANN

Woman Called Mary, Corgi, 1965.
Now Barabbas Was a Robber: The Story of the Man Who Lived that Christ Might Die, Corgi, 1967.
Song of Salome, Corgi, 1969.
Pilate's Wife, Corgi, 1977.

UNDER PSEUDONYM LOZANIA PROLE

Our Dearest Emma, Museum Press, 1949, published as *The Magnificent Courtesan,* McBride, 1950.
Pretty Witty Nell, McGraw (New York City), 1953.
Tonight, Josephine, McGraw, 1953.
King's Pleasure, McGraw, 1953.
Enchanting Courtesan, R. Hale, 1955.
My Wanton Tudor Rose: The Love Story of Lady Katheryn Howard, R. Hale, 1956.
Little Victoria, R. Hale, 1957.
Queen for England, R. Hale, 1957.
Henry's Last Love, R. Hale, 1958.
Stuart Sisters, R. Hale, 1958.
Consort to the Queen, R. Hale, 1959.
Little Wigmaker of Bread Street, R. Hale, 1959.
For the Love of the King, R. Hale, 1960.
Tudor Boy, R. Hale, 1960.
The Queen's Midwife, R. Hale, 1961.
My Love! My Little Queen!, R. Hale, 1961.
A King's Plaything, R. Hale, 1962.
Queen Guillotine, R. Hale, 1962.
The Ghost that Haunted a King, R. Hale, 1963.
The Wild Daughter, R. Hale, 1963.
Daughter of the Devil, R. Hale, 1963.
Henry's Golden Queen, R. Hale, 1964.
The Three Passionate Queens, R. Hale, 1964.
Marlborough's Unfair Lady, R. Hale, 1965.
The Haunted Headsman, R. Hale, 1965.
The Dangerous Husband, R. Hale, 1966.
Nelson's Love, R. Hale, 1966.
The Dark-eyed Queen, R. Hale, 1967.
King Henry's Sweetheart, R. Hale, 1967.
The Queen Who Was a Nun, R. Hale, 1967.
The Greatest Nurse of Them All, R. Hale, 1968.
Princess Philanderer, R. Hale, 1968.
The Loves of a Virgin Princess, R. Hale, 1968.
Sweet Marie Antoinette, R. Hale, 1969.
The Boutique of the Singing Clocks, R. Hale, 1969.
The Enchanting Princess, R. Hale, 1970.
The Last Tsarina, R. Hale, 1970.
Six Wives but One Love, R. Hale, 1972.

The Queen's Daughters, R. Hale, 1973.
Life Is No Fairy Tale, R. Hale, 1976.
Henry's Last Love, Lythway, 1978.
Judas Iscariot—Traitor?, Chivers, 1981.
Albert the Beloved, Chivers, 1982.
The Two Queen Annes, Chivers 1982.
The Last Love of a King, Chivers, 1983.
Taj Mahal, Shrine of Desire, Chivers, 1983.
A Queen for the Regent, Chivers, 1983.
The Ten-Day Queen, Chivers, 1983.
The King's Daughter, Chivers, 1984.

UNDER PSEUDONYM SARA SLOANE

Once on an Island, Arcadia House, 1950.

SIDELIGHTS: As the author of more than five hundred books, Ursula Bloom was arguably England's most prolific literary figure. She completed her first book at age seven and edited a modest children's magazine when she was only eleven. After her first husband died in 1918, Bloom began working as a crime reporter for the *Empire News.* In 1924 she started writing novels, and by 1930 she had completed eleven of them. From 1930 to 1970 Bloom worked constantly, often writing sixteen hours each day.

Bloom also designed her own needlework. She showed 150 pieces in a London exhibition in 1963.

OBITUARIES:

PERIODICALS

Chicago Tribune, November 1, 1984.
Detroit Free Press, October 31, 1984.
Los Angeles Times, November 1, 1984.
New York Times, October 31, 1984.
Newsweek, November 12, 1984.
Times (London), October 31, 1984.
Washington Post, November 1, 1984.*

*   *   *

BLYTHE, Ronald (George) 1922-

PERSONAL: Born November 6, 1922, in Acton, Suffolk, England. *Avocational interests:* Walking, music, conversation, reading.

ADDRESSES: Home—Bottengom's Farm, Wormingford, Colchester, Essex, England. *Agent*—Deborah Rogers, Coleridge & White, Ltd., 20, Powis Mews, London W11 1JN.

CAREER: Reference librarian in Colchester, England, 1947-54; writer, 1960—.

MEMBER: Colchester Literary Society (founder, 1949), Royal Society of Literature, Society of Authors, John Clare Society (president), Fabian Society.

AWARDS, HONORS: Fellow, Royal Society of Literature, 1969; Heinemann Award, 1969, for *Akenfield: Portrait of an English Village;* Society of Authors Travel Scholarship, 1970; *The View in Winter: Reflections on Old Age* was named a notable book by *Library Journal,* 1980; Angel Prize, 1986; honorary degree, University of East Anglia, 1990.

WRITINGS:

FICTION

A Treasonable Growth (novel), MacGibbon & Kee (London), 1960.

Immediate Possession (short stories), MacGibbon & Kee, 1961.

The Visitors: The Stories of Ronald Blythe, Harcourt (New York City), 1985, published as *The Stories of Ronald Blythe,* Chatto & Windus (London), 1985.

NONFICTION

The Age of Illusion (social history), Hamish Hamilton (London), 1963, Houghton (Boston, MA), 1964.

Akenfield: Portrait of an English Village (social history), Pantheon (New York City), 1969.

The View in Winter: Reflections on Old Age (social history), Harcourt, 1979.

From the Headlands, 1982, published as *Characters and Their Landscapes,* Harcourt, 1984.

Divine Landscapes (travel), Harcourt, 1986.

EDITOR

Jane Austen, *Emma,* New English Library (London), 1966.

Components of the Scene: An Anthology of the Poetry and Prose of the Second World War, Penguin (New York City), 1966.

William Hazlitt, *William Hazlitt: Selected Writings,* Penguin, 1970.

Aldeburgh Anthology (history of Aldeburgh Festival), Faber (London), 1972.

Thomas Hardy, *A Pair of Blue Eyes,* Macmillan (New York City), 1978.

Hardy, *Far from the Madding Crowd,* Penguin, 1979.

My Favourite Village Stories, Lutterworth (Cambridge, England), 1979.

Leon Tolstoy, *The Death of Ivan Illych,* Bantam (New York City), 1980.

Places: An Anthology of Britain, Viking (New York City), 1981.

Henry James, *The Awkward Age,* Penguin, 1987.

The Pleasures of Diaries, Pantheon (New York City), 1989.

Private Words: Letters and Diaries from the Second World War, Viking, 1991.

OTHER

Also author of *Each Returning Day,* 1989. Contributor of short stories, essays, and reviews to *London Magazine, Observer, New World Writing, New Statesman, Sunday Times, Harper's Bazaar, Country Life, Countryman, New York Times, Atlantic Monthly, Listener, Independent, Guardian,* and other publications. Author of scripts for British Broadcasting Corp. (BBC-TV) and New Zealand Broadcasting Co., including *Akenfield,* directed by Sir Peter Hall; *A Painter in the Country,* directed by John Read for BBC-TV; and *Constable Observed,* directed by Read for BBC-TV.

SIDELIGHTS: Ronald Blythe describes himself to *CA* as "an imaginative and poetic writer, partly a scholar." While his bibliography includes a long and diverse list of titles, his reputation rests primarily on two "oral histories," *Akenfield: Portrait of an English Village* and *The View in Winter: Reflections on Old Age.* Paul Fussel, writing in the *Times Literary Supplement,* calls *Akenfield* a "sympathetic study of village life" and *The View in Winter* a "moving inquiry into the life of the very old." Blythe, Fussel concludes, has a "talent for celebrating admirable people." Blythe's work has been compared to that of American writer John Updike by Valentine Cunningham of the *Times Literary Supplement* who observes that "it often seems that Blythe is doing for the honeysuckled ambience of unfervid village Anglicans what Updike seeks to do for their white clapboard counterparts in Lutheran North America."

Akenfield: Portrait of an English Village is an oral history of an imaginary English village in East Anglia, about ninety miles northeast of London. Blythe was born and raised in the area and still lives there. In the summer and fall of 1967 he interviewed forty-nine ordinary people about their lives, edited the transcripts, invented names for his interview subjects, and placed them in the imaginary farming village of Akenfield. The village is a composite of several of the communities in this bucolic corner of England.

Although other writers had ploughed this same literary ground, critics praised the sensitivity and eye for detail that Blythe brought to the task. Reviewer Roger Starr of the *New Republic* praises the book as "a self-portrait so artfully drawn by the writer that it appears artless." Yorick Blumenfeld of the *Atlantic* describes it as a "superb documentation of the changes which have revolutionized modern England." *Akenfield* earned a Heinemann Award as one of the best books of 1969.

Blythe employed the same interviewing techniques a decade later to create *The View in Winter,* an oral history of old age. He recorded his conversations with elderly people in East Anglia and in a Welsh mining community. Author

V. S. Pritchett, writing in the *New York Review of Books,* calls *The View in Winter* "an unflinching, inquiring, and reflective essay, graced by wide reading of the poets, novelists and philosophers and brought sharply to life by interviews in which the old cottager, farmer, miner, the matron, the nurse, and others of all classes talk about their experiences and their dreads." B. G. Harrison of the *New York Times Book Review* echoes these comments: "It does not take much imagination or courage to predict that *The View in Winter,* a wise and beautiful book, splendid in its conception, lyrical in its prose, will become a classic in the literature of old age."

According to an interview with *New York Times* reporter Richard Eder, Blythe is reluctant to be regarded as an authority on old age. "I am a poet, not an expert," he says. Indeed, Blythe's greatest strength as a writer, critics agree, is his capacity to absorb the stories that people tell him; it is the richness of everyday life which intrigues him and which he celebrates in his writings. This quality is also evident in the twenty short stories in *The Visitors: The Stories of Ronald Blythe.* As reviewer Michiko Kakutani of the *New York Times* notes, "Blythe takes on in fictional terms much the same territory he covered as a journalist, in *Akenfield.*"

Blythe once told *CA:* "Except for visits to Cambridge and London for research, I live rather quietly in the country. I work to schedules, don't travel much, read constantly and enormously, give talks, garden a great deal, talk a lot and walk long distances. . . . The country at Debach is pastoral and remote. I enjoy sophisticated breaks in London, but on the whole I am a studious countryman."

BIOGRAPHICAL/CRITICAL SOURCES:

PERIODICALS

Atlantic, September, 1969.
Christian Science Monitor, October 22, 1986, p. 21.
New Republic, October 4, 1969, p. 23; December 15, 1979, p. 39.
New York Review of Books, January 1, 1970, p. 24; November 8, 1979, p. 7.
New York Times, April 16, 1980, pp. C-1, 9; November 30, 1985.
New York Times Book Review, December 8, 1985, p. 68.
Times Literary Supplement, June 6, 1969, p. 609; November 23, 1979, p. 18; August 9, 1985, p. 874; September 27, 1991.
Washington Post, October 18, 1969.

—*Sketch by Ken Cuthbertson*

BOLES, John B(ruce) 1943-

PERSONAL: Born October 20, 1943, in Houston, TX; son of B. B. Boles (a farmer) and Mary (McDaniel) Boles; married Nancy Gaebler, September 2, 1967; children: David Christopher, Matthew Thomas. *Education:* Rice University, B.A., 1965; University of Virginia, Ph.D., 1969. *Politics:* Democrat. *Religion:* "Baptist/Lutheran."

ADDRESSES: Home—8514 Prichett, Houston, TX 77096. *Office*—Department of History, Rice University, Houston, TX 77251.

CAREER: Towson State University, Baltimore, MD, assistant professor, 1969-72, associate professor, 1972-75, professor of history, 1975-77; Rice University, Houston, TX, visiting associate professor, 1977-78, professor of history, 1981—; Tulane University, New Orleans, LA, associate professor, 1978-80, professor of history, 1980-81.

MEMBER: Organization of American Historians, Southern Historical Association, Houston Philosophical Society.

AWARDS, HONORS: National Endowment for the Humanities fellow in anthropology, 1976-77.

WRITINGS:

The Great Revival, 1787-1805: The Origins of the Southern Evangelical Mind, University Press of Kentucky (Lexington), 1972.
(Editor) *America, the Middle Period: Essays in Honor of Bernard Mayo,* University Press of Virginia (Charlottesville), 1973.
Religion in Antebellum Kentucky, University Press of Kentucky, 1976.
(Editor) *Maryland Heritage: Five Baltimore Institutions Celebrate the American Bicentennial,* Maryland Historical Society (Baltimore), 1976.
Black Southerners, 1619-1869, University Press of Kentucky, 1983.
(Editor) *Dixie Dateline: A Journalistic Portrait of the Contemporary South,* Rice University Studies (Houston, TX), 1983.
(With Fryar Calhoun and Geoff Winningham) *Rice University: A 75th Anniversary Portrait,* photographs by Winningham, Rice University Press (Houston, TX), 1987.
(Editor with Evelyn Thomas Nolen) *Interpreting Southern History: Historiographical Essays in Honor of S. W. Higginbotham,* Louisiana State University Press (Baton Rouge), 1987.
(Editor) *Masters and Slaves in the House of the Lord: Race and Religion in the American South,* University Press of Kentucky, 1988.

Also author of pamphlets *Guide to the Papers of William Wirt,* Maryland Historical Society, 1971; and *Guide to the Papers of John Pendleton Kennedy,* Maryland Historical Society, 1972. Contributor to books, including *Religion in the South: Essays,* edited by Charles Reagan Wilson, University Press of Mississippi, 1985. Contributor of articles and reviews to history journals, encyclopedias, and dictionaries. Editor, *Maryland Historical Magazine,* 1974-77; managing editor, *Journal of Southern History,* 1983—.

WORK IN PROGRESS: Research on culture and religion in the antebellum South.*

*　　*　　*

BONATTI, Walter 1930-

PERSONAL: Born June 22, 1930, in Bergamo, Italy; son of Angelo and Agostina (Appiani) Bonatti; married (separated). *Religion:* Christian.

ADDRESSES: Via Monastero, 18, 23015 Dubino, Sondrio, Italy.

CAREER: Epoca (weekly magazine), Milan, Italy, journalist and correspondent, 1965-79; writer, 1979—. *Military service:* Corpo Militare Alpini, 1951-52.

AWARDS, HONORS: Gold, silver, and bronze medals from the Italian Republic for civil valor; French Legion of Honor; gold medal from the Consiglio d'Europa; grand prize from the Sports Academy of Paris; gold medal for sports valor; Argosy Giant of Adventure Award, 1971.

WRITINGS:

(And photographer) *Le mie montagne,* Zanichelli, 1961, revised edition, Rizzoli, 1983, translation by Lovett F. Edwards published as *On the Heights,* Hart-Davis (London), 1964.
I giorni grandi, preface by Dino Buzzati, A. Mondadori, 1971, translation by Geoffrey Sutton published as *The Great Days,* Gollancz (London), 1974.
Ho vissuto tra gli animali selvaggi, Zanichelli, 1980.
Avventura, Rizzoli, 1984.
Magia del Monte Blanco, Massimo Baldini Editore, 1984, translation by Sutton published as *Magic of Mount Blanc,* Gollancz, 1985.
Processo al K2, Massimo Baldini Editore, 1985.
La mia Patagonia, Massimo Baldini Editore, 1986.
L'ultima Amazzonia, Massimo Baldini Editore, 1989.
Un modo di essere, Dall' Oglio Editore, 1989.

BIOGRAPHICAL/CRITICAL SOURCES:

PERIODICALS

Esquire, November, 1965.
Guardian Weekly, December 21, 1974.

Reader's Digest, September, 1965.
Times Literary Supplement, March 28, 1975.

*　　*　　*

BONNER, John Tyler 1920-

PERSONAL: Born May 12, 1920, in New York, NY; son of Paul Hyde (an author) and Lilly Marguerite (Stehli) Bonner; married Ruth Anna Graham, July 11, 1942; children: Rebecca, Jonathan Graham, Jeremy Tyndall, Andrew Duncan. *Education:* Phillips Exeter Academy, graduate, 1937; Harvard University, B.S. (magna cum laude), 1941, M.A., 1942, Ph.D., 1947.

ADDRESSES: Home—148 Mercer St., Princeton, NJ 08540. *Office*—Department of Ecology and Evolutionary Biology, Princeton University, Princeton, NJ 08544.

CAREER: Princeton University, Princeton, NJ, assistant professor, 1947-50, associate professor, 1950-58, professor, 1958-66, George M. Moffett Professor of Biology, 1966—, chairman of department, 1965-77, 1983-84, 1987-88. Special lecturer at Marine Biology Laboratory, Woods Hole, MA, 1951-52, University of London, winter, 1956, and Brooklyn College of the City University of New York, spring, 1966. Trustee, *Biological Abstracts,* 1958-63; advisory editor, Dodd, Mead & Co., 1962-69; member of editorial board, Princeton University Press, 1964-68, 1971, trustee, 1975. *Military service:* U.S. Army Air Forces, 1942-46; became first lieutenant.

MEMBER: American Academy of Arts and Sciences (fellow), National Academy of Sciences, American Society of Naturalists, Society for Developmental Biology, American Philosophical Society, Mycological Society of America, Phi Beta Kappa, Sigma Xi.

AWARDS, HONORS: Sheldon traveling fellow in Panama and Cuba, Harvard University, 1941; Rockefeller traveling fellow in Paris, 1953; Selman A. Waksman Award, Theobald Smith Society, 1955, for contributions to microbiology; Guggenheim fellow in Edinburgh, Scotland, 1958, 1971-72; National Science Foundation senior postdoctoral fellow in Cambridge, England, 1963; D.Sc., Middlebury College, 1970.

WRITINGS:

Morphogenesis: An Essay on Development, Princeton University Press (Princeton, NJ), 1952.
Cells and Societies, Princeton University Press, 1955.
The Evolution of Development, Cambridge University Press (New York City), 1958.
The Cellular Slime Molds, Princeton University Press, 1959, 2nd edition, 1966.

(Editor) D'Arcy Wentworth Thompson, *On Growth and Form,* abridged edition, Cambridge University Press, 1961, reprinted, 1984.

The Ideas of Biology, Harper (New York City), 1962.

Size and Cycle: An Essay on the Structure of Biology, Princeton University Press, 1965.

The Scale of Nature, Harper, 1969.

On Development: The Biology of Form, Harvard University Press (Cambridge, MA), 1974.

The Evolution of Culture in Animals, Princeton University Press, 1980.

Evolution and Development, Dahlem Workshop on Evolution and Development (Berlin), 1981, Springer-Verlag (New York City), 1982.

The Evolution of Complexity by Means of Natural Selection, Princeton University Press, 1988.

Researches on Cellular Slime Moulds: Selected Papers of J. T. Bonner, Indian Academy of Sciences (Bangalore, India), 1991.

Life Cycles: Reflections of an Evolutionary Biologist, Princeton University Press, 1993.

Also author, with T. A. McMahon, of *On Life and Size,* 1983. Contributor to books, including *Developmental Biology,* W. C. Brown (Dubuque, IA), 1966; *Chemical Ecology,* Academic Press (New York City), 1970; and *The Process of Biology: Primary Sources,* Addison-Wesley (Reading, MA), 1970.

Contributor to *Science Digest, Scientific American, Natural History,* and other periodicals. Member of editorial board, *Growth,* 1955—, *American Naturalist,* 1958-60, 1966-68, *Journal of General Physiology,* 1962-69, *Oxford Surveys in Evolutionary Biology,* 1982—; associate editor of two sections, *Biological Abstracts,* 1957—; associate editor, *American Scientist,* 1961-69, and *Differentiation,* 1976—.

The Ideas of Biology is the most translated of Bonner's books, with editions in Italian, Danish, Portuguese, German, Arabic, and Norwegian.

BIOGRAPHICAL/CRITICAL SOURCES:

PERIODICALS

American Anthropologist, September, 1981, p. 708.

Best Sellers, October 15, 1970, p. 294.

Catholic World, December, 1969, p. 134.

Library Journal, May 1, 1969, p. 1887.

Los Angeles Times Book Review, September 21, 1980, p. 12.

Nature, November 17, 1988, p. 269.

New Yorker, August 11, 1980, p. 90.

New York Review of Books, January 21, 1981, p. 42.

Science and Technology, November, 1988; October, 1990.

Times Literary Supplement, September 19, 1980, p. 1014.

BOOKCHIN, Murray 1921-
(Lewis Herber)

PERSONAL: Born January 14, 1921, in New York, NY; son of Nathan and Rose Bookchin; children: one daughter, one son.

ADDRESSES: Home—21 Alfred St., Burlington, VT 05401.

CAREER: Writer and lecturer. Professor emeritus of social ecology, Ramapo College of New Jersey, Mahwah. Director emeritus, Institute for Social Ecology, Goddard College, Rochester, VT.

WRITINGS:

(Under pseudonym Lewis Herber) *Lebensgefarlich Lebensmittel,* [Munich], 1954.

(Under pseudonym Lewis Herber) *Our Synthetic Environment,* Knopf (New York City), 1962, revised edition (under real name), Harper (New York City), 1974.

(Under pseudonym Lewis Herber) *Crisis in Our Cities,* Prentice-Hall (Englewood Hills, NJ), 1965.

Post-Scarcity Anarchism, Ramparts (San Francisco), 1971.

The Limits of the City, Harper, 1973.

Spanish Anarchists, Harper, 1978.

Toward an Ecological Society, Black Rose Books (New York City), 1980.

The Ecology of Freedom: The Emergence and Dissolution of Hierarchy, Cheshire (Palo Alto, CA), 1982.

The Modern Crisis, New Society Publishers (Philadelphia, PA), 1986.

The Rise of Urbanization and the Decline of Citizenship, Sierra Club (San Francisco), 1987.

The Philosophy of Social Ecology: Essays on Dialectical Naturalism, Black Rose Books, 1990.

Remaking Society: Pathways to a Green Future, South End Press (Boston), 1990.

(With David Foreman) *Defending the Earth: A Dialogue Between Murray Bookchin and Dave Foreman,* South End Press, 1991.

Urbanization Without Cities: The Rise and Decline of Citizenship, Black Rose Books, 1992.

Which Way for the Ecology Movement?, AK Press (San Francisco), 1993.

Also the author of *Ecology and Revolutionary Thought,* 1970, and (under pseudonym Lewis Herber) *Listen, Marxist!,* 1971. Contributor to *Hip Culture: Six Essays on Its Revolutionary Potential,* Times Change Press, 1971. Contributor to numerous anthologies and of numerous articles in periodicals and journals. Former associate editor, *Contemporary Issues* and *Radiation Information.*

SIDELIGHTS: Anarchist thinker and historian Murray Bookchin began his career with two books on the developing environmental crisis: *Our Synthetic Environment* and *Crisis in Our Cities.* Along with Rachel Carson's *Silent Spring,* these two books were among the earliest warnings that the prosperity of the post-war United States had been bought at the price of serious harm to our environment. Contemporary reviews were mixed, as some critics looked for Bookchin to supply practical solutions as well as sounding the alarm about the dangers of industrialization. But twenty years later, as many of these problems remain insufficiently explored, Stanley Aronowitz points out in the *Village Voice* that Bookchin "called the shots on an increasingly chemical-penetrated culture while most of us wallowed in the pleasures of disposable napkins and sugar-free everything."

Post-Scarcity Anarchism collected several essays from the 1960s outlining Bookchin's blend of ecological activism and anarchist philosophy. Like Marx, Bookchin argues that the human race can no longer thrive within such institutions of bourgeois life as the modern city, bureaucracy and family life. Unlike Marx, however, Bookchin does not predict the triumph of the working class over capitalism. Instead he foresees that the anti-authoritarian "younger generation" will rise up to dissolve all social hierarchies. Bookchin further makes the point that while capitalism and socialism differ in the assignment of control over the means of production, they are equally heedless of the effect that industrialized labor has on the environment. Therefore, neither can be the basis of a sustained society. People's domination over nature and their domination over each other sprang up together, argues Bookchin, and must be eliminated together.

A *Times Literary Supplement* critic finds that the essays in *Post-Scarcity Anarchism* have not held up over time. The reviewer claims that Bookchin's expectation that the "general lawlessness" of 1960s' youth culture would lead to a "liberating revolution . . . is touching, but preposterous." On the other hand, Todd Gitlin states in *Nation* that Bookchin's major point, that social problems must be considered in the context of the earth's environment, is an important contribution to revolutionary thought.

The pressing need to find new forms of living which will not destroy the planet has been a dominant theme in Bookchin's writings. *The Ecology of Freedom: The Emergence and Dissolution of Hierarchy* is devoted to Bookchin's idea that the concept of hierarchy—not simply our misuse of technology—is at the core of humanity's troubles. Bookchin's "social ecology" establishes the link "between our destructive relation with nature and our destructive human reactions," Aronowitz writes. Bookchin criticizes those "environmentalists" who are willing to leave most social institutions alone if whales can be saved and aerosol cans are banned. But the real threat to the planet's survival, claims Bookchin, is the destructive logic

behind a hierarchical social structure. Bookchin calls on the reader to appreciate the organic and harmonious societies of the past, such as the Plains Indians, and to envision a return to their way of life. "Bookchin calls for the reenchantment of nature," summarizes Aronowitz. "He wants to restore our sense of an organic life because he holds that such a life is the precondition for human survival."

According to Alan Wolfe in *Nation,* this poetic evocation of a harmonious past is more effective as a critique than as a blueprint for a new utopia. To appreciate the qualities of preliterate cultures does not show the way to cultural transformation, particularly if it is true, as Wolfe maintains, that preliterate societies "deformed human potential." "If we detest the artificial and inauthentic products of consumer capitalism run wild," Wolfe asks, "do we have to love the primitive ritual and long for states of heightened ecstasy?"

With *Remaking Society: Pathways to a Green Future,* Bookchin continues to warn of the conflict between unchecked industrialization and the health of the environment. The solution he proposes is to return to a way of life that ended with the Industrial Revolution. "He envisions confederations of small communities, governments built around town meetings, and shared labor based on the artisanal model of customized production," summarizes Michael Oppenheimer in a review for *New York Times Book Review.* Bookchin again looks to the past to argue that societies less hierarchical than ours once existed, an anthropological claim Oppenheimer finds "too sweeping to be credible." Oppenheimer concludes, nevertheless, that Bookchin "should not be ignored," because "environmentalism is no longer about wilderness protection; it's about saving the collective neck of humanity."

BIOGRAPHICAL/CRITICAL SOURCES:

BOOKS

Contemporary Issues Criticism, Volume 1, Gale, 1982.

PERIODICALS

American Anthropologist, March, 1984, p. 161.
American Political Science Review, June, 1983, p. 540.
American Spectator, December, 1982, p. 14.
Books & Bookmen, June, 1974, pp. 36-39.
Canadian Forum, March, 1993, p. 41.
Christian Century, October 6, 1965, pp. 1232-33.
Dissent, summer, 1977, pp. 538-40.
Nation, March 6, 1972, pp. 309-11; May 29, 1982, p. 660.
Natural History, January, 1963, pp. 3-5.
New York Review of Books, October 13, 1977, p. 22.
New York Times Book Review, November 8, 1987, p. 18; November 25, 1990, p. 13.
Reason, December, 1990, p. 35.

San Francisco Review of Books, November, 1982, p. 7.
Sierra, September, 1982, p. 74; July, 1991, p. 56.
Technology Review, April, 1983, p. 22.
Times Literary Supplement, June 21, 1974, p. 662.
Village Voice, July 20, 1982, p. 36.
Washington Post Book World, September 2, 1990, p. 12.*

* * *

BORETZ, Alvin 1919-

PERSONAL: Born June 15, 1919, in New York, NY; son of Samuel (a tailor) and Mollie (a shopkeeper; maiden name, Milch) Boretz; married Lucille Garson, November 1, 1942; children: Dr. Jennifer Boretz Kahnweiler, Carrie Boretz Keating. *Education:* Brooklyn College (now Brooklyn College of the City University of New York), B.A., 1942. *Politics:* Liberal. *Religion:* Jewish. *Avocational interests:* Squash; bicycling; theater, concerts, and museums; travel at home and abroad; magazines, newspapers, and people, where "the ideas come from all and crowd each other out."

ADDRESSES: Home—Woodmere, NY. *Agent*—Preferred Artists Agency, 16633 Ventura Blvd., Encino, CA 91436.

CAREER: Writer of scripts for stage, screen, radio, and television programs, including *The Alcoa Hour, Armstrong Circle Theatre, General Electric Theatre, Playhouse 90, ABC Afterschool Special, CBS Children's Hour, ABC Movie of the Week,* and *NBC World Premiere Movie. New York Evening Journal,* New York City, copy assistant, 1937; Modern Industrial Bank, New York City, credit analyst, 1937-42; freelance radio scriptwriter, 1942-54; television scriptwriter, 1954—. Adjunct professor of screenwriting at Hofstra University and of communications at Adelphi University, both 1976-78; president of board of trustees of Hewlett-Woodmere Public Library, Long Island, NY. *Military service:* U.S. Army Air Force, 1942-45; became warrant officer.

MEMBER: Writers Guild of America (member of council, 1962-74; vice president, 1969-71), Dramatists Guild, PEN American Center.

AWARDS, HONORS: Ohio State Award, Institute for Education by Radio-Television, 1956, for radio play *Little Girl Lost;* Harcourt Brace Award for best television play, 1957, for *Trial of Poznan;* Godmothers' League Public Service Award, 1961, for *Armstrong Circle Theatre* television play *The Hidden World;* first prize from Family Service Association, 1963, for *Armstrong Circle Theatre* television play *Battle of Hearts;* Christopher Award, 1973, for children's drama *Follow the North Star,* an *ABC Afterschool Special.*

WRITINGS:

Brass Target (screenplay; based on the novel *The Algonquin Project* by Frederick Nolan), United Artists, 1978.
Made in America (two-act stage play), first produced in Los Angeles at Mark Taper Forum, 1984.
I Remember You (television play; first produced on Arts and Entertainment Network, 1991) I. E. Clark (Schulenburg, TX), 1993.

Author of many documentaries, several hundred radio plays, and more than one thousand television plays, including *The Blue Men, The Desperate Season, No License to Kill, Little Girl Lost, House of Cards, Trial of Poznan, The Hidden World, Battle of Hearts,* and *Follow the North Star.* Also author of scripts for episodes of television series *The Defenders, Dr. Kildare, Medical Center,* and *Kojak,* among others.

SIDELIGHTS: Alvin Boretz is widely known as one of television's most prolific writers. With an estimated one thousand dramatic scripts to his credit, he is an industry veteran who contributed to such "Golden Age of Television" shows as *The Alcoa Hour, Playhouse 90,* and *General Electric Theatre.* He also wrote scripts for episodes of a number of television series, including *Kojak* as well as the *ABC Afterschool Special* and *NBC World Premiere Movie.* Before television became popular in the early 1950s, Boretz wrote for radio where he honed his language skills and developed a flair for writing dialogue. Additionally, he became noted for strong character development, a feature which distinguishes Boretz's work, along with his sensitive but forthright handling of themes such as divorce, suicide, and mental retardation.

One of Boretz's stage plays, *Made in America,* made its debut in 1984 at the Mark Taper Forum in Los Angeles. Dan Sullivan of the *Los Angeles Times* described it as "a big play, with no scarcity of themes." Set in middle-class Boston, the play's central character is a blue-collar, second-generation Irish American who laments the deteriorating condition of his life and his country. "Boretz shows a good grasp of his characters and . . . where he wants to go with them," stated Sullivan, adding that each of the play's scenes offers a "fresh attempt" to convey the main character's general malaise. Noting Boretz's sometimes humorous dialogue in an otherwise serious play, Sullivan suggested that "we may be dealing with an optimist here."

Boretz once told *CA:* "As a boy I began frequenting Brooklyn's first-run movie houses that also featured stage shows. That was enough to fire anyone's imagination, and I knew where my future lay. After my discharge from the army, I was still young enough and brave enough to try to make it as a dramatic writer. I managed to write a few radio plays and eventually was doing two or three a week.

Radio was a marvelous training ground and gave me a love and respect for language that has helped me immeasurably. Through language, you were shaping everything—the place, the people. And every line of dialogue not only had to impart information and show characterization, at the same time it also had to be a good line in itself. Just the alliteration of the line, or the words you chose, would convey the emotion you were trying to get.

"Writing in all three dramatic forms—television, movies, and the theater—allows me to work on a limitless range of material, as most stories naturally fall into one medium more easily than the other two. For my thematic material I look for the affirmation in most people's struggles.

"I was an original founder of United Cerebral Palsy [UCP] because I had a cerebral palsy son. A script for a radio program I wrote in 1947, *Love Is a Doctor,* played a tremendous part in helping UCP become a reality. And that's one of the reasons why, in later years, I would go to the problems of society to find a lot of my material. I felt that was part of my function as a writer. I've always felt very proud of that, and I feel very encouraged by it. It's one of the things that keeps you going in this terribly difficult business.

"When people ask me how to get started as a writer, I say that there's no rule. You write something and then you bang on doors, and if you believe in yourself, it will someday happen to you. But you can't just sit there in a tweed jacket smoking a pipe and think that someone's going to think of you and call you up. I respect talent enormously, and I firmly believe that people with talent will make it. There are very few brilliant writers in this country who are sitting at home unknown. It just does not happen, because good talent is very rare and it shines by example, because it's so singular."

BIOGRAPHICAL/CRITICAL SOURCES:

PERIODICALS

Hollywood Reporter, April 15, 1991.
Los Angeles Times, March 3, 1984.
New York Post, February 22, 1978.
New York Times, March 17, 1960; November 1, 1972; December 22, 1978.
Sun-Times (Chicago), December 26, 1978.
Variety, June 10, 1959; January 9, 1962; January 28, 1970; November 8, 1972; April 15, 1991.

*   *   *

BOSE, Tarun Chandra   1931-

PERSONAL: Born June 16, 1931, in Calcutta, India; son of B. C. and Lily (Mitra) Bose; married Zinnia Dutt (an artist), May 6, 1962. *Education:* Presidency College, B.A., (honors), 1951; University of Calcutta, M.A., 1954; University Law College, LL.B., 1955; Indian School of International Studies, Ph.D., 1961.

ADDRESSES: Home—26 Lansdowne Ter., Calcutta 700026, India. *Office*—Department of Political Science, University of Kalyani, Kalyani, 74125, West Bengal, India.

CAREER: Jadavpur University, Calcutta, India, assistant professor, 1959-64, associate professor of international law, international politics and relations, and American-Russian foreign policy, 1965-73; Dibrugarh University, Dibrugarh, India, professor of political science, 1974-80, member of the executive council, 1978-80; University of Kalyani, Kalyani, India, professor of political science and chairman of department, 1981—. Indian University Grants Commission, national lecturer, 1977-78, member, Panel of Experts in Political Science, 1978-80; visiting professor at University of Nebraska, 1980; has attended international professional congresses.

MEMBER: International Political Science Association, Indian Society of International Law, Indian Council of World Affairs, Indian Political Science Association (member of executive committee, 1976-78), American Studies Research Centre (member of board of directors, 1963-64), Indian Association for American Studies (president, 1976), Lions International.

AWARDS, HONORS: Ford Foundation research fellow at Columbia University, 1957-58; postdoctoral fellow at the University of Missouri, 1964; Fulbright-Hays senior grantee at Harvard University, 1969-70; American Council of Learned Societies fellow at the Center for International Affairs, Harvard University, 1979-80.

WRITINGS:

American-Soviet Relations, Firma K. L. Mukhopadhyay, 1967.
The Superpowers and the Middle East, Asia Publishing House, 1972.
(Editor) *Political Development in North-East India,* Dibrugarh University (Dibrugarh, India), Volume 1, 1976, Volume 2, 1978.
(Editor) *Indian Federalism: Problems and Issues,* University of Kalyani (Kalyani, India), 1987.

Contributor to *American History by Indian Historians,* Volume 2, American Studies Research Centre, 1969, and to *International Studies* and other professional journals. Member of board of editors, *Indian Journal of American Studies,* 1968-72.

WORK IN PROGRESS: Research on nuclear arms limitation, nuclear power and proliferation, and nuclear terrorism.

SIDELIGHTS: Tarun Chandra Bose has traveled in the United States, England, West Germany, the Soviet Union, France, Norway, Sweden, Denmark, Switzerland, Spain, Italy, Austria, Greece, Turkey, Egypt, Lebanon, Iran, Hong Kong, and Japan.

BIOGRAPHICAL/CRITICAL SOURCES:

PERIODICALS

American Political Science Review, September, 1974, p. 1382.
Middle East Journal, summer, 1974, p. 328.*

* * *

BOWDEN, Elbert Victor 1924-

PERSONAL: First syllable of surname rhymes with "how"; born November 25, 1924, in Wilmington, NC; son of James Owen (a seafood producer and wholesaler) and Dovie Ellen (Phelps) Bowden; married Mary Mariani, May 30, 1948 (divorced, 1950); married Doris Fales (a registered nurse), September 11, 1951 (divorced, 1977); married Marie-Louise van Laarshot (a professional dancer), June 25, 1979 (divorced, 1984); married Judith Holbert (an economist), November 25, 1984; children: (first marriage) Elbert Victor, Jr.; (second marriage) Richard A., Doris Ellen, William Austin, Jack B., Joyce Leigh; (fourth marriage) Kristen Rae, Amy LeeLani. *Education:* University of Connecticut, B.A. (with high distinction), 1950; Duke University, M.A., 1952, Ph.D., 1957.

ADDRESSES: Home—P. O. Box 1461, Boone, NC 28607. *Office*—John A. Walker College of Business, Appalachian State University, Boone, NC 28608.

CAREER: Duke University, Durham, NC, instructor in economics, 1952-54; University of Kentucky, Lexington, research associate at Bureau of Business Research, 1954-55; Duke University, Durham, instructor in economics, 1955-56; College of William and Mary in Norfolk (now Old Dominion University), Norfolk, VA, associate professor, 1956-57, professor of economics and chair of department, 1958-63; Elmira College, Elmira, NY, professor of economics, 1963-64; Upper Peninsula Committee for Area Progress, Escanaba, MI, executive director, 1964-65; Robert R. Nathan Associates (trust territory economic development team), Saipan, Mariana Islands, chief economist and chief of mission, 1965-67; Texas A & M University, College Station, associate professor of economics and research economist, 1967-70; State University of New York College at Fredonia, professor of economics,

1970-74; United Nations Fiji Regional Planning Project, Suva, Fiji, chief economic advisor and project manager, 1975-77; Appalachian State University, John A. Walker College of Business, Boone, NC, professor of economics and chair of banking department, 1977—. *Military service:* U.S. Maritime Service, instructor, 1943, student at officer's training school, 1945; U.S. Merchant Marine, 1943-45, deck officer, 1945-46; served in Atlantic, European and Pacific theaters.

Has conducted symposia, workshops, and seminars; testified at hearings of Interstate Commerce Commission and U.S. Senate committees, and presented material to Federal Communications Commission, Federal Power Commission, and U.S. Trust Territory of the Pacific Islands.

MEMBER: American Association for the Advancement of Science, American Economic Association, American Business Writers Association, American Association of University Professors, Northeast Regional Science Association (vice president, 1971-72), Rocky Mountain Social Science Association, Southern Economic Association, Southwestern Social Science Association, Western Regional Science Association, New York State Economic Association, Western Economic Association International, Midwest Finance Association, Southwestern Finance Association, Southwestern Society of Economists, Eastern Economic Association, Eastern Finance Association, Atlantic Economic Society, Southern Finance Association, Gamma Chi Epsilon, Omicron Delta Epsilon.

AWARDS, HONORS: Ford Foundation fellowship, University of North Carolina at Chapel Hill, 1960; Chancellor's Award for teaching excellence, State University of New York College at Fredonia, 1973; award for teaching excellence, Student Government Association, Appalachian State University, 1989.

WRITINGS:

(With Thomas W. Carlin) *Economics,* Alexander Hamilton Institute (New York City), 1960, revised edition, 1969.
Development Opportunities for Virginia's Eastern Shore (monograph), Area Redevelopment Administration, U.S. Department of Commerce (Washington, DC), 1963.
Multi-County Programming and Implementation for Economic Development (monograph), Robert R. Nathan Associates, 1964.
(Principal author) *Economic Development Plan for Micronesia: A Proposed Long-Rang Plan for Developing the Trust Territory of the Pacific Islands,* three volumes, Robert R. Nathan Associates for High Commissioner of Trust Territory, 1966.

Economic Development Plan for Micronesia: Summary Report (monograph), Robert R. Nathan Associates, 1967.

WIDE: A Mic-American Concept for the Economic Development of the Western Pacific Islands, Industrial Economics Research Division, Texas A & M University (College Station), 1968.

(Editor) *Urban and Regional Development Planning in Texas,* Division of Planning Coordination, Office of the Governor of Texas (Austin), 1969.

(With E. A. Copp) *The Houston-Galveston Area: An Overview of Resources, Population, Economic Activities, and Projections* (monograph), Industrial Economics Research Division, Texas A & M University, 1969.

(With Copp) *Analysis of Land Use Alternatives and Industrial Potential for the Houston Farms Properties* (monograph), Industrial Economics Research Division, Texas A & M University, 1969.

(With Copp) *Future Industry Demand and Land Development Patterns for the Houston Farms Properties* (monograph), Industrial Economics Research Division, Texas A & M University, 1969.

Location Factors for Nuclear Energy Centers (monograph), Industrial Economics Research Division, Texas A & M University, 1970.

University and Community: Principles, Issues and Case Studies of Faculty-Student Involvement in Urban and Regional Problems (monograph), Department of Economics, Texas A & M University, 1970.

Nuclear Energy Research and Development in the Pacific Northwest (monograph), Industrial Economics Research Division, Texas A & M University, 1970.

(Editor) *Intergovernmental Relations and Regional Planning in Texas* (monograph), Division of Planning Coordination, Office of the Governor of Texas, 1970.

Fundamentals of Economics: Simple Explanations of Basic Micro and Macro Concepts, privately printed, 1971.

Economics in Historical Perspective: The Continuing Evolution of Economics Conditions, Problems, Theories, and Systems, State University of New York College at Fredonia, 1973.

Economics: The Science of Common Sense, South-Western (Cincinnati), 1974, abridged edition published with *Study Guide, Instructor's Manual,* and *Test Bank,* 1975, 7th edition, 1992.

Economics through the Looking Glass, Canfield Press, 1974.

Principles of Economics: Theory, Problems, Policies, published with *Study Guide, Instructor's Manual,* and *Test Bank,* 3rd edition, South-Western, 1980, 5th edition, 1986.

Revolution in Banking: Regulatory Changes, the New Competitive Environment, and the "New World" for the Financial Services Industry in the 1980s, Robert F. Dame (Richmond, VA), 1980, 2nd edition (with wife Judith L. Holbert), Reston, 1984.

Economic Evolution: Principles, Issues, Ideas—Through the Looking Glass of Time, South-Western, 1981, 2nd edition, 1985.

Money, Banking, and the Financial System, published with *Study Guide, Instructor's Manual,* and *Test Bank,* West Publishing (St. Paul, MN), 1989.

Economics in Perspective, 3rd edition, South-Western, 1990.

Contributor to conferences, proceedings, and annals. Contributor of articles and reviews to journals, including *Land Economics, Southern Economic Review, Social Science Quarterly, American Economic Review, Journal of Economic Literature,* and *Growth and Change: A Journal of Development.*

SIDELIGHTS: Elbert Victor Bowden once told *CA:* "Economics is not noted for its simplicity nor for the clarity with which it is discussed in print. But I think the problem is more with economists than with economics. It isn't that economics is so complex that it defies explanation. It's just that economists (so often) lack either the conceptual understanding of their own theories or the communications skills required to transmit that understanding. So the singular objective of my writings in economics is to explain complex ideas and theory in easily understandable (and hopefully interesting) prose. To the extent that I succeed in doing that, I can make a contribution to economic understanding in this nation and world, and God knows, that's an objective worthy of pursuit."

In the introduction to his book *Economic Evolution: Principles, Issues, Ideas—through the Looking Glass of Time,* Bowden writes that the volume "has but one purpose: to explain the economic realities of today—the conditions, problems, and ideas—in historical perspective and thereby to provide better awareness and understanding of the present, and insight into the future. There isn't much *historical detail* in this book. The flow of thought moves rapidly from one period to another and from one developer of ideas to another, touching the highlights, gathering the threads and pulling them all together.

"The facts of history, once learned, are easily forgotten. But an awareness of the flow of history, once gained, is never lost. And an awareness of the importance of *economic forces* influencing history, once gained, is never lost. All of us can gain this awareness—can learn to see ourselves and our world as a part of this evolutionary sweep through time."

BIOGRAPHICAL/CRITICAL SOURCES:

BOOKS

Bowden, Elbert Victor, *Economic Evolution: Principles, Issues, Ideas—Through the Looking Glass of Time,* 2nd edition, South-Western, 1985.*

*   *   *

BOWERS, Fredson (Thayer)   1905-1991

PERSONAL: Born April 25, 1905, in New Haven, CT; died of arteriosclerotic vascular disease, April 11, 1991, in Charlottesville, VA; son of Fredson Eugene and Hattie (Quigley) Bowers; married Nancy Hale (a writer; died, 1988), March 16, 1942; children: Fredson, Jr., Stephen, Peter, Joan (Stout). *Education:* Brown University, Ph.B.; Harvard University, Ph.D.

CAREER: Harvard University, Cambridge, MA, instructor in English and tutor in modern languages, 1926-35; Princeton University, Princeton, NJ, instructor in English, 1936-38; University of Virginia, Charlottesville, 1938-91, began as assistant professor, became chairman of department, faculty dean, Linden Kent Memorial Professor of English, and Linden Kent Professor Emeritus, 1975-91. Sandars Reader, Cambridge University, 1958; James Lyell Reader, Oxford University, 1959. *Military service:* U.S. Naval Reserve, 1942-46; became commander; received unit decoration.

MEMBER: Modern Language Association of America (member of executive council, 1962-66), South Atlantic Modern Language Association (president, 1969), American Academy of Arts and Sciences, British Academy (corresponding fellow, 1968), Phi Beta Kappa.

AWARDS, HONORS: Fulbright fellow to United Kingdom, 1952-53; Guggenheim fellow, 1958-59, 1971-72; Poetry Society of America Award, 1960, for *Whitman's Manuscripts: Leaves of Grass (1860);* Bicentennial Medal, Brown University, 1964; Gold Medal, Bibliographical Society, London, 1968; Corresponding Fellow of the British Academy, 1968; honorary doctorates, Brown University, Clark University, both 1970; Thomas Jefferson Award, University of Virginia, 1971; research scholar, Villa Serbelloni Research Center, Bellagio, Italy, 1971-72; visiting fellow, All Souls College, Oxford University, 1972, 1974; fellow, American Academy of Arts and Sciences, 1972; honorary doctorate, University of Chicago, 1973; fellow, Commoner Churchill College, Cambridge University, 1975; Julian Boyd Award, Association of Documentary Editing, 1986; honorary member, Bibliographical Society of America, 1986.

WRITINGS:

The Dog Owner's Handbook, Houghton (Boston), 1936.
Elizabethan Revenge Tragedy: 1587-1942, Princeton University Press (Princeton, NJ), 1940, reprinted, Peter Smith, 1958.
Principles of Bibliographical Description, introduction by G. Thomas Tanselle, Princeton University Press, 1949, reprinted, Oak Knoll Press (New Castle, DE), 1994.
(With R. B. Davis) *George Sandys: A Bibliographical Catalogue of Printed Editions in England to 1700,* New York Public Library, 1950.
On Editing Shakespeare and the Elizabethan Dramatists, University of Pennsylvania Library (Philadelphia), 1955.
Textual and Literary Criticism, Cambridge University Press (Cambridge), 1959.
Bibliography and Textual Criticism, Clarendon Press, 1964.
Hamlet: An Outline Guide to the Play, Barnes & Noble (New York City), 1965.
(With Lyle H. Wright) *Bibliography,* University of California (Berkeley), 1966.
(With Charlton Hinman) *Two Lectures on Editing: Shakespeare and Hawthorne,* Ohio State University Press (Columbus), 1969.
Essays in Bibliography, Text, and Editing, University Press of Virginia (Charlottesville), 1975.
Hamlet as Minister and Scourge and Other Studies in Shakespeare and Milton, University Press of Virginia, 1989.

Also author of introduction to *Henry Fielding, Miscellanies,* Volume 1, edited by Henry K. Miller, Wesleyan University Press, 1973.

EDITOR

A Fary Knight or Oberon the Second: A Manuscript Play Attributed to Thomas Randolph, University of North Carolina Press (Chapel Hill), 1944.
Studies in Bibliography: Papers of the Bibliographical Society of the University of Virginia, thirty-five volumes, Bibliographical Society of the University of Virginia (Charlottesville), 1949-91.
The Dramatic Works of Thomas Dekker, four volumes, Cambridge University Press, 1953-61.
Whitman's Manuscripts: Leaves of Grass (1860), University of Chicago Press (Chicago), 1955.
Centenary Edition of the Works of Nathaniel Hawthorne, eleven volumes, Ohio State University Press, 1962-75.
William Shakespeare, *The Merry Wives of Windsor,* Penguin (Baltimore), 1963.

The Dramatic Works in the Beaumont and Fletcher Canon, ten volumes, Cambridge University Press, 1966-1995.

(With L. A. Beaurline) *John Dryden: Four Comedies,* University of Chicago Press, 1967.

(With Beaurline) *John Dryden: Four Tragedies,* University of Chicago Press, 1967.

The Works of Stephen Crane, ten volumes, University Press of Virginia, 1969-75.

The Complete Works of Christopher Marlowe, two volumes, Cambridge University Press, 1973, 2nd edition, 1981.

Henry Fielding, *Tom Jones, the History of a Foundling,* two volumes, Wesleyan University Press (Middletown, CT), 1974.

(Textual editor) *The Works of William James,* fifteen volumes, Harvard University Press (Cambridge, MA), 1975-87.

Vladimir Nabokov, *Lectures on Literature,* Harcourt Brace Jovanovich/Bruccoli Clark (New York City), 1980.

Vladimir Nabokov, *Lectures on Russian Literature,* Harcourt Brace Jovanovich/Bruccoli Clark, 1981.

(Textual editor) William James, *The Principles of Psychology,* three volumes, Harvard University Press, 1981.

(Textual editor) James, *Essays in Religion and Morality,* introduction by John J. McDermott, Harvard University Press, 1982.

Nabokov, *Lectures on Don Quixote,* foreword by Guy Davenport, Harcourt Brace Jovanovich/Bruccoli Clark, 1983.

(With wife, Nancy Hale Bowers) *Leon Kroll: A Spoken Memoir,* University Press of Virginia, 1983.

(Textual editor) Fielding, *Tom Jones,* introduction by Martin C. Battesin, Modern Library (New York City), 1985.

Dictionary of Literary Biography, Volume 58: *Jacobean and Elizabethan Dramatists,* Volume 62: *Elizabethan Dramatists,* Gale (Detroit), 1987.

Studies in Bibliography (hardcover text edition), University Press of Virginia, 1994.

Also textual consultant for *The Great Gatsby,* Cambridge University Press, 1991. Founded and edited *Studies in Bibliography;* contributed more than 1,200 book reviews to *Richmond Times-Dispatch.*

SIDELIGHTS: Fredson Bowers was an educator, a bibliographer, and a textual scholar of world renown. By studying earlier editions of an author's works in great detail, he was able to present new literary insights and prepare more authoritative texts. Bowers was best known for his theoretical work in descriptive bibliography and its practical applications. His system eventually became a standard for the field. His work *Principles of Bibliographi-*

cal Description was lauded as "one of the great achievements in modern scholarship . . . not likely ever to be superseded," according to G. Thomas Tanselle in *The Life and Work of Fredson Bowers.* Large collections edited by Bowers include the four-volume *Dramatic Works of Thomas Dekker,* the eleven-volume *Centenary Edition of the Works of Nathaniel Hawthorne,* and the ten-volume *Works of Stephen Crane.* He was at work on a bibliography of seventeenth-century English drama at the time of his death.

BIOGRAPHICAL/CRITICAL SOURCES:

BOOKS

Dictionary of Literary Biography, Volume 140: *American Book-Collectors and Bibliographers,* Gale (Detroit), 1994.

Dictionary of Literary Biography Yearbook: 1991, Gale, 1992.

Tanselle, G. Thomas, *The Life and Work of Fredson Bowers,* The Bibliographical Society of the University of Virginia (Charlottesville), 1993.

PERIODICALS

American Literature, November, 1971.

Los Angeles Times Book Review, December 20, 1981, p. 4.

Modern Language Review, July, 1978.

Times Literary Supplement, April 27, 1967; August 14, 1970; April 24, 1981, p. 457; June 24, 1983, p. 662; September 20, 1985, p. 1034; December 14, 1986, p. 12.

Washington Post Book World, September 19, 1982, p. 12; December 14, 1986, p. 12.

OBITUARIES:

PERIODICALS

Chicago Tribune, April 14, 1991, sec. 2, p. 6.

New York Times, April 13, 1991, p. 11.

Washington Post, April 13, 1991, p. B4.*

*   *   *

BOYD, Andrew (Kirk Henry)   1920-

PERSONAL: Born June 21, 1920, in Bournemouth, England; son of Henry Crawford and Beryl (Hylton-Foster) Boyd; married Frances Paterson, September 2, 1944; children: Lindsay. *Education:* Winchester College (England), 1933-38; Oxford University, M.A., 1940.

ADDRESSES: Home and office—25 St. James St., London SW1A 1HG, England.

CAREER: Pilot Press Ltd., London, England, editorial work, 1946-47; United Nations Association of Great Britain, London, England, editor, 1948-50; British Broadcasting Corporation (BBC), London, England, report editor, 1950-51; *Economist,* London, England, foreign affairs editor, 1951—. *Military service:* British Army, 1940-46; became captain; received Burma and Pacific stars.

MEMBER: Royal Institute of International Affairs, Travellers Club.

WRITINGS:

United Nations Organisation Handbook, Pilot Press (London), 1946.

Guide to 14 Asiatic Languages, Pilot Press, 1947.

(With Frances Boyd) *Western Union: U.N.A.'s Guide to European Recovery,* Hutchinson (London), 1948, published as *Western Union: A Study of the Trend toward European Unity,* Public Affairs Press (Washington, DC), 1949.

(With William Metson) *Atlantic Pact, Commonwealth and United Nations,* Hutchinson, 1949.

An Atlas of World Affairs, Praeger (New York City), 1957, 9th edition, Routledge (New York City), 1987.

(With Patrick van Rensburg) *An Atlas of African Affairs,* Praeger, 1962, 2nd edition, Methuen (New York City), 1965.

United Nations: Piety, Myth and Truth, Penguin (New York City), 1962, revised edition, Pelican (New York City), 1964.

Fifteen Men on a Powder Keg: A History of the U.N. Security Council, Stein & Day (Briarcliff Manor, NY), 1971, Methuen, 1973.

Contributor to various journals, including the *Listener, Nation* and *Survival.* Editor, *United Nations News,* 1948-50.

SIDELIGHTS: Andrew Boyd has traveled in Asia, Europe, North and South America, and Africa.

BIOGRAPHICAL/CRITICAL SOURCES:

PERIODICALS

Saturday Review, April 17, 1971.*

* * *

BRAGG, Melvyn 1939-

PERSONAL: Born October 6, 1939, in Wigton, Cumberland, England; son of Stanley (a shopkeeper) and Mary Ethel (Parks) Bragg; married Marie-Elisabeth Roche, June 26, 1961 (died September 1, 1971); married Catherine Mary Haste (a writer), December 18, 1974; children: (first marriage) Marie-Elsa; (second marriage) one daughter, one son. *Education:* Wadham College, Oxford, M.A.

(with honors), 1961. *Avocational interests:* Walking, books.

ADDRESSES: Home—12 Hampstead Hill Gardens, London NW3, England.

CAREER: British Broadcasting Corp. (BBC), London, England, producer, 1961-67, presenter of *Second House* series, 1973-77, presenter and editor of *Read All about It* series, 1976-77; ITV, London Weekend Television, London, presenter and editor of *South Bank Show,* 1978—, head of arts, 1982-90, controller of arts, 1992—; presenter, *Start the Week,* Radio 4, 1988—. Border Television, deputy chairperson, 1985-90, chairperson, 1990—. President, Cumbrians for Peace, 1982—, Northern Arts, 1983-87, and National Campaign for the Arts, 1986—; Arts Council Literature Panel, member, 1969—, chairperson, 1977-80.

MEMBER: Royal Society of Literature (fellow), Association of Cinematograph, Television and Allied Technicians, PEN, Garrick Club.

AWARDS, HONORS: Writers Guild Award, 1966, for screenplay; Rhys Memorial Prize, 1968; prose award, Northern Arts Association, 1970; Silver Pen Award, PEN, 1970, for *The Hired Man;* Ivor Novello Award for best British musical, 1984, for *The Hired Man: A Musical;* Broadcasting Press Guild award, 1984; D.Litt., Liverpool University, 1986, and University of Lancaster, 1990; Domus fellow, St. Catherine's College, Oxford, 1990; Richard Dimbleby Award for highest television achievement in the United Kingdom.

WRITINGS:

NOVELS

For Want of a Nail, Knopf (New York City), 1965.

The Second Inheritance, Secker & Warburg (London), 1966, Knopf, 1967.

Without a City Wall, Secker & Warburg, 1968, Knopf, 1969.

The Hired Man (first book in *The Cumbrian Trilogy;* also see below), Secker & Warburg, 1969, Knopf, 1970.

A Place in England (second book in *The Cumbrian Trilogy;* also see below), Secker & Warburg, 1970, Knopf, 1971.

The Nerve, Knopf, 1972.

Josh Lawton, Knopf, 1973.

The Silken Net, Knopf, 1974.

Speak for England, Secker & Warburg, 1976, Knopf, 1977.

Autumn Manoeuvres, Secker & Warburg, 1978.

Kingdom Come (third book in *The Cumbrian Trilogy;* also see below), Secker & Warburg, 1980.

Love and Glory, Secker & Warburg, 1983.

The Cumbrian Trilogy (contains *The Hired Man, A Place in England,* and *Kingdom Come*), Coronet (London), 1984.

The Maid of Buttermere, Putnam (New York City), 1987.

A Time to Dance, Hodder & Stoughton (London), 1990, Little, Brown (Boston), 1992.

Crystal Rooms, Hodder & Stoughton, 1992.

OTHER

(With Clive Exton and Margaret Drabble) *Isadora* (screenplay), Universal, 1968.

The Music Lovers (screenplay), United Artists, 1970.

Play Dirty (screenplay), United Artists, 1970.

Charity Begins at Home (television script), British Broadcasting Corp. (BBC), 1970.

Zinotchka (television script), BBC, 1972.

(With Norman Jewison) *Jesus Christ Superstar* (screenplay), Universal, 1973.

Mardi Gras (play), produced in London, 1976.

A Christmas Child (short story), Secker & Warburg, 1976.

Speak for England: An Essay on England 1900-1975, Secker & Warburg, 1976, revised edition published as *Speak for England: An Oral History of England 1900-1975,* Knopf, 1977.

Clouds of Glory (television script), ITV, 1978.

(Editor) *My Favorite Stories of Lakeland* (anthology), Lutterworth Press (Cambridge, England), 1981.

Land of the Lakes, Secker & Warburg, 1983, Norton (New York City), 1984, 2nd edition, Hodder & Stoughton, 1990.

Laurence Olivier (biography), Hutchinson (London), 1984, St. Martin's (New York City), 1985.

(Editor) *Cumbria in Verse,* Secker & Warburg, 1984.

(With Howard Goodall) *The Hired Man: A Musical* (libretto; produced in Southampton and London, 1984; also see below), Samuel French (New York City), 1986.

Rich: The Life of Richard Burton (biography), Hodder & Stoughton, 1988, published as *Richard Burton: A Life,* Little, Brown, 1988.

(Author of introduction) *Enid J. Wilson's Country Diary,* Hodder & Stoughton, 1989.

Also author of plays *Prince of Wales,* 1976, and *King Lear in New York,* 1992; author of teleplays *The Debussy File,* with Russell, 1965, and *Orion,* with Ken Howard and Alan Blaikley, 1977; author of a radio play, *Robin Hood,* 1971. Contributor to *Winter's Tales 18,* edited by A. D. Maclean, St. Martin's, 1972. Contributor to periodicals, including *Listener* and *New Review.*

ADAPTATIONS: *Land of the Lakes* was televised in 1983, and *A Time to Dance* was televised in 1992.

SIDELIGHTS: Widely known throughout England as both a novelist and television personality, Melvyn Bragg

brings his various interests together in his writing. He pens novels of traditional life in the English countryside as well as biographies of international film stars. His roots in the northern England area of Cumberland and the Lake District often emerge in his work, from his tales of regional historical fiction, such as *The Hired Man* and *The Maid of Buttermere,* to his treatises on both his hometown of Wigton, Cumberland, and the Lake District in general—whose natural beauty Romantic poets William Wordsworth and Samuel Taylor Coleridge immortalized. Additionally, his experience and background in the television and entertainment industry aided the research for his biographies of Laurence Olivier and Richard Burton.

In a *Publishers Weekly* interview, Michele Field notes, "Ironically, though he is an important British novelist, his reputation in the States is now chiefly as the producer and presenter of the South Bank Show on Bravo Cable TV, and as the author of *Richard Burton: A Life.*" Field adds, "In England, however, Bragg is immediately put in the traditional 'man of letters' pigeonhole (people who have been great commentators and taste-makers as well as writers). His influence in the British media, especially in the arts on television . . . has no counterpart in American TV." She claims that the success of his writing career becomes all the more "remarkable" when one considers the demands of his television profession.

In his books of historical fiction, critics note Bragg's strong interest in the English working class. "He places his characters in a particular rural and small town setting," comments John Mellors in *Listener,* "and chronicles the tensions and conflicts between different generations of the same family, between husband and wife, between individual and society." Clancy Sigal of *Saturday Review* finds that Bragg's characters express an "undercurrent of anger, even bitterness, against the centuries-old class system."

About *The Hired Man,* a novel exploring class and expectations set in Victorian Cumberland, David Pryce-Jones observes in the *New York Times Book Review,* "To dramatize the plain tale of John Tallentire, a farm laborer inseparable from his native Cumberland, Melvyn Bragg has to put back the clock to the end of the last century. That Victorian past can just be recovered." Pryce-Jones adds, "Bragg exploits the lost diversity of the past, but he is not a false romantic who would welcome old hardships for the sake of the old virtues required to overcome them." A reviewer for the *Times Literary Supplement* finds *The Hired Man* "largely concerned with the changing attitudes among working men during this century towards being 'hired'—or employed, exploited, used." The reviewer considers that "Bragg is a good novelist but his narrative is clogged by heavy phrasing, especially when trying to report the self-communication of his characters. When he tells us what they said, what they did, how they and their environment appear to the author, he is consistently successful."

Another of Bragg's historical novels, *The Maid of Buttermere,* focuses on an actual publicized 1802 event in which a young Lake District girl—Mary Robinson, the "beauty of Buttermere"—became the bride of a titled newcomer, who in fact was actually an impoverished imposter who fooled the whole town with his pretensions. The novel examines the social and emotional repercussions of such a betrayal of trust. Anna Vaux notes in the *Times Literary Supplement* that "Bragg makes use of documentary detail both to heighten the tale and to reclaim 'the real' from what has been invented." Peter Ackroyd comments in the London *Times,* "So it is that Melvyn Bragg has taken what was once a great Romantic story to explore what has now become one of the most prominent themes in his work—the virtues of failure, contrasted with the strange and diminished world of success." Ackroyd further observes that Bragg "has created a fascinating network of duplicity and adventure," adding, "This is historical fiction with a human face, as it were, rather than a period mask." Another London *Times* reviewer writes, "The novel stresses the mythical element of this encounter between Beauty and the Beast, the rooted and the feckless, but it also suggests that the protagonists embodied a change of sensibility that was occurring as the 18th century became the 19th." Mary Lide in the *Washington Post* suggests: "For readers of historical fiction this novel will have a certain appeal. Basically, however, it is a psychological study, and the historical setting and natural environment are subservient to that goal."

In *A Time to Dance,* Bragg again sets the story in a small Cumbrian town in the Lake District, although the action occurs in the present. The novel, essentially a series of graphic, sexually explicit love letters written by a staid, middle-aged married man to his teenaged mistress, "makes wild lurches," opines Richard Eder in the *Los Angeles Times Book Review.* "When the narrator gathers his wits, to recount the beginning of the affair, it is taut and absorbing." Jane O'Grady asserts in the *Times Literary Supplement* that the book "clearly purports to deliver a message for our time—that sex can provide a meaning to everything, but only when it is 'twinned' with love." Victoria Glendinning observes in the London *Times* that "this is the classic male-menopausal wish-fulfillment novel (greying, older man transformed by sensational sex with adoring bimbo), and as such a recipe for embarrassing disaster. No one can know that better than the author, so it is a brave undertaking." Glendinning adds that "Melvyn Bragg has proved that he can write about sexual love, not as dirty bits, but as world-shatteringly pleasur-

able. His novel is not world-shattering, but it's pleasurable."

For his nonfiction book *Speak for England: An Essay on England 1900-1975,* the author spent five years conducting interviews in his hometown of five thousand inhabitants. Bragg's interview subjects represented diversity in age and socio-economic status; they spoke to Bragg of their individual lives and memories, in some cases dating back to the turn of the century. A *New Yorker* reviewer finds the book "exceptionally cheerful," while *Newsweek*'s Walter Clemons, declaring that Bragg "has done his work with thoroughness and affection," compares the book to works by Ronald Blythe and Studs Terkel. Clemons concludes that "his book is most eloquent when he openly expresses his satisfaction in the tough individuality of the people he grew up among and his pride that they still consider him one in whom they can confide." In the *New York Times Book Review,* Raymond Williams writes that despite some of the inferences Bragg makes from his various conversations, he considers the work "a basically honest, careful and serious book, full of interesting detail about the lives of people in Wigton."

Bragg again pays literary homage to his birthplace in *Land of the Lakes,* "in effect a labor of love and a tribute to all that is in his blood," according to Richard Adams in the *Washington Post Book World.* Adams mentions several misgivings about the book, including "a certain hyperbolic warmth of style which at times verges on traveloguese" and that "Bragg often descends to the chatty." Yet the reviewer perceives the book overall as "a very honest piece of work, handsomely produced, lavishly illustrated with excellent photographs and reproductions and well worth the price."

Bragg's biography of actor Richard Burton, published in England as *Rich: The Life of Richard Burton* and subsequently in the United States as *Richard Burton: A Life,* relies heavily upon pages and pages of personal journals written by Burton himself and released by his fourth wife, Sally Hay, for Bragg's use. Herbert Kretzmer remarks in the *Los Angeles Times Book Review* that Burton's widow "selected Bragg as the chronicler of her husband's career and made available to him Burton's voluminous notebooks—about 350,000 words of confession, self-analysis, gossip and commentary that publishers had coveted for half a decade." John Osborne indicates in the *New York Review of Books* that "this is not so much the authorized version as the widow's version, for she it was who entrusted Bragg with Burton's unpublished notebooks and made clear her ideas of how her late, brief husband should be respected and represented." In the *Chicago Tribune,* Steve Johnson quotes Bragg's initial reaction to Burton's private thoughts: "In reading them [Burton's notebooks], 'I was terribly moved,' Bragg said recently, 'because they're so honest and they're so honest about himself. I mean he's very very tough on himself. I was just taken aback. I was astounded by the detail of the relationship with [Elizabeth] Taylor. . . . I was impressed by the range of the man, the amount of reading and then the depths of the reading. . . . And the social range of the man.' " In addition to the actor's journals, Bragg also had access to the memoirs of Philip Burton, Richard Burton's legal guardian and the father figure from whom the actor took his surname.

Most reviewers agree that Richard Burton's own words provide a compelling and intriguing glimpse into the complex man who died in 1984 at age 58. In *New York* magazine, Rita Koenig declares, "Bragg's greatest asset . . . is his access to Burton's diaries, a far cry from the usual chitchat of show-business journals." *Newsweek*'s Cathleen McGuigan remarks, "The treats here are in the diary passages—domestic poetry written in Burton's witty, often humble voice." David Kaufman asserts in the *New York Times Book Review*, "Posterity should be grateful for the handful of Burton's superb film portrayals . . . and that Sally Burton, his fourth and last wife, overrode Burton's wishes and supplied Mr. Bragg with the notebooks that corroborate his greatness as an actor even as they document his frustrations as a human being." While Richard Panek maintains in the *Chicago Tribune* that Bragg's "overheated and underattributed narrative . . . doesn't do his subject justice," he finds that "the notebooks more than compensate for Bragg's failings. . . . As the autobiography that Richard Burton never got around to writing, they prove he knew how to treat his absurd world, as a stage where he was merely a player." Similarly, in the *New York Times*, Caryn James mentions Bragg's "overwrought prose" yet commends "the journal fragments that give the book its only true value."

In the *Times Literary Supplement* John Wilders comments on Bragg's thorough research and claims that "*Rich* is an account not so much of an extraordinary actor but of an extraordinary man whose genius was displayed in his acting." An *Economist* reviewer maintains, "Melvyn Bragg makes the best case he can for him [Burton], casting him as a man who prized language and great literature above love and life, certainly above mere acting." Anthony Burgess explains in the *Washington Post Book World:* "Bragg gives us a very full and sympathetic picture in a literary style he would not bring to his novels. He lets syntax go, admits the vague terms of the showbiz world, but, cunning writer that he is, has throughout impeccably fitted narrative technique to his subject." Burgess applauds "Melvyn Bragg's wholly admirable book."

BIOGRAPHICAL/CRITICAL SOURCES:

BOOKS

Contemporary Literary Criticism, Volume 10, Gale (Detroit), 1979.
Dictionary of Literary Biography, Volume 14: *British Novelists since 1960,* Gale, 1983.

PERIODICALS

Chicago Tribune, May 19, 1985; February 26, 1989, pp. 1, 7; March 21, 1989, p. 3.
Christian Science Monitor, June 2, 1989, p. 13.
Drama, Number 171, 1989, p. 50.
Economist, October 22, 1988, pp. 99-100.
Kenyon Review, Number 127, 1971.
Listener, August 22, 1974; October 20, 1988, p. 29; June 14, 1990, p. 22.
London Review of Books, June 14, 1990, p. 22; June 25, 1992, p. 18.
Los Angeles Times Book Review, March 26, 1989, p. 2; July 8, 1990, p. 10; February 10, 1991, p. 3.
New Statesman, August 16, 1974; April 8, 1977, pp. 456-57.
Newsweek, February 28, 1977, pp. 73B-74; February 13, 1989, p. 77.
New York, February 20, 1989, p. 64.
New Yorker, March 14, 1977, p. 139.
New York Review of Books, April 27, 1989, p. 24.
New York Times, February 22, 1989, p. C21.
New York Times Book Review, March 8, 1970, p. 30; February 27, 1977, p. 3; March 12, 1989, pp. 15-16.
Observer (London), December 9, 1984, p. 22; October 2, 1988, p. 43; June 14, 1992, p. 67.
Publishers Weekly, November 18, 1988, p. 37; February 3, 1989, pp. 83-84.
Punch, July 6, 1990, p. 47.
Saturday Review, February 19, 1977.
Spectator, October 8, 1988, p. 33; June 20, 1992, p. 34.
Stand, summer, 1970, pp. 68-74.
Time, February 20, 1989, p. 101.
Times (London), September 8, 1983; April 6, 1987; April 16, 1987; June 14, 1990.
Times Literary Supplement, October 23, 1969; October 15, 1971; April 4, 1980; April 17, 1981; September 9, 1983, p. 950; December 7, 1984, p. 1418; April 24, 1987, p. 434; September 24, 1988; October 21, 1988, p. 1165; June 15, 1990, p. 653; May 29, 1992, p. 20.
Tribune Books (Chicago), July 1, 1990, p. 4.
Washington Post, June 25, 1987; March 4, 1991, p. B3.
Washington Post Book World, February 27, 1977, p. E7; August 5, 1984, p. 1; January 22, 1989, pp. 1, 8.
World and I, May, 1989, p. 370.*

—*Sketch by Michaela Swart Wilson*

BRANDON, (Oscar) Henry 1916-1993

PERSONAL: Born March 9, 1916, in Liberec, Czechoslovakia (now Czech Republic); naturalized British subject; died of a stroke, April 20, 1993, in London, England; son of Oscar and Ida Brandon; married Mabel Hobart Wentworth (a photographer and White House social secretary during Ronald Reagan's administration), April 4, 1970; children: Fiona; stepchildren: John Wentworth, Elizabeth Wentworth Yates, Alexandra Wentworth. *Education:* Attended University of Lausanne and University of London.

ADDRESSES: Home—3604 Winfield Lane N.W., Washington, DC 20007.

CAREER: Sunday Times, London, England, staff member, 1939-42, war correspondent in north Africa and western Europe, 1943-45, Paris correspondent, 1945-46, roving diplomatic correspondent, 1947-49, associate editor and chief American correspondent based in Washington, DC, 1949-83; Brookings Institution, Washington, DC, guest scholar, 1983-93.

AWARDS, HONORS: Foreign Correspondents Award, University of California, Los Angeles, 1957; journalism award, Lincoln University, 1962; Hannen Swaffer Award as reporter of the year, 1964; Commander of the Order of the British Empire, 1985.

WRITINGS:

As We Are, Doubleday (New York City), 1961.
In the Red: The Struggle for Sterling, 1964-1966, Deutsch (London), 1966, Houghton (Boston), 1967.
Conversations with Henry Brandon, Deutsch, 1966, Houghton, 1968.
The Anatomy of Error: The Inside Story of the Asian War on the Potomac, 1954-1969, Gambit (Ipswich, MA), 1969.
(With others) *American Melodrama: The Presidential Campaign of 1968,* Viking (New York City), 1969.
(Editor) *The Retreat of American Power,* Doubleday, 1973.
Special Relationships: A Foreign Correspondent's Memoirs from Roosevelt to Reagan (autobiography), Atheneum (New York City), 1988.
(Editor) *In Search of a New World Order: The Future of U.S.-European Relations,* Brookings Institution (Washington, DC), 1992.

Author of column "Inside Washington" for New York Times Syndicate, 1984-91; syndicated columnist for *Washington Star,* 1979-81. Contributor to periodicals, including *Saturday Evening Post, Washington Post, Harper's, Encounter,* and *New York Times Magazine.* Editor-at-large, *Saturday Review.*

BIOGRAPHICAL/CRITICAL SOURCES:

BOOKS

Brandon, Henry, *Conversations with Henry Brandon,* Deutsch, 1966.
Brandon, *Special Relationships: A Foreign Correspondent's Memoirs from Roosevelt to Reagan,* Atheneum, 1988.

OBITUARIES:

PERIODICALS

Los Angeles Times, April 22, 1993, p. A26.
New York Times, April 21, 1993, p. D23.
Washington Post, April 21, 1993, p. C5.*

*　　　*　　　*

BRATER, Enoch 1944-

PERSONAL: Born October 1, 1944, in New York, NY; son of Hy and Sara (Openden) Brater; married Elizabeth Schussheim, 1973; children: Jessica, Jonathan. *Education:* New York University, B.A., 1965; Harvard University, A.M., 1967, Ph.D., 1971.

ADDRESSES: Office—Department of English, University of Michigan, Ann Arbor, MI 48109.

CAREER: Harvard University, Cambridge, MA, managing director of Loeb Drama Center, 1970-71; University of Pennsylvania, Philadelphia, assistant professor of English, 1971-75, coordinator of undergraduate theater program, 1973-75; University of Michigan, Ann Arbor, assistant professor, 1975-77, associate professor, 1977-87, professor of English and theater, 1987—, director of graduate studies, 1982-85, director of summer program in London, 1982-86.

MEMBER: Modern Language Association of America, Association for Theatre in Higher Education, Samuel Beckett Society (president, 1984-86).

AWARDS, HONORS: American Philosophical Society grants, 1973 and 1975; Amoco Award for Outstanding Teaching, 1984; Excellence in Education Award, 1994.

WRITINGS:

Beckett at Eighty/Beckett in Context, Oxford University Press, 1986.
Beyond Minimalism: Beckett's Late Style in the Theater, Oxford University Press, 1987.
Why Beckett, Thames & Hudson (New York City), 1989.
Feminine Focus: The New Women Playwrights, Oxford University Press, 1989.
Approaches to Teaching "Waiting for Godot," Modern Language Association of America (New York City), 1991.

Around the Absurd: Essays on Modern and Postmodern Drama, University of Michigan Press (Ann Arbor), 1991.
The Drama in the Text: Beckett's Late Fiction, Oxford University Press, 1994.
The Critical Gamut: Notes for a Post-Beckettian Stage, University of Michigan Press, 1995.

Contributor to professional journals. Editor of *Journal of Modern Literature,* February, 1977, *Michigan Academician,* 1979-84, and *Theatre Journal,* 1987-91.

*   *   *

BRESEE, Clyde W. 1916-

PERSONAL: Surname is pronounced "bre-*see*"; born February 2, 1916, in Ulster, PA; son of Chester J. (a farmer) and Ruth (a homemaker; maiden name, Gillette) Bresee; married Elizabeth Barner (a teacher), June 19, 1941; children: Jerome S., Catherine A. *Education:* Mansfield State Teachers College (now Mansfield University), B.S., 1937; Pennsylvania State University, M.Ed., 1942; Cornell University, Ph.D., 1956. *Politics:* Democrat. *Religion:* Methodist. *Avocational interests:* "Music has always been an absorbing interest. I was a church organist for twenty-eight years and served as a choral director for half that time."

ADDRESSES: Home and office—610 North Main St., Athens, PA 18810.

CAREER: High school teacher in Ulster, PA, 1937-43; Athens High School, Athens, PA, teacher of English, 1947-53, director of guidance services, 1953-78; writer, 1978—. Visiting professor at Cornell University, 1957-75; licensed psychologist in private practice, 1974. Vice president, local affiliate of Habitat for Humanity; board member, Bradford County Regional Arts Council. *Military service:* U.S. Army, Medical Administration Corps, 1943-46; became first lieutenant.

MEMBER: American Psychological Association, American Personnel and Guidance Association.

WRITINGS:

Sea Island Yankee (reminiscences), Algonquin Books of Chapel Hill (Chapel Hill, NC), 1986.
How Grand a Flame, Algonquin Books of Chapel Hill, 1992.

Contributor to education journals.

WORK IN PROGRESS: A personal narrative sequel to *Sea Island Yankee,* tentatively titled *Finding My Way in Crisis Years,* set in northern Pennsylvania, 1930-46.

SIDELIGHTS: Clyde W. Bresee once told *CA:* "I have always been interested in writing. The one thousand letters I sent to my wife during World War II lay idle for thirty years. I have now compiled them into a substantial, bound collection for family use. I admire the clarity and singularity of C. S. Lewis and E. B. White and the beautiful sentences of Robert L. Stevenson. They, and Mozart, are high on my scale."

When Bresee was four years old, his family moved from their farm in Pennsylvania to a dairy plantation on James Island in North Carolina, and *Sea Island Yankee* is the author's memoir of those formative years in the South. The work received good notices from reviewers. Harriet Choice wrote in the *Chicago Tribune:* "From the plantation store where he sold penny candy to the edge of the creek where he fished for crabs, Bresee has crafted a journey to land now buried and forgotten in rows of subdivisions." *New York Times* critic Andrew Harvey called Bresee "a writer of distinction from whom we must hear more. His prose is transparent, supple and spare; he evokes unhurriedly the smells and textures of the Southern world of his boyhood."

Bresee added that his second book, *How Grand a Flame,* is a narrative history of the Lawton plantation and family of Charleston, South Carolina, from 1813 to 1947.

BIOGRAPHICAL/CRITICAL SOURCES:

BOOKS

Bresee, Clyde W., *Sea Island Yankee,* Algonquin Books of Chapel Hill, 1986.

PERIODICALS

Chicago Tribune, June 29, 1986.
New York Times, June 1, 1986.

*   *   *

BROEGER, Achim 1944-

PERSONAL: Born May 16, 1944, in Erlangen, Germany; son of Arnold and Anneliese Broeger; married wife, Elizabeth, October 4, 1975; children: Jonas, Grunda, Olaf.

ADDRESSES: Home—Wilhelm-Raabe-Weg 3, 3300 Braunschweig Bienrode, Germany.

CAREER: Writer. Worked for textbook publisher.

MEMBER: PEN.

AWARDS, HONORS: Selected for best European children's book list, 1976; Schallplattenpreis der Deutschen Phonoakademie for *Der Ausredenerfinder;* nominated for the Mildred L. Batchelder Award for *Good Morning,*

Whale, 1977; best German juvenile book list for *Moritz-geschichten*, 1979; and Deutscher-Jugendliteraturpreis for *Oma und Ich.*

WRITINGS:

Buchveroeffentlichungen: Raupengeschichte, (juvenile; illustrated by Gisela Brandt), Atlantis (Zurich), 1971, published as *The Caterpillar's Story*, Scroll Press (Merrick, NY), 1973.

Doppelte Ferien sind am schoensten, Thienemanns (Stuttgart), 1974.

Guten Tag, lieber Wal (juvenile; illustrated by Gisela Kalow), Thienemanns, 1974, translation by Elizabeth Shub published as *Good Morning, Whale*, Macmillan (New York City), 1974.

Taschenbuchausgabe, Arena (Wuerzburg), 1974.

Der Ausredenerfinder, juvenile; illustrated by Ronald Himler, Thienemanns, 1974, translation by Hilda van Stockum published as *Bruno*, Morrow (New York City), 1975.

Das wunderbare Bettmobil (illustrated by Kalow), Thienemanns, 1975, translation by Caroline Gueritz published as *The Wonderful Bedmobile*, Hamish Hamilton (London), 1976.

Steckst du dahinter, Kasimir? (juvenile; illustrated by Susan Jeschke), Thienemanns, 1975, translation by van Stockum published as *Outrageous Kasimir*, Morrow, 1976.

Der Saurier aus der Heinrichstrasse (illustrated by Karl Meiler), Kinderbuecher, 1976.

Kurzschluss, Thienemanns, 1976, translation by Patricia Crampton published as *Running in Circles*, Morrow, 1977.

Mensch, waer das schoen!, Thienemanns, 1977.

Bruno verreist (juvenile; illustrated by Kalow), Thienemanns, 1978, translation by Gueritz published as *Bruno Takes a Trip* (published in England as *Bruno's Journey*, Hamish Hamilton, 1978).

Moritzgeschichten, Thienemanns, 1979, translation by Elizabeth D. Crawford published as *Little Harry* (illustrated by Judy Morgan), Morrow, 1979.

Ich war einmal, (illustrated by Kalow), Thienemanns, 1980, translation published as *The Happy Dragon*, Methuen (New York City), 1980.

Kinder DUDEN, Bibliographisches Institut (Mannheim), 1981.

In Wirklichkeit ist alles ganz anders, Thienemanns, 1982.

Meyers-Grosses-Kinderlexikon, Bibliographisches Institute, 1982.

Pizza und Oskar Band 1, Arena, 1982.

Draussen ist es Dunkel (illustrated by R. Michl), Thienemanns, 1982.

Bruno und das Telefon (illustrated by Kalow), Thienemanns, 1982.

Aug Zehenspitzen und Katzenpfoten, Arena, 1983.

Pizza und Oskar Band 2 and 3, Arena, 1984.

Hallo, Pizza—Hallo, Oskar, Arena, 1984.

Der Geburtstagsriese, Ravensburger, 1984.

Tshues, lieber Wal (illustrated by Kalow), Thienemanns, 1985.

Spaetschichttage sind Spaghettitage, Arena, 1985.

Mein 24. Dezember, Arena, 1985.

Die kleine Jule, Thienemanns, 1985.

Die Weihnachtsmaenner, Middelhauve, 1985.

Ich mag dich, Thienemanns, 1986.

Oma und ich, Verlag Nagel & Kimche, 1986.

Schon, das es dich gibt, Arena, 1987.

Geschwister . . . nein, danke!?, Arena, 1987.

Broeger's works have been translated into various languages, including Japanese, Spanish, Norwegian, French, Danish, Swedish, and Finnish.*

*   *   *

BROUGHTON, T(homas) Alan   1936-

PERSONAL: Born June 9, 1936, in Bryn Mawr, PA; son of T. Robert S. and Annie Leigh (Hobson) Broughton; married Susan Becker (divorced, 1962); married Lenore Follansbee (divorced, 1969); married Mary Twitchell (divorced, 1975); married Laurel Ginter, 1982; children: (first marriage) Shannon Leigh; (second marriage) John Camm; (fourth marriage) Travers Nathaniel. *Education:* Attended Harvard University, 1954-57, and Juilliard School of Music, 1957-59; Swarthmore College, B.A. (with honors), 1962; University of Washington, Seattle, M.A., 1964. *Avocational interests:* Music.

ADDRESSES: Home—124 Spruce St., Burlington, VT 05401. *Office*—Department of English, University of Vermont, 315 Old Mill, Burlington, VT 05401.

CAREER: Private piano teacher, 1959-62; Sweet Briar College, Sweet Briar, VA, instructor in English, 1964-66; University of Vermont, Burlington, assistant professor, 1966-70, associate professor, 1970-74, professor of English, 1974—, chairperson of English department, 1994—, director of writer's workshop program. Speaker and lecturer at numerous universities in the United States and abroad.

MEMBER: Associated Writing Programs, Phi Beta Kappa.

AWARDS, HONORS: Chicago Review Fiction Contest honorable mention, 1969; *Yankee* Annual Poetry Awards, 1971, 1973, 1975, 1992; Borestone Awards, 1972, 1973, 1974; Emily Balch Award, *Virginia Quarterly Review*, 1974; National Endowment for the Arts fellowship in fiction, 1976-77; Guggenheim fellowship in fiction, 1982-83; PEN Syndicated Fiction Project, 1981, 1986, 1987.

WRITINGS:

The Skin and All (poems), George Little Press, 1972.

In the Face of Descent (poems), Carnegie-Mellon University Press (Pittsburgh), 1975.

Adam's Dream (poems), Northeast/Juniper, 1975.

A Family Gathering (novel; Book-of-the-Month Club alternate selection), Dutton (New York City), 1977.

Far from Home (poems), Carnegie-Mellon University Press, 1979.

The Man on the Moon (stories and poems), Barlenmir (New York City), 1979.

The Others We Are (poems), Northeast/Juniper, 1979.

Winter Journey (novel), Dutton, 1980.

The Horsemaster (novel), Dutton, 1981.

Dreams before Sleep (poems), Carnegie-Mellon University Press, 1982.

Hob's Daughter (novel), Morrow (New York City), 1984.

Preparing to Be Happy, Carnegie-Mellon University Press, 1988.

The Jesse Tree (stories), Northeast/Juniper, 1988.

In the Country of Elegies (poems), Carnegie-Mellon University Press, 1995.

Contributor to anthologies, including *Best Poems of 1972: Borestone Mountain Poetry Awards 1973,* Pacific Books (Palo Alto, CA), 1973; *Flowering after Frost: The Anthology of Contemporary New England Poetry,* edited by Michael McMahon, Branden Press (Brookline Village, MA), 1975; *Three Rivers, Ten Years: An Anthology of Poems from Three Rivers Poetry Journal,* edited by Gerald Costanzo, Carnegie-Mellon University Press, 1983; *Ploughshares Reader: New Fiction for the Eighties,* edited by DeWitt Henry, Pushcart (Wainscott, NY), 1985; *Contemporary New England Poetry: A Sampler,* Texas Review Press, 1987; *Prize Stories: The O'Henry Awards,* Doubleday (New York City), 1991; *The Writer's Handbook,* Writer, Inc. (Boston), 1991, revised edition, 1992; and *The Carnegie-Mellon Anthology of Poetry,* Carnegie-Mellon University Press, 1993. Contributor of short stories and poems to periodicals, including *Poetry, American Weave, Beloit Poetry Journal, Commonweal, Prairie Schooner, Yankee,* and *Cosmopolitan.*

WORK IN PROGRESS: Novels, poems, novellas, and short stories.

SIDELIGHTS: "By all odds," notes Susan Wood in the *Washington Post Book World,* "*Winter Journey* should not be a particularly successful novel. Its plot and characters are, on the surface anyway, fairly standard, if not trite. . . . Yet, thanks to T. Alan Broughton's considerable talent, these stock elements combine into a moving,

finely crafted novel, full of real people about whom the reader comes to care deeply."

Wood's comments reflect general critical reaction to Broughton's works. *New York Times* reviewer John Leonard describes *Winter Journey* as the story of a young man, an aspiring pianist, whose mother takes him to Rome after her marriage breaks up. Their journey is one of self-discovery, of maturing, a story which, as Leonard states, "has been written before and will be written again, although probably not as well as T. Alan Broughton has written this time. . . . Not the least of Mr. Broughton's accomplishments is to seize material we had thought to be worn out, used up, discarded, replaced—by a newer model of anti-story, the ironic grimace—and make it somehow lyrical all over again."

In the *New York Times Book Review* John Casey echoes the opinions of both Wood and Leonard; he finds "the effect of *Winter Journey* is that of intimate personal narration. There is a sense (historically accurate and well-rendered) that the characters are bound in by politeness and good taste from being open and easily familiar with each other." He adds that such consideration has gone out of fashion in recent literature: "This theme is most often treated comically or bitterly and ironically, so it is a pleasure to find that [Broughton] treats it lyrically and romantically."

Broughton's novel *The Horsemaster* deals with a young woman's search for her biological father and her impact on his life and the lives of those around him. Although *Washington Post* reviewer Matthew Schudel labels it "an approachable and well-written novel," he nonetheless regards the book as "a somewhat uneven accomplishment. In style and theme, Broughton resembles, say, Wallace Stegner and Frederick Busch in the way he depicts the unexpected or unexamined complexities in the lives of ordinary people in the overlooked corners of America. Unfortunately, Broughton presents too little of their daily working lives and too much of their memories, brooding and dreaming to convince us of their ordinariness. The result is an overly psychological picture of people whose primary concerns are probably much more humdrum than Broughton allows them to be."

In the *Los Angeles Times Book Review,* Ralph B. Sipper offers a different assessment; he feels that "one of Broughton's graces is to have written a psychological novel that does not psychologize or employ clinical jargon. Feelings, dreams and memories are precisely catalogued, not diluted by superficial analysis." Similarly, Alexandra Johnson observes in the *Chicago Tribune Book World* that *The Horsemaster* is "a rich and intricate story of how two strangers, grappling with their own private needs, gradually assume responsibility for the other. . . . It's a novel of intense affirmation, a hauntingly poignant study of a man growing up."

"In my childhood," Broughton told *CA*, "I had a recurrent dream, so basic that it still rules me. In my sleeping mind, deep in an area close to oblivion, I hear the sound of a tone. Sometimes that tone is accompanied by a visual counterpart in the form of perfectly arranged objects that scatter into disorder, then reform. The sound is a clear, perfectly tuned, unbroken note. In its perfection resides a dread since I know it must break. It does, and as it disintegrates I am lost in terror—a chaos beyond all light and joy. But in the noise that tone has become, I find relief since I know *that* must dissolve into order, and it does. The music and the dissolution from which it rises make a dream of paradoxes. Unbearable joy, ecstatic terror. This rhythm of death and rebirth is the dream that forms all the smaller dreams I try to write down."

BIOGRAPHICAL/CRITICAL SOURCES:

BOOKS

Contemporary Literary Criticism, Gale (Detroit), Volume 19, 1981.

PERIODICALS

Atlantic Monthly, February, 1980, p. 96.
Chicago Tribune Book World, March 23, 1980; November 8, 1981.
Los Angeles Times, January 17, 1980.
Los Angeles Times Book Review, October 18, 1981.
National Observer, June 13, 1977, p. 21.
New Yorker, February 25, 1980, p. 134.
New York Times, January 11, 1980.
New York Times Book Review, May 15, 1977, p. 13; January 20, 1980, pp. 14-15; October 14, 1984.
Ontario Review, spring-summer, 1980, pp. 94-99.
Virginia Quarterly Review, winter, 1978, p. 21.
Washington Post, October 31, 1981.
Washington Post Book World, February 3, 1980, p. 14.

*   *   *

BROWN, Drollene P. 1939-

PERSONAL: Given name is pronounced "drole-*een*"; born September 24, 1939, in South Charleston, WV; daughter of Wilson William (a firefighter and carpenter) and Evelyn (a church treasurer; maiden name, McClure) Plattner; married Charles R. Tittle, August 29, 1961 (divorced May 21, 1975); married Albert J. Brown, Jr. (an airline consultant), May 28, 1982; children: (first marriage) Mark Alan, Shauna Kay. *Education:* Ouachita Baptist University, B.A. (summa cum laude), 1961; University of Texas at Ausitn, M.A., 1963, additional graduate study, 1963-65.

ADDRESSES: Home and office—Morriston, FL.

CAREER: Indiana University, Bloomington, research assistant and associate, 1965-70; College of Boca Raton, Boca Raton, FL, assistant professor of sociology, 1973-78, director of Professional Arts Program, Wilmington College Extension, 1978; American Savings and Loan Association, Boca Raton, branch manager, 1979-81; A. J. Brown, Inc. (airline consulting firm), Boca Raton, vice president, 1981-88; freelance ghostwriter, 1989—; Distinctive Publishing Corp., Pompano Beach, FL, director of marketing and public relations, 1991-92, writer and senior editor, 1992—. Chairperson of International Playwriting Competition at Boca Raton's Caldwell Playhouse, 1981-84.

MEMBER: Alpha Chi, Phi Kappa Phi, Kappa Delta Pi.

AWARDS, HONORS: National Institutes for Mental Health fellow, 1962-64; National Endowment for the Humanities fellow, 1977.

WRITINGS:

Sybil Rides for Independence (juvenile), Albert Whitman (Niles, IL), 1985.
Belva Lockwood Wins Her Case (juvenile), Albert Whitman, 1987.
(With Abe Goldman) *Holding On to Ettie* (adult), Distinctive Publishing (Pompano Beach, FL), 1991.
Thomas and Launia, RitAmelia Press, 1994.

Also author of monographs for *Spanish River Papers.* Columnist for *Boca Raton News* and *News of Delray.* Contributor of articles and reviews to periodicals.

WORK IN PROGRESS: Three ghostwriting projects—two by victims of violent crimes and one by a political philosopher.

SIDELIGHTS: Drollene P. Brown once told *CA:* "Writing is my compulsion, and teaching is my motivation. One of the advantages of writing children's books is the opportunity to go into the schools to talk about writing and the subjects of my books. I loved college teaching when I could see young minds opening to new ideas. Much of my thrill in writing newspaper columns came when readers reported that I had told them something they hadn't known. There's contentment in seeing my words set down just so on a printed page. I've worried them and nudged them until I can do no more. I can feel pride then, too, but to know those words made a difference to someone— that's joy.

"I think it's important to show strong female role models, not only for the benefit of girls, but also for boys. Women won't have full equality until men, as well as women, expect and accept nothing else. *Sybil Rides for Independence* retells the story of a sixteen-year-old girl who rode through the night on April 26, 1777, to awaken minutemen to fight the British in the Battle of Ridgefield. *Belva Lockwood Wins Her Case* is a biography of the woman lawyer who ran for president of the United States in 1884 and 1888. A contemporary of Susan B. Anthony and Elizabeth Cady Stanton, Lockwood was a stalwart feminist and indefatigable worker for world peace."

About her later writing experiences, Brown added: "As with my work history, my writing career has taken a number of twists and turns. The heady days of visiting schools to talk to eager children about my biographies have given way to the more structured tasks of ghostwriting and editing. Always looking for new horizons, in 1994 I began a publishing effort designed to help families publish their own genealogy studies and family histories.

"One of the advantages of being a writer is that there are so many avenues to pursue, from turns onto little side roads (different reading audiences) to complete route changes (editing, rewriting, ghostwriting, publishing). No step away from the original road precludes going back to it, and each new pursuit, to me, has seemed to be a logical progression. I love to write, whether it's 'my baby' or someone else's brain child. Creating books is more than just a living; it's a way of life."

*   *   *

BROWN, Marshall 1945-

PERSONAL: Born February 9, 1945, in Los Angeles, CA; son of Louis (an attorney and professor) and Hermione (an attorney; maiden name, Kopp) Brown; married Jane Kurshan (a professor), May 21, 1967; children: Dorrit, Benedict. *Education:* Harvard University, A.B. (magna cum laude), 1965; attended Free University of Berlin, 1965-66; Yale University, M.Phil., 1969, Ph.D., 1972.

ADDRESSES: Home—8001 Lakemont Dr. N.E., Seattle, WA 98195. *Office*—Department of English, University of Washington, Seattle, WA 98195.

CAREER: Boston University, Boston, MA, instructor, 1970-71, assistant professor of English and German, 1971-74; Smith College, Northampton, MA, instructor in German, 1975; University of North Carolina, Chapel Hill, visiting assistant professor of English, 1976-77; University of Virginia, Charlottesville, lecturer in English, 1978-79; University of Colorado, Boulder, associate professor of English, 1979-88, director of comparative literature program, 1986-88; University of Washington, Seattle, professor of English and comparative literature, 1988—, adjunct

professor of music, 1991—. Member of faculty at Mount Holyoke College, 1976. Member of Boulder City Arts Commission, 1983-87.

MEMBER: International Association for Philosophy and Literature, Modern Language Association of America, American Society for Eighteenth Century Studies, North American Society for the Study of Romanticism (advisory board member, 1992—), Phi Beta Kappa.

AWARDS, HONORS: Fulbright fellow, 1965-66; Jacob van Ek Award, University of Colorado, 1981 and 1983, for teaching; William Riley Parker Prize honorable mention, Modern Language Association, 1981, for "The Logic of Realism: A Hegelian Approach," and 1984, for " 'Errours Endlesse Traine:' On Turning Points and the Dialectical Imagination"; Chancellor's Essay Prize, University of Colorado, 1983, for "The Classic Is the Baroque: On the Principle of Woelfflin's Art History"; National Endowment for the Humanities fellow, 1994-95.

WRITINGS:

The Shape of German Romanticism, Cornell University Press (Ithaca, NY), 1979.
(Editor) *La Via al sublime,* Alinea, 1988.
Preromanticism, Stanford University Press (Stanford, CA), 1991.
(Editor) *The Uses of Literary History,* Duke University Press (Durham, NC), 1995.

Also contributor to *Goethezeit: Festschrift fuer Stuart Atkins,* edited by Gerhart Hoffmeister, Francke, 1981. Contributor of articles, translations, and reviews to periodicals, including *Critical Inquiry, PMLA, Comparative Literature,* and *German Quarterly. Modern Language Quarterly,* editor, 1991—. Member of editorial board, *English Language Notes,* 1980-91, *PMLA,* 1987-89, *Studies in Romanticism,* 1989—; and *Eighteenth Century: Theory and Interpretation,* 1990—.

WORK IN PROGRESS: Turning Points: Essays in the History of Cultural Expressions for Stanford University Press; co-editing with Ernst Behler, *The Cambridge History of Literary Criticism: Romanticism;* and *Philosophy of the Gothic.*

*   *   *

BROWN, R(onald) G(ordon) S(clater) 1929-1978

PERSONAL: Born May 21, 1929, in Edinburgh, Scotland; died June 28, 1978; son of Gordon (a civil servant) and Tomima (Slater) Brown; married Jean Isobel Peebles (a teacher), August 2, 1952; children: Gordon David Alexander, Stuart Chester. *Education:* University of St. Andrews, M.A., 1951; University of Hull, Ph.D., 1972.

ADDRESSES: Home—16 Tranby Lane, Anlaby, Hull, Yorkshire, England. *Office*—Institute for Health Studies, University of Hull, Hull, England.

CAREER: Ministry of Health and Local Government, Belfast, Northern Ireland, administrator, 1953-58; University of Manchester, Manchester, England, lecturer in social administration, 1958-62; Scottish Home and Health Department, Edinburgh, Scotland, administrator, 1962-65; University of Hull, Hull, Humberside, England, senior lecturer in social administration, 1965-74, director of Institute for Health Studies, 1974-78. *Military service:* Royal Air Force, 1951-53; became flying officer.

MEMBER: Royal Institute of Public Administration.

AWARDS, HONORS: Haldane Essay Prize of Royal Institute of Public Administration, 1964.

WRITINGS:

The Administrative Process in Britain, Barnes & Noble (Totowa, NJ), 1970, 2nd edition (with D. R. Steel), Methuen (London), 1979.
The Changing National Health Service, Routledge & Kegan Paul (London), 1973, 2nd edition, 1978.
(With R. W. H. Stones) *The Male Nurse,* G. Bell (London), 1973.
The Administrative Process as Incrementalism, Open University Press, 1974.
The Management of Welfare, Martin Robertson, 1975.
Reorganising the National Health Service: A Case Study in Administrative Change, Blackwell (Oxford), 1979.

Contributor to *The Yearbook of Social Policy in Britain, 1971* edited by K. Jones, Routledge & Kegan Paul, 1972; *Management in the Social and Safety Services,* edited by W. D. Reekie and N. C. Hunt, Barnes & Noble, 1974; and *The Yearbook of Social Policy in Britain, 1975,* edited by K. Jones, Routledge & Kegan Paul, 1976. Contributor to numerous public administration, hospital, and nursing journals.

BIOGRAPHICAL/CRITICAL SOURCES:

PERIODICALS

Parnassus, January, 1973, p. 88.
Times Literary Supplement, October 16, 1970, p. 1205.

*   *   *

BROZEK, Josef (Maria) 1913-

PERSONAL: Born August 14, 1913, in Melnik, Bohemia (now Czech Republic); came to U.S. in 1939, naturalized, 1945; son of Josef Francis and Filomena (Sourek) Brozek; married Eunice Magnuson, March 23, 1945; children: Josef T., Margaret M., Peter M. *Education:* Graduated from Masaryk Realgym, 1932; Charles University (Prague), Ph.D., 1937; postdoctoral studies at University of Pennsylvania and Pendle Hill, 1939-40, and University of Minnesota, 1940-41.

ADDRESSES: Home—265 East Market St., Bethlehem, PA 18018.

CAREER: Bata Shoe Factories, Zlin, Czechoslovakia, psychotechnologist, 1937-39; University of Minnesota, Minneapolis, School of Public Health, Laboratory of Physiological Hygiene, junior psychologist, 1941-43, associate scientist, 1943-44, assistant professor, 1944-49, associate professor, 1949-56, professor of psychology, 1956-59; Lehigh University, Bethlehem, PA, professor of psychology and chairperson of department, 1959-63, research professor of psychology, 1963-79, professor emeritus, 1971, adjunct professor, 1982-84.

U.S. Office of Scientific Research and Development, researcher, 1944-46; chairperson, Symposium on Adjustment to Aging, 15th International Congress on Applied Psychology, 1964, and Kyoto Symposium on Anthropological Aspects of Human Growth, 1968; University of New Hampshire, director of summer institute, 1968; U.S.-Japan Cooperative Medical Science Program, member of U.S. Malnutrition Panel, 1973-78; National Research Council (NRC), Food and Nutrition Board, member of committee on nutrition, brain development, and behavior, 1974-79, chairperson, 1980; Institute of Psychology at the University of Wuerzburg, Fulbright senior research fellow, 1979-80; United Nations University World Hunger Program, Massachusetts Institute of Technology, resident coordinator, 1980-81; University of Passau, visiting professor, 1986-87.

MEMBER: International Society for the History of Behavioral and Social Sciences, European Society for the History of Behavioral and Social Sciences, American Psychological Association (division president, 1972-73), Archives of the History of American Psychology (on board of directors, 1971—), History of Science Society, Pavlovian Society, Deutsche Gesellschaft fuer Psychologie, Sigma Xi.

WRITINGS:

(With Ancel Keys and others) *The Biology of Human Starvation,* University of Minnesota Press (Minneapolis), 1950.
(With Francisco Grande) *Neurologicke poruchy pri nedostatecne vyzive,* State Health Publishing House (Prague), 1959.
(With F. Ashley Montagu) *A Handbook of Anthropometry,* C. C. Thomas (Springfield, IL), 1960.

Determinacion somatometrica de la composicion corporal, Instituto Nacional de Antropologia e Historia (Mexico), 1961.

Psychology in Czechoslovakia: Background, Bibliographies, Current Topics, and Perspectives for the Future, Bundesinstituts fur Ostwissenschaftliche und Internationale Studien (Koeln, Germany), 1977.

(With Solomon Diamond) *Le Origini della Psicologia obiettiva,* Editore Bulzoni (Rome), 1982.

(Translator with Simona Hoskovec), *Svetlusky,* translation from the original English manuscript, *Fireflies,* by Rabindranath Tagore, STRATOS (Prague), 1994.

EDITOR AND CONTRIBUTOR

Body Measurements and Human Nutrition, Wayne State University Press (Detroit), 1956.

(With Austin Henschel) *Techniques for Measuring Body Composition,* National Research Council (Washington, DC), 1961.

Human Body Composition: Approaches and Applications, Pergamon (Elmsford, NY), 1965.

(And translator with Ernst Simonson) A. I. Naumenko and N. N. Benua, *Physiological Mechanisms of Cerebral Blood Circulation,* C. C. Thomas, 1970.

(And translator with Maarten S. Sibinga) Johan Jacob de Jaager, *Origins of Psychometry,* B. de Graaf, 1970.

(With Dan I. Slobin) *Psychology in the USSR: An Historical Perspective,* International Arts and Sciences Press, 1972.

(With Rand B. Evans) *R. I. Watson's Selected Papers on the History of Psychology,* University of New Hampshire Press (Hanover), 1977.

Behavioral Effects of Energy and Protein Deficits, U.S. National Institutes of Health (Bethesda, MD), 1979.

(With Ludwig J. Pongratz) *Historiography of Modern Psychology: Aims, Resources, and Approaches,* C. J. Hogrefe (Toronto), 1980.

(With Beat Schurch) *Malnutrition and Behavior: Critical Assessment of Key Issues,* Nestle Foundation (Lausanne, Switzerland), 1984.

Explorations in the History of Psychology in the United States, Bucknell University Press (Lewisburg, PA), 1984.

Malnutrition and Human Behavior: Experimental, Clinical, and Community Studies, Van Nostrand Reinhold (New York City), 1985.

(With Jiri Hoskovec) *J. E. Purkyne and Psychology, with a focus on unpublished manuscripts,* Akademia (Praha, Czech Republic), 1987.

(With Hoskovec) *Thomas Garrigue Masaryk on Psychology: Six Facets of the Psyche,* Karolinum (Praha, Czech Republic), 1995.

OTHER

Also author of *Soviet Studies on Nutrition and Higher Nervous Activity,* 1962. Editor of *The Biology of Human Variation,* 1966, *Physical Growth and Body Composition,* 1970, and *G. T. Fechner and Psychology,* 1988, and collaborator of *The Influence of European Thought on the Development of American Psychology: The First Decades,* 1988. Contributor to *Industrial Hygiene and Toxicology,* Volume One, edited by Frank A. Patty, Interscience Publishers, 1948-49, and *Science in Progress,* edited by Wallace R. Brode, Yale University Press (New Haven, CT), 1964.

Contributor to various professional journals, symposia reports, and annals. Book review editor and author of book notes, *Human Biology,* 1955-65; editorial consultant, *Contemporary Psychology,* 1959-79, *Soviet Psychology and Psychiatry,* 1962-67, and *Soviet Psychology,* 1967—; consulting editor, *Psychophysiology,* 1964-66; member of editorial board, *Journal of the History of Behavioral Sciences,* 1976—, *Revista de Historia de la Psicologia,* 1980-90, *Storia e Critica della Psicologia,* 1980-84, *Archiv fuer Psychologie,* 1980-91, *Teorie e Modelli,* 1988, *Storia della Psicologia,* 1989-91, *Archivo Latino-americano de la Psicologia y Ciencias Afines,* 1989-90, and *Cuadernos Argentinos de Historia de la Psicologia,* 1995—.

*   *   *

BRUNE, Lester H(ugo) 1926-

PERSONAL: Born January 14, 1926, in Reading, OH; son of Frederick Gustave (a minister) and Marie (Bueker) Brune; married Joan Loretta Herzfeld (an educational administrator), October 21, 1950. *Education:* Elmhurst College, A.B., 1948; Bradley University, M.A., 1950; University of Rochester, Ph.D., 1959.

ADDRESSES: Home—2921 West Winterberry Lane, Peoria, IL 61604. *Office*—Department of History, Bradley University, Peoria, IL 61625.

CAREER: Elmhurst College, Elmhurst, IL, admissions counselor, 1950-51; Morris Harvey College, Charleston, WV, instructor in history, 1951-53; University of Rochester, Rochester, NY, American history fellow, 1953-56; Bradley University, Peoria, IL, assistant professor, 1956-62, associate professor, 1962-67, professor of history, 1968-86, Oglesby Chair of American Heritage, 1986—, chairman of department, 1970-78, assistant dean of College of Liberal Arts, 1962-65. Adjunct professor of history, Moorhead State College, 1971. Director, Berlin Seminar for Historians, 1981—.

MEMBER: American Historical Association, Foreign Policy Association, Society for Historians of American

Foreign Relations, Organization of American Historians, Phi Kappa Phi (secretary), Phi Alpha Theta, Pi Sigma Phi.

AWARDS, HONORS: Association for Middle-Eastern Studies fellowship at University of Illinois, summer, 1961; Harry S. Truman Institute research fellow, 1982-83.

WRITINGS:

PROGRAMMED INSTRUCTION TEXTS

Ancient History to the Fall of Rome, Media Masters, 1968.
China and Japan to 1600 A.D., Media Masters, 1968.
India and Southeast Asia to 1600 A.D., Media Masters, 1968.
The Middle East to 1600 A.D., Media Masters, 1968.
The Middle Ages and Early Modern Europe to 1700 A.D., Media Masters, 1968.
(With Charles E. P. Simmons) *Mexico and South America,* Media Masters, 1969.
The United States, Media Masters, 1969.
Europe since 1500 A.D., Media Masters, 1969.
The Mid-East since 1500 A.D., Media Masters, 1969.
China and Japan since 1600 A.D., Media Masters, 1969.
India and Southeast Asia since 1600 A.D., Media Masters, 1969.
(Editor) *Origins of Tomorrow,* two volumes, Holbrook, 1973.
The Origins of American National Security Policy: Sea Power, Air Power, and Foreign Policy, 1900-1941, MA/AH Press, 1981.
A Chronological History of U.S. Foreign Relations, 1776 to 1981, Garland (New York City), Volumes 1 and 2, 1984, Volume 3, 1991.
The Missile Crisis of October 1962: A Review of Issues and References, Regina Books (Claremont, CA), 1985.
(With Richard Dean Burns) *America and the Indochina Wars, 1945-1990: A Bibliographic Guide,* Regina Books, 1991.
America and the Iraqi Crisis, 1990-1992: Origins and Aftermath, Regina Books, 1993.
Korean War Handbook: A Guide to Literature and Research, Greenwood (Westport, CT), 1995.

Contributor to history journals. Also a contributor to *Guide to the Sources of U.S. Military History,* Anchor (New York City), 1986, and 1993 supplement.

WORK IN PROGRESS: A study relating national security policy to the Korean and Vietnam Wars.

SIDELIGHTS: Lester H. Brune once told *CA:* "My publications resulted from efforts to experiment with better methods for teaching history. The present generation of historians need more than ever to discover a better means for nourishing the vitality of the study of history as a means for continuing to provide humanistic insights in a technically oriented world.

"After completing my study of National Security Policy to 1941, I continued using the insights gained to continue past 1945 studies of National Security relative to the Cuban crisis, Vietnam and the nuclear deterrent issues seeking to prevent nuclear war by understanding how to deal with diplomacy in the nuclear era."

Brune has traveled through Europe, Japan, China, Egypt, Israel, Lebanon, Greece, the Aegean, and the Soviet Union.

*   *   *

BRYANT, James C(ecil), Jr. 1931-

PERSONAL: Born October 21, 1931, in Lake Wales, FL; son of James Cecil (a shipyard worker) and Mary Lou (McCranie) Bryant; married Marion Lois Carnett (a school teacher), June 19, 1955; children: David, Albert. *Education:* Stetson University, B.A., 1954; Southern Baptist Theological Seminary, B.D., 1958; University of Miami, M.A., 1961; University of Kentucky, Ph.D., 1967. *Politics:* Democrat.

ADDRESSES: Home—1470 Leafmore Pl., Decatur, GA 30033. *Office*—President's Office, Mercer University, Macon, GA 31207.

CAREER: Ordained minister of Baptist Church, 1952; pastor in Miami, FL, 1958-63, Corinth, KY, 1963-67, Quincy, FL, 1968-69, and Atlanta, GA, 1975-1992; Florida State University, Tallahassee, assistant professor of English, 1967-73, taught under auspices of Florida State University, Overseas Study Center in Florence, Italy, 1969-70; Mercer University, Atlanta, GA, associate professor, 1973-76, head of English department, 1973-76, professor of English, 1976-92; Mercer University, Macon, GA, currently university historian and special assistant to the president. *Military service:* U.S. Naval Reserve, 1948-52.

MEMBER: American Association of University Professors, College English Association, Modern Language Association of America, Renaissance Society of America, South Atlantic Modern Language Association, Southeastern Renaissance Conference, Council of Authors and Journalists (chair, board of trustees, 1984-90), German-American Society (board of directors, 1976), Rotary Club (board of directors, 1977), Scottish Rite Mason (KCCH), Sons of the American Revolution (treasurer and vice president, 1971, 1972, 1973), Georgia Baptist Historical Society (president, 1990-93), Georgia Writers, Inc. (founding member, 1994), YAARAB Shrine Temple, Atlanta Writers Club (second vice president, 1974-75; president, 1975-76), Atlanta Press Club, Atlanta Historical Society, Atlanta Baptist History Committee (chair, 1980—), Atlanta Union Mission (advisory board), Old Guard of the Gate City Guard (1990—).

AWARDS, HONORS: Florida Heritage Award from Colonial Dames, 1972, for *Indian Springs: The Story of a Pioneer Church;* Dixie Council of Authors and Journalists Award for fiction, 1973; Dixie Council of Authors and Journalists Award for biography, 1975, for *The Morningside Man: A Biography of James Pickett Wesberry;* Dixie Council of Authors and Journalists Special Award, 1983, International Biographical Institute fellow, Cambridge University, 1986.

WRITINGS:

New Columbus and the Baptist Church, privately printed, 1965.
Indian Springs: The Story of a Pioneer Church, Florida State University Press (Tallahassee), 1972.
Smooth Runs the Water, Broadman (Nashville), 1973.
The Morningside Man: A Biography of James Pickett Wesberry, Morningside Baptist Church (Atlanta), 1975.
(With Charlie Brown) *Charlie Brown Remembers Atlanta: Memoirs of a Public Man as Told to James C. Bryant,* R. L. Bryan Co. (Columbia, SC), 1982.
Tudor Drama and Religious Controversy, Mercer University Press (Macon, GA), 1984.
The Atlanta Baptist Association, Atlanta Baptist Association, 1984.
Mountain Island in Owen County, Kentucky: The Settlers and Their Churches, Owen County Historical Society, 1986.
James McDonald: Pioneer Missionary to East Florida, [DeLand, FL], 1986.
Capital City Club: The First One Hundred Years, 1883-1983, The Club (Atlanta), 1991.
A Gift for Giving: The Story of Lamar Rich Plunkett, Mercer University Press, 1993.

Also contributor to periodicals, including *Atlanta Journal-Constitution, American Literature, English Studies, Event, Guideposts, Renaissance Papers, Viewpoints,* and *United Daughters of the Confederacy Magazine.* Literary specialist for Youth In Action, 1972-73. Editor of *Basharat Magazine,* 1977—.

WORK IN PROGRESS: Druid Hills Golf Club of Atlanta: Backward and Forward (history), to be privately printed by Druid Hills Golf Club; *Mercer University History,* a five year project.

BRYCE, James
See MOBLEY, James Bryce

*   *   *

BUCHEISTER, Patt   1942-
(Patt Parrish)

PERSONAL: Surname is pronounced "boo-eye-ster"; born March 27, 1942, in Waterloo, IA; daughter of David M. and Elaine (Sandberg) Fluharty; married Raymond C. Bucheister (a marketing director of a computer firm), January 14, 1961; children: Scott, Todd. *Education:* Graduated from high school in Clear Lake, IA. *Religion:* Protestant.

ADDRESSES: Home—901 Shady Hollow Lane, Virginia Beach, VA 23452. *Agent*—Joyce A. Flaherty, 816 Lynda Court, St. Louis, MO 63122.

CAREER: Chamber of Commerce, Clear Lake, IA, secretary, 1959-60; artist; romance writer.

MEMBER: Romance Writers of America, National Society of Tole and Decorative Painters, Tidewater Decorative Painters (second vice president, 1983-84).

AWARDS, HONORS: Silver Palette Award, Tidewater Decorative Painters, 1985.

WRITINGS:

ROMANCE NOVELS

Night and Day, Bantam (New York City), 1986.
The Dragon Slayer, Bantam, 1987.
Touch the Stars, Bantam, 1987.
Two Roads, Bantam, 1987.
The Luck o' the Irish, Bantam, 1988.
Flynn's Fate, Bantam, 1988.
Time Out, Bantam, 1988.
Near the Edge, Bantam, 1989.
Fire and Ice, Bantam, 1989.
Elusive Gypsy, Bantam, 1989.
Once Burned, Twice As Hot, Bantam, 1990.
The Rogue, Bantam, 1990.
Relentless, Bantam, 1990.
Tropical Heat, Bantam, 1990.
Tropical Storm, Bantam, 1991.
Hot Pursuit, Bantam, 1991.
Island Lover, Bantam, 1992.
Mischief and Magic, Bantam, 1992.
Struck by Lightning, Bantam, 1992.
Tilt at Windmills, Silhouette, 1992.
Stroke by Stroke, Bantam, 1993.
Tame a Wildcat, Bantam, 1993.
Strange Bedfellows, Bantam, 1994.
Unpredictable, Silhouette, 1994.

Hot Southern Nights, Bantam, 1995.
Rascal, Bantam, 1995.
Instant Family, Silhouette, 1995.

ROMANCE NOVELS; UNDER PSEUDONYM PATT PARRISH

Make the Angel Weep, R. Hale (London), 1979, published as *His Fierce Angel,* Bantam, 1983.
Summer of Silence, R. Hale, 1980, published as *A Gift to Cherish,* Bantam, 1985.
Feather in the Wind, R. Hale, 1981, Bantam, 1982.
The Sheltered Haven, R. Hale, 1981, Bantam, 1982.
The Amberley Affair, R. Hale, 1983.
Lifetime Affair, Harlequin (Tarrytown, NY), 1985.
Escape the Past, Walker & Co. (New York City), 1985.

OTHER

Contributor of articles and stories to magazines. Editor of newsletter *Brushstrokes.*

WORK IN PROGRESS: First Steps in a New Land; Arianna.

SIDELIGHTS: Patt Bucheister told *CA:* "I began to write seriously in 1976 while living in Chesham, England. So far away from familiar art exhibits, my painting took a backseat to writing once I had my first book published in 1979 in England.

"My novels are based on the relationship between a man and a woman. They usually have interesting occupations and are warm, likable characters with a sense of humor and traditional values. My characters have a few problems in their lives and their relationships, but there is always a happy ending.

"I write six days a week from 8:00 A.M. until 6:00 P.M., occasionally working in the evenings. I try to write at least ten pages a day. My main purpose in writing novels is to entertain the reader. I don't try to solve any major universal situation; I leave that to those who are more qualified.

"Due to my husband's former career as a naval officer I have resided in various states, including Hawaii and California, and I spent four years in England. I am able to use a variety of locations in my novels, and they are based on firsthand knowledge."

*   *   *

BURKS, Arthur W(alter) 1915-

PERSONAL: Born October 13, 1915, in Duluth, MN; son of Walter Demoree and Cora Belle (Voyles) Burks; married Alice Grace Rowe, February 27, 1943; children: Edward, Nancy, Douglas. *Education:* Depauw University,

B.A., 1936; University of Michigan, M.A., 1937, Ph.D., 1941.

ADDRESSES: Home—3445 Vintage Valley Rd., Ann Arbor, MI 48105. *Office*—Department of Electrical Engineering and Computer Science, University of Michigan, Ann Arbor, MI 48109.

CAREER: High school mathematics teacher in Mount Morris, MI, 1937-38; Moore School of Electrical Engineering, University of Pennsylvania, Philadelphia, instructor in electrical engineering and research engineer, 1941-46; Swarthmore College, instructor, 1945-46; University of Michigan, Ann Arbor, assistant professor, 1946-48, associate professor, 1948-54, professor of philosophy, 1954—, professor of computer and communication sciences, 1967—, Henry Russel Lecturer, 1978, distinguished senior faculty lecturer in College of Literature, Science, and the Arts, 1982, director of Logic of Computers Group, 1956—, member of executive committee of Computing Center, 1959-60, chair of department of communication sciences, 1967-71, member of executive committee of College of Literature, Science, and the Arts, 1973-74. Research associate at University of Chicago, 1950-51, and Harvard University, 1955; visiting professor of applied mathematics at University of Illinois, autumn, 1960, Gillies Lecturer, 1983; member of committee to advise the director of research of the Atomic Energy Commission on digital computers, 1960-62; visiting professor at Indian Institute of Technology, Kanpur, India, 1965-66; fellow of Center for Advanced Study in the Behavioral Sciences, Stanford, CA, 1971-72. Consultant to Institute for Advanced Study, Princeton, NJ, 1946-48, Burroughs Corp., 1948-54, and Argonne National Laboratory, 1950-51.

MEMBER: American Philosophical Association (member of executive committee of Western Division, 1962-65; vice president, 1971-72; president, 1972-73), Association for Computing Machinery, Association of Symbolic Logic (executive committee and council member, 1956-58), Philosophy of Science Association (governor and president, 1975-76), Charles S. Peirce Society (president, 1954-55), University of Michigan Research Club, Phi Beta Kappa, Sigma Xi, Phi Eta Sigma, Delta Sigma Rho, Phi Kappa Phi, Eta Kappa Nu.

AWARDS, HONORS: Guggenheim fellowship, 1953-54; (co-recipient) Louis E. Levy gold medal, Franklin Institute, 1956, for "The Folded Tree"; American Council of Learned Societies fellowship, 1962-63; Distinguished Faculty Achievement award, University of Michigan, 1970; D.Sc. from DePauw University, 1973; National Endowment for the Humanities fellow, 1978-79.

WRITINGS:

(With John von Neumann and H. H. Goldstine) *Preliminary Discussion of the Logical Design of an Electronic Computing Instrument,* Institute for Advanced Study (Princeton, NJ), 1946, 2nd edition, 1947.

(Editor with Max Fisch and others, and contributor) *Classic American Philosophers,* Appleton (Norwalk, CT), 1951.

(Editor) *Collected Papers of Charles Sanders Peirce,* Harvard University Press (Cambridge, MA), Volume 7 (Burks was not associated with earlier volumes): *Science and Philosophy,* 1958, Volume 8: *Reviews, Correspondence, and Bibliography,* 1958.

(Editor) John von Neumann, *Theory of Self-Reproducing Automata,* University of Illinois Press (Champaign, IL), 1966.

(Editor and contributor) *Essays on Cellular Automata,* University of Illinois Press, 1970.

Robots and Free Minds, University of Michigan Press (Ann Arbor, MI), 1986.

(Editor with William Aspray) *Papers of John von Neumann on Computing and Computer Theory,* MIT Press (Cambridge, MA), 1987.

(With wife, Alice R. Burks) *The First Electronic Computer,* University of Michigan Press, 1988.

Also author of *Chance, Cause, Reason: An Inquiry into the Nature of Scientific Evidence,* University of Chicago Press (Chicago). Contributor to books, including *Academic Freedom, Logic, and Religion,* edited by Morton White, University of Pennsylvania Press (Philadelphia), 1953; *Self-Organizing Systems,* edited by Marshall Yovits and Scott Cameron, Pergamon (Elmsford, NY), 1960; *Computer Handbook,* edited by Harry Huskey and G. A. Korn, McGraw (New York City), 1962; *Computer Programming and Formal Systems,* edited by Paul Braffort and Donald Hirschberg, North-Holland Publishing (New York City), 1963; *Sequential Machines: Selected Papers,* edited by Edward F. Moore, Addison-Wesley (Reading, MA), 1964; *System Engineering Handbook,* edited by Robert Machol and others, McGraw, 1965; *The Philosophy of C. I. Lewis,* edited by Schilpp, Open Court (LaSalle, IL), 1968; *Computer Structures: Readings and Examples,* edited by C. G. Bell and Allen Newell, McGraw, 1971; *The Origins of Digital Computers: Selected Papers,* edited by Brian Randell, Springer-Verlag (New York City), 1973; *Cybernetics and Bionics: Proceedings of the Fifth Congress of the Deutsche Gesellschaft fuer Kybernetik, Nurnberg, March 28-30, 1973,* edited by W. D. Keidel, Wolfgang Handler, and M. Spreng, Oldenbourg, 1974; contributor to proceedings; contributor of about forty articles to professional journals; consulting editor of *Synthese: An International Journal for Epistemology, Methodology,* *and Philosophy of Science,* 1966—, and *Journal of Computer and System Sciences,* 1975—.

SIDELIGHTS: Arthur W. Burks is one of the principal inventors and developers of ENIAC, the first general-purpose electronic computer. The commendation accompanying his Distinguished Faculty Achievement Award from the University of Michigan reads in part: "As a principal inventor and designer or the first electronic computer, Professor Burks enjoys a happy position as a master of processes of which the rest of us are more likely to conceive ourselves the slaves. With his few peers, among whom are now numbered some of his former students, he has since extended and refined the theories underlying such computation. He has brought his distinguished capability for clarity and precision to bear, moreover, on non-mathematical aspects of former logic and on inductive logic and scientific method. For these accomplishments he is internationally honored among mathematicians, engineers, and philosophers."

Burks's books have been translated into Russian, German, and Japanese.

BIOGRAPHICAL/CRITICAL SOURCES:

BOOKS

Salmon, Merrilee H., editor, *The Philosophy of Logical Mechanism: Essays in Honor of Arthur W. Burks, with His Responses,* Kluwer Academic (Boston and Dordrecht), 1990.

*   *   *

BURNER, David (B.) 1937-

PERSONAL: Born May 10, 1937, in Cornwall, NY; son of William Arthur (a clergyman) and Beatrice (Bird) Burner; married Sandra Ayers (a college teacher), June 14, 1958; children: Diane, Eric. *Education:* Hamilton College, B.A., 1958; Columbia University, Ph.D., 1965.

ADDRESSES: Home—Private Road, Nissequogue, NY 11780. *Office*—Department of History, State University of New York, Stony Brook, NY 11794.

CAREER: Colby College, Waterville, ME, instructor in history, 1962-63; Oakland University, Rochester, MI, assistant professor of history, 1963-67; State University of New York at Stony Brook, 1967—, began as associate professor, currently professor of history.

AWARDS, HONORS: Guggenheim fellow; National Endowment for the Humanities fellow; Ford Foundation fellow, Carnegie teaching fellow.

WRITINGS:

The Politics of Provincialism: The Democratic Party in Transition, 1918-1932, Knopf (New York City), 1968.
Herbert Hoover: A Public Life, Knopf, 1979.
An American Portrait, Knopf, 1982.
(With Thomas R. West) *The Torch Is Passed: The Kennedy Brothers and American Liberalism,* Atheneum (New York City), 1984.
John F. Kennedy and a New Generation, Little, Brown (Boston), 1988.
(With Thomas R. West) *Column Right: Conservative Journalists in the Service of Nationalism,* New York University Press (New York City), 1988.
Making Peace with the 60s, Harvard University Press (Cambridge, MA), in press.

Also author and editor of textbooks. Contributor to journals.

SIDELIGHTS: Historian David Burner's biography, *Herbert Hoover: A Public Life,* is an "ample, absorbing study of the man and his times," according to Naomi Bliven in the *New Yorker.* John Bartlow Martin, commenting in the *Chicago Tribune,* writes: "As biographies go nowadays, this book is short. One might have wished for less on Hoover's early career and for more on his presidency. His private life is missing almost entirely (as the subtitle promises). The book is not exhaustive or definitive; it is, rather, analytical and judgmental. The organization is topical, not rigorously chronological. It seems a fair and balanced book, neither savagely critical of Hoover nor blindly laudatory. It ably fills a gap in the history of the modern presidency."

The book "has many excellences," claims Arthur Schlesinger, Jr. in the *New York Review of Books.* "It is diligently researched and generally well written. . . . The tone is incisive and dryly detached, and the text has sensitive and subtle insights into character and politics." In a *New York Times Book Review* article, August Heckscher adds: "Professor Burner writes for the scholar and, he hopes, for the general reader as well. The scholar will surely be satisfied; the more elusive general reader will find here much to surprise him—and perhaps something to correct earlier, uncharitable views."

In *The Torch Is Passed: The Kennedy Brothers and American Liberalism,* Burner and co-author Thomas R. West detail the rise of the John, Robert, and Edward Kennedy from their conservative family background to their eventual position in liberal politics. Based in part on newly-opened oral histories from the JFK Presidential Library, the authors present an analysis of John Kennedy's relationship to the liberalism of his times. *The Torch Is Passed* received mixed reviews from critics. *Choice* reviewer P. L. Silver praises the authors for their "clear, thoughtful, and

thought-provoking work, effective within the limits [they] set." Pointing to the clarity and liveliness of the authors' writing, *Library Journal*'s Charles DeBenedetti finds that *The Torch Is Passed* "recaptures the spirit of the main players in the Kennedy story." In contrast, *Los Angeles Times*'s Carolyn See feels the authors fail to offer any new information to readers and considers *The Torch Is Passed* dull and "preternaturally tedious." "It is when they try to account for the great change in liberals since Kennedy's day that they lose their grip," writes Walter Karp in the *New York Times Book Review.* But, Karp concedes: "In vividly recalling what they called the era of 'cold war liberalism,' the authors sharpen considerably our understanding of Kennedy's closeness to the prevailing spirit of his time."

Column Right: Conservative Journalists in the Service of Nationalism, also co-authored with Thomas R. West, examines the writings and ideas of five conservative journalists—George Will, William F. Buckley, Jr., Irving Kristol, Charles Krauthammer, and Jeane Kirkpatrick. Each writer is "scrutinized for evidence" that their conservative belief systems "underlie their day-to-day commentaries," according to *Choice* contributor K. F. Rystrom. The journalists' works analyzed by Burner and West are outdated and limited finds Rystrom; the writings selected date from 1950 to 1983—even though each author appeared in press after that time period. Although *New York Times Book Review*'s Walter Karp considers *Column Right* a "brief, thoughtful study," he faults Burner and West who "treat these conservative intellectuals as thinkers divorced from actual political life." According to Karp, this approach results in the conservative journalists appearing "so self-contradictory that they seem not to take their avowed conservative principles seriously. . . . Treating conservative intellectuals as if they had nothing to do with conservative politics misconstrues the political role they have played—providing a respectable cloak for ambitions that square ill with genuine republican virtues and abiding conservative values." But, even with its limitations, Karp concludes "*Column Right* is a useful book."

BIOGRAPHICAL/CRITICAL SOURCES:

PERIODICALS

Chicago Tribune, January 14, 1979.
Choice, February, 1985, p. 864; November, 1988, p. 569.
Kirkus Reviews, October 15, 1988, p. 1500.
Library Journal, July, 1984, p. 1333.
Los Angeles Times, August 20, 1984.
New Republic, March 10, 1979.
New Yorker, April 16, 1979.
New York Review of Books, March 8, 1979.
New York Times, January 12, 1979.

New York Times Book Review, February 4, 1979; September 9, 1984, p. 18; October 9, 1988, p. 16.
Publishers Weekly, June 1, 1984, p. 53.
Washington Post Book World, February 25, 1979.

*   *   *

BURNHAM, David (Bright) 1933-

PERSONAL: Born January 24, 1933, in Boston, MA; son of Addison Center (a publisher) and Dorothy (Moore) Burnham; married Sophy Tayloe Doub (a writer), March 12, 1960 (divorced, 1984); married Joanne Omang, October 23, 1985; children: (first marriage) Sarah Tayloe, Molly Bright. *Education:* Harvard University, B.A., 1955.

ADDRESSES: Home—524 Sixth St. S.E., Washington, DC 20003. *Office*—Suite 301, 666 Pennsylvania Ave. S.E., Washington, DC 20003-4319. *Agent*—Robin Straus, 229 East 79th St., New York, NY 10021.

CAREER: United Press International, New York City, reporter in Washington, DC, 1959-61; *Newsweek,* New York City, reporter in Washington, DC, 1961-63; Columbia Broadcasting System, Inc., New York City, writer, 1963-65; President's Commission on Law Enforcement and Administration of Justice, Washington, DC, assistant director, 1965-67; *New York Times,* New York City, reporter, 1967-80, at Washington, DC, bureau, 1974-80 and 1982-86; Aspen Institute for Humanistic Studies, journalist and writer, 1980-82; Syracuse University, associate research professor at S. I. Newhouse School of Public Communications, 1989—, codirector of Transactional Records Access Clearinghouse. Stanford University, visiting professor of journalism and ethics, spring, 1980. *Military service:* Served in 11th and 82nd Airborne Infantry.

AWARDS, HONORS: George Polk Memorial Award, Long Island University, and Silurians Award, Society of the Silurians, both 1968; Page One Award for Crusading Journalism, New York Newspaper Guild, 1969; Golden Typewriter Award for investigative reporting, New York Reporters Association, 1977; Alicia Patterson Foundation fellow, 1987; Best Investigative Book of 1990, Investigative Reporters and Editors, for *A Law unto Itself: Power, Politics and the IRS;* Rockefeller Foundation fellow, Bellagio, Italy, 1992.

WRITINGS:

The Rise of the Computer State, foreword by Walter Cronkite, Random House (New York City), 1983.
A Law unto Itself: Power, Politics and the IRS, Random House, 1990.

Work represented in anthologies, including *Crime in the Cities,* edited by Dan Glaser, Harper (New York City), 1970; and *High Technology and Human Freedom,* edited by Lewis H. Lapham, Smithsonian Institution Press (Washington, DC), 1985. Contributor of numerous articles to magazines, including *Atlantic Monthly, Nation, New York Times Magazine, Reader's Digest, Reporter, Washingtonian,* and *Washington Post.*

WORK IN PROGRESS: An investigative book on the U.S. Justice Department, for Macmillan.

SIDELIGHTS: David Burnham's *Rise of the Computer State* examines the threat to society brought about by the collection and storage of data by government agencies and public and private companies. According to Burnham, the pieces of information gathered by such organizations as the Central Intelligence Agency (CIA), the Internal Revenue Service (IRS), and American Telephone and Telegraph (AT&T) "present a threat to the continuation of the American way of life more pervasive than any foreign enemy," Harrison E. Salisbury wrote in the *Los Angeles Times Book Review.* He added that "it is Burnham's conviction that the evolution of a computerized American society . . . already is far advanced."

Burnham argues, for example, that virtually everything Americans do can now be recorded electronically: telephone calls can be monitored by the phone company, financial transactions are monitored by banks, and the use of credit cards allows the close scrutinization of buying habits. David Wise noted in his *Washington Post Book World* review that "Burnham sees us moving toward a cashless, printless society" and "has thought long and well about computers, what they are doing to our values, to our society, and to ourselves." Wise added that *The Rise of the Computer State* is a "scary yet thoughtful book."

In it, according to Salisbury, Burnham discusses the activities of the National Security Agency (NSA), a top-secret government organization that "possesses the world's largest and most sophisticated complex of computers, satellites, electronic-eavesdropping devices and other wholly unknown capabilities." The NSA "collects, through electronic espionage, so much raw data that it sometimes needs to destroy tens of thousands of pounds of excess secret paper a day," John Brooks stated in the *New York Times.* "How much, then, do they keep a day?"

Marc Granetz, writing in the *New Republic,* declared that Burnham's book is "entertaining" and "studded with anecdotes about computer-system abuses." He added, however, that "the book's organization makes it difficult to assess potential dangers to privacy." In addition, Granetz noted that Burnham "doesn't talk about remedies, which is inexcusable, because there are so many." L. D. Burnard, in his *Times Literary Supplement* review, also found some faults with *The Rise of the Computer State,* calling attention to the book's lack of discussion of the positive aspects of computers and the absence of anything "on computer fraud, which probably poses a far greater threat to society than any amount of NSA cloak-and-dagger stuff." Even so, Burnard concluded that the book was "a gold mine of anecdotal information, guaranteed to break the ice at Civil Rights gatherings."

BIOGRAPHICAL/CRITICAL SOURCES:

PERIODICALS

Chicago Tribune, August 7, 1983.
Los Angeles Times Book Review, June 5, 1983.
New Republic, October 3, 1983; April 9, 1990, p. 40.

New York Times, June 6, 1983; February 7, 1990, p. C21.
New York Times Book Review, August 21, 1983; February 11, 1990, pp. 1, 24.
Time, February 5, 1990, p. 67.
Times Literary Supplement, November 25, 1983.
Washington Post Book World, June 26, 1983; February 11, 1990, pp. 1, 8.

*   *   *

BURNS, Sheila
   See BLOOM, Ursula (Harvey)

C

CAINE, Geoffrey
See WALKER, Robert W(ayne)

*   *   *

CAMPBELL, Sid 1944-

PERSONAL: Born September 29, 1944, in Montgomery, AL; son of John Selvyn (a railroad worker) and Audress Magnolia (Langston) Campbell; married Leonor Cantu (divorced); children: Kimberlee Dawn. *Education:* Attended University of Maryland at College Park and Contra Costa College. *Avocational interests:* Motorcycling, pistol and rifle shooting, oriental weaponry.

ADDRESSES: Office—Gong Productions International, 2019 MacArthur Blvd., Oakland, CA 94602.

CAREER: Shorin Ryu Karate Studio, Oakland, CA, founder and martial arts instructor, 1966—. Founder of Movie Media Production Corp., 1978, Creative Martial Arts Productions, 1980, Coliseum Martial Arts EXPO and World Tournament, 1980, and Tonfa Police Baton Academy; coproducer of United Karate Competition and Western Pro-Am Karate Championships; official at martial arts tournaments; choreographer of action sequences for films, including *Yellow Faced Tiger, Death Machines, Weapons of Death,* and *Shadow Fight;* star or co-star of action films and instructional videos, including *The Tonfa Police Baton: Innovative Baton of Law Enforcement, Shadow Fight, Ninja Busters, Master Demon, Boots, Buckles and Blades,* and "Super Nunchaku" series; producer of films and videos, including *Eclectic Escrima,* 1990, *Sticks of Death,* 1991, *Arnis Master,* 1992, *The Master Demon, Eclectic Escrima for Self-Defense,* and *Martial Arts Expo and World Tournament;* narrator and producer

of audio-books. *Military service:* U.S. Navy, torpedoman, 1962-66.

MEMBER: U.S. Shorin Ryu Karate Association (vice president), Northern California Referees Association (secretary, 1976), Brotherhood of Martial Art Instructors, Okinawan Shorin-Ryu Shorinkan Karate Association (Japan).

AWARDS, HONORS: Golden Fist Award, Golden Fist Association, 1976; Presidential Sports Award, 1982; inducted into World Professional Black Belt Association Hall of Fame, 1982.

WRITINGS:

Johnny Learns Karate (coloring book), Dimond, 1978.
The Bay Area Roller Skaters Guide, Dimond, 1979.
2001 Martial Arts Questions Kung Fu, Karate, Tae Kwon Do, Kenpo Students Should Know, Dimond, 1980.
Falcon Claw: The Motion Picture, Dimond, 1980.
Ninja Shuriken Throwing: The Weapon of Stealth, Paladin Press, 1984.
The Shuko: Ninja Claw of Death, I & I Publishers, 1985.
The Kusarigama: Ninja Weapon of Vengeance, I & I Publishers, 1985.
(With Sonny Umpad and Gary Cagaanan) *The Butterfly Knife,* Paladin Press, 1985.
(Coauthor) *Falcon Claw* (screenplay), Movie Media Productions, 1985.
Shadows of Darkness: Secrets of the Night Fighter, Paladin Press, 1985.
The Ninja Shinobi-Ken, I & I Publishers, 1986.
(With Cagaanan and Umpad) *Balisong: The Lethal Arts of Filipino Knife Fighting,* Paladin Press, 1986.
Shadow Fight (screenplay), Movie Media Productions, 1986.
The Kusarifundo: Ninja Weapon of Illusion, I & I Publishers, 1986.

The Mercenary Tactical Handbook, J. Flores, 1988.

The Weapons of Okinawa, Paladin Press, 1988.

The Weapon Masters of Okinawa, Gong Productions, 1990.

Martial Arts Philosophy Made Easy (audio-book), Gong Productions, 1990.

Kata: The Essence and Inner Meaning (audio-book), Gong Productions, 1990.

Ancient Fighting Secrets of the Yin-Yang (audio-book), Gong Productions, 1990.

Fistload Weaponry (audio-book), Gong Productions, 1991.

Boots, Buckles and Blades (audio-book), Gong Productions, 1992.

Also author of *The Tonfa Police Baton Instructional Manual,* 1989, *The Shorin-Ryu Instructor's Handbook,* 1993, *Real Men Don't Eat Crow, The Complete Book of Ninja Weaponry, Circle and Point: The Combative Hand Science, The Ninja Sword of Doom, Bruce Lee's One and Three Inch Instructional Manual,* and *The Aerobic Speed Striking System Manual;* author of more than two hundred short stories; author of screenplays, including *Bushwhackers, China Bomb,* and (with Diana-Taylor Christopher) *Elizabeth* and *Nowhere Island;* television scriptwriter for weekly series *TUF;* writer, producer, and host of cable television show *Just for Kicks.* Contributor to martial arts magazines, including *Black Belt, Warriors, Inside Kung-fu, Fighting Stars, Inside Karate, Official Karate,* and *Karate Illustrated;* featured columnist, *Karate World Magazine,* 1993—.

WORK IN PROGRESS: The Dragon and Tiger: The Oakland Years, with Greglon Y. Lee, a book on the early life of martial arts superstar Bruce Lee; *Wingless,* with Christopher, a screenplay about William Horton, the engineer whose work led to the development of the Stealth bomber.

SIDELIGHTS: Sid Campbell has a seventh degree black belt in Shorin-Ryu karate, one of only four such black belts awarded to Americans. He has been involved in virtually every facet of the martial arts for more than thirty years. He began his training at the age of seventeen in Okinawa, Japan, under the tutelage of Grand Master Shugoro Nakazato.

Campbell was one of the first Americans to introduce the art of Shorin-Ryu karate to the United States. He has taught self-defense and the philosophy underlying the art to more than fourteen thousand martial arts practitioners. He told *CA* that he has introduced the martial arts to law enforcement agencies, fraternal organizations, clubs, recreation departments, schools, and organizations for the handicapped. He added that he was one of the first martial arts instructors to teach these skills to the deaf and blind.

Campbell and his Demo Team have been featured in several instructional self-defense public broadcast programs. He was also the featured instructor in several Gong Productions videotapes, including the "Super Nunchaku" trilogy and *The Tonfa Police Baton: Innovative Baton of Law Enforcement.* Campbell is the founder of the Tonfa Police Baton Academy, which provides local, regional, and state law enforcement agencies with instructions for the use of the side-handle police baton, a new tool introduced to reduce serious injury while allowing police officers more personal protection than they have had in the past.

Campbell once told *CA:* "My study into the fascinating field of the martial arts began at age seventeen when I was stationed in Okinawa, Japan. During my five-year stay, I had the opportunity to discover, learn, and train in the art of self-defense. While in Okinawa, I was exposed to the simplicity of the Eastern way of life and I learned the language, culture, and history of the area. That early education, in addition to the training I received in the martial arts, influenced me greatly in perpetuating that way of life in the United States after I was honorably discharged from the U.S. Navy in 1966.

"I found it surprising to discover upon my return from Okinawa that there were virtually no self-defense schools in the immediate San Francisco Bay area. It soon occurred to me that there was going to be an incredible future interest in these methods of self-defense, which prompted me to seriously consider ways in which this opening field could afford me a livelihood. It became my full-time avocation, and writing about the martial arts is an extension of more than twenty years of teaching this fantastically unique way of life. [My books] are not merely 'how-to' manuals illustrating the physical techniques; rather, my books educate people in the history, the purpose, and the philosophy behind the martial arts because I believe in the importance of Eastern thought as it applies to the art of self-defense.

"It's only a matter of time until the Western reader may begin to enjoy the physiological and psychological benefits of these treasured arts. A longer, more productive, and enriched life is possible through the study and practice of the disciplines found in self-defense and the martial arts. Not only will practitioners better understand themselves, they will better understand others.

"I've been very busy researching and documenting the chronological accounts and historical archives pertaining to two highly visible, yet truly unrecognizable individuals who have greatly contributed to changing the world with their innovative ideas and persistent determination. Bruce Lee has been heralded as the 'Greatest Martial Artist of the 20th Century,' and William Horton has been virtually forgotten despite his contributions and technological innovations, over sixty years ago, that eventually led to the 'secret stealth' concepts behind the highly classified B-2 Stealth bomber, the world's most advanced military aircraft."

*   *   *

CAROSSO, Vincent P(hillip)   1922-1993

PERSONAL: Born March 20 (one source says March 19), 1922, in San Francisco, CA; died of lung cancer, June 29, 1993, in Manhattan, NY; son of Vincent G. (in business) and Lucia M. (Barale) Carosso; married Rose Celeste Berti, August 23, 1952; children: Steven Berti. *Education:* University of California, Berkeley, A.B., 1943, M.A., 1944, Ph.D., 1948. *Avocational interests:* Music.

CAREER: Harvard University, Cambridge, MA, postdoctoral fellow in American economic and business history, 1948-49; San Jose State College (now University), San Jose, CA, instructor in history, 1949-50; Carnegie Institute of Technology (now Carnegie-Mellon University), Pittsburgh, PA, assistant professor of history, 1950-53; New York University, New York City, assistant professor, 1953-56, associate professor, 1956-61, professor of history, 1962-76, William R. Kenan Jr. Professor of History, 1976-88, Kenan Professor Emeritus, 1989-93. Columbia University, faculty member, late 1950s; Harvard University, visiting associate research professor, 1961-62, visiting research lecturer, 1964-65; Fulbright-Hays senior lecturer, Italy, 1973, 1976. Trustee of Business and Economic History Conference, 1973-76 and 1985-87.

MEMBER: American Historical Association, Economic History Association, Organization of American Historians.

AWARDS, HONORS: National Endowment for the Humanities senior fellow, 1976-77; American Council of Learned Societies grant-in-aid, 1978; John Simon Guggenheim Memorial fellow, 1980-81; Alfred P. Sloan Foundation grant, 1983; Kenan Enterprise Award, 1988.

WRITINGS:

The California Wine Industry, 1830-1895: A Study of the Formative Years, University of California Press (Berkeley), 1951.
(With George Soule) *American Economic History,* revised edition, Dryden (New York City), 1957.
(With Henry Bamford Parkes) *Recent America: A History,* two volumes, Crowell (New York City), 1963.
Investment Banking in America: A History, Harvard University Press (Cambridge, MA), 1970.
(Editor) *Wall Street and the Security Markets,* 58 volumes, Arno (New York City), 1975.

(Editor with Stuart Bruchey) *Companies and Men: Business Enterprise in America,* 38 volumes, Arno, 1976.
(Editor) *The United States in the Twentieth Century,* three volumes, St. Martin's (New York City), 1978-80.
More Than a Century of Investment Banking: The Kidder, Peabody & Co. Story, McGraw (New York City), 1979.
(Editor with Bruchey) *The Survival of Small Business,* Arno, 1979.
(With wife, Rose Carosso) *The Morgans: Private International Bankers, 1854-1913,* Harvard University Press, 1987.

Also affiliated with *Timber and Men: The Weyerhaeuser Story,* Macmillan, 1961. Contributor of articles and book reviews to professional journals. Associate editor, *Journal of Economic History,* 1955-60; member of editorial board, *Business History Review,* 1957-58, and *Journal of American History,* 1968-71.

OBITUARIES:

PERIODICALS

New York Times, July 1, 1993, p. D19.*

*   *   *

CARTWRIGHT, Vanessa
See PRESTON, Harry

*   *   *

CASELEY, Judith   1951-

PERSONAL: Surname is pronounced "*case*-ley"; born October 17, 1951, in Rahway, NJ; daughter of Lester (a writer) and Dorothy Jeanne (a professor of mathematics) Goldberg; married Roger Caseley, August 31, 1975 (divorced); married Neil Brian Curtis (an educational evaluator), August 3, 1985; children: (second marriage) Jenna Lindsay, Michael Harrison. *Education:* Syracuse University, B.F.A. (cum laude), 1973.

ADDRESSES: Home—211-06 75th Ave., No. 2E, Bayside, NY 11364.

CAREER: Sotheby Parke-Bernet, London, receptionist, 1975-80; artist, with group and solo exhibitions in New York, New Jersey, and London; paintings in private collections in France, Spain, England, Germany, and the United States.

MEMBER: Society of Children's Book Writers and Illustrators, Authors Guild.

AWARDS, HONORS: Author's Citation, New Jersey Writers Conference, 1986, for *Molly Pink* and *Molly Pink*

Goes Hiking; Children's Book of the Year citations, Child Study Children's Book Committee, c. 1987, for *When Grandpa Came to Stay* and *Apple Pie and Onions;* Pick of the Lists citation, American Booksellers, c. 1989, for *Three Happy Birthdays;* Best Book citations, American Library Association, 1991, for *Kisses,* and 1992, for *My Father, the Nutcase.*

WRITINGS:

JUVENILES; SELF-ILLUSTRATED; PUBLISHED BY GREENWILLOW, EXCEPT AS NOTED

(Illustrator) Olga Norris, *The Garden of Eden,* Abelard, 1982.
Molly Pink, 1985.
Molly Pink Goes Hiking, 1985.
When Grandpa Came to Stay, 1986.
My Sister Celia, 1986.
Apple Pie and Onions, 1987.
Silly Baby, 1988.
Three Happy Birthdays, 1989.
Ada Potato, 1989.
The Cousins, 1990.
Grandpa's Garden Lunch, 1990.
Annie's Pottie, 1990.
Kisses (young adult), Knopf (New York City), 1990.
Dear Annie, 1991.
Harry and Willy and Carrothead, 1991.
Hurricane Harry, 1991.
My Father, the Nutcase (young adult), Knopf, 1992.
Starring Dorothy Kane, 1992.
The Noisemakers, 1992.
Chloe in the Know, 1993.
Sophie and Sammy's Library Sleepover, 1993.
Harry and Arney, 1994.
Mama, Coming and Going, 1994.
Mr. Green Peas, 1994.

WORK IN PROGRESS: Priscilla Twice and *When the Big Dog Barks,* both for Greenwillow.

SIDELIGHTS: Judith Caseley once told *CA:* "After trying to sustain myself by painting pictures for gallery viewing, I began to design and sell greeting cards and received several awards for tiny watercolors. Eventually I found that writing and illustrating stories was more fulfilling work.

"*Molly Pink* is based on a traumatic experience from my own childhood—horrible stage fright. *Molly Pink Goes Hiking* recounts an adventure when I nearly drowned in a river and was saved—and embarrassed—by a boy who was *fat. When Grandpa Came to Stay* is loosely based on a period from my childhood when my sick grandfather came to stay with our family. It is the story of a young boy who must deal with grief and death. *My Sister Celia* documents parts of my own wedding and the abandoned feel-

ings of a young child. *Apple Pie and Onions* recalls some of the stories my Russian-born grandmother told us. All my books are little psychodramas for children."

*　　　*　　　*

CASSELL, Anthony K.　1941-

PERSONAL: Surname is accented on first syllable; born March 31, 1941, in Reading, England; Canadian citizen. *Education:* University of Toronto, B.A., 1963; Johns Hopkins University, Ph.D., 1969. *Politics:* Progressive Conservative. *Religion:* Anglican. *Avocational interests:* Huntseat equitation and dressage, painting, gardening.

ADDRESSES: Home—716 South Lynn St., Champaign, IL 61820. *Office*—Department of Spanish, Italian, and Portuguese, University of Illinois at Urbana-Champaign, Urbana, IL 61801.

CAREER: University of Illinois at Urbana-Champaign, Urbana, assistant professor, 1971-76, associate professor, 1976-84, professor of Italian and comparative literature, 1984—. Managing editor of *Italian Culture.*

MEMBER: American Association of Teachers of Italian, Dante Society of America (council member, 1980-83, 1992-95), American Boccaccio Association, Modern Language Association of America, Mediaeval Academy of America, American Association for Italian Studies, Renaissance Society of America.

AWARDS, HONORS: Outstanding Academic Book Award, *Choice,* 1976, for *The Corbaccio;* Aylwin M. Colton Foundation Award for Mediterranean Studies, 1984; John Simon Guggenheim fellow, 1984-85; Beckman fellow, University of Illinois, 1989-90.

WRITINGS:

(Editor and translator) Giovanni Boccaccio, *The Corbaccio,* University of Illinois Press (Urbana and London), 1975, 2nd revised edition, Pegasus (Binghamton, NY), 1993.
Dante's Fearful Art of Justice, University of Toronto Press (Toronto and London), 1984.
Lectura Dantis Americana: Inferno I, University of Pennsylvania Press (Philadelphia), 1989.
(Translation, notes, and commentary with Victoria Kirkham) *Diana's Hunt/Caccia di Diana: Boccaccio's First Fiction,* University of Pennsylvania Press, 1991.

Author of introduction to Dante's *Monarchia,* 1994. Associate editor of "Dante Studies," Dante Society of America, and *Italian Culture.* Contributor of articles on Dante and Boccaccio to journals.

WORK IN PROGRESS: Translations of Dante's *Monarchy* and Guido Vernani's *Reprobation of Dante's Monar-*

chy; study of Dante's *De Monarchia,* its history and reception, including two translations from the original Latin and critical essays.

*   *   *

CERF, Christopher (Bennett)   1941-

PERSONAL: Born August 19, 1941, in New York, NY; son of Bennett Alfred (a publisher) and Phyllis (an editor, maiden name: Fraser) Cerf; married Genevieve Charbin, July 8, 1972. *Education:* Harvard University, B.A. (cum laude), 1963. *Politics:* Democrat.

ADDRESSES: Home—146 East 62nd St., New York, NY 10021.

CAREER: Random House, New York City, editor, 1963-64, senior editor, 1965-70; *National Lampoon* magazine, contributing editor, 1970-76; Children's Television Workshop, New York City, organizer and editor-in-chief of Books, Records and Toys Division, 1970-76; Christopher Cerf Associates, Inc., New York City, 1979—. Resistance Music, Inc., partner, 1964—. Composer, lyricist, pianist, and vocalist; has written music and lyrics for television shows *Sesame Street, The Electric Co.,* and *Saturday Night Live,* as well as for *The National Lampoon Radio Hour* and the motion picture *Grease 2;* recordings have been issued by Vanitas, Jet Set records, Amy Records, and Epic Records. Consultant for the Children's Television Workshop, Fisher-Price Toys, Henson Associates, Warner Communications. Bank Street College, trustee, 1983—. *Military service:* National Guard, active duty with Army, 1964, reserve duty, 1964-70.

MEMBER: Association of International Advertising Agencies, National Academy of Recording Arts and Sciences, American Federation of Television and Radio Artists, American Federation of Musicians, National Academy of TV Arts and Sciences, American Institute of Graphics Arts.

AWARDS, HONORS: Playboy, 1979, award for best humor; Emmy Award nomination for musical composition, 1981 and 1982, both for *Sesame Street;* Grammy Award nomination for recording for children, 1983, for *Sesame Street* album *Born to Add.*

WRITINGS:

(With Michael J. Frith) *Alligator,* Vanitas (Boston, MA), 1962.

(Editor) *The Vintage Anthology of Science Fantasy,* Random House (New York City), 1966.

The Pop-Up Animal Alphabet Book (juvenile), Random House, 1967.

(Coeditor) *Andy Warhol's Index,* Random House, 1967.

Dial-an-Alphabet (juvenile), Random House, 1968.

The World's Largest Cheese, illustrated by Cerf and Frith, Doubleday (New York City), 1968.

(With Frith, Michael O'Donoghue, George Trow, and Jeffrey Steingarten) *The Official Pogroms,* Domesday (New York City), 1969.

(With Frith) *The Chicago Conspiracy vs. The Washington Kangaroos: Official Pogrom,* Grove (New York City), 1969.

(With Bill Effros) *The Official National Lampoon Bicentennial Calendar, 1976,* National Lampoon, 1975.

(With Sharon Lerner) *Star Trek: The Truth Machine,* Random House, 1977.

(Editor with Elisabeth L. Scharlatt) *Kids, Day In and Day Out,* Simon & Schuster (New York City), 1979.

(Editor with Tony Hendra and Peter Elbling) *The 80s: A Look Back at the Tumultuous Decade, 1980-1989,* Workman Publishing (New York City), 1979.

(Editor with Victor Navasky) *The Experts Speak: The Definitive Compendium of Authoritative Misinformation,* Pantheon (New York City), 1984.

(Editor with Henry Beard) *The Pentagon Catalog: Ordinary Products at Extraordinary Prices,* Workman, 1986.

(Editor with Marina Albee and Lev Gushchin) *Small Fires: Letters from the Soviet People to Ogonyok Magazine, 1987-1990,* translated by Hans Fenstermacher, Summit (New York City), 1990, published in England as *Voices of Glasnost: Letters from the Soviet People to Ogonyok Magazine, 1987-1990,* Kyle Cathie, 1990.

(Editor with Micah L. Sifry) *The Gulf War Reader: History, Documents, Opinions,* Times Books (New York City), 1991.

The Book of Sequels: The Greatest Stories Ever Retold, Random House, 1991.

(With Beard) *The Official Politically Correct Dictionary and Handbook,* Villard (New York City), 1992.

Co-author of *Not the New York Times,* 1978; author of "Random House Skilstarters," reading readiness materials prepared in collaboration with Phyllis Cerf and Firth. Contributor to *Grump, New Yorker,* and *Mademoiselle. Paris Review,* editorial assistant, 1964—.

SIDELIGHTS: Christopher Cerf, son of the famed publisher and "What's My Line?" panelist Bennett Cerf, has written and compiled a number of books that have taken the pulse of American popular culture since the 1960s. While most of the books have a humorous intent and could fairly be classified as "light reading," they often reflect serious contemporary preoccupations and are presented in an anecdotal style along with the actual words of the people with whom he is concerned.

One example of this style is *Kids, Day In and Day Out,* a lengthy compendium of child-rearing advice that Alice L. Powers of the *Washington Post* observed "has been called a cross between Studs Terkel and Hints From Heloise." The book was compiled from responses to questionnaires distributed to famous and less-famous people, including Margaret Mead and Cerf's own mother, Phyllis. A *New York Times* writer concluded: "It is like having a battalion of wise and supportive but never critical friends, who offer advice when asked but do not criticize. . . . The approach is a mixture of psychology and consumer guidance."

That *The 80s: A Look Back at the Tumultuous Decade 1980-1989* was published in 1979 is the reader's first clue that something wacky is afoot. *The 80s,* a send-up of the Time-Life decade books, is a comic compendium of predictions for the 1980s, including the death of reading, bankruptcies, the Meat Proscription Act of 1983, the use of toasters as premiums for those who bothered to vote, and the election of Walter Cronkite to the office of "Anchorman of the United States." With *The Experts Speak: The Definitive Compendium of Authoritative Misinformation,* Cerf takes a wry look at "disinformation, misunderstanding, miscalculation, egregious prognostication, booboos, and occasionally just plain lies." Typical of the 2,000 entries is the statement made in 1900 by Lord Kelvin, a respected British physicist: "X rays are a hoax."

The Pentagon was a favorite target of comics and pundits in the 1980s; Cerf takes aim with *The Pentagon Catalog: Ordinary Products at Extraordinary Prices.* In the *Village Voice Literary Supplement,* Paul Berman wrote: "The *Catalog* is a joke book based on a single joke: the Pentagon buys ordinary hardware for astronomical prices." The book documents instances of the outrageous prices the Pentagon paid for screwdrivers, wrenches, and toilet seats during the heady days of the arms buildup of the 1980s.

Such absurdities, however, were not restricted to the United States. In *Small Fires: Letters from the Soviet People to Ogonyok Magazine, 1987-1990,* Cerf documents some of the absurdities of life in the former Soviet Union, described in the words of its own citizens. The book is a compilation of letters to the editor of *Ogonyok,* a prominent Russian magazine. As *glasnost* (or "openness") took root in the late 1980s, Soviet citizens felt increasingly free to vent their frustration in public over the arcane and bewildering features of Soviet life. An *Atlantic* reviewer wrote: "It is the unnecessary and ridiculous aspect of Soviet arrangements that time and again causes a Western reader to marvel or to chuckle."

BIOGRAPHICAL/CRITICAL SOURCES:

PERIODICALS

Atlantic, February, 1991, p. 92.
Book World, March 17, 1968.
Los Angeles Times, September 19, 1984, pp. 1, 10.

Los Angeles Times Book Review, September 23, 1984, p. 11.
Newsweek, July 13, 1970; September 10, 1984, p. 66.
New York Times, November 18, 1967.
New York Times Book Review, August 26, 1984, p. 16.
Time, August 13, 1984.
Village Voice, October 16, 1984.
Village Voice Literary Supplement, July, 1986.
Washington Post, August 31, 1979; October 26, 1979, p. D11.
Washington Post Book World, January 27, 1991, pp. 4-5.*

*   *   *

CHARLES, Will
See WILLEFORD, Charles (Ray III)

*   *   *

CHASE, Emily
See SACHS, Judith

*   *   *

CHORAFAS, Dimitris N. 1926-

PERSONAL: Born March 25, 1926, in Athens, Greece; son of Nicolas (a civil engineer) and Chryssi (Sissini) Chorafas. *Education:* National Technical University, Athens, Greece, M.E., E.E., 1953; University of California, Los Angeles, M.S.E., 1954; Sorbonne, University of Paris, doctorate, 1958; additional study at George Washington University and University of Denver.

ADDRESSES: Home—Villa Romantic, Vitznau, LU 6354, Switzerland; and Villa Valmer, 06360 Saint Laurent d'Eze, France.

CAREER: Affiliated with University of California, Los Angeles, 1953-56; Catholic University of America, School of Engineering and Architecture, Washington, DC, member of faculty, 1956-63; engineering and management consultant in United States and Europe, 1961—. Visiting professor, Program in Information Science and School of Business Administration, Washington State University, Pullman, 1965-67, Georgia Institute of Technology, 1968-69, University of Florida, 1980, University of Alberta, 1982, and University of Vermont, 1982. Affiliated with International Business Machines (IBM), New York City, and IBM World Trade Europe Corp., 1957-60; director of management information systems, Booz, Allen & Hamilton International, Inc., United States and Europe, 1960-61. Organizer and contributor to executive development seminars and symposia.

MEMBER: Institute of Electrical and Electronics Engineers Computer Society, Society of Industrial and Applied Mathematics, Institute of Radio Engineers, Association for Computing Machinery, Technical Chamber of Greece.

WRITINGS:

Applied Mathematics, School of Engineering and Architecture, Catholic University of America, 1957.

Systems Engineering, School of Engineering and Architecture, Catholic University of America, 1957.

Factory Automation, School of Engineering and Architecture, Catholic University of America, 1958.

Economics for Engineers and Scientists, School of Engineering and Architecture, Catholic University of America, 1958.

Mathematical Statistics and Reliability Engineering, School of Engineering and Architecture, Catholic University of America, 1958.

Operations Research for Industrial Management, Reinhold, 1958.

Programming for Electronic Computers, School of Engineering and Architecture, Catholic University of America, 1958.

La Fonction de recherche dans l'entreprise, Editions de l'Entreprise Moderne, 1960.

Statistical Processes and Reliability Engineering, Van Nostrand (New York City), 1960.

Traite des ordinateurs, Hermann (Paris), 1960.

Les Applications des ordinateurs dans l'industrie, le commerce et les services publiques, Editions de l'Entreprise Moderne, 1961.

La Strategie industrielle, original text translated from the English by Charles Voraz, Editions de l'Entreprise Moderne, 1962.

Programming Systems for Electronic Computers, Butterworth, 1962.

Die Aufgaben der Forschung in der Modernen Unternehmung, Oldenbourg Verlag, 1963.

Nouvelles methodes d'analyse economique simulation, Dunod (Paris), 1963.

Systems and Simulation, Academic Press (San Diego), 1965.

Control Systems Functions and Programming Approaches, two volumes, Academic Press, 1966.

Sales Engineering: The Marketing of Technological Products, Cassell, 1967.

An Introduction to Product Planning and Reliability Management, Cassell, 1967.

Managing Industrial Research for Profits, Cassell, 1967.

Developing the International Executive, American Management Association (Saranac Lake, NY), 1967.

Selecting the Computer System, Gee & Co., 1967.

The Knowledge Revolution: An Analysis of the International Brain Market and the Challenge to Europe, Allen & Unwin (Winchester, MA), 1968, published as *The Knowledge Revolution: An Analysis of the International Brain Market,* McGraw (New York City), 1970.

Product Effectiveness, Editions de l'Entreprise Moderne, 1968.

The Communication Barrier in International Management, American Management Association, 1969.

La Simulation mathematique et ses applications, Dunod, 1969.

How to Manage Computers for Results, Gee & Co., 1969.

La Formation permanente des cadres, Editions d'Organisation, 1971.

Management Planning, Droeste Verlag, 1972.

Management Information Systems, Carl Hauser Verlag, 1973.

Computer in der Medizin, De Gruyter, 1973.

Die kranke Gesellschaft, Ullstein, 1974.

Warehousing: Planning, Organizing and Controlling the Storage and Distribution of Goods, American Elsevier, 1974.

Informationsspeicherung in Mikroform, Oldenbourg Verlag, 1976.

Data Communications, Petrocelli (Princeton, NJ), 1980.

Computer Networks, Petrocelli, 1980.

The Domesticated Computer: Interactive Videotext, Petrocelli, 1981.

Office Automation, Prentice-Hall (Englewood Cliffs, NJ), 1981.

Money: The Banks of the 1980s, Petrocelli, 1981.

Office Automation—The Productivity Challenge, Prentice-Hall, 1982.

Databases for Networks and Minicomputers, Petrocelli, 1982.

Database Management Systems for Distributed Computers and Networks, Petrocelli, 1983.

Information Systems in Financial Institutions: A Guide to Strategic Planning Based on the Japanese Experience, Prentice-Hall, 1983.

Microprocessors for Management: CAD, CAM, and Robotics, Petrocelli, 1983.

Interactive Message Services, McGraw, 1984.

Banking Automation, Pirola Editore (Milan), 1984.

Telephony: Today and Tomorrow, Prentice-Hall, 1984.

Local Area Networks, McGraw, 1984.

The Software Handbook: Analysis, Design, Programming, Petrocelli, 1984.

Management Workstations for Greater Productivity, McGraw, 1985.

Handbook of Data Communications and Computer Networks, Petrocelli, 1985.

Applying Expert Systems in Business, McGraw, 1986.

Fourth Generation Programming Languages: Which Unix?, McGraw, 1986.

Fourth Generation Programming Languages: Integrated Software, Database Languages and Expert Systems, McGraw, 1986.

Interactive Workstations, Petrocelli, 1986.

Personal Computers and Data Communications, Computer Science Press (Rockville, MD), 1986.

Engineering Productivity through CAD-CAM, Butterworth, 1987.

Strategic Planning for Electronic Banking, Butterworth Legal Publishers (Newton Upper Falls, MA), 1987.

Applying Expert Systems in Business, McGraw, 1987.

Membership of the Board of Directors: The Job Top Executives Want No More, International Specialized Book Services, 1988.

(With Stephen J. Legg) *The Engineering Database: Design, Normalization, and Implementation for Successful CAD-CAM Applications*, Butterworth-Heinemann, 1988.

Electronic Document Handling: The New Communications Architectures, Petrocelli, 1988.

The Handbook of Management, Petrocelli, 1988.

Electronic Funds Transfer, Butterworth Legal Publishers, 1988.

(With Heinrich Steinmann) *High Technology at UBS: For Excellence in Client Service*, Union Bank of Switzerland (Zurich), 1988.

(With Steinmann) *Implementing Networks in Banking and Financial Services*, Macmillan (London), 1988.

Handbook of Database Management and Distributed Relational Databases, Petrocelli, 1989.

Systems Architecture and Systems Design, McGraw, 1989.

Local Area Network Reference, McGraw, 1989.

Handbook of Management for Scientific and Technical Personnel, Tab Books (Blue Ridge Summit, PA), 1989.

Bank Profitability, Butterworth Legal Publishers, 1989.

(With Steinmann) *Supercomputers*, McGraw, 1990.

(With Steinmann) *Intelligent Networks: Telecommunications Solutions for the 1990s*, CRC Press, 1990.

Knowledge Engineering: Knowledge Acquisition, Knowledge Representation, the Role of the Knowledge Engineer, and Domains Fertile to AI Implementation, Van Nostrand, 1990.

The New Technology: A Survival Guide to New Materials, Supercomputers and Global Communications for the 1990s, Sigma Press (England), 1990.

Handbook of Data Communications, Tab Books, 1990, 2nd edition published as *Handbook of Data Communications and Computer Networks*, 1991.

Risk Management in Financial Institutions, Butterworth Legal Publishers, 1990.

(With Steinmann) *Expert Systems in Banking: A Guide for Senior Managers*, St. Martin's (New York City), 1990.

Expert Systems in Manufacturing, Van Nostrand, 1992.

Treasury Operations and Foreign Exchange Challenge: A Guide to Risk Management Strategies for the New World Markets, Wiley (New York City), 1992.

(With Eva Maria Binder) *Technoculture and Change*, Adamantine Press, 1992.

Simulation, Optimization and Expert Systems: How Technology Is Revolutionizing the Way Securities Are Underwritten, Analyzed and Traded, Probus Publishing, 1992.

The New Technology of Financial Management, Wiley, 1992.

New Information Technologies: A Practitioner's Guide, Van Nostrand, 1992.

The Globalization of Money and Securities: The New Products, Players and Markets, Probus Publishing, 1992.

(With Steinmann) *Do It or Die: Database Solutions for Financial Institutions*, Lafferty Publications, 1992.

(With Steinmann) *Object-Oriented Databases*, Prentice-Hall, 1993.

Manufacturing Databases and Computer Integrated Systems, CRC Press, 1993.

(With Steinmann) *Solutions for Networked Databases: How to Move from Heterogeneous Structures to Federated Concepts*, Academic Press, 1993.

Beyond LANS: Client-Server Computing, McGraw, 1993.

Measuring Return on Technology Investments, Lafferty Publications, 1993.

Intelligent Multimedia Databases: From Object Orientation and Fuzzy Engineering to Intentional Database Structures, Prentice-Hall, 1994.

Chaos Theory in the Financial Markets, Probus Publishing, 1994.

(With Steinmann) *Risk Management with Off-Balance Sheet Financial Instruments*, Probus Publishing, 1994.

Also author of *Computer Theory*, 1960, *The Influence of the Computer on the Organization*, 1964, *La Direction des produits nouveaux*, 1967, *Information Systems Design*, 1972, *The New Communications Disciplines*, 1987, and *Data Communications for Distributed Information Systems*, Petrocelli. Contributor to management magazines and technical and scholarly journals.

Chorafas's books have been translated into sixteen languages, including Russian, Polish, Swedish, Norwegian, Danish, Finnish, Greek, Portuguese, Spanish, German, French, and Japanese, and they have appeared in sixteen countries on four continents.

SIDELIGHTS: Dimitris N. Chorafas once told *CA:* "As a young faculty member at Catholic University, I started writing because there was no textbook available for my systems engineering, computers, and communications course. Since then, writing is both a pleasure and a fulfillment. It helps transmit knowledge and at the same time make one's own know-how more complete."

He added that in 1992 he "instituted the Chorafas Foundation, a nonprofit organization based in Switzerland registered under Swiss law and affiliated with the Swiss Academies of Science. The Chorafas Foundation has been endowed with one million Swiss francs and gives two yearly awards of one hundred thousand Swiss francs each. Each award is selected by the corresponding Swiss Academy of Science following an international competition. Four awards alternate two by two every two years: (1) breakthroughs in technology; (2) new, innovative financial products; (3) birth control; and (4) environmental protection."

*   *   *

CHOWDER, Ken   1950-

PERSONAL: Born October 11, 1950, in New York, NY. *Education:* Attended Reed College, 1968-70; Stanford University, B.A., 1971. *Politics:* "Correct." *Religion:* "Latent."

ADDRESSES: Office—Christianshavns Voldgade 9D, V, 1424 Copenhagen K, Denmark.

CAREER: Writer, freelance editor, and documentary film writer. Shiver Mountain Press, Washington, CT, press worker, 1972-76; National Center of Scientific Research, Paris, English language editor, 1976-77; Association Marzio, Istres, Bouches-du-Rhone, France, teacher of English as a foreign language, 1977-78; documentary film writer, 1986—.

AWARDS, HONORS: Harper-Saxton Prize, 1978, for *Blackbird Days;* fellowships from Mary Roberts Rinehart Foundation, 1980, Ingram Merrill Foundation, 1982 and 1987, Oregon Arts Commission, 1983, National Endowment for the Arts, 1986 and 1991, Shifting Foundation, 1989, and Ludwig Vogelstein Foundation, 1991; *Fiction Network* competition award, 1986, for short story "Moodring"; NEA-PEN award, 1987, for short story "We're in Sally's House," and 1991, for short story "With Pat Boone in the Pentlands"; Pushcart Prize, 1990, for "With Pat Boone in the Pentlands"; Blue Ribbon, American Film Festival, Golden Apple Award, National Educational Film Festival, Golden Gate Award, San Francisco Film Festival, Golden Plaque, Chicago Film Festival, and CINE Golden Eagle Award, all 1990, all for *The Wilderness Idea: John Muir, Gifford Pinchot, and the First Great Battle for Wilderness;* Academy Award nomination, 1992, for *Wild by Law;* O. Henry Prize, 1992, for short story "With Seth in Tana Toraja."

WRITINGS:

TELEVISION SCRIPTS; DOCUMENTARIES

The Wilderness Idea: John Muir, Gifford Pinchot, and the First Great Battle for Wilderness, Public Broadcasting Service (PBS), 1990.
Wild by Law, PBS, 1992.
Knute Rockne, PBS, 1993.
The People's Plague: Tuberculosis in America, PBS, 1995.

Also author of scripts for *The Lost Fleet of Guadalcanal,* 1993, and *Russia's Last Tsar,* 1995, both broadcast as *National Geographic* specials.

OTHER

Blackbird Days (novel), Harper (New York City), 1980.
Delicate Geometry (novel), Harper, 1982.
Jadis (novel), Harper, 1985.
(Editor and author of introduction) Mark Twain, *Gold Miners and Guttersnipes: Tales of California,* Chronicle Books (San Francisco), 1991.

Contributor to numerous periodicals, including *Yankee, Southern Review, American Short Fiction, New England Review, Harper's, Southwest Review, Boulevard, Short Story International, Smithsonian, Modern Maturity,* and *Fiction Network.*

SIDELIGHTS: Ken Chowder's debut, *Blackbird Days,* a novel about three brothers of the sixties generation and their struggles with imminent middle age, was praised by many critics who felt that Chowder displayed great promise as a novelist. Carole Cook of *Saturday Review* wrote of Chowder, "He is a tremendously satisfying writer, bringing good news, for a change, of the people who used to be called the Woodstock generation." Scott Spencer of the *New York Times Book Review,* however, indicated that though *Blackbird Days* is an exceptional first novel, Chowder still has room for improvement. "Chowder can describe nearly anything and make it live," Spencer commented. "Still, the novel lacks power in the end. My guess is that *Blackbird Days* is the warm-up exercise of a strong writer."

Despite being praised by most critics as "poetic," "unusual," and "delightfully eccentric," Chowder's third novel, *Jadis,* was not entirely admired by reviewers. *Washington Post* reviewer Christopher Schemering, who called Chowder's second effort, *Delicate Geometry,* a "thoroughbred novel," had a mixed reaction after reading *Jadis.* He explained: "Reading *Jadis,* one is alternately charmed and appalled. Chowder has the extraordinary ability to find beauty in the everyday mess of love relationships. . . . The main problem with the novel is that it's not about grown-up romance at all but about puppy love."

Chowder told *CA:* "I have always written. My novels tend to be more quiet than some, perhaps because not enough happens. It's my feeling that it isn't so much what happens that matters, but how life is lived in the mind. Real life usually includes both more and less than the serial killings and endless car chases of the stories we spend our lives watching (and reading). I don't think we always have to live so near the surface of things; language can go down and fetch things from the bottom of a pond that is both deep and still."

BIOGRAPHICAL/CRITICAL SOURCES:

PERIODICALS

Chicago Tribune, October 5, 1980, p. 10; February 13, 1983, p. 3; April 28, 1985.
Globe and Mail (Toronto), October 19, 1985.
Los Angeles Times, July 29, 1980.
Los Angeles Times Book Review, October 10, 1982, p. 3; July 14, 1985, p. 4.
New Yorker, August 4, 1980.
New York Times Book Review, September 7, 1980; April 21, 1985, p. 11.
Saturday Review, July, 1980.
Washington Post, April 20, 1985.
Washington Post Book World, October 3, 1982, p. 6.

*　　*　　*

CLARK, Ann Nolan 1896-
(Marie Dunne)

PERSONAL: Born December 5, 1896, in Las Vegas, NM; daughter of Patrick Frances (a merchant) and Mary (a teacher; maiden name, Dunne) Nolan; married Thomas Patrick Clark, August 6, 1919 (deceased); children: Thomas Patrick, Jr. (killed in World War II). *Education:* New Mexico Normal School (now New Mexico Highlands University), B.A., 1919. *Politics:* Democrat. *Religion:* Catholic.

ADDRESSES: Home—2500 North Rosemont Blvd. No. 603, Tucson, AZ 85712.

CAREER: Bureau of Indian Affairs, Washington, DC, education specialist, 1920-62; International Cooperation Administration, Washington, DC, education consultant in Latin American Bureau, 1945-50. Institute of Inter-America Affairs, former material specialist; U.S. delegate to UNESCO conference, Brazil.

MEMBER: International Council of Women, PEN, National Council of Women, Alpha Delta Kappa, Altrusa International.

AWARDS, HONORS: Spring Book Festival Awards, *New York Herald Tribune,* 1941, for *In My Mother's House,*

1952, for *Looking-for-Something: The Story of a Stray Burro of Ecuador* and *Secret of the Andes,* and 1955, for *Santiago;* Newbery Medal, 1953, for *Secret of the Andes;* Distinguished Service Award, U.S. Department of the Interior, 1962; Regina Medal, Catholic Library Association, 1963; Daughter of Mark Twain Honor, *Mark Twain Journal,* 1971; named outstanding Arizona author, 1984.

WRITINGS:

JUVENILE FICTION

Handmade Tales, [Zuni, NM], 1932.
Who Wants to Be a Prairie Dog? (reader), illustrated by Van Tishnahjinnie, U.S. Office of Indian Affairs (Phoenix), 1940.
Little Herder in Spring (reader; also see below), illustrated by Hoke Denetsosie, U.S. Office of Indian Affairs, 1940.
Little Herder in Autumn (reader; also see below), illustrated by Denetsosie, U.S. Office of Indian Affairs, 1940.
Little Boy with Three Names: Stories of Taos Pueblo (reader), illustrated by Tonita Lujan, U.S. Office of Indian Affairs (Washington, DC), 1940, 2nd edition, Ancient City Press (Santa Fe, NM), 1990.
The Pine Ridge Porcupine (reader), illustrated by Andrew Standing Soldier, U.S. Office of Indian Affairs (Lawrence, KS), 1941.
In My Mother's House (verse; earlier version privately printed as *Third Grade Home Geography;* Junior Literary Guild selection), illustrated by Velino Herrera, Viking (New York City), 1941.
(With Frances Carey) *A Child's Story of New Mexico,* University Publishing (Lincoln, NE, and New York), 1941, 3rd edition, 1960.
About the Slim Butte Raccoon (reader), illustrated by Standing Soldier, U.S. Department of the Interior, Bureau of Indian Affairs (Washington, DC), 1942.
Little Herder in Winter (reader; also see below), illustrated by Denetsosie, U.S. Office of Indian Affairs (Phoenix), 1942.
Little Herder in Summer (reader; also see below), illustrated by Denetsosie, U.S. Office of Indian Affairs (Phoenix), 1942.
Buffalo Caller: The Story of a Young Sioux Boy of the Early 1700s, before the Coming of the Horse, illustrated by Marian Hulsizer, Row, Peterson (Evanston, IL, and New York City), 1942.
There Still Are Buffalo (reader), illustrated by Standing Soldier, U.S. Office of Indian Affairs (Washington, DC), 1942.
About the Grass Mountain Mouse (reader), illustrated by Standing Soldier, U.S. Office of Indian Affairs (Washington, DC), 1942.

About the Hen of Wahpeton (reader), illustrated by Standing Soldier, U.S. Office of Indian Affairs (Lawrence, KS), 1942.

Young Hunter of Picuris, illustrated by Herrera, U.S. Office of Indian Affairs (Chilocco, OK), 1943.

Little Navajo Bluebird (Junior Literary Guild selection), illustrated by Paul Lantz, Viking, 1943.

Bringer of the Mystery Dog (reader), illustrated by Oscar Howe, Department of the Interior, Bureau of Indian Affairs (Lawrence), 1943.

Brave against the Enemy: A Story of Three Generations—of the Day before Yesterday, of Yesterday, and of Tomorrow (reader), illustrated by Helen Post, U.S. Bureau of Indian Affairs (Lawrence), 1944.

Sun Journey: A Story of the Zuni Pueblo (reader), illustrated by Percy T. Sandy, U.S. Bureau of Indian Affairs (Chilocco), 1945, 2nd edition, Ancient City Press, 1988.

Singing Sioux Cowboy Reader, illustrated by Standing Soldier, U.S. Indian Service (Lawrence), 1947.

Linda Rita (reader), Government Printing Office (Washington, DC), 1948.

Los patos son diferentes (reader), Government Printing Office (Washington, DC), 1948.

El buey que queria vivir en la casa (reader), Government Printing Office (Washington, DC), 1948.

Juan el poblano (reader), Government Printing Office (Washington, DC), 1949.

El cerdito que fue al mercado (reader), Government Printing Office (Washington, DC), 1949.

Magic Money (Junior Literary Guild selection), illustrated by Leo Politi, Viking, 1950.

Little Herder in Spring, in Summer (reader; incorporating *Little Herder in Spring* and *Little Herder in Summer*), U.S. Indian Service (Phoenix), 1950.

Little Herder in Autumn, in Winter (reader; incorporating *Little Herder in Autumn* and *Little Herder in Winter*), U.S. Indian Service (Phoenix), 1950.

Little Navajo Herder (reader; compilation of *Little Herder in Spring, Little Herder in Summer, Little Herder in Autumn,* and *Little Herder in Winter*), U.S. Indian Service (Phoenix), 1951.

Secret of the Andes (Junior Literary Guild selection), illustrated by Jean Charlot, Viking, 1952.

Looking-for-Something: The Story of a Stray Burro of Ecuador (Junior Literary Guild selection), illustrated by Politi, Viking, 1952.

Blue Canyon Horse, illustrated by Allan Houser, Viking, 1954.

Santiago, illustrated by Lynd Ward, Viking, 1955.

The Little Indian Pottery Maker, illustrated by Don Perceval, Melmont (Los Angeles), 1955.

(With Manuel Arce and Miguel Gordillo) *El maestro rural en la comunidad,* Ministerio de Educacion Publica (Guatemala), 1955.

Third Monkey (verse), illustrated by Don Freeman, Viking, 1956.

The Little Indian Basket Maker, illustrated by Harrison Begay, Melmont, 1957.

A Santo for Pasqualita, illustrated by Mary Villarejo, Viking, 1959.

World Song, illustrated by Kurt Wiese, Viking, 1960.

Paco's Miracle, illustrated by Agnes Tait, Farrar, Straus (New York City), 1962.

The Desert People, illustrated by Houser, Viking, 1962.

Tia Maria's Garden, illustrated by Ezra Jack Keats, Viking, 1963.

Medicine Man's Daughter, illustrated by Don Bolognese, Farrar, Straus, 1963.

Father Kino: Priest to the Pimas, illustrated by H. Lawrence Hoffman, Farrar, Straus, 1963.

Bear Cub (verse), illustrated by Charles Frace, Viking, 1965.

This for That, illustrated by Freeman, Golden Gate (San Carlos, CA), 1965.

Brother Andre of Montreal, illustrated by Harold Lang, Farrar, Straus, 1967.

Summer Is for Growing, illustrated by Tait, Farrar, Straus, 1967.

(With Glenna Craw) *Arizona for Young People,* Nebraska University Publishing (Lincoln), 1968.

A Child's Story of New Mexico, Nebraska University Publishing, 1968.

Along Sandy Trails, illustrated by Alfred A. Cohn, Viking, 1969.

Circle of Seasons, illustrated by W. T. Mars, Farrar, Straus, 1970.

Hoofprint on the Wind, illustrated by Robert Andrew Parker, Viking, 1972.

Year Walk, Viking, 1975.

All This Wild Land, Viking, 1976.

To Stand against the Wind, Viking, 1978.

(With Dang Manh Kha) *In the Land of Small Dragon: A Vietnamese Folktale,* illustrated by Tony Chen, Viking, 1979.

NONFICTION FOR ADULTS

Journey to the People (essays), Viking, 1969.

These Were the Valiant: A Collection of New Mexico Profiles, Calvin Horn (Albuquerque, NM), 1969.

OTHER

Also author of pamphlet *Writers and Writing of New Mexico,* Writers' Round Table of Las Vegas, NM, 1935, and of *Local Government,* United Pueblo Agency. Supervised the preparation of materials for adult literacy, Bureau of

Indian Affairs, and reading texts for several countries in Latin America, including Guatemala, Costa Rica, Ecuador, Honduras, Panama, and Peru. Contributor, sometimes under pseudonym Marie Dunne, to periodicals, including *New Mexico* and *Horn Book.*

Collections of Clark's manuscripts are located in the Kerlan Collection at the University of Minnesota and in the de Grummond Collection at the University of Southern Mississippi. A collection of Clark's books is located in the Special Collections of the New Mexico State University Library.

SIDELIGHTS: Ann Nolan Clark is an American of Irish descent who has spent much of her life writing books for Native-American and Spanish-American children. Clark was one of the first non-Indian educators to realize that Indian children needed books they could relate to, with stories reflecting their own rich heritages. The author began on a small scale, writing easy primers for her own Native-American students. Eventually, these primers—and later Clark's more sophisticated stories—became favorites among white children as well. In *Elementary English,* Evelyn Wenzel notes that Clark "feels a strong responsibility: to help Indian children understand their own problems of growing-up and to interpret to children of other cultures these people she knows and loves so well."

About Clark's writing, Claire Huchet Bishop observes in *Catholic Library World:* "Ann Nolan Clark's books are a joy to the Indians, both young and old, who recognize themselves, their traditions, their sense of values, their suffering and their hopes. Also, her books introduce the Indians to what is relevant for them in the White man's culture and which they can assimilate without betraying their own ways." In general, Clark's books relate day-to-day events in Indian society, imparting importance to daily tasks and observations. *New York Times Book Review* contributor Anne T. Eaton claims that such an approach "gives to [all] little children . . . a sense of knowing Indian boys and girls and the feeling of experiences shared."

Ann Nolan was born in 1896 in Las Vegas, New Mexico. Her own parents and grandparents were Irish, but she grew up with an Indian nurse and with friends of Indian, Spanish, and French backgrounds. In her Newbery Award acceptance speech, published in *Horn Book* magazine, the author reflects that New Mexico gave her "understanding, a tolerance and acceptance and appreciation and ease with different peoples who have other ways of thinking and other ways of living. New Mexico gave that to all her early children, and for me it has made my lifeway rich and warm and wide."

By 1923, Ann Nolan Clark was a widow with a young child to support. She had done some substitute teaching among the students of the Zuni Pueblo in New Mexico,

and officials at the Bureau of Indian Affairs urged her to take the examination for permanent employment in the Indian Service, which she then passed. Her first assignment was at the Santa Fe Boarding School for Indian children, a large and well-maintained facility. Then the Tewa Indians at the Tesuque Pueblo, near Santa Fe, asked Clark to teach in their one-room school. Despite administrative officials who believed that Clark's move to a smaller school would seriously jeopardize her career as an Indian educator, her experience in that tiny Tewa Indian school led directly to her long and fruitful writing career; many of her books were penned specifically for Native-American children.

Clark quickly discovered that her young pupils faced an extremely difficult task. They had to learn a new language—English—as well as new ways of thinking and living, and very little emphasis was put on their own culture. Instead, they were expected to learn "American" ways. Clark saw injustice in this dichotomy of heritage and education. Her students came from an ancient culture and had a right, she thought, to feel comfortable with their heritage. In her spare time, Clark began to write easy-to-read primers about the pueblo way of life, using poetic language that translated easily from English into the Tesuque dialect. Clark became a specialist in teaching children to read and write English through stories about their own familiar traditions. The resulting books not only helped Indian children to learn a second language, they also gave non-Indian children a glimpse of everyday Indian life.

Eventually Clark left teaching and became a full-time writer and educational specialist with the Bureau of Indian Affairs. Her work took her through Latin America and South America as well, where she taught local school administrators how to reach their special ethnic students. Clark's travels enriched her imagination, and soon she found herself writing stories about the children she encountered in such places as Guatemala, Peru, and Mexico.

In *Elementary English,* Wenzel describes Clark's primers, such as *In My Mother's House* and the "Little Herder" series, as "truly delightful stories telling of familiar details of the . . . Navajo, Sioux, and Pueblo children; revealing humor and sensitive understanding of these people as individual personalities as well as a minority culture with its problems; and written in simple, often poetic language which has an Indian 'flavor' even in English." May Hill Arbuthnot comments in *Children and Books* that "*In My Mother's House* is written as if a Tewa child were speaking simply and beautifully of the small world he knows and holds dear. The cadenced prose of the text is matched by the rhythmic beauty of the illustrations." Many of these easy-to-understand "Indian Life Readers" remain in print, even though they were written in the 1940s and 1950s.

Clark's stories often revolve around the conflict an Indian child feels between the traditional ways of his or her people and the demands of the alien majority culture. As Wenzel further explains in *Elementary English,* works such as Newbery Medal-winner *Secret of the Andes, Santiago,* and *Little Navajo Bluebird* "present some of the problems of the people of whom they are written. Here Ann Nolan Clark's artistry is at its best, for only a teacher who knows and loves children and a person who has lived and felt with these people could deal with such problems so simply and effectively."

In *Secret of the Andes,* an Inca boy in modern Peru becomes heir to a four-hundred-year-old secret dating to the days before the Spaniards overtook the region. The boy must choose to become guardian of the secret in his turn or forever lose the path of the ancient Inca peoples. "To my mind," claims *Catholic Library World*'s Bishop, "*Secret of the Andes* is one of the summits of American literature for the young."

Clark's most recent books include more accounts of Native Americans as well as stories about Finnish immigrants to Minnesota and Vietnamese youngsters caught in the dangers of war. The author has earned a number of prestigious awards in addition to her Newbery Medal, and in 1984 she was named an "outstanding Arizona author" by the state to which she has retired.

BIOGRAPHICAL/CRITICAL SOURCES:

BOOKS

Arbuthnot, May Hill, *Children and Books,* 3rd edition, Scott, Foresman (Glenview, IL), 1964, pp. 452-53.
Children's Literature Review, Volume 16, Gale (Detroit), 1989.
Dictionary of Literary Biography, Volume 52: *American Writers for Children since 1960: Fiction,* Gale, 1986.
Helbig, Alethea K., and Agnes Regan Perkins, *Dictionary of American Children's Fiction, 1859-1959: Books of Recognized Merit,* Greenwood Press (Westport, CT), 1985.
Sadker, Myra Pollack, and David Miller Sadker, *Now upon a Time: A Contemporary View of Children's Literature,* Harper (New York City), 1977, pp. 163-90.
Something about the Author Autobiography Series, Volume 16, Gale, 1993, pp. 33-109.

PERIODICALS

Books, September 2, 1962, p. 10.
Bloomsbury Review, October, 1992, p. 25.
Catholic Library World, February, 1963, pp. 280-86, 333.
Christian Science Monitor, May 7, 1975, p. B2; May 4, 1977, p. B2.
Elementary English, October, 1953, pp. 327-32; May, 1972, pp. 648-58.

Horn Book, June, 1952, pp. 160-61, 174; August, 1953, pp. 249-57.
Library Journal, March 15, 1953; February 15, 1963, p. 847-48.
New York Times Book Review, May 4, 1941, p. 11.
School Library Journal, February 10, 1963, p. 35-6.*

*   *   *

CLARK, James C. 1947-

PERSONAL: Born May 22, 1947, in Washington, DC; son of William E. (a cartographer) and Louise (an accountant; maiden name, Covington) Clark; married Jane E. Healy (a newspaper editor), June 4, 1977 (divorced); children: Randall Healy, Kevin Healy. *Education:* Lenoir-Rhyne College, B.A., 1975; Stetson University, M.A., 1985.

ADDRESSES: Home—633 North Orange Ave., Orlando, FL 32801.

CAREER: Associated Press, Philadelphia, PA, reporter, 1974-75; *Tampa Tribune,* Tampa, FL, editor, 1976-77; *Orlando Sentinel,* Orlando, FL, editor, 1977—.

MEMBER: Authors Guild, Society of Professional Journalists.

AWARDS, HONORS: George Polk Memorial Award, 1981; Sigma Delta Chi Award, 1982.

WRITINGS:

Last Train South, McFarland & Co. (Jefferson, NC), 1984.
Faded Glory, Praeger (New York City), 1985.
The Murder of James A. Garfield, McFarland & Co., 1994.

*   *   *

CLAVELL, James (duMaresq) 1925-1994

PERSONAL: Born October 10, 1925, in Australia; came to the United States, 1953; naturalized, 1963; died of complications from cancer, September 6, 1994, in Vevey, Switzerland; son of Richard Charles (a captain in the British Royal Navy) and Eileen (Collis) Clavell; married April Stride, February 20, 1951; children: Michaela, Holly. *Education:* Attended University of Birmingham, 1946-47. *Avocational interests:* Sailing, flying helicopters.

ADDRESSES: Agent—Foreign Rights, Inc., 400 East 58th St., #17D, New York, NY 10022; Contemporary Artists, 132 Lasky Dr., Beverly Hills, CA 90212.

CAREER: Worked as a carpenter, 1953; screenwriter, director, and producer, 1954-94; director of television programs, beginning 1958; novelist, 1962-94. *Military service:* Served as captain with the Royal Artillery, 1940-46; taken prisoner of war by Japanese.

MEMBER: Writers Guild, Authors League of America, Producers Guild, Dramatists Guild, Directors Guild.

AWARDS, HONORS: Writers Guild Best Screenplay Award, 1963, for *The Great Escape;* honorary doctorates from the University of Maryland and the University of Bradford.

WRITINGS:

NOVELS

King Rat, Little, Brown (Boston), 1962, reprinted as *James Clavell's "King Rat,"* Delacorte (New York City), 1983.
Tai-Pan: A Novel of Hong Kong, Atheneum (New York City), 1966, reprinted, Delacorte, 1983.
Shogun: A Novel of Japan, Atheneum, 1975.
Noble House: A Novel of Contemporary Hong Kong, Delacorte, 1981.
The Children's Story, Delacorte, 1981.
James Clavell's "Whirlwind," Morrow (New York City), 1986.
James Clavell's "Thrump-o-moto," illustrated by George Sharp, Delacorte, 1986.
James Clavell's Gai-Jin: A Novel of Japan, Delacorte, 1993.

SCREENPLAYS

The Fly, Twentieth Century-Fox, 1958.
Watusi, Metro-Goldwyn-Mayer, 1959.
(And producer and director) *Five Gates to Hell,* Twentieth Century-Fox, 1959.
(And producer and director) *Walk like a Dragon,* Paramount, 1960.
(And producer and director) *The Great Escape,* United Artists, 1963.
633 Squadron, United Artists, 1964.
The Satan Bug, United Artists, 1965.
(And producer and director) *Where's Jack?,* Paramount, 1968.
(And producer and director) *To Sir with Love,* Columbia, 1969.
(And producer and director) *The Last Valley,* ABC Pictures, 1969.

OTHER

Countdown to Armageddon: E=mc² (play), produced in Vancouver, British Columbia, at Vancouver Playhouse Theatre, 1966.
(Author of introduction) *The Making of James Clavell's "Shogun,"* Dell (New York City), 1980.

(Editor and author of foreword) Sun Tzu, *The Art of War,* Hodder & Stoughton (London), 1981, Delacorte, 1983.

Also author of poetry ("published and paid, by God").

ADAPTATIONS: King Rat was produced by Columbia, 1965; *Tai-Pan* was produced by DeLaurentiis Entertainment Group, 1986. *Shogun* was produced as a television miniseries, 1980 (Clavell was executive producer); *The Children's Story* was produced as a Mobile Showcase television special, 1982; *Noble House* was produced as a television miniseries under the title *James Clavell's "Noble House",* 1988; a television miniseries based on *King Rat* and one based on *Whirlwind* are planned. *Shogun* was produced for the stage at the Kennedy Center in Washington, DC, and on Broadway in 1990.

SIDELIGHTS: James Clavell, who called himself an "old-fashioned storyteller," is one of the twentieth century's most widely read novelists. His sagas of the Far East—*Tai-Pan: A Novel of Hong Kong, Shogun: A Novel of Japan,* and *Noble House: A Novel of Contemporary Hong Kong*—have each sold millions of copies and dominated bestseller lists for months, while his Iran-based adventure, *James Clavell's "Whirlwind,"* commanded a record-setting $5,000,000 advance from its publisher. In the *Los Angeles Times,* an industry insider described Clavell as "one of the very few writers . . . whose names have marquee value. Clavell's name on the cover sells enormous quantities of books." As James Vesely noted in the *Detroit News,* the author "always does one thing right: he is never boring." Indeed, Clavell combined action, intrigue, cultural conflicts, and romance to produce "event-packed books with the addictive appeal of popcorn," asserted *Detroit News* correspondent Helen Dudar. Although critics agreed that Clavell's blockbusters do not aspire to literary greatness, they also concurred that his works possess the sort of research and detail rarely found in so-called "popular novels." In the *National Review,* Terry Teachout called Clavell a "first-rate novelist of the second rank," the kind of writer "who provides genuinely stimulating literary entertainment without insulting the sensibilities."

Washington Post contributor Cynthia Gorney described the main theme of Clavell's novels as being "the enormous gulf between Asian and Occidental views of the world." Against exotic backgrounds the books explore the powerful human obsession with waging war, cornering power, or forming giant corporations. International espionage, skulduggery, and forbidden romance often round out the picture. "Each of [Clavell's] novels involves an enormous amount of research and enough plot for a dozen books," wrote Ann Marie Cunningham in the *Los Angeles Times.* "All describe strategic thinking during wartime: Teams of tough British boys try to extract themselves from tight spots, . . . often in parts of the former empire." Webster Schott in the *New York Times Book Review* noted that Clavell is "neither literary psychoanalyst nor philosophizing intellectual. He reports the world as he sees people—in terms of power, control, strength. . . . He writes in the oldest and grandest tradition that fiction knows." Likewise, *Chicago Tribune* correspondent Harrison E. Salisbury claimed that the author "gives you your money's worth if you like suspense, blood, thunder, romance, intrigue, lust, greed, dirty work—you name it—and pages. He is a generous man." Clavell has "sprayed his prose in machine-gun fashion, strafing targets the size of billboards," commented Paul King in *Maclean's.* "Still, he has learned the art of structuring convoluted plots that would have dazzled even Dickens. Above all, with lengthy tales of gut wrenching suspense, Clavell has mastered the technique of keeping readers turning pages until dawn."

"The people I write about are mostly doers," Clavell told the *Washington Post.* "They're not people who sit on their tails in New York, who are concerned about their place in life or should they get a divorce." His epics, he related to *Publishers Weekly,* concern "ordinary people placed in extraordinary circumstances and exposed to danger. They have to do something to extract themselves from this situation, and what you have, then, are heroics and a good read." In the *New York Times Magazine,* Paul Bernstein compared Clavell's characters to those of Charles Dickens. "Dickens's big-hearted orphans become Clavell's larger-than-life men of action," wrote Bernstein, "Dickens's hard-hearted villains, Clavell's hard-hearted business or political adversaries. The social commentary of Dickens becomes in Clavell cross-cultural education and reactionary political warnings." Schott admitted in the *Washington Post Book World* that some of Clavell's characters are romantic stereotypes. The critic added, however, that "others are troubled outsiders, wondering who they are and what their lives mean. Some of his villains and contemporary courtesans have distant cousins in Marvel Comics. But others are men and women painfully compromised into evil because they do not know how to fight evil without becoming it." In the same review, Schott offered further praise for Clavell: "The riches of his imagination and the reach of his authority are only the start. James Clavell tells his stories so well . . . that it's possible to miss the tough-minded intelligence at work. . . . Clavell knows people and what motivates them. He understands systems and how they work and fail. He remembers history and sees what technology has wrought. . . . James Clavell does more than entertain. He transports us into worlds we've not known, stimulating, educating, questioning almost simultaneously."

Clavell's life was almost as eventful as one of his books. He was born in Australia in 1925, the son of a British Royal Navy captain who traveled to ports all over the world. As a child, Clavell relished the swashbuckling sea tales—most of them fictional—recounted by his father and grandfather, both career military men. A career in the service seemed a natural choice for Clavell, too, and after his secondary schooling was completed, he joined the Royal Artillery in 1940. A year later, he was sent to fight in the Far East and was wounded by machine-gun fire in the jungles of Malaysia. For several months he hid in a Malay village, but he was eventually captured by the Japanese and sent to the notorious Changi prison near Singapore. The conditions at Changi were so severe that only 10,000 of its 150,000 inmates survived incarceration—and Clavell was there three and a half years. He told the *Guardian:* "Changi was a school for survivors. It gave me a strength most people don't have. I have an awareness of life others lack. Changi was my university. . . . Those who were supposed to survive didn't." The experience invested Clavell with some of the same verve and intensity which characterize his fictional protagonists. Calling Changi "the rock" on which he put his life, he said: "So long as I remember Changi, I know I'm living forty borrowed lifetimes."

Released from captivity after the war, Clavell returned to Great Britain to continue his military career. A motorcycle accident left him lame in one leg, however, and he was discharged in 1946. He attended Birmingham University briefly, considering law or engineering as a profession, but when he began to visit movie sets with his future wife, an aspiring actress, he became fascinated with directing and writing for films. He entered the movie industry on the ground floor as a distributor, gradually moving into production work. In 1953 he and his wife immigrated to the United States, where, after a period of television production in New York, they moved to Hollywood. There Clavell bluffed his way into a screenwriting contract ("They liked my accent, I suppose," he told the *Washington Post*) and set to work in the field that would bring him his first success. His first produced screenplay, *The Fly,* was based on a science fiction story about an atomic scientist whose experiments cause an exchange of heads with a housefly. The movie made a $4,000,000 profit in two years and has since become a classic genre film in its own right and the source of several sequels and remakes. Clavell won a Writers Guild Best Screenplay Award for the 1963 film *The Great Escape,* also a box-office success. Of the films the author produced, directed, and wrote, perhaps the most notable remains the 1969 hit *To Sir with Love,* starring Sidney Poitier. Created with a budget of $625,000, the movie about a black teacher's efforts to mold a class of tough British delinquents grossed $15,000,000. Both Clavell and Poitier had contracted for percentages of the profits, so the project proved lucrative.

A Hollywood screenwriters' strike brought a fortuitous change to Clavell's career in 1960. Simultaneously sidelined from his regular employment and haunted by returning memories of Changi, he began to work on a novel about his prison experiences. The process of writing released many suppressed emotions for Clavell; in twelve weeks he had completed the first draft of *King Rat.* Set in Changi, the novel follows the fortunes of an English prisoner of war and his ruthless American comrade in their struggles to survive the brutal conditions. *New York Times Book Review* contributor Martin Levin observed, "All personal relationships [in the work] pale beside the impersonal, soul-disintegrating evil of Changi itself which Mr. Clavell, himself a Japanese P.O.W. for three years, renders with stunning authority." Some critics have maintained that the book loses some impact because it is aimed at the popular audience, but Paul King of *Maclean's* called *King Rat* the work of "a sensitive craftsman." A *New York Herald Tribune Books* reviewer concluded that *King Rat* is "at once fascinating in narrative detail, penetrating in observation of human nature under survival stress, and provoking in its analysis of right and wrong." In the *Christian Science Monitor,* R. R. Bruun also noted that by virtue of his careful plotting, "Mr. Clavell manages to keep the tension wound up to the snapping point through much of the book." A bestseller, *King Rat* was adapted for film in 1965.

Clavell was still primarily a screenwriter when he penned *Tai-Pan,* a sweeping fictional account of the founding of Hong Kong. A historical novel set in 1841, the story recounts the adventures of Dirk Struan, first tai-pan, or merchant overlord, of the Noble House trading company. Struan builds his empire on the nearly deserted peninsula of Hong Kong, convinced that a British colony there would provide a power base for the growing empire. *New York Times* reviewer Orville Prescott claimed that in *Tai-Pan,* Clavell "holds attention with a relentless grip. *Tai-Pan* frequently is crude. It is grossly exaggerated much of the time. But seldom does a novel appear so stuffed with imaginative invention, so packed with melodramatic action, so gaudy and flamboyant with blood and sin, treachery and conspiracy, sex and murder." A *Time* critic labeled the work "a belly-gutting, god-rotting typhoon of a book" and added: "Its narrative pace is numbing, its style deafening, its language penny dreadful. . . . It isn't art and it isn't truth. But its very energy and scope command the eye." Since its publication in 1966 and its 44-week stay on the bestseller lists, it has sold more than 2,000,000 copies. It too has been made into a motion picture that was released in 1986.

According to the *Washington Post*'s Gorney, Clavell's best-known novel, *Shogun,* had an inauspicious beginning in the author's mind. She wrote, "James Clavell, his imagi-

nation awash with plans for the modern-day Asian chronicle that was to be his third novel, picked up one of his 9-year-old daughter's school books one afternoon in London, and came upon an intriguing bit of history." He read the following sentence from the text: "In 1600, an Englishman went to Japan and became a Samurai." Fascinated by that possibility, Clavell began to read everything he could find about medieval Japan and Will Adams, the historical figure in question. The research led Clavell into the story of *Shogun,* but it also gave him a new understanding of the culture that had kept him in captivity during the Second World War. "I started reading about Japan's history and characteristics," he told the *New York Times,* "and then the way the Japanese treated me and my brothers became clearer to me." After a year of research in the British Museum and several visits to Japan, Clavell created the tale of John Blackthorne, an Elizabethan sailor cast upon the shores of Japan during a period of internal conflict between rival warlords. Spanning all the elements of seventeenth-century Japanese society, the adventure recounts Blackthorne's transformation from a European "barbarian" into a trusted adviser to the powerful Shogun Toranaga.

Most critics have praised *Shogun* for its historical detail as well as for its riveting plot. "Clavell offers a wide-ranging view of feudal Japan at a time of crisis," stated Bruce Cook in the *Washington Post Book World,* adding, "Scene after scene is given, conversation after conversation reported, with the point not merely of advancing the narrative (which does somehow grind inexorably forward), but also of imparting to us the peculiar flavor of life in feudal Japan and the unique code of conduct (*bushido*) which dominated life there and then." Other reviewers have cited the story itself as the source of *Shogun*'s appeal. Gorney of the *Washington Post* described it as "one of those books that blots up vacations and imperils marriages, because it simply will not let the reader go," and *Library Journal* contributor Mitsu Yamamoto deemed it "a wonderful churning brew of adventure, intrigue, love, philosophy, and history." "Clavell has a gift," contended Schott in the *New York Times Book Review.* "It may be something that cannot be taught or earned. He breathes narrative. It's almost impossible not to continue to read *Shogun* once having opened it. The imagination is possessed by Blackthorne, Toranaga and medieval Japan. Clavell creates a world: people, customs, settings, needs and desires all become so enveloping that you forget who and where you are."

Critics have also praised *Noble House,* Clavell's 1981 bestseller about financial power struggles in modern Hong Kong. *Washington Post* correspondent Sandy Rovner informed readers of the mass of the novel—"1,207 pages long, 2 1/2 inches (not counting covers) thick and 3 pounds and 13 ounces"—because *Noble House* must be carried with you since "you can't put it down." Henry S. Hayward commented on the book's mass as well in the *Christian Science Monitor.* "James Clavell is a master yarn-spinner and an expert on detail," Hayward asserted. "Indeed, one sometimes feels overwhelmed with the masses of information and wishes a firmer editing pencil had been applied. But the author, nevertheless, is in a class with James Michener and Robert Elegant in his ability to handle a massive cast and hold your attention through the intricacies of a 1,200 page plot." The *National Review*'s Teachout remarked that one "races through *Noble House* like a fire engine, torn between savoring each tasty bit of local color and wanting to find out as soon as possible what new outrage [the hero] will put down next." In the *New York Times Book Review,* Schott concluded that the novel "isn't primarily about any particular story or character or set of characters. It's about a condition that's a place, Hong Kong. Mr. Clavell perceives that city to be a unique setting for extremes of greed and vengefulness, international intrigue and silky romance." Commenting on Clavell's plotting, *New York Times* columnist Christopher Lehmann-Haupt opined: "Curiously enough, its staggering complexity is one of the things that the novel has going for it. Not only is *Noble House* as long as life, it's also as rich with possibilities. . . . There are so many irons in the fire that almost anything can plausibly happen."

Noble House, the Far East trading company featured in *Tai-Pan* and *Noble House,* is also a part of *James Clavell's Gai-Jin.* Set in Japan in the 1860s, *Gai-Jin* offers a fictional chronicle concentrating on early Yokohama and its turbulent history, based on events which actually happened in the late 1800s. *Gai-Jin* introduces Malcolm Struan, twenty-year-old heir to the Far East English shipping firm Noble House. The novel received mixed reviews. Lehmann-Haupt observed, "At the start of *Gai-Jin,* which means foreigner in Japanese, *Tai-Pan* crashes into *Shogun,*" referring in part to the intermixing of characters and action between the three novels. Lehmann-Haupt added, "At its best, *Gai-Jin* achieves a grand historical perspective that makes us feel we're understanding how today's Japan came into being with its ambivalence toward outsiders." The critic questions the inclusion of Japanese dialogue, complete with its stereotypical English pronunciations, comparing it to a "World War I comic book." Lehmann-Haupt concluded that the thousand-page tome "is in the mainstream of a great and enduring storytelling tradition, full of rich characters and complicated action. It's just that modernism makes such fiction seem unreal."

Reviewer F. G. Notehelfer commented in the *New York Times Book Review,* "*Gai-Jin* is not without interest. Many of the period's colorful characters are here in thin

disguise, and so are many episodes from the early days of Yokohama." Yet the critic describes the plot and action as "a kind of comic-book portrait of Yokohama and its people," pointing out several instances of a "gap between fiction and reality." Notehelfer concluded that "such reservations do not detract from what is a well-told story, but I feel obliged to mention them because Mr. Clavell prefaces his book with the remark that his tale 'is not history but fiction,' adding that works of history 'do not necessarily always relate what truly happened.' "

Clavell's successes with his novels have not been limited to the sales of books. As Teachout noted in the *National Review,* "Even non-readers have gotten pleasure out of his lucrative knack for telling an appealing story." Through movies and television miniseries, Clavell's works have reached audiences estimated in the hundreds of millions. The best known of these efforts are *King Rat,* a film produced in 1965, *Shogun,* which aired on television in 1980, *Tai-Pan,* a 1986 movie, and *James Clavell's "Noble House,"* a 1988 television miniseries. Clavell, who served as executive producer for the *Shogun* and *Noble House* miniseries, expressed approval for the use of his work in that medium. "Television keeps you current, and so do movies," he told *Publishers Weekly.* "People are seeing your name regularly enough that they remember you. . . . In a way, it makes me almost a brand name."

The publishing industry seemed to concur that Clavell's name alone is quite appealing to book buyers. An auction of his 1986 novel *Whirlwind* brought Clavell an unprecedented $5,000,000 advance from the William Morrow Company, which had based its bid on a preview of only 10 percent of the manuscript. Morrow also ordered a first printing of 950,000 hardcover copies, another unprecedented move. Set in Iran during the hectic weeks after the overthrow of the Shah, *Whirlwind* charts the activities of a group of helicopter pilots trying to move their precious machinery out of the country before the government can seize it. Dorothy Allison described the work as "1147 pages of violence, passion, cutthroat business, religious obsession, and martyrdom—exactly what his readers expect and want along with their exotic settings." Although *Whirlwind* received mixed reviews, it was also a bestseller; a miniseries based on it has been planned.

In various interviews, Clavell discussed both his aims as a writer and his methods of putting a book together. He told the *Los Angeles Times:* "I look at storytelling in picture form," he explained. "I watch the story happen, and I describe what I see. When you write a screenplay, you write only what you can photograph and what you can hear. As a result, my books have no fat, no purple prose, and they're very visual." Writing a lengthy novel, he told the *Washington Post,* "is pertinacity, you know, grim determination. And a marvelous selfishness to finish, to exclude everything. I begrudge the time spent away from my novel. . . . I've got this need to finish, to find the last page." Clavell mentioned in the *National Review* that his basic goal was entertainment—for himself as well as his readers. "I'm not a novelist, I'm a storyteller," he contended. "I'm not a literary figure at all. I work very hard and try to do the best I can; and I try and write for myself, thinking that what I like, other people may like."

Many critics feel Clavell achieved his goal as an entertaining writer. Teachout declared: "To call Clavell a 'popular novelist' is an understatement: incredibly, he is . . . among the most widely read authors of the century." *New York Times* contributor William Grimes summarized: "Although historians sometimes disputed the historical accuracy of Mr. Clavell's novels, no one doubted his gifts as a storyteller, or his ability to draw the reader into a faraway time and place." And *National Review*'s William F. Buckley opined: "[Clavell] was the supreme storyteller."

BIOGRAPHICAL/CRITICAL SOURCES:

BOOKS

Contemporary Literary Criticism, Gale (Detroit), Volume 6, 1976, Volume 25, 1983, Volume 87, 1995.
The Making of James Clavell's "Shogun," Dell, 1980.

PERIODICALS

Best Sellers, July 15, 1966; October, 1981.
Chicago Tribune, April 12, 1981; February 18, 1982; November 21, 1986.
Christian Science Monitor, August 9, 1962; June 24, 1981, May 12, 1993, p. 13; May 13, 1994, p. 12.
Detroit News, May 3, 1981; May 12, 1993, p. 13.
Fantasy Review, June, 1987, p. 42.
Far Eastern Economic Review, May 20, 1993, p. 46.
Globe and Mail (Toronto), January 4, 1986.
Guardian, October 4, 1975.
History Today, October, 1981, pp. 39-42.
Los Angeles Times, November 7, 1986; December 11, 1986.
Maclean's, May 11, 1981; November 24, 1986.
National Review, October 12, 1982, pp. 23-24; November 12, 1982, pp. 1420-22.
New Republic, July 4, 1981.
New Statesman, November 21, 1975.
Newsweek, November 10, 1986, p. 84.
New York Herald Tribune Books, August 5, 1962.
New York Review of Books, September 18, 1975; December 18, 1986, pp. 58-60.
New York Times, May 4, 1966; April 28, 1981; May 17, 1981; February 18, 1982; December 28, 1985; January 7, 1986; January 11, 1986; November 1, 1986; November 7, 1986; November 17, 1986; May 24, 1993, p. C16.

New York Times Book Review, August 12, 1962; May 22, 1966; June 22, 1975; May 3, 1981; April 18, 1993, p. 13.
New York Times Magazine, September 13, 1981.
Observer, July 4, 1993, p. 62.
People, May 10, 1993, pp. 27, 29.
Poe Studies, June, 1983, p. 13.
Publishers Weekly, October 24, 1986; March 22, 1993, p. 69.
Saturday Review, August 11, 1962.
Time, June 17, 1966; July 7, 1975; July 6, 1981.
Times (London), November 2, 1986, pp. 41, 43-4.
Times Literary Supplement, December 5, 1986; December 26, 1986.
Village Voice, September 2, 1981, p. 37; December 16, 1986.
Wall Street Journal, October 7, 1986, p. 30.
Washington Post, February 4, 1979; May 5, 1981; November 11, 1986.
Washington Post Book World, July 13, 1975; October 26, 1986; December 7, 1986, p. 4.

OBITUARIES:

PERIODICALS

National Review, October 10, 1994, p. 23.
Newsweek, September 19, 1994, p. 75.
New York Times, September 8, 1994, p. D19.
Time, September 19, 1994, p. 27.
Times (London), September 9, 1994, p. 21.
U. S. News & World Report, September 19, 1994, p. 24.
Washington Post, September 8, 1994, p. D4.*

* * *

COLEMAN, Emmett
See REED, Ishmael

* * *

COLIN, Ann
See URE, Jean

* * *

COLLINS, Robert O(akley) 1933-

PERSONAL: Born April 1, 1933, in Waukegan, IL; son of William G. (a ceramic engineer) and Louise (Jack) Collins; married Diana R. Ware, June 22, 1955 (marriage ended); married second wife, Janyce Hutchins Monroe, October 6, 1974; children: (first marriage) Catharine Louise, Randolph Ware, Robert William. *Education:* Dartmouth College, B.A., 1954; Balliol College, Oxford University, B.A., 1956, M.S., 1960; Yale University, M.A., 1958, Ph.D., 1959.

ADDRESSES: Home—735 Calle De Los Amigos, Santa Barbara, CA 93105. *Office*—Department of History, University of California, Santa Barbara, CA 93106.

CAREER: Williams College, Williamstown, MA, instructor, 1959-61, lecturer, 1961-62, assistant professor of history, 1962-65; University of California, Santa Barbara, associate professor, 1965-69, professor of history, 1969—, director, Center for Developing Nations, 1968, associate dean, 1969, dean of graduate division, 1970-80, acting vice-chancellor for research and academic affairs, 1970-71, director, University of California Washington Center, 1992-94. Visiting assistant professor, Columbia University, 1962-63; Rockefeller scholar-in-residence, Villa Serbelloni Study Center, Bellagio, Italy, 1979; senior associate member, St. Anthony's College, Oxford, 1980-81, 1987, 1989; Trevelyan fellow, Durham University, 1986; visiting fellow, Balliol College, 1987; lifetime fellow, African and Asian Institute, University of Khartoum.

MEMBER: American Historical Association, African Studies Association, American Philosophical Society (fellow), American Council of Learned Societies, Society of Fellows (Durham University), Western River Guides Association.

AWARDS, HONORS: Ford Foundation fellowship, 1956-57, research fellow, 1979, 1981; National Defense Education Act language fellowship, 1961; Social Science Research Council fellowships, 1962-63, 1968; Gold Class Award, Order of Sciences and Arts, Democratic Republic of Sudan, 1980; Fulbright senior research fellow, 1981-82; Woodrow Wilson fellow, 1983-84; John Ben Snow Foundation prize for best book in history and social sciences in the field of British studies, 1984, for *Shadows in the Grass: Britain in the Southern Sudan, 1918-1956.*

WRITINGS:

EDITOR

(And author of introduction) *Problems in African History,* Prentice-Hall (Englewood Cliffs, NJ), 1968.
(And author of introduction) Sir Gilbert Clayton, *An Arabian Diary,* University of California Press (Berkeley), 1969.
(And author of introduction) *The Partition of Africa: Illusion or Necessity?,* Wiley (New York City), 1969.
African History: Text and Readings, Random House (New York City), 1970.
(And author of introduction) *Documents in African History,* Random House, 1970.

(And author of introduction) *Problems in the History of Colonial Africa,* Prentice-Hall, 1970.
(With Francis Deng) *British in the Sudan, 1898-1956: The Sweetness and the Sorrow,* Hoover Institution (Stanford, CA), 1984.
Western African History, Text and Readings, Markus Weiner (New York City), 1990.
Eastern African History, Text and Readings, Markus Weiner, 1990.
Central and Southern African History, Text and Readings, Markus Weiner, 1990.
The Waters of the Nile: An Annotated Bibliography, Hans Zell (Oxford, England), 1991.
Problems in African History: The Precolonial Centuries, Markus Weiner, 1993.
Historical Problems of Imperial Africa, Markus Weiner, 1994.

OTHER

The Southern Sudan, 1883-1898: A Struggle for Control, Yale University Press (New Haven, CT), 1962.
(With R. L. Tignor) *Egypt and the Sudan,* Prentice-Hall, 1967.
King Leopold: England and the Upper Nile, 1899-1909, Yale University Press, 1968.
Land beyond the Rivers: The Southern Sudan, 1898-1918, Yale University Press, 1971.
Europeans in Africa, Knopf (New York City), 1971.
The Southern Sudan in Historical Perspective, Shiloah Center for Middle Eastern and African Studies (Tel Aviv), 1975.
(With Roderick Nash) *The Big Drops: Ten Legendary Rapids,* Sierra Books (San Francisco), 1978.
Shadows in the Grass: Britain in the Southern Sudan, 1918-1956, Yale University Press, 1983.
The Waters of the Nile: Hydropolitics and the Jonglei Canal, 1900-1988, Clarendon (Oxford), 1990.

Contributor to books, including *The Transformation of East Africa: Studies in Political Anthropology,* edited by Stanley Diamond and Fred G. Burke, Basic Books, 1966; *The Nile Basin,* by Sir Richard Burton, DaCapo Press, 1967; *Sudan in Africa,* edited by Yusuf Fadl Hasan, Khartoum University Press, 1971; *Islam, Nationalism, and Radicalism in Egypt and the Sudan,* Praeger, 1983; *Double Impact: France and Africa in the Age of Imperialism,* edited by G. Wesley Johnson, Greenwood Press, 1985; and *Sudan: A Country Study,* by Helen C. Metz, Department of the Army, 1992.

Contributor to *Encyclopedia Britannica.* Contributor of articles and reviews to *American Historical Review, Bulletin of the School of Oriental and African Studies, International History Review, Journal of African History, Journal of Asian and African Studies, Journal of Modern History,*

Middle East Journal, Middle East Studies, Northeast African Studies, Revue Belge de Philologie et d'Histoire, and *Zaire.* Member of editorial boards, *Journal of African Studies* and *International Journal of African Historical Studies.*

WORK IN PROGRESS: *Requiem for the Sudan: War, Drought, and Disaster Relief on the Nile, 1983-1993* with Millard Burr, for Westview Press.

SIDELIGHTS: Robert O. Collins told *CA* that he has devoted his career "to the study of the Upper Nile Valley, particularly, the Sudan and the Sudanese people. I have been deeply involved in the disastrous events occurring in the Sudan, whereby 1.5 million people have perished through conflict and famine. The story will be published by the Westview Press, under the authorship of myself and Millard Burr, as *Requiem for the Sudan: War, Drought, and Disaster Relief on the Nile, 1983-1993.*"

BIOGRAPHICAL/CRITICAL SOURCES:

PERIODICALS

Times Literary Supplement, September 7, 1984.*

*　　　*　　　*

COLOMBO, John Robert 1936-

PERSONAL: Born March 24, 1936, in Kitchener, Ontario, Canada; son of John Anthony and Irene (Nicholson) Colombo; married Ruth Florence Brown (a professor), May 11, 1959; children: Jonathan, Catherine, Theodore. *Education:* Attended Waterloo College, 1956-57; University of Toronto, B.A. (with honors), 1959, graduate study, 1959-60. *Avocational interests:* Reading.

ADDRESSES: *Home*—42 Dell Park Ave., Toronto, Ontario, Canada M6B 2T6.

CAREER: Poet, editor, and translator. University of Toronto Press, Toronto, Ontario, editorial assistant, 1957-59; Ryerson Press, Toronto, assistant editor, 1960-63; McClelland & Stewart, Toronto, advisory editor and editor-at-large, 1964-70; Mohawk College, Hamilton, Ontario, writer in residence, 1978; host, *Colombo's Quotes* (weekly television series), Canadian Broadcasting Corp. (CBC), 1978. York University, Toronto, occasional instructor, 1963-66. Has given poetry readings throughout Canada and in New York and London; representative for Canadian poetry, Commonwealth Arts Festival, Cardiff and London, 1965; adviser, Ontario Arts Council, 1965-69; member of advisory arts panel, Canada Council, 1968-70; honorary patron, North York Arts Council.

Guest of the writers' unions of Russia, Romania, and Bulgaria.

MEMBER: PEN (Canada), Association of Canadian Television and Radio Artists (ACTRA).

AWARDS, HONORS: Centennial Medal, 1967; Philips Information Systems Literary Prize, 1985; certificate of merit, Ontario Library Association; cited for best paperback of the year, Periodical Distributors of Canada; named Esteemed Knight of Mark Twain; Order of Cyril and Methodius (first class); Laureate, Order of Cyril and Methodius.

WRITINGS:

POEMS

Fragments, privately printed, 1957.
Variations, Hawkshead Press (Kitchener, Ontario), 1958.
This Citadel in Time, Hawkshead Press, 1958.
This Studied Self, Hawkshead Press, 1958.
In the Streets, Hawkshead Press, 1959.
Poem and Other Poems, Hawkshead Press, 1959.
Two Poems, Hawkshead Press, 1959.
This Is the Work Entitled Canada, Purple Partridge Press (Toronto), 1959.
Fire Escape, Fire Esc, Fire, Hawkshead Press, 1959.
The Impression of Beauty, Hawkshead Press, 1959.
Poems to Be Sold for Bread, Hawkshead Press, 1959.
Lines for the Last Day, Hawkshead Press, 1960.
The Mackenzie Poems, Swan Publishing (Toronto), 1965.
Miraculous Montages, Heinrich Heine Press (Don Mills, Ontario), 1966.
The Great Wall of China, Delta (Montreal), 1966.
Abracadabra, McClelland & Stewart (Toronto), 1967.
William Lyon Mackenzie Rides Again!, Guild of Hand Printers (Toronto), 1967.
John Toronto: New Poems by Dr. Strachan, Found by John Robert Colombo, Oberon Press (Ottawa), 1969.
Neo Poems, Sono Nis Press (Victoria, British Columbia), 1970.
The Great San Francisco Earthquake and Fire, Fiddlehead (Fredericton, New Brunswick), 1971.
Leonardo's Lists, Weed/Flower Press (Toronto), 1972.
Praise Poems, Weed/Flower Press, 1972.
The Great Collage, Oasis Books (Toronto), 1974.
Translations from the English: Found Poems, Peter Martin Associates (Toronto), 1974.
The Sad Truths, Peter Martin Associates, 1974.
Proverbial Play, Missing Link Press (Toronto), 1975.
Mostly Monsters, Hounslow (Toronto), 1977.
Variable Cloudiness, Hounslow, 1977.
Private Parts, Hounslow, 1978.
The Great Cities of Antiquity, Hounslow, 1979.
Recent Poems, League of Canadian Poets (Toronto), 1980.

Selected Poems, Black Moss Press (Windsor, Ontario), 1982.

Selected Translations, Black Moss Press, 1982.

Off Earth, Hounslow, 1987.

Luna Park: One Thousand Poems, Hounslow, 1994.

EDITOR

Rubato: New Poems by Young Canadian Poets, Purple Partridge Press, 1958.

The Varsity Chapbook, Ryerson (Toronto), 1959.

(With Jacques Godbout) *Poesis 64/Poetry 64,* Ryerson and Editions du Jour, 1963.

(With Raymond Souster) *Shapes and Sounds: Poems of W. W. E. Ross,* Longmans, Green (Canada), 1968.

How Do I Love Thee: Sixty Poets of Canada (and Quebec) Select and Discuss Their Favorite Poems from Their Own Work, Hurtig Publishers (Edmonton), 1970.

(With Roy Bentley) *Rhymes and Reasons: Nine Canadian Poets Discuss Their Work,* Holt, 1971.

New Direction in Canadian Poetry, Holt (Toronto), 1971.

An Alphabet of Annotations, Gheerbrant (Montreal), 1972.

Colombo's Canadian Quotations, Hurtig Publishers, 1974, published as *Concise Canadian Quotations,* 1976, published as *Colombo's New Canadian Quotations,* 1987.

Colombo's Little Book of Canadian Proverbs, Graffiti, Limericks and Other Vital Matters, Hurtig Publishers, 1975.

Colombo's Canadian References, Oxford University Press (New York), 1976.

Colombo's Book of Canada, Hurtig Publishers, 1978.

The Poets of Canada, Hurtig Publishers, 1978.

Other Canadas: An Anthology of Science Fiction and Fantasy, McGraw-Hill (Toronto), 1979.

CDN SF & F: A Bibliography of Canadian Science Fiction and Fantasy, Hounslow, 1979.

Colombo's Names and Nicknames, NC Press (Toronto), 1979.

Colombo's Book of Marvels, NC Press, 1979.

Waclaw Iwaniuk, *Dark Times: Selected Poems of Waclaw Iwaniuk,* Hounslow, 1979.

Colombo's Hollywood, Collins (Toronto), 1979, published as *Popcorn in Paradise,* Holt, 1980, published as *Wit and Wisdom of the Moviemakers,* Hamlyn, 1980.

The Canada Colouring Book, with drawings by Emma Hesse, Hounslow, 1980.

222 Canadian Jokes, with drawings by Peter Whalley, Highway Book Shop, 1981.

Blackwood's Books: A Bibliography Devoted to Algernon Blackwood, Hounslow, 1981.

(With Michael Richardson) *Not to Be Taken at Night: Classic Canadian Tales of Mystery and the Supernatural,* Lester & Orpen Dennys (Toronto), 1981.

Friendly Aliens, Hounslow, 1981.

Poems of the Inuit, Oberon, 1981.

Blackwood's Books: A Bibliography, Hounslow, 1981.

Colombo's Laws, with drawings by Whalley, Highway Book Shop, 1982.

Colombo's Last Words, with drawings by Whalley, Highway Book Shop, 1982.

Years of Light: A Celebration of Leslie A. Croutch, Hounslow, 1982.

Windigo: An Anthology of Fact and Fantastic Fiction, Western Producer Prairie Books (Saskatoon), 1982.

George Faludy, *Learn This Poem of Mine by Heart,* Hounslow, 1983.

Colombo's 101 Canadian Places, with drawings by Whalley, Hounslow, 1983.

Colombo's Canadian Quiz Book, Western Producer Prairie Books, 1983.

Rene Levesque Buys Canada Savings Bonds and Other Great Canadian Graffiti, with drawings by David Shaw, Hurtig Publishers, 1983.

Songs of the Indians (two volumes), Oberon Press, 1983.

Great Moments in Canadian History, with drawings by Whalley, Hounslow, 1984.

The Toronto Puzzle Book, McClelland & Stewart, 1984.

Toronto's Fantastic Street Names, Bakka Books, 1984.

Canadian Literary Landmarks, Hounslow, 1984.

(With Michael Richardson) *We Stand on Guard: Poems and Songs of Canadians in Battle,* Doubleday (Canada) 1985.

1,001 Questions about Canada, Doubleday (Garden City, NY), 1986.

Off Earth, Hounslow, 1987.

Mysterious Canada: Strange Sights, Extraordinary Events, and Peculiar Places, Doubleday, 1988.

999 Questions about Canada, Doubleday, 1989.

Extraordinary Experiences: Personal Accounts of the Paranormal in Canada, Hounslow, 1989.

Songs of the Great Land, Oberon Press, 1989.

Quotations from Chairman Lamport, Pulp Press, 1990.

Mysterious Encounters: Personal Accounts of the Supernatural in Canada, Hounslow, 1990.

Voices of Ram, Oberon Press, 1990.

UFOs over Canada: Personal Accounts of Sightings and Close Encounters, Hounslow, 1991.

Dark Visions: Personal Accounts of the Mysterious in Canada, Hounslow, 1991.

Mackenzie King's Ghost: And Other Personal Accounts of Canadian Hauntings, Hounslow, 1991.

The Dictionary of Canadian Quotations, Stoddart, 1991.

Worlds in Small: An Anthology of Miniature Literary Compositions, Cacanadada, 1992.

Quotations on Sex and Love in Canada, Arsenal Pulp, 1992.

The Little Blue Book of Canadian UFOs, Arsenal Pulp, 1992.

(With Cyril Greenland) *Walt Whitman's Canada,* Hounslow, 1992.

The Mystery of the Shaking Tent, Hounslow, 1993.

Colombo's All-Time Great Canadian Quotations, Stoddart, 1994.

General editor, *The Canadian Global Almanac* (annual),
Macmillan, 1991—.

TRANSLATOR

Robert Zend, *From Zero to One,* Sono Nis Press, 1973.

(With Irene Currie) Paul Eluard and Benjamin Peret, *152
Proverbs Adapted to the Taste of the Day,* Oasis Press,
1975.

(With Nikola Roussanoff) *Under the Eaves of a Forgotten
Village: Sixty Poems from Contemporary Bulgaria,*
Hounslow, 1975.

(With Roussanoff) *The Balkan Range: A Bulgarian
Reader,* Hounslow, 1976.

(With Susana Wald) Ludwig Zeller, *When the Animal
Rises from the Deep the Head Explodes,* Mosaic
Press/Valley Editions, (poems), 1976.

(With Roussanoff) Lyubomir Levchev, *The Left-Handed
One: Poems of Lyubomir Levchev,* Hounslow, 1977.

George Faludy, *East and West,* Hounslow, 1978.

(With Roussanoff) Andrei Germanov, *Remember Me
Well: Poems of Andrei Germanov,* Hounslow, 1978.

(With Roussanoff) *Depths: Poems of Dora Gabe,* Hounslow, 1978.

(With Iwaniuk) Ewa Lipska, *Such Times,* Hounslow,
1981.

(With Ron D. K. Banerjee) Pavel Javor, *Far from You,*
Hounslow, 1981.

(With Robert Zend) Robert Zend, *Beyond Labels,* Hounslow, 1982.

OTHER

Also author of plays and documentaries for CBC-TV.
Contributor to *Open Poetry,* edited by Ronald Grose and
George Quasha, Simon & Schuster (New York), 1973.
Contributor of articles, art criticism, and reviews to many
periodicals. Member of editorial board, *Tamarack Review,*
1960-82. Former editor, *Montrealer* and *Exchange.*

SIDELIGHTS: John Robert Colombo is known as an an-
thologist and editor whose books of Canadiana have been
bestsellers and as an experimental writer of international
reputation. Once called a "master gatherer" by Robin
Skelton, Colombo is a devoted collector of information
which he uses in his reference and trivia books. Colombo,
who once took a speed-reading course, is a self-described
"inveterate collector and a chronic listmaker." He told M.
T. Kelly of *Toronto Life* magazine, "At any one time, I
have a half dozen books in progress. I find relief and re-
freshment in going from project to project."

Colombo's earliest published works were poetry pamphlets. During his student days at the University of Toronto, he operated the Hawkshead Press to publish his
own writings and those of other young poets; one of them
was M. E. Atwood, today better known as novelist Margaret Atwood. Colombo's first real book was an outgrowth
of his other efforts as a literary entrepreneur. He organized the first regular series of readings in a Canadian coffee house and then edited a collection of the verse read
there. *The Varsity Chapbook* appeared in 1959, the same
year Colombo received his degree from the University of
Toronto.

After a brief stint working as an editor with various Canadian book publishers, Colombo became a freelance writer
and editor. He immersed himself in the Canadian literary
community through his work as an adviser to the Canada
Council, the powerful government arts funding body, and
as a member of the editorial board of the now-defunct
Tamarack Review, a small but influential Canadian literary journal. When not otherwise engaged, Colombo wrote
newspaper and magazine articles and continued to write
and edit poetry.

While Colombo wrote some noteworthy original verse,
what attracted far more attention were his experiments in
"found poetry"—lines of other writers' prose which are
cobbled together to form poems; Colombo himself terms
the end result "redeemed prose." While the surrealist
technique originated around the time of the First World
War, it was a series of found-poem books Colombo published in the mid-1960s which revived the art form and
brought it to the attention of Canadian readers. In a review of *Abracadabra,* the first of Colombo's books of
found poetry to be printed by a major publisher, Mungo
James of *Saturday Night* called Colombo "an interesting,
inventive and original poet." James was more receptive to
the concept of found poetry than were most other critics.
As Douglas Fetherling noted in *Saturday Night,* "Some
who were not disposed toward innovations, as well as others who found nothing wrong with tricks but thought Colombo's antics a substitute for creative talent, took harshly
to the book." Undeterred, Colombo continued his experiments in the genre. As he explained in a "found introduction" to *Open Poetry,* found poetry is worthwhile in that
it teaches the reader "to respond aesthetically to the universe around us, not just to those separate parts of the
world called works of art. It is possible to act as if the universe itself were an immense piece of art, a collage perhaps."

In 1974 Colombo published *Translations from the English:
Found Poems,* a collection which moved Douglas Barbour
in the *Dictionary of Literary Biography* to call Colombo "a
master of witty juxtapositions." *The Great Cities of Antiquity* is an innovative collection of poems taken from the

Encyclopaedia Britannica. Beginning with the entries on ancient cities from the encyclopedia, Colombo "takes their words and shapes them into a variety of forms," Barbour explained. "He breaks the words down, he repeats phrases, he arranges them as visual designs or 'concrete poems,' he destroys original syntax to free the language of its referential quality and lend it poetic opaqueness."

Despite his love of poetry, in the early 1970s Colombo decided to change the direction of his work. As Barbour pointed out, Colombo is "a shrewd market analyst and salesman [who] has recognized from the first that his major product is not this book or that book but rather John Robert Colombo, the maker of all kinds of books." In addition to publishing poetry he began to publish nonfiction books. *Colombo's Canadian Quotations,* a collection of six thousand quotations from twenty-five hundred sources, was Colombo's first commercial success. Reviewer J. M. Bliss of the *Canadian Forum* commented, "This is an invaluable reference book. . . . [It] is worth more than it costs, which is the highest praise a reviewer can give these days."

Following on the success of *Colombo's Canadian Quotations,* Colombo continued to create reference books, commonplace books, and anthologies of quotations and unusual facts. Many of these books focus on Canada, its literature, history, geography, and people. Among the most popular are *Colombo's Canadian References, Colombo's Book of Canada, Colombo's Book of Marvels* and *Colombo's Laws. Other Canadas* is the country's first anthology of its fantastic literature, and *Mysterious Canada* is its first, comprehensive study of supernatural and paranormal events and experiences. These books have an audience beyond Canada, however; that was the case with *1001 Questions about Canada,* which reviewer Don James of the *Los Angeles Times* praised as "a revelation about our next-door neighbor." James predicted that "browsers, researchers, teachers or trivia buffs will recognize it as a quality reference book."

Colombo once told *CA:* "My mission (in part at least) is to make inventories and make accessible previously snubbed materials from the tributaries and mainstreams, the highways and byways of the Canadian people. Such literary material reveals the human spirit and sheds some light on life in the northern half of the North American continent."

BIOGRAPHICAL/CRITICAL SOURCES:

BOOKS

Contemporary Poets, 5th edition, St. James Press, 1991.
Dictionary of Literary Biography, Volume 53: *Canadian Writers since 1960,* Gale (Detroit), 1986.

Grose, Ronald, and George Quasha, editors, *Open Poetry,* Simon & Schuster (New York City), 1973, pp. 431-523.
Kostelanetz, Richard, editor, *Dictionary of the Avant Gardes,* A Capella Books, 1993.

PERIODICALS

Canadian Forum, June, 1975, pp. 44-45.
Canadian Literature, summer, 1966.
Essays on Canadian Writing, fall, 1976.
Globe and Mail (Toronto), June 4, 1966; March 18, 1967; January 28, 1984; November 7, 1987; January 9, 1988; January 14, 1989; April 28, 1990.
Intrinsic, autumn, 1978, pp. 176-88.
Los Angeles Times, September 21, 1986.
Maclean's, August 1, 1994, p. 2.
Montreal Gazette, October 22, 1966.
Saturday Night, May, 1967, p. 44; May, 1974, pp. 31-34.
Times Literary Supplement, May 13, 1983.
Toronto Life, January, 1983, pp. 42-43.
Toronto Star, May 24, 1987.
University of Toronto Review, July, 1959; July, 1967; July, 1968.

*   *   *

COOK, David 1940-

PERSONAL: Born September 21, 1940, in Preston, Lancashire, England; son of George T. and Beatrice (Jackson) Cook. *Education:* Attended Royal Academy of Dramatic Art, 1959-61.

ADDRESSES: Home—7 Sydney Pl., London SW7 3NL, England. *Agent*—Greene & Heaton Ltd., 37 Goldhawk Rd., London W12 8QQ, England.

CAREER: Professional actor, 1961—. St. Martin's College, Lancaster, England, writer in residence, 1982-83.

MEMBER: Writers Guild of Great Britain, Society of Authors.

AWARDS, HONORS: Writers Guild of Great Britain award, 1977, for *A Place Like Home;* E. M. Forster Prize, American Academy of Arts and Letters, 1977, for *Happy Endings;* Hawthornden Prize for Literature, Society of Authors, 1978, for *Walter;* fiction award, Arts Council, 1979, for *Winter Doves;* Southern Arts Literature Prize, 1986, for *Sunrising;* Arthur Welton Scholarship, Society of Authors, 1991; Oddfellows Social Concern Award, 1992, for *Second Best.*

WRITINGS:

NOVELS

Albert's Memorial, Secker & Warburg (London), 1972.

Happy Endings, Secker & Warburg, 1974.

Walter, Secker & Warburg, 1978, Overlook Press (Woodstock, NY), 1985.

Winter Doves (sequel to *Walter*), Secker & Warburg, 1979, Overlook Press, 1985, published as *June,* Secker & Warburg, 1989.

Sunrising, Secker & Warburg, 1984, Overlook Press, 1986.

Missing Persons, Secker & Warburg, 1986.

Crying Out Loud, Secker & Warburg, 1988.

Second Best, (also see below), Faber & Faber (Boston), 1991.

TELEVISION PLAYS

Willy, Associated Television, 1973.

Jenny Can't Work Any Faster, Associated Television, 1975.

Why Here?, Associated Television, 1976.

Repent at Leisure, Associated Television, 1978.

Mary's Wife, British Broadcasting Corp. (BBC-TV), 1980.

Singles Weekend, London Weekend Television, 1984.

Love Match, BBC-TV, 1986.

Also writer for television series *Couples* and *A Place Like Home,* both 1976; author of *Walter* and *Walter and June,* both 1982, *Missing Persons,* 1990, and *Closing Numbers,* 1993.

OTHER

Square Dance (play), first produced in London, 1968.

If Only (play; broadcast in 1984), published in *Scene Scripts 3,* edited by Roy Blatchford, Longman (London), 1982.

Second Best (screenplay), Warner Brothers, 1994.

Also author of a radio play, *Pity,* 1989.

SIDELIGHTS: David Cook's novels *Walter* and *Winter Doves* detail the unfortunate life of the mentally-impaired Walter from his birth through his parents' deaths and his resultant institutionalization and on to the impoverished existence with the suicidal June, with whom he escapes. Several critics laud Cook for his compassionate rendering of the two tales, yet a few also feel that the novels tend occasionally toward sociology. Calling *Walter* a "painful novel," Valerie Miner suggests in the *New York Times Book Review* that it is also an "authentic, sympathetic tale that finally spirals into a morass of dour determinism."

Wray Herbert comments in the *New York Times Book Review* that Cook's pessimism in *Walter* becomes utter hopelessness in *Winter Doves,* but Herbert believes, nonetheless, that Cook "wrenches us unmercifully but honestly." In a London *Observer* review, Anthony Thwaite finds *Winter Doves* the "strikingly better" novel and observes that "Cook's style—part curt demotic, part supercilious eloquent—is so achieved that it can accommodate Walter,

June, and the author's own passionate concern for the lost, the derided, the deprived, in a seamless garment." In the *Voice Literary Supplement,* Sam Tannenhaus notes Cook's "balance of piercing satire and gentle comedy" throughout both novels and adds: "His flexible prose pins the objective world firmly onto the page, then glides with effortless omniscience into the interior space of his characters' minds; and he approaches people with sympathy. . . . Cook reserves his venom for social evils."

Sunrising, Cook's first historical novel, relates the hazards and injustice encountered by a young couple on their journey to London through the Midlands in 1830. David Profumo places the novel within the picaresque genre and writes in the *Times Literary Supplement* that while it contains "some evocative set-pieces," *Sunrising* suffers from "Cook having thrown together too many diverting incidents and too much authentic detail." Profumo also sees a "histrionic touch, both in verbal mannerism and in narrative contrivance," as well as a "sentimental strain" in the novel. However, writing about Cook's "richly suggestive and often very moving descriptive style," Stephen Bann says in the *London Review of Books:* "Again and again, [Cook] brings the reader so close to an imagined scene that one's nose seems almost to be grazing against it. Also, he is capable of extending his range from the individual, pictured scene to the dynamic sequence of related events." A *Kirkus Reviews* contributor likens the novel to "a slender slice of [Charles] Dickens." And in the London *Observer,* Anthony Thwaite concludes that "as a whole, what Cook has produced is a carefully paced and convincing period portrait, in which [the protagonist's] wanderings among the down-and-outs, rogues and grotesques are movingly and entertainingly brought to life."

Cook once told *CA:* "When I am writing a book, I don't think about 'themes.' Getting inside my characters and telling a story are what concern me at the time of writing. Training and working as an actor with directors such as Vivian Matalon have helped me with the first, and with the latter I've had invaluable help from the playwright and novelist John Bowen.

"The reasons why one decides to write about such a situation or character are for me almost always accidental. Seeing a lady tramp at South Kensington Underground Station and wondering what had led up to her being there was the starting point of my first novel, *Albert's Memorial.* Meeting a mentally handicapped man who ran errands for the actors when I was playing in *Othello* at the Ludlow Festival and who reminded me of a young man with whom I'd worked twenty years earlier sparked off an obsessive wanting to know how a mentally handicapped man perceives what goes on around him and led to *Walter* and its sequel, *Winter Doves.*

"Most of my plays for television have been concerned with the 'walking wounded'—brain damage, autism, transvestism, children in care. In fact, as I look back at both the novels and the television plays, I see that there is a theme—innocence and the corruption of innocence—and since this was not intentional, it may be all the more valid as an insight into my work.

"What most of all fascinate me are relationships or the lack of them. We arrive in this world screaming and we go on screaming—for love, sex, emotional security—and we leave it whimpering at how little of any of these we've found. Although for the future I plan to write . . . maybe a thriller. I don't think this primary concern will change. I should like to write a bestseller, however. Having won a share of the Glittering Prizes, I would now exchange good reviews for higher sales figures. I write to be read."

BIOGRAPHICAL/CRITICAL SOURCES:

BOOKS

Contemporary Novelists, 5th edition, St. James Press (Chicago), 1991, pp. 208-09.

PERIODICALS

Kirkus Reviews, June 1, 1986.
London Review of Books, March 15, 1984.
Los Angeles Times Book Review, March 17, 1985.
New York Times Book Review, February 17, 1985; June 23, 1985.
Observer (London), September 23, 1979; February 19, 1984; March 15, 1984; July 27, 1986.
Times Literary Supplement, February 3, 1978; November 30, 1979; March 2, 1984; August 8, 1986.
Voice Literary Supplement, July, 1985.

* * *

CORCORAN, Barbara (Asenath) 1911-
(Paige Dixon, Gail Hamilton)

PERSONAL: Born April 12, 1911, in Hamilton, MA; daughter of John Gilbert (a physician) and Anna (Tuck) Corcoran. *Education:* Wellesley College, B.A., 1933; University of Montana, M.A., 1955; University of Denver, post-graduate study, 1965-66. *Politics:* Democrat. *Religion:* Episcopalian.

ADDRESSES: P. O. Box 4394, Missoula, MT 59806.

CAREER: Worked at a variety of jobs in New York City and Hamilton, MA, 1933-40, including writing for the Works Progress Administration, working as a theater manager, and working as a playwright and freelance writer; Celebrity Service, Hollywood, CA, researcher, 1945-53; Station KGVO, Missoula, MT, copywriter, 1953-54; University of Kentucky, Covington, instructor in English, 1956-57; Columbia Broadcasting System (CBS), Hollywood, researcher, 1957-59; Marlborough School, Los Angeles, CA, teacher of English, 1959-60; University of Colorado, Boulder, instructor in English, 1960-65; Palomar College, San Marcos, CA, instructor in English, 1965-69; author of books for children and young adults, 1967—; Austin Community College, Austin, TX, instructor in expressive writing, 1983; Women's Center, University of Montana, Missoula, instructor in writing for children, 1984—. *Wartime service:* Worked as a Navy inspector at a proximity-fuse factory in Ipswich, MA, and for the Army Signal Corps in Arlington, VA, 1940-45.

MEMBER: Authors League of America, PEN.

AWARDS, HONORS: Samuel French Award for original play, 1955; children's book of the year citation, Child Study Association, 1970, for *The Long Journey;* William Allen White Children's Book Award, 1972, for *Sasha, My Friend;* outstanding science trade book for children citations, National Science Teachers Association, 1974, for *The Young Grizzly,* and 1977, for *Summer of the White Goat;* Pacific Northwest Book Sellers' Award, 1975; Merriam Award, University of Montana, 1992; award from Western Writers of America, 1994, for *Wolf at the Door;* National Endowment for the Arts fellow.

WRITINGS:

JUVENILE NOVELS

Sam, illustrated by Barbara McGee, Atheneum (New York City), 1967.
(With Jeanne Dixon and Bradford Angier) *The Ghost of Spirit River,* Atheneum, 1968.
A Row of Tigers, illustrated by Allan Eitzen, Atheneum, 1969.
Sasha, My Friend, illustrated by Richard L. Shell, Atheneum, 1969, published as *My Wolf, My Friend,* Scholastic (New York City), 1975.
The Long Journey, illustrated by Charles Robinson, Atheneum, 1970.
(With Angier) *A Star to the North,* Thomas Nelson (Nashville), 1970.
The Lifestyle of Robie Tuckerman, Thomas Nelson, 1971.
This Is a Recording, illustrated by Richard Cuffari, Atheneum, 1971.
A Trick of Light, illustrated by Lydia Dabcovich, Atheneum, 1972.
Don't Slam the Door When You Go, Atheneum, 1972.
All the Summer Voices (historical), illustrated by Robinson, Atheneum, 1973.
The Winds of Time, illustrated by Gail Owens, Atheneum, 1974, published as *The Watching Eyes,* Scholastic, 1975.

A Dance to Still Music, illustrated by Robinson, Atheneum, 1974.

The Clown, Atheneum, 1975, published as *I Wish You Love,* Scholastic, 1977.

Axe-Time, Sword-Time (historical), Atheneum, 1976.

Cabin in the Sky (historical), Atheneum, 1976.

The Faraway Island, Atheneum, 1977.

Make No Sound, Atheneum, 1977.

(With Angier) *Ask for Love and They Give You Rice Pudding,* Houghton (Boston), 1977.

Hey, That's My Soul You're Stomping On, Atheneum, 1978.

Me and You and a Dog Named Blue, Atheneum, 1979.

Rising Damp, Atheneum, 1980.

Making It, Little, Brown (Boston), 1980.

Child of the Morning, Atheneum, 1982.

Strike!, Atheneum, 1983.

The Woman in Your Life, Atheneum, 1984.

Face the Music, Atheneum, 1985.

A Horse Named Sky, Atheneum, 1986.

I Am the Universe, Atheneum, 1986.

You Put Up with Me, I'll Put Up with You, Atheneum, 1987.

The Hideaway, Atheneum, 1987.

The Sky Is Falling, Atheneum, 1988.

The Private War of Lillian Adams, Atheneum, 1989.

The Potato Kid, Atheneum, 1989.

Annie's Monster, Macmillan (New York City), 1990.

Stay Tuned, Atheneum, 1991.

Family Secrets, Atheneum, 1992.

Wolf at the Door, Atheneum, 1993.

Some of Corcoran's novels have been translated into German, Swedish, and Spanish.

JUVENILE MYSTERY NOVELS

Meet Me at Tamerlane's Tomb, illustrated by Robinson, Atheneum, 1975.

The Person in the Potting Shed, Atheneum, 1980.

You're Allegro Dead, Atheneum, 1981.

A Watery Grave, Atheneum, 1982.

Which Witch Is Which?, Atheneum, 1983.

August, Die She Must, Atheneum, 1984.

Mystery on Ice, Atheneum, 1985.

The Shadowed Path (part of "Moonstone Mystery Romance" series), Archway (New York City), 1985.

When Darkness Falls (part of "Moonstone Mystery Romance" series), Archway, 1986.

JUVENILE NOVELS UNDER PSEUDONYM PAIGE DIXON

Lion on the Mountain, illustrated by J. H. Breslow, Atheneum, 1972.

Silver Wolf, illustrated by Ann Brewster, Atheneum, 1973.

The Young Grizzly, illustrated by Grambs Miller, Atheneum, 1974.

Promises to Keep, Atheneum, 1974.

May I Cross Your Golden River?, Atheneum, 1975, published as *A Time to Love, a Time to Mourn,* Scholastic, 1982.

The Search for Charlie, Atheneum, 1976.

Pimm's Cup for Everybody, Atheneum, 1976.

Summer of the White Goat, Atheneum, 1977.

The Loner: A Story of the Wolverine, illustrated by Miller, Atheneum, 1978.

Skipper (sequel to *May I Cross Your Golden River?*), Atheneum, 1979.

Walk My Way, Atheneum, 1980.

JUVENILE NOVELS UNDER PSEUDONYM GAIL HAMILTON

Titania's Lodestone, Atheneum, 1975.

A Candle to the Devil (mystery), illustrated by Joanne Scribner, Atheneum, 1975.

Love Comes to Eunice K. O'Herlihy, Atheneum, 1977.

HISTORICAL ROMANCE NOVELS

Abigail, Ballantine (New York City), 1981.

Abbie in Love (continuation of *Abigail*), Ballantine, 1981.

A Husband for Gail (conclusion of *Abigail*), Ballantine, 1981.

Beloved Enemy, Ballantine, 1981.

Call of the Heart, Ballantine, 1981.

Love Is Not Enough, Ballantine, 1981.

Song for Two Voices, Ballantine, 1981.

By the Silvery Moon, Ballantine, 1982.

OTHER

From the Drawn Sword (play), produced in Boston, MA, 1940.

Yankee Pine (play), produced at Bard College, Annandale-on-Hudson, NY, 1940.

The Mustang and Other Stories, Scholastic, 1978.

Contributor of radio scripts to *Dr. Christian* program; also contributor of short stories and other pieces to *Glamour, Charm, Woman's Day, Redbook, American Girl,* and *Good Housekeeping.*

WORK IN PROGRESS: Other books for young people; an autobiography told as fantasy.

SIDELIGHTS: "Hallie pressed her cheek against the window of the plane. The jagged snow-covered peaks of the Rockies seemed almost close enough to touch. She looked down at the pockets of snow caught in the black rocks and shivered. She felt as if she had left the real world behind her and had ventured into some terror-filled land of fantasy." So begins one of Barbara Corcoran's early novels, *Sasha, My Friend.* Leaving her life in California behind after her mother's death, Hallie grows and matures by the end of the novel, learning to enjoy her new life in Montana with her father. "She sat back in her chair," concludes Corcoran. "She was too tired to think much now, but it was nice to have the idea of a real school in the back of her mind. She looked over at her father. He had fallen asleep. His face had relaxed and he looked boyish, almost defenseless. She felt older than her father, almost as if the roles had been reversed and she was the parent. She leaned her head back and sighed. Growing up was strange."

Similar to many other Corcoran heroines and heroes, Hallie comes of age when confronted with new experiences that test her beliefs and endurance. It is through adventures and physical ordeals that Corcoran's characters are able to grow and reach a new level of maturity. And these growing experiences take place in mystery novels, historical novels, and contemporary novels. When not creating perceptive young adult characters, Corcoran also deals with the issue of animal welfare through wildlife books. Jean Fritz, writing in the *New York Times Book Review,* comments on one of the major messages of Corcoran's works: " 'Trust life,' she says, 'Go into the world. There'll be good people out there as well as bad. There'll be help.' She handles her theme like a prism, holding it up to catch the light at different angles, turning it this way and that so that each book is a fresh experience and a variation of the pattern."

Corcoran herself varied from the pattern as early as the day of her birth. "According to my mother," she writes in *Contemporary Authors Autobiography Series* (*CAAS*), "my arrival, in Hamilton, Massachusetts, on April 12, 1911, was not first class. I broke her pelvis, and she never quite forgave me." This rough beginning behind her, Corcoran found herself growing up in an area that had been home to her mother's family for more than 250 years; both Corcoran's maternal grandparents spent their lives in Hamilton. Remembering her grandfather in *CAAS,* Corcoran relates, "He used to regale me with stories of the Civil War, which he got from books and newspapers. He was too young even to be a drummer boy. It was the great frustration of his life." And her grandmother, she writes, "was a sweetheart. My best friend and sharer of secrets and jokes. When she died I had my first real sorrow."

Corcoran was just twelve years old when her first piece was published. "Since the first grade I had been writing 'stories' on my father's prescription pads or whatever was handy," comments Corcoran in *CAAS.* "At twelve I wrote real stories on real paper for a real magazine, *The Turret.*" One of these stories, concerning a garter snake afraid of young girls, was inspired by the summers Corcoran spent at Camp Allegro in New Hampshire, where it was most of her fellow campers who were the ones afraid of the snakes.

Adolescence found Corcoran attending Beverly High and racing around in her father's old Buick roadster, despite her lingering shyness. Dancing was another important activity, as Corcoran and her friends followed big band appearances all over the area, including Ella Fitzgerald and Benny Goodman. Scholarly success was not lost in the midst of all this activity, though. "I made the National Honor Society in spite of never understanding what algebra was all about," reveals Corcoran in *CAAS.* "And I was the class poet. My Camp Allegro friend, Frankie Jones, had introduced me to poetry, and I wallowed in Amy Lowell, Rupert Brooke, Edna Millay, Sara Teasdale, Keats, Shelley."

Breezing through her college boards—except for the chemistry section—Corcoran confidently began her freshman year at Wellesley in 1929. "Having always been the fair-haired student in English, I expected to be exempted from freshman comp, and to make the news staff," writes Corcoran in *CAAS.* "I did neither. My ego was badly dented." After a shaky sophomore year filled with too many dances and not enough studying, Corcoran pulled her grades back up and graduated two years later in 1933. The "Real World" that Corcoran then entered was still suffering the effects of the Depression, so she lived at home while searching for a job and writing plays. The Works Progress Administration Writers Project provided Corcoran with her first job, where she wrote town histories for schools. But it was her summer job as assistant stage manager and prop girl with the Oceanside Theatre that propelled Corcoran's writing forward.

Stage-struck by the whole experience with the Oceanside Theatre, Corcoran had a new desire to attend Yale Drama School. Not willing to take on such an expense, her father did finance a couple of months in New York, where Corcoran engrossed herself in numerous Broadway productions. Corcoran even sold a one-act play about the Spanish Revolution which was produced by several labor theaters. "I was beginning to sell a few pieces to magazines. The first one was a humorous essay about summer theater, sold to *Cue* for fifteen dollars," she remembers in *CAAS.* "They accepted it with a telegram, and I assumed that would be the first of many such happy telegrams, but I never got that kind of acceptance again."

Theater work and play writing also remained an important part of Corcoran's summers, while her winters were occupied by jobs in New York. Aside from plays, Corcoran wrote short pieces for magazines and play and movie reviews for an Italian-American newspaper. And the year 1940 saw two more of Corcoran's plays produced—the anti-Nazi play *From the Drawn Sword,* and *Yankee Pine,* a play relating the events of Shays' Rebellion. A play agent even tried to sell *Yankee Pine* on Broadway, but the real war that America was involved in made historical war plays less marketable.

Corcoran eventually left the New England winter behind for sunny California with her mother, her cousin Helen, and one of the author's closest friends, Rosalie. "We headed south and southwest, shedding our winter underwear and heavy socks and sweaters as we went," describes Corcoran in *CAAS*. "It took us a month to get to California. Provincial New Englanders that we were, we were fascinated by everything, from cotton fields to cactus. We encountered a flood in Mississippi, and Coolidge Dam, and an Indian reservation, desert, and Joshua trees. America in one long gulp."

A number of Corcoran's friends from the theater were already living in California when she arrived, so she joined them as a prop girl for the Phoenix Theatre in Westwood. During this time, Corcoran and her family rented the third floor of Anne Lehr's house. Associated with the Hollywood Canteen, Lehr became a close friend, and Corcoran passed many happy years in her house. Eventually buying a house in the Valley, Corcoran began working at the west coast branch of Celebrity Service, where she stayed for eight years. In the meantime, she continued to sell pieces to magazines and took a course in television writing. "Mostly I learned what not to do," Corcoran relates in *CAAS*, "like not trying to hit a trend, because by the time a script was finished, the trend was over. I find that still to be true, even in children's books, which are on the whole far less trend-influenced than adult books."

By 1953, Los Angeles was growing quickly, so after an enchanting trip to visit a friend in Missoula, Montana, Corcoran managed to get a job as a radio station copywriter and move there. Enrolling in a graduate program, Corcoran earned her M.A. and set forth for Mexico with a friend and $150. "Travelling without money is the way to have adventures," she asserts in *CAAS*. "It may be hell at the time, but it makes for good reminiscing long afterward." The fact that she had mononeucleosis at the time made the trip even more of an adventure for Corcoran: "I have never remembered how long we stayed." Returning to Los Angeles, Corcoran went through another string of jobs, including a stint as a teacher, a profession to which she has returned several times during her career.

Teaching eventually led Corcoran to Boulder, Colorado, in 1960, and it was during her first year here that she sold a novel to *Redbook*. "The long *Redbook* story, which they called 'The Runaways,' was rewritten after I started doing children's books," points out Corcoran in *CAAS*. "I went back to my original title, *A Row of Tigers*, and the only change I made was in viewpoint. I changed from the adult character's point of view to the child's." As Corcoran's writing career began to take off in a new direction, her en-

joyment of teaching also continued to grow. It was shortly after her mother died that she moved back to California to teach at Palomar College.

"During the summer I taught full time and I was also writing a novel called *Sam*," remembers Corcoran in *CAAS*. "It took me a long time to finish *Sam* because of the teaching schedule, but when it was finally done, I made an interesting discovery. My agent said I had written a good children's book. I told her that was not possible because I had no idea how to write children's books." Since this first children's book, Corcoran has written over seventy books for young people. "I talk to school children around the country quite a lot, and they always want to know where I 'get my ideas,' " she relates in *CAAS*. "I try to explain that ideas are all over the place. The trick is simply in being always on the lookout for them. It's a habit, a way of looking at the world, that writers have. Even one's own most traumatic experiences are grist for the mill. Part of every writer, I think, stands aside watching himself react and taking mental notes."

Sam is the tale of a fifteen-year-old girl who has led an isolated existence on a small island in Montana with her antisocial father. When she enters school for the first time as a high school junior, she experiences a severe culture shock and is faced with many conflicts. "Corcoran portrays Sam's problems in making decisions and choices and creates an exciting story and an appealing main character," maintains Mary Lou White in an essay for the *Dictionary of Literary Biography*. Martha Gardner, writing in the *Christian Science Monitor*, concludes that *Sam* "is a mature, wise, and well-developed story, as individual and appealing as Sam herself."

In 1969 Corcoran decided to give up teaching to write full time. That same year her novel *Sasha, My Friend* was published. Similar to the story of *Sam*, *Sasha, My Friend* follows the progress of fifteen-year-old Hallie after she moves from Los Angeles to live with her sick father on a tree farm in rural Montana. As she adapts to her new surroundings, Hallie adopts an orphaned wolf cub and eventually cultivates new friendships. "Themes of hard work, acceptance of people as they are, appreciation of nature, and family love and loyalty are well developed," notes White. And *Library Journal* contributor Cherie Zarookian asserts that *Sasha, My Friend* is written in an "unsentimental style that results in an extremely moving and sensitive story."

Corcoran used her own bout with temporary deafness to write about the experience in *A Dance to Still Music*. Published in 1974, this novel portrays fourteen-year-old Margaret's bitter struggle to accept her sudden deafness, the result of a severe illness. Margaret is also dealing with her family's recent move to Florida, eventually deciding to hitchhike back to her home state of Maine. Along the way she encounters an injured fawn and an understanding woman who cares for her until she is ready to return home. White maintains: "Corcoran grasps the feelings of anger and frustration and skillfully develops the characters." Fritz, writing in the *New York Times Book Review,* contends that *A Dance to Still Music* is "one of . . . Corcoran's most gripping stories." "I used my memory of the mastoid days to recreate what it feels like suddenly to be deaf," reveals Corcoran in *CAAS.* "It seemed to me that the deaf got a lot less sympathy than, for instance, the blind. People got tired of repeating, of having to raise their voices, of being misunderstood, and they were often impatient, or, worse, behaved as if the deaf person were not there. *A Dance to Still Music* remains my favorite of my own books."

Shortly after completing *A Dance to Still Music,* Corcoran fulfilled a life-long dream; she travelled to Europe with Jeanne Dixon and her godchildren. This lengthy trip took Corcoran and her fellow travellers to numerous cities and countries, including Finland, the Soviet Union, Samarkand (an ancient Arabic city), Budapest, and England. The time spent in Samarkand and Moscow eventually became the basis for two of Corcoran's books—*Meet Me at Tamerlane's Tomb* and *The Clown.*

Meet Me at Tamerlane's Tomb is Corcoran's first mystery; it concerns Hardy, an overweight fourteen-year-old girl vacationing in Samarkand with her parents and younger brother. During the trip she is almost deceived into helping a drug smuggler as she comes to terms with her own insecurities. "The setting is exotic," relates White, "Hardy's character is fully developed, and the story is amusing, even though the plot is improbable. The book concludes with the two siblings' journal accounts of the adventure, which make an interesting contrast of children's writing styles." Also set in the Soviet Union, Corcoran's 1975 novel *The Clown* follows an orphaned girl who travels to Moscow as a translator for her aunt and uncle. During the journey Lisa meets a young Russian clown and helps him escape to the free world by giving him her uncle's passport. *Bulletin of the Center for Children's Books* reviewer Zena Sutherland asserts that "the details of the planning and execution of the escape are intriguing," and concludes that *The Clown* is "a cracking good book."

Returning home to the United States, Corcoran finished a novel written under one of her pseudonyms—Paige Dixon. She had previously written under this name, and also writes under the name Gail Hamilton. The reasoning behind the use of pen names is directly tied to the marketing of her books. Once she became a full-time writer, Corcoran began writing more than two books a year. Most publishers prefer that their authors are not competing

against themselves for sales, so Corcoran's publishers suggested she take another name. Because she was writing a book with a male protagonist at the time, *Lion on the Mountain,* Corcoran chose a male identity. "Later I used that name for all the wild animal books I have done, and for some others as well, whenever there was an overlap," she comments in *CAAS.*

One of the wild animal tales Corcoran wrote under the pseudonym Paige Dixon is *The Young Grizzly.* Describing the first few years of a young grizzly bear's life, the novel features a bloodthirsty hunter and his hesitant son who serve to emphasize the danger threatening the animals. A *Kirkus Reviews* contributor comments that Corcoran portrays the grizzlies "with unusual immediacy." Patti Hagan, in the *New York Times Book Review,* states that *The Young Grizzly* "is a fine adventure story, giving a good accounting of mountain plants and animals."

With the animal tales of Paige Dixon, and her own novels, Corcoran sometimes writes more than four books in a year. Because of this she has also used the pseudonym Gail Hamilton. "Gail Hamilton was the pen name of a popular nineteenth-century writer in my home town . . . who was a cousin of my grandfather's," explains Corcoran in *CAAS.* "She died before I was born, but I had always been intrigued by her books. The house she had lived in stood empty during my childhood; in fact, on Halloween it was usually on our route because it qualified as a haunted house. By the time I was a teenager it had burned down, but I used to go and sit on the stones of the foundation, where some of the rose bushes she and her sister had planted still bloomed, and I would think about being a writer like Gail Hamilton."

In the years following 1975, Corcoran won an NEA fellowship and continued to travel, eventually went back to part-time teaching, wrote a series of adult romance novels, and added numerous titles to her list of works for young adults. Among these titles are historical novels, modern problem novels, and mysteries. "Corcoran writes very quickly," White asserts, "not even pausing to make an outline. She spends two hours a day at the typewriter and also puts considerable time into revising. She is a compulsive writer, claiming that she is 'restless when I'm not doing it.' "

One of the results of this restlessness is Corcoran's 1976 critically- acclaimed work, *Axe-Time, Sword-Time.* In this novel, set during World War II, eighteen-year-old Elinor overcomes a learning disability and asserts her independence by taking a war factory job as her parents start divorce proceedings. "The homefront wartime era is recreated with accuracy, and autobiographical details from Corcoran's early years as a wartime factory worker add to the book's authenticity," asserts White. *Bulletin of the*

Center for Children's Books reviewer Sutherland sees Elinor as facing common teenage problems and concludes: "The writing is subdued but not sedate, the characters and relationships perceptively depicted."

Corcoran wrote of another setting from her childhood in a series of mysteries focusing on two young sleuths, Stella and Kim. In *You're Allegro Dead*, Corcoran uses the Camp Allegro she attended as a child as the setting. In the novel, twelve-year-olds Stella and Kim are sent to a revival of Camp Allegro by their mothers, who attended the camp as children themselves. The visit becomes suspenseful when someone throws rocks at Stella and takes a shot at Kim. "Kim and Stella are believable characters and the clues are well placed," relates White. In their second adventure, *A Watery Grave*, Kim and Stella solve a murder mystery in their own New England town. "The story has suspense and smooth dialogue," states White. The two friends find suspense and mystery at Camp Allegro once again in *Mystery on Ice*. Spending a winter holiday at the camp with their families and friends, Stella and Kim uncover the culprit behind a series of troubling incidents. "There's plenty of activity and a hale and hearty cast to keep the plot skating smoothly along," comments Drew Stevenson in *School Library Journal*. Denise M. Wilms, writing in *Booklist*, contends that readers will "keep on till the villain is unveiled in the final pages."

In addition to mysteries, many of Corcoran's realistic novels focus on modern-day teenage problems. In *Family Secrets*, Tracy learns while returning to the coastal town near Boston where her father grew up, that she was adopted; her biological mother was one of her father's high school friends, Felicia Shaw. Shaw had Tracy's father and mother promise not to reveal the adoption until she died or until Tracy's eighteenth birthday; Felicia dies of cancer shortly before the family arrives, so Tracy is told. Desperate to learn everything she can about her mother, Tracy finds her answers through the delivery of a tape made by Felicia before her death. *Voice of Youth Advocates* contributor Judy Fink finds it strange that Tracy's family would move back to this town without first telling Tracy about her adoption, but also describes *Family Secrets* as "an involving and fast read, with elements of romance and suspense tied in with the theme of family being the people who care about you."

Corcoran's three young protagonists must overcome family problems in *Stay Tuned*. Unhappy in the cheap, crime-ridden New York City hotel where she is living with her father, sixteen-year-old Stevie takes an interest in two children next door: thirteen-year-old Eddie and his younger sister, Fawn. The recent death of their grandmother has left them alone. When Stevie takes it upon herself to leave her father to stay with relatives in New Hampshire, she takes Eddie and Fawn with her. Along the way they meet

Alex, an eighteen year old who has also left his father because of a disagreement concerning Alex's future. The four end up at a campsite in Maine, where Alex teaches the others how to survive while allowing them to make their own decisions. Through the course of their journey, they all experience emotional growth and develop a greater understanding of others. "Corcoran's characters are likable, and readers who favor happy endings will overlook the book's implausibilities," relates Gerry Larson in *School Library Journal*. *Stay Tuned* is "a good read for reluctant patrons," writes Margaret Galloway in *Voice of Youth Advocates*, concluding: "There are few stories that are as engrossing as surviving on your own or with friends."

Teenage growth is one of the mainstays of Corcoran's writing, as is a love of animals, and an underlying sense of mystery and suspense. Over the course of her career, she has developed from a playwright into a prolific author of realistic fiction for children and young adults. "Corcoran's strengths in writing are that she can tell an engrossing story and that she can write on many themes," relates White. "Her main characters are usually well developed, and her animal tales are compassionate." Corcoran herself views her writing in a somewhat less important light. "I don't see myself as a great writer so I don't think either the world or I is being cheated of anything," she explains in the *Missoulian*. "I think I'm a competent writer. I know the tricks of the trade."

BIOGRAPHICAL/CRITICAL SOURCES:

BOOKS

Contemporary Authors Autobiography Series, Volume 2, Gale, 1985.
Contemporary Literary Criticism, Volume 17, Gale (Detroit), 1981.
Corcoran, Barbara, *Sasha, My Friend*, Atheneum, 1969.
Dictionary of Literary Biography, Volume 52, *American Writers for Children since 1960: Fiction*, Gale, 1986.

PERIODICALS

Booklist, April 15, 1985, p. 1190; March 15, 1987, pp. 1125-26; October 1, 1993, p. 330.
Bulletin of the Center for Children's Books, January, 1976, p. 75; September, 1976, p. 6.
Christian Science Monitor, November 2, 1967, p. B11.
Kirkus Reviews, March 15, 1974, p. 305; November 1, 1993, p. 1388.
Library Journal, October 15, 1969, p. 3828; September 15, 1970, p. 3060.
Missoulian, August 29, 1981.
New York Times Book Review, January 31, 1971, p. 26; October 3, 1971, p. 8; November 3, 1974, p. 46; November 17, 1974, p. 8; January 4, 1976, p. 8.

Publishers Weekly, November 10, 1975, p. 55; August 28, 1987, p. 81.

School Library Journal, December, 1971, p. 63; May, 1985, p. 109; February, 1986, p. 94; October, 1986, pp. 171-72; March, 1987, p. 169; November, 1987, p. 114; April, 1991, p. 118; February, 1992, p. 85; September, 1993, pp. 228-29.

Voice of Youth Advocates, February, 1986, p. 391; December, 1986, p. 214; February, 1990, p. 342; June, 1991, p. 94; June, 1992, pp. 92-93; December, 1993, p. 288.

*   *   *

COURTNEY, (John) Richard 1927-

PERSONAL: Born June 4, 1927, in Newmarket, England; son of Arthur John (a teacher) and Celia Annie Courtney; married Rosemary Gale (a writer and editor); children: Anne, John. *Education:* University of Leeds, B.A., 1951, diploma in education, 1952.

ADDRESSES: Home—P.O. Box 353, Jackson's Point, Ontario, Canada L0E 1L0. *Office*—Ontario Institute for Studies in Education, 252 Bloor St. W., Toronto, Ontario, Canada M5S 1V6.

CAREER: Primary school teacher, Dalham, England, 1948; high school drama teacher, Leeds, England, 1952-55, and Colne Valley, England, 1955-59; University of London, Institute of Education, Trent Park College, senior lecturer in drama, 1959-67, warden of Sir Phillip Sassoon Hall, 1961-64; University of Victoria, British Columbia, associate professor of theatre, 1968-71; University of Calgary, Alberta, professor of drama, 1971-74, head of Developmental Drama Summer School, 1970-72; Ontario Institute for Studies in Education, Toronto and University of Toronto, Graduate Centre of Drama, professor emeritus of arts and education, 1974-94.

Goldsmith's College, London, lecturer, summers 1973-74; Melbourne State College, visiting fellow, 1979; University of Western Ontario, visiting instructor, 1980; lecturer at universities in England, Australia, the United States, and Hong Kong. Actor with British Broadcasting Corp. Northern Repertory Company, 1954-64, and English Theatre Guild; performed in repertory, music halls, and amateur productions; director of Proscenium Players, Leeds, and educational theatre productions; Four Valleys Youth Theatre, founder, 1955; Enfield Youth Theatre, co-founder, 1961; North Hertfordshire Youth Theatre, life patron. Artist, with exhibitions of paintings. Task force on arts and education in Canada, chairman, 1975-79; national inquiry into arts and education in Canada, chairman, 1979; guest on television programs in Canada, the United States, Hong Kong, and Australia; consultant to Canada Council, Design Canada, and Ontario Arts Council. *Military service:* Royal Air Force, 1945-48.

MEMBER: National Drama (United Kingdom), Canadian Conference of the Arts (member of board of governors, 1970; member of executive committee, 1971; vice-president, 1972; national president, 1973-76), Canadian Child and Youth Drama Association (member of board of directors, 1968-69; president, 1969-72), Creative Education Foundation, Educational Drama Association, Society for Teachers of Speech and Drama, Folklore Society, Royal Society of Arts (fellow), Canadian Society for Aesthetics, British Society for Aesthetics, British Children's Theatre Association, British Society of Dramatherapy, American Councils of the Arts (governor, 1974-77), American Theatre Association (member of Theatre Education Commission, 1979-81), American Society for Aesthetics.

AWARDS, HONORS: Alberta Achievement Award, government of Alberta, 1973, for services to arts and education; Canadian Silver Jubilee Medal, governor-general of Canada, 1977; fortieth anniversary award, Canadian Conference of the Arts, 1985; research awards from Social Sciences and Humanities Research Council of Canada, Design Canada, Ontario Arts Council, and Ontario Ministry of Education.

WRITINGS:

EDUCATIONAL DRAMA

(Editor) *College Drama Space,* London University Institute of Education (London), 1964.
Drama for Youth, Pitman (London), 1964.
Teaching Drama, Cassell (London), 1965.
The School Play, Cassell, 1966.
The Drama Studio, Pitman, 1967.
Play, Drama & Thought, Simon & Pierre (Toronto), 1968, 4th revised edition, 1989.
The Dramatic Curriculum, University of Western Ontario (London, ONT), 1981.
Re-Play: Studies of Human Drama in Education, Ontario Institute for Studies in Education Press, 1982.
The Rarest Dream: "Play, Drama & Thought" Re-visited, National Association for Teaching of Drama, 1984.
Drama Education Canada, Bison Books, 1987.
Dictionary of Developmental Drama, C. C. Thomas (Springfield, IL), 1987.
Drama & Intelligence, McGill-Queens University Press (Montreal), 1990.
Drama & Feeling, McGill-Queens University Press, 1995.

ARTS EDUCATION

(Editor) *Arts in Society,* Alberta Culture, 1974.
Teaching and the Arts, Melbourne College (Australia), 1979.

(Editor) *The Face of the Future,* Canadian Conference of the Arts, 1980.

(With P. Park) *Learning Through the Arts,* Ontario Ministry of Education, 1981.

Aesthetic Learning, Social Sciences and Humanities Research Council of Canada, 1985.

The Quest: Research and Inquiry in Arts Education, University Press of America, 1985.

(With David Booth, John Emerson, and Natalie Kuzmich) *Teacher Education in the Arts,* Bison Books, 1985.

(Editor with David Booth, John Emerson, and Natalie Kuzmich) *Basic Books in Arts Education,* Bison Books, 1986.

Practical Research, Bison Books, 1988.

(With David Booth, John Emerson, and Natalie Kuzmich) *No One Way of Being: Practical Knowledge of Elementary Arts Teachers,* Ontario Ministry of Education, 1988.

POETRY

Wild Eyed Girl, Stockwell, 1948.
Beasts and Other People, Bison Books, 1987.
The Turning of the World, Bison Books, 1987.
Tales of a Traveling Man, Bison Books, 1987.

OTHER

(Editor with G. Schattner) *Drama in Therapy,* 2 volumes (drama therapy), Drama Book Specialists, 1982.

Outline of British Drama (history), Littlefield Adams, 1982.

Lord of the Sky: An Ancient Egyptian Ritual Drama (drama), Bison Books, 1987.

Also author of *Shakespeare's World of War, Shakespeare's World of Death, Shakespeare's Masked World, Shakespeare's Tragic World, Shakespeare's Comic World, Shakespeare's Problem World, Shakespeare's Magic World, Shakespeare's World of Love,* all Simon & Pierre, 1994-96. Editor of monograph series "Discussions in Developmental Drama," University of Calgary, 1971-74. Contributor of more than one hundred articles, stories, poems, and reviews to scholarly journals, popular magazines, and newspapers, including *Gryphon, Players, Connecticut Review, Queen's Quarterly, Children's Theatre Review,* and *Youth Theatre Journal.* Contributing editor to *Curriculum Inquiry,* 1975-78.

WORK IN PROGRESS: Secret Spirits: Possession and Performance of Canadian Indians on Vancouver Island; The Dancing Priest: Ritual Origins of Greek Tragedy; The Birth of God: The Ritual Drama of Ancient Israel; On Theatre: The Theory of Drama in Performance; Acts of Mind; The Comic World of Carlo Goldoni; Play: From Pre-History to Post-Structuralism.

SIDELIGHTS: Richard Courtney once told *CA:* "I have always been concerned with the drama of existence. Human drama commences in the first months of life—we make sense out of the world by creating a dramatic relationship with it—and theatre is simply the tip of the iceberg of human existence.

"In a recent 'Sunrise Semester' series on CBS-TV, I explained that in order to understand this process, we have to examine it from the inside out and from the outside in. How can we understand ourselves or other people unless we do both things at the same time? Our inner world (the 'me') creates a drama between itself and other people and things. Yet, at the same time, the outer world (our society and culture) is made up of other people who are also creating their own dramas; this opens up some possibilities to us, but closes off others. This accounts for two types of my writing: studies in children's play, maturation, and education (the drama of the inner), and studies of ceremonialism and ritual (the drama of the outer).

"Yet, a play in a theatre provides human beings with models as to how to live their lives—how to relate the inner to the outer—and that is what makes theatre so significant as an art form. This accounts for my third type of writing: studies of plays and the theatre."

BIOGRAPHICAL/CRITICAL SOURCES:

BOOKS

Booth, D. and A. Martin-Smith, editors, *Re-cognizing Richard Courtney: Selected Writings on Drama & Education,* Pembroke, 1988.

PERIODICALS

Cambridge Daily News, April 18, 1968.
Canadian Theatre Review, October, 1982.
Children's Theatre Review, fall, 1981; fall, 1982.
Communication Education, 1982.
Educational Theatre Journal, March, 1976.
L'Expression, November, 1981.
Journal of Creative Behavior, spring, 1970.
Theatre Design and Technology, October, 1968.
Theatre News, fall, 1982.
Times Educational Supplement, April 8, 1983.
Times Literary Supplement, November 11, 1964; March 31, 1967; May 31, 1968.
Victoria Daily Times, January 20, 1968; July 20, 1968; May 23, 1970.

*   *   *

CRANE, Elaine Forman 1939-

PERSONAL: Born July 23, 1939, in New York, NY; daughter of Monroe A. (an attorney) and Lillian (a teacher; maiden name, Radofsky) Forman; married Stephen G. Crane (a judge), August 21, 1960; children: Melissa, Andrea. *Education:* Cornell University, B.A., 1961; New York University, M.A., 1973, Ph.D., 1977.

ADDRESSES: Home—35 East 84th St., New York, NY 10028. *Office*—Department of History, Fordham University, Rose Hill, Bronx, NY 10458.

CAREER: City University of New York, New York City, editorial fellow, working on "The Papers of Robert Morris," 1976-77; New York University, New York City, assistant editor of "The Papers of William Livingston," 1977-78; Fordham University, Bronx, NY, assistant professor, 1978-84, associate professor of history and chairperson of department, 1984-87, director of Women's Studies Program, 1981-85. Consultant to Coastal Resources Management Council of Rhode Island.

MEMBER: Organization of American Historians, Association for Documentary Editing, Newport Historical Society, Columbia University Seminar in American Civilization, Columbia University Seminar in Early American History.

AWARDS, HONORS: Grants from National Endowment for the Humanities, 1982, 1984, Barra Foundation, 1982-87, National Historical Publications and Records Commission, 1983-93, American Council of Learned Societies, 1983, and Society of American Archivists, 1992; Mellon Foundation grant, 1983; teaching award, Fordham College, 1994.

WRITINGS:

EDITOR

Growing Up Black, Morrow (New York City), 1968.
The Black Soldier, Morrow, 1971.
Living Black in White America, Morrow, 1971.
The Diary of Elizabeth Drinker, 3 volumes, Northeastern University Press (Boston), 1991.

OTHER

(Contributor) Kelly Weisberg, editor, *Women and the Law: Interdisciplinary Perspectives,* Schenkman (New York City), 1983.
A Dependent People: Newport, Rhode Island, in the Revolutionary Era, Fordham University Press (Bronx), 1985.

Also contributor to Ronald Hoffman and Peter Albert, editors, *Religion in a Revolutionary Age,* 1994. Contributor of articles and reviews to history journals.

WORK IN PROGRESS: In the Beginning: Urban Women in Colonial New England.

SIDELIGHTS: Elaine Forman Crane once told *CA:* "I am old-fashioned to the extent that I believe historical writing should be part of our literary tradition. I like to think of myself as both a writer and historian."

*   *   *

CUPITT, Don   1934-

PERSONAL: Surname is pronounced "*Kew*-pit"; born May 22, 1934, in Lancashire, England; son of Robert and Norah (Gregson) Cupitt; married Susan Marianne Day (a teacher), December 28, 1963; children: John Robert Gregson, Caroline Mary, Sarah Anne. *Education:* Trinity Hall, Cambridge, B.A., 1955, M.A., 1958; attended Westcott House, Cambridge, 1957-59. *Religion:* Church of England.

ADDRESSES: Home—62 Humberstone Rd., Cambridge CB4 1JF, England. *Office*—Emmanuel College, Cambridge University, Cambridge CB2 3AP, England.

CAREER: Cambridge University, Cambridge, England, fellow, 1965—, dean, and director of studies in theology and philosophy at Emmanuel College, 1966-91, university assistant lecturer, 1968-73, lecturer in the philosophy of religion, 1973—. Priest in the Church of England.

AWARDS, HONORS: D. Litt., Bristol, 1985.

WRITINGS:

Christ and the Hiddenness of God, Westminster (London), 1971, second edition, S.C.M. Press (London), 1985.
Crisis of Moral Authority, Westminster, 1972, second edition, S.C.M. Press, 1985.
The Leap of Reason, Westminster, 1976, second edition, S.C.M. Press, 1985.
The Worlds of Science and Religion, Seabury, 1976.
The Nature of Man, Seabury, 1979.
Jesus and the Gospel of God, Lutterworth (Cambridge), 1979.
The Debate about Christ, S.C.M. Press, 1979.
(Editor) *Explorations in Theology 6,* S.C.M. Press, 1979.
Taking Leave of God, Crossroad Publishing (London), 1980.
The World to Come, S.C.M. Press, 1982.
Only Human, S.C.M. Press, 1985.
Life Lines, S.C.M. Press, 1986.
The Long-Legged Fly, S.C.M. Press, 1987.
The New Christian Ethics, S.C.M. Press, 1988.
Radicals and the Future of the Church, S.C.M. Press, 1989.
Creation Out of Nothing, Trinity Press (Philadelphia), 1990.
What Is a Story?, S.C.M. Press, 1991.

Rethinking Religion, St. Andrew's Trust (Wellington, New Zealand), 1992.
The Time Being, S.C.M. Press, 1992.
After All, S.C.M. Press, 1994.
The Last Philosophy, S.C.M., 1995.

Also contributor to books, including *Christ, Faith and History,* edited by S. W. Sykes and J. P. Clayton, Cambridge University Press, 1972; *Incarnation and Myth,* edited by Michael Goulder, S.C.M. Press, 1979; *The Philosophical Frontiers of Christian Theology,* edited by Brian Hebblethwaite and Stewart Sutherland, Cambridge University Press, 1982; *The Trial of Faith,* edited by Peter Eaton, Morehouse-Barlow, 1988; *Humanity, Environment and God,* edited by Neil Spurway, 1993; and *Glimpses of God,* edited by Dan Cohn-Sherbok, 1994. Contributor to theology journals, including *Anglican Theological Review, Theology,* and *Journal of Theological Studies.*

TELEVISION SCRIPTS

(With Peter Armstrong; also presenter) *Who Was Jesus?,* British Broadcasting Corporation (BBC), 1977.
The Sea of Faith, BBC, 1984, Cambridge University Press (New York City), 1988.

WORK IN PROGRESS: Research on philosophical theology.

BIOGRAPHICAL/CRITICAL SOURCES:

BOOKS

Cowdell, Scott, *Atheist Priest? Don Cupitt and Christianity,* S.C.M. Press (London), 1988.
White, Stephen Ross, *Don Cupitt and the Future of Christian Doctrine,* S.C.M. Press, 1994.

PERIODICALS

Times Literary Supplement, December 5, 1980; May 28, 1982; August 2, 1985, p. 854; December 26, 1986, p. 1446; October 27-November 2, 1989, p. 1188.

*   *   *

CURNOW, (Thomas) Allen (Monro) 1911- (Whim-Wham)

PERSONAL: Born June 17, 1911, in Timaru, New Zealand; son of Tremayne Monro (an Anglican clergyman) and Jessamine Towler (Gambling) Curnow; married Elizabeth Jaumaud Le Cren, 1936 (divorced, 1965); married Jenifer Mary Tole, August 31, 1965; children: Wystan Tremayne Le Cren, Belinda Elizabeth Allen Curnow Morley, Timothy Charles Monro. *Education:* Attended St. John's College, Auckland, New Zealand, 1931-33; University of New Zealand, B.A., 1933.

ADDRESSES: Home—62 Tohunga Cres., Parnell, Auckland, New Zealand. *Agent*—Curtis Brown Ltd., P.O. Box 19, Paddington 2021, Australia.

CAREER: Press, Christchurch, New Zealand, reporter, 1936-40, sub-editor, 1941-48, drama critic, 1945-47; *News Chronicle,* London, England, reporter and sub-editor, 1949; University of Auckland, Auckland, New Zealand, senior lecturer, 1951-66, associate professor of English, 1967-76. Guest poet, Upstate New York Poetry Circuit, 1966; has given poetry readings at University of Cincinnati and University of Pennsylvania, 1966; Library of Congress, 1966, 1974; Cambridge, England, Poetry Festival, 1985; South Bank Centre, London, England, 1992.

AWARDS, HONORS: Travel award, New Zealand State Literary Fund, 1949; Carnegie grant, 1950; Jessie Mackay Memorial Prize from New Zealand branch of International PEN and State Literary Fund, 1957, for *Poems, 1949-1957,* and 1962, for *A Small Room with Large Windows: Selected Poems;* Fulbright fellowship, 1961; Institute of Contemporary Arts fellowship, Washington, DC, 1961; Litt.D., University of Auckland, 1966, and University of Canterbury, 1975; New Zealand Poetry Award, 1975, for *Collected Poems, 1933-1973,* 1979, for *An Incorrigible Music: A Sequence of Poems,* and 1983, for *You Will Know When You Get There: Poems, 1979-1981;* Dillons Commonwealth Poetry Prize, for *Continuum, New and Later Poems,* 1989; Queen's Gold Medal for Poetry, 1989; Order of New Zealand, 1990.

WRITINGS:

POETRY

Enemies: Poems, 1934-36, Caxton Press (Christchurch, New Zealand), 1937.
Not in Narrow Seas, Caxton Press, 1939.
Island and Time, Caxton Press, 1941.
(With A. R. D. Fairburn, Denis Glover, and R. A. K. Mason) *Recent Poems,* Caxton Press, 1941.
(Under pseudonym Whim-Wham) *Verses, 1941-1942,* Caxton Press, 1942.
Sailing or Drowning, Progressive Publishing Society (Wellington, New Zealand), 1943.
(Editor) *A Book of New Zealand Verse, 1923-1945,* Caxton Press, 1945, revised edition, 1951.
Jack without Magic, Caxton Press, 1946.
At Dead Low Water, and Sonnets, Caxton Press, 1949.
Poems, 1949-1957, Mermaid Press (Wellington), 1957.
(Under pseudonym Whim-Wham) *The Best of Whim-Wham,* Paul's Book Arcade, 1959.
(Editor) *The Penguin Book of New Zealand Verse,* Penguin (Harmondsworth, Middlesex, England), 1960.

A Small Room with Large Windows: Selected Poems, Oxford University Press (London), 1962.

(Under pseudonym Whim-Wham) *Whim-Wham Land,* Blackwood & Janet Paul (Auckland, New Zealand), 1967.

Trees, Effigies, Moving Objects: A Sequence of Poems, Catspaw Press (Wellington), 1972.

An Abominable Temper, and Other Poems, Catspaw Press, 1973.

Collected Poems, 1933-1973, A. H. & A. W. Reed (Australia), 1974.

An Incorrigible Music: A Sequence of Poems, Auckland University Press (Auckland), 1979.

You Will Know When You Get There: Poems, 1979-81, Auckland University Press, 1982.

The Loop in Lone Kauri Road: Poems, 1983-1985, Auckland University Press, 1986.

Continuum: New and Later Poems, 1972-1988, Auckland University Press, 1988.

Selected Poems, 1940-1989, Viking (London), 1990.

PLAYS

The Axe: A Verse Tragedy (three-act; produced in Christchurch, New Zealand, at Little Theatre, Canterbury University College, 1948), Caxton Press, 1949.

Moon Section, produced in Auckland at Aukland Festival Play, 1959.

Doctor Pom, produced in Auckland, 1964.

Four Plays (contains *The Axe,* revised version, and three radio plays, all produced by New Zealand Broadcasting Corporation: *The Overseas Expert,* broadcast 1961, *The Duke's Miracle,* broadcast 1967, and *Resident of Nowhere,* broadcast 1969), A. H. & A. W. Reed, 1972.

Il Miracolo del Duca (Italian translation of *The Duke's Miracle* by Italo Verri), Casa Editrice 'Liberty house' di Lucio Scardino, Ferrara, 1994.

OTHER

Also author of *Valley of Decision,* 1933, *Selected Poems,* 1982, and *Look Back Harder: Critical Writings, 1935-84,* 1987. Work is represented in anthologies, including *Poems from New Writing,* John Lehmann (London), 1946; *An Anthology of New Zealand Verse,* Oxford University Press, 1956; *A Garland for Dylan Thomas,* Clark and Way, (New York City), 1963, and *Seven Centuries of Poetry in English,* Oxford, 1987. Contributor to periodicals, including *Meanjin Quarterly* (Melbourne), *Poetry, New World Writing, Times Literary Supplement, London Magazine, Partisan Review,* and *London Review of Books.*

WORK IN PROGRESS: Satirical pieces and more poems.

SIDELIGHTS: Allen Curnow, one of New Zealand's best-known poets and dramatists, once told *CA:* "My first very youthful poems came from a personal religious crisis during studies for the Anglican ministry and the social crisis of the nineteen thirties depression. A few of the poems which followed touched on New Zealand life and history: a poet's attempt to solve questions about where he was, the language and tradition being almost everywhere, and his country rather inconveniently but ineluctably *somewhere.* There was *The Unhistoric Story* about Cook's first southern voyage, *The Victim* about a Dutch crewman killed in a clash with the Maori when Abel Tasman made the first European discovery of New Zealand (in 1642), and *Landfall in Unknown Seas,* written on commission by the New Zealand government to celebrate the 300th anniversary of Tasman's voyage. There was also a sonnet, *The Skeleton of the Great Moa,* about New Zealand's giant extinct bird. It pleases me that all these works have continued to be quoted, nearly forty years after their first appearance—not only in literary works, but occasionally in historical and even scientific studies. It pleased me less when one or two younger writers chose to regard me as a banner-bearer for some kind of hole-and-corner poetic nationalism. The truth was that for a few years my island nation served me the way Yeats said his 'System' served him—it 'gave me metaphors for poetry.'

"Like some other New Zealand authors," Curnow recalled, "I was to find dramatic writing (especially for the stage) a somewhat frustrating exercise in a country without dramatic tradition or well-established theatre. Since 1970 I have persisted with poems about the troublesome question of how to be in two (or more) places at once, i.e. Auckland, New Zealand, and Washington, D.C. A title like *Trees, Effigies, Moving Objects,* for instance, is an excuse for arranging in perspective a giant kauri tree, the Washington Memorial, a roadside effigy of the Virgin at Paraparaumu, and Nebuchadnezzar's golden idol. Can I perhaps unite a memory of the Duomo in Florence, by way of the assassin's dagger which killed Giuliano de'Medici in 1478, with my own rusty fishing knife and a *kahawai* landed at Kare Kare, and the chemistry of a garden poison for snails? This may sound far-fetched, but isn't it one of the tasks of a poet to transform the far-fetched into the self-evident?"

Curnow added, "Extended trips to Italy, France, and the United Kingdom (1974, 1978, 1983) must have helped to 'universalise' (if the word isn't too pretentious) my later writing, but not to obscure where it all begins, in a life and a home in the South-West Pacific."

BIOGRAPHICAL/CRITICAL SOURCES:

BOOKS

Roddick, Alan, *Allen Curnow,* Oxford University Press, 1980.

PERIODICALS

Islands, autumn, 1975.

Landfall, autumn, 1963; spring, 1983; spring, 1989; spring, 1990.

Observer (London), October 16, 1983.

Poetry Review, Volume 78, number 1, 1988.

Scripsi (Melbourne, Australia), spring, 1983.

Times Literary Supplement, July 31, 1987, p. 823; June 1, 1989, p. 593.

*　　　*　　　*

CURRAN, Charles E. 1934-

PERSONAL: Born March 30, 1934, in Rochester, NY. *Education:* St. Bernard's Seminary and College, B.A., 1955; Pontifical Gregorian University, Rome, Italy, S.T.D., 1957, S.T.L., 1959, S.T.D., 1961; Academia Alfonsiana, Rome, S.T.D., 1961.

ADDRESSES: Office—317 Dallas Hall, Southern Methodist University, P.O. Box 750235, Dallas, TX 75275-0235.

CAREER: Ordained Roman Catholic priest, 1958. St. Bernard's Seminary, Rochester, NY, professor of moral theology, 1961-65; Catholic University of America, Washington, DC, assistant professor, 1965-67, associate professor, 1967-71, professor of moral theology, 1971-89; Southern Methodist University, Dallas, TX, Elizabeth Scurlock University Professor of Human Values, 1991—. Senior research scholar, Kennedy Center for Bioethics, Georgetown University, 1972; external examiner in Christian ethics, University of the West Indies, 1982-86; visiting Kaneb Professor of Catholic Studies, Cornell University, 1987-88; visiting Brooks Professor of Religion, University of Southern California, 1988-89, visiting Firestone Professor of Religion, 1989-90; visiting Goodwin-Philpott Eminent Scholar in Religion, Auburn University, 1990-91.

MEMBER: American Society of Christian Ethics (president, 1971-72), American Theological Society (vice-president, 1988-89; president, 1989-90), Catholic Theological Society of America (vice-president, 1968-69; president, 1969-70), College Theology Society.

AWARDS, HONORS: "Man in the News" citation, *New York Times,* 1967; faculty fellowship, American Association of Theological Schools, 1971; John Courtney Murray Award, Catholic Society of America, 1972, for distinguished achievement in theology; "Person of the Week," American Broadcasting Company, August, 1986; honorary doctorate, University of Charleston, 1987, and Concordia College, 1992.

WRITINGS:

Christian Morality Today: The Renewal of Moral Theology, Fides (Notre Dame, IN), 1966.

A New Look at Christian Morality, Fides, 1968.

(Editor) *Absolutes in Moral Theology?,* Corpus Books (Washington, DC), 1968.

(With Robert E. Hunt and others) *Dissent in and for the Church: Theologians and Humanae Vitae,* Sheed & Ward (New York City), 1969.

(With others) *The Responsibility of Dissent: The Church and Academic Freedom,* Sheed & Ward, 1969.

(Editor) *Contraception: Authority and Dissent,* Herder & Herder (New York City), 1969.

Contemporary Problems in Moral Theology, Fides, 1970.

(Editor with George J. Dyer) *Shared Responsibility in the Local Church,* Catholic Theological Society of America, 1970.

Catholic Moral Theology in Dialogue, Fides, 1972.

The Crisis in Priestly Ministry, Fides, 1972.

Politics, Medicine and Christian Ethics: A Dialogue with Paul Ramsey, Fortress (Philadelphia), 1973.

New Perspectives in Moral Theology, Fides, 1974.

Ongoing Revision: Studies in Moral Theology, Fides, 1975.

Themes in Fundamental Moral Theology, University of Notre Dame Press, 1977.

Issues in Sexual and Medical Ethics, University of Notre Dame Press, 1978.

Transition and Tradition in Moral Theology, University of Notre Dame Press, 1979.

(Editor with Richard A. McCormick) *Readings in Moral Theology Number 1: Moral Norms and Catholic Tradition,* Paulist Press (Ramsey, NJ), 1979.

(Editor with McCormick) *Readings in Moral Theology Number 2: The Distinctiveness of Christian Ethics,* Paulist Press, 1980.

Moral Theology: A Continuing Journey, University of Notre Dame Press, 1982.

American Catholic Social Ethics: Twentieth-Century Approaches, University of Notre Dame Press, 1982.

(Editor with McCormick) *Readings in Moral Theology Number 3: The Magisterium and Morality,* Paulist Press, 1982.

(Editor with McCormick) *Readings in Moral Theology Number 4: The Use of Scripture in Moral Theology,* Paulist Press, 1984.

Critical Concerns in Moral Theology, University of Notre Dame Press, 1984.

Directions in Catholic Social Ethics, University of Notre Dame Press, 1985.

Directions in Fundamental Moral Theology, University of Notre Dame Press, 1985.

Faithful Dissent, Sheed & Ward (Kansas City, MO), 1986.

(Editor with McCormick) *Readings in Moral Theology Number 5: Official Catholic Social Teaching,* Paulist Press, 1986.

Toward an American Catholic Moral Theology, University of Notre Dame Press, 1988.

Sexualitat und Ethik, Athenaum (Frankfurt), 1988.

Tensions in Moral Theology, University of Notre Dame Press, 1988.

(Editor with McCormick) *Readings in Moral Theology Number 6: Dissent in the Church,* Paulist Press, 1988.

Catholic Higher Education, Theology, and Academic Freedom, University of Notre Dame Press, 1990.

(Editor) *Moral Theology: Challenges for the Future; Essays in Honor of Richard A. McCormick,* Paulist Press, 1990.

(Editor with McCormick) *Readings in Moral Theology Number 7: Natural Law and Theology,* Paulist Press, 1991.

The Living Tradition of Catholic Moral Theology, University of Notre Dame Press, 1992.

(Editor with McCormick) *Readings in Moral Theology Number 8: Dialogue about Catholic Sexual Teaching,* Paulist Press, 1993.

The Church and Morality: An Ecumenical and Catholic Approach, Fortress (Minneapolis), 1993.

Contributor to books, including *Ecumenical Dialogue at Harvard,* edited by S. H. Miller and G. E. Wright, Harvard University Press (Cambridge, MA), 1964; *Law for Liberty,* edited by James E. Biechler, Helicon (La Jolla, CA), 1967; and *The Situation Ethics Debate,* edited by Harvey Cox, Westminster (Philadelphia), 1968. Contributor to periodicals, including *Jurist, Commonweal,* and *Homiletic.* Member of editorial board, *International Christian Digest, Eglise et Theologie,* and *Horizons.*

WORK IN PROGRESS: Articles and monographs on medical ethics, Roman Catholic social ethics in the United States, and questions of fundamental moral theology.

SIDELIGHTS: In April, 1967, Charles E. Curran became a cause celebre for priestly academic freedom when he was fired by Catholic University of America, supposedly (although the university gave no reasons for the dismissal) for his liberal views on birth control. The popular teacher chose to fight the ouster, and the Catholic University faculty voted 400 to 18 not to hold classes until he was reinstated. The boycott closed the university for three days before Curran was rehired with the announcement that he would be promoted from assistant to associate professor the following semester.

In the summer of 1968, Curran was, he told *CA,* "the organizer and chief spokesman of a group of American Catholic theologians, ultimately totalling about 600, who dissented from the papal encyclical *Humanae Vitae,*"

which reaffirmed the church's traditional stand against artificial birth control. "The day after the encyclical was issued in Rome, I spoke for 89 Roman Catholic theologians . . . indicating that one could be a loyal Roman Catholic and still disagree with this particular teaching. This dissent was widely carried in the newspaper and television accounts of those days. . . . These events are recorded in . . . *Dissent in and for the Church.*"

In 1989, Curran explained further about his difficulties with the Catholic University of America and the Vatican: "The Vatican's Congregation for the Doctrine of the Faith [declared] that I was no longer suitable nor eligible to teach Catholic theology at Catholic University of America. Subsequent to that, the university said that I could not teach Catholic theology there and had to sign a statement saying I would agree with the Vatican declaration. I refused to do so, on the grounds that it was a violation of my academic freedom. I took the case to court in the Superior Court of the District of Columbia but the judge ruled that Catholic University did not always have to come down on the side of academic freedom and that I had no case against them. However, a committee of the American Association of University Professors has concluded that Catholic University has violated my academic freedom and my tenure rights."

BIOGRAPHICAL/CRITICAL SOURCES:

PERIODICALS

Christian Century, August 27, 1969.
Los Angeles Times, March 4, 1989.
National Observer, April 24, 1967; May 1, 1967.
New York Times Book Review, March 19, 1989, p. 11.
Washington Post, May 18, 1988.
Washington Post Magazine, March 22, 1987, pp. 15-19, 41-48.

*   *   *

CUTCLIFFE, Stephen H(osmer) 1947-

PERSONAL: Born January 17, 1947, in Melrose, MA; son of Woodrow A. and Elizabeth (Hosmer) Cutcliffe; married Kathlene Fekula, August 29, 1980. *Education:* Bates College, A.B., 1968; Lehigh University, M.A., 1973, Ph.D., 1976.

ADDRESSES: Home—802 Prospect Ave., Bethlehem, PA 18018. *Office*—Science, Technology, and Society Program, 327 Maginnes Hall, 9 West Packer Ave., Lehigh University, Bethlehem, PA, 18015.

CAREER: Lehigh University, Bethlehem, PA, administrative assistant to director of Science, Technology, and Society Program, 1976-83, assistant to provost for administration, 1982-83, director of Technology Studies Resource Center, 1983—, director of Lehigh University Press, 1987-90, currently director of Science, Technology, and Society Program (STS), and associate professor of STS and history. Visiting assistant professor at Lafayette College, 1980. Technology consultant to Historic Bethlehem, Inc., 1978-80, 1988-89, Rensselaer Polytechnic Institute, 1982, Monroe County Community College, 1983, Eastern Michigan University, 1985, Northwestern College, 1985, Colby College, 1986, Babson College, 1987, New Jersey Institute of Technology, 1989, Vassar College, 1992. Citizen's public advisory committee of Pennsylvania Power and Light Co., member, 1981-90, chair, 1982-84. Member of advisory council for documentary film *Bethlehem: A Search for Community,* 1977-78; member of board of directors, Historic Bethlehem, Inc., 1989-95; member, review panel, Ethics and Values Studies, National Science Foundation, 1992; member of advisory board, Attracting Minority Scholars to Ethics and Values Studies in Science and Technology, American Association for the Advancement of Science. Outside evaluator of Bachelor of Arts candidates in the College of Science in Society of Wesleyan University, 1981-82. Associated with the Lawrence Henry Gipson Institute for Eighteenth-Century Studies, 1970—, member of executive council, 1982—. *Military service:* U.S. Army, 1968-70; became sergeant.

MEMBER: History of Science Society, American Society for Environmental History, Organization of American Historians, Society for the History of Technology (chair of technology studies and education committee, 1981-83; member of executive council, 1985-87, 1991-93; member of Robinson Prize committee, 1989-91), Society for Philosophy and Technology, Society for Social Studies of Science, National Association for Science, Technology, and Society (member of board of directors, 1989-92; vice-president, 1990; president, 1991), Phi Alpha Theta.

AWARDS, HONORS: Golden Desk Award from Lehigh University, 1971-72; grant from Lawrence Henry Gipson Institute for Eighteenth-Century Studies, 1975; honorary director, Research Center of Science, Technology, Economy and Society, graduate school of Chinese Academy of Sciences, Beijing.

WRITINGS:

(With J. A. Mistichelli and C. M. Roysdon) *Technology and Human Values in American Civilization,* Gale (Detroit), 1980.

(Editor with R. C. Post) *In Context: History and the History of Technology, Essays in Honor of Melvin Kranzberg,* Lehigh University Press (Bethlehem, PA), 1989.

(Editor with S. L. Goldman, M. Medina, and J. Sanmartin) *New Worlds, New Technologies, New Issues,* Lehigh University Press, 1992.

Contributor of numerous articles to periodicals, including *Western Pennsylvania Historical Magazine, Technology in Society, Bulletin of Science, Technology, and Society, Science, Technology, and Human Values* and *Research in Philosophy and Technology.* Editor of *Science, Technology, and Society Curriculum Development Newsletter,* 1977—; co-author of the annual bibliography for the Society of the History of Technology in *Technology and Culture,* 1984-89, contributor, 1990—; editor of *Science and Technology in the Eighteenth-Century Studies,* 1984; editor of *Working Papers in Technology Studies,* 1984-88; advisory editor of *Technology and Culture,* 1989—.

SIDELIGHTS: Stephen H. Cutcliffe told *CA:* "The central theme or interpretation that comes through my writing is an understanding of science and technology as value-laden social processes. That is, neither science nor technology are autonomous juggernauts with lives of their own. Rather they are complex enterprises taking place in specific contexts shaped by, and in turn shaping, human values that are reflected and refracted through societal institutions, whether they be cultural, political, or economic. Thus, certain vested interests on the part of consumers, corporate managers, government policymakers, financiers, and others define the problems, set the parameters within which solutions to those problems will be sought, and determine what results will be acceptable. In the end, of course, science and technology affect the shaping and defining values and institutions, such that the relationship is a dynamic one of constant and complex recursive interactions."

*   *   *

CZERNIAWSKI, Adam   1934-

PERSONAL: Born December 20, 1934, in Warsaw, Poland; son of Emil Jerzy (a military officer and civil servant) and Maria (Tynicka) Czerniawski; married Ann Christine Daker (head teacher at a high school), July 27, 1957; children: Irena Christine, Stefan Mark Emil. *Education:* University of London, B.A., 1955, B.A., 1967; University of Sussex, M.A., 1968; Oxford University, B.Phil., 1970.

ADDRESSES: Home—12 Drake Court, Tylney Ave., London SE19 1LW, England.

CAREER: Freelance writer, broadcaster, lecturer, 1986—. U.S. Information Agency, Munich, Germany, broadcaster, 1955-57; Northern Assurance Co., London, England, assistant superintendent, 1957-65; Medway College of Design, Rochester, England, lecturer in philosophy and literature, 1970-74; Thames Polytechnic, London, lecturer in philosophy, 1974-77, senior lecturer and acting head of philosophy division, 1977-78, senior course tutor, 1980-81.

MEMBER: Polish Society of Arts and Sciences Abroad, Trinity College Oxford Society, United Oxford and Cambridge University Club.

AWARDS, HONORS: Second prize for young writers, Union of Polish Writers Abroad (London), 1954; Abraham Woursell Foundation grant, University of Vienna, 1966-70; poetry prize, Union of Writers Abroad, 1967; poetry award, Koscielski Foundation, Geneva, 1971; Sulkowski prize for literary criticism, Poet's & Painter's Press, 1971; L'ordre du "Merite Culturel," Polish government, 1975; Translators' Award, Arts Council of Great Britain, 1976; Polish Writers' Union Translators' Prize (Warsaw), 1977; Hawthornden Castle writing fellow, 1985.

WRITINGS:

POETRY

Polowanie na jednorozca (title means "Hunting the Unicorn"), Poets' & Painters' Press (London), 1956.
Topografia wnetrza (title means "Topography of the Interior"), Institut Litteraire (Paris), 1962.
Sen cytadela gaj (title means "A Dream, a Citadel, a Grove"), Institut Litteraire, 1966.
Widok Delft (title means "A View of Delft"), Wydawnictwo Literackie (Krakow, Poland), 1973.
Wiek zloty 1969-1981 (title means "Golden Age") Institut Litteraire, 1982.
Wladza najwyzsza (title means "Supreme Authority"), Wydawnictwo Literackie, 1982.

Also author of *Jesien* (poetry; title means "Autumn") [Krakow, Poland] 1989.

EDITOR

Ryby na piasku (poetry; title means "Fish on the Strand"), Swiderski (London), 1965.
(And translator) *The Burning Forest* (anthology of modern Polish poetry), Bloodaxe (Newcastle Upon Tyne, England), 1988.
The Mature Laurel: Essays on Modern Polish Poetry, Dufor Editions (Chester Springs, PA), 1991.

TRANSLATOR

Tadeusz Rozewicz, *Faces of Anxiety,* Rapp & Whiting (London), 1969.
Rozewicz, *The Card-Index and Other Plays,* Calder & Boyars (London), 1969.
Rozewicz, *The Witnesses and Other Plays,* Calder & Boyars, 1970.
W. Tatarkiewicz, *History of Aesthetics,* Mouton (The Netherlands), 1970.

Rozewicz, *Selected Poems,* Penguin, 1976.
Artur Sandauer, *Bialoszewski,* Authors' Agency, 1979.
Leon Stroinski, *Window,* Oasis Books (London), 1979.
Rozewicz, *Conversation with the Prince and Other Poems,* Anvil Press, (London), 1982.
Leopold Staff, *An Empty Room,* Bloodaxe Books (Chester Springs, PA), 1983.
Rozewicz, *Mariage Blanc and the Hunger Artist Departs: Two Plays,* Marion Boyars, London, 1983.
Rozewicz, *The Trap,* City University of New York, 1984.
Roman Ingarden, *The Work of Music and the Problem of Its Identity,* Jean G. Harrell, editor, University of California (Berkeley), 1986.
Leszek Kolakowski, *The Presence of Myth,* University of Chicago Press, 1989.
Wislawa Szymborska, *People on a Bridge: Poems,* Forest Books (Boston), 1990.

Also translator of *Seven Polish Canadian Poets,* edited by W. Iwaniuk and F. Smieja, [Toronto], 1984, and C. K. Norwid's, *Poems,* Krakow, 1986. Contributing translator to *Ten Contemporary Polish Stories,* edited by E. Ordon, Wayne State University Press, 1958; *Polish Writing Today,* Penguin, 1967; *Poetry of the Committed Individual,* edited by Jon Silkin, Penguin, 1973; R. Ingarden's *Selected Papers on Aesthetics,* edited by P. J. MacCormick, Catholic University Press (Washington, DC), 1985; *Voices in the Gallery,* edited by D. & J. Abse, [London], 1986.

OTHER

Czesci mniejszej calosci (short stories; title means "Parts of a Smaller Whole"), Poets' & Painters' Press, 1964.
Liryka i druk (literary criticism; title means "Poetry and Print"), Poets' & Painters' Press, 1972.
Akt (short stories), Poets' & Painters' Press, 1975.
Wiersz Wspolczsny (literary essays; title means "The Contemporary Poem"), Poets' & Painters' Press, 1977.
Scenes from a Disturbed Childhood (autobiography), Serpent's Tail (London), 1991.
Koncert zycen, Staromiejski Dom Kultury (Warsaw), 1991.

Also author of introduction to Ewa Lipska's, *Poet? Criminal? Madman?,* 1991. Contributor to anthologies, including *Opisanie z pamieci,* edited by Andrzej Lam, PIW (Warsaw), 1965; *Explorations in Freedom,* edited by L. Tyrmand, Free Press, 1970; *Kolumbowie i wspolczesni,* edited by A. Lam, Czytelnik (Warsaw), 1972, 2nd revised edition, 1976; *Een Gevecht om Lucht,* edited by Jan-Willem Overeem and Ewa Dijk-Borkowska, Corrie Zelen, 1979; *Modern Poetry in Translation: 1983,* edited by D. Weissbort, (London), 1983; *Mala muza,* edited by A. Siomkajko, (Warsaw), 1986.

BIOGRAPHICAL/CRITICAL SOURCES:

BOOKS

Czaykowski, B. *Glossy do poezji Adama Czerniawskiego,*
    Archipelag (Berlin), 1986.
Lisiecka, A, Kto jest "ksieciem poetow"? [London], 1979.
Literatura Polska, [Warsaw], 1984.
Paulin, Tom, *Ireland and the English Crisis* [Newcastle],
    1984.
Slownik wspolczesnych pisarzy polskich [Warsaw], 1977.

PERIODICALS

Times (London), November 16, 1991, p. 50.
Times Literary Supplement, September 2-8, 1988, p. 955;
    October 6-12, 1989.*

D

DABYDEEN, Cyril 1945-

PERSONAL: Born October 15, 1945, in Berbice, British Guiana (now Guyana); immigrated to Canada, 1970; naturalized citizen, 1976; son of Abel (a farmer) and Hilda (a seamstress; maiden name, Oudit) Dabydeen; children: Alana. *Education:* Lakehead University, B.A. (with honors), 1973; Queen's University, Kingston, Ontario, M.A., 1974; M.P.A., 1975. *Politics:* "Free thinker, on the left." *Religion:* Ecumenical Christian. *Avocational interests:* Swimming, reading anthropology/mythology (Claude Levi Strauss), track and field and other sports, movies, traveling.

ADDRESSES: Home—106 Blackburn, Ottawa, Ontario, Canada K1N 8A7.

CAREER: Writer and editor. Schoolteacher in Guyana, 1961-70; Algonquin College, Ottawa, Ontario, Canada, teacher of communications, 1975-81; University of Ottawa, Ottawa, teacher of creative writing, 1986—. Reviewer for *Ottawa Journal,* 1975-78; organizer of poetry readings; has given readings in Britain, Denmark, the Caribbean, and throughout Canada. City of Ottawa, race relations coordinator, 1975-78; government of Canada, writer and editorial consultant, 1975-80; City of Ottawa's Anti-Apartheid Committee, chair, 1987—; Mayor's Advisory Committee on Visible Minorities, member; has worked in the Canadian federal government on race issues; Federation of Canadian Municipalities, coordinator of race relation.

MEMBER: League of Canadian Poets (selection committee member, 1983), Canadian Association of Commonwealth Language and Literature Studies, Canadian Asian Studies Association, Ottawa Independent Writers.

AWARDS, HONORS: Sandbach Parker Gold Medal, 1964, and First A. J. Seymour Lyric Poetry Prize, 1967, both from Government of Guyana; Louise Plumb Poetry Prize, 1978; Okanagan Fiction Prize from *Canadian Author and Bookman,* 1982; Ontario Arts Council award, 1977-80; Canada Council award, 1983; Poet Laureate of Ottawa, 1984-87.

WRITINGS:

POETRY

Poems in Recession, Sadeek Press (Georgetown, Guyana), 1972.
Distances, Fiddlehead Poetry Books, 1977.
Goatsong, illustrated by Sharon Katz, Mosaic Press/ Valley Editions, 1977.
Heart's Frame, Vesta Publications, 1979.
This Planet Earth, Borealis Press, 1979.
Elephants Make Good Stepladders, Third Eye (London, Ontario), 1982.
Islands Lovelier Than a Vision, Peepal Tree Press (Yorkshire, England), 1986.
Coastland: New and Selected Poems, 1973-1987, introduction by Jeremy Poynting, Mosaic Press, 1989.
(With Seymour Mayne and others) *Six Ottawa Poets,* Mosaic Press, 1990.
Stoning the Wind, TSAR (Toronto), 1994.
Discussing Columbus, Peepal Tree Press, 1994.

NOVELS

The Wizard Swami, Peepal Tree Press, 1989.
Dark Swirl, Peepal Tree Press, 1989.
Sometimes Hard, Longmans Green (London)), 1994.

SHORT STORIES

Still Close to the Island, Commoner's Publishing, 1980.
To Monkey Jungle, Third Eye, 1988.
Jogging in Havana, Mosaic Press, 1992.
Berbice Crossing, Peepal Tree Press, 1995.

EDITOR AND AUTHOR OF INTRODUCTION

A Shapely Fire: Changing the Literary Landscape (anthology), Mosaic Press, 1987.

Another Way to Dance: Anthology of Canadian-Asian Poets, Williams-Wallace, 1990.

Also author of reports for the Canadian municipal government. Work represented in anthologies, including *Fiddlehead Greens,* Oberon Press, 1980; *Caribbean Verse,* Penguin Books, 1985; and *Arrivals: Canadian Poetry in the Eighties,* Greenfield Review Press, 1988. Contributor to numerous periodicals, including *Fiddlehead, Quarry, Ariel, Dalhousie Review, Antigonish Review, Canadian Forum, Canadian Literature, Literary Review,* and *Kunapipi.*

WORK IN PROGRESS: Two novels, *Drums of My Flesh* and *Sun's Darkness.*

SIDELIGHTS: A native of Guyana, Cyril Dabydeen immigrated to Canada while in his twenties, experiencing firsthand the process of adapting to a foreign country. In his poetry and short stories Dabydeen empathizes with the problems of people who are displaced, lonely, and homeless. His interest in these subjects has led reviewers to liken his poetry to that of famed Latin American writer Pablo Neruda. Described as an original and exciting poet, Dabydeen won admiration with the collections *Distances, Goatsong, Heart's Frame,* and *This Planet Earth* for his clear, concise language, strong emotion, and vivid depictions of Guyana and Canada

With his fiction, often set in rural Canada, Dabydeen has garnered praise for careful, detached observations about his adopted country. Many of his characters immigrate to Canada to escape the history of colonialism and the poor economic prospects of their native countries. Expecting the "promised land," they feel alienated and unwelcome once they have arrived. In his story collection *Still Close to the Island* Dabydeen attacks the notion that hunger, poverty, and prejudice do not exist in well-to-do nations like Canada. A passage from the story "Mammita's Garden Cove," reprinted in *Literary Review,* describes the thoughts of a West Indian immigrant named Max as he searches unsuccessfully for employment: "Once more he thought about a job; if he didn't find one soon he might starve. But as the reality of this dawned on him he began laughing. No! No one starved in Canada; that only happened in such places as India or Africa. But definitely not Canada! A growling in his stomach reminded him of reality. A slight panic. Max stepped quickly, walking, looking around, feeling like a fugitive."

According to *World Literature Today* contributor Peter Nazareth there are fleeting instances of sympathy and connection between Dabydeen's characters, but little ac-

tion in his dream-like stories: "There are no climaxes. . . . It is the epiphany, the moment of illumination that comes out of an ordinary experience, which gives them meaning and shape."

Dabydeen once told *CA:* "I began writing in Guyana, where I was born. Growing up in the rural world of sugar plantations and rice fields, I was close to ordinary, simple folk. At the same time, colonial experience in what was then British Guiana made me see myself ambivalently (and not without anxiety), as a sort of 'little Englishman' who sought his values overseas, often in London, and later in New York and Toronto. It was the belief while living in the colony that nothing from an indigenous source was good, was worthy of emulation, or for one to take pride in. Self-contempt was the order of the day. In my writing I aim to explore the mythology of self in the context of traumatized society and people: to grapple with those early experiences, those feelings, and to universalize that experience through transcendence.

"Having moved to Canada, I began to see things in a broader, bigger light—to see the Caribbean as a whole, and the world of interrelationships between Old and New World cultures. I worked for a while in northern Ontario (my student days) planting trees, living with the native Ojibwa and Cree Indians in bush camps. My social awareness and experience broadened even further in mixing with these people. Now I am actively involved in the West Indian-Canadian and Asian-American writing scenes and have been editing works in both areas. I have also organized readings of these groups in most of the major cities across Canada."

BIOGRAPHICAL/CRITICAL SOURCES:

PERIODICALS

Globe and Mail (Toronto), September 13, 1986.
Literary Review, summer, 1986.
World Literature Today, autumn, 1986; summer, 1989.
World Literature Written in English, spring, 1983.

*   *   *

DANIELS, Bruce C(olin) 1943-

PERSONAL: Born August 27, 1943, in Baldwin, NY; son of Howard and Willa (Stich) Daniels; children: Elizabeth Howard, Abigail Mary, Nora Kate. *Education:* Syracuse University, B.A., 1964; University of Connecticut, M.A., 1967, Ph.D., 1970.

ADDRESSES: Office—Department of History, University of Winnipeg, Winnipeg, Manitoba, Canada R3B 2E9.

CAREER: U.S. Peace Corps, Washington, DC, volunteer worker in Bihar, India, 1964-65; University of Winnipeg,

Winnipeg, Manitoba, associate professor, 1970-80, professor of history, 1980—.

MEMBER: American Historical Association, Organization of American Historians, Canadian Historical Association (member of council, 1984-87), Canadian Association for American Studies (president, 1991-93), Institute of Early American History and Culture.

AWARDS, HONORS: Canada Council fellow, 1976-77; Social Sciences and Humanities Research Council Fellow, 1983-84; Fulbright scholar, 1993-94.

WRITINGS:

Connecticut's First Family, Pequot Press, 1975.
(Editor) *Town and County: Essays on Local Government in the American Colonies,* Wesleyan University Press (Middleton, CT), 1978.
The Connecticut Town: Growth and Development, Wesleyan University Press, 1979.
Dissent and Conformity on Narrangansett Bay: The Colonial Rhode Island Town, Wesleyan University Press, 1984.
(Editor) *Power and Status: Officeholding in the American Colonies,* Wesleyan University Press, 1986.
The Fragmentation of New England: Comparative Perspectives on Economic, Political, and Social Divisions in Eighteenth-Century New England, Greenwood Press (Westport, CT), 1988.
"Sober Mirth and Fancy Frolics": Leisure and Recreation in Colonial New England, St. Martin's (New York City), 1995.

Co-editor of *Canadian Review of American Studies,* 1978-87; member of editorial boards of *Canadian Journal of History,* 1978-88, *Social Science Quarterly,* 1980—, *Urban Historical Review,* 1982-83, *Journal of Popular Culture,* 1983—, *Historical Journal of Massachusetts,* 1983—, and *Revolt Studies,* 1984—; book review editor of *Urban Historical Review,* 1983-93; associate editor, *American National Biography,* 1991—; contributing editor, *Journal of American History,* 1994. Contributor to history journals.

WORK IN PROGRESS: Urbanization in Early New England; The American Revolution in International Popular Culture.

SIDELIGHTS: Bruce C. Daniels once told *CA:* "I am increasingly interested in the views of American history and society that are held by people living outside the United States. Living and working in India and Canada most of my adult life has fundamentally shaped my understanding of America's past."

BIOGRAPHICAL/CRITICAL SOURCES:

PERIODICALS

American Historical Review, October, 1979; October, 1985.

*   *   *

d'ARGYRE, Gilles
  See KLEIN, Gerard

*   *   *

DAVIDSON, Jeffrey P(hilip)   1951-

PERSONAL: Born January 13, 1951, in Hartford, CT; son of Emanuel (a teacher and school vice-principal) and Shirley (a sales representative; maiden name, Leader) Davidson; married Susan Millard (a nurse manager), December 9, 1989 (divorced); children: Valerie Ann. *Education:* University of Connecticut, B.S., 1973, M.B.A., 1974.

ADDRESSES: Home—2417 Honeysuckle Rd., Suite 2A, Chapel Hill, NC 27514.

CAREER: Burroughs Corp., East Hartford, CT, marketing representative, 1974-75; Profiles, Inc. (management consulting firm), Vernon, CT, project manager, 1975-77; EMAY Corp. (management consulting firm), Washington, DC, senior project manager, 1977-80; IMR Systems, Inc. (management consulting firm), Falls Church, VA, vice-president of marketing, 1980-84; author and professional speaker, 1984-94; executive director, Breathing Space Institute, 1994—. Has appeared on numerous television and radio talk shows, including *CBS Nightwatch* and *America in the Morning.*

MEMBER: American Marketing Association, Institute of Management Consultants, National Speakers Association, Washington Independent Writers, Washington Area Writers.

AWARDS, HONORS: Selected one of Outstanding Young Men in America, 1982 and 1986; state winner, Small Business Media Advocate of the Year, U.S. Small Business Administration, 1983-87, for books and articles; Executive of Distinction designation, American Institute of Management, 1984; selection as a Recommended Business Book, *Library Journal,* 1985, for *Marketing Your Consulting and Professional Services,* and 1987, for both *The Achievement Challenge: How to Be a "Ten" in Business* and *Getting New Clients;* Professional Insurance Communicator's Association award, 1986, for outstanding feature article; selection as one of Best Business Books of 1992, *Library Journal,* for *The Domino Effect: How to Grow Sales, Profits, and Market Share through Super Vision.*

WRITINGS:

(With Richard A. Connor, Jr.) *Marketing Your Consulting and Professional Services,* Wiley (New York City), 1985.

Checklist Management: The Eight-Hour Manager, National Press, 1987, published in England as *Essential Management Checklists: Marketing Your Community,* Public Technology, 1987.

Blow Your Own Horn: How to Get Ahead and Get Noticed, American Management Association (New York City), 1987.

(With Connor) *Getting New Clients,* Wiley, 1987, 2nd edition, 1993.

(With Don Beveridge, Jr.) *The Achievement Challenge: How to Be a "Ten" in Business,* Business One-Irwin (Homewood, IL), 1987.

Marketing on a Shoestring, Wiley, 1988, 2nd edition, 1994.

Avoiding the Pitfalls of Starting Your Own Business, Walker, 1988.

The Marketing Sourcebook for Small Business, Wiley, 1989.

Marketing for the Home-Based Business, Bob Adams (Brighton, MA), 1990, published as *Marketing to Home-Based Businesses,* Business One-Irwin, 1991.

(With Dave Yoho) *How to Have a Good Year Every Year,* Berkley Books, 1991.

Power and Protocol for Getting to the Top, Shapolsky Publishers, 1991.

Selling to the Giants: How to Become a Key Supplier to Large Corporations, Tab Books (Blue Ridge Summit, PA)/McGraw (New York City), 1991.

You Can Start Your Own Business, Washington Publications, 1991.

Breathing Space: Living and Working at a Comfortable Pace in a Sped-Up Society, Mastermedia, 1991, 2nd edition, 1995.

Cash Traps: Small Business Secrets for Reducing Costs and Improving Cash Flow, Wiley, 1992.

(With Donald J. Vlcek) *The Domino Effect: How to Grow Sales, Profits, and Market Share through Super Vision,* Business One-Irwin, 1992.

Your Bank: How to Get Better Service, Consumer Reports Books, 1992.

Contributor of articles to numerous periodicals, including *Business and Society Review, Entrepreneur, Executive Female, Personnel, Supervisory Management, World Executive Digest,* and *Working Woman.*

Some of Davidson's work has been published in numerous foreign countries and foreign languages, including Italian, Chinese, Japanese, Spanish, Portuguese, Hebrew, Dutch, Malay, and Indonesian.

SIDELIGHTS: In *Breathing Space: Living and Working at a Comfortable Pace in a Sped-Up Society,* Jeffrey P. Davidson addresses one of his major concerns: How to live and work at a comfortable pace while remaining competitive, balanced, and happy. While his previous books have centered on career enhancement, entrepreneurism, and personal achievement, Davidson now focuses his writing and lecturing on what he sees as today's fundamental challenges to individuals.

Davidson once told *CA:* "Today everybody is under pressure both on and off the job. We exist with an overabundance of people, choices, and information. Yet, because modern technology enables us to gain new information faster, we have greater expectations about what we need to accomplish in our lives.

"Nearly every aspect of American society has become more complex even since the mid-1980s. Learning new ways to manage and new ways to increase productivity takes its toll. *Merely living* in America today and participating as a functioning member of society guarantees that your day, week, month, year, and life—and your physical, emotional, and spiritual energy—will easily be depleted without the proper vantage point from which to approach each day.

"Right now, keen focus on a handful of priorities has never been more important for each of us. Yes, some compelling issues must be given short shrift. Otherwise you run the risk of being overwhelmed by more demanding issues, and feeling overwhelmed always intensifies the feeling of being overworked. *This is not how it has to be.* As an author, I have a vision. I see Americans leading balanced lives, with rewarding careers, happy home lives, and the ability to enjoy themselves. Our ticket to living and working at a comfortable pace is to not accommodate a way of being that doesn't support us."

BIOGRAPHICAL/CRITICAL SOURCES:

PERIODICALS

ABA Journal, December, 1985.
Baltimore Sun, July 10, 1994.
Boston Herald, January 5, 1992.
Chicago Tribune, June 23, 1991; January 10, 1993.
Christian Science Monitor, May 17, 1984.
Dallas Times Herald, December 5, 1991.
Executive Excellence, May, 1994.
Harvard Courant, July 31, 1985.
Los Angeles Times, June 15, 1985; November 10, 1992.
Miami Herald, June 17, 1985.
USA Today, January 8, 1992.
Washington Post, May 20, 1985; December 14, 1989; December 21, 1992.

DAVIES, Christie 1941-

PERSONAL: Given name is John Christopher Hughes Davies; surname is pronounced "*Day*-viss"; born December 25, 1941, in Sutton, Surrey, England; son of Christopher G. H. (an inspector of schools) and Marian (a teacher; maiden name, Johns) Davies. *Education:* Emmanuel College, Cambridge, B.A. (with first class honors), 1964, M.A., 1968, Ph.D.

ADDRESSES: Home—Reading, England. *Office*—Department of Sociology, University of Reading, Whiteknights, P.O. Box 218, Reading, Berkshire RG6 2AA, England. *Agent*—Laurence Pollinger Ltd., 18 Maddox St., London W1R 0EU, England.

CAREER: British Broadcasting Corporation, London, England, radio producer for *Third Programme,* 1967-69; University of Leeds, Leeds, England, lecturer in sociology, 1969-72; University of Reading, Reading, England, lecturer, 1972-75, senior lecturer in sociology, 1975-81, acting head of sociology, 1976-77, reader in sociology, 1981-84, head of sociology 1982-94, professor of sociology, 1984—, chair in sociology, 1990. Visiting lecturer at University of Bombay and Delhi University, both 1973-74, Jagiellonian University, 1991; Distinguished Scholars Interdisciplinary Lecturer at George Mason University, 1986; lecture tours for British Council. Member of the faculty board, Letters and Social Sciences of the University of Reading, 1973-77, 1978—; external examiner for Ph.D. theses and modular degrees at various universities; external assessor for fellowships. Member of editorial board, International Steering Committee for Humor Research.

MEMBER: Union Society, Cambridge (president, 1964).

AWARDS, HONORS: Salzburg Seminar in American Studies, fellow, 1977.

WRITINGS:

(With Ruth Brandon) *Wrongful Imprisonment: Mistaken Convictions, and Their Consequences,* Allen & Unwin (London), 1973.
(With Russell Lewis) *The Reactionary Joke Book,* Wolfe, 1973.
Permissive Britain: Social Change in the Sixties and Seventies, Pitman (London), 1975.
(Editor with Rajeev Dhavan and author of introduction) *Censorship and Obscenity,* Martin Robertson (Oxford), 1978.
Welsh Jokes, John Jones (Cardiff), 1978.
Ethnic Humor around the World: A Comparative Analysis, Indiana University Press (Bloomington), 1990.
Humor, Values, and Identity, Mouton (Berlin), in press.

Also contributor to books, including *The Boundaries of the State in Modern Britain,* edited by Simon Green and Richard Whiting, Cambridge University Press, 1995, and *Contemporary Issues in the Sociology of Death, Dying and Disposal,* edited by Glennys Howarth and Peter Jupp, Macmillan, 1995. Contributor to periodicals in India, Bulgaria, Switzerland, Ireland, Wales, Canada, United States and England, including *Quest, Irish Independent, Le Devoir, Vingt, New Quest, Daily Telegraph,* and *Wall Street Journal.* Contributor to academic journals, including *American Journal of Sociology, British Journal of Sociology, Journal of Strategic Studies, Policy Review, Humor, International Journal of Human Research, Annual Review of the Social Sciences of Religion,* and *British Journal of Sexual Medicine.* Member of editorial board, *Humor, the International Journal of Humor Research* and *Sociological Papers.* Also author of a number of radio and television scripts, and contributor of humorous fiction to various periodicals.

WORK IN PROGRESS: The Strange Death of Moral England, a collection of Davies' previous work on the sociology of morality; a book on the social position of those born out of wedlock who have come to occupy high positions.

* * *

DeLONG, Lea Rosson 1947-

PERSONAL: Born June 13, 1947, in Ferriday, LA; daughter of Aaron Kenneth (a civil engineer) and Patsy Ruth (a homemaker; maiden name, Smith) Rosson; married Harris Coggeshall DeLong (a marketing representative), September 1, 1979; children: Timothy Rosson, Catherine Rosson. *Education:* Cottey College, A.A., 1969; University of Oklahoma, B.A., 1971; University of Kansas, M.A., 1973, Ph.D., 1983.

ADDRESSES: Home—Des Moines, IA. *Office*—Department of Art, Drake University, 25th and University Ave., Des Moines, IA 50311.

CAREER: University of Kansas, Lawrence, assistant curator of Spencer Museum of Art, 1974-76; Drake University, Des Moines, IA, instructor, 1976-80, assistant professor, 1980-83, associate professor, 1983-90, adjunct associate professor of art, 1990—. Des Moines Art Center, adjunct curator, 1989-91.

MEMBER: College Art Association of America.

WRITINGS:

(With Gregg Narber) *New Deal Mural Projects in Iowa,* Drake University, 1983.
Nature's Forms/Nature's Forces: The Art of Alexandre Hogue, University of Oklahoma Press (Norman, OK), 1985.

New Deal Art of the Upper Midwest, Sioux City Art Center, 1988.

Experience Art: A Young People's Guide to the Des Moines Art Center Collection, Des Moines Art Center, 1991.

Contributor to *Chemistry Imagined: Reflections of Science,* Smithsonian Institution Press, 1993, and to *Woman's Art Journal.**

*   *   *

DELORIA, Vine (Victor), Jr. 1933-

PERSONAL: Born March 26, 1933, in Martin, SD; son of Vine Victor (a minister) and Barbara (Eastburn) Deloria; married Barbara Jeanne Nystrom, June 14, 1958; children: Philip, Daniel, Jeanne Ann. *Education:* Iowa State University, B.S., 1958; Lutheran School of Theology, Rock Island, IL, M.S.Th., 1963; University of Colorado, J.D., 1970. *Politics:* Republican. *Religion:* "Seven Day Absentist."

ADDRESSES: Office—Department of History, University of Colorado, Campus Box 234, Boulder, CO 80309-0234.

CAREER: McLaughlin Body Company, Moline, IL, welder, 1959-63; United Scholarship Service, Denver, CO, staff associate, 1963-64; National Congress of American Indians, Washington, DC, executive director, 1964-67; National Congress of American Indians FUND, Denver, CO, consultant on programs, 1968; Western Washington University, Bellingham, lecturer in college of ethnic studies, 1970-72; University of California at Los Angeles, lecturer at American Indian Cultural and Research Center, 1972-73; American Indian Resource Associates, Oglala, SD, researcher, 1973-74; American Indian Resource Consultants, Denver, CO, researcher, 1974-75; Pacific School of Religion, Berkeley, CA, visiting lecturer, 1975; New School of Religion, Pontiac, MI, visiting lecturer, 1976; Colorado College, Colorado Springs, visiting lecturer, 1977-78; University of Arizona, Tucson, visiting professor, spring, 1978, professor of law and political science, 1978-90, chair of American Indian studies, 1979-82; University of Colorado, Boulder, professor of American Indian studies, professor of history, adjunct professor of law, religious studies, and political science, 1990—.

Council on Indian Affairs, vice-chair, 1965-68; Board of Inquiry into Hunger and Malnutrition in the U.S.A., member, 1967-68; Episcopal Church, chair of Ad-Hoc Committee on Indian Work and member of executive council, 1968-69; Institute for the Development of Indian Law, chair and founder, 1971-76; American Civil Liberties Union, member of Indian Committee, 1976—; Museum of the American Indian, Heye Foundation, member

of board of trustees, 1977-82, 1984—, vice-chair of collections committee, 1990-92, chair, 1992-93. KRMA-TV, script writer for Indian series, 1972-74.

Member of board of directors, White Buffalo Council, 1964-65, Citizens' Crusade Against Poverty, 1965-66, National Office for the Rights of the Indigent, 1967-68, Southwest Intergroup Council, 1969-71 (executive director, 1972), Model Urban Indian Centers Project, 1971-73, Oglala Sioux Legal Rights Foundation, 1971-74, Colorado Humanities Program, 1975-77, Denver Public Library Foundation, 1977-79, American Indian Development, Inc., 1978-82, Daybreak Films, 1979-81, Field Foundation, 1980-86, Indian Rights Association, 1980-87, Foundation for the Preservation of American Indian Art and Culture, 1985—, Institute of the North American West, 1989—, Morning Star Foundation, 1989—, Indian Law Resource Center, 1990—, Howard Simons Fund, 1990—, Native American Land Research and Policy Institute, 1991—, Southwest Voter Education Project, 1991—, and Friends of the Denver Public Library, 1992—; member of advisory council, National Indian Youth Council, 1976—, Sun Valley Center for the Arts and Humanities, 1976-78, 1980-83, Nebraska Educational Television Network, 1976-78, Center for Land Grant Studies, 1976-79, Institute of the American West, 1981-83, Disability Rights Education and Defense Fund, Inc., 1981-87 (member of National Policy Council, 1987—), and Save the Children, 1983-84. Consultant to American Lutheran Church, 1976-78, and U.S. Senate Select Committee on Aging. *Military service:* U.S. Marine Corps Reserve, 1954-56.

MEMBER: American Judicature Society, Authors Guild, Advocates for the Arts, American Indian Resource Association (vice-chair, 1973-75), Colorado Authors League.

AWARDS, HONORS: Anisfield-Wolf Award, 1970, for *Custer Died for Your Sins: An Indian Manifesto;* special citation, National Conference of Christians and Jews, 1971, for *We Talk, You Listen: New Tribes, New Turf;* D.H.Litt., Augustana College, 1972; Indian Achievement Award, Indian Council Fire, 1972; named one of eleven "Theological Superstars of the Future," Interchurch Features, 1974; D.H.L., Scholastica College, 1976, Hamline University, 1979, and Northern Michigan University, 1991; honorary professorship, Athabasca University, 1977; Distinguished Alumni Award, Iowa State University, 1977, and University of Colorado School of Law, 1985; State of Michigan Senate Resolution Number 118 named "A Resolution Honoring Vine Deloria, Jr."

WRITINGS:

EDITOR

Of Utmost Good Faith, Straight Arrow Books, 1971.

(And author of introduction) Jennings Cooper Wise, *The Red Man in the New World Drama: A Politico-Legal Study with a Pageantry of American History,* Macmillan, 1971.

(With Sandra L. Cadwalader) *The Aggressions of Civilization: Federal Indian Policy since the 1880s,* Temple University Press (Philadelphia), 1984.

A Sender of Words: Essays in Memory of John G. Neihardt, Howe Brothers (Salt Lake City), 1984.

American Indian Policy in the Twentieth Century, University of Oklahoma Press (Norman), 1984.

Frank Waters: Man and Mystic, Swallow Press (Athens, OH), 1993.

Also editor of *A Ballad of the West: Seekers of the Fleece,* by Bobby Bridger, 2nd edition, Augustine.

OTHER

Custer Died for Your Sins: An Indian Manifesto, Macmillan, 1969, with new preface by Deloria, 1988.

We Talk, You Listen: New Tribes, New Turf, Macmillan, 1970.

God Is Red, Grosset, 1973, 2nd edition published as *God Is Red: A Native View of Religion,* North American Press, 1992.

Behind the Trail of Broken Treaties: An Indian Declaration of Independence, Delacorte (New York City), 1974.

The Indian Affair, Friendship (New York City), 1974.

A Better Day for Indians, Field Foundation, 1976.

Indians of the Pacific Northwest: From the Coming of the White Man to the Present Day, Doubleday (New York City), 1977.

The Metaphysics of Modern Existence, Harper (New York City), 1979.

(With Clifford M. Lytle) *American Indians, American Justice,* University of Texas Press (Austin), 1983.

(With Lytle) *The Nations Within: The Past and Future of American Indian Sovereignty,* Pantheon (New York City), 1984.

Indian Education in America: Eight Essays by Vine Deloria, Jr., American Indian Science and Engineering Society, 1991.

Contributor to books, including *Taxing Those They Found Here,* by Jay Vincent White, Institute for the Development of Indian Law, 1972; *Damned Indians,* by Michael L. Lawson, University of Oklahoma Press, 1982; and *The Dream Seekers: Native American Visionary Traditions of the Great Plains,* by Lee Irwin, University of Oklahoma Press, 1994.

Member of editorial or advisory boards, American Indian Historical Society, 1971-72; *American Indian Cultural and Research Center Journal,* 1972—; Clearwater Press, 1972-78; *Integrateducation,* 1975-82; *Explorations in Eth-*

nic Studies, 1977-82; *The Historical Magazine of the Episcopal Church,* 1977-82; *Katallagete,* 1977-85; *Colorado,* 1979—; *Journal of International and Comparative Law,* 1980—; *Studies in American Indian Literature,* 1981—; *Shaman's Drum,* 1984—; *Winds of Change,* 1987—; and *Native Peoples Magazine,* 1989—. Contributing editor, Race Relations Information Center, 1974-75; *National Forum,* 1979-81; and *Adherent Forum,* 1981-85.

WORK IN PROGRESS: Research on Indian legends concerning the creation of mountains, rivers, and other natural phenomena; research on Indian treaties, social problems, and political history.

SIDELIGHTS: "Among his people Vine Deloria Jr. has achieved a status somewhat similar to that of Sitting Bull's leadership of the Sioux tribes a century ago," writes Dee Brown in the *New York Times Book Review.* A Standing Rock Sioux lawyer and educator, Deloria is perhaps the most prominent advocate of Native American nationalism in the country. Brought to public attention in 1969 with the publication of his first book, *Custer Died for Your Sins: An Indian Manifesto,* Deloria, says Douglas N. Mount of *Publishers Weekly,* "wants to be the red man's Ralph Nader." He must, states Nancy Oestreich Lurie in *Saturday Review,* "be considered a bona fide modern Indian and an experienced, informed activist in Indian organizational work." To that end, he has, in addition to having served as executive director of the National Congress of American Indians and chair of the Institute for the Development of Indian Law, written several books that serve as legal and historical sourcebooks as well as sharply defined statements of Indian nationalism.

Custer Died for Your Sins is both a scathing indictment of white America's treatment of Indians and an articulation of the goal of Indian activists: an existence that is culturally but not economically separate. J. A. Phillips of *Best Sellers* notes that if this book "is indicative of Deloria's methods, he's more interested in results than in being tactful. Nauseated by the traditional Indian image, he asserts the worth if not the dignity of the redman and blasts the political, social, and religious forces that perpetuate the Little Big Horn and wigwam stereotyping of his people." *Custer Died for Your Sins* "is truly an Indian book," declares Lurie. "[Deloria] should shake a patronizing public, self-righteous benefactors, and preciously scientific scholars into a realization that the day is past when we can talk or write as if Indians were either illiterate or extinct, no matter how benevolent or objective our intentions."

Yet "Deloria opposes militant confrontation with white society," observes W. Roger Buffalohead in *Pacific Historical Review.* "Rather, he argues, struggles in the 'intellectual arena' will bring about the desired aims: self-determination in all phases of Indian life and a humane and personalized alternative to contemporary industrialized urban society." "Perhaps all that Deloria is asking of . . . the government and other 'friends,' " Lurie surmises, "is that, if they cannot agree absolutely that the tribals actually will inherit the earth, they will agree to help Indians get a chance to try to inherit something."

A *Time* critic writes that what Deloria really wants to talk about, aside from the origins of scalping and the differences between Black and Indian nationalism, is something "few white Americans know anything about—termination and tribalism." Termination is a U.S. Government policy designed to cut federal aid to Indians, close down reservations, and blend all remaining Indians into the American economic and cultural mainstream. The *Time* critic says that in Deloria's opinion, "the termination policy, which implies integration of Indians, is a loser's game." Deloria sees tribalism—whereby peoplehood, land, and religion form a single covenantal relationship that gives each community unique character—as the key to the whole Indian struggle, but he adds that it may also be the Indians' greatest liability. In an interview with *Mount,* he describes tribalism as "a way of life, a way of thinking. . . . A great tradition which is timeless, which has nothing to do with the sequence of events. This creates a wonderful relaxing atmosphere, a tremendous sense of invulnerability." But he cautions that it also fosters the impression that the white man will just go away and leave the Indian alone.

Tribalism is also the subject of *We Talk, You Listen: New Tribes, New Turf.* Examining what he considers to be the deteriorating core of contemporary technological society, Deloria attacks the corporate patterns of American life, advocates a return to tribal social organization, and describes the tribal characteristics he perceives in American minority groups. Cecil Eby of *Book World* writes that in this book, as well as in *Custer Died for Your Sins,* Deloria "describes the thrust of the Red-Power movement without anointing himself as its oracle or its official spokesman. . . . [He] brings into focus the moods and habitat of the contemporary Indian as seen by a Standing Rock Sioux, not by a research anthropologist or a jobber in the basketry trades. He peels away layers of tinsel and feathers heaped upon the Indian by misinformed whites . . . and he reveals an uncanny ability for impaling them on the fine points of their own illogic." However, N. Scott Momaday, writing in the *New York Review of Books,* considers Deloria's portrayal of the contemporary Indian weak: "Deloria is a thoughtful man, and he is articulate as well; but [*Custer Died for Your Sins* and *We Talk, You Listen*] are disappointing in one respect: they tell us very little about Indians, after all. In neither book is there any real evocation of that spirit and mentality which distinguishes the Indian as a man and as a race. This seems all the more regrettable in view of the fact that he really knows something about the subject by virtue of blood as well as experience."

In *God Is Red,* Deloria, the son of an Indian Episcopalian minister and himself seminary-trained, not only attempts to evoke that spirit and mentality which is unique to the Indian but argues that its theological basis in tribal religions seems to be "more at home in the modern world than Christian ideas and Western man's traditional concepts." Asserting that Christianity inculcates and justifies imperialism, rootlessness, and ecocide, Deloria maintains that America can survive only if there is a revolution in theological concepts. "Indian people," he declares in *God Is Red,* "have the possibility of total withdrawal from American society because of their special legal status. They can, when necessary, return to a recognized homeland where time is static and the world becomes a psychic unity again." Peter Mayer says in *Best Sellers* that "Deloria could have made his point—that Indian religious practices are far more in accord with the necessities of contemporary life than are Christian—without dredging up the many failures of the sons of the Church upon earth. . . . But read the book; I found it hard to put down."

Serving as an Indian treaties expert, Deloria was the first witness for the defense in the Wounded Knee trial of 1974, held in St. Paul, Minnesota. His book *Behind the Trail of Broken Treaties: An Indian Declaration of Independence* not only surpasses prior accounts of the prolonged armed confrontation between Sioux Indians and federal forces at Wounded Knee, South Dakota, in early 1973, according to Dee Brown in the *New York Times Book Review,* but "it is also a compelling argument for a reopening of the treaty-making procedure between Indian tribes and the U.S. Government." L. A. Howard of *Best Sellers* reveals that "step by step, argument by argument, [Deloria] refutes those who would label treaty-making as an implausible way at best for the United States to conduct its relations with the American Indians." Leo E. Oliva notes in *Library Journal* that Deloria does not consider this proposal "as a panacea, but simply as a necessary first step" to insure the survival of Indian tribes, their lands, and their ways of life. What Deloria hopes for is a new treaty relationship that will give Indian tribes the status of quasi-international independence, with the United States acting as protector.

BIOGRAPHICAL/CRITICAL SOURCES:

BOOKS

Contemporary Literary Criticism, Volume 21, Gale (Detroit), 1982.
Deloria, Vine, Jr., *Custer Died for Your Sins: An Indian Manifesto,* Macmillan, 1969.

Deloria, *God Is Red,* Grosset, 1973.

Gridley, Marian E., *Contemporary American Indian Leaders,* Dodd (New York City), 1972.

Gridley, editor, *Indians of Today,* I.C.F.P., 1971.

Native North American Literature, Gale, 1994.

PERIODICALS

America, March 16, 1974, pp. 198-200; May 22, 1976, pp. 456-57.

American Anthropologist, Volume 73, number 4, 1971, pp. 953-55; Volume 77, number 1, 1975, p. 109.

American Political Science Review, December, 1976, pp. 1306-07.

Best Sellers, October 15, 1969; November 15, 1973, p. 363; September 1, 1974, p. 254.

Booklist, September 1, 1977, p. 38.

Book World, October 4, 1970, p. 4.

Choice, December, 1974, p. 1508; April, 1975, p. 256.

Christian Century, February 18, 1970, p. 213; March 7, 1984, pp. 256-57.

Christian Science Monitor, February 26, 1970; January 2, 1974, p. F7.

Commonweal, February 6, 1970, p. 515.

Ethics, January, 1985, pp. 398-99.

Harper's, November, 1970, p. 134.

Library Journal, August, 1974, p. 1923.

Mademoiselle, April, 1971.

Nation, January 26, 1970, pp. 86-88; February 9, 1974, pp. 186-87.

New Yorker, October 24, 1970, p. 76.

New York Review of Books, April 8, 1971, pp. 39-42.

New York Times Book Review, November 9, 1969, p. 46; September 13, 1970, pp. 8, 10; November 24, 1974; April 11, 1993, p. 22.

Pacific Historical Review, November, 1970, pp. 353-54.

Progressive, April, 1990, p. 24.

Publishers Weekly, December 1, 1969.

Saturday Review, October 4, 1969, pp. 39-41, 80-81.

School Library Journal, April, 1977, p. 76.

Southwest Review, autumn, 1985, pp. 550-51.

Time, October 10, 1969, p. 102.

Village Voice, January 29, 1970, pp. 8, 33, 48.

Western American Literature, spring, 1985, pp. 79-80.

Western Historical Quarterly, October, 1984, pp. 451-52; January, 1986, pp. 77-78.*

*   *   *

DIAMOND, Petra
See SACHS, Judith

DIAMOND, Rebecca
See SACHS, Judith

*   *   *

DICKEY, James (Lafayette) 1923-

PERSONAL: Born February 2, 1923, in Buckhead, GA; son of Eugene (a lawyer) and Maibelle (Swift) Dickey; married Maxine Syerson, November 4, 1948 (died October 28, 1976); married Deborah Dodson, December 30, 1976; children: (first marriage) Christopher Swift, Kevin Webster; (second marriage) Bronwen Elaine. *Education:* Attended Clemson College (now University), 1942; Vanderbilt University, B.A. (magna cum laude), 1949, M.A., 1950.

ADDRESSES: Home—4620 Lelia's Court, Lake Katherine, Columbia, SC 29206. *Office*—Department of English, University of South Carolina, Columbia, SC 29208.

CAREER: Poet, novelist, and essayist. Instructor in English at Rice Institute (now Rice University), Houston, TX, 1950 and 1952-54, and University of Florida, Gainesville, 1955-56; worked in advertising, 1956-60, first as copywriter for McCann-Erickson, New York City, then as official for Liller, Neal, Battle & Lindsey and Burke Dowling Adams, both in Atlanta, GA; poet in residence at Reed College, Portland, OR, 1963-64, San Fernando Valley State College (now California State University, Northridge), Northridge, CA, 1964-65, University of Wisconsin—Madison, 1966, University of Wisconsin—Milwaukee, 1967, and Washington University, St. Louis, MO, 1968; Georgia Institute of Technology, Atlanta, Franklin Distinguished Professor of English, 1968; University of South Carolina, Columbia, professor of English and poet in residence, 1969—. Library of Congress, consultant in poetry, 1966-68, honorary consultant in American Letters, 1968-71. *Military service:* U.S. Army Air Forces, served in World War II, flew 100 combat missions in 418th Night Fighter Squadron. U.S. Air Force, served in Korean War; awarded Air Medal.

MEMBER: American Academy of Arts and Sciences, American Academy of Arts and Letters, National Institute of Arts and Letters, Phi Beta Kappa.

AWARDS, HONORS: Sewanee Review poetry fellowship, 1954-55; *Poetry* magazine, Union League Civic and Arts Foundation Prize, 1958, Vachel Lindsay Prize, 1959, and Levinson Prize, 1982; Guggenheim fellowship, 1961-62; National Book Award for poetry and Melville Cane Award of Poetry Society of America, both 1966, for *Buckdancer's Choice;* National Institute of Arts and Letters grant, 1966; Medicis prize for best foreign book of the year (Paris), 1971, for *Deliverance;* invited to read poem "The

Strength of Fields" at Inauguration of U.S. President Jimmy Carter, 1977; *New York Quarterly* Poetry Day Award, 1977; invited to read poem "For a Time and Place" at second inauguration of Richard Riley, governor of South Carolina, 1983.

WRITINGS:

POETRY

Into the Stone, and Other Poems, Scribner (New York City), 1960.

Drowning with Others (also see below), Wesleyan University Press (Middletown, CT), 1962.

Helmets (also see below), Wesleyan University Press, 1964.

Two Poems of the Air, Centicore Press (Portland, OR), 1964.

Buckdancer's Choice, Wesleyan University Press, 1965.

Poems, 1957-1967 (selections issued as miniature edition prior to publication), Wesleyan University Press, 1968.

The Eye-Beaters, Blood, Victory, Madness, Buckhead, and Mercy, Doubleday (Garden City, NY), 1970.

Exchanges, Bruccoli Clark (Columbia, SC), 1971.

The Zodiac (long poem; based on Hendrik Marsman's poem of the same title), Doubleday and Bruccoli Clark, 1976.

The Strength of Fields (poem; also see below), Bruccoli Clark, 1977.

Tucky the Hunter (for children), Crown (New York City), 1978.

The Strength of Fields (collection; title poem previously published separately), Doubleday, 1979.

Head Deep in Strange Sounds: Improvisations from the UnEnglish, Palaemon Press (Winston-Salem, NC), 1979.

Scion, Deerfield Press (Deerfield, MA), 1980.

The Early Motion: "Drowning with Others" and "Helmets," Wesleyan University Press, 1981.

Falling, May Day Sermon, and Other Poems, Wesleyan University Press, 1981.

The Eagle's Mile (also see below), Bruccoli Clark, 1981.

Puella, Doubleday, 1982.

Vaermland: Poems Based on Poems, Palaemon Press, 1982.

False Youth: Four Seasons, Pressworks (Dallas, TX), 1983.

The Central Motion, Wesleyan University Press, 1983.

(With Sharon Anglin Kuhne) *Intervisions: Poems and Photographs,* Visualternatives, 1983.

Veteran Birth: The Gadfly Poems, 1947-1949, Palaemon Press, 1983.

Bronwen, the Traw, and the Shape Shifter: A Poem in Four Parts (for children), illustrations by Richard Jesse Watson, Harcourt, 1986.

Of Prisons and Ideas, Harcourt, 1987.

Summons, Bruccoli Clark, 1988.

The Eagle's Mile (collection), Wesleyan University Press, 1990.

The Whole Motion: Collected Poems, 1945-1992, Wesleyan University Press, 1992.

Poems represented in many anthologies, including: *Contemporary American Poetry,* edited by Donald Hall, Penguin, 1962; *Where Is Viet Nam? American Poets Respond,* edited by Walter Lowenfels, Doubleday, 1967; *The Norton Anthology of Poetry,* revised shorter edition, edited by Alexander W. Allison, Herbert Barrows, Caesar R. Blake, Arthur J. Carr, Arthur M. Eastman, and Hubert M. English, Jr., Norton, 1975; *The Norton Anthology of American Literature,* Volume 2, edited by Ronald Gottesman, Laurence B. Holland, William H. Pritchard, and David Kalstone, Norton, 1979.

PROSE

The Suspect in Poetry (criticism), Sixties Press (Madison, MN), 1964.

A Private Brinksmanship (lecture given at Pitzer College, June 6, 1965), Castle Press (Pasadena), 1965.

Spinning the Crystal Ball: Some Guesses at the Future of American Poetry (lecture given at Library of Congress, April 24, 1967), Library of Congress (Washington, DC), 1967.

Metaphor as Pure Adventure (lecture given at Library of Congress, December 4, 1967), Library of Congress, 1968.

Babel to Byzantium: Poets and Poetry Now (criticism), Farrar, Straus (New York City), 1968.

Deliverance (novel; Literary Guild selection; excerpt entitled "Two Days in September" published in *Atlantic Monthly,* February, 1970; also see below), Houghton (Boston), 1970.

Self-Interviews (informal monologues; excerpt entitled "The Poet Tries to Make a Kind of Order" published in *Mademoiselle,* September, 1970), recorded and edited by Barbara Reiss and James Reiss, Doubleday, 1970.

Sorties: Journals and New Essays, Doubleday, 1971.

(With Hubert Shuptrine) *Jericho: The South Beheld* (Book-of-the-Month Club alternate selection), Oxmoor (Birmingham, AL), 1974.

(With Marvin Hayes) *God's Images: The Bible, a New Vision,* Oxmoor, 1977.

The Enemy from Eden, Lord John Press (Northridge, CA), 1978.

In Pursuit of the Grey Soul, Bruccoli Clark, 1978.

The Water Bug's Mittens (Ezra Pound Lecture at University of Idaho), Bruccoli Clark, 1980.

The Starry Place between the Antlers: Why I Live in South Carolina, Bruccoli Clark, 1981.

Night Hurdling: Poems, Essays, Conversations, Commencements, and Afterwords, Bruccoli Clark, 1983.
Alnilam (novel), Doubleday, 1987.
Wayfarer: A Voice from the Southern Mountains, Oxmoor House, 1988.
Southern Light, with photography by James Valentine, Oxmoor House, 1991.
To the White Sea (novel), Houghton, 1993.

Contributor to books, including *Modern Southern Literature in Its Cultural Setting,* edited by Louis D. Rubin, Jr., and Robert D. Jacobs, Doubleday, 1961; *Poets on Poetry,* edited by Howard Nemerov, Basic Books, 1966; *Pages: The World of Books, Writers, and Writing,* Volume 1, Gale, 1976; *Conversations with Writers,* Volume 1, Gale, 1977; *Dictionary of Literary Biography,* Volume 5: *American Poets since World War II,* Gale, 1980; and *From the Green Horseshoe: Poems by James Dickey's Students,* University of South Carolina Press, 1987.

OTHER

(Adapter with others of English version) Evgenii Evtushenko, *Stolen Apples: Poetry,* Doubleday, 1971.
Deliverance (screenplay; based on Dickey's novel of the same title; produced by Warner Bros., 1972), Southern Illinois University Press (Carbondale), 1982.
(With Charles Fries) *Call of the Wild* (screenplay; based on the novel by Jack London), produced by National Broadcasting Co. (NBC-TV), 1976.

Also author of screenplays *To Gene Bullard* and *The Sentence.* Contributor of poems, essays, articles, and reviews to more than thirty periodicals, including *Atlantic Monthly, Harper's, Hudson Review, Nation, New Yorker, Paris Review, Poetry, Sewanee Review, Times Literary Supplement,* and *Virginia Quarterly Review.*

WORK IN PROGRESS: Crux, a novel; two books of poetry, *Real God, Roll* and *Peace-Raids;* a book on Appalachia, *The Wilderness of Heaven,* with Hubert Shuptrine.

SIDELIGHTS: James Dickey is widely regarded as a major American poet because of his unique vision and style. "It is clear," says Joyce Carol Oates in her *New Heaven, New Earth: The Visionary Experience in Literature,* "that Dickey desires to take on 'his' own personal history as an analogue to or a microscopic exploration of twentieth-century American history, which is one of the reasons he is so important a poet." Winner of both the 1966 National Book Award and the Melville Cane Award for *Buckdancer's Choice,* Dickey has been called an expansional poet, not only because the voices in his work loom large enough to address or represent facets of the American experience, but also because his violent imagery and eccentric style exceed the bounds of more traditional

norms, often producing a quality he describes as "country surrealism."

One of Dickey's principal themes, usually expressed through a direct confrontation between or a surreal juxtaposition of the world of nature and the world of civilized man, is the need to intensify life by maintaining contact with the primitive impulses, sensations, and ways of seeing suppressed by modern society. It is a theme made explicit in his internationally bestselling novel *Deliverance* and is one given much attention in critical reviews. Through his poetry and prose, Dickey has come to be known as a shaman of our culture, for as Joan Bobbitt writes in *Concerning Poetry,* he "sees civilization as so far removed from nature, its primal antecedent, that only [grotesque] aberrations can aptly depict their relationship and, as he implies, possibly restore them to harmony and order."

Although he started writing poetry in 1947 at the age of twenty-four, Dickey did not become a full-time poet until thirteen years later. After earning a master's degree in 1950, he taught and lectured at several colleges for six years, but when some of his poems were construed to be obscene, he decided to forsake academic life for the advertising business. "I thought if my chosen profession, teaching, was going to fall out to be that sort of situation," he says in *Conversations with Writers,* "I'd rather go for the buck and make some damn dough in the market place. I had the confidence of Lucifer in myself by that time, and I was beginning to appear all over the place in the *Hudson Review, Partisan* [Review], *Sewanee* [Review], *Kenyon* [Review], and so on. I figured that the kind of thing that an advertising writer would be able to write, I could do with the little finger of the left hand, and they were getting paid good dough for it. I happened to have been right."

Dickey got a job with McCann-Erickson, the biggest ad agency in New York at the time, and wrote jingles for its Coca-Cola account. Later, he went to Liller, Neal, Battle & Lindsey in Atlanta, GA, for twice the salary, working on potato chips and fertilizer accounts, and then jumped agencies again for still another increase, becoming an executive with Burke Dowling Adams, where his primary concern was the Delta Airlines account. Robert W. Hill reports in *Dictionary of Literary Biography* that by the late 1950s, Dickey was earning enough to have a secure future in the business. But after his first book, *Into the Stone, and Other Poems,* was published in 1960, Dickey left advertising to devote all his time to poetry. "There could have been no more unpromising enterprise or means of earning a livelihood than that of being an American poet," he admits in *Conversations with Writers.* "It's different now. They're still having a relatively rocky road, but it ain't like it was when I used to give readings sometimes for maybe ten or fifteen dollars, where there would be five people in the audiences, three of them relatives."

Dickey's emotional attachment to his craft—obviously great enough to lead him to abandon a lucrative career in advertising—surfaced early in his writing career. "I came to poetry with no particular qualifications," he recounts in Howard Nemerov's *Poets on Poetry.* "I had begun to suspect, however, that there is a poet—or a kind of poet—buried in every human being like Ariel in his tree, and that the people whom we are pleased to call poets are only those who have felt the need and contrived the means to release this spirit from its prison."

In seeking the means to liberate his poetic spirit, Dickey concentrated at first on rhythms, on anapests and iambs. "Although I didn't care for rhyme and the 'packaged' quality which it gives even the best poems," he says in *Poets on Poetry,* "I did care very much for meter, or at least rhythm." With his prize-winning collection, *Buckdancer's Choice,* he began using the split line and free verse forms that have come to be associated with his work. But perhaps the most recognizable feature of his stylistic development has been his ambitious experimentation with language and form—inverted or odd syntax, horizontal spaces within lines, spread-eagled and ode-like shaped poems. Dickey's poems, writes Paul Zweig in the *New York Times Book Review,* "are like richly modulated hollers; a sort of rough, American-style bel canto advertising its freedom from the constraints of ordinary language. Dickey's style is so personal, his rhythms so willfully eccentric, that the poems seem to swell up and overflow like that oldest of American art forms, the boast."

According to David Kalstone in another *New York Times Book Review* article, Dickey's "achievement has been to press the limit of language and, in his criticism, to point up the strengths of other writers who do: Hart Crane, [D. H.] Lawrence, [Theodore] Roethke." L. M. Rosenberg expresses a similar sentiment in the *Chicago Tribune Book World.* Claiming that for "sheer beauty and passion we have no greater spokesman, nor do we have any poet more powerfully, naturally musical [than Dickey]," Rosenberg maintains that Dickey's "experiments with language and form are the experiments of a man who understands that one of the strangest things about poetry is the way it looks on the page: It just isn't normal. The question of how to move the reader's eye along the page, particularly as it makes an unnatural jump from line to line . . . how to slow the reader down or speed him up, how to give words back their original, almost totemic power—that's something any poet thinks a lot about, and it's something Dickey works with almost obsessively."

Dickey's stylistic endeavors, however, only partially explain why he is, in the minds of several critics, the most frequently discussed American poet of his generation. As noted above in *Poets on Poetry,* Dickey admits that he considers style subordinate to the spirit of poetry, the "indi-

vidually imaginative" vision of the poet, and, according to William Meredith in the *New York Times Book Review,* he consequently looks "for shapes and rhythms that correspond exactly to the kind of testimony his poems have always been. When he is testifying to an experience that declares its shape and meaning eloquently—'The Shark's Parlor' and 'Falling' are examples of this—the poems have form in [Ezra] Pound's phrase, as a tree has form." But, says William Heyen in the *Southern Review,* in addition to the unity of form and content, there is in Dickey's poetry and criticism "an emphasis on the humanism, or the morality or larger concerns of poetry. There's the idea that what the poet has to reach for is not necessarily affirmation, but, yes, a kind of affirming of values."

A primary thematic concern of Dickey's, one well served by his vigorous style, is the need "to get back wholeness of being, to respond full-heartedly and full-bodiedly to experience," observes Anatole Broyard of the *New York Times.* In *Poets on Poetry,* Dickey recalls that the subject matter of his early poems came from the principal incidents of his life, "those times when I felt most strongly and was most aware of the intense reality of the objects and people I moved among. If I were to arrange my own poems in some such scheme, chronologizing them, they would form a sort of story of this kind."

Despite the many allusions to his own life which he includes in his poetry, Dickey "is able to assimilate and report the experiences of others and himself, coming to that kind of peculiarly Dickeyesque fusion of selves so powerfully worked in 'Drinking from a Helmet,' 'Slave Quarters,' and 'The Firebombing,' " claims Hill. "This aesthetic viewpoint, with the speaker self-consciously observing, knowing that he has a perspective that is momentary and unique, that the time and the place are special, that the voice of the visionary observer is the only one to deal with the striking matter before him, emphasizes Dickey's dedication to art, to the exploration of the creative process, especially with regard to the use of narrative voice under special, extreme conditions."

Extreme conditions permeate Dickey's work. "To make a radical simplification," writes Monroe K. Spears in *Dionysus and the City: Modernism in Twentieth-Century Poetry,* "the central impulse of Dickey's poetry may be said to be that of identifying with human or other creatures in moments of ultimate confrontation, of violence and truth. A good example is [the poem] 'Falling,' which imagines the thoughts and feelings of an airline stewardess, accidentally swept through an emergency door, as she falls thousands of feet to her death" in a field in Kansas. Alive as she hurtles through space, she strips and imagines making love "in a furious, death-defying motion toward fertile farms and sensuous people who must in their blood understand even such a strange, naked ritual," explains Robert

W. Hill. "Hers is a dance all the way to death; she makes a poem of her last life and a fertility prayer of her last breath: 'AH, GOD—.' "

Many of Dickey's poems explore moments of being as known by horses, dogs, deer, bees, boars, and other inhabitants of non-human worlds. In "The Sheep Child," for example, a creature half child and half sheep (the result of boys coupling with sheep) speaks out from a jar of formaldehyde. The poem "attains very nearly the power of mythic utterance," maintains Hill, for the sheep child "shows its magnified view of the truth of two worlds," the fusion of man and nature, with an "eternal, unyielding vision." In Hill's opinion, "The Sheep Child" is "the most radical expression of Dickey's sense of transcendence in fusing man and nature to achieve 'imperishable vision,' " but it is not the only such expression.

"Everywhere in [Dickey's] body of writing in-touchness with 'the other forms of life' stands forth as a primary value," asserts Benjamin DeMott in *Saturday Review.* "The strength of this body of poetry lies in its feeling for the generative power at the core of existence. A first-rate Dickey poem breathes the energy of the world, and testifies to the poet's capacity for rising out of tranced dailiness—habitual, half-lived life—into a more intense physicality, a burly appetitive wanting-ness of being. To read him is, for an instant, to share that capacity." Richard Tillinghast, writing in the *Southern Review,* agrees: "Alone among his contemporaries, Dickey has a quality of exuberance that one must go back to [Walt] Whitman to see equaled. . . . This exuberance has hurt Dickey among critics, just as it has hurt Whitman; with Randall Jarrell in his praising mood a notable exception, a critic almost by nature dislikes exuberance and rejects it when he sees it."

Along with DeMott, critics generally agree that by pressing "the neglected natural nerve in humanness" through shockingly bizarre or surreal images, Dickey seeks to depict man's proper relationship with nature. "It is rarely or never so simple as this," cautions Nemerov in *Reflexions on Poetry and Poetics,* "yet the intention seems often enough this, a feeling one's way down the chain of being, a becoming the voice which shall make dumb things respond, sometimes to their hurt or deaths, a sensing of alien modes of experience, mostly in darkness or in an unfamiliar light; reason accepting its animality; a poetry whose transcendences come of its reconciliations. Salvation is this: apprehending the continuousness of forms, the flowing of one energy through everything." "Dickey makes it clear," suggests Bobbitt, "that what seems to be unnatural is only so because of its context in a civilized world, and that these deviations actually possess a vitality which modern man has lost."

In an interview with William Heyen in the *Southern Review,* Dickey comments on the necessity for man to make some sort of connection with animal life: "I remember a quotation from D. H. Lawrence to the effect that we are in the process of losing the cosmos. We dominate it, but in a sense we've lost it or we're losing it. It's the sense of being part of what Lovejoy called 'the great chain of being.' Randall Jarrell, one of my favorite critics and poets, was a great punster, and he said that we have substituted for the great chain of being 'the great chain of buying,' which is, maybe, something that's diametrically opposed, and will be the ruination of everything."

Dickey has been widely praised for having what Herbert Leibowitz in the *New York Times Book Review* calls "a shrewd and troubled knowledge of the 'primal powers' " of nature, as well as "a dramatic skill in presenting the endless beauty of instinct, the feel of icy undertows and warm shallows, the bloodlettings which are a regular part of nature's law." But because a Dickey poem centers on "moments of ultimate confrontation," as Spears says, and because that confrontation often seems to involve a conflict with the norms of civilized society, Dickey has been criticized for what some see as an inherent preoccupation with violence that leads to a castigation of modern society. Zweig, for example, maintains that Dickey's "imagination rides the edge of violence," and James Aronson claims in the *Antioch Review* that this characteristic has given Dickey a reputation as "a kind of primitive savage" who extols the virtues of uncivilized life.

Although Dickey's images are often primitive, many reviewers consider it a mistake to see him as a spokesman for a return to savagery. Oates writes that Dickey, "so disturbing to many of us, must be seen in a larger context, as a kind of 'shaman,' a man necessarily at war with his civilization because that civilization will not, cannot, understand what he is saying." A writer in the *Virginia Quarterly Review* observes that at the heart of Dickey's work lies a "desperate insistence that every human experience, however painful or ugly, be viewed as a possible occasion for the renewal of life, [and] with Dickey any renewal inevitably requires struggle."

According to Hill and Aronson, a typical case of misinterpretation involves "The Firebombing," the first poem in *Buckdancer's Choice.* In part a result of Dickey's own experiences in the air force as a fighter-pilot, the poem presents a speaker who, in a momentary flashback, recalls that twenty years ago he was dropping 300-gallon tanks filled with napalm and gasoline on neighborhoods much like his own. Aronson reports that some readers believe the poem portrays the "joy of destroying" experienced by men at war, or even suggests that destruction itself is natural, when actually the poem expresses the complex emotion of "guilt at the inability to feel guilt." Hill concurs: "The moral indignation that might flood so readily for artists and thinkers flows less surely and less fleetingly for one whose life has depended upon a certain screening out of moral subtleties in times of actual combat. The 'luxury' of moral pangs seems to come upon the fighter-pilot in 'The Firebombing' only after his war is over, his safety and his family's restored to allow the contemplation of distant and not-to-be-altered acts of horrible proportion.''

Noting the characteristic power of Dickey's vision and the intensity of his language, Oates calls "The Firebombing" the central poem of his work. "It is," she writes, "unforgettable, and seems to me an important achievement in our contemporary literature, a masterpiece that could only have been written by an American, and only by Dickey. Having shown us so convincingly in his poetry how natural, how inevitable, is man's love for all things, Dickey now shows us what happens when man is forced to destroy, forced to step down into history and be an American ('and proud of it'). In so doing he enters a tragic dimension in which few poets indeed have operated."

In Dickey's internationally bestselling novel *Deliverance,* critics generally see a thematic continuity with his poetry. A novel about how decent men kill, it is also about the bringing forth, through confrontation, of those qualities in a man that usually lie buried. Simply put, *Deliverance* is the story of four Atlanta suburbanites on a back-to-nature canoe trip that turns into a terrifying test of survival. Dickey, who has made a number of canoe and bow-hunting trips in the wilds of northern Georgia, tells Walter Clemons in the *New York Times Book Review* that much of the story was suggested by incidents that had happened to him or that he had heard about through friends. All those experiences, according to Dickey, share the feeling of excitement and fear that "comes from being in an unprotected situation where the safeties of law and what we call civilization don't apply, they just don't. A snake can bite you and you can die before you could get treatment. There are men in those remote parts that'd just as soon kill you as look at you. And you could turn into a counter-monster yourself, doing whatever you felt compelled to do to survive."

"In writing *Deliverance,*" says the *New York Times*'s Christopher Lehmann-Haupt, "Dickey obviously made up his mind to tell a story, and on the theory that a story is an entertaining lie, he has produced a double-clutching whopper." Three ill-prepared businessmen join Lewis Medlock, an avid sportsman who constantly lectures about the purity of nature and the corruption of civilization, on a weekend escape from the banality of suburban living. Canoeing down a wild and difficult stretch of the Cahulawassee River, the men experience only the natural hazards of the river on the first day. Their idyllic sense of community with nature and of masculine camaraderie is

shattered on the second, however, when two members of the party, resting from the unaccustomed strain, are surprised by two malicious strangers coming out of the woods. Ed Gentry, the novel's narrator, is tied to a tree while Bobby Trippe is held at gunpoint and sexually assaulted by one of the mountain men. Before the attack can go much further, Lewis catches up, kills one of the assailants by shooting an arrow into his back—thereby partially avenging the homosexual rape—and scares off the other. Fearing a trial conducted by city-hating hicks, the canoeists decide to bury the body and continue down the river. But after Drew, the sole member of the party to advocate informing the authorities, accidentally drowns, and Lewis suffers a broken leg, Ed must kill the other assailant who is gunning them from the cliffs above the Cahulawassee.

Critical reactions to *Deliverance* help explain its popular success. "The story is absorbing," writes Evan S. Connell, Jr., in the *New York Times Book Review,* "even when you are not quite persuaded Dickey has told the truth. He is effective and he is deft, with the fine hand of an archer." Lehmann-Haupt gives the book similar praise, stating that Dickey "has succeeded in hammering out a comparatively lean prose style (for a man in the habit of loading words with meaning) and built the elements of his yarn into its structure. And except for one blind lead and an irritating logical discrepancy, he has built well. Best of all, he has made a monument to tall stories."

Though Christopher Ricks, critiquing the novel in the *New York Review of Books,* believes *Deliverance* is "too patently the concoction of a situation in which it will be morally permissible—nay, essential—to kill men with a bow and arrow," Charles Thomas Samuels points out in the *New Republic* that Dickey "himself seems aware of the harshness of his substructure and the absurdity of some of his details" and overcomes these deficiencies through his stylistic maneuvers: "Such is Dickey's linguistic virtuosity that he totally realizes an improbable plot. How a man acts when shot by an arrow, what it feels like to scale a cliff or to capsize, the ironic psychology of fear: these things are conveyed with remarkable descriptive writing. His publishers are right to call *Deliverance* a *tour de force.*"

Much more than a violent adventure tale, *Deliverance* is a novel of initiation that, according to William Stephenson in the *Georgia Review,* "has the potential of becoming a classic." As a result of their experience, Lewis and Ed come to a realization of the natural savagery of man in nature, says C. Hines Edwards in *Critique.* "In three days they have retraced the course of human development and have found in the natural state not the romantic ideal of beauty in nature coupled with brotherhood among men but beauty in nature coupled with the necessity to kill men, coolly and in the course of things." In line with this view, Samuels and other critics note that *Deliverance* alludes to Joseph Conrad's *Heart of Darkness.*

In *American Visionary Fiction: Mad Metaphysics as Salvation Psychology* Richard Finholt suggests that there are other literary allusions: "Ed Gentry, the quintessential contemporary American, a soft and overweight suburbanite, finds himself nonetheless [among the chosen] of Lewis. If this is not exactly the honor of being chosen by Odysseus to man the voyage to Ithaca, it is at least as good as being asked by [Ernest Hemingway] himself to join him on the 'tragic adventure' of fishing the swamp on the big two-hearted river. And since Lewis's river happens to flow through just such a dreaded underworld, his weekend canoe trip takes on an epical significance demanding an American-bred heroism that is at least Hemingwayesque, if not Homeric." Finholt considers the novel a return to a time when "the final difference between meaning and meaninglessness was the hero's ability, versus his inability, to act when the necessary time came. This is the nature of Ed's discovery after undergoing an initiation rite into heroism on the death climb up the cliff."

Consistent with this interpretation of *Deliverance* as epic, a *Times Literary Supplement* reviewer claims Lewis and Ed "are not horrified by what has happened, they are renewed by it; it was, once it became inevitable, indispensable to them. This shockingly credible insight is the central point of the book, and James Dickey reveals it with an appropriate and rewarding subtlety."

Donald W. Markos, discussing the novel in the *Southern Review,* observes that while the book "is in an obvious sense a celebration of an anachronistic concept of manhood," it is more complex than that. "It does not propose that all men embark on canoe trips or undergo a regimen of weight lifting and archery in order to salvage their manhood. An interesting conversation between Medlock and the narrator prior to the outing reveals that masculine prowess is not the primary norm of the book." Oates echoes this sentiment, noting that *Deliverance* is "about our deep, instinctive needs to get back to nature, to establish some kind of rapport with primitive energies; but it is also about the need of some men to do violence, to be delivered out of their banal lives by a violence so irreparable that it can never be confessed." Oates calls the book "a fantasy of a highly civilized and affluent society, which imagines physical violence to be transforming in a mystical—and therefore permanent—sense, a society in which rites of initiation no longer exist . . . . Dickey's work is significant in its expression of the savagery that always threatens to become an ideal, when faith in human values is difficult to come by or when a culture cannot accommodate man's most basic instincts."

Edward Doughtie concludes in the *Southwest Review* that through *Deliverance,* "Dickey shows art to be a necessary mediator between nature—both the exterior nature of woods and rivers and the interior nature of man's drives and dreams—and modern urban 'civilized' life . . . . The positive elements of nature can be stifled by civilization; but without civilization the darker, destructive natural forces may get out of hand. Art is a product of civilization, and a civilizing force, yet for Dickey genuine art never loses touch with the primitive: in short, art embraces both Dionysus and Apollo."

Deliverance represents only one of Dickey's ventures outside the realm of poetry. He not only adapted the novel for the screen but also appeared in the box-office smash as the redneck Sheriff Bullard, whom the canoeists face at the end of their journey. In addition to criticism, Dickey has published a retelling of several biblical stories, *God's Images: The Bible, a New Vision,* as well as *Jericho: The South Beheld,* an exploration of "the rich prose language and sensual impressions of the American South, which Dickey has publicly championed," writes Hill. "Like Whitman or [Mark] Twain," says Michael Dirda in the *Washington Post Book World,* "Dickey seems in a characteristic American tradition, ever ready to light out for new territories."

Dickey tells *Publishers Weekly* that he spent thirty-six years working on his lengthy World War II novel *Alnilam,* which was published in 1987. Named for the central star in the belt of the constellation Orion, *Alnilam* concerns the recently blinded Frank Cahill's search for his son, Joel, whom he has never met. Cahill slowly discovers that his son, an extraordinary pilot thought to have been killed in an aircraft-training accident, had been the leader of a mysterious, dictatorial military training cult known as Alnilam. By interviewing anyone who knew Joel, Cahill forms an impressionistic and sometimes contradictory portrait of this unusual young man. Describing the novel to R. Z. Sheppard of *Time* magazine, Dickey says, "I've tried to do for the air what [Herman] Melville did for water." Sheppard elaborates: "Flying, in the mechanical as well as transcendental sense, is basic to the action, which is surprisingly abundant for a book that is shaped by poetic impulses rather than plot."

The novel has received mixed reviews, with most critics comparing it unfavorably to the powerful *Deliverance.* As Erling Friis-Baastad puts it in the Toronto *Globe and Mail, Alnilam* "is an awkward and overworked book, but the touch of a master poet can still be experienced periodically throughout . . . at least by those who can endure the uphill read." Robert Towers, writing in the *New York Times Book Review,* says that *Alnilam* "is, for better and worse, very much a poet's novel, Mr. Dickey's extended hymn to air, light, wind and the ecstasies of flight." Although he finds Cahill an engaging character, Towers faults Dickey for the "inordinately slow pacing" of the novel. He notes that one of Dickey's innovative devices interrupts the flow of the already slow-moving narrative. Writes Towers, "On many of its pages, the symbolic contrasts between blindness and sight, between darkness and light, are typographically rendered. The page is split down the middle into two columns. The left, which represents Cahill's internal sensations and thoughts, is printed in dark type; the right, which contains the objective narration of speech and events, is printed in ordinary type. Such a device has, of course, the effect not only of dividing one's attention, but also of modifying the degree of one's involvement in what is taking place."

Although the situations in *Alnilam* sometimes seem implausible to critics, Henry Taylor believes that Dickey is able to write so convincingly that he overcomes many of these problems. In the *Los Angeles Times Book Review*, Taylor comments, "One of Dickey's great strengths as a poet has been his extraordinary ability to give plausibility to nearly incredible situations and events." Taylor concludes by saying, "There are a few brief passages in which the style becomes self-conscious, or where the intensity seems too laboriously worked up. But Dickey's ear for Southern talk, his understanding of the sensations involved in flying, and his interest in a wide array of minor characters, make the novel rich and rewarding reading. *Alnilam* is a solid achievement."

Despite his excursions into other genres, Dickey's main concern "will always be poetry," he admits in the *New York Times*. "In poetry you have the utmost concentration of meaning in the shortest space." In a 1981 *Writer's Yearbook* interview, Dickey elaborates on his devotion to verse: "Poetry is, I think, the highest medium that mankind has ever come up with. It's language itself, which is a miraculous medium which makes everything else that man has ever done possible."

Dickey once told *CA:* "I'm the same way about novels as I am about anything I write. I build them very slowly. I work on the principle that the first fifty ways I try to write a novel or a critical piece or a poem or a movie are going to be wrong. But you get a direction in some way or other. Keep drafting and redrafting and something emerges eventually. If the subject is intense, if you are intense about it, something will come. In my case, at least, the final work is nothing like what I started out with; generally I don't have a very good idea at first. But something begins to form in some unforeseen, perhaps unforeseeable, shape. It's like creating something out of nothing—creation ex nihilo, which is said to be impossible. God must have done it, I guess, but nobody else can—except poets."

BIOGRAPHICAL/CRITICAL SOURCES:

BOOKS

Authors in the News, Gale (Detroit), Volume 1, 1976, Volume 2, 1976.

Baughman, Ronald, editor, *The Voiced Connections of James Dickey: Interviews and Conversations,* University of South Carolina Press (Columbia), 1989.

Boyars, Robert, editor, *Contemporary Poetry in America,* Schocken (New York City), 1974.

Bruccoli, Matthew J., and Judith S. Baughman, *James Dickey: A Descriptive Bibliography,* University of Pittsburgh Press (Pittsburgh), 1990.

Calhoun, Richard J., editor, *James Dickey: The Expansive Imagination,* Everett/Edwards (DeLand, FL), 1973.

Carroll, Paul, *The Poem in Its Skin,* Follett, 1968.

Contemporary Authors Bibliographical Series, Volume 2, *American Poets,* Gale, 1986.

Contemporary Literary Criticism, Gale, Volume 1, 1973, Volume 2, 1974, Volume 4, 1975, Volume 7, 1977, Volume 10, 1979, Volume 15, 1980, Volume 47, 1988.

Conversations with Writers, Volume 1, Gale, 1977.

De La Fuente, Patricia, editor, *James Dickey: Splintered Sunlight,* School of Humanities, Pan American University, 1979.

Dickey, James, *Self-Interviews,* recorded and edited by Barbara Reiss and James Reiss, Doubleday, 1970.

Dictionary of Literary Biography, Volume 5: *American Poets since World War II,* Gale, 1980.

Dictionary of Literary Biography Documentary Series, Volume 7, Gale, 1989.

Dictionary of Literary Biography Yearbook, Gale, 1982, 1983, 1993, 1994.

Elledge, J., *James Dickey: A Bibliography, 1947-1974,* Scarecrow (Metuchen, NJ), 1979.

Finholt, Richard, *American Visionary Fiction: Mad Metaphysics as Salvation Psychology,* Kennikat (Port Washington, NY), 1978.

Garrett, George, editor, *The Writer's Voice: Conversations with Contemporary Writers,* Morrow (New York City), 1973.

Glancy, Eileen, *James Dickey: The Critic as Poet,* Whitston Publishing (Troy, NY), 1971.

Hill, Robert and Calhoun, *James Dickey,* Twayne, 1983.

Howard, Richard, *Alone with America: Essays on the Art of Poetry in the United States since 1950,* Atheneum (New York City), 1969.

Lieberman, Laurence, editor, *The Achievement of James Dickey,* Scott, Foresman (Glenview, IL), 1968.

Lieberman, *Unassigned Frequencies: American Poetry in Review, 1964-77,* University of Illinois Press (Champaign), 1978.

Nemerov, Howard, editor, *Poets on Poetry,* Basic Books (New York City), 1966.

Nemerov, *Reflexions on Poetry and Poetics,* Rutgers University Press (New Brunswick, NJ), 1972.

Oates, Joyce Carol, *New Heaven, New Earth: The Visionary Experience in Literature,* Vanguard, 1974.

Pages: The World of Books, Writers, and Writing, Volume 1, Gale, 1976.

Rosenthal, M. L., *The New Poets: American and British Poetry since World War II,* Oxford University Press, 1967.

Shaw, Robert B., editor, *American Poetry since 1960: Some Critical Perspectives,* Carcanet, 1973.

Spears, Monroe K., *Dionysus and the City: Modernism in Twentieth-Century Poetry,* Oxford University Press, 1970.

Stepanchev, Stephen, *American Poetry since 1945,* Harper (New York City), 1965.

Vernon, John, *The Garden and the Map: Schizophrenia in Twentieth-Century Literature and Culture,* University of Illinois Press, 1973.

Walsh, Chad, *Today's Poets,* Scribner, 1964.

Weigl, Bruce, and Terry Hummer, editors, *James Dickey: The Imagination of Glory,* University of Illinois Press, 1984.

Writer's Yearbook, Writer's Digest (Cincinnati), 1981.

PERIODICALS

Agenda, winter-spring, 1977.

American Literature, June, 1990, p. 370.

Antioch Review, fall-winter, 1970-71; spring, 1994, p. 358.

Atlantic Monthly, October, 1967; November, 1968; December, 1974; February, 1980.

Best Sellers, April 1, 1970.

Booklist, July 15, 1971.

Book World, June 30, 1968; March 15, 1970; December 6, 1970; April 25, 1971.

Bulletin of Bibliography, April-June, 1981, pp. 92-100; July-September, 1981, pp. 150-155.

Chicago Review, November 1, 1966.

Chicago Tribune, May 10, 1987.

Chicago Tribune Book World, January 27, 1980.

Christian Science Monitor, December 3, 1964; November 12, 1970; February 20, 1980.

Commonweal, December 1, 1967; February 19, 1971; September 29, 1972; December 3, 1976.

Concerning Poetry, spring, 1978.

Contemporary Literature, summer, 1975.

Critic, May, 1970.

Critique, Volume 15, number 2, 1973.

English Journal, November, 1990, p. 84; January, 1992, p. 27.

Esquire, December, 1970.

Georgia Review, spring, 1968; summer, 1969; spring, 1974; summer, 1978; fall, 1993, p. 603.

Globe and Mail (Toronto), August 15, 1987.

Hudson Review, spring, 1966; autumn, 1967; autumn, 1968; spring, 1993, p. 223; spring, 1994, p. 133.

James Dickey Newsletter, 1984—.

Life, July 22, 1966; July, 1987, p. 35.

Literary News, May-June, 1967.

Los Angeles Times, May 19, 1968; February 26, 1980; July 9, 1987; December 8, 1987.

Los Angeles Times Book Review, June 27, 1982; January 18, 1987, p. 8; June 7, 1987, p. 1.

Mademoiselle, September, 1970; August, 1972.

Milwaukee Journal, March 20, 1966.

Modern Fiction Studies, summer, 1975.

Mother Earth News, March-April, 1990.

Nation, June 20, 1966; April 24, 1967; March 23, 1970; April 6, 1970; February 5, 1983.

National Review, November 15, 1993, p. 64.

New Leader, May 22, 1967; May 20, 1968.

New Republic, September 9, 1967; June 29, 1968; April 18, 1970; December 5, 1970; August 5, 1972; November 30, 1974; November 20, 1976; January 5, 1980; January 12, 1980.

New Statesman, September 11, 1970.

Newsweek, March 30, 1970; August 7, 1972; December 6, 1976; January 31, 1977; August 30, 1993, p. 54.

New Yorker, May 2, 1970; August 5, 1972; September 27, 1993, p. 101.

New York Review of Books, April 23, 1970.

New York Times, March 16, 1966; September 10, 1966; March 27, 1970; December 17, 1971; July 31, 1972; August 20, 1972; January 22, 1977; June 1, 1987; May 19, 1988; October 27, 1990, p. 16.

New York Times Book Review, January 3, 1965; February 6, 1966; April 23, 1967; March 22, 1970; June 7, 1970; November 8, 1970; December 6, 1970; January 23, 1972; February 9, 1975; November 14, 1976; December 18, 1977; July 15, 1979; January 6, 1980; June 3, 1984, p. 23; February 15, 1987; March 8, 1987, p. 31; June 21, 1987, p. 7; September 19, 1993.

Paris Review, spring, 1976.

Partisan Review, summer, 1966.

People, July 6, 1987, p. 16; October 11, 1993, p. 29; January 31, 1994, p. 80.

Playboy, May, 1971; September, 1993, p. 78.

Poetry, October, 1966; March, 1968; July, 1971.

Publishers Weekly, May 29, 1987, p. 62; October 19, 1990, p. 52; June 7, 1993, p. 65; June 21, 1993, p. 82.

Rapport, Volume 17, number 5, 1993, p. 31.

Salmagundi, spring-summer, 1973.

Saturday Review, May 6, 1967; March 11, 1970; March 28, 1970; March 11, 1972.

Saturday Review of Science, August 5, 1972.

Sewanee Review, winter, 1963; summer, 1966; spring, 1969; summer, 1971.

Sixties, winter, 1964; spring, 1967.

Southern Review, winter, 1971; summer, 1971; winter, 1973; spring, 1973; spring, 1981; autumn, 1992, p. 971.

Southwest Review, spring, 1979.

Time, December 13, 1968; April 20, 1970; August 7, 1972; June 29, 1987; October 11, 1993, p. 88.

Times (London), February 3, 1990.

Times Literary Supplement, October 29, 1964; May 18, 1967; September 11, 1970; May 21, 1971; December 2, 1983, p. 1342; January 24, 1986, p. 95; May 10, 1991, p. 22; February 11, 1994, p. 21.

Tribune Books (Chicago), November 16, 1986, p. 4; May 24, 1987, p. 3.

Triquarterly, winter, 1968.

Village Voice, February 4, 1980.

Virginia Quarterly Review, autumn, 1967; autumn, 1968; winter, 1971; spring, 1990, p. 66; summer, 1991, p. 100; winter, 1994, p. 23.

Washington Post, March 31, 1987; May 24, 1987; December 8, 1987.

Washington Post Book World, November 21, 1976; December 30, 1979; May 24, 1987, p. 1; November 22, 1992, p. 8.

World Literature Today, summer, 1991, p. 489; spring, 1993, p. 384.

Yale Review, October, 1962; December, 1967; winter, 1968; October, 1970.

OTHER

Lord Let Me Die but Not Die Out: James Dickey, Poet (film), Encyclopaedia Britannica, 1970.

* * *

DIXON, Paige
See CORCORAN, Barbara

* * *

DOBKIN, Marjorie Housepian 1923-
(Marjorie Housepian)

PERSONAL: Born November 21, 1923, in New York, NY; daughter of Moses M. (a physician) and Makrouhie (Ashjian) Housepian; married Donald S. Johnson, 1943 (divorced, 1956); married Machbi Dobkin, March 23, 1957; children: (first marriage) Stephen Andrew; (second marriage) Daniel, Jonathan. *Education:* Attended Smith College, 1940-42; Barnard College, A.B., 1944; Columbia University, M.A., 1971.

ADDRESSES: Office—Department of English, Barnard College, 3001 Broadway, New York, NY 10027.

CAREER: Dun & Bradstreet, New York City, market researcher, 1945-46; Barnard College, New York City, sec-

retary to president, 1954-57, lecturer, 1957-67, associate in English, 1967—, associate dean of Studies, 1971-88, adjunct professor of English, 1989—.

MEMBER: International PEN, Authors League of America.

AWARDS, HONORS: Litt. D., Wilson College, 1983.

WRITINGS:

(Under name Marjorie Housepian) *A Houseful of Love,* Random House (New York City), 1957.

(Under name Marjorie Housepian) *The Smyrna Affair,* Harcourt (New York City), 1971, published in England as *Smyrna, 1922: The Destruction of a City,* Faber, 1972.

The Making of a Feminist: Early Letters and Journals of M. Carey Thomas, Kent State University Press (Kent, OH), 1980.

(With Jean Cullen) *Inside Out,* Fawcett (New York City), 1989.

Contributor to *Collier Encyclopedia.* Also contributor to various literary and popular journals, including *Atlantic, Paris Review, Commentary, Saturday Review, Vogue,* and *Ararat Quarterly.*

WORK IN PROGRESS: A historical novel set during World War II.

SIDELIGHTS: Marjorie Housepian Dobkin told *CA:* "I write when I have something to say that no one else is saying better (as far as I can tell). Judging by the current literary scene, this is not a widely held practice. More dismaying is evidence that publishers are increasingly 'merchandising' books, as though they were processing cheese, and the fact that young people who aspire to be writers—and I see this in my writing courses at Barnard—are all too seldom readers."

Housepian has traveled to Turkey, Yugoslavia, Greece, Syria, Jordan, and Lebanon, and has participated in international conferences in Cyprus, Soviet Armenia, and Israel. *A Houseful of Love* has been published in Japan, Norway, England, Germany, and Italy; *The Smyrna Affair* has been published in Greece.

BIOGRAPHICAL/CRITICAL SOURCES:

PERIODICALS

New York Times Book Review, February 24, 1980, p. 24.*

* * *

DONLEY, Carol C(ram) 1937-

PERSONAL: Born November 14, 1937, in Cleveland, OH; daughter of Spencer E. (in business) and Jean (a homemaker; maiden name, Stiven) Cram; married Alan M. Donley (in business), August 16, 1958; children: Gregory, Karen, Ted. *Education:* Hiram College, B.A., 1960; Kent State University, M.A., 1970, Ph.D., 1975.

ADDRESSES: Home—11799 Kenyon Dr., Box 903, Hiram, OH 44234. *Office*—Department of English, Hiram College, Hiram, OH 44234.

CAREER: Hiram College, Hiram, OH, assistant professor, 1974-80, associate professor, 1980-88, professor of English, 1988—. Codirector, Center for Literature, Medicine, and the Health Care Professions.

MEMBER: Modern Language Association of America (member of executive committee of Division of Literature and Science, 1981-86), College English Association, William Carlos Williams Society, Society for Literature and Science, Society for Health and Human Values.

AWARDS, HONORS: Phi Beta Kappa; National Endowment for the Humanities (NEH) grants for Institutes for Humanities and Medicine, 1988-89, 1990-91.

WRITINGS:

(With Alan J. Friedman) *Einstein as Myth and Muse,* Cambridge University Press (New York City), 1986.
(Edited with Martin Kohn and Delese Wear) *Literature and Aging: An Anthology,* Kent State University Press (Kent, OH), 1992.

Contributor to *After Einstein,* edited by Peter Barker and Cecil Shugart, Memphis State University Press, 1981; contributor to literature journals. Coeditor of Hiram Poetry Review. *Einstein as Myth and Muse,* Japanese edition, 1989.

WORK IN PROGRESS: Narrative approaches to medical ethics; interrelationships of medicine and literature; *Tyranny of the Normal,* an anthology, edited with Sheryl Buckley, for Kent State University Press, 1995.

*   *   *

DONOHUE, John J. 1926-

PERSONAL: Born January 12, 1926, in Worcester, MA; son of Florence T. (a grocer) and Helen C. (a homemaker; maiden name, Garvey) Donohue. *Education:* College of the Holy Cross, B.A., 1948; Weston College, M.A., 1950, L.T.D., 1960; Harvard University, Ph.D., 1966.

ADDRESSES: Office—P.O. Box 166-564, Center for the Study of the Modern Arab World, St. Joseph's University, Beirut, Lebanon.

CAREER: Entered Society of Jesus (Jesuits) 1948, ordained Roman Catholic priest, 1959; teacher in Baghdad,

Iraq, 1953-56 and 1966-69; St. Joseph's University, Beirut, Lebanon, director of Center for the Study of the Modern Arab World, 1970—; teacher, history and translation, Faculty of Letters, St. Joseph's University, Beirut, Lebanon. *Military service:* U.S. Navy, 1943-45; became lieutenant (junior grade).

WRITINGS:

(Editor with John L. Esposito) *Islam in Transition: Muslim Perspectives,* Oxford University Press (New York City), 1982.
The Forge of the Spirit: Structure, Motion and Meaning in the Japanese Martial Tradition, Garland Publishing (New York City), 1991.
Warrior Dreams: The Martial Arts and the American Imagination, Greenwood Press (Westport, CT), 1994.

Contributor to scholarly journals.

WORK IN PROGRESS: Research on socio-cultural developments in the Arab Middle East, focusing on political developments in Islam; *Dictionary of Contemporary Arab Authors,* in an English and an Arabic version, 1995.

SIDELIGHTS: John J. Donohue told *CA:* "A routine assignment to teach in Baghdad put me in touch with a new world that has since absorbed all my interest and efforts. Differences add a certain allure, but my basic concern is with understanding the peoples of the Middle East and what they are in the process of becoming."

*   *   *

DREXLER, K(im) Eric 1955-

PERSONAL: Born April 25, 1955, in Oakland, CA; son of Allan Barry (a management consultant) and Hazel Edna (an audiologist and speech pathologist; maiden name, Gassmann) Drexler; married Christine Louise Peterson (executive director, Foresight Institute), July 18, 1981. *Education:* Massachusetts Institute of Technology, S.B., 1977, S.M., 1979, Ph.D.

ADDRESSES: Office—P.O. Box 60775, Palo Alto, CA 94306. *Agent*—John Brockman Associates Inc., 5 East 59th St., New York, NY 10024.

CAREER: Massachusetts Institute of Technology, Cambridge, research affiliate at Space Systems Laboratory, 1980-86, research affiliate at Artificial Intelligence Laboratory, beginning 1986; currently research fellow of Institute for Molecular Manufacturing. Foresight Institute, Palo Alto, CA, director, 1986, currently chairman; visiting scholar at Stanford University, 1986-91. Chair of First Foresight Conference on Nanotechnology, 1989, Second Conference on Nanotechnology, 1991, and co-chair of

Third Conference on Nanotechnology, 1993. Gave Senate testimony on molecular manufacturing, 1992. Inventor of patented high performance solar sail and method for processing and fabricating metals in space.

MEMBER: American Association for the Advancement of Science, American Chemical Society, National Space Society (member of board of directors), American Vacuum Society, American Association for Artificial Intelligence, Authors Guild, L5 Society (member of board of directors, 1979—).

AWARDS, HONORS: Graduate fellowship in space industrialization (first fellowship granted in the field), National Science Foundation, 1977-79; Scientist/Engineer Award, National Space Society, 1991; Outstanding Computer Science Book Award, Association of American Publishers, 1992, for *Nanosystems: Molecular Machinery, Manufacturing, and Computation;* Kilby Young Innovator Award, Kilby Awards Foundation, 1993.

WRITINGS:

Engines of Creation: The Coming Era of Nanotechnology, Doubleday (New York City), 1986.
(With C. Peterson and G. Pergamit) *Unbounding the Future: The Nanotechnology Revolution,* Morrow (New York City), 1991.
Nanosystems: Molecular Machinery, Manufacturing, and Computation, Wiley (New York City), 1992.

Also contributor to *Proceedings of the National Academy of Sciences.* Contributor to periodicals, including *Smithsonian* and *CoEvolution Quarterly.* Coeditor of *L5 News,* 1983-84.

SIDELIGHTS: K. Eric Drexler describes himself as a researcher concerned with emerging technologies and their consequences for the future. This interest led him to initiate studies in the field of nanotechnology—an anticipated technology based on molecular machines able to build objects to complex atomic specifications. The possibilities he has identified include molecular manufacturing systems able to construct computers smaller than living cells, devices able to repair cells, diamond-based structural materials, and additional molecular manufacturing systems. Drexler's book *Engines of Creation: The Coming Era of Nanotechnology* addresses some of the important issues associated with nanotechnology.

In the *New York Times Book Review,* critic Terence Monmaney commented on some of the author's projections based on the use of nanotechnology: "Drexler describes a world of no pollution or disease, limitless energy and food, flawless machines and starships, and a lifespan decades, perhaps a century or two, longer than we currently enjoy." Monmaney concluded, "*Engines of Creation* is a clearly

written, hopeful forecast, remarkable for an unembarrassed faith in progress through technology."

Drexler told *CA* that reviewer Monmaney's remarks suggest "he didn't read the last third of the book, 'Dangers and Hopes,' which starts with a chapter titled 'Engines of Destruction.' I wrote the book chiefly out of a concern with the dangers, though the promise is also great."

Concerning ongoing technology research, knowledge, and information, Drexler identified the philosophy behind the Foresight Institute, a nonprofit educational organization: "The goal of the Foresight Institute is to help society prepare for new and future technologies, such as nanotechnology, artificial intelligence, and large-scale space development, by promoting an understanding of these technologies and their consequences, formulating sound policies for gaining their benefits while avoiding their dangers, informing the public and decision makers, developing an organizational base for implementing these policies, ensuring their implementation."

To help in coping with the opportunities and dangers presented by this new field, in addition to serving as chairman of the Foresight Institute, he founded the Massachusetts Institute of Technology Nanotechnology Study Group.

BIOGRAPHICAL/CRITICAL SOURCES:

PERIODICALS

New York Times Book Review, August 10, 1986.

* * *

DUBOS, Rene (Jules) 1901-1982

PERSONAL: Born February 20, 1901, in Saint Brice, France; immigrated to United States, 1924, naturalized citizen, 1938; died of heart failure, February 20, 1982, in New York, NY; son of Georges Alexandre and Adeline (DeBloedt) Dubos; married Marie Louise Bonnet, March 23, 1934 (died, 1942); married Letha Jean Porter, October 16, 1946. *Education:* College Chaptal, Paris, 1915-19; Institut National Agronomique, Paris, 1919-21; Rutgers University, Ph.D., 1927.

CAREER: International Institute of Agriculture, Rome, Italy, assistant editor, 1922-24; New Jersey Experimental Station, Rutgers University, New Brunswick, NJ, research assistant in soil microbiology and university instructor in bacteriology, 1924-27; Rockefeller Institute, New York City, Graduate University and Scientific Research Center, fellow, 1927-28, assistant, 1928-30, associate, 1930-38, associate member, 1938-41, member,

1941-42, 1944-82, professor, 1957-71, professor emeritus, 1971-82; Harvard University Medical School, Cambridge, MA, George Fabyan Professor of Comparative Pathology and professor of tropical medicine, 1942-44. *The Journal of Experimental Medicine,* editor, 1946-72. Member of the Citizens' Advisory Committee on Environmental Quality, 1970-75. *Military service:* French Army, 1921-22.

MEMBER: Harvey Society (president, 1951), Society of American Bacteriologists (president, 1951), National Academy of Sciences, American Philosophical Society, Century Association (New York).

AWARDS, HONORS: John Philips Memorial Award, American College of Physicians, 1940; Mead Johnson Award, American Academy of Pediatrics, 1940; Gordon Wilson Medal, American Clinical and Climatological Association, 1946; Lasker Award in Public Health, American Public Health Association, 1948; Trudeau Medal, National Tuberculosis Association, 1951; Award of the Pharmaceutical Industries, 1952; Triennial Prize Lecture Award, Massachusetts General Hospital, 1953; Hitchcock Award, University of California, 1954; Howard Taylor Ricketts Award, University of Chicago, 1958; Robert Koch Centennial Award, Robert Koch Institute in Berlin, 1960; Passano Foundation Award, 1960; Modern Medicine Award for Distinguished Achievement, 1961; Phi Beta Kappa Science Award, 1963, for *The Unseen World,* and 1966, for *Man Adapting;* Arches of Science Award, 1966; Pulitzer Prize for nonfiction, 1969, for *So Human an Animal;* Harold Terry Clark Award, 1970; Prix International of the Institut de la Vie, 1972; Forsythia Award, the Brooklyn Botanic Garden, 1974; Washburn Award, Boston Museum of Science, 1974; Cullum Geographical Medal, 1975; Tyler Ecology Award, 1976; Wilder Penfield Award from the Vanier Institute of the Family, 1979; American Book Award nominee, 1981, for *The Wooing of Earth.*

Honorary degrees from numerous institutions, including Rochester University, 1941, Harvard University 1942, Rutgers University, 1949, University of Paris, 1950, New School for Social Research, 1956, University College of Dublin, Yeshiva University, University of Liege, University of Rio de Janeiro, University of Alberta, 1963. Also University of Pennsylvania, University of California, L'Academie de Lille, Carleton College, Colby College, St. John's University, Beloit College, Wesleyan University, Queen's University, University of Sherbrooke, Loyola University, Clark University, Kalamazoo College, Bard College, Williams College, Marquette University, Catholic University, Fairfield University, Jefferson University, University of Calgary, Montclair State College, Rockefeller University, St. Peter's College, Kenyon College, Marietta College, University of Guelph.

WRITINGS:

The Bacterial Cell in Its Relation to Problems of Virulence, Immunity and Chemotherapy, Harvard University Press (Cambridge, MA), 1945.

(Editor) *Bacterial and Mycotic Infection of Man,* Lippincott (Philadelphia, PA), 1948.

Louis Pasteur, Free Lance of Science, Little, Brown (Boston, MA), 1950.

(With J. P. Dubos) *The White Plague: Tuberculosis, Man, and Society,* Little, Brown, 1952.

Biochemical Determinants of Microbial Diseases, Harvard University Press, 1954.

(Coeditor and translator) *Tubercle Bacillus in the Pulmonary Lesion of Man,* Springer, 1955.

Mirage of Health: Utopias, Progress and Biological Change, Harper, 1959.

Pasteur and Modern Science, Anchor (Garden City, NY), 1960, revised edition, Science Tech (Madison, WI), 1988.

The Dreams of Reason: Science and Utopias, Columbia University Press (New York City), 1961.

The Unseen World, Rockefeller Institute Press (New York City), 1962.

The Torch of Life: Continuity in Living Experience, Simon & Schuster, 1962.

Health and Disease, Time-Life (Chicago), 1965.

Man Adapting, Yale University Press (New Haven, CT), 1965, revised edition, 1980.

Man, Medicine and Environment, Praeger (New York City), 1968.

So Human an Animal, Scribner (New York City), 1968.

Reason Awake: Science for Man, Columbia University Press, 1970.

(With Maya Pines) *Health and Disease,* Time-Life, 1970, revised edition, 1980.

(With Germaine Bree and Louis B. Wright) *Essays in Honor of David Lyall Patrick,* University of Arizona (Tucson), 1971.

Man and His Environment: Biomedical and Social Action, Pan American Health Organization (Washington, DC), 1972.

A God Within, Scribner, 1972.

(With Barbara Ward) *Only One Earth: The Care and Maintenance of a Small Planet,* Norton, 1972.

Choisir d'etre humain: essai, Denoel (Paris), 1974.

Of Human Diversity, Clark University Press (Worchester, MA), 1974.

The Professor, the Institute, and DNA, Rockefeller University Press, 1975.

The Resilience of Ecosystems, Accademia Nazionale dei Lincei (Rome), 1977, published in the United States as *The Resilience of Ecosystems: An Ecological View of Environmental Restoration,* Colorado Associated University Press, 1978.

(With Jean-Paul Escande) *Chercher: des medecins, des chercheurs et des hommes,* Stock (Paris), 1979, translation by Patricia Ranum published in the United States as *Quest: Reflections on Medicine, Science, and Humanity,* Harcourt (New York City), 1980.

The Wooing of Earth, Scribner, 1980.

Celebrations of Life, McGraw, 1981.

The World of Rene Dubos: A Collection from His Writings, edited by Gerard Piel and Osborn Segerberg, Jr., Holt (New York City), 1990.

Contributor to books, including *The Nature of Life,* edited by William H. Heidcamp, University Park Press (Baltimore, MD), 1978.

SIDELIGHTS: In the tradition of writers such as Loren Eiseley and Carl Sagan, Rene Dubos was an accomplished scientist whose books found an audience with the general public. He immigrated to the United States from France in 1924, and after completing his doctorate at Rutgers University he settled into a career as a microbiologist, spending most of it at the Rockefeller Institute and Rockefeller University. Much of his research was groundbreaking; at age thirty, for example, he isolated an enzyme that was able to attack the germ that causes certain types of pneumonia. He also discovered tyrothricin, which led to the commercial production of antibiotics. Dubos's early books aimed to inform the scientific community of his research findings.

In the 1960s, however, Dubos's view of science began to encompass more than just the academic realm, and his growing body of readers began to define him as a "scientist-philosopher" and "philosopher of earth." His books were no longer scientific treatises; he explored disciplines as diverse as microbiology, anthropology, history, sociology, and theology to discuss the role and impact of human beings as part of the natural environment. In later years he wrote about environmental issues, bringing a sense of balance and optimism to the environmental movement. He told Stella Dong of *Publishers Weekly:* "I have a faith—and some people might call it a religious faith—that being human is something special, more than simply being Homo sapiens. . . . I am as conscious of the good we can do as of the bad."

One of Dubos's earliest books to take this position was *Man Adapting,* a book that Aubrey Lewis in the *New York Review of Books* called "an erudite, vigorous statement of the necessity for adaptation, its dangers and demands, and especially its medical implications." He continued to discuss these connections between people and the environment in *Man, Medicine and Environment,* which a *Times Literary Supplement* reviewer said "draws attention to the importance of the environment in which man lives to his own health and to the connexion that this environment

has to the diseases from which he may suffer." With *So Human an Animal,* which won the Pulitzer Prize in 1969, Dubos widened the scope of his concerns to "the characteristics of all living things" which "are deeply affected by the conditions of their lives." The core of his argument stated that humans have adapted to their environment very little since the Stone Age; therefore, we must engage in careful environmental planning to create a world that meets our basic biological needs. A *New Yorker* reviewer called the book "thoughtful," and a *Times Literary Supplement* writer found it "infectiously optimistic." Writing in the *Virginia Quarterly Review,* Caryl P. Haskins praised *So Human an Animal* for its "eloquent appeal for holism" and called it "a work of scientific humanism, in the truest sense."

Reason Awake: Science for Man more explicitly addressed the concerns of environmentalists. The book traces the history of people's relationship with the environment, demonstrating, for example, how agriculture, the use of tools, and the controlled use of fire have enabled humans to survive in a wider range of environments. In the twentieth century, humans have become almost entirely dependent on technology for their survival. In *Saturday Review,* Harrison Brown praised the book for the "objectivity and clarity" with which Dubos analyzes "the scientific-technological basis of our modern-day predicament."

Ultimately, Dubos offered an optimistic view of the environmental crisis. One of his most popular books was *A God Within,* which Walter Arnold in the *New York Times Book Review* called "an important . . . counterstatement to many in the conservation and ecological movements who seem soured or sick of man." Praising the author for his "sanity" and "serenity," Loren Eiseley of the *Washington Post Book World* wrote that Dubos's "book seeks above all to remind man not of a bleak deterministic world which is his master, but rather that we, all of us, carry in our bodies that mysterious creativity which the Greeks labeled *entheos*—the God within." The central message of this and later books is that human have choices and can exercise those choices for good, thus restoring ecological balance. In *Quest: Reflections on Medicine, Science, and Humanity,* Dubos engaged in thoughtful dialogues with the French writer Jean-Paul Escande, again to stress the interconnections of people and their environment. For *Saturday Review* writer Norman Cousins, the "interaction of finely honed minds . . . . [provides] the reader with rich nourishment."

Dubos's optimism was especially apparent in *The Wooing of Earth,* in which he described how people, from the ancient Greeks onward, have altered their environment and how subsequent generations have grown to appreciate these forms of "degradation." Convinced that humankind will always alter the environment for its own purposes,

Dubos stated that the goal is not necessarily for people to be in balance with nature, but for them to love it enough to preserve and improve it. At the same time, the author cautions against the imposition of authoritarian solutions to environmental problems. Joseph Kastner of the *New York Times Book Review* called Dubos's position in the book a "charitable view of man and an unhackneyed way of looking at his uses of nature," although a *Time* reviewer claimed that Dubos apparently "argues that man can have his environmental cake and eat it too."

Celebrations of Life was Dubos's final book. Once again he offered reassurance about our capacity for overcoming environmental problems. He saw cause for optimism that modern industrial societies were, however slowly, adapting to the future. Declaring Dubos "no ecological sentimentalist," Edwin M. Yoder, Jr. of the *Washington Post* called the book a "celebration of the bountiful instances in which cultural achievements, large and small, defy natural probabilities" and warned that because Dubos is a "foe of all sorts of fashionable simple-mindedness . . . we shall have to complicate our minds to get his message straight."

BIOGRAPHICAL/CRITICAL SOURCES:

BOOKS

Dubos, Rene, *So Human an Animal,* Scribner, 1968.

PERIODICALS

Antioch Review, summer, 1980, pp. 389-90.
Chicago Tribune Book World, October 18, 1981.
Christian Science Monitor, October 22, 1970.
Los Angeles Times, October 2, 1980, p. 22.
Los Angeles Times Book Review, June 1, 1986, p. 14.
New Yorker, May 24, 1969; June 13, 1970.
New York Review of Books, December 1, 1966, pp. 37-39; June 5, 1969, pp. 29-34.
New York Times, December 25, 1968, p. 29; May 27, 1970; February 21, 1982.
New York Times Book Review, February 15, 1970; December 24, 1972; June 1, 1980, pp. 7, 46.
Publishers Weekly, November 6, 1981, pp. 6-7.
Saturday Review, June 6, 1970; August, 1980, pp. 11-12.
Scientific American, May, 1991, pp. 66-67.
Time, June 9, 1980, p. 85.
Times Literary Supplement, January 16, 1969; December 25, 1970; May 2, 1971; April 5, 1974.
Virginia Quarterly Review, winter, 1969, pp. 128-35.
Washington Post, December 14, 1981.
Washington Post Book World, September 3, 1972, p. 5; June 15, 1980, pp. 1, 13.

OBITUARIES:

PERIODICALS

New York Times, February 21, 1982.
Publishers Weekly, March 5, 1982.
Time, March 1, 1982.*

*   *   *

DUBY, Georges (Michel Claude) 1919-

PERSONAL: Born October 7, 1919, in Paris, France; son of Louis and Marguerite (Dimanche) Duby; married Andree Combier, September 15, 1942; children: Jean, Catherine Kouchner, Martine Piovesan. *Education:* Universite de Lyons, agrege des lettres, 1942, docteur des lettres, 1953.

ADDRESSES: Home—Beaurecueil, 13100 Le Tholonet, France. *Office*—College de France, 11 place Marcelin Berthelot, 75231 Paris, France.

CAREER: Universite de Lyon, Lyons, France, assistant in faculty of letters, 1944-49; Universite de Besancon, Besancon, France, professor of medieval history, 1950-51; Universite d'Aix Marseille, Aix-en-Provence, France, professor of medieval history, 1951-69; College de France, Paris, professor of history of medieval societies, 1970-92. Lecturer at numerous colleges and universities in Europe, England, North Africa, Canada, China, Japan, and the United States. Director of Centre d'Etudes des Societies Mediterraneennes. *Military service:* French Army, 8th Artillery Regiment, 1940-41.

MEMBER: Institute de France, American Philosophical Society (foreign member), Medieval Academy of America (associate member), British Academy (associate member), Royal Historical Society (associate member), Academie Royale de Belgique (associate member), Accademia Nazionale dei Lincei (foreign member), Academie des Sciences de Hongrie (foreign member), Conscil Scientifique de al Fondation de France, Societe de Television Sept-Arte (president d'honneur).

AWARDS, HONORS: Premier Prix Gobert, Academie Francaise, 1953, for *La Societe aux XIe et XIIe siecles dan la region maconnaise,* and 1962, for *L'Economie rurale et la vie des campagnes dans l'occident medieval;* Fondation de France prize, 1973; Prix des Ambassadeurs, 1973, for *Le Dimanche de Bouvines,* Prix des Critiques, 1979, for *Les Trois Ordres; ou, L'Imaginaire due feodalisme;* honorary degrees from numerous universities, including Universite de Louvain, Universite de Liege, Universite de Montreal, Vrije Universiteit Amsterdam, and Harvard University; Commandeur de la Legion de Honneur; Commandeur de l'Ordre des Arts et Lettres; chevalier de l'Ordre du Merite Agricole; grand officier de l'Ordre National du Merite.

WRITINGS:

La Societe aux XIe et XIIe siecles dans la region maconnaise, A. Colin, 1953.

Recueil des pancartes de l'abbaye de la Ferte-sur-Grosne, 1113-1178, Editions Ophrys, 1953.

(With others) *Le Moyen Age: L'Expansion de l'orient et la naissance de la civilisation occidentale,* Presses Universitaires de France, 1955.

(With R. Mandrou) *Histoire de la civilisation francaise,* A. Colin, 1958, revised edition, 1968, translation by James Blakely Atkinson published as *A History of French Civilization,* Random House, 1964.

L'Economie rurale et la vie des campagnes dans l'occident medieval: France, Angleterre, Empire, IXe-XVe siecles, Aubier (Paris), 1962, translation by Cynthia Postan published as *Rural Economy and Country Life in the Medieval West,* University of South Carolina Press, 1968.

Fondements d'un nouvel humanisme, 1280-1440, (also see below), Skira, 1966, translation by Peter Price published as *Foundations of a New Humanism, 1280-1440,* World Publishing, 1966.

L'Europe des cathedrales, 1140-1280, Skira, 1966, translation by Stuart Gilbert published as *The Europe of the Cathedrals, 1140-1280,* 1966.

Adolescence de la chretiente occidentale, 980-1140 (also see below), Skira, 1967, translation by Gilbert published as *The Making of the Christian West, 980-1140,* 1967.

L'An mil, Julliard, 1967.

(Editor and author of preface) Edouard Baratier, *Atlas historique,* A. Colin, 1969.

(Editor) *Histoire de la France,* Larousse, Volume I: *Naissance d'une nation, des origines a 1348,* 1970, Volume II: *Dynasties et revolutions, de 1852 a nos jours: Fuerriers et paysans, VII-XIIE siecle,* 1972.

Premier Essor de l'economie europeenne, Gallimard (Paris), 1973, translation by Howard B. Clarke published as *The Early Growth of the European Economy: Warriors and Peasants from the Seventh to the Twelfth Century,* Cornell University Press, 1974.

Le Dimanche de Bouvines: 27 juillet 1214, Gallimard, 1973.

Hommes et structure du moyen age, Mouton, 1973.

(With wife, Andree Duby) *Les Proces de Jeanne d'Arc,* Gallimard, 1973.

Merveilleuse Notre-Dame de Lausanne: Cathedrale bourguignonne, Editions du Grand-Pont, 1975.

Saint-Bernard: L'Art cistercien, Arts et Metier Graphiques, 1976.

Le Temps des cathedrales: L'Art et la societe, 980-1420 (contains *Adolescence de la chretiente occidentale,*

980-1140, L'Europe des cathedrales, 1140-1280, and *Fondements d'un nouvel humanisme, 1280-1440*), Gallimard, 1976, translation by Eleanor Levieux and Barbara Thompson published as *The Age of the Cathedrals: Art and Society, 980-1420,* University of Chicago Press, 1981.

The Chivalrous Society (articles), translation by Postan, University of California Press, 1977.

(Editor with Jacques LeGoff) *Famille et parente dans l'occident medieval,* Ecole Francaise de Rome, 1977.

(Editor) *Atlas historique Larousse,* Larousse, 1978.

Medieval Marriage: Two Models from Twelfth-Century France (lectures), translation by Elborg Forster, Johns Hopkins Press, 1978.

Les Trois Ordres; ou, L'Imaginaire du feodalisme, Gallimard, 1978, translation by Arthur Goldhammer published as *The Three Orders: Feudal Society Imagined,* University of Chicago Press, 1980.

L'Europe au moyen age: Art roman, art gothique, Arts et Metiers Graphiques, 1979.

Dialogues: Georges Duby—Guy Lardreau, Flammarion, 1980.

Le Chevalier, la femme et le pretre, Hachette, 1981, translation by Barbara Bray published as *The Knight, the Lady and the Priest: The Making of Modern Marriage in Medieval France,* Pantheon, 1983.

Guillaume le marechal ou le meilleur chevalier du monde, Fayard, 1984, translation by Richard Howard published as *William Marshal: The Flower of Chivalry,* Pantheon, 1985.

(Editor with Philippe Aries, and contributor) *Histoire de la vie privee,* Volume I: *De l'Empire romain a l'an mil,* Volume II: *De l'Europe feodale a la Renaissance,* Editions du Seuil, 1986.

Histoire politique de la nation francaise, Volume I, Hachette, 1987.

Male Moyen Age, Flammarion, 1988.

(Editor with Michele Perrot, and contributor) *Histoire des femmes en occident,* five volumes, Editions Plon, 1991-1992.

L'Histoire continue, Editions Odile Jacob, 1991, translation published as *History Continues,* University of Chicago Press, 1994.

(With Michelle Perrot) *Images de Femmes,* Editions Plon, 1992, translation published as *Power and Beauty: Images of Women in Art,* St. Martin's, 1995.

La chevalier, Editions Perrin, 1993.

Contributor to books, including *Medieval Agriculture, 900-1500,* translated by Roger Greaves, Collins, 1969. Also editor of books in the "Historie de la France rurale" and "Historie de la France urbaine" series, Editions du Seuil. Editor of *Etudes Rurales.*

WORK IN PROGRESS: Research on family structures, history of gender, and historical memory in Europe during the Middle Ages.

SIDELIGHTS: Georges Duby has gained renown both as a medieval scholar and author. Duby's research led him to write several books on the middle ages, and these, said John Gross in the *New York Times,* make him "one of the most renowned of present-day medievalists." Although he writes primarily in French, many of Duby's works have been translated into English. Notable among these was *Le Temps des cathedrales: L'Art et la societe, 980-1420.*

Translated in 1981 as *The Age of the Cathedrals: Art and Society, 980-1420,* the work had also served as the basis for the series of television films Duby produced for Antenne 2 in Paris in 1980. A comprehensive study of the early Gothic cathedrals of France, *The Age of the Cathedrals* discusses the various building plans of the churches and explains the social and religious milieu that gave rise to their construction. *New York Times Book Review* art critic John Russell pointed out the thoroughness of Duby's scholarship. "If *The Age of the Cathedrals* has a fault," the reviewer writes, "it is that Professor Duby knows too much, has too many new ideas and takes such a delight in setting them out." This volume, in which "an exceptional intelligence marches to the beat of a kettle-drum," according to Russell, "can be read with pleasure even by those who would not normally be drawn to the subject."

Other works by Duby include *The Knight, the Lady and the Priest: The Making of Modern Marriage in Medieval France,* which traces the evolution of marriage and societal attitudes toward it through an examination of medieval romance literature, religious drama, and early church records, and *William Marshal: The Flower of Chivalry,* in which Duby examines a manuscript from the thirteenth century which contains a long poem by a French trouvere about the life of Guillaume Marechal, a knight-errant who rose to greatness and wealth in the service of kings before his death in 1219. Duby continued to write books on medieval subjects in coming years, and in 1986 he collaborated with several scholars to produce *Historie de la vie privee.* This book, said Brian Stock in the *Times Literary Supplement,* represents the combined efforts of a group of scholars who "agreed to pool their intellectual resources and to collaborate on the first systematic history of the private sphere of life in the West." The work comprises an anticipated five volumes, the first three of which were directed by Duby and the late Philippe Aries. Stock wrote of the series, "We have a cumulative history in two senses: one which not only tells an important story but which also stands back from time to time and tries to analyse the sort of story it is trying to tell." Stock affirmed that Duby "is responsible for much of the current thinking about the

rural aristocracy in medieval France" and praised Duby's contribution to *Histoire de la vie privee* for "prose as distinguished as his insights."

Duby once told *CA:* "One of my goals is to make accessible to a wide audience the findings of extensive research on the feudal society's operational structures and cultural horizons. Thus, toward this aim, I have produced a series of nine television films, entitled 'Le Temps des cathedrales,' that met with success in France and in several other European countries."

BIOGRAPHICAL/CRITICAL SOURCES:

PERIODICALS

American Historical Review, April, 1979.
Best Sellers, July 15, 1966; August 1, 1967.
Economist, March 9, 1974.
English Historical Review, July, 1979.
Newsweek, February 24, 1986.
New Yorker, November 14, 1964.
New York Review of Books, January 28, 1967; November 21, 1968.
New York Times, December 20, 1985.
New York Times Book Review, August 23, 1981; February 2, 1986.
Time, April 23, 1984.
Times (London), February 9, 1985.
Times Literary Supplement, April 14, 1978; April 24, 1981; May 4, 1984; September 5, 1986.
Virginia Quarterly Review, winter, 1968.
Yale Review, winter, 1969.

*   *   *

DUNN, Hugh Patrick 1916-

PERSONAL: Born September 29, 1916, in Tapanui, New Zealand; son of Samuel (a hotelier) and Mary (Curry) Dunn; married June Mary Grevatt, December 1, 1945; children: Patrick, Christopher, Mary Dunn Arnold, Joseph, Martin, John, Elizabeth. *Education:* Otago University, M.B., Ch.B., 1941. *Politics:* National Party. *Religion:* Roman Catholic.

ADDRESSES: Home and office—168 Upland Rd., Auckland 5, New Zealand. *Agent*—Richards Literary Agency, Box 31240, Auckland 10, New Zealand.

CAREER: Queen Charlotte's Hospital, London, England, resident medical officer, 1948-49; Radcliffe Infirmary, Oxford, England, resident medical officer, 1949-50; St. Helen's Hospital, Auckland, New Zealand, obstetrician, 1951-55; National Women's Hospital, Auckland, obstetrician and gynecologist, 1955-81. *Military service:* Royal

New Zealand Navy, surgeon, 1943-45; became lieutenant commander.

MEMBER: New Zealand Obstetrical and Gynaecological Society (president, 1960-61), Royal College of Surgeons (fellow), Royal College of Obstetricians and Gynaecologists (fellow), Royal Australasian College of Surgeons (fellow), Society for the Protection of the Unborn Child (founder, 1970), Family Rights Association (founder, 1974), Professional Club, Outboard Boating Club.

AWARDS, HONORS: Created Papal Knight of St. Sylvester by Pope Paul VI, 1974.

WRITINGS:

The Capture of Black Pete (juvenile novel), Blackwood & Janet Paul, 1968.
The School Detective (juvenile novel), Wordsworth Press, 1980.
Sex and Sensibility, E. J. Dwyer, 1982.
So You're Pregnant, E. J. Dwyer, 1986.
A Woman and Her Doctor, Little Hills Press (Sydney), 1988.
The Doctor and Christian Marriage, Alba House (New York City), 1992.
Ethics for Doctors, Nurses and Patients, Alba House, 1994.

Contributor to medical journals.

SIDELIGHTS: Hugh Patrick Dunn told *CA:* "In modern society the areas of marriage and sexuality are in a mess. Every family is afflicted by some aberration, from the Royals down to the humblest citizen. In the medical profession ethical standards have never been so confused or deplorable. The Hippocratic Oath, which has guided medical conduct for the past 24 centuries, has been largely abandoned. These books attempt to reassure readers that the only way to get back to normal decent standards is to stick to the Judaeo-Christian principles on which our civilization has been founded.

"The children's books eschew moralizing. They are mainly for fun, often at the expense of adults. Children like a good laugh, plenty of action and violence, the 'goodies' succeeding and the 'baddies' locked up."

*   *   *

DUNN, Stephen   1939-

PERSONAL: Born June 24, 1939, in New York, NY; son of Charles F. (a salesperson) and Ellen (Fleishman) Dunn; married Lois Kelly (a yoga teacher and chef), September 26, 1964; children: Andrea Ellen, Susanne. *Education:* Hofstra University, B.A., 1962; New School for Social Re-

search, graduate study, 1964-66; Syracuse University, M.A., 1970.

ADDRESSES: Home—445 Chestnut Neck Rd., Port Republic, NJ 08241. *Office*—Stockton State College, Pomona, NJ 08240. *Agent*—Philip G. Spitzer Literary Agency, 111-25 76th Ave., Forest Hills, NY 11375.

CAREER: Poet and essayist. Williamsport Billies, Williamsport, PA, semi-professional basketball player, 1962-63; National Biscuit Co., New York City, copywriter, 1963-66; Ziff-Davis Publishing Co., New York City, assistant editor, 1967-68; Southwest Minnesota State University, Marshall, assistant professor of creative writing, 1970-73; Stockton State College, Pomona, NJ, professor of creative writing and poet-in-residence, 1974—. Visiting lecturer, Syracuse University, 1973-74; visiting professor, University of Washington, 1980, and Columbia University; adjunct professor of poetry, Columbia University, 1983-87; conducted poetry workshops at Aspen Writers Conference, 1977, 1987, and Bennington Writers Workshop, 1983-87; directed Associated Writing Programs' Poetry Series, 1980-82. *Military service:* U.S. Army, 1962.

AWARDS, HONORS: "Discovery '71" Award, Academy of American Poets, New York Poetry Center; National Endowment for the Arts fellowships, 1974, 1981, 1983, 1989; Theodore Roethke Prize, 1977, and Helen Bullis Prize, 1982, both from *Poetry Northwest;* Yaddo fellowships, 1979-89; Guggenheim fellowship, 1984-85; Levinson Prize, 1987, from *Poetry.*

WRITINGS:

POETRY

Five Impersonations, Ox Head Press, 1971.
Looking for Holes in the Ceiling, University of Massachusetts Press (Amherst), 1974.
Full of Lust and Good Usage, Carnegie-Mellon University Press (Pittsburgh, PA), 1976.
A Circus of Needs, Carnegie-Mellon University Press, 1978.
Work and Love, Carnegie-Mellon University Press, 1981.
Not Dancing, Carnegie-Mellon University Press, 1984.
Local Time, Quill (New York City), 1987.
Between Angels, Norton (New York City), 1989.
Landscape at the End of the Century, Norton, 1991.
Walking Light: Essays & Memoirs, Norton, 1993.
New and Selected Poems: 1974-1994, Norton, 1994.

Also contributor of reviews, essays, and interviews to numerous magazines and anthologies.

SIDELIGHTS: Stephen Dunn's writing often celebrates both the everyday events of life and what SuAnne Doak calls in her *Dictionary of Literary Biography* essay the "inexplicable, startling, even subversive elements of human existence." Dunn's works, which include surreal and allegorical components, exhibit an inventive mixture of wit and pathos. Doak contends that a unique ability to balance seemingly opposing elements is one quality that makes Dunn "one of the best poetic voices of the late twentieth century."

Dunn once said, "My poetry must speak for itself; I have no comments about it." Critics are less reticent. Robert F. Willson, Jr., describes Dunn's collection *Looking for Holes in the Ceiling* as a book that seems "to strike a blow for life with style and grace" and notes the poet's "wit, his refreshingly oblique vision, and his faith in the vitality of poetry." Ronald Wallace, reviewing *Full of Lust and Good Usage,* states that, at its best, Dunn's work "exhilarates you with the sheer joy of his talent and craft and imagination."

With *A Circus of Needs,* declares Dave Smith in the *American Poetry Review,* "Dunn has become a philosophical poet of weight." William H. Pritchard, however, suggests in the *Hudson Review* that Dunn exercise more control over his material so that certain poems in this collection "might become more individually memorable." Similarly, *Work and Love* also met with a mixed reception. Robert B. Shaw, writing in *Poetry,* finds the poem "Late Summer" from that collection suggestive in "its amiable randomness . . . of the limitations of Dunn's esthetic, which pays more attention to the creative process than the creative product." A reviewer for the *Virginia Quarterly Review,* on the other hand, calls this collection Dunn's "finest."

Later collections reinforce Dunn's place in contemporary American poetry. *Not Dancing* elicits Jonathan Holden's pronouncement that Dunn is a "poet/seer, . . . the *real* thing." And Philip Booth couches his praise in a bit of understatement on the dustjacket for *Between Angels:* in reading Dunn's poems, he writes, "one starts to see the flowers on the kitchen table."

BIOGRAPHICAL/CRITICAL SOURCES:

BOOKS

Dictionary of Literary Biography, Volume 105: *American Poets since World War II,* Gale (Detroit), 1991.

Holden, Jonathan, *Style and Authenticity in Postmodern Poetry,* University of Missouri Press (Columbia), 1986, p. 124.

PERIODICALS

American Poetry Review, May-June, 1979, pp. 29-33.
Booklist, February 1, 1982, p. 694; May 1, 1994, p. 1577.
Chowder Review, number 8, 1977, pp. 74-76; number 12, 1979, pp. 41-45.
Georgia Review, fall, 1977; fall, 1979; summer, 1994, p. 406.
Hudson Review, summer, 1979, pp. 252-68.
Library Journal, April 1, 1993, p. 98.
Los Angeles Times Book Review, May 11, 1986, p. 1.
New Letters, June, 1975, pp. 103-7.
New Republic, June 2, 1986, pp. 39-41.
New York Times Book Review, July 6, 1986, p. 23; January 28, 1990, p. 26.
Parnassus, fall-winter, 1977, pp. 198-207.
Poetry, December, 1982.
Publishers Weekly, March 29, 1993, p. 42; March 28, 1994, p. 88.
Sewanee Review, April, 1994, p. R36.
Times Literary Supplement, January 11, 1985, p. 35.
Virginia Quarterly Review, autumn, 1982, p. 135; autumn, 1994, p. 133.
Washington Post Book World, July 6, 1986, p. 8.
Western Humanities Review, summer, 1985, pp. 162-64.
Yale Review, summer, 1979, pp. 557-77.

*　　　*　　　*

DUNNE, Marie
See CLARK, Ann Nolan

*　　　*　　　*

DUPONT, Paul
See FREWIN, Leslie Ronald

E

EDDISON, John 1916-

PERSONAL: Born September 7, 1916, in Derbyshire, England; son of Frederick William (a clergyman) and Dorothea (Buchanan-Dunlop) Eddison. *Education:* Trinity College, Cambridge, M.A., 1939.

ADDRESSES: *Home*—Durham Lodge, Crowborough, Sussex, England.

CAREER: Ordained minister in Church of England, 1939; St. John's, Tunbridge Wells, England, curate, 1939-43; Scripture Union, London, traveling secretary, 1942-80. Honorary chaplain to Bishop of Rochester, 1947-59. Member of board of directors of school companies.

MEMBER: National Club, Marylebone Cricket Club.

WRITINGS:

Search Party, Scripture Union (London), 1960.
The Troubled Mind, Scripture Union, 1963, Concordia, 1972.
Christian Answers about Doctrine, Scripture Union, 1966.
Christian Answers to Contemporary Problems, Scripture Union, 1967.
Who Died Why, Scripture Union, 1970.
God's Frontiers, Scripture Union, 1972.
To Tell You the Truth, Scripture Union, 1972.
It's A Great Life, Scripture Union, 1973.
What Makes a Leader, Scripture Union, 1974.
Understanding Bible Topics, Scripture Union, 1977.
Step by Step, Walters, 1977.
Talking to Children, Walters, 1978.
Your Money and Your Life, Walters, 1979.
What Christians Believe, Hodder & Stoughton (London), 1981.
Towards Confirmation, Marshall, 1982.
(Editor) *Bash: A Study in Spiritual Power,* Marshall, 1983.
The Bible, Scripture Union, 1984.

The Last Lap, Kingsway, 1986.

Also author of *Dictionary of Bible Words,* Scripture Union, and *Prayer by Prayer,* Marshall. Also author of booklets, including *Heart Castle* (juvenile), *Glad Tidings* (juvenile), *Newness of Life, Finding the Way,* and *Were You There?* (Christian verse).

SIDELIGHTS: John Eddison told *CA:* "In recent years I have in effect become my own publisher. With funds available for the purpose I produce small print orders of 1,000 to 3,000, relying on personal recommendations and reviews, so far with some success. I have no plans at present to produce anything bigger, though I am under some pressure to try to get reprinted some of my earlier books."

*   *   *

EDELSON, Julie 1949-

PERSONAL: Born March 26, 1949, in Brooklyn, NY; daughter of Sidney (a physician) and Virginia (a teacher; maiden name, Odle) Edelson; married Roy Hantgan (a professor of biochemistry), December 19, 1971; children: Abbie, Aaron. *Education:* Attended University of Manchester, 1969-70; Sarah Lawrence College, B.A., 1970; Cornell University, Ph.D., 1974.

ADDRESSES: *Home*—910 Carolina Ave., Winston-Salem, NC 27101.

CAREER: Artschool, Carrboro, NC, instructor and creator of Prose Workshop, 1979-83; University of North Carolina at Chapel Hill, Wilson Library, out-of-print specialist, 1981-83; Guilford Technical Community College, Jamestown, NC, coordinator of writing center, 1983-84; Wake Forest University, editor-coordinator, *Tocqueville Forum,* 1988—, instructor, short story workshop, 1994—; editor, Cut to the Quick Editorial Services, 1990—;

WRITINGS:

No News Is Good (novel), North Point Press (Berkeley, CA), 1986.
Bad Housekeeping (novel), Baskerville Publishers (Dallas), 1995.

Editor of books and other publications.

WORK IN PROGRESS: The Mortal Coil, a novel about biological scientists.

SIDELIGHTS: Julie Edelson told *CA:* "I write in order to think a question out. My questions are moral. Moral questions are like teratomas—snarled masses of randomly differentiated cells, tooth by elbow, trailing shreds of nerve, benign or malignant, and wedged into the social tissue. A novel is a good lab for poking at them without trashing your life and your loved ones. It affords the space, the time, and the leeway for trial and error and control. Characters, sensitive and refractory, are the instruments. The telling itself may be both your allowance for indeterminacy and an order that cancels it out, but you have to be lucky."

Edelson added: "When it works—when you are really on to it, up with it, off on it—the exhilaration is levitating. I mean you ditch your limitations. Like Air Jordan. Sometimes you manage to be funny."

Edelson advised aspiring writers: "Of course, don't write unless you can't help it. But the good news from my experience is you don't have to play games or collaborate with the enemy to be read. I've simply written as well as I can the thoughts that have stricken me in colloquy with the language and sent my work out myself in padded envelopes and have now scored twice. No agent and no pandering to popular inanity/insanity. Keep your day job and keep the faith."

*   *   *

ELLIS, Carolyn Sue 1950-

PERSONAL: Born October 13, 1950, in Luray, VA; daughter of Arthur (a contractor) and Mary Katherine (a secretary; maiden name, Good) Ellis; married Eugene Weinstein (a sociologist), December 25, 1984 (died February 8, 1985). *Education:* College of William and Mary, B.A. (with high honors), 1973; State University of New York at Stony Brook, M.A., 1977, Ph.D., 1981.

ADDRESSES: Home—8303 River Oaks Dr., Tampa, FL 33617. *Office*—Department of Sociology, University of South Florida, Tampa, FL 33620.

CAREER: Department of Social Services, Newport News, VA, social worker, 1973-74; State University of New York

at Stony Brook, instructor in sociology, 1977-81; University of South Florida, Tampa, assistant professor, 1981-85, associate professor, 1985-94, professor of sociology, 1994—, director of the Institute for Interpretive Studies.

MEMBER: American Sociological Association, Sociologists for Women in Society, Society for the Study of Symbolic Interaction, Speech Communication Association, Sociologists for Women in Society in the South.

WRITINGS:

Fisher Folk: Two Communities on Chesapeake Bay, University Press of Kentucky (Lexington), 1986.
Investigating Subjectivity: Research on Lived Experience, Sage Publications (Beverly Hills, CA), 1992.
Final Negotiations: A Story of Love, Loss, and Chronic Illness, Temple University Press (Philadelphia), 1995.

Also author of *Social Perspectives on Emotion,* Volume 3, JAI Press (Greenwich, CT). Contributor of articles and reviews to sociology journals.

SIDELIGHTS: Carolyn Sue Ellis told *CA* that when she, a graduate student, fell in love with her professor Gene Weinstein, he was experiencing the first stages of chronic emphysema. As Weinstein's health declined and he became increasingly disabled and immobile, they fought to maintain their love in the face of dire threats posed by the dynamics of chronic illness and romance. Fusing their skills as sociological analysts with their thirst for meaningful lived experience, Ellis and Weinstein negotiated their daily lives in a way that enabled each of them to feel sufficiently autonomous—he not always like a patient and she not always like a caretaker. Writing as a sociologist, Ellis portrays their life together as a way to understand the complexities of romance, of living with a progressive illness, and, in the final negotiation and reversal of positions, of coping with the loss of a loved one.

*   *   *

ELPHICK, Richard Hall 1943-

PERSONAL: Born May 3, 1943, in Toronto, Ontario, Canada; son of Archibald George (a manager) and Ada (Laycock) Elphick; married Ester Timbancaya (a teacher), August 24, 1968; children: Tomas Ponce de Leon, Elizabeth Alice. *Education:* University of Toronto, B.A. (with honors), 1964; University of California, Los Angeles, M.A., 1967; Yale University, Ph.D., 1972. *Religion:* Episcopal.

ADDRESSES: Home—12 Yellow Cir., Middletown, CT 06457. *Office*—Department of History, Wesleyan University, Middletown, CT 06457.

CAREER: Wesleyan University, Middletown, CT, professor of history, 1971—.

AWARDS, HONORS: Woodrow Wilson fellow, 1965-66; Canada Council fellow at Yale University, 1968-71; National Endowment for the Humanities grant, 1975; South African Research Program fellow, Yale University, 1979-80; Institute of Social and Economic Research fellow, Rhodes University, 1983-84; Social Science Research Council grant, 1987; John Simon Guggenheim fellow, 1987-88; Social Services Research Council grant, 1987.

WRITINGS:

Kraal and Castle: Khoikhoi and the Founding of White South Africa, Yale University Press (New Haven, CT), 1977.

(With Hermann Giliomee) *The Shaping of South African Society, 1652-1820,* Longman (New York City), 1977, revised and expanded edition published as *The Shaping of South African Society, 1652-1840,* Wesleyan University Press (Middletown, CT), 1989.

(Editor with Jeffrey Butler and David Welsh) *Democratic Liberalism in South Africa: Its History and Prospect,* Wesleyan University Press, 1987.

Contributor to history journals.

BIOGRAPHICAL/CRITICAL SOURCES:

PERIODICALS

American Historical Review, June, 1978.
Times Literary Supplement, January 29, 1988, p. 105.*

* * *

ESSEX, Mary
See BLOOM, Ursula (Harvey)

* * *

EVANS, Mary 1946-

PERSONAL: Born August 24, 1946, in Chelmsford, Essex, England; daughter of Francis (a banker) and Evelyn (a teacher; maiden name, Warwick) Evans; married David Morgan (a university dean), December 19, 1983; children: Thomas, James, James Alexander. *Education:* London School of Economics and Political Science, B.Sc., 1967, M.Sc., 1968; University of Sussex, D.Phil., 1975. *Politics:* Labour. *Religion:* None.

ADDRESSES: Home—Patrixbourne Lodge, Patrixbourne, Canterbury CT4 5BP England. *Office*—Darwin College, University of Kent, Canterbury CT1 1XR, England.

CAREER: University of Kent at Canterbury, Canterbury, England, lecturer, 1971-87, senior lecturer in sociology, 1987-93, professor of women's studies, 1993—.

WRITINGS:

(Editor with David Morgan) *Work on Women: Guide to the Literature,* Tavistock Publications (London), 1979.

Lucien Goldmann: An Introduction, Harvester (Brighton, England), 1981.

(Editor) *The Woman Question,* Fontana (London), 1982, second edition, Sage Publications (Beverly Hills, CA), 1994.

(With Clare Ungerson) *Sexual Divisions: Patterns and Processes,* Tavistock Publications, 1983.

Simone de Beauvoir: A Feminist Mandarin, Tavistock Publications, 1985.

(Editor with Janet Sayers and Nanneke Redclift) *Engels Revisited,* Tavistock Publications, 1986.

Jane Austen and the State, Tavistock Publications, 1987.

Battle for Britain, Routledge & Kegan Paul (London), 1993.

SIDELIGHTS: In her 1985 book, *Simone de Beauvoir: A Feminist Mandarin,* Mary Evans analyzes from a modern feminist perspective the life and works of the renowned French author. Beauvoir's *Second Sex,* a highly acclaimed 1949 study of the oppression of women in Western society, was at one time regarded as the foremost text of the feminist movement. Writing in the *Times Literary Supplement,* reviewer Anne Whitmarsh judges Evans's book a "scholarly and very readable analysis" of Beauvoir as a feminist. Although Evans sought "a contemporary feminist message" in the body of Beauvoir's work, she was ultimately disappointed, Whitmarsh suggests, because "such a message was never intended." Indeed, Whitmarsh maintains, Beauvoir's discussion of feminist issues was limited only to *The Second Sex* and many of her ideas run contrary to contemporary feminist thought. Such ideas—including her assertion that women are "willing victims" who accept the "passive and subordinate role assigned them by the dominant sex"—contribute to Evans's opinion that others who have studied Beauvoir have not reviewed her work with a strongly critical eye. Yet, Whitmarsh concludes, "like many who have studied Beauvoir in detail and found her wanting," Evans still stands in awe of her subject and carefully balances criticism with praise in her analysis.

Evans told *CA:* "My interests are primarily in gender divisions and gender differences, particularly as articulated in literature."

BIOGRAPHICAL/CRITICAL SOURCES:

PERIODICALS

Times Literary Supplement, February 5, 1982; October 4, 1985.

* * *

EVSLIN, Bernard   1922-1993

PERSONAL: Born April 9, 1922, in Philadelphia, PA; died of cardiac arrest, June 4, 1993, in Kauai, HI; son of Leo (an inventor) and Tillie (Stalberg) Evslin; married Dorothy Shapiro (a writer and teacher), April 18, 1942; children: Thomas, Lee, Pamela Evslin Zino, Janet Evslin Clinton. *Education:* Attended Rutgers University.

CAREER: Writer, screenwriter, playwright, and producer of documentaries filmed in the United States and various parts of Europe and Asia. *Military service:* U.S. Army, 1942-45.

AWARDS, HONORS: Best television film of 1959, *Variety,* for *Face of the Land;* National Education Association Award, 1961, for best television documentary on an educational theme; National Book Award nomination, 1975, for *The Green Hero;* Washington Irving Children's Book Choice Award, Westchester Library Association, 1986, for *Hercules.*

WRITINGS:

The Geranium Hat (play), produced Off-Broadway at the Orpheum Theatre, 1959.
Step on a Crack (play), produced on Broadway at the Ethel Barrymore Theatre, 1962.
The Merchants of Venus, Fawcett (New York City), 1964.
The Greek Gods (also see below), Scholastic Book Services (New York City), 1966.
Heroes and Monsters of Greek Myth (also see below), Scholastic Book Services, 1967.
Heroes, Gods and Monsters of the Greek Myths (includes *The Greek Gods* and *Heroes and Monsters of Greek Myth*), Four Winds (Bristol, FL), 1967.
Adventures of Ulysses (also see below), Scholastic Book Services, 1969.
The Trojan War (also see below), Scholastic Book Services, 1971.
Gods, Demigods and Heroes, Scholastic Book Services, 1975.
The Green Hero, Four Winds, 1975.
The Dolphin Rider, Scholastic Book Services, 1976.
Greeks Bearing Gifts (includes *Adventures of Ulysses* and *The Trojan War*), Four Winds, 1976.
Heraclea, Four Winds, 1978.
Signs and Wonders: Tales from the Old Testament, Bantam (New York City), 1979.

Hercules, Morrow (New York City), 1984.
Jason and the Argonauts, Morrow, 1986.
Gods, Demigods and Demons: An Encyclopedia of Greek Mythology, Scholastic Inc. (New York City), 1988.

"MONSTERS OF MYTHOLOGY" SERIES

The Dragon of Boeotia, Chelsea House (New York City), 1987.
Geryon, Chelsea House, 1987.
Cerberus, Chelsea House, 1987.
Procrustes, Chelsea House, 1987.
The Cyclopes, Chelsea House, 1987.
Medusa, Chelsea House, 1987.
The Minotaur, Chelsea House, 1987.
Hecate, Chelsea House, 1988.
Anteus, Chelsea House, 1988.
The Sirens, Chelsea House, 1988.
The Chimaera, Chelsea House, 1988.
The Furies, Chelsea House, 1989.
Amycus, Chelsea House, 1989.
The Calydonian Boar, Chelsea House, 1989.
The Hydra, Chelsea House, 1989.
Scylla and Charybdis, Chelsea House, 1989.
Drabne of Dole, Chelsea House, 1990.
Pig's Ploughman, Chelsea House, 1990.
Ladon, Chelsea House, 1990.
The Nemean Lion, Chelsea House, 1990.
The Sphinx, Chelsea House, 1990.

OTHER

Also author of scripts for documentaries and short films, including *Face of the Land,* 1959. Several of Evslin's books have been translated into Japanese.

SIDELIGHTS: While a producer of documentaries filmed in the United States, Europe, and Asia, Bernard Evslin also wrote stage plays and screenplays for a wider audience. His comedy *The Geranium Hat* won acclaim for productions in 1959, and in the same year, his *Face of the Land* was named best television film in a poll by *Variety.* His experiences as a screenwriter in the early 1960s served as the basis for his 1964 novel *The Merchants of Venus.* In the mid-1960s, Evslin turned to writing about mythology; some of his prolific output of books about mythology and its heroes and monsters are used in numerous schools.

OBITUARIES:

PERIODICALS

New York Times, June 26, 1993, p. 27.*

F

FACKLAM, Margery (Metz) 1927-

PERSONAL: Born September 6, 1927, in Buffalo, NY; daughter of Eduard Frederick (a civil engineer) and Ruth (Schauss) Metz; married Howard F. Facklam, Jr. (a teacher), July 9, 1949; children: Thomas, David, John, Paul, Margaret. *Education:* University of Buffalo, B.A., 1947; State University of New York College at Buffalo, M.S., 1976. *Avocational interests:* "Nature in general, animals in particular, reading, writing, my grandchildren—seven boys and one girl—family, and anything new and exciting in the world."

ADDRESSES: Home—9690 Clarence Center Rd., Clarence Center, NY 14032.

CAREER: Erie County Department of Social Welfare, Buffalo, NY, caseworker, 1948; high school teacher of science in Snyder, NY, 1949-50; Buffalo Museum of Science, Buffalo, assistant administrator of education, 1970-74; Aquarium of Niagara Falls, Niagara Falls, NY, curator of education and public relations, 1974-77; Buffalo Zoo, Buffalo, director of education, 1977-79; freelance writer and instructor for Institute of Children's Literature.

MEMBER: American Society of Journalists and Authors, Society of Children's Book Writers, National League of American Pen Women, Authors Guild.

AWARDS, HONORS: Spare Parts for People was on the New York Public Library's list of Best Books for Teenagers, 1988; Reading Magic Award, *Parenting* magazine, 1989, for *Do Not Disturb: The Mysteries of Hibernation and Sleep* and *Partners for Life: The Mysteries of Animal Symbiosis; The Trouble with Mothers* was named on the *School Library Journal*'s list of recommended books for reluctant young adult readers, 1990; *And Then There was One: The Mysteries of Animal Extinction* was cited on the *School Library Journal*'s list of best books of 1990; *Bees*

Dance and Whales Sing: The Mysteries of Animal Communication was selected for the *Boston Globe*'s list of 25 best nonfiction books of 1992; *Kid's World Almanac of Amazing Facts about Numbers, Math, and Money* was on the New York Public Library's list of Best Books for the Teen Age, 1993; *I Eat Dinner, So Can I, But Not Like Mine, Spare Parts for People, Changes in the Wind, The Brain, Magnificent Mind Machine, Wild Animals, Gentle Women, Frozen Snakes and Dinosaur Bones, Plants—Extinction or Survival?, Partners for Life: The Mysteries of Animal Symbiosis,* and *Do Not Disturb: The Mysteries of Hibernation and Sleep* were all named Outstanding Science Trade Books.

WRITINGS:

Whistle for Danger, Rand McNally (Chicago, IL), 1962.
Behind These Doors: Science Museum Makers, Rand McNally, 1968.
(With Patricia Phibbs) *Corn Husk Crafts,* Sterling (New York City), 1973.
Frozen Snakes and Dinosaur Bones (Junior Literary Guild selection), Harcourt (New York City), 1976.
Wild Animals, Gentle Women (Junior Literary Guild selection), Harcourt, 1978.
(With husband, Howard Facklam) *From Cell to Clone: The Story of Genetic Engineering* (Book-of-the-Month Club selection), Harcourt, 1979.
The Brain, Magnificent Mind Machine, Harcourt, 1982.
(With Howard Facklam) *Changes in the Wind* (Junior Literary Guild selection), Harcourt, 1986.
Spare Parts for People, Harcourt, 1987.
So Can I, Harcourt, 1987.
But Not Like Mine, Harcourt, 1987.
Do Not Disturb: The Mysteries of Hibernation and Sleep, Sierra Club Books (San Francisco, CA), 1989.
The Trouble with Mothers (fiction; Junior Library Guild selection), Clarion, 1989.

Partners for Life: The Mysteries of Animal Symbiosis, Sierra Club Books, 1989.

And Then There Was One: The Mysteries of Animal Extinction, Sierra Club Books, 1990.

(With Howard Facklam) *Plants—Extinction or Survival?,* Enslow Publishers (Hillside, NJ), 1990.

(With Howard Facklam) *Avalanche!,* Crestwood House (Mankato, MN), 1991.

(With Howard Facklam) *Healing Drugs: The History of Pharmacology,* Facts on File (New York City), 1992.

I Eat Dinner, Boyds Mills Press, 1992.

I Go to Sleep, Boyds Mills Press, 1992.

Bees Dance and Whales Sing: The Mysteries of Animal Communication, Sierra Club Books, 1992.

(With daughter Margaret Thomas) *Kid's World Almanac of Amazing Facts about Numbers, Math, and Money,* Pharos Books, 1992.

Who Harnessed the Horse?: The Story of Animal Domestication (Junior Library Guild selection), Little, Brown (Boston, MA), 1992.

The Big Bug Book, Little, Brown, 1994.

What Does the Crow Know?: The Mysteries of Animal Intelligence, Sierra Club Books, 1994.

Contributor to periodicals, including *Ranger Rick, Cricket,* and *Spider.*

WORK IN PROGRESS: Caterpillars, for Little, Brown; *The Invaders,* a four-book series about viruses, bacteria, insects, and parasites, for 21st Century Books.

SIDELIGHTS: Margery Facklam once told *CA:* "Writing is hard work, at least for me, but I can't stay away from it. I love being a writer because I'm never bored. How can you be when there are always new ideas to develop, or research to do, or revisions to work on? And I especially love writing for children just because it is a bigger challenge. My first two picture books, *So Can I* and *But Not Like Mine,* taught me that the old truism is indeed true, 'Easy reading is hard writing.' I did a lot of revising on those books.

"It was a great pleasure to be rewarded with the wonderful review in *Booklist* for the young adult book *Changes in the Wind* which said the topic (climate changes) 'is broad and complex, and [Margery and her husband, Howard,] do an admirable job of presenting its dimensions.' The reviewer added that it was 'A first rate explanation.' That's what you work for in nonfiction, a way of explaining a subject clearly yet dramatically. It's been a special thrill to see some of these books translated into Japanese, Italian, and French.

Facklam later added: "Looking back, I can now see that writing nonfiction took root very early in my childhood, when I spent every Saturday at the Buffalo Museum of Science. When I was in high school I worked Saturdays and after school in the reptile house at the Buffalo Zoo, where Marlin Perkins (of *Wild Kingdom* fame) was director. He taught me more about snakes than any number of college courses ever could do. Then I worked my way through college taking care of a colony of porcupines and other animals in the biology department. (I even know how to give a porcupine a bath!) I have finally written about porcupines, but I still haven't written about snakes. Maybe that will be next.

"The books I loved best were almost all nonfiction, especially the real life adventures of Roy Chapman Andrews, who found the first dinosaur eggs, and explorers like Osa Johnson and Richard Halliburton. We didn't have television, but books fed my imagination just as well, maybe better. Although my dreams of becoming an explorer didn't come true, I am a kind of explorer in a small way as I research books.

"I've collaborated on many books with my husband, Howard, because he knows more biology than I do, but more of the family is involved now. My daughter, Peggy (Margaret Thomas), and I collaborated on *The Kids World Almanac of Amazing Facts about Numbers, Math, and Money,* and my son, Paul, has illustrated two science-picture books, *The Big Bug Book* and *Creepy Crawly Caterpillars.*"

BIOGRAPHICAL/CRITICAL SOURCES:

PERIODICALS

Booklist, August, 1986.
Publishers Weekly, May 19, 1989.
School Library Journal, January, 1988; September, 1990.

*   *   *

FALK, Quentin 1948-

PERSONAL: Born August 22, 1948, in London, England; son of Roger Salis (a management consultant) and Margaret Helen Falk; married Anthea Sillery (a teacher), February 22, 1975; children: Benjamin Salis, Laura Valentine. *Education:* Attended Inns of Court School of Law, 1968-69. *Avocational interests:* Cricket, classical music, travel.

ADDRESSES: Old Barn Cottage, Little Marlow, Buckinghamshire SL7 3RZ, England.

CAREER: Thames Valley Newspapers, Workingham, England, reporter and film critic, 1969-73; *Screen International,* King Publications, London, England, foreign editor, 1973-76, associate editor, 1976-80, editor, 1980-82; *London Daily Mail,* London, assistant entertainments editor and film critic, 1983-84; free-lance writer and broadcaster, 1984—. Co-director of documentary film *Chocks Away: The Making of Biggles,* for Yellowbill Productions.

AWARDS, HONORS: Travels in Greeneland: The Cinema of Graham Greene was nominated for Mobil British Film Institute awards, 1985.

WRITINGS:

Travels in Greeneland: The Cinema of Graham Greene, Quartet Books (London), 1984.
(With Dominic Prince) *Last of a Kind: The Sinking of Lew Grade,* Quartet Books, 1987.
The Golden Gong: Fifty Years of Rank Films, Columbus Books (London), 1987.
Anthony Hopkins: The Authorized Biography, Virgin Books (London), 1989, revised edition, 1993.
Albert Finney: In Character, Robson Books (London), 1992.

Contributor to books, including *Anatomy of the Movies,* edited by David Pirie, Windward, 1981, and *British Cinema Now,* edited by Martyn Auty and Nick Roddick, British Film Institute, 1985. Film critic for *Sunday Mirror* and *Daily Telegraph.* Contributor to *Film Yearbook.* Contributor to magazines and newspapers, including *Today, Guardian, Punch, Sight and Sound, Radio Times, Broadcast,* and *Expression!* Editor of *Flicks* movie monthly.

BIOGRAPHICAL/CRITICAL SOURCES:

PERIODICALS

Times Literary Supplement, February 22, 1985.

*   *   *

FARRELL, C(larence) Frederick, Jr. 1934-

PERSONAL: Born November 10, 1934, in Stoughton, MA; son of Clarence Frederick and Dorothy (Dykeman) Farrell; married Edith Rodgers (a teacher and writer), June 1, 1957; children: Charles Frederick, Stephen Douglas. *Education:* University of Massachusetts at Amherst, B.A., 1956; University of Iowa, M.A., 1958; College de France, additional study, 1960-61; University of Pittsburgh, Ph.D., 1965.

ADDRESSES: Home—100 Columbia Ave., Morris, MN 56267. *Office*—Division of the Humanities, University of Minnesota, Morris, MN 56267

CAREER: Lake Forest College, Lake Forest, IL, instructor in French, 1961-65; University of Minnesota, Morris, assistant professor, 1965-68, associate professor, 1968-78, professor of French, 1978—, chairman of Division of the Humanities, 1985—. President of Friends of the Library,

Morris, 1967-71. *Military service:* U.S. Army, 1957-58 and 1961-62. U.S. Army Reserve, 1958-63.

MEMBER: Modern Language Association of America, American Association of Teachers of French, Foreign Language Association of the Red River Valley, Rocky Mountain Modern Language Association, Women in French, Societe internationale d'etudes Yourcenariennes (board of directors), North American Marguerite Yourcenar Society, Centre international de documentation Marguerite Yourcenar (founding member), Sigma Kappi Phi, Pi Delta Phi.

AWARDS, HONORS: Fulbright scholarship, 1960-61.

WRITINGS:

WITH WIFE, EDITH R. FARRELL

(Editor and translator) Emeric Cruce, *The New Cineas,* Garland Publishing (New York City), 1972.
Marguerite Yourcenar in Counterpoint, University Press of America (Lanham, MD), 1983.
(Editor) *The Complete Works of Louise Labe,* Whitston Publishing (Troy, NY), 1986.
(Editor and translator) Gaston Bachelard, *Air and Dreams,* Dallas Institute of Humanities and Culture (Dallas), 1986.
(Editor) *Les Visages de la mort dans l'oeuvre de Marguerite Yourcenar: actes d'un colloque international tenu a l'Universite du Minnesota, Morris, 7-10 juillet 1992,* University of Minnesota, Morris, 1993.
Side by Side French and English Grammar, National Textbook Co. (Lincolnwood, IL), 1994.
Side by Side Spanish and English Grammar, National Textbook Co., 1994.

Contributor to reference works, including *Dictionary of Literary Biography, French Women Writers,* and *Gay and Lesbian Literature.* Contributor of articles, poems, and reviews to newspapers and language and literature journals.

WORK IN PROGRESS: With Edith R. Farrell, continuing work on Marguerite Yourcenar.

SIDELIGHTS: C. Frederick Farrell, Jr., told *CA:* "In our research and writing my wife and I have concentrated on bringing to our colleagues and to the public authors and works that were, at the time, not well enough known. Emeric Cruce, who formulated a model United Nations in the early seventeenth century, had been mentioned by only a handful of writers in the intervening years, and there was no accurate translation of his work. Gaston Bachelard's studies of the four elements, although weil known to readers of French, were—except for the volume on fire—not available in English. While there were a number of translations of Louise Labe's love sonnets, her complete works had never been published in English, despite recently renewed interest in her work. As for Marguerite Yourcenar, although her works had been consistently reviewed in the press since the publication of her *Memoirs of Hadrian,* and while coverage was given to her election to the French Academy, no academic book on her work existed before ours. The variety that we have found among these writers, especially within the canons of Bachelard and Yourcenar, continues to provide sources for future endeavors."

*   *   *

FARRELL, Edith R(odgers) 1933-

PERSONAL: Born December 5, 1933, in Pittsburgh, PA; daughter of Charles Denver and Edna Elizabeth (Snee) Rodgers; married C. Frederick Farrell, Jr. (a teacher and writer), June 1, 1957; children: Charles Frederick, Stephen Douglas. *Education:* Allegheny College, B.A. (cum laude), 1955; University of Iowa, M.A., 1957, Ph.D., 1965; College de France, additional study, 1960-61.

ADDRESSES: Home—100 Columbia Ave., Morris, MN 56267. *Office*—Division of the Humanities, University of Minnesota, Morris, MN 56267.

CAREER: Teacher and director of foreign languages at elementary schools in Wilkinsburg, PA, 1958-60; Lake Forest College, Lake Forest, IL, instructor in French and Western civilization, 1961-65; University of Minnesota, Morris, instructor in French, 1965-71; writer, 1971-85; University of Minnesota, lecturer, 1985-92, associate professor, 1992-94, professor of French, 1994—.

MEMBER: Modern Language Association of America, American Association of Teachers of French, Foreign Language Association of the Red River Valley, Rocky Mountain Modern Language Association, Women in French, Societe internationale d'etudes Yourcenariennes (member of board of directors), North American Marguerite Yourcenar Society (president), Centre international de documentation Marguerite Yourcenar (founding member), Order of the Eastern Star (past matron), Pi Gamma Mu, Pi Delta Phi.

AWARDS, HONORS: Phi Beta Kappa.

WRITINGS:

WITH HUSBAND, C. FREDERICK FARRELL, JR.

(Editor and translator) Emeric Cruce, *The New Cineas,* Garland Publishing (New York City), 1972.
Marguerite Yourcenar in Counterpoint, University Press of America (Lanham, MD), 1983.
(Editor and translator) *The Complete Works of Louise Labe,* Whitston Publishing (Troy, NY), 1986.

(Editor and translator) Gaston Bachelard, *Air and Dreams,* Dallas Institute of Humanities and Culture (Dallas), 1986.
(Editor) *Les Visages de la mort dans l'oeuvre de Marguerite Yourcenar: actes d'un colloque international tenu a l'Universite du Minnesota, Morris, 7-10 juillet 1992,* University of Minnesota, Morris, 1993.
Side by Side French and English Grammar, National Textbook Co. (Lincolnwood, IL), 1994.
Side by Side Spanish and English Grammar, National Textbook Co., 1994.

OTHER

(Translator) Marguerite Yourcenar, *The Alms of Alcippe,* Targ Editions, 1982.
(Editor and translator) Gaston Bachelard, *Water and Dreams,* Dallas Institute of Humanities and Culture, 1983.

Contributor to reference works, including *Dictionary of Literary Biography, French Women Writers,* and *Gay and Lesbian Literature.* Contributor of articles, poems, and reviews to newspapers and language and literature journals.

WORK IN PROGRESS: With husband, C. Frederick Farrell, Jr., continuing work on Marguerite Yourcenar; with student researchers, the transcription and translation of autograph documents from archives of the Minnesota Historical Society and a collection of work by Francophone writers.

SIDELIGHTS: Edith R. Farrell and her husband have collaborated on a number of books involving little-known writers, especially foreign authors about whom little had been previously available in English.

*   *   *

FEATHER, John 1947-

PERSONAL: Born December 20, 1947, in Leeds, England; son of Harold R. and E. May (Barnett) Feather; married Sarah Rees, 1971. *Education:* Oxford University, B.A., 1968, B.Litt., 1972, M.A., 1972; Loughborough University, Ph.D., 1986.

ADDRESSES: Home—Quorn, England. *Office*—Department of Library and Information Studies, Loughborough University, Loughborough, Leicester LE11 3TU, England.

CAREER: Oxford University, Oxford, England, assistant librarian at Bodleian Library, 1972-79; Loughborough University, Loughborough, England, lecturer, 1979-84, senior lecturer in library and information studies, 1984-88, professor of information and library studies, 1988—, dean of education and humanities, 1994—. Munby Fellow in bibliography at Cambridge University, 1977-78; visiting professor at University of California, Los Angeles, 1982; consultant to British Council and UNESCO.

MEMBER: Library Association (fellow), Bibliographical Society (member of council, 1982-85), Oxford Bibliographical Society (president, 1989-93), Institute of Information Scientists.

WRITINGS:

English Book Prospectuses: An Illustrated History, Bird and Bull Press, 1984.
The Provincial Book Trade in Eighteenth-Century England, Cambridge University Press (Cambridge, England), 1985.
A Dictionary of Book History, Croom Helm (Beckenham, Kent), 1986.
(With David McKitterick) *A History of Books and Libraries: Two Views,* Library of Congress (Washington, DC), 1986.
A History of British Publishing, Routledge & Kegan Paul (London), 1988.
Preservation and the Management of Library Collections, Library Association (London), 1991.
The Information Society, Library Association, 1994.
Piracy, Publishing and Politics, Mansell (London), 1994.

Contributor of more than eighty articles and reviews to scholarly journals.

SIDELIGHTS: John Feather told *CA:* "My principal interest as a scholar is in the history of the book trade, chiefly in Britain. I am also, however, much involved with book and library development in the Third World. Because of this I have traveled widely in Asia, the Middle East, Africa, and Latin America as a consultant and an organizer of seminars, and have written on these topics. For an academic, writing is a duty; but for me, it is also a pleasure."

BIOGRAPHICAL/CRITICAL SOURCES:

PERIODICALS

Times Literary Supplement, January 17, 1986.

*   *   *

FEZLER, William 1945-

PERSONAL: Born October 30, 1945, in Melrose, MN; son of Elvin (a merchant) and Edith (a housewife; maiden name, O'Gara) Fezler. *Education:* St. Cloud State University, B.A., 1967; Arizona State University, M.A., 1968, Ph.D., 1971.

ADDRESSES: Home—8448 Harold Way, Los Angeles, CA 90069. *Office*—Institute for Comprehensive Medicine, 9735 Wilshire Blvd., No. 426, Beverly Hills, CA 90212.

CAREER: Institute for Comprehensive Medicine, Beverly Hills, CA, psychologist, 1971—.

MEMBER: American Psychological Association, American Society of Clinical Hypnosis, Society for Clinical and Experimental Hypnosis, Gerontological Society, California State Psychological Association, Southern California Society of Clinical and Experimental Hypnosis, Los Angeles County Psychological Association.

WRITINGS:

(With William S. Kroger) *Hypnosis and Behavior Modification: Imagery Conditioning,* Lippincott (Philadelphia), 1976.
Just Imagine: A Guide to Materialization Using Imagery, Citrine Press, 1980.
Breaking Free: Ninety Ways to Leave Your Lover and Survive, Acropolis Books (Washington, DC), 1985.
(With Eleanor S. Field) *The Good Girl Syndrome: How Women Are Programmed to Fail in a Man's World and How to Stop It* (Literary Guild selection), Macmillan (New York City), 1985.
Creative Imagery, Simon & Schuster (New York City), 1989.
Imagery for Healing, Knowledge and Power, Simon & Schuster, 1990.

*   *   *

FIENNES, Ranulph (Twisleton-Wykeham) 1944-

PERSONAL: Surname is pronounced Fines; born third baronet, March 7, 1944, in Windsor, England; son of Ranulph (second baronet; a lieutenant colonel and regimental commander in the Royal Scots Greys) and Audrey Joan (Newson) Twisleton-Wykeham-Fiennes; married Virginia Pepper (an explorer and the first female recipient of the Polar Medal in 1987), 1970. *Education:* Attended Eton College. *Avocational interests:* Langlauf (cross-country ski racing), photography.

ADDRESSES: Home—10 Belgrave Rd., Barnes, London SW13 9NS, England.

CAREER: Explorer, author, and lecturer. Spent childhood in South Africa. British Army, 1965-70, began as lieutenant, became captain in Royal Scots Greys; served with Special Air Service, 1966, and Sultan of Muscat's Armed Forces, 1968-70; became captain, R.A.C. Leader of British expeditions to White Nile, 1969, Jostedalsbre Glacier, 1970, and Headless Valley, British Columbia,

1971, of the first surface circumpolar journey around the earth, 1979-82 (reached South Pole December 15, 1980, and reached North Pole April 11, 1982), and of five unsupported expeditions toward the North Pole between 1985 and 1990. Has appeared on television and in documentary films; broadcasts over British Broadcasting Corporation.

AWARDS, HONORS: Dhofar Campaign Medal, 1969; Sultan's Bravery Medal, 1970; Krug Award of Excellence, 1980; Gold Medal and honorary life membership, Explorers' Club of New York, 1983; Livingstone's Gold Medal, Royal Scottish Geographic Society, 1983; Founder's Medal, Royal Geographic Society, 1984; honorary D.Sc., Loughborough, 1986; elected to Guinness Hall of Fame, 1987; Polar Medal, 1987; I.T.N. Award, 1990, for the "Event of the Decade."

WRITINGS:

A Talent for Trouble, Hodder & Stoughton (London), 1970.
Ice Fall in Norway, Hodder & Stoughton, 1972.
The Headless Valley, Hodder & Stoughton, 1973.
Where Soldiers Fear to Tread, Hodder & Stoughton, 1975.
Hell on Ice, Hodder & Stoughton, 1979.
To the Ends of the Earth: The Transglobe Expedition—The First Pole-to-Pole Circumnavigation of the Globe, Arbor House (New York City), 1983.
(With wife, Virginia Fiennes) *Bothie, the Polar Dog,* Hodder & Stoughton, 1984.
Living Dangerously (autobiography), Atheneum (New York City), 1988.
The Feather Men, Bloomsbury, 1991, Morrow (New York City), 1993.
Atlantis of the Sands, Bloomsbury, 1992.
(Photographer, with others) Mike Stroud, *Shadows on the Wasteland,* J. Cape (London), 1993.
Mind over Matter: The Epic Crossing of the Antarctic Continent, Delacorte (New York City), 1994.

ADAPTATIONS: To The Ends of the Earth: The Transglobe Expedition—The First Pole-to-Pole Circumnavigation of the Globe was adapted for film.

SIDELIGHTS: Sir Ranulph Fiennes organized and led the Transglobe Expedition, the first to cross the earth from pole to pole. Fiennes relates his experiences in *To the Ends of the Earth: The Transglobe Expedition—The First Pole-to-Pole Circumnavigation of the Globe.* "Lasting from 1979 to 1982 and preceded by four years of planning and practice, Transglobe was a stunning success, especially considering its paltry budget and hand-me-down gear," declares *Washington Post Book World* contributor Dennis Drabelle. The reviewer continues, "Fiennes may dangle too many participles, but his account of the adventure evokes it wonderfully well. In the action passages his writing is often inspired."

Fiennes told *CA* that his 1990 expedition toward the North Pole set the existing world record of reaching the furthest north—eighty-nine miles from the Pole—unassisted. He added that in 1992, he led the Ubar Expedition which discovered the lost city of Ubar in Oman, and in 1993 he led the Pentland South Pole Expedition which achieved the first crossing of the Antarctic continent unassisted, also qualifying as the longest unassisted polar journey in history.

Mind over Matter: The Epic Crossing of the Antarctic Continent describes Fiennes 1500-mile journey with Mike Stroud from Chile in November, 1992, to the South Pole 95 days later. Dragging 485-pound sleds with the necessary supplies for the entire journey, Fiennes and Stroud withstood extreme cold and wind, hazardous landscape, and hungry polar bears to complete their trek. "Another gripping account of endurance and adventure," reports a *Publishers Weekly* reviewer. *Library Journal's* Pamela Bellows points out Fiennes inclusion of the history of Antarctic exploration in his account and praises *Mind over Matter* as a "fascinating book [that] will be enjoyed by adventurers, armchair travelers, and Antarctic researchers.

BIOGRAPHICAL/CRITICAL SOURCES:

BOOKS

Fiennes, Ranulph, *Living Dangerously* (autobiography), Atheneum, 1988.

PERIODICALS

Kirkus Reviews, April 15, 1994.
Library Journal, August, 1994.
Publishers Weekly, May 16, 1994.
Washington Post Book World, September 4, 1983.

*   *   *

FINER, S(amuel) E(dward) 1915-1993

PERSONAL: Born September 22, 1915, in London, England; died June 9, 1993; son of Max and Fanny Finer; married Margaret Ann McFadyean, 1949 (divorced, 1975); married Catherine J. Jones, 1977; children: (first marriage) two sons, one daughter. *Education:* Trinity College, Oxford, B.A. (with first class honors), 1937, M.A., 1946. *Avocational interests:* Painting, writing poetry (for pleasure, not publication), and translating French poetry.

CAREER: Oxford University, Balliol College, Oxford, England, lecturer in politics, 1946-49, junior research fellow, 1949-50; University of Keele, Keele, England, professor of political institutions, 1950-66, deputy vice-chancellor, 1962-64; University of Manchester, Manchester, England, professor of government, 1966-74; Oxford University, All Soul's College, Gladstone Professor of Government and Public Administration, 1974-92, professor emeritus, 1992-93, emeritus fellow. Visiting professor and faculty member, Institute of Social Studies, The Hague, 1957-59; visiting professor at Cornell University, 1962, Hebrew University of Jerusalem, 1969, Simon Fraser University, 1976, European University Institute, 1977, Stanford University, 1979, and Hong Kong University, 1980; visiting Schweitzer Professor, Columbia University, 1982. Fellow, Royal Historical Society. *Military service:* British Army, Royal Signals, 1940-46; became captain.

AWARDS, HONORS: D.Litt., Oxford University, 1979.

WRITINGS:

A Primer of Public Administration, Muller, 1950.

The Life and Times of Sir Edwin Chadwick, Methuen (London), 1952, reprinted, Barnes & Noble (New York City), 1970.

(With Sir John P. R. Maud) *Local Government in England and Wales,* 2nd edition (Finer was not associated with earlier edition), Oxford University Press (Oxford, England), 1953.

Anonymous Empire: A Study of the Lobby in Great Britain, Pall Mall, 1958, 2nd revised and enlarged edition, Humanities (Atlantic Highlands, NJ), 1966.

Private Industry and Political Power (expansion of 1958 Ramsey Muir Memorial Lecture), Pall Mall, 1958.

(With H. B. Berrington and D. J. Bartholomew) *Backbench Opinion in the House of Commons, 1955-59,* Pergamon Press (Oxford), 1961.

The Man on Horseback: The Role of the Military in Politics, Praeger (New York City), 1962, 2nd enlarged edition, Westview Press (Boulder, CO), 1988.

(With others) *Modern Political Systems: Europe,* edited by Roy C. Macridis and R. E. Ward, Prentice-Hall (Englewood Cliffs, NJ), 1963, 4th edition, 1978.

Comparative Government, Penguin Books (Harmondsworth, Middlesex, England), 1970, Basic Books (New York City), 1971.

The Changing British Party System, 1945-1979, American Enterprise Institute for Public Policy Research (Washington, DC), 1980.

(With Vernon Bogdanor and Bernard Rudden) *Comparing Constitutions,* Oxford University Press (New York City), 1994.

EDITOR

(And author of historical notes) Emmanuel J. Sieyes, *What Is the Third Estate?,* translation from the French by M. Blondel, Pall Mall, 1963, Praeger, 1964.

(And author of introduction) Vilfredo Pareto, *Sociological Writings,* translation from the Italian by Derick Mirfin, Praeger, 1966.

Adversary Politics and Electoral Reform, Wigram, 1975.

(And author of introduction) *Five Constitutions,* Humanities, 1979.

(With Alfio Mastropaolo) Paulo Farneti, *The Italian Party System (1945-1980),* St. Martin's (New York City), 1985.

OTHER

Contributor to books, including *Studies in the Growth of 19th Century Government,* edited by Gillian Sutherland, Rowman & Littlefield (Totowa, NJ), 1972; *Participation,* edited by Geraint Parry, Manchester University Press (Manchester, England), 1972; and *The Formation of National States in Western Europe,* edited by C. Tilly, Princeton University Press (Princeton, NJ), 1975. Contributor of articles and reviews to periodicals and newspapers.

SIDELIGHTS: S. E. Finer was an innovative and influential political scientist who is remembered as much by his pupils for his passionate methods of teaching as by the political science community to whom he contributed several notable works. His books include *Anonymous Empire,* a landmark study of lobby groups and their function in modern British politics, *Man on Horseback,* which examines the military's role in various cultures and political structures, and *Britain's Changing Party System.* Before his death, Finer was nearing completion of *The History of Government from the Earliest Times,* a volume he had devoted the better part of his last years to writing and which he also considered his "magnum opus," according to a London *Times* critic.

BIOGRAPHICAL/CRITICAL SOURCES:

BOOKS

Kavanagh, Dennis, and Gillian Peele, editors, *Comparative Government and Politics: Essays in Honour of S. E. Finer,* Westview Press, 1984.

OBITUARIES:

PERIODICALS

Times (London), June 11, 1993, p. 17.*

*   *   *

FISHER, Alan (E.)   1929-

PERSONAL: Born January 25, 1929, in London, England; son of Ernest Frederick and Minnie Esther (Stevens) Fisher; married Beryl Longhorn (a housewife), September 10, 1960; children: Laurence Digby, Maurice Vincent. *Education:* Attended Avery Hill College, 1959-61; University of Sussex, postgraduate diploma in education, 1970; Open University, B.A., 1972. *Politics:* Liberal. *Religion:* Taoism.

ADDRESSES: Home and office—2 Mill Close, Hastings, East Sussex TN35 5EY, England. *Agent*—Campbell Thompson & McLaughlin Ltd., 31 Newington Green, London N16 9PU, England.

CAREER: Royal Borough of Kensington, London, England, library assistant, 1943-47, 1949-50; Lloyds of London, London, clerk, 1950-52; University of London, London, porter, 1952-53; Paddington General Hospital, London, clerk, 1953-58; schoolteacher in New Romney, England, 1961-65, and Hastings, England, 1965-69; Kent Education Committee, Ashford, England, curriculum organizer, 1969-84; writer, 1984—. *Military service:* Royal Air Force, radio operator, 1947-49.

AWARDS, HONORS: Georgette Heyer Award, Georgette Heyer Trust, 1984, for *The Terioki Crossing.*

WRITINGS:

Brief Candles (novel), R. Hale (London), 1979.
Madrid! Madrid! (novel), R. Hale, 1980.
The Midnight Men (novel), R. Hale, 1980.
The Terioki Crossing (novel), Bodley Head (London), 1984, published as *The Three Passions of the Countess Natalya,* Macmillan (New York), 1985.
Yangtze (novel), Bodley Head, 1987.
The Kazak Talisman (novel), Rampant Horse Press, 1994.
Hastings (history), Oaktree Press, 1995.

Writer for BBC-Radio. One of Fisher's novels has been translated into Danish.

SIDELIGHTS: Alan Fisher, who gave up a teaching career to write full-time, once told *CA:* "I grew up in wartime London, my part of it bounded by Portobello Road, Notting Hill, and the Great Western Railway. I showed no aptitude for learning, preferring the cinema, and I left school as soon as I possibly could. With no qualifications, I followed a number of unskilled occupations: machinist in a factory, demolition work, shop assistant. For a while, though, I worked in Kensington public libraries, and this massive exposure to books was very good for me.

"Conscripted for service in the Royal Air Force, I was a watchkeeper on communications with nothing much to do. I read for most of the two years—anything and everything—and left the service with a sort of informal education.

"I was employed as a clerk to an underwriting syndicate at Lloyds, but it went broke, then I worked as a porter at the University of London. I used to sit in the sun on the broad steps at lunchtime and read. I hadn't the faintest

idea what to do with my life. However, I started to write a novel—it was quite impossible by the time I finished it. By then I was a clerk at Paddington General Hospital. I also attended night school and, with the very basic requirements, I entered teacher training.

"Qualified, and now married, I taught history in secondary schools. My wife and I moved to the Sussex coast to bring up our sons. I gained a B.A. from the Open University and a postgraduate diploma from the University of Sussex, but I learned more in the end by reading Arthur Koestler. He was a big influence in my life.

"I began writing seriously ten years ago, and I had three novels published, one translated into Danish. The idea for *The Terioki Crossing* was in the back of my mind for a long time. I spent two years writing it, but it was rejected by a dozen publishers. My present literary agent identified a basic flaw running right through the book, so I rewrote it, and that took another two years. It was my agent who entered the novel for the Georgette Heyer Award. I couldn't have succeeded without him. My novel *The Kazak Talisman* is in the grand tradition of my award-winning book."

*   *   *

FITZ-SIMON, Christopher 1934-

PERSONAL: Born June 9, 1934, in Belfast, Northern Ireland; son of Christopher O'Connell (an army officer) and Gladys Elliott (Killen) Fitz-Simon; married Anne Makower (an opera and television director), May 15, 1965; children: Vanessa Una, Adrian Christopher. *Education:* Trinity College, Dublin, Mod.B.A., 1957, M.A., 1959.

ADDRESSES: Home—8 Richmond Hill, Monkstown, County Dublin, Ireland. *Office*—Abbey Theatre, Lower Abbey St., Dublin 1, Ireland.

CAREER: Radio Telefis Eireann (RTE), Dublin, Ireland, television drama director, 1961-79; Irish Theatre Company, Dublin, artistic director, 1979-83; Abbey Theatre, Dublin, script editor, 1983—; Trinity College, Dublin, lecturer, 1983—. Visiting lecturer at universities in Ireland, England, Italy, Brazil, Argentina, Australia, the United States, and Canada. Founding member of board of directors of Tyrone Guthrie Centre, Annaghmakerrig, Ireland; founding member of board of directors of Siamsa Tire (Ireland's national folk theatre); Irish representative on European Community (EC) Cultural Commission (theater group).

MEMBER: Irish Actors Equity Association, Irish Georgian Society, An Taisce (Ireland's National Trust), Irish Association for Political and Economic Development, Friends of the National Collections, Friends of the Monaghan Museum.

WRITINGS:

PLAYS

But Still and All, broadcast by British Broadcasting Corp.
　　(BBC), 1962.
April Fool, broadcast by BBC, 1963.
Remembrance Sunday, broadcast by RTE, 1968.
The Pool, broadcast by RTE, 1974.
A Bed in the Nettles, broadcast by RTE, 1983.
Vina, broadcast by RTE, 1990.
Johnny Sheehes, broadcast by BBC, 1994.
Ballylenon, broadcast by BBC, 1994.
Raskolnikov's Axe, broadcast by BBC, 1995.

OTHER

The Arts in Ireland, Gill & Macmillan (Dublin), 1982.
The Irish Theatre, Thames & Hudson (London), 1983.
The Irish Village, Holt (New York City), 1986.
The Boys: A Biography of Micheal MacLiammoir and Hilton Edwards, Nick Hern Books, 1994.

Also author of several dramatized documentaries, 1987—, and dramatizations of Jean Giraudoux, James Joyce, Forrest Reid, and others.

SIDELIGHTS: Christopher Fitz-Simon once told *CA:* "I am best known in Ireland as a theatre and television director. If I had to describe my own work I suppose I would say that I am a theatre practitioner and have been so since leaving Dublin University in the late 1950s. There is no common theme in my plays or short stories, except that all are set in contemporary Ireland and are in the tradition of Irish writing, whether consciously or not, comic in spite of noncomic themes.

"*The Arts in Ireland* was commissioned by the Anglo-Irish publishers Gill & Macmillan after I had complained (in an office conversation) about the difficulty of finding chronological references to events and personalities in the arts in Ireland. Michael Gill said, 'You write it.' It took several years to compile, and it covers the period from 2,500 B.C. to 1970.

"*The Irish Theatre* was a commission for the Anglo-American publisher Thames & Hudson. The objective was to show the British and American public how central the Irish theatrical tradition has been to the development of Western theatre, from 1690 to Samuel Beckett, and to formulate a consistent view of the 'Irishness' of writers like Goldsmith, Shaw, Wilde, and Beckett.

"The arts in Ireland at present are bedeviled by a well-meaning, ill-funded, and largely scatterbrained bureaucracy, but professional artists still manage to emerge in spite of this. The theatre is very strong here at present, particularly on account of the diversity and energy of the playwrights in the thirty to fifty-five age group.

"*The Boys,* though published in the UK, was among the top five Irish best-sellers for five weeks in the spring of 1994. The hardback edition sold out in four months."

　　　　*　　　*　　　*

FLYNT, Wayne 1940-

PERSONAL: Born October 4, 1940, in Pontotoc, MS; son of James H. (a manager) and Mae (Moore) Flynt; married Dorothy Smith, August 20, 1961; children: David, Sean. *Education:* Samford University, A.B. (magna cum laude), 1961; Florida State University, M.S., 1962, Ph.D., 1965. *Politics:* Democrat. *Religion:* Baptist.

ADDRESSES: Home—1224 Pene Ln., Auburn, AL 36830. *Office*—Auburn University, Department of History, Auburn, AL 36849.

CAREER: Samford University, Birmingham, AL, began as assistant professor, became professor of history, 1965-77; Auburn University, Auburn, AL, chairperson of history department, 1977-85, Hollifield Professor of History, 1985-90, distinguished university professor, 1990—.

MEMBER: Southern Historical Association.

AWARDS, HONORS: Rembert Patrick Memorial Award for best book on Florida history, and Award of Merit from Association for State and Local History, both 1971, both for *Duncan U. Fletcher: Dixie's Reluctant Progressive;* John Buchanan Award for Excellence in Classroom Teaching; Mortar Board Award for Outstanding Teacher in School of Arts and Sciences, and Faculty Achievement Award in the Humanities, both Auburn University; inducted into Alabama Academy of Distinguished Authors, 1983; Lillian Smith Award for nonfiction, Alabama Library Association award for nonfiction, and *Choice*'s outstanding academic book award, all 1990, all for *Poor but Proud: Alabama's Poor Whites;* named Alabama professor of the year, Council for Advancement and Support of Education, 1991; named Alabamian of the Year, *Mobile Press-Register,* 1992.

WRITINGS:

Duncan U. Fletcher: Dixie's Reluctant Progressive, Florida State University Press (Tallahassee), 1971.
Cracker Messiah: Governor Sidney J. Catts of Florida, Louisiana State University Press (Baton Rouge), 1977.
Dixie's Forgotten People: The South's Poor Whites, Indiana University Press (Bloomington), 1979.
Montgomery: An Illustrated History, Windsor Press (Binghamton, NY), 1980.
Southern Poor Whites: An Annotated Bibliography, Garland Publishing (New York City), 1981.

Mine, Mill & Microchip: A Chronicle of Alabama Enterprise, Windsor Publications (Northridge, CA), 1987.

Poor but Proud: Alabama's Poor Whites, University of Alabama Press (Tuscaloosa), 1989.

(With William W. Rogers, Robert D. Ward, and Leah R. Atkins) *Alabama: The History of a Deep South State,* University of Alabama Press, 1994.

Contributor to various anthologies. Also contributor of articles to history, speech, and social science journals.

BIOGRAPHICAL/CRITICAL SOURCES:

PERIODICALS

Los Angeles Times Book Review, October 29, 1989, p. 6.

*   *   *

FOGEL, Robert W(illiam)   1926-

PERSONAL: Born July 1, 1926, in New York, NY; son of Harry G. and Elizabeth (Mitnik) Fogel; married Enid Morgan, April 2, 1949; children: Michael Paul, Steven Dennis. *Education:* Cornell University, A.B., 1948; Columbia University, A.M., 1960; Johns Hopkins University, Ph.D., 1963.

ADDRESSES: Home—5321 University, Chicago, IL 60615. *Office*—Graduate School of Business, Center for Population Economics, University of Chicago, 1101 East 58th St., Chicago, IL 60637.

CAREER: Johns Hopkins University, Baltimore, MD, instructor in economics, 1958-59; University of Rochester, Rochester, NY, assistant professor of economics, 1960-64; University of Chicago, Chicago, IL, associate professor, 1964-65, professor of economics and history, 1965-75; Harvard University, Cambridge, MA, Taussig Research Professor, 1973-74, Harold Hitchings Burbank Professor of Political Economy and professor of history, 1975-81; University of Chicago, Graduate School of Business, Charles R. Walgreen Professor of American Institutions, 1981—, director of Center for Population Economics, 1981—. University of Chicago, Ford Foundation visiting research professor, 1963-64; University of Rochester, professor of economics and history, autumns, 1968-75; Cambridge University, Pitt Professor of American History and Institutions, 1975-76; Texas A & M University, centennial professor, 1976; lecturer at numerous schools in the United States, Australia, Canada, Israel, and throughout Europe. Associate of Columbia University Seminar in Economics and History; member of Mathematical Social Science Board, 1965-72; National Bureau of Economics, program director, 1978—.

MEMBER: American Academy of Arts and Sciences (fellow), National Academy of Sciences, American Associa-

tion for the Advancement of Science (fellow), American Population Society, Royal Historical Society (fellow), Econometric Society (fellow), Economic History Association (member of board of trustees, 1972-82; president, 1977-78), Social Science History Association (president, 1980-81), Economic History Society (Glasgow; honorary vice president, 1967), Phi Beta Kappa.

AWARDS, HONORS: Social Science Research Council grant, 1966; Mathematical Social Science Board grant, 1966; National Science Foundation grants, 1967, 1970, 1972, 1974, 1976, 1978; Fulbright grant, 1968; Arthur H. Cole Prize, Economic History Association, 1968; Ford Foundation fellowship, 1970; Schumpeter Prize, Harvard University, 1971; Bancroft Prize in American History, Columbia University, 1975, for *Time on the Cross;* honorary D.Sc., University of Rochester, 1987; Gustavus Myers Prize, 1990.

WRITINGS:

The Union Pacific Railroad: A Case in Premature Enterprise, Johns Hopkins University Press (Baltimore, MD), 1960.

(Editor with Stanley L. Engerman, and contributor) *The Reinterpretation of American Economic History,* Harper (New York City), 1971.

(Editor with W. O. Aydelotte and A. G. Bogue, and contributor) *The Dimensions of Quantitative Research in History,* Princeton University Press (Princeton, NJ), 1972.

Railroads and American Economic Growth: Essays in Econometric History, Johns Hopkins University Press, 1974.

(With Engerman) *Time on the Cross: The Economics of American Negro Slavery,* Volume 1: *The Economics of American Negro Slavery,* Volume 2: *Evidence and Methods—A Supplement,* Little, Brown (Boston, MA), 1974.

(Editor with E. Hatfield, S. Kiesler, and E. Shanas) *Aging: Stability and Change in the Family,* Academic Press (New York City), 1981.

(With Geoffrey Elton) *Which Road to the Past?: Two Views of History,* Yale University Press (New Haven, CT), 1984.

Without Consent or Contract: The Rise and Fall of American Slavery, Norton (New York City), 1989.

(Editor with Engerman, and contributor) *Without Consent or Contract—Technical Papers: The Rise and Fall of American Slavery,* Volume 1: *Markets and Production,* Volume 2: *Conditions of Slave Life and Transition to Freedom,* Norton, 1990.

(Editor with Ralph A. Galantine and Richard L. Manning, and contributor) *Without Consent or Contract: The Rise and Fall of American Slavery—Evidence and Methods,* Norton, 1991.

Also author of a Japanese book, the title of which means "Ten Lectures on the New Economic History", Nan-un-do, 1977. Contributor to numerous books, including *The Railroad and the Space Program,* edited by Bruce Mazlish, M.I.T. Press, 1965; *Essays in American Economic History,* edited by Ross M. Robertson and A. W. Coats, Arnold, 1969; *Philosophy and History and Contemporary Historiography,* edited by David Carr, William Dray, and Theodore Geraets, University of Ottawa Press, 1982; and *Long-Term Factors in American Economic Growth,* edited by Engerman and Robert E. Gallman, University of Chicago Press, 1986. Editor, *Long-Term Changes in Nutrition and the Standard of Living,* Ninth International Economic History Congress, 1986. General editor, "Quantitative Studies in History" series, Mathematical Social Science Board and Princeton University, 1971-76, (with S. Thernstrom) "Interdisciplinary Perspectives in Modern History" series, Cambridge University Press, 1979—, and (with C. Pope) "Long-Term Economic Growth" series, National Bureau of Economics, 1988—. Contributor to economics, history, and law journals. Member of editorial board, *Explorations in Economic History,* 1970—, and *Journal of the Social Science History Association,* 1976—.

Some of Fogel's work has been published in Spanish, Italian, and Japanese editions.

WORK IN PROGRESS: The Aging of Union Army Men: A Longitudinal Study, 1830-1940; The Economics of Mortality in the United States, 1650-1980; The Escape from Hunger and Early Death: Europe and America, 1750-2050; Business Ethics in Historical Perspective; Modeling Complex Dynamic Interactions: The Role of Intergenerational, Cohort, and Period Factors in the Political Realignment of the 1850s.

SIDELIGHTS: "Seldom has the advent of a historical study been greeted with such publicity and ballyhoo as [Robert W. Fogel and Stanley L. Engerman's *Time on the Cross: The Economics of American Negro Slavery*], which [claims] to overturn traditional interpretations of American slavery," observes *Commonweal* critic Nathan Irvan Huggins on the 1974 publication of the two-volume work. "Calling themselves cliometricians [those who address historical situations quantitatively]," Huggins adds, "the authors insist that they have cut beneath the sentimentality and moralizing that they think has plagued the historical literature. Because they find slavery to have been not only profitable but viable, . . . those who have an ideological or emotional stake in either a paternalistic master or a totally victimized slave will make these volumes the subject of heated argument."

Indeed, in producing a study based on many heretofore unknown facts and figures, the authors have reworked popular notions of slavery "so drastically . . . that 'revi-

sionist' is a feeble description of its thrust," comments Walter Clemons in *Newsweek.* As Naomi Bliven notes in the *New Yorker,* "Fogel and Engerman believe they are proving that Southern plantation slavery was an economically rational enterprise (they do not claim that it was moral), that slavery did not retard the economic growth of the South, that the slave system would not have died of its own weight, and that, as in any sensible business venture, the slaves were pulled by inducements as well as pushed by force."

In *The Economics of American Negro Slavery,* the first volume of *Time on the Cross,* the authors use government and private sources to substantiate their claims. Clemons recounts that "slave-sale records do not support abolitionist horror stories of the splitting up of black families and the stud-farm breeding of slaves for market (investigation has not turned up a single authentic instance of the latter)." The reviewer continues, "Instead, Victorian morality joined with economic interest to make stable nuclear black families the norm rather than the exception in plantation life. The extent of miscegenation was greatly exaggerated by travelers who observed an unrepresentative concentration of mulattoes in cities and among freedmen." Fogel and Engerman also examine some preconceptions about the personal lives of slaves, including the idea that slave women were sexually promiscuous from their youth. According to the authors' data, the female slave averaged twenty-two years of age at the birth of her first child, making widespread promiscuity unlikely.

Pointing out that "some of these contentions are corroborated by the works of other men which are not always statistically oriented," Bliven postulates that "when a reader adds what he has learned from other sources to what Fogel and Engerman offer, the Southern planter appears a cross between Milton Friedman and Bonnie Prince Charlie. . . . Economics may be, as the authors maintain, a 'hard' science, but it may also be that its 'hardness,' its ability to formulate exact outlines and diagrams, removes it from life; a skeleton is not a man." Similarly, *Time* critic Timothy Foote perceives limitations in the cliometric approach to historical analysis, mentioning that "traditional historians already regard the sociologist and statisticians now invading their discipline as so many Visigoths likely to ruin the already declining quality of written history, substitute accounting for breadth of vision and insight, and eventually relegate old-school historians to peripheral pursuits like intellectual history. . . . Statistics and averages are misleading."

Yet, "*Time on the Cross* is offered not as a complete history but as a corrective," explains Foote. "The authors bow to the need for psychological studies. They are clearly aware that their statistical base is sometimes small and that their inferences about average well-being on the plantation is morally irrelevant to the outrage of slavery, the psychological anguish it caused, and the agonized voices of individual slaves that have come down from the dark past."

In spite of the reservations expressed by many critics about the imperfections of the cliometric research employed in *Time on the Cross,* Clemons ultimately praises the volumes as "a rare instance of a seminal work nonspecialists can read with the most intense pleasure and interest." Bliven states that "despite its argumentative style, [the work] is continually interesting, even absorbing. And, still more important for any contribution to historical understanding, it is productive of reflection. History is concerned with what people were doing, what they thought they were doing, and, when what they did do turned out badly, what alibis they gave. Our authors want to stem one strong current in American historical theory—one that has been a sort of Confederate alibi."

Fogel's next large treatise on slavery, *Without Consent or Contract: The Rise and Fall of American Slavery,* which appeared fifteen years after *Time on the Cross,* is labelled "an act of penance" by reviewer Jonathan Clark in the (London) *Times.* Critics closely scrutinized the two books, looking for evidence that Fogel has refuted or proven the criticisms of his earlier work. While many detractors of *Time on the Cross* complain about the authors' lack of moral awareness and object to their description of slavery as the best means of improved economics for both landowners and slaves, Clark labels *Without Consent or Contract* "a superb achievement of modern quantifying research, which takes due account of humanist learning on the religious, cultural, and political dimension of American slavery from its beginnings to 1860." Eugene D. Genovese remarks in the *Los Angeles Times Book Review* that the book's "brave and thoughtful assault on the easy identification of economic with political and moral progress compels urgent attention today. This splendid book is, among other things, a powerful moral tract."

While Fogel has not departed from the statistical, quantifying approach to historical analysis of the cliometricians, Herbert Mitgang notes in the *New York Times* that *Without Consent or Contract* "is a much more humane work than his cold-blooded and controversial *Time on the Cross.*" Genovese asserts that *"Time on the Cross* was the work of economists who were learning to work as historians and who sometimes stumbled badly," but claims that Fogel has developed into a competent historian who has "written a first-rate book that deserves to rank with the best books of the greatest historians of slavery and the secession crisis."

Weighing some of the criticisms of *Time on the Cross* against this new work, C. Vann Woodward of the *New York Times Book Review* writes: "In *Without Consent or Contract* Mr. Fogel has the good judgment to moderate the polemical tone of the earlier work as well as its strident lectures to other historians." Woodward further notes that while Fogel's beliefs in some instances show moderation from those in *Time on the Cross,* "On the whole, however, he sticks to the main points of the original theses and even brings forth new evidence to strengthen them."

Without Consent or Contract received some negative reaction, however. Genovese notes that "as with every good book, this one may be criticized for matters large and small. One of the most puzzling features of Fogel's performance is the almost total absence of a consideration of Southern culture and society." Genovese further states, "The slight treatment of Southern culture and society reflects the deepest underlying flaw in this impressive book. For Fogel has modified but not abandoned the central vision of *Time on the Cross,* which views the Old South as a bourgeois society and a mere variant of a burgeoning transatlantic capitalism." Peter J. Parish comments in the *Washington Post Book World* that the book "repeats some of the bad habits of *Time on the Cross*—the erection of straw men simply for the pleasure of knocking them down again, the penchant for comparing like with unlike, and, more seriously, the practice of distancing conclusions from evidence." Mitgang echoes earlier criticism of *Time on the Cross,* asserting that Fogel "has not conceded that cliometric conclusions can be as speculative as any economic interpretation of men and events. . . . What the cliometricians fail to recognize is that there is no heartbeat inside a computer."

Overall, critics find *Without Consent or Contract* a powerful treatise on a sensitive subject. Parish observes that Fogel's "restless energy, unquenchable curiosity and almost reckless intellectual courage have kept him in the eye of the historiographical storm for almost two decades. Above all, his zeal for raising new and awkward questions, and his readiness to think the hitherto unthinkable, have shaped much of the modern agenda of historians of slavery, including those who have disagreed most profoundly with his answers." Duncan Macleod concludes in the *Times Literary Supplement* that the book's "syntheses point always to remaining problems and new questions while its account of antebellum politics is no less than a major new interpretation. A very readable account of cliometric approaches and findings, it will surely provoke discussions as deep as *Time on the Cross,* although less rancorous."

Fogel told *CA:* "Most of my work is directed to specialists in economics, history, demography, medicine, or political science. *Time on the Cross* (written with Engerman) was the first book that I directed to a general audience. However, the first volume of *Without Consent or Contract* and two other volumes now underway are also being written for general audiences. These are *Business Ethics in Historical Perspective* and *The Escape from Hunger and Early Death: Europe and America, 1750-2050.* The subtitle of the last volume is intended to indicate that even the most well-to-do classes of the most prosperous nations are only about two-thirds of the way through the escape from hunger and early death. Odd as it may seem, America today is still an underprivileged nation, and that is the way it will be viewed by 2050, if not sooner."

BIOGRAPHICAL/CRITICAL SOURCES:

BOOKS

Goldin, Claudia, and Hugh Rockoff, editors, *Strategic Factors in Nineteenth-Century American Economic History: A Volume to Honor Robert W. Fogel,* University of Chicago Press, 1992.

PERIODICALS

Commentary, August, 1974.
Commonweal, August 23, 1974.
Los Angeles Times Book Review, February 18, 1990, p. 1.
Newsweek, May 6, 1974.
New Yorker, September 39, 1974.
New York Review of Books, May 2, 1974.
New York Times, December 16, 1989.
New York Times Book Review, November 5, 1989, p. 15.
Time, June 17, 1974.
Times (London), April 14, 1990.
Times Literary Supplement, November 9-15, 1990, p. 1211.
Washington Post Book World, November 26, 1989, p. 1.*

—*Sketch by Michaela Swart Wilson*

*   *   *

FOOT, M(ichael) R(ichard) D(aniell) 1919-

PERSONAL: Born December 14, 1919, in London, England; son of Richard Cunningham (a merchant) and Nina (Raymond) Foot; married Mirjam Michaela Romme, 1972; children: (previous marriage) Sarah, Richard. *Education:* Attended New College, Oxford, 1938-39, M.A., 1945, B.Litt., 1950. *Politics:* Radical. *Religion:* Agnostic. *Avocational interests:* "Reading and trying to write good English," following contemporary English and international politics, travel, talking.

ADDRESSES: Office—45 Countess Rd., London NW5 2XH, England.

CAREER: Oxford University, Oxford, England, resident senior member in research and teaching, 1947-59; researcher, 1959-67; University of Manchester, Manchester,

England, professor of modern history, 1967-73; deputy chairman, European Discussion Centre, 1973-75; historian, 1975—. *Military service:* British Army, parachutist, 1939-45; became major; awarded French Croix de Guerre.

MEMBER: Royal Historical Society (fellow).

AWARDS, HONORS: Officer, Order of Orange Nassau, Netherlands, 1989.

WRITINGS:

(With J. L. Hammond) *Gladstone and Liberalism,* English Universities Press, 1952, Collier Books (New York City), 1966.
British Foreign Policy since 1898, Hutchinson's University Library (London), 1956.
Men in Uniform, Praeger (New York City), 1961.
SOE in France, Her Majesty's Stationery Office (HMSO; London), 1966, published as *SOE in France: An Account of the Work of the British Special Operations Executive in France, 1940-1944,* University Publications of America (Frederick, MD), 1984.
(Editor) W. E. Gladstone, *The Gladstone Diaries,* Oxford University Press (Oxford, England), Volumes 1 and 2, 1968, Volumes 3 and 4 (with H. C. G. Matthew), 1974.
(Editor) *War and Society,* Elek (London), 1973.
Resistance, Eyre Methuen (London), 1976.
Six Faces of Courage, Eyre Methuen, 1978.
(With J. M. Langley) *MI9,* Bodley Head (London), 1979, Little, Brown (Boston), 1980.
SOE: An Outline History, BBC, 1984, published as *SOE: An Outline History of the Special Operations Executive, 1940-46,* University Publications of America, 1985.
Art and War: Twentieth-Century Warfare as Depicted by War Artists, Headline (London), 1990.
(Editor) *Holland at War against Hitler: Anglo-Dutch Relations, 1940-45,* Frank Cass (Portland, OR), 1990.

Contributor to *New Cambridge Modern History,* 1960, *Encyclopaedia Britannica,* and *Dictionary of National Biography.* Contributor of articles to numerous periodicals, including *English Historical Review* and *Economist.*

WORK IN PROGRESS: SOE in the Low Countries.

BIOGRAPHICAL/CRITICAL SOURCES:

PERIODICALS

New York Times Book Review, February 8, 1981, p. 9.
Times (London), January 10, 1985.

FORTESCUE, William (Archer Irvine) 1945-

PERSONAL: Born November 10, 1945, in Quetta, Pakistan; son of William Grenville Irvine (an army officer) and Kathleen Sheila (a lecturer; maiden name, Bennett-Jones) Fortescue. *Education:* Wadham College, Oxford, B.A., 1966; Queen's University, Ontario, Canada, M.A., 1968; University College, London, Ph.D., 1973.

ADDRESSES: Office—Rutherford College, University of Kent, Canterbury, Kent CT2 7NX, England.

CAREER: University of Kent, Rutherford College, Canterbury, Kent, England, lecturer, 1971-93, senior lecturer in history, 1993—.

MEMBER: Society of Antiquaries of Scotland, Society for French Historical Studies (United Kingdom), Academy of Macon (France).

WRITINGS:

Alphonse de Lamartine: A Political Biography, Croom Helm (Beckenham, Kent, England), 1983.
Revolution and Counter-Revolution in France, 1815-1852, Basil Blackwell (Oxford, England), 1988.

Contributor to *Annual Bulletin of Historical Literature* and *Annales de l'Academie de Macon.* Contributor of articles and reviews to periodicals, including *French History, Historian, Journal of European Studies, History, English Historical Review,* and *Journal of Modern History.*

WORK IN PROGRESS: A study of French politics and political culture in 1848.

BIOGRAPHICAL/CRITICAL SOURCES:

PERIODICALS

American Historical Review, October, 1984.
Times Literary Supplement, May 20, 1983.

*   *   *

FOWLER, Marian (Elizabeth) 1929-

PERSONAL: Born October 15, 1929, in Newmarket, Ontario, Canada; daughter of Robert Daniel (a car dealer) and Dorothy Gertrude (a school teacher; maiden name, Maconachie) Little; married Rodney Fowler, September 19, 1953 (divorced, 1978); children: Timothy Evan, Caroline Jane. *Education:* University of Toronto, B.A. (with honors), 1951, M.A., 1965, Ph.D., 1970. *Religion:* Protestant. *Avocational interests:* Travel, bird-watching, antique collecting.

ADDRESSES: Home—Kilmara, Box 20, R.R.2, Lisle, Ontario, Canada L0M 1M0.

CAREER: Clarke, Irwin & Co. (publisher), Toronto, Ontario, Canada, promotion writer, 1951-53; T. Eaton Co. (department store), Toronto, advertising copywriter, 1953-54; homemaker, 1954-71; York University, Downsview, Ontario, course director and lecturer in English and Canadian studies at Atkinson College, 1971-82; full-time writer, 1982—.

MEMBER: International PEN, Writers Union of Canada, Association for Canadian Studies, Association of Canadian University Teachers of English.

AWARDS, HONORS: Governor-General's Gold Medal, 1951; Canadian Biography Award, Association for Canadian Studies, 1979, for a proposed biography of Sara Jeannette Duncan (*Redney: A Life of Sara Jeannette Duncan*).

WRITINGS:

The Embroidered Tent: Five Gentlewomen in Early Canada, House of Anansi Press, 1982.
Redney: A Life of Sara Jeannette Duncan, House of Anansi Press, 1983.
Below the Peacock Fan: First Ladies of the Raj, Viking/Penguin (New York City), 1987.
Blenheim: Biography of a Palace, Viking/Penguin, 1989.

WORK IN PROGRESS: A nonfiction book on five American heiresses who married British dukes.

SIDELIGHTS: Best known as a biographer, Marian Fowler has written absorbing accounts of the lives of several interesting people. Her best-known book is titled *Below the Peacock Fan: First Ladies of the Raj.* In this work, Fowler profiles the consorts—one sister and three wives—of four of India's Governor-Generals or Viceroys during British Colonial rule. Joanna Motion of the *Times Literary Supplement* notes, "The idea of writing the story of these eminent Victorian women was an excellent one. . . . Fowler moves easily and readably through the vignettes and social set-pieces of this high domesticity." Despite the fact that Fowler focused on these four women because they resided in India during Queen Victoria's reign, some critics have objected to her choice of only four "first ladies" when the British presence in India lasted nearly two hundred years. Audrey C. Foote observes in the *Washington Post Book World,* "It seems a shame Fowler did not complete the story with a fifth chapter on the last vicereine, Edwina, who helped Lord Mountbatten to dismantle the Raj and finally liberate India."

William French claims in the Toronto *Globe & Mail* that the book exceeds mere historical recounting: "One of the virtues of *Below the Peacock Fan* is that it's more than four mini-biographies. Fowler examines the experience of the four women in the context of the whole history of the British in India, and her book, intended or not, becomes a scathing indictment of imperialism." French, who describes Fowler as "perceptive and tough-minded," admires the author's achievement, remarking that her "prose is as colorful as her subject, and her narrative is thoroughly documented."

In 1989 Fowler issued another biography, this time detailing the life of Blenheim Palace, one of the oldest and largest castles in England. Commissioned by the first Duke of Marlborough, John Churchill, after he was awarded a thousand acres of land by Queen Anne in reward for his 1704 military victory against the French at Blenheim, the palace was designed by architect John Vanbrugh. It has become the ancestral home of the Spencer-Churchill family since then. *Blenheim: Biography of a Palace* "is an unusual book that is partly the history of a famous family, partly a chronicle of changing domestic attitudes and manners among the English aristocracy during the past 250 years, and partly, and the subtitle suggests, the biography of a building," comments Witold Rybczynski in the Toronto *Globe & Mail.* The reviewer adds, "The result is a vivid historical account which . . . provides compelling and illuminates a neglected subject—the way that the genius of a place forms the fortunes of its inhabitants." Marian Fowler once told *CA:* "My writing career began late in life, and I divide my time between Canada and England. I work long hours at my desk partly because I am very ambitious to make my name as a writer, but mainly because for me writing is a joyous and rewarding activity.

"I am interested in the kinds of social and psychological accommodations women have had to make to conform to accepted female roles. I began with a doctoral dissertation on Jane Austen, in which I looked closely at women's roles and behavior in early nineteenth-century England. I began to wonder how such upper-middle-class women, taught to be decorative and docile, adapted and developed when suddenly transplanted to a rough, Canadian frontier society.

"This interest sparked my first book, *The Embroidered Tent: Five Gentlewomen in Early Canada,* in which I examined the remarkable effects a Canadian wilderness setting had on five genteel women raised in Britain. Next, I wrote a biography of a nineteenth-century Canadian woman who was an intrepid and daring journalist, feminist, and novelist. She, too, experienced sudden cultural displacement, having spent her married life in India trying desperately to adapt and to write novels. While working on that book, *Redney: A Life of Sara Jeannette Duncan,* I became intrigued by the whole era of the British Raj in India and decided to write a book on five of the viceroys' wives and the ways in which India changed them, titled *Below the Peacock Fan.* The effect of a house on its inhabitants was my next project, resulting in *Blenheim: Biography of a Palace.*"

BIOGRAPHICAL/CRITICAL SOURCES:

PERIODICALS

Globe & Mail (Toronto), August 29, 1987; August 20, 1988; December 16, 1989.
Los Angeles Times Book Review, September 1, 1991, p. 10.
Quill and Quire, January, 1984; June, 1987, p. 33.
Times Literary Supplement, March 16, 1984; October 23, 1987, p. 1160.
Washington Post Book World, December 27, 1987, p. 7; January 1, 1989, p. 12.*

*   *   *

FOX, Anthony
    See FULLERTON, Alexander (Fergus)

*   *   *

FRASCONI, Antonio 1919-

PERSONAL: Born April 28, 1919, in Buenos Aires, Argentina; immigrated into the United States in 1945; son of Franco (a chef) and Armida (a restaurateur; maiden name, Carbonai) Frasconi; married Leona Pierce (an artist), July 18, 1951; children: Pablo, Miguel. *Education:* Attended Circulo de Bellas Artes (Montevideo); studied at Art Students League (New York), 1944-46; studied mural painting at New School for Social Research, 1947-48.

ADDRESSES: Home and studio—26 Dock Rd., South Norwalk, CT 06854. *Office*—Visual Arts Dept., State University of New York College at Purchase, Purchase, NY 10577. *Agent*—Terry Dintenfass, Inc., Gallery, 50 West 57th St., New York, NY 10019; Weyhe Gallery, 794 Lexington Ave., New York, NY 10021.

CAREER: Graphic artist, painter, and illustrator. *Marcha* and *La Linea Maginot* (weeklies), Montevideo, Uruguay, political cartoonist, 1940; New School for Social Research, New York, NY, member of art faculty, 1951-57; University of Hawaii, Honolulu, artist-in-residence, 1964; State University of New York College at Purchase, Purchase, adjunct professor, 1973-77, associate professor, 1977-79, professor of visual arts, 1979—. Has also taught at Vassar College, Brooklyn Museum, California State College at Hayward, University of California at Berkeley, and Carnegie-Mellon University; artist-in-residence, Dartmouth College, 1984, and Arizona State University, 1985; lecturer. Member of Mayor's Committee for Art in Public Places, Norwalk, CT, 1978, and of Arts review Committee, Westchester County, NY, 1980. Has had numerous one-man shows in North America, South America, and Europe; work represented in many permanent collections of museums and galleries, including Bibliotheque National (Paris, France), Casa Americas (Havana, Cuba), Museo Nacional de Bellas Artes and Museo Municipal Juan M. Blanes (Montevideo, Uruguay), University of Puerto Rico, Arts Council of Great Britain (London, England), Library of Congress, Museum of Modern Art (New York), Metropolitan Museum of Art (New York), Art Institute of Chicago, Detroit Institute of Arts, San Diego Museum of Arts, and Rhode Island School of Design.

AWARDS, HONORS: Purchase Prize, Brooklyn Museum, 1946, and University of Nebraska, 1951; Philadelphia Print Club Prize, 1951; Erickson Award, Society of American Graphic Artists, 1952; Yaddo scholarship, 1952; Guggenheim Inter-American Fellowship in graphic arts, 1952; Joseph Pennell Memorial Medal, Pennsylvania Academy of the Fine Arts, 1953; National Institute of Arts and Letters grant, 1954; American Institute of Graphic Arts "50 Books of the Year" citations, 1955, for *Twelve Fables of Aesop,* 1958, for *Birds from My Homeland: The Hand-Colored Woodcuts with Notes from W. H. Hudson's "Birds of La Plata",* 1959, for *The Face of Edgar Allan Poe: With a Note on Poe by Charles Baudelaire,* 1964, for *Known Fables,* and 1965, for *The Cantilever Rainbow; New York Times* Best Illustrated Books of the Year citations, 1955, for *See and Say: A Picture Book in Four Languages,* 1958, for *The House That Jack Built: A Picture Book in Two Languages,* 1961, for *The Snow and the Sun/La nieve y el sol: A South American Folk Rhyme in Two Languages,* and 1985, for *Monkey Puzzle and Other Poems;* First Prize for Book Illustration, Limited Editions Club and the Society of American Graphic Artists, 1956; American Institute of Graphic Art's Children's Books citations, 1958-60, for *The House That Jack Built: A Picture Book in Two Languages,* and 1970, for *Unstill Life: An Introduction to the Spanish Poetry of Latin America* and *Overhead the Sun: Lines from Walt Whitman;* Caldecott Honor Book citation, 1959, for *The House That Jack Built: A Picture Book in Two Languages;* Grand Prix, Venice Film Festival, 1960, for film, *The Neighboring Shore;* American Library Association Notable Book Award, 1961, for *The Snow and the Sun/La nieve y el sol: A South American Folk Rhyme in Two Languages;* Tamarind Lithography Workshop grant, 1962; winner of competition to design postage stamp honoring National Academy of Science, 1963; Joseph H. Hirshorn Foundation Prize, Society of American Graphic Artists, 1963; W. H. Walker Prize, Philadelphia Print Club, 1964; prize of Second Biennale d'Art Graphique, Brno, Czechoslovakia, 1966; prize of Salon Nacional de Bellas Artes, Montevideo, Uruguay, 1967; Grand Premio, Exposition de la Habana, Cuba, 1968; named National Academician by the National Academy of Design, NY, 1969; commissioned

by the Metropolitan Museum of Art, NY, for a series of Christmas ornaments "Snow Flakes," 1972.

Crickets and Frogs: A Fable in Spanish and English was included in the American Institute of Graphic Arts Children's Book Show, 1973-74; *The Elephant and His Secret* was selected one of Child Study Association's Children's Books of the Year, 1974; Connecticut Commission on the Arts grant, 1974; prize of Ninth International Biennial of Arts, Tokyo, 1975; Xerox Corporation grant, 1978, for experimentation with the Xerox Color Copier; Cannon Prize, National Academy of Design, NY, 1979; Ralph Frabrizi Prize, National Academy of Design, 1983; Chancellor's Award, State University of New York, 1983, for excellence in teaching; award from the Bienal de la Habana-Comision Nacional Cubana de la UNESCO, 1984; Meissner Prize, National Academy of Design, 1985; *Monkey Puzzle and Other Poems* was included in the American Institute of Graphic Arts Book Show, 1985; Purchase Award, American Academy and the Institute of Arts and Letters, 1986; Distinguished Teaching Professor, State University of New York College at Purchase, 1986.

WRITINGS:

SELF-ILLUSTRATED

See and Say: A Picture Book in Four Languages, Harcourt (New York City), 1955.
Woodcuts by Antonio Frasconi, Weyhe, 1957.
The House That Jack Built: A Picture Book in Two Languages, Harcourt, 1958.
The Snow and the Sun/La nieve y el sol: A South American Folk Rhyme in Two Languages, Harcourt, 1961.
A Sunday in Monterey, Harcourt, 1964.
See Again, Say Again: A Picture Book in Four Languages, Harcourt, 1964.
Kaleidoscope in Woodcuts, Harcourt, 1968.
(Editor) Walt Whitman, *Overhead the Sun: Lines from Walt Whitman,* Farrar, Straus (New York City), 1969.
(Editor) Herman Melville, *On the Slain Collegians: Selections from Poems,* Farrar, Straus, 1971.
Antonio Frasconi's World, Macmillan (New York City), 1974.
Frasconi Against the Grain: The Woodcuts of Antonio Frasconi, Macmillan, 1974.

ILLUSTRATOR

Glenway Wescott, reteller, *Twelve Fables of Aesop,* Museum of Modern Art, 1954, revised edition, 1964.
Jorge Luis Borges, *Dreamtigers,* University of Texas Press (Austin), 1964.
Ruth Krauss, *The Cantilever Rainbow,* Pantheon (New York City), 1965.

Pablo Neruda (pseudonym of Neftali R. R. Basulato), *Bestiary/Bestiario* (verse), translated by Elsa Neuberger, Harcourt, 1965.

Louis Untermeyer, editor, *Love Lyrics,* Odyssey (Indianapolis, IN), 1965.

Mario Benedetti, editor, *Unstill Life: An Introduction to the Spanish Poetry of Latin America,* Harcourt, 1969.

Isaac Bashevis Singer, *Elijah the Slave: A Hebrew Legend Retold,* Farrar, Straus, 1970.

Gabriela Mistral (pseudonym of Lucila Godoy Alcayaga), *Selected Poems of Grabriela Mistral,* Johns Hopkins (Baltimore, MD), 1970.

G. Mistral, *Crickets and Frogs: A Fable in Spanish and English,* translated by Doris Dana, Atheneum, 1972.

G. Mistral, *The Elephant and His Secret,* translated by D. Dana, Atheneum, 1974.

Myra Cohn Livingston, editor, *One Little Room, an Everywhere: Poems of Love,* Atheneum, 1975.

Penelope Farmer, compiler, *Beginnings: Creation Myths of the World,* Chatto & Windus, 1978, Atheneum, 1979.

Norma Faber, *How the Left-Behind Beasts Built Ararat,* Walker (Louisville, KY), 1978.

Jan Wahl, *The Little Blind Goat,* Stemmer House, 1981.

Merce Rodereda, *The Salamander,* Red Ozier Press, 1982.

I. B. Singer, *Yentl the Yeshiva Boy,* translated by Marion Magid and Elizabeth Pollet, Farrar, Straus, 1983.

M. C. Livingston, *Monkey Puzzle and Other Poems,* Atheneum, 1984.

Muso Soseki, *Sun at Midnight* (poems), translated from Japanese by W. S. Merwin, Nadja, 1986.

Carlos Oquendo de Amat, *Five Meters of Poems,* Turkey Press (Isla Vista, CA), 1986.

M. C. Livingston, *If the Owl Calls Again: A Collection of Owl Poems,* Macmillan, 1990.

Valerie Worth, *At Christmastime* (poems), HarperCollins (New York City), 1992.

Juan Ramon Jimenez, *Platero: Selections from Platero y yo,* translated by M. C. Livingston and Joseph F. Dominguez, Clarion Books (Boston, MA), 1993.

LIMITED EDITIONS; ILLUSTRATED WITH WOODCUTS

Aesop, *Some Well Known Fables,* privately printed, 1950.

A Book of Vegetable Plants, privately printed, 1951.

Foothill Dairy, privately printed, 1951-52.

The World Upside Down, privately printed, 1952.

The Fulton Fish Market, privately printed, 1953.

Federico Garcia Lorca, *2 Poemas de Federico Garcia Lorca: Romance de la luna, luna; Romance de la Guardia Civil Espanola,* privately printed, 1953.

Plants, Ants and Other Insects, privately printed, 1953.

Santa Barbara, privately printed, 1953.

The Acrobats, privately printed, 1954.

El Camino Real, privately printed, 1954.

Lettuce Country, privately printed, 1954.

Printing with Dough, privately printed, 1954.

A Book of Many Suns, privately printed, 1955.

Fire Island Dunes, privately printed, 1955.

High Tide, privately printed, 1955.

Abraham Lincoln, *The Fundamental Creed of Abraham Lincoln: A Selection from His Writings and Speeches,* edited by Earl Schenk Miers, privately printed, 1956.

An Old Czech Carol, Murray Printers, 1956.

Woodcuts 1957, Spiral, 1957, also published as *Woodcuts: With Comments by Antonio Frasconi,* Weyhe, 1957.

Homage to Thelonius Monk, privately printed, 1958.

Birds from My Homeland: Ten Hand-Colored Woodcuts with Notes from W. H. Hudson's "Birds of La Plata," Roodenko, 1958.

The Face of Edgar Allan Poe: With a Note on Poe by Charles Baudelaire, Roodenko, 1959.

Walt Whitman, *A Whitman Portrait,* Spiral, 1959.

A Calendar for 1960, privately printed, 1959.

Six Spanish Nursery Rhymes, privately printed, 1960.

American Wild Flowers, privately printed, 1961.

Berthold Brecht, *Das Lied vom Sa-mann,* Spiral, 1961.

Oda a Lorca, privately printed, 1962.

Known Fables, Spiral, 1964.

Six South American Folk Rhymes about Love: With Woodcuts, Spiral, 1964.

An Appointment Calendar for 1966, Baltimore Museum of Art, 1965.

Henry David Thoreau, *A Vision of Thoreau,* Spiral, 1965.

F. Garcia Lorca, *Llanto por Ignacio Sanches Mejias,* privately printed, 1967.

The Portrait, privately printed, 1967.

Quattro facciate, privately printed, 1967.

Viet Nam!, privately printed, 1967.

Vedute di Venezia, Spiral, 1969.

M. Benedetti, selector, *19 Poemas de Hispano America,* privately printed, 1969.

Fourteen Americans, privately printed, 1974.

Venice Remembered, privately printed, 1974.

A View of Tuscany, privately printed, 1974.

Cantos a Garcia Lorca, privately printed, 1974-75.

The Seasons on the Sound, privately printed, 1974-75.

The Sound, privately printed, 1974-75.

Frasconi's Composite Side Show, privately printed, 1978.

Frasconi's Night Creatures, privately printed, 1978.

The Tides at Village Creek, privately printed, 1979.

Monet Gardens, Giverny, privately printed, 1980.

The USA from the San Francisco-Oakland Bay Bridge, California to the George Washington Bridge, New York, Every Six Miles, privately printed, 1982.

Ten Views of Rome, privately printed, 1983.

Theodore Low de Vinne, *The First Editor: Aldus Pius Manutius,* privately printed, 1983.

Los Desaparecidos, privately printed, 1984.

Travels through Tuscany, privately printed, 1985.
Italo Calvino, *Prima che tu dica "Pronto,"* translated by William Weaver, Plain Wrapper Press, 1985.
Views of Venice by Day and Night, privately printed, 1986.

Also published *Outdoors,* 1953.

OTHER

The Neighboring Shore (film), Sextant, 1960.
The Woodcuts of Antonio Frasconi (film), American Federation of Arts, 1985.
Antonio Frasconi at the Library of Congress: A Lecture Presented May 18, 1989, for International Children's Book Week, edited by Sybille A. Jagusch, Library of Congress, 1993.

Contributor of illustrations to *New Republic* and *Fortune.*

ADAPTATIONS:See and Say: A Picture Book in Four Languages was adapted for sound filmstrip by Weston Woods, 1964; *Los Desaparecidos* was adapted for film by Darino Films, 1989.

Crickets and Frogs is available in Braille.

BIOGRAPHICAL/CRITICAL SOURCES:

BOOKS

Bader, Barbara, *American Picture Books from Noah's Ark to the Beast Within,* Macmillan, 1976.
Contemporary American Illustrators of Children's Books, Rutgers University Art Gallery, 1974.
Frasconi, Antonio, *Frasconi Against the Grain: The Woodcuts of Antonio Frasconi,* Macmillan, 1974.
Hurlimann, Bettina, *Picture-Book World,* World, 1969.
The Illustrator's Notebook, Horn Book, 1978.
Kingman, Lee, and others, compilers, *Illustrators of Children's Books: 1957-1966,* Horn Book, 1968.
Kingman, Lee, and others, compilers, *Illustrators of Children's Books: 1967-1976,* Horn Book, 1978.
Klemin, Diana, *The Art of Art for Children's Books,* C. N. Potter, 1966.
Klemin, Diana, *The Illustrated Book: Its Art and Craft,* C. N. Potter, 1970.
MacCann, Donnarae, and Olga Richard, *The Child's First Books,* H. W. Wilson, 1973.
Miller, Betha M., and others, compilers, *Illustrators of Children's Books: 1946-1956,* Horn Book, 1958.
Montreville, Doris de and Donna Hill, editors, *Third Book of Junior Authors,* H. W. Wilson, 1972.
Pitz, Henry C., *200 Years of American Illustration,* Clibborn, 1977.
Roginski, Jim, compiler, *Newbery and Caldecott Medalists and Honor Book Winners,* Libraries Unlimited, 1982.
Ward, Martha E., and Dorothy A. Marquardt, *Authors of Books for Young People,* 2nd edition, Scarecrow, 1971.

PERIODICALS

American Artist, October, 1974.
Americas, May, 1957.
Art in America, number 4, 1961; October, 1964.
Artist's Proof, Volume 6, numbers 9-10, 1966.
Graphis, May/June, 1958; March/April, 1962; Volume 23, number 134, 1967; March/April, 1983.
Graphis 155, Volume 27, number 155, 1971-72.
Horizon, March, 1961.
Life, October 18, 1954.
New Republic, February 29, 1964.
Newsweek, March 17, 1952; April 5, 1954.
New York Times, March 19, 1950.
Print, winter, 1950-51; August, 1955.
Print Review, numbers 16-17, 1982.
School Arts, September, 1961; May, 1966; February, 1968.
Texas Quarterly, autumn, 1962.
Time, June 15, 1953; December 20, 1963.

OTHER

Antonio Frasconi—Graphic Artist (film), Pablo Frasconi, 1976.
The Woodcuts of Antonio Frasconi (film), American Federation of Art, 1985.

*   *   *

FRASER, George MacDonald 1925-
(Dand MacNeill)

PERSONAL: Born April 2, 1925, in Carlisle, England; son of William (a doctor) and Anne Struth (Donaldson) Fraser; married Kathleen Margarette Hetherington, April 16, 1949; children: Simon, Caroline, Nicholas. *Education:* Educated in England and Scotland. *Politics:* "Totally independent and firmly opposed to all party politics." *Religion:* "Sentimental Presbyterian."

ADDRESSES: Home and office—Bungalow, Baldrine, Isle of Man 1M4 6DS, Britain. *Agent*—Curtis Brown, Haymarket House, 28/29 Haymarket, London, England.

CAREER: Carlisle Journal, Carlisle, England, reporter, 1947-49; *Leader-Post,* Regina, Saskatchewan, Canada, reporter, 1949-50; *Cumberland News,* Carlisle, reporter and subeditor, 1950-53; *Glasgow Herald,* Glasgow, Scotland, features editor, leader writer, and deputy editor, 1953-69; writer. *Military service:* British Army, 1943-45. Indian Army, Gordon Highlanders, 1945-47; became lieutenant.

MEMBER: Society of Authors, Authors Guild.

AWARDS, HONORS: British Arts Council Prize, 1972, for *The Steel Bonnets; Playboy* editorial awards, 1973 and 1975; Writers Guild of Great Britain award for best comedy screenplay, 1974.

WRITINGS:

Flashman: From the Flashman Papers, 1839-1842, World Publishing (New York City), 1969.

(Editor and arranger) *Royal Flash: From the Flashman Papers, 1842-3 and 1847-8,* Knopf (New York City), 1970.

The General Danced at Dawn (short stories), Knopf, 1970.

The Steel Bonnets, Knopf, 1971.

Flash for Freedom!, Knopf, 1971.

Flashman at the Charge, Knopf, 1973.

McAuslan in the Rough, Knopf, 1974.

Flashman in the Great Game: From the Flashman Papers, 1856-1858, Knopf, 1975.

(With others) *The World of the Public School,* St. Martin's (New York City), 1977.

Flashman's Lady, Knopf, 1977.

Mr. American, Simon & Schuster (New York City), 1980.

Flashman and the Redskins, Knopf, 1982.

The Pyrates, Knopf, 1984.

Flashman and the Dragon, Knopf, 1986.

The Hollywood History of the World: From One Million Years B.C. to Apocalypse Now (film stills), Beech Tree Books (New York City), 1988.

(Editor and arranger) *Flashman and the Mountain of Light: From the Flashman Papers, 1845-46,* Knopf, 1991.

The Candlemass Road, HarperCollins (New York City), 1993.

Quartered Safe Out Here, HarperCollins, 1994.

Flashman and the Angel of the Lord, HarperCollins, 1994.

Contributor to numerous journals and newspapers, sometimes under the pseudonym, Dand MacNeill.

SCREENPLAYS

The Three Musketeers, Twentieth Century-Fox, 1973.

The Four Musketeers, Twentieth Century-Fox, 1975.

Royal Flash (based on his novel of the same title), Twentieth Century-Fox, 1975.

Prince and the Pauper, Warner Bros., 1977, released in America as *Crossed Swords,* 1978.

Octopussy, MGM/United Artists, 1983.

Red Sonja, MGM/United Artists, 1985.

Also author of *Casanova,* 1987, and *The Return of the Musketeers,* 1989.

WORK IN PROGRESS: Continuing research on Victorian and Elizabethan history.

SIDELIGHTS: George MacDonald Fraser's novels, notes W. Keith Kraus of *Best Sellers,* are "the continuing story of Harry Flashman, a nineteenth-century rogue who zoomed to stardom in a first volume over the bodies of a few thousand Afghans . . . and a handful of reviewers.

Masquerading as a true account, *Flashman: From the Flashman Papers, 1839-1842* chronicled the misadventures of a young British captain in India who always managed to end up the hero while running from danger. The book was as funny as it was spurious and reviewers from Texas to, alas, Shippensburg, Pennsylvania, assumed the account was on the level. When the publisher, 'motivated solely by a desire to set the record aright,' broke the story in the *New York Times* the book became a best seller."

Other Flashman books feature the hero in various historical settings. In *Flashman and the Redskins,* for instance, Flashman travels to the United States and tries to persuade President Grant to give General Custer his job back. Jonathan Yardley, in *Washington Post Book World,* finds this adventure, though not "quite as hilarious as promised in the promotional material," still "consistently entertaining" and "eminently satisfying." Jack Kapica, of the Toronto *Globe and Mail,* considering the hero's exploits in *Flashman and the Dragon* less predictable than the previous Flashman books, declares that "there is a more mature hand at work here, and one that is oddly even more satisfying."

In addition to publishing volumes of his "discovery" (the memoirs of Harry Flashman, soldier), Fraser has presented stories of other rascals. Many reviewers have welcomed Fraser's work. W. F. Graham of *Best Sellers,* for example, finds *The General Danced at Dawn* a "good, humorous [collection] that keeps one pleasantly engaged during its reading. While it is not at all so gripping that you can't put it down once you start it, it is a delightful book to have around." And in the *New York Times Book Review,* Martin Levin remarks that *McAuslan in the Rough* "is loaded with good humor and Scottish charm, and if you have charm, as J. M. Barrie observed, you don't need anything else." *The Pyrates* is a high-seas lark that Flashman and McAuslan admirer John Nicolson, writing in the London *Times,* deems "not really vintage stuff." In the Toronto *Globe and Mail,* however, H. J. Kirchhoff describes the swashbuckling romp as "a rollicking good read."

Fraser's second Flashman book, *Royal Flash,* was made into a 1975 Twentieth Century-Fox movie, for which Fraser wrote the screenplay. Among his other screenplays are *The Three Musketeers,* a tongue-in-cheek version of the classic by Alexandre Dumas, and *The Four Musketeers;* the 1983 James Bond movie *Octopussy,* which Gene Siskel found weakly scripted but entertaining nonetheless and *New York Times* reviewer Vincent Canby called "actually better" than most of the previous twelve James Bond fantasies; and the less successful *Red Sonja.* Fraser's interest in movies is apparent as well in *The Hollywood History of the World: From One Million Years B.C. to Apocalypse Now,* a 1988 collection of film stills that document the movies' treatment of history through what he calls in his accompanying narrative the "Seven Ages of Hollywood."

BIOGRAPHICAL/CRITICAL SOURCES:

BOOKS

Contemporary Literary Criticism, Volume 7, Gale (Detroit), 1977.

PERIODICALS

Best Sellers, June 15, 1969; October 15, 1970; April 1, 1973.
Books and Bookmen, July, 1976.
Chicago Tribune, June 10, 1983; July 5, 1985.
Globe and Mail (Toronto), May 26, 1984; March 8, 1986; September 3, 1988.
Los Angeles Times, June 10, 1983; July 3, 1985.
Los Angeles Times Book Review, September 25, 1988.
National Review, November 8, 1974.
New Republic, November 26, 1977.
Newsweek, May 5, 1986.
New York Times, June 10, 1983; July 3, 1985.
New York Times Book Review, October 26, 1969; October 18, 1970; May 20, 1973; November 24, 1974; October 21, 1984; May 4, 1985.
Observer (London), December 18, 1977.
Saturday Review, July, 1981.
Time, August 3, 1981; June 2, 1986.
Times (London), December 1, 1983; April 1, 1989.
Times Literary Supplement, June 12, 1969; May 31, 1974; July 16, 1982; December 2, 1983; October 11, 1985.
Washington Post, October 6, 1974; June 10, 1983.
Washington Post Book World, July 12, 1981; August 25, 1982; August 26, 1984; May 4, 1986.

*   *   *

FREWIN, Leslie Ronald 1917-
(Paul Dupont, Mark Nicholls)

PERSONAL: Born August 8, 1917, in Westminster, London, England; son of William Sydney and Anne (Dorland-Cumberland) Frewin; married June Fox (a company director), April 14, 1948 (divorced, 1976); married Susan Nicholls, 1977; children: Michael Pirie, Colin, Angela (stepdaughter). *Education:* Attended St. Stephen's College.

ADDRESSES: Home—Hope Cottage, Westleigh, Bideford, North Devonshire, England. *Agent*—Julian Bach, The Julian Bach Literary Agency, 474 Third Ave., New York, NY 10017; Eric Glass, Artists' and Authors' Management, 28 Berkeley Sq., London, W1X 6HD, England; Bruce Hunter, David Higham Associates, 508 Lower

John Street, Golden Square, London, W1R 4HA, England.

CAREER: Trained for theater production with J. Foster Horsfield Theatrical Management and J. Wyndham Pemberton Management, at various London theaters; trainee executive at Gainsborough Pictures Ltd., London, England, and Gaumont-British Studios, London, where he worked on more than fifty films; Associated British at Elstree Studios, senior executive; worked for Walt Disney on loan-out, Twentieth Century-Fox, John Huston, and many others, variously in production, writing, and advertising fields. Public affairs consultant to various companies, including Texas Instruments (Europe), Caterpillar Tractors, and Grant's Whiskey; Terance Verity Associates (architectural firm), Mayfair, founder and partner; Leslie Frewin Books, founder. *Military service:* British Army, 1939-46; served with Royal Regiment of Fusiliers and in Europe.

MEMBER: Lord's Taverners (former chair), Carlton Club, St. James, M. C. C.

AWARDS, HONORS: American Export Magazine Award, for *Focus* magazine.

WRITINGS:

Battledress Ballads, W. H. Allen (London), 1943.
I Did Not Hear the Laughter, Wren Books (Kent, England), 1948.
The Legends of Rob Roy MacGregor, Rylee, 1948, published as *The Highland Rogue: The Legends of Rob Roy MacGregor,* Frewin, 1968.
Blond Venus, MacGibbon & Kee (London), 1955, revised edition published as *Dietrich: The Story of a Star,* Stein & Day (Briarcliff Manor, NY), 1967.
The Boundary Book, preface by the Duke of Edinburgh, MacDonald (Edinburgh, Scotland), 1962.
The Cafe Royal Story, preface by Graham Greene, Hutchinson (London), 1962.
The Importance of Being Oscar (Wilde), St. Martin's (New York City), 1981.
The Late Mrs. Dorothy Parker, Macmillan (New York City), 1986.
(Under pseudonym Mark Nicholls) *Investigating Gunpowder Plot,* Manchester University Press (Manchester, England), 1991.

EDITOR

The Poetry of Cricket, MacDonald, 1964.
Cricket Bag, MacDonald, 1965.
(Under pseudonym Paul Dupont) *Across a Crowded Room,* Nelson (Walton-on-Thomas, Surrey, England), 1965.
Parnassus near Piccadilly, Frewin, 1965, Soccer, 1966.
The Best of Cricket's Fiction, MacDonald, 1966.

The Saturday Men, MacDonald, 1967.
The Royal Silver Anniversary Book, 1947-1972, Frewin, 1972.

COMPILER

The Spy Trade, Frewin, 1966.
Immortal Jester: A Treasury of the Great Good Humour of Sir Winston Churchill, 1874-1965, Frewin, 1973.
More Wit of Prince Philip, Frewin, 1974.

OTHER

Dottie (play; adapted from his own novel *The Late Mrs. Dorothy Potter*), produced in London. Writer-producer of *Film Festival, Story of a Star,* and other television productions for British Broadcasting Corporation; and *Your Name in Print, Pick of the Week,* and other broadcasts for radio. Editor, *Focus* magazine.

WORK IN PROGRESS: Sarabande for a Voice from the Past, a novel.

SIDELIGHTS: Leslie Ronald Frewin's *The Late Mrs. Dorothy Parker* was the first full-length biography of the humorist and author Dorothy Parker. Frewin also adapted the work as a play, *Dottie,* which has been produced in London. Film rights to the book have been purchased for British television production. Critical response to the book was mixed. *Time* magazine described it as "a culling of choice Parkeriana, a well-considered if clumsily executed effort to evoke the pop-culture context of her times and a brief, provocative assessment of her talents."

BIOGRAPHICAL/CRITICAL SOURCES:

PERIODICALS

Globe and Mail (Toronto), June 20, 1987.
Los Angeles Times, April 10, 1987.
Time, June 15, 1987.
Times (London), August 27, 1987.
Times Literary Supplement, February 5, 1988; July 26, 1991.
Washington Post Book World, May 17, 1987.

*　　*　　*

FRIEDMAN, B(ernard) H(arper) 1926-

PERSONAL: Born July 27, 1926, in New York, NY; son of Leonard and Madeline (Uris) Friedman; married Abby Noselson, March 6, 1948; children: Jackson, Daisy. *Education:* Cornell University, B.A., 1948.

ADDRESSES: Home—439 East 51st St., New York, NY 10022-6473. *Agent*—Gunther Stuhlmann, P.O. Box 276, Becket, MA 01223.

CAREER: University Place Apartments, New York City, residential manager, 1948-49; Cross & Brown Co., New York City, real estate broker, 1949-50; Uris Buildings Corp., New York City, vice president and director, 1950-63; Cornell University, Ithaca, NY, lecturer in creative writing, 1966-67; Fine Arts Work Center, Provincetown, MA, director and staff consultant, 1968-82. Trustee of American Federation of the Arts, 1958-64, Whitney Museum of American Art, 1961—, and Broida Museum, 1983-86. Member of advisory council, Cornell University College of Arts and Sciences, 1968-83, and Herbert F. Johnson Museum, 1972-87. Founding member, Fiction Collective, 1973—. *Military service:* U.S. Navy, 1944-46.

MEMBER: PEN, Authors Guild, Dramatists Guild, Century Association (New York City).

AWARDS, HONORS: Fels Award, Coordinating Council of Literary Magazines, for story "Moving in Place"; Nelson Algren Award, 1983, for story "Duplex."

WRITINGS:

FICTION

Circles, Fleet Press (New York City), 1962, published as *I Need to Love,* Macfadden Books, 1963.
Yarborough, World Publishing (New York City), 1964.
Whispers, Ithaca House (Ithaca, NY), 1972.
Museum, Fiction Collective (Brooklyn, NY), 1974.
Almost a Life, Viking (New York City), 1975.
The Polygamist, Little, Brown (Boston), 1981.
Coming Close: A Novella and Three Stories as Alternative Autobiographies, Fiction Collective, 1982.
Between the Flags: Uncollected Stories, 1948-1990, Fiction Collective Two (Boulder, CO), 1990.

BIOGRAPHY

(Editor) *School of New York: Some Younger Artists,* Grove (New York City), 1959.
(With Barbara Guest) *Robert Goodnough,* Musee de Poche, 1962.
Lee Krasner, Whitechapel Gallery, 1965.
Jackson Pollock: Energy Made Visible, McGraw (New York City), 1972.
Alfonso Ossorio, Abrams (New York City), 1973.
Salvatore Scarpitta, Contemporary Arts Museum (Houston), 1977.
(With Flora Miller Biddle) *Gertrude Vanderbilt Whitney,* Doubleday (New York City), 1978.
Myron Stout, Whitney Museum of American Art (New York City), 1980.

OTHER

Also author of plays, including *In Search of Luigi Pirandello,* 1983, *The Critic,* 1986, *Beauty Business,* 1987, *Tony's Case,* 1991, and *Open End,* 1992; and of stories, including "Moving in Place," and "Duplex." Contributor of articles to magazines. Member of advisory board, *Cornell Review,* 1977-79.

SIDELIGHTS: B. H. Friedman's writings frequently concern the fine arts and those who are involved in them. His novels *Circles* and *Museum* are based upon his own experiences in the art world while his biographies and monographs focus on prominent artists. As Irving Malin writes in his review of *Museum,* "Friedman's knowledge of art (and the art world) is apparent on every page. [He] gives us an insider's novel." Friedman told *CA:* "I believe (hope) that in these novels the art world is a metaphor for the larger world, as are bridge-playing in *Yarborough,* photography in *Almost a Life,* and Islamic studies in *The Polygamist.*"

Friedman told *CA* that during the fifteen years he was in the real estate business he contributed many articles to literary and art magazines. "When I left business to write full time," he says, "I discovered that I did not write any more than previously but that the quality of the writing improved with greater concentration and more time for contemplation."

BIOGRAPHICAL/CRITICAL SOURCES:

BOOKS

Contemporary Literary Criticism, Volume 7, Gale, 1977.

PERIODICALS

Carolina Quarterly, spring, 1976.
Christian Science Monitor, July 9, 1975.
East Hampton Star, February 17, 1983.
Hudson Review, winter, 1975; spring, 1982.
Los Angeles Times, April 23, 1981.
Nation, December 7, 1974.
New Republic, October 19, 1974.
Newsday, May 23, 1982.
New Statesman, February 16, 1973.
New Yorker, September 8, 1975.
New York Times, December 8, 1978; March 2, 1981.
New York Times Book Review, October 13, 1974; August 24, 1975; December 24, 1978; February 22, 1981.
Observer, February 11, 1973.
Saturday Review, September 9, 1972.
Times Literary Supplement, November 9, 1973.*

*   *   *

FRIEDMAN, Ken(neth) 1939-

PERSONAL: Born September 22, 1939; son of Alfred and Bertha (Berman) Friedman. *Education:* University of Florida, B.A., 1964.

ADDRESSES: Home—330 East 33rd St., Apt. 12G, New York, NY 10016. *Agent*—Ron Bernstein, c/o Robert Lantz, 111 West 57th St., New York, NY 10022.

CAREER: Screenwriter. Longshoreman, New York City, 1964-65; social worker, New York City, 1965-67; stage manager, 1967-68; Hilda Vincent, New York City, comedy writer, 1968; National Broadcasting Company (NBC-TV), New York City, comedy writer for Johnny Carson, 1969; comedy writer for Marty Brill, beginning 1970. *Military service:* U.S. Navy, 1957-60.

WRITINGS:

The Neighbors (play), produced in New York City, November, 1966, produced Off-Broadway, 1967.
The March-March (play), produced Off-Broadway, 1967.
(With Marty Brill) *The Missing Tapes* (a record of comedy sketches), Laurie Records, 1974.

SCREENPLAYS

(With Jonathan Kaplan) *White Line Fever,* International Cinemedia Center, 1975.
(And producer with Steven Bach) *Mr. Billion,* Pantheon/ Fox, 1977.
Heart Like a Wheel, Aurora/Fox, 1983.
Johnny Handsome (based on the novel *The Three Worlds of Johnny Handsome* by John Godey), Tri-Star, 1990.
(With Nick Wechsler, and director) *Made in USA,* Nelson, 1990.
Cadillac Man, Orion, 1990.

SIDELIGHTS: Vincent Canby, writing in the *New York Times* of the film *Heart Like a Wheel,* finds that "Mr. Kaplan, the director, and Ken Friedman, who wrote the screenplay, never take their eyes off the road, which is the story, to search the stars for some great meaning. However, . . . they have made a film that is as socially instructive and moving as it is entertaining."

BIOGRAPHICAL/CRITICAL SOURCES:

PERIODICALS

Los Angeles Times, November 4, 1983; May 18, 1990.
New York Times, October 6, 1983; October 23, 1983; May 18, 1990.
Washington Post, May 18, 1990.*

*   *   *

FRY, Michael G(raham) 1934-

PERSONAL: Born November 5, 1934, in Brierley, England; son of Cyril Victor (a surveyor) and Margaret Mary (Copley) Fry; married Anna Maria Fulgoni, May, 1957; children: Michael Gareth, Gabriella, Margaret Louise.

Education: University of London, B.Sc. (with honors), 1956, Ph.D., 1963. *Religion:* Roman Catholic.

ADDRESSES: Home—444 34th St., Manhattan Beach, CA 91105. *Office*—School of International Relations, University of Southern California, Los Angeles, CA 90089.

CAREER: University of Toronto, Toronto, Ontario, lecturer in history, 1961-62; University of Saskatchewan, Saskatoon, lecturer, 1962-63, assistant professor of history, 1963-65; Carleton University, Ottawa, Ontario, assistant professor, 1965-66, associate professor, 1966-72, professor of history, 1972-78, associate director of School of International Affairs, 1973-76, director, 1976-77; School of International Affairs, University of Denver, Denver, CO, dean and professor, 1978-81; School of International Relations, University of Southern California, Los Angeles, director and professor, 1981—. Visiting professor, University of Leningrad, 1976, University of Cairo, and Middle East Center, University of Utah, 1979. *Military service:* British Army, 1956-58.

MEMBER: International Studies Association (vice-president, 1977), Society for Historians of American Foreign Relations, Royal Historical Society (fellow, 1992—).

AWARDS, HONORS: Canada Council Fellowships, 1966, 1967, 1968, 1973, and 1976; North Atlantic Treaty Organization research fellowship, 1969-70.

WRITINGS:

Illusions of Security: North Atlantic Diplomacy, 1918-1922, University of Toronto Press (Toronto), 1972.

(Editor) *"Freedom and Change": Essays in Honour of Lester B. Pearson,* McClelland & Stewart (Toronto), 1975.

Lloyd George and Foreign Policy, Volume I: *The Education of a Statesman, 1890-1916,* McGill-Queen's University Press (Montreal), 1977.

(With Itamar Rabinovich) *Despatches from Damascus: Gilbert Mackereth and British Policy in the Levant, 1933-39,* Tel Aviv University Press (Tel Aviv), 1986.

History, the White House, and the Kremlin: Statesmen as Historians, Pinter, 1991.

Power, Personalities and Policies, F. Cass, 1992.

Contributor to history and international relations journals, including *Canadian Journal of History, Journal of Modern History, Royal United States Institution Journal, Diplomatic History, Historical Journal, International Studies Quarterly, Review of International Studies, Albion,* and *International History Review.*

WORK IN PROGRESS: Lloyd George and Foreign Policy, Volume II; *The North Pacific Triangle: Canada, Japan*

and the United States and Century's End, and *The Encyclopedia of Modern Diplomacy.*

SIDELIGHTS: Michael G. Fry told *CA:* "I am a student of international history, the international relations of the great powers in the 20th century, and the functioning of the international system. I am a historian who is attempting to cross disciplinary boundaries and relate to other scholars in the field of international relations. I am also concerned with dissent about foreign and defence policies."

BIOGRAPHICAL/CRITICAL SOURCES:

PERIODICALS

Journal of American History, December, 1972.
Times Literary Supplement, August 19, 1977.

* * *

FRYDMAN, Szajko 1911-
(Zosa Szajkowski)

PERSONAL: Born January 10, 1911, in Poland; son of Chaim-Jakub and Minka (Roza) Frydman; married Chana Giterman, 1954; children: Isaac. *Education:* Studied at a religious Jewish teacher's seminary in Poland, 1922-27.

ADDRESSES: Home—200 West 108th St., New York, NY. *Office*—YIVO Institute for Jewish Research, 1048 Fifth Ave., New York, NY 10028.

CAREER: YIVO Institute for Jewish Research, New York City, staff member, 1946—. *Military service:* French Army, 1939-40; U.S. Army, 1943-45; paratrooper in Eighty-second Airborne Division.

MEMBER: American Academy for Jewish Research (fellow).

WRITINGS:

ALL UNDER PSEUDONYM ZOSA SZAJKOWSKI

(In Yiddish) *Studies of the History of Jewish Emigrations in France,* [Paris], 1936.

Di profesyonele bavegung (labor history), [Paris], 1937.

Dos lashon fun di Yidn, [New York City], 1948.

Socialists and Radicals in the Development of Antisemitism in Algeria (1884-1900), Conference on Jewish Relations, 1948.

Antisemitizm in der frantseyzisher arbeter bavegung (title means "Anti-Semitism in the French Labor Movement"), [New York City], 1948.

Agricultural Credit and Napoleon's Anti-Jewish Decrees, Editions Historiques Franco-Juives (New York City), 1953.

The Economic Status of the Jews in Alsace, Metz and Lorraine (1648-1789), Editions Historiques Franco-Juives, 1954.

Poverty and Social Welfare among French Jews (1800-1880), Editions Historiques Franco-Juives, 1954.

Ha-Komunah ha-Parisait veha-Yehudim (history), [Tel-Aviv], 1956.

Autonomy and Communal Jewish Debts during the French Revolution of 1789, Alexander Kohut Memorial Foundation, 1959.

Alsatian Jewish Inventories in the Hebrew Union College Library, Library of Hebrew Union College-Jewish Institute of Religion (Cincinnati, OH), 1959.

Bibliography of Jewish Periodicals in Belgium, 1841-1959, Library of Hebrew Union College-Jewish Institute of Religion, 1959.

The Emancipation of Jews during the French Revolution: A Bibliography of Books, Pamphlets, and Printed Documents, 1789-1800, Library of Hebrew Union College-Jewish Institute of Religion, 1959.

Franco-Judaica: An Analytical Bibliography of Books, Pamphlets, Decrees, Briefs and Other Printed Documents Pertaining to the Jews in France, 1500-1788, American Academy for Jewish Research, 1962.

Analytical Franco-Jewish Gazetteer, 1939-1945, privately printed, 1966.

Jews and the French Revolution of 1789, 1830, and 1898, Ktav (New York City), 1970.

Jews, Wars, and Communism, two volumes, Ktav, 1971-72.

The Attitude of American Jews to World War I, the Russian Revolution of 1917, and Communism (1914-1945), Ktav, 1972.

The Impact of the 1919-20 Red Scare on American Jewish Life, Ktav, 1974.

Jews and the French Foreign Legion, Ktav, 1975.

Kolchak, Jews, and the American Intervention in Northern Russia and Siberia, 1918-20, privately printed, 1977.

The Mirage of American Jewish Aid in Soviet Russia, 1917-1939, privately printed, 1977.

An Illustrated Sourcebook on the Holocaust, Ktav, 1977-79.

(Edited by Tobey B. Gitelle) *Jewish Education in France, 1789-1939,* Columbia University Press (New York City), 1980.

An Illustrated Sourcebook of Russian Antisemitism, 1881-1978, Ktav, 1980.

Writer of more than 250 papers for various journals.*

FUCHS, Daniel 1934-

PERSONAL: Born August 12, 1934, in New York, NY; son of Isaac (a manufacturer) and Sadie (Fox) Fuchs; married Cara Skoler, January 25, 1959; children: Margot Lynn, Sabrina. *Education:* Columbia University, A.B., 1955, Ph.D., 1960; Brandeis University, A.M., 1956. *Politics:* Democrat. *Religion:* Jewish. *Avocational interests:* Sports, camping, classical music, opera, enology, museums, travel.

ADDRESSES: Home—155 Elm St., Tenafly, NJ 07670. *Office*—Department of English, Speech and World Literatures, College of Staten Island of the City University of New York, 715 Ocean Terrace, Staten Island, NY 10301.

CAREER: Rensselaer Polytechnic Institute, Troy, NY, instructor in English, 1960-61; University of Michigan, Ann Arbor, instructor in English, 1961-62; University of Chicago, Chicago, IL, instructor, 1962-64, assistant professor of English, 1964-67; College of Staten Island of the City University of New York, Staten Island, NY, assistant professor, 1968-70, associate professor, 1970-82, professor of English, 1983—. Fulbright lecturer in American literature at University of Nantes, 1967-68, University of Vienna, 1975-76, John F. Kennedy Institute of American Studies, Free University of Berlin, 1987-88; Yaddo fellow, 1975, 1977. Free University of Berlin, John F. Kennedy Institute of American studies, visiting professor, 1980-81.

AWARDS, HONORS: Norman Foerster Prize, for "Ernest Hemingway: Literary Critic," an essay published in *American Literature,* 1965; City University of New York faculty research grants, 1972-73, 1979-80, 1989-90; *Choice* magazine award for an outstanding academic book, 1984-85, for *Saul Bellow: Vision and Revision.*

WRITINGS:

The Comic Spirit of Wallace Stevens, Duke University Press (Durham, NC), 1963.
Saul Bellow: Vision and Revision, Duke University Press, 1984.

Contributor to books, including *Patterns of Commitment in American Literature,* edited by Marston LaFrance, University of Toronto Press, 1967; *Ernest Hemingway,* edited by Arthur Waldhorn, McGraw, 1972; *The Stoic Strain in American Literature,* edited by Duane Macmillan, University of Toronto Press, 1977; *Critical Essays on Saul Bellow,* edited by Stanley Trachtenberg, G. K. Hall, 1979; *Nobel Prize Library,* Helveticus, 1984; *Saul Bellow, Modern Critical Views,* edited by Harold Bloom, Chelsea House, 1986; and *Saul Bellow in the 80s,* edited by G. Cronin and L. H. Goldman, Michigan State University Press, 1989. Contributor to literature journals.

WORK IN PROGRESS: A critical study, *The Limits of Ferocity.*

SIDELIGHTS: Daniel Fuchs once told *CA:* "I have for some time thought that the primary function of the scholar-critic is to bring learning to bear on contemporary literary issues. I derive this point of view, in part, from having studied (at Columbia University) with Lionel Trilling, F. W. Dupee, Richard Chase and (at Brandeis University) with Irving Howe, and in greater part, from my own temperament and inclinations."

Choice noted that Fuch's major study *Saul Bellow: Vision and Revision* "is a major contribution to Bellow scholarship. . . . It is the only critical study that deals with all of Bellow's fictional works to date." The review concluded, "Fuch's careful examination of Bellow's revisions allows the reader the unique opportunity to observe a major novelists's imagination actively struggling to discover the inner truth of his characters."

BIOGRAPHICAL/CRITICAL SOURCES:

American Literature, October, 1984, pp. 446-47.
Choice, June, 1984, p. 1465.
New York Times, March 3, 1984, p. 14.

*   *   *

FULLERTON, Alexander (Fergus) 1924-
(Anthony Fox)

PERSONAL: Born September 20, 1924, in Suffolk, England; son of John Skipwith Fullerton; married Priscilla Mary Edelston, 1956; children: John, Simon, Giles. *Education:* Attended Royal Naval College, Dartmouth, England, 1938-41, and Cambridge University, England, School of Slavonic Studies, 1946-47.

ADDRESSES: Agent—John Johnson Ltd, Clerkenwell House, 45-47 Clerkenwell Green, London EC1R 0HT, England.

CAREER: Writer. Royal Navy, regular officer in Submarine Service and Russian interpreter, 1942-49, became lieutenant; editorial director, Peter Davies Ltd. (publishers), London, England, and Arrow Books Ltd. (paperback division of Hutchinson & Co. Ltd.), London.

AWARDS, HONORS: Military: Mentioned in dispatches, Far East, 1945.

WRITINGS:

Surface!, P. Davies (London), 1953.
Bury the Past, P. Davies, 1954.
Old Moke, P. Davies, 1954.
No Man's Mistress, P. Davies, 1955.
A Wren Called Smith, P. Davies, 1957.

The White Men Sang, P. Davies, 1958, reprinted, Mayflower Books (London), 1977.
The Yellow Ford, P. Davies, 1959.
The Waiting Game, Ives Washburn, 1961.
Soldier from the Sea, P. Davies, 1962.
The Thunder and the Flame, Hodder & Stoughton (London), 1964.
Lionheart, Norton (New York City), 1965.
Chief Executive, Cassell (London), 1969, published in the United States as *The Executives,* Putnam (New York City), 1970.
The Publisher, Putnam, 1971.
Store, Cassell, 1971.
The Escapists, Cassell, 1972.
Other Men's Wives, Cassell, 1973.
Piper's Leave, Cassell, 1974.
(Under pseudonym Anthony Fox) *Threat Warning Red,* M. Joseph (London), 1979.
(Under pseudonym Anthony Fox) *Kingfisher Scream,* Viking (New York City), 1980.
Regenesis, M. Joseph, 1982.
The Aphrodite Cargo, M. Joseph, 1985.
Special Deliverance, Macmillan (New York City), 1986.
Special Dynamic, Macmillan, 1987.
Special Deception, Macmillan, 1988.
Bloody Sunset, Little, Brown (Boston), 1991.
Look to the Wolves, Little, Brown, 1992.
Love for an Enemy, Little, Brown, 1993.
Not Thinking of Death, Little, Brown, 1994.

"EVERARD" SERIES; WORLD WARS I AND II NAVAL ADVENTURE NOVELS

The Blooding of the Guns, M. Joseph, 1976.
Sixty Minutes for St. George, M. Joseph, 1977.
Patrol to the Golden Horn, M. Joseph, 1978.
Storm Force to Narvik, M. Joseph, 1979.
Last Lift from Crete, M. Joseph, 1980.
All the Drowning Seas, M. Joseph, 1981.
A Share of Honour, M. Joseph, 1982.
The Torch Bearers, M. Joseph, 1983.
The Gatecrashers, M. Joseph, 1984.

Also author of *Johnson's Bird,* 1989. The nine-book "Everard" series has been translated into Japanese.

SIDELIGHTS: Regarding Alexander Fullerton's *The Torch Bearers,* Michael Trend in the *Times Literary Supplement* writes that "Fullerton's novel makes much of how people deceive one another and themselves, both in terms of the progress of the war and in his characters' inner lives; his main theme, though, is courage—especially the courage, or the lack of it, of the individual in the face of danger."

Fullerton's novels *Special Deliverance, Special Dynamic,* and *Special Deception* form a trilogy about the Special Boat Squadron of the Royal Marines.

BIOGRAPHICAL/CRITICAL SOURCES:

PERIODICALS

Times Literary Supplement, July 23, 1970; December 23, 1983.

G

GADDIS, William 1922-

PERSONAL: Born in 1922, in New York, NY; children: one son, one daughter. *Education:* Attended Harvard College, 1941-45.

ADDRESSES: Agent—Donadio and Ashworth, 121 West 27th St., New York, NY 10001.

CAREER: New Yorker, New York, NY, fact checker, 1946-47; lived in Latin America, Europe, and North Africa, 1947-52; freelance writer of filmscripts, speeches, and corporate communications, 1956-70; novelist. Has also taught at universities. Distinguished visiting professor at Bard College, 1977.

MEMBER: American Academy of Arts and Letters.

AWARDS, HONORS: National Institute of Arts and Letters grant, 1963; National Endowment for the Arts grants, 1967 and 1974; Rockefeller grant and National Book Award for fiction, both 1976, both for *J R;* Guggenheim Fellowship, 1981; MacArthur Foundation Fellowship, 1982; nomination for PEN/Faulkner Award, 1985, for *Carpenter's Gothic;* National Book Award, 1994, for *A Frolic of His Own.*

WRITINGS:

NOVELS

The Recognitions, Harcourt (New York City), 1955, corrected edition, Penguin Books (New York City), 1993.

J R, Knopf (New York City), 1975, corrected edition, Penguin Books, 1993.

Carpenter's Gothic, Viking (New York City), 1985.

A Frolic of His Own, Simon & Schuster (New York City), 1994.

OTHER

Contributor to periodicals, including *Atlantic, Antaeus, New Yorker, New York Times,* and *Harper's.*

SIDELIGHTS: William Gaddis is one of the most highly regarded yet least read novelists in America. In 1976, *New York Times Book Review* contributor George Stade described Gaddis as "a presiding genius . . . of post-war American fiction." Although many readers remain unfamiliar with his work, certain critics have made extravagant claims for it. Richard Toney, in the *San Francisco Review of Books,* describes Gaddis's first book, *The Recognitions,* as "a novel of stunning power, 956 pages of linguistic pyrotechnics and multi-lingual erudition unmatched by any American writer in this century—perhaps in any century." L. J. Davis, in the *National Observer,* writes that Gaddis's second novel, *J R,* "is the equal of—if not superior to—its predecessor"; but the work remains, as Frederick Karl asserts in *Conjunctions,* "perhaps the great unread novel of the postwar era." With the publication in 1994 of *A Frolic of His Own,* which won a National Book Award, Gaddis's work has received wider recognition.

Gaddis has drawn heavily on his own background for the settings of his novels. Born in Manhattan in 1922, he was raised in Massapequa, Long Island, in the house that was the model for the Bast home in *J R.* Like the Basts, Gaddis's maternal relatives were Quakers, though he himself was raised in a Calvinist tradition, as is Wyatt Gwyon in *The Recognitions.* Like Otto in the same novel and Jack Gibbs in *J R,* Gaddis grew up without a father. Haunting all four novels, in fact, is the spirit of a dead or absent father who leaves a ruinous state of affairs for his children, a situation that may be extrapolated to include Gaddis's literary vision of a world abandoned by God and plunged into disorder. The writer's fifth through thirteenth years were spent at a boarding school in Berlin, Connecticut, which not only furnished the fictional Jack Gibbs with the bleak memories recalled in *J R* but also provided the unnamed New England setting for the first chapter of *The Recognitions.* Returning to Long Island to attend Farmingdale High School, Gaddis contracted the illness that debilitates Wyatt in the first novel and that kept Gaddis out of World War II. Instead he attended Harvard and edited the *Harvard Lampoon* until circumstances required him to leave in 1945 without a degree.

Back in New York, Gaddis worked as a fact checker at the *New Yorker,* a job that he later recalled as "terribly good training, a kind of post-graduate school for a writer, checking everything, whether they were stories or profiles or articles. . . . A lot of the complications of high finance and so forth in *J R*—I tried very hard to get them all right. And it was very much that two years at the *New Yorker,*" he told Miriam Berkley in a *Publishers Weekly* interview. At this time he also mingled in the Greenwich Village milieu recreated in the middle section of *The Recognitions.* Here he became acquainted with future Beat writers William Burroughs, Allen Ginsberg, Alan Ansen, Chandler Brossard and Jack Kerouac. (In fact, Kerouac converted Gaddis into a character named Harold Sand in his 1958 novel *The Subterraneans.*) In 1947 Gaddis set off on five years of wandering through Mexico, Central America, Spain, France, and North Africa until, in 1952, he returned to America to complete his first novel.

Published in 1955, *The Recognitions* is an account of personal integration amid collective disintegration, of an individual finding himself in a society losing itself. Protagonist Wyatt Gwyon, a failed seminarian, turns to forging Old Masters in an earnest but misguided attempt to return to an era when art was authentic and sanctioned by God. Gaddis sets Wyatt in stark contrast to most of the other artist figures in the novel: Otto, the playwright; Esme, the poet; Max, the painter; Sinisterra, the counterfeiter—all of whom plagiarize, falsify, or discredit the artistic process. These personages, along with the rest of the novel's large cast of characters, are representative of a society crumbling in a shoddy world so encrusted with counterfeit that "recognitions" of authenticity are nearly impossible.

The action in *The Recognitions* runs on two narrative planes that occasionally intersect. On one plane lives Wyatt, whom Karl in *Conjunctions* calls "an avenging Messiah . . . because he perceives himself as bringing a purifying and cleansing quality, a 'recognition,' to a society that has doomed itself with corruptive sophistication." But Wyatt is hobbled in his pursuit of a "vision of order" (as it is later defined in *Carpenter's Gothic*) by a psychologically crippling boyhood that has instilled in him a mixture of guilt, secrecy, and alienation. The author exposes the compromised worlds of religion and art in the first two chapters, and Wyatt's brief fling with conventionality (complete with wife and nine-to-five job) fails by chapter three, leaving him open to the temptations of the novel's Mephistopheles, Recktall Brown, a corrupt art dealer. Selling his soul to the devil, Wyatt retreats offstage for the

entrance of his parodic counterpart, Otto Pivner, whose comic misadventures in Central America and Greenwich Village constitute the second narrative plane of the novel.

Here the "corruptive sophistication" mentioned by *Conjunctions*'s Karl appear as endless discussions of art and religion are carried on through endless parties and bar conversations by those whom Gaddis lampoons as "the educated classes, an ill-dressed, underfed, overdrunken group of squatters with minds so highly developed that they were excused from good manners, tastes so refined in one direction that they were excused for having none in any other, emotions so cultivated that the only aberration was normality, all afloat here on sodden pools of depravity calculated only to manifest the pricelessness of what they were throwing away, the three sexes in two colors, a group of people all mentally and physically the wrong size."

With the realization that the major cause for the godless condition embodied by and surrounding modern humanity may be attributed to the absence of love, Wyatt abandons forgery, travels to Spain (where his mother is entombed), and finds the love necessary to baptize his new life. Spurning love, the rest of the novel's characters are last seen rushing headlong into death, madness, or disintegration.

The Recognitions presents a multi-layered complexity necessary to dramatize the novel's themes of imitation versus reality. As Tony Tanner points out in the *New York Times Book Review,* "If at times we feel lost, displaced, disoriented as we move through the complicated edifice of the book, we are only experiencing analogically a lostness that is felt in varying ways by all the characters in the book." Often eschewing traditional narrative exposition, Gaddis abandons the reader at the various scenes of action, forcing him instead to overhear the confused gropings, deliberate lies, and mistaken notions of the characters, to sort them out as best he can. In other words, the reader must participate in the novel and make the same "recognitions" demanded of its characters by the title. An immense network of allusions, references, motifs, and gestures are introduced and repeated in countless convoluted permutations, demanding much more than casual attention from the reader. The novel is also very erudite, but any negative effects of this characteristic have often been overemphasized; the sense, if not the literal meaning, of Gaddis's hundreds of references, allusions, and foreign language phrases is usually clear enough from the context.

The Recognitions had little immediate critical impact upon publication. Unfortunately, 1955 was "one of American criticism's weakest hours," as Maurice Dolbier noted in a *New York Herald Tribune* article seven years later, and most reviewers were put off by this gargantuan novel by an unknown writer. A few readers recognized its greatness immediately, but only in later years did a historical perspective allow critics to gauge its importance. In his 1975 *Saturday Review* assessment of Gaddis's second novel, John W. Aldridge, an early champion, writes from such a perspective: "As is usually the case with abrasively original work, there had to be a certain passage of time before an audience could begin to be educated to accept *The Recognitions.* The problem was not simply that the novel was too long and intricate or its vision of experience too outrageous, but that even the sophisticated reading public of the mid-Fifties was not yet accustomed to the kind of fiction it represented. . . . The most authoritative mode in the serious fiction of the Fifties was primarily realistic, and the novel of fabulation and Black Humor—of which *The Recognitions* was later to be identified as a distinguished pioneering example—had not yet come into vogue. In fact, the writers who became the leaders of the Black Humor movement had either not been heard from in 1955 or remained undiscovered. Their work over the past 20 years has created a context in which it is possible to recognize Gaddis's novel as having helped inaugurate a whole new movement in American fiction. Rereading it with the knowledge of all that this movement has taught us about modern experience and the opening of new possibilities for the novel, one can see that *The Recognitions* occupies a strikingly unique and primary place in contemporary literature."

Little was heard of Gaddis in the decade and a half after 1955. Denied the life of a "successful" novelist, he began a long line of jobs in industry, working first in publicity for a pharmaceutical firm, then writing films for the army, and later writing speeches for corporate executives (as does Thomas Eigen in *J R,* who has also published an important but neglected novel). With the 1970 appearance in the *Dutton Review* of what would later become the opening pages of his second novel, Gaddis broke his fifteen-year silence. Two more fragments from *J R* appeared, in *Antaeus* and *Harper's,* before the novel was published in the fall of 1975 to much stronger reviews than those received by *The Recognitions. J R* won the National Book Award for the best fiction of the year and has since earned the praise of such writers as Saul Bellow, Mary McCarthy, William H. Gass, Stanley Elkin, Joseph McElroy, and Don DeLillo.

Although this intricate, 726-page novel resists easy summary, it is essentially a satire of corporate America, a "country" so obsessed with money that failure is all but inevitable for anyone who doesn't sell his soul to Mammon. The first word of the novel is "money," a word that reappears throughout the novel as its debasing touch besmirches everything from education to science, from politics to marriage, from the arts to warfare. At the center

of the novel is eleven-year-old J. R. Vansant, a slovenly but clever boy who transforms a small "portfolio" of mail order acquisitions and penny stocks into an unwieldy paper empire in an improbably short time. The most radical feature of the novel is its narrative mode: except for an occasional transitional passage, the novel is composed entirely of dialogue. While novels composed totally of dialogue had been written before, none followed Gaddis's extreme format. For his dialogue is not the literary dialogue of most novels, tidied up and helpfully sprinkled with conversational conventions and explanatory asides by the author helping to clarify what the characters actually mean. Instead, *J R* reads like a tape-recorded transcription of real voices: ungrammatical, often truncated, with constant interruptions by other characters (and by telephones, radios, and televisions), with rarely an identifying or interpretive remark by the author.

Such a literary mode makes unusual demands upon the reader; it requires that he read actively with involvement and concentration, rather than passively, awaiting entertainment. Jack Gibbs, a major character, pinpoints this problem during a drunken conversation with Edward Bast, a young composer: " . . . problem most God damned readers rather be at the movies. Pay attention here bring something to it take something away problem most God damned writing's written for readers perfectly happy who they are rather be at the movies, come in empty-handed go out the same God damned way I told him Bast. Ask them to bring one God damned bit of effort want everything done for them they get up and go to the movies." In his interview with *Publishers Weekly,* Gaddis reiterated the point: "For me it is very much a proposition between the reader and the page. That's what books are about. And he must bring something to it or he won't take anything away. . . . Television is hot, it provides everything. In the so-called situation comedies, you go with a completely blank mind, which is preoccupied for a half hour, and then you turn it off. You have brought nothing to it and you take nothing home. Much bad fiction is like this. Everything is provided for you, and you forget it a week later." What the attentive reader takes home from *J R* is a ringing in the ears from what Sarah E. Lauzen, in *Postmodern Fiction,* labels "the constant cacophony of America selling America."

Just as everyone in the counterfeit cultural world of *The Recognitions* moves in relation to Wyatt, everyone in the phony paper world of *J R* moves in relation to the young title figure, who embodies what Gaddis calls, in the *Publishers Weekly* interview: "Simple naked cheerful greed, no meanness, no nastiness, and not a great deal of intelligence, as I say. Just doing what you're supposed to do." J. R. gleefully accepts the corrupt civilization handed down to him, wanting only to know how fast he can get his share. By following the letter of the law at the expense of its spirit, he is able to build his "family of companies" with the assistance of adults as amoral as he is.

The only adults who attempt to infuse a moral sense into J. R. are his teacher, Amy Joubert, and his reluctant business associate, Edward Bast, a struggling musician. But Amy is too preoccupied with her own problems to be of much help, and Bast causes more problems than he solves. Although one of the major conflicts in the novel is between such outwardly directed people as J. R. and such inwardly directed people as the book's artists, all of the latter figures have largely themselves to blame for their artistic failures rather than the crass business world to which they belong. Despite their failures, however, most are seen at work on new art projects at the novel's end, for as Johan Thielemans notes in an essay in *In Recognition of William Gaddis,* "Artistic perfection represents the only possible escape from entropic processes."

The term "entropy" is introduced in the novel almost as early as "money," and this concept—the tendency for any system to move from a state of order to one of disorder—operates throughout the novel. Nearly everyone in Gaddis's novel is caught up in a desperate attempt to hold things together in the face of encroaching disorder and dissolution. But the attempts are largely futile: families break up, artists burn out and/or commit suicide, businesses close or are swallowed up by conglomerates, children are abandoned, coitus is interrupted, and communication breaks down. In *J R,* everyone's life is chaotic, and the exclusive use of dialogue creates what Thomas LeClair describes in *Modern Fiction Studies* as "a massive consistency in which characters with different backgrounds, money-men and artists alike, come to have the same rushed habits of speech, the inability to complete a message or act." As *Saturday Review*'s Aldridge concludes about *J R:* "It is undoubtedly inevitable that the novel promises at almost every point to fall victim to the imitative fallacy, that it is frequently as turgid, monotonous, and confusing as the situation it describes. Yet Gaddis has a strength of mind and talent capable of surmounting this very large difficulty. He has managed to reflect chaos in a fiction that is not itself artistically chaotic because it is imbued with the conserving and correcting power of his imagination. His awareness of what is human and sensible is always present behind his depiction of how far we have fallen from humanity and sense."

Like its predecessor, *J R* is primarily a comic novel. As Alicia Metcalf Miller writes in the Cleveland *Plain Dealer,* "If Gaddis is a moralist, he is also a master of satire and humor. *J R* is a devastatingly funny book. Reading it, I laughed loudly and unashamedly in public places, and at home, more than once, I saw my small children gather in

consternation as tears of laughter ran down my face." Such is the reader response for which *J R* aims.

Gaddis's underground reputation surfaced somewhat following the publication of *J R* in 1975. The National Book Award for fiction was followed by a steady stream of academic essays and dissertations, culminating in 1982 with the first book on Gaddis's work, a special issue of the *Review of Contemporary Fiction,* and his receipt of a MacArthur Foundation Fellowship. Two years later, the second book on his work appeared, Gaddis was elected to the American Academy and Institute of Arts and Letters, and he finished his third novel.

For this novel—originally titled *That Time of Year: A Romance* but published in the summer of 1985 as *Carpenter's Gothic*—Gaddis turned away from the "mega-novel" and set out to write a shorter (262 pages), different sort of book. As he explained in a *Washington Post* interview with Lloyd Grove: "I wanted it to move very fast. Everything that happens on one page is preparing for the next page and the next chapter and the end of the book. When I started I thought, 'I want 240 pages'—that was what set I out for. It preserved the unity: one place, one very small amount of time, very small group of characters, and then, in effect, there's a nicer word than 'cliche,' what is it? Staples. That is, the staples of the marriage, which is on the rocks, the obligatory adultery, the locked room, the mysterious stranger, the older man and the younger woman, to try to take these and make them work."

Gaddis restores to worn-out literary cliches some of their original drama and intensity, particularly in *Carpenter's Gothic.* Like *The Recognitions,* his third novel is concerned with the ambiguous nature of reality; "there's a very fine line between the truth and what really happens" is an oft-repeated line in *Carpenter's Gothic.* It also attacks the perversions done in the name of religion. From *J R* it takes its narrative technique—an almost total dependence on dialogue—and its contempt for the motivating factor of capitalism. Sometimes seen by critics as a smaller, less important reflection of the author's two preceding novels, this novel presents Gaddis's most characteristic themes and techniques with economy and flair.

Carpenter's Gothic is rooted in a specific time and place: the action takes place over a month's time (internal references date it October-November 1983) in a "carpenter gothic" style Victorian house in a small Hudson River Valley town. (Gaddis owned just such a house on Ritie Street in Piermont, New York.) Almost continuously on stage is Elizabeth Booth: "Bibbs" to her brother Billy, "Liz" to her husband Paul, and "Mrs. Booth" to McCandless, the house's owner and a failed novelist. These men subject Liz to the bullying, self-serving dialogue that makes up the bulk of the novel and that brings the outside world onto Gaddis's one-set stage. With newspapers and telephone calls filling the roles of messengers, a complicated plot quickly unfolds concerning Christian fundamentalism, political chicanery, African mineral rights, and a half-dozen family disputes. Long-suffering Liz endures it all, helpless to prevent her men from rushing headlong into—and even creating—the Armageddon that looms on the final pages of the novel.

In *Carpenter's Gothic,* as in all of Gaddis's novels, the males do most of the talking and create most of the problems. Like Esme in *The Recognitions* and Amy in *J R,* Liz is the still point in a frantic male world, "the only thing that holds things together," as her brother Billy admits. Though flawed, she is perhaps the most sympathetic figure in all three of Gaddis's novels. For that reason, her sudden death at the end gives *Carpenter's Gothic* its bleaker, more despairing tone.

Liz's husband Paul, a Vietnam veteran once attacked by his own men, is in one sense a grown-up J. R. Vansant—an identification Gaddis encourages when someone dismisses Paul for "know[ing] as much about finance as some snot nosed sixth grader." Like J. R., Paul simply does what people do to "make it" in America, never examining for an instant the ethics or morality of his questionable dealings. But the man who brings the greatest disorder into Liz's life is McCandless, the mysterious owner of the house, whom she transforms into a wearily romantic figure out of Charlotte Bronte's *Jane Eyre* (a movie version of which serves as a backdrop to Liz and Paul's joyless lovemaking). McCandless, no longer feeling any connection between his world and himself and outraged at the stupidity that has severed that connection, can only envision a bleak future.

This vision of deep disorder and empty outlook belongs to Gaddis as well, for *Carpenter's Gothic,* as Peter Prescott declares in his *Newsweek* article, "is surely Gaddis's most pessimistic, his most savage novel." No one in the novel demonstrates any possibility of sidestepping, much less overcoming, Gaddis's vision of the world's crushing stupidity. An escape hatch through which characters such as Wyatt and Bast can save themselves is present in the first two novels, but no such option exists in *Carpenter's Gothic.* As Robert Kelly notes in *Conjunctions,* Gaddis does not seem to have "an optimistic bone in his body—at least not in his writing hand." This pessimism bothers many readers, but Kelly explains: "We are foolish if we expect the skilful anatomist who excoriates vicious folly to provide a cure for it too—and doubly foolish if we credit any panacea he does trick himself into prescribing."

In a 1986 *Listener* article, Peter Kemp describes the work as Gaddis's "grimmest book," observing, "A scathing, exacerbated *tour de force, Carpenter's Gothic* seems the last word on a society whose doomed babble it so vehemently transmits." In the *Nation,* Terrence Rafferty mentions the book's "sour, contemptuous tone and its formal bad faith," adding, "The real story of *Carpenter's Gothic* isn't the end of the world, it's the end of the imagination, the world gone dark in the writer's head." Carol Iannone remarks in *Commentary* that "Gaddis means to show us the consequences of stupidity. . . . *Carpenter's Gothic* shows that Gaddis is not so much an artist as an anti-artist, working with cartoon characters and disembodied ideas."

Even art, the panacea prescribed in the first two novels, is suspect in the third book. On one level, *Carpenter's Gothic* is a meditation on fiction, specifically on the dubious motives for writers' fiction-making impulses. For Liz—as perhaps for the younger Gaddis—fiction offers "some hope of order restored, even that of a past life in tatters, revised, amended, fabricated in fact from its very outset to reorder its unlikelihoods, what it all might have been." But McCandless insists on the suspect, compromised nature of art in his commentary on the carpenter gothic style of his house, a passage which doubles as a description of the novel itself: "All they had were the simple dependable old materials, the wood and their hammers and saws and their own clumsy ingenuity bringing those grandiose visions the masters had left behind down to a human scale with their own little inventions, . . . a patchwork of conceits, borrowings, deceptions, the inside's a hodgepodge of good intentions like one last ridiculous effort at something worth doing even on this small a scale." In this sense, any reader who flees the disorder of life for the order of art will find cold comfort in *Carpenter's Gothic.*

Throughout Gaddis's novels there is a sense of bitter disappointment at America for not fulfilling its potential, for events not working out as planned. In this regard Gaddis resembles his beloved Russian novelists of the nineteenth century; in the *New York Times Book Review* William H. Gass reports a talk of Gaddis's in Lithuania where he insisted "the comic and satiric side of his work was attempting to save his version of his country as the earlier Russian writers had endeavored to redeem theirs." In the third novel, however, America seems to have reached the bottom of the psychosocial abyss. *Carpenter's Gothic* implies that it is too late to reverse the tide, to restore the promise of the American dream, too late for anything more than "one last ridiculous effort at something worth doing."

Emphasizing litigiousness and greed as characteristics of contemporary American society, Gaddis's award-winning novel *A Frolic of His Own* focuses on Oscar Crease, his family, his friends, and the various lawsuits in which they are all enmeshed. Employing elements of humor and farce, Gaddis exhaustively details the absurdities of his characters' suits and subsequent countersuits. For example, Oscar is plaintiff in a plagiarism case he has brought against Constantine Kiester, a top Hollywood producer whose real name is Jonathan Livingston Siegal. Oscar is also, paradoxically, plaintiff and defendant in a suit concerning a hit-and-run accident in which he was hit by his own car—a Sosumi ("so sue me"). Taking its title from a British legal phrase used to describe an employee's actions which, though they resulted in on-the-job injuries, do not entitle the employee to compensation, *A Frolic of His Own* is largely noted for its satire of justice and law in contemporary American society and for its unusual narrative structure.

Except for the inclusion of excerpts from Oscar's writings, legal documents, and court opinions, the novel is told primarily through dialogue that is unattributed and only lightly punctuated. Critics have praised Gaddis's realistic depiction of everyday speech—complete with pauses, interruptions, and unfinished thoughts—and stressed the difficulty such a narrative technique, reminiscent of stream-of-consciousness writing, places on readers. Steven Moore observes in the *Nation:* "*A Frolic of His Own* is both cutting-edge, state-of-the-art fiction and a throwback to the great moral novels of Tolstoy and Dickens. That it can be both is just one of the many balancing acts it performs: It is bleak and pessimistic while howlingly funny; it is a deeply serious exploration of such lofty themes as justice and morality but is paced like a screwball comedy; it is avant-garde in its fictional techniques but traditional in conception and in the reading pleasures it offers; it is a damning indictment of the United States, Christianity and the legal system, but also a playful frolic of Gaddis's own." Zachary Leader in the *Times Literary Supplement* calls *A Frolic of His Own* a "bleak, brilliant, exhausting novel."

BIOGRAPHICAL/CRITICAL SOURCES:

BOOKS

Aldridge, John W., *In Search of Heresy,* McGraw, 1956.
Comnes, Gregory, *The Ethics of Indeterminacy in the Novels of William Gaddis,* University Press of Florida, 1994.
Contemporary Literary Criticism, Gale (Detroit), Volume 1, 1973, Volume 3, 1975, Volume 6, 1976, Volume 8, 1978, Volume 10, 1979, Volume 19, 1981, Volume 43, 1987, Volume 86, 1995.
Dictionary of Literary Biography, Volume 2: *American Novelists since World War II,* Gale, 1978.
Gaddis, William, *The Recognitions,* Harcourt, 1955, corrected edition, Penguin Books, 1985.
Gaddis, William, *J R,* Knopf, 1975, corrected edition, Penguin Books, 1985.
Gaddis, William, *Carpenter's Gothic,* Viking, 1985.
Gardner, John, *On Moral Fiction,* Basic Books, 1978.

Kuehl, John, and Steven Moore, editors, *In Recognition of William Gaddis,* Syracuse University Press, 1984.
Madden, David, *Rediscoveries,* Crown, 1971.
Magill, Frank N., editor, *Survey of Contemporary Literature,* supplement, Salem Press, 1972.
Magill, Frank N., editor, *Literary Annual,* Salem Press, 1976.
McCaffery, Larry, editor, *Postmodern Fiction,* Greenwood Press, 1986.
Moore, Steven, *A Reader's Guide to William Gaddis's "The Recognitions,"* University of Nebraska Press, 1982.
Tanner, Tony, *City of Words,* Harper, 1971.
Wiener, Norbert, *The Human Use of Human Beings,* Houghton, 1954.

PERIODICALS

Atlantic, April, 1985.
Berkeley Gazette, March 16, 1962.
Chicago Tribune Book World, July 14, 1985.
Christian Science Monitor, September 17, 1985, pp. 25-26.
Commentary, December, 1985, pp. 62-65.
Commonweal, April 15, 1955.
Conjunctions, number 7, 1985; number 8, 1985.
Contemporary Literature, winter, 1975.
Critique, winter, 1962-63; Volume 19, number 3, 1978; Volume 22, number 1, 1980.
Genre, number 13, 1980.
Hollins Critic, April, 1977.
Hungry Mind Review, spring, 1994, pp. 34, 42-43.
International Fiction Review, Volume 10, number 2, 1983.
Listener, March 13, 1986, pp. 28-29.
London Review of Books, May 12, 1994, pp. 20-21.
Los Angeles Times Book Review, July 14, 1985.
Modern Fiction Studies, number 27, 1981-82.
Nation, April 30, 1955; November 16, 1985, p. 496; April 25, 1994, pp. 569-71.
National Observer, October 11, 1975.
New Leader, January 17-31, 1994, pp. 18-19.
New Republic, September 2, 1985, pp. 30-32; February 7, 1994, pp. 27-30.
Newspaper, numbers 12-14, 1962.
Newsweek, March 14, 1955; November 10, 1975; July 15, 1985; January 17, 1994, p. 52.
New Yorker, April 9, 1955.
New York Herald Tribune, April 14, 1962.
New York Herald Tribune Book Review, March 13, 1955.
New York Review of Books, February 17, 1994, pp. 3-4, 6.
New York Times, July 3, 1985, p. C22; November 15, 1987; January 4, 1994, p. C20.
New York Times Book Review, March 13, 1955; July 14, 1974; November 9, 1975; June 20, 1976; June 6, 1982; July 7, 1985; February 2, 1986; January 9, 1994, pp. 1, 22.

New York Times Magazine, November 15, 1987.

Observer Weekend Review, September 9, 1962.

Plain Dealer (Cleveland), October, 1975.

Publishers Weekly, July 12, 1985.

Pynchon Notes, Number 11, 1983.

Queen's Quarterly, summer, 1962.

Review of Contemporary Fiction, Volume 2, number 2, 1982.

San Francisco Review of Books, February, 1976.

Saturday Review, March 12, 1955; October 4, 1975.

Scotsman, April 10, 1965.

Studies in American Humor, Number 1, 1982.

Time, March 14, 1955; July 22, 1985.

Times Literary Supplement, February 28, 1986; June 3, 1994, p. 22.

TREMA, Number 2, 1977.

United States Quarterly Book Review, June, 1955.

Village Voice, November 1, 1962.

Village Voice Literary Supplement, April, 1991, p. 26.

Virginia Quarterly Review, summer, 1976.

Wall Street Journal, August 26, 1985, p. 14.

Washington Post, August 23, 1985.

Washington Post Book World, July 7, 1985, p. 1; January 23, 1994, pp. 1, 10.

Western Review, winter, 1956.

Wisconsin Studies in Contemporary Literature, summer, 1965.

Yale Review, September, 1951.

*   *   *

GARDNER, Howard 1943-

PERSONAL: Born July 11, 1943, in Scranton, PA; son of Ralph (a businessperson) and Hilde (Weilheimer) Gardner; married Judith Krieger (a psychologist), June 9, 1966 (divorced); married Ellen Winner, November 20, 1982; children: (first marriage) Kerith, Jay, Andrew; (second marriage) Benjamin. *Education:* Harvard University, B.A. (summa cum laude), 1965, Ph.D., 1971; graduate study at London School of Economics and Political Science, London, 1966.

ADDRESSES: Home—15 Lancaster St., Cambridge, MA 02140.

CAREER: Harvard University, Cambridge, MA, research associate, 1971—, codirector, Project Zero, 1973—, professor of education, 1986—; Boston Veteran's Administration Hospital, Boston, MA, research psychologist, 1972—; Boston University School of Medicine, Boston, MA, associate professor of medicine, 1979—, professor of neurology, 1984—. Board member of Social Sciences Research Council.

MEMBER: Society for Research in Child Development, Academy of Aphasia (Chairman 1986-88), Phi Beta Kappa.

AWARDS, HONORS: Claude Bernard Journalism Award, National Society for Medical Research, 1975, for "Brain Damage: Gateway to the Mind"; MacArthur Prize fellowship, 1981; Best Book Award, 1984, American Psychological Association, for *Frames of Mind: The Theory of Multiple Intelligences.*

WRITINGS:

(With Martin Grossack) *Man and Men: Social Psychology as Social Sciences,* Intext, 1970.

The Quest for Mind: Jean Piaget, Claude Levi-Strauss, and the Structuralist Movement, Knopf (New York City), 1973, second edition, University of Chicago Press (Chicago, IL), 1982.

The Arts and Human Development, Wiley (New York City), 1973.

The Shattered Mind: The Person after Brain Damage, Knopf, 1975.

Developmental Psychology: An Introduction, Little, Brown (Boston, MA), 1978, second edition, 1982.

Artful Scribbles: The Significance of Children's Drawings, Basic Books (New York City), 1980.

Art, Mind, and Brain: A Cognitive Approach to Creativity, Basic Books, 1982.

Frames of Mind: The Theory of Multiple Intelligences, Basic Books, 1983.

The Mind's New Science: A History of the Cognitive Revolution, Basic Books, 1985.

To Open Minds: Chinese Clues to the Dilemma of Contemporary Education, Basic Books, 1989.

Art Education and Human Development, Getty Center for Education in the Arts, 1990.

The Unschooled Mind: How Children Think and How Schools Should Teach, Basic Books, 1991.

Multiple Intelligences: The Theory in Practice, Basic Books, 1993.

Creating Minds: An Anatomy of Creativity Seen through the Lives of Freud, Einstein, Picasso, Stavinsky, Eliot, Graham, and Gandhi, Basic Books, 1993.

Changing the World: A Framework for the Study of Creativity, Praeger (Westport, CT), 1994.

EDITOR

(With J. Gardner) *Classics in Psychology,* Arno, 1973.

(With D. N. Perkins) *Art, Mind, and Education: Research from Project Zero,* University of Illinois Press, 1988.

Also editor of (with J. Gardner) *Classics in Child Development,* Arno; (with E. Winner) *Fact, Fiction, and Fantasy in Childhood,* 1979; and (with H. Kelly) *Viewing Child-*

hood through Television, 1981. Contributing editor, *Psychology Today.*

OTHER

Contributor to books, including *MindScience: An East-West Dialogue,* Wisdom Publications, 1991. Contributor to professional journals. Translator and author of numerous book club adaptations.

SIDELIGHTS: Howard Gardner once told *CA:* "I am trained as a developmental psychologist. . . . I conduct basic research on the development and breakdown of the capacity to use various kinds of symbols (words, pictures, gestures, and the like). I work with normal and gifted children and with once normal adults who have suffered brain damage. . . . I enjoy the challenge of trying to make my research, and that of other social scientists, accessible to the interested layman."

During a long career as a teacher and researcher, Gardner has written numerous books on various aspects of developmental psychology, with a special emphasis on the evolution of creativity in children and adults. Reviewing Gardner's accomplishments as a researcher and writer in a *New York Times Book Review* article, Edward Rothstein describes the author as "a cognitive psychologist, a scientist concerned with the concrete ways in which people come to know the world." This interest is clearly defined in Gardner's 1980 book, *Artful Scribbles: The Significance of Children's Drawings,* where he investigates the flowering of creativity in young children, its subsequent decline as they mature, and the questions that this developmental sequence raises. Why, Gardner asks, does artistic expressiveness decline when children enter school: Should the work they produce be considered "real art"—or the domain of anthropologists? And what connection exists between children's spontaneous expressions and the deliberate work of mature artists? Writing in the *New York Times Book Review,* Marie Winn characterizes *Artful Scribbles* as "one of those studies that raises more questions than it can answer."

The work, in fact, traces the artistic development of Gardner's own son and daughter over a period of months, and then years, sounding, Winn writes, "a poignant note . . . a note of diminishment and loss." For as the children mature, their drawings become more realistic but less compelling. In Gardner's daugher's case, "dramatic scenes give way to placid bucolic compositions," which Gardner deems "predictable." But, unlike those who attribute this artistic decline to the oppressive atmosphere of schools, Gardner sees it as a natural step in development. Winn explains: "As language skills develop toward the end of early childhood, Mr. Gardner suggests, the child is able to rely more on linguistic resources for expression and no longer

feels the deep need to communicate through the nonverbal medium of drawing."

While much of his discussion in *Artful Scribbles* is theoretical, Gardner also deals with some educational issues, including, says *Times Literary Supplement* critic Peter Fuller, "the vexed question of the value of copying." "Copying," says the critic, "has been out of favour in art education in recent years, but Gardner argues that, if it is introduced at a certain stage of development, and not over-rigidly imposed, it can provide an important bridge between drawing as a 'natural' expressive activity and participation in the pictorial tradition of one's own culture."

During the 1980s Gardner continued his research on the process of learning, expanding his field of investigation to include China, a country he visited four times during the decade. During his last two trips, Gardner concentrated his research efforts to study the role played by art in the process of learning, a topic he had previously dealt with in *Artful Scribbles* and *Art, Mind, and Brain: A Cognitive Approach to Creativity,* a collection of essays referring readers to experiments conducted to unravel the nature of artistic thinking. Gardner's travels to China introduced him to a traditional system of learning and development. And while *To Open Minds: Chinese Clues to the Dilemma of Contemporary Education* compares the Chinese education system to the American, Ann-ping Chin of the *Washington Post Book World* says that the book is, in many ways, "mainly about Howard Gardner['s] . . . intellectual and spiritual journey." The first part of the book, explains Chin, is autobiographical, tracing events in the author's life until he arrives in China—and for the first time, is confronted by an opposing view of creativity and development. Unlike western education systems, which define art as an individual, cognitive act, the Chinese, says Gardner, believe "artistic activity [is] . . . the re-creation of traditional beautiful forms and the engendering of moral behavior."

While Gardner was praised for the comparisons he lays out in *To Open Minds,* some critics charge that the book is limited by the narrowness of the author's perception. Chin, for example, declares that "throughout his journal Gardner asked provocative questions although he never made any earnest effort to search for answers beyond China as he perceived it." And reviewing the book in the *Los Angeles Times Book Review* Thomas Cahill points to Gardner's lack of attention to "a raft of cultural questions" contending, that by doing so, Gardner gives the reader only "a sort of travelogue of his experiences in China, skin-deep impressions of a man who can never let go of his own identity long enough to truly comprehend another's."

In 1983 Gardner issued *Frames of Mind: The Theories of Multiple Intelligences.* Reviewing the work in the *Los Angeles Times Book Review,* Kenneth Atchity says the book "presents a suitably complex view of what's going on inside our heads." Exploring, once again, the multifarious nature of human intelligence, Gardner posits that humans have a family of seven intelligences that can be divided into three main groups: object-related intelligence, which includes mathematics and logic; object-free intelligence, including music and language; and personal intelligence, or the psychological perception we have of ourselves and others. The problem, as Gardner points out, is that our education system is not prepared to address the needs of all these intelligences, thus neglecting to address the development of some of these areas. Reviewing the work in the *Times Literary Supplement,* Philip Johnson-Laird says that Gardner has "amassed many intriguing anecdotes and case histories to support his arguments for each of the multiple intelligences" offering "a plausible analysis of types of schooling and their effects." And Jerome Bruner, writing for the *New York Review of Books,* finds *Frames of Mind* "a timely, wide-reaching, and in many ways brilliant book. His effort to bring together the data of neurology, exceptionality, development, and symbolic-cultural skills," the critic sums up, "is not only heroic but makes extremely evocative reading."

Gardner continues his exploration of human intelligence in *The Mind's New Science: A History of the Cognitive Revolution.* Based on extensive research, this historical account covers the study of cognitive skill, or intelligence, tracing its philosophical foundations as far back as the ancient Greeks and Plato to its modern beginnings in the work of Descartes, who believed that ideas innately present in the human mind are only stimulated, not produced, by human experience. Later philosophers, too, had their opinions on the question of rationalist versus empiricist orientation, and in the twentieth century, the debate has continued. A turning point in this discussion was reached in 1956 when scientists and scholars from a variety of disciplines came together to create the field of "cognitive science." The aim was to work in a more concerted way toward knowledge on intelligence and how the mind works to acquire and express knowledge. More recently, the development of computer technology has offered a means for systematic study of logical processes. In his Toronto *Globe and Mail* review of *The Mind's New Science,* David R. Olson praises Gardner for his "admirable detail and clarity, the rich range of background research and theory on which the current cognitive sciences are based."

In *The Unschooled Mind: How Children Think and How Schools Should Teach,* which Gardner issued in 1991, he builds on his theory of multiple intelligences to discuss different learning styles and calls for doing away with our

"fast-food approach to education" to accommodate all children, not just those who find it easy to learn in traditional ways. In the *New York Times Book Review,* Vivian Gussin Paley, a kindergarten teacher in Chicago, calls this book "invaluable . . . for teachers, school administrators, parents and policy makers."

BIOGRAPHICAL/CRITICAL SOURCES:

BOOKS

Gardner, Howard, *To Open Minds: Chinese Clues to the Dilemma of Contemporary Education,* Basic Books (New York City), 1989.

Gardner, Howard, *The Unschooled Mind: How Children Think and How Schools Should Teach,* Basic Books, 1991.

PERIODICALS

Discover, January 1984, p. 79.
Globe and Mail (Toronto), January 25, 1986.
Los Angeles Times Book Review, February 26, 1984; December 22, 1985. p. 9; January 28, 1990.
New Republic, February 24, 1980, pp. 38-40.
New York Review of Books, October 27, 1983.
New York Times, February 14, 1975.
New York Times Book Review, March 2, 1975; April 6, 1980; February 6, 1983; October 27, 1983; December 25, 1983; October 13, 1985; November 26, 1989; December 15, 1991.
Saturday Review, May, 1980.
Times Literary Supplement, January 20, 1978; September 19, 1980; May 11, 1984.
Washington Post Book World, December 24, 1989.*

*   *   *

GARRISON, Paul 1918-

PERSONAL: Born February 10, 1918, in Hamm, Germany; immigrated to the United States, 1937, naturalized citizen, 1943; son of Ernst (a lawyer) and Lotte (Papendieck) Garrison; married Marianne Johansen; children: Peter. *Education:* Attended secondary school in Hamm, Germany.

ADDRESSES: Home—P.O. Box 2490, Santa Fe, NM 87504.

CAREER: Fashion photographer in New York City, 1939-43; television film producer in Los Angeles, CA, 1948-54; producer of industrial motion pictures, 1954-69; *Flying* magazine, New York City, assistant editor, 1969-71; *Business and Commercial Aviation,* New York City, managing editor, 1971-73; free-lance writer, 1973—.

Military service: U.S. Army, Signal Corps, 1943-45; became staff sergeant.

MEMBER: Writers Guild of America, Aviation/Space Writers of America.

WRITINGS:

ON AVIATION

Inside Private Aviation, H & C Publishing, 1973.

Gliders: How to Build and Fly Them, Sterling Publishing (New York City), 1978.

The Encyclopedia of Hot Air Balloons, Sterling Publishing, 1978.

How the Air Traffic Control System Works, Tab Books, 1979.

Night Flying in Single Engine Airplanes, Tab Books, 1979.

The Illustrated Encyclopedia of General Aviation, Tab Books, 1979.

Cross-Country Flying, Tab Books, 1980.

Flying VFR in Marginal Weather, Tab Books, 1980.

Practical Area Navigation, Tab Books, 1980.

A Funny Thing Happened on the Way to the Airport, Tab Books, 1980.

The Complete Guide to Single-Engine Mooneys, Tab Books, 1980.

Lift, Thrust, and Drag, Tab Books, 1981.

The Corporate Aircraft Owner's Handbook, Tab Books, 1982.

Aircraft Turbocharging, Tab Books, 1982.

A Pilot's Guide to Aviation Insurance, Tab Books, 1982.

Autopilots, Flight Directors, and Flight Control Systems, Tab Books, 1985.

Flying without Wings: A Flight Simulation Manual, Tab Books, 1985.

ON MODEL RAILROADS

Model Railroad Photography, Tab Books, 1981.

Model Railroading in Small Spaces, Tab Books, 1982.

All About N Gauge Model Railroading, Tab Books, 1982.

One Hundred One Model Railroad Layouts, Tab Books, 1983.

Model Railroad Electronics, Tab Books, 1987.

ON COMPUTERS

Cockpit Computers, McGraw (New York City), 1982.

Programming the TI59 and the HP-41 Calculators, Tab Books, 1982.

How to Select and Use Computers in Real Estate, EPPCO, 1982.

Fun, Games, and Graphics for the Apple II, IIe, IIc, . . . , Tab Books, 1984.

The Last Whole TI-99/4A Book, Wiley (New York City), 1984.

Star Power: Mastering WordStar, MailMerge, SpellStar, DataStar, Supersport, CalStar, InfoStar, StarIndex, CorrectStar, StarBurst, ReportStar, and PlanStar, Tab Books, 1985.

Microcomputers and Aviation, Wiley, 1985.

Turbo Pascal for BASIC Programmers, Que (Indianapolis), 1985.

One Hundred One Personal Computer Programs for Business and Professional Use, Compute! (Greensboro, NC), 1985.

Turbo Pascal Toolbox, Tab Books, 1987.

"Publish It" Made Easy, Osborne/McGraw (Berkeley, CA), 1990.

WordPerfect Wizardry, Wordware Publications, 1991.

OTHER

How to Build Adobe Houses, Tab Books (Blue Ridge Summit, PA), 1979.

Investing in Oil in the Eighties without Spending a Fortune, Pennwell (Tulsa, OK), 1981.

Also author of poetry. Creator of computer software "One Hundred Programs for Business and Professional Use," Compute!, 1985, and "Turbo Pascal for BASIC Programmers," Que, 1985.

WORK IN PROGRESS: Research for a book on artificial intelligence.

SIDELIGHTS: Paul Garrison once told *CA:* "I started writing television filmscripts in 1948, producing the first half-hour television film series, *The Cases of Eddie Drake,* because there wasn't anyone around in those days who seemed to know how to do it. Later, I wrote a great many industrial filmscripts and eventually graduated to writing magazine articles on subjects that I was familiar with or that just interested me.

"In 1959 I became a licensed pilot, accumulating some five thousand hours in small airplanes; so it was only natural that I'd start writing about aviation. I was also an active model railroader from time to time, and as a result I wrote several books on that subject as well. Eventually, unable to think of anything else to write about either aviation or model railroading, I began looking for another subject, and computers seemed ideal. I started with programmable calculators and then graduated to more sophisticated personal computers. I found that programming is both exciting and satisfying, and I am spending a lot of time writing software in several different computer languages. Some of these programs are finding their way into my books."

GILL, Bob 1931-

PERSONAL: Born January 17, 1931, in New York, NY; son of Jacob and Frieda (Gothelf) Gill; married Elizabeth Ann Mills, 1966 (divorced, 1974). *Education:* Attended Philadelphia Museum School of Art, 1948-51, Pennsylvania Academy of Fine Arts, 1951, and City College of New York, 1952, 1955.

ADDRESSES: Home—1200 Broadway, New York, NY 10001.

CAREER: Freelance designer and illustrator in New York City, 1954-60; Charles Hobson Advertising Agency, London, art director, 1960-62; Fletcher/Forbes/Gill (later Crosby/Fletcher/Forbes/Gill; design studio), London, partner, 1962-67; freelance design consultant, illustrator, and filmmaker, London, 1967-75, New York City, 1976—. Instructor, School of Visual Arts, New York City, 1955-60, Pratt Institute, Brooklyn, 1959, Central School of Art, London, 1967-69, Chelsea School of Art, London, 1969, Royal College of Art, London, 1970-75, Hornsey School of Art, London, 1972-74, and Parsons School of Design, New York City, 1981. Work has been exhibited in the U.S. and abroad at numerous shows, including American Institute of Graphic Arts, New York City, 1966, and Stedelijk Museum, Amsterdam, 1970. Has made more than 30 documentaries and industrial film for clients, including Olivetti, Singapore Airlines, and the Lincoln Center; has also drawn record covers and created illustrations and graphics for packaging. *Military service:* U.S. Army, 1952-54.

AWARDS, HONORS: Gold medal, Art Directors Club of New York, 1956; silver medal, Design and Art Directors Association (London), 1968, 1970; has received more than 100 other awards in graphic design, including many from the American Institute of Graphic Arts and Type Directors Club.

WRITINGS:

(And illustrator) *New York: Places and Pleasures,* Simon & Schuster (New York City), 1957, 4th revised edition published as *New York, Places and Pleasures: An Uncommon Guidebook,* Davis-Poynter, 1973.
(With Alastair Reid) *The Millionaires,* Simon & Schuster, 1959.
(With Reid) *A Balloon for a Blunderbuss* (juvenile), Harper (New York City), 1961.
(And illustrator) *A to Z,* Little, Brown (Boston), 1962.
What Color Is Your World, Anthony Blond (London), 1962, Helene Obolensky (New York City), 1963.
(With Alan Fletcher and Colin Forbes) *Graphic Design: Visual Comparisons,* Studio Books, 1963, Reinhold (New York City), 1964.

(With John Lewis) *Illustration: Aspects and Directions,* Reinhold, 1964.
(With Keith Botsford) *Parade,* Curwen Press (London), 1965.
(And illustrator) *The Green-Eyed Mouse and the Blue-Eyed Mouse,* Curwen Press, 1965.
Bob Gill's Portfolio, Lund Humphries (London), 1968.
I Keep Changing (juvenile), Scroll Press (New York City), 1971.
Ups and Downs (juvenile), A. & C. Black (London), 1971, Addison-Wesley (Reading, MA), 1974.
Forget All the Rules You Ever Learned about Graphic Design, Including the Ones in This Book, Watson-Guptill (New York City), 1981.
Graphic Design Made Difficult, Van Nostrand (New York City), 1992.

Also author, with Fletcher and Forbes, of *The Present,* 1963.

Graphic Design: Visual Comparisons has been published in German. Collections of Gill's work are housed in the Museum of Modern Art, New York City, and Victoria and Albert Museum, London.

BIOGRAPHICAL/CRITICAL SOURCES:

BOOKS

Booth-Clibborn, Edward, and Daniele Baroni, *The Language of Graphics,* [London], 1980.
Gerstner, Karl, and Markus Kutter, *The New Graphic Design,* [London], 1959.

*   *   *

GINGERICH, Owen (Jay) 1930-

PERSONAL: Surname rhymes with "Singer-rich"; born March 24, 1930, in Washington, IA; son of Melvin (a historian) and Verna (Roth) Gingerich; married Miriam Sensenig, June 26, 1954; children: Jonathan C., Mark P., Peter E. *Education:* Goshen College, B.A., 1951; Harvard University, M.A., 1953, Ph.D., 1962. *Religion:* Mennonite. *Avocational interests:* Photography, rare books (Gingerich assisted American designer Charles Eames with a major Copernicus exhibition and show), travel, shell collecting.

ADDRESSES: Home—Cambridge, MA. *Office*—Harvard-Smithsonian Center for Astrophysics, 60 Garden St., Cambridge, MA 02138.

CAREER: American University, Beirut, Lebanon, director of Observatory, 1955-58, assistant professor of astronomy, 1957-58; Wellesley College, Wellesley, MA, lecturer in astronomy, 1958-59; Harvard University, Cambridge,

MA, lecturer, 1960-68, associate professor, 1968-69, professor of astronomy and history of science, 1969-92, chairperson of history of science department, 1992—. Harvard-Smithsonian Center for Astrophysics, Cambridge, astrophysicist, 1962-87, senior astronomer, 1987—; George Darwin Lecturer for Royal Astronomical Society, 1971; national lecturer for Sigma Xi, 1971; visiting fellow, St. Edmund's House, Cambridge University, 1977-78; overseas fellow, Churchill College, Cambridge University, 1985-86. Corporation member or overseer, Boston Museum of Science, 1979—; member of advisory board, Center of Theological Inquiry, Princeton, 1988-93; member of advisory committee on history of physics, American Institute of Physics, 1972-82. Member of Yale University Council's committee on the library, 1985-90, and of Library of Congress's Council of Scholars, 1986-88. Member of Harvard astronomy expeditions to Ceylon, 1955, and Beirut, 1959. Consultant to Harvard Project Physics, 1964-69, and Office of Charles and Ray Eames, 1969-77.

MEMBER: International Academy of the History of Science, International Astronomical Union (Central Bureau for Astronomical Telegrams, director, 1965-67, associate director, 1968-79; president of Commission 41, 1970-76; chairperson of U.S. national committee, 1981-83), Academie Internationale d'Histoire des Sciences, American Association for the Advancement of Science (fellow; councilor, 1971-73; chairperson of Section L, 1974; chairperson of Section D, 1980), American Association of Variable Star Observers (councilor, 1965-70), American Astronomical Society (councilor, 1973-76; chairperson of educational advisory committee, 1975-77; chairperson of Division of Historical Astronomy, 1980, 1983-85), American Academy of Arts and Sciences, American Philosophical Society (vice-president, 1982-85; councilor, 1994—), Royal Astronomical Society (vice-president of library committee, 1982-85), Royal Astronomical Society Club (honorary member), British Society for the History of Science, Royal Astronomical Society of Canada (honorary member), History of Science Society, Scientific Instruments Society, Astronomical Society of the Pacific, Phi Beta Kappa (chairperson of national science award committee, 1976), Sigma Xi, Examiner Club.

AWARDS, HONORS: John F. Lewis Prize, American Philosophical Society, 1976, for paper "From Copernicus to Kepler: Heliocentrism as Model and as Reality"; Physical and Earth Sciences Prize, Professional and Scholarly Publishing Division of Association of American Publishers, 1979, for *A Source Book in Astronomy and Astrophysics, 1900-1975;* Order of Merit, Commander Class, People's Republic of Poland, 1981; the International Astronomical Union has named Asteroid 2658 "Gingerich" in his honor.

WRITINGS:

(Translator from German) Theodore Oppolzer, *Canon of Eclipses,* Dover (New York City), 1962.

(With William Stahlman) *Solar and Planetary Longitudes for Years -2500 to +2000,* University of Wisconsin Press (Madison), 1963.

(Translator from French) Jean Dufay, *Introduction to Astrophysics: The Stars,* Dover, 1964.

(With David Godine) *Renaissance Books of Science from the Collection of Albert E. Lownes,* Dartmouth College Press (Hanover, NH), 1970.

(With Kenneth Lang) *A Source Book in Astronomy and Astrophysics 1900-1975,* Harvard University Press (Cambridge, MA), 1979.

(With Barbara L. Welther) *Planetary, Lunar, and Solar Positions A.D. 1650-A.D. 1800* (memoirs of the American Philosophical Society), American Philosophical Society (Philadelphia), 1983.

(With Robert S. Westman) *The Wittich Connection: Conflict and Priority in Late Sixteenth-Century Cosmology,* American Philosophical Society, 1988.

Album of Science: The Physical Sciences in the Twentieth Century, Scribner (New York City), 1989.

The Great Copernicus Chase and Other Adventures in Astronomical History (collection of essays and articles), Sky Publishing (Cambridge, MA), 1992.

The Eye of Heaven: Ptolemy, Copernicus, Kepler (collection of articles), American Institute of Physics (New York City), 1993.

An Annotates Census of Copernicus' "De Revolutionibus" (Nuremberg, 1543, and Basel, 1566), E. J. Brill (Long Island City, NY), 1995.

EDITOR

Theory and Observation of Normal Stellar Atmospheres, MIT Press (Cambridge, MA), 1969.

Frontiers in Astronomy, W. H. Freeman (San Francisco), 1970, revised edition published as *New Frontiers in Astronomy,* 1975.

The Nature of Scientific Discovery, Smithsonian Institution Press (Washington, DC), 1975.

(With Jerzy Dobrzycki) *The Astronomy of Copernicus and Its Background,* Ossolineum (Wroclaw), 1975.

(And author of introduction) *Cosmology + 1,* W. H. Freeman, 1977.

General History of Astronomy, Volume 4: *Astrophysics and Twentieth-Century Astronomy to 1950,* Cambridge University Press, 1984.

(And author of introduction) *Scientific Genius and Creativity,* W. H. Freeman, 1987.

(With Michael Hoskin) *Two Astronomical Anniversaries: HCO and SAO,* Harvard-Smithsonian Center for Astrophysics (Cambridge, MA), 1990.

OTHER

Contributor to *Encyclopaedia Britannica, Collier's Encyclopedia,* and *Encyclopedia Americana;* associate editor for science, medicine, and technology, *Dictionary of American History* (supplement), Macmillan (New York City), 1994. Editor, "Harvard Books on Astronomy" series, 1977-84, "Harvard Dissertations in the History of Science" series, Garland Publishing (New York City), 1990—, and "Young Oxford Scientists" series, Oxford University Press (New York City), 1994—; chairperson of editorial advisory board, *General History of Astronomy,* 1972—, and "Classics of Science Library," Gryphon Editions (New York City), 1994—. Contributor of more than 250 articles and reviews to scientific journals, including *Astrophysical Journal, Journal for the History of Astronomy, Scientific American, Atlantic, Science Year,* and *Sky and Telescope. Journal for the History of Astronomy,* member of editorial board, 1970-74, associate editor, 1975—; member of editorial board, *American Scholar,* 1975-80; *Harvard Magazine,* member of editorial advisory committee, 1976-77, director, 1978-85, incorporator, 1986—.

WORK IN PROGRESS: Nicolaus Copernicus, for Oxford University Press.

*   *   *

GINSBERG, Benjamin   1947-

PERSONAL: Born April 1, 1947, in Poking, Germany; immigrated to the United States, 1949, naturalized citizen, 1955; son of Herman (a businessman) and Anna (a homemaker; maiden name, Wolfstein) Ginsberg; married Sandra J. Brewer (a physician), December 15, 1968; children: Cynthia, Alexander. *Education:* University of Chicago, B.A., 1968, M.A., 1970, Ph.D., 1973. *Religion:* Jewish.

ADDRESSES: Home—10800 Tara Road, Potomac, MD 20854. *Office*—Department of Political Science, Johns Hopkins University, 341 Mergenthaler Hall, Baltimore, MD 21218.

CAREER: Cornell University, Ithaca, NY, instructor, 1972-73, assistant professor, 1973-78, associate professor, 1978-83, professor of government, 1983—, director of graduate studies, 1978-85, chairman of Graduate Fellowship Board for the Social Sciences, 1978-81. Public speaker on government and politics; guest on television and radio programs; consultant to Hansard Society for Parliamentary Government.

MEMBER: American Political Science Association.

AWARDS, HONORS: Trustees' scholar, University of Chicago, 1964-68; NIMH fellow, University of Chicago, 1968-72; Grant from Bureau of Justice Statistics, U.S. De-

partment of Justice, 1983-84; Jonathan Meigs grantee, Cornell University, 1985; Kellogg Foundation grantee, 1987.

WRITINGS:

(With Theodore J. Lowi) *Poliscide,* Macmillan (New York City), 1976, 2nd edition, 1990.
(Contributor) Lowi and Alan Stone, editors, *Nationalizing Government,* Russell Sage (New York City), 1978.
(Contributor) Jeff Fishel, editor, *Parties and Elections,* Indiana University Press (Bloomington, IN), 1978.
The Consequences of Consent: Elections, Citizen Control, and Popular Acquiescence, Random House (New York City), 1982.
(Contributor) Thomas Ferguson and Joel Rogers, editors, *The Political Economy: Readings in the Politics and Economics of American Public Policy,* M. E. Sharpe (Armonk, NY), 1984.
(Contributor) Michael Nelson, editor, *The Elections of 1984,* Congressional Quarterly (Washington, DC), 1985.
(Editor with Stone, and contributor) *Do Elections Matter?,* M. E. Sharpe, 1986, 3rd edition, in press.
The Captive Public: How Mass Opinion Promotes State Power, Basic Books (New York City), 1986.
(Contributor) Nelson, editor, *The Presidency and the Political System,* 2nd edition, Congressional Quarterly, 1987.
(With Lowi) *Freedom and Power in American Government* (with instructor's manual and study guide), Norton (New York City), 1989.
(With Lowi) *American Government: Freedom and Power,* Norton, 1990, 3rd edition, 1994.
(With Martin Shefter) *Politics by Other Means: The Declining Importance of Elections in America,* Basic Books, 1990.
(With Lowi and Alice Hearst) *American Government: Readings and Cases,* Norton, 1992, 2nd edition, 1994.
The Fatal Embrace: Jews and the State, University of Chicago Press (Chicago), 1993.
Democrats Return to Power: Politics and Policy in the Clinton Era, Norton, 1994.

Contributor of articles and reviews to political science journals. GINSBERG

*   *   *

GIRARD, Hazel Batten   1901-1989

PERSONAL: Born December 8, 1901, in Batten's Crossing, MI; died April 24, 1989, in Owosso, MI; daughter of

John W. (a farmer) and Johanna (Alexander) Batten; married Joseph Jerome Girard (a teacher), August 16, 1920 (died April 25, 1965); children: Victor M., Marvin Eugene. *Education:* Attended high school in Ann Arbor, MI. *Politics:* "Variable, depending on the status of the cupboard." *Religion:* "Handshaking Methodist."

ADDRESSES: Home—1019 Fletcher St., Owosso, MI 48867.

CAREER: Free-lance writer and photographer, beginning 1922. Assistant postmaster of Glennie, MI, 1927-30. Partner in family wholesale candy business. Photographs syndicated by Free-lance Photographers Guild.

MEMBER: International Platform Association, Photographic Society of America, Shiawassee Historical Society, Corunna VFW Auxiliary 4005.

WRITINGS:

A Giant Walked among Them: Half-Tall Tales of Paul Bunyan and His Loggers, Marshall Jones (Francestown, NH), 1977.

(With son, Marvin Eugene Girard) *Rail Fences and Roosters* (light verse), illustrations by M. E. Girard, Golden Quill Press (Francestown, NH), 1978.

Blow for Batten's Crossing: A Backwoods Odyssey, Glendon (Los Angeles), 1979.

Black Loam and Buttermilk (light verse), illustrations by the author and M. E. Girard, Downhome Press, 1986.

Author of "Batten Me Down," a column in *Bay City Times.* Contributor of articles and photographs to magazines and newspapers, including *Collier's, American Home, Nature, Field and Stream,* and *Outdoors.*

SIDELIGHTS: Hazel Girard once told *CA:* "Throughout my childhood, the little narrow-gauge train of the Au Sable and North Western Railroad rattled the window panes of our home at Batten's Crossing twice a day—once early in the morning when it went by with its long strings of empty flatcars for the pickup of freshly-cut logs 'further up the pike,' and again in the afternoon when it returned with its massive loads of sawlogs chained to the cars en route to the mills at Au Sable and Oscoda.

"It was the Batten farm (near Glennie, Michigan) that had been carved out of virgin wilderness by my lumberjack father, Silver Jack of the Rollways. By self-appraisal, I was easily the ugly duckling of the seven daughters at the Crossing—a restless redhead with no patience for the passive activities of dollplaying, dominoes, and such. I much preferred tagging the freshly-ploughed furrows in my bare feet, always at my dad's heels. Every few rounds of the ploughing we'd climb the nearby rail fence and discuss many topics: things we had read, who wrote them, why it was good writing—or wasn't. I didn't recognize it at the time, but Dad was like a dean of journalism sitting atop a wormy rail fence, and I was the budding author learning her craft from a master storyteller.

"We agreed we hated ponderous writing, laborious writing that went on and on with long sentences, long paragraphs, and prowling chapters. We liked concise, assertive writing that picked up its feet and got moving down the page. I have always insisted that the rail fence teachings were the best lessons I ever received about writing. Somehow, I have always been very fortunate that editors invariably leave my writing intact, exactly as submitted to them.

"The late Malcolm Bingay, editor of the *Detroit Free Press,* once told me that I wrote with cadence, with a proclivity for choosing words with 'ear appeal.' I prefer nonfiction for reading and like to stick to writing about things I know—always done concisely and with a quick wrap-up. And, oh yes, I would love to own a rail fence!"

BIOGRAPHICAL/CRITICAL SOURCES:

PERIODICALS

Detroit Free Press, August 19, 1979.

OBITUARIES:

PERIODICALS

Argus-Press (Owosso, MI), April 26, 1989.
Flint Journal (Flint, MI), April 28, 1989.*

*   *   *

GLIDEWELL, John C(alvin) 1919-

PERSONAL: Born November 5, 1919, in Okolona, MS; son of Henry Clay and Jessie Kate (Jones) Glidewell; married Frances Lee Reed, 1941; children: Pamela Lee, Janis Lynn. *Education:* University of Chicago, A.M., 1949, Ph.D., 1953.

ADDRESSES: Home—101 Longwood Pl., Nashville, TN 37215-1926. *Office*—Department of Psychology and Human Development, Vanderbilt University, Peabody Box 512, Nashville, TN 37203.

CAREER: University of Chicago, Human Dynamics Laboratory, Chicago, IL, project director, 1948-49; Meridian Public Schools, Meridian, MS, director of psychological services, 1949-51; U.S. Air Force, Maxwell Air Force Base, AK, Human Resources Research Institute, project director, 1951-53; St. Louis County Health Department, Clayton, MO, director of research and development, 1953-67; Washington University, St. Louis, MO, Medical

School, research assistant, 1954-58, research instructor, 1958-64, research assistant professor of medical psychology, 1964-67, Social Science Institute, director of training program for social science research in community mental health, 1958-66, department of sociology and anthropology, associate professor of social psychology, 1963-65, Graduate Institute of Education, associate professor of educational psychology, 1965-67; University of Chicago, professor of education and behavioral science, 1967-81, chairman of educational psychology faculty, 1970-73; Vanderbilt University, Nashville, TN, professor of psychology, 1981-90, professor emeritus, 1990—. Adjunct staff member, National Training Laboratories, National Education Association, 1950—; lecturer in public health, School of Nursing, Washington University, School of Nursing, St. Louis University, and Marilac College, 1957-65. *Military service:* U.S. Army, 1942-46; became captain. U.S. Air Force Reserve, 1946-50; active duty, 1950-52; retired as major.

MEMBER: International Association of Applied Social Scientists (member of board of directors, 1970-73), American Psychological Association (fellow), American Sociological Association (fellow), National Training Laboratories Association (fellow), American Public Health Association (fellow; Mental Health Section, secretary, 1964-66, chairperson, 1968), Society for the Psychological Study of Social Issues (fellow), Midwest Psychological Association, Sigma Xi.

AWARDS, HONORS: Award for distinguished contribution, Division 27, American Psychological Association, 1975.

WRITINGS:

(Editor and contributor) *Parental Attitudes and Child Behavior,* C. C Thomas (Springfield, IL), 1961.

(With L. M. Smith and others) *Socialization and Social Organization in Elementary Classrooms,* Social Science Research Council, 1965.

(With Martha M. Brown and others) *Nurses, Patients and Social Systems,* University of Missouri Press (Columbia), 1968.

(With C. S. Swallow) *The Prevalence of Maladjustment in Elementary Schools,* Joint Commission on the Mental Health of Children, 1968.

Choice Points: The Emotional Problems of Living with People, MIT Press (Cambridge, MA), 1970.

(Editor) *The Social Context of Learning and Development,* Gardner Press (New York City), 1977.

(Editor and contributor) *Corporate Cultures: Research Implications for Managers and Human Resource Development,* American Society for Training and Development, 1986.

(Editor with Erwin C. Hargrove, and contributor) *Impossible Jobs in Public Management,* University Press of Kansas (Lawrence), 1990.

Author of numerous research reports for various organizations, including St. Louis County Health Department and Swampscott Conference. Contributor to numerous books, including *Leadership Training for Community Health Promotion,* U.S. Public Health Service, 1957; *Community Mental Health: An International Perspective,* edited by R. Williams and L. Ozarin, Jossey-Bass (San Francisco), 1967; *Community Psychology in Transition,* edited by I. Iscoe, B. L. Bloom, and C. D. Spielberger, Hemisphere Publishing (Washington, D.C.), 1977; and *Cognitive Perspectives on Educational Leadership,* edited by R. Hallinger, K. Leithwood, and J. Murphy, Teachers College Press, Columbia University (New York City), 1993. Contributor to *Third Year Book* of the American Association of Public Schools, 1955; contributor to proceedings of the Ninth Congress of the Interamerican Society of Psychology, 1962. Contributor to psychiatry, public health, education, and sociology journals, including *Journal of Educational Research, American Journal of Orthopsychiatry, American Journal of Psychiatry, Human Organization,* and *Human Relations.* Associate editor, *Adult Leadership,* 1958-62; special issue editor, *Journal of Social Issues,* 1959; editor, *American Journal of Community Psychology,* 1976-87. Author of "Training the Trainer" (on diskette), Stonybrook Software (Mt. Juliet, TN), 1994.

WORK IN PROGRESS: Crisis and Change in a Liberal Arts College; Management of Conflict.

SIDELIGHTS: John Calvin Glidewell once told *CA:* "I try to write because ideas interest me profoundly, and I think that ideas interest everybody else. I enjoy trying to express ideas as clearly and as precisely as can be. In part, the great human capacity to communicate drives my expression, but human communication is never precise. Others' ideas stir my juices, my motives, my feelings, and my thoughts; what I absorb is my reconstruction of what I think I read or heard; it is never exactly what others said. That continuous reconstruction fires the wondrous creativity of the human exchange of thought. In fact, I think that the more precisely accurate communication becomes, the less creative it becomes; the less precisely accurate, the more creative—lots of misses, to be sure, but a few vivid, life-changing hits. That fact makes the quest for truth and love a never-ending, always fascinating quest. My profound interest in ideas, their communication, and their myriad transformations, forces me to try to write, to try to activate my reconstructions and those of others. Another force: I simply enjoy trying to express ideas."

GOLD, Susan Dudley 1949-
(Susan Dudley Morrison)

PERSONAL: Born March 18, 1949, in Portland, ME; daughter of Edward Elias (a bookkeeper and salesman) and Helyn Rose (a bookkeeper and secretary; maiden name, Walton) Dudley; married John Coopersmith Gold, September 16, 1989; children: Samuel Bowman Morrison. *Education:* Attended Brandeis University, 1967-70; University of Maine at Portland-Gorham (now University of Southern Maine), B.A., 1971. *Politics:* Democrat. *Religion:* Unitarian-Universalist.

ADDRESSES: Home—92 Franklin St., Saco, ME 04072. *Office*—Custom Communications, P.O. Box 16036, Portland, ME 04101.

CAREER: Biddeford Journal Tribune (now *Journal Tribune,*) Biddeford, ME, reporter, 1973-76; freelance writer for local and regional publications, 1976-87; *Commercial Fisheries News,* Stonington, ME, correspondent, 1976-87; *Business Digest,* staff writer, 1981-87; coordinator for *Maine Fishermen's Forum,* 1984-87; *Maine Enterprise,* Portland, ME, editor, 1987-89; *Munjoy Hill Observer,* editor and production manager, 1988—; Custom Communications (desktop publisher), Portland, ME, owner and manager, 1989—. Member of Old Orchard Beach Planning Board, 1984-85; president of Action for Child Transportation Safety, 1984-85. Delegate, Maine Democratic Convention, 1988; member and paper editor, Munjoy Hill Neighborhood Association; member of board of directors, Unitarian-Universalist Church, Saco-Biddeford, 1990-91; board member, Greater Biddeford-Saco Aspirations Compact, 1992—.

MEMBER: National Press Women's Association, The Literary Network, Society of Children's Book Writers, New England Business Association, Maine Media Women, Maine Writers and Publishers Alliance, Biddeford-Saco Chamber of Commerce and Industry (membership director).

AWARDS, HONORS: Third-place award for feature writing, New England Press Association, 1975; first-place awards, Maine Media Women, 1984, for feature story "Cole-Haan Is Walking Away with the World's Quality Shoe Market," and 1985, for interview "Jimmy Odlin," 1991, for brochure design, nondaily newspaper editing and children's book categories; bronze award, national Ozzie Award for Design Excellence, 1988, as member of four-person team that redesigned *Maine Enterprise;* first-place awards for brochure design, nondaily newspaper editing, newsletter, editorial writing, and children's book categories, National Press Women's Association-Northeast Region, 1993.

WRITINGS:

UNDER NAME SUSAN DUDLEY MORRISON; JUVENILE

Balls, Crestwood (New York City), 1983.
Shoes for Sport, Crestwood, 1983.
The Alligator, Crestwood, 1984.
The Passenger Pigeon, Crestwood, 1989.
(With Jamie Malanowski and the editors of *Spy*) *Spy High: A Make-Believe Yearbook of America's Rich and Famous,* Doubleday (New York City), 1991.

UNDER NAME SUSAN DUDLEY GOLD; JUVENILE

The Pharoah's Curse ("Incredible Histories" series), illustrated by Sandy Rabinowitz, Crestwood House, 1990.
Toxic Waste ("Earth Alert" series), Crestwood House, 1990.
Countdown to the Moon ("Adventures in Space" series), Crestwood House, 1992.
The Kennedy Space Center: Gateway to Space ("Adventures in Space" series), Crestwood House, 1992.
To Space and Back: The Story of the Shuttle ("Adventures in Space" series), Crestwood House, 1992.
Roe vs. Wade: Abortion, Twenty-First Century Books (New York City), 1994, also published as *Roe vs. Wade (1973): Abortion,* Macmillan Children's Book Group, 1994.

OTHER

Producer, director and writer of video *The Tenth Year: Maine's Fishing Industry,* 1976-85.

*   *   *

GOLDBERG, R. A.
See GOLDBERG, Ray A(llan)

*   *   *

GOLDBERG, Ray A(llan) 1926-
(R. A. Goldberg)

PERSONAL: Born October 19, 1926, in Fargo, ND; son of Max and Anne Libby (Paletz) Goldberg; married Thelma Ruth Englander, May 20, 1956; children: Marc Evan, Jennifer Eve, Jeffrey Lewis. *Education:* Harvard University, A.B. (cum laude), 1948, M.B.A., 1950; University of Minnesota, Ph.D., 1952.

ADDRESSES: Home—975 Memorial Dr., Apt. 701, Cambridge, MA 02138. *Office*—Harvard Graduate School of Business Administration, Soldiers Field, Boston, MA 02163.

CAREER: Moorhead Seed & Grain Co., Minneapolis, MN, chief of public relations, 1952-56, member of board of directors until 1962; Harvard University, Cambridge, MA, lecturer, 1955-57, assistant professor, 1960-66, associate professor of business administration, 1966-70, George M. Moffett Professor of Agriculture and Business, 1970—. Goldena Mills, Inc., officer and member of board of directors, 1952-62; Experience, Inc., secretary and member of board of directors, 1963-78; member of board of directors, Red River Elevator Co., Sola Basic Industries, 1965-67, Mid-America Foods, Inc., 1969-72, International Development Foundation, 1969—, Tri/Valley Growers, 1973—, and other companies; John Hancock Insurance Co., Inc., member of agricultural investment commission, 1971—. National Commission on Productivity, chair of panel on food processing, 1972; National Research Council, member of study team and subgroup chair, world food and nutritional study, 1975—, member of commission on industrial policy for developing countries, Commission on Engineering and Technical Systems, 1982—; National Academy of Engineering, member of commission on technical factors contributing to nation's foreign trade positions, 1976—; Government of Canada, International Development Research Center, member of board of governors, 1978—; Fowler-McCracken Commission, member of task force on agriculture, 1984—; member of U.S. Presidential Economic Delegation to Poland, 1989; chair of Massachusetts Governor's Emergency Commission on Food. Adviser and consultant to foundations, associations, government organizations, and agribusiness firms in the United States and Latin America, 1955—; U.S. Department of Agriculture, chair of agribusiness advisory committee on Caribbean Basin, 1982—. Roxbury Latin School, trustee, 1973-76; New England Conservatory of Music, member of advisory committee to preparatory school, 1974—, associate trustee, 1978—; Beth Israel Hospital, trustee, 1978—, chair of gerontology committee, 1991—.

MEMBER: International Agribusiness Management Association (president, 1990—), American Agricultural Economics Association (editorial council, 1974-78), American Dairy Science Association, American Marketing Association, American Society of Animal Science (national agribusiness educational commission, 1988—), Food Distribution Research Society, Canadian Agricultural Economics Society, V. I. Lenin All-Union Academy of Agricultural Sciences, Agribusiness Institute of Cambridge (chair of the board and treasurer, 1991—), Harvard Club (Boston and New York City).

AWARDS, HONORS: Uhlmann Grain Award, 1952.

WRITINGS:

The Soybean Industry, with Special Reference to the Competitive Position of the Minnesota Producer and Proces-

sor, University of Minnesota Press (Minneapolis), 1952.

(With John H. Davis) *A Concept of Agribusiness,* Division of Research, Graduate School of Business Administration, Harvard University (Cambridge, MA), 1957.

(Under name R. A. Goldberg; with H. B. Arthur and K. M. Bird) *The United States Food and Fiber System in a Changing World Environment,* National Advisory Commission on Food and Fiber (Washington, DC), 1967.

Dynamic Brand Strategies (published with "Brand Strategy in United States Food Marketing: Perspectives on Food Manufacturers" and "Distributors Brands in the United States," by William Applebaum), Division of Research, Graduate School of Business Administration, Harvard University, 1967.

Agribusiness Coordination: A Systems Approach to the Wheat, Soybean, and Florida Orange Economies, Division of Research, Harvard University, 1968.

(With Arthur) *Identifying Management Problems of Agribusiness Firms,* three volumes in one, Division of Research, Graduate School of Business Administration, Harvard University, 1968.

Advanced Agribusiness Management Seminar Philippine Casebook, [Manila], 1969.

(With Lee F. Schrader) *Federal Income Taxes and Farmers' Cooperatives,* Harvard Graduate School of Business Administration, 1973.

(With Leonard M. Wilson and others) *Agribusiness Management for Developing Countries—Latin America,* Ballinger (Cambridge, MA), 1974.

(With Schrader) *Farmers' Cooperatives and Federal Income Taxes,* Ballinger, 1975.

(With Richard C. McGinity, Wilson, Jose D. Drilon, and others) *Agribusiness Management for Developing Countries: Southeast Asian Corn System and American and Japanese Trends Affecting It,* Ballinger, 1979.

(Editor) *Research in Domestic and International Agribusiness Management,* Jai Press (Greenwich, CT), Volume 1, 1980, Volume 2, 1981, Volume 3, 1982, Volume 4, 1983, Volume 5, 1984, Volume 6, 1986, Volume 7, 1987, Volume 8, 1988, Volume 9, 1989, Volume 10, 1990.

(Editor with Gerald E. Gaull) *New Technologies and the Future of Food and Nutrition: Proceedings of the First Ceres Conference, Williamsburg, VA, October 1989,* Wiley (New York City), 1991.

(Editor with Gaull) *The Emerging Global Food System: Public and Private Sector Issues,* Wiley, 1993.

Also author of *The Nonpartisan League in North Dakota,* 1948, (with others) *Agribusiness Management for Developing Countries: With Special Reference to the Central American Fruit and Vegetable Commodity System,* 1973. Contributor to proceedings, symposia, and journals in his field. Chair of editorial advisory board, *Agribusiness: An International Journal,* 1983—.

*   *   *

GOLDMAN, Albert   1927-1994

PERSONAL: Born April 15, 1927, in Dormont, PA; died of a heart attack, March 28, 1994; son of Harry Benjamin and Marie (Levenson) Goldman. *Education:* Attended Carnegie Institute of Technology (now Carnegie-Mellon University), 1944-45, 1946-47; University of Chicago, A.M., 1950; Columbia University, Ph.D., 1961.

ADDRESSES: Agent—Deborah Karl, William Morrow and Co., 105 Madison Ave., New York, NY 10016.

CAREER: Writer. Columbia University, New York City, associate professor of English, 1963-72; moderator and writer of *Wednesday Review,* weekly television cultural program, WNDT, New York, 1966-67; popular music critic, *Life* magazine, 1970-73. *Military service:* U.S. Navy, 1945-46.

MEMBER: Phi Beta Kappa.

WRITINGS:

(Editor with Everet Sprinchorn) *Wagner on Music and Drama,* Dutton (New York City), 1964.
The Mine and the Mint: Sources for the Writings of Thomas De Quincey, Southern Illinois University Press (Carbondale), 1965.
Freakshow: The Rocksoulbluesjazzsickjewblackhumorsexpoppsych Gig and Other Scenes from the Counterculture, Atheneum (New York City), 1971.
Ladies and Gentlemen—Lenny Bruce!!, Random House (New York City), 1974.
Carnival in Rio, Hawthorn (New York City), 1978.
Grass Roots: Marijuana in America Today, Harper (New York City), 1979.
Disco, Hawthorn, 1979.
Elvis, McGraw (New York City), 1981.
The Lives of John Lennon, Morrow (New York City), 1988.
Elvis: The Last 24 Hours, St. Martin's (New York City), 1991.
Sound Bites, Turtle Bay Books, 1992.

Editor-in-chief of *Cultural Affairs.*

WORK IN PROGRESS: A biography of singer Jim Morrison for Ballantine Books.

SIDELIGHTS: After writing books on classical composer Richard Wagner and Thomas De Quincey, Albert Goldman became a best-selling author in the early 1970s when he started focusing on popular culture. Annie Gottlieb,

writing in the *New York Times Book Review,* describes *Freakshow: The Rocksoulbluesjazzsickjewblackhumorsexpoppsych Gig and Other Scenes from the Counterculture* as "a decade's worth of [Goldman's] reviews, interviews and musings on rock music, jazz, comedy and the pop sensibility." Gottlieb says the book "reads like a travel guide to a modern Inferno, whose Virgil spiels with the authority of an anthropologist turned carnival barker"; she concludes that "Goldman comes across uncommonly well—as a stand-up critic who combines the fan's talent for being swept off his feet with the connoisseur's for keeping his head." Richard Locke, in his review for the *New York Times,* thinks less highly of the book, calling Goldman's "taste and point of view . . . extremely erratic" and faulting the author for being "self-absorbed."

Christopher Lehmann-Haupt of the *New York Times* says that in *Ladies and Gentlemen—Lenny Bruce!!,* Goldman "has given us Lenny Bruce in all his many guises—showman, jazzman, hipster and whore; scam-artist, liar, fink and junkie; schlemiel, meshugana, tummuler and naar; genius, rebel, artist and hero." In praising the book, Lehmann-Haupt notes that "what is most extraordinary about Mr. Goldman's biography is the sense he conveys of simultaneous involvement in Mr. Bruce's life and objectivity about its meaning."

Goldman's best-selling biography of the late Elvis Presley, simply called *Elvis,* is "undeniably the most ambitious, the most comprehensive, and the most grotesquely fascinating picture to emerge of the man and the myth," according to Lynn Van Matre of the *Chicago Tribune Book World.* The book has generated controversy since its publication in late 1981, not only because of the fame of its subject, but because of what many critics see as Goldman's unfair treatment of Presley's life and work. As Blake Morrison comments in the *Times Literary Supplement,* "reviewers on both sides of the Atlantic have been quick to point out [that] Goldman's [book] is one of the most vengeful and cannibalistic biographies ever written." A London *Times* reviewer says that "critics have fallen over themselves to get at [Goldman]. . . . Even critics whose normal aloofness from popular culture suggests they'd be hard-pressed to tell a hound dog from a blue suede shoe."

Commenting on this criticism, Goldman tells Tim Grobaty in a *Chicago Tribune* interview: "What was particularly terrible was that the people who were really out to get me were not the fans. . . . The real grim reapers were your 35- or 38-year-olds, you know, with an M.A. in American Studies from Berkeley, rock and roll intellectual types. They really had the knife out." Greil Marcus speculates about Goldman's motives in a *Village Voice* article, maintaining that Goldman meant "to entirely discredit Elvis Presley, the culture that produced him, and the culture he helped to create—to altogether dismiss and condemn, in other words, not just Elvis Presley, but the white working-class South from which Presley came, and the pop world which emerged in Presley's wake." Furthermore, says Marcus, "what is at stake is this: any book that means to separate a people from the sources of its history and its identity, that means to make the past meaningless and the present incomprehensible, is destructive of that people's ability to know itself as a people, to determine the things it might do as a people, and to discover how and why those things might be done. This is precisely the weight of the cultural genocide he wishes to enact."

"Greil went nuts," Goldman tells Grobaty, responding to the *Village Voice* article. "He accused me of ethnogenocide! Try that one out. Ethnogenocide! It's what Hitler did, right? Wiping out whole peoples, right? . . . If I respected [my critics] as writers or people of intelligence, I guess I would go out and cut my throat. The truth, though, is most of them are morons. I respect very few of them."

Many critics find the amount and type of detail revealed about Elvis in the book to be excessive. Morrison believes that "it is the graphic portrait of Presley's last years . . . that makes *Elvis* so offensive." The information Goldman gathered from more than six hundred interviews he conducted with Presley's friends and acquaintances "often gleefully [crosses] the bounds of good taste into a posthumous invasion of privacy," says Van Matre. "One gets the distinct impression that it's the sleaze that really sets [Goldman] off." Jim Miller writes in *Newsweek* that because Goldman "savers that 'there is absolutely no poignance in this history' . . . he savors the sheer vulgarity of Presley's long decline."

Goldman again reacts to this criticism in an interview with Carol Lawson in the *New York Times Book Review*. "It's absurd to believe that I wanted to trash Elvis," says Goldman. "One of the greatest problems was trying to find something positive to say about this man. Every time I started investigating a given area, even one that promised to make him look good, it always ended up making him look bad." In a *Washington Post Book World* interview, Jonathan Yardley acknowledges Goldman's attempt to present a balanced picture of Presley's life. "Though Goldman makes a halfhearted effort to argue to the contrary, the Elvis Presley who emerges from this book is a person wholly without redeeming virtue. He was selfish, greedy, stupid and lazy. That he was so widely and passionately adored says more about us than it does about him. . . . Because [Goldman] is a conscientious biographer he tries to like his subject, . . . but all the evidence that he so forthrightly presents damns the effort; what he demonstrates is that there was scarcely enough art in Presley to justify the contemptible life."

In spite of the revelations about Elvis that Goldman's book provides, some critics believe it does little to mar Elvis's image in the public eye. "When Goldman finishes his juicy recounting of Elvis Presley's life," says J. D. Reed in *Time,* "the mystery of the King's fascination remains. For that, fans and readers should rejoice." Similarly, Morrison writes that "harsh things might be said, then, but Goldman vents his spleen in the wrong place, on the suffering man rather than on the artist, and at the end of this book Elvis Presley's reputation is as secure as ever." Miller points out that "Elvis Presley was, after all, the most exciting pop singer of his generation—even if Albert Goldman can't figure out why."

The publication of Goldman's *The Lives of John Lennon* occurred shortly after writer Joyce Carol Oates, as quoted by James Atlas in a *New York Times Magazine* article, coined the word "pathography," to describe a genre of biography defined by an emphasis on motifs of "dysfunction and disaster, illnesses and pratfalls, failed marriages and failed careers, alcoholism and breakdowns and outrageous conduct." That new word is cited by several critics in response to Goldman's biography of Lennon.

Mark Breslin, in a review for the Toronto *Globe and Mail,* provides a concise description of the book: "The myth of John Lennon was that he was a working-class hero who dedicated his life to peace, art and equality, precisely the values of the sixties. The reality, according to Goldman's book, is that Lennon was a spoiled, egocentric opportunist who was a bullying, bisexual drug addict whose life had spun out of control." Breslin, however, is one of only a few critics satisfied with the biography; he calls it "strident and aggressively shocking," praising the author's description of the 1960s Liverpool music scene and "the psychology that created and destroyed his subject—Lennon's mother complex and the subsequent tendency to abdicate responsibility to a succession of mentors. If not precisely accurate, the book nevertheless gets inside the fallen hero's tortured soul, imagining his struggle to give peace a chance."

Time reviewer Paul Gray likewise finds the book worthy of praise: "Goldman deserves considerable credit for making such sordid, depressing material compulsively readable. *The Lives of John Lennon* is a far more balanced and objective biography than his *Elvis*." As David Gates of *Newsweek* sees it, though he has questions about the book, it should not be discounted altogether: the "misanthropic tone of *The Lives of John Lennon* should make even the least dainty reader question its fairness; and its small, careless errors of fact cast doubt on its overall accuracy. So why should anyone be taking this book seriously? Mostly because of the sheer boldness of its allegations—and because it's possible some could be true."

However, such critical commentary is overshadowed by the torrent of negative response that greeted the book. Many reviewers object to the Lennon biography for the reasons set out by *New York Review of Books* critic Luc Sante: "[Goldman's] research mostly consisted of interviews with single-incident witnesses and with former underlings and sometime pals with axes to grind, as well as of selected readings in and wholesale and uncredited derivations from previously published books by other hands." In addition, Sante complains that "Goldman embroidered upon and distorted the stories he heard to make them more scurrilous, and . . . when he had to choose between two or more versions of an incident, he invariably chose the one that showed his subject in the worse light. Since the book is not annotated, it is largely impossible to tell where given anecdotes or details originated." Writing in the *Washington Post Book World,* Charles Kaiser sees the author's unprofessionalism as even more blatant than does Sante: "Goldman has described himself as a 'very good researcher,' but this book is an appalling combination of uncorroborated accusation and outright invention. Not once does Goldman ever give the reader any indication of the relative credibility of his various informants."

Many see in the book a distortion of Lennon's life. According to Louis Menand of the *New Republic,* "[w]hat is offensive to Lennon's admirers about Goldman's account is that he ignores or downplays the rest of the public testimony, which is that Lennon was a well-intentioned public figure, a despiser of cant, an astute analyst of his own contradictions and the culture's, fundamentally humane, sensible about his foolishness, witty, articulate, and truthful."

John Lahr, in an article in the *New York Times Book Review,* labels the book "an inept account." He further asserts that Goldman's "massive biography has the ring not of trenchancy but of tittle-tattle. His pages are filled with trivia and bad writing. The prose is abstruse when it strains to be hip and laughable when it tries to be matter-of-fact." Michiko Kakutani of the *New York Times* also complains about the writing, calling it "some of the most overheated prose to be found outside a cheap romance novel."

During the controversy over *The Lives of John Lennon,* Goldman himself became an object of scrutiny and analysis. Sante, in another *New York Review of Books* article speculates that the "relentlessness with which Goldman pursues every shade and suspicion of vice, weakness, and neurosis goes well beyond mere sensationalism and takes on the contours of a world view. In Goldman's universe every man and woman is a tyrant or a patsy (or, optimally, both), every closet is thick with skeletons, every eccentricity is a sickness, all creative work is a confidence game. His outlook has perhaps never been what might be called

sunny, or generous . . . but his work has been growing visibly more bitter over the years."

Following publication of *The Lives of John Lennon,* Goldman spoke with reporter Rosemary Bailey in an interview published by the *Chicago Tribune.* On the subject of deciding whether or not to publish unflattering information about a subject, he says, "The worse the story looks, the more pressure you're under to suppress it, not to publish it. People are always saying, 'Look, er, we don't really want to know where the bodies are buried, okay? You just keep that to yourself.' So many times in my life as a journalist, editors have said to me: 'Now that'll be enough, Al. I don't think we want to know any more.'" When asked about his attitude toward John Lennon, he responds: "I thought that I had sympathy for Lennon. I think that this book presents things that will disturb people and startle them, but I don't feel it's devoid of sympathy at all."

Goldman's next book, *Elvis: The Last 24 Hours,* follows Presley, hour by hour, through the final day of his life. *Sound Bites* is a collection of Goldman's journalism from the past twenty-five years. Goldman died in 1994 while traveling from Miami to London; at the time he had been working on a biography of Doors lead singer and songwriter, Jim Morrison.

BIOGRAPHICAL/CRITICAL SOURCES:

PERIODICALS

Chicago Tribune, March 23, 1982; August 10, 1988; August 26, 1988.
Chicago Tribune Book World, November 15, 1981.
Esquire, January, 1982, p. 15.
Globe and Mail (Toronto), October 8, 1988.
Los Angeles Times Book Review, September 4, 1988, p. 9.
New Republic, October 31, 1988, p. 30.
Newsweek, November 2, 1981; October 3, 1988, p. 46; October 17, 1988, p. 64.
New York Review of Books, December 17, 1981, p. 22; December 22, 1988, p. 30.
New York Times, April 24, 1971; May 31, 1974; November 2, 1981; August 31, 1988; September 12, 1988.
New York Times Book Review, May 23, 1971, p. 38; May 26, 1974; October 25, 1981, p. 3; December 13, 1981; September 25, 1988, p. 7; December 12, 1988, p. 30.
New York Times Magazine, November 6, 1988, p. 40.
Rolling Stone, October 20, 1988, p. 42.
Time, November 2, 1981, p. 116; September 12, 1988, p. 77.
Times (London), December 23, 1981.
Times Literary Supplement, January 29, 1982; September 23, 1988, p. 1053.
Tribune Books (Chicago), September 4, 1988, p. 3; January 27, 1991, p. 8; February 2, 1992, p. 8.
Village Voice, September 27, 1988, p. 53.

Village Voice Literary Supplement, December, 1981.
Washington Post Book World, October 18, 1981; January
    22, 1989, p. 10; August 9, 1992, p. 6.

OBITUARIES:

PERIODICALS

Chicago Tribune, March 31, 1994, p. 13.
New York Times, March 30, 1994, p. D19.*

*   *   *

GORAN, Lester   1928-

PERSONAL: Born May 16, 1928; son of Jacob (a banker)
and Tillie; married Edythe McDowell; children: Robert,
William, John. *Education:* University of Pittsburgh, B.A.,
1951, M.A., 1960. *Politics:* Democrat.

ADDRESSES: Home—810 Paradiso, Coral Gables, FL
33146. *Office*—Department of English, University of
Miami, Coral Gables, FL 33124. *Agent*—Wendy Weil, Julian Bach Literary Agency Inc., 747 Third Ave., New
York, NY 10017.

CAREER: University of Miami, Coral Gables, FL,
1960—, became professor of English. *Military service:* U.S.
Corps of Engineers and Military Police.

AWARDS, HONORS: Research project grant, University
of Miami, 1977.

WRITINGS:

The Paratrooper of Mechanic Avenue (novel), Houghton
    (Boston, MA), 1960.
Maria Light (novel), Houghton, 1962.
The Candy Butcher's Farewell (novel), McGraw (New
    York City), 1964.
The Stranger in the Snow (novel), New American Library
    (New York City), 1966.
The Demon in the Sun Parlor (novel), New American Li-
    brary, 1968.
The Keeper of Secrets (novel), McCall Publishing, 1971.
Mrs. Beautiful, New Horizon Press (Far Hills, NJ), 1985.
*The Bright Streets of Surfside: The Memoir of a Friendship
    with Isaac Bashevis Singer,* Kent State University
    Press (Kent, OH), 1994.

Also author of *This New Land,* 1980, and musical *Razzle
Dazzle,* 1976. Contributor of nonfiction to periodicals.

WORK IN PROGRESS: Once the Sweet Birds Sang, for
New American Library, the first novel in the Holtsweg
family saga trilogy.

BIOGRAPHICAL/CRITICAL SOURCES:

PERIODICALS

New Yorker, October 14, 1985, p. 142.
New York Times Book Review, April 21, 1968, p. 54; Janu-
    ary 11, 1981, p. 8.*

*   *   *

GOREN, Charles H(enry)   1901-1991

PERSONAL: Born March 4, 1901, in Philadelphia, PA;
died of a heart attack, April 3, 1991, in Encino, CA; son
of Jacob (a writer) and Rebecca Goren. *Education:* Mc-
Gill University, LL.B., 1922, LL.M., 1923. *Avocational interests:* Golf, theater, symphony.

CAREER: Bridge player, lawyer, and writer. Worked in
furniture sales, 1918; admitted to Pennsylvania Bar, 1923;
attorney in private practice in Philadelphia, PA, 1923-36;
master of ceremonies and commentator on television program *Championship Bridge with Charles Goren,* 1959-62;
Goren Enterprises, founder.

MEMBER: American Contract Bridge League (honorary
member; law commissioner).

AWARDS, HONORS: Contract Bridge Championship of
the World, 1942-43; won various other bridge championships, including world championship, 1950, national
bridge championship (more than thirty times), and more
than two thousand bridge trophies, including McKenney
Trophy (eight times); Life Masters Pair Gold Cup, 1958;
named "Mr. Bridge" by American Contract Bridge
League, 1969; honorary doctor of laws, McGill University, 1973.

WRITINGS:

*Winning Bridge Made Easy: A Simplified Self-Teaching
    Method of Contract Bidding Combining All the Princi-
    ples of the New Culbertson System with the Principal
    Features of the Four Aces System,* foreword by E. Hall
    Downes, Telegraph Press (Harrisburg, PA), 1936,
    new edition published as *Contract Bridge Made Easy:
    A Self-Teacher,* Doubleday (Garden City, NY), 1948,
    revised edition, 1953.
Better Bridge for Better Players: The Play of the Cards
    (also see below), introduction by Ely Culbertson, fore-
    word by George S. Kaufman, Doubleday, 1942.
The Standard Book of Bidding (also see below), introduc-
    tion by W. Somerset Maugham, Doubleday, 1944, re-
    vised edition, 1947.
Contract Bridge in a Nutshell, Doubleday, 1946, published
    as *Charles H. Goren's New Contract Bridge in a Nut-
    shell,* 1959, updated edition, 1986.

Point Count Bidding in Contract Bridge, Simon & Schuster (New York City), 1949, revised edition, 1958.

Bridge Quiz Book, Permabooks (New York City), 1949.

(With Ralph Michaels) *The Complete Canasta,* Pellegrini & Cudahy (New York City), 1949.

Canasta Up-to-Date, Permabooks, 1950.

The Fundamentals of Contract Bridge, Permabooks, 1950.

The New Canasta and Samba: Including the New Official International Code of Laws, Simon & Schuster, 1951.

Contract Bridge Complete (includes *Better Bridge for Better Players* and *The Standard Book of Bidding*), Doubleday, 1951, revised edition published as *New Contract Bridge Complete,* 1957, revised edition published as *Goren's Bridge Complete: A Major Revision of the Standard Work for All Bridge Players,* 1963, revised edition published as *Goren's Bridge Complete,* 1971, revised edition, with Omar Sharif, 1980, new revised edition published as *Goren's New Bridge Complete,* 1985.

Contract Bridge for Beginners: A Simple, Concise Guide for the Novice, Including Point Count Bidding, Simon & Schuster, 1953.

New Way to Better Bridge, Simon & Schuster, 1958.

Goren Presents the Italian Bridge System, Doubleday, 1958.

An Evening of Bridge with Charles H. Goren, Simon & Schuster, 1959.

The Elements of Bridge, Doubleday, 1960.

Goren's Point Count System Made Easy, Doubleday, 1960, published as *Goren's Point Count Bidding Made Easy,* 1975.

(With the editors of *Sports Illustrated*) *The "Sports Illustrated" Book of Bridge,* Time, Inc. (New York City), 1961.

Goren's Winning Partnership Bridge, Random House (New York City), 1961.

Goren's Hoyle Encyclopedia of Games: With Official Rules and Pointers on Play, Including the Latest Laws of Contract Bridge, Greystone Press (New York City), 1961.

Advanced Bidding, Doubleday, 1963.

Goren's Easy Steps to Winning Bridge, F. Watts (New York City), 1963.

Championship Bridge with Charles Goren, foreword by Walter Schwimmer, Doubleday, 1964.

(With Jack Olsen) *Bridge Is My Game: Lessons of a Lifetime,* Doubleday, 1965.

Goren's Bridge Quizzes, Doubleday, 1966.

Bridge Players Write the Funniest Letters to Charles H. Goren, edited by Bill Adler, Doubleday, 1968.

Go with the Odds: A Guide to Successful Gambling, Macmillan (New York City), 1969.

Charles H. Goren Presents the Precision System of Contract Bridge Bidding: Instructions for the Precision System,

Bridge Hands, and Quizzers, edited by Robert B. Ewen, Doubleday, 1971, published in England as *The Precision System of Bidding,* R. Hale (London), 1972, published as *Charles H. Goren Presents the Precision System of Contract Bidding,* Simon & Schuster, 1984.

Play Winning Bridge with Any Partner, Even a Stranger, Cornerstone Library (New York City), 1972.

Goren on Play and Defense: All of Play—The Technique, the Logic, and the Challenge of Master Bridge, Doubleday, 1974.

Goren Settles the Bridge Arguments: Authoritative Answers to Knotty Problems That Are the Cause of Frequent Misunderstandings at the Bridge Table, Hart Publishing (New York City), 1974.

Goren's Modern Backgammon Complete, Doubleday, 1974.

Charles H. Goren's One Hundred Challenging Bridge Hands for You to Enjoy: Test Your Skill against the Master's Winning Way to Play and Defend, introduction by Sharif, Doubleday, 1976.

(With C. C. Wei) *Precision Bridge for Everyone,* Doubleday, 1978.

Play as You Learn Bridge, Doubleday, 1979.

(With Ronald P. Von der Porten) *Introduction to Competitive Bidding,* Doubleday, 1984.

Also author with Effie L. Long of *Your First Introduction to Bridge: Student Text for Goren Manual,* published by Barclay Bridge. Author of daily column "Goren on Bridge," *Chicago Tribune* Syndicate, 1944-91, weekly column in *Sports Illustrated,* beginning 1944, and column in *McCall's.* Contributor to periodicals, including *Good Housekeeping* and *Woman's Home Companion.* Contributing editor, *Bridge World;* member of editorial advisory board, *Bridge Encyclopedia.*

SIDELIGHTS: Although he worked as a lawyer for thirteen years, Charles H. Goren earned an international reputation as one of the world's top contract bridge players during the 1940s and 1950s. Goren simplified and popularized point-count bidding, a system in which a bridge hand's strength is evaluated by assigning different numbers of points to face cards and certain card configurations, and claimed numerous bridge championships. During his career, Goren received the McKenney Trophy—annually awarded to the top master-point winner—eight times. His writings on the game often became best-sellers, and in 1969 he was officially named "Mr. Bridge."

OBITUARIES:

PERIODICALS

Chicago Tribune, April 12, 1991.
Los Angeles Times, April 12, 1991.
New York Times, April 12, 1991.
Times (London), April 13, 1991.*

GRAHAM, George J(ackson), Jr. 1938-

PERSONAL: Born November 12, 1938, in Dayton, OH; son of George Jackson and Mary E. (McBride) Graham; married Scarlett Colone Gower, September 10, 1966; children: Carmen Michelle. *Education:* Wabash College, B.A., 1960; Indiana University, Ph.D., 1965. *Avocational interests:* Photography, painting.

ADDRESSES: Home—224 Dogwood Dr., Mt. Juliet, TN 37122. *Office*—Department of Political Science, Vanderbilt University, Nashville, TN 37235.

CAREER: Vanderbilt University, Nashville, TN, instructor, 1963-64, assistant professor, 1965-71, associate professor, 1971-77, professor of political science, 1977—, director of Politics Study Center, 1970-78.

MEMBER: International Political Science Association, American Society for Legal and Political Philosophy, American Political Science Association, Foundations of Political Theory Group (founder; organizing director, 1974—), Midwest Political Science Association, Southern Political Science Association.

AWARDS, HONORS: National Humanities Institute fellow, 1976-77.

WRITINGS:

Methodological Foundations for Political Analysis, Ginn (Lexington, MA), 1971.
(Editor with George W. Carey) *The Post-Behavioral Era: Perspectives on Political Science,* McKay (New York City), 1972.
(Editor with wife, Scarlett G. Graham, and contributor) *Founding Principles of American Government: Two Hundred Years of Democracy on Trial,* Indiana University Press (Bloomington), 1977, revised edition, Chatham House (Chatham, NJ), 1984.

Also contributor to *Problems of Theory in Policy Analysis,* edited by Philip Gregg, Lexington Books (Lexington, MA), 1976. Contributor to periodicals, including *Political Science Quarterly, American Political Science Review, American Journal of Computational Linguistics, Political Theory, Midwest Journal of Political Science, Revista Italiana di Scienza-Politica,* and *Political Science Reviewer.*

BIOGRAPHICAL/CRITICAL SOURCES:

PERIODICALS

American Political Science Review, March, 1979, p. 206.
Choice, March, 1973, p. 180.*

GRANICK, Harry 1898-
(Harry Taylor)

PERSONAL: Born January 23, 1898, in Nova Kraruka, Russia; immigrated to the United States in 1905, became naturalized citizen, 1918; son of Joseph (a worker) and Elizabeth (Tishkofsky) Granick; married Ray Weiss (a librarian), February 3, 1924; children: David. *Education:* "Like many writers of my generation, self-taught."

ADDRESSES: Home—100 La Salle St., New York, NY 10027. *Agent*—Bertha Klausner International Literary Agency Inc., 71 Park Ave., New York, NY 10016.

CAREER: Playwright and critic. Freelance radio writer, 1934-46, and television writer, 1950-52. *Military service:* British Army, Jewish Legion, Royal Fusiliers, 1918-19; served in Palestine and Egypt.

MEMBER: Authors League of America, Dramatists Guild, American Society of Composers, Authors, and Publishers (ASCAP), New Playwrights Committee.

AWARDS, HONORS: Peabody Broadcasting Award, Academy of Television Arts and Sciences, 1944, for radio series *Great Adventure Series;* Sergel Prize from National Theatre Conference, 1949, and first prize from Five Arts Contest, 1952, both for *Witches' Sabbath;* award for best Vermont play, Valley Players of Vermont, 1984, for *And Still Is Love.*

WRITINGS:

Run, Run! (juvenile), Simon & Schuster (New York City), 1941.
Underneath New York, Rinehart (New York City), 1947.

PLAYS

(Co-author) *Dear Mother* (three acts), produced in New York City at Master Arts Theater, 1937.
Age of the Common Man (choral tone poem; music by S. Morgenstern), produced in New York City at Carnegie Hall, 1943.
Warsaw Ghetto (choral tone poem; music by S. Morgenstern; produced by the Dean Dixon Orchestra in New York City at Carnegie Hall, 1946) Fordham University Press (New York City), 1991.
Reveille Is Always (three acts), produced in New York City at Young Men's Hebrew Association, 1947.
The Criminals (three acts), produced in Smithtown, NY, 1949.
Witches' Sabbath (three acts; produced in Syracuse, NY, at Syracuse University, 1951, produced Off-Broadway, 1962) First Stage, 1961.
The Guilty (three acts), first produced in Dallas, TX, at Margo Jones Theater, 1953.
The Hooper Law (three acts), produced in Dallas, TX, at Margo Jones Theater, 1955, revised version entitled

It Happened in Kansas City produced in New York City by Morningside Players, 1987.

The Bright and Golden Land (two acts), produced in Huntington, NY, at PAF Playhouse, 1978.

The Man Who Knew Ole Abe (one act), produced in Randolph, VT, by Chandler Players, 1984.

Florabelle for President (one act), produced in New York City by Morningside Players, 1984.

And Still Is Love (one act), produced in Vermont by Valley Players, 1984.

The Long Smoldering (two acts), produced in New York City at Riverside Church Theater, 1985.

Shall We Ever Know (one act), produced in New York City by Morningside Players, 1985.

Let's All Take a Ride (one act), produced in New York City by Morningside Players, 1987.

The Hells of Dante, produced in New York City by Morningside Players, 1990.

OTHER

Also author of unproduced plays, including *Promenade and Around We Go* (three acts), 1968; *Pigeons* (three acts), 1972; *The Jew of Venice* (three acts), 1975; and *Two for One,* 1978; also author of radio series *Great Adventure Series,* 1934-54. Work is represented in anthologies, including *American Stuff,* Viking (New York City), 1937, and *First Stage,* Purdue University (West Lafayette, IN), 1961-62. Drama critic under pseudonym Harry Taylor for *Masses, Masses and Mainstream,* 1938-48, and *New Theater,* 1945-51. Contributor of poems, stories, and articles to magazines. Some of Granick's work has been recorded on *Yank and Christopher Columbus,* music by Alex North, Keystone, 1937, and *Are You the One?,* music by Irma Jurist, Columbia, 1960.

The Guilty has also been produced in Germany, Austria, Switzerland, and Spain.

WORK IN PROGRESS: Another play; a family memoir.

SIDELIGHTS: Harry Granick once told *CA:* "I fought in Palestine and Egypt, and revisited Israel in 1965. My wife and I have visited England, France, Italy, Greece, Japan, the People's Republic of China, and the Soviet Union. My most consistent interest has been in the social and political environments of peoples everywhere and in the life of the individual coping with that and with his near ones."

BIOGRAPHICAL/CRITICAL SOURCES:

PERIODICALS

New York Times, April 4, 1978.

GRATUS, Jack 1935-

PERSONAL: Born in 1935, in Johannesburg, South Africa; son of Victor and Flora (Maneshewitz) Gratus; married wife, Estelle, 1959 (divorced); married wife, Christine (an advertising executive), October, 1971; children: David, Jonathan. *Education:* King Edward VII School, B.A., 1955, LL.B., 1958.

ADDRESSES: Home—32 The Grove, Ealing, London W5 5LH, England. *Agent*—Murray Pollinger, 4 Garrick St., London WC26 9BH.

CAREER: Pritchard Englefield & Co., London, England, legal executive, 1960-62; Oxford College, Johannesburg, South Africa, deputy principal and teacher of English and commercial law, 1963-66; freelance writer, 1967—; Glamorgan Summer School, South Wales, England, organizing tutor of creative writing course, 1968-77; City Literary Institute, London, tutor in charge of nonfiction writing, 1974—. Senior tutor at Regent Institute, 1973-76; member of faculty at London extension of University of California, Los Angeles; Antioch International, London, England, degree committee chairperson, 1982—; executive training consultant, 1990—.

MEMBER: Writers Guild of Great Britain (co-chair, 1980-81; former member of executive council, member of finance and other committees).

WRITINGS:

(With Estelle Gratus) *Cooking in Season,* edited by P. H. Hargreaves, L. Hill, 1967.

A Man in His Position (novel), Hutchinson, 1968.

The Victims (nonfiction), Hutchinson, 1969.

Mister Landlord Appel (novel), Hutchinson, 1971.

(With Trevor Preston) *Night Hair Child* (novel), Sphere Books (London), 1971.

The Great White Lie: Slavery, Emancipation, and Changing Racial Attitudes, Hutchinson, 1973.

The False Messiahs: Prophets of the Millenium, Gollancz (London), 1975, 2nd edition, Taplinger (New York City), 1976.

The Jo'burgers (novel), Corgi, 1979.

The Redneck Rebel (novel), Corgi, 1980.

Successful Interviewing: How to Find and Keep the Best People, Penguin Books (New York City), 1988.

Give and Take, BBC Books, 1990.

Sharpen Up Your Interviewing, Mercury Business Books, 1991.

Facing Your Next Interview with Confidence, Mercury Business Books, 1992.

Author of numerous plays for British Broadcasting Corporation (BBC); also creator short documentaries for radio. Author of two three-video series, *Successful Inter-*

viewing and *Give and Take,* both for BBC Training Videos.

SIDELIGHTS: Jack Gratus told *CA:* "I started as a fiction writer (of very small books written for proud parents) when I was about eight or nine, but a university education in an English department put an end temporarily to any ambitions as a writer. So I became a lawyer instead. After a few years of this and then another few years of teaching, I realized that I could not avoid my destiny. The call to write was too strong to be ignored any longer and I started writing short stories, which won prizes in the *Transatlantic Review,* and then my first novel, which was praised for its 'psychological insights,' among other things.

"Financial needs drove me to journalism, which in turn led to a desire to find out about things, such as the effect of slavery on race relations (*The Great White Lie*), what makes people victim-prone (*The Victims*), and the kind of people who claim to be gods (*The False Messiahs*). But I wanted to return to my original love, the novel, so I combined my research techniques with my fiction writing to produce a historical novel set in the early mining camp days of my home town, Johannesburg.

"The eighties proved to be difficult years for me as a novelist, for personal as well as professional reasons. I suffered the kind of crisis of confidence that one reads other writers may suffer from, but I never expected it to happen to me. For this reason, as well as to experiment with the medium, I turned my talents to radio and wrote plays and documentaries for the British Broadcasting Corporation, which I very much enjoyed doing. I also became involved in the writing and presenting of two series for BBC-television; one on interviewing, the other on meetings, which became world best-sellers as training videos.

"I am concerned about the writing profession in general and that is why I joined and actively support the Writers' Guild of Great Britain, which represents writers of all kinds and which strives to improve their lot."

*   *   *

GREAVES, Percy L(aurie), Jr. 1906-

PERSONAL: Born August 24, 1906, in Brooklyn, NY; son of Percy Laurie (an accountant) and Grace I. (Dodge) Greaves; married Edith Leslye Platt, August 23, 1930 (divorced, 1971); married Bettina Herbert Bien (an economist), June 26, 1971; children: (first marriage) Richard Laurie, Muriel Ann, Charles Flint. *Education:* Syracuse University, B.S. (magna cum laude), 1929; Columbia University, graduate study, 1933-34. *Politics:* American Party. *Religion:* Episcopalian.

ADDRESSES: Home—19 Pine Lane, Irvington-on-Hudson, NY 10533. *Office*—P.O. Box 298, Dobbs Ferry, NY 10522.

CAREER: American Trading Co., New York, NY, bookkeeper, 1923-25; Gillette Safety Razor Co., Boston, MA, 1929-32, began as executive trainee, became assistant advertising manager; Young Men's Hebrew Association, New York, NY, instructor in economics and foreign trade, 1933-34; *U.S. News* (now *U.S. News & World Report*), Washington, DC, financial editor and research economist, 1934-36; European subsidiaries of Pet and Carnation Milk Cos., advertising manager, 1936-38; Metropolitan Life Insurance Co., New York, NY, advertising and public relations executive, 1938-43; Republican National Committee, Washington, DC, associate research director, 1943-45; U.S. Joint Congressional Committee for the Investigation of Pearl Harbor Attack, chief of minority staff, 1945-46; Foundation for Freedom, Inc., Washington, DC, executive director, 1946-48; economic consultant, writer, and lecturer, 1948—. U.S. House of Representatives, Committee on Education and Labor, consulting expert, 1947; participant in Ludwig von Mises' Graduate Seminar at New York University, 1950-69; Christian Freedom Foundation, economic advisor, 1950-58; The Freedom School, Inc., guest lecturer, 1957-60; Foundation for Economic Education, Inc., seminar speaker and discussion leader, 1962-67; University of Plano, Texas, Armstrong Professor of Economics, 1965-71.

MEMBER: American Economic Association, American Historical Association, American Military Institute, Naval Historical Foundation, United States Naval Institute, Beta Gamma Sigma, Phi Kappa Phi.

WRITINGS:

Operation Immigration, Foundation for Freedom, Foundation for Freedom Inc., 1947.

Algunos principios fundamentales de la ciencia economica, Centro de Estudios Sobre la Libertad (Buenos Aires), 1969.

(With others) *Toward Liberty: Essays in Honor of Ludwig von Mises on the Occasion of His 90th Birthday, September 29, 1971,* Institute for Humane Studies, Inc., 1971.

Understanding the Dollar Crisis, Western Islands (Boston, MA), 1973, 2nd edition Free Market Books (Dobbs Ferry, NY), 1984.

Mises Made Easy: A Glossary of Mises' "Human Action", Free Market Books, 1974.

(Editor and contributor) Ludwig von Muses, *On the Manipulation of Money and Credit,* translated by Bettina Bien Greaves, Free Market Books, 1978.

Contributor to books, including *Perpetual War for Perpetual Peace,* edited by H. E. Barnes, Caxton, 1952; and *On Freedom and Free Enterprise: In Honor of Ludwig von Mises,* edited by Mary Sennholz, Van Nostrand, 1956. Also author of numerous articles on economics, history, and public affairs. Columnist, *Christian Economics,* 1950-58.

SIDELIGHTS: Percy L. Greaves, Jr. has written: "I always stress, as simply as I can, that sound economics is the science which reveals that the voluntary social cooperation of a free market economy provides the greatest human satisfaction for all moral persons. Conversely, every use of force, coercion or political intervention, other than for the equal protection of life, property and free market operations, must inevitably result in a decrease in the satisfactions of all moral persons. My specialty is exploding the myth that we tried free enterprise in the twenties and that it failed in 1929, making New Deal interventions necessary."

*   *   *

GREGORY, Jean
    See URE, Jean

*   *   *

GRILLO, Ralph David   1940-

PERSONAL: Born April 23, 1940, in Watford, England; son of Ralph (a tradesperson) and Muriel May (Harries) Grillo; married Bronacha Frances Ryan, August 7, 1968; children: Claudia Serafina, Philippa Frances, Ioan Benedict. *Education:* King's College, Cambridge, B.A., 1963, Ph.D., 1968. *Politics:* Green Party. *Religion:* None.

ADDRESSES: Home—21 Bradford Rd., Lewes, Sussex, England. *Office*—School of African and Asian Studies, University of Sussex, Falmer, Brighton BN1 9QN, England.

CAREER: Queen's University, Belfast, Northern Ireland, assistant lecturer, 1967-69, lecturer in social anthropology, 1969-70; University of Sussex, Brighton, Sussex, England, lecturer in social anthropology, 1970-78, reader, 1978-88, professor, 1988—.

MEMBER: International African Institute, Association of Social Anthropologists of United Kingdom (honorary secretary, 1978—), Royal Anthropological Institute.

WRITINGS:

African Railwaymen: Solidarity and Opposition in an East African Labour Force, Cambridge University Press (Cambridge, England), 1973.

Race, Class, and Militancy: An African Trade Union, 1939-1965, Chandler Publishing (Sussex, England), 1974.

(Editor) *Nation and State in Europe: Anthropological Perspectives,* Academic Press (London), 1980.

Ideologies and Institutions in Urban France: The Representation of Immigrants, Cambridge University Press, 1985.

(Editor with Alan Rew) *Social Anthropology and Development Policy,* Tavistock (London), 1985.

Dominant Languages: Language and Hierarchy in Britain and France, Cambridge University Press, 1989.

(Editor) *Social Anthropology and the Politics of Language,* Routledge (London), 1989.

Contributor to *Africa, Man,* and other journals.

SIDELIGHTS: Ralph David Grillo has done fieldwork in East Africa in 1964-65, in the Republic of Ireland, and in France in 1975-76. He is interested as a spectator in films, cricket, and politics.

BIOGRAPHICAL/CRITICAL SOURCES:

PERIODICALS

Choice, June, 1974, p. 639; December, 1985, p. 640; October, 1990, p. 301.

*   *   *

GRIMES, Alan P.   1919-

PERSONAL: Born February 3, 1919, in Staten Island, NY; son of Willard Mudgette and Mildred (Staples) Grimes; married Margaret E. Whitehurst, 1942; children: Margaret G. Wallace, Alan P., Jr., Katherine Grimes Green, Peter E. *Education:* University of North Carolina, A.B., 1941, M.A., 1946, Ph.D., 1948.

ADDRESSES: Home—728 Lantern Hill Dr., East Lansing, MI 48823. *Office*—Department of Political Science, Michigan State University, East Lansing, MI 48824.

CAREER: University of North Carolina at Chapel Hill, instructor, 1946-48, assistant professor, 1948-49; Michigan State University, East Lansing, assistant professor, 1949-51, associate professor, 1951-57, professor of political science, beginning 1957, currently professor emeritus. *Military service:* U.S. Navy, 1941-45; became lieutenant.

MEMBER: American Political Science Association.

AWARDS, HONORS: Michigan State University Distinguished Faculty Award, 1969.

WRITINGS:

The Political Liberalism of the New York Nation, 1865-1932, University of North Carolina Press (Chapel Hill), 1953.

American Political Thought, Holt (New York City), 1955, revised edition, 1960, reprinted, University Press of America (Lanham, MD), 1983.

(With Robert Horwitz) *Modern Political Ideologies,* Oxford University Press (New York City), 1959.

(Editor and author of introduction) L. T. Hobhouse, *Liberalism,* Oxford University Press, 1964.

Equality in America, Oxford University Press, 1964.

The Puritan Ethic and Woman Suffrage, Oxford University Press, 1967, reprint, Greenwood (Westport, CT), 1980.

Democracy and the Amendments to the Constitution, Heath (Lexington, MA), 1978, reprint, University Press of America, 1987.

Contributor to various publications, including *Two Hundred Years of the Republic in Retrospect,* edited by William C. Havard and Joseph L. Bernd, University Press of Virginia (Charlottesville), 1976; *Dictionary of American Biography,* edited by John A. Garraty, Scribner (New York City), *Supplement Five, 1951-55,* 1977, *Supplement Seven, 1961-65,* 1981, *Supplement Eight, 1966-70,* 1988, *Supplement Nine, 1971-75,* 1994; and *Encyclopedia of Democracy,* edited by Seymour M. Lipset, Congressional Quarterly Books (Washington, DC), 1995.

SIDELIGHTS: Alan P. Grimes once told *CA:* "My recent books have usually been a record of my thinking as I have attempted to understand a political question and explain a political settlement. *Equality in America* developed out of my effort to understand why Supreme Court decisions of the Warren court in religion, race, and representation favored the principle of equality. *The Puritan Ethic and Woman Suffrage* arose out of my curiosity as to why the woman suffrage movement in America achieved its early success in the West rather than the East. *Democracy and the Amendments to the Constitution* is my explanation for the success of the movement toward democratic equality in enacting amendments to the Constitution. In each instance the research and writing followed from curiosity as to why some pattern in politics had developed where it did, and when it did."

In his book, *The Puritan Ethic and Woman Suffrage,* Grimes attempts to disprove the widely-held belief that giving women the right to vote drastically changed the American political system. In truth, he claims, social and political leaders of the time who were in favor of the movement (including the suffragettes themselves) saw it as a way to double the voting power of the white Protestant ruling class and thus maintain the *status quo.* Milton Viorst of *Book Week* writes that "as a study of power, [*The Puritan Ethic and Woman Suffrage*] well deserves to be read. For Grimes challenges some of the mythology and shatters some of the complacency about the virtues of American society. He replaces a widely popular misconception with a glimmer of truth that gives us a sounder perspective on ourselves." Christopher Lasch of the *New York Review of Books* praises Grimes for writing "one of the few studies of women and woman suffrage that advances beyond guesswork and anecdote to real historical analysis."

BIOGRAPHICAL/CRITICAL SOURCES:

PERIODICALS

American Political Science Review, Volume 73, 1979.
Book Week, May 7, 1967.
Choice, January, 1979.
New York Review of Books, July 13, 1967.

H

HAERTLING, Peter 1933-

PERSONAL: Born November 13, 1933, in Chemnitz, (now Karl-Marx-Stadt) Germany; son of Rudolf (a lawyer) and Erika (Haentzschel) Haertling; married Mechthild Maier, July 3, 1959; children: Fabian, Friederike, Clemens, Sophie. *Education:* Educated in Germany. *Religion:* "Evangelic." *Avocational interests:* "Reading, conversing with wife, children and friends."

ADDRESSES: Home—Finkenweg 1, 64546 Moerfelden-Walldorf, Germany.

CAREER: Writer. *Deutsche Zeitung und Wirtschaftzeitung* (newspaper), Stuttgart and Cologne, West Germany (now Germany), literary editor, 1955-62; *Der Monat* (magazine), West Berlin, West Germany (now Berlin, Germany), editor and copublisher, 1962-70; S. Fischer Verlag (publisher), Frankfurt am Main, West Germany (now Germany), editor and managing director, 1967-74.

MEMBER: PEN, Akademie der Kuenste, Akademie der Wissenschaften und der Literatur, Deutsche Akademie fuer Sprache und Dichtung.

AWARDS, HONORS: Literaturpreis des deutschen Kritikerverbandes, 1964, for *Niembsch oder Der Stillstand: Eine Suite;* Literaturpreis des Kulturkreises der deutschen Industrie, 1965; Literarischer Foerderungspreis des landes Niedersachen, 1965; Prix du meilleur livre etranger, 1966, for *Niembsch oder Der Stillstand: Eine Suite;* Gerhart Hauptmann Preis, 1971, for *Gilles: Ein Kostuemstuck aus der Revolution;* Schubart Prize of the City of Aalen, 1973; Deutscher Jugendbuchpreis, (German children's book award) 1976; Wilhelmine Luebke Prize, 1978; Stadtschreiber von Bergen-Enkheim, 1978-79; Poetik-Dozentur, Universitaet Frankfurt, 1983-84; Hermann Sinsheimer Prize of the City of Freinsheim and Holderlin Prize of the City of Bad Homburg, both 1987; Mildred Batchelder Prize for best children's book translation, 1989, for *Crutches;* Andreas-Gryphius Preis, 1990; Poetik-Dozentur, 1994.

WRITINGS:

IN ENGLISH TRANSLATION; JUVENILE

Oma: Die Geschichte von Kalle, der seine Eltern verliert und von seiner Grossmutter aufgenommen wird, Beltz & Gelberg (Weinheim), 1975, translation by Anthea Bell published as *Oma,* Harper (New York), 1977, published in England as *Granny: The Story of Karl, Who Loses His Parents and Dogs to Live with His Grandmother,* Hutchinson (London), 1977.

Theo haut ab: Kinderroman, Beltz & Gelbert, 1977, translation by Bell published as *Theo Runs Away,* Andersen Press (London), 1978.

Ben liebt Anna, Beltz & Gelberg, 1979, translation by J. H. Auerbach published as *Ben Loves Anna,* Overlook Press (New York City), 1990.

Alter John, Beltz & Gelberg, 1981, translation by Elizabeth D. Crawford published as *Old John,* Lothrop (New York City), 1990.

Krucke, Beltz & Gelberg, 1986, translation by Crawford published as *Crutches,* Lothrop, 1988.

NOVELS

Im Schein des Kometen: Roman, Goverts (Stuttgart), 1959.

Niembsch oder Der Stillstand: Eine Suite, Goverts, 1964.

Janek: Portraet einer Erinnerung, Goverts, 1966.

Das Familienfest oder Das Ende der Geschichte: Roman, Goverts, 1969.

Ein Abend, eine Nacht, ein Morgen: Eine Geschichte, Luchterhand (Berlin), 1971.

Zwettl: Nachpruefung einer Erinnerung, Luchterhand, 1973.

Das war der Hirbel: Wie Hirbel ins Heim kam, warum er anders ist als andere und ob ihm zu helfen ist (childrens), Beltz & Gelberg (Weinheim), 1973.

Eine Frau: Roman, Luchterhand, 1974, translation by Joachim Neugroschel published as *A Woman,* Holmes & Meier (New York City), 1988.

Hoelderlin: Ein Roman, Luchterhand, 1976.

Hubert; oder, Die Rueckkehr nach Casablanca, Luchterhand, 1978.

Nachgetragene Liebe: Erzahlung, Luchterhand, 1980.

Die dreifache Maria, Luchterhand, 1982.

Das Windrad, Luchterhand, 1983.

Felix Guttmann: Roman, Luchterhand, 1985.

Waiblingers Augen (biographical novel), Luchterhand, 1987.

Herzwand, Luchterhand, 1990.

Schubert, Luchterhand, 1992.

Schubert: Twelve Moments Musicaux and a Novel (biographical novel), translated by Rosemary Smith, Holmes & Meier, 1995.

POETRY

Poems and Songs, Bechtle (Esslingen), 1953.

Yamins Stationen, Bechtle, 1955.

Unter den Brunnen: Neue Gedichte, 1959-1961 Bechtle, 1958.

Spielgeist, Spiegelgeist: Gedichte, 1959-1961, Goverts, 1962.

Yamins Stationen: Gedichte, Bechtle, 1965.

Neue Gedichte, Blaschke (Darmstadt), 1972.

Zum laut und leise lesen: Geschichten und Gedichte fuer Kinder (juvenile), Luchterhand, 1975.

Anreden: Gedichten aus den Jahren, 1972-1977, Luchterhand, 1977.

Ausgewaehlte Gedichte, 1953-1979, Luchterhand, 1979.

Vorwarnung: Gedichte, Luchterhand, 1983.

Ich rufe die Woerter zusammen: Gedichte, 1983-84, Radius, 1984.

Die Moersinger Pappel, Luchterhand, 1987.

Die Gedichte, 1953-1987, Luchterhand, 1988.

Das Land, das id erdachte, Radius, 1993.

OTHER

In Zeilen zuhaus: Vom Abenteuer des Gedichts, des Gedichteschreibens und Gedichtelesens (essays), Neske (Pfullingen), 1957.

Palmstroem gruesst Anna Blume: Essay und Anthologie der Geister aus Poetia (essays), Goverts, 1961.

Vergessene Buecher: Hinweise und Beispiele (essays), Goverts, 1966.

Das Ende der Geschichte: Ueber die Arbeit an einem historischen Roman, Verlag der Akademie der Wissenschaften und der Literatur (Mainz), 1968.

(Editor) Christian Friedrich Damiel Schubart, *Gedichte,* Fischer (Frankfurt am Main), 1968.

(Editor) Nicolaus Lenau, *Briefe an Sophie von Loewenthal, 1834-1845,* Koesel Verlag (Munich), 1968.

(Compiler) *Die Vaeter: Berichte und Geschichten,* Fischer, 1968.

. . . und das ist die ganze Familie: Tageslaeufe mit Kindern, Bitter (Recklinghausen), 1970.

Gilles: Ein Kostuemstuck aus der Revolution (twenty-two act play; produced in Hamburg, Germany, September 26, 1973), Goverts, 1970.

(Compiler) *Leporello faellt aus der Rolle: Zeitgenoessische Autoren erzaehlen das Leben von Figuren der Weltliteratur weiter,* Fischer, 1971.

(Contributor) Willy Michel, *Die Aktaulitaet des Interpretierens ,* Quelle & Meyer, 1978.

(Author of introduction) *Die Kopfkissen-Gans und andere Geschichten von grossen Dichtern fuer kleine Leute,* Hueber (Frauenfeld), 1978.

Sophie macht Geschichten (juvenile), Beltz & Gelberg, 1980.

Der wiederholte Unfall (stories), Reclam, 1980.

Meine Lektuere: Literatur als Widerstand (essays), edited by Klaus Siblewski, Luchterhand, 1981.

(Editor and author of afterword) Eduard Friedrich Morike, *Du bist Orplid, mein Land,* Luchterhand, 1982.

Ueber Heimat (essay), Verlag der Buchhandlung Aigner, 1982.

Jakob hinter der blauen Tuer (juvenile), Beltz & Gelberg, 1983.

Der spanische Soldat oder Finden und Erfinden: Frankfurter Poetik-Vorlesungen, Luchterhand, 1984.

Fuer Ottla (story), Radius, 1984.

(Compiler) *Helft den Buechern, helft den Kindern!* (essays), Hanser (Munich), 1985.

Zueignung (essays), Radius, 1985.

Briefe an meine Kinder, Radius, 1986.

Die kleine Welle (stories), Radius, 1987.

Der Wanderer (stories and essays), Luchterhand, 1988.

Das Wandesnde Wance (essays), Radius, 1994.

Also contributor to books, including *Fuenfzehn Autoren suchen sich selbst,* edited by U. Schultz, List (Munich), 1967. Author of introduction for *Die Kopfkissen-Gans und andere Geschichten von grossen Dichtern fuer kleine Leute.* Contributor to periodicals, including *Der Monat, Akzente,* and *Stuttgarter Zeitung.*

ADAPTATIONS: Oma: Die Geschichte von Kalle, der seine Eltern verliert und von seiner Grossmutter aufgenommen wird was adapted for television as *Oma,* 1976; *Ben liebt Anna,* was adapted for television, 1982; *Jakob hinter der blauen Tuer* was adapted for film, 1987.

WORK IN PROGRESS: Bozena, a novel.

SIDELIGHTS: Peter Haertling is a versatile German author of poetry, novels, and children's books. In his novels Haertling explores the ways that people remember and seeks to show that it is impossible to truly understand the past. His children's books often relate in some way to his own childhood experiences.

Haertling was born in 1933 in Chemnitz, Germany. While he was growing up he was deeply affected by the turmoil of Nazi Germany. His father died in a Russian prisoner of war camp in 1945, when the author was twelve years old. At this time his mother moved the family to Zwettl, Austria, and then to Nuertingen in southwest Germany. A year later, overcome by grief, she took her own life. From then on Haertling was raised by his grandmother. He attended high school in Nuertingen but did not graduate. Instead he worked for a short time in a factory, then began a career in journalism that would last for more than twenty years.

Throughout these years Haertling also published a great deal of poetry and fiction. His first poetry collection appeared in 1953, when he was only twenty years old. He published several other highly regarded poetry collections and essays on the subject during the 1950s and early 1960s. Haertling published his first novel, *Im Schein des Kometen,* which states for the first time his ideas about memory. Continuing this theme in his second novel, *Niembsch oder der Stillstand: Eine Suite* in 1964, "Haertling proved he had mastered the novel," wrote Egbert Krispyn in the *Dictionary of Literary Biography.* Both *Niembsch* and a later novel, *Hoelderlin: Eine Roman,* describe the lives of German writers of the 1800s and demonstrate that a biographer cannot completely reconstruct a person's life, even with the aid of documents.

In 1966 *Niembsch* was chosen in France as the best foreign novel of the year. Its main rival was Saul Bellow's *Herzog.* Deemed "a subtle and fascinating work" by Mark Slonim in the *New York Times Book Review,* Haertling's book is the story of Nikolaus Franz Niembsch von Strehlenau, an Austrian poet who wrote under the pseudonym Lenau in the early nineteenth century and became associated with the German romantics in the 1830s. Slonim explained that the work is not a biography but rather "a fictional narrative, based on some factual material, and revolving around two major themes: the metaphysical concept of time, and erotic experience as a way toward individual fulfillment."

Among his other novels for adults, *Janek: Portraet einer Erinnerung* and *Zwettl: Nachpruefung einer Erinnerung* draw directly from the author's life. The main character is a young boy whose father, like Haertling's, died in Russia at the end of World War II. The story relates the boy's obsessive desire to know about his father and to find his grave.

Some of the author's books for children—begun after deciding to devote himself to writing full-time in 1974—are set in Germany in the aftermath of the World War II, reflecting the author's early years and the troubles of this period. Families during this time were sometimes separated and food and shelter were scarce. Several of Haertling's children's books have been published in English translation, including *Oma, Crutches,* and *Old John.*

The award winning *Oma,* also translated as *Granny,* is the tale of a young boy named Kalle, who lives with his grandmother after his parents die in a car crash. The book describes how the two relatives adapt to this major change in their lives, cope with poverty, and grow in their relationship with each other. Oma is a hearty, courageous person but far from perfect, and she sometimes embarrasses and angers Kalle by talking to herself, wearing funny clothes, or making unkind remarks about his mother. After five years together, Oma has a heart attack, forcing them both to face fears about the possibility of Oma dying. Oma's reflections about Kalle at chapter ends are considered a highlight of the book. Marilyn Sachs asserted in the *New York Times Book Review* that the story "manages to make a warm human statement about ordinary people who love each other." Elinor Lyon wrote in the *Times Literary Supplement* that the book "should give its readers or hearers new ideas about their relations with old people."

Haertling's second book for children, *Crutches* (*Krucke*) is set in Vienna, Austria, in 1945. The book describes the adventures of thirteen-year-old Thomas Schramm, whose father has been killed and who has been separated from his mother. He succeeds, eventually, in gaining the help of a one-legged man called Crutches, who travels with him until they find the boy's mother. In the *Bulletin of the Center for Children's Books* Betsy Hearne praised the author's portrayal of the two characters as well as the tension of the war-torn country. Hearne was most impressed with the author's depiction of Crutches, "an embittered, anti-Hitlerian ex-soldier who tries to protect his battered heart . . . but who cannot resist getting involved" in aiding the boy. During their journey, Thomas learns from Crutches a new view of Nazism, which he had been taught to admire. Their parting, when Thomas is at last reunited with his mother, makes the book's ending "bittersweet" and "tinged with sadness," noted Mary M. Burns in *Horn Book.*

Like *Oma, Old John* (*Alter John*), describes a relationship between young and old. In this story, though, it is Jacob's lively, independent-minded, and cranky grandfather who comes to live with the family, causing them quite a bit of excitement. Old John finds entertainment in town with his friends and announces that he has fallen in love with a local schoolteacher. While filling the book with humorous episodes, Haertling portrays Old John with affection and sympathy. John's illness and death are strongly felt by not only the family, but the reader as well, a reviewer for *Horn Book* noted.

BIOGRAPHICAL/CRITICAL SOURCES:

BOOKS

Dictionary of Literary Biography, Volume 75: *Contemporary German Fiction Writers,* Second Series, Gale, 1988, pp. 92-96.
Duecker, Burckhard, *Peter Haertling,* Beck (Munich), 1983.

PERIODICALS

Bookbird, September 15, 1977, pp. 2-7; June 15, 1980, pp. 21-25.
Booklist, February 1, 1989.
Books Abroad, autumn, 1967; spring, 1970.
Bulletin of the Center for Children's Books, November, 1988, p. 74; July/August, 1990, pp. 266-67; April 1991, pp. 193-94.
Horn Book, November/December, 1988, pp. 787-88; July/August, 1990, p. 456.
Kirkus Reviews, April 15, 1990, p. 577; March 1, 1991, p. 317.
New York Times Book Review, November 20, 1977, p. 30; March 12, 1967.
Publishers Weekly, February 15, 1991, p. 90; March 27, 1995, p. 75.
School Library Journal, July, 1990, p. 76.
Times Literary Supplement, December 2, 1977, p. 1412; October 14, 1983.
World Literature Today, autumn, 1983; winter, 1984; spring, 1986; autumn, 1989.

*   *   *

HAHN, Mary Downing 1937-

PERSONAL: Born December 9, 1937, in Washington, DC; daughter of Kenneth Ernest (an automobile mechanic) and Anna Elisabeth (a teacher; maiden name, Sherwood) Downing; married William E. Hahn, October 7, 1961 (divorced, 1977); married Norman Pearce Jacob (a librarian), April 23, 1982; children: (first marriage) Katherine Sherwood, Margaret Elizabeth. *Education:* University of Maryland at College Park, B.A., 1960, M.A., 1969, doctoral study, 1970-74. *Politics:* Democrat. *Avocational interests:* Reading, walking, photography, and riding trains.

ADDRESSES: Home—9746 Basket Ring Rd., Columbia, MD 21045.

CAREER: Art teacher at junior high school in Greenbelt, MD, 1960-61; Hutzler's Department Store, Baltimore, MD, clerk, 1963; correspondence clerk for Navy Federal Credit Union, 1963-65; homemaker and writer, 1965-70; Prince George's County Memorial Library System, Laurel Branch, Laurel, MD, children's librarian associate, 1975-91; writer, 1991—. Free-lance artist for *Cover to Cover,* WETA-TV, 1973-75.

MEMBER: Society of Children's Book Writers and Illustrators, Authors Guild, PEN, Washington Children's Book Guild.

AWARDS, HONORS: William Allen White Children's Choice Award, William Allen White Library (Kansas), 1986, for *Daphne's Book;* Dorothy Canfield Fisher Award, Vermont, 1988, Children's Choice Award, Utah, 1988, Bluebonnet Award, Texas, 1989, Children's Choice Award, Pacific Northwest, 1989, Young Hoosier Award, Indiana, 1989, Young Reader's Award, Virginia, 1989, Volunteer State Award, Tennessee, 1989, Maud Hart Lovelace Award, Minnesota, 1990, Rebecca Caudill Award, Illinois, 1990, Children's Choice Award, Iowa, 1990, and Golden Sowers Children's Choice Award, Nebraska, 1990, all for *Wait Till Helen Comes: A Ghost Story;* Child Study Association Award, 1989, Jane Addams Peace Association honor book, 1989, and Young Reader's Medal, California, 1991, all for *December Stillness.*

Children's Book Award, Maryland, Sequoyah Children's Choice Award, Oklahoma, William Allen White Award Children's Choice Award, William Allan White Library (Kansas), Young Reader's Award, Virginia, Mark Twain Award, Missouri, Prairie Pasque Award, South Dakota, and Children's Choice Award, Georgia, all 1992, all for *The Doll in the Garden;* selection as one of American Library Association Books for the Reluctant Reader, 1990, Children's Choice Award, Utah, 1993, Maud Hart Lovelace Award, Minnesota, 1993, Children's Choice Award, South Carolina, 1993, Young Hoosier Award, Indiana, 1993, and Young Reader's Award, Virginia, 1994, all for *The Dead Man in Indian Creek;* selection as an American Library Association notable book, 1992, Scott O'Dell Award for Historical Fiction, 1992, Joan G. Sugarman Award, 1992, Hedda Seisler Mason Award, 1993, Black-Eyed Susan Award, Maryland, 1994, Children's Choice Award, South Carolina, 1994, and Golden Sower Children's Choice Award, Nebraska, 1994, all for *Stepping on the Cracks;* selection as one of YALSA Best Books for Young Adults, 1993, and as one of New York Public Library Books for the Teen Age, 1994, both for *The Wind Blows Backward.*

WRITINGS:

JUVENILE

The Sara Summer, Clarion Books (Boston), 1979.
The Time of the Witch, Clarion Books, 1982.
Daphne's Book, Clarion Books, 1983.
The Jellyfish Season, Clarion Books, 1985.
Wait Till Helen Comes: A Ghost Story, Clarion Books, 1986.
Tallahassee Higgins, Clarion Books, 1987.
December Stillness, Clarion Books, 1988.
Following the Mystery Man, Clarion Books, 1988.
The Doll in the Garden, Clarion Books, 1989.
The Dead Man in Indian Creek, Clarion Books, 1990.
The Spanish Kidnapping Disaster, Clarion Books, 1991.
Stepping on the Cracks, Clarion Books, 1991.
The Wind Blows Backward, Clarion Books, 1993.
Time for Andrew, Clarion Books, 1994.
Look for Me by Moonlight, Clarion Books, 1995.
The Gentleman Outlaw and Me, Eli, Clarion Books, in press.

WORK IN PROGRESS: Following My Own Footsteps, a companion to *Stepping on the Cracks,* which follows Gordy Smith to his grandmother's house in North Carolina.

SIDELIGHTS: Children's book author Mary Downing Hahn told *CA:* "I began to write before I knew how—that is, I drew pictures and told myself stories to go with them. Until I was in junior high school, I thought putting the words down was the boring part. My penmanship was poor, and my hand tired quickly. Plus I had a vague idea outlining was required, a skill I never mastered. What I wanted was to illustrate other people's stories. Let the authors do the hard work, not me.

"Over the years my attitude gradually changed. In junior high school, I realized pictures were fine for action stories, but what if you wanted to show thoughts and feelings? You needed words for that. I began keeping a diary in which I faithfully recorded my adventures as well as my misadventures, illustrating them with quick doodles labeled 'not my best drawing.' I also started writing a book. *Small Town Life* recounted the happy life of Susan, a girl who was all I wanted to be—funny, brave, and popular, a leader admired by everyone. I was too shy and self-conscious to reveal my new ambition. What if I wasn't smart enough to be a writer? After all, I still detested outlining, received Bs in English, and was never encouraged to do anything but draw.

"By the time I entered the University of Maryland, I was convinced my only talent was art. But something funny happened. I received Bs from art professors and As from my English professors. After the campus literary maga-

zine published two of my short stories, I began to entertain secret hopes of becoming the J. D. Salinger of my generation. However, I never sent anything to a real magazine for fear of being rejected.

"After graduating, I continued to draw and paint, write short stories, and experiment with poetry, but I let years go by without making a serious effort to become either an artist or a writer. It's amazing how long you can sit around imagining what you'd accomplish if only you had more time. When my daughters were preschoolers, I wrote and illustrated several picture books which I actually mailed to various publishers but gave up quickly when they were returned.

"Then, after years in English graduate school, I found myself working in the children's department of a public library, an unplanned career I fell into when my stipend ran out. As part of my training, I read tons of juvenile novels. Some were wonderful; others were not. Wanting something beyond library work, I decided to try writing a book for young readers. It took at least a year to put a manuscript together. I mailed it only to see it return several weeks later. Like my earlier picture books, my novel didn't meet the publisher's 'present needs.' Refusing to be discouraged again, I picked another house and tried again. Again and again and again. If nothing else, I'd learned perseverance.

"Finally, my manuscript landed on the desk of James Cross Giblin, then editor and publisher of Clarion Books. He returned it with a long letter detailing the novel's many problems which I attempted to correct. After seven rewrites, Jim accepted *The Sara Summer.* A year later, I had the pleasure of seeing my own book on the library shelf. Fearing I might not be able to go on producing publishable manuscripts, I kept my job until Sara had eleven companions. Taking a deep breath, I left the library in 1991, the year *Stepping on the Cracks* was published.

"Since then, I've been writing (and re-writing) full time. My editor is still Jim Giblin. His uncanny ability to find the story I'm trying to tell is as invaluable to me as his friendship."

BIOGRAPHICAL/CRITICAL SOURCES:

BOOKS

Something about the Author Autobiography Series, Volume 12, Gale (Detroit), 1991.

PERIODICALS

Book Links, September, 1994.
New York Times, October 23, 1983.

OTHER

A Visit with Mary Downing Hahn (video), Kit Morse Productions, Houghton Mifflin, 1994.

*   *   *

HAILEY, Elizabeth Forsythe 1938-

PERSONAL: Born August 31, 1938, in Dallas, TX; daughter of Earl Andrew (an attorney) and Janet (Kendall) Forsythe; married Oliver Daffan Hailey (a writer), June 25, 1960 (died, 1993); children: Elizabeth Kendall, Melinda Brooke. *Education:* University of Paris, Sorbonne, diploma, 1958; Hollins College, B.A., 1960. *Politics:* Democrat. *Avocational interests:* travel, cooking.

ADDRESSES: Home—11747 Canton Place, Studio City, CA 91604. *Agent*—Molly Friedrich, Aaron M. Priest Literary Agency, 122 East 42nd Street, Suite 3902, New York, NY 10168.

CAREER: Writer. *Dallas Morning News,* Dallas, TX, reporter, summers, 1956-60; Yale University Press, New Haven, CT, editorial assistant, 1961-62; Tandem Productions, creative consultant for syndicated television series *Mary Hartman, Mary Hartman,* 1976; Columbia Broadcasting System, Inc. (CBS), co-producer of television series *Another Day,* 1977.

MEMBER: PEN, Authors League of America, Writers Guild of America West.

AWARDS, HONORS: Silver Medal for best first novel, Commonwealth Club of California, and nominee for best work of fiction, Texas Institute of Arts and Letters, both 1978, both for *A Woman of Independent Means;* L.A. Drama Critics Award for the play *A Woman of Independent Means,* 1983.

WRITINGS:

NOVELS

A Woman of Independent Means (also see below), Viking (New York City), 1978.
Life Sentences, Delacorte (New York City), 1982.
Joanna's Husband and David's Wife (also see below), Delacorte, 1986.
Home Free, Delacorte, 1991.

PLAYS

A Woman of Independent Means (based on Hailey's own novel), first produced in Los Angeles, CA, produced on Broadway at the Biltmore Theater, May, 1984.
Joanna's Husband and David's Wife (based on Hailey's own novel), first produced in Los Angeles, 1989.

OTHER

Contributor to books, including *Her Work: Stories by Texas Women,* edited by Lou Halsell Rodenberger, Shearer, 1982; *A Texas Christmas,* Volume 2, edited by John Edward Weems, Pressworks, 1986; *An Apple for My Teacher,* edited by Louis D. Rubin Jr., Algonquin Books of Chapel Hill, 1987; *New Growth,* edited by Lyman Grant, Corona, 1989; and *West Winds Four,* Strawberry Hill Press, 1989. Contributor of reviews to *Washington Post* and *Dallas Morning News.*

ADAPTATIONS: A Woman of Independent Means was adapted for television as a miniseries by the National Broadcasting Company, February, 1995.

SIDELIGHTS: Elizabeth Forsythe Hailey began writing fiction at age thirty-five, and her first novel, *A Woman of Independent Means,* fast became a national bestseller. Hailey originally planned to call the novel *Letters from a Runaway Wife.* The title was "indicative of the mood I was in at the time," she says in a *Contemporary Authors Autobiography Series (CAAS)* article. "I was thirty-five. Our younger daughter had just started nursery school. I had begun to feel that everyone in the family but me had somewhere to go each day, work awaiting them, friends expecting them." It was her husband, playwright Oliver Hailey, who suggested that there might be a relevant story in the life of Hailey's maternal grandmother, Bess Kendall Jones.

The story of free-spirited Bess Steed Garner, born at the turn of the century, *A Woman of Independent Means* is a thinly-disguised interpretation of Bess Kendall Jones's life. Hailey once told *CA:* "I used the real facts of her life as a framework for the fiction of the book, and the large events of the book are all taken from her life, all the tragedies." Researching her grandmother's life for the book "was like doing detective work in my family. The more I invented, the more I wanted to know what had really happened. I asked my mother hundreds of questions it probably never would have occurred to me to ask otherwise, and I found intriguing clues buried in the entries of my grandmother's travel diaries," notes Hailey in her *CAAS* essay. She points to one of Jones's trips, on the ocean-liner *Lusitania* in 1913, as an example of her grandmother's spirit: "Reading her day-by-day account of that trip—how she had to amuse her children and look after her mother-in-law—I saw her for the first time not as my grandmother but as a woman my age, facing the same daily crises I was facing. It gave me a perspective I never had from just being her grandchild. And her courage and independence made her a better role model for me than anyone I was reading about in *Ms.* magazine."

A Woman of Independent Means is an epistolary novel. While "the device of letter writing is not an unusual vehicle for writing a novel," remarks *Best Sellers* critic Emily W. Weir, the author nonetheless "has used it particularly well." Weir likens reading the novel to "[sitting] down on a quiet day and [looking] through your grandmother's photograph album." According to a *Ms.* critic, "the letters are a tour de force that unfolds a multiple view of Bess. . . . Without the benefit of a single word from the other 'characters,' we know exactly how they see her. What emerges is a complex, moving, and entertaining portrait." That *A Woman of Independent Means* includes letters from only one person forces the reader to play detective and fill in some of the gaps. A *West Coast Review of Books* critic notes that while "at times we may wish to hear the 'other side,' [we don't] for long, for Bess' rationale is really all we need. She may have her faults but her quick wit and intelligence keep us on her side all the way. When we read her final letter (handled beautifully by Hailey) it is with a sense of loss for a dear friend."

Hailey understands that her novel is one-sided. In *CAAS* she notes: "I was writing about a woman who was much more interested in what she had to say than in what people said to her in reply." As Anne Tyler notes in the *New York Times Book Review*, "Bess is so memorable a character that I seem here to be reviewing not *A Woman of Independent Means* but the woman herself, which speaks well for Elizabeth Forsythe Hailey's writing. The book becomes Bess's own; the author backs out, giving her the floor."

In *CAAS* Hailey describes her second book, *Life Sentences*, as a "novel of reconciliation." To Susan Slocum Hinerfeld, a *Los Angeles Times Book Review* contributor, the book is a novel of "fecundity. There are side issues: the nature of marriage and friendship; visions of Utopia, where child care is shared. But mostly and relentlessly, the book is about child bearing." Beginning with the lead character's rape, *Life Sentences* goes on to describe how she seeks the support of those closest to her in the aftermath of the crime.

While *Life Sentences* enjoyed a fourteen-week appearance on the *New York Times* bestseller list, critical reaction to the novel was less enthusiastic than for *A Woman of Independent Means*. Citing the implausibility of a woman's decision to bear her rapist's child, *Washington Post* reviewer Susan Jacoby says that "the deficiencies of this novel cannot be attributed solely to the predictable difficulties of a writer whose first book has aroused extraordinarily high expectations. Hailey's stylistic gifts have not deserted her, but she seems to have been infected by the contempt for causality that has made so many readers forsake serious fiction in favor of romantic sagas that . . . at least have the virtue of internal logic."

"Such is the authority of the writing, however, and its sheer momentum, that *Life Sentences* becomes a kind of

closed system," Cyra McFadden maintains in the *San Francisco Chronicle Review*. "One accepts its 'givens' as [the protagonist] accepts the events of her life." "In lesser hands than Hailey's," Allen Lacy points out in *Dallas Morning News*, "*Life Sentences* might have turned out to be a soap opera—momentarily engrossing, but ultimately forgettable. But it isn't soap opera, for it moves in a moral dimension that soap operas never strive for, much less attain." In McFadden's opinion, "It's a considerable feat, this novel, the work of a writer firmly in control of risky material." *Life Sentences* "isn't a perfect novel," Lacy asserts. "But it's a very good novel, a very thoughtful novel, and a very rich novel, even despite its economy and restraint."

With her next novel, *Joanna's Husband and David's Wife*, Hailey again employs an original framing device. Consisting entirely of journal entries, this novel tells the story of a marriage from the points of view of both a husband and a wife. The book begins when Joanna's daughter finds her mother's diary with a cover letter inviting her to read the journal of her twenty-five-year marriage. Joanna's diary, however, has also been read by her husband, David, who has annotated the entries with his comments and reactions to many of her records. Writing in the *Los Angeles Times Book Review*, Shelby Hearon comments that although the diary is meant to convey a record of the couple's life together, the framing device is somewhat unbalanced because David's entries are responses to Joanna's journal rather that a record of his own recollections of the marriage. "The result," says Hearon, "is that instead of seeing the same span of years from two different points of view, we are left with a great deal of information about her, her children, her work, and a sketchy impression of him, mostly as an emotionally controlling and parsimonious cad." Other critics have also noted this imbalance in the book. Writing in the *Washington Post Book World*, Elizabeth Ward praises Hailey for resurrecting the literary device she had so successfully used in *A Woman of Independent Means*. And yet, while Ward praises the author for "the substance of the theme . . . [and] the suitability of this theme to the novel's form," she nevertheless feels that "since the novel is largely composed of . . . [Joanna's] reflections, this indicates something of what is wrong with it."

Home Free, Hailey's next novel, is vastly different in both subject matter and style from her previous work. In this book Hailey deals with the theme of homelessness. The novel begins one Christmas Eve when Kate, a wealthy, middle-aged woman who has just been abandoned by her film-director husband, meets Ford, a homeless man who gets stranded in front of Kate's house. Lonely and depressed, Kate offers the homeless man, his wife, and two children the family's Christmas dinner, as well as the presents intended for her husband. In return, Ford will repair Kate's home, thus enabling her to sell it in order to gain financial independence. Calling *Home Free* a "heartwarming story about the real meaning of 'home' and 'family,' " Chicago *Tribune Books* contributor Joyce R. Slater praises Hailey for "avoiding a stereotypical portrait of the homeless as worthless people." Other critics, however, were less complimentary, charging that Hailey does not present any real solutions in *Home Free,* also faulting her for presenting an unrealistic picture of the plight of the homeless. Writing in the *Washington Post Book World,* Pat Dowell feels that despite the relevance of the theme, the characters of *Home Free* "seem to have been drawn from television-movie cliches about the deserving poor" and "seem merely convenient pegs for a genteel homily about house-sitting as a way to empty homeless shelters." And similarly, while praising Hailey for tackling the enormously important issue of homelessness, Judith Freeman also finds the situation in the novel far-fetched and simplistic. The story, Freeman notes in the *Los Angeles Times Book Review,* "feels stuck in another time loaded with sentimentality, a kind of Lassie-goodness that undermines credibility." In an interview with her publisher, Hailey explains the genesis of the novel: "I decided I would write about what 'home' means, 'homeless' being the other side of the coin. In essence, these are two worlds in collision." In conclusion, Hailey encourages readers to "open your front door and look around."

BIOGRAPHICAL/CRITICAL SOURCES:

BOOKS

Contemporary Authors Autobiography Series, Volume 1, Gale (Detroit), 1984.
Contemporary Literary Criticism, Volume 40, Gale, 1986.

PERIODICALS

Best Sellers, October, 1978.
Christian Science Monitor, June 14, 1978.
Dallas Morning News, October 24, 1982.
Globe & Mail (Toronto), April 6, 1991.
Harper's, October, 1982.
Los Angeles Times, February 27, 1984; March 29, 1986; August 20, 1989.
Los Angeles Times Book Review, October 31, 1982; March 23, 1986; February 3, 1991.
Ms., July, 1978; November, 1982.
New York Times Book Review, May 28, 1978; November 14, 1982; February 23, 1986; March 1, 1987.
Observer, November 21, 1982.
Publishers Weekly, March 7, 1986.
Richmond Times-Dispatch, October 17, 1982.
San Francisco Chronicle Review, October 31, 1982.
Times Literary Supplement, January 21, 1983.
Tribune Books (Chicago), February 24, 1991.

Virginia Quarterly Review, autumn, 1978.
Washington Post, October 11, 1982.
Washington Post Book World, June 4, 1978; March 9, 1986, p. 3; April 7, 1991.
West Coast Review of Books, summer, 1978.*

*   *   *

HAILEY, Johanna
   See JARVIS, Sharon

*   *   *

HALE, Glenn
   See WALKER, Robert W(ayne)

*   *   *

HAMILTON, Gail
   See CORCORAN, Barbara

*   *   *

HANNA, Paul R(obert)   1902-1988

PERSONAL: Born June 21, 1902, in Sioux City, IA; died April 8, 1988; son of George Archibald and Regula (Figi) Hanna; married Jean Shuman (a writer of textbooks; deceased), August 20, 1926; married Aurella Klipper, December 26, 1987; children (first marriage): Emily-Jean Hanna Johnson, John Paul, Robert Shuman. *Education:* Hamline University, A.B. (magna cum laude), 1924; Columbia University, A.M., 1925, Ph.D., 1929. *Politics:* Republican. *Religion:* Methodist.

CAREER: Superintendent of schools, West Winfield, NY, 1925-27; Columbia University, New York City, research associate, Lincoln School, 1928-35, assistant professor of education, Teachers College, 1930-35; Stanford University, Stanford, CA, associate professor, 1935-37, professor of education, 1937-54, director of Stanford Services (war contracts—research and training), 1942-44, Lee L. Jacks Professor of Child Education, 1954-68, founder and director of Stanford International Development Education Center, 1954-68, emeritus Jacks Professor and emeritus director of International Development Education Center, 1968-88, senior research fellow, Hoover Institution on War, Revolution, and Peace, 1972-88.

National director of U.S. Council for Conservation Education, 1936-39; U.S. Agency for International Development (originally U.S. Mutual Security Agency), director of Educational Division, Philippines, 1952-53, coordinator of University of the Philippines-Stanford University Contract, 1953-56, coordinator of Philippine Department of Education-Stanford University Contract, 1956-60; U.S. Department of State, chairperson of educational and cultural exchanges team to Yugoslavia, 1966, specialist-consultant to four African governments on educational reform, 1967. American Council on Education, member of Commission on International Education, 1964-68; Atlantic Council and Atlantic Institute, member of committee on Atlantic studies, 1964-72. Educational consultant to U.S. National resources Planning Board, 1939-42, War Department, 1942-44, War Relocation Authority, 1942-45, U.S. Secretary of War (on German education), 1947, U.S. Office of Education, 1963-70, to universities and colleges in United States and abroad, and U.S. school systems. Member of international board, Atlantic Colleges, 1966-69; member of board of directors, W. Clement and Jessie V. Stone Foundation, 1969-72, Videorecord Corp. of America, 1970-72, Infomedia, Inc. (also secretary), 1972-88, U.S. National Commission for UNESCO, 1972-76; member of Presidential Task Force on Humanities, 1981-82; trustee of Castilleja School and United World Colleges.

MEMBER: Childhood Education Association International, National Education Association, American Educational Research Association (chairperson of committee on international relations, 1964-66), National Society for the Study of Education, American Association for the Advancement of Science (fellow), American Overseas Educators Association, Society for International Development, Comparative Education Society (member of board of directors), American Academy of Political and Social Science, National Planning Association, Asia Society, John Dewey Society, Society for the History of Technology, Society for Architectural Historians, American Institute of Biological Sciences, National Council of Teachers of English, Foreign Policy Association (member of national council), World Affairs Council, American Forestry Association, Phi Delta Kappa, Kappa Delta Pi, Phi Gamma Mu, Theta Chi, Cosmos Club (Washington, DC), Bohemian Club (San Francisco).

AWARDS, HONORS: D.Ped., Hamline University, 1937; senior fellow, East-West Center, University of Hawaii, 1965.

WRITINGS:

(With others) *Youth Serves the Community,* Appleton, for Progressive Education Association, 1936.

(Editor) *Aviation Education Source Book,* Hastings House (New York City), 1946.

(Editor) *Education: An Instrument of National Goals,* McGraw (New York City), 1962.

(With others) *Geography in the Teaching of Social Studies: Concepts and Skills,* Houghton (Boston), 1966.

(With others) *Phoneme-Grapheme Correspondences as Cues to Spelling Improvement,* U.S. Office of Education, 1966.

(With wife, Jean S. Hanna, and Richard E. Hodges) *Spelling: Structure and Strategies,* Houghton, 1971, revised edition, University Press of America (Lanham, MD), 1982.

(With Jean S. Hanna) *Frank Lloyd Wright's Hanna House: The Client's Report,* Architectural History Foundation/MIT Press (Cambridge, MA), 1981, revised edition, Southern Illinois University Press (Carbondale), 1987.

Assuring Quality for the Social Studies in Our Schools, Hoover Institution Press (Stanford, CA), 1987.

Civic Education: The Critical Core of our School Curriculum, Hoover Institution Press, 1987.

TEXTBOOKS

(With Mary Elizabeth Barry) *Wonder Flights of Long Ago,* Appleton, 1930.

(With Jesse H. Newlon) *The Newlon-Hanna Speller,* Houghton, 1933, and other variously titled spellers, including *The Day-by-Day Speller,* seven books, 1942.

(With Genevieve Anderson and William S. Gray) *Peter's Family,* Scott, Foresman, 1935, 4th edition, 1949.

(With Anderson and Gray) *David's Friends at School,* Scott, Foresman, 1936, revised edition published as *Hello, David,* 1943.

(With Anderson and Gray) *Susan's Neighbors at Work,* Scott, Foresman, 1937, revised edition published as *Someday Soon: A Study of a Community and Its Workers,* 1947.

(With Anderson and Gray) *Centerville,* Scott, Foresman, 1938, revised edition published as *New Centerville,* 1948.

(With Gray and Gladys Potter) *Without Machinery,* Scott, Foresman, 1939.

(With Potter and I. James Quillen) *Ten Communities,* Scott, Foresman, 1940.

(With Paul B. Sears) *This Useful World,* Scott, Foresman, 1941.

(With Edward A. Krug) *Marketing the Things We Use,* Scott, Foresman, 1943, 2nd edition, 1953.

(With Quillen and Sears) *Making the Goods We Need,* Scott, Foresman, 1943, 2nd edition, 1953.

(With Clyde F. Kohn) *Cross-Country: Geography for Children,* Scott, Foresman, 1950.

(With Genevieve Anderson and William S. Gray) *Tom and Susan,* Scott, Foresman, 1951.

(With Edna Fay Campbell) *Our World and How We Use It,* Scott, Foresman, 1953.

(With Jean S. Hanna) *Building Spelling Power,* seven books, Houghton, 1956.

(With Anderson and Gray) *At School,* Scott, Foresman, 1956.

(With Anderson and Gray) *At Home,* Scott, Foresman, 1956.

(With Anderson and Gray) *In the Neighborhood,* Scott, Foresman, 1958.

(With Anderson and Kohn) *In City, Town, and Country,* Scott, Foresman, 1959.

(With Kohn and Robert A. Lively) *In All Our States,* Scott, Foresman, 1960.

(With Kohn, Lively, and Helen F. Wise) *In the Americas,* Scott, Foresman, 1962.

(With Kohn, Lively, and Helen F. Wise) *Living and Learning Together,* Scott, Foresman, 1962.

(With Jean S. Hanna) *First Steps: A Speller for Beginners,* Houghton, 1963.

(With Kohn and Lively) *Beyond the Americas,* Scott, Foresman, 1964.

(With others) *Power to Spell,* eight books, Houghton, 1967.

Coauthor of teacher's editions and guidebooks accompanying many of the textbooks above.

OTHER

Member of editorial board, *Building America,* 1930-44, *World Book Encyclopedia,* 1936-66, *Review of Educational Research,* 1961-65, American Educational Press, 1964-70, *My Weekly Reader,* Field Education Enterprises, and Encyclopaedia Britannica Films; editorial adviser, "Elementary School Professional Textbook" series, Houghton, 1964-69.

BIOGRAPHICAL/CRITICAL SOURCES:

PERIODICALS

Choice, April, 1967, p. 190.
Library Journal, October 1, 1981, p. 1917.
Los Angeles Times Book Review, May 9, 1982, p. 12.
Publishers Weekly, August 28, 1981, p. 385.*

*   *   *

HARARY, Keith 1953-
(Stuart Blue Harary)

PERSONAL: Born February 9, 1953, in New York, NY; son of Victor (a salesman) and Lillian (a saleswoman; maiden name, Mazur) Harary; married Darlene Moore (a writer), October 22, 1985. *Education:* Duke University, B.A. (magna cum laude), 1975; Union Institute, Ph.D., 1986.

ADDRESSES: Office—Institute for Advanced Psychology, 2269 Chestnut St., No. 875, San Francisco, CA 94123. *Agent*—Roslyn Targ, Roslyn Targ Literary Agency, Inc., 105 West 13th St., New York, NY 10011.

CAREER: Research consultant at American Society for Psychical Research, 1970-72; research consultant at Institute for Parapsychology, 1972; research associate at Psychical Research Foundation, 1973-76; research associate in department of psychiatry at Maimonides Medical Center, 1976-79; director of counseling, Human Freedom Center, 1979; research consultant at SRI International, 1980-82; design consultant, Atari Corporation, 1983-85; research director, Institute for Advanced Psychology, San Francisco, 1986—; free-lance science journalist, 1988—. Crisis and suicide counselor at Durham Mental Health Center, 1972-76. Adjunct professor at Antioch University, 1985, 1986. Guest lecturer at Smithsonian Institution, Esalen Institute, United Nations, and at universities and colleges, including Stanford University, Duke University, University of North Carolina, University of California at Berkeley, at Los Angeles, and Santa Barbara, and Syracuse University; lecturer at conferences, including U.S.S.R. Academy of Sciences and Swiss Industries Fair. Has made guest appearances on over two hundred television and radio shows, including *Phil Donahue Show, 20/20, 60 Minutes, Oprah Winfrey Show, CNN News, Michael Jackson Show* (radio), and *Barry Farber Show* (radio).

MEMBER: American Psychological Society, American Psychological Association, Association for Media Psychology, American Association of Applied and Preventive Psychology, American Society for Psychical Research (member, board of directors, 1993—).

WRITINGS:

(With Russell Targ) *The Mind Race: Understanding and Using Psychic Abilities,* Random House (New York City), 1984.

(With Pamela Weintraub) *The Creative Sleep Program,* St. Martin's (New York City), 1989.

(With P. Weintraub) *The Free Flight Program,* St. Martin's, 1989.

(With P. Weintraub) *The Erotic Fulfillment Program,* St. Martin's, 1990.

(With P. Weintraub) *The Higher Consciousness Program,* St. Martin's, 1990.

(With P. Weintraub) *The Total Recall Program,* St. Martin's, 1991.

(With P. Weintraub) *The Whole Mind Program,* St. Martin's, 1991.

(With Eileen Donohue) *Who Do You Think You Are?: Explore Your Many-Sided Self with the Berkeley Personality Profile,* Harper (San Francisco), 1994.

Also author of two manuals: *Suicidal Calling as Crisis-Coping Behavior* and *Suicide Intervention: Answering the Cry for Help.* Contributor of articles on experimental psychology, psychical research, philosophy of science, ethics, and counseling, some under pseudonym Stuart Blue Harary, to periodicals and journals, including *Journal of the American Society for Psychical Research, Research in Parapsychology, Skeptical Inquirer, Omni, Psychology Today,* and *Cosmopolitan.* Contributor to reference books and anthologies, including *Phantastische Phanomene,* Herbig, 1993, *Psychic Dreaming,* Warner Books, 1991, *Psychic Voyages,* Time-Life, 1988, and *Psychic Powers,* Time-Life, 1987. Scientific editor, *Psi Research,* 1983-86.

WORK IN PROGRESS: Continued work on an autobiography; a clinical anthology on reported psychic experiences; several journal articles on a new approach to personality testing.

SIDELIGHTS: Keith Harary told *CA:* "My current thinking about experimental research on reported psychic experiences and the clinical treatment of those who have such experiences is that we frequently allow our perspective to be clouded by stereotypical attitudes and misconceptions. We invite those who share the intimate details of their psi experiences to lose their perspective along with the rest of us. Perhaps the most familiar example of this destructive tendency is our eagerness to label selected individuals as 'psychic,' and the ardent manner in which many people embrace and even compete for the dubious honor of this questionable label.

"I call for a more balanced and scientific treatment of these experiences. To label anyone a psychic is to deny the limits of our understanding and pretend to have answers to questions that have yet to be asked. That the mind is capable of remarkable feats is undeniable. Exploring the implications of this realization does not require resorting to extremes. It should encourage us to create a middle ground—one that defines human potential in human terms. If a higher perceptual, communicative and thinking capability exists within us, then it cannot be consigned to the realm of the psychic and paranormal. It must be understood within the context of normal experience and achievable human potential and considered within the emerging framework of mainstream science. Rather than approaching this exploration as a conflict between an occult versus a materialistic ideology, we may then embrace a balanced vision of human potential and investigate the mysteries of nature with a truly open mind."

*   *   *

HARARY, Stuart Blue
See HARARY, Keith

HARMON, Robert Bartlett   1932-

PERSONAL: Born November 29, 1932, in Helper, UT; son of John Harold (a salesman) and Winnie Ethlynn (Bartlett) Harmon; married Merlynn Swensen, August 18, 1961; children: Marriner John, Jane Anne, David Wright, James Bartlett, Nancy Louise. *Education:* Brigham Young University, B.A., 1958, M.A., 1960; Rutgers University, M.L.S., 1962; graduate study at San Jose State University, 1966-68. *Politics:* Republican. *Religion:* Church of Jesus Christ of Latter-day Saints (Mormon).

ADDRESSES: Home—964 Chapel Hill Way, San Jose, CA 95122. *Office*—Library, San Jose State University, San Jose, CA 95122.

CAREER: San Jose State University, San Jose, CA, librarian II, 1962-65, senior assistant librarian, 1969-75, associate librarian, 1975—, reference librarian, 1979—, Library Education and Assistance Program lecturer in Graduate School of Librarianship, head of acquisitions department, 1969-79. Editor and publisher, Dibco Press, 1966—; founder and research bibliographer, Bibliographic Research Library, 1970—.

MEMBER: American Library Association (founder and director of Bibliographic Information Center for the Study of Political Science, 1970—), Association for the Bibliography of History, Bibliographical Society of America, American Printing History Association, John Steinbeck Society of America, Mormon History Association, Kappa Delta Pi.

WRITINGS:

The Cole Family: A Brief Bibliography, privately printed, 1964.
A Preliminary Checklist of Materials on Harman-Harmon Genealogy, privately printed, 1964.
Political Science: A Bibliographical Guide to the Literature, four volumes, Scarecrow (Metuchen, NJ), 1965-74.
(With John Ray Harmon) *Descendants of Charles Claymore Bartlett and Annie Katrine Jensen,* Harmonart, 1965.
Sources and Problems of Bibliography in Political Science, Dibco, 1966.
Suggestions for a Basic Political Science Library, Bibliographic Information Center for the Study of Political Science, 1970.
Political Science Seminar Research Methods Manual, Bibliographic Information Center for the Study of Political Science, 1970.
Imperialism as a Concept of Political Science: Essay and Bibliography, Bibliographic Information Center for the Study of Political Science, 1971.
Art and Practice of Diplomacy, Scarecrow, 1971.

Methodology and Research in Political Science: An Annotated Bibliography, Bibliographic Information Center for the Study of Political Science, 1972.

Elementary Cataloging Manual for Small Libraries, Dibco, 1972.

Earthquakes: Toward a Bibliography of Bibliographies, Dibco, 1972.

John Steinbeck: Toward a Bibliography of Bibliographies, Dibco, 1973.

Georgette Heyer: A Preliminary Checklist, Dibco, 1974.

The Ghostly Bibliography, Dibco, 1975.

Selected Guide to Annotated Sources of Information in Political Science, General Learning Press, 1975.

Simplified Cataloging Manual for Small Libraries and Private Collections, Bibliographic Research Library, 1975.

Developing the Library Collection in Political Science, Scarecrow, 1976.

(With Margaert A. Burger) *An Annotated Guide to the Works of Dorothy L. Sayers,* Garland Publishing (New York City), 1977.

Understanding Ernest Hemingway: A Study and Research Guide, Scarecrow, 1977.

The First Editions of Ernest Hemingway, Hermes House (Niles, IL), 1978.

The First Editions of William Faulkner, Hermes House, 1978.

The First Editions of John Steinbeck, Hermes House, 1978.

The First Editions of Robinson Jeffers, Hermes House, 1978.

The First Editions of Gertrude Stein, Hermes House, 1978.

The First Editions of F. Scott Fitzgerald, Hermes House, 1978.

Elements of Bibliography: A Simplified Approach, Scarecrow, 1981.

A Collector's Guide to the First Editions of John Steinbeck, Opuscala Press, 1985.

The Collectible John Steinbeck: A Practical Guide, McFarland & Co. (Jefferson, NC), 1986.

(Compiler with Robert L. Lauritzen) *Index to the Steinbeck Research Center at San Jose State University: A Descriptive Catalogue,* Steinbeck Research Center, 1987.

Steinbeck Bibliographies: An Annotated Guide, Scarecrow, 1987.

Elements of Bibliography, Scarecrow, 1989.

The Grapes of Wrath: A Fifty Year Bibliographic Survey, San Jose State University (San Jose, CA), 1990.

Steinbeck Editions, Bibliographic Research Services, 1992.

Also author of bibliographies for "Public Administration and Architecture" series, Vance Bibliographies, 1974. Editor, *Steinbeck Collector,* 1979—, and a series on state government and politics for Vance Bibliographies, 27 volumes, 1990-91.

WORK IN PROGRESS: Annotated Guide to Steinbeck Biographical Sources.

SIDELIGHTS: Robert Bartlett Harmon wrote *CA:* "I continue to attempt what seems at times to be the impossible, to compile bibliographic instruments that most users will find valuable in their research endeavors. As bridges to information, bibliographies, if compiled effectively, offer unexcelled opportunities for researchers to uncover gold mines of unsuspected information related to their interests. With the advent of machine-readable databases and means to access them via computers with modems, the use of bibliographic information becomes more widely disseminated and thus more valuable to users at all levels.

"With the advent of the information superhighway, the value of published bibliographies in the minds of many seems to be diminishing. It is my firm belief, however, that non-electronic bibliographic record will serve a useful purpose in a published format for some time to come, with respect to developmental research in all areas and the dissemination of information generally."

*   *   *

HARRIGAN, Stephen 1948-

PERSONAL: Born October 5, 1948, in Oklahoma City, OK; son of Thomas F. (an independent oil operator) and Marjorie (an educator in family planning; maiden name, Berney) Harrigan; married Sue Ellen Line (a homemaker), September 6, 1975; children: Marjorie Rose, Dorothy, Charlotte. *Education:* University of Texas, B.A., 1970.

ADDRESSES: Home—2801 Clearview, Austin, TX 78703. *Agent*—Esther Newberg, International Creative Management, 40 West 57th St., New York, NY 10019.

CAREER: Worked as a yardman and later as a free-lance writer in Austin, TX; *Texas Monthly,* Austin, senior editor, 1983-91; free-lance novelist, journalist, and screenwriter, 1991—.

MEMBER: Texas Institute of Letters (past president), Philosophical Society of Texas.

AWARDS, HONORS: Dobie-Paisano fellow, 1977; National Endowment for the Arts grant in creative writing, 1979; Headliner's Award for year's best magazine article; Wrangler Award, National Cowboy Hall of Fame; selection as a notable book of 1980, *New York Times,* for *Aransas;* selection as one of year's best books, *Washington Post* and *Dallas Morning News,* both 1984, both for *Jacob's Well.*

WRITINGS:

Aransas (novel), Knopf (New York City), 1980.

Jacob's Well: A Novel, Simon & Schuster (New York City), 1984.

(Author of introduction) Martha A. Sandweiss, Roy Flukinger, and Anne W. Tucker, editors, *Contemporary Texas: A Photographic Portrait,* Texas Monthly (Austin), 1986.

A Natural State (collection of his *Texas Monthly* essays), Texas Monthly, 1988.

Water and Light: A Diver's Journey to a Coral Reef, Houghton (Boston), 1992.

The Last of His Tribe (screenplay), Home Box Office (HBO), 1992.

Comanche Midnight (essay collection), University of Texas Press (Austin), 1995.

The O. J. Simpson Story (teleplay), Fox-TV, 1995.

Also author of an episode for television series *Ned Blessing;* also author of screenwriting assignments, including *Sister Walks Ahead, The Donner Party, Huey Long,* and *Rin Tin Tin.* Contributor of articles to periodicals, including *Atlantic, Esquire, Travel Holiday, New Yorker, Audubon, Life,* and *Outside.*

WORK IN PROGRESS: A novel, *The Gates of the Alamo,* for Houghton; a screenplay, *Ocean of Storms,* with Lawrence Wright, for development with Warren Beatty.

SIDELIGHTS: Stephen Harrigan's first novel, *Aransas,* chronicles the story of Jeff Dowling, who returns to his hometown of Port Aransas, Texas, after an eleven-year absence to help run a dolphin circus. Dowling comes home primarily because, according to a *Village Voice* critique, he "just wanted to live in the world again" after years of drifting through life as a disaffected refugee from the counterculture of the early 1970s. While working with the dolphins Dowling notices that he shares certain personality traits with them, and he eventually becomes infatuated with the aquatic mammals. "Like them, Jeff feels but seems unable to express emotions," Nancy Naglin notes in the *Chicago Tribune Book World,* adding, "The Dolphins, Wanda and Sammy, slowly kindle the curiosity, passion, and sense of commitment that an oddly jaded Jeff Dowling lacks."

Critics praised *Aransas* for its realism and for Harrigan's characterization of Wanda and Sammy. In the *New York Times Book Review,* Michael Malone describes Harrigan's successful authenticity: "That we believe and share Jeff's feelings is the quiet accomplishment of [*Aransas*]." *Newsweek's* Walter Clemons lauds Harrigan for giving "his porpoises [dolphins] such distinct personalities," and labels *Aransas* "an elegant debut" and "solidly convincing." In addition, the reviewer states that "the sureness

and poise of this first novel are as remarkable as the sharpness, oddity and clarity of its feelings."

Although Clemons appreciates the "excitingly detailed" descriptions of the dolphins' training process that Harrigan includes in *Aransas, Village Voice* critic John Calvin Batchelor believes Harrigan's descriptions "continually [threaten] to overpower his drama." Yet, Batchelor declares *Aransas* a "fine first novel" and its author "literate and clever."

Harrigan's second novel, *Jacob's Well,* revolves around an artesian well and, like *Aransas,* takes place in Texas. When geologist Sam Marsh and his wife, Libby, separate after the death of their young son, Libby becomes involved with Rich Trammel, a professional diver who is fascinated by the well. He introduces both Libby and Sam to the well's mysteries, and the three of them explore its passage together. In the *Washington Post Book World* Dennis Drabelle points out that the novel's plot—"the combination of love triangle plus outdoor adventure"—may be "staple," but that "Harrigan . . . makes every page of his book seem new. . . . Reading *Jacob's Well* is a pleasure of the first magnitude."

Harrigan once told *CA:* "I make my living as a journalist, and I've come to realize over the years that that's not a bad profession for a novelist. (Being a novelist, we may assume, is rarely much of a profession in itself.) My novels are filled with scraps of information and otherwise useless detail I picked up while reporting articles, so I am warmly disposed toward journalism. Fiction, I think requires a deeper sensibility, an eagerness to deal with information that is murky and half-understood and often disturbing. But it is information nonetheless, and in that sense a novelist's work, like a journalist's, must begin with facts."

BIOGRAPHICAL/CRITICAL SOURCES:

PERIODICALS

Chicago Tribune Book World, April 27, 1980.
Newsweek, April 21, 1980.
New York Times Book Review, June 15, 1980; May 6, 1984.
Village Voice, April 7, 1980.
Washington Post Book World, May 6, 1984.

*   *   *

HARRIS, Jonathan 1921-

PERSONAL: Surname legally changed in 1954; born November 13, 1921, in New York, NY; son of Morris (in sales) and Becky (Plutt) Awerbach; married Martha Sheffer (a school librarian), February 22, 1948; children: Paul Julian, Seth David. *Education:* College of the City of New

York (now City College of the City University of New York), B.A., 1941; Institut d'Etudes Politiques, Paris, France, Diploma, 1952; Harvard University, M.A.T., 1962; New York University, Ph.D., 1972. *Avocational interests:* Travel, with extended trips to Japan and France, shorter trips to Mexico, Canada, Israel, Greece, England, Scotland, Spain, and Sicily.

ADDRESSES: Home and office—78 Hillside Ave., Roslyn Heights, NY 11577. *Agent*—Edite Kroll, 31 East 31st St., New York, NY 10016.

CAREER: International News Service, New York City, foreign news rewriter, 1953-54; advertising copywriter and copy chief for agencies in New York City and Boston, MA, 1954-60; Paul D. Schreiber High School, Port Washington, NY, social studies teacher and department chairman, 1962-83; writer, 1983—. *Military service:* U.S. Army, 1943-46; became technical sergeant.

MEMBER: Authors Guild, Authors League of America, American Civil Liberties Union.

WRITINGS:

FOR YOUNG ADULTS

Hiroshima: A Study in Science, Politics, and the Ethics of War, Addison-Wesley (Reading, MA), 1970.
Scientists in the Shaping of America, Addison-Wesley, 1971.
Judgment: A Simulated Trial of Harry S. Truman, Interact, 1977.
The New Terrorism: Politics of Violence, Messner (New York City), 1983.
Super Mafia, Messner, 1984.
A Statue for America: The First One Hundred Years of the Statue of Liberty (Junior Literary Guild selection), Macmillan (New York City), 1986.
Drugged Athletes: The Crisis in American Sports, Macmillan, 1987.
The Land and the People of France, Lippincott (New York City), 1988.
Drugged America, Four Winds Press (New York City), 1991.
This Drinking Nation, Macmillan, 1994.

SIDELIGHTS: Jonathan Harris told *CA:* "My first books for teenagers were published during the twenty-one richly rewarding years I spent teaching social studies to high school students. I retired from teaching in 1983 in order to write full time.

"I feel strongly that the conceptual content of books for young people should never be watered down in any condescending way. Any and all ideas, however subtle or complex, can and should be expounded clearly and simply.

"Since my writings tend to deal with broad historical subjects that have been treated by other authors, I get a special kick out of discoveries—which often happen through the mysterious process of serendipity—of precious nuggets of information that have never been published before."

*   *   *

HARRISON, Barbara Grizzuti 1934-

PERSONAL: Born September 14, 1934, in Brooklyn, NY; daughter of Dominick (a printer) and Carmela (Di Nardo) Grizzuti; married W. Dale Harrison, July, 1960 (divorced, 1968); children: Joshua Paul, Anna Edyth. *Religion:* Roman Catholic.

ADDRESSES: Home—Brooklyn, NY. *Agent*—Georges Borchardt, Inc., 136 East 57th St., New York, NY 10022.

CAREER: Writer. Worked as secretary, 1958-60.

MEMBER: PEN, Authors Guild, Authors League of America.

AWARDS, HONORS: American Book Award, Before Columbus Foundation, for *Italian Days;* recipient of an O'Henry award for short fiction, a MacDowell fellowship, and a Yaddo fellowship.

WRITINGS:

Unlearning the Lie: Sexism in School, Liveright (New York City), 1969.
Visions of Glory: A History and a Memory of Jehovah's Witnesses, Simon & Schuster (New York City), 1978.
Off Center: Essays, Dial (New York City), 1980.
Foreign Bodies (novel), Doubleday (New York City), 1984.
Italian Days, Weidenfeld & Nicolson (New York City), 1989.
The Islands of Italy: Sicily, Sardinia, and the Aeolian Islands, Ticknor & Fields (New York City), 1991.
The Astonishing World: Essays, Ticknor & Fields, 1992.
All Her Dreams, Severn House (New York City), 1994.

Also contributor to books, including the introduction to *The Spirit's Pilgrimage,* by Mirabehn, Great Ocean (Arlington, VA), 1984. Contributor to numerous periodicals, including *Esquire, European Travel and Life, Harper's, Mademoiselle, McCall's, Nation, New Republic, Newsday, New York, New York Times Book Review, Ms., New York Times Magazine, Redbook, Saturday Review, Traveler, Village Voice,* and *Vogue.*

SIDELIGHTS: Hard-edged journalism and autobiography often combine in the nonfiction writing of Barbara Grizzuti Harrison. Her first book, *Unlearning the Lie:*

Sexism in School, grew out of an article about an experiment at her child's school; her second book is a theological and historical explanation of Jehovah's Witnesses, a religious group with which Harrison was involved for eleven years. Such personal involvement with her subjects might seem likely to weaken Harrison's objectivity, but according to Lore Dickstein in the *New York Times Book Review,* it does not. Dickstein writes: "Harrison's style demonstrates the strength of personal journalism in the hands of a skilled, compassionate and open-minded writer. Mrs. Harrison is always a presence in her work and while she has strong opinions (freely acknowledged), she comes to her subjects with receptivity, energy and a critical awareness of human fallibility."

One of Harrison's most widely-reviewed works is *Visions of Glory: A History and a Memory of Jehovah's Witnesses.* The seeds for this book were planted when the author was nine years-old and converted, along with her mother, to the Witness faith. Witnesses emphasize self-discipline and strict codes of behavior. For example, they are not allowed to salute the flag, take blood transfusions, or serve in the army of any country. Instead, they concentrate on the "New Eden" that they believe will be created on this earth after a bloody Armageddon destroys the existing society. All non-Witnesses will perish in this disaster, which will supposedly take place within our lifetime. The unorthodox ways of the Witness sect made Harrison feel like an outsider during her school years; still, she became so devoted to the religion that at the age of nineteen she went to live and work in its giant Watchtower Bible and Tract Society headquarters in Brooklyn Heights, New York. After three years there, she renounced the faith and left, although advised that anyone who does so will be ostracized by their former brothers in this life and by God in the next.

Harrison's book portrays the Witnesses as racist, sexist, and totalitarian. However, she also details their kindness to one another, the pains they take to assure that their elderly are well cared for, and their tremendous courage in the face of the many persecutions they have suffered through the years. The author's well-rounded description of the religion, in spite of her own negative experience with it, is noted by Lisa Gubernick in the *Nation:* "[Harrison's] memories do not make her history suspect; instead, the autobiographical fragments give the book balance and weight. . . . Indeed, the tremendous success of the Witnesses—there are at present more than 2 million followers—would be scarcely credible without Harrison's personal testimony, for the origins of the sect and its makeshift theology seem on the face of things banal and uninviting."

Vivian Gornick writes in the *New York Times Book Review* that *Visions of Glory* is "well written, contains a mass

of absorbing information, and the personality of its author is extremely appealing. Barbara Harrison seems to be a warm, intelligent woman with a disarming street-smart sense of humor." The author's intelligence and integrity have been remarked upon by other reviewers as well. In a *Washington Post Book World* review, Allen Lacy writes: "Harrison knows her own mind and expresses it with force and good humor. . . . [She] does not subscribe to the doctrine promulgated by contemporary pop psychology that the chief virtue is to be 'accepting,' the worst vice is to be 'judgmental.' To the contrary: 'The judgements I make,' she writes, 'are the person I am.' That's a marvelous sentence and a succinct definition of the nature of moral experience. To refuse to make essential discriminations, to abdicate the responsibility of judgement, is to lessen one's being as a person."

Harrison does not shy away from tackling difficult subjects or offering unpopular opinions. For example, her book *Off Center: Essays* contains some harsh criticism of Joan Didion, a writer highly regarded by many readers. According to Dickstein, the essay is "a brilliant hatchet job. . . . Despite its excess, you have to admire its iconoclastic daring. Mrs. Harrison describes Miss Didion as a 'neurasthenic Cher' rather than 'America's finest woman prose stylist.'" Harrison offers a challenge to readers with her strong opinions and intelligent argument, notes Suzanne Fields in the *Los Angeles Times Book Review:* "She makes us think while other writers are content to invite us to join them in merely feeling good."

Similarly, *Italian Days*—an account of the four years Harrison spent travelling through Italy, living in large cities like Venice and Rome and in places where her parents' families were born and raised—is not a conventional travel book. *Italian Days* includes quotations from various writers, as well as Harrison's personal encounters with distant relatives. Writing in the *New York Times,* Eva Hoffman observes: "Ms. Grizzuti Harrison's peasant relatives, and Italy on the whole, are a sort of counterpoint to her American self, and in part *Italian Days* is her dialogue with American culture." In a review for the *Los Angeles Times,* Elaine Kendall describes *Italian Days* as "a sometimes joyous, often arduous diary of a search for an essential self, recounted by a mature and sophisticated essayist. Though the Italy presented here is uniquely Harrison's, she shows readers the way to find their own."

Harrison's collection of essays, reports, and interviews entitled *The Astonishing World: Essays* served only to strengthen her already-high standing with critics. In her description of Harrison's talent for interviewing, *Washington Post Book World* reviewer Abigail McCarthy explains, "[Harrison] seems to have the gift of instant intimacy. Her method of interviewing, which she says is simply talking with people, and the basic empathy with which she approaches her subjects result in portraits of striking wholeness." John F. Baker, writing in the *Village Voice,* similarly applauds Harrison as "one of the best essayists around," praising her as "a thoroughly savvy contemporary woman with a gift for informed enthusiasm and occasional necessary malice." In an interview for *CA,* Harrison explains that one of her "tricks" to conducting a successful interview is "to pay absolute attention when you're with that person. Usually when I interview, the person I'm interviewing is the most interesting person in the world to me at that moment. . . . [Moreover] that person has to be more interesting to you than you are to yourself."

BIOGRAPHICAL/CRITICAL SOURCES:

PERIODICALS

America, September 23, 1978.
Chicago Tribune Book World, May 21, 1981.
Choice, November, 1980.
Globe and Mail (Toronto), July 21, 1984; August 11, 1984.
Los Angeles Times, September 22, 1989.
Los Angeles Times Book Review, June 1, 1980; February 16, 1992.
Nation, January 6, 1979; May 14, 1980; October 3, 1981.
New York Review of Books, October 26, 1978.
New York Times, June 12, 1980; August 23, 1989.
New York Times Book Review, November 19, 1978; June 15, 1980; July 1, 1984; December 1, 1991.
Publishers Weekly, July 27, 1992.
Tribune Books, July 26, 1992.
Village Voice, February 16, 1993.
Wall Street Journal, August 4, 1992.
Washington Post, May 16, 1980; May 23, 1984.
Washington Post Book World, July 19, 1981; July 12, 1992.*

*　　　*　　　*

HARRISON, James P.
　See HARRISON, James Pinckney

*　　　*　　　*

HARRISON, James Pinckney　1932-
　(James P. Harrison)

PERSONAL: Born July 20, 1932, in Richmond, VA; son of Pinckney and Nellie (Meade) Harrison. *Education:* Yale University, B.A., 1954; Columbia University, M.A., 1960, Ph.D., 1965.

ADDRESSES: Home—322 West 57th St., No. 33A, New York, NY 10019. *Office*—Department of History, Hunter

College of the City University of New York, New York, NY 10021.

CAREER: Richmond News Leader, Richmond, VA, reporter, 1957-58; Hunter College of the City University of New York, New York City, professor of history, 1965—. Barnard College, part-time visiting lecturer in history, 1966; Columbia University, visiting professor of political science, 1969-71. *Military service:* U.S. Air Force, pilot, 1955-57.

MEMBER: American Historical Association, Association of Asian Studies, Amnesty International (chair of board of directors, 1971-73).

AWARDS, HONORS: Ford Foundation fellowship in Hong Kong, 1962-63; Fulbright travel grant for exchange teaching in Paris, 1985-86.

WRITINGS:

(Under name James P. Harrison) *The Communists and Chinese Peasant Rebellions: A Study in the Rewriting of Chinese History,* Atheneum (New York City), 1968.
(Under name James P. Harrison) *Modern Chinese Nationalism,* Hunter College of the City University of New York (New York City), 1969.
The Long March to Power: A History of the Chinese Communist Party, 1921-1972, Praeger (New York City), 1972.
The Endless War: Fifty Years of Struggle in Vietnam, Free Press (New York City), 1982, published as *The Endless War: Vietnam's Struggle for Independence,* McGraw (New York City), 1983, with new preface, Columbia University Press (New York City), 1989.

WORK IN PROGRESS: The Miracle of Flight: A History of Aviation.

SIDELIGHTS: James Pinckney Harrison told *CA:* "In my research and writings on Chinese Communism, I have attempted to understand the forces which created the huge Chinese revolution and how the Communists were able to take leadership of that revolution against overwhelming odds. Similarly my work on the victory of the Vietnamese communists against even greater odds aims to examine similar interactions of economic and social conditions with ideology and leadership. I have sought interviews with participants in these extraordinary events in China and Vietnam and have made trips to both countries. But the students of these complex and highly controversial revolutions must rely primarily on research in such documents as exist, and on the scholarly studies of these documents. I am able to pursue these in English, French, Russian, and Chinese."

BIOGRAPHICAL/CRITICAL SOURCES:

PERIODICALS

New York Times Book Review, April 24, 1966; May 20, 1973, p. 52; May 2, 1982, p. 3.
Times Literary Supplement, August 14, 1970, p. 898; September 21, 1973, p. 1076.
Washington Post Book World, February 21, 1982, p. 7.

*   *   *

HARRISON, Roland Kenneth 1920-

PERSONAL: Born August 4, 1920, in Lancashire, England; son of William (a civil servant) and Hilda Mary (Marsden) Harrison; married Kathleen Beattie, October 18, 1945; children: Charmian Felicity and Hermione Judith (twins), Graham Kenneth. *Education:* University of London, B.D., 1943, M.Th., 1947, Ph.D., 1952. *Politics:* Progressive Conservative.

ADDRESSES: Home—41 Cuthbert Crescent, Toronto, Ontario M4S 2G9, Canada. *Office*—Wycliffe College, University of Toronto, Toronto, Ontario M5S 1H7, Canada.

CAREER: Ordained Anglican priest, 1943; Clifton Theological College, Bristol, England, chaplain, 1947-49; Huron College, London, Ontario, Canada, professor of Biblical Greek, 1949-52, Hellmuth Professor of Old Testament, 1952-60; University of Toronto, Wycliffe College, Toronto, Ontario, Bishops Frederick and Heber Wilkinson Professor of Old Testament, 1960-86, professor emeritus, 1986—.

MEMBER: Worshipful Society of Apothecaries (London), Canadian Psychiatric Association.

AWARDS, HONORS: D.D. from Huron College, London, Ontario, 1963.

WRITINGS:

Teach Yourself Hebrew, McKay (New York City), 1955, reprinted as *Teach Yourself Biblical Hebrew,* Lincolnwood (Chicago), 1993.
A History of Old Testament Times, Marshall, Morgan & Scott (Basingstoke, England), 1957, revised edition published as *Old Testament Times,* Eerdmans (Grand Rapids, MI), 1970.
The Dead Sea Scrolls, English Universities Press, 1961.
Introduction to the Old Testament, Eerdmans, 1969.
Jeremiah and Lamentations, Tyndale Press (Downer's Grove, IL), 1973.
(With Peter C. Craigie) *Book of Deuteronomy,* Eerdmans, 1976.
(With L. C. Allen) *Books of Joel, Obadiah, Jonah, and Micah,* Eerdmans, 1976.

Biblical Criticism: Historical, Literary, and Textual, Zondervan (Grand Rapids, MI), 1978.
Leviticus: An Introduction and Commentary, Inter-Varsity (Downer's Grove, IL), 1980.
(Editor with Edward M. Blaiklock) *The New International Dictionary of Biblical Archaeology,* Zondervan, 1983.
(Editor) *Major Cities of the Biblical World,* T. Nelson (Nashville, TN), 1985.
(Consulting editor) *International Children's Bible Dictionary,* Sweet Publishing (Fort Worth, TX), 1987.
(Editor) *Encyclopedia of Biblical and Christian Ethics,* T. Nelson, 1987, revised edition, 1992.
(Editor) Merrill F. Unger, *The New Unger's Bible Dictionary,* Moody Press (Chicago), 1988.
Numbers, Moody Press, 1990.

Also author of *The Ancient World,* 1971. Editor of *New International Commentary on the Old Testament,* 1969—.

SIDELIGHTS: Roland Kenneth Harrison told *CA:* "My writing career began at an early stage in my professional career. Most of my books were written in order to supplement courses that I was teaching. But as well as this, they served to enlarge the range of my teaching."

Some of Harrison's books have been translated into Italian, French, and Spanish.*

*   *   *

HARTMAN, John J(acob) 1942-

PERSONAL: Born August 13, 1942, in Detroit, MI; son of Manuel and Eleanor (Jacob) Hartman; married Julia Carlin, 1968; children: Michelle, Amanda. *Education:* Harvard University, A.B. (magna cum laude), 1964; University of Michigan, M.A., 1969, Ph.D., 1969.

ADDRESSES: Home—3689 Middleton Dr., Ann Arbor, MI 48105. *Office*—Department of Psychiatry, University of Michigan Medical Center, 220 Riverview Bldg., Ann Arbor, MI 48109.

CAREER: University of California, Los Angeles, assistant professor of psychology, 1969-71; University of Michigan, Neuropsychiatric Institute, Ann Arbor, assistant professor, 1971-74, associate professor of psychology, 1974—.

MEMBER: International Psychohistory Association, American Psychological Association, Society for the Psychological Study of Social Issues, American Group Psychotherapy Association, Michigan Psychological Association.

AWARDS, HONORS: Woodrow Wilson fellow, 1964-65; Prytanean Distinguished Service Award for teaching from University of California at Los Angeles, 1971.

WRITINGS:

(With R. D. Mann and G. S. Gibbard) *Interpersonal Styles and Group Development,* Wiley (New York City), 1967.

(With M. J. Goldstein and H. S. Kant) *Pornography and Sexual Deviance,* University of California Press (Berkeley), 1973.

(Editor with Gibbard and Mann, and contributor) *Analysis of Groups: Contributions to Theory, Research, and Practice,* Jossey-Bass (San Francisco), 1974.

Methods for the Social Sciences: A Handbook for Students and Non-Specialists, Greenwood (Westport, CT), 1979.

Contributor to *New Directions in Teaching, American Journal of Orthopsychiatry, Contemporary Psychoanalysis, International Journal of Group Psychotherapy, Behavioral Science, Small Group Behavior,* and *Michigan Medicine.**

*   *   *

HARTNETT, D(avid) W(illiam) 1952-

PERSONAL: Born September 4, 1952, in London, England; son of James Arthur (a company chairman) and Audrey Julia (Briggs) Hartnett; married Margaret Rosamond Newton Thomas, August 26, 1976; children: Edward, Sarah. *Education:* Exeter College, Oxford, B.A. (with first class honors), 1975, D.Phil., 1986.

ADDRESSES: c/o Jonathan Cape, 20, Vauxhall Bridge Road, London, SW1V 25A England.

CAREER: Freelance writer, 1993—

*AWARDS, HONORS: Times Literary Supplement/*Cheltenham Festival of Literature Poetry Prize, 1989.

WRITINGS:

A Signalled Love (poems), Anvil Press (London), 1985.
House of Moon (poems), Secker & Warburg (London), 1988.
Dark Ages (poems), Secker & Warburg, 1992.
Black Milk (novel), Jonathan Cape (London), 1994.

WORK IN PROGRESS: A second novel, a collection of short stories and a fourth collection of poems for Jonathan Cape; a critical study of the poetry of James Merrill; a collection of essays on twentieth century poets.

SIDELIGHTS: D. W. Hartnett told *CA:* "I regard all my work—in poetry and fiction—as an attempt to marry the personal with the historical, the domestic movement with vaster processes of accident and necessity. Themes in my poetry range from childhood and birth to the twentieth century nightmare of total war. I have published poems about animals, requiems for dead artists (Rilke, Gurney); love poems and poems about the origins and burdens of creativity.

"More recently I have turned to fiction as a way of grounding these insights in a particular social and historical milieu. *Black Milk,* my first novel, is set in a fictional Jewish ghetto in Eastern Europe during the Second World War. The novel plunges the reader into a world of terror and guilt, even as it tenderly evokes the intimacies of family life. Novelists I admire include Hawthorne, Joyce, Patrick White and William Golding."

BIOGRAPHICAL/CRITICAL SOURCES:

PERIODICALS

Guardian, October 17, 1985.
Listener, April 10, 1986.
PN Review, Volume XIII, number 1, 1986.
Sunday Telegraph, August 21, 1994.
Times (London) August 11, 1994.

*   *   *

HARVEY, Anne 1933-

PERSONAL: Born April 27, 1933, in London, England; daughter of Charles (a banker) and Rose (Humphreys) Lewis; married Alan Harvey (a lecturer; deceased); children: Matthew Damian Lewis, Charlotte Olivia Anne. *Education:* Guildhall School of Music and Drama, L.G.S.M., 1953, A.G.S.M., 1954. *Religion:* Roman Catholic. *Avocational interests:* "My hobbies are reading, theatre, and people. I am the organizer of a local group of the National Schizophrenia Fellowship, and I counsel parents and sufferers on a voluntary basis."

ADDRESSES: Home—37 St. Stephen's Rd., Ealing, London W13 8HJ, England.

CAREER: Guildhall Players, Perranporth, England, actress and director, 1954-56; private drama teacher and coach, 1962-86; Notting Hills Ealing (girls' high school), London, England, drama teacher and coach, 1978—. Director of Pegasus (professional theatre company). Freelance writer and broadcaster.

AWARDS, HONORS: Leverhulme fellow, 1983; Compton Poetry Fund Award, 1984, 1986-87; Signal Poetry Award, 1992.

WRITINGS:

A Present for Nellie (juvenile), Julia Macrae (London), 1981.
Flora's Red Socks (picture book), Blackie & Son (Glasgow), 1991.
He Said, She Said, They Said, Blackie & Son, 1993.

EDITOR

(With Mary Greenslade) *Scenes for Two,* Books I-II, Samuel French (New York City), 1969.

Solo (dramatic monologues), Samuel French, 1973.

Take Two, Samuel French, 1980.

Jewels, Hutchinson (London), 1981.

Poets in Hand, Puffin (London), 1985.

Caterpillars, Cats, and Cattle (poetry), Kestrel (London), 1987.

In Time of War (poetry), Blackie & Son, 1987.

Something I Remember: Selected Poems of Eleanor Farjeon, Blackie & Son, 1987.

A Picnic of Poetry, Blackie/Puffin, 1988.

Six of the Best, Puffin, 1989.

Occasions, Blackie/Puffin, 1989.

The Language of Love, Penguin (New York City), 1990.

Faces in a Crown, Viking (New York City), 1990.

(With Virginia McKenna) *Headlines from the Jungle,* Viking, 1990.

Poetry Originals, Blackie & Son, 1990.

Shades of Green, Julia MacRae/Red Fox, 1991.

Elected Friends: Poems for and about Edward Thomas (adult), Enitharmon Press (London), 1990.

Solo Audition Speeches for Young Actors, Methuen (New York City), 1993.

Criminal Records, Viking, 1994.

Also author of *A Life Kept Always Young* (radio play), 1981.

WORK IN PROGRESS: Research into diaries by young girls; editing a second drama book for young actors; researching and lecturing on the history of children's poetry.

SIDELIGHTS: Anne Harvey told *CA:* "The idea for *A Present for Nellie* is from a childhood incident in the life of Eleanor Farjeon, the famous English children's poet and storyteller. I have spent many years researching her life and wrote a radio program about her—*A Life Kept Always Young*—for her centenary in 1981. I give talks on her in schools and to literary groups and have presented stage performances about her. I have also edited a new selection of her poems called *Something I Remember* and would like to come to the States to give presentations about her. There is something of a revival of Farjeon here in England, with the reprinting of many of her books.

"One of my main interests is Pegasus, a professional theatre company. The actors are both well-known stars, including Roger Rees, Virginia McKenna, and Eileen Atkins, and promising beginners. The company's aim is to present literature on stage faithfully. We work closely with publishers, often basing a program on a book and selling the book at the performances. These are presented all over the country at theatres, art festivals, churches, and colleges. In 1994 a programme in which I play Christina Rossetti during the centenary of her death was very popular.

"My life is busy—too busy—and my aim is to cut out some of the demanding activities that take me from home and to concentrate on my writing, editing, and performing. I am filled with ideas for the future.

"I frequently give talks and readings, and am involved in Poetry Days in schools. My concern is to introduce young people to the best of the past and present and to be an influence in guiding them subtly away form some of the very poor poetry (or doggerel) offered to children to-day."

*   *   *

HARVEY, Rachel
See BLOOM, Ursula (Harvey)

*   *   *

HASHMI, Aurangzeb Alamgir   1951-

PERSONAL: Born November 15, 1951, in Lahore, Pakistan; came to the United States in 1974; son of Sharif Ahmed (a professor) and Naseem (Akhter) Hashmi; married Beatrice Stoerk, December 15, 1978; children: Aniq, Cyril, Celine. *Education:* University of the Punjab, M.A., 1972; University of Louisville, M.A., 1977. *Avocational interests:* Walking, cricket.

ADDRESSES: Home—House 162, Street 64, Ramna 8/1, Islamabad, Pakistan; and c/o S. S. Sirajuddin, 30-C Sarwar Rd., Lahore Cantt., Pakistan.

CAREER: Pakistan Broadcasting Corp., Lahore, Pakistan, broadcaster, lecturer, compere, and translator on Radio Pakistan, 1968-74; Government College, Lahore, instructor, 1971-72, tutor in English, 1972-73; Forman Christian College, Lahore, lecturer in English, 1973-74; University of North Carolina, Davidson International Visiting Scholar from Pakistan, 1974-75; University of Louisville, Louisville, KY, lecturer in English, 1975-78; University of Bahawalpur, assistant professor of English, Pakistan, 1979-80; University of Zurich and Volkshochschule Zurich, Zurich, Switzerland, lecturer in English, 1980-85; International Islamic University, Islamabad, Pakistan, associate professor of English, 1985-86; University of Azad Jammu and Kashmir, Muzaffarabad, Pakistan, professor of English and head of department, 1986-87; Pakistan Broadcasting Corp., broadcaster, lecturer, compere, and translator, 1988—; Pakistan Ministry of Foreign Affairs, Islamabad, course director at Foreign Service Training Institute, 1988—; Pakistan Futuristics Institute, Islamabad, professor of English and comparative literature, 1990.

Course director in Foreign Service Training Institute, Pakistan Ministry of Foreign Affairs, Islamabad, 1988—; literary editor and chief of Publications Division, Pakistan

Institute of Development Economics, Islamabad, 1988—. Lecturer at University of Bern and University of Basel, Switzerland, 1982; visiting lecturer in English, University of Zurich, 1982—; visiting professor of English, University of Fribourg, Switzerland, 1985—; visiting professor of English literature, Federal Government Postgraduate College for Men, Islamabad, 1986; visiting professor of American literature, Quaid-i-Azam University, Islamabad, 1986. Chairperson, Standing International Conference Committee on English in South Asia, 1989—. Founder of Townsend Poetry Prize, 1986; judge, Commonwealth Writers Prize, 1990. Has given poetry readings on Radio Pakistan and on the campuses of several Pakistani and American colleges and universities, 1973-78; has given poetry readings at other colleges, universities, and institutions throughout Asia, Europe, and North America, 1978-91. Sector warden, Civil Defense, Multan Cantonment, 1965-66. Adviser, National Book Council of Pakistan, 1989.

MEMBER: International Association of University Professors of English, International PEN (fellow), International Centre for Asian Studies (fellow), Modern Language Association of America, Associated Writing Programs, Poetry Society, Council on National Literatures, Centre for Research in the New Literatures in English (Flinders University, Australia), Association for Commonwealth Literature and Language Studies, Association for Asian Studies, South Asian Area Center.

AWARDS, HONORS: First prize, All-Pakistan Creative Writing Contest at University of Lyallpur, 1972, for *The Telegram;* certificate of merit, University of the Punjab (Lahore), 1973; D.Litt., Centre Universitaire de Luxembourg, 1984; Litt.D., San Francisco State University, 1984; Patras Bokhari Award (national literature prize), Pakistan Academy of Letters, 1985.

WRITINGS:

The Oath and Amen: Love Poems, Dorrance (Bryn Mawr, PA), 1976.

(Editor) *Pakistani Literature,* two volumes, [New York], 1978, 2nd edition published as *Pakistani Literature: The Contemporary English Writers,* Gulmohar (Islamabad, Pakistan), 1987.

America Is a Punjabi Word (poetry), Limmat Editions (Lahore, Pakistan), 1979.

An Old Chair (poetry), Xenia Press, 1979.

My Second in Kentucky (poetry), Vision Press (London), 1981.

This Time in Lahore (poetry), Vision Press, 1983.

Commonwealth Literature (literary criticism), Vision Press, 1983.

(Editor with Les Harrop and others) *Ezra Pound in Melbourne,* Helix, 1983.

Neither This Time/Nor That Place (poetry), Vision Press, 1984.

(Editor and contributor) *The Worlds of Muslim Imagination* (anthology), Gulmohar, 1986.

Inland and Other Poems, Gulmohar, 1988.

The Commonwealth, Comparative Literature and the World (literary criticism), Gulmohar, 1988.

The Poems of Alamgir Hashmi, National Book Foundation (Islamabad), 1992.

OTHER

Also author of *Sun and Moon and Other Poems,* 1992, and *Others to Sport with Amaryllis in the Shade* (poetry), 1992. Also editor, *Pakistani Short Stories in English,* 1992, and *Studies in Pakistani Literature,* 1992. Editor and advisor, *The Routledge Encyclopaedia of Commonwealth Literature, The Blackwell Companion to Twentieth-Century Theatre,* and *The Oxford Companion to Twentieth-Century Poetry.* Also contributor to numerous books, including *Four Young Poets of Pakistan,* [Karachi], 1972; *Three Poets,* [Winterthur, Switzerland], 1979; *Soundings,* [Deerfield, IL], 1985; and *Epistolary Fiction and the Letter as Artifact,* [Youngstown, OH], 1991. Contributor to annuals, including *Annual Bibliography of English Language and Literature* and *Annual of Urdu Studies.* Contributor of articles, reviews, poetry, and translations of modern Urdu and Punjabi poetry to numerous periodicals throughout the world, including *MLA International Bibliography, International Poetry Review, Pacific Quarterly, Translation, Journal of South Asian Literature, World Literature Written in English,* and *Chicago Review.* Assistant editor, associate editor, corresponding editor, member of editorial board, correspondent, or staff reviewer of numerous periodicals throughout Pakistan and Asia. Has recorded on tape a reading of selected poems for the contemporary English poetry archives of the Library of Congress, 1989.

WORK IN PROGRESS: A comparative study of poetry and the novel in English; critical work on modern Urdu poetry; verse translation from Urdu and Punjabi; editorial work on social sciences, humanities, and contemporary literary scholarship; new poems.

SIDELIGHTS: Aurangzeb Alamgir Hashmi told *CA:* "I grew up in my parents' home with its three spoken (English, Urdu, Punjabi) and two half-spoken (Persian, Arabic) languages. The classics of each language were a sort of collar that one had to wear for a time. I flirted with several but English won out early enough. I chose it or perhaps it chose me; I don't write in any other language. As it happened, French and German were later to complicate both love and life.

"I started writing around 1962 and began to show my work to friends around 1964-65. My first book, *The Oath and Amen* (1976), was a thematic collection subtitled 'Love Poems,' though it contained a counter-movement, *Distractions,* in the last section; and I had indeed written by then at least as many poems which would be described differently. Love, nevertheless, is a theme and a quality that runs through my work, as a question or an answer or the distance between them—the role and the play that it must have in personal relations and the world formed so. Time, place, distance, and closeness—and their personal, geographical, natural, and cultural *relations*—all matter in ordinary life, as well as in dimensions that cannot actually be *lived* (in the real world).

"*America Is a Punjabi Word* (1979) followed several years' residence in the United States, which had increasingly become a second home. This long poem established the loss of *America* as a personal loss, retaining what one could of it in an imaginative world not entirely devoid of humour and even self-mockery. As a lyric-narrative, a long poem on a short scale, it explores the same concerns in a stretchable form and a new setting, language and feeling being a further equation of relevance. *My Second in Kentucky* (1981), containing much of my best work done till the end of 1977 (I moved the following year), has three divisions by setting, corresponding to three different movements in my life as in my book: poems in America, poems in Pakistan, and poems in America-Pakistan.

"Moving to Europe in the late 1970s, necessitated by the martial law in Pakistan, proved to be a mixed blessing; one had to adjust now, additionally, to the *appearance* of freedom. I began to re-examine my Swiss existence and the overall human issues involved in the light of my commitments and values. Two major books are from this period: *This Time in Lahore* (1983) and *Neither This Time/Nor That Place* (1984). In both of these I have generally dropped the traditional verse forms and tried to develop a *vers libre* drawing on the poetic resources of natural speech as far as my linguistic access and (educated) inclination would allow. As I have personally moved house several times, many of my poems have been seen to be set in here, or there, or nowhere in particular, leading to appropriate observations and generalization. Some of the poems in the books, in fact, have omissions and deletions of lines or whole stanzas so that the poetry could be kept in circulation in the face of censorship. Only the earlier published versions in the magazines and journals, or the author's own records, in such cases, could help retrieve the objective text.

"All these features—of form, language, theme, and setting—can also be seen in *Inland and Other Poems* (1988), the last poetry book completed in Switzerland. My 1992 book of poems, *Others to Sport with Amaryllis in the Shade,* contains poems written in Pakistan, and I believe that this word represents a turning-point of a life in art, in such forms as will not defeat the experience; one kind of exile has led to another and found its home in the only words and rhythms possible for it.

"I continue to see man/woman in nature, in the world, and in the society with as much wonder as the fun of the world will elicit, though touched by a sense of the tragic, which is too personal—and, I feel, cosmic—to have a long span in any narrative. My work is one of celebration, analysis, and integration, looking out for possibility and seeking the joy that comes from the discovery of the common natural and human element across each Berlin Wall that has been built upon the foundation of our own inhibitions or fears.

"I have been increasingly drawn lately to the study of imaginative literature as a function of language study rather than only as a national or ethnic construct; the latter category exists only to obviate its own necessity. Comparative studies and translation are also strong current interests. I was trained as a scholar, and I have taught English and comparative literature for the past twenty years in North America, Europe, and Asia. My scholarly and critical work is part of my total experience as a writer. I find the practice of poetry enriches the critical understanding of literature, which I teach as a form of knowledge about being human and as a language to understand with pleasure."

BIOGRAPHICAL/CRITICAL SOURCES:

PERIODICALS

Asiaweek (Hong Kong), October 5, 1985, p. 62; May 10, 1987, p. 64.
CRNLE Reviews Journal (Australia), number 2, 1982, pp. 72-73; number 2, 1986, pp. 87-88; number 2, 1990, pp. 93-96.
Explorations (Pakistan), Volume 6, number 2, 1980, pp. 28-31; winter, 1987; summer, 1991, pp. 51-63.
Journal of Indian Writing in English: Writing in English from Pakistan, Sri Lanka and Bangladesh (India), July, 1988, pp. 55-68.
Journal of South Asian Literature, Volume 22, number 1, 1987, pp. 248-49; Volume 23, number 1, 1988, pp. 146-50.
New Literature Review (Australia), number 15, 1988, pp. 33-39.

Orbis, summer, 1983.
Thinker, March-April, 1980, p. 18.
Third World Quarterly, October, 1987, pp. 1412-14.
Viewpoint, January 21, 1982.
World Literature Today, autumn, 1985, p. 661; Volume 62, number 4, 1988, pp. 731-32; winter, 1990, pp. 203-04.*

*   *   *

HASKINS, James S. 1941-
(Jim Haskins)

PERSONAL: Born September 19, 1941, in Demopolis, AL; son of Henry and Julia (Brown) Haskins. *Education:* Georgetown University, B.A. (psychology), 1960; Alabama State University, B.S. (history), 1962; University of New Mexico, M.A. (social psychology), 1963; graduate study at New School for Social Research, 1965-67, and Queens College of the City University of New York, 1968-70.

ADDRESSES: Home—325 West End Ave., Apt. 7D, New York, NY 10023. *Office*—Department of English, University of Florida, Gainesville, FL 32611.

CAREER: Smith Barney & Co., New York City, stock trader, 1963-65; New York City Board of Education, New York City, teacher, 1966-68; New School for Social Research, New York City, visiting lecturer, 1970-72; Staten Island Community College of the City University of New York, Staten Island, NY, associate professor, 1970-77; University of Florida, Gainesville, professor of English, 1977—. New York *Daily News,* reporter, 1963-64. Visiting lecturer at Elisabeth Irwin High School, 1971-73, Indiana University/Purdue University—Indianapolis, 1973-76, and College of New Rochelle, 1977. Director, Union Mutual Life, Health and Accident Insurance, 1970-73; member of board of directors, Psi Systems, 1971-72, and Speedwell Services for Children, 1974-76. Member of Manhattan Community Board No. 9, 1972-73, academic council for the State University of New York, 1972-74, New York Urban League Manhattan Advisory Board, 1973-75, and National Education Advisory Committee and vice director of Southeast Region of Statue of Liberty—Ellis Island Foundation, 1985-86. Consultant, Education Development Center, 1975—, Department of Health, Education and Welfare, 1977-79, Ford Foundation, 1977-78, National Research Council, 1979-80, and Grolier, Inc., 1979-82. Member of National Education Advisory Committee, Commission on the Bicentennial of the Constitution, 1987-92.

MEMBER: National Book Critics Circle, Authors League of America, Authors Guild, New York Urban League, 100 Black Men, Civitas, Phi Beta Kappa, Kappa Alpha Psi.

AWARDS, HONORS: Notable children's book in the field of social studies citations from *Social Education,* 1971, for *Revolutionaries: Agents of Change,* from *Social Studies,* 1972, for *Resistance: Profiles in Nonviolence* and *Profiles in Black Power,* and 1973, for *A Piece of the Power: Four Black Mayors,* from National Council for the Social Studies—Children's Book Council book review committee, 1975, for *Fighting Shirley Chisholm,* and 1976, for *The Creoles of Color of New Orleans* and *The Picture Life of Malcolm X,* and from Children's Book Council, 1978, for *The Life and Death of Martin Luther King, Jr.;* World Book Year Book literature for children citation, 1973, for *From Lew Alcindor to Kareem Abdul Jabbar;* Books of the Year citations, Child Study Association of America, 1974, for *Adam Clayton Powell: Portrait of a Marching Black* and *Street Gangs: Yesterday and Today;* Books for Brotherhood bibliography citation, National Council of Christians and Jews book review committee, 1975, for *Adam Clayton Powell;* Spur Award finalist, Western Writers of America, 1975, for *The Creoles of Color of New Orleans;* Coretta Scott King Award, and children's choice citation, Children's Book Council, both 1977, both for *The Story of Stevie Wonder;* Carter G. Woodson Outstanding Merit Award, National Council for the Social Studies, 1980, for *James Van DerZee: The Picture Takin' Man;* Deems Taylor Award, American Society of Composers, Authors and Publishers, 1980, for *Scott Joplin: The Man Who Made Ragtime;* Ambassador of Honor Book, English-Speaking Union Books-Across-the-Sea, 1983, for *Bricktop;* Coretta Scott King honorable mention, 1984, for *Lena Horne;* American Library Association (ALA) best book for young adults citation, 1987, and Carter G. Woodson Award, 1988, both for *Black Music in America: A History through Its People;* Alabama Library Association best juvenile work citation, 1987, for "Count Your Way" series; Coretta Scott King honor book, 1991, for *Black Dance in America: A History through Its People;* Carter G. Woodson Award, 1994, for *The March on Washington; Washington Post*/Children's Book Guild award, 1994, for body of work in nonfiction for young people; "Bicentennial Reading, Viewing, Listening for Young Americans" selections, ALA and National Endowment for the Humanities, for *Street Gangs, Ralph Bunche: A Most Reluctant Hero,* and *A Piece of the Power;* certificate of appreciation, Joseph P. Kennedy Foundation, for work with Special Olympics.

WRITINGS:

JUVENILE

Resistance: Profiles in Nonviolence, Doubleday (New York City), 1970.

Revolutionaries: Agents of Change, Lippincott (Philadelphia), 1971.

The War and the Protest: Vietnam, Doubleday, 1971.

Religions, Lippincott, 1971, revised edition as *Religions of the World,* Hippocrene (New York City), 1991.

Witchcraft, Mysticism and Magic in the Black World, Doubleday, 1974.

Street Gangs: Yesterday and Today, Hastings House (New York City), 1974.

Jobs in Business and Office, Lothrop (New York City), 1974.

The Creoles of Color of New Orleans, Crowell (New York City), 1975.

The Consumer Movement, F. Watts (New York City), 1975.

Who Are the Handicapped?, Doubleday, 1978.

(With J. M. Stifle) *The Quiet Revolution: The Struggle for the Rights of Disabled Americans,* Crowell, 1979.

The New Americans: Vietnamese Boat People, Enslow Pubs. (Hillside, NJ), 1980.

Black Theatre in America, Crowell, 1982.

The New Americans: Cuban Boat People, Enslow Pubs., 1982.

The Guardian Angels, Enslow Pubs., 1983.

(With David A. Walker) *Double Dutch,* Enslow Pubs., 1986.

Black Music in America: A History through Its People, Crowell, 1987.

(With Kathleen Benson) *The Sixties Reader,* Viking (New York City), 1988.

India under Indira and Rajiv Gandhi, Enslow Pubs., 1989.

Black Dance in America: A History through Its People, Crowell, 1990.

(With Rosa Parks) *The Autobiography of Rosa Parks,* Dial (New York City), 1990.

The Methodists, Hippocrene, 1992.

The March on Washington, introduction by James Farmer, HarperCollins (New York City), 1993.

(Reteller) *The Headless Haunt and Other African-American Ghost Stories,* illustrated by Ben Otera, HarperCollins, 1994.

Freedom Rides, Hyperion (Westport, CT), 1994.

(With Joann Biondi) *From Afar to Zulu: A Dictionary of African Cultures,* Walker, 1995.

JUVENILE BIOGRAPHIES

From Lew Alcindor to Kareem Abdul Jabbar, Lothrop, 1972.

A Piece of the Power: Four Black Mayors, Dial, 1972.

Profiles in Black Power, Doubleday, 1972.

Deep Like the Rivers: A Biography of Langston Hughes, 1902-1967, Holt (New York City), 1973.

Adam Clayton Powell: Portrait of a Marching Black, Dial, 1974.

Babe Ruth and Hank Aaron: The Home Run Kings, Lothrop, 1974.

Fighting Shirley Chisholm, Dial, 1975.

The Picture Life of Malcolm X, F. Watts, 1975.

Dr. J: A Biography of Julius Irving, Doubleday, 1975.

Pele: A Biography, Doubleday, 1976.

The Story of Stevie Wonder, Doubleday, 1976.

Always Movin' On: The Life of Langston Hughes, F. Watts, 1976, revised edition, Africa World Press (Trenton, NJ), 1992.

Barbara Jordan, Dial, 1977.

The Life and Death of Martin Luther King, Jr., Lothrop, 1977.

George McGinnis: Basketball Superstar, Hastings House, 1978.

Bob McAdoo: Superstar, Lothrop, 1978.

Andrew Young: Man with a Mission, Lothrop, 1979.

I'm Gonna Make You Love Me: The Story of Diana Ross, Dial, 1980.

"Magic": A Biography of Earvin Johnson, Enslow Pubs., 1981.

Katherine Dunham, Coward-McCann, 1982.

Sugar Ray Leonard, Lothrop, 1982.

Donna Summer, Atlantic Monthly Press, 1983.

About Michael Jackson, Enslow Pubs., 1985.

Diana Ross: Star Supreme, Viking, 1985.

Leaders of the Middle East, Enslow Pubs., 1985.

Corazon Aquino: Leader of the Philippines, Enslow Pubs., 1988.

The Magic Johnson Story, Enslow Pubs., 1988.

Shirley Temple Black: From Actress to Ambassador, illustrated by Donna Ruff, Puffin Books (New York City), 1988.

Sports Great Magic Johnson, Enslow Pubs., 1989, revised and expanded edition, 1992.

Thurgood Marshall: A Life for Justice, Holt, 1992.

Colin Powell: A Biography, Scholastic Inc. (New York City), 1992.

I am Somebody! A Biography of Jesse Jackson, Enslow Pubs., 1992.

The Scottsboro Boys, Holt, 1994.

JUVENILE; UNDER NAME JIM HASKINS

Jokes from Black Folks, Doubleday, 1973.

Ralph Bunche: A Most Reluctant Hero, Hawthorne (New York City), 1974.

Your Rights, Past and Present: A Guide for Young People, Hawthorne, 1975.

Teen-Age Alcoholism, Hawthorne, 1976.

The Long Struggle: The Story of American Labor, Westminster (Philadelphia), 1976.

Real Estate Careers, F. Watts, 1978.

Gambling—Who Really Wins, F. Watts, 1978.

James Van DerZee: The Picture Takin' Man, illustrated by James Van DerZee, Dodd (New York City), 1979.

(With Pat Connolly) *The Child Abuse Help Book,* Addison Wesley (Reading, MA), 1981.

Werewolves, Lothrop, 1982.

(Editor) *The Filipino Nation,* three volumes, Grolier (Danbury, CT), 1982.

(With Stifle) *Donna Summer: An Unauthorized Biography,* Little, Brown (Boston), 1983.

(With Benson) *Space Challenger: The Story of Guion Bluford, an Authorized Biography,* Carolrhoda (Minneapolis, MN), 1984.

Break Dancing, Lerner Publications (Minneapolis, MN), 1985.

The Statue of Liberty: America's Proud Lady, Lerner, 1986.

Bill Cosby: America's Most Famous Father, Walker, 1988.

(With Helen Crothers) *Scatman: An Authorized Biography of Scatman Crothers,* Morrow (New York City), 1991.

Christopher Columbus: Admiral of the Ocean Sea, Scholastic, 1991.

Outward Dreams: Black Inventors and Their Inventions, Walker, 1991.

I Have a Dream: The Life and Words of Martin Luther King, Millbrook Press, 1992.

The Day Martin Luther King, Jr. Was Shot: A Photo History of the Civil Rights Movement, Scholastic, 1992.

Amazing Grace: The Story Behind the Song, Millbrook Press, 1992.

Against All Opposition: Black Explorers in America, Walker, 1992.

One More River to Cross: The Story of Twelve Black Americans, Scholastic, 1992.

Get On Board: The Story of the Underground Railroad, Scholastic, 1993.

Black Eagles: African Americans in Aviation, Scholastic, 1995.

The Day They Fired on Fort Sumter, Scholastic, 1995.

"COUNT YOUR WAY" SERIES; UNDER NAME JIM HASKINS

Count Your Way through China, illustrated by Martin Skoro, Carolrhoda, 1987.

Count Your Way through Japan, Carolrhoda, 1987.

Count Your Way through Russia, Carolrhoda, 1987.

Count Your Way through the Arab World, illustrated by Skoro, Carolrhoda, 1987.

Count Your Way through Mexico, illustrations by Helen Byers, Carolrhoda, 1989.

Count Your Way through Canada, illustrations by Steve Michaels, Carolrhoda, 1989.

Count Your Way through Africa, illustrations by Barbara Knutson, Carolrhoda, 1989.

Count Your Way through Korea, illustrations by Dennis Hockerman, Carolrhoda, 1989.

Count Your Way through Israel, illustrations by Rick Hanson, Carolrhoda, 1990.

Count Your Way through India, illustrations by Liz Brenner Dodson, Carolrhoda, 1990.

Count Your Way through Italy, illustrations by Beth Wright, Carolrhoda, 1990.

Count Your Way through Germany, illustrations by Byers, Carolrhoda, 1990.

NONFICTION; UNDER NAME JIM HASKINS

Diary of a Harlem School Teacher, Grove (New York City), 1969, 2nd edition, Stein & Day (Briarcliff Manor, NY), 1979.

(Editor) *Black Manifesto for Education,* Morrow, 1973.

(With Hugh F. Butts) *The Psychology of Black Language,* Barnes & Noble (New York City), 1973, enlarged edition, Hippocrene, 1993.

Snow Sculpture and Ice Carving, Macmillan (New York City), 1974.

The Cotton Club, Random House (New York City), 1977, 2nd edition, New American Library (New York City), 1984, revised edition, Hippocrene, 1994.

(With Benson and Ellen Inkelis) *The Great American Crazies,* Condor Publishing (Ashland, MA), 1977.

Voodoo and Hoodoo: Their Tradition and Craft as Revealed by Actual Practitioners, Stein & Day, 1978.

(With Benson) *The Stevie Wonder Scrapbook,* Grosset & Dunlap, 1978.

Richard Pryor, a Man and His Madness: A Biography, Beaufort Books (New York City), 1984.

Queen of the Blues: A Biography of Dinah Washington, Morrow, 1987.

NONFICTION; UNDER NAME JAMES HASKINS

Pinckney Benton Stewart Pitchback: A Biography, Macmillan, 1973.

A New Kind of Joy: The Story of the Special Olympics, Doubleday, 1976.

(With Benson) *Scott Joplin: The Man Who Made Ragtime,* Doubleday, 1978.

(With Benson) *Lena: A Personal and Professional Biography of Lena Horne,* Stein & Day, 1983.

(With Bricktop) *Bricktop,* Atheneum (New York City), 1983.

(With Benson) *Nat King Cole,* Stein & Day, 1984, updated and revised edition, Scarborough House, 1990.

Mabel Mercer: A Life, Atheneum, 1988.

Winnie Mandela: Life of Struggle, Putnam (New York City), 1988.

Mr. Bojangles: The Biography of Bill Robinson, Morrow, 1988.

(With Lionel Hampton) *Hamp: An Autobiography* (with discography), Warner Books (New York City), 1989, revised edition, Amistad Press, 1993.

(With Benson) *Nat King Cole: A Personal and Professional Biography*, Scarborough House, 1990.

(With Joann Biondi) *Hippocrene U.S.A. Guide to the Historic Black South: Historical Sites, Cultural Centers, and Musical Happenings of the African-American South*, Hippocrene, 1993.

(With Biondi) *Hippocrene U.S.A. Guide to Black New York*, Hippocrene, 1994.

OTHER

Editor of Hippocrene's "Great Religions of the World" series. Contributor to books, including *Children and Books*, 4th edition, 1976; Emily Mumford, *Understanding Human Behavior in Health and Illness*, 1977; *New York Kid's Catalog*, 1979; *Notable American Women Supplement*, 1979; Jerry Brown, *Clearings in the Thicket: An Alabama Humanities Reader*, 1985; and *Author in the Kitchen*.

Contributor of articles and reviews to periodicals, including *American Visions, Now, Arizona English Bulletin, Rolling Stone, Children's Book Review Service, Western Journal of Black Studies, Elementary English, Amsterdam News, New York Times Book Review, Afro-Hawaii News*, and *Gainesville Sun*.

ADAPTATIONS: Diary of a Harlem Schoolteacher has been recorded by Recordings for the Blind; *The Cotton Club* inspired Francis Ford Coppola's film of the same name, produced by Orion in 1984.

SIDELIGHTS: Born in the rural South at a time when African Americans did not receive the full rights of American citizenship, James S. Haskins absorbed the hard realities of life around him, translated them into a fascination with fact, and, as an adult, became the author of over 100 works of nonfiction. "It has always seemed to me that truth is not just 'stranger than fiction,' but also more interesting," Haskins explained in an essay for *Something about the Author Autobiography Series (SAAS)*. Haskins also cites the desire to provide information as another reason for writing only nonfiction, and further explains his commitment to facts by writing: "I was born into a society in which blacks were in deep trouble if they forgot about the real world. For if they daydreamed and were caught off-guard, they could pay dearly."

Demopolis, Alabama, in 1941, the year of Haskins's birth, was a segregated community. Because there were no adequate medical facilities for African Americans, Haskins was born at home, where, appropriately, he locates the literary lessons of his early childhood. Haskins recalled for *SAAS* that a strong tradition of storytelling existed in his family and among his relatives. "My Aunt Cindy was the greatest storyteller who ever lived," he declared, describing her mixed-up versions of traditional folktales as ones in which Hansel and Gretel meet the Three Little Pigs. Haskins credits these stories with stimulating an interest in the unseen, complex "goings on under the surface of the real world." Among these interests was Voodoo, which the Haskins family regarded with skepticism, but which was a real part of everyday life for many people in the black community. Like other interests he developed as child, Haskins continued to think about the belief and practice of such mysticism, and later wrote a book about the subject.

Once he began reading, however, Haskins encountered obstacles to the pursuit of his interests. "There was not a lot of money for books, and the Demopolis Public Library was off limits to blacks," Haskins remembered in *SAAS*. His mother managed to get him an encyclopedia, one volume at a time, from a local supermarket. This constituted the majority of his reading, until a white woman for whom his mother worked learned of his interest in books. With access to the library, the woman checked out books for Haskins once a week, which she passed along through his mother. In this way, Haskins was able to read a wide assortment of fiction. "I enjoyed these stories," Haskins noted in *SAAS*, "but since my first major reading was the encyclopedia, this is probably another reason why I prefer nonfiction."

Haskins attended a segregated elementary school. The district did not have the most recent textbooks or best sports equipment, but, Haskins points out, there was an atmosphere of respect between teachers and students that transcended the limits of the environment. Because teaching was the highest profession African Americans had entry to at the time, they were greatly respected in black community. They "earned that respect," Haskins reasoned in *SAAS*, "by caring about their students as if it were their mission in life to educate us." In particular, Haskins's teachers departed from standard lessons and emphasized African-American contributions to American history. "In fact, if my teachers had followed the official curriculum, I would have grown up thinking that blacks had never done anything in the history of the world except be slaves," he wrote. "But they taught us that there had been many important black heroes in history."

As a teenager, Haskins and his mother moved to Boston, where he was admitted to the prestigious Boston Latin School. While attending school with a majority of white students was a new experience for Haskins, he quickly made the adjustment, and did well academically. After graduating from high school, Haskins decided to return to Alabama to attend Alabama State University in Montgomery. Haskins admitted in his autobiographical essay to being somewhat lonely in Boston, and he wanted once again to be surrounded by people like himself. He drew additional incentive to return to Alabama from the recent activities of the civil rights movement, which had its roots in that state.

As Haskins explained, the protests began over the segregation of Montgomery city buses, and gained such momentum that leaders of the cause formed the Montgomery Improvement Association to unite African Americans on issues of common concern. A young Martin Luther King Jr. was chosen to head the association, and his charismatic leadership attracted Haskins and others to Montgomery to take part in the struggle for equal rights for all. Haskins contacted King shortly after his enrollment at Alabama State. The young student was soon "putting leaflets under doors in the dormitories at Alabama State and stuffing envelopes and doing other fairly innocent tasks," he recalled in *SAAS*. Even this level of activism, however, was met with opposition by the university administration, and when Haskins was arrested for marching on downtown Montgomery, he was expelled from Alabama State.

Haskins then went to Georgetown University in Washington, D.C., where he graduated with a bachelor's degree in psychology in 1960. In the years since his expulsion from Alabama State, public sentiment toward the civil rights movement had improved, and Haskins returned to Montgomery to pick up the work he had left behind. Haskins also returned to Alabama State, where he earned a second bachelor's degree, this time in history. Haskins continued his education at the University of New Mexico, earning a graduate degree in social psychology.

Haskins worked for a time in New York City at the brokerage house of Smith Barney & Co. as a stock trader, but found that he wasn't quite satisfied with his career. "And then, gradually, it dawned on me that what I wanted to be was like the people who had made the strongest impression on me," Haskins commented in his *SAAS* essay, "and those people were teachers." Haskins took a job teaching special education at Public School 92 in Harlem. His students were challenged by a variety of handicaps, he noted, but most simply lacked the kind of supportive environment necessary to develop as individuals. Haskins undertook a variety of alternative teaching methods, including bringing newspapers to class for his students to read in place of outdated textbooks, and taking his students on learning excursions outside school.

"While I could not do much about their home lives, I worried about my students constantly and wondered what kind of future awaited them," Haskins confessed in his *SAAS* essay. He shared his concerns with friends and associates, and one, a social worker named Fran Morill, suggested that he keep a record of his feelings. She gave him

a diary, and Haskins kept a daily journal of his experiences at P.S. 92. The result was Haskins's first publication, *Diary of a Harlem School Teacher*. Ronald Gross of the *New York Times Book Review* characterized the work as "plain, concrete, unemotional, and unliterary. . . . By its truthfulness alone does it command our concern. The book is like a weapon—cold, blunt, painful."

Following the publication of *Diary of a Harlem School Teacher*, Haskins was approached by publishers who wondered if he might be interested in writing books for children. "I knew exactly the kind of books I wanted to do—books about current events and books about important black people so that students could understand the larger world around them through books written at a level they could understand," Haskins told *SAAS*.

Published in 1970, *Resistance: Profiles in Nonviolence* was Haskins' first book for children. With this work Haskins tried to place nonviolence in a historical context culminating in, but not exclusive to, Martin Luther King, Jr. Shortly after *Resistance,* Haskins published *A Piece of the Power: Four Black Mayors,* which chronicles the political successes of Carl Stokes, Richard Hatcher, Charles Evers, and Kenneth Gibson. In addition to telling how these men began their careers and ultimately came to hold power, "James Haskins tells us something about what happens next and it is interesting and useful information," asserted Fred and Lucille Clifton in the *New York Times Book Review.* A *Kirkus Reviews* writer took issue, however, with the fact that the book provides little guidance to the complex issues surrounding the men profiled, calling the work "competent but totally non-interpretive."

In 1975 Haskins published another work with an historical emphasis, *The Creoles of Color of New Orleans.* In this book Haskins examines the culture of Louisiana's Creoles, a mixed population of African-American descent which was exempt from slavery. In the absence of any definitive political freedom, the Creoles embraced the values of slave-owning whites, and set themselves up in differentiation and opposition to black slaves. In an *Interracial Books for Children Bulletin,* Patricia Spence credited Haskins for dealing openly with the prejudices of the Creoles, but faulted him for failing to locate Creoles in the larger context of a racially segregated society: "Such a framework is necessary to foster understanding of the Creole's value system as the product of a racist environment." *The Creoles of Color of New Orleans* attracted the attention of other readers and critics, and was selected as a Spur Award finalist by the Western Writers of America.

In *Street Gangs: Yesterday and Today* Haskins studies the history of organized violence among adolescents and teenagers to explain the gang culture which absorbs so many young Americans. Haskins concludes that gang membership brings a sense of inclusion and a feeling of worth that is otherwise lacking in the gang member's life. This has been true, he claims, throughout American history. "The strength of Haskins' book is in its historical material," wrote Colman McCarthy in a *Washington Post Book World* review. McCarthy notes, in particular, the descriptions of street gangs that formed in the new states following the revolutionary war, and the notorious Bowery Boys of nineteenth-century New York City. In a *Bulletin of the Center for Children's Books* review, Zena Sutherland praised the "strong direct prose" of *Street Gangs,* and credited the book with linking the problems of contemporary youth to the past. For the insight it provided into a disturbing aspect of American urban life, *Street Gangs* received a Books of the Year citation from the Child Study Association of America.

Haskins has, since 1970, taught writing and lectured on literature for young readers at several colleges and universities. Haskins began teaching at this level at the New School for Social Research, in New York City. He then taught at Staten Island Community College of the City University of New York, Indiana University—Purdue University in Indianapolis, and the State University of New York at New Paltz. In 1977, Haskins assumed his current post as a professor of English at the University of Florida in Gainesville. Commenting on the development of his career in his *SAAS* essay, Haskins observed that he really has two careers. Teaching is Haskins' primary career, while writing remains a fascinating sideline that allows him to simultaneously pursue his own interests, and share them with others.

In 1977 Haskins published an adult book, *The Cotton Club,* an in-depth account of a night club in Harlem that showcased African-American entertainers for a white audience during the 1920s. Among the luminaries that performed in this segregated setting were Cab Calloway, Lena Horne, and Duke Ellington. In the *New York Times Book Review,* Jervis Anderson concluded that the *Cotton Club* "memorializes that Harlem nightspot—one of the classiest joints in the history of New York late-night entertainment. It is a detailed, instructive and entertaining work." *The Cotton Club* inspired a 1984 movie of the same name. Although the melodramatic film departed greatly from Haskins's book, he was invited to visit the movie set, and also met the actors and actresses who starred in the film. "I even got a director's chair with my name on it," he recalled fondly in *SAAS,* "though I had nothing really to do with the movie."

Among Haskins's more recent historical works for young readers is *The Sixties Reader,* which he co-wrote with Kathleen Benson. The reader is an attempt to present some of the major social movements of the 1960s through documentary evidence, with little interpretation. In a

Voice of Youth Advocates review of the book, Patrick Jones compared it to other works which deal with the same period for young readers, pointing out that the strength of *The Sixties Reader* is a reliance on fact and a desire to present information rather than anecdotes. "The book is a starting point," Jones wrote. "Each of the chapters focuses on a movement, then important documents, statements, lyrics, or interviews are presented." This allows readers to appreciate not only the events of the period, but how those events were shaped in the minds of those present, concluded Jones.

As a writer, Haskins has a professed interest in biography. "It seemed to me that young people ought to have some living black heroes to read about," he noted in *SAAS,* "and because of the gains made by black people there were more black heroes to write about." Haskins was reluctant at first to write about African-American sports stars, however, because he felt that children needed role models other than athletes. But when professional baseball player Hank Aaron was on the verge of breaking Babe Ruth's career mark for home runs, Haskins noticed a debate emerging over who was the better athlete and the better person. Inspired by the need for fairness in this dialogue, Haskins wrote his first sports biography, *Babe Ruth and Hank Aaron: The Home Run Kings.* Several other sports biographies followed, and they have been among Haskins's more popular works, a fact the writer has come to accept. "I realized that it doesn't matter so much *what* kids read as it does *that* they read," he proclaimed.

Among Haskins's later sports biographies is *Sports Great Magic Johnson.* From high school championships in Lansing, Michigan, to professional championships with the Los Angeles Lakers, basketball superstar Earvin "Magic" Johnson has a remarkable record of winning. Well before the emergence of Michael Jordan as the dominant player in the National Basketball Association (NBA), critics and fans hailed Magic Johnson as the greatest player ever to play the game. In a *School Library Journal* review, Tom S. Hurlbut characterized Haskins's work as straightforward, and noted that Johnson's personal and family life are covered, "keeping the biography focused on the person rather than just the athlete." In 1992 Haskins updated the volume to reflect the emergence of Johnson, who is infected with HIV, as an activist in the fight against AIDS.

Haskins has also written biographies of entertainment celebrities as well. To research *The Story of Stevie Wonder,* Haskins traveled to Los Angeles to spend a couple of days with the musician. "He made music all the time and everywhere," Haskins recalled of Wonder in *SAAS,* "beating on the table with a fork or making rhythms with his feet on the steps." Haskins has also written a biography of pop superstar Michael Jackson. In *About Michael Jackson,* Haskins provides a glimpse of the childhood and personal life of the intensely private and reclusive star. In a *Voice of Youth Advocates* review, Jerry Grim wrote that although he found the writing "trite" in places, "the artist comes out looking like a human being and not a two-dimensional poster." Hurlbut's *School Library Journal* review of the book faulted Haskins, however, for skirting the more controversial issues of Jackson's life, including his plastic surgery and family difficulties, saying they are "only dealt with in passing."

Haskins's biography of Bill Cosby, *Bill Cosby: America's Most Famous Father,* attempts to reveal the early influences that gave direction to the comedian's life. "Young people will relate to the impatience with school that brought on bad grades and dropping out of high school," commented Luvada Kuhn in a *Voice of Youth Advocates* review. They will also respect the struggle Cosby faced to pass his GED (General Equivalency Diploma) test and go on to college, Kuhn concluded. In a *School Library Journal* review Todd Morning noted that Cosby's career is surveyed in detail, and credits Haskins for presenting the charge that "there is a certain amount of anger and arrogance beneath the affable surface" of the actor.

Haskins's recent profiles of blacks in positions of leadership include books about Jesse Jackson, Winnie Mandela, Colin Powell, and Thurgood Marshall. *I Am Somebody! A Biography of Jesse Jackson* tells of Jackson's childhood in rural Greenville, South Carolina, of the determination that led Jackson to succeed in sports and academics and win a college scholarship, of his rise to the forefront of the civil rights movement, and his eventual prominence among black political figures. Jeanette Lambert, in a *School Library Journal* review, called the book "incisive," and credited Haskins with providing a fair portrait of Jackson, in which both strengths and flaws of character are discussed "in a balanced manner." In a *Voice of Youth Advocates* review of *I Am Somebody,* Alice M. Johns appreciated Haskins's depiction of Jackson as a leader who increased his power and influence by helping "people to participate in full citizenship."

Winnie Mandela: Life of Struggle is similar to the Jackson biography in that its subject has been intimately involved in a civil rights struggle, this time in South Africa. Born in a remote village, Winnie Mandela became the first black medical social worker in South African history. In the process of her education she was introduced to the ideology of African nationalism, which she soon advocated. This advocacy became the determining factor in her life after her marriage to the former leader of the once-outlawed African National Congress, Nelson Mandela. After his imprisonment, Winnie continued to oppose apartheid and to keep the vision of a democratic South Africa alive. To promote her cause, Winnie has "endured police harassment, numerous arrests, physical mistreatment,

solitary confinement, and banishment to a community with a language different from her own," pointed out Virginia B. Moore in a *Voice of Youth Advocates* review, making for an "easy-to-read, fast-paced and gripping profile." In a *School Library Journal* review Nancy J. Schmidt praised Haskins's facility for connecting "Mandela's personal story with that of milestones in the black South African struggle." In the "moving" portrayal that results, Schmidt remarked, Mandela is both a person and the leader of a globally significant social movement.

Colin Powell takes a look at the life of the first African American to head the Joint Chiefs of Staff of the United States. Hazel Moore, in a *Voice of Youth Advocates* review, found the description of Powell's struggle to succeed academically sufficiently inspiring to recommend the book. "The person, more than the military leader, emerges from the portrait Haskins paints," she added. *Thurgood Marshall: A Life for Justice* follows a similar format, emphasizing Marshall's beginnings in the Civil Rights movement, then following him through his years as attorney to the National Association for the Advancement of Colored People (NAACP), and finally, to the bench of the United States Supreme Court. In a *School Library Journal* review, Mary Mueller particularly appreciated the "discussion of the difference between Marshall's constitutional tactics and those used by the Direct Actions Civil Rights Movement, led by Martin Luther King, Jr."

Haskins returned to the subject of overall black contributions to history with *Against All Opposition: Black Explorers in America.* From the seafaring adventurers of the African nation of Mali in the 1300s, to the Arctic travels of Matthew Henson, and the experiences of astronauts Ronald McNair and Guion Stewart Bluford, Jr., Haskins sheds light on accomplishments which racism has suppressed. In *Voice of Youth Advocates,* Diane Yankelevitz found the work informative, but asserted that the specificity that makes the work valuable as a reference prevents it from being "very interesting as general reading." A similar work, *Get on Board: The Story of the Underground Railroad,* recounts the history of the network of abolitionists and free African-American men and women who helped escaped slaves flee north. In addition to describing the organization and structure of the railroad, the roles played by the "conductors," who provided safe passage, and the "stationmasters," who provided shelter, Haskins includes accounts from men and women who "rode" the railroad to freedom. "Although the firsthand stories are interesting on their own, the book is not successful" because of its organization, wrote Elizabeth M. Reardon in a *School Library Journal* review. A reviewer for *Chicago Tribune Books* concluded, however, that the book was successful in evoking the "significant" courage of those involved, especially the fugitives themselves.

Haskins captures one of the greatest days of the Civil Rights movement in *The March on Washington.* Haskins points out that a nonviolent march on Washington, D.C., had been proposed as early as 1941 by labor organizer A. Phillip Randolph, but it was not until 1963, after enormous coordination and compromise, that 250,000 people marched from the Washington Monument to the Lincoln Memorial. While the nation watched, Martin Luther King, Jr., delivered his famous "I Have a Dream" speech. Haskins also goes into the planning and logistics of the march, from provisions for sanitation and food to the clean-up following one of the country's largest public demonstrations. Offering high praise in a *Booklist* review, Sheilamae O'Hara wrote, "the narrative is eminently readable as a story of what may be regarded as one of the great days in American history." Similarly, Judy Silverman remarked in a *Voice of Youth Advocates* review that "Haskins manages to make this history come very much alive." "Haskins provides a lucid, in-depth, and moving study of the 1963 March on Washington for jobs and freedom," Helen Fader declared in a *Horn Book* review.

Haskins often uses his credibility as a writer to support personal causes, such as the restoration of the Statue of Liberty. It is his writing for children, however, that Haskins gives greatest importance. In his *SAAS* essay he wrote: "Most of my books are about black subjects—black history, black people. Partly that's because I remember being a child and not having many books about black people to read. I want children today, black and white, to be able to find books about black people and black history in case they want to read them. . . . And when, some day, the missing second date after that '1941-' gets filled in, I will know that I have not only done something worthwhile in the years between, but also that I have had a good time doing it."

BIOGRAPHICAL/CRITICAL SOURCES:

BOOKS

Brown, Jerry, *Clearings in the Thicket: An Alabama Humanities Reader,* Mercer University Press (Macon, GA), 1985.
Children's Literature Review, Volume 3, Gale (Detroit), 1978, pp. 63-69.
Something About the Author Autobiography Series, Volume 4, Gale, 1987, pp. 197-209.

PERIODICALS

Booklist, September 15, 1974, p. 100; January 1, 1977, p. 666; July 15, 1979, p. 1618; January 15, 1983, p. 676; September 1, 1984, p. 65; February 15, 1992, p. 1097; May 15, 1993, p. 1691.
Bulletin of the Center for Children's Books, January, 1975, p. 78; September, 1983, p. 9; June, 1988, p. 205; July, 1988, p. 229.
Christian Science Monitor, March 12, 1970, p. 9; February 21, 1990, p. 13.
Horn Book, August, 1993, pp. 477-478.
Interracial Books for Children Bulletin, Volume 7, No. 5, 1976, pp. 12-13.
Kirkus Reviews, June 1, 1972, p. 631; May 1, 1974, p. 492; June 15, 1979, p. 692; August 1, 1979, p. 862; November 1, 1984, p. 1036; April 15, 1988, p. 618.
Los Angeles Times Book Review, July 24, 1983, p. 8; March 11, 1984, p. 9; January 20, 1985, p. 6; July 17, 1988, p. 10; February 23, 1992, p. 10.
New York Times Book Review, February 8, 1970, pp. 6-7; May 7, 1972, Part 2, p. 30; May 5, 1974, p. 22; August 4, 1974, p. 8; November 20, 1977, pp. 13, 58; September 23, 1979, p. 26; October 7, 1979, p. 34; January 25, 1981, p. 31; March 4, 1984; May 17, 1987, p. 51; September 13, 1987, p. 48; February 28, 1988, p. 21; June 26, 1988, p. 45.
School Library Journal, January, 1986, pp. 67-68; June-July, 1988, p. 111; June-July, 1988, p. 123; July, 1989, pp. 85-86; August, 1992, p. 181; February, 1993, p. 98.
Times Literary Supplement, May 24, 1985, p. 583.
Tribune Books (Chicago), February 14, 1993, p. 5.
Voice Literary Supplement, October, 1988, p. 5.
Voice of Youth Advocates, February, 1986, p. 40; August, 1988, p. 146; April, 1989, p. 58; June, 1992, p. 125; August, 1992, p. 188; December, 1992, pp. 300-301; August, 1993, p. 177.
Washington Post Book World, November 10, 1974, p. 8; February 5, 1978, p. G4; September 11, 1977, p. E6; August 17, 1983; December 9, 1984, p. 15; January 16, 1985; May 10, 1987; May 13, 1990, p. 17; September 1, 1991, p. 13.

*   *   *

HASKINS, Jim
See HASKINS, James S.

*   *   *

HASTINGS, (Macdonald) Max   1945-

PERSONAL: Born December 28, 1945, in London, England; son of Macdonald (a writer) and Anne (a writer; maiden name, Scott-James) Hastings; married Patricia Mary Edmondson, May 27, 1972; children: Charles, Charlotte, Harry. *Education:* Attended University College, Oxford, 1964-65. *Religion:* Church of England. *Avocational interests:* Shooting, fishing.

ADDRESSES: Home—Guilsborough Lodge, Guilsborough, Northamptonshire, England. *Office*—*Daily Telegraph,* South Quay Plaza, London E14, England. *Agent*—A. D. Peters, 10 Buckingham St., London WC1, England.

CAREER: British Broadcasting Corp. (BBC), London, researcher for television historical documentaries, 1963-64; *Evening Standard,* London, reporter, 1965-67, foreign correspondent, 1968-70; BBC, current affairs commentator for television program *Twenty-Four Hours* (covering southeast Asia, the Middle East, southern Africa, China, and India), 1970-73; freelance foreign correspondent for television and newspapers, 1973-86; *Daily Telegraph,* editor, 1986-89, director, 1989—, editor-in-chief, 1990—. Trustee, Game Conservancy, 1987—, Liddell-Hart Archives, 1988—. Member, Press Complaints Commission, 1991—. *Military service:* British Army, Parachute Regiment, 1963.

MEMBER: Beefsteak Club, Brooks's Club, Saintsbury Club.

AWARDS, HONORS: Fellowship from World Press Institute, 1967; British Press Award, 1973, for coverage of "Yom Kippur War," and 1980, 1982; Somerset Maugham Prize for nonfiction, 1980, for *Bomber Command: The British Bombing of Germany in World War II;* Journalist of the Year, 1982; Granada TV Reporter of the Year, 1982, for coverage of the Falklands War; *Yorkshire Post* Book of the Year Award, 1983, for *The Battle for the Falklands,* and 1989, for *Overlord: D-Day and the Battle for Normandy;* NCR Prize shortlist, 1987, for *The Korean War;* named Editor of the Year, 1988.

WRITINGS:

The Fire This Time: America in 1968, Taplinger (New York City), 1968.
Barricades in Belfast: The Struggle for Civil Rights in Northern Ireland, Taplinger, 1970.
Montrose: The King's Champion, Gollancz (London), 1977.
Yoni: The Hero of Entebbe, Dial (New York City), 1979.
Bomber Command: The British Bombing of Germany in World War II, Dial, 1979, reprint, Touchstone (New York City), 1989.
Game Book: Sporting around the World, M. Joseph (London), 1979.
(With Len Deighton) *The Battle of Britain,* Rainbird (London), 1980.
Das Reich: Resistance and the March of the 2nd Panzer Division through France, June 1944, M. Joseph, 1981, Holt (New York City), 1991.

The Shotgun, David & Charles (Newton Abbot, England), 1981.
(With Simon Jenkins) *The Battle for the Falklands,* Norton (New York City), 1983.
Overlord: D-Day and the Battle for Normandy, Simon & Schuster (New York City), 1984, 2nd edition, 1989.
(Editor) *The Oxford Book of Military Anecdotes,* Oxford University Press (Oxford, England), 1985.
Victory in Europe: D-Day to V-E Day, photographs by George Stevens, Little, Brown (Boston), 1985.
The Korean War, Simon & Schuster, 1987.
(Contributor) *The Daily Telegraph Record of the Second World War: Month by Month from 1939 to 1945,* Sidgwick & Jackson/Daily Telegraph (London), 1989.
(Editor) *Robert Churchill's Game Shooting: The Definitive Book on the Churchill Method of Instinctive Wingshooting for Game and Sporting Clays,* revised edition, Countrysport Press (Traverse City, MI), 1990.

Author of scripts for television reports and special programs, including *The Korean War,* BBC-TV, 1988. Contributor to various magazines, including *Field, Spectator, DNB, Country Life, Shooting Times,* and *Economist.* Columnist, London *Standard,* 1973—, and *Daily Express,* 1981-83.

SIDELIGHTS: Journalist and nonfiction writer Max Hastings has received much attention for his works of military history focusing on World War II, including *Bomber Command: The British Bombing of Germany in World War II, Das Reich: Resistance and the March of the 2nd Panzer Division through France, June 1944,* and *Overlord: D-Day and the Battle for Normandy.* Perhaps best-known for his 1983 collaboration with Simon Jenkins, the political editor for the *Economist,* entitled *The Battle for the Falklands,* Hastings has won numerous awards not only for his writings, but also for his reporting both in print and for television.

Bomber Command: The British Bombing of Germany in World War II examines the British campaign of "area bombing" against German cities during World War II. Begun in 1940 when British intelligence saw no other way of defeating the quickly-advancing German forces, the Bomber Command's five-year air offensive resulted not only in the destruction of many German cities and the killing of some 600,000 German civilians, but also left over 50,000 British aircrew dead. Such casualties caused Geoffrey Wheatcroft in a *Spectator* review of *Bomber Command* to call the bombings "the greatest war crime of the Second World War." Although C. M. Woodhouse of the *Times Literary Supplement* faulted Hastings for what he termed "sometimes inadequate and sometimes misleading references," he pronounced *Bomber Command* "a brilliant *tour de force* for a man born after the events he describes." Michael Howard of the *New Republic* offered similar praise, calling the work "careful without being dull, vivid without being overwritten," and "popular history at its best."

Hastings' historical account *Das Reich: Resistance and the March of the 2nd Panzer Division through France, June 1944* garnered admiration from Woodhouse, who judged the "well-documented combination of oral history with documentary records" even "maturer than [*Bomber Command*]" because its author is "less passionately concerned to prove a thesis." In the *Spectator,* Richard Cobb noted that "some questions do remain unanswered in this crisp and enjoyable narrative," but Hastings displays a "skillful use of a series of personal case histories," by which he reduces "Hitler's *corps d'elite*" to "feasible persons rather than abstract machines."

Frequently touted as the best source to date written about the Falklands War, *The Battle for the Falklands* brought Hastings and coauthor Jenkins a prestigious award and generally favorable reviews. In Christopher Wain's assessment for the *Listener,* the account is "outstanding" in that it "pulls together the complex strands of the history of the dispute . . . and weaves them into a pattern which has few obvious flaws." According to *New York Times* reviewer Drew Middleton, who called the account "war correspondence in the great tradition of Bill Stoneman and Ernie Pyle," *The Battle for the Falklands* "probably will endure as the standard history of the campaign because of the happy combination of two authors, each a master in his field."

Neal Ascherson's opinion in the *Observer* was less glowing. He dubbed *The Battle for the Falklands* "a meticulous war history," but thought the book lacked Hastings' "natural bounce." He went on to accuse Hastings and Jenkins of often lapsing into a "three-piece-suit language," making them "sound as if they had just laid down high offices of state." In the consideration of Charles Carter in the *Los Angeles Times,* "the book is crammed with facts, coherently told and immensely aided by maps," but "the writing declines to merely competent." Carter complained that an "inherent weakness of such a book is its form, a journalistic effort relying partly on the statements of anonymous interviewees," but conceded that "the strength of this one is that the narrative is plausible and the conclusions are intelligent."

As for the interviews that Carter labeled a weakness, Robert Fox writing in the *Times Educational Supplement* believed that the Hastings and Simon report represents "the weightiest of the new books [on the Falklands War] in content and reputation." Specifically, Fox contended that Hastings "has carried out a *tour de force* in interviewing nearly every key commander from all three services" involved in the war. *Time* reviewer Donald Morrison also

lauded *The Battle for the Falklands,* describing it as "a poignant memorial," while Reid Beddow writing in the *Washington Post Book World* called it "a small gem of military and naval history."

In his review of *Overlord: D-Day and the Battle for Normandy,* Michael Carver wrote in the *Times Literary Supplement* that Hastings' book "combines serious historical and critical comment with brilliant reportage," bringing "both the arguments between higher commanders and the fighting on the battlefield itself to life more vividly than any previous books." Middleton, again writing in the *New York Times,* explained that the central theme of the book is "that whenever Allied troops met Germans on anything like equal terms, the Germans nearly always prevailed." Hastings explains that the German army represented one of the finest military forces the world has ever known. He warns that any future defense of Europe will need to look not to the Allied invasion of Normandy for a model, but to the resourceful defensive tactics of the German forces who fought "in the face of all the odds against them and in spite of their own demented Fuehrer." Such a no-nonsense approach led *Detroit News* reviewer Al Stark to conclude: "I began to see [Hastings' treatment of Normandy] for what it is, an unvarnished look at one of the greatest military missions of all time. . . . It is refreshing to find [a book] that describes Normandy straight up, with all the human failure, and still does not diminish the achievement."

BIOGRAPHICAL/CRITICAL SOURCES:

PERIODICALS

Chicago Tribune, December 23, 1987.

Detroit News, July 29, 1984.

Economist, November 14, 1981, p. 113.

Globe and Mail (Toronto), January 9, 1988.

Listener, April, 1979, p. 463; October 4, 1979; November 12, 1981, p. 580; March 3, 1983, p. 20.

London Review of Books, March 4, 1982, p. 20.

Los Angeles Times, August 21, 1983, p. 3.

Los Angeles Times Book Review, December 20, 1987.

New Republic, February 16, 1980, pp. 34-5.

New Statesman, February 21, 1969, p. 263; November 19, 1982.

Newsweek, November 25, 1985.

New York Times, July 6, 1983, p. C22; May 18, 1984, p. 23; November 14, 1987.

New York Times Book Review, August 1, 1982; November 29, 1987.

Observer, May 20, 1979, p. 37; February 13, 1983.

Spectator, February 26, 1977; September 29, 1979, pp. 18-21; May 8, 1982, pp. 19-20; March 12, 1983, p. 20.

Time, August 8, 1983, pp. 74-5.

Times (London), February 17, 1983; October 17, 1985; October 3, 1987.

Times Educational Supplement, March 4, 1983.

Times Literary Supplement, January 30, 1969, p. 103; June 18, 1970, p. 651; April 29, 1977, p. 519; December 14, 1979, p. 136; December 25, 1981, p. 1486; May 13, 1983; June 8, 1984, p. 634; May 17, 1985, p. 555; November 29, 1985; December 11, 1987.

Washington Post Book World, June 3, 1984; July 10, 1984; June 9, 1985; December 22, 1985; January 10, 1988.*

* * *

HASTINGS, Robert J. 1924-

PERSONAL: Born May 17, 1924, in Marion, IL; son of George E. (a miner) and Ruby (a housewife; maiden name, Gordon) Hastings; married Bessie Ruth Emling, April 1, 1945; children: Ruth Hastings Jessup, Nancy Hastings Schumacher, Timothy L. *Education:* Southern Illinois Normal University (now Southern Illinois University at Carbondale), B.A. (with honors), 1945, and graduate study; Southwestern Baptist Theological Seminary, B.D., 1948, Th.D., 1950.

ADDRESSES: Home—98 Laconwood, Springfield, IL 62703.

CAREER: Ordained Baptist minister, 1943; pastor of University Baptist church in Carbondale, IL, 1950-55, 1965-67; Southern Baptist Convention, Nashville, TN, assistant director of church finance, 1955-60; Kentucky Baptist Convention, Middletown, KY, director of stewardship, 1960-65; *Illinois Baptist,* Springfield, IL, editor, 1967-84; writer, 1984—. Storyteller on "Tinyburg Tales," a weekly program on WIBI-Radio. Lecturer at New Orleans Baptist Theological Seminary, Golden Gate Baptist Theological Seminary, Southwestern Baptist Theological Seminary, Midwestern Baptist Theological Seminary, Regents Park College, Oxford, London Bible College, and Spurgeon's College, as well as seminaries in Colombia, Chile, and Argentina; lecturer at Pacific Union College, Judson College (Elsah, IL), Southern Illinois University at Carbondale, Campbellsville College, Wayland Baptist College (now University), McKendree College, Hannibal-La Grange College, and Illinois State University.

MEMBER: National Association for the Preservation of Storytelling in America, Southern Baptist Press Association.

AWARDS, HONORS: Editorial advocacy award from Associated Church Press, 1970; award from Illinois State Historical Society, 1973, for *A Nickel's Worth of Skim Milk, We Were There,* and a series of photo-essays on Illinois churches; Billy Graham Evangelistic Association award for excellence in Christian journalism, 1974, for *A Nickel's Worth of Skim Milk;* award from Southern Baptist Historical Commission, 1976, for *We Were There;* D.Letters from Judson College (Elsah, IL), 1977.

WRITINGS:

Jesus Is Calling, privately printed, 1955.

Broadman Sermon Outlines, Broadman (Nashville, TN), 1960.

My Money and My God, Broadman, 1961.

A Word Fitly Spoken, Broadman, 1962.

The Christian Man's World, Brotherhood Commission (Memphis, TN), 1964.

The Christian Faith and Life, Broadman, 1965.

How to Manage Your Money, Broadman, 1965.

How to Live with Yourself, Broadman, 1966.

(Contributor) William S. Cannon, editor, *Everyday Five Minutes with God,* Broadman, 1967.

Take Heaven Now, Broadman, 1968.

Devotional Talks on Everyday Objects, Broadman, 1968.

Hastings' Illustrations, Broadman, 1971.

A Nickel's Worth of Skim Milk: A Boy's View of the Great Depression, Southern Illinois University Press (Carbondale, IL), 1972.

How I Write: A Manual for Beginning Writers, Broadman, 1973.

We Were There: An Illinois Oral History, Illinois Baptist State Association, 1976.

Just Folks from the Midwest, Broadman, 1979.

(Contributor) Jas. C. Barry, editor, *Award Winning Sermons,* Broadman, 1979.

How to Help Yourself, Broadman, 1981.

(Contributor) James Hightower, editor, *Illustrating the Gospel of Matthew,* Broadman, 1982.

Tinyburg Tales, Broadman, 1983.

Glorious Is Thy Name!, Broadman, 1986.

A Penny's Worth of Minced Ham: Another Look at the Great Depression, Southern Illinois University Press, 1986.

Tinyburg Revisited, Broadman, 1988.

The Answer Book for Writers and Storytellers, privately printed, 1991.

O Happy Day and Other Tinyburg Tales, Broadman, 1992.

The Station and Other Gems of Joy (booklet), privately printed, 1993.

Illinois Snapshots (booklet), Southern Illinois University Press, 1994.

Author of "Perspective," a column distributed by Kentucky Baptist Convention to Kentucky newspapers, 1964-65, and "A Letter from Home," syndicated by Illinois Baptist State Association to sixty newspapers in Illinois, 1973-79. Contributor to church publications. Author of short stories for radio.

WORK IN PROGRESS: "I continue to write about twenty-five short stories a year for radio."

SIDELIGHTS: Robert J. Hastings told *CA:* "Stories have fascinated me since I was a child. I made up stories for our own children while they were growing up.

"My two most popular books—*A Nickel's Worth of Skim Milk* and *A Penny's Worth of Minced Ham*—are collections of true stories about my boyhood written against the backdrop of the Great Depression. About 1974, the Christian Herald Family Bookshelf selected *Nickel* for its book club members and reprinted it in paperback.

"Around 1980, I started writing short fiction about a mythical village named Tinyburg, population 1,473, which I describe as 'the only city in the U.S. with an unlisted zip code.' As these proved popular with readers, I started telling them to church, club, and school groups. I continue to do so. The stories are very popular with senior adults but appeal to all ages, including children.

"My most widely reprinted piece is a three hundred-word essay, 'The Station.' Ann Landers gave the piece its first national exposure in her column and since then it has been reprinted three times, including in the June, 1988, issue of *Readers Digest.* ABC newscaster Paul Harvey read it on one of his shows, and it has continued to be reprinted in magazines, anthologies, and high school year books. Since it is so popular, I included it in *Penny* so it would have permanent cataloging."

*   *   *

HAWKING, S. W.
See HAWKING, Stephen W(illiam)

*   *   *

HAWKING, Stephen W(illiam) 1942-
S. W. Hawking

PERSONAL: Born January 8, 1942; son of Frank (a research biologist) and E. Isobel (a secretary) Hawking; married Jane Wilde (a linguist), 1965; children: Robert, Lucy, Timothy. *Education:* Oxford University, B.A., 1962; Cambridge University, Ph.D., 1966.

ADDRESSES: Office—Department of Applied Mathematics and Theoretical Physics, Cambridge University, Silver St., Cambridge CB3 9EW, England.

CAREER: Theoretical physicist. Cambridge University, Cambridge, England, research fellow at Gonville and Caius College, 1965-69, member of Institute of Theoretical Astronomy, 1968-72, research assistant at Institute of Astronomy, 1972-73, research assistant in department of applied mathematics and theoretical physics, 1973-75, reader in gravitational physics, 1977-79, Lucasian Professor of Mathematics, 1979—. Fairchild Distinguished Scholar at California Institute of Technology, 1974-75.

MEMBER: Royal Society of London (fellow), Pontifical Academy of Sciences, American Academy of Arts and Sciences, American Philosophical Society, Royal Astronomical Society of Canada (honorary member).

AWARDS, HONORS: Eddington Medal, Royal Astronomical Society, 1975; Pius IX Gold Medal, Pontifical Academy of Sciences, 1975; Dannie Heinemann Prize for mathematical physics, American Physical Society and American Institute of Physics, 1976; William Hopkins Prize, Cambridge Philosophical Society, 1976; Maxwell Medal, Institute of Physics, 1976; Hughes Medal, Royal Society of London, 1976; honorary fellow of University College, Oxford, 1977; Albert Einstein Award, Lewis and Rosa Strauss Memorial Fund, 1978; Albert Einstein Medal, Albert Einstein Society (Berne), 1979; Franklin Medal, Franklin Institute, 1981; Commander of the British Empire, 1982; honorary fellow of Trinity Hall, Cambridge, 1984; Royal Astronomical Society Gold Medal, 1985; Paul Dirac Medal and Prize, Institute of Physics, 1987; Wolf Foundation Prize for physics, 1988; named a Companion of Honour on the Queen's Birthday Honours List, 1989. Honorary degrees from various universities, including Oxford, 1978; Chicago, 1981; Leicester, Notre Dame, and Princeton, 1982; Newcastle and Leeds, 1987; and Tufts, Yale, and Cambridge, 1989.

WRITINGS:

A Brief History of Time: From the Big Bang to Black Holes, introduction by Carl Sagan, Bantam Books (New York City), 1988.
Black Holes and Baby Universes and Other Essays, Bantam Books, 1993.

ACADEMIC WRITINGS; UNDER NAME S. W. HAWKING

(With G. F. R. Ellis) *The Large Scale Structure of Space-Time,* Cambridge University Press (Cambridge, England), 1973.
(Editor with Werner Israel) *General Relativity: An Einstein Centenary Survey,* Cambridge University Press, 1979.
Is the End in Sight for Theoretical Physics? An Inaugural Lecture, Cambridge University Press, 1980.
(Editor with M. Rocek) *Superspace and Supergravity: Proceedings of the Nuffield Workshop, Cambridge, June 16-July 12, 1980,* Cambridge University Press, 1981.
(Editor with G. W. Gibbons and S. T. C. Siklos) *The Very Early Universe: Proceedings of the Nuffield Workshop,*

Cambridge, 21 June to 9 July 1982, Cambridge University Press, 1983.

(Editor with Gibbons and P. K. Townsend) *Supersymmetry and Its Applications: Superstrings, Anomalies, and Supergravity: Proceedings of a Workshop Supported by the Ralph Smith and Nuffield Foundations, Cambridge, 23 June to 14 July 1985,* Cambridge University Press, 1986.

(Editor with Werner Israel) *Three Hundred Years of Gravitation,* Cambridge University Press, 1987.

(Editor with Gibbons and T. Vachaspati) *The Formation and Evolution of Cosmic Strings; Proceedings of a Workshop supported by the SERC and held in Cambridge, 3-7 July, 1989,* Cambridge University Press, 1990.

OTHER

Author and editor of many articles for scientific journals. *A Brief History of Time: From the Big Bang to Black Holes* has been translated into over thirty languages.

ADAPTATIONS: Errol Morris directed a film version of *A Brief History of Time* for Anglia Television, 1991; *Black Holes and Baby Universes and Other Essays,* read by Simon Prebble, was adapted for audio cassette, Bantam, 1993.

SIDELIGHTS: "Where did the universe come from, and where is it going? Did the universe have a beginning, and if so, what happened *before* then? What is the nature of time? Will it ever come to an end?" These are the questions that absorb physicist Stephen W. Hawking, questions posed in his best-selling book, *A Brief History of Time.* Queries such as these drive the scientist towards his goal of helping to create a "Theory of Everything" (known to physicists as "TOE," or the "Grand Unification Theory," or "GUT"). Hawking believes that such an all-encompassing explanation may be worked out within the lifetime of many of his readers.

Hawking made it to University College, Oxford, when he was seventeen years old. He wanted to study mathematics and physics, but his father wanted him to go into biology (the senior Hawking felt that teaching would be the only opportunity in his son's future if he studied math). So Hawking compromised, taking chemistry in addition to physics. In *Black Holes and Baby Universes,* Hawking notes that, though he is now a professor of mathematics, he had no "formal instruction in mathematics since I left St. Albans school. . . . I have had to pick up what mathematics I know as I went along." The problem with biology, Hawking felt, was that it was not an exact enough science, like physics or math. Besides, he writes in *Black Holes and Baby Universes,* "it also had a rather low status at school. The brightest boys did mathematics and physics; the less bright did biology."

Hawking estimates he did about one thousand hours of work during his three years at Oxford, "an average of an hour a day," he tells Gene Stone in *Stephen Hawking's a Brief History of Time: A Reader's Companion* "I'm not proud of this lack of work, I'm just describing my attitude at the time, which I shared with most of my fellow students: an attitude of complete boredom and feeling that nothing was worth making an effort for." He didn't have many friends his first year or so; many of his classmates were older, having done national service before college. By his third year, though, Hawking was experiencing his happiest time at Oxford, discussing ideas and partying with friends, and rowing for the boat club.

When it came time to choose an academic specialty, Hawking was sure it would be physics, but his interests within physics lay in cosmology and elementary particles—the very large and the very small. He finally decided on cosmology, since that field was governed by Einstein's "General Theory of Relativity" (there was no comparable theory in elementary particles). Eventually, Hawking would pull these interests together again with his renowned theory about black holes.

Along with choosing his specialty came the sticky business of where to pursue that specialty. At Oxford, the program of study was set up so that the only examination was at the end of a student's three years of study. Hawking did not do well on his test, scoring on the borderline between a first and second class degree. This put him in the unenviable position of having to undergo an interview with the examiners so that they could decide which he should get. At one point in the interview, Hawking says in *Black Holes and Baby Universes,* "they asked my about my future plans. I replied that I wanted to do research. If they gave me a first, I would go to Cambridge. If I only got a second, I would stay in Oxford. They gave me a first."

Having earned his bachelor's degree from Oxford, Hawking went on to Cambridge to study for his doctorate. He took a break, however, to visit Iran with a friend. His mother recalls for Stone that while Hawking was there, a severe earthquake struck between Tehran and Tabriz. At the time, Hawking was riding a bus to Tabriz. Apparently the ride was so bumpy that neither he nor his friend noticed the earthquake, and no one told them it had occurred. Hawking's family waited anxiously for three weeks to hear from him. "He had been ill well before" the trip, his mother recalls, but "when he finally came home he looked very much worse for wear."

During his last year at Oxford, Hawking remembers in *Black Holes and Baby Universes,* "I seemed to be getting clumsier, and I fell over once or twice for no apparent reason." While he was at Cambridge, his mother noticed his problems, and the family ended up at a specialist who put Hawking in the hospital for tests. He remembers: "They took a muscle sample from my arm, stuck electrodes into me, injected some radio-opaque fluid into my spine, and watched it going up and down with X-rays as they tilted the bed." The diagnosis was amyotrophic lateral sclerosis (ALS) or motor neuron disease, known in the United States as Lou Gehrig's disease (named after the New York Yankee player who died of the illness in 1941).

Hawking was given two and one-half years to live. He gradually lost the use of his body as it deteriorated. The long-term prognosis was grim: eventually, only his lungs and heart would work. His brain, however, would be totally unaffected to the end. At first, Hawking was extremely depressed. He spent a lot of time listening to classical music by Richard Wagner, a longtime family favorite, and sitting in his room. "But," he asserts in *Black Holes and Baby Universes,* "reports in magazine articles that I drank heavily are an exaggeration." He also remembers having troubling dreams at that time. A couple of them made a tremendous impact on his outlook: "I dreamt that I was going to be executed. I suddenly realized that there were a lot of worthwhile things I could do if I were reprieved. Another dream that I had several times was that I would sacrifice my life to save others."

Just before being diagnosed, Hawking met Jane Wilde at a New Year's party. The two fell in love and got engaged. The scientist told Kitty Ferguson, in *Stephen Hawking: Quest for a Theory of Everything,* that "the engagement changed my life. It gave me something to live for. It made me determined to live. Without the help that Jane has given I would not have been able to carry on, nor would I have had the will to do so."

After an engagement during which they commuted between London and Cambridge, the couple was married in July, 1965, after Hawking won his fellowship to work at Gonville and Caius College at Cambridge. They eventually found a house conveniently located near the Department of Applied Mathematics and Theoretical Physics where Hawking would work. He lived by himself during the week, and Jane commuted on weekends to Cambridge until she finished her degree. Over the years, the Hawkings had three children—Robert, born in 1967; Lucy, born in 1970; and Timothy, born in 1979.

Hawking soon found that he needed a wheelchair to get around; he also required nursing care around the clock. When he contracted pneumonia in 1985, an operation was necessary to save his life; it also removed his voice. A computer programmer in California sent Hawking a program called Equalizer, which, Hawking says "allowed me to select words from a series of menus on the screen, by pressing a switch with my hand." When he has completed his statement, the computer attached to his wheelchair sends

it to a speech synthesizer. "The only problem," says Hawking, "is that it gives me an American accent."

Before his impending marriage, Hawking realized he needed to finish his doctorate and get a job. He looked for a thesis topic. In Ferguson's *Stephen Hawking: Quest for a Theory of Everything,* Hawking says, "I started working hard for the first time in my life. To my surprise, I found I liked it. Maybe it is not really fair to call it work." His imagination was caught after reading Roger Penrose's ideas about collapsing stars that turn into black holes, or singularities (tiny but incredibly dense points of mass in spacetime from which not even light can escape due to the immense gravitational pull). Hawking asked: if stars gradually burn out and collapse under their own gravity into singularities, what happens if one looks back in time, to the beginning of the universe? What if the universe began as a singularity and then exploded in what is called the Big Bang?

Hawking worked with Penrose to prove that there must be a singularity in spacetime if general relativity is correct and the universe contains as much matter as scientists have observed. This bit of information was not completely well-received. Hawking says in *A Brief History of Time* that the opposition was "partly from the Russians because of their Marxist belief in scientific determinism [the idea that everything in the universe can be predicted], and partly from people who felt that the whole idea of singularities was repugnant and spoiled the beauty of Einstein's theory." Now, Hawking's theory is generally accepted; as he put it, "one cannot really argue with a mathematical theorem."

By the 1970s Hawking's work led him to study elementary particles in more depth, to see how they might contribute to an understanding of the cosmos. That study is now known as quantum mechanics, or the scientific theories dealing with the behavior of very small particles, such as photons and electrons, which make up larger particles, such as atoms. The basic rule of quantum mechanics is the uncertainty principle, formulated by the German physicist Werner Heisenberg. The uncertainty principle showed that some things in the universe just can not be predicted—in particular, the behavior of small particles. Heisenberg found, and many researchers have since confirmed, that one can never know both the position and speed, or velocity, of a particle. Scientists can measure one, but not the other. Hawking explains why in *Black Holes and Baby Universes:* "You had to use at least one packet, or quantum [of light] to try to measure the position of a particle. This packet of light would disturb the particle and cause it to move at a speed in some direction. The more accurately you wanted to measure the position of the particle, the greater the energy of the packet you would have to use and thus the more it would disturb the particle." The best scientists can do with these particles is to predict for them to be in a number of possible "quantum states" along the spacetime continuum.

In 1973, Hawking discovered that black holes appear to emit particles. In *A Brief History of Time,* he writes that he was surprised and annoyed, but every time he redid the calculations, he came up with the same result. Knowing that nothing can escape from a black hole, Hawking theorized that what must be happening is that the particles come from the space just outside the event horizon (the boundary of a black hole).

At first, Hawking told only a few close colleagues about his discovery. In *RC,* he remembers Roger Penrose calling him about it on his birthday. Penrose "was very excited and he went on so long that my dinner was quite cold. It was a great pity, because it was goose, which I'm very fond of." When Hawking presented his results to an audience at the Rutherford-Appleton Laboratory near Oxford, "people were flabbergasted. I remember someone getting up and saying, 'You must be wrong, Stephen. I don't believe a word of it'."

But physicists around the world began checking Hawking's findings on their own and, when they reached the same conclusions, they agreed he was correct. Hawking tells Stone that "Einstein never accepted quantum mechanics, because of its element of chance and uncertainty. He said, 'God does not play dice.' It seems that Einstein was doubly wrong. The quantum effects of black holes suggest that not only does God play dice, he sometimes throws them where they cannot be seen."

Hawking is not known as a particularly religious man. He once commented on a BBC broadcast, *Master of the Universe: Stephen Hawking,* that "we are such insignificant creatures on a minor planet of a very average star in the outer suburbs of one of a hundred thousand million galaxies. So it is difficult to believe in a God that would care about us or even notice our existence." Yet the name comes up somewhat often in Hawking's writings and interviews. Tensions between science and the Roman Catholic church go back to Galileo's time. One of Hawking's experiences illustrates one reason why. He attended a cosmology conference at the Vatican in 1981 and gave a paper called, "The Boundary Conditions of the Universe," in which he proposed that space and time in the universe were similar to the earth's surface—finite in area but without boundaries or edges. Pope John Paul II granted the conference participants an audience. In his interview for Stone, Hawking recalls that the Pope "told us that it was all right to study the evolution of the universe after the big bang, but we should not inquire into the big bang itself because that was the moment of creation and therefore the work of God." He continues, "I was glad then that he did

not know that subject of the talk I had just given at the conference was the possibility that space-time was finite but had no boundary, which means that it had no beginning, no moment of creation."

Hawking has made a number of provocative comments about the impact the current state of physics might have on the existence of God. In the chapter called "The Origin and Fate of the Universe" in *A Brief History of Time,* Hawking theorizes that "if the universe is really completely self-contained, having no boundary or edge, it would have neither beginning nor end: it would simply be. What place, then, for a creator?" Some of the physicist's most well-known queries conclude the book: "Why does the universe go to all the bother of existing? Is the unified theory so compelling that it brings about its own existence? Or does it need a creator, and, if so, does he have any other effect on the universe? And who created him?" Hawking continues that if a unified theory is found, everyone will "be able to take part in the discussion of the question of why it is that we and the universe exist. If we find the answer to that, it would be the ultimate triumph of human reason—for then we would know the mind of God."

Michael D. Lemonick, writing in *Time,* notes that many *Brief History* readers have the impression that Hawking is trying to disprove the existence of God. Hawking responds, "You don't need to appeal to God to set the initial conditions for the universe, but that doesn't prove there is no God—only that he acts through the laws of physics."

Though *A Brief History of Time* is certainly Hawking's most popular book, it was not his first. *The Large Scale Structure of Space-Time,* co-written with G.F.R. Ellis, deals with classical cosmological theory and is filled with equations. But Hawking wanted to write a book that would be sold at airport newsstands. He chose to submit his manuscript to Bantam, a publisher specializing in popular books, because "I wanted to explain how far I felt we had come in our understanding of the universe: how we might be near finding a complete theory that would describe the universe and everything in it. . . . I wanted it to get to as many people as possible," he writes in *Black Holes and Baby Universes.* Toward that end, his editor advised him that every equation he put in the book would halve the sales. Hawking managed with only $E = mc^2$.

In *A Brief History of Time,* Hawking gives an overview of the history of physics, relying heavily on pictorial diagrams and examples using everyday objects and ideas to explain the nature of spacetime and imaginary time (which Hawking now wishes he had explained more thoroughly), general relativity, the uncertainty principle and elementary particles, black holes, the origin and possible future of the universe. In the process, he discusses his own theories and ideas on black holes, Hawking Radiation, the Big Bang, and the still elusive "Theory of Everything."

Jeremy Bernstein, writing in the *New Yorker,* compares *A Brief History of Time* to Steven Weinberg's *The First Three Minutes.* One problem in the book, he says, is some inaccuracy in Hawking's account of physicist George Gamow's work—Gamow's 1948 paper was on "The Origin of Chemical Elements," not microwave radiation. But Bernstein also points out that "very few active scientists . . . actually take the trouble to read the papers of their early predecessors. A kind of folklore builds up which bears only a tangential relationship to reality." Martin Gardner spots a couple of other historical errors in the *New York Review of Books:* 1. That Newton believed in absolute time, not absolute space, and 2. That it was not Berkeley who believed that " 'all material objects . . . are an illusion'." In an aside, Gardner considers "The Origin and Fate of the Universe" chapter "the book's centerpiece."

Taking the book as a whole, Jeffrey Marsh of *Commentary* calls it "a concise, firsthand account of current scientific thinking," and A.J. Ayer, in the *London Review of Books,* writes that "Hawking gives a more lucid account than any that has yet come my way" of the complicated world of modern physics.

When producer Gordon Freeman and Hawking decided to make a film of *A Brief History of Time,* they went to Steven Spielberg for financing assistance. Errol Morris would direct, Gerald Peary would write the film, and Hawking would contribute to the narrative of the film and helped edit the final product. The movie was filmed in a studio made to resemble Hawking's office in Cambridge. Writer Peary interviewed director Morris for *Interview.* When asked if Hawking disliked anything in the film, Morris replied that "he was always opposed to the chicken at the very beginning of the movie." Asked what brought Hawking the "most immediate pleasure" about the film, "he thanked me for making his mother into a movie star."

In a review of the film, *Time*'s Richard Schickel sees the "bottom line" as: "The real world and the theoretical universe of a physicist are explored with simplicity and elegance." The film is a series of short scenes focussing on Hawking, family members, Hawking, colleagues, old friends, Hawking—all having to do with Hawking's life and work in physics. Schickel writes that in watching the film "one begins to perceive a powerful analogy between Hawking's condition and the thrust of his thought. His disease seems to have affected him much as loss of energy affects a failing star."

All the reviews are not yet in for Hawking's latest book, *Black Holes and Baby Universes,* but critics who complained that the author did not reveal enough of himself in *A Brief History of Time* will not be disappointed. The first three essays in the book are autobiographical. The last chapter is a transcript of Hawking's appearance on BBC's *Desert Island Discs* program in 1992. And in between are more essays on cosmology and quantum mechanics. A reviewer in *Publishers Weekly* writes that Hawking "sheds light" on his personal life, and his "mind sparks in" the scientific essays that comprise the rest of the book. Michael D. Lemonick, writing in *Time,* quotes Hawking's answer to the question, "Why, when his days are already overcrowded with scientific meetings, lecture tours and the occasional sit-down with disabled kids, did he take the time to write a new book? 'I had to pay for my nurses.' "

BIOGRAPHICAL/CRITICAL SOURCES:

BOOKS

Ferguson, Kitty, *Stephen Hawking: Quest for a Theory of Everything,* Bantam Books, 1992.

Hawking, Stephen, *A Brief History of Time,* Bantam Books, 1988.

Hawking, Stephen, *Black Holes and Baby Universes and Other Essays,* Bantam Books, 1993.

Stone, Gene, *Stephen Hawking's a Brief History of Time: A Reader's Companion,* Bantam Books, 1992.

White, Michael, and John Gribbin, *Stephen Hawking: A Life in Science,* Dutton, 1992.

PERIODICALS

Commentary, September, 1988.

Forbes, March 23, 1987, p. 142.

Interview, September 1992.

London Review of Books, January 5, 1989.

New Statesman & Society, June 24, 1988, p. 39.

Newsweek, June 13, 1988, p. 56.

New Yorker, June 6, 1988, p. 117.

New York Review of Books, June 16, 1988.

People, September 11, 1989, p. 11.

Publishers Weekly, November 1, 1993, p. 33.

Time, February 8, 1988, p. 58; August 31, 1992; September 27, 1993.

—*Sketch by Helene Henderson*

*   *   *

HAZLITT, Henry   1894-1993

PERSONAL: Born November 28, 1894, in Philadelphia, PA; died July 9, 1993, in Fairfield, CT; son of Stuart Clark and Bertha (Zauner) Hazlitt; married Frances S. Kanes, July, 1936 (died in 1991). *Education:* Attended City College (now City College of the City University of New York), 1912.

CAREER: Editor and writer, New York City, beginning 1913. *Wall Street Journal,* reporter, 1913-16; *New York Evening Post,* member of financial staff, 1916-18; Mechanics and Metals National Bank, writer of monthly financial letter, 1919-20; *New York Evening Mail,* financial editor, 1921-23; *New York Herald,* editorial writer, 1923-24; *New York Sun,* editorial writer, 1924-25, literary editor, 1925-29; *Nation,* literary editor, 1930-33; *American Mercury,* editor, 1933-34; *New York Times,* member of editorial staff, 1934-46; *Newsweek,* writer of "Business Tides" column, 1946-66; *Freeman,* co-founder and co-editor, 1950-52, president and editor-in-chief, 1953; syndicated columnist for Los Angeles Times Syndicate, 1966-69. Lecturer at colleges and universities in the United States, Mexico, Peru, Netherlands, and Austria. Radio and television panelist and debater with government officials on national issues. Trustee, Foundation for Economic Education. *Military service:* U.S. Aviation Service, World War I.

MEMBER: Century Association, Dutch Treat Club (New York), Authors Club (London).

AWARDS, HONORS: Twice received the George Washington Honor Medal from Freedom Foundation; Litt.D., Grove City College, 1958; LL.D., Bethany College, Bethany, WV, 1961; S.Sc.D., Universidad Francisco Marroquin, 1976.

WRITINGS:

Thinking as a Science, Dutton (New York City), 1916.
The Way to Will-Power, Dutton, 1922.
(Editor) *A Practical Program for America* (essays), Harcourt (New York City), 1932.
The Anatomy of Criticism: A Trialogue, Simon & Schuster (New York City), 1933.
Instead of Dictatorship, John Day (New York City), 1933.
A New Constitution Now, McGraw (New York City), 1942, 2nd edition, Arlington House (New Rochelle, NY), 1974.
The Full Employment Bill, American Enterprise Association (New York City and Washington, DC), 1945.
Economics in One Lesson, Harper (New York City), 1946, revised edition, Arlington House, 1979.
Will Dollars Save the World?, Foundation for Economic Education (Irvington-on-Hudson, NY), 1947.
Illusions of Point Four, Foundation for Economic Education, 1950.
The Great Idea (novel), Appleton-Century-Crofts (New York City), 1951, revised edition published as *Time Will Run Back,* Arlington House, 1966.
The Free Man's Library: A Descriptive and Critical Bibliography, Van Nostrand (Princeton, NJ), 1956.
The Failure of the "New Economics": An Analysis of the Keynesian Fallacies, Van Nostrand, 1959.

What You Should Know about Inflation, Van Nostrand, 1960, 2nd edition, 1965.
(Editor) *The Critics of Keynesian Economics,* Van Nostrand, 1960, reprinted with new preface, Arlington House, 1983.
The Foundations of Morality, Van Nostrand, 1964, 2nd edition, Nash Publishing, 1972.
Life and Death of the Welfare State, La Jolla Rancho Press (La Jolla, CA), 1968.
Man vs. the Welfare State, Arlington House, 1969.
The Conquest of Poverty, Arlington House, 1973.
(With others) *Champions of Freedom* (lectures), Hillsdale College Press (Hillsdale, MI), 1974.
The Inflation Crisis and How to Resolve It, Arlington House, 1978.
From Bretton Woods to World Inflation: A Study of the Causes and Consequences, Regnery Gateway (Chicago), 1984.
(Editor with wife, Frances Hazlitt) *The Wisdom of the Stoics: Selections from Seneca, Epictetus, and Marcus Aurelius,* University Press of America (Lanham, MD), 1984.

Also author of pamphlets on government and economics. Member of editorial board, *American Scholar,* 1941-44. Hazlitt's books have been translated into foreign languages, including German, Japanese, Swedish, and Spanish.

WORK IN PROGRESS: A book, tentatively entitled *Is Politics Insoluble?*

SIDELIGHTS: Henry Hazlitt once told *CA:* "I think I have been extremely fortunate, for many reasons, in having been a newspaper man. A journalist forms the habit of writing often several thousand words a week. When he has become accustomed to this, he never has a 'writing block,' which some of my non-journalistic friends used to complain about. One reason he never has it is that he never fears it. More important, habit and necessity have solved that problem for him."

OBITUARIES:

PERIODICALS

New York Times, July 10, 1993, p. 27.
Washington Post, July 11, 1993, p. B7.*

*   *   *

HEANEY, Seamus (Justin) 1939-

PERSONAL: Name is pronounced "*Shay*-moos *Hee*-knee"; born April 13, 1939, in County Derry, Northern Ireland; son of Patrick (a farmer) and Margaret Heaney; married Marie Devlin, 1965; children: Michael, Christopher, Catherine. *Education:* Attended St. Columb's College, Derry; Queen's University of Belfast, B.A. (first class honors), 1961, St. Joseph's College of Education, teacher's certificate, 1962.

ADDRESSES: Office—Department of English and American Literature and Language, Harvard University, Warren House, 11 Prescott St., Cambridge, MA 02138.

CAREER: Poet, 1960—. Worked as secondary school teacher in Belfast, 1962-63; St. Joseph's College of Education, Belfast, Northern Ireland, lecturer, 1963-66; Queen's University of Belfast, lecturer in English, 1966-72; freelance writer, 1972-75; Carysfort College, Dublin, Ireland, lecturer, 1976-82; Harvard University, Cambridge, MA, visiting lecturer, 1979, visiting professor, 1982-86, Boylston Professor of Rhetoric and Oratory, 1986—; Oxford University, Oxford, England, professor of poetry, 1990—. Visiting lecturer, University of California, Berkeley, 1970-71. Has given numerous lectures and poetry readings at universities in England, Ireland, and the United States.

MEMBER: Irish Academy of Letters.

AWARDS, HONORS: Eric Gregory Award, 1966, Cholomondeley Award, 1967, Somerset Maugham Award, 1968, and Geoffrey Faber Memorial Prize, 1968, all for *Death of a Naturalist;* Poetry Book Society Choice citation, 1969, for *Door into the Dark;* writer in residence award from American Irish Foundation and Denis Devlin Award, both 1973, both for *Wintering Out;* E. M. Forster Award from American Academy and Institute of Arts and Letters, 1975; W. H. Smith Award, Duff Cooper Memorial Prize, and Poetry Book Society Choice citation, all 1976, all for *North;* Bennett Award from *Hudson Review,* 1982; D.H.L. from Fordham University and Queen's University of Belfast, both 1982; *Los Angeles Times* Book Prize nomination, 1984, and PEN Translation Prize for Poetry, 1985, both for *Sweeney Astray: A Version from the Irish;* Whitbread Award, 1987, for *The Haw Lantern;* Lannam Foundation award, 1990.

WRITINGS:

POETRY COLLECTIONS

Death of a Naturalist, Oxford University Press (New York City), 1966.
Door into the Dark, Oxford University Press, 1969.
Wintering Out, Faber & Faber (London), 1972, Oxford University Press, 1973.
North, Faber & Faber, 1975, Oxford University Press, 1976.
Field Work, Farrar, Straus (New York City), 1979.
Poems: 1965-1975, Farrar, Straus, 1980 (published in England as *Selected Poems, 1965-1975,* Faber & Faber, 1980).
(Adapter) *Sweeney Astray: A Version from the Irish,* Farrar, Straus, 1984, revised edition, with photographs by Rachel Giese, published as *Sweeney's Flight,* 1992.

Station Island, Farrar, Straus, 1984.
The Haw Lantern, Farrar, Straus, 1987.
New and Selected Poems, 1969-1987, Farrar, Straus, 1990, revised edition published as *Selected Poems, 1966-1987,* 1991.
Seeing Things: Poems, Farrar, Straus, 1991.

POETRY CHAPBOOKS

Eleven Poems, Festival Publications (Belfast), 1965.
(With David Hammond and Michael Longley) *Room to Rhyme,* Arts Council of Northern Ireland, 1968.
A Lough Neagh Sequence, edited by Harry Chambers and Eric J. Morten, Phoenix Pamphlets Poets Press (Manchester), 1969.
Boy Driving His Father to Confession, Sceptre Press (Surrey), 1970.
Night Drive: Poems, Richard Gilbertson (Devon), 1970.
Land, Poem-of-the-Month Club, 1971.
Servant Boy, Red Hanrahan Press (Detroit), 1971.
Stations, Ulsterman Publications (Belfast), 1975.
Bog Poems, Rainbow Press (London), 1975.
(With Derek Mahon) *In Their Element,* Arts Council of Northern Ireland, 1977.
After Summer, Deerfield Press, 1978.
Hedge School: Sonnets from Glanmore, C. Seluzichi (Oregon), 1979.
Sweeney Praises the Trees, [New York], 1981.

PROSE

The Fire i' the Flint: Reflections on the Poetry of Gerard Manley Hopkins, Oxford University Press, 1975.
Robert Lowell: A Memorial Address and Elegy, Faber & Faber, 1978.
Preoccupations: Selected Prose, 1968-1978, Farrar, Straus, 1980.
The Government of the Tongue: Selected Prose, 1978-1987, Farrar, Straus, 1988.
The Place of Writing, Scholars Press, 1989.

EDITOR

(With Alan Brownjohn) *New Poems: 1970-71,* Hutchinson (London), 1971.
Soundings: An Annual Anthology of New Irish Poetry, Blackstaff Press (Belfast), 1972.
Soundings II, Blackstaff Press, 1974.
(With Ted Hughes) *The Rattle Bag: An Anthology of Poetry* (juvenile), Faber & Faber, 1982.
The Essential Wordsworth, Ecco Press (New York City), 1988.

Also editor of *The May Anthology of Oxford and Cambridge Poetry,* 1993.

OTHER

(With John Montague) *The Northern Muse* (sound recording), Claddagh Records, 1969.

(Contributor) *The Writers: A Sense of Ireland,* O'Brien Press (Dublin), 1979.

Advent Parish Programme, State Mutual Book & Periodical Service, 1989.

Lenten Parish Programme: Renewal of Personal and Community Life through Prayer and Scripture, State Mutual Book & Periodical Service, 1989.

The Cure at Troy: A Version of Sophocles Philotetes (drama), Farrar, Straus, 1991.

Contributor of poetry and essays to periodicals, including *New Statesman, Listener, Guardian, Times Literary Supplement,* and *London Review of Books.*

SIDELIGHTS: Seamus Heaney is widely recognized as one of Ireland's finest living poets. A native of Northern Ireland who divides his time between a home in Dublin and a teaching position at Harvard University, Heaney has attracted a readership on two continents and has won prestigious literary awards in England, Ireland, and the United States. As Blake Morrison notes in his work *Seamus Heaney,* the author is "that rare thing, a poet rated highly by critics and academics yet popular with 'the common reader.'" Part of Heaney's popularity stems from his subject matter—modern Northern Ireland, its farms and cities beset with civil strife, its natural culture and language overrun by English rule. *Washington Post Book World* contributor Marjorie Perloff suggests that Heaney is so successful "because of his political position: the Catholic farm boy from County Derry transformed into the sensitive witness to and historian of the Irish troubles, as those troubles have shaped and altered individual lives." Likewise, *New York Review of Books* essayist Richard Murphy describes Heaney as "the poet who has shown the finest art in presenting a coherent vision of Ireland, past and present." Heaney's "is, after all," writes Robert Buttel in the *Concise Dictionary of British Literary Biography (CDBLB),* "a poetry manifestly regional and largely rural in subject matter and traditional in structure—a poetry that appears to be a deliberate step back into a premodernist world of William Wordsworth and John Clare and to represent a rejection of most contemporary poetic fashions."

To call Heaney a poet of the Irish countryside is to oversimplify his sensibility, however. According to Robert Pinsky in the *New Republic,* the author also incorporates "a *literary* element into his work without embarrassment, apology, or ostentation." Indeed, Heaney takes delight in the sounds and histories of words, using language to create "the music of what happens," to quote from one of his poems. "The poet's triumph is to bring the ingredients of history and biography under the control of his music," writes Irvin Ehrenpreis in the *New York Review of Books.* "Heaney's expressive rhythms support his pleasure in re-echoing syllables and modulating vowels through a series of lines to evoke continuities and resolutions." Nor is Heaney's subject matter merely provincial and pastoral, insulated from broader human perspectives. Morrison notes: "One does not have to look very deeply into Heaney's work . . . to see that it is rather less comforting and comfortable than has been supposed. Far from being 'whole,' it is tense, torn, divided against itself; far from being straightforward, it is layered with often obscure allusions; far from being archaic, it registers the tremors and turmoils of its age, forcing traditional forms to accept the challenge of harsh, intractable material. . . . A proper response to Heaney's work requires reference to complex matters of ancestry, nationality, religion, history, and politics." This is not to say that Heaney's work is difficult or inaccessible, though. Pinsky concludes that the poems "give several kinds of pleasure: first of all, [Heaney] is a talented writer, with a sense of language and rhythm as clean, sweet, and solid as new-worked hardwood. Beyond that, . . . his talent [has] the limberness and pluck needed to take up some of the burden of history—the tangled, pained history of Ireland. Heaney's success in dealing with the murderous racial enmities of past and present, avoiding all the sins of oratory, and keeping his personal sense of balance, seems to me one of the most exhilarating poetic accomplishments in many years."

Inevitably, Heaney has been compared with the great Irish poet William Butler Yeats; in fact, several critics have called Heaney "the greatest Irish poet since Yeats." Such praise-by-comparison makes the poet uncomfortable, and it serves to obscure the uniqueness of his work. *New York Review of Books* contributor Richard Ellmann once wrote: "After the heavily accented melodies of Yeats, and that poet's elegiac celebrations of imaginative glories, Seamus Heaney addresses his readers in a quite different key. He does not overwhelm his subjects; rather he allows them a certain freedom from him, and his sharp conjunctions with them leave their authority and his undiminished." Elizabeth Jennings makes a similar observation in the *Spectator.* To Jennings, Heaney is "an extremely Irish poet most especially in language, but he is not a poet in the Yeatsian mould; not for him high-mannered seriousness or intentional rhetoric. He is serious, of course, but it is the gravity which grows in his roots, not one which is obtrusive in the finished artefact." In the *Listener,* Conor Cruise O'Brien analyzes the source from which the comparison might have stemmed. "Heaney's writing is modest, often conversational, apparently easy, low-pitched, companionably ironic, ominous, alert, accurate and surprising," notes O'Brien. "An Irish reader is not automatically reminded of Yeats by this cluster of characteristics, yet an English reader may perhaps see resemblances that are there but overlooked by the Irish—resemblances coming, perhaps, from certain common rhythms and hesitations of Irish speech and non-speech." *Newsweek* correspondent Jack Kroll finds similarities in Heaney's subject matter: "Like Yeats, Heaney combines all the conflicting poles of the Irish experience into a rich, embattled language: paganism and Christianity, repression and expansion, desire and chastity, country and city, ignorance and enlightenment, hope and despair."

Kroll is not the only critic who notes "the conflicting poles of Irish experience" in Heaney's work. London *Times* contributor Bel Mooney also delineates the inner divisions that define and intensify the poet's writing. "Again and again," contends Mooney, "we observe him poised on a pivot, a one-man dialectic in whom opposites are—uncomfortably—unified. Ulster v Eire; English learning v Irish culture; education v roots; the language of debate v silence and acceptance; liberalism v Catholicism; comfort v guilt; love v loneliness and restlessness; belonging v exile. . . . It is all there. He knows it well." Ehrenpreis elaborates: "Speech is never simple in Heaney's conception. He grew up as an Irish Catholic boy in a land governed by Protestants whose tradition is British. He grew up on a farm in his country's northern, industrial region. As a person, therefore, he springs from the old divisions of his nation. At the same time, the theme that dominates Heaney's work is self-definition, the most natural subject of the modern lyric; and language, from which it starts, shares the old polarities. For Heaney, it is the Irish speech of his family and district, overlaid by British and urban culture which he had acquired as a student." In a *Harper's* essay, Terrence Des Pres suggests that Heaney has had "to accommodate, but also shove against, the expansive beauty of the conqueror's tongue in order to recover the rooted speech of his own society and place." *Critical Quarterly* correspondent John Wilson Foster describes how Heaney remains "suspended between the English and (Anglo-) Irish traditions and cultures. Correlatives of ambivalence proliferate in his verse: the archetypal sound in his work (and to be savoured in the reading) is the guttural spirant, half-consonant, half-vowel; the archetypal locale is the bog, half-water, half-land; the archetypal animal is the eel which can fancifully be regarded (in its overland forays) as half-mammal, half-fish."

Heaney is well aware of the dual perspective afforded him by his upbringing and subsequent experiences. He once described himself in the *New York Times Book Review* as one of a group of Catholics in Northern Ireland who "emerged from a hidden, a buried life and entered the realm of education." This process began for Heaney at age eleven; that year he left the family farm to study on scholarship at a boarding school in Belfast. Access to the world

of English, Irish, and American letters—first at St. Columb's College and then at Queen's University of Belfast—was "a crucial experience," according to the poet. He was especially moved by artists who created poetry out of their local and native backgrounds—authors such as Ted Hughes, Patrick Kavanagh, and Robert Frost. Heaney said: "From them I learned that my local County Derry [childhood] experience, which I had considered archaic and irrelevant to 'the modern world' was to be trusted. They taught me that trust and helped me to articulate it." Searching his cultural roots, but also letting his English literary education enrich his expression, Heaney began to craft "a poetry concerned with nature, the shocks and discoveries of childhood experience on a farm, the mythos of the locale—in short, a regional poetry," to quote Robert Buttel in his book *Seamus Heaney.* This sort of poetry, Buttel continues, was, in the early 1960s, "essentially a counter-poetry, decidedly not fashionable at the time. To write such poetry called for a measure of confidence if not outright defiance."

According to Morrison, a "general spirit of reverence towards the past helped Heaney resolve some of his awkwardness about being a writer: he could serve his own community by preserving in literature its customs and crafts, yet simultaneously gain access to a larger community of letters." Indeed, Heaney's earliest poetry collections—*Death of a Naturalist* and *Door into the Dark*—evoke "a hard, mainly rural life with rare exactness," in the words of *Parnassus: Poetry in Review* contributor Michael Wood. Using descriptions of rural laborers and their tasks and contemplations of natural phenomena—filtered sometimes through childhood and sometimes through adulthood—Heaney seeks the self by way of the perceived experience, celebrating the life force through earthly things. Buttel writes in *Seamus Heaney:* "Augmenting the physical authenticity and the clean, decisive art of the best of the early poems, mainly the ones concerned with the impact of the recollected initiatory experiences of childhood and youth, is the human voice that speaks in them. At its most distinctive it is unpretentious, open, modest, and yet poised, aware." Kroll notes that in these first poems, Heaney "makes you see, hear, smell, taste this life, which in his words is not provincial, but parochial; provincialism hints at the minor or the mediocre, but all parishes, rural or urban, are equal as communities of the human spirit. So Heaney's poems dig away, filled with a grunting vowel music that evokes the blunt ecstasy of physical work."

In *Northern Voices: Poets from Ulster,* Terence Brown expresses the view that it is a mistake "to think of Heaney as merely a descriptive poet, endowed with unusual powers of observation. From the first his involvement with landscape and locale, with the physical world, has been both more personal and more remarkable in its implications than any mere act of observation and record could be." Heaney's early poems are not burdened with romantic notions about nature; rather they present nature "as a random power that sometimes rewards but more often frustrates human [efforts]," to quote Arthur E. McGuinness in *Eire-Ireland. New York Times Book Review* correspondent Nicholas Christopher likewise finds "no folksy, down-home or miniaturist tendencies in [Heaney's] presentation of natural subjects. His voice is complex and his eye keen, but as with any inspired poet, he is after transformations, not reproductions. Nature is neither antagonist nor sounding board but a component of the human imagination." This latter description outlines the direction Heaney's poetry has taken since he "began to open, both to the Irish, and to his own abyss," in the words of *Times Literary Supplement* reviewer Harold Bloom. In the poems collected in *Wintering Out* and *North,* according to Des Pres, "rural integrity remains intact, but images of violent intent intrude all the same. Which is to say that the structure of Heaney's poetry reflects the shape of life as he knows it to be, a fusion of history and the land, politics colliding with life's daily round. This could hardly be otherwise for a poet growing up in Northern Ireland, where religious and political tensions always threatened to break, as they have since 1969, into madness and bloodshed."

"Seamus Heaney comes from the north of Ireland, and his career has almost exactly coincided with the present span of the 'troubles,'" claims Seamus Deane in the *Sewanee Review.* The "troubles" to which Deane refers are, of course, the violent political struggles between Northern Ireland's Protestants and their British allies and the militant Irish Republican Army. Heaney was living in Belfast when the fighting erupted in 1969; as a Catholic partisan, notes Morrison, "he felt the need to write poetry that would be not necessarily propagandist but certainly urgent in tone." In *Critical Quarterly,* Damian Grant suggests that Heaney "is no protest poet, but nor can he remain indifferent to the bombs, snipers, and internment camps that maim the body of his land." The poet has sought, therefore, to weave the current Irish troubles into a broader historical frame embracing the general human situation. Deane writes that in *Wintering Out* and *North,* "the ancient past and the contemporary present, myth and politics, are in fact analogues for one another. . . . Mr. Heaney is very much in the Irish tradition in that he has learned, more successfully than most, to conceive of his personal experience in terms of his country's history. . . . Accent, etymologies, old ritual murders and invasions, contemporary assassinations and security systems—these and other related elements swarm now more and more thickly, the lethal infusoria in this pellucid verse." *New York Review of Books* correspondent Richard Murphy suggests that the poetry "is seriously attempting to purge

our land of a terrible blood-guilt, and inwardly acknowledging our enslavement to a sacrificial myth. I think it may go a long way toward freeing us from the myth by portraying it in its true archaic shape and color, not disguising its brutality."

Heaney has found a powerful metaphor for current violence in the archaeological discoveries made in peat bogs in Ireland and northern Europe. The chemical nature of the water in the bogs preserves organic material buried in them—including human beings. In 1969 Heaney read *The Bog People,* by P. V. Glob, an archaeologist who had unearthed the preserved remains of several ritually slaughtered Iron Age Europeans. Des Pres quotes Heaney on the impact this work had on his poetry: "The unforgettable photographs of these victims blended in my mind with photographs of atrocities, past and present, in the long rites of Irish political and religious struggles." Although the first of the well-known "bog poems" appeared in *Wintering Out,* published in 1972, Heaney continued the sequence in *North,* published in 1975. Eight of the poems in that sequence were brought together in a limited edition entitled *Bog Poems* that same year.

Heaney's bog poems, according to Murphy, trace "modern terrorism back to its roots in the early Iron Age, and mysterious awe back to the 'bonehouse' of language itself. . . . He looks closely . . . at our funeral rites and our worship of the past. . . . The central image of this work, a symbol which unifies time, person, and place, is bogland: it contains, preserves, and yields up terror as well as awe." "What makes Heaney different is the archetypal dimension of his poetic involvement with Irish culture," writes Gregory A. Schirmer in *Eire-Ireland.* "Nowhere is this more evident—and nowhere is Heaney's art more transcendent—than in the poems that Heaney has written about the peat bogs of Ireland and Jutland and the treasures and horrors that they have preserved. Heaney has developed the image of the bog into a powerful symbol of the continuity of human experience that at once enables him to write about the particularities of his own parish, past and present, and to transcend, at the same time, those particularities." In 'Punishment,' for instance, Heaney interprets one of the victims (a young girl) as an adulteress. Buttel explains in *CDBLB,* "The speaker's sympathy for the [young girl] pulls him erotically: 'I almost love you'; 'I am the artful voyeur / of your brain's exposed / and darkened combs, / your muscles' webbing.' But as he compares her with 'your betraying sisters' in the present who have presumably been punished, 'cauled in tar,' for consorting with British soldiers, he feels himself caught between the 'civilized outrage' at which he 'would connive' and his understanding of 'the exact / and tribal, intimate revenge' to which the Iron Age adulteress had been subjected."

Some critics have detected another dimension to the bog imagery in Heaney's poems. According to Helen Vendler in the *New Yorker,* these works "represent Heaney's coming to grips with an intractable element deep both in personal life (insofar as the bog and its contents represent the unconscious) and in history. They lift him free from a superficial piety that would put either sectarian or national names to the Ulster killings, and they enable a hymn to the 'ruminant ground.' . . . He remarks dissolution and change by tasting things as they grow sour, feeling them sink in himself, losing part of himself bubbling in the acrid changes of fermentation." *Stand* contributor Terry Eagleton likewise feels that the bog landscape "furnishes the imagery for a self-exploration, as the movement of sinking into the bog becomes symbolic of a meditative psychological return to the roots of personal identity; and it does all this while preserving and deepening the kind of discourse which has always been Heaney's chief poetic strength—the discourse of material Nature itself." Brown writes: "The imagination has its dark bog-like depths, its sediments and strata from which images and metaphors emerge unbidden into the light of consciousness. . . . Such a sense of self as bound up with, and almost indistinguishable from, the dense complex of Irish natural and historical experience, obviously allows Heaney to explore Ulster's contemporary social and political crisis through attending to his own memories and obsessions." McGuinness suggests that digging into the "bog" of his imagination as well as into the sediments of the real bog "has convinced Heaney that, even in these desperate times, one might hope to connect with life-enhancing elemental powers and, through the discipline of language, to give these connections shape." However, Heaney dropped the bog imagery in his poetry after the publication of *North.* Buttel explains in *CDBLB:* "The intensity of the poems derives from what Heaney has referred to as his entrancement with the material, but at the same time the interest led to a near surfeit of archeological imagery and Nordic vocabulary. Having completed *North,* he came to feel a 'self-consciousness about the bogs and so forth.' He also felt a need to open up the narrow poetic lines of two and three stresses and escape from a 'sense of constriction.' "

Morrison suggests that the role of political spokesman has never particularly suited Heaney. The author "has written poems directly about the Troubles as well as elegies for friends and acquaintances who have died in them; he has tried to discover a historical framework in which to interpret the current unrest; and he has taken on the mantle of public spokesman, someone looked to for comment and guidance," notes Morrison. "Yet he has also shown signs of deeply resenting this role, defending the right of poets to be private and apolitical, and questioning the extent to which poetry, however 'committed,' can influence the course of history." In the *New Boston Review,* Shaun

O'Connell contends that even Heaney's most overtly political poems contain depths that subtly alter their meanings. "Those who see Seamus Heaney as a symbol of hope in a troubled land are not, of course, wrong to do so," O'Connell states, "though they may be missing much of the undercutting complexities of his poetry, the backwash of ironies which make him as bleak as he is bright." Deane makes a similar assessment, claiming that under sustained reading "the poems express no politics and indeed they flee conceptual formulations with an almost indecent success. Instead they interrogate the quality of the relationship between the poet and his mixed political and literary traditions. . . . Relationship is unavoidable, but commitment, relationship gone sour, is a limiting risk." *Partisan Review* contributor Deborah Tall feels that, in Heaney's poetry, "the burden is not so much to act politically as to speak for his unspoken-for peasant countrymen."

In 1972 Heaney left Belfast for the opportunity to live in a cottage outside Dublin, where he could write full time. The move had political overtones even though Heaney made it for financial reasons; Morrison observes that the subsequent poetry in *Field Work* "is deeply conscious of that move into the countryside." Morrison adds: "It was not surprising that the move should have been seen by some as a betrayal of the Northern Catholic community and should have aroused in Heaney feelings of unease and even guilt. One important consequence was the new seriousness he brought to his thinking about the writer and his responsibilities." At his retreat in Glanmore, Heaney reasserted his determination to produce fresh aesthetic objects, to pursue his personal feelings as member of—and not spokesman for—church, state, and tribe. Denis Donoghue suggests in the *New York Times Book Review* that in *Field Work* "Heaney is writing more powerfully than ever, more fully in possession of his feeling, more at home in his style. He has given up, at least for the moment, the short line of his earlier poems, which often went along with a brittle, self-protective relation to his experience. The new long line is more thoughtful, it brings a meditative music to bear on fundamental themes of person and place, the mutuality of ourselves and the world."

A further liberating experience occurred at Glanmore when Heaney began to undertake the translation and adaptation of the Irish lyric poem *Buile Suibhne.* The work concerns an ancient king who, cursed by the church, is transformed into a mad bird-man and forced to wander in the harsh and inhospitable countryside. Heaney's translation of the epic was published as *Sweeney Astray: A Version from the Irish;* in the *Dictionary of Literary Biography* Buttel contends that the poem "reveals a heartfelt affinity with the dispossessed king who responds with such acute sensitivity, poetic accuracy, and imaginative force to his landscape." *New York Times Book Review* contributor

Brendan Kennelly also deems the poem "a balanced statement about a tragically unbalanced mind. One feels that this balance, urbanely sustained, is the product of a long, imaginative bond between Mr. Heaney and Sweeney." Indeed, this bond is extended into Heaney's 1984 volume *Station Island,* where a series of poems entitled "Sweeney Redivivus" take up Sweeney's voice once more. Buttel sees these poems as part of a larger theme in *Station Island;* namely, "a personal drama of guilt, lost innocence, and lost moral and religious certainty played against the redemptions of love, faith in the integrity of craft and of dedicated individuals, and ties with the universal forces operating in nature and history."

Station Island also introduces a spiritual theme that Heaney had not developed strongly before. "The tone," declares Buttel in *CDBLB*, "is devout and properly purgatorial." Buttel quotes *Times Literary Supplement* contributor Blake Morrison as calling the volume "a religious book and no getting around it—intense, superstitious, pantheistic, even mystical, and at times very difficult to decipher. . . . it gives us a rather different poet from the one we thought we knew." "Actually," Buttel continues, "the poet is not very different: we still hear the essential Heaney voice . . . and find not unusual variations on his central themes." Instead, the *CDBLB* contributor continues, "the sequence becomes a complex though accessible narrative concerned not only with spiritual inadequacy, which includes a failure of personal response to the pattern of violence in the North [of Ireland], but also with atonement. The sequence is also a pilgrimage of the persona as poet coming to terms with himself, attempting to perfect his artistic sensibility. It is fitting in this regard that his penance is to translate a poem by Saint John of the Cross, which is just what he does in section 9—the spiritual and poetic acts thus conjoined."

Language—and the action of writing—have always been central preoccupations for Heaney, but especially so in his more recent works. Morrison contends that the author's poetry has been shaped "by the modes of post-war Anglo-American poetry" as well as by the romantic tradition. Moreover, continues Morrison, "Heaney's preoccupation with language and with questions of authorial control makes him part of a still larger modern intellectual movement which has emphasized that language is not a transparent medium by means of which a writer says what he intends to, but rather something self-generating, infinitely productive, exceeding us as individuals." As A. Alvarez puts it in the *New York Review of Books,* Heaney "is not rural and sturdy and domestic, with his feet planted firmly in the Irish mud, but is instead an ornamentalist, a word collector, a connoisseur of fine language for its own sake." *Washington Post Book World* contributor John B. Breslin writes: "Like every poet, Heaney is a professional deceiver, saying one thing and meaning another, in a timeless effort at rescuing our language from the half-attention we normally accord it. Words matter because they are his matter, and ours, the inescapable medium of exchange between two otherwise isolated sets of experience."

This fascination with words is evident in *The Haw Lantern,* published in 1987; *Times Literary Supplement* reviewer Neil Corcoran feels that the poems in that work "have a very contemporary sense of how writing is elegy to experience." W. S. DiPiero explains Heaney's intent in the *American Scholar:* "Whatever the occasion—childhood, farm life, politics and culture in Northern Ireland, other poets past and present—Heaney strikes time and again at the taproot of language, examining its genetic structures, trying to discover how it has served, in all its changes, as a culture bearer, a world to contain imaginations, at once a rhetorical weapon and nutriment of spirit. He writes of these matters with rare discrimination and resourcefulness, and a winning impatience with received wisdom." Heaney, declares Buttel in *CDBLB*, remains "in a long tradition of Irish writers who have flourished in the British literary scene, showing the Britons new possibilities for poetry in their mother tongue."

With the publication of *Selected Poems, 1966-1987,* Heaney marked the beginning of a new direction in his career. Michael Dirda, writing in the *Washington Post Book World,* notes that a collection of "selected poems" is almost redundant for a poet of Heaney's stature and popularity. The reviewer points out that "where a 'Collected Poems' is a monument, a 'Selected' is an invitation, a sometimes needed ice-breaker for shy new readers." "In truth," Dirda concludes, Heaney "is probably one of the few poets who doesn't really need a Selected Poems. Anyone who cares for poetry already knows that he should be reading him. And anyone who likes his work will want to own it all." *Poetry* contributor William Logan questions how successful the poet has been in this new direction, saying, "The younger Heaney wrote like a man possessed by demons, even when those demons were very literary demons; the older Heaney seems to wonder, bemusedly, what sort of demon he has become himself." Another critic also notices that some of the material in *Selected Poems* marks a significant departure from Heaney's established earlier work, but holds a higher opinion of Heaney's success than does Logan. "After a while," declares Richard Eder in the *Los Angeles Times Book Review,* "a poet moves on or risks becoming Poet Laureate of himself. The moving-on is tough. It is not, like the pioneer's, necessarily to greener or more promising land. Departure may be from the poet's best work." This new collection, Eder explains, "is a record of triumph, but the risks show themselves too. Dry spots, elaborations, explorations that seem unrevealing, and even a turn or two of Self-Laureating while the strength gathers for another mortal departure." Yet this is a strength, both of the poet and of his poetry, Eder declares. Heaney "has a belief about a poet's progress. He suggests that the early and middle stages have to do with finding and mastering the individuality of roots, experience and voice; with becoming wonderfully oneself." Once this is accomplished, Eder concludes, the poet can then "work free of it—free of [his] images, landscapes, battlefields and perfected complexities."

In another poetry collection, *Seeing Things,* Heaney demonstrates even more clearly the direction in which he is taking his career. Jefferson Hunter, reviewing the book for the *Virginia Quarterly Review,* shows that in some of the poems in *Seeing Things* Heaney has taken a more spiritual, less concrete approach than had been his habit previously. "Words like 'spirit' and 'pure,' as opposed to words like 'reek' and 'hock,' have never figured largely in Heaney's poetry," the critic explains. In the portion of the book titled "Squarings," "they create a new distanced perspective and indeed a new mood . . . [in which] 'things beyond measure' or 'things in the offing' or 'the longed-for' can sometimes be sensed, if never directly seen." Heaney also creates a direct link between himself and some of his ancient predecessors, Hunter continues. " 'The Golden Bough' translates the famous passage of *Aeneid* VI wherein the Sybil tells the hero what talisman he must carry on his trip to the underworld, while 'The Crossing' translates Dante's and Virgil's confrontation with the angry Charon in *Inferno* III." In another poem, "Heaney recalls being carried piggyback by his father; a simile compares himself as a child to 'a witless elder rescued from the fire'; but that simile in turn recalls Aeneas carrying his father Anchises away from burning Troy." Hunter concludes, "No previous Heaney volume—not even *Station Island,* with its *terza rima* Dantesque encounters with older poets—has been so literary, so determined to establish lines of poetic affiliation."

Critical reaction to Heaney's work has been almost universally positive. "Only the most gifted poets can start from their peculiar origin in a language, a landscape, a nation, and from these enclosures rise to impersonal authority," writes Ehrenpreis. "Seamus Heaney has this kind of power. . . . One may enter his poetry by a number of paths, but each joins up with others. Nationality becomes landscape; landscape becomes language; language becomes genius." Des Pres concludes that Heaney's audience should "read him for his excellence, and then for the way he meets the challenge of politics and manages to honor beauty's plea. Then read him again for a perspective on our own predicament. For to judge from most recent American poetry, we stick to flowers and sidestep the rage, ignoring *what we know* or turning it to metaphor merely. . . . What we need is what he gives—a poetry

that allows the spirit to face and engage, and thereby transcend, or at least stand up to, the murderous pressures of our time. This need is not a question of praxis or ideology, but of imagination regaining authority and of spirit bearing witness to its own misfortune and struggle." In *Seamus Heaney,* Buttel remarks: "Heaney continues to write his own poetry, carrying on his essential contribution to the flourishing state of Irish poetry today. For all its native authenticity, however, his is not an insular poetry. Seamus Heaney's best poems define their landscape and human experience with such visceral clarity, immediacy, and integrity of feeling that they transcend their regional source and make a significant contribution to contemporary poetry written in English."

In an interview published in *Viewpoints: Poets in Conversation with John Haffenden,* Heaney offered some insight into his craftsmanship. "One thing I try to avoid ever saying at readings is '*my* poem,' " he said, "—because that sounds like a presumption. The poem *came, it came.* I didn't go and fetch it. To some extent you wait for it, you coax it in the door when it gets there. I prefer to think of myself as the host to the thing rather than a big-game hunter." Elsewhere in the same interview he commented: "You write books of poems because that is a fulfillment, a making; it's a making sense of your life and it gives achievement, but it also gives you a sense of growth."

BIOGRAPHICAL/CRITICAL SOURCES:

BOOKS

Abse, Dannie, editor, *Best of the Poetry Year 6,* Robson (London), 1979.

Begley, Monie, *Rambles in Ireland,* Devin-Adair (Old Greenwich, CT), 1977.

Broadbridge, Edward, editor, *Seamus Heaney,* Danmarks Radio (Copenhagen), 1977.

Brown, Terence, *Northern Voices: Poets from Ulster,* Rowman & Littlefield (Totowa, NJ), 1975.

Buttel, Robert, *Seamus Heaney,* Bucknell University Press (Cranbury, NJ), 1975.

Concise Dictionary of British Literary Biography: Contemporary Writers, 1960 to the Present, Gale, 1992.

Contemporary Literary Criticism, Gale (Detroit), Volume 5, 1976, Volume 7, 1977, Volume 14, 1980, Volume 25, 1983, Volume 37, 1986.

Curtis, Tony, editor, *The Art of Seamus Heaney,* Poetry Wales Press, 1982.

Dictionary of Literary Biography, Volume 40: *Poets of Great Britain and Ireland since 1960,* Gale, 1985.

Harmon, Maurice, editor, *Image and Illusion: Anglo-Irish Literature and Its Contexts,* Wolfhound Press (Dublin), 1979.

Longley, Michael, editor, *Causeway: The Arts in Ulster,* Arts Council of Northern Ireland, 1971.

Morrison, Blake, *Seamus Heaney,* Methuen (London), 1982.

Viewpoints: Poets in Conversation with John Haffenden, Faber & Faber, 1981.

Weathers, William, editor, *The Nature of Identity: Essays Presented to Donald E. Haydon by the Graduate Faculty of Modern Letters,* University of Tulsa Press, 1981.

PERIODICALS

American Scholar, autumn, 1981.

Antioch Review, spring, 1993.

Chicago Tribune Book World, April 19, 1981; September 9, 1984.

Crane Bag, Volume 1, number 1, 1977; Volume 3, number 2, 1979.

Critical Inquiry, spring, 1982.

Critical Quarterly, spring, 1974; spring, 1976.

Eire-Ireland, summer, 1978; winter, 1980.

Encounter, November, 1975.

Fortnight, December, 1980.

Globe and Mail (Toronto), September 3, 1988.

Harper's, March, 1981.

Hollins Critic, October, 1970.

Honest Ulsterman, winter, 1975.

Irish Times, December 28, 1973; December 6, 1975.

Listener, December 7, 1972; November 8, 1973; September 25, 1975; December 20-27, 1984.

London Review of Books, November 1-14, 1984.

Los Angeles Times, May 16, 1984; January 5, 1989.

Los Angeles Times Book Review, March 2, 1980; October 21, 1984; June 2, 1985; October 27, 1987; August 26, 1990; December 27, 1992.

Midwest Quarterly, summer, 1974.

Nation, November 10, 1979.

New Boston Review, August-September, 1980.

New Republic, March 27, 1976; December 22, 1979; April 30, 1984; February 18, 1985.

New Review, August, 1975.

New Statesman, July 11, 1975.

Newsweek, February 2, 1981; April 15, 1985.

New Yorker, September 28, 1981; September 23, 1985.

New York Review of Books, September 20, 1973; September 30, 1976; March 6, 1980; October 8, 1981; March 14, 1985; June 25, 1992.

New York Times, April 22, 1979; January 11, 1985.

New York Times Book Review, March 26, 1967; April 18, 1976; December 2, 1979; December 21, 1980; May 27, 1984; March 10, 1985; March 5, 1989.

New York Times Magazine, March 13, 1983.

Observer, June 22, 1969; November 4, 1979; November 11, 1979.

Parnassus: Poetry in Review, spring-summer, 1974; fall-winter, 1977; fall-winter, 1979.

Partisan Review, Number 3, 1986.

Philadelphia Inquirer, January 24, 1988.

Phoenix, July, 1973.

Ploughshares, Volume 5, number 3, 1979.

Poetry, June, 1992.

Quest, January-February, 1978.

Saturday Review, July-August, 1985.

Sewanee Review, winter, 1976.

Shenandoah, summer, 1974.

Southern Review, January, 1980.

Spectator, September 6, 1975; December 1, 1979; November 24, 1984; June 27, 1987.

Stand, Volume 17, number 1, 1975-76; Volume 22, number 3, 1981.

Time, March 19, 1984; February 25, 1985.

Times (London), October 11, 1984; January 24, 1985; October 22, 1987; June 3, 1989.

Times Literary Supplement, June 9, 1966; July 17, 1969; December 15, 1972; August 1, 1975; February 8, 1980; October 31, 1980; November 26, 1982; October 19, 1984; June 26, 1987; July 1-7, 1988; December 6, 1991.

Tribune Books (Chicago), November 8, 1987; November 25, 1990.

Twentieth Century Studies, November, 1970.

Virginia Quarterly Review, autumn, 1992.

Washington Post Book World, January 6, 1980; January 25, 1981; May 20, 1984; January 27, 1985; August 19, 1990.

World Literature Today, summer, 1977; autumn, 1981; summer, 1983.

*   *   *

HEARON, Shelby 1931-

PERSONAL: Born January 18, 1931, in Marion, KY; daughter of Charles B. (a geologist) and Evelyn (Roberts) Reed; married Robert J. Hearon, Jr. (an attorney), June 15, 1953 (divorced, 1977); married Billy Joe Lucas (a philosopher), April 19, 1981; children: (first marriage) Anne, Reed. *Education:* University of Texas, B.A. (with honors), 1953.

ADDRESSES: Home—5 Church St., North White Plains, NY 10603. *Agent*—Wendy Weil, Weil Agency, 232 Madison Ave., #1300, New York, NY 10016; (lecture agent) Bill Thompson, BWA, 61 Briarwood Circle, Needham Heights, MA 02194.

CAREER: Freelance writer, 1966—. Visiting lecturer, University of Texas at Austin, 1978-80; teacher, Bennington College Summer Program fiction workshop, summer, 1980; visiting associate professor, University of Houston, spring, 1981, and University of California at Irvine, 1987;

writer in residence, Wichita State University, spring, 1984, Clark University, spring, 1985, and Ohio Wesleyan University, spring, 1989; visiting professor, University of Illinois at Chicago, spring, 1993; visiting distinguished professor, Colgate University, fall, 1993, and University of Miami, Coral Gables, spring, 1994. Member of judging panel for numerous fiction and nonfiction awards.

MEMBER: Authors Guild, Authors League of America, PEN American Center, Poets & Writers, Inc., Associated Writing Programs, Texas Institute of Letters (president, 1979-81).

AWARDS, HONORS: Jesse H. Jones fiction award, Texas Institute of Letters, 1973, for *The Second Dune,* and 1978, for *A Prince of a Fellow;* New York Guggenheim fellowship, 1982; National Endowment for the Arts fellowship, 1983; PEN Syndication fiction prize, 1983, for "Missing Kin," 1984, for "The Undertow of Friends," 1985, for "Vast Distances," 1987, for "Growing Boys," and 1988, for "I've Seen It Twice"; Women in Communications award, 1984; Ingram Merrill grant, 1987; American Academy of Arts and Letters literature award, 1990; University of Texas distinguished alumnus, 1993.

WRITINGS:

NOVELS

Armadillo in the Grass, Knopf (New York City), 1968.
The Second Dune, Knopf, 1973.
Hannah's House, Doubleday (New York City), 1975.
Now and Another Time, Doubleday, 1976.
A Prince of a Fellow, Doubleday, 1978.
Painted Dresses, Atheneum (New York City), 1981.
Afternoon of a Faun, Atheneum, 1983.
Group Therapy, Atheneum, 1984.
A Small Town, Atheneum, 1985.
Five Hundred Scorpions, Atheneum, 1987.
Owning Jolene, Knopf, 1989.
Hug Dancing, Knopf, 1991.
Life Estates, Knopf, 1994.

OTHER

(With Barbara Jordan) *Barbara Jordan* (biography), Doubleday, 1979.

Contributor of short stories to anthologies, including "Order," published in *Her Work: Stories by Texas Women,* edited by Lou Rodenberger, Shearer (Bryan, TX), 1982; "Missing Kin," published in *Available Stories,* Ballantine (New York City), 1985; "The British Museum," published in *New Growth,* edited by Lyman Grant, Corona (San Antonio, TX), 1989; and "The Undertow of Friends," published in *Common Bonds,* edited by Suzanne Comer, Southern Methodist University Press (Dallas, TX), 1990. Contributor of short fiction to *Southwest Re-*

view, Mississippi Review, Southern Review, Cosmopolitan, and *Shenandoah.* Contributor of articles and features to periodicals, including *Publishers Weekly, Writer, Washington Post, Texas Monthly, GQ, Harper's Bazaar, Cosmopolitan,* and *Family Circle.* Contributor of book reviews to *Dallas Morning News,* 1979—, *New York Times, Washington Post,* and *Houston Post.* Member of advisory board and contributing editor, *American Literary Review,* 1991—, and *Shenandoah,* 1992—.

SIDELIGHTS: Much of Shelby Hearon's fiction is set in Texas, where the author lived for several years, and she usually writes about strong female protagonists. Described as a "female Larry McMurtry" by Marilyn Murray Willison in a *Los Angeles Times Book Review* article, Hearon is a writer whose novels "come off full but somehow uncrowded," notes *Dallas Morning News* interviewer Mary Brinkerhoff, "despite all the mothers, daughters, grandparents, husbands, ex-husbands, lovers, . . . ancestral memories, adolescent crises, family rituals, professional 'do-gooders,' partly liberated females, [and] freshly integrated schools. Also," adds Brinkerhoff, "each novel is illuminated by a feeling for context which evades too many writers—what [the author] herself calls 'an enormous sense of place,' an equally powerful flow of time (domestic or geologic) and a vividness of physical perception—the way food tastes, the way skin feels, the way a garden smells." On this point, Hearon told *CA,* "I always start a novel with place. I think to build a fictional world you have to walk where you have walked before: the building of a concrete and fictional world rests solidly on the grounding of remembrance and recollection. To rewalk the past is to rewrite the past. To return is to consider what might have been."

In *Painted Dresses* Hearon tells the story of a bittersweet romance between artist Nell and chemist Nick, two middle-aged characters who "have been stifled by early experiences in their family lives, and spend years trying to work them out," according to *Washington Post Book World* critic David Guy. "Like the lives she is describing," Guy says, "Shelby Hearon's narrative grows more satisfactory as it goes along; its early episodes can seem fragmentary and puzzling." And while he further criticizes some of Hearon's characters—"Nell's family is too cutely eccentric to be believed"—Guy ultimately praises *Painted Dresses* as the work of an author who "writes with the buoyant, precise prose of a veteran novelist. If her story is unsatisfactory at first, it builds in momentum once her characters reach adulthood, and ends wonderfully."

"A feel-good book" is the way Carolyn Banks, in a *Washington Post* review, describes Hearon's *Group Therapy,* the story of Lutie, a divorced Texas woman who moves to New York City to start a new life. Feeling out of place among the East Coast sophisticates, Lutie enrolls in a group therapy class that focuses on image. "Therapy saves Lutie," says Banks. "She learns that what is appropriate garb in the South is overdressing in the North." And then Lutie falls in love with Joe, one of her therapists. "Their romance generates the story's suspense—is [Lutie] indelibly Southern or has she been seduced by the North?," as Valerie Miner explains in the *New York Times Book Review. Group Therapy,* continues Miner, is "intelligent, witty, and tightly written," although "if anything, it is too compressed and needs more description of Lutie's work and her complex family." To Willison, in the *Los Angeles Times Book Review* article, the novel leaves "a warm, soft feeling of having shared chunks of the characters' lives."

Hearon's *A Small Town* is set in Venice, Missouri, a village on the Mississippi described by James Kaufmann in the *Los Angeles Times* as "the kind of place where what goes around comes around generation after generation." In fact, he indicates, "the burden of Hearon's novel is," as the main character tells it, "that 'history repeats.' " The book's narrator is Alma, who, according to Elizabeth Tallent in the *New York Times Book Review,* "grows from an abused child with a Huckleberry Finn spunkiness into a high-school Lolita, from a principal's dutiful wife into a trailer-park adulteress, handling each role with an equanimity she never admits to."

Janice Greene in the *San Francisco Chronicle Review* calls *A Small Town* "a delightfully entertaining novel," while Kaufmann points out that the book alternates between "humor and quiet wisdom—it has a friendly and even tone." "Fey, funny and sometimes sad," the book "is recommended reading," writes George Bulanda in the *Detroit News.* "It isn't without its faults, but the weaknesses pale in comparison to the strengths." In *A Small Town,* Greene concludes, "[Hearon's] writing is tight and clean and her craft so unobtrusive we hardly know it's there. She sets up a scene or builds a character as quietly as a weaving spider—a tightly drawn line here, a connecting thread there. Then light falls on the web and the whole pattern is revealed in its beauty and intricacy."

In *Five Hundred Scorpions* a disillusioned husband leaves his family to join an anthropological expedition in Mexico that turns out to have a distinctly feminist agenda. The novel is described by Lowry Pei in the *New York Times Book Review* as a graceful mixture of "bittersweet domestic comedy," intrigue, realism, and the "magical and fantastic." James Park Sloan, in the *Chicago Tribune,* finds that "the price of heightened sensitivity" in the book "is a feeling of limited depth." Pei, however, concludes that, "if its narration sometimes becomes too benign, . . . that is directly related to the risk Ms. Hearon takes which makes this book unique: the demonic and the domestic inhabit the novel together in a struggle that denies neither and intensifies both."

The title of *Owning Jolene* is a reference to the battle that a pair of divorced parents wage for possession of their daughter, the nineteen-year-old heroine of what James N. Baker calls in *Newsweek* "another penetrating comedy of Texas manners" that "seriously explores how fragile human self-perception can be" while taking "some entertaining satirical swipes at several cultural artifacts of the 1980s." Jolene is described by several reviewers as a passive character, but, affirms Tim Sandlin in the *New York Times Book Review,* "after 11 novels, Ms. Hearon has become very good at avoiding the pitfalls of passivity. Above all else, Jolene is likeable."

Hug Dancing, declares Penelope Rowlands in the *San Francisco Chronicle Review,* "seduces the reader with well-drawn characters who continually manage to surprise, yet remain believable, and a plot that may falter at times, yet always regains momentum." The plot revolves around what happens when an old sweetheart returns to disrupt Cile Tate's marriage to a Presbyterian minister, and "the entire experience," Dabney Stuart relates in the *Roanoke Times & World-News,* "evokes the essence of Greek tragedy, lightened." "Despite the quality of [Hearon's] past books," Stuart concludes, *Hug Dancing* "surpasses them in balance, grace, and acceptance." *Life Estates* follows lifelong friends Sarah and Harriet, both widowed in their fifties, as they reshape their lives without their husbands. While Sarah thrives, continuing as head of her own wallpaper business and beginning a new relationship, Harriet struggles to cope, terrified that she will become a stereotypical widow and at the same time unable to find purpose outside of the role of wife. A crisis forces the two to reevaluate their friendship. The book is "a wise, melancholy, glowing appreciation of middle age and after, a pleasure to read," Rebecca Radner comments in the *San Francisco Chronicle Review.* A *Publishers Weekly* reviewer finds *Life Estates* "a thoughtful and honest book" that speaks "of grace under pressure, of carrying on after loss and grief, of affirming the day and looking bravely into the future." *New York Times Book Review*'s Lee Smith concludes, "*Life Estates* is a quietly told novel of compassion and great charm."

BIOGRAPHICAL/CRITICAL SOURCES:

BOOKS

Contemporary Authors Autobiography Series, Volume 11, Gale (Detroit), 1990.

PERIODICALS

Chicago Tribune, April 26, 1987, Section 14, p. 6.
Dallas Morning News, March 6, 1976; October 13, 1985.
Detroit News, January 19, 1985.
Los Angeles Times, March 22, 1979; November 27, 1985.

Los Angeles Times Book Review, April 3, 1983; May 27, 1984; November 11, 1985.

Newsweek, July 3, 1978; December 2, 1985; April 17, 1989.

New Yorker, June, 1978.

New York Times Book Review, September 22, 1968; October 7, 1973; June 15, 1975; February 18, 1979; August 2, 1981; March 18, 1984; October 20, 1985; May 10, 1987, p. 7; January 22, 1989; February 13, 1994.

People, April 23, 1984; October 28, 1985.

Picture Week, November 25, 1985.

Publishers Weekly, December 13, 1993.

Roanoke Times & World-News, January 12, 1992.

San Francisco Chronicle Review, October 13, 1985; February 2, 1992; February 13, 1994, p. 3.

Washington Post, April 9, 1984; December 20, 1985.

Washington Post Book World, April 2, 1978; June 14, 1981; April 10, 1983.

*   *   *

HEERESMA, Heere   1932-
(Heeresma Inc., a joint pseudonym)

PERSONAL: Born March 9, 1932, in Amsterdam, Netherlands; son of Heere and Hendrika (van der Zwan) Heeresma; married Els Overvliet; married second wife, Louise Cornets de Groot, August 23, 1961; children: (first marriage) Marijne; (second marriage) Heere. *Education:* Studied layout at an engraving school in the Netherlands and took a two-year course in gardening and flower decorating. *Politics:* "Ultra Left and Right." *Religion:* "Thora and Tradition."

ADDRESSES: Home—Haagen Veld 187, Amsterdam-Bijlmermeer, Netherlands.

CAREER: Author.

MEMBER: Vereniging voor Letterkundigen, Maatschappij voor Nederlandse Letterkunde.

WRITINGS:

Bevind van Zaken (short stories), Contact (Amsterdam), 1962.

Een dagje naar het strand (novella), Contact, 1962, translation by James Brockway published as *A Day at the Beach,* Alan Ross, 1967.

De Vis (allegory), Contact, 1963.

Juweeltjes van Waterverf (short stories), Contact, 1965, 2nd edition published as *Slapstick,* Striptease, 1970.

De verloedering van de Swieps (film scenario), Contact, 1967.

De Roadman (novel), Polak & van Gennep, 1968.

Geef die mok eens door, Jet! Een avontuurlijk verhaal vol gruwel en geweld, Contact & van Gennep, 1968.

Werk van Heere Heeresma, Contact, 1968.

Hip Hip Hip voor de AntiKrist (novel), Contact, 1969.

(Under pseudonym Heeresma Inc.) *Teneinde in Dublin,* Bruna (Utrecht, Netherlands), 1969.

Han de wit gaat in ontwikkelingshulp, Rap (Amsterdam), 1972.

Langs berg en dal klinkt hoorngeschal, Contact, 1972.

Zwaarmoedige verhalen voor bij de centrale verwarming, Rap, 1973.

Vader vertelt, Rap, 1974.

Mijmeringen naast m'n naaimachine: Over het leed in het algemeen en de rijpere vrouw vaak in het bizonder, Rap, 1975.

Waar het fruit valt, valt het nergens: Rijp en rot, wijs en zot, treur en spot, Rap, 1976.

Enige portretten van een mopperkont, Athenaeum/Loeb (Amsterdam), 1977.

Heeresma helemaal: Verzamelde verhalen, Loeb & Van der Velden (Amsterdam), 1978.

(With Laurie Langenbach) *Hier mijn hand en daar je wang: Wat intieme correspondentie,* Loeb, 1978.

Eens en nooit weer, Loeb & Van der Velden, 1979.

(With Hans Dutting) *Heere Heeresma—en greep me duchtig bij de keel: Confrontaties met de schrijver,* Van der Velden, 1981.

Autobiografisch, Villa (Bussum, Netherlands), 1983.

Beuk en degel, Villa, 1983.

Spreekt met winter en 't komt in orde, Prom (Baarn, Netherlands), 1986.

(With others) *Gelukkig gescheiden: Echtscheiding in de Nederlandse literatuur* (fiction), Novella (Amersfoort, Netherlands), 1992.

Also author of screenplays for films, including *De verloedering van de Swieps* and *De Roadman,* both directed by Erik Terpstra, and *A Day at the Beach,* produced by Gutowski-Cadre Films; and of teleplays, including *Met z'n allen door de vloer,* 1967, *De wereld heeft een prachtkamar,* 1968, and *Mijn vriend de kommissaris,* 1968. Also writer for radio program *Radiorama.*

Heeresma's writings have been translated into German, French, Danish, Slovak, Finnish, and Romanian.

SIDELIGHTS: Kay Dick writes of Heere Heeresma's novel *A Day at the Beach:* "With admirable precision and a fine edge of humor, it conveys the drama of a man who deliberately chooses to waste himself. . . . Short though it is, it contains more wisdom, and art, than many novels self-consciously worked out at full length." Rivers Scott calls it "a tour de force of such intensity that its horror is almost unbearable." "I do not think that the extinction of the modern novel is such a real possibility." writes Campbell Black. "Every so often a work appears which, to some extent, reaffirms one's faith in the art of fiction . . . *A Day at the Beach* strikes me as one of these." Black continues:

"Such a situation could, in the hands of a lesser writer, have developed into dreadful melodrama, but because the author's main focal point is the drunk, Bernard, and not the child, he has written a novel which is essentially tragic. . . . This novel is a considerable achievement and is certain to make the author's name better known." Speaking of Bernard and the child, Gabriel Fielding writes: "The pain is as luminous as the pleasure and both are informed by a wit so singular that it is the other 'normal' people who appear pitiable."

BIOGRAPHICAL/CRITICAL SOURCES:

PERIODICALS

Catholic Herald, August 4, 1967.
Observer (London), June 11, 1967.
Ons erfdeel, December, 1967.
Queen, June 7, 1967.
Spectator, June 10, 1967.
Sunday Telegraph (London), May 28, 1967.
Sunday Times (London), June 11, 1967.*

* * *

HEERESMA INC.
See HEERESMA, Heere

* * *

HEINRICHS, Waldo H(untley), Jr.   1925-

PERSONAL: Born July 19, 1925, in New York, NY; son of Waldo Huntley; married, 1949; children: four. *Education:* Harvard University, B.A., 1949, Ph.D., 1960; Oxford University, B.A., 1951.

ADDRESSES: Office—Department of History, San Diego State University, San Diego, CA 92182-0380.

CAREER: Wheelock College, Wheelock, WV, instructor in history, 1959-60; Johns Hopkins University, Baltimore, MD, assistant professor of history, 1960-66; University of Tennessee, Knoxville, associate professor of history, 1966-68; University of Illinois at Urbana-Champaign, Urbana, professor of history, 1968-74; Temple University, Philadelphia, PA, professor of history, 1974-91; San Diego State University, San Diego, CA, professor of history and holder of Dwight E. Stanford Chair in American Foreign Relations, 1991—. Visiting lecturer at Harvard University, 1963-64. Appeared on *Today Show,* NBC-TV, during anniversary of World War II's Pearl Harbor invasion, 1991. Consultant to British Broadcasting Corp. (BBC).

MEMBER: Society of Historians of American Foreign Relations.

AWARDS, HONORS: Allan Nevins Prize, Society for American Historians, 1960; fellowship, Woodrow Wilson Center for International Scholars, 1985-86.

WRITINGS:

American Ambassador: Joseph C. Grew and the Development of the U.S. Diplomatic Tradition, Little, Brown (Boston), 1966.
(Editor with Dorothy Borg) *Uncertain Years: Chinese-American Relations, 1947-1950,* Columbia University Press (New York City), 1980.
Threshold of War: Franklin D. Roosevelt and American Entry into World War II, Oxford University Press (New York City), 1988.

Contributor to books, including *Twentieth-Century American Foreign Policy,* edited by John Braeman and others, Ohio State University Press (Columbus), 1971; *Dragon and Eagle: Sino-American Relations in Historical Perspective,* edited by Michel Oxenberg and Robert Oxnam, Basic Books (New York City), 1978; *New Frontiers in Chinese-American Relations,* edited by Warren Cohen, Columbia University Press, 1985; *Pearl Harbor Reexamined,* edited by Hilary Conroy and Harry Wray, University of Hawaii Press (Honolulu), 1990; and *Pearl Harbor Fifty Years After* (in Japanese), edited by Hosoya Chihiro, Kodansha Press, 1993. Contributor to periodicals. Member of board of editors, *Pacific Historical Review, Diplomatic History,* and *Journal of American-East Asian Relations.*

WORK IN PROGRESS: A book on the end of World War II.

BIOGRAPHICAL/CRITICAL SOURCES:

PERIODICALS

American Historical Review, July, 1967.
Annals of the American Academy of Political and Social Science, January, 1968.
Saturday Review, February 4, 1967.

* * *

HELBLING, Robert E(ugene)   1923-

PERSONAL: Born May 6, 1923, in Lucerne, Switzerland; immigrated to United States, 1948, naturalized citizen, 1954; son of Emil (a librarian) and Senta (Lamm) Helbling; married Suzanne O. Ottinger (an office manager), June 9, 1956. *Education:* Handelsschule, Lucerne, diploma, 1943; University of Utah, M.A., 1949; Columbia University, graduate study, 1951; Stanford University, Ph.D., 1958; University of California, Berkeley, postdoctoral study, 1961. *Politics:* Independent.

ADDRESSES: Home—3018 St. Mary's Circle, Salt Lake City, UT 84108. *Office*—Department of Languages, University of Utah, Salt Lake City, UT 84112.

CAREER: R. I. Geigy, Inc. Chemical Works, Basel, Switzerland, junior executive for foreign trade, 1945-47; University of Utah, Salt Lake City, instructor in French and German, 1950-57, assistant professor, 1958-61, associate professor, 1962-65, professor of French, German, and comparative literature, 1966—, coordinator of humanities program, 1958-76, director of honors program, 1964-66; chair of department of languages, 1965-77, Reynolds lecturer and distinguished honors professor, 1983—. Visiting associate professor, Long Island University, summer, 1962; occasional reader for Oxford University Press, New Directions Press, and Holt, Rinehart, Winston. *Military service:* Swiss Army, 1943-45.

MEMBER: Association of Departments of Foreign Languages (member of executive committee, 1973-75, president, 1974—), Modern Language Association of America, American Association of Teachers of German, American Association of Teachers of French, American Association of University Professors (president of Salt Lake City Chapter, 1963-64), Joint National Council for Languages, (chair, 1975), Phi Kappa Phi (president of local chapter, 1973-74), Phi Delta Phi, Phi Sigma Iota, Sigma Delta Pi, Delta Phi Alpha.

AWARDS, HONORS: Named one of the Outstanding Educators in America, 1971.

WRITINGS:

(Editor with Andree M. L. Barnett) Pierre Daninos, *Les Carnets du Major Thompson* (title means "The Notebooks of Major Thompson"), Holt (New York City), 1959.

(With Barnett) *Le Language de la France Moderne* (title means "The Language of Modern France"), Holt, 1961.

(Editor and author of essay) Friedrich Duerrenmatt, *Die Physiker*, Oxford University Press (New York City), 1965.

(With Barnett) *L'Actualite Francaise* (title means "The Contemporary French Presence"), Holt, 1967.

(Editor and author of essay) *Heinrich von Kleist: Novellan und Aesthetische Schriften* (title means "Heinrich von Kleist: Novellas and Aesthetic Writings"), Oxford University Press, 1967.

(With Morton Donner and Kenneth E. Eble) *The Intellectual Tradition of the West*, Scott, Foresman (Glenview, IL), Volume I: *From Hesiod to Calvin*, 1967, Volume II: *From Copernicus to Kafka*, 1968.

(With Barnett) *Introduction au Francais Actuel* (title means "Introduction to Contemporary French"), Holt, 1973.

The Major Works of Heinrich von Kleist, New Directions (New York City), 1975.

(With Wolf Gewehr and Wolff A. von Schmidt) *First-Year German*, Holt, 1975, 3rd edition, 1983.

(With Gewehr and von Schmidt) *Current Issues: Basic German Readings*, Holt, 1975, 2nd edition, 1979.

(With Gewehr and von Schmidt) *Arts and Letters*, Holt, 1975, 2nd edition, 1979.

The Power of "Negative" Thinking: The Grotesque in the Modern World (45th Annual Frederick William Reynolds lecture), F. W. Reynolds Association (Salt Lake City, UT), 1982.

(Editor) Heinrich von Kleist, *Erzahlungen* (German text with notes in English), Suhrkamp/Insel (Boston, MA), 1983.

(With others) *Aspekte: Kultur, Politik, Alltag, Literatur* (German and English text), Holt, 1984.

(With Franz R. Kempf) *Deutsche Gegenwart* (German and English text), Holt, 1985.

Also coeditor, with Morton Donner and Kenneth E. Eble, of *Readings in the History of Ideas*, University of Utah Press. Contributor to books, including *Friedrich Duerrenmatt: Studien zu seinem Werk* (title means "Friedrich Duerrenmatt: Studies on His Work"), Lothar Stiehm (Heidelberg), 1976. Contributor to *Heinrich von Kleist Studies*, Hofstra University Cultural and Intercultural Studies. Book reviewer for *Language Quarterly* and *Monostshefte*.

BIOGRAPHICAL/CRITICAL SOURCES:

PERIODICALS

Times Literary Supplement, March 12, 1976.

*   *   *

HELLYER, Paul (Theodore) 1923-

PERSONAL: Born August 6, 1923, in Waterford, Ontario, Canada; son of Audrey Samuel (a farmer) and Lulla Maude (Anderson) Hellyer; married Ellen Jean Ralph, June 1, 1945; children: Mary Elizabeth, Peter Lawrence, David Ralph. *Education:* Curtiss-Wright Technical Institute of Aerodynamics, diploma in aeronautical engineering, 1941; University of Toronto, B.A., 1949. *Religion:* United Church. *Avocational interests:* Swimming, water-skiing, skin and scuba diving, stamp collecting.

ADDRESSES: Home—506-65 Harbour Square, Toronto, Ontario, Canada M5J 2L4. *Office*—302-99 Atlantic Ave., Toronto, Ontario, Canada M6K 3J8.

CAREER: Fleet Aircraft Manufacturing Co. Ltd., Fort Erie, Ontario, 1942-44, began as junior draftsperson, became group leader in engineering department; House of

Commons, Ottawa, Ontario, representative from Davenport riding, 1949-57, and Trinity riding, 1958-74; *Toronto Sun,* Toronto, Ontario, author of syndicated column "Comment—Paul Hellyer," 1974-84. Proprietor of Mari-Jane Fashions (Toronto), 1945-56; president of Curran-Hall Ltd., 1951-62, Trepil Realty Ltd., 1951-62, and Hendon Estates Ltd., 1959-62; distinguished visitor at York University, 1969-70. Member of Canadian Privy Council and Associate Minister of National Defence, 1957, Minister of National Defence, 1963-67, Minister of Transport, 1967-69, minister responsible for housing and urban affairs, 1968-69, acting Prime Minister, 1968-69; founding chairperson of Action Canada (populist movement), 1971—; committee chairperson and opposition spokesperson on industry, trade, and commerce for Progressive Conservative Caucus, 1973. *Military service:* Royal Canadian Air Force, 1944. Canadian Army, Royal Canadian Artillery, 1945-46; received Coronation medal, Centennial medal, Jubilee medal, and commemorative medal for the 125th anniversary of the Confederation of Canada.

MEMBER: North Atlantic Treaty Organization (NATO) Parliamentary Association, Commonwealth Parliamentary Association, Royal Society for the Encouragement of Arts, Manufactures and Commerce (fellow), Canadian Institute of International Affairs, Association of Canadian Television and Radio Artists, National Ballet of Canada, Canadian Association for Adult Education, Canadian Authors Association, Ontario Club, Ontario Art Gallery, Royal Ontario Museum.

WRITINGS:

Agenda: A Plan for Action, Prentice-Hall (Englewood Cliffs, NJ), 1971.
Exit Inflation, Nelson (Scarborough, Ontario), 1981.
Jobs for All: Capitalism on Trial, Methuen (Scarborough, Ontario), 1984.
Canada at the Crossroads, Chimo Media, 1990.
Damn the Torpedoes: My Fight to Unify Canada's Armed Forces, McClelland and Stewart (Toronto, Ontario), 1990.
Funny Money: A Common Sense Alternative to Mainline Economics, Chimo Media, 1994.

Contributor to *Queen's Quarterly.*

SIDELIGHTS: A Canadian politician who once served as a Liberal Cabinet minister, Paul Hellyer is also the author of several books on politics and economics. Hellyer once told *CA:* "My central thesis has been that the division between Left and Right in politics, between East and West in the world, is based on a false premise, i.e., that it is not possible to operate a decentralized private capital system with full employment and stable prices. If the premise is wrong, as I believe, then the whole superstructure of band-aid programs designed to alleviate the symptoms has to be

re-examined. While, theoretically, politics is the vehicle for the re-examination, the rigidity of bureaucracies and the reluctance to innovate makes the introduction of new ideas difficult."

In his *Globe and Mail* review of Hellyer's *Jobs for All: Capitalism on Trial,* Charles Taylor explains, "In presenting his own solution, Hellyer maintains that the main cause of inflation [in Canada] is the widening gap between wage increases and productivity." Despite dismissing Hellyer's idea to unify the Canadian armed forces as "one of the Liberals' more bone-headed decisions of recent decades," Taylor offers the following endorsement of Hellyer's economic approach: "If *Jobs for All* could spark a serious debate on economic priorities . . . then Hellyer would have done his party, and the nation, some real service."

BIOGRAPHICAL/CRITICAL SOURCES:

PERIODICALS

Globe and Mail (Toronto), February 18, 1984.
Toronto Sun, March 12, 1995, p. 15.

*   *   *

HELMS, Randel   1942-

PERSONAL: Born November 16, 1942, in Montgomery, AL; son of Loyce Virgil (a contractor) and Vernell Helms; married Penelope Palmer, August 1, 1964; children: Katherine. *Education:* University of California, Riverside, B.A. (magna cum laude), 1964; University of Washington, Seattle, Ph.D., 1968.

ADDRESSES: Home—6514 North 87th Pl., Scottsdale, AZ 85253. *Office*—Department of English, Arizona State University, Tempe, AZ 85287.

CAREER: University of California, Los Angeles, assistant professor of English, beginning 1968; Arizona State University, Tempe, associate professor of English.

MEMBER: Modern Language Association of America.

WRITINGS:

Tolkien's World, Houghton (Boston), 1974.
Tolkien and the Silmarils, Houghton, 1981.
Gospel Fictions, Prometheus Books (Buffalo), 1988.

Contributor to literature journals.

WORK IN PROGRESS: Intellectual Warfare, a monograph on William Blake's use of the Bible; *The Prophetic Book,* a monograph on Old Testament prophecy.

HENDERSON, Bill
See HENDERSON, William Charles

*　　*　　*

HENDERSON, William Charles 1941-
(Bill Henderson; Luke Walton, a pseudonym)

PERSONAL: Born April 5, 1941, in Philadelphia, PA; son of Francis Louis (an engineer) and Dorothy Price (a teacher; maiden name, Galloway) Henderson; married September 29, 1983; wife's name, Genie (a writer); children: Lily. *Education:* Hamilton College, B.A., 1963; graduate study, Harvard University, 1963, and University of Pennsylvania, 1965-66. *Politics:* Independent. *Religion:* Independent.

ADDRESSES: Home and office—P.O. Box 380, Wainscott, NY 11975.

CAREER: Nautilus Books, cofounder, c. 1971; Doubleday & Co., New York City, associate editor, 1972-73; Pushcart Press, Wainscott, NY, publisher, 1972—; Coward, McCann & Geoghegan, senior editor, 1973-75; Harper & Row, consulting editor, 1975—. Guest lecturer at Harvard University, summer, 1974, Columbia University, 1976-79, Sarah Lawrence College, University of Rochester, summers, 1978 and 1987, Princeton University, 1983, 1986, and 1987, Johns Hopkins University, 1989, and Radcliffe Publishing Course, 1989; Library of Congress, Center for the Book, member of national advisory board, 1979; Pushcart Foundation, president, 1984-87.

MEMBER: PEN, Lead Pencil Club (founder).

AWARDS, HONORS: Citation, New Jersey Association of Teachers of English, 1972, for *The Galapagos Kid;* Newsboy Award, Horatio Alger Society, 1973; Carey-Thomas Award, *Publishers Weekly,* 1978, for creative publishing.

WRITINGS:

EDITOR

The Publish-It-Yourself Handbook—Literary Tradition and How-To without Commercial or Vanity Publishers, Pushcart (Yonkers, NY), 1973, revised edition, 1980.
The Pushcart Prize: Best of the Small Presses (annual anthology), Pushcart, 1976—.
The Art of Literary Publishing: Editors on Their Craft, Pushcart, 1980.
Rotten Reviews: A Literary Companion, introduction by Anthony Brandt, illustrations by Mary Kornblum, Pushcart, 1986.

Rotten Reviews II: A Literary Companion, introduction by Brandt, illustrations by Kornblum, Pushcart (Wainscott, NY), 1987.
Love Stories for the Time Being, Pushcart, 1987.
(With Genie D. Chipps) *Love Stories for the Rest of Us,* Pushcart, 1994.

OTHER

(Under pseudonym Luke Walton) *The Galapagos Kid* (novel), Nautilus Books, 1971.
His Son: A Child of the Fifties (memoir), Norton (New York City), 1981.
Her Father (memoir), Faber & Faber (Winchester, MA), 1995.

Also author of *The Kid That Could,* 1990. Contributor to books, including *Lost in Cyberspace: Essays and Far-Fetched Tales,* edited by Val Schaffner, Bridge Works Publishing, 1993. Contributor of short stories and essays to periodicals, including *Carolina Quarterly, Chicago Review, Ontario Review,* and *New York Times Book Review.*

SIDELIGHTS: After finding no one to publish his first novel, *The Galapagos Kid,* William Charles Henderson teamed up with his uncle and they founded their own small publishing house, Nautilus Books. Although Nautilus soon folded, Henderson launched the small-but-well-regarded Pushcart Press in 1973 with a book that he felt sure people needed: *The Publish-It-Yourself Handbook—Literary Tradition and How-To without Commercial or Vanity Publishers.* One chapter was contributed by Anais Nin, who published all her own work during the 1940s, and other chapters were written by editors, publishers, Henderson, and other self-published authors. The volume was favorably reviewed and sold better than Henderson expected; his initial cautious printing of one thousand copies soon turned into multiple reprintings.

In a *Publishers Weekly* interview with Robert Dahlin, Henderson discusses the functions of small presses, including his own Pushcart Press: "Most small presses, even if they are good, never make it out of the garage. But they provide a great chance for the writer to write freely, without commercial restraint. They are just about the only place a new writer can get a hearing, the only place a writer can learn." Critics, including Stephen Stark, agree. Reviewing a Pushcart Prize anthology in the *New York Times Book Review,* Stark called it "a testament to the way literature has survived, even flourished, beyond the high-walled island of commercial publishing."

BIOGRAPHICAL/CRITICAL SOURCES:

BOOKS

Dictionary of Literary Biography Yearbook: 1987, Gale (Detroit), 1988, pp. 47-51.

PERIODICALS

Chicago Tribune, March 14, 1991, section 2, p. 3.
Los Angeles Times, March 11, 1981.
New York Times Book Review, January 7, 1990.
Poets and Writers, May/June, 1995, p. 63.
Publishers Weekly, June 5, 1978; August 28, 1989.
Tribune Books (Chicago), January 29, 1989, p. 4.
Washington Post, March 26, 1981, p. D13.

* * *

HERBER, Lewis
See BOOKCHIN, Murray

* * *

HIGHSMITH, (Mary) Patricia   1921-1995
(Claire Morgan)

PERSONAL: Born January 19, 1921, in Fort Worth, TX; daughter of Jay Bernard Plangman and Mary (Coates) Highsmith; died February 4, 1995, in Locarno, Switzerland. *Education:* Barnard College, B.A., 1942. *Avocational interests:* Drawing, painting, carpentering, snail watching, traveling by train.

ADDRESSES: Agent—Marianne Ligginstorfer, Diogenes Verlag, Sprechtstrasse 8, 8032 Zurich, Switzerland.

CAREER: Writer, 1942-95.

MEMBER: Detection Club.

AWARDS, HONORS: Mystery Writers of America Scroll and Grand Prix de Litterature Policiere, both 1957, both for *The Talented Mr. Ripley;* Silver Dagger Award for best crime novel of the year, Crime Writers Association of England, 1964, for *The Two Faces of January;* Officer l'Ordre des Arts es des Lettres, 1990.

WRITINGS:

NOVELS

Strangers on a Train (also see below), Harper (New York City), 1950.
(Under pseudonym Claire Morgan) *The Price of Salt,* Coward-McCann (New York City), 1952, reprinted as *Carol* under the name Patricia Highsmith with a new afterword by the author, Naiad Press (Tallahassee, FL), 1984.
The Blunderer (also see below), Coward-McCann, 1954, published as *Lament for a Lover,* Popular Library, 1956, reprinted under original title, Hamlyn (London), 1978.
The Talented Mr. Ripley (also see below), Coward-McCann, 1955.

Deep Water, Harper, 1957, published in England as *Deep Water: A Novel of Suspense,* Heinemann (London), 1957.
A Game for the Living, Harper, 1958.
This Sweet Sickness (also see below), Harper, 1960.
The Cry of the Owl, Harper, 1962.
The Two Faces of January, Doubleday (New York City), 1964.
The Glass Cell, Doubleday, 1964.
The Story-Teller, Doubleday, 1965, published in England as *A Suspension of Mercy,* Heinemann, 1965.
Those Who Walk Away, Doubleday, 1967.
The Tremor of Forgery, Doubleday, 1969.
Ripley under Ground (also see below), Doubleday, 1970.
A Dog's Ransom, Knopf (New York City), 1972.
Ripley's Game (also see below), Knopf, 1974.
Edith's Diary, Simon & Schuster (New York City), 1977.
The Boy Who Followed Ripley, Crowell, 1980.
People Who Knock on the Door, Heinemann, 1983, Mysterious Press, 1985.
The Mysterious Mr. Ripley (contains *The Talented Mr. Ripley, Ripley under Ground,* and *Ripley's Game*), Penguin, 1985.
Found in the Street, Heinemann, 1986, Atlantic Monthly Press (New York City), 1987.
Mermaids on a Golf Course, Mysterious Press, 1988.
Ripley under Water, Knopf, 1991.
The Boy Who Followed Ripley, Vintage (New York City), 1993.

SHORT STORIES

(With Doris Sanders) *Miranda the Panda Is on the Veranda* (juvenile), Coward-McCann, 1958.
The Snail-Watcher, and Other Stories, Doubleday, 1970 (published in England as *Eleven: Short Stories,* Heinemann, 1970).
Little Tales of Misogyny (in German), Diogenes Verlag (Zurich), 1974, English language edition, Heinemann, 1977, Mysterious Press, 1987.
The Animal-Lover's Book of Beastly Murder (young adult), Heinemann, 1975.
Slowly, Slowly in the Wind, Heinemann, 1979, Mysterious Press, 1987.
The Black House, David & Charles, 1979, published in England as *The Black House, and Other Stories,* Heinemann, 1981.
Mermaids on the Golf Course, and Other Stories, Heinemann, 1985, Mysterious Press, 1988.

OTHER

Plotting and Writing Suspense Fiction, Writers Inc., 1966, enlarged and revised edition, St. Martin's (New York City), 1981.

Tales of Natural and Unnatural Catastrophes, Heinemann, 1987, Atlantic Monthly Press, 1989.

Also author of material for television, including the "Alfred Hitchcock Presents" series.

ADAPTATIONS: Strangers on a Train was made into a film directed by Alfred Hitchcock, produced by Warner Brothers in 1951, and it also served as the basis for another Warner Brothers movie in 1969, entitled *Once You Kiss a Stranger; The Talented Mr. Ripley* was filmed as *Purple Noon* by Times Film Corp. in 1961; *The Blunderer* was first filmed as *Le Meurtrier* in 1963 and then as *Enough Rope* by Artixo Productions in 1966; *This Sweet Sickness* inspired the French film *Tell Her That I Love Her* in 1977; and *Ripley's Game* was filmed as *The American Friend* in 1978. Many other novels by Highsmith have been optioned for film.

SIDELIGHTS: The author of numerous short story collections and novels, including the well-known *Strangers on a Train,* American-born Patricia Highsmith enjoyed greater critical and commercial success in England, France, and Germany than in her native country. As Jeff Weinstein speculates in the *Village Voice Literary Supplement,* the reason for this is that Highsmith's books have been "misplaced"—relegated to the mystery and suspense shelves instead of being allowed to take their rightful place in the literature section. As far as her ardent admirers in the United States and abroad are concerned, Highsmith was more than just a superb crime novelist. In fact, declares Brigid Brophy in *Don't Never Forget: Collected Views and Reviews,* "there's the injustice. . . . As a novelist *tout court* [Highsmith is] excellent. . . . Highsmith and Simenon are alone in writing books which transcend the limits of the genre while staying strictly inside its rules: they alone have taken the crucial step from playing games to creating art."

Reviewer Robert Towers, however, sees signs of a turn in the American reception of Highsmith's work. Writing in the *New York Review of Books,* he observes that Highsmith "has had enthusiastic [American] readers ever since her first book, *Strangers on a Train,* which was filmed by Hitchcock," and that although her "literary reputation is fairly recent" in this country, it "seems just now to be gaining momentum."

The art in Highsmith's work springs from her skillful fusion of plot, characterization, and style, with the crime story serving primarily "as a means of revealing and examining her own deepest interests and obsessions," according to a *Times Literary Supplement* reviewer. Among her most common themes are the nature of guilt and the often symbiotic relationship that develops between two people (almost always men) who are at the same time fascinated and repelled by each other. Highsmith's works therefore

"dig down very deeply into the roots of personality," says Julian Symons in the *London Magazine,* exposing the darkside of people regarded by society as normal and good. Or, as Thomas Sutcliffe explains in the *Times Literary Supplement,* Highsmith wrote "not about what it feels like to be mad, but what it feels like to remain sane while committing the actions of a madman."

Also in the *Times Literary Supplement,* James Campbell states that "the conflict of good and evil—or rather, simple decency and ordinary badness—is at the heart of all Highsmith's novels, dramatized in the encounters between two characters, often in an exotic locale, where it is easier to lose one's moral bearings. Usually, we see events from the point of view of the innocent, the blind, as they stumble towards doom."

Highsmith's preoccupations with guilt and contrasting personalities surfaced as early as her very first novel. *Strangers on a Train* chronicles the relationship between Guy Haines, a successful young architect, and Charles Bruno, a charming but unstable man slightly younger than Haines. The two men first meet on a train journey when Bruno repeatedly tries to engage his traveling companion in conversation. He eventually persuades Haines to open up and talk about feelings he usually keeps to himself—including the fact that he harbors resentment toward his wife. Bruno, who has long fantasized about killing his much-hated father, then suggests to Haines that they rid themselves of the "problems" once and for all: Bruno will kill Haines's wife for him, and Haines in turn will kill Bruno's father. Since there is no connection between the victims and their killers, Bruno theorizes, the police will be at a loss to solve the murders. With more than a hint of reluctance, Haines rejects the plan, but to no avail; Bruno remains intrigued by it and proceeds to carry out his part.

As Paul Binding observes in a *Books and Bookmen* article, "the relation of abnormal Bruno to normal [Haines] is an exceedingly complex one which is to reverberate throughout Patricia Highsmith's output. On the one hand Bruno is a *doppelgaenger* figure; he embodies in repulsive flesh and blood form what [Haines's] subconscious has long been whispering to him. . . . On the other hand Bruno exists in his own perverse right, and [Haines] can have no control over him. . . . As a result of [Bruno's] existence, and of its coincidence with [Haines's] own, the rational, moral [Haines] becomes entangled in a mesh which threatens to destroy his entire security of identity. . . . [Haines is a man] tormented by guilt—guilt originally inspired by interior elements. Yet [he becomes], in society's eyes, guilty for exterior reasons." With the exception of the Ripley books (*The Talented Mr. Ripley, Ripley under Ground, Ripley's Game, The Boy Who Followed Ripley,* and *Ripley under Water*), which focus on the activities of the opportunistic and amoral Tom Ripley, a man incapable of feeling guilt, these themes are at the heart of Highsmith's fiction.

According to Symons, Highsmith typically launched her stories with the kind of "trickily ingenious plot devices often used by very inferior writers." He hastens to add, however, that these serve only as starting points for the "profound and subtle studies of character that follow." As Burt Supree observes in the *Village Voice Literary Supplement,* most of Highsmith's characters—none of whom are "heroes" in the conventional sense—are likely to be "obsessive, unquestioning, humdrum men with no self-knowledge, no curiosity, and Byzantine fantasy-lives—respectable or criminal middle-class, middle-brow people of incredible shallowness. Nowhere else will you find so many characters you'd want to smack. . . . Like lab animals, [they] come under careful scrutiny, but [Highsmith] doesn't care to analyze them or beg sympathy for them. They go their independent ways with the illusion of freedom. Contact seems only to sharpen their edges, to irk and enrage." Yet as Craig Brown points out in the *Times Literary Supplement,* "it is a rare villain or psychopath [in Highsmith's fiction] whom the reader does not find himself willing toward freedom, a rare investigator whom the reader is unhappy to see dead. Those she terms her 'murderer-heroes' or 'heropsychopaths' are usually people whose protective shells are not thick enough to deaden the pain as the world hammers at their emotions. . . . Some live, some die, some kill, some crack up."

Sutcliffe echoes this assessment of Highsmith's characters as basically sane people who commit apparently insane acts, usually while under considerable strain. "What she observes so truthfully is not the collapse of reason but its persistence in what it suits us to think of as inappropriate conditions," Sutcliffe assesses. He continues: "Even Ripley, the least scrupulous and likeable of her central characters, has motives for his actions, and though they are venal and vicious they are not irrational. Her suburban killers remain calculatingly evasive until the end. . . . They don't hear voices and they don't have fun. Indeed in the act of killing their attitude is one of dispassionate detachment, of a sustained attempt to rationalize the intolerable. . . . In all the books death is contingent and unsought, almost never meticulously planned and very rarely the focus for our moral indignation."

In the eyes of most critics, it is Highsmith's skill at depicting a character's slide into derangement or death that distinguishes her "in a field where imitative hacks and dull formula-mongers abound," remarks a *Times Literary Supplement* reviewer. Symons declares, "The quality that takes her books beyond the run of intelligent fiction is not [the] professional ability to order a plot and create a significant environment, but rather the intensity of feeling that she brings to the problems of her central figures. . . . From original ideas that are sometimes far-fetched or even trivial she proceeds with an imaginative power that makes the whole thing terrifyingly real." The world she creates for her characters has a "relentless, compulsive, mutedly ominous quality," asserts Hermione Lee in the *Observer,* one that leaves the reader "in a perpetual state of anxiety and wariness."

The prose Highsmith uses to communicate a sense of chilling dread and almost claustrophobic desperation is flat and plain, devoid of jargon, cliches, and padding. Some find it reminiscent of a psychological case history—a detailed and dispassionate account of a life moving out of control. According to Reg Gadney in *London Magazine,* "It is a characteristic skill of Miss Highsmith to convey unease and apprehension with an understated narrative style and painstaking description of domestic practicalities. Her characters often seem to counterbalance their expectation of fear by entrenching themselves in domestic routines. . . . [Their] tenacious efforts . . . to keep hold of everyday reality and logic serve to heighten the menace and chaos." *New Statesman* reviewer Blake Morrison, in fact, believes Highsmith is "at her most macabre when most mundane."

In Brown's opinion, "her style, on the surface so smooth and calm, underneath so powerful and merciless," is precisely what "entices the reader in and then sends him, alongside the 'psychopath-hero,' tumbling against the rocks." Weinstein agrees that "the reader has no choice but to follow the work, nothing could go another way. You are trapped in the very ease of the reading. The result is like suffocation, losing breath or will." Orhan Pamuk, reviewing the "Ripley" books in the *Village Voice,* describes the fascination: "To know that people really will be hurt bonds the reader, with an almost self-destructive joy, to Highsmith's novels. For the reader has already discovered that the banality and pettiness, which spread like an epidemic in every one of her books, are those of his own life. He might as well begin to loathe himself. We rediscover, in each novel, the vulnerability of our existence."

Symons identifies several qualities in Highsmith's work that make her, in his words, "such an interesting and unusual novelist." He has particular praise for "the power with which her male characters are realized" as well as for her ability to portray "what would seem to most people abnormal states of minds and ways of behavior." Symons continues: "The way in which all this is presented can be masterly in its choice of tone and phrase. [Highsmith's] opening sentences make a statement that is symbolically meaningful in relation to the whole book. . . . The setting is also chosen with great care. . . . [She seems to be making the point that] in surroundings that are sufficiently strange, men become uncertain of their personalities and question the reason for their own conduct in society." In short, remarks Symons, Highsmith's work is "as serious in its implications and as subtle in its approach as anything being done in the novel today."

A *Times Literary Supplement* reviewer reflects on the dilemma facing those who attempt to evaluate Highsmith's work, explaining that, in essence, "it is difficult to find ways of praising [her] that do not at the same time do something to diminish her. . . . With each new book, she is ritually congratulated for outstripping the limitations of her genre, for being as much concerned with people and ideas as with manipulated incident, for attempting a more than superficial exploration of the psychopathology of her unpleasant heroes—for, in short, exhibiting some of the gifts and preoccupations which are elementarily demanded of competent straight novelists." According to the same reviewer, Highsmith can best be described in the following terms: "She is the crime writer who comes closest to giving crime writing a good name." And J. M. Edelstein in a *New Republic* article sums up: "Low-key is the word for Patricia Highsmith. . . . Low-key, subtle, and profound. It is amazing to me that she is not better known for she is superb and is a master of the suspense novel. . . . [The body of her work] should be among the classics of the genre."

BIOGRAPHICAL/CRITICAL SOURCES:

BOOKS

Brophy, Brigid, *Don't Never Forget: Collected Views and Reviews,* Holt, 1966.
Contemporary Literary Criticism, Gale (Detroit), Volume 2, 1974, Volume 4, 1975, Volume 14, 1980, Volume 42, 1987.
Symons, Julian, *Mortal Consequences: A History—From the Detective Story to the Crime Novel,* Harper, 1972.

PERIODICALS

Books and Bookmen, March, 1971; March, 1983.
Globe and Mail (Toronto), January 21, 1984.
Listener, July 9, 1970; February 17, 1983.
London Magazine, June, 1969; June-July, 1972.
Los Angeles Times Book Review, November 1, 1987; March 13, 1988; February 5, 1989; January 17, 1993.
New Republic, May 20, 1967; June 29, 1974.
New Statesman, May 31, 1963; February 26, 1965; October 29, 1965; January 25, 1969; March 30, 1979; October 2, 1981.
Newsweek, July 4, 1977.
New Yorker, May 27, 1974.
New York Herald Tribune Books, February 7, 1960.
New York Review of Books, September 15, 1974; March 31, 1988, pp. 36-37.

New York Times Book Review, January 30, 1966; April 1, 1967; April 30, 1967; July 19, 1970; July 7, 1974; April 6, 1986; July 19, 1987; November 1, 1987; April 3, 1988; December 18, 1988; January 29, 1989; September 17, 1989; December 24, 1989; October 18, 1992.
Observer, February 12, 1967; January 19, 1969; July 12, 1970; January 9, 1983.
Publishers Weekly, November 2, 1992, pp. 46-47.
Punch, January 29, 1969; March 10, 1971; June 2, 1982.
Spectator, February 21, 1969; December 5, 1981; February 12, 1983; October 13, 1990, p. 33; December 7, 1991, p. 34.
Times (London), February 24, 1983; April 3, 1986.
Times Literary Supplement, June 1, 1967; September 24, 1971; April 25, 1980; October 2, 1981; February 4, 1983; September 27, 1985; April 18, 1986; December 6, 1987, p. 1227; October 4, 1991, p. 26.
Tribune Books (Chicago), October 4, 1992.
Village Voice, November 17, 1992.
Village Voice Literary Supplement, August, 1982.
Washington Post, June 28, 1980.
Washington Post Book World, September 15, 1985; October 6, 1985; October 18, 1992.
Washington Star-News, November 25, 1973.

*   *   *

HILL, L(eslie) A(lexander) 1918-

PERSONAL: Born January 6, 1918, in Athens, Greece; son of Arthur Edwin and Anastasia (Tsaoussopoulou) Hill; married Margaret Beryl Barrett, September 26, 1946 (marriage ended); married Jane Elizabeth Hose, January 14, 1963; children: (first marriage) Rosemary Anne, Julian Alexander, Judith Mary, Katherine Jane. *Education:* Cambridge University, B.A. (with honors), 1939, M.A., 1948; University of London, B.A. (with first class honors), 1953, M.A. (with mark of distinction), 1956, Ph.D., 1978. *Avocational interests:* Travel (especially in the Mediterranean and Southeast Asia), music (chiefly pre-1800 and classical Indian), photography.

ADDRESSES: Home and office—La Prairie, St. Mary, Jersey JE3 3EH, Channel Islands.

CAREER: British Council, service in Kavalla, Greece, 1941-42, Tehran, Iran, 1946-49, Isfahan, Iran, 1949-51, Indonesia, 1951-58, and India, 1958-61; University of Indonesia, Djakarta, professor of English and head of department, 1953-58; Oxford University Press, Oxford, England, adviser on the teaching of English as a second language, 1961-71; full-time writer, 1961—. Chairperson, Hill Publications Ltd., 1967—. Head of British translators and interpreters at Nuremberg Trials, 1945-46; adviser,

Oxford University Press, 1961-71; English language adviser, United Nations Development Programme, South Pacific, 1971-72. *Military service:* British Army, 1941-46; became major; received Military Cross.

MEMBER: International Phonetic Association, International Association of Teachers of English as a Foreign Language, Mensa, Linguistic Circle of New York.

WRITINGS:

Comprehension and Precis Pieces for Overseas Students, Longmans, Green (Essex, England), 1950.

The Teaching of English in Indonesia: Problems and Suggestions, Wolters (Djakarta, Indonesia), 1955.

(With others) *Indonesian Ministry of Education's English Language Syllabus,* Year 1, with *Teacher's Guide and Drill Book,* Indonesian Ministry of Education, 1955, Years 2-3, 1957.

(With R. D. S. Fielden) *Further Comprehension and Precis Pieces for Overseas Students,* Longmans, Green, 1956.

A Corrective Course for Indonesian Students of English, Ganaco (Bandung, Indonesia), 1957.

(With Fielden) *Vocabulary Tests and Exercises for Indonesian Students of English,* Ganaco, 1958.

Picture Stories for Composition and Teacher's Guide, Longmans, Green, 1960.

Drills and Tests in English Sounds, Longmans, Green, 1961.

(With Derwent J. May) *Advanced Comprehension and Appreciation Pieces,* Oxford University Press, 1962.

(With J. M. Ure) *English Sounds and Spellings,* Oxford University Press, 1962, with *Tests,* 1963, and *Dictation Pieces,* 1964.

(With Fielden) *Vocabulary Tests and Exercises,* Oxford University Press, 1962.

(With May) *Literary Comprehension and Appreciation Pieces,* Oxford University Press, 1963.

Letter Writing, Oxford University Press, 1963.

Elementary Comprehension Pieces, Oxford University Press, 1963.

Elementary Composition Pieces, Oxford University Press, 1964.

An Elementary Refresher Course, Oxford University Press, 1964.

An Intermediate Refresher Course, Oxford University Press, 1964.

English Letters for All Occasions, Diesterweg (Frankfurt, Germany), 1965.

An Advanced Refresher Course, Oxford University Press, 1965.

A Picture Vocabulary, with Student's Book and Teacher's Book, Oxford University Press, 1965.

A Guide to Correct English, Oxford University Press, 1965, 2nd edition, 1968.

Stress and Intonation, Step by Step, with Workbook and Companion, Oxford University Press, 1965.

Elementary Stories for Reproduction, Oxford University Press, 1965, Series 2, Oxford University Press (Tokyo), 1977, original edition published as *Elementary Anecdotes in American English,* 1980.

Advanced Stories for Reproduction, Oxford University Press, 1965, Series 2, Oxford University Press (Tokyo), 1977.

Outline Composition Book, Oxford University Press, 1966.

Free Composition Book, Oxford University Press, 1966.

Intermediate Stories for Composition, with Workbook and Companion, Oxford University Press, 1967.

Selected Articles on the Teaching of English as a Foreign Language, Oxford University Press, 1967.

Note-Taking Practice, Oxford University Press, 1968.

(With Prema Popkin) *A First Crossword Puzzle Book,* Oxford University Press, 1968.

Exercises for Senior Pupils, Verlag Moritz Diesterweg, 1968.

Easy Pieces, Gleerups (Sweden), 1968.

Prepositions and Adverbial Particles, Oxford University Press, 1968.

Intermediate Comprehension Pieces, Oxford University Press, 1969.

A First Reader, Oxford University Press, 1969, 2nd edition, two volumes, 1973.

A Prelude to English, Oxford University Press, 1969.

(With Popkin) *A Second Crossword Puzzle Book,* Oxford University Press, 1969.

(With Popkin) *A Third Crossword Book,* Oxford University Press, 1970.

Contextualized Vocabulary Tests, three books, Oxford University Press, 1970-75.

Contemporary Short Stories, Oxford University Press, 1970.

(With M. Sinha) *Elementary Stories for Translation into Hindi or English,* Oxford University Press, 1970.

(With Popkin) *A Fourth Crossword Puzzle Book,* Oxford University Press, 1970.

(With K. Shimizu and T. Shimaoka) *Study Guide to Elementary Stories for Reproduction: Spoken English through Humorous Stories,* Oxford University Press, 1970.

(With Shimizu and Shimaoka) *Study Guide for Intermediate Stories for Reproduction,* Oxford University Press, 1971.

(With others) *English Language Course for Colleges,* Oxford University Press, Book 1, 1971, Book 2, 1974, Book 3, 1975.

A Second Reading Book, Oxford University Press, 1972.

A Third Reading Book, Oxford University Press, 1972.

A Fourth Reading Book, Oxford University Press, 1972.

A Fifth Reading Book, Oxford University Press, 1972.

(With D. Mallet and Shimizu) *English through Cartoons,* Oxford University Press, Book 1, 1973, Book 2, 1975.

English Language Teaching Games for Adult Students, Book 1: *Elementary,* Book 2 (with Fielden): *Advanced,* Evans Brothers (London), 1974.

(With O. Dunn) *Japanese Talking Workbook,* Oxford University Press, 1974, revised edition, 1975.

What Would You Say?, Evans Brothers, 1975.

(With K. Ando and Shimizu) *Listen and Speak* (with ten cassettes), Oxford University Press, 1975.

Niagara Falls and Other Stories, Nelson, 1976.

UFOs and Other Stories, Nelson, 1976.

(With S. Kawabe) *Elementary Comprehension Topics* (with two cassettes and answer key), Oxford University Press (Tokyo), 1976, new edition, 1980.

(With T. Watanabe) *Elementary Revision Course* (with two cassettes and answer key), Oxford University Press (Tokyo), 1976.

A Day at the Races and Other Stories, Nelson, 1977.

Old Towns and New Towns, Nelson, 1977.

I Have Run away from Home, Nelson, 1977.

Leonardo, Michelangelo, and Raphael, Nelson, 1977.

Intermediate Stories for Reproduction, Series 2, Oxford University Press (Tokyo), 1977, American Series, Oxford University Press (New York City), 1980.

(With Shimizu) *Junior Listen and Speak: Student's Book and Teacher's Book* (with ten cassettes), Oxford University Press (Tokyo), 1977.

(With S. Chehan) *From Comprehension to Composition,* Evans Brothers, 1978.

(Adapter) Dick Francis, *Bonecrack,* Nelson-Getaway Books, 1978.

Writing for a Purpose, Oxford University Press, 1978.

The Ghost and Other Stories, Nelson, 1978.

Superconductivity and Other Articles, Nelson, 1978.

Freedom and Other Articles, Nelson, 1978.

(Adapter) Paul Gallico, *Trial by Terror,* Nelson Streamline Books, 1978.

(Adapter) David Howarth, *The Shetland Bus,* Nelson Streamline Books, 1978.

(Adapter) Madelaine Duke, *Death at the Wedding,* Nelson Streamline Books, 1978.

(With Michael Dobbyn) *A Teacher Training Course: Lecturer's Book,* Cassell (London), 1979.

(With Dobbyn) *A Teacher Training Course: Trainee's Book,* Cassell, 1979.

Your Shopping List from Outer Space and Other Articles (adapted from *Sunday Telegraph Magazine*), Nelson, 1979.

Kind Words and Other Stories, Efstathiadis & Sons (Greece), 1979.

Don't Jump and Other Stories, Efstathiadis & Sons, 1979.

The Elephant in Pyjamas and Other Stories, Efstathiadis & Sons, 1979.

Trees in the Sahara and Other Stories, Efstathiadis & Sons, 1979.

The Flying Doctor and Other Stories, Efstathiadis & Sons, 1979.

Donkey's Ears and Other Stories, Efstathiadis & Sons, 1979.

Dear God and Other Stories, Efstathiadis & Sons, 1979.

The Cat's Plate and Other Stories, Efstathiadis & Sons, 1979.

How Good Is Your English? Vocabulary and Structures, Max Hueber Verlag (Munich, Germany), 1980.

Techniques of Discussion, Evans Brothers, 1980.

Intermediate Anecdotes in American English, Oxford University Press (New York City), 1980.

(With Kawabe) *Intermediate Comprehension Topics* (with answer key), Oxford University Press (Kuala Lumpur, Malaysia), 1980, revised edition, 1982.

Introductory Stories for Comprehension (with answer key), Oxford University Press (Kuala Lumpur), 1980.

Elementary Stories for Comprehension (with answer key), Oxford University Press (Kuala Lumpur), 1980.

Intermediate Stories for Comprehension (with answer key), Oxford University Press (Kuala Lumpur), 1980.

Introductory Steps to Understanding (with cassette), Oxford University Press (Tokyo), 1980.

Intermediate Steps to Understanding (with cassette), Oxford University Press (Tokyo), 1980.

Advanced Steps to Understanding (with cassette), Oxford University Press (Tokyo), 1980.

Stories from Ancient Greece, Oxford University Press, 1981.

Let's Get It Right, Max Hueber Verlag, 1981.

Advanced Anecdotes in American English, Oxford University Press (New York City), 1981.

Advanced Stories for Reproduction, Oxford University Press (New York City), 1981.

Oxford Children's Picture Dictionary, Oxford University Press, 1981.

Introductory Stories for Reproduction (with cassette and answer key), Series 1 and 2, Oxford University Press (Tokyo), 1982.

Word Power 1500 (with answer key), Oxford University Press (Tokyo), 1982, British English edition, [Hong Kong], 1985.

Word Power 3000 (with answer key), Oxford University Press (Tokyo), 1982, British English edition, [Hong Kong], 1985.

Word Power 4500 (with answer key), Oxford University Press (Tokyo), 1983, British English edition, [Hong Kong], 1985.

Elementary Conversation Topics (with cassette and teacher's guide), Oxford University Press (Singapore), 1983.

Oxford Children's Picture Dictionary (Welsh edition), Oxford University Press, 1984.

Intermediate Conversation Topics (with cassette and teacher's guide), Oxford University Press (Singapore), 1984.

Advanced Conversation Topics (with cassette and teacher's guide) Oxford University Press (Singapore), 1984.

Stories for Reading Comprehension 1 (with cassette), Longmans, Green, 1985.

Stories for Reading Comprehension 2 (with cassette), Longmans, Green, 1985.

Stories for Reading Comprehension 3 (with cassette), Longmans, Green, 1985.

Best Funny Stories 1: Elementary (with answer key), Kirihara Shoten/Oxford University Press (Tokyo), 1985.

Best Funny Stories 2: Intermediate (with answer key), Kirihara Shoten/Oxford University Press (Tokyo), 1985.

Best Funny Stories 3: Advanced (with answer key), Kirihara Shoten/Oxford University Press (Tokyo), 1986.

A Descent into the Maelstrom, Alhambra (Madrid), 1986.

The Gold Bug, Alhambra, 1987.

The Deerslayer, Alhambra, 1987.

Dracula, Alhambra, 1987.

Further Stories for Reading Comprehension A, Longmans, Green, 1988.

Further Stories for Reading Comprehension B, Longmans, Green, 1988.

(With Toshio Shiozawa) *Shorter College Listening Course,* Kirihara Shoten/Oxford University Press (Tokyo), 1988.

College Comprehensive Course, Kirihara Shoten/Oxford University Press (Tokyo), 1988.

(With others) *Amusing Stories for Comprehension,* Eichosha Longman (Tokyo), 1989.

(Adapter) *Uncle Tom's Cabin,* Alhambra, 1989.

(Adapter) *Kim,* Alhambra, 1989.

(With Kenichi Ando) *Twenty Tales* (student's book, teacher's book, and cassettes), Seibido (Tokyo), 1991.

Penguin English Student's Dictionary, Penguin (London), 1991.

(Adapter) *Jane Eyre,* Alhambra Longman (Madrid), 1991.

Happy Readers, eight books, Efstathiadis Group (Greece), 1991.

(With Laurin F. Lewis) *Contextualized Vocabulary Tests, Books 1-4* (CD-ROM; Russian, Arabic, and Hebrew versions), Linguatech (Israel), 1992.

(With Ando) *Amusing Tales,* Seibido, 1993.

Far from the Madding Crowd, Oxford Progressive English Readers/Oxford University Press (Hong Kong), 1994.

(Adapter) *Dracula,* Oxford Progressive English Readers/Oxford University Press (Hong Kong), 1994.

(Adapter) *The Picture of Dorian Gray,* Oxford Progressive English Readers/Oxford University Press (Hong Kong), 1994.

(With Ikuo Uchida) *Wit and Humor through Listening* (student's book, teacher's book, and cassette), Seibido, 1995.

(Adapter) *The Old Wives' Tale,* Oxford Progressive English Readers/Oxford University Press (Hong Kong), 1995.

EDITOR, "OXFORD GRADED READERS" SERIES, JUNIOR LEVEL, STAGE 1

The Three Goats and the Dwarf, Oxford University Press, 1971.

The Grasshopper and the Ant, Oxford University Press, 1971.

The Lion, the Wolf, and the Fox, Oxford University Press, 1971.

The Eagle, the Pig, and the Cat, Oxford University Press, 1971.

The Boy in the Moon, Oxford University Press, 1971.

The Old Woman and Her Pig, Oxford University Press, 1971.

The Father, His Son and Their Donkey, Oxford University Press, 1971.

Goldilocks and the Three Bears, Oxford University Press, 1971.

The Happy Dragon, Oxford University Press, 1971.

Hansel and Gretel, Oxford University Press, 1971.

The Ugly Duckling, Oxford University Press, 1971.

The Boy and the Ice, Oxford University Press, 1971.

EDITOR, "OXFORD GRADED READERS" SERIES, JUNIOR LEVEL, STAGE 2

The Tin Soldier, Oxford University Press, 1971.

Red Shoes, Oxford University Press, 1971.

Big Claus and Small Claus, Oxford University Press, 1972.

Thumbelisa, Oxford University Press, 1972.

The Piper of Hamelin, Oxford University Press, 1972.

Beauty and the Beast, Oxford University Press, 1972.

Snow-White and Rose-Red, Oxford University Press, 1972.

Donkey Boy, Oxford University Press, 1972.

EDITOR, "OXFORD GRADED READERS" SERIES, JUNIOR LEVEL, STAGE 3

The Tinder Box, Oxford University Press, 1972.

Nasreddin, Oxford University Press, 1972.

The Ruined House, Oxford University Press, 1973.

The Dragon's Head, Oxford University Press, 1975.

The Muster, Oxford University Press, 1975.

He Cannot Really Read, Oxford University Press, 1975.

Moses, Oxford University Press, 1975.

The Happy Prince, Oxford University Press, 1980.

EDITOR, "OXFORD GRADED READERS" SERIES, JUNIOR LEVEL, STAGE 4

Another Adventure in London, Oxford University Press, 1978.
Missing, Oxford University Press, 1978.

EDITOR, "OXFORD GRADED READERS" SERIES, SENIOR LEVEL, STAGE 1

The Good Man, Oxford University Press, 1973.
Black Beauty, Oxford University Press, 1973.
A Message from Mars, Oxford University Press, 1976.

EDITOR, "OXFORD GRADED READERS" SERIES, SENIOR LEVEL, STAGE 2

Funny Stories, Oxford University Press, 1972.
How Much Land Does a Man Want?, Oxford University Press, 1972.
Heidi, Oxford University Press, 1972.
Buffalo Bill, Oxford University Press, 1972.
Gulliver's Travels, Oxford University Press, 1972.
Smugglers' Island, Oxford University Press, 1973.
Fire in the Bush, Oxford University Press, 1973.
Kit Carson, Oxford University Press, 1973.
The Magician, Oxford University Press, 1976.
In the New Forest, Oxford University Press, 1976.
In Portobello Road, Oxford University Press, 1976.
More Funny Stories, Oxford University Press, 1978.

EDITOR, "OXFORD GRADED READERS" SERIES, SENIOR LEVEL, STAGE 3

The Story of Trains, Oxford University Press, 1975.
Little Women, Oxford University Press, 1975.
The Black Cane, Oxford University Press, 1975.
Joan of Arc, Oxford University Press, 1975.
To Catch a Thief, Oxford University Press, 1975.
Adventure in London, Oxford University Press, 1975.
A Little Princess, Oxford University Press, 1980.
Adventure in Tokyo, Oxford University Press, 1981.
Adventure in New York, Oxford University Press, 1981.

EDITOR, "OXFORD GRADED READERS" SERIES, SENIOR LEVEL, STAGE 4

A Life of Her Own, Oxford University Press, 1978.

OTHER

Also author or editor of other series, including "Programmed English Course," student and teacher books 1-12, 1966-68; "Books Adapted for Use with the Stillitron Teaching Machine," eight books, Stillit Books, 1967-68; (with Derwent J. May) "A New Introduction to English Literature," five books, 1969-73; "Cartoons for Students of English," five books, 1972; scriptwriter for radio series *Ear and Speech Training,* British Broadcasting Corp. (BBC), 1961, and television series *English for Everyone,* Center for Educational Television Overseas, 1963-65.

Contributor to books, including *Recent Trends in Educational Practice,* Longmans, Green, 1961; and *Teaching English as a Second Language,* edited by H. B. Allen, McGraw (New York City), 1965. Educational sound materials include *Stress and Intonation, Step by Step* (recordings), Oxford University Press, 1965, and *Drills and Tests in English Sounds* (tapes), Longmans, Green, 1966-67. Contributor of more than sixty articles to professional journals in England, United States, Taiwan, India, France, Japan, Ethiopia, Peru, Singapore, Nigeria, and Germany. Editor, *Teaching English* (Calcutta), 1959-61.

Some of Hill's books have been published in other languages, including Danish, Greek, Italian, Japanese, Indonesian, and Spanish.

WORK IN PROGRESS: English as a Foreign Language Dictionary, for Penguin Books.

SIDELIGHTS: L. A. Hill is fluent in German, modern Greek, French, and Italian; he has some competence in Spanish, Russian, and Dutch; he considers himself "rusty" in Persian and Indonesian. He has studied about ten other languages. Hill's interest in linguistics extends to "human behavior and its similarities/variations between different cultures."

*   *   *

HILLGRUBER, Andreas (Fritz) 1925-1989

PERSONAL: Born January 18, 1925, in Angerburg, Germany (now Wegorzewo, Poland); died after a long illness, May 8, 1989, in Cologne, West Germany (now Germany); son of Andreas (a high school teacher) and Irmgard (Schilling) Hillgruber; married Karin Zierau, January 11, 1960; children: Michael, Christian, Gabriele. *Education:* University of Goettingen, Ph.D., 1952. *Religion:* Evangelical.

ADDRESSES: Office—Department of History, University of Cologne, Albertus-Magnus-Platz, D-5000 Cologne 41, Germany.

CAREER: High school history teacher in Wiesbaden, West Germany, 1954-58, Darmstadt, West Germany, 1958-61, and Marburg/Lahn, West Germany, 1961-64; University of Marburg/Lahn, Marburg/Lahn, West Germany, instructor, 1965-67, professor of modern history, 1967-68; University of Freiberg/Breisgau, Freiburg/ Breisgau, West Germany, professor of modern and contemporary history, 1968-72; University of Cologne, Cologne, West Germany, professor of modern and contemporary history, 1972-89. *Military service:* German Army, 1943-45, prisoner of war in France, 1945-48.

WRITINGS:

IN ENGLISH

Hitler, King Carol, and Marshall Antonescu, Franz Steiner Verlag, 1954, 2nd edition, 1965.

Hitler's Strategy, Politics, and War, 1940-1941, Bernard & Graefe, 1965, 2nd edition, 1982.

The Role of Germany in the History Preceding the Two World Wars, Vandenhoeck & Ruprecht, 1967, 2nd edition, 1979.

Continuity and Discontinuity in German Foreign Politics from Bismarck to Hitler, Droste Verlag, 1969, 3rd edition, 1971.

Bismarck's Foreign Policy, Verlag Rombach, 1972, 2nd edition, 1981.

German History, 1945-1972, Ullstein, 1974, 3rd edition, 1980.

Germany and the Two World Wars, Harvard University Press (Cambridge, MA), 1981.

IN GERMAN

Der Zweite Weltkrieg 1939-1945: Kriegsziele und Strategie der grossen Maechte, Kohlhammer (Stuttgart, Germany), 1982, 4th edition, 1985.

Endlich genug uber Nationalsozialismus und Zweiten Weltkrieg?: Forschungsstand und Literatur, Droste (Dusseldorf, Germany), 1982.

Deutsche Geschichte 1945-1982: die "deutsche Frage" in der Weltpolitik, W. Kohlhammer, 1983.

(With Volker Rittberger) *1933: Wie die Republik der Diktatur erlag,* W. Kohlhammer, 1983.

(With Theodor Schieder) *Theodor Schieder zum 75. Geburtstag; Akademische Festveranstaltung in der Universitat zu Koln am 16. April 1983: Ansprachen, Festvortrag von Andreas Hillgruber, "Revisionismus," Kontinuitat und Wandel in der Aussenpolitik der Weimarer Rupublik,* University of Cologne (Cologne, Germany), 1983.

(With Josef Becker) *Die Deutsche Frage in 19. und 20. Jahrhundert; Referate und Diskussionsbeitrage eines Augsburger Symposions, 23. bis 25. September 1981,* E. Vogel (Munich, Germany), 1983.

Die Last de Nation; funf Beitrage uber Deutschland und die Deutschen, Droste, 1984.

(With Inge Auerbach and Gottfried Schramm) *Felder und Vorfelder russischer Geschichte; Studien zu Ehren von Peter Scheibert,* Rombach (Germany), 1985.

(With Theodor Schieder) *Vom Beruf des Historikers in einer Zeit beschleunigten Wandels; Akademische Gedenkfeier fur Theodor Schieder am 8. February 1985 in der Universitat zu Koln,* Oldenbourg (Munich, Germany), 1985.

(With Klaus Hildebrand and Reiner Pommerin) *Deutsche Frage und europaisches Gleichgewicht; Festschrift fur Andreas Hillgruber zum 60,* Bohlau (Cologne, Germany), 1985.

Zweierlei Untergang; die Zerschlagung des Deutschen Reiches und das Ende des europaischen Judentums (title means "The Destruction of the German Reich and the End of European Judaism") W. J. Seidler (Berlin), 1986.

Alliierte Plane fur eine "Neutralisierung" Deutschlands, 1945-1955, Westdeutscher Verlag (Opladen, Germany), 1987.

Europa in der Weltpolitik der Nachkriegszeit, 1945-1963, Oldenbourg, 1987.

Die Zerstorung Europas; Beitrage zue Weltkriegsepoche 1914 bis 1945, Propylaen (Frankfurt, Germany), 1988.

(With Jost Dulffer, Bernd Martin and Gunter Wollstein) *Deutschland in Europa; Kontinuitat und Bruch: Gedenkschrift fur Andreas Hillgruber,* Propylaen, 1990.

OTHER

Also editor of *Probleme des Zweiten Weltkrieges* (title means "Problems of the Second World War"). Contributor to history journals.

SIDELIGHTS: Andreas Hillgruber once told *CA:* "My specialty is research into the history of Germany as a great power in international politics between 1871 and 1945, from Bismarck to Hitler. My particular focus is on the problem of continuity and discontinuity in the major trends in German foreign policy during Bismarck's epoch, the Wilhelmine era, the First World War, the Weimar Republic, the Third Reich, and the Second World War. I consider the result of my research 'political history' in a modern sense: the emphasis is on understanding the sequence of great decisions by working out the alternatives. Intellectual and social history supplement my study of political outcomes, but are not central points."

BIOGRAPHICAL/CRITICAL SOURCES:

PERIODICALS

Times Literary Supplement, May 15, 1987.

OBITUARIES:

BOOKS

International Authors and Writers Who's Who, 10th edition, International Biographical Centre (England), 1986.

PERIODICALS

Los Angeles Times, May 26, 1989.
New York Times, May 25, 1989.
Times (London), May 31, 1989.
Washington Post, May 27, 1989.*

HILLMAN, James 1926-

PERSONAL: Born April 12, 1926, in Atlantic City, NJ; married Catharina Kempe, 1952 (marriage ended, 1974); married Patricia Berry, 1976; children: three daughters, one son. *Education:* Attended Georgetown University, 1943; Sorbonne, University of Paris, certificate, 1948; Trinity College, Dublin, B.A., 1950, M.A., 1953; University of Zurich, Ph.D. (summa cum laude), 1958.

CAREER: C. G. Jung Institute, Zurich, analytical psychologist and director of studies, 1959-69; Spring Publications, New York City, editor, 1970-78, publisher, 1978—; University of Dallas, professor, senior fellow of Institute for Philosophic Studies, and graduate dean, 1979—. Armed Forces Network, newswriter, 1946-47. *Military service:* U.S. Navy, 1944-46.

MEMBER: Swiss Society for Analytical Psychology.

WRITINGS:

Emotion: A Comprehensive Phenomenology of Theories and Their Meanings for Therapy, Routledge & Kegan Paul (London), 1960, revised edition, Northwestern University Press (Evanston, IL), 1963.

Suicide and the Soul, Harper (New York City), 1964.

(Contributor) Gopi Krishna, *Kundalini: The Evolutionary Energy in Man,* Ramadhar & Hopman, 1967.

Insearch: Psychology and Religion, Scribner (New York City), 1968.

The Feeling Function, Spring Publications (Dorset, England), 1971.

(With Marie-Louise von Franz) *Lectures on Jung's Typology,* Spring Publications, 1971.

The Myth of Analysis, Northwestern University Press, 1972.

Pan and the Nightmare, Spring Publications, 1972.

Loose Ends, Spring Publications, 1975.

Revisioning Psychology, Harper, 1975.

The Dream and the Underworld, Harper, 1979.

(Editor and contributor) *Puer Papers,* Spring Publications, 1979.

(Editor and contributor) *Facing the Gods,* Spring Publications, 1980.

(With Laura Pozzo) *Inter Views: Conversations with Laura Pozzo on Psychotherapy, Biography, Love, Soul, Dreams, Work, Imagination, and the State of the Culture,* Harper, 1983.

Healing Fiction, Station Hill (Barrytown, NY), 1983.

Anima: An Anatomy of a Personified Notion, illustrated by Mary Vernon, Spring Publications, 1985.

(Editor with Charles Boer) *Freud's Own Cookbook,* illustrated by Jeff Fisher, Harper, 1985.

(Contributor) Gaston Bachelard, *Lautreamont,* translated from the French by Robert S. Dupree, Dallas Institute Publications, 1986.

A Blue Fire: Selected Writings, edited by Thomas Moore, Harper, 1989.

(With Karl Kerenyi) *Oedipus Variations: Studies in Literature and Psychoanalysis,* translated by Jon Solomon, Spring Publications, 1991.

The Thought of the Heart [and] *The Soul of the World,* Spring Publications, 1992.

(With Michael Ventura) *We've Had a Hundred Years of Psychotherapy—and the World's Getting Worse,* HarperSanFrancisco, 1992.

(Editor with Robert Bly and Michael Meade) *The Rag and Bone Shop of the Heart: Poems for Men,* HarperCollins (New York City), 1992.

Kinds of Power, Doubleday (New York City), 1995.

Contributor of many articles and translations to various publications, including *Eranos Jarhbuecher.* Founding associate editor of *Envoy: An Irish Review of Literature and the Arts,* 1949-51; editor of *Studies in Jungian Thought* for Bucknell University Press.

SIDELIGHTS: Jungian psychoanalyst James Hillman writes for both general and specialized audiences. His forays into theology, mythology, and popular culture and his efforts to develop a modern theory of the soul and a contemporary definition of human spirituality have been praised by reviewers. Annie Gottlieb wrote in a *New York Times Book Review* of *A Blue Fire: Selected Writings,* "Mr. Hillman's work, throughout his life, has been to bring us knowledge of the soul, both our own and the world's (*anima mundi*), so that we may care for it, not as a patient needing cure, but as a poet seeking to sing our lives into beauty and meaning."

Hillman's early interest in the religious aspects of psychoanalysis was apparent in *Insearch: Psychology and Religion,* a book addressed to pastoral counselors seeking to apply modern psychoanalytic insight to their work. The book was praised by a reviewer for the *Times Literary Supplement,* who cited Hillman's notion that "human problems are not something which people have, but something people are." Reviewers generally lauded Hillman's attempts to bring psychoanalysis and religion together on an equal footing, rather than using modern science to explain away traditional religious notions like the soul.

In *The Dream and the Underworld,* Hillman continued his project of applying psychoanalytic theory to spiritual matters. As Edgar Levenson wrote in the *New York Times Book Review,* Hillman reached beyond dream theories of Freud and Jung in an attempt "to place dreams in the mainstream of myth, specifically the myth of the underworld." Levenson remarked that Hillman's theory, in which the "dream qua myth taps a rich underworld of imagery and experience" in the dreamer, is an "extraordinarily rich concept."

Hillman made a foray into humorous writing in 1985 with the publication of *Freud's Own Cookbook,* which he edited with Charles Boer. Presented as a collection of recipes with commentary by the founder of psychoanalysis, Sigmund Freud, the cookbook abounds in such puns and wordplay as "Erogenous Scones," "Incredible Oedipal Pie," and "Momovers." The commentary both reflects and satirizes Freudian thought, analyzing matzoh balls, for example, as "the ego in the midst of the primal broth." Writing in the *New York Times Book Review,* Fred Ferretti praised the book as "utter hilarity" and noted that the recipes could actually be prepared with good results.

An overview of Hillman's concerns can be found in *A Blue Fire: Selected Writings,* which spans thirty years of Hillman's work to offer "a rich and provocative introduction," according to Gottlieb. As she wrote in the *New York Times Book Review,* "Hillman frankly abducts psychology from the scientific and medical realm, claiming it, in [editor Thomas] Moore's words, as 'an art of the soul.' " Gottlieb noted the breadth of Hillman's interests and concerns, commenting that his mind "ranges easily from the arcana of alchemy to the discomforts of a bus ride. . . . He can write as breathtakingly as a poet and, at times, as unintelligibly as a philosopher."

An equally wide-ranging collection is Hillman's 1992 work, *We've Had a Hundred Years of Psychotherapy—and the World's Getting Worse,* written with Michael Ventura. The title itself suggests Hillman's iconoclastic relationship with psychoanalysis, as well as his ongoing quest to apply its insights to modern life. The book takes the form of letters, interviews, and conversations between Hillman and Ventura, a filmmaker and columnist for *LA Weekly.* Reviewing the book in the *Los Angeles Times Book Review,* Mihaly Csikszentmihalyi found its style reminiscent of a "college bull session. . . . But beneath the banter, there is a desperate seriousness that tries honestly to come to terms with the sense of alienation—from government, community, and nature—that seems to be at the root of our problems." Perhaps ironically, given his profession, Hillman joins Ventura in a critique of psychoanalysis. As Csikszentmihalyi noted, "Both believe that modern psychotherapy, with its emphasis on introspection, self-pity and individual solutions, is more a part of the problem than the cure." Instead, "Both look for help to animism, deep ecology, ecofeminism and radical therapy (Freud is out, Jung and Laing are in)," Csikszentmihalyi commented.

Throughout his career, Hillman has won critical acclaim for his depth of insight, his open-mindedness, and his respect for the mysteries of the human condition. As Gottlieb noted, "To read Mr. Hillman is to see the world anew through the eyes of soul, and the sight astonishes and consoles."

BIOGRAPHICAL/CRITICAL SOURCES:

BOOKS

Encyclopedia of Occultism and Parapsychology, third edition, Gale (Detroit), 1991.

PERIODICALS

Christian Century, February 21, 1968.
Encounter, spring, 1969.
Los Angeles Times Book Review, June 5, 1983, p. 11; May 31, 1992, pp. 2, 10.
New York Times Book Review, August 26, 1979; May 26, 1985, p. 15; March 11, 1990, p. 22; September 15, 1991, p. 34.
Times Literary Supplement, June 8, 1967.*

—*Sidelights by Rachel Kranz*

*   *   *

HINGLEY, Ronald F(rancis)   1920-

PERSONAL: Born April 26, 1920, in Edinburgh, Scotland; son of Robert Henry and Ruth Esther (Dye) Hingley; married August 30, 1953 (wife's maiden name, Wyatt); children: Peter James, Richard Charles, Joseph Martin, Andrew John, Victoria Frances, Helen Ann, Thomas William. *Education:* Attended Kingswood School, Bath, England; Corpus Christi College, Oxford University, B.A., M.A., 1946; University of London, Ph.D., 1951.

ADDRESSES: Home—Frilford Grange, Abingdon, Berkshire, England. *Agent*—A. D. Peters Ltd., 10 Buckingham St., Adelphi, London WC2, England.

CAREER: University of London, School of Slavonic and East European Studies, London, England, assistant lecturer, 1947-50, lecturer, 1950-55, director of studies, joint services language course, 1951-55; Oxford University, Oxford, England, university lecturer in Russian, 1955—, research fellow of St. Antony's College, 1961-65, fellow, 1965—. *Military service:* British Army, 1940-45; became captain.

WRITINGS:

Chekhov: A Biographical and Critical Study, Allen & Unwin (London), 1950, 2nd edition, Barnes & Noble (New York City), 1966.
Up Jenkins (novel), Longmans, Green (London), 1956.
Soviet Prose, Allen & Unwin, 1959.
(Author of preface) Aleksandr Pushkin, *Eugene Onegin,* Blackwell (London), 1960, reprinted, 1987.
Under Soviet Skins, Hamish Hamilton (London), 1961.
(With T. J. Binyon) *Russian: A Beginner's Course,* Allen & Unwin, 1962.
The Undiscovered Dostoyevsky, Hamish Hamilton, 1962.

(Translator with Max Hayward) Alexander Solzhenitsyn, *One Day in the Life of Ivan Denisovich,* Praeger (New York City), 1963.

(Translator with Hayward) Abram Tertz, *Fantastic Stories,* Pantheon (New York City), 1963.

(Translator and editor) *The Oxford Chekhov,* Oxford University Press (New York City), Volume III, 1964, Volume VIII, 1965, Volume II, 1967, Volume IX, 1975, Volume VII, 1978.

(Translator) Anton Chekhov, *Uncle Vanya* [*and*] *the Cherry Orchard,* Oxford University Press, 1965.

(Translator and author of introduction and notes) Chekhov, *The Princess and Other Stories,* Oxford University Press, 1965, reprinted, 1990.

Russian Writers and Society, 1825-1904, McGraw-Hill (New York City), 1967, 2nd revised edition published as *Russian Writers and Society in the Nineteenth Century,* Weidenfeld & Nicolson (London), 1977.

Nihilists, Weidenfeld & Nicolson, 1967, Delacorte (New York City), 1969.

(Translator) Chekhov, *Ivanov; The Seagull;* [*and*] *Three Sisters,* Oxford University Press, 1968.

The Tsars, 1533-1917, Macmillan (New York City), 1968.

(Author of introduction) Dostoevsky, *Great Short Works,* Harper (New York City), 1968.

Russian Revolution, Bodley Head (London), 1970.

The Russian Secret Police: Muscovite, Imperial Russian and Soviet Political Security Operations, 1565-1970, Hutchinson, 1970, Simon & Schuster (New York City), 1971.

A Concise History of Russia, Viking (New York City), 1972, revised edition, Thames & Hudson, 1991.

Joseph Stalin: Man and Legend, Hutchinson, 1974.

(Translator) Chekhov, *Eleven Stories,* Oxford University Press, 1976.

A Life of Anton Chekhov, Oxford University Press, 1976, reprinted, 1989.

The Russian Mind, Scribner (New York City), 1977.

Dostoyevsky: His Life and Work, Scribner, 1978.

Russian Writers and Soviet Society, 1917-1978, Random House (New York City), 1979.

(Translator and author of introduction) Chekhov, *Five Plays,* Oxford University Press, 1980.

Nightingale Fever: Russian Poets in Revolution, Knopf (New York City), 1981.

Pasternak: A Biography, Knopf, 1983.

(Editor) Fedor Dostoevsky, *Memoirs from the House of the Dead,* translated by Jessie Coulson, Oxford University Press, 1983.

(Translator and author of introduction and notes) Chekhov, *The Russian Master and Other Stories,* Oxford University Press, 1984.

(Translator and author of introduction) Chekhov, *Ward Number Six and Other Stories,* Oxford University Press, 1988.

(Translator and author of introduction and notes) Chekhov, *A Woman's Kingdom and Other Stories,* Oxford University Press, 1989.

(Translator and author of introduction and notes) Chekhov, *Twelve Plays,* Oxford University Press, 1992.

Author of forty scripts on Russian language for beginners broadcast by British Broadcasting Corp. (BBC), 1959-60, 1960-61. Editor, *Modern Russian Reader,* published by New American Library. Commentator on Communist affairs, *Sunday Times* (London); editor, Allen & Unwin's "Russian Language" series. Contributor to *Punch, Spectator, Encounter, Forum, Tatler, Survey, Problems of Communism, Slavonic and East European Review, Russian Review,* and *Listener.*

SIDELIGHTS: According to Kay Dick in the London *Times,* Ronald F. Hingley's "authority in the field of Russian literature is of high distinction, as biographer and translator." The author of several biographies of major Russian writers and a translator of the works of Fedor Dostoyevsky, Alexander Solzhenitsyn, and, most notably, Anton Chekhov, Hingley has also distinguished himself as the writer of many studies of the history, culture, and leaders of Russia.

In *The Russian Secret Police: Muscovite, Imperial Russian and Soviet Political Security Operations, 1565-1970,* Hingley analyzes the terrorist security forces that have arisen repeatedly over the course of three centuries to keep the Russian people in check—regardless of the changes in ruling structure the country has undergone. Despite criticism that the book lacks the sense of perspective that would bring its subject into focus against the backdrop of Russian history, *The Russian Secret Police* is considered by many to be a useful study. "As it is," a reviewer for the *Times Literary Supplement* remarks, "the work is very easily written: it is precise where it can be precise; and it brings out several valuable themes, often overlooked." Robert Conquest, writing in the *New Statesman,* remarks: "Above all, what emerges from this history is the extravagant flavour of the Russian style, the shock of a strange culture on to which one cannot simply project one's own preconceptions."

In his conception of *The Tsars, 1533-1917,* Tibor Szamuely writes in the *Spectator,* "Mr. Hingley has had the splendid idea of writing a history of the extraordinary set of men and women who ruled Russia for four centuries in accordance with their private whims and fancies, and whose personal eccentricities (and what eccentricities!) to a great extent determined the policies and events of their reigns."

"Mr. Hingley," the reviewer concludes, "has acquitted himself of the task masterfully."

Hingley's accomplishment with the publication of *Nihilists,* in the eyes of several reviewers, is to have complemented and supplemented the more exhaustive studies of its subject—"pre-Marxist revolutionism in Russia," according to George Woodcock in *Commentary*—that already exist. "Although the whole subject . . . has been dealt with very fully in Ranco Venturi's massive study, *Roots of Revolution,*" Woodcock notes, "there is still room for a knowledgeable and brightly written short account, and this Mr. Hingley . . . has given us." Also comparing Hingley's book to other volumes on the same subject, Paul Green of the *New Statesman* describes *Nihilists* as "a more varied and balanced treatment of Russian Radicals and Revolutionaries in the reign of Alexander II."

A lecturer in Russian literature at Oxford University, Hingley has earned critical favor for his many studies of Russia's important literary figures. Of *Nightingale Fever: Russian Poets in Revolution,* Susan Jacoby asserts in the *New York Times Book Review* that "Ronald Hingley's concise, elegantly written study offers to those who do not read Russian new insights into the lives and work of the four poets [Boris Pasternak, Marina Tsvetayeva, Anna Akmatova, and Osip Mandelstam]." While the work has been criticized as gossipy by some, most critics find it a valuable biography. Peter France of the *Times Literary Supplement* writes: "Making good use of the important studies which already exist on each individual poets, the author weaves together four different destinies into a single story. This is told in a rather brisk way, but it is a powerful story none the less." Decrying the absence of an appendix and what she feels are confusing reference notes in an otherwise "excellent book," Jacoby adds: "This is a book that deserves to be fully understood, because it explains why four great poets came into inexorable conflict with their terrible age—and why they were able to survive as artists in spite of the odds in favor of silence."

In the *Los Angeles Times Book Review,* Neil M. Heyman intimates that Hingley's subject in *Pasternak: A Biography* is often associated only with his novel *Doctor Zhivago* and his rejection, in the face of vast criticism by his countrypeople, of the 1958 Nobel Prize for literature earned by that work. Noting that "Hingley's readable biography revolves around [that] phenomenon" as well, Heyman continues: "But Hingley . . . sees Pasternak as far more than international celebrity of a brief moment. . . . Moreover, Hingley's Pasternak is infinitely more complex an individual than the cartoon image many foreigners perceived in the late 1950s." For John Glad, writing in the *Washington Post Book World,* the style of Hingley's book is also of interest, as it "attempts to pick up the peculiar lilt of Pasternak's own prose—a sort of ecstatic and impressionistic

manner which gradually reverts to a more dispassionate tone as the study progresses."

BIOGRAPHICAL/CRITICAL SOURCES:

PERIODICALS

American Spectator, January, 1984, p. 38.
Best Sellers, July 15, 1971; February, 1984, p. 412.
British Book News, December, 1983, p. 781.
Christian Science Monitor, May 19, 1982, p. 17.
Commentary, August, 1969, p. 64.
Economist, February 20, 1982, p. 92.
History Today, April, 1983, p. 42.
Los Angeles Times Book Review, November 20, 1983, p. 15.
Modern Fiction Studies, winter, 1984, p. 734.
Modern Language Review, October, 1983, p. 1003; October, 1984, p. 1005.
National Review, September 16, 1983, p. 1150.
New Scientist, April 28, 1990, p. 75.
New Statesman, December 15, 1967; October 9, 1970.
New York Times, August 20, 1979, p. C18.
New York Times Book Review, December 20, 1981, p. 6; October 30, 1983, p. 7.
Observer, November 15, 1970; November 24, 1985, p. 28; May 7, 1989, p. 45.
Progressive, May, 1984, p. 45.
Spectator, November 22, 1968; February 6, 1982, p. 21.
Times (London), August 4, 1983.
Times Literary Supplement, September 28, 1967; October 16, 1970; March 12, 1982, p. 275.
Virginia Quarterly Review, spring, 1984, p. 53.
Washington Post Book World, December 18, 1983, p. 4.
World Literature Today, winter, 1983, p. 129.*

* * *

HINNELLS, John R(ussell) 1941-

PERSONAL: Born August 27, 1941, in Derby, England; son of William and Lilian (Jackson) Hinnells; married Marianne Grace Bushell (a teacher), July 24, 1965; children: Mark Julian, Duncan Keith. *Education:* King's College, London, B.D., 1964, graduate study, 1965-67. *Politics:* Moderate. *Avocational interests:* Soccer, gardening.

ADDRESSES: Home—10 St. Brannock's Rd., Chorlton-cum-Hardy, Manchester 21, England. *Office*—Department of Comparative Religion, University of Manchester, Manchester M13 9PL, England.

CAREER: Teacher of art in Ambleside, England, 1960-61, of social studies in Burton-on-Trent, Staffordshire, England, 1964-65; University of Manchester, Manchester, England, lecturer in comparative religion,

1970-80, senior lecturer, 1980—; Open University, visiting senior lecturer, 1975-77.

MEMBER: International Association for History of Religions, Society for Mithraic Studies (treasurer, 1971—), British Institute of Persian Studies, Society for Afghan Studies, New Testament Studies, Royal Asiatic Society (fellow), Shap Working Party (vice-chair, 1969—).

WRITINGS:

Persian Mythology, Hamlyn (Twickenham, England), 1974, revised edition, P. Bedrick Books (New York City), 1985.

Spanning East and West, Open University Press, 1978.

Parsis and the British, K. R. Cama Oriental Institute (Bombay), 1978.

A History of the Parsis in British India, Manchester University Press (Manchester, England), 1982.

Religion and the Arts, Allen Lane, 1983.

Zoroastrianism and the Parsis, Ward Lock (London), 1985.

EDITOR

Comparative Religion in Education, Oriel Press, 1970.

(With E. J. Sharpe) *Hinduism,* Oriel Press, 1972, 2nd edition, Routledge & Kegan Paul (London), 1973.

(With Sharpe) *Man and His Salvation: Studies in Memory of S. G. F. Brandon,* Manchester University Press, 1973.

Mithraic Studies, Rowman & Littlefield (Totowa, NJ), 1975.

The Facts on File Dictionary of Religions, Facts on File (New York City), 1984.

The Penguin Dictionary of Religions, Penguin (New York City), 1984.

A Handbook of Living Religions, Penguin, 1985.

Mary Boyce, *Zoroastrians,* Routledge & Kegan Paul, 1986.

Who's Who of World Religions, Macmillan (London), 1991, Simon & Schuster (New York City), 1992.

A New Dictionary of Religions, revised edition, Blackwell, 1995.

OTHER

Editor of a number of book series, including "Makers of New Worlds," Scribner (New York City), "Library of Religious Beliefs and Practices," Routledge & Kegan Paul, and "Sources for the Study of Religion," Manchester University Press. Contributor to *Numen, Religion, Journal of K. R. Cama Oriental Institute,* and *Journal of Mithraic Studies.* Editorial secretary of *Religion,* 1970-72.*

HINTON, John (Mark) 1926-

PERSONAL: Born March 5, 1926, in London, England; son of Albert George and Winifred Alice (Bray) Hinton; married Moira Patricia Watkins, August 15, 1950; children: Ruth Frances, Peter John. *Education:* King's College Hospital Medical School, University of London, M.B., B.S., 1949, D.P.M., 1958, M.D., 1961.

ADDRESSES: Home—99 Auckland Rd., London, SE19 2DT, England.

CAREER: King's College Hospital, London, England, medical registrar, 1949, 1952-54; Maudsley Hospital, London, senior registrar, 1955-61; Middlesex Hospital Medical School, London, senior lecturer and professor of psychiatry, 1961-83, head of academic department of psychiatry, 1966-83; University of London, professor emeritus in psychiatry, 1983—; St. Christopher's Hospice, London, England, senior research fellow, 1984—. *Military service:* British Army, Medical Corps., 1950-52; became captain.

MEMBER: Royal Society of Medicine (president, psychiatry section, 1974), Royal College of Physicians (fellow), Royal College of Psychiatrists (fellow).

WRITINGS:

Dying, Penguin (London), 1967, 2nd edition, 1972.

(With Arnold Toynbee and others) *Man's Concern with Death,* Hodder & Stoughton (London), 1968, McGraw (Berkshire), 1969.

(With Ray Fitzpatrick) *The Experience of Illness,* Methuen (London), 1985.

Contributor of articles on terminal care, depression and reactions to cancer to medical journals.

Dying has been translated into Spanish, Swedish, Finnish and Japanese.

WORK IN PROGRESS: Continued research in terminal care.*

*   *   *

HIRSCH, Monroe J(erome) 1917-1982

PERSONAL: Born March 6, 1917, in New York, NY; died, January, 1982; son of Stanley (a publisher) and Anna (Mandell) Hirsch; married Winifred Maud Wilson (a teacher), May 4, 1940; children: Geoffrey Alan. *Education:* Attended College of the City of New York (now City College of the City University of New York), 1934-37; University of California, Berkeley, A.B., 1940, certificate in optometry, 1940; Stanford University, Ph.D., 1947.

CAREER: Private practice in optometry in Oakland, CA, 1940-45; University of California, clinical instructor in optometry, 1941-45; Ohio State University, Columbus, assistant professor of optometry, 1947-48; Stanford University, Stanford, CA, acting assistant professor of physiology, 1948-49; Los Angeles College of Optometry, Los Angeles, CA, associate professor of optometry, 1949-51, professor and director of graduate education and research, 1951-53; private practice in optometry in Ojai, CA, beginning 1953; University of California, Berkeley, clinical instructor, 1954-66, Thomas H. Peters Memorial Lecturer in School of Optometry, c. 1956, lecturer, 1966-69, professor of optometry and physiological optics, 1969-78, director of clinics, 1970-74, dean of School of Optometry, 1974-78.

Alameda County Hospital, refractionist, 1943-44; worked in Office of Science Research and Development and Wright Field contracts, 1944-47; Pacific University, member of faculty, summer, 1946; member of advisory committees for American Foundation for the Blind, 1952-59, California Department of Education, 1960-62, California Department of Public Health, 1961-63, University of California, 1970-74, and National Research Council, beginning 1974; University of Auckland, George Cox Memorial Lecturer, 1969; University of Waterloo, Squarebriggs Memorial Lecturer, 1972. Member of city council in Ojai, CA, 1956-60 and 1966-70; mayor of Ojai, 1958; member of County Democratic Central Committee, 1960-64, and California Democratic Central Committee, 1962-64.

MEMBER: American Academy of Optometry (fellow; vice president, 1964-66; president, 1966-68), American Optometric Association, American Association for the Advancement of Science (fellow), American Association of University Professors, California Optometric Association, Sigma Xi.

AWARDS, HONORS: Silver Medal for distinguished service, Foundation in Optometry, 1960; Alumnus of the Year, University of California Optometry Alumni Association, 1962; distinguished service award, U. S. C. of C., 1967; California Optometric Association, Optometrist of the Year, 1969, citation, 1979; Berkeley optometry citation, 1978; Charles F. Prentice Medal, American Academy of Optometry, 1978; honorary doctorate, Illinois College of Optometry, 1979.

WRITINGS:

EDITOR

(With Ralph E. Wick) *Vision of the Aging Patient: An Optometric Symposium,* Chilton (Philadelphia), 1960.
(With Wick) *Vision of Children: An Optometric Symposium,* Chilton, 1963.
Synopsis of the Refractive State of the Eye, Burgess (Minneapolis), 1967.

(And author of historical commentary) H. A. Thomson, *Dr. Thomson's 1895 Correspondence Course in Optics,* Professional Press (Chicago), 1975.
Wallace M. Handeland and John E. Staroba, *Optometric and Medical Terminology: A Programmed Text,* Multimedia Center, School of Optometry, University of California (Berkeley), 1976.

OTHER

(With Wick) *The Optometric Profession,* Chilton, 1968.

Contributor of about two hundred papers to optometry journals. *Archives of American Academy of Optometry,* associate editor, 1953-68, editor, 1968-78; *American Journal of Optometry and Physiological Optics,* editor, 1968-78.*

[Death information provided by widow, Winifred W. Hirsch.]

*   *   *

HOCHMAN, Stanley Richard   1928-

PERSONAL: Born October 15, 1928, in New York, NY; son of Isador and Rose (Merman) Hochman; married Gloria S. Honickman, October 30, 1961; children: Anndee Elyn. *Education:* New York University, B.A., 1948, M.A., 1950.

ADDRESSES: Home—44 Trent Rd., Wynnewood, PA 19096. *Office*—*Philadelphia Daily News,* 400 North Broad St., Philadelphia, PA 19101.

CAREER: Member of staff of *Brownsville Herald,* Brownsville, TX, 1953-54, *Corpus Christi Caller-Times,* Corpus Christi, TX, 1954-56, *Waco News-Tribune,* Waco, TX, 1956-58, and *San Bernardino Sun,* San Bernardino, CA, 1958-59; *Philadelphia Daily News,* Philadelphia, PA, member of staff, 1959—, sports editor, 1971-74. *Military service:* U.S. Army, 1951-53.

WRITINGS:

Mike Schmidt: Baseball's King of Swing (for children), Random House (New York City), 1983.
(With Max Patkin) *The Clown Prince of Baseball,* foreword by Joe Garagiola, WRS Group (Waco, TX), 1994.

*   *   *

HODGES, H(erbert) A(rthur)   1905-1976

PERSONAL: Born January 4, 1905; died October 4, 1976, in England; son of Willis and Lily Malaingre (Dyson) Hodges; married Vera Joan Willis, 1939; children: two sons, one daughter. *Education:* Balliol College, Oxford, B.A., 1926; University of Reading, M.A., D.Phil., 1932.

CAREER: University of Reading, Reading, Berkshire, England, professor of philosophy, 1934-69, professor emeritus, 1969-76. Member of Royal Commission on Betting, Lotteries, and Gaming, 1949-51. Master, Guild of St. George, 1954-73.

WRITINGS:

Wilhelm Dilthey: An Introduction, K. Paul, Trench, Trubner & Co., 1944, reprinted, Fertig (New York City), 1969.

Christianity and the Modern World View, SCM Press (London), 1949.

The Philosophy of Wilhelm Dilthey, Routledge & Kegan Paul (London), 1952, reprinted, Greenwood Press (Westport, CT), 1974.

Languages, Standpoints, and Attitudes, Oxford University Press (Oxford, England), 1953.

Anglicanism and Orthodoxy: A Study in Dialectical Churchmanship, SCM Press, 1955.

The Pattern of Atonement, SCM Press, 1955.

Death and Life Have Contended, SCM Press, 1964.

God beyond Knowledge (essays and lectures), edited by W. D. Hudson, Barnes & Noble (New York City), 1979.

Angels and Human Knowledge, Community of the Servants of the Will of God (Crawley, West Sussex, England), 1982.

Also author of *A Rapture of Praise,* with A. M. Allchin, 1966; also author of pamphlets.

OBITUARIES:

PERIODICALS

AB Bookman's Weekly, October 4, 1976.*

*   *   *

HOLL, Kristi D(iane) 1951-

PERSONAL: Surname is pronounced "hall"; born December 8, 1951, in Guthrie Center, IA; daughter of Delbert Richard and Melva (a real estate agent; maiden name, Hanysh) Couchman; married Randy Holl (a landscape nursery owner), June 17, 1973; children: Matthew (adopted), Jennifer, Laurel, Jacqueline. *Education:* University of Northern Iowa, B.A., 1974. *Religion:* Baptist. *Avocational interests:* Civil War era, *Gone with the Wind* memorabilia, camping, hiking, reading, museums, steamboat rides on the Mississippi River.

ADDRESSES: Home and office—340 Grant, Story City, IA 50248.

CAREER: Reading teacher at elementary school in Waterloo, IA, 1972; writer, 1980—. Institute of Children's Literature, correspondence instructor, 1983-90.

MEMBER: Society of Children's Book Writers and Illustrators, Mystery Writers of America, Authors Guild.

AWARDS, HONORS: The Rose beyond the Wall was named a Notable Children's Trade Book in the field of social studies by the joint committee of the National Council of Social Studies and the Children's Book Council, 1985; Maryland Children's Book Award, 1990, for *The Haunting of Cabin 13.*

WRITINGS:

FICTION FOR CHILDREN

Just like a Real Family, Atheneum (New York City), 1983.

Mystery by Mail, Atheneum, 1983.

Footprints up My Back (Junior Literary Guild selection), Atheneum, 1984.

The Rose beyond the Wall, Atheneum, 1985.

Cast a Single Shadow, Atheneum, 1986.

First Things First, Atheneum, 1986.

Perfect or Not, Here I Come (Junior Literary Guild selection), Atheneum, 1986.

The Haunting of Cabin 13, Atheneum, 1987.

Patchwork Summer, Atheneum, 1987.

No Strings Attached, Atheneum, 1988.

Hidden in the Fog, Atheneum, 1989.

Danger at Hanging Rock, David Cook (Elgin, IL), 1989.

Two of a Kind, Standard Publishing (Cincinnati, OH), 1990.

Trusting in the Dark, Standard Publishing, 1990.

A Change of Heart, Standard Publishing, 1991.

A Tangled Web, Standard Publishing, 1991.

OTHER

Contributor of articles and stories to magazines, including *Child Life, Children's Digest, Children's Playmate, Family Life Today, Health Explorer, Jack and Jill, Living with Children, SCBW Bulletin, Touch, Vibrant Life, Writer,* and *Your Life and Health.*

WORK IN PROGRESS: Four more books for Standard Publishing.

SIDELIGHTS: Kristi D. Holl learned to write from a correspondence course provided by the Institute of Children's Literature. Three of her stories were sold while she was still a student. "It was gratifying," she once told *CA,* "to see that, after years of full-time mothering, I remembered a few words longer than two syllables. My instructor's encouragement was the single most important factor in my success. She helped me stretch beyond what I considered to be my capabilities." Holl went on to encourage other writers in the same way by teaching the correspondence course herself.

The author once commented: "When people ask me if I hope someday to write for adults, they're often surprised when I say no. I much prefer to write for children. Kids have the ability to believe in 'impractical' ideas, in fantastic places and people. Children are fun to write for because they still believe all things are possible. When I write, I enjoy becoming a child again, letting down all the barriers adults build up. When I was a child, I thought writers who actually got paid to stay home and make up stories must be the luckiest people in the world. I still think so.

"My advice to aspiring writers: The one factor I think you must have in order to succeed in writing is this—a strong belief in your ability. You must believe in the value of your work. You must believe that you have something to say to readers. Each writer has a unique perspective and unique experiences to bring to his writing. I think you get this belief in yourself by writing about what you care about. If you write about something you care deeply about, you will write with enthusiasm. This enthusiasm will be transmitted to your readers. So I advise a student not to write science fiction if he hates to read it, and not to write romances if a swooning heroine turns his stomach. Don't jump on bandwagons, writing something just because you think it will sell. Your 'lukewarm-ness' will show in your writing—your readers will feel about it as you do."

BIOGRAPHICAL/CRITICAL SOURCES:

PERIODICALS

Times-Republican (Marshalltown, IA), March 17, 1984.

*   *   *

HOPKINS, David   1948-

PERSONAL: Born September 11, 1948, in Salisbury, Wiltshire, England; son of Clifford (a schoolmaster) and Marjorie (a schoolmistress; maiden name, Gay) Hopkins; married Sandra Harmer (a university continuing education tutor), July 31, 1971; children: Kate, James. *Education:* St. Catharine's College, Cambridge, B.A., 1969, M.A., 1973; University of Leicester, Ph.D., 1979.

ADDRESSES: Home—89 Hill View, Henleaze, Bristol, Avon BS9 4QQ, England. *Office*—Department of English, University of Bristol, 3/5 Woodland Rd., Bristol, Avon BS8 1TB, England.

CAREER: University of Bristol, Bristol, England, lecturer in English, 1977—, reader in English poetry, 1993—.

WRITINGS:

(Author of introduction) John Wilson, *Specimens of the British Critics,* Scholars' Facsimiles and Reprints (Delmar, NY), 1979.
(Editor with Thomas Mason) *The Beauties of Dryden,* Bristol Classical Press (Bristol, England), 1982.
John Dryden, Cambridge University Press (Cambridge, England), 1986.
(Editor with Charles Martindale) *Horace Made New,* Cambridge University Press, 1993.
(With Tom Mason) *The Story of Poetry,* Broadcast Books, 1993.
(Editor) *The Routledge Anthology of Poets on Poets,* Routledge & Kegan Paul (London), 1994.
(Editor with Tom Mason) *Abraham Cowley: Selected Poems,* Carcanet Press (Manchester, England), 1994.

Contributor to periodicals, including *Modern Language Review, Review of English Studies, Yearbook of English Studies, Notes and Queries, Comparative Literature, Translation and Literature,* and *Cambridge Quarterly.* Member of editorial board, *Translation and Literature.*

WORK IN PROGRESS: Currently co-editing (with Paul Hammond) volumes three and four of *The Poems of John Dryden* for the Longman Annotated English Poets series.

SIDELIGHTS: In *John Dryden,* David Hopkins explains that Dryden's poetry has been neglected primarily because of late Victorian judgments. Though Dryden's reputation is based mainly upon a few of his satires, Hopkins claims that Dryden's genius is more evident in his translations of such authors as Virgil, Juvenal, Chaucer, and Boccaccio. He takes a somewhat dim view of Dryden's plays, and sees Dryden's shift from playwriting to religious and philosophical verse as an important point in the poet's career. John Dryden has "the virtues of energy and clarity," wrote David Nokes for the *Times Literary Supplement,* adding that Hopkins's "enthusiasm" for his subject "is refreshing."

Hopkins told *CA:* "My research and teaching are motivated by a desire to communicate the pleasure and power of English literature (particularly English poetry). I wish to explain literature's capacity, in the words of Samuel Johnson, 'to enable readers better to enjoy life, or better to endure it.' Since I believe English literature is the birthright of all, not merely the preserve of the academy, I try to work on assumptions and employ arguments that might have an appeal for any serious readers of the works I discuss—not merely for 'students' or 'scholarly specialists.'

"My main aims are first, to present the work of certain neglected (or misunderstood) English poets of the past in ways that make them intelligible and attractive to modern readers, and second, to explore the relations between English poetry (especially that of the 17th and 18th Centuries) and that of Classical Greece and Rome."

BIOGRAPHICAL/CRITICAL SOURCES:

PERIODICALS

Times Literary Supplement, August 8, 1986.

*   *   *

HORWITZ, Richard P(aul) 1949-

PERSONAL: Born October 12, 1949, in New Britain, CT; son of Sydney Jonas (a dentist) and Shirley (a homemaker; maiden name, Brander) Horwitz; married Ilona Rifkin (a physical therapist), August 24, 1969; children: Carl Allen. *Education:* University of Pennsylvania, B.A. (cum laude), 1971, M.A., 1972, Ph.D., 1975. *Politics:* "Left-of-center." *Religion:* Jewish.

ADDRESSES: Home—3431 480th St., S.W., Iowa City, IA 52240. *Office*—American Studies Department, 202 Jefferson Building, University of Iowa, Iowa City, IA 52242.

CAREER: Colby College, Waterville, ME, assistant professor of history and American studies, 1975-76; University of Minnesota, Minneapolis, assistant professor of American studies, 1976-77; University of Iowa, Iowa City, assistant professor, 1977-81, associate professor, 1981-87, professor of American studies, 1987—, director of undergraduate program in American studies, 1982-86, chair of undergraduate program in American studies, 1986-90, director of graduate studies in American studies, 1993—. Visiting scholar in the Republic of China, Republic of Korea, Japan, and India, 1984-85, and distinguished senior lecturer for Netherlands American Commission for Educational Exchange, 1990-91. Speaker at conventions and conferences.

MEMBER: American Anthropological Association, American Studies Association, Organization of American Historians, American Folklore Society, Popular/American Culture Association, Mid-America American Studies Association (president, 1992-93), Heartland Folklorists.

AWARDS, HONORS: Old Gold summer fellowship, 1980, 1981; U.S.I.S. and Fulbright grants to Japan, India, and Republic of Korea, 1985, Switzerland, 1990, Denmark, Finland, Germany, the Netherlands, and Portugal, 1991; fellowship from National Science Council, 1984-85; University House interdisciplinary research grant, 1987; fellow, National Endowment for the Humanities, 1990, 1992; development assignment, University of Iowa, 1990-91.

WRITINGS:

Anthropology Toward History: Culture and Work in a Nineteenth-Century Maine Town, Wesleyan University Press (Middletown, CT), 1978.
The Strip: An American Place, photographs by Karin E. Becker, University of Nebraska Press (Lincoln, NE), 1985.
(Editor and contributor) *Exporting America: Essays on American Studies Abroad,* Garland Publishing (New York City), 1993.

Also contributor to books, including *Exploring Society Photographically,* edited by Howard S. Becker, Mary & Leigh Block Gallery, Northwestern (Chicago, IL), 1981; *When They Read What We Write: The Politics of Ethnography,* edited by Caroline B. Brettell, Bergin and Garvey (Westport, CT), 1993; *The Fulbright Difference, 1948-1992,* edited by Richard T. Arndt and David L. Rubin, Transaction (New Brunswick, NJ), 1993; and *Multiculturalism and the Canon of American Culture,* edited by Hans Bak, VU University Press (Amsterdam), 1993.

Contributor of articles and reviews to *American Studies, American Studies International, American Quarterly, Ethnohistory, Journal of the Society for the Humanities and Technology, North Dakota Quarterly,* and *Winterthur Portfolio.*

WORK IN PROGRESS: A book on farmers, pigs, and disease in American culture.

SIDELIGHTS: Richard P. Horwitz researched *Anthropology Toward History: Culture and Work in a Nineteenth-Century Maine Town* by living in Winthrop, Maine, for three years. He perused the local records for material that would reveal to him what life had been like in the town between 1820 and 1850, years during which Winthrop changed from a farming village to a mill town. "By piling up . . . instances of vivid, ordinary language," a reviewer for the *New York Times Book Review* said, "Professor Horwitz produces a basic and apparently objective picture of the past in one place."

Horwitz carefully researches the subjects of his anthropological work. For instance, he once told *CA:* "With the help of photographer and journalism professor Karin Becker I spent more than three years cruising for burgers and chatting with strip-side workers to assess roadside commerce for *The Strip.*" More recently, Horwitz commented: "I have spent 15 years working part-time as a hired hand on a 2000-acre hay-grain-cattle farm in Iowa, a source and resource for my latest obsession."

BIOGRAPHICAL/CRITICAL SOURCES:

PERIODICALS

New York Times Book Review, March 19, 1978.

HOSPITAL, Janette Turner 1942-
(Alex Juniper)

PERSONAL: Born November 12, 1942, in Melbourne, Australia; daughter of Adrian C. (a painter) and Elsie (Morgan) Turner; married Clifford G. Hospital (a professor), February 5, 1965; children: Geoffrey, Cressida. *Education:* University of Queensland, St. Lucia, Brisbane, Australia, B.A., 1966; Queen's University, Kingston, Ontario, Canada, M.A., 1973; doctoral study, 1974-75. *Politics:* Democrat.

ADDRESSES: Home—Boston, MA; Brisbane, Australia; and Kingston, Ontario, Canada. *Agent*—Jill Hickson Associates, P.O. Box 271, Woollahra, New South Wales 2025, Australia; and Molly Friedrich, Aaron Priest Agency, 708 Third Ave., 23rd Floor, New York, NY 10017.

CAREER: Writer, 1982—. High school teacher of English in Brisbane, Australia, 1963-66; Harvard University, Cambridge, MA, librarian, 1967-71; teacher of English at several institutions, including St. Lawrence College and Queen's University, 1973-82; writer in residence, Massachusetts Institute of Technology, 1985-86, 1987, 1989, University of Ottawa, 1987, University of Sydney, 1989, La Trobe University, 1989, and Boston University, fall, 1991; La Trobe University, adjunct professor of English, 1991-93.

AWARDS, HONORS: Citation from *Atlantic Monthly*, 1982, for story "Waiting"; Seal First Novel Award, Seal Books, 1982, for *The Ivory Swing*; Fellowship of Australian Writers award, 1988, for *Dislocations*; gold medal, Canadian National Magazine Awards, 1980, for travel writing.

WRITINGS:

NOVELS

The Ivory Swing, McClelland & Stewart (Toronto), 1982, Dutton (New York City), 1983.
The Tiger in the Tiger Pit, Dutton, 1983.
Borderline, Dutton, 1985.
Charades, Bantam (New York City), 1989.
(As Alex Juniper) *A Very Proper Death*, Penguin (Melbourne), 1990, Scribner (New York City), 1991.
The Last Magician, Holt (New York City), 1992.

SHORT STORIES

Dislocations, Norton (New York City), 1986.
Isobars, University of Queensland Press (New York City), 1990.

Work represented in anthologies, including *CBC Anthology*. Contributor of stories to magazines in Canada, the United States, England, and Australia, including *Atlantic*

Monthly, Canadian Forum, Commonweal, North American Review, Queen's Quarterly, Saturday Night, and *Yale Review.*

WORK IN PROGRESS: An untitled novel; a screenplay, *Suicide of a Gentleman.*

SIDELIGHTS: Janette Turner Hospital once told *CA:* "I have lived for extended periods in Australia, the United States, Canada, England, and India, and I am very conscious of being at ease in many countries but belonging nowhere. All my writing reflects this. My characters are always caught between worlds or between cultures or between subcultures."

"All my writing," she commented in *Contemporary Novelists,* "in a sense, revolves around the mediation of one culture (or subculture) to another." It is, Helen Daniel observed in the same source, "intellectually sophisticated writing which spirals through mysteries and indeterminacies but never loosens its tug on the senses. Much of [Hospital's] work is about the borderlines of things, of art and self, of time and space. . . . Intellectually compelling yet fiery and dynamic, her work is baroque, elegant yet with a sensuous energy and immediacy."

Hospital's first novel, *The Ivory Swing*, tells the story of a university professor's wife who goes with her husband and children to India for a year and wrestles during that time with the questions of love and marriage, and of freedom—both her own and what the concept means in another culture. Christopher Schemering, writing in the *Washington Post Book World*, described it as "a disturbing meditation on the clash of cultures and the rebellion and feminine rage in each." Reviewing the book in *Maclean's,* Marni Jackson faulted Hospital for prose that sometimes "runs perilously close to Ladies' Home Daydream" but concluded that *The Ivory Swing* deserved its Seal Award for turning "the shopworn plot of Canadians in exile into a romantic, intelligent, well-written first novel." Gail Pearce, writing for *Quill and Quire*, called *The Ivory Swing* "compelling and enjoyable reading" and reported that "the plot is well constructed [and] the characters are plausible and sympathetic."

The Tiger in the Tiger Pit, Hospital's second novel, derives its name from T. S. Eliot's "Lines for an Old Man," the author once told *CA.* The story centers on the members of the unhappy, patriarchal Carpenter family, who, as Judith Fitzgerald noted in *Books in Canada,* "display a perverse tendency for chaos." Mona Simpson, in the *New York Times Book Review,* found the story unsuited for treatment as a novel, noting that "the book feels more like a play." Clare Colvin, however, in a review for *Books and Bookmen,* remarked that Hospital "portrays the claustrophobic web of family relationships with perception."

Hospital's fascination with borders is obvious not only in the title of her third novel, *Borderline*, but in its plot as well, in which a couple help an injured South American woman who is attempting to cross the border between the United States and Canada. In the *New York Times Book Review*, Cheri Fein labeled Hospital's third novel "by far her most complex and disturbing." M. G. Vassanji observed in *Books in Canada* that *Borderline* contains "echoes . . . of Conrad, parallels in theme and form with Renaissance art, allusions to Indian mythology" and interpreted the borderline of the title as "a metaphor for other barriers," particularly in interpersonal relationships. Writing in *Saturday Night*, Elspeth Cameron called *Borderline* "a coup" in which Hospital "brings to the fore political issues that seemed slight and redundant in her first two novels (though not in some of her stories), and through symbolic parallels integrates their startling relevance with her almost existentialist musings on the nature of reality, perception, and art."

Hospital's novel *Charades*, in the words of *New York Times Book Review* writer Ron Loewinsohn, "manages to combine images from our Judeo-Christian myth of origin—the Garden of Eden story—with metaphors and concepts from quantum physics and cosmology" in the tale of a young Australian graduate student who seeks to piece together her sketchy past during an affair she initiates with a professor of cosmology. She does this by entertaining her lover, a la Scheherazade, with nightly stories—her guesses about her past, her parents, her life—and by the end has woven together an incomplete but acceptable truth for herself. Valerie Miner, in the *Los Angeles Times Book Review*, maintained that "Hospital writes with luminous wit and ripe sensuality about the sublime and the wretched. . . . It is a measure of [her] lush talent that none of this seems contrived. She takes the reader on an exuberant tour of quantum physics, Middle Eastern mythology, [and] the comparative cultural legacies of British imperialism and still leaves you caring about her characters." Linda Barrett Osborne in the *Washington Post Book World* described Hospital's writing in *Charades* as "clever and lyrical, and her characterization superb," and Alan Cheuse, writing for the *Chicago Tribune*, praised the novel's "mixture of intelligence and sensuality, idea and deeply felt drama."

The Last Magician begins with strong Dantean allusions that foreshadow the hellish Sydney catacombs that house the Quarry, an area of destitution and depravity where the "last magician," photographer and filmmaker Charlie Chang, and other characters go in search of Cat, the lost figure around whom the story revolves. The first of Hospital's novels to be set wholly in Australia, where the author has tended to spend more and more of her time through the years, garnered praise from major review journals. In the opinion of Aamer Hussein in the *Times Literary Supplement*, *The Last Magician* surpassed "even the excellent *Borderline*, and should establish [Hospital] as one of the most powerful and innovative writers in English today."

Hussein found the book "unashamedly dense with ideas: reflections on the art of photography collide with meditations on science; Taoist citations . . . intertwine with a critique of contemporary literary norms (many of which Hospital challenges and brilliantly contravenes)." Writing in the *New York Times Book Review*, Edward Hower lauded Hospital for knowing "how to cast a spell that makes us as eager as her narrator to uncover the truth," and added that Hospital "fills her novel with evocative settings, characters we care deeply about and language that is entrancingly lyrical." In the *Washington Post Book World*, Carol Anshaw criticized Hospital's lapses into overwrought writing but acknowledged that risk as inherent in "trying to pull off a highwire act." However, Anshaw added, "The up-side of the author's full-tilt style is that, when the prose and ideas of this book resonate against each other, the result is passages of stunning clarity and beauty."

Comparing Hospital's novels with the short stories in her second collection, *Isobars*, Hussein noted that the latter "collide with, and diverge from, her novels, finishing incomplete phrases, casting light on distant corners, indicating new projects." In the *New York Times Book Review*, Richard Burgin found the prose in these stories "too feverish and preachy" at times and the irony "too heavy-handed." He concluded, however, that "much more often [Hospital is] able to fuse her disparate talents and concerns to create an original, convincing vision of our struggles with ourselves and others, and with our memories and dreams." Michael Harris of the *Los Angeles Times Book Review*, in addition, commended Hospital's "strengths as a writer: a lyrical style, a wide range, a gift for compression, and the ability to get down and dirty when lyricism doesn't cut it."

BIOGRAPHICAL/CRITICAL SOURCES:

BOOKS

Contemporary Literary Criticism, Volume 42, Gale (Detroit), 1987.
Contemporary Novelists, fifth edition, St. James (Detroit), 1991.

PERIODICALS

Books and Bookmen, August, 1984, pp. 33-34.
Books in Canada, November 9, 1983, p. 33; January-February, 1986, p. 27.
Chicago Tribune, March 13, 1989.

Los Angeles Times Book Review, May 29, 1983, p. 8; January 19, 1986, p. 10; April 23, 1989, pp. 3, 7; September 8, 1991, p. 6; September 20, 1992, pp. 3, 12.
Maclean's, May 3, 1982; October 4, 1982, p. 72; September 26, 1983, p. 62.
Ms., July, 1983, p. 21.
New York Times Book Review, April 15, 1984, p. 22; September 1, 1985, p. 8; December 25, 1988, p. 9; March 12, 1989, p. 14; September 29, 1991, p. 18; September 13, 1992, p. 15.
Quill and Quire, October, 1982, p. 31.
Saturday Night, April, 1986, pp. 57-59.
Times Literary Supplement, July 3, 1992, p. 25.
Toronto Star, April 21, 1982.
Washington Post Book World, June 5, 1983, p. 10; February 26, 1989, p. 8; August 30, 1992, p. 8.

*   *   *

HOUSEPIAN, Marjorie
See DOBKIN, Marjorie Housepian

*   *   *

HOWARD, Alyssa
See TITCHENER, Louise

*   *   *

HUMPHREY, James H(arry) 1911-

PERSONAL: Born February 26, 1911, in Marietta, OH; son of Harry and Nellie (Pugh) Humphrey; married Frances Drokopil, March 29, 1945; children: Joy Nell. *Education:* Denison University, B.S., 1933; Western Reserve University (now Case Western Reserve University), M.S., 1946; Boston University, Ph.D., 1951. *Religion:* Protestant.

ADDRESSES: Home—9108 St. Andrews Pl., College Park, MD 20740. *Office*—Department of Physical Education, University of Maryland, College Park, MD 20740.

CAREER: Bedford Board of Education, Bedford, OH, director of health and physical education, 1937-49; Michigan State University, East Lansing, assistant professor of health and physical education, 1951-53; University of Maryland, College Park, associate professor, 1953-56, professor of physical education and health, 1956-81, professor emeritus, 1981—. Distinguished visiting scholar, University of Delaware, 1965, University of Northern Colorado, 1967, University of Hawaii, 1968, and Texas A & M University, 1971. Lecturer to learned societies and

educational groups. *Military service:* U.S. Naval Reserve, 1943-45.

MEMBER: American Academy of Physical Education, American Alliance for Health, Physical Education, and Recreation, American School Health Association (fellow; past chair of research council), Society for Research in Child Development (fellow), Society of Children's Book Writers, Science for the Handicapped Association, Association for Anthropological Study of Play.

AWARDS, HONORS: American Alliance for Health, Physical Education, Recreation National Honor Award, 1972; selected for inclusion in the *International Compendium of Eminent People in the Field of Exceptional Education,* 1975; R. Tait McKenzie Award of the American Alliance for Health, Physical Education, Recreation and Dance, 1976; Alumni Citation, Denison University; elected to Fellowship in the American Institute of Stress, 1984.

WRITINGS:

Elementary School Physical Education: With Emphasis upon Its Integration in Other Curriculum Areas, Harper (New York City), 1958.
Read and Play (series of six books for 6-8 year olds) Garrard (Easton, MD), 1962.
Child Learning through Elementary School Physical Education, W. C. Brown (Dubuque, IA), 1966, 2nd edition (with daughter, Joy N. Humphrey), 1974.
Teaching Elementary School Science through Motor Learning, C. C. Thomas (Springfield, IL), 1975.
Education of Children through Motor Activity, C. C. Thomas, 1975.
Improving Learning Ability through Compensatory Physical Education, C. C. Thomas, 1976.
Physical Education as a Career, C. C. Thomas, 1978.
Child Development through Physical Education, C. C. Thomas, 1980.
Ted Learns About Stress, Kimbo (Long Branch, NJ), 1980.
A Textbook of Stress for College Students, C. C. Thomas, 1982.
Teaching Gifted Children through Motor Learning, C. C. Thomas, 1985.
Profiles in Stress, AMS Press (New York City), 1986.
Children and Stress, AMS Press, 1987.
Children Development and Learning through Dance, AMS Press, 1987.
Stress in Coaching, C. C. Thomas, 1988.
Stress in the Nursing Profession, C. C. Thomas, 1988.
Teaching Children to Relax, C. C. Thomas, 1988.
Helping Learning Disabled Gifted Children Learn through Compensatory Active Play, C. C. Thomas, 1990.

Integration of Physical Education in the Elementary School Curriculum, C. C. Thomas, 1990.

An Overview of Childhood Fitness, C. C. Thomas, 1991.

Health and Fitness for Older Persons, AMS Press, 1992.

Stress among Older Adults, AMS Press, 1992.

Stress among Women in Modern Society, AMS Press, 1992.

Motor Learning in Childhood Education, C. C. Thomas, 1992.

Stress Management for Elementary Schools, C. C. Thomas, 1993.

Elementary School Child Health: For Parents and Teachers, C. C. Thomas, 1993.

Sports for Children: A Guide For Adults, C. C. Thomas, 1993.

Physical Education for the Elementary School, C. C. Thomas, 1994.

Supervision in Health Education: Principles and Techniques, C. C. Thomas, in press.

COAUTHOR

(With Harris F. Beeman) *Intramural Sports: A Text and Study Guide,* W. C. Brown, 1954, 3rd edition, Princeton Book (Princeton, NJ), 1980.

(With Leslie W. Irwin) *Principles and Techniques of Supervision in Physical Education,* Mosby (St. Louis, MO), 1954, 3rd edition, Princeton Book, 1980.

(With Irwin and Warren R. Johnson) *Methods and Materials in School Health Education,* Mosby, 1956.

(With W. R. Johnson and Granville Bradley Johnson) *Your Career in Physical Education: An Introduction to the Profession for Young Men and Women,* Harper, 1957.

(Editor with Edwina Jones and Martha J. Haverstick) *Readings in Physical Education for the Elementary School,* National Press (Plymouth, England), 1958, 2nd edition, 1960.

(With W. R. Johnson and Virginia D. Moore) *Elementary School Health Education: Curriculum, Methods, Integration,* Harper, 1962.

(With W. R. Johnson and others) *Health Concepts for College Students,* Ronald (New York City), 1962.

(Compiler with Doris E. Terry and Howard S. Slusher) *Readings in Health Education: A Collection of Selected Articles for Use in Personal Health and Health Education Courses,* W. C. Brown, 1964.

(With Anne Gayle Ingram) *Introduction to Physical Education for College Students,* Holbrook (Boston), 1969.

(With Dorothy D. Sullivan) *Teaching Slow Learners through Activity Games,* C. C. Thomas, 1970.

(With Sullivan) *Teaching Reading through Motor Learning,* C. C. Thomas, 1973.

(With J. N. Humphrey) *Learning to Listen and Read through Movement,* Kimbo, 1974.

(With others) *Health Teaching in Elementary Schools,* C. C. Thomas, 1975.

(With R. B. Ashlock) *Teaching Elementary School Mathematics through Motor Learning,* C. C. Thomas, 1976.

(With Humphrey) *Sports Skills for Boys and Girls,* C. C. Thomas, 1980.

(With Humphrey) *Help Your Child Learn the 3 R's through Active Play,* C. C. Thomas, 1980.

(With Humphrey) *Reducing Stress in Children through Creative Relaxation,* C. C. Thomas, 1981.

(With others) *Coping with Stress in Teaching,* AMS Press, 1986.

(With others) *Child Development during the Elementary School Years,* C. C. Thomas, 1989.

(With others) *Reading Can Be Child's Play,* C. C. Thomas, 1990.

(With others) *Mathematics Can Be Child's Play,* C. C. Thomas, 1990.

(With others) *Developing Elementary School Science Concepts through Active Games,* C. C. Thomas, 1991.

RECORDINGS; ALL PRODUCED BY KIMBO EDUCATIONAL

Teaching Children Mathematics through Games, Rhythms and Stunts, 1968.

Stunts and Tumbling for Elementary School Children, 1969.

(With others) *Teaching Reading through Creative Movement,* 1969.

(With Humphrey) *Helping Children Understand about Stress,* 1980.

OTHER

Contributor to books, including *Games in Education and Development,* edited by Loyda M. Shears and Eli M. Bower, C. C. Thomas, 1974; and *Selye's Guide to Stress Research,* Volume III, edited by Hans Selye, Van Nostrand (New York City), 1983.

Also contributor to proceedings of professional organizations, including International Reading Association, International Seminar on Play, and National Science Teachers Association. Contributor to professional journals, including *Stress, Perceptual and Motor Skills, Research Quarterly,* and *Academic Therapy.* Member of board of associate editors, *Research Quarterly,* 1954-59 and 1960-63; research editor, *Journal of School Health,* 1962-65.

SIDELIGHTS: James H. Humphrey is widely known for his writing of and contributions to over forty textbooks used at colleges and universities throughout the world. In addition, he has written books for children and issued a series of educational recordings. Humphrey, who has been professor emeritus of Physical Education and Health at the University of Maryland since 1981, is renowned as one of the world's leading researchers in the area of child learning through motor activities.

BIOGRAPHICAL/CRITICAL SOURCES:

PERIODICALS

Children Today, July, 1971; May, 1986.
Choice, November, 1969.
Contemporary Psychology, May, 1986; June, 1989.
Grade Teacher, February, 1967.
Instructor, May, 1989.
Journal of Education, November, 1977.
School Library Journal, December, 1980.

I-J

IRWIN, Robert (Graham) 1946-

PERSONAL: Born August 23, 1946, in Guildford, Surrey, England; son of Joseph Alan (a psychiatrist) and Wilhemina (a homemaker; maiden name, Drapers) Irwin; married Helen Elizabeth Taylor (a parliamentary clerk), September 30, 1972; children: Felicity Anne. *Education:* Merton College, Oxford, B.A., 1967; graduate study at School of Oriental and African Studies, London, 1967-72. *Religion:* Monotheist. *Avocational interests:* Juggling, roller-skating.

ADDRESSES: Home—39 Harleyford Rd., London SE 11, England. *Agent*—Juri Gabriel, 35 Camberwell Grove, London, England.

CAREER: University of St. Andrews, St. Andrews, Fife, Scotland, lecturer in medieval history, 1972-77; part-time teacher of Arabic and Middle Eastern history at Cambridge University, Oxford University, and University of London, 1977—.

MEMBER: Royal Asiatic Society (fellow), Society of Antiquarians (fellow).

WRITINGS:

The Arabian Nightmare (novel), Dedalus (London), 1983, revised edition, Viking (New York City), 1987.
The Limits of Vision (novel), Viking, 1986.
The Middle East in the Middle Ages: The Early Mamluk Sultanate, 1250-1382 (nonfiction), Southern Illinois University Press (Carbondale), 1986.
The Mysteries of Algiers (novel), Viking, 1988.
The Arabian Nights: A Companion, Viking, 1994.
Exquisite Corpse (novel on surrealism), Dedalus, in press.

Contributor of book reviews and articles to periodicals, including *Times Literary Supplement* and *Washington Post.*

WORK IN PROGRESS: A book on Islamic art; a historical novel about England in the fifteenth century.

SIDELIGHTS: In *The Limits of Vision* Robert Irwin tells the story of Marcia, a South London housewife who is obsessed with grime. The novel depicts Marcia's typical day, from the time her husband goes to work until the time he returns home. During this period Marcia does her household duties, but, according to Stephen Dobyns in the *New York Times Book Review,* imagination—not housework—is the main subject of *The Limits of Vision.* Reviewer Jeanette Winterson agrees, writing in the *Times Literary Supplement* that Irwin's book "ranks as a genuine (and rare) work of the imagination."

Irwin lets Marcia's imagination run wild throughout *The Limits of Vision.* One day Marcia is led by a distracting dustball "into the fantastic landscape" of her tattered, filthy carpet, Nadia Cowen explains in the *Chicago Tribune.* "Like Alice in a weird, primeval wonderland of grime," Cowen continues, "she is led by a white mite to a meeting with her nemesis—'Mucor, Lord of the Dust.' " In addition, to help her through her day of cleaning, Marcia invents illustrious historical visitors—artist and scientist Leonardo da Vinci, artist and poet William Blake, writer Charles Dickens, and naturalist Charles Darwin, for example—with whom she converses on the subject of dirt. "This quirky book . . .is witty, sometimes uproariously funny," Cowen states. Dobyns concurred, declaring *The Limits of Vision* "an immensely intelligent and delightful novel that constantly jumps and turns through level after level of humor and invention while managing to hold at bay those enemies of comedy—the cute, the winsome and the arch." Dobyns added that "the book is very short . . .yet so dense with wit and surprise that it seems longer."

Irwin told *CA:* "I have traveled extensively in the Middle East and all aspects of its history and culture are of interest to me. So are dreams and hypnagogic imagery, which provide a lot of the material for my novels, all of which deal with obsessional states. I am currently combining a career as a part-time academic, specializing in the Middle Ages and Islamic society, with a career as a novelist. I gave up being a full-time historian to write novels. I am competent in French and Arabic, and incompetent in most Western European languages."

BIOGRAPHICAL/CRITICAL SOURCES:

PERIODICALS

Chicago Tribune, July 11, 1986.
New York Times Book Review, August 24, 1986.
Times Literary Supplement, April 25, 1986; July 25, 1986.
Washington Post, August 23, 1986.

*   *   *

JACOBSEN, Josephine   1908-

PERSONAL: Born August 19, 1908, in Cobourg, Ontario, Canada; daughter of Joseph Edward (a doctor) and Octavia (Winder) Boylan; married Eric Jacobsen, March 17, 1932; children: Erlend Ericsen. *Education:* Educated by private tutors and at Roland Park Country School, 1915-18. *Politics:* Democrat. *Religion:* Roman Catholic.

ADDRESSES: Home—220 Stony Ford Rd., Baltimore, MD 21210. *Office*—Poetry Office, Library of Congress, Washington, DC 20540. *Agent*—McIntosh & Otis Inc., 475 Fifth Ave., New York, NY 10017.

CAREER: Library of Congress, Washington, DC, poetry consultant, 1971-73, honorary consultant in American letters, 1973-79. Lecturer for the American Writers Program annual meeting, Savannah, GA, 1984. Member of the literature panel, National Endowment for the Arts, 1979-83, and of the poetry committee of Folger Library.

MEMBER: Poetry Society of America (vice-president, 1978-79), PEN, Corporation of Yaddo, Baltimore Citizens' Planning and Housing Association, Baltimore Center Stage Association, Baltimore Museum of Art, Walters Art Gallery, Hamilton Street Club.

AWARDS, HONORS: The Shade-Seller: New and Selected Poems was nominated for a National Book Award; *A Walk with Raschid and Other Stories* was selected one of the Fifty Distinguished Books of the Year by *Library Journal;* recipient of award from the American Academy and Institute of Arts and Letters for Service to Literature; received fellowships from Yaddo, the Millay Colony for the Arts, and the MacDowell Colony; Doctor of Humane

Letters from Towson State University, Goucher College, College of Notre Dame of Maryland, and Johns Hopkins University; Literary Lion, New York Public Library, 1985; Shelley Memorial Award for lifetime service to literature, Poetry Society of America, 1992; inducted into the American Academy of Arts and Letters, 1994.

WRITINGS:

POETRY

For the Unlost, Contemporary Poetry, 1946.
The Human Climate, Contemporary Poetry, 1953.
The Animal Inside, Ohio University Press (Athens, OH), 1966.
(Editor) *From Anne to Marianne: Some American Women Poets,* Library of Congress (Washington, DC), 1972.
The Instant of Knowing, Library of Congress, 1974.
The Shade-Seller: New and Selected Poems, Doubleday (New York City), 1974.
One Poet's Poetry, Agnes Scott College, 1975.
The Chinese Insomniacs: New Poems, University of Pennsylvania Press (Philadelphia), 1981.
The Sisters: New and Selected Poems, Bench Press (Oakland, CA), 1987.
Distances, Bucknell University Press (Cranbury, NJ), 1992.
Collected Poems, Johns Hopkins University Press (Baltimore), 1995.

SHORT STORIES

A Walk with Raschid and Other Stories, Jackpine (Winston-Salem, NC), 1978.
Adios, Mr. Moxley, Jackpine, 1986.
On the Island, Ontario Review Press, 1989.

OTHER

(With William R. Mueller) *The Testament of Samuel Beckett* (dramatic criticism), Hill & Wang (New York City), 1964.
(With Mueller) *Ionesco and Genet: Playwrights of Silence* (dramatic criticism), Hill & Wang, 1968.
Substance of Things Hoped For, Doubleday, 1987.

Also contributor to books and anthologies, including *The Way We Live Now,* Ontario Press, 1986; *Best American Short Stories,* 1966; *O. Henry Prize Stories,* 1967, 1971, 1973, 1976, 1985, and 1993; *Fifty Years of the American Short Story,* 1970; *A Geography of Poets,* edited by William Field; *A Treasury of American Poetry,* edited by Nancy Sullivan; *Night Walks: Short Stories,* edited by Joyce Carol Oates; *A Treasury of American Short Stories,* edited by Sullivan; *Pushcart Prizes Six; Belles Lettres,* 1986; *Best American Poetry,* 1991 and 1993; *Scarecrow Poetry; Diamonds Are a Girl's Best Friend; No More Masks;* and *A Formal Feeling Comes,* 1993 and 1994.

ADAPTATIONS: Three poems from *The Chinese Insomniacs: New Poems* were set to Jean Eigelberger Ivey's composition "Notes toward Time," March, 1984; the poem "The Monosyllable" from *The Chinese Insomniacs* was performed at the Baltimore Museum of Art, Baltimore, MD, 1987.

SIDELIGHTS: Josephine Jacobsen is "extremely interested" in the theatre, and has acted with the Vagabond Players in Baltimore. Equally interested in travel, she has visited Mexico, Guatemala, Venezuela, the Caribbean Islands, France, Italy, Greece, Morocco, Kenya, Tanzania, Portugal, Madeira, Spain, and Canada.

BIOGRAPHICAL/CRITICAL SOURCES:

PERIODICALS

New York Times Book Review, April 4, 1982.
Poetry, March, 1983.

*   *   *

JANGER, Allen R(obert)   1932-

PERSONAL: Born September 5, 1932, in Chicago, IL; son of Max and Myrtle (Levy) Janger; married Inez Kurn, September 11, 1960; children: Edward, Matthew, Michael. *Education:* Attended University of Chicago, 1949-55, and London School of Economics and Political Science, 1955-56.

ADDRESSES: Office—The Conference Board, 845 Third Ave., New York, NY 10022.

CAREER: The Conference Board (formerly National Industrial Conference Board), New York City, research specialist, research analyst, and research assistant, 1960-65, director of information services, 1965-68, senior specialist in organization and developmental research, 1968-75, senior research associate in management research, 1975-81, director of management research, 1981-82, executive director of management system programs, 1982-86, senior research associate, 1986—.

WRITINGS:

PUBLISHED BY NATIONAL INDUSTRIAL CONFERENCE BOARD (NEW YORK CITY)

(With Harold Steiglitz) *Top Management Organization in Divisionalized Companies,* 1965.
Personnel Administration: Changing Scope and Organization, 1966.
Managing Programs to Employ the Disadvantaged, 1970.

PUBLISHED BY THE CONFERENCE BOARD (NEW YORK CITY)

(With Ruth G. Shaeffer) *Employing the Disadvantaged: A Management Perspective,* 1972.

Corporate Organization Structures, Volume 1: *Manufacturing,* 1973, Volume 2: *Financial Enterprises,* 1974, Volume 3: *Service Companies,* 1977.
The Personnel Function: Changing Objectives and Organization, 1977.
Matrix Organization of Complex Businesses, 1978.
Organization of Joint Ventures, 1980.
(With Ronald E. Berenbeim) *External Forces on Corporate Decision Making: A Growing International Problem,* 1981.
(With Shaeffer) *Who Is Top Management?,* 1982.
Management Outlook (series), 1983.
Organizing for Flexibility in Financial Services, 1989.
Measuring Managerial Layers and Spans, 1989.
How European Companies Organize in the United States, 1990.*

*   *   *

JARCHOW, Merrill E(arl)   1910-

PERSONAL: Surname pronounced "Jarko"; born September 25, 1910, in Stillwater, MN; son of Louis D. (a sheriff) and Elsie (Bruntlett) Jarchow; married Doris A. Vrenegor (a dance teacher), March 21, 1943; children: Barbara (Mrs. Keith Slater), Susan (Mrs. William Alrich). *Education:* University of Minnesota, A.B., 1930, M.A., 1933, Ph.D., 1941. *Politics:* Republican. *Religion:* Methodist.

ADDRESSES: Home—203 Oak, Northfield, MN 55057. *Office*—Carleton College, Northfield, MN 55057.

CAREER: South Dakota State College (now University), Brookings, instructor, 1935-37, assistant professor, 1937-40, associate professor of history, 1940-41; Carleton College, Northfield, MN, associate professor, 1946-67, historian-in-residence, 1967—, dean of men, 1946-67. Trustee, Shattuck School, Faribault, MN, 1954-74. *Military service:* U.S. Navy, 1943-46; became lieutenant.

MEMBER: Organization of American Historians, National Association of Deans and Advisers of Men (member of executive committee, 1948-50), Minnesota Historical Society (member of council, 1954-62), Phi Beta Kappa, Northfield Golf Club (president, 1961).

AWARDS, HONORS: L.L.D., Carleton College, 1988.

WRITINGS:

(With R. W. Murchie) *Population Trends in Minnesota,* University of Minnesota Press (Minneapolis, MN), 1936.
The Earth Brought Forth, Minnesota Historical Society (St. Paul, MN), 1949.
(With L. A. Headley) *Carleton: The First Century,* Carleton College (Northfield, MN), 1966.

Minnesota's Private Liberal Arts Colleges: Their History and Contributions, Minnesota Historical Society, 1973.

Donald J. Cowling, Carleton College, 1974.

In Search of Fulfillment: Episodes in the Life of D. Blake Stewart, North Central Publishing, 1974.

(With William M. Werber) *Circling the Bases,* [Naples], 1978.

Amherst H. Wilder and His Enduring Legacy to Saint Paul, [St. Paul, MN], 1981.

Letters to Alice: Life at Carleton from Strong to Sallmon, Carleton College, 1982.

Like Father, Like Son: The Gilfillan Story, Ramsey County Historical Society (St. Paul, MN), 1986.

(Editor with David H. Porter), *Carleton Remembered, 1909-1986,* Carleton College, 1987.

Neither Trivial nor Frivolous: A History of the Tatman Foundation, The Foundation (Webster Groves, MO), 1991.

Carleton Moves Confidently into Its Second Century, 1966-1992, Carleton College, 1992.

Contributor to *The Navy's Air War,* edited by A. R. Buchanan, Harper (New York City), 1946.

WORK IN PROGRESS: A book based on the diary of Winifred Fairbank, 1907-1940.*

*   *   *

JARVIS, Sharon   1943-
(Johanna Hailey, H. M. Major, joint pseudonyms)

PERSONAL: Born October 1, 1943, in Brooklyn, NY; daughter of Joseph and Ethel (Karger) Jarvis. *Education:* Hunter College of the City University of New York, B.F.A., 1964.

ADDRESSES: Home and office—Sharon Jarvis & Co., Toad Hall, Inc., Rural Route 2, Box 16B, Laceyville, PA 18623.

CAREER: Ace Books, New York City, copy editor and copywriter, 1969-70; assistant managing editor for Popular Library, 1970-71; Ballantine Books, Inc., New York City, editor, 1971-74; Doubleday & Co., New York City, editor, 1974-77; Playboy Books, New York City, senior editor, 1977-82; Jarvis, Braff Ltd. (literary agency), Staten Island, NY, vice president, 1978-82; Sharon Jarvis & Co. (literary agency), Laceyville, PA, president, 1983—.

MEMBER: International Fortean Organization, Association of Author's Representatives, Science Fiction Writers of America, Holistic Consortium.

WRITINGS:

WITH KATHLEEN BUCKLEY UNDER JOINT PSEUDONYM H. M. MAJOR

The Alien Trace, New American Library (New York City), 1984.

Time Twister, New American Library, 1984.

WITH MARCIA HOWL UNDER JOINT PSEUDONYM JOHANNA HAILEY

Enchanted Paradise, Zebra Books (New York City), 1985.

Crystal Paradise, Zebra Books, 1986.

Beloved Paradise, Zebra Books, 1987.

EDITOR

True Tales of the Unknown, Bantam (New York City), 1985.

Inside Outer Space: Science Fiction Professionals Look at Their Craft, Frederick Ungar (New York City), 1985.

The Uninvited, Bantam, 1989.

Beyond Reality, Bantam, 1991.

Dark Zones, Warner Books (New York City), 1992.

Dead Zones, Warner Books, 1992.

OTHER:

Author of columns for *Mystery Scene Magazine.*

WORK IN PROGRESS: True Tales of the Unknown, Volume 2.

SIDELIGHTS: Sharon Jarvis told *CA:* "We do a lot of New Age and nonfiction occult, in addition to genre fiction."

*   *   *

JEANSONNE, Glen   1946-

PERSONAL: Born November 13, 1946, in New Orleans, LA; son of R.J. (in agriculture) and LaNelle S. (a housewife) Jeansonne; married Sharon Pace (a college teacher); children: Leah, Hannah. *Education:* University of Southwestern Louisiana, B.A., 1968; Florida State University, M.A., 1969, Ph.D., 1973. *Politics:* Democrat. *Religion:* Jewish.

ADDRESSES: Home—4060 North Farwell Ave., Milwaukee, WI 53211. *Office*—Department of History, University of Wisconsin—Milwaukee, Milwaukee, WI 53201.

CAREER: University of Southwestern Louisiana, Lafayette, assistant professor of history, 1973-75; Williams College, Williamstown, MA, assistant professor of history, 1975-78; University of Wisconsin—Milwaukee, assistant professor, 1978-81, associate professor, 1981-88, professor of history, 1988—, Morris Fromkin Memorial Lecturer,

1979. Visiting associate professor at University of Michigan, 1985. Member of National Coordinating Committee for the Promotion of History.

MEMBER: American Historical Association, Organization of American Historians, Oral History Association, Popular Culture Association, Southern Historical Association, Louisiana Historical Association, Wisconsin State Historical Society, Wisconsin Association for the Promotion of History (vice-president, 1985-88), Milwaukee Metropolitan Historians Association, Milwaukee County Historical Society.

AWARDS, HONORS: Woodrow Wilson fellow, 1972; grant from American Philosophical Society, 1975, 1982, Wisconsin Humanities Committee, 1982, Earhart Foundation of Michigan, 1984, 1991, and University of Wisconsin—Milwaukee; fellow of American Council of Learned Societies, 1977; Albert J. Beveridge grant from American Historical Association, 1982, 1986; John D. and Catherine T. MacArthur Foundation Fellow, 1987-88; *Gerald L. K. Smith: Minister of Hate* was awarded first place for best scholarly book by the Wisconsin Council of Writers, was nominated for a Pulitzer Prize in biography, and was awarded the Gustavus Myers citation for books dealing with race relations; Alumni Association Teaching Award, University of Wisconsin—Milwaukee, 1992.

WRITINGS:

Race, Religion, and Politics: The Louisiana Gubernatorial Elections of 1959-1960, University of Southwestern Louisiana Press (Lafayette, LA), 1977.
Leander Perez: Boss of the Delta, Louisiana State University Press (Baton Rouge, LA), 1977.
Gerald L. K. Smith: Minister of Hate, Yale University Press (New Haven, CT), 1988.
Messiah of the Masses: Huey P. Long and the Great Depression, HarperCollins (New York City), 1992.
Transformation and Reaction: America, 1921-1945, HarperCollins, 1994.
Women of the Far Right: The Mothers' Movement and World War II, University of Chicago Press (Chicago, IL), 1995.

SCREENPLAYS

Papa Perez, Cecropia Films, 1980.
The Ends of the Earth (television documentary), broadcast by PBS-TV, Louisiana, 1982.

EDITOR

(With Light T. Cummins) *A Research Guide to the History of Louisiana,* Greenwood Press (Westport, CT), 1982.
Huey at 100: Centennial Essays on Huey P. Long, Louisiana Tech University (Ruston, LA), 1994.

OTHER

Also contributor to books, including *Readings in Louisiana History,* edited by Glenn R. Conrad and others, University of Southwestern Louisiana Press, 1977; *The Quest for Social Justice,* edited by Ralph M. Alderman, University of Wisconsin Press, 1982; and *Anti-Semitism in American History,* edited by David A. Gerber, University of Illinois Press, 1986.

Contributor of articles, poems, a story, and reviews to history journals. Associate editor of *Louisiana History,* 1973-75. General co-editor of series "Reference Guide to State and Local History," Greenwood Press; editor of monograph series "The Right Wing in America," M. E. Sharpe.

WORK IN PROGRESS: A Time of Paradox: America 1900-2000, HarperCollins.

SIDELIGHTS: Glen Jeansonne told *CA:* "My teaching encompasses 20th-century American political, social, cultural, and intellectual history. Research interests include the above, as well as biography, the history of the right in America, history of racism and anti-Semitism, Southern history, and Louisiana history. I am also doing research in women's history. Future projects include a history of hate groups in America, a history of the 1980s, and several biographies. I have published about 50 scholarly and popular articles and about 100 reviews in newspapers, magazines, and scholarly journals. I make frequent appearances on public television and radio, as well as commercial radio and television and the journalistic media to comment on contemporary events."

BIOGRAPHICAL/CRITICAL SOURCES:

PERIODICALS

New York Times Book Review, January 8, 1978.

*   *   *

JOHANSON, Donald C(arl) 1943-

PERSONAL: Born June 28, 1943, in Chicago, IL; son of Carl Torsten (a barber) and Sally Eugenia (Johnson) Johanson; married Lenora Carey, 1988. *Education:* University of Illinois, B.A. (with honors), 1966; University of Chicago, M.A., 1970, Ph.D., 1974.

ADDRESSES: Home—Berkeley, CA. *Office*—Institute of Human Origins, 2453 Ridge Rd., Berkeley, CA 94709. *Agent*—Don Cutler, Bookmark, P. O. Box 170, Irvington, NY 10021.

CAREER: University of Illinois, Urbana, teaching assistant in anthropology, 1966; University of Chicago, Chicago, IL, teaching assistant in anthropology, 1969 and 1971-72; Cleveland Museum of Natural History, Cleveland, OH, associate curator of anthropology, 1972-74, curator of physical anthropology, 1974-81; director of scientific research and director of laboratory of physical anthropology, 1976-81; Institute of Human Origins, Berkeley, CA, founding director, 1981—. Case Western Reserve University, assistant professor, 1972-76, associate professor, 1976-78, adjunct professor of anthropology, 1978-81; Northeastern Ohio Universities College of Medicine, research associate professor of anatomy, 1977—; Sweet Briar College, visiting professor of anthropology, 1978; Kent State University, adjunct professor of anthropology, 1978-82; University of California, Berkeley, research associate in anthropology, 1982; Stanford University, professor of anthropology, 1984-90.

City of Clinton, IA, archaeologist, 1965; University of Illinois, archaeological field assistant, 1965; state of Illinois, survey and salvage archaeologist, summer, 1966; Kodiak Island, AK, research assistant, summer, 1967; Omo Research Expedition, Ethiopia, summers, 1970-72; International Afar Research Expedition, paleoanthropologist in Ethiopia, 1972, director of American contingent of expedition, autumn, 1973-76; conductor of field surveys and research in Yemen, autumn, 1977, Saudi Arabia, spring, 1978, and Ethiopia, 1980. Host of thirteen-week television series, "Nature," for WNET, Public Broadcasting Service (PBS-TV), 1982; host, narrator, and coauthor of "In Search of Human Origins," *NOVA,* PBS-TV, 1994. Lecturer at numerous universities and colleges, including California Institute of Technology, University of California, Berkeley, Stanford University, and the universities of Denver, New Orleans, Colorado, and Frankfurt am Mainz, Germany; also lecturer in Yemen, Turkey, Kenya, South Africa, China, France, Japan, Sweden, Canada, and England. Participant in Nobel Symposium, Sweden, 1978. Fellow of Rochester Museum of Natural History, 1982.

MEMBER: International Association for Dental Research, International Association of Human Biologists, International Association for the Study of Human Paleontology, American Association for the Advancement of Science (fellow), American Association of Physical Anthropologists, Royal Geographical Society (fellow), Association of Africanist Archaeologists, Society of Vertebrate Paleontology, Society for the Study of Human Biology, California Academy of Sciences (fellow), Societe de l'Anthropologie de Paris, Centro Studie Ricerche Ligabue (Venice, Italy), National Center for Science Education (supporting scientist), Founders Council, Explorers Club (honorary board), Bohemian Club.

AWARDS, HONORS: Grants from Wenner-Gren Foundation for Anthropological Research, 1970 and 1973; grants in anthropology from National Science Foundation, 1973-74, 1975-77, 1979-81, and 1987-88; grants from George Gund Foundation, 1974-75; special grant from Cleveland Foundation, 1975, grant, 1980-81; grants from National Geographic Society, 1975-76 and 1980-81; grants from L. S. B. Leakey Foundation, 1975-78 and 1980-81; golden plate award from American Academy of Achievement, 1976; grant from Roush Foundation, 1977-78; D.Sc. from John Carroll University, 1979; Jared Potter Kirtland Award from Cleveland Museum of Natural History, 1979, for outstanding scientific achievement; professional achievement award from University of Chicago Alumni Association, 1980; American Book Award, 1982, for *Lucy: The Beginnings of Humankind;* Houston International Film Award, 1982, for "Lucy in Disguise"; Humanist Laureate award, Academy of Humanism, 1983; distinguished service award, American Humanist Association, 1983; D.Sc., College of Wooster, 1985; San Francisco Exploratorium Award, 1986; International Premio Fregene Award, 1987.

WRITINGS:

(Editor) *Festschrift Albert Dahlberg,* OSSA, International Journal of Skeletal Research, 1979.
(With Maitland A. Edey) *Lucy: The Beginnings of Humankind,* Simon & Schuster (New York City), 1981.
(With Edey) *Blueprint: Solving the Mystery of Evolution,* Little, Brown (Boston), 1989.
(With James Shreeve) *Lucy's Child: The Discovery of a Human Ancestor,* Morrow (New York City), 1989.
(With Kevin O'Farrell) *Journey from the Dawn: Life with the World's First Family,* Villard, 1990.
(With Lenora E. Johanson and Blake Edgar) *Ancestors: In Search of Human Origins,* Villard, 1994.

FILMS

The First Family, PBS-TV, 1981.
Lucy in Disguise, PBS-TV, 1982.

OTHER

(With others) "In Search of Human Origins" (three-hour television special), *NOVA,* PBS-TV, 1994.

Also author of "Mysteries of Mankind" National Geographic Special, 1988. Contributor to *Earliest Man and Environments in the Lake Rudolf Basin,* edited by Yves Coppens, F. C. Howell, G. L. Isaac and R. E. F. Leakey, University of Chicago Press, 1976; *Geographical Background to Fossil Man,* edited by W. W. Bishop, Scottish Academic Press, 1978; *The Encyclopedia of Ignorance,* edited by Ronald Duncan and Miranda Weston-Smith, Pergamon (Elmsford, NY), 1978; *Early Hominids of Africa,* edited by C. J. Jolley, St. Martins (New York City), 1978; *Current Argument on Early Man,* edited by Lars-Konig Koenigsson and Stephan Sundstrom, Pergamon, 1980.

Also contributor of more than seventy-five articles to periodicals, including *American Journal of Physical Anthropology, Explorer, Science, Anesthesiology, Nature,* and *National Geographic.* General editor of *Paleoanthropology;* editor of *Reviews in Anthropology. Lucy: The Beginnings of Humankind* has been translated into Dutch, French, German, Hebrew, Italian, Japanese, Russian, Spanish, and Swedish.

SIDELIGHTS: Donald C. Johanson once told *CA:* "My research in human origins is motivated by the strong urge to know our beginnings. We are all fascinated by knowing how we got here and where we come from. It adds a very valuable perspective to all humankind. Human evolution is now fully documented and evolution is fact and not fantasy. It is important that people know this and learn that it is not something we should be ashamed of nor should it be ignored."

Johanson's fossil discoveries have caused a major revision in the theory of human origins. In a scientific field dependent on the scant fossil remains of creatures long since disappeared, the paleoanthropologist's finds provided a wealth of new information for incorporation into the human evolutionary scheme. As a result of his work, Johanson has named a new species, altered humankind's proposed family tree, and excited much debate among his colleagues.

In 1972 Johanson first explored the fossil-rich Afar Triangle of Ethiopia with French geologist Maurice Taieb. Combining forces in 1973 to create the International Afar Research Expedition, the scientists began excavating the site. In late October of the same year Johanson unearthed his first major find—a perfectly preserved knee joint dating back 3.5 million years. The scientist called the fossil "a historic discovery" because "it is the oldest anatomical evidence for man's bipedal stature and locomotion, the hallmark of mankind."

Returning to the same area in 1974 Johanson and one of his students uncovered the oldest, most complete skeleton known to anthropologists. Forty percent extant, the skeleton indicated a creature entirely new to scientists. Study determined it to be female, about twenty-five years old, and three and a half feet tall. Johanson nicknamed the creature Lucy after the Beatles' song "Lucy in the Sky with Diamonds," the tape that played in the expedition's camp. Lucy exhibited other, more remarkable physical characteristics: she had a small skull, walked upright, and was approximately 3.5 million years old. Her cranium the size of a softball, Lucy could not be considered human, yet as a biped, she could not be labeled an ape. Michael Bishop explained in the *Washington Post Book World* that "these two points—upright walking and a decidedly apelike brain—strongly suggest that she belonged to a species an-

cestral to both the earliest humans and our extinct austrolopithecine [sic; australopithecine means 'southern ape'] cousins."

This conclusion, reached after years of research and laboratory analysis of Lucy's remains, prompted Johanson and his colleagues to name Lucy a member of a new species of pre-human creatures called *Australopithecus afarensis* ("Afar southern apes"). The addition of this new species to humankind's family tree reverberated throughout the scientific community. Lucy became the "missing link" joining the separate evolutionary paths of the *Australopithecus* species and the *Homo* species. "If Johanson is right about Lucy and her relatives," related Suzanne Fields of the *Los Angeles Times Book Review,* "he halts the backward march of *Homo* and sets the divergence between ape and humans somewhere between 3 and 4 million years ago." Such an emendation of the evolutionary theory "is controversial," noted Kubet Luchterhand in the *Chicago Tribune Book World,* "because it requires substantial changes in many older ideas about the nature of our earlier ancestors."

One major reassessment concerns the relationship between brain enlargement and the advent of bipedalism. Traditional theory holds that brain enlargement came before bipedalism, or that the two developed together. "One idea had been that as four-legged primates began to make and use tools, their tool-rich environment favored larger brains," disclosed Boyce Rensberger in the *New York Times Book Review.* "This, in turn, had led to better tool making, which had then favored still bigger brains. According to this theory, the forelimbs had eventually . . . [become] so specialized for tool making that locomotion was relegated to the hind legs." Lucy's presence debunked this theory: her bipedalism and small brain preceded the use of tools by approximately 1.5 million years. Johanson and his associates thereupon advanced another hypothesis. They attributed the development of the nuclear family and pair bonding as the reasons for walking upright. Bipedalism allowed pre-humans to gather more food at one time and to more easily nurture their young. Fields pointed out that "Lucy thus carried the seeds of the nuclear family."

Johanson's discoveries and theories have brought him into conflict with the doyens of his field, the Leakeys. His find, declared Bishop, "establishes the advent of bipedalism approximately 1.75 million years earlier than does Richard Leakey's important 1972 discovery of a representative of *Homo habilis,* an early hominid . . . not quite 2 million years old." Furthermore, Lucy "casts suspicion on some of Richard Leakey's own fossil work, making the Leakey '1470' skull a million years more recent than he claims," commented Fields. Johanson's view of humankind's evolution also runs contrary to the Leakey's theories. Bishop elucidated: "Today, Johanson and the Leakeys hold mutually exclusive opinions about Lucy's significance. . . . Johanson has challenged two of the Leakeys entrenched beliefs about human evolution: first, that human beings are descended from an earlier variety of the genus *Homo* rather than from the australopithecines . . . ; and, second, that the genus *Homo* has bona fide representatives much older than 2 million years, whose remains have not yet been discovered."

In 1981 Johanson and science writer Maitland A. Edey published *Lucy: The Beginnings of Humankind.* The book described the discovery of Lucy and puts forth the paleoanthropologist's ideas about her significance. *Time* magazine contributor Peter Stoler observed that the two told their story "like polished mystery writers." Rensberger asserted that *Lucy* "is a fascinating, candid and scientifically reliable account of one of the most compelling scientific investigations ever undertaken—the effort to understand how human beings evolved." "Perhaps the most notable thing about this book," claimed Luchterhand, "is the skill and clarity of the authors' scientific explanations." Bishop stated that "in any event, this is an exciting, informative, mind-rocking, and important book."

Johanson's contributions to the field of paleoanthropology did not slow after finding Lucy. While again surveying the Afar region in November, 1975, the scientist came upon a site in which the remains of at least thirteen beings were found. Examination of the fossils revealed that they all died at about the same time, perhaps in some natural disaster. Johanson explained the importance of the find. "This discovery stunned the anthropological world because for the first time, an associated group of individuals had been recovered. It was a chance of nature that these individuals were fossilized in sediments 3.5 million years old." The group of fossils, which includes the remains of men, women, and children, appears to be those of a single family. As a result, they have been dubbed "the first family."

In the summer of 1986, Johanson's field team of ten U.S. and Tanzanian scientists, working at Olduvai Gorge, Tanzania, made another dramatic discovery: a 1.8 million-year-old partial skeleton of modern humans' earliest direct ancestor, *Homo habilis.* Assembled from 302 fragments of skull and limb bones and teeth, OH62 suggests that *Homo habilis* was much smaller and more apelike than previously thought; that the human body type probably did not evolve until *Homo erectus* emerged some 1.6 million years ago, and that it happened fairly rapidly. The proportions of the skeleton were a surprise to scientists and seem to indicate a major transition in human evolution.

This second remarkable breakthrough by the Johanson team, on the very site of the earlier Leakey discoveries, fanned the flames of the controversy that had broken out in the late 1970s over Johanson's claim that Lucy was the mother of all hominids. The Leakeys disputed his contention, maintaining that the "missing link," a separate *Homo habilis* ancestor, remained to be discovered. For more than a decade this dispute raged among paleoanthropologists, but by 1989 Johanson could state that "almost everybody who draws a family tree for hominids now uses Lucy—*Australopithecus afarensis*—as the common ancestor," the *Chicago Tribune* quoted him as saying. Then, at the old Leakey site, the Olduvai Gorge in Tanzania, Johanson's group uncovered humanlike fossils within a few days. The arm and leg bones of *Homo habilis* (never found by the Leakeys) resembled Lucy's, which strongly suggested that Johanson's original claim was correct: that Lucy was indeed the ancestor of humans. This finding prompted Johanson to cowrite *Lucy's Child: The Discovery of a Human Ancestor.*

Although Marvin Harris in the *Washington Post Book World* took exception to some personal remarks Johanson made about the Leakeys in the book, he calls *Lucy's Child: The Discovery of a Human Ancestor* "an exciting, fast-moving, nuts-and-bolts narrative of how Lucy's child was discovered." John Noble Wilford, writing for the *New York Times Book Review,* commented that "the descriptions of digging fossils are rich in detail and dialogue, conveying a sense of the gritty, sweaty reality of paleontological fieldwork," but added that "the book's real value lies elsewhere, in the lengthy digressions" on new theories of human origin and Johanson's relations with the Leakeys.

BIOGRAPHICAL/CRITICAL SOURCES:

BOOKS

Contemporary Issues Criticism, Volume 1, Gale (Detroit), 1982.

PERIODICALS

Chicago Tribune, December 3, 1989.
Chicago Tribune Book World, March 22, 1981; April 18, 1982.
Los Angeles Times, June 9, 1989.
Los Angeles Times Book Review, March 15, 1981.
National Geographic, December, 1976.
New York Times, February 22, 1981; April 25, 1982.
New York Times Book Review, February 18, 1979; February 19, 1981, April 20, 1982; November 12, 1989, p. 14; October 7, 1990, p. 38.
Time, March 16, 1981; June 1, 1987.
Times Literary Supplement, January 22, 1982; January 25, 1991, p. 25.

Washington Post Book World, March 15, 1981; October 22, 1989, p. 1.

*   *   *

JOHNSON, Haynes Bonner 1931-

PERSONAL: Born July 9, 1931, in New York, NY; son of Malcolm Malone (an editor and writer) and Ludie (Adams) Johnson; married Julia Ann Erwin, September 21, 1954 (divorced); children: Katherine Adams, David Malone, Stephen Holmes, Sarah Brooks, Elizabeth Haynes. *Education:* University of Missouri, B.J., 1952; University of Wisconsin at Madison, M.S., 1956. *Politics:* Independent. *Religion:* Episcopalian.

ADDRESSES: Office—Washington Post, 1150 15th St. N.W., Washington, DC 20071.

CAREER: Wilmington News-Journal, Wilmington, DE, reporter, 1956-57; *Washington Star,* Washington, DC, began as reporter, successively became national rewriteman, assistant city editor, and national assignments reporter, 1957-69; *Washington Post,* Washington, DC, national correspondent, 1969-73, assistant managing editor, 1973-77, columnist, 1977—. Lecturer at colleges and universities; Ferris Professor of Journalism at Princeton University, 1975 and 1978. Commentator on television programs *Today* and *Washington Week in Review. Military service:* U.S. Army, 1952-55; became first lieutenant.

MEMBER: National Press Club, Phi Gamma Delta, Gridiron Club (Washington, DC), Nassau Club (Princeton, NJ).

AWARDS, HONORS: Grand Award for reporting and Public Service Award, Washington Newspaper Guild, 1962 and 1968; Front Page Award, American Newspaper Guild, 1964, for political reporting; Pulitzer Prize in national reporting, 1966, for coverage of the civil rights demonstrations in Selma, AL; Headliners Award for national reporting, 1968; Sigma Delta Chi Award for general reporting, 1969; Duke University fellow in communications, 1973-74.

WRITINGS:

Dusk at the Mountain—The Negro, the Nation, and the Capital: A Report on Problems and Progress, Doubleday (New York City), 1963.

(With Manuel Artime, Jose Perez San Roman, Erneido Oliva, and Enrique Ruiz-Williams) *The Bay of Pigs: The Leaders' Story of Brigade 2506,* Norton (New York City), 1964, published in England as *The Bay of Pigs: The Invasion of Cuba by Brigade 2506,* Hutchinson (London), 1965.

(Author of introduction and epilogue) David Lowe, *Ku Klux Klan: The Invisible Empire,* Norton, 1967.

(With Bernard M. Gwertzman) *Fulbright: The Dissenter,* Doubleday, 1968.

(With George C. Wilson, Peter A. Jay, and Peter Osnos) *Army in Anguish* (articles originally published in *Washington Post,* September-October, 1971), Pocket Books (New York City), 1972.

(With Richard Harwood) *Lyndon,* Praeger (New York City), 1973.

(Editor) *The Fall of a President,* introduction by Benjamin C. Bradlee and Howard Simons, Delacorte (New York City), 1974.

The Working White House, illustrated with photographs by Frank Johnston, Praeger, 1975.

In the Absence of Power: Governing America, Viking (New York City), 1980.

(With Howard Simons) *The Landing* (novel), Villard Books (New York City), 1986.

(Editor with others) *Evolution and Revolutions: The World in Change,* Rhodes College (Memphis, TN), 1990.

Sleepwalking through History: America in the Reagan Years, Anchor Books (New York City), 1991.

SIDELIGHTS: The son of the late Pulitzer Prize-winning reporter and editor Malcolm Johnson, Haynes Bonner Johnson has distinguished himself as a newspaperman and political commentator in his own right. Whereas his father was awarded the 1948 Pulitzer Prize in local reporting for his "Crime on the Water Front" series in the *New York Sun,* Johnson himself won the 1966 Pulitzer in national reporting for his coverage of the civil rights demonstrations in Selma, Alabama. The Johnsons are the only father and son to receive Pulitzers in the history of American journalism. A thirty-year veteran newsman in the nation's capital—first for the *Washington Star,* then the *Washington Post*—Johnson is considered "one of the most perceptive, the best-informed, and the most level-headed reporters in Washington," says former London *Times* editor Godfrey Hodgson in the *Washington Post Book World.* Presidents and congressional leaders have sought his advice and help, and thousands of television viewers know him for his reports on the Public Broadcasting Service (PBS) program *Washington Week in Review.* Johnson's books on affairs of national interest, particularly *The Bay of Pigs: The Leaders' Story of Brigade 2506, In the Absence of Power: Governing America,* and *Sleepwalking Through History: America in the Reagan Years,* have accordingly attracted much attention.

The Bay of Pigs is the story of "Brigade 2506," the task force of Cuban exiles organized, trained, and directed by the U.S. Central Intelligence Agency (CIA) to overthrow Premier Fidel Castro in April, 1961. The book "is not, and does not purport to be, a complete history of the [disastrous] invasion and of the events that led up to it," notes

Ernest Halperin in the *New York Review of Books.* "The reader is mercifully spared an account of the various political groups in Miami, their complicated maneuvers and intrigues, their combinations and internal disputes."

Basing his report largely on interviews with the four principal brigade leaders and other survivors of the invasion force, Johnson "offers what unquestionably is the most coherent, detailed and complete account of the brigade's adventures," writes Tad Szulc in the *New York Times Book Review.* "In putting it all together as a narrative told in terms of individual and recognizable human beings, instead of the previous treatments of the expeditionary force as a faceless and anonymous entity, Mr. Johnson has done a superb and exciting job of writing. . . . He has not sought to embellish his story with adjectives and superfluous comments, but lets it tell itself in crisp dialogue of the shouted commands and of the commonplace remarks that men in battle make to each other."

Despite his appreciation for Johnson's style and research, Halperin disagrees with the author's claim that the CIA was ultimately responsible for the Bay of Pigs fiasco: "The basic fact is that all the important decisions concerning the invasion were made by the top policymakers of two administrations, and not by the CIA. The CIA was entrusted with the execution of these decisions." Harold Lavine, however, maintains in *Saturday Review* that "there is ample evidence in Johnson's book to support the belief that, after a while, the [CIA agents] became so obsessed with the idea of invading Cuba they were ready to lie to anyone, the President, the Cuban exile leaders, the brigade leaders, anyone, to carry out their plans."

Szulc, too, points out that Johnson "documents his charges abundantly, describing how the CIA inexplicably changed an earlier plan for multiple guerrilla landings, which might have succeeded, into the blueprint for the one-thrust invasion, which never had a reasonable chance of victory." Lavine concludes that though there are minor gaps in the story, "Johnson has written a powerful and convincing book that will long remain a definitive one."

In the Absence of Power: Governing America, an examination of President Jimmy Carter's experiences with Congress, the bureaucracy, and the press during his first thirty months in office, suggests that Carter's inability to get key legislation through Congress reflects a nationwide breakdown of party loyalty, discipline, and power. Johnson found the breakdown "so severe and so ominous," says Walter Karp in a 1980 review for *New Republic,* "that America today stands in imminent danger of becoming ungovernable."

Though many reviewers share Johnson's concern, several dismiss his explanation of Carter's legislative failures. Lowell Ponte, for example, writes in the *Los Angeles Times Book Review* that despite the diminishing authority of political machines, labor unions, and Capitol Hill bosses, "power seems not so much absent as up for grabs." Ponte believes that Johnson, "in his criticisms of Carter, . . . unwittingly reflects the mind-set of those Washington Old Insiders the voters elected Carter to replace." According to Karp, Johnson's explanation "not only contradicts the facts, it contradicts itself. . . . Carter's failure, in Johnson's view, stems in large measure from his unwillingness to cooperate with Democratic leaders. The implication of this is obvious. Democratic leaders are powerful men and Carter's defiant conduct turned them into powerful adversaries."

Godfrey Hodgson resolves the apparent conflict in the book this way: "I happen to believe Haynes Johnson is right in his judgment that the American people show some signs of being unwilling to govern themselves. As he points out, they certainly show every sign of being unwilling to be taxed adequately to provide the services they expect. But I also believe that these problems go further back in time, and deeper into the structure of the society, than Jimmy Carter's experience in his first thirty months in office."

Sleepwalking through History: America in the Reagan Years examines and frequently condemns the state of American government during the Reagan administration. Johnson looks at some infamous highlights of Reagan's tenure, tracing events like the Savings and Loan fiasco, the Wedtech scandal, the Wall Street crash of 1987, and the Iran-contra controversy. John Kenneth Galbraith explains in his *Washington Post Book World* review that Johnson's intent "was to see and describe just as much as possible of what happened during this decade, and in impressive measure he succeeds." Although he finds fault with the book's conclusion that all of America is responsible and to blame for the shortcomings of its government, Galbraith praises Johnson for his sharp journalism and willingness to insert opinion: "Johnson is no dry, detached observer, content to tell what happened without passing judgment. On the contrary, there is judgment on almost every page and certainly in every chapter."

BIOGRAPHICAL/CRITICAL SOURCES:

PERIODICALS

Book World, August 18, 1968.
Los Angeles Times Book Review, April 27, 1980.
New Republic, June 27, 1964; April 5, 1980.
Newsweek, May 18, 1964.
New Yorker, April 1, 1991.
New York Review of Books, July 9, 1964.
New York Times, March 20, 1991, p. C15.
New York Times Book Review, May 24, 1964; September 22, 1968; April 27, 1980; July 13, 1986, p. 12; Febru-

ary 24, 1991, p. 7; June 9, 1991, p. 34; March 22, 1992, p. 28.

Reporter, June 18, 1964.

Saturday Review, May 25, 1963; May 16, 1964.

Times Literary Supplement, February 18, 1965; August 7, 1969.

Tribune Books (Chicago), March 24, 1991, p. 6; April 5, 1992, p. 2.

USA Today, July 3, 1986, p. 2D; December 19, 1986, p. 4D.

Village Voice Literary Supplement, May, 1992, p. 28.

Washington Post Book World, April 6, 1980; June 22, 1986, p. 1; May 29, 1988, p. 12; February 24, 1991, p. 1; April 26, 1992, p. 12.*

*   *   *

JOHNSON, Joan J. 1942-

PERSONAL: Born September 8, 1942, in Norwalk, CT; daughter of John Lincoln (a corporation president) and Edith (a homemaker; maiden name, Wood) Irving; divorced; children: Jedidiah Lincoln David, Nathan Azariah Jacob. *Education:* Bethany College (Bethany, WV), B.A., 1964; University of Pennsylvania, graduate study, 1964-65; Fairfield University, M.A., 1983. *Politics:* Independent.

ADDRESSES: Home—Norwalk, CT. *Office*—Darien High School, School Lane, Darien, CT 06820.

CAREER: High school English teacher, Ipswich, MA, 1966-70; Stauffer Chemical Co., Westport, CT, assistant records administrator, 1978-79; Darien High School, Darien, CT, teacher of English and of talented and gifted students, 1979—.

WRITINGS:

YOUNG ADULT

The Cult Movement, F. Watts (New York City), 1984.

America's War on Drugs, F. Watts, 1989.

Kids without Homes, F. Watts, 1991.

Teenage Prostitution, F. Watts, 1992.

JUVENILE

Justice, F. Watts, 1985.

WORK IN PROGRESS: Not in My Backyard!

*   *   *

JOHNSON, Loch K. 1942-

PERSONAL: Given name is pronounced "lock"; born February 21, 1942, in Auckland, New Zealand; immi-

grated to the United States, 1946, naturalized citizen, 1969; son of Roland (in the military) and Kathleen (a homemaker) Johnson; married Leena Sepp (a librarian), March 22, 1969; children: Kristin Elizabeth. *Education:* University of California, Davis, A.B., 1965; University of California, Riverside, M.A., 1967, Ph.D., 1969. *Politics:* Democrat. *Religion:* Presbyterian. *Avocational interests:* Painting, drawing, long distance running.

ADDRESSES: Home—150 Sunnybrook Dr., Athens, GA 30605. *Office*—Department of Political Science, 104 Baldwin, University of Georgia, Athens, GA 30602.

CAREER: Visiting assistant professor of political science at University of North Carolina, 1970-71; Ohio University, Athens, associate professor of political science, 1971-75; U.S. Senate, Washington, DC, staff member of Intelligence Committee and Foreign Relations Committee, 1975-77; U.S. House of Representatives, Washington, DC, staff director of Sub-committee on Oversight Intelligence, 1977-79; University of Georgia, Athens, associate professor, 1979-85, professor of political science, 1985-90, Regents professor, 1990—. Member of national advisory board of Center for National Policy; local political campaign coordinator.

MEMBER: International Studies Association (president, Southern Region, 1993), American Political Science Association (secretary, 1994-95).

AWARDS, HONORS: Haynes Foundation fellow, 1966; U.S. Congressional fellow, 1969; named Outstanding Teacher by Pi Sigma Alpha, University of Georgia, 1980, 1981; Outstanding Honors Professor, University of Georgia, 1981, 1982, 1985; certificate of distinction from the National Intelligence Study Center, 1985, for *A Season of Inquiry;* V. O. Key Award, 1993, for *Runoff Elections in the United States.*

WRITINGS:

The Making of International Agreements, New York University Press (New York City), 1984.

A Season of Inquiry: The Senate Intelligence Investigation, University Press of Kentucky (Lexington, KY), 1985, Dorsey Press (Chicago, IL), 1987.

Democracy and the CIA, Oxford University Press (New York City), 1987.

Arms Control: Issues and Prospects, University of Georgia Press (Athens, GA), 1987.

America's Secret Power: The CIA in a Democratic Society, Oxford University Press, 1989.

America as a World Power: Foreign Policy in a Constitutional Framework, McGraw-Hill (New York City), 1990, 2nd edition, 1994.

(With Charles S. Bullock III) *Runoff Elections in the United States,* University of North Carolina Press (Chapel Hill, NC), 1992.

Intelligence and the State, Yale University Press (New Haven, CT), 1995.

EDITOR

(With Paul F. Diehl) *Through the Straits of Armageddon: Arms Control Issues and Prospects,* University of Georgia Press, 1987.

(With Karl F. Inderfurth) *Decisions of the Highest Order,* Brooks/Cole (Pacific Grove, CA), 1988.

Also contributor to professional journals.

SIDELIGHTS: Loch K. Johnson told *CA:* "My writing revolves around executive-legislative relations and ways to maintain the balance between national security and civil liberties. I have a special interest in the conduct of American foreign policy and the proper role of Congress in this process. Much of my research and writing grows out of my work as an investigator for Congress into the operations of the Central Intelligence Agency. I am searching for the right mix of the openness necessary for a democratic society and the secrecy necessary for some forms of intelligence activity."

BIOGRAPHICAL/CRITICAL SOURCES:

PERIODICALS

New York Times Book Review, December 21, 1986.

*   *   *

JONES, Douglas C(lyde) 1924-

PERSONAL: Born December 6, 1924, in Winslow, AR; son of Marvin Clyde (an auto mechanic) and Bethel (Stockburger) Jones; married Mary Arnold (a sales clerk), January 1, 1949; children: Mary Glenn, Martha Claire, Kathryn Greer, Douglas Eben. *Education:* University of Arkansas, B.A., 1949; graduate study at U.S. Army Command and General Staff College, 1961; University of Wisconsin—Madison, M.S., 1963.

CAREER: Writer and artist. U.S. Army, career officer, 1943-68, retiring as lieutenant colonel; served in Pacific Theater during World War II, later as commander of infantry rifle companies in Europe and Korea, and as information officer with Philadelphia Army Air Defense Command; chief of Armed Forces Press Branch, Office of Assistant Secretary of Defense for Public Affairs, the Pentagon, Washington, DC, 1966-68. University of Wisconsin—Madison, member of faculty in School of Journalism and Mass Communication, 1968-74, visiting lecturer, 1974—. Has exhibited paintings of Plains Indians

in one-man show at Washington Gallery of Art, 1967, and in Fayetteville, AR, and Tulsa, OK.

AWARDS, HONORS: Military: Army Commendation medal (three citations); Legion of Merit, 1968. Civilian: Golden Spur Award, Western Writers of America, 1976, for *The Court-Martial of George Armstrong Custer,* 1984, for *Gone the Dreams and Dancing,* and 1986, for *Roman;* Best Novel of the Year award, Friends of American Writers, 1980, for *Elkhorn Tavern.*

WRITINGS:

NOVELS

The Court-Martial of George Armstrong Custer, Scribner (New York City), 1976.

Arrest Sitting Bull, Scribner, 1977.

A Creek Called Wounded Knee, Scribner, 1978.

Winding Stair, Holt (New York City), 1979 (published in England as *The Winding Stair Massacre,* Allen & Unwin, 1980).

Elkhorn Tavern, Holt, 1980.

Weedy Rough, Holt, 1981.

The Barefoot Brigade, Holt, 1982.

Season of Yellow Leaf, Holt, 1983.

Gone the Dreams and Dancing, Holt, 1984.

Roman, Holt, 1986.

Remember Santiago, Holt, 1988.

Come Winter, Holt, 1989.

The Search for Temperance Moon, Holt, 1991.

This Savage Race, Holt, 1993.

OTHER

The Treaty of Medicine Lodge (nonfiction), University of Oklahoma Press (Norman, OK), 1966.

(Photographer) *Edison and His Invention Factory: A Photo Essay,* Eastern National Park and Monument Association, 1986.

(And illustrator) *Hickory Cured* (short stories), Holt, 1987.

Also contributor of articles and reviews to periodicals, including *Kansas Historical Quarterly* and *Journalism Quarterly.*

ADAPTATIONS: The Court-Martial of George Armstrong Custer was adapted for television and broadcast on "Hallmark Hall of Fame," NBC-TV, 1978, and released on cassette, Books on Tape, 1979.

SIDELIGHTS: Douglas C. Jones "has to be one of the most knowledgeable and imaginative writers of the American West," says Jay Daly in the *School Library Journal.* A retired army officer, Jones became a best-selling author in 1976 with the publication of *The Court-Martial of George Armstrong Custer,* an "obviously well-researched and unquestionably readable first novel," according to

James R. Frakes in the *New York Times Book Review.* Since then, Jones has produced a string of successful novels that Jeff Nathan claims in the *Los Angeles Times Book Review* demonstrate his skills as "a superb storyteller and authentic chronicler of the American West."

The Court-Martial of George Armstrong Custer and the two novels that followed it, *Arrest Sitting Bull* and *A Creek Called Wounded Knee,* form a "de facto trilogy," notes Alan Cheuse in the *New York Times Book Review,* since they chronologically deal with U.S.-Indian relations. *The Court-Martial of George Armstrong Custer* is an exercise in the historical imagination—the premise being that Custer somehow survived the Little Big Horn massacre, only to be court-martialed for his actions. Though Walter Clemons maintains in *Newsweek* that the "initial gimmick remains merely a gimmick" and says "Custer is hauled back from the grave and never brought to convincing life in any of the book's invented scenes," Robert McGeehin states in *Best Sellers* that the "setting, personalities, and testimony are convincing and suspenseful."

James R. Frakes also considers *The Court-Martial of George Armstrong Custer* exceptional. Calling it a "harbinger of a new fictional genre—the imaginative staging of a whole series of trials that *might* have occurred," he praises Jones's handling of the subject: "Douglas C. Jones is not untalented; he apparently knows military law and American Indians, and his present-tense style is taut and disciplined. His subject here is unusually provocative. Besides its political implications and its elements of Greek tragedy, 'there are more intrigues in this case . . . than in the Arabian Navy.' "

Arrest Sitting Bull further develops the matter of the Little Big Horn and its aftermath: the quelling of the Indian uprising and the death of Sitting Bull. Noting that the book "avoids both cowboy movie cliches and racist formulations about the Rapacious White Usurper," Jane Larkin Crain says in the *New York Times Book Review* that it "is written with supple and effective simplicity; the narrator's stoic awareness of the enormity of history itself gives this narrative a compelling dignity that distinguishes it from more run-of-the-mill popularizing treatments of the American West."

A Creek Called Wounded Knee reenacts what Sylvia Martin describes in the *Chicago Tribune Book World* as "the definitive last scene in the tragedy of the American Indian." Though Martin believes Jones's use of the present tense occasionally forces him to "sink into a mire of 'had had's," she nevertheless points out the merit of Jones's rendering: "Excellence rears up now and again like a struggling stallion. Jones depicts each side, placing us now with the Indians, now with the whites, so that we approach the fatal rendezvous with the fears, confusions,

and misunderstandings of both. He does not disguise the fact that his sympathies are with the Indians . . . but avoids the pit of sentimentality, taking his cue from that great Indian history by Dee Brown, *Bury My Heart at Wounded Knee.* That was a broad canvas. Here we see as through an enlarging glass the clash of two incompatible cultures." Alan Cheuse has similar praise for the book: "The pages describing the battle . . . , if not some of the laconic scenes leading up to it, will burn into your mind. Mr. Jones's prose here is less fine than in his earlier novels, but *A Creek Called Wounded Knee* is 'honest civilized work with a hammer and forge.' "

Although Jones is best known for his U.S. Cavalry-Sioux Indian trilogy, his other novels exhibit the same level of skill and authenticity, according to critics. *Winding Stair,* for example, is "a significant and highly entertaining contribution to the popular literature of the West," writes Brian Garfield in the *New York Times Book Review.* "The historical research is seamless—the story never slows down to admit dull exposition. *Winding Stair* convinces the reader, utterly, that this is how life must have been in that place at that time."

"The realism evoked by [*Weedy Rough*] is as strong as that in [Jones's] historical novels," says John Thomas Stovall in the *Chicago Tribune Book World.* Set in a small Southern town in the years following World War I, *Weedy Rough* is a departure from the time and place that Jones's readers have come to expect. But Stovall believes the book "isn't that radical a departure" for Jones, because "his narrative technique and thorough depiction of people and place make the novel seem realistic, almost factual. Even though *Weedy Rough* is a change, Jones's skill is still there."

Elkhorn Tavern, moreover, "has the makings of a classic Western," insists Michael Malone in the *New York Times Book Review.* "It has the beauty of *Shane* and the elegiac dignity of *Red River* without the false glamour or sentimentality of those classic Western films. . . . Mr. Jones is at home among the ridges and hardwoods of a frontier valley; he knows what moves in its forests, how the land changes under the seasons. He holds us still and compels us to notice what we live in."

The sights, sounds, smells and pains of the Civil War are evoked in Jones's novel *The Barefoot Brigade,* in which a squad of rough farmers, enlisted into the Confederate army, fight their way through different battles. The book's power, explains Mary Lee Settle of the *New York Times Book Review,* "lies in small events, individual antagonisms, boredom, waiting, slogging, hunger."

In his novel *Season of Yellow Leaf* and its sequel, *Gone the Dreams and Dancing,* Jones focuses on the ways a Comanche tribe collides with white culture. In *Season of Yellow*

Leaf, a white woman who had been captured by the Indians as a child confronts her conflicting feelings about being "rescued." In *Gone the Dreams and Dancing* Jones tells about the Antelope group that decides to give up fighting in 1875 and manages to adapt to the ways of the white world. Focusing on characters Kwahadi, who leads the band, and Liverpool Morgan, a former Confederate soldier in the Civil War, author Jones tells how the two become friends. Morgan, whose life grows closer and closer to the Comanches, helps Kwahadi find out what happened to his white mother—the one who was kidnapped from her people and then rescued. A *Publishers Weekly* reviewer calls *Gone the Dreams and Dancing* "wonderfully written" but observes that even though Jones has a "detailed appreciation" for the Indian ways, he "overlooks many of the difficulties" the race actually must face in white society. The reviewer continues, saying Jones describes the era and the events "with great poignancy and effectiveness."

The character Roman Hasford, whom Jones first introduced in his novel *Elkhorn Tavern,* reappears in *Roman,* a novel that tells how he leaves his family's isolated Arkansas hill cabin and comes of age. Moving from St. Louis to the bustling new town of Leavenworth, Kansas, Roman eventually makes it big in the unlikely businesses of raising pigs and picking up garbage. The contradictory world of the West after the Civil War, with stylish parties one day and shoot-outs with Indians the next, "is sketched in all its strange variety" says Tom Nolan in the *New York Times Book Review. Roman,* he says, brings out a "realistic texture of life" back then and characters who, by the end, have "earned the reader's affection and respect." This novel won Jones one of his Golden Spur awards from the Western Writers of America.

Jones departs from his long form of fiction in *Hickory Cured,* a collection of short stories set mostly in the 1930s Arkansas back-country town of Weedy Rough (site of a previous Jones novel). The narrator for these stories is Shanks Caulder, "a one-time professional soldier who retired after a generation in the service, came home to sit in his store between the cracker box and yellow rat-cheese wheel on the counter 'and tell stories about the way things used to be' "—a character who sounds very much like Jones himself, according to Michael J. Bandler in *Tribune Books.* Other characters include law officer Leo Sparks, who feuds with a family despised in the town, and the slipshod Slaven Budd, whose only talent is that he can "talk dog." In the *Los Angeles Times Book Review,* C. A. Wedlan concludes that in *Hickory Cured,* "You'd be hard pressed to find a better account of whistle-stop America 50 years ago."

Jones turned his attention to the 1898 period of the Spanish-American War in his novel *Remember Santiago,* pre-

senting the invasion of Cuba while introducing both real and fictitious characters from the historic conflict: Teddy Roosevelt, nurse Clara Barton of the Red Cross, and Gen. William Shafter, who is "the most sympathetic and most entertaining of the lot," reports Rory Quirk in the *Washington Post Book World.* Caught between a confused Washington headquarters and an untrustworthy Navy, thrown into combat with a former enemy, the out-of-shape Shafter is "a creaking Civil War relic, . . . no match for the murderous Cuban heat" who doesn't exactly inspire his troops. Shafter embodies the whole invasion that, as *Remember Santiago* makes clear, was a "poorly conceived, artlessly executed bloody mess that succeeded in spite of itself," Quirk remarks. This was also a war between rival newspapers, with William Randolph Hearst and Joseph Pulitzer competing for headlines, and Quirk points out that "Jones is hitting on all cylinders when he juxtaposes the horror of a combat assault . . . with the frenzied efforts of the newspaper flacks."

The period after the Civil War and leading up to the Spanish American War is captured in Jones's *Come Winter,* where the character of Roman Hasford returns, now a wealthy patriarch. Owner of the bank in the "vividly realized fictional backwater community of Gourdville," as Bob Allen puts it in the *Washington Post Book World,* Hasford, "the most powerful man" in the growing Arkansas town, "is also a troubled, solitary, dangerously eccentric man." Jones "plumbs the uneasy secrets, conflicted spirits, shady motives, misguided loyalties and desperate duplicities" of both the men and women who lead the town, comments Allen. Jones is "a strong storyteller who knows the territory" of the Western novel, Herbert Mitgang remarks in a *New York Times* review of *Come Winter.*

Jones once told *CA:* "From my earliest recollection, I have been a history buff. Especially as it deals with the nineteenth-century frontier in the United States. This really began for me when my family lived in Ft. Smith, Arkansas, between the years 1927 and 1933. Ft. Smith had been a pretty wild frontier town and was just across the river from what had been the Cherokee Nation until 1907 when all that area became part of the state of Oklahoma.

"My mother's family had been residents of the Ozark hills of northwest Arkansas since two generations before the Civil War. I heard a lot of stories from many of them about how things were in that area in the nineteenth century. I began to visualize story ideas from that time and place as early as 1958. The first novel on related subjects appeared in 1980 with *Elkhorn Tavern.*

"I write historical novels which I research as thoroughly as possible so that I can set my fictional characters down in a real situation. I try to make all my stories ring clear for the time and place in which they occur, to include how things look, smell, taste, sound and feel from the touch of your fingers."

BIOGRAPHICAL/CRITICAL SOURCES:

PERIODICALS

Armchair Detective, winter, 1992, p. 59.

Best Sellers, April, 1977; December, 1977; February, 1985, p. 407; October, 1986, p. 249.

Chicago Tribune Book World, November 5, 1978; December 28, 1980; October 25, 1981; July 12, 1987, p. 6.

Kirkus Reviews, September 1, 1984, p. 816; April 15, 1986, p. 570; May 1, 1987, p. 667; September 1, 1988, p. 1266; August 1, 1989, p. 1099; April 1, 1991, p. 423; April 15, 1993, p. 478.

Library Journal, October 15, 1984, p. 1959; June 15, 1986, p. 78; July, 1987, p. 95; September 1, 1989, p. 216; May 1, 1991, p. 108; October, 1991, p. 160; September 1, 1992, p. 244.

Los Angeles Times, October 1, 1980.

Los Angeles Times Book Review, November 11, 1979; December 30, 1984, p. 5; July 26, 1987, p. 4; January 8, 1989, p. 2.

Newsweek, December 20, 1976.

New York Times, December 2, 1989, p. 19.

New York Times Book Review, November 21, 1976; December 11, 1977; November 19, 1978; October 28, 1979; November 16, 1980; October 3, 1982; December 11, 1983, p. 18; January 13, 1985, p. 34; July 13, 1986, p. 18; December 10, 1989, p. 32; June 16, 1991, p. 21.

Publishers Weekly, September 28, 1984, p. 97; May 16, 1986, p. 68; May 22, 1987, p. 66; May 29, 1987, p. 73; September 2, 1988, p. 85; August 11, 1989, p. 443; April 26, 1991, p. 44; April 19, 1993, p. 48.

School Library Journal, January, 1981; October, 1986, p. 194; October, 1987, p. 146; October, 1991, p. 160.

Tribune Books (Chicago), July 12, 1987, p. 6.

Voice of Youth Advocates, June, 1985, p. 132; August, 1986, p. 145; December, 1987, pp. 235, 257; June, 1989, p. 102; June, 1990, p. 93.

Washington Post, December 20, 1979; December 30, 1988.

Washington Post Book World, October 5, 1980; January 13, 1985, p. 12; December 30, 1988; October 8, 1989, p. 5.

Western American Literature, winter, 1985, p. 329; spring, 1986, p. 66; summer, 1992, p. 172.*

* * *

JONES, Geoffrey (Gareth) 1952-

PERSONAL: Born July 8, 1952, in Birmingham, England; son of Cyril Gareth and Alice May Jones; married Frances Celia Moss (a company director), May 30, 1981, marriage ended; married Fabienne Hedwige Debrunner, September 21, 1992. *Education:* Corpus Christi College, Cambridge, B.A., 1974, Ph.D., 1978. *Avocational interests:* Wine, Chinese astrology, running a housing management company.

ADDRESSES: Home—Flat 1, 32 Leinster Gardens, London W2 3AN, England. *Office*—Economics Department, University of Reading, Faculty of Letters & Social Sciences, P.O. Box 218, Whiteknights, Reading RG6 2AA, England.

CAREER: Cambridge University, Cambridge, England, research fellow at Corpus Christi College, 1977-79; University of London, London School of Economics and Political Science, London, England, research officer in business history unit, 1979-81, lecturer in economic history, 1981—; University of Reading, England, professor in business history, 1988—.

MEMBER: Association of Business Historians, Business History Conference, Economic History Society, Royal Historical Society (fellow).

AWARDS, HONORS: Newcomen Prize, 1985, for article "The Gramophone Company: An Anglo-American Multinational, 1898-1931"; Harold F. Williamson Jr. Prize, 1993.

WRITINGS:

The State and the Emergence of the British Oil Industry, Macmillan (New York City), 1981.

British Multinationals: Origins, Management, and Performance, Gower (Brookfield, VT), 1986.

Banking and Empire in Iran: The History of the British Bank of the Middle East, volume 1, Cambridge University Press (Cambridge), 1986.

Banking and Oil: The History of the British Bank in the Middle East, volume 2, Cambridge University Press, 1987.

Banks as Multinationals, Routledge & Kegan Paul (London), 1990.

British Multinational Banking, 1830-1990, Clarendon Press (Oxford), 1993.

EDITOR

(With Peter Hertner) *Multinationals: Theory and History,* Gower, 1986.

(With R. Davenport-Hines) *British Business in Asia since 1860,* Cambridge University Press, 1989.

(With F. Bostock), *Planning and Power in Iran,* Frank Cass, 1989.

(With Harm Schroeter) *The Rise of Multinationals in Continental Europe,* Edward Elgar, 1993.

(With Richard Tedlow) *The Rise and Fall of Mass Marketing*, Routledge & Kegan Paul, 1993.

(With Nicholas J. Morgan) *Adding Value: Brands and Marketing in Food and Drink*, Routledge & Kegan Paul, 1994.

Contributor to business and economic journals. Editor of *Business History*.

WORK IN PROGRESS: The Development of International Business, forthcoming, 1995.

SIDELIGHTS: Geoffrey Jones told *CA:* "I enjoy writing in the area of business history, which has grown in recent years from a preoccupation with writing in-depth studies of single companies to pursuing a more holistic vision to understand the role and performance of business in our society, past and present. An important development in recent years has been the recognition that the business and history of individual countries, even important ones such as the United States and Japan, cannot be studied in isolation. International and cross-cultural comparisons are challenging but offer the way forward to real understanding. I hope to encourage this approach further in my own writings and through my role as a journal editor."

*   *   *

JONES, Kathleen 1922-

PERSONAL: Born April 7, 1922, in London, England; daughter of William Robert and Kate Lilian (Barnard) Savage; married David Gwyn Jones, July 22, 1944 (deceased); children: Stephen Gwyn. *Education:* University of London, B.A., 1943, Ph.D., 1953. *Politics:* Liberal Democrat. *Religion:* Anglican.

ADDRESSES: Home—44 West Moor Lane, Heslington, York YO1 5ER, England. *Office*—Goodricke College, University of York, York YO1 5DD, England.

CAREER: University of Manchester, Manchester, England, research assistant, 1952-54, assistant lecturer in history, 1954-55; Victoria Institution, Kuala Lumpur, Malaysia, senior historian, 1956-58; University of Manchester, lecturer, 1958-62, senior lecturer, 1962-65; University of York, York, England, professor of social policy and head of department, 1965-89, professor emeritus, 1989—. Maudsley Lecturer for Royal College of Psychiatrists, 1977. Chairman of the UNESCO United Kingdom social sciences committee, 1968-72; chairman of Mental Health Commission Act, Northeastern Region, 1983-85. *Military service:* Auxiliary Territorial Service, welfare worker, 1946-47.

MEMBER: Association of Psychiatric Social Workers of Great Britain (chairman, 1968-70), Royal College of Psychiatrists (fellow), Social Administration Association (chairman, 1980-83).

WRITINGS:

Lunacy, Law and Conscience, Routledge & Kegan Paul (London), 1955.

Mental Health and Social Policy, Routledge & Kegan Paul, 1960.

(With R. Sidebotham) *Mental Hospitals at Work*, Routledge & Kegan Paul, 1962.

The Teaching of Social Studies in British Universities, G. Bell (London), 1965.

The Compassionate Society, S.P.C.K., 1965.

A History of the Mental Health Services, Routledge & Kegan Paul, 1972.

Opening the Door: A Study of New Policies for the Mentally Handicapped, Routledge & Kegan Paul, 1975.

(With John Brown and Jonathan Bradshaw) *Issues in Social Policy*, Routledge & Kegan Paul, 1978, revised edition, 1983.

(Editor) *Living the Faith: A Call to the Church*, Oxford University Press (Oxford), 1980.

(With A. J. Fowles) *Ideas on Institutions: Analysing the Literature on Long-Term Care and Custody*, Routledge & Kegan Paul, 1984.

Experience in Mental Health: Community Care and Social Policy, Sage Publications (London), 1988.

The Making of Social Policy in Britain, 1830-1990, Athlone Press, (London), 1991, 2nd edition, 1994.

Asylums and After: A Revised History of the Mental Health Services from the Early 18th Century to the 1990s, Athlone Press, 1993.

(Translator and author of introduction) *The Poems of St. John of the Cross*, Benns & Oates/Search Press (Kent, England), 1993.

General editor of "International Library of Social Policy." Contributor to medical, social studies, and health services journals. Editor of *Yearbook of Social Policy in Britain*, 1971-76.

SIDELIGHTS: Kathleen Jones once told *CA:* "My values are those of the Declaration of Human Rights, 1948: I am against racism, sexism, and ageism, and in favour of liberty, equality, and fraternity (though the three are unfortunately not always compatible, hence the need for the academic study of social policy and administration). These I believe to be the values of the Gospel."

*   *   *

JONES, Malcolm V(ince) 1940-

PERSONAL: Born January 7, 1940, in Stoke-sub-Hamdon, England; son of Reginald Cross (in life insurance) and Winifred Ethel (Vince) Jones; married Jennifer Rosemary Durrant, July, 1963. *Education:* University of Nottingham, B.A. (with first class honors), 1962, Ph.D., 1966.

ADDRESSES: Home—Nottingham, England. *Office*—Department of Slavonic Studies, University of Nottingham, Nottingham NG7 2RD, England. *Agent*—Frances Kelly, 9 King Edward Mansions, 629 Fulham Rd., London SW6, England.

CAREER: University of Sussex, Brighton, England, assistant lecturer in Russian, 1965-67; University of Nottingham, Nottingham, England, lecturer, 1967-73, senior lecturer, 1973-80, professor of Slavonic studies, 1980—, head of department, 1980-95, vice-dean of faculty of arts, 1976-79, dean of faculty of arts, 1982-85, pro-vice-chancellor, 1987-92, associate dean of graduate school, 1994—.

MEMBER: International Dostoyevsky Society (member of executive committee; vice president, 1986-89), Association of Teachers of Russian (honorary vice president; president, 1985-86), British Association for Soviet, Slavonic and East European Studies (vice president, 1988-90), British Universities Association of Slavists (president, 1986-88).

WRITINGS:

Dostoyevsky: The Novel of Discord, Barnes & Noble (New York City), 1976.
(Editor) *New Essays on Tolstoy,* Cambridge University Press (Cambridge, England), 1978.
(Editor with G. Terry) *New Essays on Dostoyevsky,* Cambridge University Press, 1983.
Dostoyevsky after Bakhtin: Readings in Dostoyevsky's Fantastic Realism, Cambridge University Press, 1990.

General editor of "Cambridge Studies in Russian Literature," 1985—. Contributor to Slavic studies and history journals; member of editorial board of *Birmingham Slavonic Monographs.*

WORK IN PROGRESS: Editing *Cambridge Companion to the Russian Novel.*

SIDELIGHTS: Malcolm V. Jones once told *CA:* "I first took up the study of Russian not only because of its intrinsic interest and its cultural, economic, and political importance, but also because I am convinced that an almost exclusive concentration on French and German in the British educational system is an inadequate response to the complexity of international and intercultural relations in the modern world."

BIOGRAPHICAL/CRITICAL SOURCES:

PERIODICALS

Times Literary Supplement, March 9, 1984, p. 249.

*   *   *

JONES, P(eter) M(ichael) 1949-

PERSONAL: Born April 19, 1949, in Birmingham, England; son of Ronald Arthur and Ethel Constance (Jesper) Jones; married Carolyn Margot Ford (a school teacher), August 3, 1973; children: Nicholas, Anna, Isobel. *Education:* University of Leeds, B.A. (with honors), 1970; Oxford University, D.Phil., 1977; attended University of Toulouse le Mirail, 1971-72.

ADDRESSES: Office—School of History, University of Birmingham, Edgbaston, Birmingham B15 2TT, England.

CAREER: University of Leicester, Leicester, England, tutorial assistant, 1973-74; University of Birmingham, Birmingham, England, lecturer in history, 1974-88, reader in French history, 1988—.

WRITINGS:

Politics and Rural Society: The Southern Massif Central, ca. 1750-1880, Cambridge University Press (Cambridge), 1985.
The Peasantry In the French Revolution, Cambridge University Press, 1988.

WORK IN PROGRESS: Reform and Revolution in France, 1774-1791: An Essay in the Politics of Transition, forthcoming from Cambridge University Press.

SIDELIGHTS: P. M. Jones once told *CA:* "My fascination with things French burgeoned in the 1960s as a result of camping holidays spent on the Atlantic coast. My professional connection with France dates back to 1970, when I began doctoral research under the guidance of an Oxford-based historian of France. As the student of an endangered species (the French peasantry), I elected to trace it to one of its last known habitats—the Massif Central. The result was my first book, which explores the impact of a century of political change on the country dwellers of southern central France. This was followed by a textbook study of the peasantry during the revolution."

*   *   *

JONES, Reginald L(anier) 1931-

PERSONAL: Born January 21, 1931, in Clearwater, FL; son of Moses (a musician) and Naomi (Henry) Jones; married Johnette Turner (an artist), September 8, 1959; children: Juliette Melinda, Angela Michele, Cynthia Ann, Sjaun, Leasa. *Education:* Morehouse College, A.B., 1952; Wayne State University, M.A., 1954; Ohio State University, Ph.D., 1959.

ADDRESSES: Office—Department of Psychology, Hampton University, Hampton, VA 23668.

CAREER: Miami University, Oxford, OH, research assistant professor in instructional research service, 1959-63; Fisk University, Nashville, TN, associate professor of psychology, 1963-64; University of California, Los Angeles, assistant professor of education, 1964-66; Ohio State University, Columbus, professor of psychology, 1966-69, vice-chairman of department, 1968-69; University of California, Riverside, professor of education, 1969-73, chairman of department, 1971-72; University of California, Berkeley, professor of education and ethnic studies, 1973-75, chairman of Department of Afro-American Studies and professor of education, 1975-78, 1985-87, faculty, assistant to the vice chancellor, 1982-84, 1987-90; Hampton University, Hampton, VA, chairman, Department of Psychology, 1990—. Haile Selassie I University, director of university testing center, 1972-74; vice-chairman of school board at American Community School (Addis Ababa, Ethiopia); National Institute of Mental Health and U.S. Office of Education, consultant. *Military service:* U.S. Army, Medical Corps, clinical psychologist, 1954-56.

MEMBER: American Psychological Association (fellow), Association of Black Psychologists (national chair, 1971-72), American Association on Mental Deficiency, American Educational Research Association, Western Psychological Association.

AWARDS, HONORS: Scholarship Award, Association of Black Psychologists, 1979 and 1986; J. E. Wallace Wallin Award, Council for Exceptional Children, 1983; Citation for Distinguished Achievement, Ohio State University, 1983; Education Award, American Association on Mental Retardation, 1988; Berkeley Citation, University of California, Berkeley, 1991.

WRITINGS:

(With Marilyn Lucas) *Attitudes of Teachers of Mentally Retarded Children,* Ohio State University (Columbus), 1968.

The Impact of Newborn Sickle Cell Testing on Maternal Attitudes toward Child Rearing: A Simulation Study, (Ph.D. thesis), University of Cincinnati, 1980.

EDITOR

New Directions in Special Education, Allyn & Bacon (Boston, MA), 1970.

Problems and Issues in the Education of Exceptional Children, Houghton (Burlington, MA), 1971.

Black Psychology, Harper (New York City), 1972, 3rd edition, 1991.

(With I. H. Hendrick) *Student Dissent in the Schools,* Houghton, 1972.

(With Donald L. Macmillan) *Special Education in Transition,* Allyn & Bacon (Boston, MA), 1974.

Mainstreaming and the Minority Child, Council for Exceptional Children (Reston, VA), 1976.

(And compiler) *Sourcebook on the Teaching of Black Psychology,* Association of Black Psychologists (Washington, DC), 1978.

Reflections on Growing Up Disabled: A Product of the ERIC Clearinghouse on Handicapped and Gifted Children, Council for Exceptional Children, 1983.

Attitudes and Attitude Change in Special Education: Theory and Practice, Council for Exceptional Children, 1984.

Psychoeducational Assessment of Minority Group Children: A Casebook, Cobb & Henry, (Richmond, CA), 1988.

Black Adult Development and Aging, Cobb & Henry (Berkeley, CA), 1989.

Black Adolescents, Cobb & Henry, 1989.

Also editor of *Mental Retardation,* 1979-83. Guest editor, *Journal of Black Psychology.* Associate editor, *American Journal of Mental Deficiency.* Consulting editor, *Contemporary Psychology, Journal of School Psychology, Journal of Social Issues, Professional Psychology,* and *Rehabilitation Psychology.*

*   *   *

JOOSSE, Barbara M(onnot) 1949-

PERSONAL: Born February 18, 1949, in Grafton, WI; daughter of Robert Elmer (a banker) and M. Eileen (Hutmacher) Monnot; married Peter Clifford Joosse (a psychiatrist), August 30, 1969; children: Maaike Sari, Anneke Els, Robert Collin. *Education:* Attended University of Wisconsin—Stevens Point, 1966; University of Wisconsin—Madison, B.A., 1970; graduate study at University of Wisconsin—Milwaukee, 1977-80. *Avocational interests:* Reading, jogging, biking, baking.

ADDRESSES: Home and office—2953 Kettle Moraine Dr., Hartford, WI 35027.

CAREER: Associated with Stephan & Brady, Madison, WI, 1970-71; Waldbillig & Besteman, Madison, copywriter, 1971-74.

MEMBER: Society of Children's Book Writers.

AWARDS, HONORS: Picture Book Award, Council of Wisconsin Writers, 1983, for *The Thinking Place,* and 1985, for *Fourth of July.*

WRITINGS:

JUVENILE

The Thinking Place, illustrated by Kay Chorao, Knopf (New York City), 1982.
Fourth of July, illustrated by Emily Arnold McCully, Knopf, 1983.
Spiders in the Fruit Cellar, illustrated by Chorao, Knopf, 1985.
Jam Day, illustrated by McCully, Harper (New York City), 1987.
Anna, The One and Only, illustrated by Gretchen Will Mayo, Lippincott (New York City), 1988.
Better with Two, illustrated by Catherine Stock, Harper, 1988.
Dinah's Mad, Bad Wishes, illustrated by McCully, Harper, 1989.
Pieces of the Picture, Lippincott, 1989.
Mama, Do You Love Me?, illustrated by Barbara Lavallee, Chronicle Books (San Francisco, CA), 1991.
The Pitiful Life of Simon Schultz, HarperCollins (New York City), 1991.
Nobody's Cat, illustrated by Marcia Sewall, HarperCollins, 1992.
Anna and the Cat Lady, illustrated by Mayo, HarperCollins, 1992.
Wild Willie and King Kyle Detectives (mystery), illustrated by Sue Truesdell, Clarion Books (New York City), 1993.
The Losers Fight Back: A Wild Willie Mystery, illustrated by Truesdell, Clarion Books, 1994.

Contributor of fiction to *Cricket Magazine.* Contributor of adult humor to *Milwaukee Magazine.*

SIDELIGHTS: Barbara M. Joosse told *CA:* "I have always liked to write. Upon the birth of my second daughter (and with it, full-time homemaker status), it became important for me to have another niche. I wanted to take writing as seriously as I took mothering, so I enrolled in the master's degree program in creative writing at the University of Wisconsin—Milwaukee.

"Early in the program, I discovered writing for children to be the most natural and exciting form for me. Writing for children combines the word power and rhythms of poetry, another form of writing I have loved. It demands absolute honesty in dialogue and characterization. There is plenty of psychology, fantasy, and drama. You have the opportunity to work with another medium (illustration), and your words will be read and, hopefully, cherished by small people. Words have added impact and incorporation

when they are read repeatedly and by someone who loves you.

"My own daughters and son are frequently a source of inspiration for my stories. Both girls are also apt critics, quick to point out when a story gets boring or when they don't like an ending.

"My childhood was secure and loving. I draw on this to write for children. Since we write what we know, and I have known happiness and dignity, this is the feeling I want to create for my readers. This secure environment gave me another advantage. Because there were no cataclysmic events that overshadowed my childhood, like serious illness or parental separation, I was able to concentrate on universal childhood problems. I could devote full energy (and now, clear memories) to the fear of the spiders in my fruit cellar or how I might survive jealousy of Suzanne Smith's white tennis shoes (mine were navy blue because I got mine dirty).

"I write about heroes. Heroes are people who do something that is beyond comfort. Heroes stretch themselves, solving their own problems with dignity. That is the story I celebrate, most of all, in *Fourth of July.* I want children to feel the pageantry and honor in Ross doing something that was very difficult, which will, of course, apply to them when they do something difficult.

"I remember that my picture books are for a 'reading partnership.' The child is the listener and the reader is often someone the child loves. The job I love is creating shared experience between these two people.

"Now . . . I'm starting to write for older children. I find the problems and rhythms of these older children as interesting as younger children. I plan to write for both."

BIOGRAPHICAL/CRITICAL SOURCES:

PERIODICALS

Los Angeles Times Book Review, December 20, 1987, p. 28.
Milwaukee, May, 1984.
Tribune Books, September 10, 1989, p. 4.

*   *   *

JORDAN, Alexis Hill
 See TITCHENER, Louise

*   *   *

JOSEPHY, Alvin M., Jr. 1915-

PERSONAL: Surname is accented on second syllable, "Jo-*seph*-y"; born May 18, 1915, in Woodmere, NY; son of Alvin M. (a businessman) and Sophia C. (Knopf) Josephy; married Elizabeth C. Peet, March 13, 1948; children: Diane, Alvin M. III, Allison, Katherine. *Education:* Attended Harvard University, 1932-34. *Politics:* Democrat.

ADDRESSES: Home—4 Kinsman Lane, Greenwich, CT 06830; and Box 62, Joseph, OR 97846.

CAREER: New York Herald-Tribune, New York City, reporter and correspondent, 1937-38; WOR-Mutual, New York City, director of news and special features, 1938-42; Office of War Information, Radio Bureau, Washington, DC, chief of special events, 1942-43; Metro-Goldwyn-Mayer (MGM) Studios, Culver City, CA, screenwriter, 1945-51; *Time,* New York City, associate editor, 1951-60; American Heritage Publishing Co., New York City, vice president and senior editor of American Heritage books, 1960-76, editor of *American Heritage* magazine, 1976-78; editor-in-chief, 1978-79. Commissioner of Indian Arts and Crafts Board, Department of Interior, 1966-70; author of Report on Indian Affairs for President Nixon, 1969; trustee of National Resources Defense Council, 1977-81, Museum of the American Indian, 1977—, Environmental Policy Institute, 1978-89, and Friends of the Earth, 1989—. Democratic state central committee member, Connecticut, 1956-60; Democratic candidate for Connecticut Legislature, 1958 and 1960; consultant to National Congress of American Indians, 1958-65, Secretary of the Interior, 1963, and Public Land Law Review Commission, 1970; member of Connecticut Small Business Advisory Committee, 1961-63; member of National Advisory Committee on Indian Work, Episcopal Church, American Association for State and Local History (member of council), 1976-79. *Military service:* U.S. Marine Corps, combat correspondent, 1943-45; became master sergeant; received Bronze Star (action at Guam).

MEMBER: Institute of the American West (president of national council, 1981-86), Institute of the North American West (member of the board, 1986—), Association on American Indian affairs (member of the executive committee, 1971—), American Antiquarian Society, U.S. Capitol Historical Association, Western History Association (president, 1993-94), New York Westerners, Third Marine Division Association, Harvard Club (New York City).

AWARDS, HONORS: Awards from National Cowboy Hall of Fame and Western Heritage Center, 1961 and 1965, for best books on the American West; Western writers of America Golden Spur and Golden Saddleman Awards, 1965; New York Westerners Buffalo Award, 1965 and 1968, for best books on the American West; American Association for State and Local History national award of merit, 1966; Guggenheim fellowship, 1966-67; National Book Award nominee for history, 1968;

National Magazine Award for Excellence in Reporting, 1976.

WRITINGS:

(Coauthor) *The U.S. Marines on Iwo Jima,* Dial (New York City), 1945.

The Long and the Short and the Tall: The Story of a Marine Combat Unit in the Pacific, Knopf (New York City), 1946.

(Coauthor) *Uncommon Valor,* Infantry Journal Press, 1946.

(Coauthor) *The American Heritage Book of the Pioneer Spirit,* American Heritage Publishing (New York City), 1959.

The Patriot Chiefs: A Chronicle of American Indian Leadership, Viking (New York City), 1961.

Chief Joseph's People and Their War, Yellowstone Library (Yellowstone Park, WY), 1964.

The Nez Perce Indians and the Opening of the Northwest, Yale University Press (New Haven, CT), 1965, abridged edition, Yale University Press, 1971, reprint edition, University of Nebraska Press (Lincoln), 1979.

(Coauthor) *The American Heritage Pictorial Atlas of United States History,* American Heritage Publishing, 1966.

The Artist Was a Young Man, Amon Carter Museum of Western Art (Fort Worth, TX), 1970.

Red Power: The American Indians' Fight for Freedom, American Heritage Publishing, 1971, reprint edition, University of Nebraska Press, 1985.

(Reviser) Oliver La Farge, *The Pictorial History of the American Indian,* Crown (New York City), 1974.

History of the Congress of the United States, McGraw (New York City), 1975.

Black Hills, White Sky, New York Times (New York City), 1979.

On the Hill, Simon & Schuster (New York City), 1979.

Now That the Buffalo's Gone: A Study of Today's American Indians, Knopf, 1982, reprint edition, University of Oklahoma Press (Norman), 1984.

The Civil War in the American West, Knopf, 1991, reprint edition, Vintage Trade (New York City), 1992.

500 Nations, Knopf, 1994.

EDITOR

The American Heritage Book of Indians, American Heritage Publishing, 1961.

The American History of Flight, American Heritage Publishing, 1962.

The American Heritage Book of Natural Wonders, American Heritage Publishing, 1962.

The American Heritage History of World War I, American Heritage Publishing, 1964.

The American Heritage History of the Great West, American Heritage Publishing, 1965.

RFK: His Life and Death, Dell (New York City), 1968.

The Horizon History of Africa, American Heritage Publishing, 1971.

American Heritage History of Business and Industry, American Heritage Publishing, 1972.

The Horizon History of Vanishing Primitive Man, American Heritage Publishing, 1973.

The Law in America, American Heritage Publishing, 1974.

The Cold War, American Heritage Publishing, 1982.

(And author of introduction) *America in 1492,* Knopf, 1992.

OTHER

Chief consultant and author of introduction, *The Native Americans,* Knopf, 1992. Contributor to various books, including *My Favorite Love Story,* Whittlesey House, 1946; *Semper Fidelis,* Sloane, 1947; *The Red Man's West,* Hastings House, 1965; *The Mountain Men,* Volume III, Arthur H. Clark, 1966; *The Indian Heritage of America,* Knopf, 1968; *Great Adventures of the Old West,* American Heritage Press, 1969; *The United States Marine Corps in World War II,* Random House, 1969; *Nez Perce Country,* National Park Service, 1983; *A Sender of Words,* Howe Bros., 1984; *Arizona, The Land and the People,* University of Arizona Press, 1986; *Indian Self-Rule,* Howe Bros., 1986; *War on the Frontier: The Trans-Mississippi West* for Time-Life Books' series on the Civil War, 1986; and *Frank Waters: Man and Mystic,* Swallow Press, 1993.

Also author of screenplays for MGM, 1945-51. Contributor to *Collier's Encyclopedia* and *Brand Book.* Also contributor to numerous periodicals, including *Life, Atlantic, New York Times Sunday Magazine, American West,* and *Audubon.* Contributing editor, *American West* magazine, 1980-88.

SIDELIGHTS: Alvin M. Josephy, Jr.'s historical studies of Native Americans have been praised for their value to scholars and general readers alike. Additionally, critics have applauded Josephy's fair and compassionate treatment of the Native American experience. In a *New York Times* review of *Now That the Buffalo's Gone: A Study of Today's American Indians,* Herbert Mitgang commended the author for his realistic presentation of the Native Americans' "struggle for recognition" in modern America. In Mitgang's opinion, Josephy is the "leading non-Indian writer about Native Americans."

In a *Los Angeles Times* review of Josephy's respected work, *Now That the Buffalo's Gone,* George P. Horse Capture noted the author's scholarly approach to recounting the lives of Native Americans through "tribal oral histories, first person accounts, [and] historical and anthropo-

logical works." Praising the author for his ability to encapsulate the Native American experience, Horse Capture cited Josephy's "constant exposure to the Indian people and the many phases of their situation." This is why Josephy has "amassed rare knowledge about the First People," wrote Horse Capture, who recommended the book "to be read as a 'starter' by those just beginning to learn about Indian people, and by the hard-core devotees to sharpen their knowledge with this unique perspective."

A later work, *The Civil War in the American West,* focuses on a number of forgotten battles that took place west of the Mississippi River, including campaigns in Texas, New Mexico, and California. The narrative strategy in this book, according to the author, is to deal with military operations that have attracted "comparatively little notice." Reviews of *The Civil War in the American West* were mixed. In the *Washington Post Book World,* David Herbert Donald noted that Josephy's handling of the material is competent and professional, but that "doubtless because he has to cover so much ground, his prose is flat." Herbert added: "Probably only a handful of the most devoted local historians will be able to assimilate so much detail about campaigns that were, after all, quite minor." Conversely, David Haward Bain in the *New York Times Book Review* argued: "Inescapably, the entire era—especially the war that rocked and shaped us—is cast into a different, clearer light by this powerfully wrought narrative." In addition, Bain declared that Josephy, a "veteran of the role of the American Indian in Western History," had done the Native Americans justice with his "clear-eyed, evenhanded scholarship about the part Indians played in the Civil War."

Josephy is also the editor of *America in 1492,* "a quincentennial anthology celebrating the range of native cultures in the Western Hemisphere at the time of first contact with Europeans," according to Philip Burnham in the *Washington Post Book World.* Essays on topics ranging from Incan colonization to Inuit hunting methods are provided by such noted authors and scholars as N. Scott Momaday, Peter Nabokov, and Vine Deloria, Jr. Chris Goodrich in the *Los Angeles Times Book Review* remarked that *America in 1492* is "so packed with information" that it would be "more effective in five volumes" rather than having the reader reach "critical overload a hundred pages in." Burnham observed that while "there are discussions of kinship, trade, language and art, one might wonder why there isn't an in-depth analysis of pre-Columbian environmental practices. Nothing could be more topical in Indian studies today—and controversial—than native attitudes towards land." However, Burnham concluded that "*America in 1492* fills a niche. It's nice to have an Indian overview that includes both North *and* South America."

BIOGRAPHICAL/CRITICAL SOURCES:

PERIODICALS

American Historical Review, June, 1969.
Antioch Review, summer, 1976.
Books and Bookmen, November, 1972.
Los Angeles Times, March 31, 1983.
Los Angeles Times Book Review, January 19, 1992.
Nation, December 23, 1968.
New York Times, January 11, 1983.
New York Times Book Review, November 7, 1965; February 15, 1970; August 29, 1971; May 8, 1983, p. 14; March 8, 1992.
Time, December 1, 1961; November 19, 1965.
Washington Post Book World, September 22, 1968; November 24, 1991; January 19, 1992.

*   *   *

JUERGENSEN, Hans   1919-

PERSONAL: Born December 17, 1919, in Myslowitz, Germany (now Myslowice, Poland); naturalized U.S. citizen; foster son of Hermann Anton and Dora (Grossmann) Juergensen; married Ilse Dina Loebenberg (a poet and teacher of poetry in elementary schools), October 27, 1945; children: Claudia Jeanne. *Education:* Upsala College, B.A., 1942; Johns Hopkins University, Ph.D., 1951. *Religion:* Jewish.

ADDRESSES: Home—7815 Pine Hill Dr., Tampa, FL 33610. *Office*—Department of Humanities, University of South Florida, Tampa, FL 33620.

CAREER: University of Kansas, Lawrence, instructor in German, 1951-53; Quinnipiac College, Hamden, CT, 1953-61, began as assistant professor, became associate professor of English and chairperson of department; University of South Florida, Tampa, assistant professor, 1961-63, associate professor, 1963-68, professor of humanities, 1968—. Silvermine College of Art, lecturer in humanities, 1958-61, acting dean and member of board, 1960-61. Coordinator, Poetry in the Schools, Hillsborough County, FL, 1972-76; member of nominating committee, Nobel Prize in literature, 1975-80. Has exhibited his works of graphic art at a number of one-person shows. Special consultant to U.S. Holocaust Memorial Council, 1981-85. *Military service:* U.S. Army, 1942-45; served in three campaigns; wounded at Anzio; received Purple Heart and Unit Citation.

MEMBER: International Poetry Society (fellow), National Federation of State Poetry Societies (president, 1968-70), Poetry Society of America, Academy of American Poets, Poetry Society of Florida, Connecticut Academy of Arts and Science (fellow).

AWARDS, HONORS: Florida poet of the year award, 1965; Stephen Vincent Benet Award, 1970 and 1974; award for services to American literature, Hayden Library, Arizona State University, 1970; special arts award, State of Florida, 1980.

WRITINGS:

I Feed You from My Cup (poetry), Quinnipiac College Press (Hamden, CT), 1958.
In Need for Names (poetry), Linden Press (Interlaken, NY), 1961.
Existential Canon, and Other Poems, South & West, 1965.
Florida Montage (poetry), South & West, 1966.
Sermons from the Ammunition Hatch of the Ship of Fools (poetry), Vagabond (Ellensburg, WA), 1968.
From the Divide (poetry), Olivant (Homestead, FL), 1970.
Hebraic Modes (poetry), Olivant, 1972.
Journey toward the Roots (poetry and drawings), Valkyrie Press (St. Petersburg, FL), 1976.
(Translator) Heinrich von Kleist, *The Broken Jug,* Olivant, 1977.
California Frescoes (poetry and drawings), American Studies Press (Tampa, FL), 1980.
General George H. Thomas: A Summary in Perspective, American Studies Press, 1980.
The Record of a Green Planet (poetry), Linden Press, 1982.
Fire-Tested (chapbook), Lieb-Schott, 1983.
Beachheads and Mountains: Campaigning from Sicily to Anzio, A Journal, American Studies Press, 1984, 3rd edition, 1987.
The Ambivalent Journey, American Studies Press, 1986.
Roma, Cerews Press, 1987.
Testimony: Selected Poems, 1954-1986, University of South Florida Press (Tampa, FL), 1989.

OTHER

Also contributor to various publications, including *Where Is Vietnam?,* Doubleday (New York City), 1967; *Ipso Facto* (poetry anthology), edited by Robin Gregory, Hud Publications, 1975; *For Neruda, For Chile,* edited by Walter Lowenfels, Beacon Press (Boston, MA), 1975; *The Anthology of American Magazine Verse,* edited by Alan F. Pater, Monitor (Beverly Hills, CA), 1982; *Perigraph* (poetry anthology), edited by Michael Cummings and John A. Kantor, University of South Florida, 1987; *Encore* (anthology), edited by Alice Briley, [Albuquerque, NM] 1987; and *American Poets on the Holocaust,* edited by Charles A. Fishman, Avon (New York City), 1987.

Also author of essays on Germany from 1918-1939 for archives of U.S. Holocaust Memorial Council, 1982; editor of *Children's Poetry Anthology,* 1975. Contributor of art criticism to *Tampa Times,* 1961-67. Coeditor, *Orange Street Poetry Journal,* 1958-62, and *University of South Florida Language Quarterly,* 1961-74; editor, *Gryphon* (University of South Florida), 1974—.

SIDELIGHTS: "The more I write and publish," observed Hans Juergensen, "the more reluctant I become about pronouncing artistic maxims. There is stark necessity in me to create. It is my hope that my skill complements that need."

Juergensen further commented to *CA:* "Archibald Mac-Leish defined art as 'Experience that is recuperated.' My experiences in Germany as a boy, nature, America, the WWII and my psychic as well as philosophical experiences determine my poetic expression. My first poem was 'Farewell to Germany', written in December of 1933, under the stress of Nazi oppression. Quite a few of my poems have been set to music—both in groups and singly."

Juergensen cited as influences: "Goethe, Heine, Whitman, Rilke, T. S. Eliot, and contemporaries like Anne Sexton, Wallace Stevens, Richard Eberhart." He added: "The current scene is as pluralistic in literature as in every other endeavor. Existentialism informs much of our best work."

Juergensen's manuscripts are deposited in a special collection at University of Florida Libraries. In addition to English and his native German, he is competent in French and has some knowledge of Latin and Hebrew.

BIOGRAPHICAL/CRITICAL SOURCES:

PERIODICALS

Bitterroot, winter, 1989-90.
Choice, September, 1977; January, 1990.
St. Louis Post-Dispatch, April 8, 1984.
Small Pond Magazine of Literature, spring, 1990.
Tampa Tribune, August 6, 1989.
Thirteen Poetry, July, 1989.

*   *   *

JUNGE, Mark G(ene)   1943-

PERSONAL: Surname is pronounced "young-ee"; born June 5, 1943, in Chicago, IL; son of Mark C. (a meat packinghouse foreman) and Louise (a homemaker and waitress; maiden name, Schacht) Junge; married Ardath Loretta Kuennen (a schoolteacher), December 27, 1966; children: Andrew Benedict, Daniel Jerome. *Education:* Western State College of Colorado, B.A., 1965, M.A., 1966; University of Wyoming, graduate study, 1967-68, 1970-71. *Politics:* Democrat. *Religion:* Lutheran

Church—Missouri Synod. *Avocational interests:* Family, sports and performing arts photography, reading, travel, fishing, sports of all kinds—particularly jogging, swimming, and biking.

ADDRESSES: Home—543 Baldwin Dr., Cheyenne, WY 82001. *Office*—Editor, *Wyoming Annals,* Department of commerce, Barrett Building, Cheyenne, WY 82002.

CAREER: Sheridan College, Sheridan, WY, instructor in social studies 1968-70; State of Wyoming, Cheyenne, historian, 1971-81, deputy state historic preservation officer, 1981-87; *Wyoming Album,* project director, 1987-92; *Wyoming Annals,* Cheyenne, state historian and editor, 1992—. *Wyoming State Tribune,* Cheyenne, free-lance photographer, 1975-90.

MEMBER: Wyoming State Historical Society, Young Men's Christian Association (member of board of directors of Cheyenne branch, 1977-83).

WRITINGS:

(With Ned Frost) *At Noon We Reached Independence Rock . . . ,* Central Duplicating Plant of the State of Wyoming, 1973.
Wyoming: A Guide to Historic Sites, Big Horn Books, 1976.
J. E. Stimson: Photographer of the West, University of Nebraska Press (Lincoln), 1985.
Wyoming: A Pictorial History, Donning (Norfolk, VA), 1989.

WORK IN PROGRESS: A Wyoming Album, a book of photographs and narrative biographical sketches of a cross section of the Wyoming populace.

SIDELIGHTS: Mark G. Junge's *J. E. Stimson: Photographer of the West* assembles 231 photographs taken by Stimson during the late nineteenth and early twentieth centuries. The book won acclaim not only for Junge and Stimson, but also for its publisher, the University of Nebraska Press, to which Nikon, Inc., awarded the 1986 Publisher of the Year Award.

The photographs in *J. E. Stimson* reveal the western United States at a turning point in history, when the region was no longer the mythic Old West nor yet fully developed. As Junge writes, "What Stimson offers is a frontal view of the American West as it wanted to see itself, at a time when it was proudly emerging from rude, frontier beginnings." Drake Hokanson of *Photographer's Forum* called the book's photographs—of railroads, industry, towns, agriculture, mines, and other subjects—"a delight to look at not just for historical information, but for their inherent beauty." He deemed the volume "well written, beautifully designed and splendidly reproduced." And as Lee Milazzo observed in the *Southwest Review,* Junge "rescues" Stimson, whose "superb" work was virtually unknown before the book's publication, "from oblivion."

Junge once told *CA:* "Photography, writing, and history have intertwined during my life in a variety of ways. Writer by intention, historian by training, historic preservationist by circumstance, and photographer by obsession, I am interested in producing narrative and photographic publications.

"Writing is such difficult work that I write only when I absolutely have to, even though I am aware of the joy caused by occasionally being able to write well. Producing a well-researched, well-written essay or a dynamic photograph is rewarding, and yet it is not the product but rather the creative act itself that is inwardly most satisfying."

Junge added: "It is my belief that entirely new points of view are created when combining illustrative materials with historical writing and that neither, apart from one another, can penetrate history as deeply as when the two are used together. As I become more involved with oral history, I also see more clearly the need for historians to use all of their investigative tools, including that of listening, in order to create the work of art that is history."

BIOGRAPHICAL/CRITICAL SOURCES:

PERIODICALS

Newsday, December 14, 1985.
Photographer's Forum, May, 1986.
PhotoGraphic, May, 1986.
Southwest Review, spring, 1986.

*   *   *

JUNIPER, Alex
See HOSPITAL, Janette Turner

K

KAKONIS, Thomas E. 1930-
(Tom Kakonis, Tom E. Kakonis)

PERSONAL: Born November 13, 1930, in Long Beach, CA; son of Gus Peter and Olive (Woodward) Kakonis; married Judith J. Whitlock (a reading consultant), May 29, 1971; children: Tom D., Daniel J. *Education:* University of Minnesota, B.A., 1952; South Dakota State University, M.S., 1958; University of Iowa, Ph.D., 1965. *Politics:* None. *Religion:* None.

ADDRESSES: Home—630 Clark St., Big Rapids, MI 49307. *Office*—School of General Education, Ferris State College, Big Rapids, MI 49307.

CAREER: University of Idaho, instructor in English, 1958-59; Mankato State College, instructor, 1959-60; Northern Illinois University, DeKalb, English instructor, 1964-66; Wisconsin State University, Whitewater, associate professor, 1966-68, 1969-72; South Dakota State University, Brookings, associate professor, 1968-69; Ferris State College, Big Rapids, MI, head of department of languages and literature, 1972—, associate dean of general education, 1978—. Film Counselors, Inc., education consultant, 1970—; Brevet International, Inc., editorial consultant, 1970—; National Endowment for the Humanities, member of National Board of Consultants, 1977—. *Military service:* U.S. Army, 1953-55; became first lieutenant.

MEMBER: Modern Language Association of America, Popular Culture Association.

AWARDS, HONORS: National Endowment for the Humanities grant, 1974-75.

WRITINGS:

NONFICTION

(As Tom E. Kakonis, with Donald K. Hanzek) *A Practical Guide to Police Reporting,* McGraw-Hill (New York City), 1978.
(With John Scally) *Writing in an Age of Technology,* Macmillan (New York City), 1978.

NOVELS; ALL UNDER NAME TOM KAKONIS

Michigan Roll, St. Martin's (New York City), 1988.
Criss Cross, St. Martin's, 1990.
Double Down, Dutton (New York City), 1991.
Shadow Counter, Dutton, 1993.

EDITOR; ALL UNDER NAME TOM E. KAKONIS

(With Louis E. Glorfeld) *The Short Story: Ideas and Backgrounds,* C. E. Merrill (Columbus, OH), 1967.
(With Glorfeld) *Language, Rhetoric, and Idea,* C. E. Merrill, 1967.
(With others) *Plays by Four Tragedians,* C. E. Merrill, 1968.
(With Barbara Demarais) *The Literary Artist as Social Critic,* Glencoe Press (New York City), 1969.
(With James C. Wilcox) *Forms of Rhetoric,* McGraw (New York City), 1969.
(With others) *Strategies in Rhetoric from Thought to Symbol,* Harper (New York City), 1971.
(With David A. Evans) *Statement and Craft,* Prentice-Hall (Englewood Cliffs, NJ), 1971.
(With Evans) *From Language to Idea: An Integrated Rhetoric,* Holt (New York City), 1971.
(With Wilcox) *Now and Tomorrow,* Heath, 1971.
(With Ralph Demarais) *America: Involvement of Escape,* Cummings, 1971.
(With Richard Shereikis) *Scene Seventy: Nonfiction Prose,* Houghton (Burlington, MA), 1972.

(With Wilcox) *Crossroads: Quality of Life through Rhetorical Modes,* Heath, 1972.

(With John Scally) *We Have But Faith,* Brevet Press (Sioux Falls, SD), 1975.

Contributor of reviews to *Minneapolis Tribune* book section.

* * *

KAKONIS, Tom
See KAKONIS, Thomas E.

* * *

KAKONIS, Tom E.
See KAKONIS, Thomas E.

* * *

KANE, Robert S. 1925-

PERSONAL: Born April 19, 1925, in Albany, NY; son of Samuel Charles and Stella (Weiss) Kane. *Education:* Syracuse University, B.S., 1947; University of Southampton, graduate study, 1948.

ADDRESSES: Home and office—311 East 72nd St., New York, NY 10021. *Agent*—Anita Diamant, 310 Madison Ave., New York, NY 10017.

CAREER: Started as reporter for *Daily Tribune,* Great Bend, KS, later worked in New York City for *Staten Island Daily Advance* and *New York Herald Tribune,* then for *New York World-Telegram* and *Sun,* 1954-59; *Playbill,* New York City, travel editor, 1961-63; *Cue,* New York City, travel editor, 1963-73; *50 Plus,* New York City, travel editor, 1982-85. Working-party member, President Johnson's Task Force on Travel, 1968. *Military service:* U.S. Navy, World War II; served in Pacific.

MEMBER: Society of American Travel Writers (regional secretary, 1962-63; national secretary, 1963-64; national president, 1968-69; chairman of board, 1970), National Press Club, PEN, American Society of Journalists and Authors, Authors Guild, New York Travel Writers' Association (president, 1977-79), Society of Professional Journalists/Sigma Delta Chi.

AWARDS, HONORS: Hedman Award, 1967; Austrian Gold Medal of Touristic Merit, 1969; Best Travel Book of the Year Award, Society of American Travel Writers, 1981.

WRITINGS:

Africa A to Z: A Guide for Travelers—Armchair and Actual, Doubleday (New York City), 1961, revised edition, 1972.

South America A to Z, Doubleday, 1962, revised edition, 1971.

Asia A to Z, Doubleday, 1963.

Canada A to Z, Doubleday, 1964, revised edition, 1976.

South Pacific A to Z, Doubleday, 1966.

Eastern Europe A to Z, Doubleday, 1968.

(Contributor) *Around the World with the Experts,* Doubleday, 1969.

Grand Tour A to Z: The Capitals of Europe, Doubleday, 1972.

London A to Z, Doubleday, 1974, revised edition, 1990.

Paris A to Z, Doubleday, 1974, revised edition, 1991.

Hawaii A to Z, Doubleday, 1975, revised edition, 1981.

Italy A to Z: A Grand Tour of the Classic Cities, Doubleday, 1977.

Germany A to Z Guide, Rand McNally (Chicago, IL), 1980.

Spain A to Z Guide, Rand McNally, 1980.

Great Britain A to Z Guide, Rand McNally, 1982.

"WORLD AT ITS BEST" SERIES

Germany at Its Best, Passport Books (Moscow, VT), 1985, revised edition, 1994.

Italy at Its Best, Passport Books, 1985, revised edition, 1993.

Spain at Its Best, Passport Books, 1985.

Hawaii at Its Best, Passport Books, 1985, revised edition, 1992.

Britain at Its Best, Passport Books, 1986.

France at Its Best, Passport Books, 1986.

London at Its Best, Passport Books, 1987, revised edition, 1990.

Paris at Its Best, Passport Books, 1987.

Switzerland at Its Best, Passport Books, 1987, revised edition, 1995.

Holland at Its Best, Passport Books, 1987.

New York at Its Best, Passport Books, 1990.

Washington at Its Best, Passport Books, 1991.

Hong Kong at Its Best, Passport Books, 1992.

San Francisco at Its Best, Passport Books, 1994.

OTHER

Contributor to periodicals, including *Atlantic, Family Circle, Globe and Mail* (Toronto), *Los Angeles Times, Newark Star Ledger, Newsweek, New York Post, New York Times, Saturday Review,* and *Travel & Leisure.*

SIDELIGHTS: Robert S. Kane has visited well over one hundred countries on six continents and frequently discusses the travel scene on television and radio talk shows.

KAPLAN, Abraham 1918-1993

PERSONAL: Born June 11, 1918, in Odessa, Ukraine; immigrated to the United States, 1923, naturalized U.S. citizen, 1930; Israeli citizen, 1972; died of a heart attack, June 19, 1993, in Los Angeles, CA; son of Joseph J. (a rabbi) and Chava (Lerner) Kaplan; married Iona Judith Wax (a child psychologist), November 17, 1939; children: Karen Eva Kaplan Diskin, Jessica Aryia Kaplan Symonds. *Education:* College of St. Thomas, St. Paul, MN, B.A., 1937; University of Chicago, graduate study, 1937-40; University of California, Los Angeles, Ph.D., 1942. *Politics:* Democrat. *Religion:* Jewish.

CAREER: New York University, New York City, instructor in philosophy, 1940-45; University of California, Los Angeles, assistant professor, 1946-49, associate professor, 1949-52, professor of philosophy, 1952-63, chair of department, 1952-65; University of Michigan, Ann Arbor, professor of philosophy, 1962-72; University of Haifa, Mount Carmel, Haifa, Israel, professor of philosophy, 1972-78, Gruenblat Professor of Social Ethics and chair of philosophy department, beginning 1978, dean of faculty of social sciences, beginning 1972. Faculty member at Brandeis Institute, 1954-62, and Hebrew Union College, 1959-62; California Institute of Technology, Andrew Mellon visiting professor, 1977-78; visiting or adjunct professor at University of Cincinnati, Harvard University, Columbia University, University of Hawaii, University of Southern California, Oregon State University, Hebrew University, Union Graduate School, and Antioch College; fellow, Center for Advanced Study in Behavioral Sciences, 1960-61, Center for Advanced Studies, Wesleyan University, 1962-63, and Institute for Social and Behavioral Pathology; visiting fellow, Western Behavioral Sciences Institute, 1966. Director, Fifth East-West Philosophers' Conference; RAND Corp., consultant, 1952-64, member of academic advisory board of RAND Graduate Institute for Policy Sciences; Adolf Meyer Lecturer, American Psychiatric Association; delegate to World Congress for Soviet Jewry and White House Conference on Youth.

MEMBER: International Association of Applied Scientists (charter member), American Philosophical Association (president of Pacific Division, 1947-58), Israel Philosophical Association (president, beginning 1976), Academy of Psychoanalysis, Institute of Social and Behavioral Pathology, Association for Jewish Philosophy, American Society for Aesthetics, Association for Legal and Political Philosophy.

AWARDS, HONORS: Guggenheim fellow, 1945-46; Rockefeller fellow, 1957-58; D.H.L., University of Judaism, 1962, Hebrew Union College (now Hebrew Union College-Jewish Institute of Religion), 1971; named one of the ten best college professors in the United States, *Time* magazine, 1966.

WRITINGS:

(With H. D. Laswell) *Power and Society,* Yale University Press (New Haven, CT), 1960.
New World of Philosophy, Random House (New York City), 1962.
American Ethics and Public Policy, Oxford University Press (New York City), 1963.
The Conduct of Inquiry, Chandler, 1964.
(Editor) *Individuality and the New Society,* University of Washington Press (Seattle, WA), 1970.
Love . . . and Death: Talks on Contemporary and Perennial Themes (originally presented as an eleven-part television series *The Worlds of Abraham Kaplan*), University of Michigan Press (Ann Arbor), 1973.
In Pursuit of Wisdom: The Scope of Philosophy, Glencoe Press (Beverly Hills, CA), 1977.

Member of editorial board, *Inquiry, Journal of Applied Behavioral Science, Journal of Humanistic Psychology.*

SIDELIGHTS: Abraham Kaplan traveled and studied in Israel, India, and Japan.

BIOGRAPHICAL/CRITICAL SOURCES:

PERIODICALS

National Observer, July 20, 1964.
Newsweek, August 21, 1961.

OBITUARIES:

PERIODICALS

Los Angeles Times, June 22, 1993, p. A22.
New York Times, June 24, 1993, p. B10.*

*   *   *

KAPLAN, Fred 1937-

PERSONAL: Born November 4, 1937, in Bronx, NY; son of Isaac (an attorney) and Bessie (Zwirn) Kaplan; married Gloria Taplin (a teacher), May 28, 1959 (divorced, 1989); children: Benjamin, Noah, Julia. *Education:* Brooklyn College (now Brooklyn College of the City University of New York), B.A., 1959; Columbia University, M.A., 1961, Ph.D., 1966.

ADDRESSES: Home—151 Bergen Street, Brooklyn, NY 11217. *Office*—Department of English, Queens College of the City University of New York, Flushing, NY 11367; Graduate School and University Center of the City University of New York, 33 West 42nd St., New York, NY 10036.

CAREER: Lawrence University, Appleton, WI, instructor in English, 1962-64; California State College (now University), Los Angeles, assistant professor of English, 1964-67; City University of New York, Queens College, Flushing, NY, associate professor, 1967-71, professor of English, 1971-90; Queens College and Graduate Center, New York City, distinguished professor of English, 1990—. Graduate School and University Center, New York City, professor of English, 1979—. University of Copenhagen, Fulbright professor, 1973-74; University of Paris, visiting professor, 1986-87; Bar-Ilan University, Israel, visiting professor, 1987.

MEMBER: International Association of University Professors of English, Modern Language Association of America, Dickens Society (president, 1990-91), PEN.

AWARDS, HONORS: City University of New York research grant, 1968-69, 1976-78, 1980-85; Guggenheim fellow, 1976-77; National Endowment for the Humanities, fellowship at Huntington Library, 1981-82, grant, 1983; *Thomas Carlyle: A Biography* was a nominee for National Book Critics Circle award, 1983, and a jury-nominated finalist for Pulitzer Prize, 1984; fellow at National Humanities Center, NC, 1985-86; fellow, Rockefeller Study Center, Bellagio, Italy, 1990.

WRITINGS:

NONFICTION

Miracles of Rare Device: The Poet's Sense of Self in Nineteenth-Century Poetry, Wayne State University Press (Detroit, MI), 1972.
Dickens and Mesmerism: The Hidden Springs of Fiction, Princeton University Press (Princeton, NJ), 1975.
Thomas Carlyle: A Biography, Cornell University Press (Ithaca, NY), 1983.
(With Michael Goldberg and K. J. Fielding) *Lectures on Carlyle & His Era,* edited and compiled by Jerry D. James and Rita B. Bottoms, University of California Press (Santa Cruz, CA), 1985.
Sacred Tears: Sentimentality in Victorian Literature, Princeton University Press, 1985.
Dickens: A Biography, Morrow (New York City), 1988.
Henry James: The Imagination of Genius, Morrow, 1992.

EDITOR

Dickens' Book of Memoranda: A Photographic and Typographic Facsimile of the Notebook Begun in January, 1855, New York Public Library (New York City), 1981.
John Elliotson on Mesmerism, Da Capo Press (New York City), 1982.
(General editor) *The Readers' Advisor: A Layman's Guide to Literature,* 13th edition, Bowker (New York City), 1985.

Carlyle's "The French Revolution," annotated edition, University of California Press, 1990.
Charles Dickens, *Oliver Twist: Authoritative Text, Backgrounds and Sources, Early Reviews, Criticism,* Norton Critical Education (New York City), 1993.
Traveling in Italy with Henry James (essays), Morrow, 1994.

Editor, *Dickens Studies Annual,* 1980—.

OTHER

Contributor to *Carlyle Newsletter, Dickens Studies Annual, Journal of the History of Ideas, Journal of Narrative Techniques, New York Times Book Review, Nineteenth-Century Fiction, Studies in English Literature,* and *Victorian Newsletter.*

SIDELIGHTS: Fred Kaplan's *Thomas Carlyle: A Biography,* "tells the story of Carlyle's life with descriptive skill, conviction and a sure sense of history," comments Donald Thomas in a *New York Times Book Review* article. As John Clive notes in the *Times Literary Supplement,* Kaplan focuses on Carlyle's childhood in Scotland, his strained marriage, and his chronic gastric disorders, but offers little detail of his works. Carlyle's complicated personality has inspired extreme opinions on his life and works, but of Kaplan Clive writes, "He is sympathetic to his subject, but at the same time does not let his judgements depend on any particular bias." Maureen Corrigan observes in a *Village Voice* article that Kaplan's *Thomas Carlyle* "doubtless will be the definitive [Carlyle] biography for decades, displacing the one written by James Anthony Froude in 1884."

BIOGRAPHICAL/CRITICAL SOURCES:

PERIODICALS

Los Angeles Times Book Review, January 29, 1984; October 23, 1988, p. 3.
Modern Language Review, April, 1978.
New Yorker, January 16, 1984.
New York Times Book Review, January 8, 1984; November 13, 1988, p. 3; April 29, 1990, p. 37.
Sewanee Review, October, 1977.
Times (London), November 17, 1988.
Times Literary Supplement, April 2, 1976, June 3, 1983, April 20, 1984.
Village Voice, February 21, 1984.
Washington Post Book World, August 15, 1982.

*   *   *

KATZ, Michael B(arry) 1939-

PERSONAL: Born April 13, 1939, in Wilmington, DE; son of George J. (a chemical engineer) and Beatrice (Goldstein) Katz; married Edda Gering (a teacher), August 27, 1970; children: Paul, Rebecca, Sarah. *Education:* Harvard University, B.A., 1961, M.A.T., 1962, Ed.D., 1966. *Politics:* Democrat.

ADDRESSES: Office—Graduate School of Education, Urban Studies Program, University of Pennsylvania, Philadelphia, PA 19104.

CAREER: Ontario Institute for Studies in Education, Toronto, associate professor of educational theory, 1966-74; University of Toronto, Toronto, Ontario, associate professor of history, 1966-74; York University, Toronto, professor of history, 1974-78; University of Pennsylvania, Philadelphia, professor of history and education, and director of urban studies program, 1978—. Ontario Institute for Studies in Education, speaker of the Institute Assembly, Social Science Research Council Committee on the Urban Underclass, archivist, 1988—; Russell Sage Foundation, visiting scholar, 1989-90.

MEMBER: Canadian Historical Association, American Historical Society, History of Education Society (director; president, 1975-76), Organization of American Historians, Social Science History Association.

AWARDS, HONORS: Fellow, Institute for Advanced Studies, Princeton University, 1973-74; Guggenheim fellow, 1973-78; Albert C. Cory Award, American and Canadian Historical Foundation, 1978; fellow, Shelby Cullom Davis Center for Historical Studies, Princeton University, 1984-85.

WRITINGS:

The Irony of Early School Reform: Educational Innovation in Mid-Nineteenth Century Massachusetts, Harvard University Press (Cambridge, MA), 1968.

School Reform: Past and Present, Little, Brown (Boston, MA), 1971.

Class, Bureaucracy and Schools: The Illusion of Educational Change in America, Praeger (New York City), 1971, revised edition, 1973.

(Editor) *Education and American History,* Praeger, 1973.

(With Paul Mattingly) *Education and Social Change: Themes from Ontario's Past,* New York University Press (New York City), 1975.

The People of Hamilton, Canada West: Family and Class in a Mid-Nineteenth-Century City, Harvard University Press, 1976.

(With Michael J. Doucet and Mark J. Stern) *The Social Organization of Early Industrial Capitalism,* Harvard University Press, 1982.

Poverty and Policy in American History, Academic Press (San Diego, CA), 1983.

In the Shadow of the Poorhouse: A Social History of Welfare in America, Basic Books (New York City), 1986.

Reconstructing American Education, Harvard University Press, 1987.

The Undeserving Poor: From the War on Poverty to the War on Welfare, Pantheon Books (New York City), 1990.

(Editor) *The "Underclass" Debate: Views from History,* Princeton University Press (Princeton, NJ), 1993.

BIOGRAPHICAL/CRITICAL SOURCES:

PERIODICALS

Globe and Mail (Toronto), September 10, 1988.

New York Times Book Review, April 24, 1988; January 21, 1990, p. 29.

Village Voice Literary Supplement, April, 1990, p. 12.

Washington Post Book World, January 4, 1987, p. 6; January 7, 1990, p. 11.

*　　*　　*

KAVALER, Lucy 1930-

PERSONAL: Born August 29, 1930, in New York, NY; daughter of L. I. (a banker) and Helen (Vishniac) Estrin; married Arthur R. Kavaler (a publisher), November 9, 1949; children: Roger, Andrea. *Education:* Oberlin College, B.A. (magna cum laude), 1949.

ADDRESSES: Home—103 E. 86th St., New York, NY 10028. *Agent*—Claire Smith, Harold Ober Associates, 425 Madison Ave., New York, NY 10017.

CAREER: Maher-Wade Publishing Co., New York City, senior editor of medical publications, 1970-75; P. W. Communications, New York City, executive editor of *The Female Patient,* 1975-84, associate editorial director, 1984-89; AIN Co., New York City, editorial director, 1989-91; Skin Cancer Foundation, senior editor/writer, 1992—.

MEMBER: American Medical Writers Association, American Society of Journalists and Authors, Authors Guild, Authors League of America, National Association of Science Writers, PEN American Center (member of executive board, 1972-77).

AWARDS, HONORS: Advanced science writing fellowship from Columbia University Graduate School of Journalism, 1969-70; citations from *Library Journal* for outstanding titles in science-technology; several titles named Outstanding Book of the Year by American Library Association.

WRITINGS:

NONFICTION

The Private World of High Society, McKay (New York City), 1960.

Mushrooms, Molds, and Miracles: The Strange Realm of Fungi, John Day (New York City), 1965.

The Astors: A Family Chronicle of Pomp and Power, Dodd (New York City), 1966 (published in England as *The Astors: A Family Chronicle,* Harrap, 1966), abridged juvenile edition published as *The Astors: An American Legend,* 1966.

Freezing Point, John Day, 1970.

Noise: The New Menace, John Day, 1975.

A Matter of Degree: Heat, Life, and Death, Harper (New York City), 1981.

NOVELS

The Secret Lives of the Edmonts, Dutton (New York City), 1989.

Heroes and Lovers, Dutton, 1995.

JUVENILES

The Wonders of Algae, John Day, 1961.

The Artificial World around Us, John Day, 1963.

The Wonders of Fungi, John Day, 1964.

Dangerous Air, John Day, 1967.

Cold against Disease, John Day, 1971.

Life Battles Cold, John Day, 1973.

The Dangers of Noise, Crowell (New York City), 1978.

Green Magic, Crowell, 1983.

OTHER

Contributor to anthologies, including *New Worlds of Literature,* Harcourt (New York City), 1970; *The Young Americans,* Lyons & Carnahan, 1972; *How Many Miles?,* Gage, 1974; *Crimson Hills,* Economy (Oklahoma City, OK), 1986; *Pageants,* Houghton, 1986; *Riverside Reader,* Houghton, 1993.

Contributor of articles to magazines, including *McCall's, Memories, Natural History, Redbook, Smithsonian,* and *Woman's Day.*

Kavaler's works have been translated into Spanish, French, and Arabic. Collections of her manuscripts are preserved in the Kerlan Collection at the University of Minnesota, the Archive of Contemporary History at the University of Wyoming, and the Grummond Collection at the University of Southern Mississippi.

SIDELIGHTS: Lucy Kavaler told *CA* that she has been writing professionally "since I first learned to write at all. My first sale—for one dollar—was of a poem to a children's magazine. I was six years old. The books and countless magazine and newspaper articles I have written have taken me into very diverse areas. When I was eighteen and in college, I had a summer job as a cub reporter on the New York Journal of Commerce and was assigned to write about grocery markets—nuts, salt fish, brewery products. And it was then that I discovered that no topic

is boring when you know enough about it. I've tried to put this across in my writing—to make readers see that heat, fungi, and debutante balls all have the potential to interest and excite."

Kavaler added: "After 15 nonfiction books, I made the switch to fiction—planned from the start of my writing career, but postponed from one year to the next by one nonfiction book to the next. Each of the two novels I've written was inspired by the historical and geographical research I had done for my nonfiction books."

BIOGRAPHICAL/CRITICAL SOURCES:

PERIODICALS

New York Times, July 27, 1981.

New York Times Book Review, August 2, 1981.

*   *   *

KEITH, Harold (Verne) 1903-

PERSONAL: Born April 8, 1903, in Lambert, Oklahoma Territory (now Oklahoma); son of Malcolm Arrowwood (a grain buyer) and Arlyn (Kee) Keith; married Virginia Livingston, August 20, 1931; children: John Livingston, Kathleen Ann. *Education:* Attended Northwestern State Teachers College (now Northwestern State College); University of Oklahoma, B.A., 1929, M.A., 1938, special courses in professional writing, 1953-56. *Politics:* Independent. *Religion:* Episcopalian. *Avocational interests:* Long-distance running, quail hunting, trout fishing, singing in a barbershop quartet.

ADDRESSES: Home—2318 Ravenwood Lane, Hall Park, Route 4, Norman, OK. *Office*—Faculty Exchange, University of Oklahoma, Norman, OK. *Agent*—Oliver G. Swan, Collier Associates, 280 Madison Ave., New York, NY 10016.

CAREER: Amorita Consolidated School System, Amorita, OK, seventh-grade teacher, 1922-23; *Daily Oklahoman, Oklahoma City, Tulsa World, Kansas City Star,* and *Oklahoma World-Herald,* sports correspondent, 1922-29; Red Star Milling Co., Hutchinson, KS, assistant to grain buyer, 1929-30; University of Oklahoma, Norman, sports publicity director, 1930-69; College Sports Information Directors, president, 1964-65.

MEMBER: College Sports Information Directors of America (president, 1964-65), National Collegiate Athletic Association (member of public relations committee, 1960-69), Norman Kiwanis Club (member of board of directors for eleven years).

AWARDS, HONORS: Helms Foundation Sports Publicist of Year, 1950; John Newbery Medal for the most distinguished contribution to literature for American children, 1958, for *Rifles for Watie;* Arch Ward Memorial Trophy for outstanding achievement in sports publicity, 1961; Charlie May Simon Award for *The Runt of Rogers School;* Spur Award and Western Heritage Award for *Susy's Scoundrel;* Western Heritage Award for *The Obstinate Land.*

WRITINGS:

JUVENILE; ALL PUBLISHED BY CROWELL (NEW YORK CITY), EXCEPT AS INDICATED

Boys' Life of Will Rogers, illustrated by Karl S. Woerner, 1936, revised edition published as *Will Rogers, A Boy's Life: An Indian Territory Childhood,* Levite of Apache Publishing (Norman, OK), 1991.
Sports and Games (Junior Literary Guild selection), 1940.
Shotgun Shaw: A Baseball Story, illustrated by Mabel Jones Woodbury, 1949.
A Pair of Captains, illustrated by Woodbury, 1951.
Rifles for Watie, 1957.
Komantcia (novel about Comanche Indians), Levite of Apache Publishing, 1965, 2nd edition, 1991.
Brief Garland, 1971.
The Runt of Rogers School, Lippincott (Philadelphia, PA), 1971.
The Bluejay Boarders, illustrated by Harold Berson, 1972.
Go Red, Go!, illustrated by Ned Glattauer, Nelson (Nashville, TN), 1972.
Susy's Scoundrel, illustrated by John Schoenherr, 1974.
The Obstinate Land, 1977.
The Sound of Strings, Levite of Apache Publishing, 1992.

OTHER

Sports and Games, Crowell, 1941, revised edition, 1960.
Oklahoma Kickoff: An Informal History of the First Twenty-Five Years at the University of Oklahoma, & of the Amusing Hardships that Attended Its Pioneering (on football), privately printed, 1948, University of Oklahoma Press, 1978.
(With Wilkinson's players of the University of Oklahoma Football Team) *Forty-Seven Straight: The Bud Wilkinson Era at Oklahoma,* University of Oklahoma Press, 1984.

Contributor of sports fiction to *American Boy* and *Bluebook,* sports articles to *Esquire* and *Saturday Evening Post.*

Collections of Keith's manuscript collections are housed at Northwestern State College Library, Alva, OK and University of Oklahoma Library, Norman, OK.

SIDELIGHTS: Harold Keith's books for young people are noted for their accuracy and attention to detail. A thorough researcher, Keith once commented that he drew material for *The Runt of Rogers School* partly from talks with "five runtish Oklahomans who won their spurs as

athletes . . . and several elementary school football coaches." For *Rifles for Watie,* his Newbery-winning book about the Civil War set in Oklahoma, he interviewed twenty-two veterans of that conflict, each nearly one hundred years old. His material has come primarily from his involvement in sports, both personally and professionally, and from his fascination with local history.

Keith's first book, *Boys' Life of Will Rogers,* grew out of his master's thesis on Rogers's father, Clem Rogers, and his influence on Oklahoma history. The inspiration for *Komantcia,* based on the true story of a young Spaniard's captivity by the Comanches in 1865, came from Keith's extensive reading about "these fascinating people," as he once called them, "as well as [from] personally visiting several Comanches still living in Oklahoma, one of them Topay, seventh and last living wife of War Chief Quanah Parker." *Oklahoma Kickoff* is a history of another kind: an account of the first twenty-five years of University of Oklahoma football. And the later book *Forty-Seven Straight* is a biography of Oklahoma football coach Bud Wilkinson as told by his players and by Keith.

In the years before his retirement, Keith wrote at night and on weekends. *Rifles for Watie* was a five-year labor that led him to compare writing to long-distance running: "You had to learn to punish yourself and keep going even after you grew dead tired. But each night I sat down to write, I felt enthusiasm about this story. I never grew tired of it nor doubted for a moment that it would be accepted," he explained in an interview in the *Wilson Library Bulletin.* The novel's plot involves a young Union soldier, Jefferson Davis Bussey, who spies behind Confederate lines to find a Cherokee, Stand Watie, who is intercepting rifles intended for the Union Army. Jeff is captured by the Confederates and successfully pretends to be one of them for a time, thus learning, as Zena Sutherland notes in *Twentieth-Century Children's Writers,* that "his enemies . . . are young men much like himself." In this "substantial historical fiction," as Sutherland and May Hill Arbuthnot call it in *Children and Books,* Keith presents "unforgettable characters . . . and all the hunger, dirt and weariness of war to balance the heroism." In his Newbery Medal acceptance speech for *Rifles for Watie,* Keith credited his professional writing experience at the University of Oklahoma for teaching him the skills that critics found so evident in the book.

When he retired from the University of Oklahoma, Keith no longer had to fit his writing into the hours he was away from work. At that time he explained his new writing schedule: "I like to start writing early in the morning and work steadily for four hours, then join my friends for a long-distance run, then drive home for a short nap, then return to my library sanctum to work two additional hours in the afternoon. . . . I compose by hand-writing and triple space on the typewriter and my first drafts are as rough as you'll find anywhere.''

Among his own favorite authors Keith names Charles Dickens, O. Henry, and Mark Twain.

BIOGRAPHICAL/CRITICAL SOURCES:

BOOKS

Arbuthnot, May Hill and Zena Sutherland, *Children and Books,* 8th edition, HarperCollins, 1991, p. 436.
Carlson, G. Robert, *Books and the Teen-Age Reader,* Harper, 1967.
Hack, Charlotte S., editor, *Newbery and Caldecott Medal Books: 1956-1965,* Horn Book, 1965.
Twentieth-Century Children's Writers, 3rd edition, St. Martin's, 1989.

PERIODICALS

Horn Book, August, 1958.
Wilson Library Bulletin, June, 1958.

*   *   *

KESSLER, Ethel   1922-

PERSONAL: Born January 7, 1922, in Pittsburgh, PA; daughter of J. Karney (a mining engineer) and Rachel (a homemaker; maiden name, Basin) Gerson; married Leonard Kessler (a writer and illustrator of children's books), January 23, 1946; children: Paul, Kim. *Education:* Carnegie-Mellon University, B.A., 1944; graduate study at Bank Street College of Education, 1955-56; Saint Thomas Aquinas College, teacher certification, 1965. *Avocational interests:* Visiting art galleries and museums, herb gardening, swimming, tennis, walking.

ADDRESSES: Home and office—6 Stoneham Lane, New City, NY 10956.

CAREER: Social worker in Pennsylvania and New York, 1944-53; summer camp program director, 1944-53; Summit Park School, Pomona, NY, kindergarten and first grade teacher, 1965-78; writer of books for children in collaboration with husband, Leonard Kessler, 1954—.

MEMBER: Authors League of America, Authors Guild.

AWARDS, HONORS: Big Red Bus was chosen by the *New York Times* as one of the best illustrated children's books of the year, 1957; Child Study Association Children's Book of the Year, 1977, for *What Do You Play on a Summer Day?,* and 1982, for *Night Story;* Child Study Committee Children's Book of the Year, 1986, for *The Sweeneys from 9D; Stan, the Hot Dog Man* was selected by *Parenting Magazine* as a Book of the Year, 1989.

WRITINGS:

FOR CHILDREN; WITH HUSBAND, LEONARD KESSLER

Plink, Plink! Goes the Water in My Sink, illustrations by L. Kessler, Doubleday (New York City), 1954.
Crunch, Crunch, illustrations by L. Kessler, Doubleday, 1955.
Peek-a-Boo: A Child's First Book (Junior Literary Guild selection), illustrations by L. Kessler, Doubleday, 1956.
Big Red Bus, illustrations by L. Kessler, Doubleday, 1957.
The Day Daddy Stayed Home, illustrations by L. Kessler, Doubleday, 1959.
I Have Twenty Teeth—Do You?: A First Visit to the Dentist, illustrations by L. Kessler, Dodd, Mead (New York City), 1959.
Kim and Me, illustrations by L. Kessler, Doubleday, 1960.
Do Baby Bears Sit in Chairs?, illustrations by L. Kessler, Doubleday, 1961.
All Aboard the Train (Junior Literary Guild Selection), illustrations by L. Kessler, Doubleday, 1964.
Are You Square?, illustrations by L. Kessler, Doubleday, 1966.
Our Tooth Story: A Tale of Twenty Teeth, illustrations by L. Kessler, Dodd, Mead, 1972.
Slush, Slush!, illustrations by L. Kessler, Parents Magazine Press (New York City), 1973.
Splish, Splash, illustrations by L. Kessler, Parents Magazine Press, 1973.
All for Fall, illustrations by L. Kessler, Parents Magazine Press, 1974.
What's Inside the Box?, illustrations by L. Kessler, Dodd, Mead, 1976.
What Do You Play on a Summer Day?, illustrations by L. Kessler, Parents Magazine Press, 1977.
Two, Four, Six, Eight: A Book about Legs, illustrations by L. Kessler, Dodd, Mead, 1980.
Grandpa Witch and the Magic Doobelator, illustrations by L. Kessler, Macmillan (New York City), 1981.
Night Story, illustrations by L. Kessler, Macmillan, 1981.
Baby-Sitter, Duck, illustrations by Pat Paris, Garrard (Easton, MD), 1981.
The Big Fight, illustrations by Paris, Garrard, 1981.
Pig's New Hat, illustrations by Paris, Garrard, 1981.
Pig's Orange House, illustrations by Paris, Garrard, 1981.
The Sweeneys from 9D, illustrations by L. Kessler, Macmillan, 1984.
Is There an Elephant in Your Kitchen?, illustrations by L. Kessler, Simon & Schuster (New York City), 1987.
Stan, the Hot Dog Man, illustrations by L. Kessler, Harper (New York City), 1987.
Are There Hippos on the Farm?, illustrations by L. Kessler, Simon & Schuster, 1987.

Is There a Horse in Your House?, illustrations by L. Kessler, Simon & Schuster, 1990.

Are There Seals in the Sandbox?, illustrations by L. Kessler, Simon & Schuster, 1990.

Is There a Gorilla in the Band?, illustrations by L. Kessler, Simon & Schuster, 1994.

Is There a Penguin at Your Party?, illustrations by L. Kessler, Simon & Schuster, 1994.

SIDELIGHTS: Ethel Kessler told *CA:* "I have been fortunate that I have had four careers—social worker, camp program director, elementary school teacher, and author of books for young readers. All of my work experiences have one common characteristic. They involved me in close relationships with children in their formative years. The experiences have been paramount in my commitment to writing for the preschool child and the beginning reader. It's a challenge to write and then rewrite by cutting the text to the bone.

"My husband Len and I have traveled across the country presenting programs at elementary schools. We use slides and read from our books as Len sketches at the easel. We talk about our families and the life of freelancers. Our presentation ends with a lively question-and-answer session. One of our favorite questions came from a first grader who inquired, 'Does a writer make money?' "

BIOGRAPHICAL/CRITICAL SOURCES:

PERIODICALS

New York Times Book Review, June 9, 1985.

*   *   *

KESSLER, Jascha (Frederick) 1929-

PERSONAL: Born November 27, 1929, in New York, NY; son of Hyman (a furrier) and Rosella (Bronsweig) Kessler; married Julia Braun (a freelance editor and writer), July 17, 1950; children: Margot Lucia Braun, Adam Theodore Braun, William Alessandro Braun. *Education:* New York University, B.A., 1950; University of Michigan, M.A., 1951, Ph.D., 1955. *Politics:* Independent.

ADDRESSES: Office—Department of English, University of California, Los Angeles, CA 90024-1530.

CAREER: New York University, New York City, instructor in English, 1954-55; Hunter College (now Hunter College of the City University of New York), New York City, instructor in English, 1955-56; Harcourt, Brace & Co. (publishers), New York City, educational research director, 1956-57; Hamilton College, Clinton, NY, assistant professor of English, 1957-61; University of California, Los Angeles, assistant professor, 1961-64, associate professor, 1964-70, professor of English, 1970—, director of Institute of Government and Public Affairs research project "Culture in Los Angeles: A Study of Its Problems, Resources, Potentialities," 1967-68. Visiting poet, Seminar of the President of Israel, Haifa, Tel Aviv, and Jerusalem, Israel, 1964, 1970; Fulbright professor of American literature and director of American studies seminar at Centro di Studi Americani, Rome, Italy, 1970; Seminar Professor of American Literature, University of Urbino, Urbino, Italy, 1970; lecturer and translator of contemporary poetry, PEN (Hungary), 1972, 1974, 1977, 1979; program development writer, lecturer in western United States, and member of advisory panel of Western Center for Program Development, National Humanities Series, National Endowment for the Humanities, 1973-75; U.S. Department of State lecturer in Belgium and Iran, 1974; lecturer in Hungary, Israel, Austria, and Yugoslavia, 1979; guest poet, XIXth Struga Festival of Poetry, Yugoslavia, 1980; member of literature panel, California Council for the Arts, 1982-85; speaker and participant at international writers conferences in Ireland, Israel, France, Finland, and Bulgaria. Reviewer, KUSC-FM, Los Angeles, 1979-85.

MEMBER: American Society of Composers, Authors, and Publishers (ASCAP), Poetry Society of America, American Literary Translators Association, Los Angeles PEN Center.

AWARDS, HONORS: Avery and Jule Hopwood Award in Poetry, Major Division, University of Michigan, 1952; poetry prizes, Heptagon Club (New York), 1954, and Ellis Bush Foundation, 1958; writing fellowships, Yaddo Foundation, 1958, Danforth Foundation, 1960, Helene Wurlitzer Foundation, 1961, Institute for the Creative Arts, University of California, 1963-64, 1974, and 1978, and National Endowment for the Arts, 1974-75; D. H. Lawrence fellowship, University of New Mexico, 1961; Fulbright research fellowship, 1963-64, to Florence, Italy; American Place Theater playwriting fellowship, 1967; Popular Panel Awards Prize, American Society of Composers, Authors, and Publishers (ASCAP), 1968-75; Academy Award ("Oscar") nomination, Academy of Motion Picture Arts and Sciences, 1970, for film *A Long Way from Nowhere;* regents fellowship in the humanities, University of California, 1977; translation award, Translation Center of Columbia University, 1978, for *The Magician's Garden;* Rockefeller Foundation fellowship, 1978, to Bellagio, Italy; PEN (Hungary) Memorial Medal, 1979, for "outstanding translation of Hungarian poetry and service to Hungarian literature in the United States"; Artisjus Award, Artisjus: Agence Litteraire, de Musique et Theatrale (Budapest), 1980, for work in Hungarian literature; Shirley Collier Award for fiction, 1986, for *Classical Illusions;* George Soros Foundation Prize, 1989.

WRITINGS:

POETRY

(Editor and author of introduction) *American Poems: A Contemporary Collection,* Southern Illinois University Press (Carbondale), 1964.

Whatever Love Declares, Plantin (Los Angeles), 1969.

After the Armies Have Passed, New York University Press (New York City), 1970.

In Memory of the Future, Kayak (Santa Cruz, CA), 1976.

Bearing Gifts: Two Mythologems, Treacle Press, 1979.

Transmigrations: Eighteen Mythologems, Jazz (Santa Cruz), 1985.

PLAYS

Perfect Days (one-act; first produced at University of California, Los Angeles, 1965), published in *Modern Occasions,* edited by Philip Rahv, Farrar, Straus (New York City), 1966.

The Dummy (one-act), first produced at University of California, Los Angeles, 1965.

Crane, Crane, Montrose and Crane (one-act), first produced in New York City at American Place Theatre, 1968.

Also author of *The Cave* (libretto for an opera in two acts), 1963, and *Exodus,* 1966.

TRANSLATOR

(Contributor of translations) David Ray, editor, *From the Hungarian Revolt,* Cornell University Press (Ithaca, NY), 1966.

(With Charlotte Rogers; from the Hungarian) Geza Csath, *The Magician's Garden* (stories), Columbia University Press (New York City), 1980.

(With Amin Banani; from the Persian) Forugh Farrokhzad, *Bride of Acacias: The Selected Poems of Forugh Farrokhzad,* Caravan (Delmar, NY), 1983.

(With Kenneth and Zita McRobbie; from the Hungarian) Miklos Radnoti, *Under Gemini: A Prose Memoir and Selected Poetry,* Ohio University Press (Athens, OH), 1985.

(With Julia Kada and Maria Korosy; from the Hungarian) *The Face of Creation: Contemporary Hungarian Poetry,* Coffee House Press (Minneapolis, MN), 1986.

(With Alexander Shurbanov; from the Bulgarian) *Medusa: The Selected Poetry of Nicolai Kantchev,* Quarterly Review of Literature Press (Princeton, NJ), 1986.

(With Korosy; from the Hungarian) Sandor Rakos, *Cattulan Games,* Marlboro Press (Marlboro, VT), 1989.

OTHER

An Egyptian Bondage and Other Stories, Harper (New York City), 1967.

Lee Mullican, Galerie Schreiner, 1980.

Death Comes for the Behaviorist and Other Stories, illustrated by Kathy Jacobi, Lexis Press (San Francisco, CA), 1983.

Classical Illusions (stories), McPherson & Co. (New Paltz, NY), 1985.

Siren Songs and Classical Illusions, McPherson (Kingston, NY), 1992.

Also author of teaching films *Autistic Children,* 1968, *Reaching Them with Reward-Punishment Therapy,* 1969, and *The Fire of the Gods,* 1974, and documentaries *The Tender Power,* 1969, *A Long Way from Nowhere,* 1970, and *An American Family,* 1971. Author of *Technology, Prometheus, and Future Human Values,* readings and commentary to accompany lecture series. Contributor to periodicals, including *Encounter, Poetry, Kayak, Midstream, Centennial Review, West Coast Poetry Review, Southwest Review, Saturday Review, Emerson Review, Los Angeles Times,* and *Parnassus: Poetry in Review;* contributor of translations to *Hungarian Pen, Mundis Artium, New Hungarian Quarterly,* and *Modern Poetry in Translation.*

SIDELIGHTS: "Like all of the best literature, Jascha Kessler's fiction homes in on the two central issues of human life—morality and mortality—and pits one against the other," Susannah H. Stone remarks in a *San Francisco Chronicle* review of *Death Comes for the Behaviorist and Other Stories.* In doing so, Kessler's work occasionally employs deceptive subjects. The author, observes *New York Times Book Review* critic Laurence Lafore, "writes about the death of mice; simple domestic events. The simplicity is ironic, of course; mice and their deaths are subjects of infinite complexity."

In his short stories and in his poetry, Kessler endeavors to infuse the commonplace with "cosmic meanings," as Lafore points out in a review of *An Egyptian Bondage and Other Stories.* Kessler's subjects are ordinary people and ordinary events that, through some quirk of fate or idiosyncrasy of character, become extraordinary. Kessler's ability to draw universal conclusions from the particulars of everyday occurrences leads Robert Kirsch to write in the *Los Angeles Times:* "[Kessler's] experience is individual; his evocation universal. . . . He celebrates the private voice, the individual history. And yet, its overtones seem to have resonance in us."

At times, Kessler's attempts to imbue the "simple domestic events" of his fiction with deeper significance have earned some negative criticism. For Lafore, the effect can be writing that is too heavy-handed; for one *Choice* critic, the result is a lack of the tension that makes fiction compelling. Yet while he agrees that Kessler's stories "sometimes tend to reach too far for too little, or for too little that is defined," *New York Times* contributor Eliot Fremont-Smith finds *An Egyptian Bondage and Other Stories* "never without interest." "That is not a backhanded compliment," Fremont-Smith continues. "The interest comes repeatedly as a surprise, and even the most tenuous of the stories keeps poking around inside one's head long after the book is done."

The stories collected in *Classical Illusions* give a contemporary spin to the myths of antiquity, but they "are much more than reworkings of classical themes," Don Meredith notes in *Short Story Review.* "They are powerful, terse, contemporary statements." Unlike many works rooted in literary allusion, the collection's stories can stand alone. "Kessler's inventions are never pedantic parables or thinly cloaked allegories," Kenneth Funsten argues in the *Los Angeles Times Book Review.* The collection "yields a literary and modern anthropology that can be read without a knowledge of classical mythology," writes R. Eric Staley in the *New York Times Book Review.*

Classical Illusions earns critical favor as much for the style and tone of its writing as for its ability to transcend time in renewing ancient tales. At times, a reviewer for *Publishers Weekly* asserts, the stories "have sharp-edged wit; the irony is trenchant, the intelligence incisive, the writing stylish." According to Warren Bargad in *Midstream,* "Kessler's zest for writing, his satiric deftness, and his unabashed revival of existential issues make for a most enjoyable—often moving, often raucous—reading experience."

Some of Kessler's poetry has been recorded for broadcast and for the National Poetry Archives. Kessler's own work has been translated into Italian and Hungarian, and his translations of the writings of Persian, Hungarian, and Bulgarian authors have prompted positive reviews. Clara Gyorgyey asserts in *Midstream* that the translation efforts of Kessler as well as Kenneth and Zita McRobbie for *Under Gemini: A Prose Memoir and Selected Poetry* "reveal an acumen in the art of transplanting even the most complex, foreign concepts into smooth English with amazing authenticity." Kessler's work with Amin Banani in *Bride of Acacias: The Selected Poems of Forugh Farrokhzad* has "set a new standard for the translation not only of Forugh's poetry, but for that of modern Persian poetry generally," writes Jerome W. Clinton in the *International Journal of Middle East Studies.* "That [Kessler and Banani] have at times fallen short of the standard they themselves set only points up how considerable their accomplishment is, and how much will be expected of those who wish to equal, or better their work."

Commenting on his work, Kessler once told *CA:* "I have always written down what has been given to me, and my word, such as it is, seems to be given over to past and future, the dead and the not-yet-living. One listens, then, for it, and waits, more or less patiently, perhaps stoically.

Force and violence are of little use, though they have been the means of too many of us scribblers in this long period of the last hundred years, though many of us are easily inclined towards such instruments, and tempted continually to avail ourselves of them. As for the present, the long present that is the lot of some of us, perhaps I am occasionally overheard. Certainly glad of it when I am, as who would not be? ('Wouldn't you?' The most powerful question asked in this time, and that is the motto and moral of Burroughs's *Naked Lunch.* . . . 'Wouldn't you?' He should be remembered for that! It may be that some phrase of mine will be remembered as I remember his, something better and tending more towards hope, I pray.) At any rate, we are always in the present, the ever-present, and I can be found there these days."

BIOGRAPHICAL/CRITICAL SOURCES:

BOOKS

Contemporary Literary Criticism, Volume 4, Gale, 1975.

PERIODICALS

Choice, July/August, 1968.
International Journal of Middle East Studies, November, 1984, pp. 570-573.
Library Journal, March 1, 1970.
Los Angeles Herald Examiner, September 18, 1983.
Los Angeles Times, March 13, 1970; December 8, 1971; July 27, 1977, p. 4.
Los Angeles Times Book Review, August 28, 1983, p. 6; September 8, 1985, p. 7; January 26, 1986, p. 6.
Midstream, June/July, 1986, p. 62; November, 1986.
New Leader, February 12, 1968.
New York Times, November 10, 1967.
New York Times Book Review, September 24, 1967; November 24, 1985, p. 24.
Publishers Weekly, July 17, 1967; September 13, 1985, p. 124.
San Francisco Chronicle, December 25, 1983.
Short Story Review, winter, 1986-87.*

*   *   *

KING-SMITH, Dick 1922-

PERSONAL: Born March 27, 1922, in Bitton, Gloucestershire, England; son of Ronald (a paper mill director) and Grace (Boucher) King-Smith; married Myrle England, February 6, 1943; children: Juliet Clare (Mrs. Jeremy Hurst), Elizabeth Myrle (Mrs. David Rose), Giles Anthony Beaumont. *Education:* Attended Marlborough College, 1936-40; Bristol University, B.Ed., 1975.

ADDRESSES: Home—Diamond's Cottage, Queen Charlton, near Keynsham, Avon BS18 2SJ, England. *Agent*—

Caradoc King, A. P. Watt & Son, 26/28 Bedford Row, London WC1R 4HL, England.

CAREER: Farmer in Gloucestershire, England, 1947-67; sold asbestos suits and worked in a shoe factory; Farmborough Primary School, near Bath, Avon, England, teacher, 1975-82; writer, 1978—. Writer and presenter of Yorkshire Television's *Tumbledown Farm* series for children, beginning 1983; presenter of *Rub-a-Dub-Dub* for TVAM and *Pob's Programme* for Channel 4. *Military service:* Grenadier Guards, 1941-46; became lieutenant; mentioned in dispatches.

AWARDS, HONORS: Guardian Award runner-up, 1981, for *Daggie Dogfoot;* American Library Association Notable Book citations, 1982, for *Pigs Might Fly,* 1985, for *Babe: The Gallant Pig,* and 1987, for *Harry's Mad;* Guardian Award, 1984, for *The Sheep-Pig; Boston Globe-Horn Book* Honor Book, and Parents' Choice Award for Literature, both 1985, both for *Babe: The Gallant Pig;* Children's Author of the Year, British Book Awards, 1991.

WRITINGS:

JUVENILES

The Fox Busters, illustrated by Jon Miller, Gollancz, 1978, Delacorte (New York City, NY), 1988.

Daggie Dogfoot, illustrated by Mary Rayner, Gollancz, 1980, published as *Pigs Might Fly,* Viking (New York City, NY), 1982.

The Mouse Butcher, illustrated by Wendy Smith, Gollancz, 1981, illustrated by Margot Apple, Viking, 1982.

Magnus Powermouse, illustrated by Rayner, Gollancz, 1982, Harper (New York City, NY), 1984.

The Queen's Nose, illustrated by Jill Bennett, Gollancz, 1983, Harper, 1985.

The Sheep-Pig, illustrated by Rayner, Gollancz, 1983, published as *Babe: The Gallant Pig,* Crown (New York City, NY), 1985.

Harry's Mad, illustrated by Bennett, Gollancz, 1984, Crown, 1987.

Saddlebottom, illustrated by Alice Englander, Gollancz, 1985.

Lightning Fred, illustrated by Michael Bragg, Heinemann, 1985.

Noah's Brother, illustrated by Ian Newsham, Gollancz, 1986.

Pets for Keeps (nonfiction), illustrated by Alan Saunders, Puffin (New York City, NY), 1986.

H. Prince, illustrated by Martin Honeysett, Walker Books, 1986.

Yob, illustrated by Abigail Pizer, Heinemann (New York City, NY), 1986.

E.S.P., illustrated by Peter Wingham, Deutsch, 1986.

Dumpling, illustrated by Jo Davies, Hamilton, 1986.

Farmer Bungle Forgets, illustrated by Honeysett, Walker Books, 1986, Atheneum (New York City, NY), 1987.

Town Watch (nonfiction), illustrated by Catherine Bradbury, Penguin Books (New York City, NY), 1987.

Country Watch: Animals to Look out for in the Countryside (nonfiction), illustrated by Bradbury, Penguin Books, 1987.

Tumbleweed, illustrated by Newsham, Gollancz, 1987.

The Hodgeheg, illustrated by Linda Birch, Hamilton, 1987.

Cuckoobush Farm, illustrated by Kazuko, Orchard, 1987, Greenwillow (New York City, NY), 1988.

Friends and Brothers, illustrated by Susan Hellard, Heinemann, 1987.

Martin's Mice, illustrated by Jez Alborough, Gollancz, 1988, Crown, 1989.

George Speaks, illustrated by Judy Brown, Viking, 1988.

The Jenius, illustrated by Peter Firmin, Gollancz, 1988.

Emily's Legs, illustrated by Katinka Kew, Macdonald, 1988.

Water Watch (nonfiction), illustrated by Bradbury, Penguin Books, 1988.

Dodo Comes to Tumbledown Farm, illustrated by John Sharp, Heinemann, 1988.

The Toby Man, illustrated by Newsham, Gollancz, 1989, illustrated by Lynette Hemmant, Crown, 1991.

Alice and Flower and Foxianna, Heinemann, 1989.

Beware of the Bull!, Heinemann, 1989.

Henry Pond Poet, Hodder & Stoughton, 1989.

Dodos Are Forever, illustrated by David Parkins, Viking, 1989.

Sophie's Snail, illustrated by Claire Minter-Kemp, Delacorte, 1989.

Ace, the Very Important Pig, illustrated by Hemmant, Crown, 1990.

Dick King-Smith's Alphabeasts, illustrated by Quentin Blake, Gollancz, 1990, Macmillan, 1992.

Paddy's Pot of Gold, illustrated by Parkins, Crown, 1990.

Sophie's Tom, illustrated by Parkins, Candlewick Press, 1991.

The Cuckoo Child, illustrated by Leslie Bowman, Hyperion Books (Westport, CT), 1991.

The Animal Parade: A Collection of Stories and Poems, illustrated by Jocelyn Wild, Tambourine Books, 1992.

Pretty Polly, illustrated by Marshall Peck, Crown, 1992.

Alphabeasts, illustrated by Quentin Blake, Macmillan (New York City, NY), 1992.

Sophie Hits Six, illustrated by Parkins, Candlewick Press, 1993.

Lady Daisy, illustrated by Jan Naimo Jones, Delacorte, 1993.

The Invisible Dog, illustrated by Roger Roth, Crown, 1993.

Find the White Horse, illustrated by Larry Wilkes, Chivers, 1993.

All Pigs Are Beautiful, illustrated by Anita Jeram, Candlewick Press, 1993.

The Swoose, Hyperion Press, 1994.

Sophie in the Saddle, illustrated by Parkins, Candlewick Press, 1994.

OTHER

Contributor to periodicals, including *Punch, Blackwood's Magazine,* and *Field.*

ADAPTATIONS: The Sheep-Pig was released as a 2-cassette set, Cover to Cover Cassettes, 1988, and *Tumbleweed* was released as a 2-cassette set, Chivers Press, 1988.

SIDELIGHTS: British author Dick King-Smith began writing for children later in life, after pursuing careers in farming and teaching. He has been prolific since the late 1970s, and has earned acclaim for his novels about animals, including *Pigs Might Fly, Babe: The Gallant Pig,* and *Harry's Mad.* As Keith Barker mentions in the *Times Literary Supplement,* King-Smith possesses "a consistent and well-deserved reputation as a writer of good readable stories for eight- to twelve-year-olds." His successful characteristic of imbuing farm animals with human qualities endears him to juvenile readers. He has also written texts for picture books, as well as authored nonfiction works for children.

Although King-Smith explained in a *Junior Literary Guild* article that he had written "reams of what might most comfortably be called verse, ranging from the romantically pastoral to vulgar lampoonery," he did not begin his career as a novelist until the mid-1970s. Though his teaching career, which he began at the age of fifty-three, had provided insight into the type of material children liked to read, he received equal inspiration from his days as a farmer, for the tales he most enjoys creating concern farm animals. In 1978 King-Smith published his first book for children, *The Fox Busters,* which centers on a family of chickens who plot to drive the local foxes away from their henhouse. Anne Carter in the *Times Literary Supplement* labels it "a good, fast-moving story with sound characterization and an ability to be funny without condescension or whimsicality."

Many of King-Smith's animal novels for children focus on "a single hero, whom we grow to love, [who] fight desperately against a terrifying enemy in a genuinely exciting plot, while the style, dialogue, and characterisation remain light and playful," comments Stephanie Nettell in *Twentieth-Century Children's Writers.* For instance, Daggie Dogfoot, the piglet protagonist of *Pigs Might Fly* whose unusually webbed feet allow him to become a

skilled swimmer, saves the entire farm, including the slaughterer, during a flood by swimming for help. His actions ensure that he will never be butchered by the farmer for food and serve to educate other characters metaphorically about inner values versus exterior appearances. About *Pigs Might Fly,* Arthur Arnold remarks in *Children's Literature in Education* that "King-Smith's writing stands comfortably alongside the more celebrated E. B. White's, sustained by his own inimitable wry sense of humour." Another of King-Smith's noteworthy animal books, *Harry's Mad,* chronicles the adventures of Madison, an intelligent, talking African grey parrot bequeathed by his American professor owner to a young English boy. Karla Kuskin of the *New York Times Book Review* observes that "Dick King-Smith, as articulate in English as Madison is in American, is mostly to be congratulated. The characters in *Harry's Mad* have wit and are good, lively company."

Not all of King-Smith's juvenile novels center on animal characters, however. The well-received *Noah's Brother* takes liberties with the Biblical tale to present the story of Noah's brother, Hazardikladoram, who is ordered about and otherwise abused by his family and in particular, Noah. Alice H. G. Phillips notes in the *Times Literary Supplement* that "the majority of parents will smile at the biblical jokes and approve King-Smith's gentle revisionism. Children . . . will appreciate in *Noah's Brother* the eternal myth of wicked authority figures making life hard for an innocent child (in this case, for a childlike 708-year-old man)." Phillips describes the book's moral as "funny and true: Count your blessings—you're alive, you have your animal friends, and your family has left you." Another of King-Smith's efforts, *The Queen's Nose,* concerns a little girl who receives a magic wishing coin from her uncle and how she manages the seven wishes allotted by the coin.

About his reasons for writing, King-Smith once told *CA:* "I write for the simplest and best of reasons—because I enjoy it. I write for children for a number of reasons: my level of humor is pretty childish (both my grandfathers were punsters of the worst kind, which is the best kind); I think I know what children like to read (teaching helps here); I like to write about animals (farming helps here), whereas adults on the whole prefer to read novels about people; I think an ounce of fantasy is worth a pound of reality; and anyway I wouldn't possibly write a modern sort of novel for grown people—I should get the giggles.

"If there is a philosophical point behind what I write, I'm not especially conscious of it; maybe I do stress the need for courage, something we all wish we had more of, and I also do feel strongly for underdogs.

"As for trying to fill a need in children's literature, if I am, it is to produce books that can afford adults some pleasure when they read to their children. I write for fun."

BIOGRAPHICAL/CRITICAL SOURCES:

BOOKS

Chevalier, Tracy, editor, *Twentieth-Century Children's Writers*, St. James Press, 1989, pp. 527-528.

PERIODICALS

Bulletin of the Center for Children's Books, July/August, 1984; July/August, 1985; May, 1987.
Children's Literature in Education, Volume 19, number 2, 1988, p. 81.
Junior Literary Guild, March, 1984.
New York Times Book Review, May 17, 1987.
Times Literary Supplement, July 7, 1978, p. 770; November 30, 1984, p. 1383; August 16, 1985; January 3, 1986; October 17, 1986.*

*   *   *

KLEHR, Harvey 1945-

PERSONAL: Born December 25, 1945, in Newark, NJ; son of Samuel (a candy store owner) and Shirley (Brummer) Klehr; married Elizabeth Jordan Turner, July 26, 1970; children: Benjamin, Gabriel, Joshua. *Education:* Franklin and Marshall College, B.A., 1967; University of North Carolina, Ph.D., 1971.

ADDRESSES: Home—168 East Parkwood Rd., Decatur, GA 30030. *Office*—Department of Political Science, Emory University, Atlanta, GA 30322.

CAREER: Emory University, Atlanta, GA, assistant professor, 1971-77, associate professor, 1977-83, professor of political science, 1983-85, Samuel Candler Dobbs Professor of Politics, 1985—. Historians of American Communism, president, 1985-87.

WRITINGS:

Communist Cadre: The Social Background of the CPUSA Elite, Hoover Institute (Stanford, CA), 1978.
The Heyday of American Communism: The Depression Decade, Basic Books (New York City), 1984.
(Editor with Bernard Johnpoll) *Biographical Dictionary of the American Left,* Greenwood Press (Westport, CT), 1986.
Far Left of Center: The American Radical Left Today, Transaction (New Brunswick, NJ), 1988.
The Secret World of American Communism: Documents from the Soviet Archives, Yale University Press (New Haven, CT), 1991.

Contributor to *American Spectator, Commentary, Encounter,* and *New Republic.*

BIOGRAPHICAL/CRITICAL SOURCES:

PERIODICALS

New York Times Book Review, January 29, 1984.

*   *   *

KLEIN, Gerard 1937-
(Gilles d'Argyre)

PERSONAL: Born May 27, 1937, in Neuilly, France; son of Paul (an executive) and Antoinette (Lahure) Klein. *Education:* University of Paris, Institut d'Etudes Politiques, diploma, 1957, Institut de Psychologie, diploma, 1959. *Avocational interests:* Modern art and music.

ADDRESSES: Home—25 Rue de Jussieu, Paris, France.

CAREER: Economist specializing in the savings field; writer, principally of science fiction. Societe d'Etudes pour le Development Economique et Social (Society for the Study of Economic and Social Development), Paris, France, consultant economist, 1963-76; Editions Robert Laffont (publisher), Paris, France, editor, 1976—; Editions Seghers, director, 1979—; Laboratoire de prospective appliquee ("Laboratory for applied prospective"), vice president, Paris, France. *Military service:* French Air Force, 1961-62.

MEMBER: Societe Francaise de Psychologie.

WRITINGS:

SCIENCE FICTION

Le Gambit des Etoiles (novel), Hachette, 1958, translation by C. J. Richards published as *Starmasters' Gambit,* DAW Books (New York City), 1973.
Les Perles du Temps (short stories; title means "The Pearls of Time"), Denoel, 1958.
Le Temps n'a Pas D'odeur (novel), Denoel, 1963, translation by P. J. Sokolowski published as *The Day before Tomorrow,* DAW Books, 1972.
Un Chant de Pierre (short stories; title means "The Song of Peter"), Losfeld, 1966.
Les Seigneures de la Guerre, Laffont, 1970, translation by John Brunner published as *The Overlords of War,* Doubleday (New York City), 1973.
La Loi du Talion (short stories; title means "The Law of Retaliation"), R. Laffont (Paris, France), 1973.
(Under pseudonym Gilles d'Argyre) *Les Tueurs de Temps* (title means "The Time-Killers"), translation by Richards published as *The Mote in Time's Eye,* DAW Books, 1975.

Histoires Comme Si (novel; title means "Histories since If "), Union generale d'editions (Paris), 1975.

La Ligne Bleue des Momes (collection of novels, narratives and stories; title means "The Blue Line of Urchins"), M. Favre (Lausanne, Switzerland), 1982.

Also author, under pseudonym Gilles d'Argyre, of other science-fiction novels, including *Chirurgiens d'une planete* (title means "Surgeons of a World"), *Les Voiliers du soleil* (title means "The Sun-Sailors"), *Le Long Voyage* (title means "The Long Journey"), and *Le Sceptre du hasard* (title means "The Scepter of Chance").

EDITOR

(With Jacques Goimard and Demetre Ioakimidis) *Histoires de Machines* (anthology; title means "Histories of Machines"), Le Livre de Poche (Paris, France), 1974.

(With Monique Battestini) *Le Grandiose Avenir: Anthologie de la Science-fiction Francaise: Les Annees 50* (title means "The Grand Future: An Anthology of French Science Fiction from the 1950s"), Seghers (Paris), 1975.

En un Autre Pays: Anthologie de la Science-fiction Franciase: 1960-1964 (anthology; title means "In Another Land"), Seghers, 1976.

Ce Qui Vient des Profondeurs: Anthologie de la Science-fiction Francaise: 1965-1970 (title means "That Which Were Living the Depths"), Seghers, 1977.

OTHER

(With Francois Nedelec) *Avant Charlemagne: Au Temps des Rois Barbares,* (title means "Before Charlemegne: To the Time of the Barbarian Kings"; role-playing game based upon the author's ideas; includes maps), R. Laffont, 1986.

(Author of introduction) *Ailleurs et Demain a Vingt Ans* (title means "Elsewhere and Tomorrow to Twenty Years"), R. Laffont, 1990.

Author of over sixty science-fiction short stories. Contributor of articles on economics, on utopias, on science fiction and the supernatural to periodicals. Editor of *Ailleurs et Demain* (title means "Elsewhere and Tomorrow"), Laffont, 1969—.

WORK IN PROGRESS: A novel; research on the sociology of literature, imagination, and society.

SIDELIGHTS: As an economist and as a writer, Gerard Klein finds "most important the ability of man to conceive things apparently outside his common experience and especially about his future, near or far." He has traveled widely in Europe, the United States, and North Africa.

KOENIG, Louis William   1916-

PERSONAL: Born May 28, 1916, in Poughkeepsie, NY; son of Casper and Pauline (Graf) Koenig; married Eleanor White, 1945; children: Juliana. *Education:* Bard College, B.A., 1938; Columbia University, M.A., 1940, Ph.D., 1944. *Avocational interests:* Gardening, stamp collecting.

ADDRESSES: Home—135 Chestnut St., Garden City, NY 11530. *Office*—Department of Politics, 715 Broadway, New York University, New York, NY 10003-6806; Political Science Department, C. W. Post, Long Island University, Brookville, NY 11548.

CAREER: U.S. Bureau of the Budget, Washington, DC, administrative analyst, 1941-42; Office of Price Administration, Washington, DC, administrative analyst, 1942-44; Bard College, Annandale-on-Hudson, NY, assistant professor of government, 1944-50; New York University, New York City, professor of government, 1950-86, adjunct professor, 1986, professor emeritus, 1986. Hoover Commission, member of Foreign Affairs Task Force, 1948-49; Breadloaf Writers Conference, Middlebury College, 1960; C. W. Post, Long Island University, visiting distinguished professor of political science, 1986—; teacher of nonfiction writing.

MEMBER: American Political Science Association, American Society for Public Administration, Phi Beta Kappa.

AWARDS, HONORS: L.H.D., Bard College, 1960; grants from the National Endowment of the Humanities, 1976, 1977, 1979, and 1981, to conduct summer seminars for college teachers on the American presidency.

WRITINGS:

(Editor) *The Truman Administration: Its Principles and Practice,* New York University Press (New York City), 1956.

The Presidency Today, New York University Press, 1956.

Public Administration, Holt (New York City), 1958.

The Invisible Presidency, Rinehart (Boulder, CO), 1960.

The Chief Executive, Harcourt (San Diego, CA), 1964, 6th edition, 1996.

Bryan: A Political Biography of William Jenings Bryan, Putnam (New York City), 1971.

Toward a Democracy: A Brief Introduction to American Government, Harcourt, 1973.

(With others) *Congress, the Presidency, and the Taiwan Relation Act,* Greenwood, 1985.

An Introduction to Public Policy, Prentice-Hall (Englewood Cliffs, NJ), 1986.

Contributor to *The Centers of Power,* edited by Alan F. Westin, Harcourt, 1964. Also contributed to *American*

Heritage, New York Times Magazine, Virginia Quarterly, Saturday Review, and *Nation.* President of board of editors, *Presidential Studies,* 1978-93.

BIOGRAPHICAL/CRITICAL SOURCES:

PERIODICALS

American History Review, fall, 1973, p. 172.
Booklist, September 1, 1971, p. 30; October 1, 1971, p. 436.
Choice, May, 1965, p. 192; December, 1966, p. 959; September, 1971, p. 904; April, 1978, p. 197.
Kirkus Reviews, January 15, 1971, p. 90.
Library Journal, April 1, 1971, p. 1257.

* * *

KONING, Hans 1924-
(Hans Koningsberger)

PERSONAL: Original name, Hans Koningsberger; name legally changed in 1977; born July 12, 1924, in Amsterdam, Netherlands; came to United States in 1951; son of Daniel and Elizabeth (Van Collem) Koningsberger; married Henriette Waterland; married Elizabeth Sutherland Martinez, March, 1952; married Katherine Scanlon, September, 1963; children: (first marriage) Ellen; (second marriage) Tessa Sutherland; (third marriage) Christina, Andrew. *Education:* Attended University of Amsterdam, 1939-41, University of Zurich, 1941-43, and Sorbonne, University of Paris, 1945.

ADDRESSES: Agent—Frances Goldin, 305 East 11th St., New York, NY 10003.

CAREER: Editor of Amsterdam, Netherlands weekly, 1947-50; radio director in Indonesia, 1950-51; freelance writer. *Military service:* British Liberation Army, 1943-45; became sergeant.

AWARDS, HONORS: Two-time recipient of fellowship for creative writers, National Endowment for the Arts, for fiction.

WRITINGS:

UNDER NAME HANS KONINGSBERGER

Modern Dutch Painting: An Introduction, Netherlands Information Service, c. 1955, 3rd edition, 1960.
The Golden Keys (young adult historical novel), Rand McNally (Chicago, IL), 1956.
The Affair (novel), Knopf (New York City), 1958.
(Translator) Carlo Coccioli, *Manuel the Mexican,* Simon & Schuster (New York City), 1958.
(Translator) Maria Dermout, *Ten Thousand Things,* Simon & Schuster, 1958.
An American Romance (novel), Simon & Schuster, 1960.

A Walk with Love and Death (novel; also see below), Simon & Schuster, 1961.
Hermione (play), first produced in Stockholm, Sweden, 1963.
I Know What I'm Doing (novel), Simon & Schuster, 1964.
Love and Hate in China (travel), McGraw (New York City), 1966.
The World of Vermeer, 1632-1675, Time-Life (Alexandria, VA), 1967.
The Revolutionary (novel; also see below), Farrar, Straus (New York City), 1967.
Along the Roads of the New Russia (travel), Farrar, Straus, 1968.
The Future of Che Guevara, Doubleday (New York City), 1971.

UNDER NAME HANS KONING

The Almost World, Dial (New York City), 1972.
Death of a Schoolboy (historical novel), Harcourt (New York City), 1974.
The Petersburg-Cannes Express (novel), Harcourt, 1975.
A New Yorker in Egypt (travel), Harcourt, 1976.
Columbus; His Enterprise: Exploding the Myth, Monthly Review Press (New York City), 1976.
Amsterdam, Time-Life, 1977.
America Made Me (novel), Gollancz, 1979, Thunder's Mouth Press (New York City), 1983.
The Kleber Flight, Atheneum (New York City), 1981.
De Witt's War (novel), Pantheon (New York City), 1983.
Acts of Faith, Gollancz, 1986, Holt (New York City), 1988.
Nineteen Sixty-Eight: A Personal Report, Norton (New York City), 1987.
The Conquest of America: How the Indian Nations Lost Their Continent, Monthly Review Press, 1993.

OTHER

Also author of screenplays, based on his novels of the same titles, *A Walk with Love and Death,* Twentieth Century-Fox, 1969, *The Revolutionary,* United Artists, 1970, and *Death of a Schoolboy,* Miran Films, 1983, and of screenplay *The Wind in the Pines,* 1961. Author of *Aquarel of Holland,* published in 1950, and *The Iron Age,* published in 1990. Author of plays *The Blood-Red Cafe,* 1957, *A Day in the Life of Alexander Herzen,* 1978, and *A Woman of New York,* 1984. Editor and translator of *Modern Dutch Poetry,* Netherlands Information Service. Contributor to *New York Times, New Yorker, Harper's,* and other periodicals.

SIDELIGHTS: Hans Koning is a critically favored and often political author of plays, screenplays, travel books, young adult books, and novels. A native Netherlander, Koning has also translated the works of Dutch writers into English. With the exception of a self-imposed ten-year exile in protest of the Vietnam War, Koning has made the United States his home since 1951. Newgate Callendar of the *New York Times Book Review* calls Koning "a cosmopolite with a wry, realistic attitude toward life."

Koning's travel books have been praised by reviewers for their authentic depictions, compelling style, and personal touch. *Love and Hate in China,* according to Eliot Fremont-Smith in the *New York Times,* "is particularly sensitive and intelligent, and, quite aside from the extra-literary importance of the subject, it is personal travel-writing in the grand tradition, a compact and beautiful book." *Along the Roads of the New Russia* recounts Koning's 1967 travels so vividly, according to Thomas P. Whitney's review for the *New York Times Book Review,* that his "reader will complete his literary journey . . . with a sense of how it really feels to take such a trip." In *Best Sellers,* David Bianco comments on the merits of Koning's *A New Yorker in Egypt.* "Meticulously avoiding the tourist path," the critic writes, "the author travels on native trains, stays in out-of-the-way places, and wanders in and out of native slums and villages. . . . Politically sophisticated and socially aware, Hans Koning has put together a very readable, up-to-date account of Egypt today." Eric Pace asserts in the *New York Times Book Review* that the book "provides a graceful, impressionistic sketch" of the Egypt its author saw in 1975.

With *Columbus; His Enterprise: Exploding the Myth,* Koning turns to the history of his adoptive country for a different kind of travel book. In recounting the explorer's arrival in the New World, Christopher Hill explains in the *New York Review of Books,* "the author consciously and deliberately emphasizes the negative aspects of the conquest, the greed, cruelty, and treachery of the conquistadores, their utter contempt for the rights of the native peoples." For Hill and others, "this makes fascinating reading."

Like his nonfiction, Koning's novels often trace politically charged paths. According to Paul Berman in the *Village Voice Literary Supplement,* Koning's "favorite topic is dreamy-eyed young revolutionaries on the verge of throwing a bomb." For many critics, these revolutionaries are sympathetic characters, their stories compellingly told. Of Koning's *I Know What I'm Doing,* a novel published in 1964, a *Times Literary Supplement* reviewer remarks: "The spareness of Mr. [Koning's] style is remarkably successful in showing the extreme thinness of his heroine's emotional life." *Death of a Schoolboy,* the tale of Gavrilo Princip, the student who assassinated Archduke Franz Ferdinand of Austria in 1914, elicits this comment from *Atlantic* reviewer Phoebe Adams: "The author succeeds brilliantly in making Princip and his friends convincing and their story provocative and significant in contempo-

rary terms. There is nothing long ago and far away about the tale." Likewise, Callendar finds that *The Petersburg-Cannes Express,* a story about two young leftists who attempt to kidnap a Russian official in 1900, "is part an exercise in nostalgia, part a sly look at Czarist Russia and turn-of-the-century Europe, part a train ride, and altogether a delightful break from the usual mystery or espionage novel."

Koning's *The Revolutionary* received a mixed response. Some critics found its depiction of an anonymous man ("A.") in an anonymous Socialist state too spare to be compelling. According to Peter Berek's review for the *Nation,* the problem stems from the good intentions of its author: "In his praiseworthy desire to keep our attention focused on the notion of a revolutionary temperament or set of mind, rather than on the details of any particular time and place, [Koning] has given up most of the resources of the conventional realistic novel." Berek concludes that there is an "honesty of imagination" to Koning's vision as revealed in the novel, adding: "Perhaps [it] is more important than some partial failures of craft."

The Kleber Flight, published after Koning's return from his exile to London, features David Chandler Lum, a "middle-aged American protagonist," in the words of *New York Times* critic Christopher Lehmann-Haupt. While Lehmann-Haupt questions the resolution of the "moral dilemma" the novel raises, he adds that "when all is said and done, there is reason to be glad for David Lum's existence as a literary character." In a review for the *Nation* of several thrillers published in 1983, Robert Lekachman puts *De Witt's War,* a novel set in Holland at the time of Hitler, "at the top of my hit parade for the novelty of the setting, Hans Koning's ironic character sketches and the infallible grip of a well-told contest against massive odds."

Koning's *Nineteen Sixty-Eight: A Personal Report* explores the activity of a nonfictional revolutionary—the author himself. Abe Peck deems the book "an impressionistic which-side-are-you-on memoir" and calls Koning "an unrepentant radical" in a review for the Chicago *Tribune Books.* As such, it appears that Koning's nonfiction is fulfilling similar goals to those he sets for his novels: "In my fiction of the last few years," he told *CA,* "I am trying to be 'political' in the sense of reflecting the crucial issues of our days . . .; I am trying to do this without writing propaganda or message novels; I'm aiming for novels which will do this and yet remain literature. Such novels are often called 'downbeat' and have a hard life on the current literary scene which is becoming ever more commercial and entertainment-minded, but it seems crucial to me that the modern American novel gets away from the purely individualistic issues . . . and deals with our common fate."

BIOGRAPHICAL/CRITICAL SOURCES:

PERIODICALS

Atlantic, August 4, 1974.

Best Sellers, April, 1977.

Booklist, March 1, 1988, p. 1095; October 15, 1991, p. 371.

Books, June, 1989, p. 11; August, 1989, p. 19; November, 1989, p. 21.

Books & Bookmen, March, 1986, p. 31.

Christian Science Monitor, June 3, 1988, p. B3.

Commonweal, March 1, 1968.

Contemporary Review, September, 1992, p. 136.

History Today, May, 1992, p. 58.

Interracial Books for Children Bulletin, Volume 14, number 7, 1983, p. 35.

Journal of American History, September, 1988, p. 678.

Kirkus Reviews, September 1, 1987, p. 1294; January 1, 1988, p. 9.

Library Journal, November 1, 1987, p. 110; March 1, 1988, p. 77; August, 1991, p. 120.

Listener, June 1, 1989, p. 27.

London Review of Books, May 8, 1986, p. 20; March 17, 1988, p. 10.

Nation, October 16, 1967, p. 376; September 17, 1983, p. 214.

National Observer, November 13, 1967.

New Republic, January 27, 1973, p. 29.

New Statesman, February 21, 1986, p. 26.

New Statesman and Society, September 20, 1991, p. 43.

New Yorker, May 6, 1974, p. 142; June 9, 1975, p. 126.

New York Herald Tribune Book Review, June 8, 1958; April 10, 1960.

New York Review of Books, January 4, 1968, p. 21; November 25, 1976, p. 43.

New York Times, May 25, 1958; May 18, 1966; October 27, 1976; November 16, 1981; January 6, 1985; October 15, 1987, p. 23; October 12, 1992, p. 1.

New York Times Book Review, July 31, 1966, p. 7; October 15, 1967; November 17, 1968; March 25, 1973; April 7, 1974; August 24, 1975; January 23, 1977, p. 4.

Observer (London), March 2, 1986, p. 29; November 10, 1991, p. 59.

Publishers Weekly, October 2, 1987, p. 92; February 12, 1988, p. 72; May 17, 1991, p. 62.

Saturday Review, May 28, 1960; July 23, 1966, p. 52; August 26, 1967, p. 35; October 7, 1967, p. 43; October 30, 1976, p. 48.

Social Studies, January, 1992, p. 27.

Spectator, February, 1977, p. 24.

Time, May 26, 1958.

Times Literary Supplement, March 10, 1966, p. 185; September 28, 1967; November 17, 1968; April 7, 1974; August 24, 1975; January 23, 1977; June 17, 1977, p.

740; April 25, 1986, p. 453; December 30, 1988, p. 1439.

Tribune Books, October 25, 1987, p. 1.

Village Voice Literary Supplement, October, 1983, p. 3.

*   *   *

KONINGSBERGER, Hans
See KONING, Hans

*   *   *

KOSS, Stephen E(dward) 1940-1984

PERSONAL: Born May 25, 1940, in New York, NY; died after heart surgery, October 25, 1984, in New York, NY; son of J. H. (a businessperson) and Ceal (Greenberg) Koss; married Elaine Rosenfield, August 19, 1962; children: Richard Andrew, Juliet Anne. *Education:* Columbia University, B.A., 1962, M.A., 1963, Ph.D., 1966. *Avocational interests:* Theater and, in particular, the opera, literature, cinema.

ADDRESSES: Office—Department of History, Barnard College, Columbia University, New York, NY 10027.

CAREER: Historian, educator, author, journalist and critic. University of Delaware, Newark, instructor in history, 1956-66; Columbia University, Barnard College, New York City, associate professor 1966-68, professor of history, 1968-84.

MEMBER: American Historical Association, Royal Historical Society (fellow), Conference on British Studies, Reform Club (London).

AWARDS, HONORS: Fulbright Foundation fellowship, 1964-65; Guggenheim Foundation fellowship, 1972-73; Netherlands Institute of Advanced Study research fellowship, 1975-76; visiting fellow at All Souls College, Oxford University, 1979 and 1983.

WRITINGS:

Lord Haldane: Scapegoat for Liberalism, Columbia University Press (New York City), 1969.

John Morley at the India Office, 1905-1910, Yale University Press (New Haven, CT), 1969.

Sir John Brunner: Radical Plutocrat, Cambridge University Press (New York City), 1970.

Fleet Street Radical, Allen Lane (London), 1973.

Nonconformity in Modern British Politics, Botsford (London), 1975.

Asquith, Allen Lane, 1976, Columbia University Press, 1985.

The Rise and Fall of the Political Press in Britain, University of North Carolina Press (Chapel Hill, NC), Volume I, 1981, Volume II, 1984.

Contributor to historical journals, and regular reviewer for the *Times Literary Supplement.* Frequent radio commentator for BBC.

SIDELIGHTS: A specialist in British politics, Stephen E. Koss began his teaching career in 1956 and was a professor of history at Columbia University at the time of his death in 1984. Summarizing his career for the London *Times* a critic described Koss as "one of the most distinguished Americans of his generation to devote himself to the study of modern British political history." Koss's best-known work was the two-volume history *The Rise and Fall of the Political Press in Britain,* the first volume of which traced the rise of such liberal newspapers such as the *Telegraph* during nineteenth-century England. Koss continued the story in the second volume, focusing mostly on twentieth-century national newspapers in England. Michael Ratcliffe reviewed both volumes of *The Rise and Fall* for the London *Times,* and praised Koss for writing an "exceptionally well written" book that "will be devoured by politicians and journalists." Ratcliffe also felt that the scope of *The Rise and Fall,* "its mind and references are broad enough for it to be enjoyed by the general reader who will frequently read amazed."

BIOGRAPHICAL/CRITICAL SOURCES:

BOOKS

Bean, J. M. W., editor, *The Political Culture of Modern Britain: Studies in Memory of Stephen Koss,* Hamish Hamilton (London), 1987.

PERIODICALS

New York Times Book Review, May 20, 1984, p. 32.
Times (London), May 29, 1981, p. 593; March 29, 1984.
Time Literary Supplement, May 29, 1981, p. 593; April 6, 1984, p. 361; July 12, 1985, p. 783.
Washington Post Book World, July 14, 1985, p. 12; August 4, 1985, p. 12.

OBITUARIES:

PERIODICALS

AB Bookman's Weekly, December 17, 1984.
New York Times, October 27, 1984.
Times (London), October 29, 1984.
Washington Post, October 29, 1984.*

*   *   *

KOVEL, Ralph

PERSONAL: Surname is pronounced "Cove-*el*"; born in Milwaukee, WI; son of Lester (a clothing manufacturer) and Dorothy (Bernstein) Kovel; married Terry Horvitz (a writer), June 27, 1950; children: Lee Ralph, Kim (daughter). *Education:* Attended Ohio State University, 1939.

ADDRESSES: Office—30799 Pinetree Rd., Suite 127, Pepper Pike, OH 44124.

CAREER: Writer on antiques, in collaboration with wife, 1952—; Ralph M. Kovel & Associates (food brokers), Cleveland, OH, president, beginning 1958; Sar-a-Lee (salad dressing manufacturer later sold to Sara Lee Inc.), Cleveland, president, beginning 1974; also senior vice president of Superior Coffee and Foods, a division of Sara Lee Co., president of U.S. Brands Inc., and vice president of Antiques, Inc. Instructor in American decorative arts, Cleveland College, Western Reserve University (now Case Western Reserve University), 1958-63. Co-host and producer, with wife, of syndicated commercial television spots, *Kovels on Collecting,* 1981; co-host, with wife, of thirteen half-hour shows, *Kovels on Collecting,* broadcast by Public Broadcast Service (PBS-TV), 1987; co-host, with wife, of 26 shows, *Collector's Journal with Ralph and Terry Kovel,* The Discovery Channel, 1990. President, East End Neighborhood House, Cleveland, 1962-63; director, Wholesome & Hearty Foods.

MEMBER: Western Reserve Historical Society (board member), Union League Club of Chicago, Oakwood Club, Whitehall Club.

AWARDS, HONORS: Cleveland Area Television Academy Award, 1971; National Antiques Show Annual Award, 1974; Louis S. Peirce Award for outstanding community service from WVIZ-TV public television; Emmy Award for cultural affairs programming, 1988, and for outstanding program achievement, both from the National Academy of Television Arts and Sciences, Cleveland area; national Lane Bryant award for distinguished volunteer; American Carnival Glass Association certificate of award.

WRITINGS:

WITH WIFE, TERRY KOVEL

Dictionary of Marks: Pottery and Porcelain, Crown (New York City), 1953.
Directory of American Silver, Pewter and Silver Plate, Crown, 1958.
American Country Furniture, 1780-1875, Crown, 1963.
Kovels' Know Your Antiques (Book-of-the-Month Club selection), Crown, 1967, 3rd edition, (Book-of-the-Month Club selection) 1981.
The Kovels' Collector's Guide to Limited Editions, Crown, 1974.
Kovels' Collector's Guide to American Art Pottery, Crown, 1974.

Kovels' Price Guide for Collector Plates, Figurines, Paper- weights and Other Limited Edition Items, Crown, 1978.

Kovels' Organizer for Collectors, Crown, 1978, revised edi- tion, 1983.

Kovels' Illustrated Price Guide to Royal Doulton, Crown, 1980, 2nd edition, 1984.

Kovels' Depression Glass and American Dinnerware Price List, Crown, 1980, 2nd edition, 1983.

Kovels' Know Your Collectibles, Crown, 1981.

Kovels' Book of Antique Labels, Crown, 1982.

Kovels' Collectors' Source Book, Crown, 1983.

Kovels' New Dictionary of Marks, Pottery and Porcelain, 1850 to Present, Crown, 1985.

Kovels' Advertising Collectibles Price List, Crown, 1986.

Kovels' Guide to Selling Your Antiques and Collectibles, Crown, 1987.

Kovels' American Silver Marks 1650 to the Present, Crown, 1989.

Kovels' Antiques and Collectibles Fix-It Source Book, Crown, 1990.

Kovels' American Art Pottery, Crown, 1993.

Also author of *Kovels' Antiques Price List,* 1968-81, pub- lished as *Kovels' Antiques and Collectibles Price List,* 1982—, and of *Kovels' Bottles Price List,* published bian- nually since 1971.

OTHER

Kovels' Picture-a-Day Collectibles Calendar, Workman Publishing (New York City), 1990.

Also author, with T. Kovel, of monthly newsletters, *Ko- vels on Antiques and Collectibles,* 1974—, and *Kovels Sports Collectibles,* 1993—, and of monthly columns, "Kovels Antiques and Collecting," for Features Syndi- cate, New York, 1954—, and "Ask the Experts," *House Beautiful,* 1979—. Contributor to magazines, including *Family Circle, House Beautiful, Redbook, Town and Country,* and *Woman's Day.*

SIDELIGHTS: In 1950 Ralph and Terry Kovel were pay- ing monthly installments on a $15 music box, their first antique. Today, according to a *New York Times Book Re- view* critic, their books on antiques and collectibles are re- garded "as bibles in their field" and have sold more than one million copies. "There was an explosion in antiques in the 1950s," Ralph Kovel's wife and co-author Terry Kovel said in a *Publishers Weekly* interview with Robert Dahlin. "The United States was finally old enough to have a history and to have something to look back on."

Many of the Kovels' books are price guides—compilations of current prices for antiques and collectibles. Their first book, however, was an alphabetical listing of the marks on the bottom of glassware and pottery. "Terry was in New

York with her parents, so I decided to put all the A's and B's [of the pottery marks] together in straight alphabetical order," Ralph Kovel told *Smithsonian* reporter Scott Eyman. "When my wife and her father came home and I showed them my work, he looked at me in disbelief and asked, 'Is that the best way you can spend a weekend of your time?' " The book, *Dictionary of Marks: Pottery and Porcelain,* is now in its thirty-second printing.

The Kovels and their staff of twelve gather information on prices quoted for items throughout the country and feed them into a computer. "We don't write books, we report prices," Ralph Kovel said in *Publishers Weekly.* Terry Kovel agrees. In *Smithsonian* she commented: "We are re- porters and researchers; we never make value judgements. A lot of what we do is like biology, devising categories and subcategories for things that have never been categorized before. As far as prices go, we just tell people what's being asked and gotten; prices obviously out of line, we don't use."

The Kovels are themselves avid antique collectors. The basement of their home has been turned into a "country store" museum, writes Eyman, and their house is "fur- nished in a profusion of heavy styles that should, theoreti- cally, clash [but instead] is a perfect representation of their personalities. Its air of lived in comfort is typical of the un- pretentiousness familiar to anyone who has ever seen [the Kovels] on television." Terry Kovel remarked in *Publish- ers Weekly:* "Any antique dishes that can't go through my dish washer, I can't live with." The most valuable item they own is an eighteenth-century silver sugar castor made by Paul Revere's father. The Kovels bought it at a house sale for $12; it is actually worth close to $10,000, Ralph Kovel said.

"If you are destined to own an antique, it will wait for you," Ralph Kovel commented in *Smithsonian.* "It's really almost mystical, the sense of union you experience when you first see the antique you've been looking and waiting for. That satisfaction is very, very special. It's what makes all the hard work—the tramping through the woods and dirty shops—more than worthwhile. It's all part of the search for something forgotten and wonder- ful."

BIOGRAPHICAL/CRITICAL SOURCES:

PERIODICALS

New York Times Book Review, January 25, 1981.
Publishers Weekly, September 25, 1981.
Smithsonian, November, 1980.

KOVEL, Terry 1928-

PERSONAL: Surname is pronounced "Cove-*el*"; born October 27, 1928, in Cleveland, OH; daughter of Isadore (a publisher) and Rix (Osteryoung) Horvitz; married Ralph Kovel (a writer and businessman), June 27, 1950; children: Lee Ralph, Kim (daughter). *Education:* Wellesley College, B.A., 1950; University of Illinois, graduate study, 1961.

ADDRESSES: Office—30799 Pinetree Rd., Suite 127, Pepper Pike, OH 44124.

CAREER: Writer on antiques, in collaboration with husband, 1952—; part-time teacher in Lyndhurst, OH, 1959-72. Instructor in American decorative arts, Cleveland College, Western Reserve University (now Case Western Reserve University), 1958-63. Co-host and producer, with husband, of syndicated commercial television spots, *Kovels on Collecting,* 1981; co-host, with husband, of thirteen half-hour shows, *Kovels on Collecting,* broadcast by Public Broadcast Service (PBS-TV), 1987; co-host, with husband, of 26 shows, *Collector's Journal with Ralph and Terry Kovel,* The Discovery Channel, 1990.

MEMBER: Ohio Newspaper Women's Association.

AWARDS, HONORS: Louis S. Peirce Award for outstanding community service from WVIZ-TV public television; Emmy Award for cultural affairs programming, 1988, and for outstanding program achievement, both from the National Academy of Television Arts and Sciences, Cleveland area; Laurel School, Cleveland, OH, alumna of the year; American Carnival Glass Association certificate of award; annual award, National Antiques Show; Hiram Fellow.

WRITINGS:

WITH HUSBAND, RALPH KOVEL

Dictionary of Marks, Pottery and Porcelain, Crown (New York City), 1953.
Directory of American Silver, Pewter and Silver Plate, Crown, 1958.
American Country Furniture, 1780-1875. Crown, 1963.
Kovels' Know Your Antiques (Book-of-the-Month Club selection), Crown, 1967, 3rd edition (Book-of-the-Month Club selection), 1981.
The Kovels' Collector's Guide to Limited Editions, Crown, 1974.
Kovels' Collector's Guide to American Art Pottery, Crown, 1974.
Kovels' Price Guide for Collector Plates, Figurines, Paperweights and Other Limited Edition Items, Crown, 1978.
Kovels' Organizer for Collectors, Crown, 1978, revised edition, 1983.

Kovels' Illustrated Price Guide to Royal Doulton, Crown, 1980, 2nd edition, 1984.
Kovels' Depression Glass and American Dinnerware Price List, Crown, 1980, 2nd edition, 1983.
Kovels' Know Your Collectibles, Crown, 1981.
Kovels' Book of Antique Labels, Crown, 1982.
Kovels' Collectors' Source Book, Crown, 1983.
Kovels' New Dictionary of Marks, Pottery and Porcelain, 1850 to Present, Crown, 1985.
Kovels' Advertising Collectibles Price List, Crown, 1986.
Kovels' Guide to Selling Your Antiques and Collectibles, Crown, 1987.
Kovels' American Silver Marks 1650 to the Present, Crown, 1989.
Kovels' Antiques and Collectibles Fix-It Source Book, Crown, 1990.
Kovels' American Art Pottery, Crown, 1993.

Also author of *Kovels' Antiques Price List,* 1968-81, published as *Kovels' Antiques and Collectibles Price List,* 1982—, and of *Kovels' Bottles Price List,* published biannually since 1971.

OTHER

Kovels' Picture-a-Day Collectibles Calendar, Workman Publishing (New York City), 1990.

Also author, with R. Kovel, of monthly newsletters, *Kovels on Antiques and Collectibles,* 1974—, and *Kovels Sports Collectibles,* 1993—, and of monthly columns, "Kovels Antiques and Collecting," for Features Syndicate, New York, 1954—, and "Ask the Experts," *House Beautiful,* 1979—. Contributor to magazines, including *Family Circle, House Beautiful, Redbook, Town and Country,* and *Woman's Day.*

SIDELIGHTS:

See *CA* entry for Ralph Kovel, in this volume.

BIOGRAPHICAL/CRITICAL SOURCES:

PERIODICALS

New York Times Book Review, January 25, 1981.
Publishers Weekly, September 25, 1981.
Smithsonian, November, 1980.

*   *   *

KURZ, Paul Konrad 1927-

PERSONAL: Born April 4, 1927, in Bad Schussenried, Germany; son of Paul and Paula (Hingele) Kurz. *Education:* Stanislaus College, Ireland, Lic. Phil., 1953; Innsbruck University, Lic. Theol., 1957; University of Munich, Ph.D., 1964. *Religion:* Roman Catholic.

ADDRESSES: Home—Josef-Gerstnerstrasse 3, D-8033 Planegg near Munich, Germany.

CAREER: Roman Catholic priest, member of Society of Jesus (Jesuits), 1947-72; lecturer in modern German literature at University of Munich, Munich, Germany, 1964-72; free-lance writer in Munich, 1972—.

MEMBER: International PEN, Verband deutscher Schriftsteller.

AWARDS, HONORS: Golden Quill Award, 1973, from International Conference of Weekly Newspaper Editors.

WRITINGS:

Denn Er ist da: Verse zu Advent und Weihnacht (poems), Ehrenwirth, 1963.

Wer bist Du? Verse des Anfanga (poems), Ehrenwirth, 1964.

Gegen die Mauer: Verse zu Passion und Ostern (poems), Ehrenwirth, 1966.

Kuenstler, Tribun, Apostel: Heinrich Heines Auffassung vom Beruf des Dichters, W. Fink, 1967.

Ueber moderne Literatur, Volume 1, 1967, Volume 2, 1969, Volume 3, 1971, Volume 4, 1973, translation by Sister Mary Frances McCarthy published as *On Modern German Literature,* University of Alabama Press (University, AL), Volume 1, 1970, Volume 2, 1971, Volume 3, 1973, Volume 4, 1976.

(With others) *Moderne Literature und christlicher Glaube,* Echter-Verlag, 1968.

Strukturen christlicher Existenz, Echter-Verlag, 1968.

(With others) *La Nueva novela europea,* Ediciones Guardarama, 1969.

Zwischen Entfremdung und Utopie, Knect, 1975.

Wir wissen dass wir sterben muessen, Guetercloher Verlaghaus, 1975.

Psalmen vom Expressionismus bis zur Gegenwart, Basel, Wien, Herder (Freiburg, Germany), 1978.

Die Liebe ist ein Hemd aus Feuer: Gedichtzyklus, F. H. Kerle (Freiburg, Germany), 1981.

Zwischen Widerstand und Wohlstand: Zur Literatur der fruhen 80er Jahre, Knecht (Frankfurt, Germany), 1986.

Also author of *Nichts und doch alles haben,* Evangelischer Verlag, and of *Gott in der Literatur,* Oberoesterreischer Landesverlag.

WORK IN PROGRESS: Niemand knetet uns wieder: Lyrik und Psalm im 20 Jahrhundert, for Krenz-Verlag and Koesel-Verlag.

SIDELIGHTS: Paul Konrad Kurz tries "to observe, interpret and diagnose contemporary German literature, with a special view on the antagonism of modern literature and Christianity."*

L

LaFEBER, Walter (Fredrick) 1933-

PERSONAL: Born August 30, 1933, in Walkerton, IN; son of Ralph Nichols (a merchant) and Helen (Lidecker) LaFeber; married Sandra Gould, September 11, 1955; children: Scott Nichols, Suzanne Margaret. *Education:* Hanover College, A.B., 1955; Stanford University, M.A., 1956; University of Wisconsin—Madison, Ph.D., 1959. *Religion:* Presbyterian.

ADDRESSES: Home—24 Cornell St., Ithaca, NY 14850. *Office*—Cornell University, Department of History, McGraw Hall, Ithaca, NY 14853-4601.

CAREER: Cornell University, Ithaca, NY, assistant professor of history, 1959-63, associate professor, 1963-67, professor, 1967-68, Noll Professor of History, 1968—. University of London, London, England, commonwealth lecturer, 1973; University of Aberdeen, Callander lecturer, 1987; Johns Hopkins University, Shaw lecturer, 1989; Amherst University, Landmark professor, 1992; University of California, Jefferson lecturer, Berkeley, 1992. Member of advisory committee historical division of the State Department, 1971-75.

MEMBER: American Academy of Arts and Sciences, American Historical Association, Organization of American Historians, Society of Historians of American Foreign Policy.

AWARDS, HONORS: Albert J. Beveridge Prize for best manuscript submitted to American Historical Association, 1962, for *The New Empire: An Interpretation of American Expansion, 1860-1898;* Gustavus Myers prize, 1985, for *Inevitable Revolutions: The United States in Central America;* Guggenheim fellow, 1992.

WRITINGS:

The New Empire: An Interpretation of American Expansion, 1860-1898, published for American Historical Association by Cornell University Press (Ithaca, NY), 1963.

America, Russia and the Cold War, 1945-1966, Wiley (New York City), 1967, 7th edition published as *America, Russia, and the Cold War, 1945-1992,* McGraw-Hill (New York City), 1993.

Origins of the Cold War, 1941-1947, Wiley, 1971.

(With Lloyd Gardner and Thomas McCormick) *Creation of American Empire,* Wiley, 1973, revised edition, 1976.

(With Richard Polenberg and Nancy Woloch) *The American Century: A History of the United States since the 1890s,* Wiley, 1975, 4th edition, McGraw-Hill, 1992.

The Panama Canal: The Crisis in Historical Perspective, Oxford University Press (New York City), 1978, updated edition, 1989.

Inevitable Revolutions: The United States in Central America, Norton (New York City), 1983, expanded edition, 1984, 2nd edition, 1993.

The American Age: United States Foreign Policy at Home and Abroad since 1970, Norton, 1989, 2nd edition, 1994.

EDITOR

John Quincy Adams and American Continental Empire, Quadrangle, 1965.

America in the Cold War: Twenty Years of Revolution and Response, 1947-1967, Wiley, 1969.

(With William Appleman Williams, McCormick and Gardner) *America in Vietnam,* Doubleday (New York City), 1985.

(With McCormick) *Behind the Throne: Servants of Power to Imperial Presidents, 1898-1968,* University of Wisconsin Press (Madison, WI), 1993.

OTHER

Contributor to books, including *The Cambridge History of American Foreign Relations,* edited by Warren I. Cohen, Cambridge University Press (New York City), 1993. Contributor of articles to professional and popular journals. Member of board of editors, *Diplomatic History, International History Review, Political Science Quarterly,* and *World Politics.*

WORK IN PROGRESS: Post-1750 U.S. diplomatic history; *U.S.-Russia to 1914.*

SIDELIGHTS: In *The Panama Canal: The Crisis in Historical Perspective,* Walter LaFeber surveys the history of the Panama Canal, concentrating on the events which led to the 1974-77 treaty negotiations between Panama and the United States. The *Christian Science Monitor*'s J. N. Goodsell calls the book, which was written before the treaties turning control of the canal over to the Panamanian government were ratified, "small and timely. [The book] goes a long way in clearing up the confusion. It disabuses concepts on both sides of the debate and comes up with an extremely readable, cogent argument for the new treaties. . . . This may not convince all U.S. citizens, . . . but it is a powerful argument for ratification."

Conversely, Daniel Oliver of the *National Review* calls LaFeber's grammar "revisionist. . . . LaFeber arrives, predictably, at the government position. . . . True, past U.S. behavior may, as he says, justify the present fierce nationalistic desire of the Panamanians to own the canal. But that behavior—and this book—hardly disposes of the appropriate military concerns, and does not support provisions in the proposed treaty requiring the U.S. to pay reparations, or to forswear building a sea-level canal elsewhere."

Summarizing the book's importance, Terry Thometz of the *Nation* writes: "Although [*The Panama Canal* was] written as a diplomatic history, evidence of 'diplomacy' is scant, for this is a history of treachery, colonialism and racism, of one power's domination of another—politically, economically, militarily, psychologically. . . . LaFeber's recognition that U.S.-Panamanian history cannot be reduced to the Canal itself, to deadweight tonnage, toll revenues and property titles—is an important contribution to the political polemics."

BIOGRAPHICAL/CRITICAL SOURCES:

PERIODICALS

Chicago Tribune, May 4, 1989.
Christian Science Monitor, February 23, 1978.
Los Angeles Times, June 14, 1984.
Los Angeles Times Book Review, April 28, 1985, p. 4.
Nation, April 15, 1968; March 11, 1978.
National Review, February 17, 1978.
Newsweek, April 16, 1984, p. 85.
New York Review of Books, March 23, 1978.
New York Times, May 2, 1968; May 3, 1968.
New York Times Book Review, February 19, 1978; November 6, 1983, p. 12.
Times Literary Supplement, August 14, 1990, p. 601.
Washington Post Book World, November 6, 1983, p. 5.

*   *   *

LAURENTIN, Rene   1917-

PERSONAL: Born October 19, 1917, in Tours, France; son of Maurice (an architect) and Marie (Jactel) Laurentin. *Education:* Institut catholique de Paris, Licence en Philosophie thomiste, 1938, Licence en Theologie, 1946, Docteur en Theologie (with high honors), 1953; Sorbonne, Universite de Paris, Licence es-Lettres Philosophie, 1938, Docteur es-Lettres (with high honors), 1952. *Religion:* Roman Catholic.

ADDRESSES: Home—La Solitud, Grand Bourg, Rue du General San Martin, BP 808, 91001 Evry Cedex, France. *Office*—Universite Catholique d'Angers, 49000 Angers, France. *Agent*—Georges Borchardt, Inc., 136 East 5th Street, New York, NY 10022.

CAREER: Ordained Roman Catholic priest, December 8, 1946; Universite Catholique de l'Ouest, Angers, professor of theology, 1955—; Institut Catholique de Paris, Paris, France, professor of theology, 1975—. Visiting professor at universities in cities including Dayton, Montreal, Florence, Milan, and Rome. Member of l'Academie Mariale Internationale de Rome, 1955; vice president of Societe Francaise d'Etudes Mariales, 1962. Consultant to the preparatory commissions for Vatican II, 1960-61, and expert of the Council, 1962-65. Professional journalist; editorialist for *Le Figaro;* radio and television broadcaster; lecturer. *Military service:* French Army, 1939-45; became captain; taken prisoner in Belgium, held for five years in German prison camp; awarded Croix de Guerre (two citations), Chevalier of French Legion of Honor.

MEMBER: Greci-Marino International Academy (associate member), European Academy (corresponding member), National Center of Scientific Research (elector member).

AWARDS, HONORS: Prix Ferrieres, Academie Francaise, 1954, for *Marie, l'Eglise, et le sacerdoce;* Prix Lods de Wagmann, Academie Francaise, 1958, for *Lourdes, dossier des documents authentiques;* Marian Award, University of Dayton, 1965, for his writings on the Virgin Mary; Wlodzimierz Pietrzak literary prize, 1974, for book translated into Polish; Prix Cardinal Grente, Academie Francaise, 1979, for *Vie de Bernadette;* Prix Broquette Gonin, Academie Francaise, 1983, for *Les Evangiles de l'enfance du Christ;* Prix oeucumenique Sapienza (Italy), 1984; Prix Magnificat, 1987, for his writings on theology; Plume d'or des Amities Franco Yougoslaves, 1988.

WRITINGS:

IN FRENCH

Le titre de Coredemptrice, etude historique, Lethielleux (Paris), 1951.

Marie, l'Eglise, et le Sacerdoce, Volume 1: *Histoire,* Volume 2: *Theologie,* Lethielleux, 1953.

Courte traite sur la Vierge Marie, Lethielleux, 1953.

(Editor with others) *Lourdes, dossier des documents authentiques,* seven volumes, Lethielleux, 1957-66.

Structure et theologie de Luc 1-2, Gabalda, 1957.

Message de Lourdes, Bonne Presse, 1958.

Lourdes, l'Eglise et la science, Albin Michel, 1958.

(Editor) *Les Apparitions recontees par Bernadette,* Lethielleux, 1958.

Bernadette raconte les apparitions, Lethielleux, 1958.

Lourdes, histoire authentique des apparitions, six volumes, Lethielleux, 1961-64, Volumes 2, 4, 5 and 6 reprinted as *Les Apparitions de Lourdes: Recit authentique,* 1966.

L'Enjeu du Concile (also see below), Editions du Seuil (Paris), 1962-65.

Bilan de la premiere session (also see below), Editions du Seuil, 1963.

Bilan de la deuxieme session (also see below), Editions du Seuil, 1964.

Bilan de la troisieme session (also see below), Editions du Seuil, 1965.

La Vierge au Concile: Presentation, texte et traduction du chapitre VIII de la Constitution dogmatique Lumen gentium consacre a la Bienheureuse Vierge Marie, Mere de Dieu dans le mystere de l'Englise, Lethielleux, 1965.

Bilan du Concile: Histoire, textes, commentaires avec une chronique de la quatrieme session, Editions du Seuil, 1966, also published in *Bilan du Concile Vatican II: Histoire, textes, commentaries* (also see below).

Le premier Synode: histoire et bilan, Editions du Seuil, 1966.

Jesus au temple: Mystere de Paques et foi de Marie, en Luc 2, 48-50, Librairie Lecoffre, 1966, published as *Jesus et le Temple,* Gabalda, 1966.

Flashes sur l'Amerique latine, suivis de documents, supplementary material by Jose De Broucker, Editions du Seuil, 1966.

L'Enjeu du Synode: Suite de Concile, Editions du Seuil, 1967.

L'Eglise et les Juifs a Vatican II, Castermann, 1967, reprinted from *The Declaration on the Relation of the Church to Non-Christian Religions, Promulgated by Pope Paul VI, October 28, 1965.*

Bilan du Concile Vatican II: Histoire, textes, commentaires (contains condensed versions of *L'Enjeu du Concile, Bilan de la premiere session, Bilan de la deuxieme session, Bilan de la troisieme session,* and *Bilan du Concile: Histoire, textes, commentaires avec une chronique de la quatrieme session*), Editions du Seuil, 1967.

L'Amerique latine a l'heure de l'enfantement, Editions du Seuil, 1968.

Enjeu du deuxieme Synode et contestation dans l'Eglise, Editions du Seuil, 1969.

Le Synode permanent: naissance et avenir, Editions du Seuil, 1970.

(With Albert Durand) *Pontmain, histoire authentique,* three volumes, Apostolat des Editions, 1970.

Nouvelles dimensions de la charite, Apostolat des Editions, 1970.

Crise et promesses d'Eglise aux USA, Apostolat des Editions, 1971.

(With Marie-Therese Bourgeade) *Logia de Bernadette: Etude critique de ses paroles de 1866 a 1870,* three volumes, Apostolat des Editions, 1971.

Nouveaux ministeres et fin du clerge devant le IIIe Synode, Editions du Seuil, 1971.

Flashes sur l'Extreme Orient, Editions du Seuil, 1972.

Bernadette vous parle, two volumes, Apostolat des Editions, 1972.

Nouvelles dimensions de l'Esperance, Editions du Cerf, 1972.

Reorientation de l'Eglise apres le troisieme Synode, Editions du Seuil, 1972.

Therese de Lisieux: Mythe et realite, Beauchesne, 1972.

Renaissance des eglises locales: Israel, Editions du Seuil, 1973.

(With Jean-Francois Six) *Therese de Lisieux: Verse et controverse,* Beauchesne, 1973.

(With Jean Fourastie) *L'Eglise a-t-elle trahi? Verse et controverse,* Beauchesne, 1974.

L'Evangelisation apres le quatrieme Synode, Editions du Seuil, 1975.

(With P. Roche) *Catherine Laboure et la medaille miraculeuse: Documents authentiques, 1830-1876,* Lethielleux, 1976.

Chine et christianisme: Apres les occasions manquees, Desclee de Brouwer (Paris), 1977.

Lourdes, pelerinage pour notre temps, Editions du Chalet, 1977.

Proces de Catherine Laboure: Documents authentiques, Lethielleux, 1978.

(With others) *L'Esprit Saint,* Facultes Universitaires Saint-Louis, 1978.

Visage de Bernadette, two volumes, Lethielleux, 1978.

Jesus Christ present, Desclee de Brouwer, 1980.

Qu'est-ce que l'Eucharistie?, Desclee de Brouwer, 1981.

Trois charismes: Discnement. Guerisons. Don de Science, Pneumatheque (Paris), 1982.

L'Annee Sainte, F. X. de Guibert, 1983.

Les Evangiles de Noel, Editions Desclee, 1983.

Les routes de Dieu, F. X. de Guibert, 1984.

Marie-Mere du Seigneur, Editions Desclee, 1984.

Dieu seul est ma tendresse: Grignion de Montfort, F. X. de Guibert, 1984.

Dernieres nouvelles de Medjugorje no .1, F. X. de Guibert, 1984, *Dernieres nouvelles de Medjugorje no. 2: Autopsie des fausses nouvelles,* 1985, *Dernieres nouvelles de Medjugorje no. 3,* 1985, *Dernieres nouvelles de Medjugorje no. 4 et 4 bis: Vers la fin des apparitions,* 1985, *Dernieres nouvelles de Medjugorje no. 5: Prolongation des apparitions* (also see below), 1985, *Dernieres nouvelles de Medjugorje no. 6: 6 annees d'apparitions* (also see below), 1987, *Dernieres nouvelles de Medjugorje no. 7: 7 annees d'apparitions,* 1988, *Dernieres nouvelles de Medjugorje no. 8: 8 annees d'apparitions,* 1989, *Dernieres nouvelles de Medjugorje no. 9: Vers la revelation des 10 secrets,* 1990, *Dernieres nouvelles de Medjugorje no. 10: Croissance et reconnaissance des pelerinages,* 1991, *Dernieres nouvelles de Medjugorje no. 11: La traversee du desert: Guerre, famine, priere,* 1992, *Dernieres nouvelles de Medjugorje no. 12: Dans l'honneur de la guerre, l'amour des ennemis,* 1993, *Dernieres nouvelles de Medjugorje no. 13: Approndissement dans la guerre,* 1994.

Comment reconcilier l'exegese at la foi, F. X. de Guibert, 1984.

Le secret de Marie, F. X. de Guibert, 1984.

Vingt ans apres le Concile: un synode extraordinaire, F. X. de Guibert, 1984.

(With Henri Joyeux) *Etudes medicales et scientifiques sur les apparitions de Medjugorje,* F. X. de Guibert, 1985.

Un amour extraordinaire: Yvonne-Aimee de Malestroit, F. X. de Guibert, 1985.

Bernadette et ses juges. Scenario-testament d'un historien pour un film sur Lourdes, F. X. de Guibert, 1986.

Alphonse Ratisbonne, vie authentique, F. X. de Guibert, Part 1: *La jeunesse,* two volumes, 1986, Part 2: *L'apparition a Alphonse Ratisbonne,* two volumes, 1993.

Medjugorje: recit et chronologie des apparitions, F. X. de Guibert, 1986.

Predictions de Mere Yvonne-Aimee: cas unique de verification scientifique, F. X. de Guibert, 1987.

Ecrits spirituels de Mere Yvonne-Aimee de Malestroit, F. X. de Guibert, 1987.

Petite vie de Bernadette, Desclee de Brouwer, 1987.

Vie de Marie, F. X. de Guibert, 1987.

Yvonne-Aimee: priorite aux pauvres en zone rouge et dans la Resistance, F. X. de Guibert, 1988.

Le voeu de Louis XIII, F. X. de Guibert, 1988.

Je vous salue Marie, Desclee de Brouwer, 1988.

Petite vie de Catherine Laboure, Desclee de Brouwer, 1988.

El Paso: le miracle continue, Desclee de Brouwer, 1988.

Multiplication des apparitions de la Vierge aujourd'hui. Est-ce Elle?, Fayard, 1988.

(With R. Lejeune) *Message et Pedagogie de la Vierge a Medjugorje,* F. X. de Guibert, 1988.

Stigmates de Mere Yvonne-Aimee, F. X. de Guibert, 1988.

Eglise qui vient: Au-dela des crises, Editions Desclee, 1989.

Un Avent avec Marie vers l'an 2000, Fayard, 1990.

Formation spirituelle et discernement chez Mere Yvonne-Aimee de Malestroit, F. X. de Guibert, 1990.

Bilocations de Mere Yvonne-Aimee, F. X. de Guibert, 1990.

San Nicolas en Argentine: des apparitions assumees par l'Eglise, F. X. de Guibert, 1990.

Magnificat: Action de grace de Marie, Desclee de Brouwer, 1991.

Les chretiens detonateurs des liberations a l'Est: l'irresistible action de Dieu sur trois axes convergents, F. X. de Guibert, 1991.

Comment Marie leur a rendu la liberte, F. X. de Guibert, 1991.

Petite vie de saint Pierre, Desclee de Brouwer, 1992.

Petite vie de saint Jean-Baptiste, Desclee de Brouwer, 1993.

Petite vie de Marie-Louise Trichet, Desclee de Brouwer, 1993.

Dieu existe en voici les preuves, Brechant, 1993.

L'amour plus fort que la souffrance: Dossier medical d'Yvonne-Aimee, en collaboration avec le Dr Maheo, F. X. de Guibert, 1993.

Lire la Bible avec Marie, F. X. de Guibert, 1993.

Les Apparitions de Scottsdale, F. X. de Guibert, 1993.

Quand Dieu fait signe. Reponse aux objections contre Vassula, F. X. de Guibert, 1993.

La passion de Madame R.: Editions du Journal d'une mystique, Plon, 1993.

Marie, cle du mystere chretien, Fayard, 1994.

Qui est Vassula?, F. X. de Guibert, 1995.

Le diable, mythe ou realite, Fayard, 1995.

IN ENGLISH TRANSLATION

Notre Dame et la messe au service de la paix du Christ, Desclee de Brouwer, 1954, translation by Francis McHenry published as *Our Lady and the Mass, in the Service of the Peace of Christ,* Macmillan (New York City), 1960.

Court Traite de theologie mariale, Lethielleux, 1954, fifth edition revised after the Vatican Council, 1968, translation by Gordon Smith of first edition published as *Queen of Heaven: A Short Treatise on Marian Theology,* Clonmore & Reynolds, 1956, Macmillan, 1961.

Sens de Lourdes, preface by P. M. Theas, Lethielleux, 1955, translation published as *Meaning of Lourdes,* Clonmore & Reynolds, 1959.

La question mariale, Editions du Seuil, 1963, translation by I. G. Pidoux with preface by Hilda Graef published as *The Question of Mary,* Holt (New York City), 1965, published in England as *Mary's Place in the Church,* Burns & Oates (Kent), 1965.

(Commentator with Joseph Neuner) *The Declaration on the Relation of the Church to Non-Christian Religions, Promulgated by Pope Paul VI, October 28, 1965* (also see below), Paulist Press (Ramsey, NJ), 1966.

Dieu est-il mort?, Apostolat des Editions, 1968, translation by Sister Mary Dominic published as *Has Our Faith Changed?: Reflections on the Faith for Today's Adult Christian,* Alba House (Staten Island, NY), 1972.

Developpement et Salut, Editions du Seuil, 1969, translation by Charles Underhill Quinn published as *Liberation, Development, and Salvation,* Orbis Books (Maryknoll, NY), 1972.

Pentecotisme chez les catholiques: Risques et avenir, Beauchesne, 1974, translation by Matthew J. O'Connell published as *Catholic Pentecostalism,* Doubleday (New York City), 1977.

Vie de Bernadette, Desclee de Brouwer, 1978, translation by John Drury published as *Bernadette of Lourdes: A Life Based on Authenticated Documents,* Winston Press (Minneapolis, MN), 1979.

Vie de Catherine Laboure, two volumes, Desclee de Brouwer, 1980, translation published as *The Life of Catherine Laboure, 1806-1876,* Collins (London), 1983.

Miracle a El Paso, Desclee de Brouwer, 1981, translation published as *Miracles in El Paso?,* Servant Books (Ann Arbor, MI), 1982.

La Vierge apparait-elle a Medjugorje?, F. X. de Guibert, 1984, translation published as *Is The Virgin Mary Appearing At Medjugorje?,* Word Among Us Press (Washington, DC), 1984.

Les Evangiles de l'Enfance du Christ, Editions Desclee, 1985, translation published as *The Truth of Christmas Beyond the Myths,* St. Bede's (Petersham, MA), 1986.

The Apparitions at Medjugorje Prolonged (translation of *Dernieres Nouvelles de Medjugorje, no. 5*), Riehle Foundation (Milford, OH), 1987.

Latest News of Medjugorje, June 1987 (translation of *Dernieres nouvelles de Medjugorje, no. 6*), Riehle Foundation, 1987.

Apparitions de Marie a Medjugorje. Ou est la verite?, F. X. de Guibert, 1987, translation published as *Learning from Medjugorje,* Word Among Us Press, 1988.

Une annee de grace avec Marie, Fayard (Paris), 1987, translation published as *A Year of Grace with Mary,* Veritas (Dublin), 1987.

A Short Treatise on the Virgin Mary, translated from the French by Charles Neumann, AMI Press, 1991.

Retour a Dieu avec Marie: de la secularisation a la consecration, F. X. de Guibert, 1991, translation by Kenneth D. Whitehead published as *The Meaning of Consecration Today: A Marian Model for a Secularized Age,* Ignatius Press (San Francisco, CA), 1992.

Our Lord and Our Lady in Scottsdale: Fruitful Charisms in a Traditional American Parish, translated from the French by Doris Laguette and Ernesto V. Laguette, Faith Publishing (Milford, OH), 1992.

The Way of the Cross in Santa Maria, CA, translated from the French by Suzanne Shutte, Anik Alvarez, and Francois Nielson, Queenship Publishing (Santa Barbara, CA), 1993.

The Cause of Liberation of the USSR, translated from the French by Leslie Schlesinger Turner, Queenship Publishing Co., 1993.

Editorial director for Desclee de Brouwer of the collection "Sanctuaires, Pelerinages, Apparitions," 1980—. Contributor to *Le Figaro, Concilium,* and *Chretiens.*

WORK IN PROGRESS: The Birth Gospels, an exegetical study; theological work on Mary; a study of miracles, healings and apparitions; a Christian history.

SIDELIGHTS: Rene Laurentin once told *CA:* "I began my career with long years of obscure research. I became ecumenical without knowing it, because my 'Catholic' works were biblical, and well-received by Protestants, and this is a difficult era. I wish to reconcile rigorous scientific research with faith, which is a profound and discreet light. Theology does not have to be pure abstraction, but the evaluation of the impact of God in the lives of men. I consider journalism and contemporary history as dimensions of my theological work."

Laurentin participated in and documented the proceedings of Vatican Council II from 1962 to 1965, and has since chronicled many such gatherings of the Roman Catholic Church. Much of Laurentin's work has been in the area of mariology, the study of the Virgin Mary, and has included the investigation of accounts of visitations such as those reported at Lourdes, France.

BIOGRAPHICAL/CRITICAL SOURCES:

PERIODICALS

America, February 26, 1966, p. 298; May 13, 1972, p. 519; May 20, 1972, p. 548.

Best Sellers, July, 1977, p. 124; October, 1985, p. 275.
Choice, June, 1967, p. 437; December, 1972, p. 1301.
Christian Century, August 2, 1972, p. 806; June 22, 1977, p. 598.
French Review, October, 1989, p. 188.
Kirkus Reviews, February 15, 1977, p. 214.
Library Journal, August, 1977, p. 1660; June 1, 1979, p. 1265.
Publishers Weekly, February 14, 1977, p. 73.
Review for Religious, September, 1972, p. 896; January, 1979, p. 158; May, 1992, p. 476.
Times Literary Supplement, May 6, 1965, p. 357; December 11, 1970, p. 1469; May 14, 1971, p. 572.

*   *   *

LAWSON, Steven F(red)   1945-

PERSONAL: Born June 14, 1945, in New York, NY; son of Murray and Ceil (Parker) Lawson. *Education:* City College of the City University of New York, B.A., 1966; Columbia University, M.A., 1967, Ph.D., 1974.

ADDRESSES: Office—Department of History, University of North Carolina—Greensboro, Greensboro, NC 27412-5001.

CAREER: City College of the City University of New York, New York, NY, lecturer in history, 1970-72; University of South Florida, Tampa, FL, instructor, 1972-74, assistant professor, 1974-86, professor of history, 1986-92, chair of department, 1983-86; University of North Carolina—Greensboro, Greensboro, NC, professor and head of department, 1992—. Managing editor of *Tampa Bay History,* 1979-83.

MEMBER: American Historical Association, Organization of American Historians, Southern Historical Association.

WRITINGS:

Black Ballots: Voting Rights in the South, 1944-1969, Columbia University Press (New York City), 1976.
In Pursuit of Power: Southern Blacks and Electoral Politics, 1965-1982, Columbia University Press, 1985.
Running for Freedom: Civil Rights and Black Politics since 1941, McGraw (New York City), 1991.

Contributor to books, including *Exploring the Johnson Years,* edited by Robert A. Divine, University of Texas Press (Austin, TX), 1981; *Southern Businessmen and Desegregation,* edited by Elizabeth Jacoway and David R. Colburn, Louisiana State University Press (Baton Rouge, LA), 1982; *American Choices: Social Dilemmas and Public Policy Since 1960,* Volume 1, edited by Robert H. Bremner, Richard J. Hopkins, and Gary W. Reichard,

Ohio State University Press (Columbus, OH), 1986. Contributor to history journals.

SIDELIGHTS: Steven F. Lawson told *CA:* "I became interested in the history of civil rights as a result of my 'coming of age' during the 1960s when social activism was at the forefront. Though not a leading participant in the movement, I greatly admired the courage and dedication of those who toiled in the South for racial equality.

"My book *Black Ballots* concludes that from massive and sustained pressure from civil rights advocates the government slowly but surely took the necessary action to enfranchise the majority of blacks in the South. Politics combined with principle to provide the incentive for reform. The process was painful and although striking successes were achieved, it left a legacy of disillusionment among civil rights activists.

"My sequel, *In Pursuit of Power,* concludes that while the 'second Reconstruction' has persisted and the ballot has improved the lives of southern blacks, black involvement in the political process has been hindered by continued economic deprivation and the vestiges of a century of discrimination. Despite the significant accomplishments blacks still stand on the threshold of political power, waiting to participate more fully in their own governance.

"*Running for Freedom* surveys the impact of the civil rights movement and the development of black electoral politics since World War II. It focuses on the connection between activities at the local and national levels. It is primarily designed for use in college classrooms and for informed general readers."

BIOGRAPHICAL/CRITICAL SOURCES:

PERIODICALS

American Historical Review, October, 1977.
Annals of the American Academy of Political and Social Science, November, 1977.
Journal of American History, December, 1977.
Political Science Quarterly, summer, 1977.
Times Literary Supplement, May 20, 1977.

*   *   *

LEEDY, Loreen (Janelle)   1959-

PERSONAL: Born June 15, 1959, in Wilmington, DE; daughter of James Allwyn (an auditor) and Grace Anne (Williams) Leedy. *Education:* Attended Indiana University—Bloomington, 1978-79; University of Delaware, B.A. (cum laude), 1981.

ADDRESSES: Home—P.O. Box 165, Winter Park, FL 32790.

CAREER: Craftsperson, specializing in jewelry, 1982-84; writer and illustrator, 1984—. Lecturer at writing workshops. Speaker for schools and conventions.

MEMBER: Authors Guild, Authors League of America, Society of Children's Book Writers and Illustrators.

AWARDS, HONORS: Parents' Choice Award for Illustration, 1987, for *Big, Small, Short, Tall;* Parents' Choice Award in Learning and Doing, 1989, for *The Dragon Halloween Party;* Ezra Jack Keats Award for excellence in the arts, 1989; Best Books Award, *Parents Magazine,* 1990, for *The Furry News,* and 1992, for *The Monster Money Book; Fraction Action* included in the Society of Illustrators' Original Art show, New York City, 1994; art depicting sea turtles, from *Tracks in the Sand,* shown at the Greensburgh Nature Center in Scarsdale, NY.

WRITINGS:

SELF-ILLUSTRATED CHILDREN'S BOOKS

A Number of Dragons, Holiday House (New York City), 1985.
The Dragon ABC Hunt, Holiday House, 1986.
The Dragon Halloween Party, Holiday House, 1986.
Big, Small, Short, Tall, Holiday House, 1987.
The Bunny Play, Holiday House, 1988.
A Dragon Christmas: Things to Make and Do, Holiday House, 1988.
Pingo the Plaid Panda, Holiday House, 1988.
The Potato Party and Other Troll Tales, Holiday House, 1989.
A Dragon Thanksgiving Feast: Things to Make and Do, Holiday House, 1990.
The Furry News: How to Make a Newspaper, Holiday House, 1990.
The Great Trash Bash, Holiday House, 1991.
Messages in the Mailbox: How to Write a Letter, Holiday House, 1991, 2nd edition, 1994.
Blast off to Earth!: A Look at Geography, Holiday House, 1992.
The Monster Money Book, Holiday House, 1992.
Postcards from Pluto: A Tour of the Solar System, Holiday House, 1993.
The Race, Scott Foresman (Glenview, IL), 1993.
Tracks in the Sand, Doubleday (New York City), 1993.
The Edible Pyramid: Good Eating Every Day, Holiday House, 1994.
Fraction Action, Holiday House, 1994.
Who's Who in My Family?, Holiday House, 1995.

ILLUSTRATOR

David A. Adler, *The Dinosaur Princess and Other Prehistoric Riddles,* Holiday House, 1988.
Tom Birdseye, *Waiting for Baby,* Holiday House, 1991.

WORK IN PROGRESS: 2 X 2 =BOO!, a set of multiplication tables (with a Halloween theme), of which the author says, "When I was struggling to learn the multiplication tables in fourth grade, I never dreamed they could be the inspiration for writing!"

SIDELIGHTS: Loreen Leedy told *CA:* "Reading, writing, and making art have been important to me throughout my lifetime. The picture book is a unique art form in which the words and artwork work together to tell the story or convey information. When developing a book, I work back and forth between the text and the illustrations to create a unified whole. Most of my books incorporate humor to engage the young reader, and many are informational.

"I choose a subject such as writing letters, then devise a set of characters and a setting for the action to take place. In *Messages in the Mailbox,* Mrs. gator and her students write busily in a swampy Florida classroom. In *The Edible Pyramid,* a suave feline waiter shows his customers the variety of foods available in the restaurant, thereby exploring the U.S.D.A.'s newly developed Food Guide Pyramid.

"Other interesting subjects that may inspire future books include computers, cats, fashion, cars, exercise, genealogy, and color."

BIOGRAPHICAL/CRITICAL SOURCES:

PERIODICALS

Delaware Today, October, 1986.

*   *   *

LEKSON, Stephen H(enry)   1950-

PERSONAL: Born May 18, 1950, in West Point, NY; son of John Stephan (in U.S. Army) and Gladys Mae (a housewife) Lekson; married Catherine M. Cameron (an archaeologist), January 12, 1979. *Education:* Case Western Reserve University, B.A., 1972; Eastern New Mexico University, M.A., 1978; University of New Mexico, Ph.D., 1988.

ADDRESSES: Home—7279 West Kentucky #B, Lakewood, CO 80226. *Office*—Crow Canyon Archaeological Center, 23390 County Rd. K, Cortez, CO 81321.

CAREER: Case Western Reserve University, project director of Upper Gila Project, 1971-73, principal investigator for Redrock Valley Survey, 1974; University of Tennessee, crew chief for Columbia Reservoir Survey Project, 1973, project director of Hartsville Reactor Mitigation Project, 1973; Eastern New Mexico University, Portales, NM, assistant director of ceramics laboratory of San Juan Valley Archaeological Project, 1974, and Puerco River

Valley Project, 1975; National Park Service, Chaco Canyon National Monument, archeologist, 1976-86; Arizona State Museum, research associate, 1986-90; Museum of New Mexico, curator of archaeology, 1991-92; Crow Canyon Archaeological Center, president, 1992—. Chairperson or organizer of various archaeological conferences and symposia.

MEMBER: World Archaeological Congress, American Anthropological Association, American Association of Museums, Archaeological Institute of America (Denver Chapter), Council for Museum Anthropology, Society for American Anthropology, Archaeological Society of New Mexico, Arizona Archaeological and Historical Society, Arizona Archaeological Council, Colorado Archaeological Society, Colorado Council of Professional Archaeologists, New Mexico Archaeological Council.

WRITINGS:

The Architecture and Dendrochronology of Chetro Ketl, U. S. Government Printing Office (Washington, DC), 1983.

Great Pueblo Architecture of Chaco Canyon, University of New Mexico Press (Albuquerque), 1986.

Nana's Raid: Apache Warfare in Southern New Mexico, 1881, Texas Western Press (El Paso, TX), 1987.

Mimbres Archaeology of the Upper Gila, New Mexico, University of Arizona Press (Tucson), 1990.

Ethnohistory of the Warm Spring Apache Reservation and Its Region (prepared for the National Park Service Southwestern Region), Human Systems Research (Las Cruces, NM), 1992.

(With Rina Swentzell and Catherine M. Cameron) *Ancient Land, Ancestral Places,* Museum of New Mexico Press (Santa Fe, NM), 1993.

Archaeological Overview of Southwestern New Mexico, New Mexico Historic Preservation Division (Santa Fe, NM), in press.

Also author of research papers and reports. Contributor to books. Contributor to scholarly journals and popular periodicals, including *American Antiquity, Archaeology, Artifact, Expedition, Kiva, New Mexico Magazine, New Mexico Archaeological Council Newsletter, New Mexico Journal of Science, El Palacio, Pottery Southwest, Scientific American,* and *Southwestern Lore.*

WORK IN PROGRESS: Editing, with Michael Adler and William Lipe, *Anasazi Societies in Transition: The Great Pueblo Period in the American Southwest.*

SIDELIGHTS: Stephen H. Lekson told *CA:* "I am primarily a research archaeologist, working with the Pueblo Indian ruins of the North American Southwest. My principal writings, about places like Chaco Canyon and Mesa Verde, have been monographs and articles in scholarly journals. For the last five years, however, I've devoted about one-third of my time to non-technical works: essays in photo books, magazine articles, copy for museum exhibits. Archaeology has a great deal to say to our times, and I plan to write more for larger audiences."

*   *   *

LEONARD, Thomas M. 1937-

PERSONAL: Born November 8, 1937, in Elizabeth, NJ; son of Edward C. (in sales) and Amelia T. (a homemaker; maiden name, Chap) Leonard; married Yvonne Ann Marie Clements (self-employed), August 13, 1960; children: Thomas, Robert, Randall, Edward, David, Stacy. *Education:* Mount St. Mary's College, Emmitsburg, MD, B.S., 1959; Georgetown University, M.A., 1963; American University, Washington, DC, Ph.D., 1968. *Politics:* "No preference." *Religion:* Catholic. *Avocational interests:* Travel (Central America).

ADDRESSES: Home—1104 Pono View Court, Fruit Cove, FL 32224. *Office*—Department of History, University of North Florida, Jacksonville, FL 32209.

CAREER: Weston Instruments, Newark, NJ, sales expeditor, 1955-60; Baltimore County Board of Education, Towson, MD, social studies teacher, 1960-63; St. Joseph College (closed in 1973), Emmitsburg, MD, associate professor of history, 1963-73; University of North Florida, Jacksonville, professor of history, 1973—, distinguished professor, 1985—. Visiting professor in Mexico and Argentina. Consultant to Florida State Department of Education and to Jacksonville Chamber of Commerce's Caribbean Task Force. Member of Florida Advisory Board that links the State University System of Florida to the National University System of Costa Rica.

MEMBER: Belize Studies Association (president, 1993-95), American Historical Association, Latin American Studies Association, Society for Historians of American Foreign Relations, First Coast International Affairs Forum (president, 1986-90), Southeast Council on Latin American Studies president, 1992-93), Florida College Teachers of History Association (president, 1981-82), Phi Kappa Phi, Knights of Columbus, Loyal Order of the Moose.

WRITINGS:

(Editor) *Proceedings: Communications Media and Their Responsibilities to the Public,* University of North Florida, 1977.

Day by Day: The Forties, edited by Richard Burbank and Steven L. Goulden, Facts on File (New York City), 1977.

United States and Central America, 1944-1949: Perceptions of Political Dynamics, University of Alabama Press (University, AL), 1984.

Central America and United States Policies, 1820s-1980s: A Guide to Issues and References, Regina Books (Claremont, CA), 1985.

(With Cynthia Crippen and Marc Aronson) *Day by Day: The Seventies,* Facts on File, 1988.

Central America and the United States: The Search for Stability, University of Georgia Press (Athens, GA), 1991.

Panama and the United States: Guide to Issues and Sources, Regina Books, 1993.

Guide to Archival Material in the United States on Central America, Greenwood Press (Westport, CT), 1994.

Contributor to books, including *Political Profiles: The Truman Years,* edited by Eleanora W. Schoenebaum, Facts on File, 1978; *Political Profiles: The Nixon Years,* edited by Schoenebaum, Facts on File, 1979; *Guide to American Foreign Relations since 1700,* edited by Richard Dean Burns, American Bibliographical Center-Clio Press (Santa Barbara, CA), 1982; *The Church and Society in Latin America,* edited by Jeffrey A. Cole and Richard Greenleaf, Tulane University Press (New Orleans, LA), 1983; *Growth and Conflict: America, 1898-1945,* edited by John M. Carroll, Kendall/Hunt (Dubuque, IA), 1986; *The Perils of Limited War: Vietnam, Central America and the Limited Arms Race,* edited by Howard Jones, University of Alabama Press, 1988; *Central America: Historical Perspectives on the Contemporary Crisis,* edited by Ralph Lee Greenwood, Jr., Greenwood Press, 1988; *Oral Tradition and Oral History in Africa and the Diaspora,* edited by E. J. Alagoa, University of Lagos (Nigeria), 1990; *Historia General de Guatemala,* five volumes, edited by Jorge Lujan Munoz, Fundacion Para La Cultura y El Desarrollo (Guatemala City), 1993-95; *Hispanic Almanac,* edited by Nicolas Kanellos, Gale, 1993; *Latin America in Transition,* edited by Robert P. Watson and Donald C. Simmons, Troy State University Press (Troy, AL), 1994.

Contributor to *Encyclopedia of Arms Control and Disarmament,* edited by Richard Dean Burns, Charles Scribner's Sons (New York City), 1993.

Contributor to periodicals, including *Americas, Interdisciplinary Essays, Journal of Caribbean Studies, Journal of Third World Studies, Mid America, SECOLAS Annals, Towson State Journal of International Affairs, Valley Forge Journal,* and *War and Diplomacy Proceedings.*

WORK IN PROGRESS: The United States and Latin America, 1850-1903, for University of Alabama Press. Contributions forthcoming to: *American National Biography,* edited by Norman Armour, James R. Partidge and John A. Garraty, Oxford University Press; *Encyclopedia*

of Latin American History, edited by Barbara A. Tenenbaum, Scribner.

SIDELIGHTS: Thomas M. Leonard told *CA:* "I enjoy researching to determine the attitudes and perceptions U.S. policy makers had toward Central America. Their attitudes and perceptions contributed significantly to policy decisions."

BIOGRAPHICAL/CRITICAL SOURCES:

PERIODICALS

American Historical Review, October, 1985.
Hispanic American History Review, May, 1986.
History: Review of New Books, February, 1985.
Journal of American History, June, 1985.
Times Literary Supplement, June 16, 1978.

*   *   *

LITTLE, David 1933-

PERSONAL: Born November 21, 1933, in St. Louis, MO; son of Henry, Jr. (a minister) and Agathe (Daniel) Little; married Priscilla Cortelyou, August 18, 1956; children: Jonathan, Martha, Kathryn. *Education:* College of Wooster, B.A., 1955; Union Theological Seminary, B.D., 1958; Harvard University, Th.D., 1963.

ADDRESSES: Office—Department of Religious Studies, University of Virginia, Charlottesville, VA 22904.

CAREER: Harvard University, Divinity School, Cambridge, MA, instructor, 1963; Yale University, Divinity School, New Haven, CT, assistant professor, 1963-69, associate professor of Christian ethics, beginning 1969; University of Virginia, Charlottesville, member of department of religious studies.

AWARDS, HONORS: Kennedy traveling fellowship of Harvard University, 1961-62; Morse fellowship of Yale University, 1968-69.

WRITINGS:

American Foreign Policy and Moral Rhetoric: The Example of Vietnam, Council on Religion and International Affairs (New York), 1969.

Religion, Order and Law: A Study in Pre-Revolutionary England, Harper (New York City), 1969, edition with foreword by Robert N. Bellah and with new preface, University of Chicago Press (Chicago, IL), 1984.

(With Sumner B. Twiss, Jr.) *Comparative Religious Ethics,* Harper, 1978.

(Editor with R. S. Khare) *Leadership—Interdisciplinary Reflections,* University Press of America (Lanham, MD), 1984.

(With John Kelsay and Abdulaziz A. Sachedina) *Human Rights and the Conflict of Cultures: Western and Islamic Perspectives on Religious Liberty,* University of South Carolina Press (Columbia, SC), 1988.

The Tabernacle in the Wilderness, Loizeaux Bros. (Neptune, NJ), 1989.

Ukraine: The Legacy of Intolerance, United States Institute of Peace Press (Washington, DC), 1991.

Sri Lanka: The Invention of Enmity, United States Institute of Peace Press, 1994.

Sri Lanka: The Legacy of Intolerance, foreword by Richard H. Solomon, United States Institute of Peace Press, 1994.

Also author of *Tabernacle in the Wilderness,* for Loizeaux.*

*   *   *

LONG, Robert Emmet 1934-

PERSONAL: Born June 7, 1934, in Oswego, NY; son of Robert Emmet (a retail merchant) and Verda (Lindsley) Long. *Education:* Columbia University, B.A., 1956, Ph.D., 1968; Syracuse University, M.A., 1964. *Politics:* Democrat. *Religion:* Episcopalian.

ADDRESSES: Home—254 South Third St., Fulton, NY 13069.

CAREER: Insurance investigator in New York, NY, and San Francisco, CA, 1957-60; State University of New York College at Cortland, instructor in English, 1962-64; Queens College of the City University of New York, Flushing, NY, assistant professor of English, 1968-71; writer, 1971—.

WRITINGS:

The Great Succession: Henry James and the Legacy of Hawthorne, University of Pittsburgh Press (Pittsburgh, PA), 1979.

The Achieving of "The Great Gatsby": F. Scott Fitzgerald, 1920-1925, Bucknell University Press (Cranbury, NJ), 1979.

Henry James: The Early Novels, G. K. Hall (Boston, MA), 1983.

John O'Hara, Ungar (New York City), 1983.

Nathaniel West, Ungar, 1985.

Barbara Pym, Ungar, 1986.

James Thurber, Continuum (New York City), 1988.

James Fenimore Cooper, Continuum, 1990.

The Films of Merchant Ivory, Abrams (New York City), 1991.

Ingmar Bergman: Film and Stage, Abrams, 1994.

EDITOR

American Education, H. W. Wilson (Bronx, NY), 1984.

Drugs and American Society, H. W. Wilson, 1985.

Vietnam Ten Years After, H. W. Wilson, 1986.

Mexico, H. W. Wilson, 1986.

AIDS, H. W. Wilson, 1987.

The Farm Crisis, H. W. Wilson, 1987.

The Problem of Waste Disposal, H. W. Wilson, 1989.

Gun Control, H. W. Wilson, 1989.

The Welfare Debate, H. W. Wilson, 1989.

Energy and Conservation, H. W. Wilson, 1989.

Japan and the U. S., H. W. Wilson, 1990.

Censorship, H. W. Wilson, 1990.

The Crisis in Health Care, H. W. Wilson, 1991.

The State of U. S. Education, H. W. Wilson, 1991.

The Reunification of Germany, H. W. Wilson, 1992.

Immigration to the United States, H. W. Wilson, 1992.

Drugs in America, H. W. Wilson, 1993.

Banking Scandals: The 5th and BCCI, H. W. Wilson, 1993.

Religious Cults in America, H. W. Wilson, 1994.

OTHER

Contributor of approximately four hundred articles, stories, and reviews to magazines, including *Commonweal, Nation, Saturday Review,* and to newspapers. Drama critic for *North American Review,* 1968-71.

WORK IN PROGRESS: A critical study.

SIDELIGHTS: Robert Emmet Long informed *CA:* "By the time I was eight or nine, I had the notion that my life as an adult would have to do with books, that I would be a writer of some kind. Some of the adults thought that I might become an actor, because I performed on local stages, but this was a passing phase. When I was in high school I had a brilliant and witty English teacher named Rose Mary O'Connor, who informed me that since I was going to be a writer I should apply to Columbia, where writers were produced in droves. That was how it was that I went to Columbia College, where cultural achievement had a very high priority. Mark Van Doren was a highlight in those years; I took all of his courses, and even a tutorial with him. The theater in New York was also suddenly available to me, and became a kind of student avocation. For better or worse and even if I have lived far away from them, I have never left Columbia and New York behind me.

"I was a somewhat reluctant literary critic, and did not begin publishing right away. When I did, however, I had no trouble being published wherever I sent a manuscript. My first books were on F. Scott Fitzgerald and Henry James because they were favorites of mine. An odd thing about the composition of the Fitzgerald book, or at least about the Fitzgerald-Conrad section, was that the whole idea, which was very complicated, came to me in a matter of seconds. The James book evolved more slowly, and was more challenging because I had come to know Marius Bewley, who had written brilliantly on the same subject. The subjects of later books—from James Thurber to James Fenimore Cooper—were chosen because they were very involving to me; but I have very versatile interests and could just as easily have written on other figures. My criticism doesn't belong to any school that I know of; I've tried to avoid association with the school of the deadly dull and pedantic.

"The performing arts have always been a side interest of mine, but in the last few years they have come to the forefront in my writing. Preparing the book on the films of Merchant Ivory was a fascinating experience that plunged me into the middle of the film world. I traveled with Merchant and Ivory, and watched them shoot their films on location. They gave me unlimited cooperation and access. When the book was published, just before the release of *Howards End,* it received an enormous amount of publicity and attention. Preparing a follow-up book on Ingmar Bergman and his long career was also an adventurous experience that took me to Sweden. Right now I am looking at the Broadway theatre, but I am not sure if my writing on the performing arts is a congenial detour or a second career."

The Great Succession was the first book to concentrate solely on the influence of Nathaniel Hawthorne on the writing of Henry James. Long has analyzed this relationship in detail, beginning with the stories James wrote in the 1860s and concluding with *The Bostonians.* According to critic David Seed, writing in the *Times Literary Supplement,* "One of the most original and rewarding chapters of Long's book shows how W. D. Howells channeled Hawthorne into James's fiction." The reviewer added that one of the richest chapters of the book is the author's analysis of James's "Hawthorne."

Long's study, *John O'Hara,* is, according to Marcelle Thiebaux, a portrayal of O'Hara "as a writer who ceaselessly experimented with form." Thiebaux commented in the *New York Times Book Review* that Long "puts O'Hara's American nightmare in . . . a subtle light," providing "a fresh guide to O'Hara's fiction."

BIOGRAPHICAL/CRITICAL SOURCES:

PERIODICALS

Christian Science Monitor, May 11, 1994.
New York Review of Books, July 9, 1994.
New York Times Book Review, March 4, 1984.
Times Literary Supplement, May 8, 1981.
Washington Post Book World, July 3, 1994.

LUTTWAK, Edward N(icholae) 1942-

PERSONAL: Surname is pronounced Loo-twack; born November 4, 1942, in Arad, Rumania; came to the United States, 1972; naturalized citizen, 1981; son of Joseph (a businessman) and Clara (Baruch) Luttwak; married Dalya Iaari, December 14, 1970; children: Yael Rachel, Joseph Emannuel. *Education:* Attended schools in Palermo and Milan, Italy, 1949-55, and Carmel College in England; London School of Economics and Political Science, B.Sc., 1964; Johns Hopkins University, Ph.D., 1975. *Politics:* Republican. *Religion:* Jewish.

ADDRESSES: Office—Center for Strategic and International Studies, Georgetown University, 1800 K St. NW, Washington, DC 20006-2202.

CAREER: Worked in Eastern Europe for CBS-TV, 1964-65; University of Bath, Bath, England, lecturer, 1965-67; Walter J. Levy, London, England, oil consultant, 1967-68; consultant to Naval War College, O.S.D./ Department of Defense, 1973—; Washington Center of Foreign Policy Research, Washington, DC, associate director, 1972-75; Georgetown University, Center for Strategic and International Studies, Washington, DC, senior fellow, 1976-87, research professor in international security affairs, 1978-82, Arlelyh Burke chair in strategy, 1987—, director of geo-economics, 1991—. Visiting professor of political science, Johns Hopkins University, 1973-78; Nimitz lecturer, University of California at Berkeley, 1987; Tanner Lecturer, Yale University, 1989.

WRITINGS:

Coup D'Etat—A Practical Handbook, Allen Lane, 1968, Knopf (New York City), 1969.
A Dictionary of Modern War, Harper (New York City), 1971, new edition with Stuart Koehl, published as *The Dictionary of Modern War,* HarperCollins, 1991.
The Strategic Balance, 1972, Library Press (LaSalle, IL), 1972.
The Political Uses of Sea Power, Johns Hopkins University Press (Baltimore, MD), 1974.
The US-USSR Nuclear Weapons Balance, Sage (Beverly Hills, CA), 1974.
(With Dan Horowitz) *The Israeli Army,* Harper, 1975.
Strategic Power: Military Capabilities and Political Utility, Sage, 1976.
The Grand Strategy of the Roman Empire: From the First Century A.D. to the Third, Johns Hopkins University Press, 1976.
(Editor with Herbert Block and contributor) *The Economic and Military Balance between East and West, 1951-1978,* American Bar Association (Chicago, IL), 1978.
(With R. G. Weinland) *Sea Power in the Mediterranean,* Sage, 1979.

Strategy and Politics: Collected Essays, Transaction Books (New Brunswick, NJ), 1980.

The Grand Strategy of the Soviet Union, St. Martin's (New York City), 1983.

The Pentagon and the Art of War: The Question of Military Reform, Simon & Schuster (New York City), 1985.

Strategy and History, Transaction Books, 1985.

On the Meaning of Victory: Essays on Strategy, Simon & Schuster, 1986.

(Editor with Barry M. Blechman) *Global Security: A Review of Strategic and Economic Issues,* Westview (Boulder, CO), 1987.

Strategy: The Logic of War and Peace, Belknap Press (Cambridge, MA), 1987.

The Endangered American Dream: How to Stop the United States from Becoming a Third World Country and How to Win the Geo-Economic Struggle for Industrial Supremacy, Simon & Schuster, 1993.

OTHER

Contributor to many books, including *World Politics and the Jewish Condition,* edited by Louis Henkin, Quadrangle, 1972; *Military Aspects of the Israeli-Arab Conflict,* edited by Louis Williams, University Publishing Projects, 1975; *The Middle East: Critical Choices for the United States,* edited by Eugene Rostow, Westview, 1976; *Decline of the West? George Kennan and His Critics,* edited by Martin F. Herz, Ethics and Public Policy Center, Georgetown University, 1978; *Struggling for Change in Mainland China: Challenges and Implications,* Institute of International Relations (Taipei), 1980; *NATO: The Next Thirty Years,* edited by Kenneth A. Myers, Center for Strategic and International Studies, 1980; *Reforming the Military,* edited by Jeffrey G. Barlow, Heritage Foundation (Washington, DC), 1980; *Planning U.S. Security,* edited by Philip S. Wronenberg, National Security Affairs Institute, National Defense University, 1981.

Also author of several research papers and contributor to conferences and proceedings. Contributor to periodicals, including *Commentary, Esquire, International Security, Survival,* and *Times Literary Supplement. Coup D'Etat—A Practical Handbook* has been published in several languages, including Dutch, Swedish, and Arabic. Some of Luttwak's other books have been published in Spanish, Italian, and Chinese.

WORK IN PROGRESS: The Emerging Post-Nuclear Era.

SIDELIGHTS: Edward N. Luttwak is a leading analyst of political, military and economic trends as they relate to the United States and its relations with other countries. His books on the Cold War, his history of the Roman Empire, and his book *The Endangered American Dream: How to Stop the United States from Becoming a Third World Country and How to Win the Geo-Economic Struggle for*

Industrial Supremacy, a study of American economic decline, have contributed to the ongoing debate on America's role in the world.

For his study *The Grand Strategy of the Roman Empire: From the First Century A.D. to the Third,* Luttwak drew partly upon his expertise in the fields of modern military and political issues. E. Badian, in the *New York Review of Books,* admires the author's foray into early Roman history: "[Luttwak] provides reassuring demonstration of the fact that, in our depressingly fragmented scholarly world, an outsider, trained in a totally different field, but trained in rigorous thought and endowed with controlled creative imagination, can lovingly steep himself in the mass of technical publications with their minutiae of fact and reasoned conjecture produced by 'the archaeologists, epigraphists, numismatists, and textual critics' (as he, tongue half in cheek, describes modern historians of Rome)—and come up with a fascinating scholarly synthesis that teaches them how they ought to be doing their job."

"Diehard classicists may remain skeptical, may doubt the existence of a grand strategy at all and raise their eyebrows whenever Luttwak uses a jargon more familiar to people working in institutes for modern strategic studies than to scholars accustomed to learned journals in classical philology," states *New Republic* critic Z. Yavetz. "Those who have difficulty understanding Luttwak's terminology in phrases like 'the input and output of the system are finally equated' should start reading the book with his appendix on power and force: 'definitions and implications.' But no classicist will find it easy to contradict [the author's] basic assumption that the Romans had no need of a Clausewitz [the Russian army officer noted for his books on war strategy] to subject their military energies to the discipline of political goals, and that without the knowledge of 'systems analysis' they were capable of designing a large and complex security system."

Badian contends that "Luttwak has done scholarship an immense service by propounding and carefully documenting these stimulating ideas. Every page brings detailed insights into the working of Roman military organization, in strategy and tactics, which, even when not wholly original, draw together and unify what is fragmented in obscure canons of strategic interpretation in terms of rigid categories of peace and war, offense and defense, that have beset Roman (indeed, all ancient) history. A century after Theodor Mommsen first provided the ancient Romans with their treatise on public law, Luttwak has now provided them with the comprehensive theoretical treatment of their strategy and foreign policy. Roman statesmen and commanders, on the whole devoid of the gift for either acute analysis or bold synthesis, would have been equally puzzled by both. They were given to proceeding by practical experience and precedent as recorded and remembered; and the powerful individual, Republican noble or emperor, had full freedom to mold tradition to his personality."

In *The Endangered American Dream* Luttwak turns his attention to contemporary America, offering "a vividly written and cogently reasoned . . . survey of America's economic polarization and decline," as Christopher Byron states in *New York*. In this study Luttwak argues that the United States exhibits many of the attributes of a Third World nation, including chronic high levels of national debt, stagnating living standards, and high unemployment. One chief reason for this situation is the overspending of average Americans and the resulting lack of savings which could be used towards long-term research and development, the infrastructure and industrial equipment. The pathologies of the inner-cities, the decline of public schools, and increasing racial and ethnic tensions also play a part in the decline Luttwak warns against. "Even at the end of his new book, it's not clear where Edward Luttwak is coming from, as they say in his country," remarks Geoffrey Hawthorn in the *London Review of Books*. "He leaves no doubt, however, about where he dreads coming to."

BIOGRAPHICAL/CRITICAL SOURCES:

BOOKS

Luttwak, Edward N., *The Grand Strategy of the Roman Empire: From the First Century A.D. to the Third*, Johns Hopkins University Press, 1976.

PERIODICALS

Booklist, October 1, 1993, p. 223.
Business Book Review, Volume 11, number 1, 1994, p. 3.
Foreign Affairs, Volume 72, number 5, 1993, p. 150.
Fortune, November 15, 1993, p. 196.
Insight, June 1, 1987, p. 61.
London Review of Books, May 26, 1994, p. 12.
Los Angeles Times Book Review, February 17, 1985, p. 3; May 18, 1986, p. 10.
New Republic, November 15, 1975; May 21, 1977.
New Statesman, December 6, 1968.
Newsweek, April 1, 1985.
New York, October 11, 1993, p. 22.
New Yorker, July 19, 1969.
New York Review of Books, June 23, 1977; December 16, 1993, p. 7.
New York Times, February 25, 1985.
New York Times Book Review, February 25, 1984, p. 29; March 10, 1985; June 15, 1986, p. 24; August 30, 1987, p. 22; December 5, 1993, p. 54.
Reason, March, 1994, p. 62.
Spectator, December 13, 1968.
Times Literary Supplement, February 20, 1976; February 10, 1978; August 26, 1983; September 18, 1987, p. 1007; February 4, 1994, p. 6.
Washington Post Book World, March 25, 1984, p. 13; March 3, 1985, p. 1; January 12, 1986, p. 12; May 4, 1986, p. 6; December 12, 1993, p. 4.
World and I, February, 1994, p. 316.

M

MacCARTHY, Fiona 1940-

PERSONAL: Born January 23, 1940, in London, England; daughter of Gerald (an army officer) and Yolande (de Belabre) MacCarthy; married David Mellor (a designer), August 19, 1966; children: Corin, Clare. *Education:* Oxford University, M.A., 1961.

ADDRESSES: Home and office—The Round Building, Hathersage, Sheffield, Yorks S30 1BA, England.

CAREER: Guardian, London, England, features writer, 1963-69; *Evening Standard,* London, features writer, 1969-72; freelance writer, 1972—; *Times,* London, reviewer of books, 1981-92; *Observer,* London, reviewer of books, 1992—.

AWARDS, HONORS: Royal Society of Arts Bicentennial Medal, 1987; Honorary fellowship, Royal College of Arts, 1990.

WRITINGS:

All Things Bright and Beautiful: Design in Britain, University of California Press (Santa Cruz, CA), 1972.
A History of British Design: 1830 to Today, Allen & Unwin (London), 1979.
The Simple Life: C. R. Ashbee in the Cotswolds, University of California Press, 1981.
The British Tradition in Design: From 1880, Humphries (London), 1981.
British Design since 1880: A Visual History, Humphries, 1982.
(Author of introduction and cataloguer, with Patrick Nuttgens) *Eye for Industry: Royal Designers for Industry, 1936-1986,* Humphries/Royal Society of Arts, 1986.
Eric Gill: A Lover's Quest for Art and God, Dutton (New York City), 1989, published in England as *Eric Gill,* Faber and Faber (London), 1989.

William Morris: A Life for Our Time, Faber and Faber, 1994, Knopf (New York City), 1995.

Also author of introduction and cataloguer for *The Omega Workshops,* (London), 1984.

SIDELIGHTS: Fiona MacCarthy told *CA:* "For a century or more, from William Morris onwards, there has been an easily identifiable strain in society in Britain concerned with the improvement of the objects which we use and live with. This movement for reform has, through the years, developed certain ideas on the designer's social role as well as recognizable criteria on aesthetics.

"The intensely idealistic early twentieth-century phase of British design history especially fascinates me. This was the background to my book on C. R. Ashbee, arts and crafts architect and designer, and friend of Frank Lloyd Wright. This was a subject that aroused great public interest: the search for the ideal of a creative life is very much still with us. I have since then developed the theme in two much larger scale biographies of Eric Gill and William Morris, whose ideas about proper human occupation and the relation of art to society are of immense importance to us now. I like to write about *big* subjects, enjoying the challenge of providing a readable, accessible narrative from a mountain of research.'

BIOGRAPHICAL/CRITICAL SOURCES:

PERIODICALS

New York Times Book Review, May 7, 1989, p. 11.
Times (London), April 23, 1980; April 29, 1982; January 26, 1989; March 13, 1989; November 10, 1994.
Times Literary Supplement, November 9, 1984, p. 1280; February 17-23, 1989, p. 160; November 25, 1994, p. 3.
Washington Post Book World, April 9, 1989, p. 3.

MACDONALD, Malcolm
   See ROSS-MACDONALD, Malcolm J(ohn)

*   *   *

MacNEILL, Dand
   See FRASER, George MacDonald

*   *   *

MAIROWITZ, David Zane   1943-

PERSONAL: Born in 1943.

CAREER: Editor and playwright. Visiting professor of theatre at University of California, 1967; *Village Voice*, New York, NY, London drama critic, 1968-76; *Plays and Players*, London, England, drama critic, 1975-80. Visiting professor at Stanford University, 1975. University of Avignon, France, teacher, 1982—. Holds periodical workshops in radio drama and writing, 1982—.

AWARDS, HONORS: Giles Cooper Award, British Broadcasting Corp. (BBC), best radio play of 1989, for *The Stalin Sonata;* Special Recommendation of Jury, Prix Futura, Berlin, 1993, for radio musical *Dictator Gal;* Selection Prix Italia, 1993, for radio play *Fragments in a Vulgar Tongue.*

WRITINGS:

Some of IT, introduction by William S. Burroughs, Knullar, 1969.
(Editor with Peter Stansill) *BAMN (By Any Means Necessary): Outlaw Manifestos and Ephemera, 1965-1970,* Penguin (New York City), 1971.
The Radical Soap Opera: An Impression of the American Left from 1917 to the Present, Wildwood House, 1974, Penguin, 1976, reprinted as *The Radical Soap Opera: Roots of Failure in the American Left,* Avon (New York City), 1976.
(Editor and author of introduction) Rosa Levine Meyer, *Inside German Communism,* Pluto Press (New York City), 1976.
In the Slipstream (stories), Chicago Review Press (Chicago, IL), 1977.
(With German Gonzales) *Reich for Beginners,* Writers and Readers (New York City), 1984.
(With Robert Crumb) *Kafka for Beginners,* Icon Books (London), 1993, published as *Introducing Kafka,* Totem Books, 1994.

RADIO SCRIPTS

Rivers to Cross, British Broadcasting Corp. (BBC), 1982.
Silent Wing, BBC, 1983.
Azari's Aerial Theatre, BBC, 1984.

Transhumance, BBC, 1985.
Chopin's Piano, BBC, 1986.
Maker of Angels, BBC, 1987.
The Stalin Sonata, BBC, 1989.
The Far Cry, BBC, 1990.
The Withering Woman, BBC, 1990.
The Inner Courtyard, BBC, 1991.
Heart of April, BBC, 1992.
Laura Singer, BBC, 1992.
Dictator Gal (radio musical), BBC, 1993.
Fragments in a Vulgar Tongue, BBC, 1993.
Planet of Ashes, BBC, 1993.
The Voluptuous Tango (radio opera), BBC, 1995.

Contributor of *The Stalin Sonata* to *Best Radio Plays of 1989,* Methuen (London), 1990.

OTHER

Also author of *The Law Circus,* 1969, *That Was Laura, But She's Only a Dream,* 1976, *Landscape of Exile,* 1979, and the play *Flash Gordon and the Angels.* Editor of *Running Man,* 1968-69. Contributor of story "Hector's Letter" to the *Pushcart Prize Anthology,* 1988-89, and to *The Best of the Missouri Review,* 1991.

Most of Mr. Mairowitz's radio plays, originally produced in English, have been subsequently translated and produced by the national radios of Belgium, Croatia, Denmark, Finland, France, Germany, Holland, Ireland, Israel, Norway, Poland, Slovenia, South Africa, Sweden, and Switzerland.

SIDELIGHTS: In *The Radical Soap Opera,* David Zane Mairowitz relates some of the highlights in the history of the American political Left. The book is written in the style of a comic soap opera, observed David Caute in *New Statesman,* and focuses on the years between 1917 and 1974. While Caute expressed disappointment with the book's first half, which treated the Old Left, the reviewer remarked that Mairowitz's exploration of the New Left era "is something else, a brilliantly sustained and sympathetic essay about the triumphs and tribulations of the author's own generation. It is the best thing I have read on the subject and shows that Mairowitz possesses a rare literary gift, a marvellous empathy for the rapid fluctuations in social psychology so rampant in recent years."

BIOGRAPHICAL/CRITICAL SOURCES:

PERIODICALS

New Statesman, October 25, 1974.
Times Literary Supplement, November 18, 1977.
Washington Post Book World, May 16, 1976.

MAJOR, H. M.
See JARVIS, Sharon

*   *   *

MAKKREEL, Rudolf A.   1939-

PERSONAL: Born May 29, 1939, in Antwerp, Belgium; immigrated to United States, 1951, naturalized citizen, 1964; son of Leendert (a businessman) and Maria (Struyk) Makkreel; married Frances Tanikawa (a scholar), 1967; children: Karen. *Education:* Columbia University, B.A., 1960, Ph.D., 1966.

ADDRESSES: Office—Department of Philosophy, Emory University, 1365 Clifton Rd. N.E., Atlanta, GA 30322.

CAREER: University of California, San Diego, assistant professor of philosophy, 1966-73; Emory University, Atlanta, GA, associate professor, 1973-85, professor of philosophy, 1985-91, Charles Howard Chandler Professor of Philosophy, 1991—.

MEMBER: American Philosophical Association, American Psychological Association (member of Philosophy of Psychology Division), American Society of Aesthetics, Society for the Study of the History of Philosophy.

AWARDS, HONORS: Fellow of Humboldt Foundation, 1978-79; grants from Thyssen Foundation, 1979-84, and National Endowment for the Humanities, 1981-84.

WRITINGS:

Dilthey, Philosopher of the Human Studies, Princeton University Press (Princeton, NJ), 1975, 3rd edition, 1992.
(Author of introduction) W. Dilthey, *Descriptive Psychology and Historical Understanding,* Nijhoff (Dordrecht, Netherlands), 1977.
(Editor and translator with Frithjof Rodi) *Selected Works of Wilhelm Dilthey,* Volume 5, Princeton University Press, 1986, Volume 1: *Introduction to the Human Sciences,* 1989.
(Editor with John Scanlon) *Dilthey and Phenomenology,* Center for Advanced Research in Phenomenology, 1987.
Imagination and Interpretation in Kant: The Hermeneutical Import of the 'Critique of Judgment', University of Chicago Press (Chicago, IL), 1990.

Contributor to philosophy journals. *Journal of the History of Philosophy,* book review editor, 1981-83, editor, 1983—.

WORK IN PROGRESS: Editing, with Jacob Owensby, *Approaches to Dilthey's Philosophy,* publication by Center for Advanced Research in Philosophy; *Interpretation and Historical Judgment* and Volume 4 of *Selected Works of*

Wilhelm Dilthey (The History of Hermeneutics and the Understanding of History).

SIDELIGHTS: Rudolf A. Makkreel told *CA:* "My interests in aesthetics and epistemology have intersected in the topic of imagination, which is central to both my books, *Dilthey, Philosopher of the Human Studies* and *Imagination and Interpretation in Kant: The Hermeneutical Import of the 'Critique of Judgment'.* Another central interest is hermeneutics and the status of the human sciences. Wilhelm Dilthey, a German philosopher and historian who lived from 1833 to 1911, is especially relevant to my work because of his important contributions to aesthetics, hermeneutics and the human sciences."

BIOGRAPHICAL/CRITICAL SOURCES:

PERIODICALS

American Historical Review, October, 1976.

*   *   *

MALLEY, Ern
See STEWART, Harold Frederick

*   *   *

MANDEL, Oscar   1926-

PERSONAL: Born 1926, in Antwerp, Belgium; U.S citizen; married Adriana Schizzano, 1960. *Education:* New York University, B.A., 1947; Columbia University, M.A., 1948; Ohio State University, Ph.D., 1951.

ADDRESSES: Office—Division of Humanities and Social Sciences, California Institute of Technology, Pasadena, CA 91125.

CAREER: Affiliated with University of Nebraska, Lincoln, 1955-60; University of Amsterdam, The Netherlands, Fulbright lecturer, 1960-61; California Institute of Technology, Pasadena, associate professor, 1961-65, professor of humanities, 1966—. *Military service:* U.S. Army, 1953-55.

MEMBER: Modern Language Association of America, Dramatists Guild, Societe des Auteurs et Compositeurs Dramatiques, College Art Association.

WRITINGS:

FICTION AND POETRY

Chi Po and the Sorcerer: A Chinese Tale for Children and Philosophers, Tuttle (Ruttland, VT), 1964.
Gobble-Up Stories (fables), Bruce Humphries, 1966.
Simplicities (poems), Spectrum Productions (Los Angeles), 1974.

Collected Lyrics and Epigrams, Whitmarsh (Hollywood), 1981.

The Kukkurrik Fables (fiction), Spectrum Productions, 1987.

LITERARY CRITICISM

A Definition of Tragedy, New York University Press (New York City), 1961.

(Editor) *The Theatre of Don Juan: A Collection of Plays and Views, 1930-1963,* University of Nebraska Press (Lincoln), 1963.

(Editor and translator) Pierre De Marivaux, *Seven Comedies by Marivaux,* Cornell University Press (Ithaca, NY), 1968.

(Compiler, translator, and author of introduction) *Five Comedies of Medieval France,* Dutton (New York City), 1970.

(Editor and author of introduction) *Three Classic Don Juan Plays,* University of Nebraska Press, 1971.

(Translator and author of introduction) Ludwig Tieck, *The Land of Upside Down,* Fairleigh Dickinson University Press (East Brunswick, NJ), 1978.

Philoctetes and the Fall of Troy: Plays, Documents, Iconography, Interpretations, Including Versions by Sophocles, Andre Gide, Oscar Mandel, and Heiner Muller, University of Nebraska Press, 1981.

Annotations to "Vanity Fair," University Press of America (Lanham, MD), 1981.

(Translator and author of introduction) *Thomas Corneille's Ariadne,* University Presses of Florida (Gainsville), 1982.

The Book of Elaborations: Essays, New Directions Publishing (New York City), 1985.

August von Kotzebue: The Comedy, the Man, Pennsylvania State University Press (University Park), 1988.

PLAYS

Island, produced in Amherst, MA, 1961.

Dance to No Music, produced in Pasadena, CA, 1965.

The Monk Who Wouldn't, first produced in Pasadena, CA, 1964; produced Off-Broadway, 1965.

The Virgin and the Unicorn (also see below), produced in Santa Monica, CA, 1966.

The Fatal French Dentist (one-act; produced in Santa Monica, CA, 1966), Samuel French, 1967.

Of Angels and Eskimos, produced at Melrose Theatre, 1969.

Collected Plays, Unicorn Press, Volume 1, 1970, Volume 2, 1972.

The Playboy of Seville, produced Off-Broadway, 1971.

Living Room with Six Oppressions, produced in New York City, 1972.

The Patriots of Nantucket: A Romantic Comedy of the American Revolution (produced in Los Angeles, 1976), Spectrum Productions, 1976.

Moliere's "Amphitryon," in a Licentious Translation (produced in Pasadena, CA, 1972), Spectrum Productions, 1976.

(Translator) De Marivaux, *The False Confessions,* produced in Edinburgh, Scotland, at Royal Lyceum Theatre, May, 1977.

L'Arc de Philoctete, first produced in Paris, broadcast by Radio-France, 1985.

Sigismund, Prince of Poland: A Baroque Entertainment, University Press of America, 1988.

The Virgin and the Unicorn: Four Plays by Oscar Mandel, Spectrum Productions, 1993.

OTHER

Contributor to *The Pushcart Prize, VIII: Best of the Small Presses,* edited by Bill Henderson, Pushcart (Wainscott, NY), 1983. Contributor of articles to professional journals, including *American Scholar, Antioch Review, Centennial Review, Comparative Literature, Dalhousie, South Atlantic Quarterly,* and *Virginia Quarterly Review.*

SIDELIGHTS: Oscar Mandel's *The Book of Elaborations: Essays* is a collection of essays that evolved from the author's poems. As Yaffa Draznin notes in the *Los Angeles Times Book Review,* the human condition is Mandel's subject matter. "With fetching humility," writes Draznin, "Oscar Mandel offers his views as supplications rather than defiances, responses of his own admittedly peculiar personality to experiences and conditioning. He invites his readers to engage in civilized discussion where disagreement need not lead to judgment, disparagement or, God forbid, an aggressive spring to the jugular."

BIOGRAPHICAL/CRITICAL SOURCES:

PERIODICALS

Los Angeles Times, December 18, 1981.
Los Angeles Times Book Review, November 10, 1985.*

*   *   *

MANN, Deborah
    See BLOOM, Ursula (Harvey)

*   *   *

MARCH, Josie
    See TITCHENER, Louise

MARIAS (AGUILERA), Julian 1914-

PERSONAL: Born June 17, 1914, in Valladolid, Spain; son of Julian and Maria (Aguilera) Marias; married Dolores Franco (a professor and author), August 14, 1941 (died December 24, 1977); children: Miguel, Fernando, Javier, Alvaro. *Education:* University of Madrid, Lic.Fil., 1936, Ph.D., 1951. *Religion:* Catholic. *Avocational interests:* Photography, searching for and buying old books.

ADDRESSES: Home—Vallehermoso 34, Madrid 28015, Spain.

CAREER: Aula Nueva, Madrid, Spain, professor of philosophy, 1940-48; Instituto de Humanidades, Madrid, cofounder and professor, 1948-50; professor of Spanish at several American colleges in Madrid, Smith College, San Francisco College for Women (now Lone Mountain College), Middlebury College, Tulane University, and Mary Baldwin College, 1952-71; University of Puerto Rico, Rio Piedras, visiting professor and research professor, 1956-64; Seminario de Estudios de Humanidades, Madrid, director, 1960-70. Universidad Nacional de Educacion a Distancia, Madrid, Jose Ortega y Gasset Professor of Spanish Philosophy, 1980-84. Visiting professor at Wellesley College, 1951-52, Harvard University, 1952, University of California, Los Angeles, 1955, Yale University, 1956, Mary Baldwin College, 1966, Indiana University, 1967, 1969, 1970, 1972-76, and University of Oklahoma, 1968 and 1971. Member of Spanish Cortes (Parliament), 1977-78. Lecturer (in Spanish, French, English, German) in most countries of western Europe, United States, Puerto Rico, Mexico, South America, India, and Israel. *Military service:* Spanish Republic Army, 1937-39.

MEMBER: International Institute of Philosophy, International Society for the History of Ideas, Hispanic Society of America, Fundacion de Estudios Sociologicos (president), Sociedad Peruana de Filosofia, Sociedad Espanola de Psicologia, Instituto Brasileiro de Filosofia, Real Academia Espanola, Real Academia de Bellas Artes.

AWARDS, HONORS: Fastenrath Prize, Royal Academy of Spain, 1947, for *Miguel de Unamuno;* Rockefeller Foundation fellow, 1957-60; John F. Kennedy Prize for intellectual achievement, North American Studies Institute of Barcelona, 1964; Juan Palomo Prize, 1971, and Gulbenkian Essay Award, Academy of the Latin World (Paris), 1972, both for *Antropologia metafisica: La estructura empirica de la vida humana;* Ramon Godo Lallana Prize for Journalism, 1976, for series of articles; Leon Felipe Prize, 1979, for "Una jornada muy particular"; Great Cross of Alfonso X el Sabio and of Isabel la Catolica; Officier de la Legion d'Honneur; doctor honoris causa from University of Buenos Aires, National University of Tucuman, Catholic University of Tucuman, and University of Montevideo.

WRITINGS:

IN ENGLISH TRANSLATION

Historia de la filosofia (also see below), Revista de Occidente (Madrid), 1941, 32nd edition, 1980, translation by Stanley Appelbaum and Clarence C. Stowbridge published as *History of Philosophy,* Dover (New York City), 1967.

Miguel de Unamuno (also see below), Espasa-Calpe (Madrid), 1943, 2nd edition, 1968, translation by Frances M. Lopez-Morillas, Harvard University Press (Cambridge, MA), 1966.

Introduccion a la filosofia (also see below), Revista de Occidente, 1947, 12th edition, 1979, translation by Kenneth S. Reid and Edward Sarmiento published as *Reason and Life: The Introduction to Philosophy,* Yale University Press (New Haven, CT), 1956.

El metodo historico de las generaciones (also see below), Revista de Occidente, 1949, 5th edition, 1970, translation by Harold C. Raley published as *Generations: A Historical Method,* University of Alabama Press (University, AL), 1970.

Idea de la metafisica (also see below), Columba (Buenos Aires), 1954, 3rd edition, Revista de Occidente, 1958, translation by A. R. Caponigri published in *Contemporary Spanish Philosophy,* University of Notre Dame Press (Notre Dame, IN), 1967.

Biografia de la filosofia (also see below), Emece (Madrid), 1954, 6th edition, Revista de Occidente, 1980, translation by Raley published as *A Biography of Philosophy,* University of Alabama Press, 1984.

Los Estados Unidos en escorzo (also see below), Emece (Buenos Aires), 1956, 5th edition, 1972, translation by Blanche de Puy and Raley published in *America in the Fifties and Sixties: Julian Marias on the United States,* Pennsylvania State University Press (University Park, PA), 1972.

Don Quijote as Seen by Sancho Panza (also see below; originally published in Spanish as "Don Quijote visto desde Sancho Panza" as a prologue to *Biografia de Sancho Panza: Filosofo de la sensatez* [also see below]), Indian Institute of Culture, 1956.

(Editor and author of introduction) *Jose Ortega y Gasset, Meditaciones del Quijote,* Ediciones de la Universidad de Puerto Rico (Rio Piedras), 1957, 3rd edition, 1985, translation by Evelyn Rugg and Diego Marin published as *Meditations on Quijote,* Norton (New York City), 1961.

Ortega, Volume 1: *Circunstancia y vocacion* (also see below), Revista de Occidente, 1960, 3rd edition, 1983, translation by Lopez-Morillas published as *Ortega y Gasset: Circumstances and Vocation,* University of Oklahoma Press (Norman, OK), 1970.

Analisis de los Estados Unidos (also see below), Guadarrama, 1968, 2nd edition, Revista de Occidente, 1970, translation by de Puy and Raley published in *America in the Fifties and Sixties: Julian Marias on the United States,* Pennsylvania State University Press, 1972.

Antropologia metafisica: La estructura empirica de la vida humana (also see below), Revista de Occidente, 1970, 3rd edition, 1983, translation by Lopez-Morillas published as *Metaphysical Anthropology: The Empirical Structure of Human Life,* Pennsylvania State University Press, 1971.

Philosophy as Dramatic Theory (collection of fourteen essays originally published in Spanish), translated by James Parsons, Pennsylvania State University Press, 1971.

Espana inteligible, Revista de Occidente, 1985, 4th edition, 1986, translation by Frances M. Lopex-Morillas published as *Understanding Spain,* University of Michigan Press (Ann Arbor, MI), 1990.

IN SPANISH

(With Carlos Alonso del Real and Manuel Granell) *Juventud en el mundo antiguo: Crucero universitario por el Mediterraneo,* Espasa-Calpe (Madrid), 1934.

La filosofia del Padre Gratry (also see below), Ediciones Escorial, 1941, 5th edition, Revista de Occidente, 1972.

El tema del hombre, Revista de Occidente, 1943, 7th edition, Espasa-Calpe, 1981.

San Anselmo y el insensato (also see below), Revista de Occidente, 1944, 5th edition, 1973.

(Editor and author of prologue) Miguel de Unamuno, *Obras selectas,* Pleyade (Madrid), 1946.

(Editor) Plato, *Fedro,* Revista de Occidente, 1948.

Ortega y la idea de la razon vital, A. Zuniga (Madrid), 1948.

La filosofia espanola actual (also see below), Espasa-Calpe (Buenos Aires), 1948, 7th edition, 1977.

(Editor with German Bleiberg) *Diccionario de literatura espanola,* Revista de Occidente, 1949, 4th edition, 1972.

Ortega y tres antipodas: Un ejemplo de intriga intelectual (also see below), Revista de Occidente (Buenos Aires), 1950.

(Compiler and author of introduction and notes) *La filosofia en sus textos* (anthology), two volumes, Labor (Barcelona), 1950, 2nd edition, three volumes, 1963.

(Author of prologue) *Biografia de Sancho Panza: Filosofo de la sensatez,* Aedos, 1952.

El existencialismo en Espana (also see below), Universidad Nacional de Colombia, 1953.

La universidad: Realidad problematica, Cruz del Sur (Santiago), 1953.

Ensayos de teoria (also see below), Barna (Barcelona), 1954, 2nd edition, Revista de Occidente, 1959.

Aqui y ahora (also see below), Espasa-Calpe, 1954, 2nd edition, Revista de Occidente, 1959.

Universidad y sociedad en los Estados Unidos, Langa (Madrid), 1954.

Ensayos de convivencia (also see below), Sudamericana (Buenos Aires), 1955, 3rd edition, 1966.

La estructura social (also see below), Sociedad de Estudios y Publicaciones (Madrid), 1955, 6th edition, 1972, new edition, Alianza Editorial, 1993.

La imagen de la vida humana (also see below), Emece, 1955, 2nd edition, Revista de Occidente, 1960.

El intelectual y su mundo (also see below), Atlantida (Buenos Aires), 1956, 2nd edition, Revista de Occidente, 1959.

Ataraxia y alcionismo, Instituto Ibys (Madrid), 1957.

El espiritu europeo, Guadarrama (Madrid), 1957.

El oficio del pensamiento: Ensayos (includes "Don Quijote visto desde Sancho Panza"), Biblioteca Nueva (Madrid), 1958, 4th edition, Revista de Occidente, 1970.

El lugar del peligro (also see below), Taurus (Madrid), 1958.

(With others) *Experiencia de la vida,* Revista de Occidente, 1960.

Imagen de la India (also see below), includes photographs by Marias, Revista de Occidente, 1961, 3rd edition, 1970.

Ortega ante Goethe, Taurus, 1961.

Los espanoles (also see below), Revista de Occidente, 1962, 3rd edition, 1966.

La Espana posible en tiempo de Carlos III (also see below), Sociedad de Estudios y Publicaciones, 1963, 2nd edition, Revista de Occidente, 1966.

El tiempo que ni vuelve ni tropieza, Editora y Distribuidora Hispano Americana (Barcelona), 1964, 3rd edition, Revista de Occidente, 1966.

(With Pedro Lain Entralgo) *Historia de la filosofia y de la ciencia,* Guadarrama, 1964, 4th edition, 1968.

Observador espanol en los Estados Unidos (contains selections from *Los Estados Unidos en escorzo*), edited by Edward R. Mulvihill and Roberto G. Sanchez, Oxford University Press, 1964.

Sobre la piel de toro, Ayma (Barcelona), 1965.

Nuestra Andalucia (also see below), watercolors by Alfredo Ramon, R. Diaz-Casariego (Madrid), 1966, 2nd edition, Revista de Occidente, 1970.

Consideracion de Cataluna (also see below; contains articles originally published in *El Noticiero Universal,* 1965), Ayma, 1966, 2nd edition, Revista de Occidente, 1970.

El uso linguistico (address given at Real Academia Espanola in Madrid, June 20, 1965), Columba, 1966.

Meditaciones sobre la sociedad espanola (also see below), Alianza Editorial, 1966, 3rd edition, Revista de Occidente, 1970.

Al margen de estos clasicos: Autores espanoles del siglo XX, A. Aguado (Madrid), 1966.

Valle-Inclan en el ruedo iberico, Columba, 1967.

(Editor and author of prologue) Gaspar Melchor de Jovellanos, *Diarios,* Alianza Editorial (Madrid), 1967.

Israel: Una resurreccion (also see below), Columba, 1968, 5th edition, Revista de Occidente, 1970.

Nuevos ensayos de filosofia (also see below), Revista de Occidente, 1968, 3rd edition, 1970.

Esquema de nuestra situacion, Columba, 1970.

Visto y no visto: Cronicas de cine, two volumes, Guadarrama, 1970.

Acerca de Ortega, Revista de Occidente, 1971.

Tres visiones de la vida humana, Salvat, 1972.

Innovacion y arcaismo, Revista de Occidente, 1973.

J. Soler Planas: El pensamiento de Julian Marias, Revista de Occidente, 1973.

La justicia social y otras justicias, Espasa-Calpe, 1973, 2nd edition, Revista de Occidente, 1979.

Sobre Hispanoamerica: Con varias meditaciones argentinas, Revista de Occidente, 1973, enlarged edition, Alianza Editorial, 1986.

Literatura y generaciones, Espasa-Calpe, 1975.

La Espana real, Espasa-Calpe, Volume 1: *La Espana real,* 1976, 6th edition, 1979, Volume 2: *La devolucion de Espana,* 1977, 2nd edition, 1979, Volume 3: *Espana en nuestras manos,* 1978, Volume IV: *Cinco anos de Espana,* 1981, 3rd edition, 1982.

(With Alain Michel and Carlos Miralles) *Estudios sobre humanismo clasico,* Fundacion Pastor de Estudios Clasicos (Madrid), 1977.

(With others) *Higiene preventiva de la tercera edad,* Karpos (Madrid), c. 1979.

Problemas del cristianismo, Biblioteca de Autores Cristianos (Madrid), 1979, 3rd edition, 1982.

La mujer en el siglo XX, Alianza, 1980, 5th edition, 1982.

(With others) *Libertades personales y convivencia social,* Karpos, c. 1980.

(With others) *La droga y la juventud,* Karpos, 1981.

Ortega: Las trayectorias, Revista de Occidente, 1983.

Breve tratado de la ilusion, Revista de Occidente, 1984, 2nd edition, 1985.

Cara y cruz de la electronica, Revista de Occidente, 1985.

Hispanoamerica, Revista de Occidente, 1986.

La libertad en juego, Revista de Occidente, 1986.

La mujer y su sombra, Alianza Editorial, 1986, 2nd edition, 1987.

La felicidad humana, Alianza Editorial, 1987, 4th edition, 1994.

Una vida presente, Memorias I-III, Alianza Editorial, 1988-89.

Generaciones y constelaciones (new edition of *El metodo historico de las generaciones,* see below), Alianza Editorial, 1989.

Domingo Henares: Hombre y sociedad en Julian Marias, Diputacion de Albacete, 1991.

La educacion sentimental, Alianza Editorial, 1992.

Razon de la filosofia, Alianza Editorial, 1993.

Mapa del mundo personal, Alianza Editorial, 1993, 2nd edition, 1994.

OMNIBUS VOLUMES

La filosofia espanola actual [and] *Existencialismo en Espana,* Revista de Occidente, 1955, enlarged edition published as *La Escuela de Madrid* (also see below), Emece, 1959, 2nd edition, Revista de Occidente, 1960.

Obras, Revista de Occidente, Volume 1: *Historia de la filosofia,* 1958, Volume 2: *Introduction a la filosofia, Idea de la metafisica,* [and] *Biografia de la filosofia,* 1958, Volume 3: *Aqui y ahora, Ensayos de convivencia,* [and] *Los Estados Unidos en escorzo,* 1959, Volume 4: *San Anselmo y el insensato, La filosofia del Padre Gratry, Ensayos de teoria,* [and] *El intelectual y su mundo,* 1959, Volume 5: *Miguel de Unamuno, La Escuela de Madrid,* [and] *La imagen de la vida humana* (also see below), 1960, Volume 7: *Los espanoles, La Espana posible en tiempo de Carlos III,* [and] *El tiempo que ni vuelve ni tropieza,* 1966, Volume 6: *El metodo historico de las generaciones, La estructura social,* [and] *El oficio del pensamiento,* 1970, Volume 8: *Analisis de los Estados Unidos, Israel: Una resurreccion, Imagen de la India, Meditaciones sobre la sociedad espanola, Consideracion de Cataluna, Nuestra Andalucia,* [and] *Nuevos ensayos de filosofia,* 1970, Volume 9: *Ortega y tres antipodas, El lugar del peligro, Ortega: Circumstancia y vocacion,* [and] *Ensayos,* 1982, Volume 10: *Antropologia metafiscia,* [and] *Ensayos,* 1982.

La imagen de la vida humana y dos ejemplos literarios: Cervantes, Valle-Inclan, Revista de Occidente, 1971.

Nuestra Andalucia [and] *Consideracion de Cataluna,* Revista de Occidente, 1972.

Imagen de la India [and] *Israel: Una resureccion,* Revista de Occidente, 1973.

Also contributor to *Interpretation: The Poetry of Meaning,* edited by S. R. Hopper and D. L. Miller, Harcourt (New York City), 1967; *International Encyclopedia of Social Sciences,* edited by David L. Sills, Macmillan and Free Press (New York City), 1968; *This Land of Europe: A Photographic Exploration,* edited by Dennis Stock, Kodansha International (Tokyo), 1976; and *Un siglo de Ortega y Gasset,* Mezquita (Madrid), 1984. Contributor to numerous other journals, including *ABC, El Noticiero Universal*

(Barcelona), *La Nacion* (Buenos Aires), *Gaceta Ilustrada* (Madrid), *Insula* (Madrid), *La Vanguardia* (Barcelona), and *Commonweal.*

TRANSLATOR

Hermann Hoepker-Aschoff, *El dinero y el oro,* Revista de Occidente, 1940.

Max Scheler, *De lo eterno en el hombre: La esencia y los atributos de Dios,* [Madrid], 1940.

R. Lehmann, *Introduccion a la filosofia,* Losada, 1941.

Alphonse Gratry, *El conocimiento de Dios,* Pegaso (Madrid), 1941.

Paul Hazard, *La crisis de la conciencia europea* (1680-1715), Pegaso, 1941.

(And editor) G. W. Leibnitz, *Discurso de metafisica,* Revista de Occidente, 1942.

(And editor) Seneca, *Sobre la felicidad,* Revista de Occidente, 1943.

(And editor) Wilhelm Dilthey, *Teoria de las concepciones del mundo,* Revista de Occidente, 1944.

Paul Hazard, *El pensamiento europeo en el siglo XVIII,* [Madrid], 1946.

Eduard Spranger, *Cultura y educacion,* [Buenos Aires], 1948.

Karl Buehler, *Teoria del lenguaje,* [Madrid], 1950.

Wilhelm Dilthey, *Introduccion a las ciencias del espiritu,* Revista de Occidente, 1956.

(With Araujo) Aristotle, *Etica a Nicomaco,* Instituto de Estudios Politicos, 1960.

Also translator and author of introduction and notes, *Aristotle's Politica,* edited by Maria Araujo, Instituto de Estudios Politicos; translator of works by Auguste Comte and Immanuel Kant; literary advisor and contributor to *Revista de Occidente.*

WORK IN PROGRESS: Las trayectorias del siglo XX.

SIDELIGHTS: In 1939, Spanish philosopher Julian Marias spent three months in prison after being denounced for anti-Franco activities during the Spanish Civil War. Although charges against Marias were eventually dropped, he soon discovered that political pressure led the University of Madrid to refuse him the doctorate degree that he had expected to receive and kept any Spanish university from offering him a teaching position.

In *Responsible Vision: The Philosophy of Julian Marias,* Harold Raley speculates that Marias's inability to find a university position sparked the philosopher's prolific writing career. Raley comments: "Denied access to other fora, Marias had only the written word. . . . He became a writer in the true sense, and this means that he is not simply a man who writes but a man who can be himself only by writing."

While he devoted much of his time to writing, Marias earned a living by teaching at private schools and conducting courses for American university programs in Madrid. He later was invited to the United States and Hispanic America for the first of many trips abroad as a visiting professor.

Marias's inability to find an adequate position in Spain seems to have brought good fortune into his life. In his book *Julian Marias,* Anton Donoso remarks, "Coming to the United States was a decisive experience in Marias' life for from that time forward the country was one more factor in his work." According to Donoso, Marias believes his first visit to the United States helped him complete one of his most important books, *The Structure of Society* [in Spanish, *La estructura social*]. Donoso quotes Marias's recollection of the trip: "When I went [to the United States] for the first time, I already had spent a few years reflecting on the problem of what . . . is the structure of society. The book entitled *The Structure of Society* that I was able to publish at the end of 1955 was born of my profound experiences of the United States as seen from Spain, of a constant comparison of social structures so different that they permitted me to see that very reality that had previously escaped me." Marias also filled two volumes with essays concerning his trips to America. A selection of his comments was translated into English as *America in the Fifties and Sixties: Julian Marias on the United States.*

Perhaps the greatest influence on Marias's writing has been the work of Spanish philosopher Jose Ortega y Gasset, with whom Marias was associated for twenty-three years. In her *Library Journal* review of Marias's book on his mentor, *Ortega y Gasset: Circumstances and Vocation,* Rosemary Neiswender notes: "Marias' patient, deeply considered study of Ortega contributes significantly to the analysis of this thinker. . . . The entire range of his work is scrutinized with an awareness only possible in a devoted pupil who was later both colleague and friend."

Marias's close association with Ortega may explain why very little has been written about Marias's work. As Raley points out, many critics erroneously feel that anything Marias writes is just a repetition of Ortega's thought. On the contrary, Raley believes, "Marias has not only expanded certain Ortegan concepts but surpassed Ortega completely in others. [Ortega's] tentative concepts of generations and circumstances, for instance, are definitively treated in Marias."

Some critics maintain that the two philosophers could not have worked together for such a long time without in some way influencing each other. For instance, Donoso identifies many similarities between Marias and Ortega, including the emphasis in their writings on man's search for the truth. According to Donoso, both Marias and Ortega agree "that philosophy's only method is that of Jericho, that is, the making of repeated circles—ever more narrow—around things, approaching them until they reveal themselves, until the 'walls' that hide them crumble . . . to expose their truth."

The University of Madrid finally granted Marias his doctorate in 1951 based on his original dissertation, which had been published ten years before. Vindication for earlier hardships came in 1977 when Spain's King Juan Carlos appointed Marias to the Cortes (Spanish parliament) to assist other senators in drafting a new constitution. Despite years of political pressure that threatened to ruin his career aspirations, Marias has become "a major figure in the intellectual life of Spain," notes Raley.

Raley summarizes Marias's philosophic thought and emphasizes the important role Marias gives to truth in his writings. "As Marias sees it," Raley comments, "to seek and tell the truth is still the greatest mission of man. . . . The philosophy of Julian Marias is a clear and rare vision of truth. In these fearful times of chilling hatreds and titantic dooms, surely such an example of intellectual brilliance and decency is worthy of our attention."

BIOGRAPHICAL/CRITICAL SOURCES:

BOOKS

Donoso, Anton, *Julian Marias,* Twayne, 1982.
Raley, Harold, *Responsible Vision: The Philosophy of Julian Marias,* American Hispanist, 1980.

PERIODICALS

America, January 14, 1967.
Books Abroad, winter, 1970.
Christian Century, September 9, 1970.
Library Journal, November 1, 1970.
Times Literary Supplement, June 15, 1967.
University Bookman, summer, 1972.
Yale Review, autumn, 1972.

—*Sketch by Marian Gonsior*

*　　*　　*

McCULLOCH, Sarah
    See URE, Jean

*　　*　　*

MILES, Betty   1928-

PERSONAL: Born May 16, 1928, in Chicago, IL; daughter of David D. (an editor) and Helen (an editor; maiden name, Otte) Baker; married Matthew B. Miles (a social psychologist), September 27, 1949; children: Sara, David Baker, Ellen. *Education:* Antioch College, B.A., 1950.

ADDRESSES: Home—94 Sparkill Ave., Tappan, NY 10983.

CAREER: New Lincoln School, Manhattan, New York, began as secretary, became assistant kindergarten teacher, 1950-51; Bank Street College of Education, New York City, publications associate, 1958-65; instructor in children's language and literature 1971—. Freelance writer, 1965—. Consultant to Random House Beginner Books, National Coordinating Council on Drug Education, and the Children's Television Workshop for series *Sesame Street.*

MEMBER: PEN, Authors Guild, Authors League of America.

AWARDS, HONORS: Distinguished Achievement Award, Educational Press Association, 1973; Child Association Book of the Year and Outstanding Science Books for Children Award, both 1974, both for *Save the Earth: An Ecology Handbook for Kids;* Child Association Book of the Year, 1974, for *The Real Me;* Mark Twain Award, 1984, and Georgia Children's Book Award, 1986, both for *The Secret Life of the Underwear Champ.*

WRITINGS:

PICTURE BOOKS

A House for Everyone, illustrated by Jo Lowrey, Knopf (New York City), 1958.
What Is the World?, illustrated by Remy Charlip, Knopf, 1958.
The Cooking Book, illustrated by Lowrey, Knopf, 1959.
Having a Friend, illustrated by Eric Blegvad, Knopf, 1959.
A Day of Summer, illustrated by Charlip, Knopf, 1960.
A Day of Winter, illustrated by Charlip, Knopf, 1961.
Mr. Turtle's Mystery, illustrated by Margot Tomes, Knopf, 1961.
The Feast on Sullivan Street, illustrated by Kurt Werth, Knopf, 1963.
(With Joan Blos) *Joe Finds a Way,* illustrated by Lee Ames, Singer, 1967.
A Day of Autumn, illustrated by Marjorie Auerbach, Knopf, 1967.
A Day of Spring, illustrated by Auerbach, Knopf, 1970.
(With Blos) *Just Think,* illustrated by Pat Grant Porter, Knopf, 1971.
Around and Around—Love, Knopf, 1975.
Hey! I'm Reading!, illustrated by Sylvie Wickstrom, Knopf, 1995.

YOUNG ADULT FICTION

The Real Me, Knopf, 1974.
All It Takes Is Practice, Knopf, 1976.

Just the Beginning, Knopf, 1976.
Looking On, Knopf, 1978.
The Trouble with Thirteen, Knopf, 1979.
Maudie and Me and the Dirty Book, Knopf, 1980.
The Secret Life of the Underwear Champ, Knopf, 1981.
I Would If I Could, Knopf, 1982.
Sink or Swim, Knopf, 1986.

OTHER

Save the Earth: An Ecology Handbook for Kids, Knopf, 1974, revised edition published as *Save the Earth: An Action Handbook for Kids,* 1991.

Also editor and author of film and television scripts and pamphlets, including *Super Me,* written for the National Coordinating Council on Drug Education in 1975, and *Little Miss Muppet Fights Back,* Feminists on Children's Media. Contributor of articles to numerous magazines; contributor of story to *Free to Be You and Me,* McGraw, 1974. Associate editor of *The Bank Street Readers,* Macmillan, 1965-69.

SIDELIGHTS: "I always hope, when my ideas have become a book, that my readers will enjoy sharing experiences and feelings with my characters—and with me," Betty Miles once commented. Miles has provided her readers with a wide range of experiences through her books, which include fiction and nonfiction for various ages. Miles's work touches on topics of current interest, such as ecology, censorship, and discrimination, as well as subjects of perennial interest for young people: growing pains, social adjustment, personal responsibility, and self-esteem. "I always hope that what I write will be useful to children," the author wrote in *Something about the Author Autobiography Series* (*SAAS*). "I hope that reading will help them, as it has helped me, to find what all of us are searching for, which is ourselves."

Stories played an important role in the author's childhood. Even before she learned to read, Miles enjoyed listening to the tales and poems her parents recited to her. "Just the sound of the words pleased me," she remarked. Books were important to the young Miles while she was growing up in Baghdad, Iraq, where her parents served as missionaries. When she was six, Miles's family returned to the United States; the move, while exciting, was a big adjustment, she recalled: "The sudden, hearty American strangeness of small-town Ohio to a shy, only child with an English accent, golden curls, and a total innocence of American ways remains sharp in my memory."

Miles soon adjusted, however, and excelled as a student. Her early literary influences were Lewis Carroll, Edward Lear, James Thurber, and P. G. Wodehouse, primarily writers with a humorous or satirical edge. A year as coeditor of her high school paper led to an interest in journal-ism, and later at Antioch College she edited the school paper and worked on a small town newspaper.

While working as a teacher's assistant in Manhattan's New Lincoln School, Miles became interested in writing her own books for young people. She enrolled at Bank Street College of Education where she joined the Writers' Laboratory, a group of children's book authors who critiqued each others' manuscripts and provided support and encouragement. During this period, Miles took time off from work to raise a family, which gave her another perspective on children's books. "Matt and I read to them for endless hours—the rhythms of Farmer Small and Little Bear and so many others still resonate in my memory— and I learned about picture books from the real experts in children's literature," the author recalled in *SAAS.* She continued working on her own manuscripts and collected three years' worth of rejection slips before her first book, *A House for Everyone,* was accepted by Knopf, which has been her publisher ever since.

That book, which explains how different kinds of families live together, shows what Miles calls her "didactic streak." "I think young readers deserve to have their questions taken seriously in books," she commented in her autobiographical essay. Thus, a much later novel, *The Trouble with Thirteen,* deals with the growing pains of twelve-year-old Annie, whose parents are separating. As Annie must deal with her upcoming move and separation from her best friend Rachel, as well as the death of her pet dog, she learns to accept the troubles life brings. Calling the book "fresh, funny, [and] tightly crafted," *Christian Science Monitor* reviewer Christine McDonnell notes that Miles "has written a convincing, satisfying story of friendship and puberty." M. B. Nickerson similarly comments that Annie and Rachel "are distinct, fully drawn characters" who make the plot "balanced and believable. . . . The book is a winner."

Dealing with the ordinary problems that Annie and Rachel experience is a central concern of Miles's work, along with young peoples' concern with fairness and social justice. As an editor of the Bank Street Readers, she helped to create one of the first multicultural primer series in the United States. Later, with the group Feminists on Children's Media, she pressed for fairer representation of girls and women in children's literature at a time when most standard texts showed boys in active, positive roles and girls in silent, supportive positions.

But while Miles continued to present good role models for girls through her books, stereotypes of women persisted in real life. She recalled in *SAAS,* "Women who wanted to change things were damned as strident and unnatural and ridiculed in flippant jokes." Tired of having requests for fairness characterized as "radical," Miles was inspired to write her first novel for young readers, *The Real Me.* In the book, Barbara Fisher is an ordinary middle-schooler who becomes involved in women's liberation issues when she questions why girls are denied paper routes and are not allowed to take tennis for their physical education class.

Barbara's triumph over these issues is told in "a breezy, pert, first-person chronicle" that is "fast-paced and funny," according to a *Horn Book* contributor. A *Publishers Weekly* reviewer similarly comments that *The Real Me* is a "low-keyed, attractively paced . . . uncontrived picture" of a "believable" heroine. Readers also find Barbara's achievements inspiring; as Miles related in *SAAS,* "from the letters I got and still get about that book, it is clear that it does provide support and reassurance to many young readers. I feel good about that."

In keeping with her desire to present the real world to young readers, Miles dealt with racial discrimination in *All It Takes Is Practice,* a story of an interracial family that moves into a white, middle-class neighborhood. And Kate Harris of *Maudie and Me and the Dirty Book* faces censorship when she reads a book about a puppy's birth to a first grade class. Miles's 1974 nonfiction book *Save the Earth: An Ecology Handbook for Kids* was one of the first books for kids on helping the environment. "I wanted to show . . . how knowledge, forward planning and hard work can lead to useful solutions," she once wrote. In 1991, she published the more comprehensive *Save the Earth: An Action Handbook for Kids,* which includes a report on significant environmental projects carried out by young people.

Miles writes out of her own experience and passion, but she finds that writing changes the very things she writes about. *I Would If I Could,* the story of a girl who does not know how to ride a bike, began as a reminiscence from Miles's own childhood. "I remember—I could never forget—how awful I felt to be ten years old and unable to ride a bike," the author recalled in *SAAS.* But when she began to set down her memories of that time in her life, she discovered "that memory doesn't make good fiction: it is selective, unreliable, fragmentary and, often, unbelievable. Right away, I found I had to jog mine" by conducting research. The experience taught her that "fiction is always a mix of reality and imagination."

"In the end," Miles concluded in *SAAS,* "I write about things I care about—like friendship, and the complicated love of people living together in families. Like the pressures children feel to grow up fast, and the losses they face as they grow. . . . Like the ordinary goodness of people, so common and so often unremarked, which is the theme of *Sink or Swim.* And like the lifelong process of changing and growing."

BIOGRAPHICAL/CRITICAL SOURCES:

BOOKS

Something about the Author Autobiography Series, Volume 9, Gale, 1990.

PERIODICALS

Bulletin of the Center for Children's Books, January, 1975, p. 83; February, 1977, p. 95; February, 1980, p. 113; June, 1980, p. 197; April, 1986, p. 154.
Christian Science Monitor, October 15, 1979, p. B2.
Horn Book, April, 1975, p. 150; June, 1980, p. 300; June, 1982, p. 290.
New York Times Book Review, April 21, 1974, p. 8; July 27, 1980, p. 22.
Publishers Weekly, October 28, 1974, p. 49.
School Library Journal, April, 1976, p. 76; December, 1976, p. 70; October, 1979, p. 153; May, 1980, p. 69; April, 1982, p. 73; March, 1986, p. 168.

* * *

MILLGATE, Michael (Henry)   1929-

PERSONAL: Born July 19, 1929, in Southampton, England; son of Stanley (a civil servant) and Marjorie Louisa (Norris) Millgate; married Eunice Jane Barr (a university teacher), February 27, 1960. *Education:* St. Catharine's College, Cambridge, B.A., 1952, M.A., 1956; University of Michigan, graduate study, 1956-57; University of Leeds, Ph.D., 1960.

ADDRESSES: Home—75 Highland Ave., Toronto, Ontario, Canada M4W 2A4. *Agent*—Peter H. Matson, Literistic, Ltd., 32 West 40th St., New York, NY 10018. *Office*—Department of English, University of Toronto, Toronto, Ontario, Canada M5S 1A1.

CAREER: Workers' Educational Association, tutor and organizer in South Lindsey, England, 1953-56; University of Leeds, Leeds, England, lecturer in English literature, 1958-64; University of Peshawar, visiting professor, 1961; York University, Toronto, Ontario, professor of English and chairman of department, 1964-67; University of Toronto, Toronto, professor of English, 1967—; University of Queensland, S. W. Brooks fellow, 1971; Ohio Wesleyan University, Carpenter Lecturer, 1978. *Military service:* Royal Air Force, 1947-49.

AWARDS, HONORS: Killam senior research scholarship, 1974-76; Guggenheim fellowship, 1977-78; Connaught senior fellowship, 1979-80; elected Fellow of the Royal Society of Canada, 1981.

WRITINGS:

William Faulkner, Grove (New York City), 1961.

(Editor and author of introduction) Alfred Tennyson, *Selected Poems,* Oxford University Press (New York City), 1963.

American Social Fiction: James to Cozzens, Barnes & Noble (New York City), 1964.

(Editor and author of introduction) Theodore Dreiser, *Sister Carrie,* Oxford University Press, 1965.

(Editor with Paul F. Mattheisen) *Transatlantic Dialogue,* University of Texas Press (Austin, TX), 1965.

The Achievement of William Faulkner, Random House (New York City), 1966.

(Editor with James B. Meriwether) *Lion in the Garden: Interviews with William Faulkner, 1926-1962,* Random House, 1968.

Thomas Hardy: His Career as a Novelist, Random House, 1971.

(Editor with Richard L. Purdy) *The Collected Letters of Thomas Hardy,* Oxford University Press, Volume 1, 1978, Volume 2, 1980, Volume 3, 1982.

Thomas Hardy: A Biography, Random House, 1982.

Also contributor of articles on English and American literature and of reviews to journals.

WORK IN PROGRESS: More work on Thomas Hardy; essays on William Faulkner.

BIOGRAPHICAL/CRITICAL SOURCES:

PERIODICALS

Books, October, 1971.
Contemporary Literature, spring, 1968.
Economist, May 23, 1966; June 12, 1971.
Globe and Mail (Toronto), October 24, 1987.
London Review of Books, October 7, 1982.
New Republic, August 31, 1968.
New Yorker, July 30, 1966; June 15, 1968.
New York Review of Books, October 7, 1982.
New York Times Book Review, September 4, 1966; June 30, 1968; May 9, 1982.
Nineteenth-Century Fiction, March, 1983.
Times Literary Supplement, March 10, 1978.*

*   *   *

MILLS, Watson Early 1939-

PERSONAL: Born August 13, 1939, in Martinsville, VA; son of James Claiborne (a salesman) and Martha (a teacher; maiden name, Watson) Mills; married Joyce Hawkins (a teacher), December 19, 1959; children: Michael Arthur. *Education:* University of Richmond, B.A., 1961; Southern Baptist Seminary, B.D., 1964, Th.M., 1965, Th.D., 1968; University of Louisville, M.A., 1967; Baylor University, Ph.D., 1973; University of North Car-

olina, postdoctoral study, 1970-71. *Avocational interests:* Travel (Japan, Thailand, India, Israel, Greece, Mexico, Scandinavia, Russia, Spain, North Africa, England, Italy, Belgium, Holland, France, Scotland, Norway, Netherlands, Austria, Hungary, Poland, Germany, Yugoslavia, Egypt, Turkey, New Zealand, and Australia), flying (holds private pilot's license).

ADDRESSES: Home—1586 River North Court, Macon, GA 31211. *Office*— Department of Religion, Mercer University, Macon, GA 31207.

CAREER: Ordained Baptist clergyman, 1961; pastor of Baptist churches in Virginia, Kentucky, and Indiana, 1961—; Southern Baptist Seminary, instructor in New Testament Greek, 1964; University of Louisville, Louisville, KY, lecturer in humanities and philosophy, 1966-68; Averett College, Danville, VA, assistant professor, 1968-70, associate professor of religion and philosophy, 1970-78; Mercer University, Macon, GA, professor of New Testament, 1979—. Visiting professor at Harvard University, 1984, Yale University, 1985, and Oxford University, 1992.

MEMBER: Society of Biblical Literature, National Association of Baptist Professors of Religion, Society of New Testament Studies, Catholic Biblical Association, Phi Delta Kappa.

WRITINGS:

Understanding Speaking in Tongues, Eerdmans (Grand Rapids, MI), 1972.

Speaking the Truth in Love: A Professor Looks at the Gospel, Averett College Press (Danville, VA), 1972.

(Editor and contributor) *Speaking in Tongues: Let's Talk About It,* Word Books, 1973.

(Editor with M. Thomas Starkes, and contributor) *The Lure of the Occult: A Christian Response,* Home Mission Board, 1974.

Speaking in Tongues: A Classified Bibliography, Society for Pentecostal Studies, 1974.

Review of New Testament Books between 1900-1950, National Association of Baptist Professors of Religion, 1977.

Charismatic Religion in Modern Research: A Bibliography, National Association of Baptist Professors of Religion, 1984.

A Theological/Exegetical Approach to Glossolalia, University Press of America, 1985.

Glossolalia: A Bibliography, Mellen, Edwin (Lewiston, NY), 1985.

New Testament Greek: An Introductory Grammar, Edwin Mellen (Lewiston, NY), 1985.

New Testament Greek: An Introductory Grammar, Edwin Mellen, 1985, revised edition, 1988.

New Testament Greek: An Introductory Grammar Instructor's Manual, Edwin Mellen, 1986.

A Classified Bibliography of Periodical Literature on the Acts of the Apostles: 1960-1985, Supplement to Novum Testamentum, #58, E. J. Brill (Long Island City, NY), 1986.

Speaking in Tongues: A Guide to Research on Glossolalia, Eerdmans, 1986.

Council of Societies for the Study of Religion Directory of Departments and Programs of Religious Studies in North America (annual), Council of Societies for the Study of Religion, 1987-92.

Council of Societies for the Study of Religion Directory of Faculty of Departments and Programs of Religious Studies in North America, Council of Societies for the Study of Religion, 1988.

Bibliography on the Holy Spirit, Hendrickson Publishers, 1989.

Perspectives on Religious Studies Review 15-Year Index, National Association of Baptist Professors of Religion, 1988.

Religious Studies Review 15-Year Index, Council of Societies for the Study of Religion, 1989.

Mercer Dictionary of the Bible, Mercer University Press (Macon, GA), 1990.

Index to Periodical Literature on the Apostle Paul, E. J. Brill, 1993.

Bibliographies for Biblical Research, Edwin Mellen, Volume 1: *The Gospel According to Matthew,* 1993, Volume 2: *The Gospel According to Mark,* 1994, Volume 3: *The Gospel According to Luke,* 1994, Volume 4: *The Gospel According to John,* 1994.

A Bibliography of Twentieth Century Writings on the Holy Spirit, Edwin Mellen, 1993.

Index to Novum Testamentum E. J. Brill, 1994.

Mercer Commentary on the Bible, Mercer University Press, 1994.

Contributor of more than 150 articles and reviews to theology journals.

*   *   *

MINARIK, Else Holmelund   1920-

PERSONAL: Born September 13, 1920, in Aarhus, Denmark; daughter of Kaj Marius and Helga Holmelund; immigrated to the United States, 1925; married Walter Minarik, July 14, 1940 (died, 1963); married Homer Bigart (a journalist), October 3, 1970 (deceased); children: (first marriage) Brooke Ellen. *Education:* Attended Paltz College of the State University of New York; Queens College (now Queens College of the City University of New York), B.A., 1942. *Avocational interests:* Gardening.

ADDRESSES: Home—Rural Delivery, Barrington, NH 03825. *Office*—c/o Greenwillow Books, 105 Madison Ave., New York, NY 10016.

CAREER: Children's author. Reporter for *Daily Sentinel,* Rome, NY, 1940s; first-grade and art teacher in Commack Public Schools, Commack, Long Island, NY, 1950-54.

MEMBER: PEN.

AWARDS, HONORS: Best Illustrated Children's Books of the Year, *New York Times,* 1959, for *Father Bear Comes Home,* and 1968, for *A Kiss for Little Bear; Little Bear's Visit* was named a Caldecott honor book, 1962.

WRITINGS:

FOR CHILDREN

Little Bear, illustrated by Maurice Sendak, Harper (New York), 1957, with audiocassette, HarperCollins (New York), 1986.

No Fighting, No Biting!, illustrated by Sendak, Harper, 1958, HarperCollins, 1978.

Father Bear Comes Home, illustrated by Sendak, Harper, 1959, HarperCollins, 1978.

Cat and Dog, illustrated by Fritz Siebel, Harper, 1960.

Little Bear's Friend, illustrated by Sendak, Harper, 1960, with audiocassette, HarperCollins, 1985.

Little Bear's Visit, illustrated by Sendak, Harper, 1961, with audiocassette, HarperCollins, 1985.

The Little Giant Girl and the Elf Boy, illustrated by Garth Williams, Harper, 1963.

The Winds That Come from Far Away, and Other Poems, illustrated by Joan P. Berg, Harper, 1964.

A Kiss for Little Bear, illustrated by Sendak, Harper, 1968.

(Translator) Jan Loeoef, *My Grandpa Is a Pirate,* Harper, 1968.

What If?, illustrated by Margaret Bloy Graham, Greenwillow (New York), 1987, with audiocassette, Random House, 1988.

It's Spring!, illustrated by Graham, Greenwillow, 1989.

Percy and the Five Houses, illustrated by James Stevenson, Greenwillow, 1989.

The Little Girl and the Dragon, illustrated by Martine Gourbault, Greenwillow, 1991.

Am I Beautiful?, illustrated by Yossi Abolafia, Greenwillow, 1992.

Some of Minarik's books have appeared in Spanish and Braille editions.

SIDELIGHTS: Else Holmelund Minarik has written many acclaimed books for children, but she is probably best known for her beloved "Little Bear" series, which began with *Little Bear,* published in 1957. Her work has attracted some of the most outstanding children's illustrators, including Maurice Sendak and Garth Williams. In addition to the "Little Bear" books, Minarik has charmed children and critics with titles including *No Fighting, No Biting!, Cat and Dog,* and *Percy and the Five Houses.* Christine McDonnell notes in *Twentieth-Century Children's Writers,* "Minarik's genius lies in her ability to create three-dimensional characters and humorous plots within the limits of a very simple text, accessible to beginning readers."

Minarik's daughter, Brooke, first inspired her to write for children. When Brooke expressed an early interest in reading, Minarik discovered a shortage of easy-to-read children's books for her. She began writing books for Brooke and continued the practice with the first-graders she was then teaching. She considered it especially important that young readers have books to read during the summers, so as not to lose the skills they had gained during the school year.

Eventually, Minarik submitted some of the stories she had written to Ursula Nordstrom of Harper and Row. Nordstrom was impressed and used Minarik's *Little Bear* to begin the publisher's "I Can Read" series. *Little Bear,* illustrated by Maurice Sendak, noted illustrator of *Where the Wild Things Are,* features a bear cub who acts much like a child of preschool age. The book quickly stole the hearts of readers and critics alike. Though Minarik's next effort, *No Fighting, No Biting!,* centered on tales of an alligator family rather than Little Bear, she continued his story with her third book, *Father Bear Comes Home.* Other titles about Little Bear include *Little Bear's Friend,* in which he becomes friends with a little girl named Emily; *Little Bear's Visit,* in which he goes to see his grandparents; and *A Kiss for Little Bear,* which chronicles his grandmother's attempts to send him a kiss via some animal friends. *Little Bear's Visit* was named a runner-up for the prestigious Caldecott Medal in 1962.

Minarik's *Percy and the Five Houses* uses the enticement of the "House of the Month Club" to teach Percy the beaver, and in turn, youthful readers, that "there's no place like home." In the *New York Times Book Review,* Daniel Meier compares it to the "Little Bear" series: "I grew up on Else Holmelund Minarik's classic 'Little Bear' books for beginning readers. As a teacher, I have shared all her books with my young students. Her direct yet gentle language can inject interest into even the most ordinary of Little Bear's adventures. . . . I was pleased to find some of these qualities in *Percy and the Five Houses.*"

BIOGRAPHICAL/CRITICAL SOURCES:

BOOKS

Twentieth-Century Children's Writers, 3rd edition, St. James Press (Chicago), 1989, pp. 684-685.

PERIODICALS

Commonweal, November 22, 1968.
New Yorker, November 23, 1957.
New York Times, September 8, 1957; October 5, 1958.
New York Times Book Review, March 25, 1990.
Storytime, spring, 1987.*

*   *   *

MOBLEY, James Bryce   1934-
(James Bryce)

PERSONAL: Born August 29, 1934, in Newport, AK. Married wife, Isabel, April 15, 1984; divorced; children: Michael, Christopher, Lewis. *Education:* Attended Valley College, Los Angeles, CA, 1952-53, received A.A.; attended University of California, Los Angeles, 1957-58.

ADDRESSES: Home—San Francisco, CA. *Office*—P.O. Box 1834, Carson City, NV 89702. *Agent*—Paul Leserman, 3700 Wilshire Blvd., Suite 575, Los Angeles, CA 90010.

CAREER: Writer for television, film, and radio, 1961—. Worked as a television dialogue director, 1958-61, film and television producer and writer, 1968-79 and 1980-90, for television shows, including *Leave It to Beaver* and *Mr. Magoo;* head writer for Educational Film Services, 1976-78; Monroe Institute of Applied Sciences, Faber, VA, media director, 1977-79; writer and producer of children's television series *One of a Kind,* Public Broadcasting Service and syndication, 1978-85. *Military service:* U.S. Army, 1953-55.

MEMBER: Writers Guild of America East, Washington Independent Writers.

AWARDS, HONORS: Second Best Book of the Year, American Association of Racing Writers, 1987, for *Sports Autoracing;* two silver medals from New York Motion Picture and Television Festival, 1979 and 1981, and Emmy Award nomination, 1980, both for *One of a Kind.*

WRITINGS:

UNDER NAME JAMES BRYCE

Reincarnation Now!, Fforbez, 1979.
(With Bill Polick) *Power Basics of Soccer,* Prentice-Hall (Englewood Cliffs, NJ), 1985.
(With Polick) *Power Basics of Football,* Prentice-Hall, 1985.
(With Polick) *Power Basics of Basketball,* Prentice-Hall, 1985.
(With Kay Presto) *Power Basics of Auto Racing,* Hope Publishing House (Pasadena, CA), 1986.

OTHER

Also author of other works under names James Bryce and James Bryce Mobley, including a home video series *Power Basics of Sports,* 1985, a book *Sports Autoracing,* 1987, and a television series *Sports Training Camp,* 1989. Author of screenplays, including *Crowfoot* (with Ray Hoy), *The Mystery of Four Crowns* and *Rock Fantasy: Make Believe.* Contributor to magazines, including *Expansion, Fate,* and *Rehabilitation World.*

WORK IN PROGRESS: A medical health series featuring Dr. Bill Schul; a television screenplay, *An Early Dawn: The Ed Burk Story,* to air in 1996.

SIDELIGHTS: James Bryce Mobley gave *CA* his advice for other writers: "Diversity. Don't be afraid to try other fields of writing that interest you. If you think a subject is of interest to you and to potential readers, then go after it. Many times you can co-author a book or screenplay when the co-author has a deeper understanding of the subject and can be matched with your creative writing abilities."

*   *   *

MOFFETT, Judith   1942-

PERSONAL: Born August 30, 1942, in Louisville, KY; daughter of James S. (a commercial artist) and Margaret (a secretary; maiden name, Cowherd) Moffett; married Edward B. Irving, Jr., March 17, 1983. *Education:* Hanover College, A.B. (cum laude), 1964; Colorado State University, M.A., 1966; University of Wisconsin—Madison, further graduate study, 1966-67; University of Pennsylvania, M.A., 1970, Ph.D., 1971.

ADDRESSES: Home—951 East Laird Ave., Salt Lake City, UT 84105.

CAREER: University of Lund, Lund, Sweden, Fulbright lecturer in American studies, 1967-68; Pennsylvania State University, Behrend College, Erie, assistant professor of English, 1971-75; writer, 1975—; University of Iowa, Iowa City, teacher of writing, 1977-78; University of Pennsylvania, Philadelphia, assistant professor, 1978-86, adjunct assistant professor, 1987-88, adjunct associate professor, 1988-93, adjunct professor of English, 1993.

AWARDS, HONORS: Eunice Tietjens Memorial Prize from *Poetry,* 1973, for two poems; grants from Pennsylvania State Institute for the Arts and Humanistic Studies, 1973, American Philosophical Association, 1973, Nathhorsts Foundation, 1973, Swedish Institute, 1973 and 1976, and Ingram Merrill Foundation, 1976, 1980, and 1991; Fulbright travel grant, 1973-74; Borestone Mountain Poetry Award, 1975, for "Cecropia Terzine"; Levin-

son Prize from *Poetry,* 1976; University of Pennsylvania faculty research grant, 1979 and 1983; translation prize from Swedish Academy, 1982, for translation of *Gentleman, Single, Refined and Selected Poems, 1937-1959* by Hjalmar Gullberg; National Endowment for the Humanities translation grant, 1983, for an anthology of nineteenth-century Swedish poetry; National Endowment for the Arts creative writing fellowship, 1984; Theodore Sturgeon Memorial Award for best science fiction story of the year, 1987; nominated for Nebula Award in short science fiction, 1987, 1989, 1990; John W. Campbell Award for best new writer in science fiction, 1988; translation grant from Swedish Academy, 1994.

WRITINGS:

Keeping Time (poems), Louisiana State University Press (Baton Rouge, LA), 1976.

(Translator from the Swedish) Hjalmar Gullberg, *Gentleman, Single, Refined and Selected Poems, 1937-1959,* Louisiana State University Press, 1979.

James Merrill: An Introduction to the Poetry (criticism), Columbia University Press (New York City), 1984.

Whinny Moor Crossing (poems), Princeton University Press (Princeton, NJ), 1984.

Pennterra (science fiction), Congdon & Weed/Davis Publications (Chicago), 1987.

The Ragged World: A Novel of the Hefn on Earth (science fiction), St. Martin's (New York City), 1991.

Two That Came True (science fiction), Pulphouse Press (Eugene, OR), 1991.

Time, Like an Ever-Rolling Stream: A Sequel to the Ragged World (science fiction), St. Martin's, 1992.

Homestead Year: Back to the Land in the Suburbs (nonfiction), Lyons & Burford (New York City), 1995.

WORK IN PROGRESS: Translations, introduction, and notes for an anthology of nineteenth-century Swedish poetry containing selections from the work of seven poets; a new novel.

BIOGRAPHICAL/CRITICAL SOURCES:

PERIODICALS

New York Times Book Review, February 3, 1991, p. 33.
Times Literary Supplement, November 9, 1984, p. 1290.

*   *   *

MOLARSKY, Osmond   1909-

PERSONAL: Born November 17, 1909, in Boston, MA; son of Abram and Sarah Ann (Shreve) Molarsky; married Aileen Olsen (an author), December 23, 1951 (divorced, 1965); married Margaret G. Hindes, December, 1971. *Education:* Swarthmore College, B.A., 1934. *Avocational in-*

terests: Yachting, soccer, legislative action on environmental issues.

ADDRESSES: Home—P.O. Box 286, Ross, CA 94957.

CAREER: Producer of marionette shows, 1929-36, traveling with the Swarthmore Chautauqua troupe; writer of scripts for documentaries for U.S. Office of Education, 1938-39; J. Walter Thompson Agency, New York City, advertising copywriter, 1953-57; KVIE-TV (educational television), Sacramento, CA, writer-producer, 1966; KNEW (radio), Oakland, CA, commentator and host of a telephone talk program, beginning 1968. *Military service:* U.S. Naval Reserve, 1943-46; became lieutenant senior grade.

AWARDS, HONORS: First place, *Stage* Magazine one-act play contest, 1937, for *No! Not the Russians!;* Reader's Digest Foundation awards for best educational television programs, 1966, for *Gold Was Where You Found It,* and 1967, for *Secrets of the Brook.*

WRITINGS:

FOR CHILDREN

Piper, the Sailboat That Came Back, New York Graphic Society (Boston, MA), 1965.
(With Virginia Brown, Billie Phillips, and Jo Paul) *Out Jumped Abraham,* McGraw (New York City), 1967.
Song of the Empty Bottles, Walck (New York City), 1968.
Right Thumb, Left Thumb, Addison-Wesley (Reading, MA), 1969.
Where the Good Luck Was, Walck, 1970.
The Bigger They Come, Walck, 1971.
Take It or Leave It, Walck, 1972.
Song of the Smoggy Stars, Walck, 1973.
The Good Guys and the Bad Guys, Walck, 1974.
Montalvo Bay, Walck, 1976.
The Fearless Leroy, illustrated by Robert Bartram, Walck, 1977.
Robbery in Right Field, illustrated by Rob Sauber, Walck, 1978.
A Different Ball Game, illustrated by James Zingarelli, Coward, McCann (New York City), 1979.
The Peasant and the Fly, illustrated by Katherine Coville, Harcourt (New York City), 1980.
Scrappy, Dodd, Mead (New York City), 1983.
A Sky Full of Kites, Tricycle Press, in press.

OTHER

(Editor and contributor) *Best Plays from Stage* (anthology), Dodd (New York City), 1938.

Also author of play *No! Not the Russians!* and television documentaries *Gold Was Where You Found It* and *Secrets of the Brook.* Writer of documentary film scripts for industry, government, and labor unions. Writer with Hardie Gramatky of a monthly children's feature, "Letters from Ellsworth Elephant," in *Family Circle,* 1960-63. Work published in anthologies.

WORK IN PROGRESS: Juvenile books.

SIDELIGHTS: Osmond Molarsky's emphasis in his juvenile books is on subjects and themes of special interest to minority children living in urban environments.

Molarsky told *CA:* "I had the idea for *Scrappy* from observing the antics of my eleven-year-old granddaughter and some of her friends. And I expect a certain amount of indignation and violent outcry when the book comes out. But that's how it seems to go—what I write grows naturally out of where I happen to be living at the time, and the conditions of my life. When I lived in a lighthouse in Maine, and was doing a lot of sailing, I wrote *Piper, the Sailboat That Came Back.* As a denizen of the inner city areas of Washington, D.C., and San Francisco, I wrote *Song of the Empty Bottles* and *The Fearless Leroy.* Now *Scrappy*—a dozen books later—emerges from Marin County, California, just north of the Golden Gate, fabled land of redwood hot tubs and peacock feathers and over-privileged youngsters. . . .

"My first professional exposure to children was as producer of 'Molarsky's Marionettes,' which toured extensively in the 1930s, with James A. Michener as an assistant puppeteer, an experience that Michener builds upon in his early novel, *Fires of Spring.*"

"Probably the most satisfying writing I ever did," Molarsky reflected, "was published in the Congressional Record—testimony presented by an environmental group before the Senate Subcommittee on Public Lands, on a bill to save from logging 32,000 acres of virgin forest in California's Sierra Nevada. The bill passed, and the area now is wilderness, legally exempt from desecration by man. I'm proud of that."

Molarsky recalls that his parents "were artists, and [I] grew up in what [I would] describe as 'an atmosphere of feverish creativity.' He adds that "This is depicted in [my] one-act farce, *No! Not the Russians!,* [which was] written as a college exercise but later published and performed widely by community and college theaters in the U.S. and Canada."

BIOGRAPHICAL/CRITICAL SOURCES:

PERIODICALS

Children's Book World, November 3, 1968.
Young Readers Review, October, 1969.

MOLINARO, Ursule

PERSONAL: Full name Ursule Molinaro Herndon. *Avocational interests:* Painting (neo-Haitian primitive; oil on wood) and philosophy (any system of self-knowledge).

ADDRESSES: Home—New York City.

CAREER: United Nations, New York City, multilingual proofreader, 1946-51; writer, 1950—. Teacher of creative and literary translation at Ecole libre des Hautes Etudes, New York, 1971-72; member of creative writing workshop at University of Idaho, Moscow, ID, 1979.

MEMBER: Coordinating Council of Literary Magazines.

AWARDS, HONORS: Creative Artists Public Service grants, 1972-73 and 1980-81; MacDowell fellowship, 1977; National Endowment for the Arts grant, 1981-82.

WRITINGS:

POETRY

Rimes et raisons, Regain (Monte Carlo), 1954.
Mirrors for Small Beasts, Noonday, 1960.

NOVELS

L'Un pour l'autre, translation from the English manuscript by Edith Fournier, Julliard (Paris), 1964, manuscript published as *The Borrower: An Alchemical Novel,* Harper (New York City), 1970.
Green Lights Are Blue: A Pornosophic Novel, New American Library (New York City), 1967.
Sounds of a Drunken Summer, Harper, 1969.
The Autobiography of Cassandra, Princess and Prophetess of Troy, Archer Editions Press (Danbury, CT), 1979.
Positions with White Roses, McPherson (New Paltz, NY), 1983.
The New Moon with the Old Moon in Her Arms: A True Story Assembled from Scholarly Hearsay, Women's Press Ltd. (London), 1990, McPherson (Kingston, NY), 1993.
Power Dreamers: The Jocasta Complex, McPherson, 1994.

Also author of unpublished novel "That Which Is Bright Rises Twice," excerpts from which have appeared in *The Little Magazine,* Volume 10, numbers 3-4, 1976, and in *Gallimaufry,* 1978.

COLLECTIONS

Encores for a Dilettante, Braziller (New York City), 1978.
Bastards: Footnotes to History (two short stories; illustrated), Treacle Press, 1979.
Nightschool for Saints, Second Floor, Ring Bell: 11 Short Stories, Archer Editions Press, 1981.
Thirteen: Stories, McPherson, 1989.

A Full Moon of Women: 29 Word Portraits of Notable Women from Different Times and Places, Dutton (New York City), 1990.

NONFICTION

The Zodiac Lovers, Avon (New York City), 1969.
Life by the Numbers: A Basic Guide to Learning Your Life through Numerology, Morrow (New York City), 1971.

PLAYS

The Abstract Wife, Hill & Wang (New York City), 1961.
Breakfast Past Noon (one-act), published in *New Women's Theatre,* Random House (New York City), 1977.

Also author of one-act plays *The Engagement, After the Wash,* and *The Sundial,* all published or produced; author of unpublished and unproduced plays "The Mine" (one-act), "Antiques" (one-act), "The Great Emancipation," and "The Happy Hexagon."

OTHER

Translator from German, Italian, Spanish, and Portuguese into French and English of work by Dino Buzzati, Ugo Carrega, Hermann Hesse, Michael Horbach, Uwe Johnson, Reinhard Lettau, Claude Ollier, Nathalie Sarraute, Jean Vauthier, Christa Wolf, and many others. Also translator of film subtitles from and into French and from Italian into English. Work represented in anthologies, including *Statements 1,* Braziller, 1975, *Statements 2,* Braziller, 1977, both compiled by Jonathan Baumbach, and *Superfiction,* edited by Joe David Bellamy, Vintage, 1975. Contributor of short stories and articles to journals, including *Benzene, Contemporary Quarterly, Epoch, Evergreen, Fiera letteraria, Iowa Review, Lettres nouvelles, New Boston Review, New Directions, Panache, Top Stories, TriQuarterly,* and *Village Voice.*

SIDELIGHTS: Ursule Molinaro once told *CA* that her basic interest is "the position of the individual, regardless of ethnic background, sex or age."

BIOGRAPHICAL/CRITICAL SOURCES:

PERIODICALS

Book World, September 7, 1969.
New Yorker, June 24, 1967.
New York Review of Books, August 24, 1967.
New York Times, August 25, 1971.
New York Times Book Review, May 21, 1967; September 2, 1990, p. 24.
Village Voice, December 19, 1968.*

MOMEN, Moojan 1950-

PERSONAL: Given name is pronounced "*Moo*-zhane"; born January 25, 1950, in Tabriz, Iran; son of Sedratu'llah (an airplane pilot) and Gloria (a fashion designer; maiden name, Iman) Momen; married Wendi Worth (a volunteer organizer), June 12, 1971; children: Sedrhat (son), Carmel (daughter). *Education:* St. John's College, Cambridge, B.A., 1971, M.A., 1974; Guy's Hospital, London, B.Chir., 1974, M.B., 1975. *Politics:* None. *Religion:* Baha'i.

ADDRESSES: c/o George Ronald Publishers, 46 High St., Kidlington, Oxford OX5 2DN, England.

CAREER: Guy's and St. Olave's Hospitals, London, England, house officer, 1974-75; Plymouth General Hospital, Plymouth, England, senior house officer, 1976-78; general medical practitioner, 1980—.

MEMBER: British Society for Middle East Studies, British Society for Persian Studies, Society for Iranian Studies, Association for Baha'i Studies, Fellow of the Royal Asiatic Society.

WRITINGS:

Dr. J. E. Esslemont, Baha'i Publishing Trust, 1975.
(Translator) Muhammad Labib, *The Seven Martyrs of Hurmuzak,* George Ronald, 1981.
The Babi and Baha'i: Religions, 1844-1944; Some Contemporary Western Accounts, George Ronald, 1981.
(Editor and contributor) *Studies in Babi and Baha'i History* (vol. I), Kalimat Press (Los Angeles), 1982, vol. II (with Juan R. Cole), 1984.
Introduction to Shi'i Islam: The History and Doctrines of Twelver Shi'ism, Yale University Press (New Haven, CT), 1985.
(Editor) *Selections From the Writings of E. G. Browne on the Babi and Baha'i Religions,* George Ronald, 1987.
(Editor) *Studies in Honor of the Late Hasan M. Balyuzi* (*Studies of the Babi and Baha'i Religions,* vol. 5.), Kalimat Press (Los Angeles), 1988.

CONTRIBUTOR

Peter Smith, editor, *Studies in Babi and Baha'i History* (vol. III), Kalimat Press (Los Angeles), 1986.
S. Akiner, editor, *Central Asia Tradition and Change,* Kegan Paul International (London), 1991.
Asghar Fathi, editor, *Iranian Refugees and Exiles Since Khomeni,* Mazda Publications (London), 1991.

OTHER

Editor of the *The Bahahi Encyclopedia,* first volume in press. Contributor of articles to a number of books, including *Islamic Fundamentalism,* edited by R. M. Burrell; *Royal Asiatic Seminar Papers No. 1,* Royal Asiatic Society, 1989. Contributor to *Encyclopaedia Iranica* and *Encyclo-*
pedia of the Modern Islamic World. Contributor to scholarly journals, including *Iran, International Journal of Middle East Studies, Past and Present,* and *Religion.* Book reviews in *Bulletin of the British Society for Middle Eastern Studies, American Historical Review, Middle East Journal, Journal of the Royal Asiatic Society, Iranian Studies,* and *Journal of Semitic Studies.*

WORK IN PROGRESS: Research on Bahahi social history, and on comparative religion.

SIDELIGHTS: Moojan Momen explained to *CA* that he began writing because "I felt there was no adequate, scholarly book on the history of the Baha'i faith. My interest in the subject was increased because most previous works on the Baha'i faith had been written polemic either for or against the religion. Though I am a Baha'i myself, I hope that my own books are sufficiently objective to be useful additions to the knowledge of the subject.

"My first books are the result of research undertaken in the Public Records Office and elsewhere while I was assisting H. M. Balyuzi in his own research. My book on Shi'i Islam came about because the roots of the Baha'i faith are in Shi'ism, and there was no comprehensive survey of this aspect of Islam.

"The Baha'i faith began in the middle of the last century in Iran. Its roots are in Shi'i Islam, although it claims to be a world religion completely independent of Islam. Its founder took the title Baha'u'llah (meaning Glory of God) and claimed that he was the fulfillment of the messianic prophecies of all religions: Islam, Christianity, Judaism, Zoroastrianism, etc. Baha'u'llah was exiled from Iran and, after successive banishments, finally came to Akka in Palestine.

"Baha'u'llah's central teaching is that all the religions of the world have been part of an evolutionary and progressive process culminating in the present age which is the age in which God intends to establish the unity of the world. This will occur upon the basis of such social teachings as universal education, equality between men and women, and a world government. However, it also requires the spiritual development of the individual in order that he or she can initiate and participate in this process.

"The Baha'i faith has no priesthood and is administered by elected bodies. It has few rituals but has a number of personal laws such as daily private prayer. It has now spread to most parts of the world with large communities of Baha'is in many parts of the Third World: India, Africa, South America, and the Pacific."

BIOGRAPHICAL/CRITICAL SOURCES:

PERIODICALS

America, May 3, 1986.

Books and Religion, January, 1986.
Library Journal, October-December, 1985.
Listener, July 18, 1985.
Perspective, Volume 110, no. 6, 1985.
Times Higher Education Supplement, September 20, 1985.
Times Literary Supplement, October 4, 1985.

*   *   *

MONTGOMERY, Marion H., Jr. 1925-

PERSONAL: Born April 16, 1925, in Thomaston, GA; son of Marion H. and Lottie Mae (Jenkins) Montgomery; married Dorothy Carlisle, January 20, 1951; children: Priscilla, Lola Dean, Marion III, Heli, Lewellyn. *Education:* University of Georgia, 1947-53, A.B., M.A. *Politics:* "Independent conservative." *Religion:* "Anglo Catholic."

ADDRESSES: Home—Box 115, Crawford, GA 30630. *Office*—Department of English, University of Georgia, Athens, GA 30602.

CAREER: University of Georgia, Athens, assistant director of university press, 1950-52, business manager of *Georgia Review,* 1951-53, instructor, 1954-60, assistant professor, 1960-67, associate professor, 1967-70, professor of English, 1970—. Darlington School for Boys, instructor, 1953-54; Converse College, writer-in-residence, 1963. *Military service:* U.S. Army, 1943-46; became sergeant.

AWARDS, HONORS: Eugene Saxton Memorial Award, Harper, 1960; Georgia Writers Association award for fiction, 1964, for *Darrell;* award for poetry, 1970, for *The Gull and Other Georgia Scenes;* award for poetry from *Carlton Miscellany,* 1967; Earhart Foundation grant for critical work.

WRITINGS:

FICTION

The Wandering of Desire (novel), Harper (New York City), 1962.
Darrell (novel), Doubleday (New York City), 1964.
Ye Olde Bluebird (novella), New College Press (Sarasota, FL), 1967.
Fugitive (novel), Harper, 1974.

POETRY

Dry Lightening, University of Nebraska Press (Lincoln, NE), 1960.
Stones from the Rubble, Argus Books, 1965.
The Gull and Other Georgia Scenes, University of Georgia Press (Athens, GA), 1969.

CRITICISM

Ezra Pound: A Critical Essay, Eerdmans (Grand Rapids, MI), 1970.

T. S. Eliot: An Essay on the American Magus, University of Georgia Press, 1970.
The Reflective Journey toward Order: Essays on Dante, Wordsworth, Eliot, and Others, University of Georgia Press, 1973.
Eliot's Reflective Journey to the Garden, Whitston Publishing, 1978.
The Prophetic Poet and the Spirit of the Age, Sherwood Sugden (La Salle, IL), Volume I: *Why Flannery O'Connor Stayed Home,* 1980, Volume II: *Why Poe Drank Liquor,* 1983, Volume III: *Why Hawthorne Was Melancholy,* 1984.
Virtue and Modern Shadows of Turning: Preliminary Agitations, Intercollegiate Studies Institute, University Press of America (Lanham, MD), 1990.

NONFICTION

Possum, and Other Receipts for the Recovery of "Southern" Being, University of Georgia Press (Athens), 1987.
The Trouble with You Innerleckchuls, Christendom College Press (Front Royal, VA), 1988.
The Men I have Chosen for Fathers: Literary and Philosophical Passages, University of Missouri Press (Columbia, MO), 1990.
Liberal Arts and Community: The Feeding of the Larger Body, Louisiana State University Press (Baton Rouge, LA), 1990.

OTHER

Contributor to anthologies, including *Best Poems of 1958* and *Best Short Stories of 1971.* Contributor of poetry and short stories to periodicals. Managing editor, *Western Review,* 1957-58.

SIDELIGHTS: A prominent Southern writer, Marion H. Montgomery Jr.'s fiction often contrasts characters who are leaving the rural South for success in the city with those who, having achieved that success, are trying to recapture their rural beginnings. This particular theme comes from Montgomery's interest in the Agrarian writers of the thirties who advocated an artistic return to the land in order to establish a mutually supportive culture and agriculture.

Montgomery's 1962 novel, *The Wandering of Desire* reflects his interests in agrarian themes, telling the story of two men, Wash Mullis and Doc Blalock, and their ultimately failed attempts to conquer the land. Writing about Montgomery's work in *Dictionary of Literary Biography,* Thomas Landers notes that the novel "is a complex work in which the diversity of characters and actions . . . suggests the author's wide knowledge of his region and its lore." Reviewer Walker Percy, reviewing *The Wandering of Desire* in *Commonweal* calls the work "a chronicle, a country epic, a first novel sprung forth whole and entire with full Faulknerian panoply of legends, yarns, family tales, and a command of country epithet unsurpassed since *The Hamlet.*"

Discussing Montgomery's second novel, *Darrell,* Landers says that the work "is simpler in its plot structure than *The Wandering of Desire . . . .*" In *Darrell,* Landers argues, the "action is uncomplicated and is rendered sequentially. Indeed the novel is Montgomery's only conventional fictional narrative." In this novel Montgomery tells the tale of a country-born and country-raised man called Darrell, who convinces his aged grandmother to move with him from their small town to the city. The two end up settling, not in the heart of the city, but on its perimeter, in the Atlanta suburbs. Eventually, Darrell's obsession to fulfill the wish of a dying girl, Sandra Lee, to visit the Atlanta zoo, leads both of them to their deaths in a motorcycle crash. Landers concludes: "Beneath this straightforward plot—which is no more than a situation out of which grows the final tragic consequence—the reader finds a statement of Montgomery's view of urban life. Suburbia is rendered as kind of a banal hell in which people are manipulated by forces beyond their control." O. B. Emerson, writing in *Critique: Studies in Modern Fiction,* says of *Darrell*: "With his clear voice, insight, and vision, Marion Montgomery is one of the most appealing spokesmen for the new South as well as the old." And in *Best Seller,* Brother Luke M. Grande assesses the book as "one of those flawless works of art being turned out by Southern writers as only they, apparently, can." He proceeds to laud Montgomery's "technical skill," calling him "an accomplished storyteller," and praises "his penetrating vision of the tragicomedy of life with rare effectiveness."

In 1974 Montgomery published *Fugitive,* which Landers considers "his most overtly Agrarian" work. *Fugitive* tells the story of Walt Mason, a successful songwriter in Nashville, who moves to the small town of Weaverton, Tennessee, in search of rural simplicity. The town, however, is far from the idyllic country community Mason seeks. Like other cities, Weaverton is plagued by commercialism and a dependence on technology. According to Landers, *Fugitive* will present "some difficulties for the critic or reader who expects a conventional plot composed of sequential events." Montgomery's style in this novel includes numerous digressions, the relevance of which may not be immediately apparent to the reader. The work demands from the reader, says Landers, " a willing suspension of disbelief." On the other hand, *New York Times Book Review* critic Shirley Ann Grau finds Montgomery's *Fugitive* "difficult, crabbed, full of half-disclosed meanings." For Grau "the experimental structure . . . makes unnecessary demands on the reader," and she finds that this "desperately

serious literary venture" "leaves the impression of a simple story complicatedly told." Thomas H. Landess of the *Georgia Review* cites Montgomery as "one of a handful of writers whose work belies the prophecies of sociological critics that the epoch of significant Southern fiction has come to and end," and deems *Fugitive* "a work as ambitious in its own way as anything yet attempted by a Southerner of his generation." And although he finds the book's shifting point of view "tricky," and expresses the concern that Montgomery "here is so bold in his aspirations that throughout the novel the reader spends much of his time wondering if the action, however skillfully rendered, can possibly bear the burden of the author's weighty thematic substance." He concludes: "the work is extraordinarily successful, which is to say that it represents a substantial literary achievement." Landess summarizes: "what Montgomery has written here is the American success story played backwards, a tale of a hero who leaves fame and fortune in the city to seek a humdrum life on the farm. . . . For these and many other reasons his trip is well worth the time and trouble, however tortuous the turns in the road. I suspect that this is the first novel of a kind, and as such it deserves our most serious and respectful attention."

BIOGRAPHICAL/CRITICAL SOURCES:

BOOKS

Contemporary Literary Criticism, Volume 7, Gale, 1977.
Dictionary of Literary Biography, Volume 6: *American Novelists Since World War II,* Second Series, Gale, 1980.
Encyclopedia of Short Fiction, Salem Press, 1981.
Separate Country: A Literary Journey through the American South, Paddington Press, 1979.

PERIODICALS

American Literature, January, 1971.
Best Sellers, May 15, 1964.
Commonweal, May 11, 1962.
Courier-Journal & Times (Louisville, KY), September 1, 1974.
Critique, Volume VIII, number 1, 1965.
Georgia Review, spring, 1967; summer, 1974; fall, 1985.
National Review, August 11, 1970.
New Republic, July 27, 1974.
New York Times Book Review, June 9, 1974.
Poetry, October, 1966.
Recherches Anglaises et Americaines, IX, 1976.
Sewanee Review, spring, 1965.
Southern Review, autumn, 1970, winter, 1975.
Times Literary Supplement, January 1, 1971.
Writer, December, 1969.

MORELLA, Joe
   See MORELLA, Joseph (James)

* * *

MORELLA, Joseph (James) 1949-
   (Joe Morella)

PERSONAL: Born November 19, 1949, in Nutley, NJ; son of Patrick Emil and Mary (Bonavita) Morella.

ADDRESSES: Home—63 Highfield Lane, Nutley, NJ 07110.

CAREER: Variety, New York, NY, reporter and critic, 1970-73; freelance writer, 1973—.

WRITINGS:

BOOKS

(With Edward Z. Epstein) *Judy: The Films & Career of Judy Garland,* L. Frewin, 1969.

(With Epstein) *Judy: The Films of Judy Garland,* Citadel (Secaucus, NJ), 1970.

(With Epstein) *Rebels: The Rebel Hero in Films,* Citadel, 1971.

(With Epstein) *Brando: The Unauthorized Biography,* Nelson, 1973.

(With others) *The Films of WW2,* introduction by Judith Crist, Citadel, 1973.

(With Epstein) *Lucy,* Lyle Stuart (Secaucus, NJ), 1973.

(With others) *The Amazing Careers of Bob Hope: From Gags to Riches,* W. H. Allen, 1974.

(With Epstein) *Lucy: The Bittersweet Life of Lucille Ball,* W. H. Allen, 1974.

(With Epstein) *Gable & Lombard & Powell & Harlow,* Dell (New York City), 1975.

(With Richard J. Turchetti) *Nutrition and the Athlete,* foreword by James F. Fixx, Van Nostrand (New York City), 1976.

(With Epstein) *The It Girl: The Story of Clara Bow,* Delacorte (New York City), 1976.

(With Epstein) *The Ince Affair* (novel), New American Library (New York City), 1978.

(With James Bliss) *The Left-Hander's Handbook,* A & W Publishers (New York City), 1980.

(With Epstein) *Rita: The Life of Rita Hayworth,* Delacorte Press, 1983.

(With Epstein) *Jane Wyman: A Biography,* Delacorte Press, 1985.

(With Epstein) *Paulette: The Adventurous Life of Paulette Goddard,* St. Martin's (New York City), 1985.

(With Epstein) *Forever Lucy: The Life of Lucille Ball,* L. Stuart, 1986.

(With Epstein) *Loretta Young: An Extraordinary Life,* Delacorte Press, 1986.

(With Epstein) *Paul and Joanne: A Biography of Paul Newman and Joanne Woodward,* Delacorte Press, 1988.

(With Patricia Barey) *Simon and Garfunkel: Old Friends,* Carol Publishing Group (New York City), 1991.

(With Epstein) *Mia: The Life of Mia Farrow,* Delacorte Press, 1991.

PLAYS

(Coauthor) *Pennyman,* first produced in Los Angeles, CA, 1979.

The Rape of Maria Perez, first produced in Los Angeles, 1980.

WORK IN PROGRESS: Show Business Dictionary, with Bill Edwards; *Caves of America,* with James Bliss; *No Illusions,* a play.

SIDELIGHTS: Joseph Morella commented: "Self-discipline is a hundred times harder than having a steady job. Friendships are all important. Travel (to Europe and South America) is necessary and welcome."

BIOGRAPHICAL/CRITICAL SOURCES:

PERIODICALS

Globe and Mail (Toronto), August 10, 1991, p. C8.
Los Angeles Times Book Review, September 1, 1985, p. 7.
Nw York Times Book Review, October 30, 1983, p. 9.
Washington Post Book World, August 9, 1985.

* * *

MORGAN, Christopher 1952-

PERSONAL: Born September 30, 1952, in Perth Amboy, NJ; son of George Leon and Helen Ann (Gecek) Morgan; married Patricia Roehrich, August 7, 1971 (divorced); married Margaret Corlett, December 24, 1978 (divorced); married Kathleen Carroll, October 23, 1982. *Education:* Rutgers University, B.A., 1974; also attended San Francisco State University, 1979-80.

ADDRESSES: Home—Edison, NJ.

CAREER: Freelance writer, 1978—. Affiliated with Mid-Day Channel 12, Monterey Peninsula, CA, 1975-76, with Gibbs & Soell Public Relations, 1979-80, and with the American Broadcasting Corp. (ABC) Television Network, 1984—; producer/director, Army Birthday Celebration, 1975. *Military service:* U.S. Army, Infantry, 1974-75, in public affairs, 1975-78. U.S. Army Reserve, 1978-85.

MEMBER: Authors Guild.

AWARDS, HONORS: Keith L. Ware Award for excellence in military journalism from U.S. Army, 1977.

WRITINGS:

The Rich and the Lonely (novel), Beaufort Book Co. (New York City), 1981.

(Ghostwriter for Lynda Van Devanter) *Home before Morning: The Story of an Army Nurse in Vietnam* (nonfiction), Beaufort Book Co., 1983.

Also author of *Facts and Fallacies: A Book of Definitive and Misguided Predictions,* St. Martin's (New York City). Contributor to newspapers and magazines. Editor of *Fort Ord Panorama;* associate editor of *Army Reserve;* editor of newsletters.

SIDELIGHTS: Christopher Morgan told *CA:* "A lot of writers give the profession a bad name because they take themselves too seriously and speak of their scribblings in pompous terms. Whenever I get that kind of urge, I remind myself that we're all descended from the guy who sat by the campfire in his prehistoric BVDs telling his friends about the dinosaur that got away. If he had been talented enough to actually catch the dinosaur, he would have been too busy making dino-burgers to do much talking.

"In my case, the writing impulse began for less than artistic reasons. In high school all the guys getting the girls were varsity athletes, except for this one who wrote a column for the school newspaper. The athletes had to go through grueling practices every day. All the columnist had to do was write five hundred words once a month. Was there really any choice? Unfortunately, before I learned that most sane girls weren't crazy about writers, I was hooked."

BIOGRAPHICAL/CRITICAL SOURCES:

PERIODICALS

Army Reserve, spring, 1981.
Library Journal, February 1, 1981, p. 381.
Los Angeles Times Book Review, March 7, 1982, p. 7.
Washington Post, April 11, 1983.*

*   *   *

MORGAN, Claire
   See HIGHSMITH, (Mary) Patricia

*   *   *

MORRIS, David Brown   1942-

PERSONAL: Born August 11, 1942, in New York, NY; married, 1979; children: one. *Education:* Hamilton College, B.A., 1964; University of Minnesota, Ph.D., 1968.

ADDRESSES: Home—3215 Magnolia Circle, Kalamazoo, MI 49008.

CAREER: University of Virginia, Charlottesville, assistant professor of English, 1968-72; American University, Washington, DC, associate professor of literature, 1972-74; University of Iowa, Iowa City, professor of English, 1974-82; writer, 1982—. Visiting professor, Michigan State University, 1988 and 1989, Milton S. Hershey Medical Center, 1990; distinguished visiting professor, Kalamazoo College, 1991 and 1992; visiting lecturer, University of Virginia, 1993.

MEMBER: Modern Language Association of America, American Society for Eighteenth-Century Studies, International Association for the Study of Pain, American Pain Society.

AWARDS, HONORS: National Endowment for the Humanities fellow, 1972-73, 1986-1987; Guggenheim fellow, 1976-77; American Council of Learned Societies fellow, 1980-81; National Science Foundation/National Endowment for the Humanities interdisciplinary fellow, 1982-83; Gottschalk Prize, American Society for Eighteenth-Century Studies, 1984; PEN/Spielvogel-Diamonstein Prize, 1992, for *The Culture of Pain.*

WRITINGS:

The Religious Sublime: Christian Poetry and Critical Tradition in Eighteenth-Century England, University Press of Kentucky (Lexington, KY), 1972.
Alexander Pope: The Genius of Sense (essays), Harvard University Press (Cambridge, MA), 1984.
The Culture of Pain, University of California Press (Berkeley, CA), 1991.
Earth Warrior, Fulcrum Press, in press.

Contributor to books, including *The Art of Alexander Pope,* edited by Howard Erskine-Hill and Anne Smith, Vision Press, 1979; *Exploring the Concept of Mind,* edited by Richard M. Caplan, University of Iowa Press (Iowa City, IA), 1986; *Alexander Pope,* edited by Harold Bloom, Chelsea House (New York City), 1986; *The Enduring Legacy: Alexander Pope Tercentenary Essays,* edited by G. S. Rousseau and Pat Rogers, Cambridge University Press (New York City), 1988; *Languages of Psyche: Mind and Body in Enlightenment Thought,* edited by Rousseau, University of California Press, 1990; *Teaching Eighteenth-Century Poetry,* edited by Christopher Fox, AMS Press (New York City), 1990; *The Profession of Eighteenth-Century Literature: Reflections on an Institution,* edited by Leopold Damrosch, University of Wisconsin Press, 1992; and *Teaching Approaches to Pope's Poetry,* edited by Wallace Jackson and Paul Yoder, Modern Language Association (New York City), 1992. Also contributor to language and literature journals.

The Culture of Pain has been translated into Spanish and German.

SIDELIGHTS: In his essay collection *Alexander Pope: The Genius of Sense,* David Brown Morris "lays the groundwork for a sophisticated reading of Pope," writes Douglas Lane Patey in the *Virginia Quarterly Review.* Patey adds: "[Morris] has much to say on such matters as the occasional nature of many Augustan poems, Pope's habits of revision, and his concept of imitation as a procedure not merely of refinement but in a deeper sense as 'a mode of learning—a source of knowledge.' "

While Patey finds Morris's treatment of individual poems disappointing, *Southern Humanities Review* contributor Peter Thorpe maintains that Morris's "readings of 'The Rape of the Lock' and 'The Dunciad' are particularly original and convincing." Adds Thorpe: "He is successful in demonstrating how Pope's very early work served as a springboard to the refinements of his later verse and as a lead-in to the mature poetic statements about sense and genius that occur mostly after 1730. Thus, although it does not always deliver what it promises, Morris's book deserves to be read."

In *The Culture of Pain* Morris examines the history of pain and its place in society from both medical and anthropological viewpoints to put forth the idea that physical and mental pain are inseparable. From historical figures such as the Marquis de Sade and Leopold von Sacher-Masoch, who lent their names to specific types of pain, to the exploration of medication (or lack of it) used to treat terminally ill patients, Morris illustrates how pain is a fact of everyday life—"an inevitable part of the awkward human condition, as relentless as sex, death and taxes," states *New York Times Book Review* writer Melvin Konner. Konner further writes that "Morris does not dispel the mystery of pain. . . . His message for doctors is that they should stop . . . insisting that pain is a mere biological puzzle. . . . His message for patients in pain is that the mind has many roles to play—from insistence on adequate medication to prayer."

David Brown Morris told *CA:* "My writing has taken me from eighteenth-century minor poetry (*The Religious Sublime*) to a voyage with environmental activist Paul Watson on an anti-driftnet campaign in the North Pacific (*Earth Warrior*). There must be a connection, but I'm not sure I want to know what it is. Perhaps it's enough to say that I like to encounter new bodies of knowledge, to cross disciplines, to mix forms. My wife claims that—no matter what I call them—I don't write books but collections of essays. Maybe so. The essay no doubt stands behind most of my writing. I like nonfiction, I suspect, because I feel about ideas the way some writers feel about character or language or plot."

BIOGRAPHICAL/CRITICAL SOURCES:

PERIODICALS

English Language Notes, June, 1985, pp. 69-71.
Journal of English and Germanic Philology, July, 1985.
Journal of the American Medical Association, January 15, 1992, p. 432.
New York Times Book Review, October 13, 1991, p. 13.
Southern Humanities Review, winter, 1986.
Times Higher Education Supplement, January 4, 1985.
Times Literary Supplement, February 8, 1985.
Virginia Quarterly Review, winter, 1985.*

*   *   *

MORRISON, J. S.
See MORRISON, John (Sinclair)

*   *   *

MORRISON, John (Sinclair)   1913-
(J. S. Morrison)

PERSONAL: Born June 15, 1913, in Lindfield, England; son of Sinclair (a civil servant) and Maria Elsie (a homemaker; maiden name, Lamaison) Morrison; married Elizabeth Helen Sulman (a homemaker), April 16, 1942; children: Andrew, Simon, Thomas, Annis Morrison Garfield, Kate Morrison Musgrave. *Education:* Trinity College, Cambridge, B.A., 1935. *Politics:* Conservative. *Religion:* Church of England.

ADDRESSES: Home—Granhams, Granhams Rd., Great Shelford, Cambridge CB2 5JX, England.

CAREER: Victoria University of Manchester, Manchester, England, assistant lecturer in classics, 1937-39; British Council, London, England, representative in Cairo, Zagazig, and Baghdad, 1941-42, service representative in Palestine and Trans-Jordan, 1942-45; University of Durham, Durham, England, professor of Greek and head of department of classics and ancient history, 1945-50; Cambridge University, Cambridge, England, fellow tutor and senior tutor of Trinity College, 1950-60, vice-master and senior tutor of Churchill College, 1960-65, president of Wolfson College, 1966-80; writer and scholar, 1980—. Research fellow of Churchill College; Reed College, Mellon Professor, 1976-77, Kenan Professor, 1981-82. Member of Sierra Leone Education Commission, 1954, Annan Committee on the Teaching of Russian, 1961, Hale Committee on University Teaching Methods, 1961, and Schools Council, 1965-67; governor of Bradfield College and Wellington College, 1963-83, and Charterhouse School, 1970-93. Member of board of trustees of National Maritime Museum, 1975-82; chairman of Trireme Trust, 1984-94, president, 1994—; member of Bell Educational Trust, 1983-88. *Military service:* Royal Navy, 1940-41.

AWARDS, HONORS: Leverhulme fellow, 1966, emeritus fellow, 1984-86; D.Litt., Davidson College, 1987, and University of Bath, 1988; named Commander of the British Empire, 1991.

WRITINGS:

(Under name J. S. Morrison, with R. T. Williams) *Greek Oared Ships, 900-323 B.C.,* Cambridge University Press (New York City), 1968.
The Ship, Volume 2: Long Ships and Round Ships: Warfare and Trade in the Mediterranean, 3000 B.C.-500 A.D., H.M.S.O., 1980.
(Under name J. S. Morrison, with J. F. Coates) *The Athenian Trireme: The History and Reconstruction of an Ancient Greek Warship,* Cambridge University Press, 1986.
(Consultant, editor and contributor) *The Age of the Galley,* Conway Maritime Press, 1994.
(Under name J. S. Morrison, with J. F. Coates) *Greek and Roman Oared Warships,* Oxbow Books, 1994.

Contributor of articles and reviews to classical and philosophy journals. Editor of *Cambridge Review,* 1939-40; co-editor of *Classical Review,* 1968-75.

WORK IN PROGRESS: The Wisdom of the Greeks: Poets and Philosophers, Eighth to Fourth Centuries B.C.

SIDELIGHTS: John Morrison told *CA:* "My main scholarly interests are in fifth and fourth century Greek philosophy and religion. However, publishers are studiously disinterested in books on such subjects, particularly if they are (as mine would be) heretical. Heresy in Greek and Roman maritime history is more viable commercially, especially if it is backed up (as mine has been) by full-scale reconstruction. This kind of evidence is more difficult to produce in ancient philosophy or religion."

With the support of the Greek Navy, Morrison, his co-author J. F. Coates, and the Trireme Trust have built an authentic reproduction of an ancient Athenian warship. The ship was launched in July, 1987, and given sea trials by a crew recruited by the Trireme Trust in August, 1987. Further trials were held in the summers of 1988, 1989, 1990, 1991, 1992, and 1994. In June, 1993, the ship was brought to England and rowed on the Thames by an international crew including many Americans. The occasion was the celebration of the birth of democracy 2,500 years previously in Athens, Greece.

Since archaeological evidence of the unsinkable trireme ranges from slim to nonexistent, the authors have had to rely on exhaustive research of classical literature, art, and

architecture. In *The Athenian Trireme,* Morrison and Coates have provided what London *Times* reviewer Peter Jones called "a detailed and commendably lucid account of the history of the trireme from its invention in the Seventh Century B.C. down to the Fourth Century."

BIOGRAPHICAL/CRITICAL SOURCES:

PERIODICALS

Times (London), October 9, 1986.
Times Literary Supplement, May 15, 1987.

*   *   *

MORRISON, Susan Dudley
   See GOLD, Susan Dudley

*   *   *

MUIR, Lynette R(oss) 1930-

PERSONAL: Born December 30, 1930, in Eastbourne, England; daughter of Harold George (in business) and Magdalen Gertrude (a caterer; maiden name, Rolfe) Muir. *Education:* University of Exeter, B.A. (with first class honors), 1951; University of London, Ph.D., 1956. *Religion:* Anglican.

ADDRESSES: Home—Leeds, England. *Office*—Department of French, University of Leeds, Leeds LS2 9JT, England.

CAREER: University College of Ghana, Accra, lecturer in French, 1959-61; University of Leeds, Leeds, England, lecturer, 1961-73, reader in French, 1973-86, director of Centre for Medieval Studies, 1980-85; writer, 1986—.

MEMBER: International Society for the Study of the Medieval Theatre.

WRITINGS:

(Editor and author of introduction) Pierre Sala, *Tristan: Roman d'adventures du seizieme siecle* (title means "Tristan: A Sixteenth-Century Adventure Story"), Droz, 1958.
(Translator and author of introduction and notes) *Adam* (play), Leeds Philosophical and Literary Society, 1970.
Liturgy and Drama in the Anglo-Norman Adam, Oxford University Press (New York City), 1973.
(Contributor of translations and author of introduction) *William, Count of Orange: Four Old French Epics,* Dent, 1975.
(Editor and author of introduction and notes) P. T. Durbin, *Le Passion de Semur* (title means "The Passion

Play from Semur"), Centre for Medieval Studies, University of Leeds, 1981.

(Translator) Peter Meredith and John Tailby, editors, *The Staging of Religious Drama in Europe in the Later Middle Ages: Texts and Documents in English Translation,* Western Michigan University (Kalamazoo), 1983.

Literature and Society in Medieval France: The Mirror and the Image, 1100-1500, Macmillan (New York City), 1985.

(Contributor) Clifford Davidson, editor, *The Saint Play in Medieval Europe,* Western Michigan University (Kalamazoo), 1986.

(Contributor) *Cambridge Guide to World Theatre,* Cambridge University Press (New York City), 1988.

The Biblical Drama of Medieval Europe, Cambridge University Press, 1995.

JUVENILES

The Unicorn Window, Abelard, 1961.
Nicholas and the Devils, Anchor Publications, 1985.
The Girls of St. Cyr, Merlin Books, 1994

OTHER

Contributor to language, literature, and medieval studies journals.

WORK IN PROGRESS: Contributions on early vernacular drama and fifteenth-century French drama, to be included in *Theatre in Europe: A Documentary History,* Vol. III, edited by William Tydeman for Cambridge University Press.

SIDELIGHTS: Lynette R. Muir told *CA:* "My two primary interests are the Middle Ages and the theatre. I especially enjoy working on medieval religious drama. I have been involved in several modern performances, notably the first staging of the complete medieval English cycles on wagons in Leeds and Wakefield. My children's book *Nicholas and the Devils* was an attempt to 'stage' a French passion play: they are too huge for normal modern performance.

"Literature is the reflection of the society in which it is created. I am very interested, therefore, in parallels between modern and medieval literary forms; for example, between *Star Trek* and medieval Arthurian literature; or a consideration of *Godspell* and the film *King of Kings* as successors to the medieval passion plays.

"My other, related interests include opera, iconography, medieval art and architecture, historical fiction for children, and school stories. Since I had the opportunity to take early retirement in 1983, I have had more time for writing and lecturing on some of these topics."

Muir's book *Literature and Society in Medieval France* was described in the *Times Literary Supplement* as "a mixture of generalisation and particular detail" intended "to give a picture of medieval society in France as it saw itself." Critic D.D.R. Owen especially enjoyed the author's "liberal use of plot summary and quotation," the sections on devotional literature and the theatre, and Muir's attention to the minute details of everyday life and attitudes in medieval times. The review concluded: "Throughout she has provided a lively and amiable guide, whose conversation is never dull and succeeds in imparting something of her own enthusiasm."

BIOGRAPHICAL/CRITICAL SOURCES:

PERIODICALS

Times Literary Supplement, May 16, 1986.

*   *   *

MULHOLLAND, Jim   1949-

PERSONAL: Born October 27, 1949, in New York, NY; son of Edward Charles and Dolores Mulholland. *Education:* Rutgers University, B.A., 1971.

CAREER: National Broadcasting Co. (NBC), New York City, writer for television program *The Tonight Show,* 1970-73; American Broadcasting Co. (ABC), New York City, writer for television programs *The Dick Cavett Show,* 1973, and *The Jack Paar Show,* 1974; freelance writer, 1974—; monologue writer for Johnny Carson for *Tonight Show,* beginning c. 1978. Television writing also includes material for comedy programs *Mary Tyler Moore* and *All in the Family.*

AWARDS, HONORS: Writers Guild Award (with Michael Barrie), for comedy anthology, 1986, for *The Ratings Game,* four Academy Awards for television writing.

WRITINGS:

The Abbott and Costello Book, Popular Library (New York City), 1975.
(With Michael Barrie) *The Ratings Game* (teleplay), Showtime/The Movie Channel, 1986.
(With Barrie) *Amazon Women on the Moon* (screenplay), Universal, 1987.

Also author of play *Good Evening, Ladies and Gentlemen . . . ,* produced in New York.

WORK IN PROGRESS: A film entitled *Many Happy Returns,* for CBS Theatricals.

BIOGRAPHICAL/CRITICAL SOURCES:

PERIODICALS

Los Angeles Times, March 24, 1986; September 15, 1987; September 18, 1987.
New York Times, September 18, 1987.
Time, September 28, 1987.*

*   *   *

MURDOCK, Eugene C(onverse) 1921-

PERSONAL: Born April 30, 1921, in Lakewood, OH; son of Stanley Howard and Elizabeth (Carter) Murdock; married Margaret Bowes McColl, October 7, 1950 (died June 14, 1987); children: Gordon Graham, Kathryn Carter. *Education:* College of Wooster, A.B., 1943; Columbia University, M.A., 1948, Ph.D., 1951.

ADDRESSES: Home—415 Columbia Ave., Williamstown, WV 26187. *Office*—Department of History, Marietta College, Marietta, OH 45750.

CAREER: Rio Grande College, Rio Grande, OH, professor of history, 1952-56; Marietta College, Marietta, OH, assistant professor, 1956-60, associate professor, 1960-63, professor of history, 1963-86, chairman of department, 1972-86. *Military service:* U.S. Army, 1943-46; served in Europe.

MEMBER: Ohio Academy of History (executive council, 1970-73; president, 1984-85), Society for American Baseball Research (president, 1976-78), North American Society for Sport History.

AWARDS, HONORS: Distinguished service awards, 1991, from Marietta College and the Ohio Academy of History.

WRITINGS:

Ohio's Bounty System in the Civil War, Ohio State University Press (Columbus, OH), 1963.
Patriotism Limited, Kent State University Press (Kent, OH), 1967.
One Million Men: The Civil War Draft in the North, State Historical Society of Wisconsin (Madison, WI), 1972.
(Coauthor) *Fenton Glass,* Richardson Printing (Marietta, OH), three volumes, 1978, 1980, 1989.
(Contributor) *The Encyclopedia of Southern History,* edited by Robert W. Twyman and David C. Roller, Louisiana State University Press (Baton Rouge, LA), 1979.
Ban Johnson: Czar of Baseball, Greenwood Press (Westport, CT), 1982.
(Contributor) *Insider's Baseball,* edited by L. Robert Davids, Scribner (New York City), 1983.
Mighty Casey, All-American, Greenwood Press, 1984.

The Civil War in the North: A Selective Annotated Bibliography, Garland (New York), 1987.
(Contributor) *Biographical Dictionary of American Sport: Baseball,* edited by David L. Porter, Greenwood Press, 1987.
The Buckeye Empire: An Illustrated History of Ohio Enterprise, Windsor Publications (Northridge, CA), 1988.
(Contributor) *Dictionary of American Biography,* eighth supplement, edited by John Garraty, Scribner, 1988.
(Contributor) *Ohio's Western Reserve: A Regional Reader,* edited by Harry F. Lupold and Gladys Haddad, Kent State University Press, 1988.
Bernard P. McDonough: The Man and His Work, Richardson Printing (Marietta, OH), 1989.
Baseball Players and Their Times: Oral Histories of the Game, 1920-1940, Meckler (Westport, CT), 1991.
Baseball between the Wars: Memories of the Game by the Men Who Played It, Meckler, 1992.
Tom Johnson of Cleveland, Wright State University Press (Dayton, OH), 1993.

Also author of *A History of the People's Banking and Trust Company,* 1991. Reviewer for *Choice,* 1964-67; member of editorial board, *Ohio History,* 1964-74, *Pro Football Digest,* 1967-69, and *Journal of Sport History,* 1973-78.*

*   *   *

MYERS, Bernard S(amuel) 1908-1993

PERSONAL: Born May 4, 1908, in New York, NY; died of pneumonia, February 28, 1993, in Brooklyn, NY; son of Louis (a businessman) and Dora (Waxenberg) Myers; married Shirley Levene (an editor of art books), August 11, 1938; children: Peter Lewis, Lucie Ellen. *Education:* New York University, Sc.B. (cum laude), 1928, M.A., 1929, Ph.D., 1933; also attended the Sorbonne, University of Paris, summer, 1931. *Avocational interests:* Travel throughout the world.

CAREER: New York University, New York City, lecturer in architecture, 1930-33, lecturer in education, 1930-43, 1945-48, instructor in fine arts, 1933-43; Rutgers University, New Brunswick, NJ, assistant professor of art history, 1946-47; University of Texas, Austin, guest professor of art history, 1948-50; New York University, New York City, lecturer in fine arts, 1951; City College of New York (now City College of the City University of New York), New York City, lecturer in fine arts, 1952-58; McGraw-Hill Book Co., New York City, editor-in-chief and manager of art books department, 1958-70, consultant, 1970-75; Rizzoli International Publications, New York City, publishing consultant, 1976-93. Lecturer at Art Students League (New York City), 1946-48; visiting associate professor at University of Southern California, summer, 1948; visiting professor at University of Colorado, summer, 1951. Education director of National Committee for Art Appreciation, 1937-39; member of executive committee of Citizens' Committee for the Arts, 1940-43; member of New York City's National Art Week Committee, 1940-41; member of an advisory committee of Princeton University, 1969-75, and of art advisory committee of New York Health and Hospitals Corp., 1971-93. Led summer art tours through Europe, 1934-36, 1947.

AWARDS, HONORS: Bollingen Foundation grant, 1950-51; Rockefeller Foundation grant, 1953-56.

WRITINGS:

(Editor with H. E. Barnes and others, and contributor) *An Intellectual and Cultural History of the Western World,* Cordon, 1937, revised edition in three volumes, Dover (New York City), 1965.

(Editor and contributor) *Forty-Eight Famous Paintings* (portfolio with text), National Committee for Art Appreciation, 1938.

(Editor and contributor) *American Art Today* (portfolio with text), New York World's Fair (New York City), 1939.

The Pageant of Art (listener's guide to accompany National Broadcasting Corp. program), Columbia University Press (New York City), 1940.

(Editor and contributor) *Roubillac, Eighteenth-Century Printmaker* (portfolio with text), Fischer, 1942.

Modern Art in the Making (college text), McGraw (New York City), 1950, 2nd edition, 1959.

Fifty Great Artists, Bantam (New York City), 1953.

(Editor and contributor) *Encyclopedia of Painting,* Crown (New York City), 1955, 4th edition, 1979.

Mexican Painting in Our Time, Oxford University Press (New York City), 1956.

Problems of the Younger American Artist, City College Press, 1957.

Art and Civilization (college text), McGraw, 1957, revised edition, 1967.

The German Expressionists, Praeger (New York City), 1957.

Understanding the Arts (college text), Holt (New York City), 1958, 3rd edition, 1977.

(Consulting editor and contributor) *Encyclopedia of World Art,* 17 volumes, McGraw, 1959-87.

(General editor with S. D. Myers) *McGraw-Hill Dictionary of Art,* five volumes, McGraw, 1969.

(Co-editor) *Dictionary of Twentieth Century Art,* McGraw, 1974.

(Senior consulting editor) *Random House Companion to Painting and Sculpture,* four volumes, Random House (New York City), 1981.

(Editor) *Encyclopedia of World Art Supplement,* McGraw, 1983.

Editor and contributor to portfolios for *Scribner's* (magazine) "American Painter's Series," 1938. Contributor of articles and reviews to art magazines, to *Saturday Review,* and to newspapers.

Myers' books were published in Germany, Italy, France, Spain, and Yugoslavia.

SIDELIGHTS: Bernard S. Myers wrote *CA* that he was "very much concerned by the tendency of younger people to forget that they were not the first to inhabit this planet—some feel that everything that came before them is not worth bothering with. Both as teacher and writer I am very much concerned with the backgrounds of culture, with the importance of tradition as it affects the present-day cultural world and, finally, with the possibility of our judging art as good or bad, effective or ineffective, a decent work of art or a failure."

OBITUARIES:

PERIODICALS

New York Times, March 3, 1993, p. B12.*

N

NEUMAN, Shirley Carol 1946-

PERSONAL: Born October 10, 1946, in Edmonton, Alberta, Canada; daughter of Herman (a farmer) and Ferdi (a nurse; maiden name, Wiethold) Neuman; married Paul Swartz, October 10, 1967 (divorced, 1979); married Jorge Frascara (a graphic designer and professor), April 8, 1982. *Education:* University of Alberta, B.A., 1968, M.A., 1969, Ph.D., 1976. *Avocational interests:* Gardening.

ADDRESSES: Home—7322 118A St., Edmonton, Alberta, Canada T6G 1V2. *Office*—Department of English, University of Alberta, Edmonton, Alberta, Canada T6G 2E9.

CAREER: University of Alberta, Edmonton, assistant professor, 1977-81, associate professor, 1981-86, professor of English, 1986—, chair of women's studies, 1987-89, chair of English, 1992—. Member of board of directors of NeWest Press and Longspoon Press, 1976-86.

MEMBER: Association of Canadian University Teachers of English (president, 1990-92), Association of Canadian and Quebecois Literature, Canadian Comparative Literature Association, Modern Language Association of America, Canadian Association of Chairs of English (president, 1993-94).

AWARDS, HONORS: Gabrielle Roy Prize from Association of Canadian and Quebecois Literature, 1984, for essay "Allow Self, Portraying Self, Autobiography in *Field Notes;*" fellow, Royal Society of Canada (1989); president, Academy II, Royal Society of Canada, 1994-96.

WRITINGS:

NONFICTION

Gertrude Stein: Autobiography and the Problem of Narration (monograph), English Literary Studies, 1979.

Some One Myth: Yeats' Autobiographical Prose, Dolmen Press, 1982.
(With Robert Wilson) *Labyrinths of Voice: Conversations With Robert Kroetsch,* NeWest Press (Edmonton), 1982.

EDITOR

Another Country: Writings by and About Henry Kreisel, NeWest Press (Edmonton), 1986.
(With Smaro Kamboureli) *A Mazing Space: Writing Canadian Women Writing,* NeWest Press, 1986.
(With Ira B. Nadel) *Gertrude Stein and the Making of Literature,* Macmillan (Basingstoke, Hampshire), 1987.
Watson, Wilfred, *Plays at the Iron Bridge, or, The Autobiography of Tom Horror,* Longspoon/NeWest (Edmonton, Alberta), 1989.
(And author of introduction) *Autobiography and Questions of Gender,* Frank Cass (London), 1992.
(With Glennis Stephenson; also author of introduction) *ReImagining Women: Representations of Women in Culture,* University of Toronto Press (Toronto, Ontario), 1993.

Contributor to books, including *Literary History of Canada,* volume 10, edited by W. H. New, University of Toronto, 1989; *Teaching Canadian Literature,* edited by Arnold E. Davidson, Modern Language Association, 1990. Contributor to literature journals.

WORK IN PROGRESS: Research on autobiography and gender construction, as well as Canadian literary history.

*   *   *

NICHOLLS, Mark
See FREWIN, Leslie Ronald

NODDINGS, Nel 1929-

PERSONAL: Born January 19, 1929, in Irvington, NJ; daughter of Edward and Nellie (Connors) Rieth; married James A. Noddings (an engineer and director of marketing), August 20, 1949; children: Laura Langer, James, Nancy, William, Victoria, Chris Wallace, Howard, Edward, Timothy, Sharon Miller. *Education:* Montclair State Teachers College (now Montclair State College), B.A., 1949; Rutgers University, M.A., 1964; Stanford University, Ph.D., 1973.

ADDRESSES: Home—340 Arboleda Drive, Los Altos, CA 94022. *Office*—School of Education, Stanford University, Stanford, CA 94305.

CAREER: Junior high school teacher in Woodbury, NJ, 1949-52; Matawan Regional High School, Matawan, NJ, mathematics teacher, department chair, and assistant principal, 1957-69; worked as curriculum supervisor in Montgomery Township, NJ, 1970-72; Pennsylvania State University, University Park, PA, assistant professor of education, 1973; University of Chicago, Chicago, IL, director of precollegiate education, 1975-76; Stanford University, Stanford, CA, acting assistant professor, 1977-79, assistant professor, 1979-83, associate professor and director of teacher education, 1983-86, professor of education, 1986—, associate dean, 1990—. Educational consultant. Phi Beta Kappa visiting scholar, 1989-90.

AWARDS, HONORS: Excellence in teaching award, Stanford University School of Education, 1981, 1982.

MEMBER: Philosophy of Education Society (president, 1991-92), American Philosophical Association, American Educational Research Association, California Association for Philosophy of Education, Society for Women in Philosophy, North American Society for Social Philosophy.

WRITINGS:

NONFICTION

Caring: A Feminine Approach to Ethics and Moral Education, University of California Press (Berkeley), 1984.
(With Paul J. Shore) *Awakening the Inner Eye,* Teachers College Press, Columbia University (New York City), 1984.
Women and Evil, University of California Press, 1989.
The Challenge to Care in Schools: An Alternative Approach to Education, Teachers College Press, Columbia University, 1992.
Educating for Intelligent Belief or Unbelief, Teachers College Press, Columbia University, 1993.

EDITOR

(With Robert B. Davis and Carolyn A. Maher) *Constructivist Views on the Teaching and Learning of Mathe-* *matics,* National Council of Teachers of Mathematics (Reston, VA), 1990.
(With Carol Witherell) *Stories Lives Tell: Narrative and Dialogue in Education,* Teachers College Press, Columbia University, 1991.

Contributor to books, as well as to education and philosophy journals.

SIDELIGHTS: Nel Noddings once told *CA:* "My current work involves bringing my philosophical training to bear on the central interests of human (mainly feminine) experience: love, morality, caring, nurturance, family life, virtue, and peace."

BIOGRAPHICAL/CRITICAL SOURCES:

PERIODICALS

Ethics in Education, January, 1985.
Times Literary Supplement, February 16-22, 1990, p. 166.*

*   *   *

NORTON, Augustus Richard 1946-

PERSONAL: Born September 2, 1946, in Brooklyn, NY; son of Augustus, Jr. (a blue collar worker) and Marion (Walsh) Norton; married Deanna J. Lampros (a freelance researcher), December 27, 1969; children: A. Timothy. *Education:* Student in Infantry Advanced Course, Fort Benning, GA, 1971-72; University of Miami, B.A. (magna cum laude) and M.A., both 1974; student in Foreign Area Officer Command and Staff Course, Fort Bragg, NC, 1978; attended Defense Language Institute (for Arabic), Presidio of Monterey, CA, 1978-79; attended Armed Forces Staff College, Norfolk, VA, 1979-80; University of Chicago, Ph.D., 1984.

ADDRESSES: Home—65 Eliot Hill Rd., South Natick, MA 01760. *Office*—Department of International Relations, Boston University, 152 Bay State Rd., Boston, MA 02215.

CAREER: U.S. Army career officer, 1966-93, basic training at Fort Gordon, GA, 1966, advanced infantry training at Fort Dix, NJ, 1966, candidate school at Fort Benning, GA, 1966-67, company executive officer at Fort Monmouth, NJ, 1967-68, platoon leader in 173rd Airborne Brigade in Republic of Vietnam, 1968-69, company commander and brigade operations officer of 82nd Airborne Division at Fort Bragg, NC, 1969-70, senior adviser to First Battalion of Vietnamese Airborne Division in Vietnam, 1970-71, assistant professor of military science and adjunct professor of political science at University of Illinois at Chicago, 1974-77, seconded to United Nations

Truce Supervision Organization headquartered in Jerusalem, served in south Lebanon, 1980-81, stationed at U.S. Military Academy at West Point, NY, assistant professor, 1981-84, associate professor of comparative politics and Middle Eastern studies, 1984-90, professor of political science, 1990-93, retired with rank of colonel, 1993.

MEMBER: International Institute for Strategic Studies, American Political Science Association, American Research Center in Egypt, Middle East Institute at Columbia University, Middle East Studies Association, Inter-University Seminar on Armed Forces and Society (associate chairman, 1982—), Council on Foreign Relations, Conference Group on the Middle East (cofounder), Phi Kappa Phi, Pi Sigma Alpha.

AWARDS, HONORS: Grantee of National Endowment for the Humanities, summer, 1986, MacArthur Foundation, 1989-90 and 1991-92, Ford Foundation, 1990-91 and 1992-95, and Rockefeller Foundation, 1993-94; Woodrow Wilson national fellow and International Peace Academy senior research fellow, both 1990-92. Military: Three Bronze Stars; Purple Heart; Combat Infantryman's Badge; Parachutist's Badge; four commendation medals; Air Medal; Vietnamese Cross of Gallantry; Honor Medal.

WRITINGS:

NONFICTION

(With Martin H. Greenberg) *International Terrorism,* Westview (Boulder, CO), 1980.

(With Ronald McLaurin, Lewis Snider, and Paul Jureidini) *The Emergence of a New Lebanon,* Praeger (New York City), 1984.

Amal and the Shi'a: Struggle for the Soul of Lebanon, University of Texas Press (Austin), 1987.

(With Thomas George Weiss) *UN Peacekeepers: Soldiers with a Difference,* Foreign Policy Association (New York City), 1990.

(With Muhammad Muslih) *Political Tides in the Arab World,* Foreign Policy Association, 1991.

EDITOR

(With Greenberg, and contributor) *Studies in Nuclear Terrorism: An Annotated Bibliography and Research Guide,* G. K. Hall (Boston), 1979.

(With R. A. Friedlander, Greenberg, and D. S. Rowe) *NATO: A Bibliography and Resource Guide,* Garland Publishing (New York City), 1984.

(With Greenberg) *Touring Nam: The Vietnam War Reader,* Morrow (New York City), 1984.

(With Greenberg) *The International Relations of the Palestine Liberation Organization,* Southern Illinois University Press (Carbondale), 1989.

Civil Society in the Middle East, Brill (Leiden, NY), 1994.

OTHER

Contributor to magazines, including *Middle East Journal, New Leader, Shofar,* and *Survival,* as well as to newspapers. Member of editorial board, *Ethics and International Affairs,* 1990—, *Current History,* 1992—, *Global Governance,* 1994—, and *al-Abhath.*

SIDELIGHTS: Augustus Richard Norton told *CA:* "After a dozen years of teaching at West Point, a site of incredible natural beauty, I moved to Boston, a city of enormous charm and character. Though the pristine calm of a Hudson valley promontory is certainly a world away from the intellectual archipelago of Boston-Cambridge, both locales offer wonderful inspiration to the writer. Beginning in the early 1990s, I have been possessed with trying to understand whether there is hope for liberal values in an increasingly illiberal world, especially in regions like the Middle East where kings, sultans, and dictators hold sway. Boston is the perfect place for this sort of reflection and writing. Thus far, I have been able to sustain a good ration of optimism, as my recent writing on civil society in the Middle East reflects. As the millennium approaches, I shall be interested to discover if global and regional trends validate my optimism."

BIOGRAPHICAL/CRITICAL SOURCES:

PERIODICALS

Los Angeles Times Book Review, April 28, 1985, p. 4.
Times Literary Supplement, September 4, 1987, p. 943.

O-P

ORLOCK, Carol (Ellen) 1947-

PERSONAL: Surname originally Gibson; name legally changed in 1965; born February 17, 1947, in San Diego, CA; daughter of James C. and Anna Elizabeth (Saylor) Gibson. *Education:* Pennsylvania State University, B.A., 1968; San Francisco State College (now University), M.A. (with honors), 1970. *Avocational interests:* Computers and computer programming.

ADDRESSES: Home—920 Second Ave. W., Seattle, WA 98119.

CAREER: Second Storey Gallery, Seattle, WA, founder and owner, 1970-72; Olympic College, Bremerton, WA, instructor in composition and creative writing, 1974-78; University of Washington, Seattle, extension lecturer in composition and fiction writing, beginning 1976; Shoreline Community College, Seattle, faculty member and adviser to *Spindrift* art and literary magazine, 1988—. Presents writing workshops; gives readings of poetry and prose throughout the western United States.

AWARDS, HONORS: Grant, National Endowment for the Arts, 1975; fellow, Washington State Arts Commission, 1984-85; semifinalist, University of Iowa Award for Short Fiction, 1986; King County Publication Award, Governor's Award for the State of Washington, and Pacific Booksellers Award, 1986-87, all for *The Goddess Letters;* Western States Book Award, 1993, for *The Hedge, the Ribbon.*

WRITINGS:

The Goddess Letters (novel), St. Martin's (New York City), 1987.
The Hedge, the Ribbon (novel), Broken Moon (Seattle, WA), 1993.
Inner Time: The Science of Body Clocks and What Makes Us Tick, Birch Lane Press, 1993.

Work is represented in anthologies, including *Backbone II: New Fiction by Northwest Women,* Seal Press (Seattle), 1980; *Hyperion Anthology,* 1980; and *Anthology of Magazine Verse and Yearbook of American Poetry,* 1981. Contributor of poems, stories, articles, and reviews to periodicals, including *Arthritis Today, Fitness, Ms., Sesame Street Parents, Greenfield Review, Lear's, Boston Phoenix, Arts,* and *Calyx.* Coeditor of *Crab Creek Review.*

WORK IN PROGRESS: A nonfiction book, tentatively titled *The End of Aging,* for Birch Lane Press.

SIDELIGHTS: Carol Orlock's novel *The Goddess Letters* retells the myth of Demeter, goddess of the earth and agriculture, and her daughter Persephone, in which Persephone is abducted and raped by Hades, god of the Underworld, and made his queen of the Underworld. Demeter's immense grief at her daughter's loss causes her to ignore the earth and its growing seasons; her bitter tears produce a reversal of the earth's lush vegetation and abundant food production, and mortals die from lack of food and water. Demeter pleads with Persephone's father, Zeus, king of the gods, for her daughter's return, and he agrees that Persephone be allowed to visit the earth for six months each year; in those six months the earth flourishes and crops grow—creating spring and summer—whereas in the six months Persephone spends in the lower region the earth withers and crops die—hence fall and winter. Orlock once described *The Goddess Letters* to *CA* as "a series of imagined correspondences between the Greek goddesses Demeter and Persephone, covering a period of two thousand years. The book has been called 'an evocative dream,' which is an apt description for much of my work."

Susan Landgraf writes in *Calyx* that "Demeter and Persephone's story—about mothers and daughters, suffering and loss, joy and love—is our history as women, individual and collective." Madelyn M. Arnold observes in *Belles*

Lettres, "Sometimes deadpan and sometimes with a hoo-haw belly laugh, [Orlock] lampoons such things as rhetoric, the arbitrary nature of moral philosophy, and sex." The critic continues, "*The Goddess Letters* articulates the complex interaction of mother and daughter in the process of becoming peers and friends—of becoming mothers, and women, together." The letters address issues which universally affect mothers and daughters as well as historic events which occur over the centuries. Eventually, according to Judith Roche in the *Seattle Times/Seattle Post-Intelligencer,* "the new ways of law, justice and punishment, which will lead to our modern world view, win out over Demeter's matriarchal wisdom and earthy sensuality." In the novel, Demeter finally realizes her dwindling strength and impact on an increasingly Christian-oriented culture; she turns away from her official duties as a goddess, relinquishing her control over her world. Christine Hunsicker and Brian Erwin assert in the *San Francisco Chronicle* that *The Goddess Letters* "is a lively and enjoyable retelling of Greek mythology," and a critic for the *New Times* concludes that the book "is a lively, lyrical and thought-provoking novel whose appeal is truly enduring."

Orlock's next novel, *The Hedge, the Ribbon,* "blends contemporary realism with the fantastic thread so integral to storytelling traditions," explains Joan Hinkemeyer in the *Rocky Mountain News.* In a series of visits to an elderly patient, a caregiver weaves interconnected stories about young Angela Maxwell and her fellow inhabitants of the town of Millford. Throughout the tales, the caregiver incorporates a piece of ribbon, which serves as an element in each story. As the visits continue, the lives and activities of the residents of Millford are revealed to be as intertwined as the elderly woman's hedge. Nancy Pearl comments in the *Seattle Times* that *The Hedge, the Ribbon* reveals life's transitory nature and shows "how transforming events—falling in love, choosing a career, having a baby, dying—happen in mysterious and magical ways."

Orlock once told *CA:* "For me, writing is an extremely trying way of having dandy fun. I probably started doing it with crayon, by now have graduated to a word processor, but the miserable delight in it remains the same. I write because I don't know how not to and maybe never did. This arduous fun occasionally leads to publication; my stories and poems have appeared in literary quarterlies and in regional magazines.

"I like imagining what couldn't possibly happen, then filling in all the fine details of exactly how it did. This makes for magical characters in everyday situations, or for ordinary folk confronted by a playful universe. I never quite know what will happen. But my themes—relationships and their quiet signal nets—always surface somehow in the midst of it all. We may be magic critters or simply more of nature's breeding fodder. Writing is, for me, a painfully pleasant way of toying with the questions.

"I admire the craft of Truman Capote, Joan Didion, and John Fowles. I write and teach with such standards in mind."

BIOGRAPHICAL/CRITICAL SOURCES:

PERIODICALS

Belles Lettres, January, 1988, p. 7.
Calyx, winter, 1987-88.
Los Angeles Times, November 26, 1993.
New Times, July, 1987.
New York Times Book Review, August 9, 1987.
Rocky Mountain News, October 8, 1993.
San Francisco Chronicle, August 16, 1987.
Seattle Times, January 2, 1994.
Seattle Times/Seattle Post-Intelligencer, August 23, 1987.

*   *   *

PANNENBERG, Wolfhart (Ulrich) 1928-

PERSONAL: Born October 2, 1928, in Stettin, Germany (now Szczecin, Poland); son of Kurt Bernhard Siegfried (a customs officer) and Irmgard (Kersten) Pannenberg; married Hilke Schuette, May 3, 1954. *Education:* Attended Universities of Berlin, Goettingen, Basel, and Heidelberg, 1947-53; University of Heidelberg, Th.D., 1953. *Avocational interests:* History, music, philosophy.

ADDRESSES: Home—Sudetenstrasse 8, 82166 Graefelfing, Germany. *Office*—Schellingstrasse 3, Institut fuer Fundamentaltheologie, 8000 Munich, Germany.

CAREER: Professor of systematic theology at University of Heidelberg, Heidelberg, Germany, 1955-58, Kirchliche Hochschule Wuppertal, Wuppertal, Germany, 1958-61, University of Mainz, Mainz, Germany, 1961-67, and University of Munich, Munich, Germany, 1967—; head of Institute of Ecumenical Theology, Munich, 1967—. Visiting professor at University of Chicago, 1963, Harvard University, 1966-67, and Claremont School of Theology, 1967 and 1975.

MEMBER: Bavarian Academy of Science.

AWARDS, HONORS: Honorary D.D. theology, University of Glasgow, 1972, University of Manchester, 1977, and University of Dublin, 1979.

WRITINGS:

Die Praedestinationslehre des Duns Skotus, Vandenhoeck & Ruprecht (Goettingen), 1954.
(Editor with Rolf Rendtorff and others) *Offenbarung als Geschichte,* Vandenhoeck & Reprecht, 1961, 5th edi-

tion, 1982, translation by David Granskou published as *Revelation as History,* Macmillan (New York City), 1969.

Was ist der Mensch?: Die Anthropologie der Gegenwart im Lichte der Theologie, Vandenhoeck & Ruprecht, 1962, translation published as *What Is Man?,* Fortress (Philadelphia, PA), 1970.

(Editor with Wilfried Joest) *Dogma und Denkstrukturen,* Vandenhoeck & Ruprecht, 1963.

Grundzuege der Christologie, Guetersloher Verlagshaus Gerd Mohn, 1964, translation by Lewis L. Wilkins and Duane A. Priebe published as *Jesus: God and Man,* Westminster (Philadelphia, PA), 1968.

Grundfragen Systematischer Theologie, Vandenhoeck & Ruprecht, Volume 1, 1967, Volume 2, 1980, translation by George Kehm published as *Basic Questions in Theology,* Fortress, Volume 1, 1970, Volume 2, 1971.

Theology and the Kingdom of God, Westminster, 1969.

(With Avery Dulles and Carl E. Braaten) *Spirit, Faith, and Church,* Westminster, 1970.

(With A. M. K. Mueller) *Erwaegungen Zur Theologie der Natur,* Guetersloher Verlagshaus Gerd Mohn, 1970.

Thesen Zur Theologie der Kirche, Claudius, 1970.

Das Glaubensbekenntnis, Siebenstern, 1972, translation by Margaret Kohl published as *The Apostles' Creed in the Light of Today's Questions,* Westminster, 1972.

Gottesgedanke und Menschliche Freiheit, Vandenhoeck & Ruprecht, 1972, translation by R. H. Wilson published as *The Idea of God and Human Freedom,* Westminster, 1972.

Wissenschaftstheorie und Theologie, Suhrkamp, 1973, translation by Francis McDonagh published as *Theology and Philosophy of Science,* Westminster, 1976.

Human Nature, Election, and History, Westminster, 1977.

Ethik und Ekklesiologie, Vandenhoeck & Ruprecht, 1977, translation by Keith Crim published in two volumes, Westminster, Volume 1: *Ethics,* 1981, Volume 2: *The Church,* 1983.

Theological Issues in Christian Spirituality, Westminster, 1983.

Anthropologie in Theologischer Perspective, Vandenhoeck & Ruprecht, 1983, translation by Matthew J. O'Connell published as *Anthropology in Theological Perspective,* Westminster Press, 1985.

(With others) *Die Erfahrung der Abwesenheit Gottes in der modernen Kultur,* Vandenhoeck & Ruprecht, 1984.

(With Arthur Kaufmann) *Gesetz und Evangelium,* Verlag der Bayerischen Akademie der Wissenschaften (Munchen), 1986.

(With Karl Lehmann) *Lehrverurteilungen, kirchentrennend?* Vandenhoeck & Ruprecht, 1986, translation by Kohl published as *The Condemnations of the Reformation Era: Do They Still Divide?* Fortress Press (Minneapolis), 1990.

(With Helmut Baitsch) *Sind wir von Natur aus Religios?,* Patmos (Dusseldorf), 1986.

(With Venanz Schubert) *Der Mensch und Seine Arbeit,* EOS Verlag (St. Ottilien), 1986.

(With Mathew Vekathanam and Karl Rehner) *Christology in the Indian Anthropological Context; Man-History-Christ: Christ, the Mystery of Man, and of the Human History: An Evaluative Encounter with K. Rehner and W. Pannenberg,* P. Lang (New York City), 1986.

(Contributor) *Etica e pragmatica,* Cedam (Padova), 1987.

Christentum in Einer Sakularisierten Welt, Herder (Freiberg), 1988, translation published as *Christianity in a Secularized World,* Crossroad (New York City), 1989.

Metaphysik und Gottesgedanke, Vandenhoeck & Ruprecht, 1988, translation by Philip Clayton published as *Metaphysics and the Idea of God,* Eerdmans (Grand Rapids, MI), 1990.

Systematische Theologie, Volume 1, Vandenhoeck & Ruprecht, 1988, translation by Geoffrey W. Bromiley published as *Systematic Theology,* Volume 1, Eerdmans, 1991.

The Theology of Wolfhart Pannenberg: Twelve American Critiques, with an Autobiographical Essay and Response, edited by Carl E. Braaten and Clayton, Augsburg (Minneapolis), 1988.

An Introduction to Systematic Theology, Eerdmans, 1991.

Toward a Theology of Nature: Essays on Science and Faith, edited by Ted Peters, Westminster/J. Knox Press (Louisville, KY), 1993.

Contributor to books, including *Verbindliches Zeugnis,* edited by K. S. Frank, Vandenhoeck & Ruprecht, 1992, and *Fides Quaerens Intellectum: Beitrage zur Fundamentaltheologie,* Francke (Tubingen), 1992.

Coeditor of *Kerygma und Dogma.*

WORK IN PROGRESS: Volumes 2 and 3 of *Systematische Theologie.*

BIOGRAPHICAL/CRITICAL SOURCES:

BOOKS

Berten, Ignace, *Die Theologie Wolfhart Pannenberg,* Claudius, 1970, translation by E. Frank Tupper, published as *The Theology of Wolfhart Pannenberg,* Westminster, 1973.

Braaten, Carl E., *History and Hermeneutics,* Westminster, 1967.

Galloway, Allan D., *Wolfhart Pannenberg,* Allen & Unwin (Winchester, MA), 1973.

Robinson, James M., and John B. Cobb, editors, *New Frontiers in Theology,* Harper, 1967.

PERIODICALS

Christian Century, March 19, 1969.
Encounter, summer, 1969.
Times Literary Supplement, October 27, 1989, p. 1188.*

*   *   *

PARKER, Julia (Louise)   1932-

PERSONAL: Born July 27, 1932, in Plymouth, England; daughter of Lester Francis and Edna Charity (Tapson) Lethbridge; married Derek William George Parker (an author), July 27, 1957. *Education:* Attended Plymouth College of Art, 1946-52; Faculty of Astrological Studies, D.F.Astrol.S., 1967. *Politics:* Liberal. *Religion:* Agnostic.

ADDRESSES: Home—41 Elsham Rd., London W14 8HB, England. *Agent*—David Higham Associates Ltd., 5-8 Lower John St., Golden Square, London W1R 4HA, England.

CAREER: Plymouth College Prepatory School, arts and crafts teacher, 1953-57; Hammersmith Girls' Comprehensive School, London, England, art and dance teacher, 1959-64; Faculty of Astrological Studies, London, secretary, 1967-72, president, 1973-79. Professional dancer, 1953-57; set designer for TWW-TV, Cardiff, Wales, 1957.

MEMBER: Society of Authors, Astrological Association.

WRITINGS:

WITH HUSBAND, DEREK PARKER

The Compleat Astrologer, McGraw, 1971, reprinted as *The New Compleat Astrologer,* Crown, 1984, Random House Value, 1990.
The Compleat Lover, McGraw, 1972.
The Natural History of the Chorus Girl, Bobbs-Merrill, 1975.
The Immortals, McGraw, 1976.
The Story and the Song, Elm Tree, 1979.
How Do Know Who You Are?, Thames & Hudson, 1980.
Do It Yourself Health, Thames & Hudson, 1982.
A History of Astrology, Deutsch, 1983.
Dreaming: Remembering, Interpreting, Benefitting, Crown, 1985.
The Traveller's Guide to the Nile Valley, J. Cape, 1986.
The Traveller's Guide to Cyprus, J. Cape, 1988.
The Future Now: How to Use All Methods of Prediction from Astrology to Tarot to Discover Your Future, Prentice-Hall (New York City), 1988.
Atlas of the Supernatural, Prentice Hall (New York City), 1990.
The Secret World of Your Dreams: A Complete A-to-Z Dictionary of Dream Interpretations, Perigree Books (New York City), 1990.

Parker's Astrology: The Essential Guide to Using Astrology in Your Daily Life, Dorling Kindersley (New York City), 1991.
The Power of Magic: Secrets and Mysteries Ancient and Modern, Simon & Schuster (New York City), 1992.
The Sun and Moon Signs Library (one book for each of the twelve signs of the zodiac), Dorling Kindersley, 1992.

SOLE AUTHOR

The Pocket Guides to Astrology, Simon & Schuster, 1981.
The Zodiac Family, Overlook Press (Woodstock, NY), 1988.
Women and Welfare: Ten Victorian Women in Public Social Service, St. Martin's Press (New York City), 1989.
Zodiac Family: How Astrology Can Help You Understand and Raise Your Child, Overlook Press, 1992.

SIDELIGHTS: Julia Parker wrote: "I am concerned to further a much wider knowledge of astrology, educating the public away from the simplistic Sun-sign columns common in newspapers and magazines. I see astrology as a helpful discipline, furthering man's awareness of himself and his potential, making life generally easier, pointing out how we can best develop our talents, develop positive characteristics, and negate negative traits.

"Astrology apart, my interests center around the arts: I paint and sculpt, and have been involved in classical ballet, teaching, choreographing, and performing for almost all my life. For the past six years I have been studying classical guitar.

"I feel strongly there should be a change in educational methods: with increasing leisure time becoming available, the only possible way to fulfillment is going to be in increased education for leisure, and an early encouragement of skills. Often the approach in art training, in particular, is far too narrow; greater versatility should be encouraged and aimed for, and the more attention that can be given to the development of new techniques in varying media the better for all concerned."

*   *   *

PARRISH, Patt
See BUCHEISTER, Patt

*   *   *

PERERA, Thomas Biddle   1938-

PERSONAL: Born November 20, 1938, in New York, NY; son of Lionel Cantoni (a banker) and Dorothy Perera; married Gretchen Gifford (a nurse), August 28, 1960; children: Daniel Gifford, Thomas Biddle, Jr. *Education:* Columbia University, A.B., 1961, M.A., 1963, Ph.D., 1968. *Avocational interests:* Ham radio, flying, scuba diving, spelunking, and computers.

ADDRESSES: Home—11 Squire Hill Rd., North Caldwell, NJ 07006. *Office*—Department of Psychology, Montclair State College, Upper Montclair, NJ 07043.

CAREER: Columbia University, Barnard College, New York, NY, instructor, 1966-68, assistant professor of psychology, 1968-74, founder and director of psychophysiology laboratory, 1969—, visiting associate professor, 1974-81, visiting professor, 1981—; Montclair State College, Upper Montclair, NJ, associate professor and director of psychophysiology laboratory, 1974-81, professor of psychology and head of the experimental program, 1981—. Senior research scientist, New York State Psychiatric Institute, 1964-71. Licensed psychologist in State of New York. Camp counselor, Camp Killooleet, 1956—. Consultant to American Association of State Psychology Boards, 1974—, to National Science Foundation, and to various colleges and organizations.

MEMBER: American Psychological Association, American Association for the Advancement of Science (life member), National Speleological Society, Biofeedback Research Association, Amateur Radio Relay League, Aircraft Owners and Pilots Association, MENSA, Eastern Psychological Association, New York Academy of Sciences, Sigma Xi.

WRITINGS:

(With Wallace Orlowsky) *Who Will Wash the River?,* Coward, 1970.
(With Orlowsky) *Who Will Clean the Air?,* Coward, 1971.
(With wife, Gretchen G. Perera) *Louder and Louder,* F. Watts (New York City), 1973.
(With G. G. Perera) *Your Brain Power,* Coward, 1975.
(With G. G. Perera) *The Evolution of the Eye,* Coward, in press.

AUDIO-VISUAL AND COMPUTERIZED INSTRUCTIONAL MODULES

The Electrical Stimulation of the Brain, Volume I: *Methodology and Techniques for Implanting Electrodes,* Volume II: *Conditioned Suppression of Hypothalamically Induced Eating, Perfusion, and Histological Verification of Electrode Loci,* Life Science Associates, 1974.
General Introduction to the Physiological Psychology Laboratory, Life Science Associates, 1974.
Tracheal Cannulation, Life Science Associates, 1974.

Perfusion of the Circulatory System with Formalin and Removal of the Central Nervous System, Life Science Associates, 1974.
Exposure of the Sciatic Nerve, Nerve-muscle Physiology, Removal and Stimulation of a Segment of the Sciatic Nerve and Clinical and Morphological Observation of Peripheral Nerve Regeneration, Life Science Associates, 1974.
Observation of Image Formation and Dissection of the Bovine Eye, Life Science Associates, 1974.
Direct Observation of a Subject's Retina and External Ear, Plotting the Blind Spot, and Direct Observation of One's Own Blind Spot and Retina, Life Science Associates, 1974.
Exposure of the Spinal Cord, Stimulation of Spinal Nerves and Removal of the Entire Intact Central Nervous System, Life Science Associates, 1974.
Removal of the Lamb Brain from the Skull and Dissection of the Brain, Life Science Associates, 1974.
The Anatomy of the Human Brain, Life Science Associates, 1974.
Stimulating and Lesioning the Brain with Clinical and Gross Histological Follow-up, Life Science Associates, 1974.
Methodology and Techniques for Stereotaxically Implanting Electrodes into the Hypothalamus of the Rat, the Production of Hypothalamically Induced Eating Behavior through Stimulation of the Hypothalamus, and Procedures for the Histological Verification of Electrode Loci, Life Science Associates, 1974.
Recording and Biofeedback of Electrophysiological Signs from Humans, Life Science Associates, 1974.
Sequential Gross Coronal Sections of the Human Brain, Life Science Associates, 1974.
Sequential Coronal Sections of the Baboon Brain, Life Science Associates, 1974.
(With M. Muller) *Construction of a Three-Dimensional Model of the Human Brain,* Life Science Associates, 1974.
Dark Adaptation, Life Science Associates, 1975.
Production of the Stabilized Retinal Image in Humans, Life Science Associates, 1975.
Computer Programs for Experimental Psychology: The TIP-500 System, Life Science Associates, 1979.
Reaction Time, Life Science Associates, 1979.
Quantification of the Muller-Lyer Illusion, Life Science Associates, 1979.
Quantification of the Horizontal-Vertical Illusion, Life Science Associates, 1979.
Quantification of the Poggendorf Illusion, Life Science Associates, 1979.
Quantification of Line Length Judgments, Life Science Associates, 1979.

Quantification of Size of Rectangle Judgments, Life Science Associates, 1979.

Concept Formation, Life Science Associates, 1979.

Verbal Learning, Life Science Associates, 1979.

Visual Illusion Demonstrations, Life Science Associates, 1979.

Operant Conditioning, Life Science Associates, 1979.

Latency Analyzer and Histogram Plotter, Life Science Associates, 1979.

Interresponse Time Analyzer and Plotter, Life Science Associates, 1979.

Event Recorder, Life Science Associates, 1979.

Cumulative Recorder, Life Science Associates, 1979.

Human Maze Learning, Life Science Associates, 1979.

Signal Detection, Life Science Associates, 1979.

Pursuit Rotor, Life Science Associates, 1979.

Mirror Tracing, Life Science Associates, 1979.

Operant Conditioning Laboratory Control System, Life Science Associates, 1979.

Multiple-Field Tachistoscope, Life Science Associates, 1979.

Psychophysical Scaling of Line Length Using, Life Science Associates, 1979.

Visual Acuity, Life Science Associates, 1979.

Difference Limens for Auditory Frequency, Life Science Associates, 1993.

Psychological Seating of Auditory Frequency, Life Science Associates, 1993.

OTHER

Contributor to books, including *Thinking: Studies of Covert Language Processes,* edited by F. J. McGuigan, Appleton-Century-Crofts (East Norwalk, CT), 1966; *Careers in Psychology,* edited by F. J. Mandriota, Life Science Associates, 1974,. Also author of numerous scientific papers presented to learned societies. Contributor to professional journals.

WORK IN PROGRESS: Research on the electrical activity of the human nervous system, environmental pollution, and developing computerized psychological testing and neuropsychological rehabilitation software.

SIDELIGHTS: Thomas Biddle Perera told *CA:* "My wide ranging interests have motivated me to study and research many different fields of science and to explore the mysteries of solo journeys into uncharted territories."

*   *   *

PERRETT, Bryan   1934-

PERSONAL: Born July 9, 1934; son of Thomas Edgar and Ellen (Nicholson) Perrett; married Anne Catherine

Trench, August 13, 1966. *Education:* Educated in Liverpool, England.

ADDRESSES: Home—7 Maple Ave., Burscough, near Ormskirk, Lancashire L40 5SL, England.

CAREER: Bentalls Ltd. (department store), Kingston, Surrey, England, trainee buyer, 1955-56; Lloyds Brokers, London, England, broker, 1956-60; Griffiths & Armour (insurance broker), Liverpool, England, broker and claims adjustor, 1960-77; professional author, 1977—. *Military service:* British Regular Army, 1952-54; Territorial Army, 1954-67; Army Emergency Reserve, Royal Tank Regiment, 1967-71, became captain.

MEMBER: Rotary Club of Ormskirk (Lancashire), Royal United Services Institute (London).

AWARDS, HONORS: Awarded Territorial Decoration, 1970, by Army Emergency Reserve, Royal Tank Regiment.

WRITINGS:

Fighting Vehicles of the Red Army, Ian Allen, 1969, Arco (New York City), 1970.

NATO Armour, Ian Allen, 1971.

The Valentine in North Africa, 1942-43, Ian Allen, 1972.

The Matilda, Ian Allen, 1973.

The Churchill, Ian Allen, 1974.

Through Mud and Blood, foreword by Field Marshal Sir Michael Carver, R. Hale (London), 1975.

The Lee/Grant Tanks in British Service, Osprey (London), 1978.

Tank Tracks to Rangoon, R. Hale, 1978, revised version, 1992.

Allied Tank Destroyers, Osprey, 1979.

Wavell's Offensive, Ian Allen, 1979.

Sturmartillerie and Panzerjager, Osprey, 1979.

The Churchill Tank, Osprey, 1980.

The Panzerkampfwagen III, Osprey, 1980.

The Stuart Light Tank Series, Osprey, 1980.

The Panzerkampfwagen IV, Osprey, 1980.

The Tiger Tanks, Osprey, 1981.

The Panzerkampfwagen V Panther, Osprey, 1981.

British Tanks in North Africa 1940-42, Osprey, 1981.

The Czar's British Squadron, foreword by His Royal Highness The Duke of Edinburgh, Kimber & Co. (London), 1981.

German Armoured Cars and Reconnaissance Half-Tracks 1939-45, Osprey, 1982.

Weapons of the Falklands Conflict, Blandford (New York City), 1982.

German Light Panzers, 1932-42, Osprey, 1983.

A History of Blitzkrieg, foreword by General Sir John Hackett, Stein & Day (Briarcliff Manor, NY), 1983

(published in England as *Lightning War*, Granada Publishing (London), 1983).

Mechanised Infantry, Osprey, 1984.

The Hawks: A Short History of the 14th/20th King's Hussars, Picton (Chippenham, Wiltshire, England), 1984.

Allied Armour in Italy 1943/45, Arms & Armour Press (London), 1985.

Allied Armour in North Africa 1942-43, Arms & Armour Press, 1986.

A Hawk at War: The Peninsular Reminiscences of General Sir Thomas Brotherton, Picton, 1986.

Knights of the Black Cross: Hitler's Panzerwaffe and Its Leaders, foreword by General F. M. von Senger und Etterlin, R. Hale, 1986, St. Martin's (New York City), 1987.

Hitler's Panzers: The Years of Aggression, Arms & Armour Press, 1987.

Soviet Armour since 1945, Blandford Press, 1987.

Desert Warfare: From Its Roman Origins to the Gulf Conflict, foreword by Field Marshal Lord Carver, P. Stephens (New York City), 1988.

(With Ian Hogg) *Encyclopaedia of the Second World War*, Presidio Press (Novato, CA), 1989.

Tank Warfare, Arms & Armour Press, 1990.

Liverpool: A City at War, R. Hale, 1990.

Canopy of War: Jungle Warfare from the Earliest Days of Forest Fighting to the Battlefields of Vietnam, foreword by General Sir Walter Walker, P. Stephens, 1990.

Last Stand: Famous Battles against the Odds, Arms & Armour Press, 1991.

The Battle Book: Crucial Conflicts in History from 1469 B.C. to the Present, Arms & Armour Press, 1992.

Churchill Infantry Tank 1941-1951, Osprey, 1993.

At All Costs: Stories of Impossible Victories, Arms & Armour Press, 1993.

Seize & Hold: Master Strokes on the Battlefield, Sterling (New York City), 1994.

Iron Fist: Classic Armoured Warfare Engagements, Sterling, 1995.

Against the Odds: Famous Defensive Engagements, Arms & Armour Press, in press.

Contributor to *The Korean War*, Orbis, 1984; *Elite Fighting Units*, Arco, 1984; *Guinness Encyclopedia of Warfare*, Guinness (London), 1991; *The World's Armies*, Salamander Books (London), 1991; and *The Hitler Options: Alternate Decisions of World War II*, Greenhill, 1995.

Also author of children's stories. Defense correspondent to *Liverpool Echo* during Falklands and Gulf Wars. Contributor to periodicals, including *Army Quarterly, Military History, U.S. Army Defense Review, War Monthly, Defence Update, Born in Battle, British Army Review, War in Peace, The Elite, Jane's Military Review*.

SIDELIGHTS: Bryan Perrett once told *CA:* "I am not sure that I can offer anything more than the obvious advice to aspiring writers of military history. One may receive many conflicting opinions concerning the conduct of any one operation, since this is seen by every man from a different standpoint. . . . It is the historian's duty to sift the merits of the case impartially, and to write what he believes to be the honest truth. Trust no one source—experts are frequently wrong, particularly as to detail; famous names are quite as capable of making mistakes as anyone else. To obtain the truth, one must play the Devil's Advocate with one's own sources, until one is absolutely satisfied that they are accurate; any historian who does less faces the uncomfortable prospect of living with his mistakes.

"I do not believe that any writer can succeed without the most ruthless self-discipline. The military historian in particular must establish an iron routine for himself, and maintain his effort until he has achieved his objective. Waiting for inspiration and working by fits and starts will not finish the job—like any artist, you are working because an inner drive compels you to do so. If that drive is so weak that you are unable to apply yourself continuously, I think you would do well to find some other way of passing your time.

"Finally, remember that criticism is only another man's opinion. It can be constructive or destructive, and should be assessed in its turn as to whether it contains merit. There is an element of the frustrated performer in most critics, and one should not become either unduly depressed or elated by what they say."

*   *   *

PIERCE, Meredith Ann 1958-

PERSONAL: Born July 5, 1958, in Seattle, WA; daughter of Frank N. (a professor of advertising) and Jo Ann (an editor and professor of agriculture; maiden name, Bell) Pierce. *Education:* University of Florida, B.A., 1978, M.A., 1980. *Avocational interests:* Music (composition, harp, and voice), picture book collecting, film and theater, anthropology, archaeology, languages, folklore and mythology, cats, science fiction, fantasy, and children's literature.

CAREER: Writer. University of Florida, instructor in creative writing, 1978-80; Bookland, Gainesville, FL, clerk, 1981; Waldenbooks, Gainesville, clerk, 1981-87; Aluchua County Library District, FL, library assistant, 1987—. Treasurer, Children's Literature Association Conference, Gainesville, 1982.

MEMBER: Phi Beta Kappa.

AWARDS, HONORS: First prize, Scholastic/Hallmark Cards creative writing contest, 1973; Best Books for Young Adults citation and Best of the Best Books 1970-1982 citation, both from the American Library Association (ALA), *New York Times* Notable Children's Book citation, and Parents' Choice Award Superbook citation, all 1982, Children's Book Award from the International Reading Association, 1983, California Young Reader Medal, 1986, and *Booklist* Best Books of the Decade (1980-89) list, all for *The Darkangel;* Jane Tinkham Broughton Fellow in writing for children, Bread Loaf Writers' Conference, 1984; Best Books for Young Adults semifinalist, ALA, 1985, for *A Gathering of Gargoyles;* Parents' Choice Award for Literature citation, 1985, and New York Public Library Books for the Teen Age exhibit citation, 1986, both for *The Woman Who Loved Reindeer;* Individual Artist Fellowship Special Award for Children's Literature, Florida Department of State, Division of Cultural Affairs, 1987; Best Books for Young Adults citation, ALA, 1991, for *The Pearl of the Soul of the World.*

WRITINGS:

YOUNG ADULT FANTASY NOVELS

The Darkangel (first novel in the "Darkangel" trilogy; also see below), Little, Brown (Boston, MA), 1982.
A Gathering of Gargoyles (second novel in the "Darkangel" trilogy; also see below), Little, Brown, 1984.
Birth of the Firebringer (first novel of the "Firebringer" trilogy), Macmillan (New York City), 1985.
The Woman Who Loved Reindeer, Little Brown, 1985.
The Pearl of the Soul of the World (third novel in the "Darkangel" trilogy; also see below), Little, Brown, 1990.
The Darkangel Trilogy (contains *The Darkangel, A Gathering of Gargoyles,* and *The Pearl of the Soul of the World*), Doubleday, 1990.
Dark Moon (second novel in the "Firebringer" trilogy), Little, Brown, 1992.

OTHER

Where the Wild Geese Go (picture book), illustrated by Jamichael Henterly, Dutton, 1988.

Contributor of novella "Rampion" to *Four from the Witch World,* edited by Andre Norton, Tor Books, 1989. Contributor to anthologies and to periodicals, including *Mythlore, Horn Book, ALAN Review, Voice of Youth Advocates,* and *New Advocate.*

WORK IN PROGRESS: The third installment of the "Firebringer" trilogy.

SIDELIGHTS: "Like good baklava, a work of fiction should be multilayered. If it doesn't have its components properly situated in correct proportion, the taste and texture will be off. Plot is like the pastry: The body and support. Theme is the nut: The kernel and the heart. Style is the savor, blending honey and spice. Nothing is more delicious either to fashion or to devour," Meredith Ann Pierce once commented. From her first novel, *The Darkangel,* to the more recent *Dark Moon,* Pierce has sought to present her readers with fantasies that have as many levels as a delicate pastry. She has established herself as "one of the foremost young authors of fantasy today. Her work combines a mythic inventiveness with such elemental themes as love, conflict and quest," according to Joan Nist in the *ALAN Review. Fantasy Review* contributor Walter Albert thinks Pierce's "Darkangel" trilogy "will surely be ranked with the small number of enduring fantasy classics."

Describing fantasy worlds full of strange beings, creatures, and places, Pierce works hard on creating the details of history, structure, and motivation for her characters. Sometimes her explanations and discussions have led critics to call her prose style awkward. For example, in her review of *Birth of the Firebringer,* Hazel Rochman notes in *Booklist* that the "language is poetic, with a wonderful rhythm and sweeping images of sky and plain, but it is sometimes overheightened and awkwardly archaic." Pierce answers her critics by refusing to simplify her complex language. In an interview for *Something about the Author* conducted by Diane Telgen, the author defends her writing: "I can't change the way I think and I can't change my vocabulary and pretend that I don't know words that I know. . . . There are lots of word games in my stories, coined words and made up words, compound words, because I like doing that, it's very enjoyable."

Born in Seattle, Washington, Pierce says that as a child she spent hours talking and playing with imaginary companions. She also joined her brothers and sister in their own make-believe games. A precocious child who began to read at the age of three, Pierce did not have to depend on her parents or any other adults for information. The advantage of this, she says, was that "I could feed myself information." One book that had a decided influence on Pierce was Lewis Carroll's *Alice in Wonderland;* the movie *The Wizard of Oz*—based on the L. Frank Baum book—also had a strong effect on her. "*Alice in Wonderland* is like my religion," she tells Telgen. "It was introduced into my system before my immune system was complete, so it's wired into my psyche. I can't distinguish between my own mythology and early influences like *Alice in Wonderland* or the movie *The Wizard of Oz.* Some of the stuff that I saw really impressed me when I was very little and just went straight into my neurons—it's inseparable from my way of thinking."

Pierce first realized writing could be a serious career when she took a class taught by children's author Joy Anderson at the University of Florida. "Through her I got a much better idea of what writing is all about," says Pierce. Anderson gave constructive criticism and encouragement as Pierce wrote her first novel, *The Darkangel,* a fantasy that takes place on the moon. The basic idea for the book, according to Nancy Willard in her review for the *New York Times Book Review,* "came to the writer 'all of a piece' during a long bus ride." Pierce was inspired by a real-life case she read about in the autobiography of psychiatrist Carl Jung. One of Jung's patients told him how she had once lived on the moon, where she met a handsome vampire who took her captive. "Jung's account of his patient and her fascinating delusion," Pierce relates in a *Horn Book* article, "served as the germinal model for [the main character] Aeriel and the first two chapters of *Darkangel.*" Later parts of the tale borrow from the fairy tale "Beauty and the Beast" and the Greek myth of Psyche and Eros. Critics also note how Pierce—either consciously or unconsciously—borrows from other stories. For example, in a *New York Times Book Review* critique of the sequel to *The Darkangel, A Gathering of Gargoyles,* Eleanor Cameron sees echoes of other fantasies: "From Le Guin's Orm Embar and Pendor come Miss Pierce's Orm and Pendar; from the cycles of Susan Cooper and Jane Louise Curry come the precognitive riddling rhyme that structures Aeriel's searches as she carries out her task."

In *The Darkangel,* readers are introduced to the young servant girl Aeriel, who struggles to destroy the vampire who has kidnapped her mistress and helps to prevent evil from taking over her world. Aeriel marries the vampire Irrylath and makes him human by exchanging her heart for his. In the second volume of the trilogy, *A Gathering of Gargoyles,* Irrylath is still bound to the evil White Witch and cannot love anyone else. To help him, Aeriel searches the moon to find their world's Ions, ancient animal guardians who will lead the battle against the Witch's forces. In the last novel of the series, *The Pearl of the Soul of the World,* Aeriel sets out to defeat the White Witch once and for all. But after a silver pin is driven into her skull, Aeriel wanders through underground caves, unaware of who she is and unable to speak. She is finally rescued by Ravenna, the last of the ancient wise ones who created the world. Removing the pin and placing all her knowledge and powers into the luminous pearl Aeriel wears around her neck, Ravenna tells her to use the pearl in her final confrontation with the witch.

The strength and courage that Aeriel shows in confronting evil has been noted by several reviewers. *Signal Review* contributor Elizabeth Hammill, for one, sees Aeriel as "a brave and resourceful heroine—fascinating because she possesses that fairy-tale compassion for apparently base

creatures which enables her to recognize their true nature and, hence, to redeem them." Hammill goes on to say that the book effectively shows an adolescent developing a meaningful adult identity, in terms of her relationships with others. Aeriel's determination to stand her ground in the face of danger is a reflection of Pierce's own childhood experiences, as the author writes in her *Horn Book* article. Pierce once had to cope with an alcoholic and abusive relative who one day "had made up his mind to do me violence." But the author refused to be bullied by the relative who, faced with such determination, backed off. It was "a little bit of a revelation—that a lot of human relationships are bluff, and that's an important thing to know," she concludes.

Several critics have commented on Pierce's use of language in the "Darkangel" books. Cameron describes the author's style as "intensely visual, even poetic, in her descriptions and imaginative in her surprising plot turns." Walter Albert of *Fantasy Review* also points out Pierce's poetic language in *A Gathering of Gargoyles.* "As in the earlier book," Albert attests, "one of her great strengths is her ability to capture the colors and textures of the physical world." Albert also admires her secure handling of characters and commends the book's conclusion as "exhilarating and moving." Ann A. Flowers notes in her *Horn Book* review of *The Pearl of the Soul of the World,* "The great strength of the story . . . is the style, with shimmering, fragile textures and delicate, shadowy descriptions." Some critics have pointed out that Pierce's writing helps make her imaginary world more believable. "Pierce's thoughtful characterization and well-constructed plot lead to a poignant and believable conclusion," a *Publishers Weekly* reviewer notes about *The Pearl,* going on to praise her "meticulous, creative use of language." In *School Library Journal* Ruth Vose similarly comments on Pierce's creativity: "Pierce continues to have the power to capture the imagination of her readers. Her creativity never falters."

"As with *Darkangel,*" Pierce reveals in her *Horn Book* article, "the inception of [*The Woman Who Loved Reindeer*] was sudden, taking place on the last day of either my first or second year of high school. As I stood looking out over the flat, barren, empty playing field, a vivid image came to mind of a woman dressed in doeskin standing stock still, her mouth open, her hands reaching out after a great stag that is carrying away her child. . . . The woman is speechless, but the child is screaming . . . with delight." Pierce later developed this vision into a story by building on the Native American husk-myth in which an animal can cast off its skin to take human form; then she set her tale on an imaginary world.

The Woman Who Loved Reindeer begins by telling how young Caribou, who lives alone after her father's death, is given her sister-in-law's baby. Caribou cares for the newborn—whom she calls Reindeer—taking herbs to cause her milk to flow, even though she feels he is not quite human. She finally realizes he is a "trangl"—one who can take on the form of an animal or a human. When he grows old enough, Reindeer runs off to join his people—the other reindeer—but occasionally returns as a golden-eyed young man and becomes Caribou's lover. He changes from man to deer several times as he helps Caribou lead her people from their homes, which have been ruined by earthquakes and eruptions, to a place on the other side of the world beyond the Land of the Broken Snow. Pregnant with Reindeer's child, Caribou now must decide whether or not to follow Reindeer by becoming a trangl herself.

"The author," McConnell concludes in her *School Library Journal* review of *The Woman Who Loved Reindeer*, "convincingly and poetically portrays [the characters'] lives and adventures." A reviewer in the *Bulletin of the Center for Children's Books* sees the love story as "convincing, the dangers . . . suspenseful," but finds the writing "overdramatic" and marred by "unnecessary exposition." In another *Horn Book* article, however, Flowers sees the romance as "believable and satisfying." She deems the setting "an intriguing combination of realistic, folkloric, and fantastic elements; her style is smooth, clear, and elegant, with never a word in the wrong place. A remarkably fine fantasy by an emerging master of the genre."

With *The Birth of the Firebringer* Pierce began a second trilogy that paints an elaborate picture of a world inhabited by unicorns. Jan, a young unicorn, proves his worth to his father, Prince of the Unicorns, and is allowed to accompany the initiates on their pilgrimage to the ancient homeland now inhabited by evil wyverns. Jan sees no vision as the others do in the sacred well and runs away, but as he flees he runs into a wyvern who tries to get him to betray his people. When Jan kills the wyvern, his noble deed results in his being able to see visions concerning his destiny as firebringer of the unicorns.

Pierce's use of language is again praised in reviews of *The Birth of the Firebringer*. For example, one *Kirkus Reviews* contributor writes: "The language here is as elegant as the unicorn people it chronicles. Unicorn rituals and mythology are woven skillfully into the story, strengthening characterization and making the fantasy believable." *School Library Journal* contributor Holly Sanhuber also comments on Pierce's use of language in her review: "The untangling of the satisfying plot and Pierce's ability to foster belief in her unicorns . . . are enhanced by her stately use of language."

Dark Moon, the second work in the trilogy, finds Jan falling in love and taking a mate named Tek. However, Jan's happiness is cut short when he and the other unicorns are attacked by harpies and Jan is swept out to sea. It seems to the other unicorns that Jan has perished, and his father goes berserk with grief, almost bringing disaster upon the entire herd. Escaping the fury of Jan's father, Tek escapes to the home of her mother—a healer—in time to give birth to two foals. Meanwhile, Jan is saved by some human unicorn worshippers who put him on a boat and take him to their city, where he is penned up with a harem of mares. Although she is not a unicorn, a mare befriends Jan and accompanies him back to his own land when they escape their human captors. He and the mare are taken home across the sea on the backs of narwhals, or sea unicorns. Realizing that the only way to rid his land of the wyverns is for the unicorns to unite with all the other creatures with whom the unicorns have fought, Jan decides in the end that they must make peace with the harpies.

Pierce is currently working on the third novel that will conclude the "Firebringer" trilogy. In addition to her writing, she works full-time at her local county library. As she tells Telgen, she has "a reasonably good time telling little children to quit running on the stairs and helping them look for the shark books." But although she enjoys working in the library, she prefers writing, comparing it to "going to sleep and dreaming a wonderful dream." "To write a novel," she concludes in *Horn Book,* "is to be in love."

BIOGRAPHICAL/CRITICAL SOURCES:

BOOKS

Authors and Artists for Young Adults, Volume 13, Gale, 1994.
Children's Literature Review, Volume 20, Gale, 1990.
Hammill, Elizabeth, *The Signal Review: A Selective Guide to Children's Books,* edited by Nancy Chambers, Thimble Press, 1984, pp. 49-50.
Something about the Author, Volume 67, Gale, 1992, pp. 160-65.

PERIODICALS

ALAN Review, winter, 1986, p. 31.
Booklist, October 15, 1985, p. 330; February 15, 1986, p. 870; January 1, 1990; January 15, 1990, p. 991; March 1, 1990, p. 1356; March 15, 1991, p. 1478; May 15, 1992, p. 1674.
Book Report, May, 1986, p. 32; May, 1990, p. 49.
Bulletin of the Center for Children's Books, July/August, 1982; February, 1985, p. 114; December, 1985, p. 75; January, 1986, p. 94.

English Journal, April, 1985, p. 84; January, 1991, p. 80.

Fantasy Review, May, 1985, p. 20; April, 1986, p. 31.

Horn Book, August, 1982, p. 416; September, 1983, p. 245; October, 1984, p. 765; March/April, 1986, p. 208-209; January/February, 1988, pp. 35-41; May/June, 1988, p. 349; May/June, 1990, p. 340.

Horn Book Guide, January, 1990, p. 254.

Journal of Reading, November, 1990, p. 234.

Kirkus Reviews, September 15, 1985, p. 992; October 1, 1985, p. 1090; February 1, 1988, p. 205; January 1, 1990, p. 49; May 15, 1992, p. 674.

Locus, January, 1990, p. 52; July, 1990, p. 15; October, 1990, p. 53; October, 1991, p. 52; June 1992, p. 56.

Magazine of Fantasy and Science Fiction, November, 1984, p. 38.

New York Times Book Review, April 25, 1982, pp. 35, 47; November 30, 1982; December 30, 1984, p. 19; February 16, 1986, p. 22.

Publishers Weekly, November 30, 1984, p. 92; June 7, 1985, p. 80; December 20, 1985, p. 65; February 12, 1988, p. 82; February 9, 1990, p. 63.

School Library Journal, December, 1984; December, 1985, p. 104; January, 1986, p. 70; June/July, 1988, p. 94; April, 1990, p. 145; June, 1992, pp. 139-40.

Voice of Youth Advocates, April, 1986, p. 41; June, 1990, p. 138; August, 1992, p. 178.

Wilson Library Bulletin, March, 1986, pp. 50-51.*

—*Sketch by Hazel K. Davis*

*   *   *

POLLAK, Michael   1918-

PERSONAL: Born January 5, 1918, in New York, NY; son of Charles Jacob and Helen (Meyerowitz) Pollak; married wife, Barbara, September 12, 1946; children: Julia P. Trilling, Nancy P. Weiss, Mark D., Susan T. *Education:* City College (now City College of the City University of New York), B.S., 1938. *Religion:* Jewish.

ADDRESSES: Home—7816 Midbury Dr., Dallas, TX 75230. *Office*—Wayside Press, Inc., 2005 Farrington St., Dallas, TX 75207.

CAREER: Wayside Press, Dallas, TX, president, 1955—.

MEMBER: American Printing Historical Society, Printing Historical Society, Sino-Judaic Institute.

WRITINGS:

The Discovery of a Missing Torah Scroll, Bridwell Library, Southern Methodist University (Dallas, TX), 1973.

The Torah Scrolls of the Chinese Jews: The History, Significance, and Present Whereabouts of the Sifrei Torah of the Defunct Jewish Community of Keifeng, Bridwell Library, Southern Methodist University, 1975.

Mandarins, Jews, and Missionaries: The Jewish Experience in the Chinese Empire, Jewish Publication Society (Philadelphia, PA), 1980, 2nd edition, enlarged, 1984.

(Author of introduction) *The Jews of Kaifeng: Chinese Jews on the Bank of the Yellow River* (exhibition catalog), Beth Hatefutsoth, 1984.

(Editor) *The Sino-Judaic Bibliographies of Rudolf Loewenthal,* Hebrew Union College and Sino-Judaic Institute (Cincinnati, OH), 1988.

The Jews of Dynastic China: A Critical Bibliography, Hebrew Union College Press, and Sino Judaic Institute, 1993

Also contributor of numerous articles to scholarly journals, including *Printing Impressions, Gutenberg Jahrbuch, La Revista de Historia de America, Library Quarterly, Visible Language, Printing History, Jewish Book Annual,* and *Studies in Bibliography and Booklore;* contributor of articles of Judaic and printing history interest to non-scholarly periodicals.

WORK IN PROGRESS: Studies in the history of Chinese Jewish settlements of the past thousand years, and a novel entitled *The Dragon and Star,* to be published in 1995 or 1996.

SIDELIGHTS: In *Mandarins, Jews, and Missionaries: The Jewish Experience in the Chinese Empire,* Michael Pollak surveys the history of the Chinese Jews, focusing on the central Chinese city of Kaifeng, where Jews succeeded in maintaining some sense of their cultural identity until recent times. The date of the first Jewish settlement in China has been lost to history, but such communities existed there by 1126 A.D. and may predate the year 1000. Jews from the Middle East reached China by going overland through Central Asia and/or by taking the sea route around the south of the continent. While freely practicing their religion, the Jews of China gradually absorbed many aspects of the culture of their new homeland, taking on Chinese names, intermarrying, and in some cases holding senior government positions. Accepted by Chinese society and largely cut off from Jews in the rest of the world, the communities began to assimilate so totally that by the 1600s few of their members could read Hebrew or display a thorough knowledge of Judaism. By 1900 the Chinese Jews had essentially ceased to constitute a distinct subculture, although some still remain aware of their ancestry, and maintain a nostalgic interest in it.

Asserting that *Mandarins, Jews, and Missionaries* "can be unreservedly recommended," British historian Charles R. Boxer, writing in the *Times Literary Supplement,* said that the book "is written with humour and gusto, as well as with erudition." Richard Shepard in the *New York Times Book Review* stated that "Mr. Pollak's book . . . tells the story of the Kaifeng Jews in a serious but by no means academic way, and the tale is fascinating."

Pollak told *CA:* "My publications about Chinese Jewry resulted from an interest I developed in the subject when I was able to identify a Torah scroll at the Bridwell Library of Southern Methodist University as one that was written in Hebrew for a synagogue located in Kaifeng, Henan province, China, during or slightly before 1663. My interest in printing history stems from my work as a publisher and printer. I should make it clear, however, that I write as an avocation. I rather suspect that I would find it difficult (and also tedious) to do it on a full-time basis."

BIOGRAPHICAL/CRITICAL SOURCES:

PERIODICALS

New York Times Book Review, February 22, 1981.
Times Literary Supplement, October 31, 1980.

*   *   *

PORTER, Robert 1946-

PERSONAL: Born in 1946, in London, England; son of Ronald (a worker) and Susan (a cleaner; maiden name, Barber) Porter; married Lissy Kvols (a doctor), August 25, 1978; children: Nadia, Camilla. *Education:* University of Leeds, B.A., 1968; University of Bristol, Ph.D., 1993.

ADDRESSES: Office—Department of Russian Studies, University of Bristol, Bristol BS8 1TE, England.

CAREER: Senior lecturer in Russian studies at University of Bristol, Bristol, England.

MEMBER: British Association of Slavonic and East European Studies.

WRITINGS:

Milan Kundera: A Voice From Central Europe, Arkona, 1981.
Understanding Soviet Politics Through Literature, Allen & Unwin (Winchester, MA), 1984.
(Editor) *Seven Soviet Poets,* Blackwell, 1988.
Four Contemporary Russian Writers, Berg (Atlanta, GA), 1989.
Russia's Alternative Prose, Berg, 1994.

Translator from Russian, Czech, and Danish.

WORK IN PROGRESS: Research on modern Russian literature.

*   *   *

PRESTON, Harry 1923-
(Vanessa Cartwright)

PERSONAL: Born September 4, 1923, in Howick, Natal, South Africa; naturalized U.S. citizen, 1956; son of Richard Henry (a chemist) and Lilian Catherine (Walter) Pimm. *Education:* University of Natal, B.A., 1942. *Religion:* "Truth and honesty." *Avocational interests:* Cooking and gardening.

ADDRESSES: Home—4413 Clemson Dr., Garland, TX 75042.

CAREER: Singer, dancer, actor, and musician in South Africa, 1939-48; Cactus State Radio Network, Big Spring, TX, program director, 1950-51; Big D Film Studio, Dallas, TX, writer and director, 1952-55; WFAA-TV, Dallas, news editor, 1956-58; Metro-Goldwyn-Mayer Studios, Culver City, CA, editorial analyst, 1959; Jam Handy Organization, Detroit, MI, writer and director, 1960-62; independent film producer and director in Detroit, 1962-67; Bill Bailey Productions, Hollywood, CA, writer and director, 1968; Harris-Tuchman Productions, Hollywood, writer and director, 1969; United States Air Force, Norton Air Force Base, California, writer, 1970-76; The Image House, Dallas, writer, 1977; *Spotlight Magazine,* Dallas, drama reviewer, 1978; *Dallas Times-Herald,* Dallas, book reviewer and feature writer, 1978-83; Omega Cinema Productions, Dallas, writer and director, 1980; Intowne Publications, Dallas, editor, 1985-86. Literary consultant to Stanton & Associates International Literary Agency, Garland, TX.

AWARDS, HONORS: Sylvania Award, 1957, for documentary film *Tornado;* Best Play, Texas Playwrights Contest, 1958, for comedy *Time for Madness;* Best Supporting Actor in Southwest, 1959, for portrayal of Lord Brockhurst in Breck Wall's production of *The Boy Friend;* Life Achievement Award, Corpus Christi Film Festival, 1989.

WRITINGS:

Time for Madness (play), first produced in Dallas at Dallas Institute of Performing Arts, 1958, produced in Dallas at Haymarket Theatre, 1980.
(With Vila Briley) *Housewives Guide to Extra Income: How to Make Your Spare Time Work for You,* Books for Better Living, 1972.
(With Jeanette Margolin) *Everything a Teenager Wants to Know about Sex and Should,* Books for Better Living, 1973.
Kicking Your Sex Hangups, Academy, 1973.

Erotic Africa, Academy, 1973.

(With Emil Halley) *The Natural Food Reducing Diet,* Books for Better Living, 1974.

Crucifixion of a Closet Queen, Academy, 1974.

How to Teach Your Children about Sex, Books for Better Living, 1974.

Queen of Darkness, Manor (New York City), 1976.

(With Ned Fritz) *The Sterile Forest,* Eakin (Austin, TX), 1983.

(With John Marion Ellis) *Free of Pain,* Southwest Publishing, 1983.

(Editor) Stan DeFreitas, *Stan DeFreitas' Complete Guide to Florida Gardening,* Taylor, 1984.

(With Paul Rollins) *I Plead Insanity: When Manic Depression Turns Violent,* Odenwald (Dallas), 1993.

SATIRICAL REVUES

Bubblegum, first produced in Cape Town, South Africa, at Hofmeyr Theatre, 1944.

You Gotta Be Kidding, first produced in Detroit, MI, 1965, produced in Hollywood, 1967, produced in Dallas, 1980.

ROMANCE NOVELS; UNDER PSEUDONYM VANESSA CARTWRIGHT

Indigo Encounter, McFadden, 1978.

Wine of Love, McFadden, 1978.

Legacy of Love, McFadden, 1978.

Appointment in Antibes, McFadden, 1978.

Winter Wish, McFadden, 1978.

Summer in Stockholm, McFadden, 1978.

Escape to Happiness, McFadden, 1978.

OTHER

Also author, with Max Morales, of *The Other Side of the Alamo,* 1984; author of pilot for *The Nostalgia Channel,* 1984. Author of screenplays *Blood of the Wolf Girl* (and director), 1990, *Adam Clayton Powell,* 1992, and *The Deeds,* 1993; rewriter of screenplays *All the Man I Need* (Denmark), 1991, *The Myth,* 1992, *Belle and Her Boys,* 1993, and *No Tears for a Hero,* 1993, and of more than four hundred industrial and documentary film scripts. Author of seven book-length children's stories serialized in South African newspapers, 1936-39. Contributor of more than two hundred short stories to newspapers and magazines.

WORK IN PROGRESS: Omar Sharif Loved My Cheesecake, an autobiography; *Shot in Dallas,* a novel set in Dallas dealing with the feature film industry in Texas; *Faces of Angels,* a novel dealing with the relationship between a middle-aged homosexual and a young male hustler; a musical version of *Time for Madness.*

SIDELIGHTS: Harry Preston once told *CA:* "As an eternal optimist, I find my hopes for harmony between the

many races in South Africa more idealistic than realistic. This is sad, because the country is one of the most beautiful in the world, and could be a paradise if people could only live together in peace, respecting each other's customs and cultures." Preston began writing at the age of ten, and was first published when he was fourteen. He reports he now writes an average of six hours a day, weekends included.

*   *   *

PROLE, Lozania
See BLOOM, Ursula (Harvey)

*   *   *

PURRINGTON, Robert Daniel 1936-

PERSONAL: Born April 11, 1936, in Alamosa, CO; son of Robert George P. and Edith Brooke (Meanley) Purrington; married Ethel Loraine Smith, September 12, 1959; children: Jaqueline Brooke, Stephen Daniel, Jennifer Ann, Christopher Wilson. *Education:* Texas A & M University, B.S., 1958, M.S., 1963, Ph.D., 1966. *Politics:* Democrat. *Religion:* Episcopalian.

ADDRESSES: Home—4700 Bissonet Dr., Metairie, LA 70003. *Office*—Department of Physics, Tulane University, New Orleans, LA 70118.

CAREER: Tulane University, New Orleans, LA, assistant professor, 1966-70, associate professor, 1970-75, professor of physics, 1975—, chairman of department, 1979-85, director of Cunningham Observatory, 1972—. Trainee at National Aeronautics and Space Administration (NASA), 1961-64. *Military service:* U.S. Army, 1958-59; became second lieutenant.

MEMBER: American Physical Society, American Association for the Advancement of Science, National Audubon Society, Sierra Club, Nature Conservancy, Society for History of Physics, Sigma Xi, Phi Eta Sigma, Phi Kappa Phi.

AWARDS, HONORS: Woodrow Wilson fellow, 1958; fellow of National Science Foundation, 1961.

WRITINGS:

(With Frank Durham) *Frame of the Universe: A History of Physical Cosmology,* Columbia University Press, 1983.

Trama del Universo, Fondo de Cultura Economica, 1989.

Some Truer Method, Columbia University Press, 1990.

Also contributor to scientific journals of physics, history of science, and ornithology; regional editor of *American Birds.*

WORK IN PROGRESS: Triumph and Transformation: A History of Nineteenth Century Physics, in press; also a survey of archaestronomy, and a pedestrian's guide to the literature of quantum theory.

Q-R

QUIRK, Thomas Vaughan 1946-
(Tom Quirk)

PERSONAL: Born December 28, 1946, in Houston, TX; son of Edward L. and Virginia (Carter) Quirk; married, 1970 (divorced); married Catherine Parke (an English professor), 1986; children: (first marriage) Laura Elizabeth; (second marriage) Ann Neal. *Education:* Arizona State University, B.A., 1970; University of New Mexico, M.A., 1972, Ph.D., 1977.

ADDRESSES: Office—Department of English, University of Missouri, 107 Tate Hall, Columbia, MO 65211.

CAREER: Navajo Community College, Tsaile, AZ, instructor in English, 1974 and 1976; College of Ganado, Ganado, AZ, instructor in English, 1976; University of New Mexico, Gallup, assistant professor, 1978-79; University of Missouri, Columbia, assistant professor, 1979-84, associate professor of English, 1984—; professor of English, 1989—; Catherine Paine Middlebush Professor of English, 1991-94.

MEMBER: American Literature Association, Melville Society, Mark Twain Circle, Willa Cather Society.

WRITINGS:

UNDER NAME TOM QUIRK

Melville's Confidence Man: From Knave to Knight, University of Missouri Press (Columbia, MO), 1982.
(Contributor) Walter Daniel, editor, *Black Journals of the United States,* Greenwood Press (Westport, CT), 1982.
(Editor with James Barbour) *Romanticism: Critical Essays in American Literature,* Garland Publishing (New York City), 1986.

(Editor with Barbour) *Essays on Puritans and Puritanism,* University of New Mexico Press (Albuquerque, NM), 1986.
(Editor with Barbour) *The Unfolding of Moby Dick: Seven Essays in Evidence* (monograph), Melville Society, 1987.
(Editor with Barbour) *Writing the American Classics,* University of North Carolina Press (Chapel Hill, NC), 1990.
Bergson in American Culture: The Worlds of Willa Cather and Wallace Stevens, University of North Carolina Press, 1990.
(Explanatory notes and commentary) Herman Melville, *Moby Dick,* introduction by Andrew Delbanco, Viking/Penguin, 1992.
Coming to Grips with "Huckleberry Finn": Essays on a Book, a Boy, and a Man, University of Missouri Press, 1993.
(Editor, with Gary Scharnhorst) *Realism and the Canon: A Collection of Essays,* University of Delaware Press (East Brunswick, NJ), 1994.
(Editor) *Selected Tales, Essays, Speeches, and Sketches of Mark Twain,* Viking/Penguin, 1994.

Contributor of essays to literature journals. Guest editor, *American Literary Realism,* special issue on canon reformation in the realist era, spring, 1991.

WORK IN PROGRESS: Editor, with Robert Sattlemeyer of a special issue of *Studies in Literary Imagination,* 1996; editor with James Barbour, of *The Path of the Creator: The Composition of Notable American Writings,* 1996; *Mark Twain: A Study of the Short Fiction,* MacMillan, 1997.

SIDELIGHTS: Thomas Vaughan Quirk told *CA:* "Temperamentally and methodologically, I am inclined to study imaginative writing as the resultant effort and genuinely creative act of actual human beings rather than as disembodied linguistic constructs. In my first book I sought to trace the contours of Melville's *The Confidence Man* as they probably developed in the author's creative imagination. In *Bergson in American Culture: The Worlds of Willa Cather and Wallace Stevens* I attempted an 'experiment' in literary history by examining an important transitional period in American culture and by employing an equal mix of intellectual, social, and literary history as a way of framing a discussion of the literary careers of two 'case studies' who were deeply influenced by these cultural changes. I meant to correct by example rather than by polemical argument what I take to be certain deficiencies of both old and 'new' historicism. And in *Coming to Grips With "Huckleberry Finn": Essays on a Book, a Boy, and a Man,* I examined Twain's novel from a variety of critical angles in order to account for its origins in his imagination and its subsequent effects on several generations of readers. In a word, I am sceptical of PostModern presuppositions about language and literature that, so far as I can see, are not borne out by experience, common sense, history, or philosophy. I have always believed that the human origins of literature are finally more interesting than the sorts of nimble interpretive ventures, no matter how eloquent, that deny or exclude this quality. Most recently, I have spent less time writing and more time pondering the ways that genuinely humanistic values might achieve practical results in the classroom. Higher education, I believe, has suffered too long from what I call the cult of the expert, the cultivation of an arcane sophistication that, ironically, often serves to shore up the exclusionary cultural dominance that its practitioners avowedly wish to dethrone."

BIOGRAPHICAL/CRITICAL SOURCES:

PERIODICALS

Times Literary Supplement, July 15, 1983.

*   *   *

QUIRK, Tom
See QUIRK, Thomas Vaughan

*   *   *

RAAT, W(illiam) Dirk   1939-

PERSONAL: Born July 1, 1939, in Ogden, UT; son of Elmer W. (a plumber) and Iris (Calkins) Raat; married Geraldine (Koba) Corter, 1984; children: Kelly, David. *Education:* University of Utah, B.S., 1961, Ph.D., 1967; also attended National University of Mexico and Center for Intercultural Documentation, Cuernavaca, Mexico.

ADDRESSES: Home—132 Center St., Fredonia, NY 14063. *Office*—Department of History, State University of New York College at Fredonia, Fredonia, NY 14063.

CAREER: Moorhead State College, Moorhead, MN, assistant professor, 1966-68, associate professor of history, 1968-70; State University of New York College at Fredonia, associate professor, 1970-77, professor of history, 1977—, chair of department, 1973-74. University of Utah, visiting professor of history, 1984-85. Consultant to National Endowment for the Humanities. Television documentary commentator. *Military service:* Utah National Guard, 1954-64.

MEMBER: World History Association, Borderlands History Association.

AWARDS, HONORS: James A. Robertson Award, Conference on Latin American History, 1968, for article "Leopoldo Zea and Mexican Positivism"; grant-in-aid, State University of New York, 1973, 1975, 1979; American Council of Learned Societies fellowship, 1976-77; Edwin Lieuwen Memorial Prize, RMCAS, 1988; SUNY Faculty Exchange Scholar.

WRITINGS:

El positivismo durante el Porfiriato (title means "Positivism during the Porifiriato"), SepSetentas, 1975.
Revoltosos: Mexico's Rebels in the United States, 1903-23, Texas A & M University Press, 1981.
Mexico: From Independence to Revolution, 1810-1910, University of Nebraska Press, 1982.
The Mexican Revolution: Historiography and Bibliography, G. K. Hall, 1982.
(With William Beezley) *Twentieth-Century Mexico,* University of Nebraska Press, 1986.
Mexico and the United States: Ambivalent Vistas, University of Georgia Press (Athens, GA), 1992.
People of the Edge: A Photohistory of the Sierra Tarahumara, University of Oklahoma Press (Norman, OK), 1994.

Also author of *Fonda de Cultura Economica: Ambivalent Vistas,* published 1988. Contributor of over 35 articles and essays to history journals and books.

WORK IN PROGRESS: People of the Edge, a television documentary on the Sierra Tarahumara.

SIDELIGHTS: W. Dirk Raat told *CA:* "Anyone desiring to be a historian should like to travel, have an excellent command of foreign languages, and be independently wealthy. As for myself, I do like to travel.

"More seriously, I believe that the historian has a special task to perform. Like the philosopher, he is analytical; unlike the great philosophers, he is seldom speculative. Like the social scientist, he is a researcher; unlike the sociologist, the historian has a story to tell. The telling of history is both a craft and an art. To create and publish a historical work is to engage in craftsmanship. To write well and effectively is the task of the artist."

*   *   *

RAWLS, Walton (Hendry) 1933-

PERSONAL: Born May 28, 1933, in Charleston, SC; son of Lucian Russell (an army officer) and Mary Louise (a teacher; maiden name, Hendry) Rawls; married Mary Jane Harley, February 14, 1965 (died December, 1970); married Brenda Jean Hart (a teacher), March 14, 1982; children: Anna Harley. *Education:* Harvard University, B.A., 1955; postgraduate studies at University of South Carolina, 1955-56; attended New York University and New School for Social Research, 1961-65.

ADDRESSES: Home—3065 Arden Rd., NW, Atlanta, GA 30305. *Office*—1050 Techwood Dr., NW, Atlanta, GA 30318.

CAREER: Charles E. Tuttle Co., Tokyo, Japan, editorial trainee, 1958, sales promotion manager in Rutland, VT, 1958-60; Twayne Publishers, New York City, advertising and promotion director, 1961-66; McGraw-Hill Book Co., New York City, editor, 1966-70, editor in chief, 1970-73; Rawls & Moskof, Inc., New York City, president, 1974-77; Harry N. Abrams, Inc., New York City, senior editor, 1977-78; Abbeville Press, Inc., New York City, senior editor, 1979-92; Turner Publishing, Inc., Atlanta, GA, vice president, 1993. *Military service:* U.S. Army, 1956-58.

MEMBER: Harvard Club (New York City), The Century Association (New York City).

WRITINGS:

The Great Book of Currier & Ives' America, Abbeville Press, 1979 (New York City).
Wake Up, America!: World War I and the American Poster, Abbeville Press, 1988.
Disney Dons Dogtags: The Best of Disney Military Insignia, Abbeville Publishing Group, 1992.

EDITOR

(And author of introduction) *The Century Book,* Long Island Historical Society, 1963.
Charles Lockwood, *Bricks and Brownstone,* Abbeville Press, 1981.
Roger T. Peterson and Virginia M. Peterson, *The Audubon Society Baby Elephant Folio: Audubon's Birds of America,* Abbeville Press, 1981.
Frank Thomas and Ollie Johnston, *Disney Animation: The Illusion of Life,* Abbeville Press, 1981.

John Baeder, *Gas, Food, and Lodging,* Abbeville Press, 1982.
Rebecca Zurier, *The American Firehouse: An Architectural and Social History,* Abbeville Press, 1982.
John Canemaker, *Treasures of Disney Animation,* Abbeville Press, 1982.
Naomi Rosenblum, *A World History of Photography,* Abbeville Press, 1984.
(And author of introduction) *Great Civil War Heroes and Their Battles,* Abbeville Press, 1985.
Clay Lancaster, *The American Bungalow,* Abbeville Press, 1985.
Edgar Kaufman, Jr., *Fallingwater,* Abbeville Press, 1986.
A Century of American Sculpture: Treasures from Brookgreen Gardens, Abbeville Press, 1988.

WORK IN PROGRESS: The Hotchkiss Maps of Stonewall Jackson's Campaigns, publication by Abbeville Press expected in 1989.

SIDELIGHTS: The Great Book of Currier & Ives' America by Walton Rawls celebrates the business team of Nathaniel Currier and James M. Ives, whose lithographs were at one time the standard pictures for both advertisement and ornamentation. Beloved for their witty, accurate, and occasionally sentimental depictions of life in nineteenth-century America, the prints were sold by street peddlers and department stores and advertised by Currier and Ives as "the best, the cheapest, and the most popular pictures in the world."

The Great Book has reproductions of more than four hundred of the original Currier and Ives lithographs, three-quarters of which are reprinted in "large-size and with technical brilliance, bringing out the lavish coloring and the abundant details of the originals," according to Eric F. Goldman in the *New York Times Book Review.* Goldman and other critics praised the author for choosing a collection of prints that is representative of the various themes found in the originals and for supplementing it with relevant and interesting historical text. "Nathaniel Currier and James M. Ives had played a unique role in expressing the era," Goldman stated. "*The Great Book of Currier and Ives' America* is a monument worthy of them."

Rawls told *CA:* "As a full-time editor in a very demanding field—heavily illustrated books—I find it difficult to keep my own works 'in progress.' Still, there is a good bit of creative satisfaction in the everyday work of choosing what to publish out of hundreds of submissions, commissioning book subjects that should be published, and putting others' words and pictures together in the best possible way.

"*Wake Up, America!* was a long time 'in progress' because I wasn't content to do the usual poster book collection. As with the Currier & Ives book, I sought to place these masterworks of popular art securely within the ethos of their time. The posters of the World War I era were the last of the genuine, hand-prepared commercial lithographs (before four-color process, photographically prepared advertising posters priced them out of business) and the last of all posters to singlehandedly perform their historic function of providing important information quickly and effectively—just before the advent of radio broadcasting and mass-market illustrated magazines. As Milton Glaser wrote about this book, '[These posters] perfectly reflect the values of our culture at an important moment of our history.' It was my job to evocatively tie the posters into this very complex period, to help the reader experience the best of them with something of the same impact they had on our ancestors. It wasn't easy!"

BIOGRAPHICAL/CRITICAL SOURCES:

PERIODICALS

New Republic, December 1, 1979.
New York Times Book Review, November 25, 1979.
New Yorker, December 24, 1979.
Times Literary Supplement, November 27, 1981.

*   *   *

REED, Ishmael 1938-
(Emmett Coleman)

PERSONAL: Born February 22, 1938, in Chattanooga, TN; son of Henry Lenoir (a fundraiser for YMCA) and Thelma Coleman (a homemaker and salesperson); stepfather, Bennie Stephen Reed (an auto worker); married Priscilla Rose, September, 1960 (divorced, 1970); married Carla Blank (a modern dancer); children: (first marriage) Timothy, Brett (daughter); (second marriage) Tennessee Maria (daughter). *Education:* Attended State University of New York at Buffalo, 1956-60. *Politics:* Independent.

CAREER: Writer. Yardbird Publishing Co., Inc., Berkeley, CA, cofounder, 1971, editorial director, 1971-75; Reed, Cannon & Johnson Communications Co. (a publisher and producer of video cassettes), Berkeley, cofounder, 1973—; Before Columbus Foundation (a producer and distributor of work of unknown ethnic writers), Berkeley, cofounder, 1976—; Ishmael Reed and Al Young's *Quilt* (magazine), Berkeley, cofounder, 1980—. Teacher at St. Mark's in the Bowery prose workshop, 1966; guest lecturer, University of California, Berkeley, 1968—, University of Washington, 1969-70, State University of New York at Buffalo, summer, 1975, and fall, 1979, Yale University, fall, 1979, Dartmouth College, summers, 1980-81, Sitka Community Association, summer, 1982, University of Arkansas at Fayetteville, 1982, Columbia University, 1983, Harvard University, 1987, and Regents

lecturer, University of California, Santa Barbara, 1988. Judge of National Poetry Competition, 1980, King's County Literary Award, 1980, University of Michigan Hopwood Award, 1981. Chair of Berkeley Arts Commission, 1980 and 1981. Coordinating Council of Literary Magazines, chair of board of directors, 1975-79, advisory board chair, 1977-79.

MEMBER: Authors Guild of America, PEN, Celtic Foundation.

AWARDS, HONORS: Certificate of Merit, California Association of English Teachers, 1972, for *19 Necromancers from Now;* nominations for National Book Award in fiction and poetry, 1973, for *Mumbo Jumbo* and *Conjure: Selected Poems, 1963-1970;* nomination for Pulitzer Prize in poetry, 1973, for *Conjure;* Richard and Hinda Rosenthal Foundation Award, National Institute of Arts and Letters, 1975, for *The Last Days of Louisiana Red;* John Simon Guggenheim Memorial Foundation award for fiction, 1974; Poetry in Public Places winner (New York City), 1976, for poem "From the Files of Agent 22," and for a bicentennial mystery play, *The Lost State of Franklin,* written in collaboration with Carla Blank and Suzushi Hanayagi; Lewis Michaux Award, 1978; American Civil Liberties Award, 1978; Pushcart Prize for essay "American Poetry: Is There a Center?," 1979; Wisconsin Arts Board fellowship, 1982; associate fellow of Calhoun College, Yale University, 1982; A.C.L.U. publishing fellowship; three New York State publishing grants for merit; three National Endowment for the Arts publishing grants for merit; California Arts Council grant; associate fellow, Harvard Signet Society, 1987—.

WRITINGS:

FICTION

The Free-Lance Pallbearers, Doubleday (New York City), 1967.
Yellow Back Radio Broke-Down, Doubleday, 1969.
Mumbo Jumbo, Doubleday, 1972.
The Last Days of Louisiana Red, Random House (New York City), 1974.
Flight to Canada, Random House, 1976.
The Terrible Twos, St. Martin's/Marek (New York City), 1982.
Reckless Eyeballing, St. Martin's, 1986.
The Terrible Threes, Atheneum (New York City), 1989.
Japanese by Spring, Atheneum, 1993.

NONFICTION

Shrovetide in Old New Orleans (essays; original manuscript entitled *This One's on Me*), Doubleday, 1978.
God Made Alaska for the Indians: Selected Essays, Garland (New York City), 1982.

Writin' Is Fightin': Thirty-Seven Years of Boxing on Paper, Atheneum, 1990.

Airing Dirty Laundry, Addison-Wesley (Reading, MA), 1993.

Contributor to numerous volumes, including *Armistad I: Writings on Black History and Culture,* Vintage Books, 1970; *The Black Aesthetic,* Doubleday, 1971; *Nommo: An Anthology of Modern Black African and Black American Literature,* Macmillan, 1972; *Cutting Edges: Young American Fiction for the 70s,* Holt, 1973; *Superfiction; or, The American Story Transformed: An Anthology,* Vintage Books, 1975; and *American Poets in 1976,* Bobbs-Merrill (New York), 1976.

EDITOR

(Under pseudonym Emmett Coleman) *The Rise, Fall, and . . . ? of Adam Clayton Powell,* Beeline (Albany, NY), 1967.

(Also author of introduction, and contributor) *19 Necromancers from Now,* Doubleday, 1970.

(With Al Young) *Yardbird Lives!,* Grove (New York City), 1978.

(And contributor) *Calafia: The California Poetry,* Y-Bird Books, 1979.

(With Kathryn Trueblood and Shawn Wong) *The Before Columbus Foundation Fiction Anthology: Selections from the American Book Awards, 1980-1990,* Norton (New York City), 1992.

POETRY

catechism of d neoamerican hoodoo church, Paul Breman (London), 1970, Broadside Press (Highland Park, MI), 1971.

Conjure: Selected Poems, 1963-1970, University of Massachusetts Press (Amherst, MA), 1972.

Chattanooga: Poems, Random House, 1973.

A Secretary to the Spirits, illustrations by Betye Saar, NOK Publishers (New York City), 1977.

New and Collected Poems, Atheneum, 1988.

Poetry also represented in anthologies, including *Where Is Vietnam? American Poets Respond: An Anthology of Contemporary Poems,* Doubleday, 1967; *The New Black Poetry,* International Publishers (New York City), 1969; *The Norton Anthology of Poetry,* Norton, 1970; *The Poetry of the Negro, 1746-1970,* Doubleday, 1970; *Afro-American Literature: An Introduction,* Harcourt, 1971; *The Writing on the Wall: 108 American Poems of Protest,* Doubleday, 1971; *Major Black Writers,* Scholastic (New York City), 1971; *The Black Poets,* Bantam (New York City), 1971; *The Poetry of Black America: Anthology of the 20th Century,* Harper, 1972; and *Giant Talk: An Anthology of Third World Writings,* Random House, 1975.

OTHER

Ishmael Reed Reading His Poetry (cassette), Temple of Zeus, Cornell University Press (Ithaca, NY), 1976.

Ishmael Reed and Michael Harper Reading in the UCSD New Poetry Series (reel), University of California, San Diego, 1977.

(Author of introduction) Elizabeth A. Settle and Thomas A. Settle, *Ishmael Reed: A Primary and Secondary Bibliography,* G. K. Hall (Boston, MA), 1982.

Cab Calloway Stands In for the Moon, Bamberger, 1986.

Also author, with wife, Carla Blank, and Suzushi Hanayagi, of a bicentennial mystery play, *The Lost State of Franklin.* Executive producer of pilot episode of soap opera *Personal Problems* and co-publisher of *The Steve Cannon Show: A Quarterly Audio-Cassette Radio Show Magazine.*

Contributor of fiction to such periodicals as *Fiction, Iowa Review, Nimrod, Players, Ramparts, Seattle Review,* and *Spokane Natural;* contributor of articles and reviews to numerous periodicals, including *Black World, Confrontation: Journal of Third World Literature, Essence, Le Monde, Los Angeles Times, New York Times, Playgirl, Rolling Stone, Village Voice, Washington Post,* and *Yale Review;* and contributor of poetry to periodicals, including *American Poetry Review, Black Scholar, Black World, Essence, Liberator, Negro Digest, Noose, San Francisco Examiner, Oakland Tribune, Life, Connoisseur,* and *Umbra.* Cofounder of periodicals *East Village Other* and *Advance* (Newark community newspaper), both 1965. Editor of *Yardbird Reader,* 1972-76; editor-in-chief, *Y'Bird* magazine, 1978-80; and co-editor of *Quilt* magazine, 1981.

Mumbo Jumbo was translated into French and Spanish, 1975.

ADAPTATIONS: Some of Reed's poetry has been scored and recorded on *New Jazz Poets;* a dramatic episode from *The Last Days of Louisiana Red* appears on *The Steve Cannon Show: A Quarterly Audio-Cassette Radio Show Magazine,* produced by Reed, Cannon & Johnson Communications.

SIDELIGHTS: The novels of contemporary black American writer Ishmael Reed "are meant to provoke," writes *New York Times* contributor Darryl Pinckney. "Though variously described as a writer in whose work the black picaresque tradition has been extended, as a misogynist or an heir to both [Zora Neale] Hurston's folk lyricism and [Ralph] Ellison's irony, he is, perhaps because of this, one of the most underrated writers in America. Certainly no other contemporary black writer, male or female, has used the language and beliefs of folk culture so imaginatively, and few have been so stinging about the absurdity of American racism." Yet this novelist and poet is not simply a voice of black protest against racial and social injustices but instead a confronter of even more universal evils, a purveyor of even more universal truths.

Reed's first novel, *The Free-Lance Pallbearers,* introduces several thematic and stylistic devices that reappear throughout his canon. In this novel, as in his later works, Reed's first satirical jab is at the oppressive, stress-filled, Western/European/Christian tradition. But in *The Free-Lance Pallbearers,* the oppressor/oppressed, evil/good dichotomy does not absolve blacks. While Reed blames whites, called HARRY SAM in the novel, for present world conditions, he also attacks culpable individuals from different strata in the black community and satirizes various kinds of black leaders in the twentieth century. Reed implies that many such leaders argue against white control by saying they want to improve conditions, to "help the people," but that in reality they are only waiting for the chance to betray and exploit poor blacks and to appropriate power.

Leaders of the black movement at the time of the novel's publication regarded as permissible the ridiculing of the white, Christian Bible, as in this grotesque caricature of St. John's vision and the Four Horsemen of the Apocalypse: "I saw an object atop the fragments of dead clippings. I waded up to my knees through grassy film and the phlegm-covered flags and picked up an ivory music box. On the cover done in mother-of-pearl was a picture of Lenore in her Bickford's uniform. I opened the music box and heard the tape of the familiar voice: ROGER YOUNG IN THE FIRST AT SARATOGA / ROGER YOUNG IN THE NINTH AT CHURCHILL DOWNS / ROGER YOUNG IN THE FOURTH AT BATAVIA / ROGER YOUNG IN THE FIFTH AT AQUEDUCT / ANNOUNCED BY RAPUNZEL." But the inclusion of negative black characters was thought by critics such as Houston Baker, Amiri Baraka, and Addison Gayle to be the wrong subject matter for the times. Reed, however, could never agree to rigid guidelines for including or excluding material from the novel form. As he would say later in *Shrovetide in Old New Orleans* concerning his battle with the critics, "The mainstream aspiration of Afro-Americans is for more freedom—and not slavery—including freedom of artistic expression."

Among the black characters whom Reed puts into a negative light in *The Free-Lance Pallbearers* are Elijah Raven, the Muslim/Black Nationalist whose ideas of cultural and racial separation in the United States are exposed as lies; Eclair Pockchop, the minister fronting as an advocate of the people's causes, later discovered performing an unspeakable sex act on SAM; the black cop who protects white people from the blacks in the projects and who idiotically allows a cow-bell to be put around his neck for "meritorious service"; Doopeyduk's neighbors in the proj-

ects who, too stupid to remember their own names, answer to "M/Neighbor" and "F/Neighbor"; and finally Doopeyduk himself, whose pretensions of being a black intellectual render all his statements and actions absurd. Yet Reed reserves his most scathing satire for the black leaders who cater to SAM in his palace: "who mounted the circuitous steps leading to SAM'S, assuring the boss dat: 'Wasn't us boss. 'Twas Stokely and Malcolm. Not us, boss. No indeed. We put dat ad in da *Times* repudiating dem, boss? Look, boss. We can prove it to you, dat we loves you. Would you like for us to cook up some strange recipes for ya, boss? Or tell some jokes? Did you hear the one about da nigger in the woodpile? Well, seems dere was this nigger, boss. . . .' "

The rhetoric of popular black literature in the 1960s is also satirized in *The Free-Lance Pallbearers.* The polemics of the time, characterized by colloquial diction, emotionalism, direct threats, automatic writing, and blueprints for a better society, are portrayed by Reed as representing the negative kind of literature required of blacks by the reading public. Reed suggests that while literature by blacks might have been saying that blacks would no longer subscribe to white dictates, in fact the converse was true, manifested in the very literature that the publishing houses generally were printing at the time.

Furthermore, *The Free-Lance Pallbearers* fully exemplifies Reed's orthographic, stylistic, and rhetorical techniques. He prefers phonetic spellings to standard spellings, thus drawing special attention to subjects otherwise mundane. He also uses capitalization for emphasis, substitutes numerals for words (1 for one) when including number references in the text, borrows Afro-American oral folklore as a source for his characters (as when Doopeyduk acts the part of "Shine" of the old crafty black tale), and utilizes newsflashes and radio voice-overs to comment on the book's action.

In his second novel, *Yellow Back Radio Broke-Down,* Reed begins to use at length Hoodoo (or Voodoo) methods and folklore as a basis for his work. Underlying all of the components of Hoodoo, according to scholars, are two precepts: 1) the Hoodoo idea of syncretism, or the combination of beliefs and practices with divergent cultural origins, and 2) the Hoodoo concept of time. Even before the exportation of slaves to the Caribbean, Hoodoo was a syncretic religion, absorbing all that it considered useful from other West African religious practices. As a religion formed to combat degrading social conditions by dignifying and connecting man with helpful supernatural forces, Hoodoo is said to thrive because of its syncretic flexibility, its ability to take even ostensibly negative influences and transfigure them into that which helps the "horse," or the one possessed by the attributes of a Hoodoo god. Hoodoo is bound by certain dogma or rites, but such rules are easily changed when they become oppressive, myopic, or no longer useful.

Reed turns this concept of syncretism into a literary method that combines aspects of "standard" English, including dialect, slang, argot, neologisms, or rhyme, with less "standard" language, whose principal rules of discourse are taken from the streets, popular music, and television. By mixing language from different sources in popular culture, Reed employs expressions that can both evoke interest and humor through seeming incongruities and create the illusion of real speech. In *Black American Literature Forum,* Michel Fabre draws a connection between Reed's use of language and his vision of the world, suggesting that "his so-called nonsense words raise disturbing questions . . . about the very nature of language." Often, "the semantic implications are disturbing because opposite meanings co-exist." Thus Reed emphasizes "the dangerous interchangeability of words and of the questionable identity of things and people" and "poses anguishing questions about self-identity, about the mechanism of meaning and about the nature of language and communication."

The historical sense of time in Reed's discourse, based on the African concept of time, is not linear; dates are not generally ascribed to the past, and past events overlap with those in the present. Berndt Ostendorf in *Black Literature in White America* notes that the African time sense is "telescoped," that it contains no concept of a future, only the certainty that man's existence will never end. Reed's version of this concept of synchronicity or simultaneity incorporates a future by positing a time cycle of revolving and re-evolving events but maintains an essentially African concept of the past/present relationship, as characters treat past and present matters as though they were simultaneous.

Syncretism and synchronicity, along with other facets of Hoodoo as literary method, are central to *Yellow Back Radio Broke-Down.* The title is street-talk for the elucidation of a problem, in this case the racial and oligarchical difficulties of an Old West town, Yellow Back Radio; these difficulties are explained, or "broke down," for the reader. The novel opens with a description of the Hoodoo fetish, or mythical cult figure, Loop Garoo, whose name means "change into." Loop embodies diverse ethnic backgrounds and a history and power derived from several religions.

At least one of Reed's themes from *The Free-Lance Pallbearers* is reworked in *Yellow Back Radio Broke-Down,* as Christianity is again attacked. Three Horsemen of the Apocalypse are represented by the Barber, Marshall, and Doctor, criminals, hypocrites, and upholders of the one-

and-only-way-of-doing-things, that is, the way which materially benefits them; and the fourth Horseman is embodied in the Preacher Reverend Boyd, who will make a profit on guilt with the volume of poetry he is putting together, *Stomp Me O Lord.* Loop calls his own betrayal by other blacks—Alcibiades and Jeff—and his resurrection a parody of "His Passion." The Pope, who appears in Yellow Back Radio in the 1880s, is revealed as a corrupt defender of the white tradition, concerned only with preventing Loop's magic from becoming stronger than his own.

The year 1972 saw the publication of Reed's first major volume of poetry, *Conjure: Selected Poems, 1963-1970,* followed in 1973 by *Chattanooga: Poems,* and in 1977 by *A Secretary to the Spirits.* Although the poem in *Conjure* beginning "I am a cowboy in the boat of Ra" continues an earlier Reed interest in Egyptian symbolism, after this work he lyrically draws his symbols from Afro-American and Anglo-American historical and popular traditions—two distinct but intertwined sources for the Afro-American aesthetic. "Black Power Poem" succinctly states the Hoodoo stance in the West: "may the best church win. / shake hands now and come out conjuring"; a longer poem, "Neo-Hoodoo Manifesto," defines all that Hoodoo is and thus sheds light on the ways Reed uses its principles in writing, primarily through his absorption of material from every available source and his expansive originality in treating that material.

The theme of *Mumbo Jumbo,* Reed's 1972 novel, is the origin and composition of the "true Afro-American aesthetic." Testifying to the novel's success in fulfilling this theme, Houston Baker in *Black World* calls *Mumbo Jumbo* "the first black American novel of the last ten years that gives one a sense of the broader vision and the careful, painful, and laborious 'fundamental brainwork' that are needed if we are to define the eternal dilemma of the Black Arts and work fruitfully toward its melioration. . . . [The novel's] overall effect is that of amazing talent and flourishing genius." *Mumbo Jumbo*'s first chapter is crucial in that it presents the details of the highly complex plot in synopsis or news-flash form. Reed has a Hoodoo detective named Papa LaBas (representing the Hoodoo god Legba) search out and reconstruct a black aesthetic from remnants of literary and cultural history. Lending the narrative authenticity, Reed inserts various scholarly devices: facts from nonfictional, published works; photographs and historical drawings; and a bibliography.

At the opening of *Mumbo Jumbo,* set in New Orleans in the 1920s, white municipal officials are trying to respond to "Jes Grew," an outbreak of behavior outside of socially conditioned roles; white people are "acting black" by dancing half-dressed in the streets to an intoxicating new loa (the spiritual essence of a fetish) called jazz. Speaking in tongues, people also abandon racist and other oppressive endeavors because it is more fun to "shake that thing." One of the doctors assigned to treat the pandemic of Jes Grew comments, "There are no isolated cases in this thing. It knows no class no race no consciousness. It is self-propagating and you can never tell when it will hit." No one knows where the germ has come from; it "jes grew." In the synoptic first chapter, the omniscient narrator says Jes Grew is actually "an anti-plague. Some plagues caused the body to waste away. Jes Grew enlivened the host. Other plagues were accompanied by bad air (malaria). Jes Grew victims said the air was as clear as they had ever seen it and that there was the aroma of roses and perfumes which had never before enticed their nostrils. Some plagues arise from decomposing animals, but Jes Grew is electric as life and is characterized by ebullience and ecstasy. Terrible plagues were due to the wrath of God; But Jes Grew is the delight of the gods."

In the novel, Christianity is called "Atonism," a word with its origin in the worship of the sun-god, Aton, of ancient Egypt. Atonists are forever at war to stamp out Jes Grew, as it threatens their traditions and their power. The word *Atonism* is also a cognate of the word *atone,* with its connotations of guilt. The Atonists do not simply wage war against nonwhites and non-Christians. Anyone who opposes their beliefs is attacked. When a white member of a multi-ethnic gang, Thor Wintergreen, sides with nonwhites, he is first duped and then killed by Atonist Biff Musclewhite. Though Musclewhite is initially being held captive by Wintergreen, the prisoner persuades Wintergreen to release him by giving the following explanation of the Atonist cause: "Son, this is a nigger closing in our mysteries and soon he will be asking our civilization to 'come quietly.' This man is talking about Judeo-Christian culture, Christianity, Atonism, whatever you want to call it. . . . I've seen them, son, in Africa, China, they're not like us, son, the Herronvolk. Europe. This place. They are lagging behind, son, and you know in your heart this is true. Son, these niggers writing. Profaning our sacred words. Taking them from us and beating them on the anvil of BoogieWoogie, putting their black hands on them so that they shine like burnished amulets. Taking our words, son, these filthy niggers and using them. . . . Why 1 of them dared to interpret, critically mind you, the great Herman Melville's *Moby Dick!!*" *Mumbo Jumbo* thus presents a battle for supremacy between powers that see the world in two distinct, opposed ways, with the separate visions endemic to the human types involved: one, expansive and syncretic; the other, impermeable and myopic.

Hoodoo time resurfaces in *Mumbo Jumbo.* Certain chapters which have detailed past events in the past tense are immediately followed by chapters that begin with present-tense verbs and present-day situations, mirroring Hoodoo/oral culture. The juxtaposition links all of the actions within a single narrative time frame. Commenting on his use both of time and of fiction-filled news-flashes, Reed says in *Shrovetide in Old New Orleans* that in writing *Mumbo Jumbo,* he "wanted to write about a time like the present or to use the past to prophesy about the future—a process our ancestors called necromancy. I chose the twenties because they are very similar to what's happening right now. This is a valid method and has been used by writers from time immemorial. Nobody ever accused James Joyce of making up things. Using a past event of one's country or culture to comment on the present."

The close of *Mumbo Jumbo* finds Jes Grew withering with the burning of its text, the Book of Thoth, which lists the sacred spells and dances of the Egyptian god Osiris. LaBas says Jes Grew will reappear some day to make its own text: "A future generation of young artists will accomplish this," says LaBas, referring to the writers, painters, politicians, and musicians of the 1960s, "the decade that screamed," as Reed termed it in *Chattanooga.*

In the course of the narrative, Reed constructs his history of the true Afro-American aesthetic and parallels the uniting of Afro-American oral tradition, folklore, art, and history with a written code, a text, a literate recapitulation of history and practice. By calling for a unification of text and tradition, Reed equates the Text (the Afro-American aesthetic) with the Vedas, the Pentateuch, the Koran, the Latin Vulgate, the Book of Mormon, and all "Holy" codifications of faith. *Mumbo Jumbo,* which itself becomes the Text, appears as a direct, written response to the assertion that there is no "black" aesthetic, that black contributions to the world culture have been insignificant at best.

As seen in *Mumbo Jumbo,* Reed equates his own aesthetic with other systems based on different myths. Then he insists that his notion of an aesthetic is more humanistic than others, especially those based on Americanized, Christian dogma. Finding its spiritual corollary in Hoodoo, Reed's method achieves a manual of codification in *Mumbo Jumbo.* This code also is used in his next two novels, *The Last Days of Louisiana Red* and *Flight to Canada,* reaffirming his belief that Hoodoo, now understood as a spiritual part of the Afro-American aesthetic, can be used as a basis for literary response.

The Last Days of Louisiana Red consists of three major story lines that coalesce toward the close of the novel to form its theme. The first and main plot is the tale of Ed Yellings, an industrious, middle-class black involved in "The Business," an insider's term for the propagation of

Hoodoo. Through experimentation in his business, Solid Gumbo Works, Yellings discovers a cure for cancer and is hard at work to refine and market this remedy and other remedies for the various aspects of Louisiana Red, the Hoodoo name for all evil. When he is mysteriously murdered, Hoodoo detective Papa LaBas appears, and the stage is set for the major part of the action. This action involves participants in the novel's second and third story lines, the tale of the Chorus and the recounting of the mythical Antigone's decision to oppose the dictates of the state. The Chorus symbolizes black Americans who will not disappear. Even though they are relegated by more powerful forces to minor roles, they work for the right to succeed or fail depending upon their merits. Therein lies Reed's theme in *The Last Days of Louisiana Red.*

In *Flight to Canada* Reed explores Hoodoo as a force that gives his black protagonists the strength to be hopeful and courageous in the face of seemingly hopeless situations. Canada has, in this novel, at least two levels of meaning. It is, first of all, a literal, historical region where slaves might flee to freedom. Second, it becomes a metaphor for happiness; that is, anything that makes an individual character happy may be referred to as "Canada."

The major plot of *Flight to Canada* involves the escape of Raven Quickskill from his owner, Massa Arthur Swille, and Swille's efforts to return Quickskill to captivity. The historical Canada is the eventual destination where Quickskill and other slaves wish to arrive when they flee from Swille in Virginia, but this historical Canada is not the heaven slaves think, and pray, it will be. Yet in the face of the depressing stories about Canada from his friends Leechfield, Carpenter, Cato, and 40s, Quickskill will not relinquish his dream. For him, Canada is personified beyond the physical plane. Refuting those who would deny or degrade the existence of the Canada that his reading tours have allowed him to see as well as the Canada that he must invent to live in peace, Quickskill reflects: "He was so much against slavery that he had begun to include prose and poetry in the same book, so that there would be no arbitrary boundaries between them. He preferred Canada to slavery, whether Canada was exile, death, art, liberation, or a woman. Each man to his own Canada. There was much avian imagery in the poetry of slaves. Poetry about dreams and flight. They wanted to cross that Black Rock Ferry to freedom even though they had different notions as to what freedom was. They often disagreed about it, Leechfield, 40s. But it was his writing that got him to Canada. 'Flight to Canada' was responsible for getting him to Canada. And so for him, freedom was his writing. His writing was his Hoodoo. Others had their way of Hoodoo, but his was his writing. It fascinated him, it possessed him; his typewriter was his drum he danced to."

In *Flight to Canada* Hoodoo becomes a kind of faith that sustains and uplifts without necessarily degrading those to whom it is opposed. Unable to explain how he has attained success, Quickskill can only attribute his freedom to things unseen. Ultimately, all of the black characters turn to this transcendent vision as their shield against the harsher aspects of reality. As is true with Quickskill when he is confronted with the truth about Canada, the black characters' ability to rely upon the metaphysical saves their lives as well as their dreams.

In *The Terrible Twos,* Reed maintains the implicit notions of Hoodoo while using his main story line to resurrect another apocryphal tale: the legend of Santa Claus and his assistant/boss, Black Peter. The time frame of the novel is roughly Christmas 1980 to Christmases of the 1990s, covering the years during and after Ronald Reagan's presidency. The evil of *The Terrible Twos* is selfishness fed by an exclusive monetary system, such as capitalism. Yet Reed does not endorse any other sort of government now in existence but criticizes any person or system that ignores what is humanly right in favor of what is economically profitable. Santa Claus (actually an out-of-work television personality) exemplifies the way Hoodoo fights this selfish evil: by bringing those who were prosperous to the level of those who have nothing and are abandoned. Santa characterizes American capitalists, those with material advantages, as infantile, selfish and exclusionary because their class station does not allow them to empathize with those who are different: " 'Two years old, that's what we are, emotionally—Americans, always wanting someone to hand us some ice cream, always complaining, Santa didn't bring me this and why didn't Santa bring me that.' People in the crowd chuckle. 'Nobody can reason with us. Nobody can tell us anything. Millions of people staggering about passing out in the snow and we say that's tough. We say too bad to the children who don't have milk. I weep as I read these letters the poor children send me at my temporary home in Alaska.' " The story continues in *The Terrible Threes,* set in the late 1990s and featuring many of the characters who populate *The Terrible Twos.* In the sequel, John O'Brien reveals in *Washington Post Book World,* "the country is in a state of chaos, having chased its president into a sanatorium after he revealed on national television a White House conspiracy to purge America of its poor and homeless, as well as to destroy Nigeria." "Reed's eerie, weird, implausible world has a way of sounding all too real, too much like what we hear on the evening news," O'Brien concludes. "And Reed has an unnerving sense of what will show up next on our televisions. He is without doubt our finest satirist since Twain."

In *The Terrible Twos* Reed leaves overt Hoodoo references as a subtext and focuses on the Rasta and Nicolaite myths, two conflicting quasi-religious cults revitalized by Black

Power. He also concentrates on the myths of power and privilege created by "the vital people," those who are white and wealthy. However, the racist policies of the Nicolaites are eventually thwarted by inexplicable circumstances that stem from the supernatural powers of Hoodoo and from the Hoodoo notion that time is circular and that therefore the mighty will possibly—even probably—fall.

Reed uses the concept of truth as stranger than fiction in conveying his vision in *The Terrible Twos.* The first chapter is almost all factual reportage about Christmas and related matters, thus laying the foundation of belief for the fantastic Christmas Reed is about to construct. But is it fact or fantasy that around Christmas of 1980 the *Buffalo Evening News* put under the headline "The Wild West is Back in the Saddle Again" the story of "First Actor" campaigning in cowboy attire in the West and a Confederate uniform in the South; is it fact or fantasy that a 6,000-pound ice sculpture of Santa and his reindeer carved by Andrew Young appears in a San Francisco Christmas parade? As John Leonard declares in his *New York Times* review of the book: "Mr. Reed is as close as we are likely to get to a Garcia Marquez, elaborating his own mythology even as he trashes ours. . . . *The Terrible Twos* tells many jokes before it kills, almost as if it had been written with barbed wire."

Several critics warn that readers will find *Threes* near-incomprehensible without first reading *Twos.* Further, *New York Times Book Review* critic Gerald Early observes, "The major problem with *The Terrible Threes* is that it seems to vaporize even as you read it; the very telling artifices that held together Mr. Reed's novelistic art in previous works, that cunning combination of boundless energy and shrewdly husbanded ingenuity, are missing here. . . . I like *The Terrible Threes,* but it seems more a work for Reed fans among whom I count myself." *Los Angeles Times Book Review* contributor Jacob Epstein finds that "Reed's vision of the future (and our present and past) is original and subversive. Subversion is out of style these days, but unfashionable or not, Reed is an always interesting writer and this book deserves to be read."

Reckless Eyeballing is a satiric allegory. Ian Ball, a black male writer, responds to the poor reception of his earlier play, *Suzanna,* by writing *Reckless Eyeballing,* a play sure to please those in power with its vicious attacks against black men. ("Reckless eyeballing" was one of the accusations against Emmett Till, the young Chicago black who was murdered in Mississippi in 1953 for "looking and whistling at a white woman.") Tremonisha Smarts, a black female writer whose first name is drawn from a Scott Joplin opera of that title, is alternately popular and unpopular with the white women who are promoting her books.

The battle for whose vision will dominate in the literary market and popular culture is fierce.

In Joplin's opera, the character Tremonisha represents the powers of assimilation into American culture in opposition to the "powers of the Hoodoo men." Thus, not only does Reed's version of the Tremonisha character allude to the original Tremonisha's disagreement with early African American currents, but she also becomes one of the critical forces that Reed has long opposed. While this allusive connection suggests that Reed is covering the same, familiar Hoodoo ground covered before, he moves in this novel toward unearthing the universal structures of Hoodoo, which are rooted in the apocryphal rites of other religions.

For example, Reed found connections between the shared traditions of Judaism and Hoodoo in *The Legends of Genesis* by Hermann Gunkel, in David Meltzer's magazine *TREE,* and in Mike Gold's *Jews without Money,* the last of which includes a description of a Jewish woman similar to the Mambos and Conjure Women of Hoodoo origin. Reed thus reminds readers that Hoodoo is ever-changing by constantly absorbing materials from diverse cultures. He also warns his readers that he, too, is ever-changing and that a sure way to be misled is to believe that one has Hoodoo's concepts (and Reed's) pinned down as to their "one true" meaning.

Syncretic and synchronic in form, Reed's novels focus most often on social circumstances that inhibit the development of blacks in American society. As satire is usually based on real types, the writer draws in part from history and the news to satirize America's cultural arrogance and the terrible price paid by those who are not "vital people," members of the dominant culture or the moneyed class. His assertion, in a *Review of Contemporary Fiction* interview with Reginald Martin, that Hoodoo is "solidly in the American tradition" is supported by his collation of myth, fact, and apocryphal data into a history; from that history, a method or aesthetic is drawn not only for formulating art and multi-ethnic cultural standards but also for developing a different and more humane way of experiencing and influencing the world.

BIOGRAPHICAL/CRITICAL SOURCES:

BOOKS

Bellamy, Joe David, editor, *The New Fiction: Interviews with Innovative American Writers,* University of Illinois Press (Champaign, IL), 1974.

Bruck, Peter, and Wolfgang Karrer, editors, *The Afro-American Novel since 1960,* B. R. Bruener (Amsterdam), 1982.

Contemporary Literary Criticism, Gale (Detroit), Volume 2, 1974, Volume 3, 1975, Volume 5, 1976, Volume 6, 1976, Volume 8, 1980, Volume 32, 1985.

Conversations with Writers, Volume 2, Gale, 1978.

Dictionary of Literary Biography, Gale, Volume 2: *American Novelists since World War II,* 1978, Volume 5: *American Poets since World War II,* 1980, Volume 33: *Afro-American Fiction Writers after 1955,* 1984.

Klinkowitz, Jerome, *Literary Subversions: New American Fiction and the Practice of Criticism,* Southern Illinois University Press (Carbondale, IL), 1985.

Martin, Reginald, *Ishmael Reed and the New Black Aesthetic Critics,* Macmillan (London), 1987.

O'Brien, John, *Interviews with Black Writers,* Liveright (New York), 1973.

O'Donnell, Patrick, and Robert Con Davis, editors, *Intertextuality and Contemporary American Fiction,* Johns Hopkins University Press (Baltimore, MD), 1989.

Ostendorf, Berndt, *Black Literature in White America,* Noble, 1982.

Reed, Ishmael, *The Free-Lance Pallbearers,* Doubleday, 1967.

Reed, Ishmael, *Yellow Back Radio Broke-Down,* Doubleday, 1969.

Reed, Ishmael, *Conjure: Selected Poems, 1963-1970,* University of Massachusetts Press, 1972.

Reed, Ishmael, *Mumbo Jumbo,* Doubleday, 1972.

Reed, Ishmael, *Chattanooga: Poems,* Random House, 1973.

Reed, Ishmael, *The Last Days of Louisiana Red,* Random House, 1974.

Reed, Ishmael, *Flight to Canada,* Random House, 1976.

Reed, Ishmael, *A Secretary to the Spirits,* NOK Publishers, 1977.

Reed, Ishmael, *Shrovetide in Old New Orleans,* Doubleday, 1978.

Reed, Ishmael, *The Terrible Twos,* St. Martin's/Marek, 1982.

Reed, Ishmael, *Reckless Eyeballing,* St. Martin's, 1986.

Settle, Elizabeth A., and Thomas A. Settle, *Ishmael Reed: A Primary and Secondary Bibliography,* G. K. Hall (Boston, MA), 1982.

PERIODICALS

Afriscope, May, 1977.

American Book Review, May/June, 1983.

American Poetry Review, May/June, 1976; January/February, 1978.

Arizona Quarterly, autumn, 1979.

Arts Magazine, May, 1967.

Berkeley News, April 10, 1975.

Black American Literature Forum, Volume 12, 1978; spring, 1979; spring, 1980; fall, 1984.

Black Books Bulletin, winter, 1976.

Black Creation, fall, 1972; winter, 1973.

Black Enterprise, January, 1973; December, 1982; April, 1983.

Black History Museum Newsletter, Volume 4, number 3/4, 1975.

Black Scholar, March, 1981.

Black Times, September, 1975.

Black World, October, 1971; December, 1972; January, 1974; June, 1974; June, 1975; July, 1975.

Changes in the Arts, November, 1972; December/January, 1973.

Chicago Review, fall, 1976.

Chicago Tribune Book World, April 27, 1986.

Critical Inquiry, June, 1983.

Essence, July, 1986.

Fiction International, summer, 1973.

Harper's, December, 1969.

Iowa Review, spring, 1982, pp. 117-131.

Journal of Black Poetry, summer/fall, 1969.

Journal of Black Studies, December, 1979.

Journal of Negro History, January, 1978.

Los Angeles Free Press, September 18, 1970.

Los Angeles Times, April 29, 1975.

Los Angeles Times Book Review, April 20, 1986; June 4, 1989; April 14, 1991, p. 10.

MELUS, spring, 1984.

Mississippi Quarterly, winter, 1984-85, pp. 21-32.

Mississippi Review, Volume 20, numbers 1-2, 1991.

Modern Fiction Studies, summer, 1976; spring, 1988, pp. 97-123.

Modern Poetry Studies, autumn, 1973; autumn, 1974.

Nation, September 18, 1976; May 22, 1982.

Negro American Literature Forum, winter, 1967; winter, 1972.

Negro Digest, February, 1969; December, 1969.

New Republic, November 23, 1974.

New Yorker, October 11, 1969.

New York Review of Books, October 5, 1972; December 12, 1974; August 12, 1982; January 29, 1987; October 12, 1989, p. 20.

New York Times, August 1, 1969; August 9, 1972; June 17, 1982; April 5, 1986.

New York Times Book Review, August 6, 1972; November 10, 1974; September 19, 1976; July 18, 1982; March 23, 1986; May 7, 1989; April 7, 1991, p. 32.

Nickel Review, August 28-September 10, 1968.

Obsidian: Black Literature in Review, spring/summer, 1979; spring/summer, 1986, pp. 113-127.

Parnassus: Poetry in Review, spring/summer, 1976.

Partisan Review, spring, 1975.

People, December 16, 1974.

PHYLON: The Atlanta University Review of Race and Culture, December, 1968; June, 1975.

Postmodern Culture, May, 1991.

Review of Contemporary Fiction, summer, 1984; spring, 1987.

San Francisco Review of Books, November, 1975; January/February, 1983.

Saturday Review, October 14, 1972; November 11, 1978.

Southern Review, July, 1985, pp. 603-614.

Studies in American Fiction, Volume 5, 1977.

Studies in the Novel, summer, 1971.

Times Literary Supplement, May 18, 1990, p. 534.

Tribune Books (Chicago), April 11, 1993, p. 3.

Twentieth Century Literature, April, 1974.

Village Voice, January 22, 1979.

Virginia Quarterly Review, winter, 1973.

Washington Post Book World, March 16, 1986; June 25, 1989, pp. 4, 6; November 12, 1989, p. 16; April 14, 1991, p. 12; January 26, 1992, p. 12; March 21, 1993, p. 6.

World Literature Today, autumn, 1978; autumn, 1986.*

*   *   *

REIDENBAUGH, Lowell (Henry) 1919-

PERSONAL: Born September 7, 1919, in Lititz, PA; son of Harry Martin (a machinist) and Marian Marie (a homemaker; maiden name, Nies) Reidenbaugh; married Ruth Elizabeth Cameron (a homemaker), November 23, 1944; children: Karen Lee, Kathy Jean. *Education:* Elizabethtown College, A.B., 1941. *Religion:* Protestant.

CAREER: Intelligencer Journal, Lancaster, PA, general reporter, 1941-42; *Philadelphia Inquirer,* Philadelphia, PA, sportswriter, 1944-47; *Sporting News,* St. Louis, MO, 1947-89, served as managing editor, 1962-79, senior editor, 1980-83, corporate editor, 1983-89. *Military service:* U.S. Army, 1942-43.

WRITINGS:

One Hundred Years of National League Baseball, 1876-1976, Sporting News Publishing (St. Louis), 1976.

(With Dave Klein) *The Sporting News Super Bowl Book,* Sporting News Publishing, 1981.

The Sporting News: Take Me Out to the Ball Park, edited by Craig Carter, illustrated by Amadee Wohlschlaeger, Sporting News Publishing, 1983, revised edition, 1987.

Cooperstown: Where Baseball's Legends Live Forever, edited by Joe Hoppel, Sporting News Publishing, 1983, revised edition published as *Baseball's Hall of Fame—Cooperstown: Where the Legends Live Forever,* Arlington House (New York City), 1986.

The Sporting News: First Hundred Years, 1886-1986, edited by Hoppel and Mike Nahrstedt, Sporting News Publishing, 1985.

Baseball's Fifty Greatest Games, edited by Hoppel, Sporting News Publishing, 1986.

33rd Virginia Infantry, H. E. Howard (Lynchburg, VA), 1987.

The Sporting News Selects Baseball's 25 Greatest Pennant Races, edited by Nahrstedt, Steve Zesch, and Carter, Sporting New Publishing, 1987.

The Sporting News Selects Baseball's 25 Greatest Teams, edited by Hoppel, Zesch, and Carter, Sporting News Publishing, 1988.

Also author of *27th Virginia Infantry,* 1993.

SIDELIGHTS: In *The Sporting News: Take Me Out to the Ball Park* Lowell Reidenbaugh examines the history of major league baseball stadiums. In addition to describing newer stadiums, such as Cincinnati's Riverfront Stadium, and the memorable moments that have occurred in them, he looks at the most celebrated modern-day parks— Boston's Fenway Park, New York's Yankee Stadium, Chicago's Wrigley Field, and Tiger Stadium in Detroit, for example—and at stadiums that are no longer in existence, including the Polo Grounds in New York City and Ebbets Field, the home of the old Brooklyn Dodgers. Jonathan Yardley, reviewing *Take Me Out to the Ball Park* in the *Washington Post,* found the chapters on the extinct arenas "most interesting precisely because the parks themselves are gone forever." While Yardley described the work of Reidenbaugh and illustrator Amadee Wohlschlaeger as "mixed," he declared their efforts "earnest and honorable."

BIOGRAPHICAL/CRITICAL SOURCES:

PERIODICALS

Washington Post, December 7, 1983.*

*   *   *

REILLY, John M(arsden) 1933-

PERSONAL: Born February 18, 1933, in Pittsburgh, PA; son of John Francis (in business) and Virginia (Marsden) Reilly; married Joyce Whisler (an office worker), 1952 (divorced); married Janet Potter (a librarian), 1994; children: (first marriage) John David, Bridget Anne, Michael Timothy. *Education:* West Virginia University, B.A. (with high honors), 1954; Washington University, St. Louis, MO, M.A., 1963, Ph.D., 1967.

ADDRESSES: Home—7 State St. W-3, Oneonta, NY 13820. *Office*—Department of English, Howard University, Washington, DC 20059.

CAREER: Washington University, St. Louis, MO, instructor in English, 1960-61; University of Puerto Rico, San Juan, assistant professor of English, 1961-63; State University of New York at Albany, assistant professor, 1963-70, associate professor, 1970-83, professor of English, 1983-94; Howard University, Washington, DC, visiting professor, 1994, professor of English, 1994—. Visiting assistant professor at University of Oregon, 1970.

MEMBER: United University Professions (chief negotiator, 1982-93; executive board, 1983-93; president, 1987-93), American Federation of Teachers (vice-president, 1987-93), American Studies Association, Modern Language Association of America, Mystery Writers of America, College Language Association, Popular Culture Association, Society for the Study of the Multi-Ethnic Literature of the United States, New York State United Teachers (board of directors, 1984-93), Society for the Study of Southern Literature, Northeastern Modern Language Association, Phi Beta Kappa.

AWARDS, HONORS: Woodrow Wilson fellow, 1954-55; National Endowment for the Humanities Younger humanist fellow, 1960-61; Edgar Allan Poe Award, Mystery Writers of America, 1981, for *Twentieth-Century Crime and Mystery Writers; Twentieth-Century Crime and Mystery Writers* was named outstanding reference book by Reference and Adult Services Division of American Library Association, 1981, John Ben Snow prize, Syracuse University Press, shared with other contributors to *Upstate Literature,* 1985.

WRITINGS:

(Editor) *Twentieth-Century Interpretations of Invisible Man,* Prentice-Hall (Englewood Cliffs, NJ), 1970.

Nagayo Honma and Shunsuke Kamei, editors, *Amerika no Taisha Bunka,* (title means "American Popular Culture"), Kenkyusha, 1974.

(Editor) *Richard Wright: The Critical Reception,* Burt Franklin (New York City), 1978.

(Editor) *Twentieth-Century Crime and Mystery Writers,* St. Martin's (New York City), 1980, second revised edition, 1985.

(Editor with others) *Oxford Companion to Crime and Mystery Writing,* Oxford University Press (New York City), in press.

Contributor to various anthologies, including *Contemporary Novelists,* edited by James Vinson, St. Martin's, 1972, 1975, 1982, 1986; *Black American Writers,* edited by M. Thomas Inge, Maurice Duke, and Jackson Bryer, St. Martin's, 1978; *American Literary Scholarship,* edited by James Woodress, Duke University Press (Durham, NC), 1979, 1982, 1983, 1984, 1985; *Seasoned Authors for a New Season,* edited by Louis Filler, Bowling Green University (Bowling Green, OH), 1980; *Ten Women of Mystery,* edited by Earl Bargainnier, Bowling Green University, 1981; *Critical Essays on Richard Wright,* edited by Yoshinobu Hakutani, G.K. Hall (Boston), 1981; *Upstate Literature,* edited by Frank Bergmann, Syracuse University Press (Syracuse, NY), 1985; *Speaking for You: Ralph Ellison's Cultural Vision,* edited by Kimberly Benston, Howard University Press (Washington, DC), 1986; and *Studies in Black American Literature,* edited by Joe Weixlman and Chester Fontenot, Penkevill Publishing, 1986. Also contributor of about forty articles and reviews to literature journals and popular magazines, including *Armchair Detective, Georgia Review, Alternative Futures, Minority Voices, Black American Literature Forum, Callaloo: Journal of the Black South* and *Clues: Journal of Detection.*

SIDELIGHTS: John M. Reilly once told *CA:* "A good deal of my writing represents an attempt to apply the training I have received as an academic to the principles I have found in popular political practice; thus, the choice of African-American writing as subject matter for my first publication originally derived from experience in the civil rights movement. As a participant in the St. Louis chapter of CORE during the 1950s I thought it necessary to unite what I was learning about the brave efforts of people to live the construction of a democratic society with the techniques of the profession I wanted to enter. Later, the fight against racism evolved into a movement for social reconstruction, and the thrill of that development stimulated me to seek additional subjects that would integrate action and investigation. So, I read social reform literature only to discover that the institution I work in (the university) is itself in need of reform as much as any other. In 1970, therefore, I did what many others at that time did—joined the strike. The consequence for my professional work was an interest in revising the subjects of literary study—particularly the canon of 'acceptable' works—and participating as I could in humanizing the relationships within the university and between the university and broader society. This purpose has now led me to become a union activist and a participant in the labor movement's effort to improve the conditions of work for the growing numbers of organized public employees.

"All this sounds neatly linear, and a mite too simple, for there is also a motive of pleasure to account for. My work on popular literature may have something to do with smashing the pantheon of greats, but it also has a lot to do with delight in storytelling—the means for establishing consciousness of our communities—and with reading that, appearing to have no utility, testifies on another level to the wonderful ability of people to make the world for themselves."

BIOGRAPHICAL/CRITICAL SOURCES:

PERIODICALS

Armchair Detective, winter, 1981.
Black American Literature Forum, fall, 1982.
Ellery Queen's Mystery Magazine, December 1, 1980.
Enigmatika, February, 1981.
MELUS, winter, 1983.
Mississippi Quarterly, fall, 1980.
Mystery Fancier, September-October, 1980; January-February, 1981.
New Republic, October 11, 1980.
New York Times Book Review, December 28, 1980.
Poisened Pen, July-August, 1980.
Reference Quarterly, December, 1980.
Southern Humanities Review, spring, 1980.
Times Literary Supplement, June 5, 1981.
Wilson Library Bulletin, January, 1981.

*   *   *

RENNICK, Robert M(orris) 1932-

PERSONAL: Born June 28, 1932, in New York, NY; son of Dan (a journalist) and Betty (a homemaker) Rennick; married Elizabeth McComb (a kindergarten teacher), June 27, 1964. *Education:* University of Wisconsin (now University of Wisconsin—Madison), B.S., 1954, M.S., 1958; began graduate study at University of North Carolina at Chapel Hill, 1956, Ph.D. candidate, 1959.

ADDRESSES: Home—61 Riverside Dr., Prestonsburg, KY 41653. *Office*—Kentucky Cabinet for Human Resources, 75 University Dr., Prestonsburg, KY 41653.

CAREER: Berea College, Berea, KY, instructor in sociology, 1960-61; Mary Washington College, Fredericksburg, VA, assistant professor of sociology, 1962-63; State University of New York, State University College at Cortland, assistant professor of sociology, 1963-65; Central Michigan University, Mount Pleasant, assistant professor of sociology, 1965-67; DePauw University, Greencastle, IN, assistant professor of sociology, 1967-70; Prestonsburg Community College, Prestonsburg, KY, assistant professor of sociology, 1970-72; Kentucky Cabinet for Human Resources, Prestonsburg, licensing specialist, 1972—. Chairman of Kentucky Committee on Geographic Names, 1985—.

MEMBER: American Folklore Society, American Name Society, Tennessee Folklore Society, New York Folklore Society, North Carolina Folklore Society, Kentucky Historical Society, Hoosier Folklore Society, Filson Club (Kentucky history).

WRITINGS:

Kentucky Place Names, University Press of Kentucky, 1984.
The Place Names of Pike County, Kentucky, Depot (Nashville, TN), 1991.
Kentucky's Bluegrass: A Survey of its Post Offices, The Depot, 1993.

Contributor of articles and book reviews to folklore and onomastics journals, including *Appalachian Notes, Comments on Etymology, Journal of Kentucky Studies, Tennessee Folklore Society Bulletin, Indiana Names, Indiana Folklore, Journal of American Folklore,* and *Midwest Journal of Language and Folklore.* Editor of *Newsletter of the Place Name Survey of the United States, 1972-73.* Occasional guest editor of the *American Name Society Bulletin.*

WORK IN PROGRESS: Continuing research on Kentucky place names, Appalachian place and folk narratives, and personal names.

SIDELIGHTS: Robert M. Rennick told *CA:* "My long-term goal has been to assist in the compilation and analysis of the estimated six million place names in the United States; my past and current efforts have been directed toward this end. This study has been under the sponsorship of the American Name Society since 1969.

"*Kentucky Place Names* is based on more than ten years of intensive library and field research in each of the state's 120 counties. It is one of a series of volumes encouraged by and affiliated with the ongoing *Place Name Survey of the United States,* which aims to compile and analyze the estimated six million place names in the country. My book, a description and explanation of some two thousand named communities and post offices, was designed to benefit historians, folklorists, and geographers as well as interested citizens of Kentucky. In addition, I hope that it will serve as a guide and inspiration for my life's ambition—a more systematic and comprehensive survey of all Kentucky place names, a cooperative effort of a number of the state's residents and institutions.

"My recent research has resulted in the publication of a number of scholarly and popular articles on Kentucky and other place names. The revision of the state's gazetteer—based on contemporary maps—and model dictionaries of Kentucky counties are anticipated future publications along with a series of books locating, describing and presenting the histories of Kentucky's 7,800 post offices. As a member of the National Commission for a Place Name Survey of the U.S., I continue to prepare research and training methodologies for persons planning and carrying out surveys of the place names of other states."

*   *   *

RICHARDS, Clare
See TITCHENER, Louise

*   *   *

RICHMOND, Claire
See TITCHENER, Louise

*   *   *

RITCHIE, Donald A(rthur) 1945-

PERSONAL: Born December 23, 1945, in New York, NY; son Arthur V. and Jeannette (Kromm) Ritchie; married Patricia A. Cooper, July 14, 1973 (divorced, 1986); married Anne Glackin Campbell, June 20, 1988; children: (second marriage) Jennifer Campbell Hannon, Andrea Campbell (stepdaughters). *Education:* City College of the City University of New York, B.A., 1967; University of Maryland at College Park, M.A., 1969, Ph.D., 1975.

ADDRESSES: Home—6033 Avon Dr., Bethesda, MD 20814. *Office*—Senate Historical Office, U.S. Senate Building, Washington, DC 20510.

CAREER: University of Maryland at College Park, instructor in history, 1974-76; Northern Virginia Community College, Alexandria, VA, instructor in history, 1975; George Mason University, Fairfax, VA, instructor in history, 1976; U. S. Senate, Washington, DC, associate historian at Senate Historical Office, 1976—. Adjunct assistant professor, Cornell in Washington Program, 1990—. Leti-

tia Woods Brown Memorial Lecturer, Historical Society of Washington, DC, 1990. *Military service:* U.S. Marine Corps, 1969-71.

MEMBER: American Historical Association (chairman of congressional fellowship committee, 1982-84; council member, 1992-96), National Council on Public History (chairman of nominating committee, 1994-95), Organization of American Historians (member of nominating committee, 1985-87; chairman of committee on research and access to historical documentation, 1993), Oral History Association (president, 1986-87), Society for History in the Federal Government (council member, 1989-91).

AWARDS, HONORS: Forrest C. Pogue Award, Oral History in the Mid-Atlantic Region, 1984; Henry Adams Prize, Society for History in the Federal Government, 1992, for *Press Gallery;* Richard W. Leopold Prize, Organization of American Historians, 1992, for *Press Gallery.*

WRITINGS:

(Editor) *Executive Sessions of the Senate Foreign Relations Committee (Historical Series),* Volumes VIII-XV, U.S. Government Printing Office (Washington, DC), 1978-93.

James M. Landis: Dean of the Regulators, Harvard University Press (Cambridge, MA), 1980.

Press Gallery: Congress and the Washington Correspondents, Harvard University Press, 1991.

The Young Oxford Companion to the Congress of the United States, Oxford University Press (New York City), 1993.

History of a Free Nation (high school textbook), Glencoe (New York City), 1994.

Doing Oral History, Twayne (Boston), 1994.

Profiles of American Journalists, Oxford University Press, 1996.

Contributor to history journals. Editor of *Maryland Historian,* 1972-73. Editor of "Oral History Series," Twayne, 1988—.

SIDELIGHTS: Donald A. Ritchie told *CA:* "While researching in the manuscript collection of James M. Landis, a leading regulatory adviser to presidents Franklin D. Roosevelt, Harry S Truman, and John F. Kennedy, I discovered the last thirty pages of an oral history interview that Landis had given shortly before his death. Further hunting located the complete seven-hundred-page manuscript at the Columbia Oral History Office. This was a magnificent find for a biographer: the subject's life in his own words. Even relatively well-known facts and incidents took on a new immediacy when presented in the first person, but, although the oral history illuminated Landis's long career as a lawyer, dean of the Harvard Law School, and government official, it revealed little about his private life. He made almost no mention of his two marriages, his children, or the income tax delinquency that eventually sent him to jail. I began to conduct my own interviews, with Landis's family, friends, colleagues, and even his psychiatrist. These oral histories significantly influenced my writing of the biography.

"I carried my interest in oral history to the Senate Historical Office, where I conduct interviews with former senators and members of the Senate staff. Oral history also influenced my writing of a high school textbook, *History of a Free Nation.* Using first-person accounts helped to enliven the narrative and to capture the attention of adolescents. After speaking about oral history at various conferences and workshops, I compiled my recommendations into an introductory guidebook, *Doing Oral History.*

"Conducting interviews raised my curiosity about other professional interviewers, particularly the journalists who regularly call the Senate Historical Office for information. Their requests made me aware of the working conditions under which journalists operate—particularly their reliance on oral rather than written sources. This led to *Press Gallery,* a study of how Washington correspondents historically gathered and reported news of the federal government to the general public."

In a review in the *New York Times,* George P. Will describes *Press Gallery* as "sometimes startling, sometimes dismaying and constantly illuminating. . . . [Ritchie] is a scrupulous historian whose fine book brings back the powerful aroma of a past too raw to be romanticized. Thus does memory help reconcile us to current discontents."

BIOGRAPHICAL/CRITICAL SOURCES:

BOOKS

Howe, Barbara J. and Emory L. Kemp, editors, *Public History: An Introduction,* Robert E. Krieger, 1986.

PERIODICALS

Booknotes, July 7, 1991.
New York Times, June 30, 1991.
OHMAR Newsletter, fall, 1984.

*   *   *

ROBERTSON, Stephen
See WALKER, Robert W(ayne)

*   *   *

ROOP, Peter (G.) 1951-

PERSONAL: Born March 8, 1951, in Winchester, MA; son of Daniel Morehead (an engineer) and Dorothy (a homemaker; maiden name, Danenhower) Roop; married Constance Betzer (an educator and author), August 4, 1973; children: Sterling Gray, Heidi Anne. *Education:* Lawrence University, B.A., 1973; Simmons College, M.A., 1980; also attended University of Wisconsin—Madison. *Politics:* Independent.

ADDRESSES: Home and office—2601 North Union St., Appleton, WI 54911.

CAREER: Appleton Area School District, Appleton, WI, teacher, 1973—. Fulbright exchange teacher at primary school in Kington, England, 1976-77; instructor at University of Wisconsin—Fox Valley, 1983-84, and University of Wisconsin School of the Arts, Rhinelander, 1986—. Member of board of directors of Friends of the Appleton Library, 1974-84, and board of trustees of Appleton Public Library, 1983-90. Educational consultant, *Booklinks Magazine.*

MEMBER: Children's Literature Association, Society of Children's Book Writers, National Council of Teachers of English, National Education Association, Wisconsin Regional Writers Association (president, 1983-86), Council for Wisconsin Writers, Chicago Reading Roundtable.

AWARDS, HONORS: Jade Ring Award from Wisconsin Regional Writers Association, 1979, for play *Who Buries the Funeral Director?,* and 1982, for *The Cry of the Conch;* named reading teacher of the year by Mideast Wisconsin Reading Council, 1983; Children's Choice Awards from International Reading Association and Children's Book Council, 1985, for *Out to Lunch!* and *Space Out!;* named Teacher of the Year and Outstanding Elementary Educator for Wisconsin by Wisconsin Department of Public Instruction, both 1986; *Keep the Lights Burning, Abbie* was named Children's Book of the Year and Irma Simonton Black Honor Book by Bank Street College of Education in 1986 and an "outstanding trade book in the language arts" by the National Council of Teachers of English, and was chosen as a 1987 feature book for Public Broadcasting System's "Reading Rainbow" program; Notable Trade Book award, National Council for the Social Sciences, for *Ahyoka and the Talking Leaves* and *Off the Map: The Journals of Lewis and Clark;* Notable Trade Book award, National Science Teachers Association, for *Seasons of the Cranes; I, Columbus* was an International Reading Association Teachers Choice and the American Library Association Young Adult Editor's Choice Book, and was named Book of the Year by the Library of Congress.

WRITINGS:

The Cry of the Conch, Press Pacifica (Waipahu, HI), 1984.
Little Blaze and the Buffalo Jump, Montana Council for Indian Education (Billings, MT), 1984.
Siskimi, Montana Council for Indian Education, 1984.

Natosi, Montana Council for Indian Education, 1984.

(With Rick McCown and Marcy Driscoll) *Educational Psychology,* 2nd edition (Roop not associated with earlier edition), Allyn & Bacon (Newton, MA), 1996.

CHILDREN'S; WITH WIFE, CONNIE ROOP

Space Out!, Lerner Publications (Minneapolis, MN), 1984.

Go Hog Wild!, Lerner Publications, 1984.

Out to Lunch!, Lerner Publications, 1984.

Keep the Lights Burning, Abbie, Carolrhoda (Minneapolis, MN), 1985.

Buttons for General Washington, Carolrhoda, 1986.

Stick Out Your Tongue!, Lerner Publications, 1986.

Going Buggy!, Lerner Publications, 1986.

Let's Celebrate!, Lerner Publications, 1986.

The Extinction of the Dinosaurs, Greenhaven Press (St. Paul, MN), 1987.

Poltergeists, Greenhaven Press, 1987.

Mysteries of the Solar System, Greenhaven Press, 1987.

We Sought Refuge Here, Appleton Schools (Appleton, WI), 1987.

Seasons of the Cranes, Walker & Co. (New York City), 1989.

I, Columbus, Walker & Co., 1990.

Ahyoka and the Talking Leaves, Lothrop (New York City), 1992.

One Earth, A Multitude of Creatures, Walker & Co., 1992.

Discovering Sea Creatures, Perfection Learning, 1992.

Discovering the Solar System, Perfection Learning, 1992.

Discovering Flowering Plants, Perfection Learning, 1992.

Discovering Insects and Spiders, Perfection Learning, 1992.

Discovering Dinosaurs, Perfection Learning, 1992.

Off the Map: The Journals of Lewis and Clark, Walker & Co., 1993

Capturing Nature: The Art and Writings of Audubon, Walker & Co., 1993.

David Farragut, Lothrop, 1995.

Goodbye for Today, Puffin Books (New York City), 1995.

Mary Jemison, Puffin Books, 1995.

The Pilgrims' Voices, Walker & Co., 1995.

San Francisco Earthquake, Lothrop, in press.

Small Deer and the Buffalo Jump, Northland Press (Flagstaff, AZ), in press.

OTHER

Also author of one-act play *Who Buries the Funeral Director?* Contributor to Harcourt's reading texts. Contributor of articles and reviews to newspapers and magazines, including *Cobblestone, Jack and Jill, Cricket, History Today,* and *Language Arts.*

SIDELIGHTS: "My work in the elementary classroom is one of the prime motivations for my writing for children

and now adults as well," Peter Roop told *CA.* "Although I had written many short stories in college, I had never considered writing for publication until I began teaching.

"When I began teaching, I was reading numerous children's books to my students. We were also doing a lot of writing. I said to myself, 'I can write these stories.' Little then did I realize the scope of children's literature and the skills it would take to write quality stories for children. The easy appearance of many children's books hides the hours of hard work involved in creating a worthwhile book for young readers.

"In 1980, to enhance my knowledge of children's books for my work as an educator, as well as for my writing, I completed my master's degree in children's literature at the Center for the Study of Children's Literature at Simmons College in Boston. The work at Simmons was pivotal to my understanding of the genre and in writing for children. There I studied with noted authors Nancy Bond and Scott O'Dell. The books of O'Dell, especially *Island of the Blue Dolphins,* have been the mainstay of my perspective on writing for children. O'Dell's style, sensitivity, and adept mixing of history and fiction are models for my own efforts.

"An intense interest in history has led me to write historical stories, articles, and books. As a writer on assignment for *Cobblestone* I researched and wrote about topics ranging from the origins of Native Americans to the creation of video games. Fascinated with the lives of pre-European peoples [of the Americas], I have written three books for the Blackfeet Nation. A fourth book, *The Cry of the Conch,* is about ancient Hawaii.

"After I had been writing by myself for about six years, my wife, Connie, and I began collaborating. Inspired by a walk by the ocean, we wrote a joke and riddle book about the seashore. This idea developed into a six-book series. Playing with words has long been a family tradition, one which we turned into six 'Reading Rainbow' books.

"Our abiding interest in Maine led us to write *Keep the Lights Burning, Abbie,* a historical story about Abbie Burgess, a brave young woman who singlehandedly kept two lighthouses going during a month-long siege of bad weather in 1856. This book, featured on the Public Broadcasting System's 'Reading Rainbow' in 1987, will hopefully create more opportunities for our future.

"We are interested in writing the stories of children who, like, Abbie, are 'footnotes in history.' John Darraugh in *Buttons for General Washington* is one such footnote. *Ahyoka and the Talking Leaves* is another. These were real children who through courage and effort overcame major obstacles.

"Our combined background in science has involved us in writing nonfiction books as well. We completed a four-book series of 'great mysteries,' followed by five teaching guides highlighting teaching science through nonfiction books.

"One area of great interest for us is primary source material and making it available for young readers. To this end, we have edited the journals of Columbus, Lewis and Clark, and John James Audubon. Our interest in travel has provided the backdrop for many books. As a writer I believe that getting the right sense of setting is critical to the impact of a story. Experiencing the sight of fifty whooping cranes at dawn for *Seasons of the Cranes,* feeling the chilling blasts of a nor'easter for *Keep the Lights Burning, Abbie,* walking the cobbled streets of Philadelphia for *Buttons for General Washington,* camping at the actual campsites of Lewis and Clark for *Off the Map:* all of the experiences have added an element of place to our stories that book research cannot provide.

"One unexpected spin-off of our writing has been the opportunity to talk to students and teachers around the country. In the past five years, I have given presentations in more than 100 schools and at various conferences. There is nothing like hearing a young reader say, 'Your book is my favorite!'

"Writing the best books possible for young readers is my goal. By providing the best for children, I can open more vistas and distant horizons to their wondering eyes and minds. What better role for a writer?"

*   *   *

ROSENBERG, Norman L(ewis) 1942-

PERSONAL: Born February 15, 1942, in Lincoln, NE; son of Joseph (in sales) and Dorothea (Anderson) Rosenberg; married Emily Schlaht (a teacher and writer), June 4, 1966; children: Sarah, Molly, Ruth, Joseph. *Education:* University of Nebraska—Lincoln, B.A. (with distinction), 1964, M.A., 1967; State University of New York at Stony Brook, Ph.D., 1972. *Religion:* Jewish.

ADDRESSES: Home—1072 Goodrich, St. Paul, MN 55105. *Office*—Department of History, Macalester College, 1600 Grand Ave., St. Paul, MN 55105.

CAREER: Central Michigan University, Mount Pleasant, assistant professor of history, 1971-73, assistant professor in honors programs, 1973-74; Macalester College, St. Paul, MN, assistant professor, 1975-80, associate professor, 1980-84, professor of history, 1984-93; DeWitt Wallace professor of history, 1993—. Assistant professor at University of Nebraska—Lincoln, summer, 1972; member

of sociology faculty at Hamline University, 1975; assistant professor at University of California, Berkeley, summer, 1976; lecturer at World Press Institute, 1978—. Member of Judicial Education Commission of Minnesota, 1985—.

MEMBER: American Historical Association, Organization of American Historians, American Society for Legal History, American Culture Association, Popular Culture Association, Phi Beta Kappa.

AWARDS, HONORS: Jerome Foundation grants, 1976-77 and 1978-79; fellow of National Endowment for the Humanities, 1977; Bush Foundation grant, 1983, 1984, 1994; Wallace Sabbatical Grant, 1987-88; Mellon Foundation grant, 1994.

WRITINGS:

(With wife, Emily Rosenberg, and others) *America: A Portrait in History,* Prentice-Hall (Englewood Cliffs, NJ), 1973, revised edition, 1978.
(With Keith Polakoff and others) *Generations of Americans,* St. Martin's (New York City), 1976.
(Editor with E. Rosenberg) *Postwar America: Readings and Reminiscences,* Prentice-Hall, 1976.
(With E. Rosenberg) *In Our Times: America Since 1945,* Prentice-Hall, 1976, 5th edition, 1995.
Protecting the "Best Man": An Interpretive History of the Law of Libel, University of North Carolina Press (Chapel Hill), 1986.
(With John Murin and others) *Liberty, Equality, and Power,* Harcourt (New York City), 1995.

Contributors of articles and reviews to books, journals, and newspapers.

WORK IN PROGRESS: Re-Inventing the First Amendment, 1940-1964.

SIDELIGHTS: Norman L. Rosenberg told *CA:* "I am interested in exploring the relationship between popular culture (past and present—especially Hollywood films) and legal culture. I have published work that deals with both the legal thought of Oliver Wendell Holmes, Jr., and his popular Hollywood bio-pic, *The Magnificent Yankee* (1950). I share both a history teaching position and a writing career with my wife, Emily. Ours is the longest-lasting 'joint-appointment professorship' in academic life."

*   *   *

ROSS, Malcolm
See ROSS-MACDONALD, Malcolm J(ohn)

ROSS-MACDONALD, Malcolm J(ohn) 1932-
(Malcolm Macdonald, Malcolm Ross)

PERSONAL: Name originally Malcolm John Ross Macdonald; name legally changed in 1947; born February 29, 1932, in Chipping Sodbury, England; son of Alan Ross (an engineer) and Brenda (a secretary; maiden name, Edwards) Macdonald; married Ingrid Giehr, March 17, 1962; children: Petra Brigid, Candida Judith. *Education:* Attended Falmouth School of Art, 1950-54; University College, London, Slade Diploma, 1958. *Politics:* "A sort-of far-right marxist—broad enough to offend all enthusiasts." *Religion:* "Atheist, humanist." *Avocational interests:* Personal computing.

ADDRESSES: Home—Ireland. *Agent*—David Higham Associates, Ltd., 5-8 Lower John St., Golden Sq., London W1R 4HA, England.

CAREER: Freelance writer, editor, and graphic designer. Folkuniversitet, Umeaa, Sweden, lecturer, 1959-61; Aldus Books Ltd., London, began as caption writer, became executive editor, 1961-65; visiting lecturer, Hornsey College of Art, 1966-69. Consultant to publishing companies. *Military service:* British Army, 1954-56.

MEMBER: Society of Authors, Radio Writers Association, Authors Guild, Authors League of America.

WRITINGS:

The Big Waves (novel), J. Cape (London), 1962.
(With Donald Longmore) *Spare Part Surgery,* Doubleday (New York City), 1968.
(With Longmore) *Machines in Medicine,* Doubleday, 1969.
(With Longmore) *The Heart,* McGraw (New York City), 1971.
The World Wildlife Guide, Viking (New York City), 1971.
Beyond the Horizon (history), Grolier (Danbury, CT), 1971.
Every Living Thing (ecology), Danbury (Suffern, NY), 1974.
Doors Doors Doors (closed circulation book for architects), Viking Aluminum, 1974.
The Origin of Johnny (human biology and evolution), foreword by Francis Crick, Knopf (New York City), 1975.
Life in the Future, Danbury, 1975.

UNDER NAME MALCOLM MACDONALD, EXCEPT AS INDICATED; HISTORICAL NOVELS

World from Rough Stones (also see below), Hodder & Stoughton (London), 1974, published as *The World from Rough Stones,* Knopf, 1975.
The Rich Are with You Always, Knopf, 1976.
Sons of Fortune, Knopf, 1978.

Abigail, Knopf, 1979.
(Under name Malcolm Ross) *The Dukes,* Simon & Schuster (New York City), 1981.
Goldeneye, Knopf, 1982.
Tessa d'Arblay, Hodder & Stoughton, 1983.
For They Shall Inherit, St. Martin's (New York City), 1984, originally published in England as *In Love and War.*
On a Far Wild Shore, St. Martin's, 1986, originally published in England as *Mistress of Pallas.*
The Silver Highways, St. Martin's, 1987.
Honour and Obey, St. Martin's, 1988, originally published in England as *The Sky with Diamonds.*
A Notorious Woman, St. Martin's, 1988.
His Father's Son, St. Martin's, 1989.
An Innocent Woman, St. Martin's, 1989.
Hell Hath No Fury, St. Martin's, 1990.
A Woman Alone, St. Martin's, 1990.
The Captain's Wives, Hodder & Stoughton, 1991.
A Woman Scorned, St. Martin's, 1991.
A Woman Possessed, St. Martin's, 1992.
All Desires Known, St. Martin's, 1994.
To the End of Her Days, St. Martin's, 1994.
Dancing on Snowflakes, St. Martin's, 1994.
For I Have Sinned, St. Martin's, 1995.

RADIO PLAYS

Kristina's Winter, British Broadcasting Corp. (BBC), 1972.
Conditional People, BBC, 1973.
(Under name Malcolm Macdonald) *World from Rough Stones* (radio trilogy based on his novel of the same title), BBC, 1974.

OTHER

Founding and consulting editor of "Living World" series, twenty volumes, Aldus Books (London), 1972.

WORK IN PROGRESS: Kernow & Daughter and *Crissy's Family,* both for St. Martin's; "there's always a story growing on the hard disk and half a dozen more in the queue."

SIDELIGHTS: Malcolm J. Ross-Macdonald once told *CA:* "I set out to become the very opposite of what 'novelist' has come to mean—to become, instead, a simple storyteller." His thirteen years as a nonfiction writer have heavily influenced his stories. Though his main characters and plots are all invented, Ross-Macdonald commented that he does not invent a "fact" if the truth will serve as well, and that his stories are made more vivid because of his obsession with history. He has collected an extensive library of Victorian source books, British and American guidebooks, and autobiographies, from which he draws material for his stories.

"I would like people to be, above all, entertained and enthralled by my stories," Ross-Macdonald explained. "I would like them to gain a new understanding of why we are where we are now—to see that the problems which beset us have not simply sprung up in the last few years. Indeed, those problems were often worse a hundred years ago, and I hope to dramatize that—but without making the difference merely sensational. We live in an age rich in communication, crammed with today's and even tomorrow's news. Perspective gets crowded out. Judgement gets warped in ways our forefathers would find ludicrously pessimistic. If one of the effects of my entertainments is to restore that perspective and straighten that judgement, I would be content."

*   *   *

ROUECHE, Berton   1911-1994

PERSONAL: Surname is pronounced "Roo-*shay*"; born April 16, 1911, in Kansas City, MO; died of a shotgun wound to the head in an apparent suicide, April 28, 1994, in Amagansett, NY; son of Clarence Berton (a business executive) and Nana Marie (Mossman) Roueche; married Katherine Eisenhower, October 28, 1936; children: Bradford. *Education:* University of Missouri, B.J., 1933.

CAREER: Kansas City Star, Kansas City, MO, reporter, 1934-41; *St. Louis Globe-Democrat,* St. Louis, MO, reporter, 1941-42; *St. Louis Post-Dispatch,* St. Louis, MO, reporter, 1942-44; *New Yorker,* New York City, staff writer, 1944-94, originator and sole proprietor of "Annals of Medicine" department. Faculty member, Bread Loaf Writers' Conference, Middlebury, VT, 1958, and Indiana University Writer's Conference, Bloomington, 1962; Trustee of Guild Hall, East Hampton, NY, 1960-76, and National Foundation for Infectious Diseases, 1976-94; member of executive committee, Health Research Council, New York City, 1966-72.

MEMBER: American Epidemiological Society (honorary member), Kansas City Academy of Medicine (fellow), Preservation Society of the East End (past president), Sigma Alpha Epsilon, Devon Yacht Club (Amagansett, NY), Coffee House Club (New York City).

AWARDS, HONORS: Albert Lasker Medical Journalism Award, 1950, for "The Fog," and 1960, for *The Neutral Spirit;* Mystery Writers of America Award, 1954; National Council of Infant and Child Care annual award, 1956; American Medical Writers Association annual award, 1963 and 1978; American Medical Association annual journalism award, 1970; William E. Leidt Award, Episcopal Church, 1973, for religious reporting; J. C. Penney-University of Missouri annual journalism award,

1978; University of Missouri honor award, 1981, for distinguished service in journalism; American Academy and Institute of Arts and Letters award in literature, 1982; New York Public Library Literary Lion Award, 1985; Lewis Thomas Communications Award, American College of Physicians, 1987.

WRITINGS:

FICTION

Black Weather, Reynal (New York City), 1945.
The Greener Grass, Harper (New York City), 1948.
The Last Enemy, Grove (New York City), 1956.
Feral, Harper, 1974.
Fago, Harper, 1977.

NONFICTION

Eleven Blue Men, Little, Brown (Boston), 1953.
The Incurable Wound, Little, Brown, 1958.
The Delectable Mountains, Little, Brown, 1959.
The Neutral Spirit, Little, Brown, 1960.
(Editor) *Curiosities of Medicine,* Little, Brown, 1963.
A Man Named Hoffman, Little, Brown, 1965.
Annals of Epidemiology, Little, Brown, 1967.
Field Guide to Disease, Little, Brown, 1967.
What's Left: Reports on a Diminishing America, Little, Brown, 1969.
The Orange Man and Other Narratives of Medical Detection, Little, Brown, 1971.
The River World and Other Explorations, Harper, 1978.
The Medical Detectives, Times Books (New York City), 1980.
Special Places: In Search of Small Town America, Little, Brown, 1982.
The Medical Detectives, Volume II, Dutton (New York City), 1984.
Sea to Shining Sea: People, Travels, Places, Dutton, 1985.
The Man Who Grew Two Breasts: And Other True Tales of Medical Detection, Dutton, 1995.

ADAPTATIONS: "A Ride into Town" (short story on cassette), Miller-Brody, 1975.

SIDELIGHTS: Despite publishing five well-received novels, Berton Roueche is perhaps best-remembered for the medical and travel writing he produced during his fifty-year career as a columnist for the *New Yorker.* In an interview with Sam Staggs for *Publishers Weekly,* Roueche explained how his well-respected *New Yorker* column, "The Annals of Medicine," came to be. Hired to write humor pieces, Roueche wrote a story about an unusual pest-control man who had an odd theory about an outbreak of disease in a Queens housing project. "Then I began to get letters from public health people around the country pointing out that there was no popular writing about health matters. One local letter said that if I was interested in more unusual cases to go to the New York City Health Department and ask them about the 11 Bowery bums who turned blue after eating oatmeal. When I wrote this case up, Harold Ross [*New Yorker* editor at the time] . . . ran it under the title of 'The Case of the Eleven Blue Men.' Later [in 1947] he invented 'Annals of Medicine' as the overall department for my medical reporting."

Roueche published a collection of these "Annals of Medicine" pieces in his volume entitled *The Medical Detectives* in 1980. *Newsweek* writer Jean Strouse said, "These tales of epidemiological sleuthing have exactly the right title. They read like mystery thrillers—only the bad guys turn out to be the anthrax bacillus, a fungus called *Histoplasma capsulatum*, jimson weed, rabies, the voracious endoparasitic trichina worm, organic phosphate insecticides, and acetylsalicylic acid, otherwise known as aspirin." Strouse found that Roueche "brings scientific facts alive with an elegant, light touch." The writer of a brief blurb in the *Washington Post Book World* agreed: "For their superb style and elegant coating of solid medical facts and procedures, these essays can hardly be topped."

Upon the release of a second volume of *The Medical Detectives*, Elaine Kendall writing in the *Los Angeles Times* shed some light on what she felt made Roueche's medical writing so fascinating: "The author chooses his cases meticulously, selecting those offering the maximum amount of suspense, confusion and peril before being brought to bay by a combination of deductive reasoning, hard work and pure serendipity. . . . Roueche's magic is to make these stories of dogged scientific inquiry, endless patience and intellectual insight compelling as any espionage thriller. His research is so thorough that the books are useful to health professionals; his witty urbane prose thoroughly captivates the general reader."

Several reviewers praised Roueche for the prose style in his medical reporting. Writing in the *Washington Post*, Robin Marantz Henig commented, "The Roueche style includes some deft touches. His best tales begin almost clinically, in unemotional prose that seems to say that the facts of the story are themselves so incredible that just stating them will capture your rapt attention. In most cases this is absolutely true."

What's Left: Reports on a Diminishing America is a collection of eight of Roueche's nature reports originally published in the *New Yorker*. These reports include accounts of a walk along the Chesapeake & Ohio Canal in Washington, DC; a day on a river in the Ozark Mountains; and a trip through the Sonoran Desert. A reviewer for the *New York Times Book Review* found most of the pieces "informed by a devoted admiration of the natural world and a firm dedication to the importance of keeping it natural."

The River World and Other Explorations was also compiled from *New Yorker* pieces, among them portraits of a country doctor in New Mexico and a Congregational minister in Massachusetts, as well as reports of a voyage to a Bering Sea island in an Eskimo open boat and one by towboat down the Missouri and the Mississippi rivers to New Orleans. *Time* reviewer Peter Stoler recommended it: "Roueche leaves no doubt that he hates to see any journey, any visit, any encounter end. Readers who pick up *The River World* are likely to have the same feeling about his book."

Benjamin DeMott, a reviewer for the *New York Times Book Review*, wrote, "At its core *The River World* is a celebration of the unbeaten path . . . and the homely pleasure. . . . The human virtues most admired are kindness and candor." DeMott happened to know one of the people Roueche wrote about in this book, and, while he claimed that Roueche wrongly characterized the man, he still liked the author's writing: "If on occasion [Roueche is] overreductive, he's never less than firm in his determination to give the provinces a fair shake, and that makes him almost unique. Read *The River World* in a spirit of *gentle* wariness, and you won't go wrong; at its best it charms and calms."

In a *Publishers Weekly* interview, Roueche spoke about how he came to write *Special Places: In Search of Small Town America*: "Flying home from the West Coast, he would often look down and see a little patch of light far below. 'I wondered what it was like down there,' he recalls. 'Looking down on western Nebraska, I thought it would be interesting to investigate those little towns. That was the beginning of a *New Yorker* series. I told William Shawn, the editor, that I'd like to go out and live for a month in one of those towns or villages and write a story about it." The book collects profiles of seven towns with populations ranging from 303 to 10,290, including Stapleton, Nebraska; Welch, West Virginia; Hermann, Missouri; Crystal City, Texas; Corydon, Indiana; Pella, Iowa; and Hope, Arkansas.

In a review for the *Washington Post Book World*, Vic Sussman described the author's approach in *Special Places: In Search of Small Town America*: "Roueche's elegantly written essays . . . have a cinematic quality. Each shifts smoothly between settings and speakers, never losing track of the central question: what makes this town so different? . . . Particularly appealing is his ability to reproduce voices. Farmers, teachers, shopkeepers, and teenagers talk to Roueche, revealing much about small town life and the human condition." *Los Angeles Times Book Review* writer Michael Parfit praised the book for a similar reason: "Roueche is deft, kind and gentle, in both style and content. His judgment is warm but invisible, hidden in the great rivers of dialogue he draws from the people he meets." Richard Lingeman, writing in the *New York Times Book Review,* also liked *Special Places: In Search of Small Town America:* "If you wish to savor the qualities of small-town life, let this gracefully written book be your guide to the kinds of places that 30 percent of the American people live in or around. You will find it a pleasure."

Sea to Shining Sea: People, Travel, Places is another volume of travel and nature pieces. Jack Schneider of the *New York Times Book Review* found five chapters set in Europe "bland"; nevertheless he commented, "This is really a book for nibbling, because even its less interesting sections contain refreshing observations and conversations." *Washington Post* reviewer T. H. Watkins had less qualified praise: "Roueche has a penetrating eye for detail and a sharp ear for dialogue, and he invests both the places he has seen and the people he has observed with a meaty verisimilitude. . . . [He] brings to [each] experience a sympathetic intelligence and a gift of language that fixes it in your memory just as surely as it is fixed in his."

Beaufort Cranford, who reviewed *The Medical Detectives, Volume II* for the *Detroit News,* mulled over the question of whether to categorize Roueche as an essayist or a journalist: "Roueche . . . is made less an essayist than a journalist by a strict attention to what happened and why. . . . But it is . . . unfair simply to call Roueche a journalist and leave it at that. . . . Roueche has consistently shown a talent for evoking a particular mood and using it to generate interest in readers. This capacity to call forth an intended emotional response is, I think, what most distinguishes a piece of writing from a piece of art. The best of journalists are artists too, and Roueche is high among that company."

BIOGRAPHICAL/CRITICAL SOURCES:

PERIODICALS

Atlantic, January, 1975, p. 91.
Detroit Free Press, May 4, 1986.
Detroit News, January 27, 1985.
Globe and Mail (Toronto), August 17, 1985; February 21, 1987.
Los Angeles Times, December 18, 1984.
Los Angeles Times Book Review, July 25, 1982, p. 11; March 24, 1991, p. 10.
New York Times, August 4, 1982.
New York Times Book Review, July 6, 1969, p. 13; September 19, 1971, p. 36; December 29, 1974, p. 20; December 28, 1975, p. 21; October 16, 1977, p. 32; January 21, 1979, p. 12; July 25, 1982, p. 8; January 26, 1986, p. 21.
New Yorker, December 11, 1971, p. 165; November 11, 1974, p. 215.
Newsweek, January 12, 1981, p. 79; January 21, 1985, p. 72.

Publishers Weekly, January 31, 1986.
Time, November 27, 1978, p. 104.
Village Voice Literary Supplement, December, 1985, p. 3.
Washington Post, October 26, 1984; February 8, 1986.
Washington Post Book World, May 16, 1982, p. 12; August 1, 1982, p. 7; January 1, 1984, p. 12; February 9, 1986, p. 12; March 10, 1991, p. 12.

OBITUARIES:

PERIODICALS

Chicago Tribune, April 30, 1994, p. 19.
Los Angeles Times, April 30, 1994, p. A24.
New York Times, April 29, 1994, p. B8.
Washington Post, April 30, 1994, p. B6.*

* * *

RUHLEN, Merritt 1944-

PERSONAL: Surname is pronounced "Roo-len"; born May 10, 1944, in Washington, DC; son of Frank Merritt (a lawyer) and Florence (a homemaker; maiden name, Ennis) Ruhlen; married Anca Popescu (a librarian), December 24, 1970; children: Ricky and Johnny (twins). *Education:* Rice University, B.A., 1966; attended University of Paris, 1966-67, University of Illinois, 1968-69, and University of Bucharest, 1969-71; Stanford University, Ph.D., 1973. *Avocational interests:* Basketball, tennis, classical guitar.

ADDRESSES: Home and office—4335 Cesano Court, Palo Alto, CA 94306.

CAREER: Stanford University, Stanford, CA, research associate, 1973-77. Interpreter for U.S. Department of State, 1975, 1977, 1981; instructor in French, College of San Mateo, 1979, lecturer in human biology, Stanford University, 1994.

MEMBER: Linguistic Society of America.

AWARDS, HONORS: Stanford University fellow, 1967-69, 1971-72; California State fellow, 1968-69; American Council of Learned Societies grant, 1968; NDEA Title VI grant, 1969; Fulbright fellow in Romania, 1969-71.

WRITINGS:

A Guide to the Languages of the World, privately printed, 1975.
A Guide to the World's Languages, Volume 1: *Classification,* Standford University Press (Stanford, CA), 1987.
The Origin of Language, Wiley (New York City), 1994.
On the Origin of Languages, Stanford University Press, 1994.

Contributor of articles and reviews to magazines.

WORK IN PROGRESS: Preparing *A Guide to the World's Languages,* Volume 2: *Language Data;* investigating the classification of American Indian Languages; exploring the linguistic evidence for the origin and spread of modern humans.

SIDELIGHTS: Merritt Ruhlen commented: "One of my interests is twins, since I am myself a twin and a father of twins.

"My work on linguistic classification has recently been the subject of stories in the *Atlantic Monthly, U.S. News and World Report,* and *Scientific American.* In 1992, I was also a participant in television documentaries on the origin of language, for the BBC and North German television. The BBC show is scheduled to appear on American television in 1994 on public television's *NOVA* program."

*   *   *

RUUD, Charles A(rthur) 1933-

PERSONAL: Surname is pronounced "rude"; born May 5, 1933, in Marietta, MN; son of Paul F. (a publisher) and Eva K. (in public relations; maiden name, Carlson) Ruud; married Marjorie Leonard (a teacher), August 14, 1955; children: Paul A., Kristi Ruud Cohen, Karen. *Education:* Willamette University, B.A., 1955; Harvard University, M.A., 1957; University of California, Berkeley, Ph.D., 1965.

ADDRESSES: Home—London, Ontario. *Office*—University of Western Ontario, London, Ontario, Canada.

CAREER: University of Western Ontario, London, lecturer, 1963-65, assistant professor, 1965-69, associate professor, 1969-83, professor of history, 1983—.

MEMBER: Canadian Slavic Association, American Association for the Advancement of Slavic Studies.

AWARDS, HONORS: Fighting Words named outstanding academic book by *Choice* magazine, 1982.

WRITINGS:

Fighting Words: Imperial Censorship and the Russian Press, 1804-1906, University of Toronto Press (Buffalo, NY), 1982.
Russian Entrepreneur: Publisher I.D. Sytin of Moscow, 1851-1934, McGill-Queen's University Press, 1990.
(With S. G. Stepanov) *Fontonka, 16, Politicheskii sysk pri tsariakh* (title means "Fontonka, 16, Political Investigation Under the Czars"), Mysl Publishers, 1993.

Contributor of articles and book reviews to magazines and journals, including *American Historical Review, Canadian Historical Review, Canadian and International Education, Canadian Journal of History, Kritika, Middle East Focus, History and Social Science Teacher, Journalism Quarterly, Russian History, Canadian Review of Studies in Nationalism, Slavonic and East European Review, California Slavic Studies,* and *Canadian Slavic Studies.*

SIDELIGHTS: In *Fighting Words: Imperial Censorship and the Russian Press, 1804-1906* Charles A. Ruud looks at a century of print censorship in czarist Russia. Examining censorship legislation and enforcement and attempts at reform, Ruud reveals that "as in the West, the government eventually found censorship a political liability, abolished it and introduced press freedom, in turn making greater use of judicial restraint on the printed word." Writing in the *Times Literary Supplement,* Kyril FitzLyon deemed *Fighting Words* "a reliable reference work" that will dispel "wrong assumptions" about Russian censorship.

In *Russian Entreprenuer: Publisher I. D. Sytin of Moscow, 1851-1934* (published in Moscow as *Russkii Predprinimatel*), Rudd describes how an unlettered villager used the skill of an entrepreneur to become the premier publisher of the Russian Empire in the last decades before the Russian Revolution of 1917. The review in *Slavic Review* calls this work a "highly readable, meticulously researched account of Sytin's rise from apprentice . . . to Russia's most powerful publishing magnate . . . [Sytin] is chiefly interesting for his contribution to Russian culture, at last documented in this impeccably crafted, absorbing biography."

Fontanka, 16, Politicheskii sysk pri tsariakh traces the evolution and policies of the czarist system of secret police that culminated in the force commonly known as the Okhranka, which was headquartered at Fontanka, 16, in Moscow. This work, jointly authored by historian S. G. Stepanov is one of the few book-length scholarly studies to appear in Russia in 1993.

BIOGRAPHICAL/CRITICAL SOURCES:

PERIODICALS

American Historical Review, December, 1983.
Canadian Journal of History, April, 1983.
History, October, 1983.
Journal of Modern History, September, 1985.
Slavic Review, spring, 1992.
Times Literary Supplement, October 7, 1983.

S

SAAL, Jocelyn
See SACHS, Judith

*   *   *

SACHS, Judith 1947-
(Petra Diamond, Rebecca Diamond, Jocelyn Saal, Jennifer Sarasin; Antonia Saxon, a joint pseudonym; Emily Chase, a house pseudonym)

PERSONAL: Born February 13, 1947, in New York, NY; daughter of E. Milton (a physician) and Naomi (a social worker) Sachs; married Anthony Bruno (a writer), February 6, 1982; children: Mia Miriam. *Education:* Brandeis University, B.A., 1968. *Religion:* Jewish. *Avocational interests:* Travel, music (formerly a choral singer), martial arts.

ADDRESSES: Home—404 Burd St., Pennington, NJ 08534. *Office*—Writers House, 21 West 26th St., New York, NY 10010.

CAREER: The Magazine, New York City, editorial assistant, 1969-70; *Saturday Review Press,* New York City, began as assistant, associate editor, 1970-73; Arbor House Publishing Co., New York City, managing editor, 1973; Delacorte Press, New York City, senior editor, 1973-77; Hawthorn Books, New York City, senior editor, 1977-79; writer, 1979—. Trenton State College, adjunct professor of health and physical education, 1994—.

MEMBER: American Society of Journalists and Authors, Author's Guild, North American Menopause Society.

WRITINGS:

(Under pseudonym Rebecca Diamond) *Summer Romance* (young adult), Silhouette, 1982.
(Under pseudonym Jocelyn Saal) *Dance of Love* (young adult), Bantam (New York City), 1982.

(Under Saal pseudonym) *Trusting Hearts* (young adult), Bantam, 1982.
(Under Saal pseudonym) *Running Mates* (young adult), Bantam, 1983.
(Under Saal pseudonym) *On Thin Ice* (young adult), Bantam, 1983.
(With husband, Anthony Bruno, under joint pseudonym Antonia Saxon) *Paradiso* (romance novel), Silhouette, 1983.
(Under pseudonym Jennifer Sarasin) *Spring Love* (young adult), Scholastic Inc. (New York City), 1983.
(With Bruno) *Smoky Joe's High Ride* (screenplay), HPS Productions, 1983.
(With Bruno, under Saxon pseudonym) *Above the Moon* (romance novel), Silhouette, 1984.
(Under Sarasin pseudonym) *The Hidden Room* (young adult), Scholastic Inc., 1984.
(Under house pseudonym Emily Chase) *The Big Crush* (young adult), Scholastic Inc., 1984.
(Under pseudonym Petra Diamond) *Confidentially Yours* (romance novel), Jove (New York City), 1984.
(With Bruno) *Just Another Friday Night* (screenplay), HPS Productions, 1984.
(Under pseudonym Petra Diamond) *Night of a Thousand Stars* (romance novel), Jove, 1985.
(Contributor) Peggy J. Schmidt and M. J. Territo, editors, *Career Choices for Studies of Art,* Walker & Co. (New York City), 1985.
(Under Chase pseudonym) *With Friends Like That,* (young adult), Scholastic Inc., 1985.
(Under Sarasin pseudonym) *Splitting* (young adult), Scholastic Inc., 1985.
(Under Sarasin pseudonym) *Cheating* (young adult), Scholastic Inc., 1985.
(Under Sarasin pseudonym) *Living It Up* (young adult), Scholastic Inc., 1986.

(Under pseudonym Petra Diamond) *Play It Again, Sam* (romance novel), Jove, 1986.

(Under Sarasin pseudonym) *Taking Over* (young adult), Scholastic Inc., 1987.

(Under Sarasin pseudonym) *Together Again* (young adult), Scholastic Inc., 1987.

Rites of Spring (novel), Pocket Books (New York City), 1988.

What Women Can Do about Chronic Endometriosis, Dell (New York City), 1991.

What Women Should Know about Menopause, Dell, 1991.

(With Art Mollen) *Dr. Mollen's Anti-Aging Diet: The Breakthrough Program for Easy Weight Loss and Longevity,* Dutton (New York City), 1992.

What You Can Do About Osteoporosis, Dell, 1993.

The Healing Power of Sex, Paramount/Prentice-Hall (Englewood Cliffs, NJ), 1994.

(Co-author with Phillip Sinaikin) *Fat Madness: How to Stop the Diet Cycle and Achieve Permanent Well-Being,* Berkley Publishing (New York City), 1994.

(Co-author with Leanne Domash) *Wanna Be My Friend?: How to Strengthen Your Child's Social Skills,* Hearst, 1994.

When Someone You Love Has AIDS: A Caregivers Guide, Dell Medical Library, 1995.

Healing the Female Heart, Pocket Books, 1995.

The Natural Health Guide to Pregnancy and Childbirth, Pocket Books, in press.

Also author of young adult novel *Burning Secrets* under Sarasin pseudonym; author of television screenplay "Aimee: The Sultan's Mistress". Co-author with Dr. Michael Schwartzman of *The Anxious Parent,* Simon & Schuster, in press; co-author with Dr. Philip Sinaikin, *After the Fast,* Doubleday, in press. Ghostwriter. Contributor to magazines and newspapers, including *On Film, Harper's, Backpaper,* and *New York Times.*

SIDELIGHTS: Judith Sachs told *CA:* "I grew up in Manhattan in the fifties and sixties. I was a real city child, the daughter of a physician. Achievement was praised highly, any interest was worthy of pursuit if it would 'get you somewhere in life.'

"Because of my parents' difficult marriage, I used my imaginative life as a substitute for real family life. My teenage years, I think, were the most formative. The adolescents I write about are often parts of me, struggling to find out how to become an adult. I became involved in theater when I was a teenager, because playing parts provided a way to explore myself. Later, I became a writer so that I could play all the parts and write the script as well.

"My interest in health and healing goes beyond the medical establishment. The authority of the physician in America—how he evolved to the godlike character everyone

trusted has been challenged in recent years—and so it should be. Doctors really don't know everything, which is what makes the vocation such an interesting double-edged one.

"As a writer, I try hard to communicate the intricate, varied states of the human condition. My personal view is that we all make our own misery in life, mostly by not trusting ourselves, and we can all make our own joy by recognizing that we are, in fact, a little bit like everyone else we know—even those we loathe and despise. If there is a theme common to most of my books, I suppose it's that we have to learn to laugh at ourselves and be flexible. The stronger and more resilient we get, the easier it is to grow up and grow old."

* * *

St. JOHN, Leonie
See BAYER, William

* * *

SARASIN, Jennifer
See SACHS, Judith

* * *

SARGENT, Alvin   1927-

PERSONAL: Born April 12, 1927, in Philadelphia, PA.

CAREER: Screenwriter and television writer.

AWARDS, HONORS: Academy Award nomination for best screenplay from Academy of Motion Picture Arts and Sciences, 1973, for *Paper Moon;* Academy Awards for best screenplay based on material from another medium, 1977, for *Julia,* and 1980, for *Ordinary People.*

WRITINGS:

SCREENPLAYS

(With Jack Davies) *Gambit* (adapted from the short story "Who Is Mr. Dean?" by Sidney Carroll), Universal, 1966.

(With Wendell Mayes) *The Stalking Moon* (adapted from the novel of the same title by Theodore V. Olsen), National General, 1968.

The Sterile Cuckoo (adapted from the novel of the same title by John Nichols), Paramount, 1969.

I Walk the Line (adapted from the novel *An Exile* by Madison Jones), Columbia, 1970.

The Impatient Heart (made-for-television movie), first broadcast by National Broadcasting Company (NBC-TV), October 8, 1971.

The Effect of Gamma Rays on Man-in-the-Moon Marigolds (adapted from the play of the same title by Paul Zindel), Twentieth Century-Fox, 1972.

Love and Pain and the Whole Damn Thing (original screenplay), Columbia, 1973.

Paper Moon (adapted from the novel *Addie Pray* by Joe David Brown), Paramount, 1973.

Bobby Deerfield (adapted from the novel *Heaven Has No Favorites* by Erich Maria Remarque), Columbia, 1977.

Julia (adapted from the story of the same title in *Pentimento: A Book of Portraits,* the memoirs of Lillian Hellman), Twentieth Century-Fox, 1977.

(With Edward Bunker and Jeffrey Boam) *Straight Time* (adapted from the novel *No Beast So Fierce* by Bunker), Warner Bros., 1978.

Ordinary People (adapted from the novel of the same title by Judith Guest), Paramount, 1980.

(With Tom Topor and Darryl Ponicsan) *Nuts* (adapted from the play of the same title by Topor), Warner Bros., 1987.

(With Corey Blechman) *Dominick and Eugene* (adapted from a story by Danny Porfirio), Orion, 1988.

(With Ted Tally) *White Palace* (adapted from a novel of the same title by Glenn Savan), Universal, 1990.

Other People's Money (adapted from the play of the same title by Jerry Sterner), Warner Bros., 1991.

(With Tom Schulman) *What about Bob?,* Touchstone, 1991.

Also author of television film *Footsteps.* Author of numerous scripts for television series including *The Naked City, Route 66, Ben Casey, Alfred Hitchcock Presents, The Nurses, Mr. Novak,* and *Empire.*

SIDELIGHTS: After writing for television until the mid-1960s, Alvin Sargent began a successful screenwriting career that has earned him two Academy Awards and one other Academy Award nomination. Sargent is considered particularly adept at creating memorable characters, ranging from the insecure and slightly manic college freshman in *The Sterile Cuckoo* to the guilt-ridden and anguished boy in *Ordinary People.* Additionally, he is often thought to depict situations in which characters are engaged in a struggle with themselves or their loved ones as they work through times of transition. "You just can't get through life happily without experiencing some degree of love and pain," Sargent was quoted in Donald Chase's book *Filmmaking: The Collaborative Art.* "That theme is something I could deal with forever."

Sargent shared screenwriting credits with Jack Davies for his first screenplay, *Gambit,* released in 1966. One of the many spy spoofs to emerge in the 1960s, *Gambit* is both farce and thriller. Based on a short story by Sidney Carroll, the film features Michael Caine as Harry Dean, an antithetical James Bond figure who bumbles his way through an art theft. Capitalizing on Caine's sophisticated screen presence to accentuate Harry's deficiencies, the film parodies the urbane manners and impossible resourcefulness of the stereotypical secret agent. Similarly, his accomplice, Nicole Chang, portrayed by Shirley MacLaine, serves as a sharp contrast to the sultry women in spy movies; she is a bright and boisterous nightclub dancer who proves more adept at spying than the spy does. Though Harry succeeds in his crime, he exhibits less skill and cunning than Nicole, who continually rescues the plan from failure.

Sargent told Chase that he was called in to work on *Gambit* ten days before shooting began. The plot was already written, but the characters needed work, related Sargent, who added that he "never saw another writer." He concentrated on the role of Nicole, which, according to Sargent, had previously been modified for MacLaine and "needed shaking up a little." He also worked briefly on Caine's character, though Sargent admitted to Chase that his rewrite for the character Harry Dean "wasn't what I would call good writing—all surface."

The Stalking Moon, for which Sargent wrote his next screenplay, is a Western, "classically pure and simple in outline," assessed Vincent Canby of the *New York Times.* Set in the late 1800s, the story depicts a retired army scout who helps a white woman and her half-Indian son escape from the Apache warrior who has held her captive for ten years. Writing for *Films in Review,* Page Cook praised Sargent's screenplay, noting that it allowed ample time for character development. Canby, however, asserted that the characters lacked depth and failed to hold his interest, while Joseph Morgenstern of *Newsweek* claimed that the "script has holes big enough to drive several stagecoaches through" and drew attention to the "thoroughly embarrassing pseudo-poetry" that comprises the female lead's lines. Countering these assessments and noting Sargent's "laconic" and "ever-taut script," Arthur Knight of the *Saturday Review* described the film as a "good, old-fashioned story excitingly told."

Sargent's talent for characterization is perhaps nowhere more apparent than in his screen adaptation for the 1969 film *The Sterile Cuckoo.* Pookie Adams, the central character, is a verbose, lonely, and insecure college freshman who encounters problems adjusting to campus life. She attaches herself to Jerry, a quiet entomology major who is initially overwhelmed by her madcap antics but eventually succumbs to her advances simply because he cannot avoid her. As their relationship develops, Pookie becomes increasingly possessive and fearful of losing Jerry, who cools toward her until they eventually break up.

Though *The Sterile Cuckoo* met with mixed reviews, most critics agreed that Pookie Adams, as played by actress Liza Minelli, was an absorbing character. Sargent, who told Chase that he generally does not fashion characters with a particular star in mind, admitted that he "couldn't help it" after being introduced to Minelli by the film's producer and director, Alan J. Pakula. Sargent claimed, "I could never get her out of my head. From then on, I could see her move, I could hear her voice, I could overhear that kind of manic thinking that goes on in her head, and applied all that to the character. I can't imagine anyone else playing that role." The result, reported Paul Warshow of *Film Quarterly,* is "a complicated and original character [that] makes this seriously flawed, sometimes cliched film into one of the most interesting and moving American films of the last couple years." Stephen Farber, also writing in *Film Quarterly,* assessed Pookie as a "potentially striking, complex character" who is treated too simplistically by Pakula and Sargent. But Morgenstern commented in *Newsweek* that the screenwriter avoids explaining Pookie's behavior with "standard-brand neuroses and convenient catch phrases. Instead of giving us a diagnosis of the girl, Sargent gives us the girl."

Sargent's next screenwriting effort, the 1970 film *I Walk the Line,* was adapted from the novel *An Exile* by Madison Jones. Set in the Cumberland Mountains of Tennessee, the story concerns a married sheriff's obsession with a moonshiner's young daughter. Reviewed by Howard Thompson in the *New York Times,* the film was judged to be a disappointment. After a promising start, wrote Thompson, the film "flattens into tedium and starts churning around in clanky melodrama." He added that Sargent's adaptation "sends the picture careening over a bumpy road."

Two years later Sargent wrote the filmscript version of the Pulitzer Prize-winning play *The Effect of Gamma Rays on Man-in-the-Moon Marigolds.* The film relates the story of Beatrice Hunsdorfer, who, after being abandoned by her husband, struggles to earn a living and constructs grandiose schemes in the hope of procuring enough money to start her own business. Her failed attempts at realizing her dreams cause her to vent her frustrations on her two daughters, Ruth and Matilda. Ruth is a bold and brassy teenager who shows signs of becoming just as obnoxious and abusive as her mother. Matilda, however, displays a sensitivity and intelligence that flourish despite the discord around her and lend the film its one hopeful note. The story is a "superior drama," judged Joseph Gelmis in *Newsday,* "because it's about basic human needs and thwarted desires and stunted emotional growth." Gelmis claimed that Beatrice "is so pathetic she makes you feel embarrassment and then anger and then pity." Gary Arnold of the *Washington Post* felt that Beatrice is a "stunted vision of a human being," a caricature incapable of arous-

ing anyone's sympathies. He faulted Paul Zindel, author of the original play, for creating "an essentially unsympathetic character" and asserted that Sargent did not add any insight into Beatrice's character with additions of new scenes that fail "in the same way Zindel's original scenes failed." Farber, however, held that the director and Sargent "intelligently refashioned the play," providing "insights into character" while eliminating "melodramatic excesses."

Sargent's first original screenplay, *Love and Pain and the Whole Damn Thing,* was written with the encouragement of Pakula, with whom Sargent had already worked on the films *The Stalking Moon* and *The Sterile Cuckoo.* Released in 1973, the film was described by Canby as a "funny and eccentric romantic comedy" that follows the developing and awkward love affair between a scatterbrained spinster and an insecure college student. "The movie is at its quiet best, funny and affectionate, as it chronicles their unlikely courtship," observed Jay Cocks of *Time.* Canby concurred, reporting that "the film is charming so long as it focuses on the details of their growing love and need for each other." Sargent credits Pakula for encouraging him to try "bold strokes" in the film. "There was a real collaboration there with Alan," Sargent told Chase, adding that he and Pakula understand each other very well in that they "have similar views on a lot of things—humor, pathos—and we really are kind of in sync."

Paper Moon, adapted from Joe David Brown's novel *Addie Pray,* was also released in 1973 and earned Sargent his first Academy Award nomination. The film recounts the adventures of small-time con artist Moses Pray and his accomplice, a nine-year-old orphaned girl, Addie Pray. Their collaboration in crime begins when Moses pays his respects at his former girlfriend's funeral, only to be burdened with transporting her daughter, Addie, to her aunt's house in distant Missouri. Moses soon discovers that in addition to the physical resemblance she bears to him, Addie displays an aptitude for swindling that neatly complements his own routines, and while traveling across the depressed Midwest, they become inseparable partners in numerous con games. Though they never openly express love for each other or acknowledge the probability that Addie is Moses's daughter, a bond grows out of their adventures, and when they reach Missouri Addie chooses to stay with Moses.

Sargent worked with director Peter Bogdanovich on *Paper Moon.* According to Chase, Bogdanovich claimed that the scenes which most interested him were the ones that Sargent had added to the original novel. Sargent, in turn, credited Bogdanovich with teaching him about "getting to the point" in his writing and explained to Chase, "I tend to overwrite." Sargent added that the director was largely responsible for keeping the relationship between Addie and Moses uncompromisingly tough and unsentimental throughout *Paper Moon.* "He saw where they were tough with one another, and he wanted to keep that conflict always going throughout the film," Sargent reflected. "I tended to be a bit more sentimental, more painful, in the sense that I wanted to show her looking for something a little more obviously, more openly, more needfully."

Sargent's screenplay for the 1977 film *Bobby Deerfield* was based on the novel *Heaven Has No Favorites* by Erich Maria Remarque. The film revolves around the relationship between Bobby, a self-engrossed racing car driver, and Lillian, a terminally ill woman who retains her zest for life. Writing in *Saturday Review,* Arthur Schlesinger, Jr., deemed the film an "old-fashioned tearjerker decked out in smart and stylish modernity," while observing that "some of the scenes have the ring of human truth nevertheless." Richard Schickel of *Time* called the film "adult entertainment in the best sense of the word." Commenting that the main theme in *Bobby Deerfield* operates neither as an "obsession nor nasty surprise" in the characters' lives, Schickel lauded the film's poignant and balanced view of the "chancy, mysterious, unfair workings of mortality."

Sargent won his first Academy Award in 1977 for *Julia,* a film adapted from sections of playwright Lillian Hellman's autobiographical *Pentimento.* Through a series of flashbacks woven into a central story line, the film recounts Hellman's recollections of her twenty-year friendship with a childhood friend, Julia. The main incident involves a smuggling operation in which Hellman, at Julia's request, transports money into Nazi Germany. At considerable risk to herself because of her Jewish heritage, Hellman successfully delivers the money to Julia, who, along with other members of an antifascist underground organization, intends to use it to secure the release of political prisoners in Germany. The intermittent flashbacks, beginning with scenes from Hellman's and Julia's childhoods, reveal the deep affection and intense loyalty that span both the distance and changes that separate the friends.

Julia contains "some shrewd, taut writing," wrote Pauline Kael in the *New Yorker,* though it ultimately "fails to draw you in." Noting that "Sargent has demonstrated his craftsmanship in the past," Kael suggested that the screenwriter was hampered by the autobiographical material that precluded his filling in gaps in the story. Yet Martin Knelman of the *Atlantic Monthly* praised Sargent for filling out the story by incorporating material from Hellman's other writings in *Pentimento,* and Vincent Canby of the *New York Times* concurred, saying Sargent and director Fred Zinneman "amplified the story with solemn care, in good taste."

Many critics hailed *Julia* for opening a new era for women in films. One of several films in the 1970s to feature strong female protagonists, *Julia,* according to *Newsweek* reviewer Jack Kroll, "heralds a swarm of films that purport to treat women as human beings with feelings, fantasies, and fates of their own." Susan Braudy and Harriet Lyons of *Ms.* judged that while *Julia* is "not the woman's film we were promised," it is "by far the most interesting film about women to come along in a while." Audiences and critics agreed, for the film was not only a box-office success, but it also garnered several Academy Awards, was named one of the ten best films of 1977 by the National Board of Review, and was voted best film of 1978 by the British Academy of Film and Television Arts.

Straight Time, a film released less than a year after Sargent's success with *Julia,* was adapted by Sargent, Jeffrey Boam, and Edward Bunker from Bunker's novel *None So Fierce.* The story centers around Max Dembo, a habitual criminal who gains his prison release only to break parole and return to crime. "A more polished, dynamic adaptation of Edward Bunker's feloniously wise novel . . . is hard to imagine," assessed Tom Allen of the *Village Voice,* adding that the film is a "revelation" in its approach to the popular genre of the crime drama. "The vision of crime" in *Straight Time,* concluded Allen, "consists of surprisingly hard labor as well as jagged nerves that become an addictive edge against the straight life."

Sargent earned his second Academy Award with the screenplay for *Ordinary People,* adapted from the novel by Judith Guest. The story centers around the Jarretts, a white, upper-middle-class family brought to a crisis by the elder son's death in a boating accident. As the film opens, the younger boy, Conrad, has just been released from a psychiatric hospital after attempting suicide in his guilt for surviving the accident in which his brother perished. The film's central conflict springs from the characters' inabilities to reach out to one another—emotionally and physically—for support. Beth, Conrad's mother, is devastated by the loss of her favorite son and is unable to show Conrad any tenderness, while Calvin, his father, struggles to come to terms with the changes within his family—particularly those concerning his relationship with Beth. Straining to feel comfortable in the increasingly tense atmosphere of his home, Conrad eventually sees a psychiatrist who helps him to deal with his feelings concerning his brother's death. Though Conrad gradually recovers, Calvin and Beth cannot salvage their relationship, and Beth leaves her family.

The power of *Ordinary People,* opined Schickel, "does not lie in originality but in the way it observes behavior, its novelistic buildup of subtly characterizing details." Writing in *New York* magazine, David Denby concurred, saying that the screenwriter's "somber, persistent probing of the characters' emotional lives holds our attention." Canby asserted that the film is "far more effective than the novel" in its expression of the characters' inability to communicate with one another, and he lauded the film's treatment of the Jarrett family, who "become important people without losing their ordinariness, without being patronized or satirized." The film was a critical and a popular success, and some critics pointed to its "ordinary" subject matter to explain its broad appeal to audiences. Lawrence O'Toole of *Maclean's* predicted that it would "probably move a lot of people . . . concerned as it is with people we all know, or might well be," and Schickel observed that *Ordinary People* is not "show-bizzy stuff " but "addresses itself quietly and intelligently to issues everyone who attempts to raise children must face."

Barbra Streisand produced and starred in *Nuts,* the 1987 film Sargent, Darryl Ponicsan, and Tom Topor adapted from the latter's 1980 Off-Broadway play. Dave Kehr, writing in the *Chicago Tribune,* called this movie "an amazingly accurate re-creation of the shape and spirit of the 1950s TV drama" for its structure as a series of dramatic revelations, its courtroom-drama format, and the "edgy, vocal" performances of its actors, many of whom were regulars in the live television series *Playhouse 90.* Claudia Draper, the Streisand character in *Nuts,* is a pricey prostitute who has been accused of killing a client and later committed to a state mental institution.

While the story of *Nuts* raises and should address questions such as the rights of the mentally ill and society's tendency to label people it finds otherwise difficult to assimilate, Kehr noted, these issues were treated too simply, and the supporting roles were undifferentiated in writing and acting, producing in sum a "lack of emotional dimension that finally limits [the movie] to the realm of TV: There's no world here, only a painted backdrop." Janet Maslin, in the *New York Times,* found the movie lacking in direction ("almost entirely adrift") and momentum, though she concluded that Streisand was "every inch the star."

Dominick and Eugene, which Sargent wrote with Corey Blechman, is a study of twin brothers whose mother died in childbirth: Gino, who is studying to be a brain surgeon and facing the question of going away to a prestigious university for his internship; and Nicky, handicapped by a childhood accident but nonetheless supporting himself and Gino by working as a garbage collector. Sheila Benson pointed out in the *Los Angeles Times* that the director, Robert M. Young, shaped this "potentially sticky material" into a "story of relationships that rings pure and fine as crystal" and praised the writers for a script that "shades Nicky and Gino's closely knit lives with interesting darknesses." Rita Kempley, writing for the *Washington Post,* felt the movie was weakened by its love story but said in

summary, "This thoughtful little piece is . . . sensitive without being sentimental."

White Palace, adapted by Sargent and Ted Tally from Glenn Savan's novel of the same title, fared less well with critics. Maslin deemed the story "no more convincing on screen than it was on the page" but found it "greatly helped" by the performances of James Spader and Susan Sarandon, who played the principals in the May-December romance. It was Hal Hinson's opinion in the *Washington Post* that Sarandon's "brilliantly vital" interpretation of her role fell far short of saving the film, which he perceived as a "rehashed '30s melodrama [that] is a study in Jewish self-hatred."

In their screenplay for the 1991 *What about Bob?,* Sargent and his collaborator Tom Schulman created an ideal medium for comedian Bill Murray. Murray plays the title role of a desperate multiphobic who follows his self-absorbed psychiatrist (Richard Dreyfuss) on his month-long vacation in New Hampshire and thoroughly ingratiates himself with the furious doctor's family, thus ensuring his stay. Kempley labeled the film more than just a movie, "a hilarious brain-teaser" that offers "sweet revenge" for patients of high-priced psychiatrists whose ongoing response to them is "What do *you* think it means?"

Other People's Money, Jerry Sterner's Off-Broadway play, was adapted for the screen by Sargent in 1991. Sargent's filmscript softened the leading character, corporate takeover artist Lawrence Garfield (played with "wicked clowning," in Maslin's view, by Danny DeVito), to a less abrasive, more charming version of Sterner's Larry Garfinkle and added characters to the play's five. In Kempley's opinion, this addition destroyed the original play's cohesiveness and, with other changes, caused *Other People's Money* to lose "its gist in translation." Peter Rainer for the *Los Angeles Times* disliked the "moist moralism that seeps into the film around its edges, most particularly in the Hallmark card manner in which the victims of Larry's machinations are portrayed." Maslin found the closing debate "about old-fashioned business versus the corporate takeover" to be "speechy but effective," though she thought it—"like the rest of the film—too genial to be hard-hitting."

BIOGRAPHICAL/CRITICAL SOURCES:

BOOKS

Chase, Donald, *Filmmaking: The Collaborative Art,* Little, Brown, 1975.
Kael, Pauline, *Deeper into the Movies,* Warner Books, 1973.

PERIODICALS

Atlantic Monthly, November, 1977.

Chicago Tribune, November 20, 1987.

Film Comment, January/February, 1981.

Film Quarterly, spring, 1970.

Films and Filming, February, 1967; July, 1971.

Films in Review, March, 1969; November, 1969.

Los Angeles Times, March 17, 1988; June 5, 1990; October 18, 1991.

Maclean's, October 6, 1980.

Ms., October, 1977.

New Leader, November 24, 1969.

New Republic, January 20, 1973; June 9, 1973; October 15, 1977; April 29, 1978; September 27, 1980.

Newsweek, January 2, 1967; February 3, 1969; November 3, 1969; January 1, 1973; May 28, 1973; October 3, 1977; October 10, 1977; April 3, 1978; September 22, 1980.

New York, May 21, 1973; September 29, 1980.

New Yorker, January 7, 1967; December 5, 1970; December 23, 1972; May 26, 1973; October 3, 1977; October 10, 1977; October 13, 1980.

New York Times, December 22, 1966; January 23, 1969; November 20, 1970; December 20, 1972; January 28, 1973; April 20, 1973; May 17, 1973; September 30, 1977; October 3, 1977; March 17, 1978; September 19, 1980; January 18, 1981; November 20, 1987; October 9, 1990.

Saturday Review, January 7, 1967; February 1, 1969; December 9, 1972; September 29, 1977; November 26, 1977.

Sight and Sound, spring, 1969; winter, 1969/70; summer, 1971; spring, 1981.

Time, January 6, 1967; February 14, 1969; October 31, 1969; January 1, 1973; May 14, 1973; May 28, 1973; October 10, 1977; April 3, 1978; September 22, 1980.

Village Voice, April 3, 1978.

Washington Post, March 18, 1988; October 19, 1990; May 17, 1991; October 18, 1991.

*   *   *

SASSER, Charles W(ayne) 1942-

PERSONAL: Born January 3, 1942, in Sallisaw, OK; son of Ben G. (a laborer) and Mary (a homemaker; maiden name, Cantrell) Sasser; married Dianne Carol Riley, October 8, 1965 (divorced June 22, 1978); married Kathy Renee Pitts (a photographer), February 2, 1979 (divorced December 10, 1986); married Juanita Marie Jackson (a nurse), May 20, 1991 (divorced December 21, 1992); children: (first marriage) David Charles, Michael Wayne; (second marriage) Joshua Dale. *Education:* Attended Miami-Dade Community College, 1966-67; Florida State University, B.A., 1969. *Politics:* Republican. *Religion:* Protestant.

ADDRESSES: Home and office—14406-D East 23rd Pl., Tulsa, OK 74134. *Agent*—Ethan Ellenberg, 548 Broadway, 5-C, New York, NY 10012.

CAREER: Writer. Miami Police Department, Miami, FL, officer, 1965-68; Tulsa Police Department, Tulsa, OK, homicide detective, 1969-79; instructor in sociology at Tulsa Junior College and director of criminal justice department at American Christian College, Tulsa, 1975-78; president of Cedar Press Publishing Co., 1981—. *Military service:* U.S. Navy, 1960-64; became journalist second class. U.S. Army, 1965-83, medic with U.S. Army Special Forces (Green Berets) in Southeast Asia and Central and South America; became sergeant first class. U.S. Army Reserve, 1983—, combat tactics instructor. Military Police Company, first sergeant, 1991.

MEMBER: Oklahoma Sociological Association, Oklahoma Criminal Justice Educators Association (founding member), Oklahoma Writers Federation, Tulsa Night Writers, Fraternal Order of Police, Special Forces Association, National Association for Crime Victims Rights (member of board of directors, 1978); Keystone Crossroad Historical Society (president, 1975).

WRITINGS:

NOVELS

No Gentle Streets, Ashley Books (Port Washington, NY), 1984.

The 100th Kill, Pocket Books (New York City), 1992.

The War Chaser, Northwest Publishing, in press.

NONFICTION

I Have Come to Step Over Your Soul, Stein & Day (New York City), 1987.

The Girl Scout Murders, Pocket Books, 1989.

The Walking Dead, Pocket Books, 1989.

One Shot—One Kill, Pocket Books, 1990.

Homicide!, Pocket Books, 1990.

The New Face of War, Time-Life (New York City), 1991.

Always a Warrior, Pocket Books, 1994.

Shoot to Kill, Pocket Books, 1994.

(With son Michael Sasser) *Last American Heroes,* Pocket Books, 1994.

In Cold Blood: Oklahoma's Most Notorious Murders, Consolidated Press, 1994.

Contributor of articles to Pinnacle Books' anthology series on true crime, 1990-94. Also author of police training film *Stopping Felony Suspects.* Contributor of more than 2,500 articles and short stories to periodicals, including *Parents, Writer's Digest, Guideposts, Official Detective, Survive, Soldier of Fortune, Family Life, Eagle, New Breed, Vietnam Combat, Old West, Rider, Florida Keys, Law and Order, Ozark Mountaineer, Gent, Teacher,* and *Miami Herald.*

Feature editor, *Prop Wash* (U.S. Navy newspaper), 1962-64; editor, *Whidbey Approach* (aviation safety bulletin), 1962-64; associate editor, *Law Enforcement News,* 1969-82; managing editor, *Keystone Sportsman* (regional monthly), 1975-76; associate editor, *Police Journal,* 1975-80. Author of column for *Oklahoma Police Journal,* 1980-85.

WORK IN PROGRESS: Smokejumpers, a nonfiction book on parachutists who fight fires, for Simon & Schuster; *Caribbean Snow,* a nonfiction work on the U.S. Coast Guard; *Cherry Street,* a mystery novel.

SIDELIGHTS: For his first novel, *No Gentle Streets,* Charles W. Sasser calls upon his past experiences as a homicide investigator. Weaving a suspense tale about a tough homicide detective bent on finding a mutilating murderer of young girls, the author also looks at the price such an occupation—dealing daily with the worst in humanity—exacts from its practitioner. Reflecting on the craft of writing in a *Library Journal* interview, Sasser related: "Craft for a writer is nuance and sound and feel and rhythm of works brought together so that they breathe and live for others."

Sasser told *CA:* "As a poor Okie kid picking cotton in the Arkansas River 'bottoms,' I vowed not to live just one life, but many lives. The wide span of my writings indicates this desire. I have pursued a number of careers and interests simultaneously—policeman, educator, airplane pilot, Golden Gloves boxer, paratrooper, sailor, rodeo bronco rider, rancher, fur trapper, newspaperman. I once spent a year traveling on an 80cc Yamaha motorbike—living in a tent—and have just returned from a free-lance job as a war correspondent in El Salvador.

"For stories I have parachuted into Korea's demilitarized zone, rode buses from the United States through Central America, chased after pirate treasure in the Caribbean, canoed 700 miles solo across the Yukon territory, chased wild mustangs, raft-floated the Mississippi River, solo-sailed the Caribbean in a 17-foot sailboat, searched for 'lost cities' in Central American jungles, hunted bear, caribou, and other big game.

"The first books I ever owned—when I was six years old—were Ernest Hemingway's *For Whom the Bell Tolls,* Steinbeck's *Grape of Wrath,* and *Robinson Crusoe,* gifts from an eccentric aunt who believed poor hill kids who lived in tin-roofed barns should read in order to open doors for themselves to the world. The books opened doors to my becoming a writer. I sold my first piece at age 15 and have been writing since. Ernest Hemingway remains my favorite author, closely followed now by Pat Conroy and John Irving.

"Motivation? I want to live, live truly, as Hemingway would have put it, and to experience literally *everything* in life, and then to share my experiences with others through my writings."

BIOGRAPHICAL/CRITICAL SOURCES:

PERIODICALS

Army Reserve Magazine, November 3, 1987.
Farmstead Magazine, summer, 1981.
Guideposts, June, 1982; June, 1983.
Library Journal, October 1, 1984.
Miami Herald, August 9, 1968; August 10, 1968.
Mostly Murder, July-September, 1990.
Muskogee Phoenix, September 8, 1983; August 26, 1984; April 17, 1986.
Oklahoma Publisher, May, 1986.
Publishers Weekly, March 20, 1987; May 5, 1989; August 3, 1990.
Rider, February, 1984.
Sequoyah County Times, July 17, 1984; April 20, 1986.
Soldier of Fortune, March, 1992.
Stars & Stripes, June 18, 1994.
Sunday Oklahoman, May 4, 1986.
True Detective, February, 1980; September, 1980.
Tulsa Tribune, April 1, 1976; September 20, 1978.
Tulsa World, January 17, 1971; September 24, 1984; May 14, 1986; May 6, 1992; May 4, 1994.
Wall Street Journal, January 14, 1994.
Yukon Reader, October, 1991.

*   *   *

SASSOON, Rosemary   1931-

PERSONAL: Born February 19, 1931, in London, England; daughter of Frank Raphael and Olga (Wilenkin) Waley; married John Philip Sassoon (an educationist and writer), March 31, 1958; children: Caroline, Joanna Sassoon Whitten, Kathryn Sassoon Cameron. *Education:* Attended Tunbridge Wells Art School, 1946-48; studied under textile master scribe M. C. Oliver. *Religion:* Jewish.

ADDRESSES: Home—Sevenoaks, Kent, England. *Office*—c/o Thames & Hudson, 30 Bloomsbury St., London WC1B 3QP, England.

CAREER: Lettering, packaging, and textile designer, 1948—; teacher of calligraphy, 1975—; researcher, lecturer, and consultant in handwriting problems, 1980—; type designer, 1985—.

MEMBER: Internationale, Graphonomics Association, Association Typographique Internationale, The Letter Exchange.

AWARDS, HONORS: University of Reading, honorary doctorate in philosophy, 1988.

WRITINGS:

The Practical Guide to Calligraphy, Thames & Hudson (London, England), 1982.

The Practical Guide to Children's Handwriting, Thames & Hudson, 1983.

(With G. S. E. Briem) *Teach Yourself Handwriting,* Hodder & Stoughton, 1984.

The Practical Guide to Lettering, Thames & Hudson, 1985.

Helping Your Handwriting, Arnold-Wheaton/Nelson, 1986.

Handwriting: The Way to Teach It, Stanley Thornes (Cheltenham, England), 1990.

Handwriting: A New Perspective, Stanley Thornes, 1990.

Creating Letterforms: Calligraphy and Lettering for Beginners, Thames & Hudson (New York City), 1992.

Computers and Typography, Intellect, 1993.

The Art and Science of Handwriting, Intellect, 1993.

Writing Systems, Intellect, in press.

Contributor to periodicals, including *Times Educational Supplement.*

WORK IN PROGRESS: Developing typefaces for computer screens, newspapers and books to improve legibility for young children and older readers. Researching writing systems from the Pacific Basin and Latin America.

SIDELIGHTS: A lettering designer turned educator and author, Rosemary Sassoon told Helen Mason in a London *Times* interview that at one time she believed that "beautiful lettering was the most important thing." Yet when asked by an education official to create a remedial handwriting course she changed that emphasis; Sassoon was stunned by the extent of the difficulties experienced by children who lacked proper handwriting instruction. "Beauty in writing will emerge as a result of doing things properly," Sassoon amended.

Sassoon's *Practical Guide to Children's Handwriting* is a manual for teachers and parents on how to teach handwriting. Concentrating on a relaxed grip, flowing movement, correctly-formed letters, and repetitive patterns that program the mind and hand, the Sassoon method also encourages a personal, creative hand once legibility and speed have been attained. "I don't expect everyone to agree with the book, but I hope it will make people think," Sassoon stated. Mason remarked, "It is difficult to imagine any teacher resisting the lucidity and joy of writing, the logic and flexibility of the manual she has produced."

Sassoon told *CA:* "Being one of the last to enjoy a traditional training in lettering, I felt that there was an obligation to pass this on. A request to run remedial handwriting

courses showed the need in this area and led to a shift in career emphasis—finally pointing to a research degree and a more scientific approach to this neglected subject."

BIOGRAPHICAL/CRITICAL SOURCES:

PERIODICALS

Times (London), September 30, 1983.

*   *   *

**SAXON, Antonia
   See SACHS, Judith**

*   *   *

SCHISGAL, Murray (Joseph) 1926-

PERSONAL: Born November 25, 1926, in Brooklyn, NY; son of Abraham (a tailor) and Irene (Sperling) Schisgal; married Reene Schapiro, June 29, 1958; children: Jane, Zachary. *Education:* Quit high school in 1943 to join the Navy but earned diploma later in night school; attended Brooklyn Conservatory of Music and Long Island University; Brooklyn Law School, LL.B., 1953, New School for Social Research, B.A., 1959.

ADDRESSES: Home—275 Central Park West, New York, NY 10024. *Agent*—Arthur B. Greene, 101 Park Ave., New York, NY 10178.

CAREER: Worked at odd jobs to support his studies and writing, including pin-setter in a bowling alley, hand trucker in the garment district, dress racker at Klein's Department Store, saxophone and clarinet player in a small band, all in New York City, 1947-50; practiced law in New York City, 1953-55; James Fenimore Cooper Junior High School, East Harlem, NY, English teacher, 1955-60; writer, 1960—. Lecturer and instructor in playwriting at colleges and universities. *Military service:* U.S. Navy, 1944-46; became radio operator, third class.

AWARDS, HONORS: Vernon Rice Award, Outer Circle Award, and Saturday Review Critics Poll Award, 1963, all for *The Typists* [and] *The Tiger;* Los Angeles Film Critics, New York Film Critics, National Society of Film Critics, and Writers Guild of America Awards for screenwriting, with Larry Gelbart, 1982, all for *Tootsie;* Academy Award nomination for Best Original Screenplay, with Gelbart, 1982, for *Tootsie.*

WRITINGS:

PLAYS

The Typists [and] *The Tiger* (one-acts; *The Tiger* first produced under the title *The Postman* with *The Typists* and *A Simple Kind of Love Story* in London, December 11, 1960; both produced Off-Broadway, February, 1963), Coward, 1963.

Luv (first produced in London, April 18, 1963, produced on Broadway, November 11, 1964; also see below), Coward, 1963; reprinted in *Luv and Other Plays,* Dodd, Mead, 1983.

Fragments, Windows and Other Plays (contains *Windows,* produced in Los Angeles, 1965; *Reverberations, The Old Jew,* and *Fragments,* produced in Stockbridge, MA, August, 1967; *Reverberations* produced as *The Basement,* with *Fragments,* under program title *Fragments,* Off-Broadway, October, 1967; *Memorial Day,* first produced in Baltimore, 1968), Coward, 1965.

Jimmy Shine (two-act; produced on Broadway, December 5, 1968; also see below), Atheneum, 1969.

Ducks and Lovers (first produced in London, October 19, 1961; also see below), Dramatists Play Service, 1972.

The Chinese and Doctor Fish (*The Chinese* first produced in Paris, 1968; produced with *Doctor Fish* on Broadway, March 10, 1970), published in *Best Short Plays of the World Theatre, 1968-1973,* Crown, 1973.

An American Millionaire (produced on Broadway, 1974), Dramatists Play Service, 1974.

All over Town (produced on Broadway, 1974), Dramatists Play Service, 1975.

A Simple Kind of Love Story (produced in London, with *The Postman* and *The Typists,* December 11, 1970), published in *The Pushcart Peddlers, The Flatulist and Other Plays,* Dramatists Play Service, 1980.

The Pushcart Peddlers, The Flatulist, and Other Plays (*The Pushcart Peddlers* produced Off-Broadway, 1979; *Walter and the Flatulist* produced Off-Off-Broadway, 1980), Dramatists Play Service, 1980.

Twice around the Park (two one-act plays, *A Need for Brussels Sprouts* and *A Need for Less Expertise* produced on Broadway, 1982), Samuel French, 1983.

Popkins (produced in Dallas, TX, 1978), Dramatists Play Service, 1984, reprinted 1990.

Closet Madness and Other Plays (includes *The Rabbi and the Toyota Dealer,* produced at the New Mayfair Theatre, 1985; and *Summer Romance*), Samuel French, 1984.

Jealousy, and There Are No Sacher Tortes in Our Society!, Dramatists Play Service, 1985.

Old Wine in a New Bottle, Dramatists Play Service, 1987.

Road Show (produced Off-Broadway, 1987), Dramatists Play Service, 1987.

Man Dangling: Three Short Plays, Dramatists Play Service, 1988.

74 Georgia Avenue, (produced in West Bloomfield, MI, 1992), Dramatists Play Service, 1988.

Oatmeal and Kisses, Dramatists Play Service, 1990.

Extensions, published in *The Best American Short Plays, 1991-1992,* Applause Theatre & Cinema, 1992.

The Cowboy, the Indian and the Fervent Feminist, (produced in Westbeth, New York, 1993), Applause Theatre & Cinema, 1993.

Sexaholics and Other Plays, Dramatists Play Service, 1994.

UNPUBLISHED PLAYS

Knit One Purl Two, produced in Boston, March 27, 1963.

The Downstairs Boys, produced in East Hampton, NY, 1980.

An Original Jimmy Shine (musical version of *Jimmy Shine*), produced in Los Angeles, 1981.

Harry, Ellen and Milt (musical of *Luv*), produced in New Haven, CT, 1982.

The New Yorkers, produced Off-Broadway, 1984.

The Songs of War, produced in Garden Grove, CA, 1989.

Play Time, produced by the Denver Center Theatre Company, 1991.

The Japanese Foreign Trade Minister, produced at the Cleveland Playhouse, 1992.

Circus Life, produced in Sag Harbor, Long Island, 1992.

Angel Wings, produced at the Circle in the Square, 1994.

SCREENPLAYS

(Coadaptor) *Ducks and Lovers* (based on play of the same title), Association of British Pictures, 1962.

The Love Song of Barney Kempenski, produced by American Broadcasting Companies (ABC-TV), 1966.

The Tiger Makes Out (based on the play *The Tiger*), Columbia Pictures, 1967.

Natasha Kovolina Pipishinsky, ABC-TV, 1976.

(With Larry Gelbart) *Tootsie,* Columbia Pictures, 1982.

OTHER

Days and Nights of a French Horn Player (novel), Little, Brown, 1980.

ADAPTATIONS: Luv was filmed by Columbia Pictures, 1967; *Love,* musical based on *Luv,* produced Off-Broadway, 1984, (produced as *What about Luv* in London, 1986), Music Theatre International, 1984.

SIDELIGHTS: "I like Murray Schisgal because he is one step ahead of the avant-garde," wrote Walter Kerr. "If the avant-garde, up to now, has successfully exploded the bright balloons of cheap optimism, Mr. Schisgal is ready to put a pin to the soapy bubbles of cheap pessimism. . . . Mr. Schisgal's knife—a very funny one, glinting brightly as it digs—is out for people who wear black on black while lovingly congratulating themselves upon the profundity of their losses."

Despite frequent praise for his "funny concepts" and ability to create "comic situations and offbeat characters,"

Schisgal has received mixed criticism of his many plays and other works for over thirty-five years. Commenting on *Fragments,* Robert Graham Kemper contended: "It is a funny concept and one that is theatrically inventive and psychologically sound. But cash-paying customers expect more for their money than a concept. They want characters, plot and dialogue." However, Edith Oliver wrote that *Fragments* appears to be more than simply a "funny concept": "There are a number of hints here and there, that this play is an early effort of Mr. Schisgal's, too many lines are high-flown or obvious, and too many attempts at humor misfire. Nevertheless, I'm for any author who tries to use comedy as a means of getting at something serious, so I'm for Mr. Schisgal, win or lose."

Differences in critical opinion are present in many other reviews of Schisgal's plays. Commenting on *The Chinese* and *Dr. Fish,* Alan Bruce noted that "behind the laughs that undeniably fill Murray Schisgal's latest comedies a nagging disappointment persists. The material is still unsatisfactorily skimpy and appears to be put together with a dangerous disregard for its relationship to human truths." A *National Observer* reviewer wrote, however, that "for that matter, you wouldn't swear that Mr. Schisgal's [*The Chinese*] isn't saying something profound about brotherhood." Discussing specific elements of Schisgal's work, Frederick Lumley wrote that Schisgal's theatre "is like a puppet one where the characters act out different changes of fortune, exchange roles and become the mouthpiece of their author's type of ventriloquistic wit." But Haskel Frankel, who has experienced the "laughter that leaves a bitter aftertaste," cited with admiration "that special half-cracked dialog that is a Schisgal specialty. The talk is interesting, often funny and always revealing."

Several critics caustically attributed the impressive success of Schisgal's *Luv* to Mike Nichols' direction of the play. Specifically, many critics argued that Schisgal's script by itself was sketchy and inadequate. John Simon wrote: "What this is, of course, is not devastating social satire, still less avant-garde theatre; it is plain and simple burlesque or vaudeville. . . . One of the troubles is that Schisgal is not quite up to what he is trying to poke fun at." Simon continued: "The playwright scatters his shots in all directions, in an attempt to puncture whatever he can hit, without committing himself to any point of view. And that, in anything but a piece of unpretentious zaniness, is simply immoral." Schisgal answered such criticism in an interview with Ira Peck, indicating that his "sketchy" theme had, in fact, been carefully developed from a well-defined notion. "The emotion of love," he told Peck, "has been perverted and misused to such an extent that it can only be defined by using another word which comes closer to what we experience, to what we think, and how we behave. It can be l-u-v, l-o-v, or x-y-z, but it cer-

tainly can't be a word that has been abused as much as l-o-v-e. L-u-v is the perversion of l-o-v-e. . . . Love has become a commodity rather than an emotion."

Schisgal's *The Pushcart Peddlers* is "a short vignette about an old immigrant and a new immigrant, a graybeard and a greenhorn, who compete for the best banana concession and the admiration of a flower girl on the Lower East Side of Manhattan," wrote Mel Gussow in a *New York Times* review. When the supposedly blind flower girl suddenly reveals her dream to be a leading lady on the musical stage, the three characters indulge in a fairy-tale fantasy life of show business producers. While Gussow complained about the play's predictability, he did compliment the author on managing "a few variations on the old tune."

Schisgal's *The Downstairs Boys,* first produced in 1980, prompted critic Jay Carr to complain in the *Detroit News* about the play's "dated point of view," notably that a highly educated woman should complain about a need to marry. "These days, a talented woman executive doesn't have to stop working in order to marry," wrote Carr. The reviewer found that the idea of three men, joined by working downstairs at a department store, "coming to grief by pursuing their dreams, and this woman who is miserable because she doesn't pursue hers, is sound enough." But he faulted the play's driving crisis as "implausible." Still, wrote Carr, "the viewpoint spawns some nice conceits," and he credits the playwright's insight: "Schisgal knows that people not only don't listen to one another but never even listen to themselves."

In a switch from writing for the stage, Schisgal published a novel entitled *Days and Nights of a French Horn Player.* He told *Library Journal:* "After working in the theater for over 20 years, I was suddenly driven by a need . . . to speak directly to an audience. . . . To speak without requiring the craft and loquaciousness of another's tongue." The book's main character, Eddie Davis, is taught French horn at age twelve by a schoolmate with a hunchback. Eventually giving up his musical studies, Eddie strikes it rich producing television game shows. However, by age forty-five Eddie's marriage and career are shot and, in a ritzy hotel room, he renews his love affair with the horn. For the *New York Times Book Review*'s Martin Levin, the book is enlivened by the author's "lust for the offbeat," such as the hunchback character and Eddie's father, who wants to become a transsexual. Levin continued: "Mr. Schisgal's characters may be grotesque, but they aren't sick. They affirm life; even those who have been maimed by it. . . . The author may be fond of cheap jokes . . . but he is definitely on the side of truth and beauty." Reviewer Barbara A. Bannon, writing in *Publishers Weekly,* was less impressed, saying Shisgal writes "a brand of black humor that has worked well on the stage but comes across as less than sparkling on the printed page and not particularly moving."

Two more of Schisgal's one-act plays opened to mixed reviews. Actors Eli Wallach and Anne Jackson, who starred in his 1964 Broadway hit *Luv,* rejoined Schisgal to play a pair of warring neighbors in *A Need for Brussels Sprouts* and a couple trying to rescue their long marriage in the companion piece *A Need for Less Expertise.* Reviewer David Richards, writing in the *Washington Post,* said Schisgal "knows what is ludicrous about his characters. Logical argument is not their strong suit. Their emotions are in a perpetual flip-flop." But, complained Richards, "I'm not sure he knows—or even cares—what might make these creatures endearing."

For Frank Rich, writing in the *New York Times,* Schisgal "has always been an exasperatingly uneven writer, so it's no surprise that . . . his pair of one-act comedies . . . splits directly down the middle." Rich described *A Need for Brussels Sprouts,* which features an out-of-work actor who rehearses too loudly for his cat food commercials and his policewoman neighbor who cites him for disturbing the peace, as "strained." But Rich also believed that Schisgal "gets us laughing, freely and almost continuously, with his loony and shrewdly crafted second sketch, *A Need for Less Expertise.*"

Widespread success arrived for Schisgal in 1982 in the form of several awards, including a Writers Guild screenwriting award and an Oscar nomination for Best Original Screenplay with cowriter Larry Gelbart, for the movie script *Tootsie.* The hit movie packed houses coast-to-coast with its situation based on a frustrated actor, Michael Dorsey (played by Dustin Hoffman), who decides he is such a talented actor he can audition and win a role on a television soap opera made up as a woman. Critic Vincent Canby, writing in the *New York Times,* noted that "*Tootsie* has a lot more going for it than its gimmick." He goes on to praise the writers of the screenplay as having "taken a wildly improbable situation and found just about all of its comic possibilities, not by exaggerating the obvious, but by treating it with inspired common sense."

Returning to Off-Broadway in 1987 with the full-length play *Road Show,* Schisgal granted an interview to writer David Kaufman in the *New York Times.* Kaufman noted: "In person Mr. Schisgal looks and behaves like a vaudeville rabbi. He combines comic comebacks with earnest delivery; at times he seems like a belligerent neighbor, at others a concerned, benevolent uncle." Confessing his "addiction" to writing plays, Schisgal, despite the frustrations, concluded, "Don't for a minute think it is not terrifically gratifying to see something written done well onstage."

Describing *Road Show* as "a four-character theatrical collage that tells of an unusual meeting between two high school lovers 20 years later," Schisgal went on to describe his sentiments as the show was about to open: "Here I am Off Broadway where I started 30 years ago and I feel very good about it . . . I'm still in the ring, man. And in the ring, in the theater, you get no points for experience, you get no points for anything beyond what you're putting on the line today." In the play, an essayist, Andy Broude, who has decided to move to Hollywood for a high-paying movie executive job, is driving across country with his ambitious wife. Stopping in a small Indiana town, Andy encounters his long-lost college sweetheart, Evelyn, and her druggist husband. The four embark on a soul-searching coming of age complete with dance, music and vaudeville. Reviewer Mel Gussow noted in the *New York Times* that "with its brief, episodic scenes, the play itself has the watermark of a wayward screenplay. . . . Two scenes that are sustained—a comic one between the two husbands, a wistful one between the two lovers—are easily the most involving aspects of the evening. But the play itself is fragmentary." Disappointed in the work, Gussow summarized: " 'Life is treacherous' says the hero towards the end of the ramshackle *Road Show*—and, as Mr. Schisgal knows, so is the theater."

BIOGRAPHICAL/CRITICAL SOURCES:

BOOKS

Contemporary Literary Criticism, Volume 6, Gale, 1976.
Lumpley, Frederick, *New Trends in Twentieth Century Drama,* Oxford University Press, 1967.

PERIODICALS

Christian Century, January 3, 1968.
Christian Science Monitor, March 16, 1970.
Detroit News, April 27, 1980, p. 6F.
Hudson Review, spring, 1965.
Library Journal, June 15, 1980.
Los Angeles Times, April 8, 1983; October 3, 1985.
Nation, October 23, 1967.
National Observer, October 9, 1967; March 16, 1970.
New Yorker, October 14, 1967.
New York Herald Tribune Magazine, November 8, 1964.
New York Times, November 22, 1964; November 22, 1979, p. 22.; October 31, 1982, p. 1; November 5, 1982; November 14, 1982, p. 5; December 17, 1982; April 16, 1984; May 17, 1987, p. 5; May 22, 1987.
New York Times Book Review, June 8, 1980, p. 14.
Newsweek, October 16, 1967.
Publishers Weekly, April 4, 1980, p. 62.
Time, October 6, 1967.

Times (London), December, 15, 1986.
Village Voice, September 7, 1967; October 12, 1967.
Washington Post, December 27, 1967; August 8, 1982; August 28, 1982, p. C1; August 30, 1982.

*   *   *

SCOTT, Jack Denton   1915-1995

PERSONAL: Born in 1915, in Elkins, WV; died January 3, 1995 in Corning, NY; married Maria Luisa Limoncelli (a photographer), June 22, 1942. *Education:* Attended night classes at Columbia University; attended Oxford University.

ADDRESSES: Home—11 Skyline Dr., Corning, NY 14830.

CAREER: Writer for *Fort Bragg News;* reporter for American and European editions and editor of Middle East edition, *Yank* army weekly, 1942-45; syndicated newspaper columnist of "Adventure Unlimited," *New York Herald-Tribune,* 1957-59; monthly columnist of "World's Largest Outdoor Column," *American Legion Magazine;* restaurant columnist, *Connecticut.* Editor, *Field and Stream;* outdoor editor, *Esquire* and *Sport;* roving editor, *Sports Afield, National Wildlife,* and *International Wildlife.* Writer of children's nonfiction, travel biographies, natural history, cookbooks, and contributor to magazines and anthologies.

MEMBER: Cordon Bleu de France.

AWARDS, HONORS: Loggerhead Turtle; Survivor from the Sea named a *Kirkus* Choice Book, a *School Library Journal* Best Book of the Year and Best of the Best Book, and Outstanding Science Trade Book for Children, all 1974; *That Wonderful Pelican* named a *Kirkus* Choice Book, a *School Library Journal* Best Book of the Year and Best of the Best Book, and Outstanding Science Trade Book for Children, all 1975; *Canada Geese* named a Junior Literary Guild Selection, Library of Congress Children's Book of the Year, *School Library Journal* Best Book of the Year, all 1976; American Institute of Graphics Arts Book Show Award, 1976, for *Discovering the American Stork; Return of the Buffalo* named a *Kirkus* Choice Book and Outstanding Science Trade Book for Children, both 1976; *The Gulls of Smuttynose Island* named a Junior Literary Guild Selection, Library of Congress Children's Book of the Year, *School Library Journal* Best Book of the Year, and Child Study Children's Book Committee Book of the Year, all 1977; *Little Dogs of the Prairie* named American Library Association Notable Children's Book, Outstanding Science Trade Book for Children, 1977; *Island of Wild Horses* named a Junior Literary Guild election and Outstanding Science Trade Book for Children, 1978; *City of*

Birds and Beasts named a *School Library Journal* Best Book of the Year, 1978; *The Book of the Goat* named a Junior Literary Guild Selection and Child Study Children's Book Committee Book of the Year, both 1979; *The Submarine Bird* named a Junior Literary Guild Selection, 1979; *The Book of the Pig* named Outstanding Science Trade Book for Children and American Library Association Children's Book, both 1981; *Moose* named American Library Association Notable Children's Book and Outstanding Science Trade Book for Children, both 1981; *Orphans from the Sea* named Outstanding Science Trade Book for Children, 1982; *The Fur Seals of Pribilof* named Outstanding Science Trade Book for Children, 1982; *Alligator* named Outstanding Science Trade Book for Children, 1984; *Swans* named a Junior Literary Guild Selection, 1987.

WRITINGS:

(With Donald Ewin Cooke) *Pug Invades the Fifth Column,* D. McKay Co., 1943.
(With Anne Damer) *Too Lively to Live* (detective novel), Doubleday, 1943.
The Weimaraner, Fawcett-Dearing Printing, 1953.
All Outdoors: Hunting and Fishing with the Author of America's Largest Outdoor Column (essays), Stackpole, 1956.
(Editor) *Your Dog's Health Book,* Macmillan, 1956.
Forests of the Night, photographs of India's jungles by wife, Maria Luisa Scott, Rinehart, 1959.
How to Write and Sell for the Out-of-Doors, Macmillan, 1962.
Marvels and Mysteries of Our Animal World, Reader's Digest Association, 1964.
The Duluth Mongoose, illustrated by Lydia Fruhauf, Morrow, 1965.
Passport to Adventure, photographs by M. L. Scott, Random House, 1966.
Speaking Wildly (essays), illustrated by Lydia Rosier, Morrow, 1966.
Elephant Grass (novel), Harcourt, 1969.
Spargo: A Novel of Espionage, World Publishing, 1971.
The Survivors: Enduring Animals of North America (essays), illustrated by Daphne Gillen, Harcourt, 1975.
Journey into Silence, Reader's Digest Press, 1976.
Discovering the Mysterious Egret, illustrated by Pamela S. Distler, Harcourt, 1978.
Window on the Wild (essays), illustrated by Geri Greinke, Putnam, 1980.
Curious Creatures, Reader's Digest Books, 1981.
The Sea File (novel), McGraw, 1981.

JUVENILE NONFICTION; PHOTOGRAPHS BY OZZIE SWEET

Loggerhead Turtle; Survivor from the Sea, Putnam, 1974.
That Wonderful Pelican, Putnam, 1975.

Canada Geese, Putnam, 1976.

Discovering the American Stork, Harcourt, 1976.

Return of the Buffalo, Putnam, 1977.

The Gulls of Smuttynose Island, Putnam, 1977.

Little Dogs of the Prairie, Putnam, 1977.

Island of Wild Horses, Putnam, 1978.

City of Birds and Beasts: Behind the Scenes at the Bronx Zoo, Putnam, 1978.

The Book of the Goat, Putnam, 1979.

The Submarine Bird, Putnam, 1979.

The Book of the Pig, Putnam, 1981.

Moose, Putnam, 1981.

Orphans from the Sea, Putnam, 1982.

The Fur Seals of Pribilof, Putnam, 1983.

Alligator, Putnam, 1984.

Swans, Putnam, 1987.

COOKBOOKS

The Complete Book of Pasta: An Italian Cookbook, illustrated by Melvin Klapholz; photographs by Samuel Chamberlain, Morrow, 1968, revised edition, Bantam, 1983, published as *The New Complete Book of Pasta: A Classic Revisited,* Morrow, 1985.

(With Antoine Gilly) *Antoine Gilly's Feast of France: A Cookbook of Masterpieces in French Cuisine,* illustrated by William Toedecki, Crowell, 1971.

(With M. L. Scott) *Cook Like a Peasant, Eat Like a King,* Follett, 1976.

(With M. L. Scott) *Mastering Microwave Cooking,* Bantam, 1976, revised edition, Consumer Reports Books, 1988.

Best of Pacific Cookbook, Bantam, 1977.

(With M. L. Scott) *A World of Pasta: Unique Pasta Recipes from Around the World,* McGraw, 1978.

(With M. L. Scott) *The Great Potato Cookbook,* Bantam, 1980.

(With M. L. Scott) *The Chicken and Egg Cookbook,* Bantam, 1981.

(With M. L. Scott) *The Complete Convection Oven Cookbook,* Bantam, 1981.

(With M. L. Scott) *The Book of Pies,* Bantam, 1985.

(With M. L. Scott) *Rice: More Than 250 Unexpected Ways to Cook the Perfect Food,* Times Books, 1985.

(With M. L. Scott) *The Great American Family Cookbook,* Bantam, 1986.

(With M. L. Scott) *Meat and Potatoes Cookbook,* Farrar, 1988.

(With M. L. Scott) *Rice: A Cookbook,* Consumer Reports Books, 1989.

(With M. L. Scott and the editors of Consumer Reports Books) *The Bean, Pea, and Lentil Cookbook,* Consumer Reports Books, 1991.

(With M. L. Scott and the editors of Consumer Reports Books) *The Incredible Potato Cookbook,* Consumer Reports Books, 1992.

OTHER

Contributor to anthologies, including *Thirty-four True Tales by Famous American War Reporters,* compiled by the editors of *Look* magazine, Whittlesey House/McGraw-Hill, 1945, and *The American Sportsman,* Ridge Press, 1968. Collaborator with playwright Sir Basil Bartlett and novelist Hilary St. George Saunders on the history of the Battle of Britain.

Contributor of articles and essays to educational textbooks, including *Spectrum I: Literature, Language, and Composition,* Ginn & Co., 1969; *Isn't That What Friends Are For?,* Houghton, 1972; *All of Us Together,* Bank Street College of Education, 1979; *Through the Eyes of a Child: An Introduction to Children's Literature,* Merrill, 1983; *Houghton Mifflin Reading Triumphs,* Houghton, 1986. Contributor of over 1,500 articles to numerous periodicals, including *American Heritage, Argosy, Audubon, Bon Appetit, Collier's, Coronet, Cosmopolitan, Family Circle, Holiday, Liberty, Outdoor Life, Prism, Reader's Digest, Redbook, Saturday Evening Post, Scouting Magazine,* and *Smithsonian.*

SIDELIGHTS: Jack Denton Scott was an award-winning author of nonfiction books for children and writer of numerous articles and books for adults, including cookbooks, travel, and fiction. In the realm of children's literature he specialized in life histories of animals. Most of the author's detailed and carefully crafted texts for children are enhanced by the black-and-white photographs of Ozzie Sweet. Critics have indicated that Scott's explorations of the animal kingdom both entertain and educate middle grade and high school readers, often clarifying misconceptions carelessly handled in other books.

Scott's travels through India with his wife, Maria Luisa, resulted in a book offer from Random House; they returned to India and Scott recorded his observations in the travel biography *Passport to Adventure,* in collaboration with his wife who provided photographs. The Scotts' arctic voyage in search of a lost lake and their attempt to reach the North Pole provided the material for *Journey into Silence.*

With his wife, Scott has also co-authored several cookbooks, of which *The Complete Book of Pasta* and *Mastering Microwave Cooking* have each undergone more than twenty printings. "Cooking, and especially writing cookbooks," wrote the author in *Something about the Author Autobiography Series (SAAS),* "is excellent training ground for the writer. Cooking, first, is a creative art, probably one of the most important acts of a civilized man or woman. It is important to note that people who read cookbooks physically act upon the words that they read. Thus, the words and instructions must be clear and concise, always the mark of good writing."

For his children's books Scott frequently concentrated on a certain species of mammal, bird, or reptile. Usually he described the evolutionary history, physical characteristics, habitat, diet, mating, and reproduction of his subject. Among the animals to receive such attention are the swan, cormorant, egret, Canada goose, buffalo, moose, turtle, alligator, horse, pig, and goat. Scott teamed up with photographer Ozzie Sweet to produce books with what he described in an essay for *Through the Eyes of a Child* as "action, constant movement, words flowing into photographs, photographs flowing into words, no labored captions, no slowing of pace. Almost as cinematic technique." Scott was a careful researcher and worked closely with Sweet to meld text and photographs. "It is teamwork of the highest order, as is our friendship, which goes back many years," Scott once remarked.

In his books on the cormorant (*The Submarine Bird*) and loggerhead turtle, Scott introduces the reader to little-known animals. A critic in *Publishers Weekly* noted about *Loggerhead Turtle* that "Scott's visual account of the loggerhead's fight for survival sparkles with wit and admiration for a creature which has remained unaffected by evolution. And Sweet's photos make the most of the text." In other books the author debunks the stereotypes about such common animals as pigs and goats. In *The Book of the Goat,* "The author first tries to undo some negative stereotypes about goats and challenges the dog's position as human's best and oldest friend. He does this by tracing the goat through history where it obviously held a popular place, even achieving divinity among the Egyptians, Greeks, and Romans," wrote Marilyn R. Singer in *School Library Journal.*

In *Through the Eyes of a Child,* Scott explained the demands of writing for children: "Be accurate. Be relaxed; write fluently; never write down to your readers; never try to write up either. Know your audience; also know your subject; but even if you do know it, research it so that you will know perhaps more than you or anyone else will want to know. Put these all together and they be an axiom for writing nonfiction for your readers. But there is more: There can be no cloudy language; writing must be simple, crisp, clear. This . . . should be a primer for all writing. Children demand the best from a writer."

Scott was a renowned naturalist and gained the reputation of a creator of high-quality instructional nature books for children in which he expressed his respect for animals and concern for endangered species. "Scott has both a profound knowledge of the animal world and a writing style that is both spontaneous and fluent," wrote Zena Sutherland in a review of *The Survivors* for *Bulletin of the Center for Children's Books.* "The admiration he feels for wild creatures is never excessive; his views on conservation or respect for animals never become didactic." His books have earned numerous awards, but most telling is the approval of his readership. In *Through the Eyes of a Child,* Scott recalled: "One ten-year-old boy wrote me that while he was reading our book, *Canada Geese,* he actually flew south with the geese. I bet he did. I *hope* he did."

BIOGRAPHICAL/CRITICAL SOURCES:

BOOKS

Children's Literature Review, Volume 20, Gale, 1990.
Norton, Donna E., *Through the Eyes of a Child: An Introduction to Children's Literature,* second edition, Merrill, 1987, pp. 590-91.
Something about the Author Autobiography Series, Volume 14, Gale, 1992.

PERIODICALS

Bulletin of the Center for Children's Books, April, 1976, p. 133.
New York Review of Books, December 19, 1968.
New York Times Book Review, May 15, 1966.
Publishers Weekly, February 18, 1974, p. 74.
School Library Journal, October, 1979, p. 162.

*   *   *

SCOTTI, R. A. 1946-

PERSONAL: Born December 25, 1946, in Providence, RI, to Ciro O. (a physician) and Rita (in business; maiden name, Dwyer) Scotti; children: Francesca Chigounis, Ciro E. D. Chigounis. *Education:* Loyola University, Chicago, IL, B.S., 1965. *Religion:* Roman Catholic. *Avocational interests:* Travel to Italy.

ADDRESSES: Home and office—224 East 18th St., New York, NY 10003.

CAREER: Star-Ledger, Newark, NJ, editor, 1967-68. Worked as publicist for Holt, Rinehart & Winston, and as copywriter for the Book-of-the-Month Club.

WRITINGS:

The Kiss of Judas (thriller; Book-of-the-Month Club alternate selection), Donald I. Fine, 1985.
The Devil's Own (thriller), Donald I. Fine, 1985.
Cradle Song (nonfiction), Donald I. Fine, 1987.
The Hammer's Eye (thriller), Knightsbridge, 1988.
Lambs Eat Ivy (novel), Donald I. Fine, 1995.

SIDELIGHTS: R. A. Scotti's 1985 thriller *The Kiss of Judas* is a fictionalized account of events following the

1978 terrorist kidnap/murder of Italy's prime minister and details a subsequent plot to seize the Roman Catholic pope. Critiquing *The Kiss of Judas* for the *New York Times Book Review,* Jacqueline Austin determined that "more complexity and imagination" might be desired from a suspense novel based on actual happenings and people. Austin nevertheless cited *The Kiss of Judas* for its vivid descriptions and lively dialogue while tracking the terrorists through Rome's streets.

Like Scotti's first book, the second, *The Devil's Own,* "is a fast-paced juxtaposition of fact and fiction," observed *Los Angeles Times Book Review* critic Mark Schorr. Apparently patterned after a true-to-life scandal, the book presents a character who exploits his friendship with the pope and builds an international empire by looting millions of dollars from Italian banks. According to Schorr, the work provides an "understandable explanation of the sophisticated world of moneylaundering."

Scotti told *CA:* "*The Kiss of Judas*—or the idea for it—came to me while on a trip to Rome when Italy's Prime Minister Aldo Moro was kidnapped by the Red Brigades. The logical question seemed to be: Who would be the next target? There could be only one answer: The pope.

"My research for *Judas* led me to *The Devil's Own,* which centers around the financial chicanery of a man who served as banker to both the Vatican and the Mafia."

Scotti later added: "There is an eerie footnote to my novel, *The Devil's Own,* an intricately plotted financial thriller in which three stories are woven together: importing drugs from Afghanistan through Europe to the United States; the rise and fall of the international financier Stefano Carlatti, who is patterned after Sindona, the Milanese banker responsible for the failure of the Franklin National Bank; and the involvement of the bishop who served as head of the Vatican Bank. At the end of the book, I have Carlatti/Sindona extradited to Italy and held in jail. While awaiting trial, he mysteriously dies in his cell from poisoning. A few months after *The Devil's Own* was published the real Sindona was extradited to Italy and held in jail. While awaiting trial, he mysteriously died in his cell, a victim of poisoning."

BIOGRAPHICAL/CRITICAL SOURCES:

PERIODICALS

Los Angeles Times Book Review, November 3, 1985.
New York Times Book Review, March 31, 1985.

SHANGE, Ntozake 1948-

PERSONAL: Original name Paulette Linda Williams; name changed in 1971, pronounced "En-to-zaki Shong-gay"; born October 18, 1948, in Trenton, NJ; daughter of Paul T. (a surgeon) and Eloise (a psychiatric social worker and educator) Williams; married second husband, David Murray (a musician), July, 1977 (divorced). *Education:* Barnard College, B.A. (with honors), 1970; University of Southern California, Los Angeles, M.A., 1973, and graduate study. *Avocational interests:* Playing the violin.

ADDRESSES: Home—231 North Third St., No. 119, Philadelphia, PA 19106. *Office*—Department of Drama, University of Houston, University Park, 4800 Calhoun Rd., Houston, TX 77004.

CAREER: Writer, performer, and teacher. Faculty member in women's studies, California State College, Sonoma Mills College, and the University of California Extension, 1972-75; associate professor of drama, University of Houston, beginning in 1983; artist in residence, New Jersey State Council on the Arts; creative writing instructor, City College of New York. Lecturer at Douglass College, 1978, and at many other institutions, such as Yale University, Howard University, Detroit Institute of Arts, and New York University. Dancer with Third World Collective, Raymond Sawyer's Afro-American Dance Company, Sounds in Motion, West Coast Dance Works, and For Colored Girls Who Have Considered Suicide (Shange's own dance company); has appeared in Broadway and Off-Broadway productions of her own plays, including *For Colored Girls Who Have Considered Suicide/When the Rainbow Is Enuf* and *Where the Mississippi Meets the Amazon.* Director of several productions including *The Mighty Gents,* produced by the New York Shakespeare Festival's Mobile Theatre, 1979, *A Photograph: A Study in Cruelty,* produced in Houston's Equinox Theatre, 1979, and June Jordan's *The Issue* and *The Spirit of Sojourner Truth,* 1979. Has given many poetry readings.

MEMBER: Actors Equity, National Academy of Television Arts and Sciences, Dramatists Guild, PEN American Center, Academy of American Poets, Poets and Writers Inc., Women's Institute for Freedom of the Press, New York Feminist Arts Guild, Writers' Guild.

AWARDS, HONORS: Obie Award, Outer Critics Circle Award, Audience Development Committee (Audelco) Award, Mademoiselle Award, and Tony, Grammy, and Emmy award nominations, all 1977, all for *For Colored Girls Who Have Considered Suicide/When the Rainbow Is Enuf;* Frank Silvera Writers' Workshop Award, 1978; *Los Angeles Times* Book Prize for Poetry, 1981, for *Three Pieces;* Guggenheim fellowship, 1981; Medal of Excellence, Columbia University, 1981; Obie Award, 1981, for *Mother Courage and Her Children;* Nori Eboraci Award,

Barnard College, 1988; Lila Wallace-Reader's Digest Fund annual writer's award, 1992; Paul Robeson Achievement Award, 1992; Arts and Cultural Achievement Award, National Coalition of 100 Black Women, Inc. (Pennsylvania chapter), 1992; Living Legend Award, National Black Theatre Festival, 1993; Claim Your Life Award, WDAS-AM/FM, 1993; Monarch Merit Award, National Council for Culture and Art, Inc.; Pushcart Prize.

WRITINGS:

For Colored Girls Who Have Considered Suicide/When the Rainbow Is Enuf: A Choreopoem (first produced in New York City at Studio Rivbea, July 7, 1975; produced Off-Broadway at Anspacher Public Theatre, 1976; produced on Broadway at Booth Theatre, September 15, 1976), Shameless Hussy Press (San Lorenzo, CA), 1975, revised edition, Macmillan (New York City), 1976.

Sassafrass (novella), Shameless Hussy Press, 1976.

Melissa & Smith, Bookslinger (St. Paul, MN), 1976.

A Photograph: A Study of Cruelty (poem-play), first produced Off-Broadway at Public Theatre, December 21, 1977, revised edition, *A Photograph: Lovers in Motion* (also see below), produced in Houston, TX, at the Equinox Theatre, November, 1979.

(With Thulani Nkabinde and Jessica Hagedorn) *Where the Mississippi Meets the Amazon,* first produced in New York City at Public Theatre Cabaret, December 18, 1977.

Natural Disasters and Other Festive Occasions (prose and poems), Heirs International (San Francisco, CA), 1977.

Nappy Edges (poems), St. Martin's (New York City), 1978.

Boogie Woogie Landscapes (play; also see below; first produced in New York City at Frank Silvera Writers' Workshop, June, 1979, produced on Broadway at the Symphony Space Theatre, produced in Washington, DC, at the Kennedy Center), St. Martin's, 1978.

Spell #7: A Geechee Quick Magic Trance Manual (play; also see below), produced on Broadway at Joseph Papp's New York Shakespeare Festival Public Theater, July 15, 1979.

Black and White Two Dimensional Planes (play), first produced in New York City at Sounds in Motion Studio Works, February, 1979.

(Adapter) Bertolt Brecht, *Mother Courage and Her Children,* first produced Off-Broadway at the Public Theatre, April, 1980.

Three Pieces: Spell #7; A Photograph: Lovers in Motion; Boogie Woogie Landscapes (plays), St. Martin's, 1981.

A Photograph: Lovers in Motion, Samuel French (New York City), 1981.

Spell #7: A Theatre Piece in Two Acts, Samuel French, 1981.

Sassafrass, Cypress & Indigo: A Novel, St. Martin's, 1982.

Three for a Full Moon [and] *Bocas,* first produced in Los Angeles, CA, at the Mark Taper Forum Lab, Center Theatre, April 28, 1982.

(Adapter) Willy Russell, *Educating Rita* (play), first produced in Atlanta, GA, by Alliance Theatre Company, 1982.

A Daughter's Geography (poems), St. Martin's, 1983.

See No Evil: Prefaces, Essays and Accounts, 1976-1983, Momo's Press (San Francisco, CA), 1984.

From Okra to Greens: Poems, Coffee House Press, 1984.

From Okra to Greens: A Different Kinda Love Story; A Play with Music and Dance (first produced in New York City at Barnard College, November, 1978), Samuel French, 1985.

Betsey Brown: A Novel, St. Martin's, 1985.

(Author of foreword) Mapplethorpe, Robert, *The Black Book,* St. Martin's, 1986.

Three Views of Mt. Fuji (play), first produced at the Lorraine Hansberry Theatre, June, 1987, produced in New York City at the New Dramatists, October, 1987.

Ridin' the Moon in Texas: Word Paintings (responses to art in prose and poetry), St. Martin's, 1987.

(Contributor) Jules Feiffer, *Selected from Contemporary American Plays: An Anthology,* Literacy Volunteers of New York City, 1990.

The Love Space Demands: A Continuing Saga, St. Martin's, 1991.

Three Pieces, St. Martin's, 1992.

I Live in Music (poem), edited by Linda Sunshine, illustrated by Romare Bearden, Stewart, Tabori & Chang (New York City), 1994.

Liliane (fiction), St. Martin's, 1994.

Also author of *Some Men* (poems in a pamphlet that resembles a dance card), 1981. Author of the play *Mouths* and the operetta *Carrie,* both produced in 1981. Has written for a television special starring Diana Ross, and appears in a documentary about her own work for WGBH-TV (Boston). Work represented in several anthologies, including *"May Your Days Be Merry and Bright" and Other Christmas Stories by Women,* edited by Susan Koppelman, Wayne State University Press (Detroit, MI), 1988; *New Plays for the Black Theatre,* edited by Woodie King, Jr., Third World Press (Chicago, IL), 1989; *Breaking Ice: An Anthology of Contemporary African American Fiction,* edited by Terry McMillan, Penguin Books (New York City), 1990; *Yellow Silk: Erotic Arts and Letters,* edited by Lily Pond and Richard Russo, Harmony Books (New York City), 1990; *Daughters of Africa: An International Anthology,* edited by Margaret Bushby, Pantheon (New York City), 1992; *Erotique Noire—Black Erotica,* edited by Miriam DeCosta-Willis, Reginald Martin, and Roseann P. Bell, Anchor (New York City), 1992; *Resurgent: New Writing by Women,* edited by Lou Robinson and Camille Norton, University of Illinois Press (Champaign, IL), 1992; and *Wild Women Don't Wear No Blues: Black Women Writers on Love, Men and Sex,* edited by Marita Golden, Doubleday (New York City), 1993. Author of preface to *Plays by Women, Book Two: An International Anthology,* Ubu Repertory Theater Publications (New York City), 1994. Contributor to periodicals, including *Black Scholar, Third World Women, Ms.,* and *Yardbird Reader.*

ADAPTATIONS: A musical-operetta version of Shange's novel *Betsey Brown* was produced by Joseph Papp's Public Theater in 1986.

WORK IN PROGRESS: In the Middle of a Flower, a play; a film adaptation of her novella *Sassafrass;* a novel.

SIDELIGHTS: Born to a surgeon and an educator, Ntozake Shange—originally named Paulette Williams—was raised with the advantages available to the black middle class. But one by one, the roles she chose for herself—including war correspondent and jazz musician—were dismissed as "no good for a woman," she told Stella Dong in a *Publishers Weekly* interview. She chose to become a writer because "there was nothing left." Frustrated and hurt after separating from her first husband, Shange attempted suicide several times before focusing her rage against the limitations society imposes on black women. While earning a master's degree in American Studies from the University of Southern California, she reaffirmed her personal strength based on a self-determined identity and took her African name, which means "she who comes with her own things" and she "who walks like a lion." Since then she has sustained a triple career as an educator, a performer/director in New York and Houston, and a writer whose works draw heavily on her experiences and the frustrations of being a black female in America. "I am a war correspondent after all," she told Dong, "because I'm involved in a war of cultural and esthetic aggression. The front lines aren't always what you think they are."

Though she is an accomplished poet and an acclaimed novelist, Shange became famous for her play *For Colored Girls Who Have Considered Suicide/When the Rainbow Is Enuf.* A unique blend of poetry, music, dance and drama called a "choreopoem," it was still being produced around the country more than ten years after it "took the theatre world by storm" in 1975. Before it won international acclaim, *For Colored Girls,* notes Jacqueline Trescott in the *Washington Post,* "became an electrifying Broadway hit and provoked heated exchanges about the relationships between black men and women. . . . When [it] debuted, [it] became the talk of literary circles. Its form—seven

women on the stage dramatizing poetry—was a refreshing slap at the traditional, one-two-three-act structures." Whereas plays combining poetry and dance had already been staged by Adrienne Kennedy, Mel Gussow of the *New York Times* states that "Miss Shange was a pioneer in terms of her subject matter: the fury of black women at their double subjugation in white male America."

Shange's anger was not always so evident. "I was always what you call a nice child," she told *Time* magazine contributor Jean Vallely. "I did everything nice. I was the nicest and most correct. I did my homework. I was always on time. I never got into fights. People now ask me, 'Where did all this rage come from?' And I just smile and say it's been there all the time, but was just trying to be nice."

Shange's childhood was filled with music, literature, and art. Dizzy Gillespie, Miles Davis, Chuck Berry, and W. E. B. Du Bois were among the frequent guests at her parents' house. On Sunday afternoons Shange's family held variety shows. She recalled them in a self-interview published in *Ms.:* "my mama wd read from dunbar, shakespeare, countee cullen, t.s. eliot. my dad wd play congas & do magic tricks. my two sisters & my brother & i wd do a soft-shoe & then pick up the instruments for a quartet of some sort: a violin, a cello, flute & saxophone. we all read constantly. anything. anywhere. we also tore the prints outta art books to carry around with us. sounds/ images, any explorations of personal visions waz the focus of my world."

However privileged her childhood might have seemed, Shange felt that she was "living a lie." As she explained to *Newsday* reviewer Allan Wallach: "[I was] living in a world that defied reality as most black people, or most white people, understood it—in other words, feeling that there was something that I could do, and then realizing that nobody was expecting me to do anything because I was colored and I was also female, which was not very easy to deal with."

Writing dramatic poetry became a means of expressing her dissatisfaction with the role of black women in society. She and a group of friends, including various musicians and the choreographer-dancer Paula Moss, would create improvisational works comprised of poetry, music, and dance, and they would frequently perform them in bars in San Francisco and New York. When Moss and Shange moved to New York City, they presented *For Colored Girls* at a Soho jazz loft, the Studio Rivbea. Director Oz Scott saw the show and helped develop the production as it was performed in bars on the Lower East Side. Impressed by one of these, black producer Woodie King, Jr., joined Scott to stage the choreopoem Off-Broadway at the New Federal Theatre, where it ran successfully from November, 1975, to the following June. Then Joseph Papp became the show's producer at the New York Shakespeare Festival's Anspacher Public Theatre. From there, it moved to the Booth Theatre uptown. "The final production at the Booth is as close to distilled as any of us in all our art forms can make it," Shange says of that production in the introduction to *For Colored Girls,* published in 1976. "The cast is enveloping almost 6,000 people a week in the words of a young black girl's growing up, her triumphs and errors, [her] struggle to be all that is forbidden by our environment, all that is forfeited by our gender, all that we have forgotten."

In *For Colored Girls,* poems dramatized by the women dancers recall encounters with their classmates, lovers, rapists, abortionists, and latent killers. The women survive the abuses and disappointments put upon them by the men in their lives and come to recognize in each other, dressed in the colors of Shange's personal rainbow, the promise of a better future. As one voice, at the end, they declare, "i found god in myself / and i loved her / . . . fiercely." To say this, remarks Carol P. Christ in *Diving Deep and Surfacing: Women Writers on Spiritual Quest,* is "to say . . . that it is all right to be a woman, that the Black woman does not have to imitate whiteness or depend on men for her power of being." "The poetry," says Marilyn Stasio in *Cue,* "touches some very tender nerve endings. Although roughly structured and stylistically unrefined, this fierce and passionate poetry has the power to move a body to tears, to rage, and to an ultimate rush of love."

While some reviewers are enthusiastic in their praise for the play, others are emphatically negative. "Some Black people, notably men, said that . . . Shange broke a taboo when her *For Colored Girls . . .* took the theatre world by storm," Connie Lauerman reports in the *Chicago Tribune.* "[Shange] was accused of racism, of 'lynching' the black male." But the playwright does not feel that she was bringing any black family secrets to light. She told Lauerman, "Half of what we discussed in *For Colored Girls* about the dissipation of the family, rape, wife-battering and all that sort of thing, the U.S. Census Bureau already had. . . . We could have gone to the Library of Congress and read the Census reports and the crime statistics every month and we would know that more black women are raped than anyone else. We would know at this point that they think 48 per cent of our households are headed by single females. . . . My job as an artist is to say what I see."

If these conditions are unknown to some, Shange feels it is all the more important to talk about them openly. Defending her portrayal of the acquaintance who turned out to be a rapist, she told interviewer Claudia Tate that men

who deal with the issues by saying they have never raped anyone trouble her: "Maybe we should have a Congressional hearing to find out if it's the UFOs who are raping women. . . . After all, that is a denial of reality. It does *not* matter if you did or not do something. . . . When is someone going to take responsibility for what goes on where we live?" In the same interview, printed in *Black Women Writers at Work,* Shange explained that she wrote about Beau Willie Brown, a war veteran who is on drugs when he drops two small children off a high-rise balcony, because she "refuse[s] to be a part of this conspiracy of silence" regarding crimes that hurt black women.

Some feminist responses to the play were negative, reports *Village Voice* critic Michele Wallace, who suspects "that some black women are angry because *For Colored Girls* exposes their fear of rejection as well as their anger at being rejected. They don't want to deal with that so they talk about how Shange is persecuting the black man." Sandra Hollin Flowers, author of the *Black American Literature Forum* article " 'Colored Girls': Textbook for the Eighties," finds most inappropriate the charges that Shange portrays black men as stupidly crude and brutal. "Quite the contrary, Shange demonstrates a compassionate vision of black men—compassionate because though the work is not without anger, it has a certain integrity which could not exist if the author lacked a perceptive understanding of the crisis between black men and women. And there is definitely a crisis. . . . This, then is what makes *Colored Girls* an important work which ranks with [Ralph] Ellison's *Invisible Man,* [Richard] Wright's *Native Son,* and the handful of other black classics—it is an artistically successful female perspective on a longstanding issue among black people."

"Shange's poems aren't war cries," Jack Kroll writes in a *Newsweek* review of the Public Theatre production of *For Colored Girls.* "They're outcries filled with a controlled passion against the brutality that blasts the lives of 'colored girls'—a phrase that in her hands vibrates with social irony and poetic beauty. These poems are political in the deepest sense, but there's no dogma, no sentimentality, no grinding of false mythic axes." Critic Edith Oliver of the *New Yorker* remarks: "The evening grows in dramatic power, encompassing, it seems, every feeling and experience a woman has ever had; strong and funny, it is entirely free of the rasping earnestness of most projects of this sort. The verses and monologues that constitute the program have been very well chosen—contrasting in mood yet always subtly building."

While Wallace was not completely satisfied with *For Colored Girls* and complained of the occasional "worn-out feminist cliches," she was still able to commend Shange. She wrote: "There is so much about black women that needs retelling; one has to start somewhere, and Shange's exploration of this aspect of our experience, admittedly the most primitive (but we were all there at some time and, if the truth be told, most of us still are) is as good a place as any. All I'm saying is that Shange's *For Colored Girls* should not be viewed as the definitive statement on black women, but as a very good beginning." She continued: "Very few have written with such clarity and honesty about the black woman's vulnerability and no one has ever brought Shange's brand of tough humor and realism to it."

Reviews of Shange's next production, *A Photograph: A Study of Cruelty,* were less positive, although critics were generally impressed with the poetic quality of her writing. "Miss Shange is something besides a poet but she is not—at least not at this stage—a dramatist," Richard Eder declares in a *New York Times* review. "More than anything else, she is a troubadour. She declares her fertile vision of the love and pain between black women and black men in outbursts full of old malice and young cheerfulness. They are short outbursts, song-length; her characters are perceived in flashes, in illuminating vignettes."

Shange's next play, *Spell #7: A Geechee Quick Magic Trance Manual,* more like *For Colored Girls* in structure, elicits a higher recommendation from Eder. Its nine characters in a New York bar discuss the racism black artists contend with in the entertainment world. At one point, the all-black cast appears in overalls and minstrel-show blackface to address the pressure placed on the black artist to fit a stereotype in order to succeed. "That's what happens to black people in the arts no matter how famous we become. . . . Black Theatre is not moving forward the way people like to think it is. We're not free of our paint yet," Shange told Tate. "On another level, *Spell #7* deals with the image of a black woman as a neutered workhorse, who is unwanted, unloved, and unattended by anyone," notes Elizabeth Brown in the *Dictionary of Literary Biography.* "The emphasis is still on the experiences of the black woman but it is broadened and deepened, and it ventures more boldly across the sexual divide," Eder writes in the *New York Times.* Don Nelson, writing in the *New York Daily News,* deems the show "black magic. . . . The word that best describes Shange's works, which are not plays in the traditional sense, is power."

To critics and producers who have complained that Shange's theater pieces do not present an easily marketable issue or point, Shange responds that a work's emotional impact should be enough. As she told Tate, "Our society allows people to be absolutely neurotic and totally out of touch with their feelings and everyone else's feelings, and yet be very respectable. This, to me, is a travesty. So I write to get at the part of people's emotional lives that they don't have control over, the part that can and will respond. . . . *For Colored Girls* for me is not an issue play. . . . There are just some people who are interesting. There's something there to make you feel intensely. Black writers have a right to do this," she said, although such works are not often rewarded with financial success. She names a number of successful plays that don't have a point except to celebrate being alive, and claims, "Black and Latin writers have to start demanding that the fact we're alive is point enough!" Furthermore, works which rely on emotional appeal reach a larger audience, she maintains in the same interview: "The kind of esteem that's given to brightness/smartness obliterates average people or slow learners from participating fully in human life. But you cannot exclude any human being from emotional participation."

Shange writes to fulfill a number of deeply felt responsibilities. Describing the genesis of *For Colored Girls,* for instance, Shange told Tate that she wrote its poems because she wanted young black women "to have information that I did not have. I wanted them to know what it was truthfully like to be a grown woman. . . . I don't want them to grow up in a void of misogynist lies." It is her commitment to break the silence of mothers who know, but don't tell their daughters, that "it's a dreadful proposition to lose oneself in the process of tending and caring for others," she said. The play "calls attention to how male-oriented black women . . . [and] women in general are," and how their self-esteem erodes when they allow themselves to be exploited, writes Tate. Says Shange, "When I die, I will not be guilty of having left a generation of girls behind thinking that anyone can tend to their emotional health other than themselves."

Speaking of her works in general, she said, "I think it was Adrienne Rich or Susan Griffin who said that one of our responsibilities as women writers is to discover the causes for our pain and to respect them. I think that much of the suffering that women and black people endure is not respected. I was also trained not to respect it. For instance, we're taught not to respect women who can't get their lives together by themselves. They have three children and a salary check for $200. The house is a mess; they're sort of hair-brained. We're taught not to respect their suffering. So I write about things that I know have never been given their full due. . . . I want people to at least understand or have the chance to see that this is a person whose life is not only valid but whose life is valiant. My responsibility is to be as honest as I can and to use whatever technical skills I may possess to make these experiences even clearer, or sharper, or more devastating or more beautiful." Shange contends that women writers should also demand more respect for writing love poems, for seeing "the world in a way that allows us to care more about people than about military power. The power we see is the power to feed, the power to nourish and to educate. . . . It's part of our responsibility as writers to make these things important."

Shange's poetry books, like her theater pieces, are distinctively original. *Nappy Edges,* containing fifty poems, is too long, says Harriet Gilbert in the *Washington Post Book World;* however, she claims, "nothing that Shange writes is ever entirely unreadable, springing, as it does, from such an intense honesty, from so fresh an awareness of the beauty of sound and of vision, from such mastery of words, from such compassion, humor and intelligence." Alice H. G. Phillips relates in the *Times Literary Supplement,* "Comparing herself to a jazzman 'takin' a solo,' she lets go with verbal runs and trills, mixes in syncopations, spins out evocative hanging phrases, variations on themes and refrains. Rarely does she come to a full stop, relying instead on line breaks, extra space breaking up a line, and/or oblique strokes. . . . She constantly tries to push things to their limit, and consequently risks seeming over-enthusiastic, oversimplistic or merely undisciplined. . . . But at its best, her method can achieve both serious humour and deep seriousness."

In her poetry, Shange takes many liberties with the conventions of written English, using nonstandard spellings and punctuation. Some reviewers feel that these innovations present unnecessary obstacles to the interested readers of *Nappy Edges, A Daughter's Geography,* and *From Okra to Greens: Poems.* Explaining her "lower-case letters, slashes, and spelling" to Tate, she said that "poems where all the first letters are capitalized" bore her; "also, I like the idea that letters dance. . . . I need some visual stimulation, so that reading becomes not just a passive act and more than an intellectual activity, but demands rigorous participation." Her idiosyncratic punctuation assures her "that the reader is not in control of the process." She wants her words in print to engage the reader in a kind of struggle, and not be "whatever you can just ignore." The spellings, she said, "reflect language as I hear it. . . . The structure is connected to the music I hear beneath the words."

Shange's rejection of standard English serves deeper emotional and political purposes as well. In a *Los Angeles Times Book Review* article on Shange's *See No Evil: Prefaces, Essays and Accounts, 1976-1983,* Karl Keller relates, "[Shange] feels that as a black performer/playwright/poet, she has wanted 'to attack deform n maim the language that i was taught to hate myself in. I have to take it apart to the bone.' " Speaking to Tate, Shange declared, "We do not have to refer continually to European art as the standard. That's absolutely absurd and racist, and I won't participate in that utter lie. My work is one of the few ways I can preserve the elements of our culture that need to be remembered and absolutely revered."

Shange takes liberties with the conventions of fiction writing with her first full-length novel, *Sassafrass, Cypress & Indigo.* "The novel is unusual in its form—a tapestry of narrative, poetry, magic spells, recipes and letters. Lyrical yet real, it also celebrates female stuff—weaving, cooking, birthing babies," relates Lauerman. Its title characters are sisters who find different ways to cope with their love relationships. Sassafrass attaches herself to Mitch, a musician who uses hard drugs and beats her; she leaves him twice, but goes back to him for another try. To male readers who called Mitch a "weak" male character, Shange replied to Lauerman, "[He] had some faults, but there's no way in the world you can say [he wasn't] strong. . . . I think you should love people with their faults. That's what love's about." Cypress, a dancer in feminist productions, at first refuses to become romantically involved with any of her male friends. Indigo, the youngest sister, retreats into her imagination, befriending her childhood dolls, seeing only the poetry and magic of the world. The music she plays on her violin becomes a rejuvenating source for her mother and sisters. "Probably there is a little bit of all three sisters in Shange," Lauerman suggests, "though she says that her novel is not autobiographical but historical, culled from the experiences of blacks and from the 'information of my feelings'."

Critics agree that Shange's poetry is more masterfully wrought than her fiction, yet they find much in the novel to applaud. Writes Doris Grumbach in the *Washington Post Book World,* "Shange is primarily a poet, with a blood-red sympathy for and love of her people, their folk as well as their sophisticated ways, their innocent, loving goodness as much as their lack of immunity to powerful evil. . . . But her voice in this novel is entirely her own, an original, spare and primary-colored sound that will remind readers of Jean Toomer's *Cane.*" In Grumbach's opinion, "Whatever Shange turns her hand to she does well, even to potions and recipes. A white reader feels the exhilarating shock of discovery at being permitted entry into a world she couldn't have known" apart from the novel.

"There is poetry in . . . *Sassafrass, Cypress & Indigo:* the poetry of rich lyrical language, of women you want to know because they're so original even their names conjure up visions," comments Joyce Howe in the *Village Voice.* *Betsey Brown: A Novel* "lacks those fantastical qualities, yet perhaps because this semi-autobiographical second novel is not as easy to love, it is the truer book." Betsey is thirteen, growing into young womanhood in St. Louis during the 1950s. "An awakening sense of racial responsibility is as important to Betsey as her first kiss," relates Patchy Wheatley, a *Times Literary Supplement* reviewer.

As one of the first students to be bused to a hostile white school, Betsey learns about racism and how to overcome it with a sense of personal pride. Says the reviewer, "By interweaving Betsey's story with those of the various generations of her family and community, Shange has also produced something of wider significance: a skillful exploration of the Southern black community at a decisive moment in its history."

"Black life has always been more various than the literature has been at liberty to show," comments Sherley Anne Williams in a *Ms.* review. Though she is not impressed with *Betsey Brown* "as a literary achievement," she welcomes this important-because-rare look at the black middle class. In a *Washington Post* review, Tate concurs, and notes the differences between *Betsey Brown* and Shange's previous works: "Shange's style is distinctively lyrical; her monologues and dialogues provide a panorama of Afro-American diversity. Most of Shange's characteristic elliptical spelling, innovative syntax and punctuation is absent from *Betsey Brown*. Missing also is the caustic social criticism about racial and sexual victimization. . . . *Betsey Brown* seems also to mark Shange's movement from explicit to subtle expressions of rage, from repudiating her girlhood past to embracing it, and from flip candor to more serious commentary." Shange told Dong that she is as angry and subversive as ever, but does not feel as powerless, she said, "because I know where to put my anger, and I don't feel alone anymore."

In *The Love Space Demands,* a choreopoem published in 1991, Shange returns to the blend of music, dance, poetry and drama that characterized *For Colored Girls Who Have Considered Suicide*. "I've gone back to being more like myself," Shange explains to *Voice Literary Supplement* interviewer Eileen Myles. "I'm working on my poetry with musicians and dancers like I originally started." Described by Myles as "a sexy, discomfiting, energizing, revealing, occasionally smug, fascinating kind of book," *The Love Space Demands* includes poems on celibacy and sexuality, on black women's sense of abandonment by black men, on a crack-addicted mother who sells her daughter's virginity for a hit and a pregnant woman who swallows cocaine, destroying her unborn child, to protect her man from arrest. The lead poem of the book, "irrepressibly bronze, beautiful & mine," was inspired by Robert Mapplethorpe's photographs of black and white gay men. The artist's task, Shange tells Myles, is "to keep our sensibilities alive. . . . To keep people alive so they know they can feel what is happening as opposed to simply trying to fend it off." "I would rather you not think about how the poem's constructed but simply be in it with me," she adds. "That's what it's for, not for the construction, even for the wit of it. It's for actual, visceral responses."

BIOGRAPHICAL/CRITICAL SOURCES:

BOOKS

Betsko, Kathleen, and Rachel Koenig, editors, *Interviews with Contemporary Women Playwrights,* Beech Tree Books, 1987.

Christ, Carol P., *Diving Deep and Surfacing: Women Writers on Spiritual Quest,* Beacon Press (Boston, MA), 1980.

Contemporary Literary Criticism, Gale (Detroit, MI), Volume 8, 1978, Volume 25, 1983, Volume 38, 1986.

Dictionary of Literary Biography, Volume 38: *Afro-American Writers after 1955: Dramatists and Prose Writers,* Gale, 1985.

Shange, Ntozake, *For Colored Girls Who Have Considered Suicide/When the Rainbow Is Enuf,* Shameless Hussy Press, 1975, Macmillan, 1976.

Shange, Ntozake, *See No Evil: Prefaces, Essays and Accounts, 1976-1983,* Momo's Press, 1984.

Squier, Susan Merrill, editor, *Women Writers and the City: Essays in Feminist Literary Criticism,* University of Tennessee Press (Knoxville, TN), 1984.

Tate, Claudia, editor, *Black Women Writers at Work,* Continuum (New York City), 1983.

PERIODICALS

African American Review, spring, 1992; summer, 1992.

American Black Review, September, 1983; March, 1986.

Black American Literature Forum, summer, 1981; fall, 1990.

Black Scholar, March, 1979; March, 1981; December, 1982; July, 1985.

Booklist, April 15, 1987; May 15, 1991.

Chicago Tribune, October 21, 1982.

Chicago Tribune Book World, July 1, 1979; September 8, 1985.

Christian Science Monitor, September 9, 1976; October 8, 1982; May 2, 1986.

Cue, June 26, 1976.

Detroit Free Press, October 30, 1978.

Ebony, August, 1977.

Essence, November, 1976; May, 1985; June, 1985; August, 1991.

Freedomways, third quarter, 1976.

Horizon, September, 1977.

Kliatt Young Adult Paperback Book Guide, January, 1989.

Library Journal, May 1, 1987.

Los Angeles Times, October 20, 1982; June 11, 1985; July 28, 1987.

Los Angeles Times Book Review, August 22, 1982; October 20, 1982; January 8, 1984; July 29, 1984; June 11, 1985; July 19, 1987.

Mademoiselle, September, 1976.

Ms., September, 1976; December, 1977; June, 1985; June, 1987.

New Leader, July 5, 1976.

Newsday, August 22, 1976.

New Statesman, October 4, 1985.

Newsweek, June 14, 1976; July 30, 1979.

New York Amsterdam News, October 9, 1976.

New York Daily News, July 16, 1979.

New Yorker, June 14, 1976; August 2, 1976; January 2, 1978.

New York Post, June 12, 1976; September 16, 1976; July 16, 1979.

New York Theatre Critics' Reviews, September 13, 1976.

New York Times, June 16, 1976; December 22, 1977; June 4, 1979; June 8, 1979; July 16, 1979; July 22, 1979; May 14, 1980; June 15, 1980.

New York Times Book Review, June 25, 1979; July 16, 1979; October 21, 1979; September 12, 1982; May 12, 1985; April 6, 1986.

New York Times Magazine, May 1, 1983.

Plays and Players, December, 1979.

Publishers Weekly, May 3, 1985.

Saturday Review, February 18, 1978; May/June, 1985.

Time, June 14, 1976; July 19, 1976; November 1, 1976.

Times (London), April 21, 1983.

Times Literary Supplement, December 6, 1985; April 15-21, 1988.

Variety, July 25, 1979.

Village Voice, August 16, 1976; July 23, 1979; June 18, 1985.

Village Voice Literary Supplement, August, 1991; September, 1991.

Washington Post, June 12, 1976; June 29, 1976; February 23, 1982; June 17, 1985.

Washington Post Book World, October 15, 1978; July 19, 1981; August 22, 1982; August 5, 1984.

Wilson Library Bulletin, October, 1990.*

*   *   *

SHIELDS, David 1956-

PERSONAL: Born July 22, 1956, in Los Angeles, CA; son of Milton (a journalist) and Hannah (a journalist; maiden name, Bloom) Shields. *Education:* Brown University, B.A., 1978; University of Iowa, M.F.A. (with honors), 1980.

ADDRESSES: Home—4235 Interlake North, Seattle, WA 98103. *Office*—English Department, University of Washington, Seattle, WA 98195.

CAREER: University of Iowa, Iowa City, research assistant, 1978-79, teaching assistant in literature, 1979-80, instructor in creative writing and literature, 1980; researcher and writer for former California governor, Pat Brown, 1984; visiting lecturer in creative writing at University of California, Los Angeles, 1985; St. Lawrence University, Canton, NY, visiting assistant professor, 1985-86, 1987-88; University of Washington, Seattle, assistant professor, 1988-92, associate professor of English, 1992—. Preliminary judge for Drue Heinz Award, University of Pittsburgh Press, 1992; juror for Barnard College undergraduate fiction writing competition, 1993; juror for Ragdale Foundation artists' colony, 1993.

MEMBER: International PEN, Authors Guild, Writers Guild of America, Modern Language Association of America, Poets and Writers, Associated Writing Programs, Phi Beta Kappa.

AWARDS, HONORS: James Michener fellowship, Iowa Writers' Workshop, 1980-82; James D. Phelan Award Literary Award, San Francisco Foundation, 1981; National Endowment for the Arts Fellowship in Fiction, 1982 and 1991; Residency fellowships at Corporation of Yaddo, MacDowell Colony, Virginia Center for the Creative Arts, Ragdale Foundation, Millay Colony, Cummington Community of the Arts, Centrum, 1982-91; Authors League Fund grant, 1983; PEN Writers Fund grant, 1983, 1986, and 1987; Ingram-Merrill Foundation award, 1983; Carnegie Fund for Authors grant, 1984 and 1987; Change Inc. grant, 1985; winner of PEN Syndicated Fiction Project Competition, 1985 and 1988; Faculty Research grant, St. Lawrence University, 1986; Ludwig Vogelstein Foundation grant, 1986; William Sloane Fellowship in Prose, Bread Loaf Writers' Conference, 1986; Carnegie Fund for Authors grant, 1987; Pushcart Prize nomination, 1987, 1988, 1989, 1992, and 1993; New York Foundation for the Arts Fellowship, 1988; Graduate School Research Fund grant, University of Washington, 1989; "Audrey" chosen one of "Ten Best" stories, PEN Syndicated Fiction Project, 1989; Silver Medal, Commonwealth Club of California Book Awards, 1989, and Washington State Governor's Writers Award, 1990, both for *Dead Languages;* Artist Trust Fellowship for Literature, 1991; PEN/Revson Foundation Fellowship, 1992; King County Arts Commission Independent Artist New Works award, 1992; Seattle Arts Commission fellowship, 1992; Distinguished Author's Award, Brandeis University National Women's Committee (Seattle chapter), 1993; Graduate School Research Fund grant, University of Washington, 1994.

WRITINGS:

Heroes (novel), Simon & Schuster (New York City), 1984.

Dead Languages (novel), Knopf (New York City), 1989.

A Handbook for Drowning (stories), Knopf, 1992.

Contributor of articles and stories to periodicals, including *Harper's, Village Voice, Utne Reader, Threepenny Review, Story, Witness,* and *Conjunctions.*

WORK IN PROGRESS: Remote: A Cultural Autobiography is scheduled for publication in 1996.

SIDELIGHTS: In his first novel, *Heroes,* David Shields writes about "those two great American preoccupations, Lost Innocence and Sports," recounted James Marcus in the *Philadelphia Inquirer.* Similar themes of spent youth and missed opportunity are also featured in this story that dramatizes the mid-life crisis and ultimate self-realization of a Midwestern sportswriter, Al Biederman. A former college basketball star whose career was prematurely ended by an injury sustained on the court, Biederman turned to journalism when he could no longer participate physically in the game. While reporting on basketball for a small-town newspaper in Iowa, he discovers a talented college athlete who reminds the middle-aged Biederman of his now diminished athletic prowess. Clinging to a romanticized vision of the past, Biederman sees the young transfer student Belvyn Menkus as the epitome of everything the unsuccessful sportswriter once hoped to become. Ironically, however, Menkus is entangled in some illegal recruiting practices. The admiring Biederman is torn between exposing the wrongdoing—and possibly gaining a more prestigious post on a big city paper—and turning away, thus sacrificing personal attainment for the good of the game. Complicating Biederman's decision-making are several other conflicts such as resentment for his wife's success, intolerance for his son's frail health, and an affair with an enamored journalism student.

Heroes garnered favorable reviews from a number of critics and likewise impressed Marcus as a celebration of "the subtler brand of heroism." It "makes a particular virtue of showing how . . . ideals run aground, but nonetheless survive intact," he added. A critic for the *Chicago Tribune* called Shields "a keen observer of humanity," and in a later Chicago *Tribune Books* review of *Heroes,* Clarence Petersen stated that the questions Shields raises "are important and eternal and have almost nothing to do with any game." Diana L. Smith, writing in the *Fort Worth Star Telegram,* opined that Shields "has an engaging way of incorporating important events . . . with a pleasant mix of hilarity and pathos." Noting that the clarity of the characters and scenes is "excellent," she concluded that *Heroes* "is a thoroughly enjoyable book."

Shields' acclaimed second novel, *Dead Languages,* concerns young Jeremy Zorn, a stutterer who lives with his domineering mother and manic-depressive father, and his efforts to overcome his disability. Eva Hoffman, writing in the *New York Times,* observed that "much of the novel . . . consists of inventive, often lyrical reflections on how

language can become a diversion from communication rather than a means to it," and *Boston Review* contributor Pagan Kennedy noted: "*Dead Languages* is a novel-long stutter, hemming and hesitating, titillating with its titubation. The language of the book is not just decoration, it is part of the plot."

Evelyn Toynton, writing for the *New York Times Book Review,* found *Dead Languages* intelligent and humorous: "Mr. Shields's own language is wonderfully fluent—colloquial and elegiac by turns—and when his sense of the ridiculous comes to the fore, as it does in deadpan descriptions of Jeremy's stint as a teacher's aide in a summer school program for black children and his romance with a cheerful illiterate druggy, his character's dilemma seems both touching and wryly comic." In the *Los Angeles Daily News,* Danielle Roter admitted that "Jeremy may be a prickly and morbidly self-absorbed character, but he is rooted in truth. And that makes him irresistible." Finally, Matthew Gilbert of the *Boston Globe* stated: "As he narrates his history, with a wry good humor that belies his constant pain, Jeremy transforms his lifelong antagonism with language into a universal plight: the failure to be understood."

A later work titled *A Handbook for Drowning* is a collection of interlinked stories focusing on Walter Jaffe, a young man struggling to come to terms with his family neuroses as well as the complexities of his own life. Like Jeremy Zorn in *Dead Languages,* Walter grows up under the shadow of a strong, activist mother and an ineffectual father who obsesses about the Ethel and Julius Rosenberg trial. Michiko Kakutani of the *New York Times* noticed the similarities between the books, stating: "Mr. Shields works a variation on the material in *Dead Languages,* stripping away the more symbolic aspects of the story to focus on the coming of age of a young man. . . . Mr. Shields again demonstrates his ability to conjure up the past using lyrical, rhythmic language to relate ordinary domestic events. He possesses a gift for taking a seemingly mundane moment . . . and investing it with layers of psychological resonance."

Commenting on *A Handbook for Drowning*'s unorthodox narrative style, Robert Taylor wrote in the *Boston Globe:* "A structure of connecting though nonchronological stories dispenses with the yoke of time. It also abolishes the drudgery of detailed exposition and character development in a conventional cause-and-effect manner; instead, juxtaposition provides contrast and sudden flashes of insight reveal an extensive landscape of feeling." In *Newsday,* Dan Cryer noted that "Shields has the latitude not to flesh out a character's background or fill in plot lines or aim toward an identifiable climax. The short-story format permits, even luxuriates in, a pointillist mysteriousness regarding all these elements." Cryer later assessed that "even if some of the stories by themselves are rather slight, their cumulative effect is powerful." "*A Handbook for Drowning* is sometimes excessively sensitive," remarked Rhoda Koenig in her *New York* review, "but it does chronicle painfully, accurately the endemic disease of our time: the difficulty of feeling."

BIOGRAPHICAL/CRITICAL SOURCES:

PERIODICALS

Bloomsbury Review, June, 1992.
Boston Globe, May 24, 1989; January 22, 1992.
Boston Review, August, 1989.
Chicago Tribune, January 20, 1985; January 28, 1985; May 1, 1989; December 26, 1991.
Cleveland Plain Dealer, July 30, 1989; January 12, 1992.
Fort Worth Star-Telegram, December 16, 1984.
Houston Chronicle, August 20, 1989.
Iowa City Press-Citizen, April 3, 1985; November 14, 1988.
Lake Effect, fall, 1989.
Los Angeles Daily News, August 20, 1989.
Los Angeles Times, May 26, 1989.
Los Angeles Times Book Review, June 25, 1989.
Newsday, April 22, 1990; January 20, 1992.
New York, January 13, 1992, p. 62.
New Yorker, July 3, 1989.
New York Review of Books, July 20, 1989.
New York Times, April 26, 1989; December 27, 1991.
New York Times Book Review, February 3, 1985; April 26, 1989; June 18, 1989; July 9, 1982; April 15, 1990; January 19, 1992.
Philadelphia Inquirer, December 8, 1984.
Pittsburgh Press, July 23, 1989.
Review of Contemporary Fiction, spring, 1992.
San Francisco Chronicle, June 11, 1989.
San Francisco Review of Books, March/April, 1995, pp. 17-19.
San Mateo Times, August 22, 1984.
Santa Monica Evening Outlook, May 7, 1985.
Seattle Times/Seattle Post-Intelligencer, May 14, 1989; December 31, 1989.
Tribune Books (Chicago), November 27, 1988, p. 7.
Writing, October, 1989.

*　　*　　*

SHOUMATOFF, Alex(ander) 1946-

PERSONAL: Born November 4, 1946, in Mount Kisco, NY; son of Nicholas (an engineer) and Nina (Adamovitch) Shoumatoff; married second wife, Ana Dos Santos, April 9, 1977 (marriage ended); married Rosette Rwigamba, 1990; children: Andre Luis, Nicholas; (with Rwigamba) Oliver Shema, Zachary Shyaka. *Education:* Harvard University, B.A., 1968.

ADDRESSES: P.O. Box 151, Keene, NY 12942.

CAREER: Washington Post, Washington, DC, reporter and book reviewer, 1968-69; variously employed as songwriter, freelance writer, and instructor in French at New England College, Henniker, NH, 1969-73; natural history teacher in private school in Bedford, NY, 1973-78; *New Yorker,* New York City, staff writer, 1980-90. Executive director and resident naturalist, Marsh Sanctuary, 1973-78; member of board of trustees, Butler Sanctuary. Minister of Universal Life Church. *Military service:* U.S. Marine Corps, 1969-70.

MEMBER: Bedford Audubon Society (member of board of directors).

AWARDS, HONORS: Woodrow Wilson fellowship, 1968; Guggenheim fellowship, 1984-85.

WRITINGS:

Florida Ramble, Harper (New York City), 1974, Vintage (New York City), 1990.
The Rivers Amazon, Sierra Books (San Francisco), 1978.
Westchester: Portrait of a County, Coward, 1979, Vintage, 1990.
The Capital of Hope: Brasilia and Its People, Coward, 1980, Vintage, 1990.
Russian Blood: A Family Chronicle, Coward, 1982, Vintage, 1990.
The Mountain of Names: A History of the Human Family, Simon & Schuster (New York City), 1985, Vintage, 1990.
In Southern Light: Trekking through Zaire and the Amazon, Simon & Schuster, 1986, Vintage, 1990.
African Madness, Knopf (New York City), 1988, Vintage, 1990.
The World Is Burning: Murder in the Rain Forest, Little, Brown (Boston), 1990, published in England as *Murder in the Rain Forest: The Chico Mendes Story,* 4th Estate (London), 1991.

Contributor to newspapers and magazines.

WORK IN PROGRESS: Prowling the Desert Southwest.

SIDELIGHTS: Part naturalist, part journalist, Alex Shoumatoff is, according to a *New York Times Book Review* critic, "a very *New Yorker* kind of writer [who is] civilized, observant to a fault, and low-key in style." Sam Staggs, in a *Publishers Weekly* interview with the author, describes Shoumatoff as being "his generation's version of a Hemingway hero: a sensitive outdoorsman who watches animals instead of shooting them." Shoumatoff's portraits of such diverse areas as the Amazon River basin, New York's Westchester County, and Brazil's capital city are testimony to what he once told *CA* was his "abiding interest in the relationship of man and nature; in the type of writing that conveys the total picture of a place, both its natural and social history." Summing up his interests, Shoumatoff told *CA:* "My recurrent subjects are natural history, local history, family history, and tribal people."

Often, Shoumatoff's subjects are inextricably linked. *Florida Ramble,* Shoumatoff's first book, is grounded in local and natural history. "An agreeably unstructured account of one man's random travels in Florida during the early '70s," in the words of a reviewer for the *Los Angeles Times Book Review,* the book warns of "the incipient ecological disaster caused by unchecked development." That theme underlies much of Shoumatoff's later writing as well, especially *The World Is Burning: Murder in the Rain Forest.*

In *Russian Blood: A Family Chronicle,* Shoumatoff makes family history (his own, that is) his central topic. A blend of personal anecdotes (gathered primarily from the author's two grandmothers), history, and photographs, *Russian Blood* is, in the words of a *Best Sellers* reviewer, "a fascinating story told by a man who has true artistic talent and the storyteller's gift of communicating his own enthusiasm to his readers." Despite feeling that Shoumatoff's many details are gathered at the expense of a deeper exploration of their significance, Herbert Gold comments in the *Los Angeles Times Book Review* that "the resonance of strong autobiographical writing—of strong writing in general—occasionally stirs from the account of Shoumatoff's shimmering, unforgettable characters." Though S. Frederick Starr finds a few "plaster props and cliches" in *Russian Blood,* he asserts in his *Washington Post* review that "Shoumatoff is a writer of exceptional sympathy and grace. The world may be full of people like his grandparents, cultured folk uprooted from their cozy environments and thrown into alien and indifferent worlds. But few of them are fortunate enough to have a writer of Shoumatoff's gifts to trace their steps. . . . He achieves just the right balance of objectivity and love."

In *The Mountain of Names: A History of the Human Family,* Shoumatoff adds the study of tribal people to the subject of family history, exploring the changing nature of kinship in the Western world. According to Neil Postman in the *Washington Post Book World,* "Shoumatoff argues that a radically different mental order—self-centered instead of kin-centered—has taken over in America and Europe and in most countries that are developing along European lines." The book contains "a torrent of information, much of which is fascinating," Postman notes.

But some like other critics, Postman also asserts that the book's encyclopedic structure works against it, straining the memory of its reader and undercutting the "moving and well focused" denouement. For John Gross of the

New York Times, the weakness of *The Mountain of Names* lies in Shoumatoff's tendency to fall back upon "pop psychology and pop sociology" in his analyses. Nevertheless, Gross confesses that he finds "something attractive about [Shoumatoff's] curiosity, and about the zest with which he falls on a picturesque piece of information." Robert Dawidoff calls *Mountain of Names* "a terrific book" in the *Los Angeles Times Book Review,* describing it as giving "contemporary issues of family a pre-history, a history, and all sorts of mediating contexts." For Dawidoff, like Gross, Shoumatoff's style is particularly appealing. "The effect of his lively and idiosyncratic discussion," the reviewer writes, "is to make his subject seem more fascinating than plaguing, more human than personal."

Among the subjects of the essays collected in *African Madness* are the AIDS epidemic, the murder of primatologist Dian Fossey, and a portrait of the self-proclaimed, despotic emperor of the Central African Republic, Jean-Bedel Bokassa. The collection was well received upon its initial publication in 1988, and it continued to find favor upon its reissue with several of Shoumatoff's earlier works by Vintage Books in 1990. "It is hardly news that catastrophes, man-made and otherwise, are pummeling Africa," Paul Gray acknowledged in *Time* magazine in 1988. "But Shoumatoff's first-person reports do not simply catalogue misery." In Gray's opinion, *African Madness* reaches the implicit conclusion that "once an incubator of life, Africa today offers a panorama of possible deaths." Calling its author "the most engaging and accessible of America's peripatetic explorers," the *Los Angeles Times Book Review* found much to praise in the "rich mosaics of history, geology and culture" Shoumatoff creates in *African Madness.* In 1990, a Chicago *Tribune Books* writer compared the author's style to that of other travel writers, deeming Shoumatoff's "a decided, always welcome departure."

The book for which Shoumatoff has received the greatest attention thus far is 1990's *The World Is Burning.* The story of the murder of rubber tapper, union leader, and Amazon rain forest defender Chico Mendes in Brazil in 1988, the book has met with a wide spectrum of responses. At one end, Roger Cohen takes the author to task in a *New York Times* review for his "hip" language and a lack of carefulness in structuring his material and giving clear and accurate information. "That is a pity," Cohen writes, "because Mr. Shoumatoff, an old Brazil hand, has a sharper journalistic eye for the country than [Andrew] Revkin," author of *Burning Season: The Murder of Chico Mendes and the Fight for the Amazon Rain Forest,* which was published around the same time as Shoumatoff's book. But at the other end of the spectrum, John Hemming pronounces both "excellent books" in a review for the *Washington Post Book World.* "Shoumatoff writes vividly about the wrangles between rival movie makers [for rights to the Mendes story], the squabbling environmentalists, and the sometimes sleazy world of the Brazilian interior," Hemming adds.

In between, Elio Gaspari finds favor with the first half of *The World Is Burning,* but sees its second half as flawed. In the *Los Angeles Times Book Review,* Gaspari describes the book's first half as "a competent blend of good reporting, serious research and novel ideas. Shoumatoff masterfully paints the tableau in which Mendes fell." Once the author leaves the tale of the murder and the destruction of the rain forest behind, however, he loses both pace and accuracy, and his accounts tend toward the self-indulgent, Gaspari asserts.

Many critics draw the line not between halves, but between Shoumatoff's style and his knowledge of his subject. A *Newsweek* article describes Shoumatoff as "a crossover artist" whose contributions to both *Vanity Fair* and the more staid *New Yorker* have "muddled his style some." Praising Shoumatoff for his "good eye and a way with the odd detail," the article questions the farcical tone of *The World Is Burning,* which it describes as a "prankish new book." In the *New York Times Book Review,* James Brooke complains that Shoumatoff "crashes around" in his narrative "like a third-world Hunter Thompson," adding: "But Mr. Shoumatoff, a student of Brazilian society . . . excels at explaining that country's culture."

For others, Shoumatoff's unusual style in *The World Is Burning* is a mixed blessing in itself. "Shoumatoff's account at times reads like undigested field notes, and he can be too flippant," James North concedes in the Chicago *Tribune Books.* "But, in places, Shoumatoff's meandering manner is extremely effective, as when he paints a chilling portrait of the ranchers [who murdered Mendes] in their favorite bar, with violence and arrogance thick in the air." "It is because . . . Shoumatoff's own feelings are rather admirably confused that his book is stimulating and amusing," writes Philip Glazebrook in the *Spectator.* "I like his incautious way of describing how contradictory it all is. . . . He is very human."

Many critics cite Shoumatoff's humanity as the factor that sets his travel writing apart from that of other authors. Shoumatoff himself told Staggs: " 'My favorite kind of writing is straightforward, compassionate prose. I think something is essentially wrong with the travel genre—so much of it is based on first impressions, which don't necessarily turn out to be accurate. And the attitude is often: "I'm going from a superior society to this exotic place to look at these savages." ' "

New York Times reviewer Michiko Kakutani indicates that the author is in no danger of assuming such an attitude. Comparing him to a character from the novels of Graham Greene, Kakutani asserts that "Shoumatoff seems drawn to hot, bug-ridden places, tropical backwaters of the third world, where the superficial comforts and rules of the West do not apply. He is not, however, a skeptical observer . . . constantly on the lookout for signs of backwardness and corruption, but rather an old-fashioned traveler, beguiled by the exotic romance of such unfamiliar places." Zuckerman writes that "Mr. Shoumatoff achieves the difficult task of getting beyond that sector of the country [in this case, Zaire] that faces West and into the lives of the 95 percent or so of its residents who ordinarily live out of the sight of visitors. Better yet, he does this without falling into the hard-to-avoid role of slumming white man, or angel of mercy."

Answering the question "What is the most pressing problem in the world today?," Shoumatoff told *CA:* "Eliminating what I call *la difference*—between white and black, rich and poor, the United States and the rest of the world, and achieving an equitable sharing of the world's resources and opportunities."

BIOGRAPHICAL/CRITICAL SOURCES:

PERIODICALS

Best Sellers, July, 1982.
Los Angeles Times Book Review, July 11, 1982; October 20, 1985, p. 11; December 11, 1988, p. 4; April 8, 1990, p. 10; August 26, 1990, p. 2; September 16, 1990, p. 10.
Newsweek, September 3, 1990, p. 62.
New York Review of Books, March 28, 1991, p. 39.
New York Times, July 2, 1985; December 3, 1988; August 14, 1990.
New York Times Book Review, July 29, 1979; November 2, 1980; July 28, 1985, p. 11; March 16, 1986, p. 10; January 22, 1989, p. 23; April 15, 1990, p. 22; August 19, 1990, p. 7; September 9, 1990, p. 42.
Publishers Weekly, March 28, 1986, p. 41.
Sewanee Review, October 1992, p. 715.
Spectator, September 28, 1991, p. 40.
Time, November 21, 1988, p. 134.
Times Literary Supplement, May 16, 1980; August 21, 1987, p. 895; July 5, 1991, p. 18.
Tribune Books (Chicago), April 22, 1990, p. 5; September 23, 1990, p. 6.
Washington Post, December 5, 1978; June 25, 1982; March 18, 1986.
Washington Post Book World, July 28, 1985, p. 3; August 12, 1990, p. 1; May 19, 1991, p. 12.

—Sketch by Heather Aronson

SILVERLOCK, Anne
See TITCHENER, Louise

*   *   *

SILVERWOOD, Jane
See TITCHENER, Louise

*   *   *

SIMPSON, John (Andrew) 1953-

PERSONAL: Born October 13, 1953, in Cheltenham, Gloucestershire, England; son of Robert Morris (in the Foreign Office) and Joan Margaret (a teacher; maiden name, Sersale) Simpson; married Hilary Croxford (a local government officer), September 25, 1976; children: Katharine Jane; Eleanor Grace. *Education:* University of York, B.A., 1975; University of Reading, M.A., 1976.

ADDRESSES: Home—36 Kennett Rd., Headington, Oxford OX3 7BJ, England. *Office—Oxford English Dictionary,* Oxford University Press, Walton St., Oxford, England.

CAREER: Oxford English Dictionaries, Oxford University Press, Oxford, England, editorial assistant, 1976-78, assistant editor, 1978-81, senior editor, 1982-86, co-editor, 1986-93, chief editor, *Oxford English Dictionary,* 1993—. Visiting assistant professor at University of Waterloo, autumn, 1985. Fellow, Kellogg College, Oxford, 1991—. Faculty member, English University of Oxford, 1993—.

WRITINGS:

(Senior editor) *Supplement to the Oxford English Dictionary,* Oxford University Press (Oxford, England), Volume 3, 1982, Volume 4, 1986.
(Co-editor) *The Oxford English Dictionary,* 2nd edition, Oxford University Press, 1989.
(Editor) *The Concise Oxford Dictionary of Proverbs,* Oxford University Press, 1982, 2nd edition, 1992.
(Co-editor) *The Oxford Dictionary of Modern Slang,* Oxford University Press, 1992.
(Editor) *The Oxford English Dictionary Additions,* Volumes 1 and 2, Oxford University Press, 1993.

Contributor to scholarly journals.

SIDELIGHTS: John Simpson told *CA:* "*The New Oxford English Dictionary* (OED) project was established to take the OED (published 1884-1928) out of the nineteenth century and into the twenty-first by making the dictionary available on computer (on-line and on CD-ROM), enabling it to be revised and continually updated as the historical dictionary of record for the English language in Britain, America, and throughout the world.

"I came to lexicography through studying English literature and philology, especially that of the medieval period. But much of the major lexicographical work in this early period of the language was at the time being undertaken in the United States and Canada, and (along with working on neologisms for the Supplement to the OED) I soon found myself applying the same analytical and historical techniques to modern-day English. Interestingly, the historical techniques employed to define and describe the early stages of the language—that is, recording instances of actual usage as it appears in printed and written documents—are not dissimilar to those used to portray the language of today.

"It is often held that in a multi-media environment, the influence of the book as a touchstone of our culture is diminishing. Whatever the truth of that, the capacity of the written word to adapt to the times is as strong as ever. The book may not be such a formal document as it used to be, but from the standpoint of the lexicographer the enormous variety of languages portrayed in books, magazines, and newspapers mirrors very closely that actually used in the real world. An informal neologism is soon picked up by the popular press of today—far more quickly, in fact, that it was in the days of the medieval scribe, when parchment was a precious resource unsuitable for the retailing of colloquial tittle-tattle.

"The lexicographer's problem today lies in the proliferation of text available for analysis, much of it in electronic form. In the reasonably near future, we can look forward to many of the original manuscript sources being accessible in bitmapped and searchable form across the Internet. But amongst all of this data, it is still the editor's task to provide a careful summary of the facts, acting as an intermediary between documentation of the language and the scholarly and reading public curious about the history and meaning of words."

*   *   *

SISSON, C(harles) H(ubert) 1914-

PERSONAL: Born April 22, 1914, in Bristol, England; son of Richard Percy and Ellen Minnie (Worlock) Sisson; married Nora Gilbertson, 1937; children: Janet, Hilary. *Education:* University of Bristol, B.A., 1934; graduate study at University of Berlin and University of Freiburg, 1934-35, and the Sorbonne, University of Paris, 1935-36.

ADDRESSES: Home—Moorfield Cottage, The Hill, Langport, Somerset TA10 9PU, England.

CAREER: Ministry of Labour/Department of Employment, London, England, assistant principal, 1936-42, principal, 1945-53, assistant secretary, 1953-62, undersecretary and director of Establishments/Ministry of Labour, 1962-68, assistant undersecretary of state, 1968-71, director of Occupational Safety and Health, 1971-73. *Military service:* British Army, Intelligence Corps, 1942-45; served in the ranks, mainly in India; became sergeant.

AWARDS, HONORS: Senior Simon research fellow, University of Manchester, beginning 1956; Fellow of the Royal Society of London, 1975; D.Litt., University of Bristol, 1980; Companion of Honour, 1993.

WRITINGS:

POETRY

Poems, Peter Russell, 1959.
Twenty-one Poems, privately printed, 1960.
The London Zoo, Abelard-Schuman (New York, NY), 1961.
Numbers, Methuen (New York, NY), 1965.
The Discarnation: Or, How the Flesh Became Word and Dwelt Among Us, privately printed, 1967.
Metamorphoses, Methuen, 1968.
Roman Poems, privately printed, 1968.
In the Trojan Ditch: Collected Poems and Selected Translations, Carcanet, 1974.
The Corridor, Mandeville Press, 1975.
Anchises, Carcanet, 1976.
Exactions, Carcanet, 1980.
Selected Poems, Carcanet, 1981.
Night Thoughts and Other Poems, illustrated by Annie Newnham, Inky Parrot Press, 1983.
Collected Poems, 1943-1983, Carcanet, 1984.
God Bless Karl Marx! Carcanet, 1987.
Antidotes, Carcanet, 1991.
Nine Sonnets, Greville Press, 1991.
The Pattern, Enitharmon, 1993.
What and Who, Carcanet, 1994.

NOVELS

An Asiatic Romance, Gaberbocchus, 1953.
Christopher Homm, Methuen, 1965.

NONFICTION

The Spirit of British Administration and Some European Comparisons, Faber & Faber, Inc. (London), 1959, 2nd edition, 1966.
Art and Action (essays), Methuen, 1965.
Essays, privately printed, 1967.
English Poetry, 1900-1950: An Assessment, Hart-Davis, 1971, Carcanet, 1981.
The Case of Walter Bagehot, Faber & Faber Inc., 1972.
David Hume, Ramsay Head Press, 1976.
The English Sermon: An Anthology, Volume 2, Carcanet, 1976.

The Avoidance of Literature: Collected Essays, Carcanet, 1978.
Anglican Essays, Carcanet, 1983.
The Poet and the Translator (Jackson Knight Memorial Lecture), University of Exeter, 1985.
On the Look-Out: A Partial Autobiography, Carcanet, 1989.
In Two Minds: Guesses at Other Writers, Carcanet, 1990.
English Perspectives: Essays on Liberty and Government, Carcanet, 1992.
Is There a Church of England?, Carcanet, 1993.

TRANSLATOR

Versions and Perversions of Heine, Gaberbocchus, 1955.
The Poetry of Catullus, MacGibbon & Kee, 1966, Orion (Columbus, OH), 1967.
The Poetic Art: A Translation of Horace's "Ars Poetica," Carcanet, 1975.
Lucretius, *De Rerum Natura: The Poem on Nature,* Carcanet, 1976.
Jean de La Fontaine, *Some Tales,* Carcanet, 1979.
Dante Alighieri, *The Divine Comedy,* Carcanet, 1980, Regnery Gateway, 1981, Oxford University Press (New York City, NY), 1993.
The Song of Roland, Carcanet, 1983.
Joachim du Bellay, *The Regrets,* Carcanet, 1984.
Virgil, *The Aeneid,* Carcanet, 1986.
Jean Racine, *Britannicus, Phaedra, Athaliah,* Oxford University Press, 1987.

EDITOR

David Wright, *South African Album* (poems), Philip Publisher (Cape Town, South Africa), 1976.
Jonathan Swift, *Selected Poems,* Carcanet, 1977.
Thomas Hardy, *Jude the Obscure,* Penguin (New York, NY), 1979.
Philip Mairet, *Autobiographical and Other Papers,* Carcanet, 1981.
Christina Rossetti, *Selected Poems,* Carcanet, 1984.
Jeremy Taylor, *Selected Writings,* Carcanet, 1990.

OTHER

Also contributor to *New English Weekly,* 1937-49, *X,* 1960-62, *Poetry Nation* and *Poetry Nation Review,* 1973—, *Times Literary Supplement,* 1975—, and *Agenda,* 1979—. Co-editor, *Poetry Nation Review,* 1976-84.

SIDELIGHTS: C. H. Sisson did not begin to publish his poetry until he was well into middle-age. He once told *CA:* "I wrote verse as a child and as an adolescent; I gave it up; I started again when I was a soldier during the war; gave it up again; started again; have often resolved to give it up but never quite succeeded." Until his retirement, Sisson was employed as a civil servant in the Ministry of Labor. "It has never occurred to me," he maintains, "that

I could earn my living by writing, or that it would be desirable to put myself in a position where I had to do so. Most of my life has been spent in practical affairs, and in a sense all my writing has been occasional." Sisson believes that "ideally, one should speak, whether in prose or verse, because one has something to say, and not otherwise."

Upon publication of Sisson's *Collected Poems, 1943-1983,* Cairns Craig noted in the *Times Literary Supplement* that Sisson "is not a comfortable writer. His poetry is brusque, edgy, assertive and aggressive; it is self-lacerating, continually unbuttoning the pretensions of humanity to display the vile body underneath." Craig recognized two schools of thought in the consideration of Sisson's poetry: "There are those who see in Sisson's commitment to the poetic craft, and in his unrelenting campaign against humanity's self-delusions, a recovery of values which had been almost swept aside in an uncritical acceptance of contemporaneity both poetic and moral. . . . On the other side, however, there are those who see in Sisson only the symptom of a period of reaction, his values nostalgic, his stance an elitist denial of common humanity."

Dominic Hibberd observed in the *Times Literary Supplement* that "there can be few collections of poems about old age as impressive as *God Bless Karl Marx!,*" published when the author was seventy-three. In this volume, Hibberd continued, "age has brought a change of focus though not of personality. . . . Sisson's outlook is bleak, but he resists the suggestion that he is a despairer, saying rather that he is an observer of things which other people may or may not agree to be there."

BIOGRAPHICAL/CRITICAL SOURCES:

BOOKS

Contemporary Literary Criticism, Volume 8, Gale, 1978.
Contemporary Authors Autobiography Series, Volume 3, Gale, 1986.
Dictionary of Literary Biography, Volume 27: *Poets of Great Britain and Ireland, 1945-1960,* Gale, 1984.

PERIODICALS

Agenda, summer-autumn, 1970; autumn-winter, 1970, pp. 207-214; autumn, 1974, pp. 45-49; autumn, 1975, pp. 5-17.
Booklist, March 15, 1985, p. 1032.
Books and Bookmen, July, 1984, p. 30; October, 1984, p. 37.
British Book News, April, 1981, p. 245; May, 1982, p. 317; June, 1982, p. 340; July, 1982, p. 399; September, 1983, p. 544; October, 1984, p. 624; August, 1987, p. 528.
Chicago Tribune, April 1, 1987.
Choice, July, 1981, p. 1549; February, 1985, p. 819.
Christian Science Monitor, November 7, 1984, p. 76.

Church History, December, 1984, p. 570.
Critical Quarterly, autumn, 1979, pp. 73-81.
Dalhousie Review, spring, 1990, p. 136.
Encounter, September, 1984, p. 40; November, 1989, p. 59.
Hudson Review, spring, 1988, p. 231.
Kirkus Reviews, February 1, 1985, p. 109.
Library Journal, May 15, 1981, p. 1082; April 15, 1985, p. 110.
Listener, May 9, 1974; June 14, 1984, p. 26; December 18, 1986, p. 50.
London Magazine, October-November, 1974.
London Review of Books, April 5, 1984, p. 18; September 20, 1984, p. 16; October 11, 1990, p. 22; May 23, 1991, p. 10.
New Statesman, April 22, 1977; January 1, 1982, p. 18.
New Statesman and Society, October 13, 1989, p. 32; March 22, 1991, p. 45.
New York Times Book Review, December 18, 1977; April 27, 1980; July 15, 1984, p. 13; May 5, 1985, p. 31.
Observer, May 5, 1974; December 2, 1984, p. 19.
Parnassus, spring, 1982, p. 75.
Publisher's Weekly, April 10, 1981, p. 68; August 3, 1984, p. 57; February 8, 1985, p. 71.
Punch, March 27, 1968.
Spectator, November 28, 1981, p. 22; February 7, 1987, p. 33; November 28, 1987, p. 35; March 26, 1988, p. 32; October 14, 1989, p. 36; December 2, 1989, p. 39; April 20, 1991, p. 33; April 23, 1994, p. 41.
Times (London), March 20, 1980; July 26, 1984; October 24, 1986; November 29, 1986; January 7, 1988; June 13, 1991; June 20, 1994.
Times Educational Supplement, August 13, 1982, p. 26.
Times Literary Supplement, February 15, 1968; November 29, 1974; January 28, 1977; July 18, 1980; September 26, 1980; August 14, 1981; April 23, 1982, p. 457; February 17, 1984; October 26, 1984, p. 1210; January 8, 1988, p. 39; February 26, 1988; October 6, 1989, p. 1091.
Times Saturday Review, November 30, 1991.
Washington Post Book World, August 4, 1985, p. 9.

*   *   *

SITARZ, Paula (Gaj) 1955-

PERSONAL: Born May 25, 1955, in New Bedford, MA; daughter of Stanley (a business executive) and Pauline (a secretary; maiden name, Rocha) Gaj; married Michael James Sitarz (a business executive), August 26, 1978; children: Andrew Michael, Kate Elizabeth. *Education:* Smith College, B.A. (cum laude), 1977; Simmons College, M.S., 1978.

ADDRESSES: Home and office—25 Stratford Dr., North Dartmouth, MA 02747.

CAREER: Thomas Crane Public Library, Quincy, MA, children's librarian and producer of weekly children's programs for local cable television channel, 1978-84; freelance writer and storyteller, 1984—. Director of Reader's Theater Workshop at Thomas Crane Public Library, summer, 1985.

MEMBER: New England Library Association, Massachusetts Library Association, Beta Phi Mu.

WRITINGS:

Picture Book Story Hours: From Birthdays to Bears, Libraries Unlimited (Littleton, CO), 1987.
More Picture Book Story Hours, Libraries Unlimited, 1990.
The Curtain Rises, Betterway (Whitehall, VA), Volume 1: *A History of Theater from its Origins in Greece and Rome through the English Restoration,* 1991, Volume 2: *A History of European Theater from the Eighteenth Century to the Present,* 1993.

Reporter for *Dartmouth Chronicle,* summer, 1976. Columnist on children's books for *Bristol County Baby Journal, First Teacher,* and *South Shore Baby Journal.* Contributor of articles to *Cobblestone, South Seventeen* and *Turtle.*

WORK IN PROGRESS: The Curtain Rises: A History of the American Theater.

SIDELIGHTS: Paula Sitarz told *CA:* "I started writing when I was twelve years old and have always enjoyed nonfiction. Early breaks with *Seventeen* and *Alive!,* a stint as news editor of the Smith College newspaper, *The Sophian,* and a summer internship for a local newspaper spurred my efforts as a writer. My first two books, *Picture Book Story Hours* and *More Picture Book Story Hours,* were based on my work as a children's librarian. I wanted to provide other children's librarians and educators with literature-based program plans. *The Curtain Rises,* my three-volume history of the theater for ages ten to adult was sparked by my love of the theater and my degree in theater history. The series was ten years in the making. I enjoy writing articles as much as I do books so I am thrilled to be writing two regular columns on children's books."

*   *   *

SLOANE, Sara
    See BLOOM, Ursula (Harvey)

SPIELBERG, Peter 1929-

PERSONAL: Born July 2, 1929, in Vienna, Austria; son of Henry and Erna (Kulka) Spielberg; married Elaine Konstant (a teacher), March 31, 1956; children: Christine, Ivan. *Education:* City College (now City College of the City University of New York), B.A., 1952; New York University, M.A., 1957; University of Buffalo (now State University of New York at Buffalo), Ph.D., 1961. *Politics:* "Antiestablishmentarianism."

ADDRESSES: Office—Department of English, Brooklyn College, City University of New York, Brooklyn, NY 11210.

CAREER: University of Buffalo (now State University of New York at Buffalo), instructor in English, 1958-61; Brooklyn College of the City University of New York, Brooklyn, NY, 1961—, began as assistant professor, currently professor of English and American literature and creative writing.

MEMBER: PEN, American Civil Liberties Union.

AWARDS, HONORS: National Endowment for the Arts creative writing fellow, 1979-80; New York Foundation for the Arts fellowship in fiction, 1987.

WRITINGS:

James Joyce's Manuscripts and Letters at the University of Buffalo: A Catalogue, State University of New York Press (Albany, NY), 1962.
(With Saul Galin) *Reference Books: How to Select and Use Them,* Random House (New York City, NY), 1969.
Bedrock: A Work of Fiction Composed of Fifteen Scenes from My Life (short stories), Crossing Press (Trumansburg, NY), 1973.
Twiddledum Twaddledum (novel), Fiction Collective (Brooklyn, NY), 1974.
The Hermetic Whore (short stories), Fiction Collective, 1977.
(Editor with Jonathan Baumbach) *Statements 2: New Fiction* (anthology), with introduction by Robert Coover, Fiction Collective, 1977.
Crash-Landing (novel), Fiction Collective, 1985.
Hearsay (novel), Fiction Collective Two, 1992.

Contributor to *Modern Occasions,* edited by Philip Rahv, Farrar Straus, 1966, *Statements 1: New Fiction,* Braziller, 1975, and *American Made,* edited by Mark Leyner and others, Fiction Collective, 1986.

WORK IN PROGRESS: Cry Wolf, a novel.

SIDELIGHTS: Nightmarish, shocking, surrealistic—these are a few of the words reviewers have used to describe novelist and short story writer Peter Spielberg's "fiction of depression." Characterized by themes of loneliness and alienation, as well as by the presence of a macabre blend of humor and biting satire, his works seek to expose and attack ridiculous and hypocritical facets of contemporary life. The overall mood the author evokes has often been compared to that found in the works of Franz Kafka.

Spielberg's first work of fiction, a collection of "fifteen scenes from my life" entitled *Bedrock,* prompted C. Webster Wheelock of *Fiction International* to remark: "Here is a writer of wit, erudition, precision, and large imagination . . . [His book is] nothing if not original—in voice, tone, and subject. . . . Spielberg's strength lies in his use of an absolutely lucid, tensile prose style—none of the gadgets or gimmickry of self-indulgent experimentalism here—for bold and sometimes brilliant flights of imagination." The *West Coast Review*'s Barbara McDaniel reports that *Bedrock* "has a way to disturb everyone. . . . The author freezes his unnamed, utterly flat characters in pointed, highly compressed descriptions that convey the futility and emptiness of existence. Such symbolic pictures, and incidents heightened by their repetition from different vantage points or with details slightly changed, characterize Spielberg's technique. He also interlaces nightmares and fantasies, the credible and the surrealistic, the mundane and the startling, fortunately relieving his depressing tone somewhat by diverting some attention to his devices. . . . Separately *Bedrock*'s 'scenes' are often impressive: together they are dizzying, sometimes overwhelming. But there is no question of Spielberg's talent for fiction."

Twiddledum Twaddledum, Spielberg's first published novel, is more or less a parody of the traditional Bildungsroman or "formation novel." By means of a somewhat loosely developed plot, it traces the farcical adventures of a Viennese Jewish boy who is spirited away to a new home in the United States in order to escape from the Nazis. Much of the book's "action" stems from the protagonist's bizarre fantasies, a device Spielberg uses to draw attention to the young man's almost total lack of connection to the real world.

Beyond a simple plot synopsis, however, critics begin to disagree somewhat as to the point the author is trying to make during the course of his narrative. Christopher Lehmann-Haupt, for example, speculates that Spielberg is demonstrating the life-long effects a traumatic childhood can have on a person despite that person's frantic attempts to overcome the past—a premise the reviewer finds "not quite interesting enough to justify the length to which Mr. Spielberg goes to illustrate it." The *New Republic*'s Irving Malin sees the book as "a comedy directed against [the notion of] 'progress'," but, unlike Lehmann-Haupt, he believes that the "shrewd flexibility" of Spielberg's elliptical approach "makes [*Twiddledum Twaddledum*] hard to resist." In a *Contemporary Literature* review, Larry McCaf-

fery describes Spielberg's book as a symbolic portrayal of "a victim who searches for love, beauty, and sexual fulfillment but accepts his punishment and constant rejections without question"; according to McCaffery, such a painful, futile search for happiness makes for a "grimly funny, often frightening, but beautifully written novel." Finally, the *Carolina Quarterly*'s John Agar, who views *Twiddledum Twaddledum* as an examination of "opposites which are never reconciled and always destructive," remarks that it is rare to encounter "such a powerfully negative statement in fiction. . . . The energy of Spielberg's language and of his cynicism makes *Twiddledum Twaddledum* a bracing, exciting novel."

Both Patricia Meyer Spacks of the *Yale Review* and Michael Mewshaw of the *New York Times Book Review* seem to have difficulty finding much meaning at all in *Twiddledum Twaddledum.* Though Spacks admits that the book has its share of "high-spirited moments," she believes that implying life has no "ultimate meaning" is too "easy" a message. Explains the reviewer: "To assert that events contain no meaning is infinitely simpler than to discover what meaning they offer. Not that Spielberg's book lacks discipline: its careful pattern of self-mirroring happenings manifests intricate planning. But the patterning is verbal rather than substantial, and so are the satisfactions the book supplies. . . . Spielberg at his best vividly evokes the mood and the limited possible alternatives to it. But he accomplishes little more." Mewshaw reports having trouble "distinguishing the jokes from the serious sections, since Spielberg can't decide whether to be realistic or surrealistic, whether to write a picaresque or a Bildungsroman." Noting that the novel "might still have survived had the author possessed the style or technical virtuosity to compensate for the absence of conventional narrative, consistency in point of view and structural coherence," Mewshaw concludes instead that "Spielberg loses control of the material and lets it slip into sloughs of sophomoric humor, pointless anecdotes and passages that sound more self-parodic than satirical."

The Hermetic Whore, Spielberg's second short story collection, strikes reviewer McCaffery as "more relaxed and playful" than the author's previous works. Furthermore, he states in the *American Review,* "[it] also demonstrates a wider range of his talents. . . . While [Spielberg] occasionally returns to the somber tone and obsessional motifs of his first two books . . . , the stories here tend to be more broadly comic and topical. . . . [He] manages to construct a world in his stories which is never safe or bland but which somehow seems familiar. . . . Relying on a deadpan tone and familiar literary conventions, [the author] catches the reader off guard by introducing material which is absurd or ridiculous." The final product, says McCaffery, "offers the sorts of challenges and rewards that the best contemporary innovative fiction often provides." "Most of the stories," a *Best Sellers* critic notes, "are startling, offbeat, and interesting. . . . The irony, wit, and satire [they contain] will provoke laughter and outrage." Though warning readers they may find some of Spielberg's material "shocking" and "crude," the critic emphasizes that his stories are worth reading, for they "consistently puncture hypocrisy, expose insincerity and nonsense, and make us think about where we may be headed as individuals in an increasingly irrational society devoid of deep and loving relationships."

McDaniel, commenting once again in the *West Coast Review,* echoes the views of both McCaffery and the *Best Sellers*' critic. She asserts that the variety of stories contained in *The Hermetic Whore* make it a good introduction to Spielberg's work, and that the collection "demonstrates a versatility in style and a maturity in vision that should dispel most of the uncertainty about his capability as a writer." McDaniel admits that certain stories "will cause some readers to find his work more offensive than funny" and that the book's "serious undertone will make others complain again that Spielberg is depressing." But, like McCaffery, she believes Spielberg has tempered the "pain or shock in his new stories" with elements of "wit or irony (most often both)." Concludes the reviewer: "At base Spielberg is always questioning the value and quality of existence; always, at the same time, questioning the role of the artist, the writer, himself. . . . Taking nothing (and everything) seriously, Peter Spielberg comprehends, yet laughs at life and, graciously, at how he functions in it. The stories of *The Hermetic Whore* beg to be reread, shared and compared."

Crash-Landing, Spielberg's second novel, deals with the breakup of protagonist and first-person narrator Chuck Burg's marriage. The opening scene finds Burg among a group of recently divorced men aboard a chartered airplane destined for a week-long retreat at the "Human Rehabilitation Center" in France. The story unfolds in a series of flashbacks, a retrogression of events detailing his wife securing the divorce, their futile bouts of marriage counseling, his wife's unfaithfulness, the Burgs' marriage and courtship—even then foreshadowed by ultimate failure—and culminating with their first meeting, the two attracted by their shared quest to be perceived as cultured. A *Booklist* contributor remarks that Spielberg's "reverse-narrative technique . . . gives the novel a bright and unpredictable energy," and a *Publishers Weekly* critic states: "Alternately full of pathos and dark comedy, the story is effective in depicting Chuck's anguish."

However, many of the same elements reviewers lauded in discussing Spielberg's earlier books—his flat, alienated characters and bleak tone, for instance—have, in the case of *Crash-Landing,* been perceived as weaknesses. Carolyn

See, reviewing *Crash-Landing* in the *Los Angeles Times,* asserts, "It's not simply that it's a 'bad' book, but that it doesn't claim to be anything else. Any real attempt at characterization, at a 'story,' at making the character empathetic or lovable in any way, would be absolutely antithetical to the purpose here. [It] would cease to be avant-garde." Robert P. Mills, reviewing *Crash-Landing* in the *New York Times Book Review,* describes the book as "basically plotless" and opines that "despite the occasional felicitous phrase, thumbnail characterizations of an interesting character and insightful look at dismal circumstances, the reader is not convinced that any of this is significant."

BIOGRAPHICAL/CRITICAL SOURCES:

BOOKS

Contemporary Literary Criticism, Volume 6, Gale, 1976.

PERIODICALS

American Book Review, April, 1978.
Best Sellers, November, 1977.
Booklist, December 15, 1984.
Carolina Quarterly, winter, 1975.
Contemporary Literature, winter, 1977-78.
Fiction International, December, 1974.
Los Angeles Times, February 25, 1985.
Los Angeles Times Book Review, March 31, 1985.
Nation, December 7, 1974.
New Republic, October 19, 1974.
New York Times, October 17, 1974.
New York Times Book Review, October 13, 1974.
Publishers Weekly, February, 1985.
West Coast Review, February, 1976; January, 1978.
Yale Review, summer, 1975.

*   *   *

STAPP, William B. 1929-

PERSONAL: Born June 17, 1929, in Cleveland, OH; son of Philip B. (a businessman) and Sally (Clapp) Stapp; married Gloria Duwe, August 13, 1955; children: Deborah, Richard, David. *Education:* University of Michigan, B.A., 1951, M.A., 1958, Ph.D., 1963.

ADDRESSES: Home—2050 Delaware, Ann Arbor, MI 48103. *Office*—School of Natural Resources, University of Michigan, Ann Arbor, MI 48109.

CAREER: Cranbrook School, Bloomfield Hills, MI, science instructor, 1951-52, biology instructor, 1954-58; Aullwood Audubon Center, Dayton, OH, field naturalist, 1958-59; University of Michigan, Ann Arbor, instructor, 1959-61, lecturer in conservation, 1963-64, associate professor of resource planning and conservation, 1966-71, professor of natural resources, 1971—, chairman of environmental education and outdoor recreation program, 1971-74, chairman of behavior and environmental program, 1976—. Summer teaching positions include instructor, National Audubon Camp of Maine, 1955-56, and National Audubon Camp of Wisconsin, 1957-58; instructor in ecology, Miami University (Oxford, OH), 1959-63; visiting professor at Eastern Michigan University, 1963-65, and Western Washington University, spring, 1978. Staff member of the Arctic Exploration of Greenland and the Northwest Passage on the World Discover Society Expedition, 1986-87.

Member of advisory committees and boards of directors of and consultant to numerous international, national, state, and local government agencies and private environmental organizations, including governor's committee on natural beauty and conservation, Lansing, MI, 1965-66; conservation committee, Michigan Department of Public Instruction, 1965-68; Gill Institute of Environmental Studies, 1970-73; U.S. Department of Health, Education, and Welfare, 1970-75; National Environmental Education Committee, 1973, United Nations Education, Scientific, and Cultural Organization (UNESCO), 1974-76, National Leadership Conference on Environmental Education, 1978, International Union of Conservation of Nature and Natural Resources, 1979, United Nations Environment Programme (UNEP), 1985, Project Planet Rescue, 1991, Global Rivers Environmental Education Network (GREEN), 1991—, and National Consortium of Environmental Education and Training, 1993. *Military service:* U.S. Marine Corps, educational services, 1952-54.

MEMBER: International Union for the Conservation of Natural Resources, North American Association for Environmental Education (president, 1984-85), American Society for Ecology Education (director of educational affairs, 1972-82), National Association of Interpretive Naturalists (member of board of directors, 1966-68; vice-president, 1970-71), American Nature Study Society (vice-president, 1966-67; president, 1969-70), American Association for the Advancement of Science, National Association of Environmental Education (member of board of directors, 1977-83; president, 1983), Michigan Association of Conservation Ecologists, Michigan United Conservation Club (member of advisory board, 1972-74), Michigan Audubon Society (member of board of directors, 1967-69), Washtenaw Land Conservancy (member of board of directors, 1972-74), Citizens' Association for Area Planning (Ann Arbor; member of executive board, 1966-68; president, 1968-70), Sigma Xi, Phi Delta Kappa.

AWARDS, HONORS: Samuel Trask Dana Award in Conservation, 1962; outstanding young man of America award, 1964; conservation educator of the year award from State of Michigan, 1966; Ford Foundation grant to study conservation for the urbanite, 1968-70; certificate of merit for serving as president of the American Nature Study Society, 1969; Key Man Award, National Conservation Education Association, 1972; American Men of Science award, 1972; special recognition awards, 1974 and 1978, both from Michigan Environmental Health Association; Lorado Taft Special Recognition Award, 1977, for furthering environmental education internationally; award for international leadership in environmental education, 1978, and certificate of merit award, 1981, both from National Association of Environmental Education; Appreciation Award, University of Michigan Alumni Association, 1980; Fulbright senior scholar award, Australian-American Educational Foundation, 1982; named honorary life member of New South Wales Environmental Education Association, Australia, 1983; certificates of appreciation, 1983 and 1984, for services rendered to the North American Association for Environmental Education; certificate of outstanding service to Partners for Excellence Program, Ann Arbor Board of Education, 1985; certificate of merit, Ecology Center of Ann Arbor, 1986, for "Thinking Internationally and Acting Locally"; Distinguished Service Award for Environmental Education, North American Association for Environmental Education, 1987; Amoco Foundation Outstanding Teaching Award of the University of Michigan in recognition of contributions to undergraduate education, 1987; Walter Jeskie Award for Outstanding Contribution to the Field of Environmental Education, 1988; American Men and Women of Science Award, 1988; Thurnau Professorship for Outstanding Contribution to Undergraduate Education, 1988, 1989, 1990, from University of Michigan; named Environmental Educator of the Year in the state of Michigan, Michigan Alliance for Environmental and Outdoor Education, 1989; Partners for Excellence Program Award, Ann Arbor Public Schools, 1989-90 and 1990-91; Fulbright Senior Scholar Award, Australian-American Educational Foundation, 1990; Environmental Education Achievement Award for Outstanding Contribution to the Promotion of Environmental Education in Queensland, Australia, Australian Associations for Environmental Education, 1990; Science and Technology Quest Award, Michigan Technology Council, 1990, for the Global Rivers Environmental Education Network (GREEN), certificate of appreciation in honor of outstanding contribution in pursuit of creative and critical thinking through application of scientific skills in furthering education in the State of Michigan, from Governor James J. Blanchard, 1990; Environmental Achievement Award, National Environmental Awards Council of

Renew America, 1990, for GREEN; Fund United Nations Environment 500 Award, United Nations Environment Program, Nairobi, Kenya, 1990, for GREEN; award for contribution to environmental education in Queensland, Australia, 1990; International Award for the Continued Support and Contributions to Environmental Education in Australia, Department of Education, Australia, 1991; National Conservation Achievement Award in Education, National Wildlife Federation, 1991; Conservationist of the Year, Detroit Audubon Society, 1991, for GREEN and the Rouge River Program; named United States/United Nations Environment 500 Environmental Achiever, United States Committee for the United Nations Environment Program, 1991, for GREEN; United States National Stream and Wetland Protection award winner, Renew America, 1991, for GREEN; Environment and Conservation Challenge Award from the President of the United States, 1991, for GREEN; Environmental Education for Global Responsibility Award, Ohio Environmental Education Association, 1992; special recognition from Partners for Excellence Program, 1992; named honorary professor of Australian environmental studies, Griffith University (Brisbane, Australia), 1992; environmental education award from the State of Michigan, 1992; special tribute from the Eighty-Sixth Legislature of the State of Michigan, 1992, for GREEN; United States Environmental Protection Agency Administrator's Award for recognition of excellence in effort and significant contributions to environmental improvement through pollution prevention, 1992.

WRITINGS:

Integrating Conservation and Outdoor Education into the Curriculum: K-12, Burgess (Minneapolis, MN), 1965.

(Editor) *Environmental Projects,* Boy Scouts of America, 1971.

(Editor with James Swan) *Environment and the Citizen: Opportunities for Effective Action,* fourteen volumes, University of Michigan Press (Ann Arbor, MI), 1972.

Developing an Environmental Education Program: K-12, Michigan Environmental Education Association, 1972.

(Editor with Swan, and contributor) *Environmental Education: Strategies toward a More Livable Future,* Sage Publications (Beverly Hills, CA), 1974.

(With Mary Dawn Liston) *Environmental Education Instructional Materials,* Gale (Detroit, MI), 1974.

(Editor with Dorothy Cox) *Environmental Education Activity Manuals,* six volumes, Thomson-Shore (Dexter, MI), 1974, 3rd edition, 1981.

(With L. A. Bertrand and B. Ray Horn) *Environmental Education Needs and Priorities: A World Survey,* United Nations Educational, Scientific, and Cultural Organization (Paris, France), 1975.

(Editor with Lori Mann) *Environmental Education Teaching Activities for Global Education,* Education Resources Information Center (Columbus, OH), 1983.

(Editor with Margaret Cowan, and contributor) *International Case Studies in Environmental Education,* Educational Resources Information Center, 1983.

(Editor with Cox) *Proceedings of the 13th Annual Conference of the North American Association for Environmental Education,* Education Resources Information Center, 1986.

(With Martha Monroe) *An Action Curriculum toward Resolving Hazardous Materials Issues,* Ohio Environmental Protection Agency, 1988.

(With Mark Mitchell) *Field Manual for Water Quality Monitoring: An Environmental Education Program for Schools,* Thomson-Shore, 1987, sixth edition, 1993.

(With Jim Bull and others) *Education in Action: Community Problem Solving for Schools,* Thomson-Shore, 1988.

(With Mitchell and Kevin Bixby) *Manual de Campo de Projects del Rio: Una guia para moniorear la calidad del aqua en Rio Bravo,* Rosita Press (Las Cruces, NM), 1992.

OTHER

Also author of *Michigan's Environmental Future: A Master Plan for Environmental Education,* 1973. Contributor to books, including *Outdoor Laboratories,* National Audubon Society, 1968; *What Makes Education Environmental?,* Data Courier, 1975, *International Actions Research Case Studies Manual,* edited by Ortrum Zuber-Skerritt, Center for the Advancement of Learning and Teaching, Queensland, Australia, 1991; and *The New Explorers Program,* Weldon Owen, 1992. Author of numerous audiovisual programs including films, videos, and filmstrips. Contributor of articles and reviews to professional journals, including *Environment and Behavior, Science Teacher, American Biology Teacher,* and *National Audubon Magazine.* Consulting editor, *Journal of Environmental Education,* 1969, Cornet Instructional Films, 1971, and *Journal of Environmental Education,* 1985-87 and 1991; advisory editor, *Environmental Conservation,* 1985-87.

*   *   *

STAVROU, Theofanis G(eorge) 1934-

PERSONAL: Born July 12, 1934, in Dhiorios, Cyprus; son of George (a merchant) and Olga (Charalambous) Stavrou; married Freda Lorene Condon, 1955; children: Gregory, Niki Lynn, Christo Michael. *Education:* Indiana

University, M.A., 1957, Ph.D., 1961. *Religion:* Greek Orthodox.

ADDRESSES: Home—5433 Clinton Ave. S., Minneapolis, MN 55419. *Office*—Department of History, University of Minnesota, Minneapolis, MN 55455.

CAREER: University of Minnesota, Minneapolis, instructor, 1961, assistant professor, 1961-64, associate professor, 1964-70, professor of Russian and Near Eastern history, 1970—. Administrator of Minnesota Student Project for Amity among Nations (SPAN), 1964—. Consultant to International Research and Exchanges Board.

MEMBER: American History Association, American Association for the Advancement of Slavic Studies, Society for Cyprus Studies, Institute for Balkan Studies.

AWARDS, HONORS: McKnight Foundation Humanities Award, 1962, for *Russian Interests in Palestine, 1882-1914: A Study in Religious and Educational Enterprise;* travel and research grant for Leningrad, Inter-University cultural exchange program, 1963-64; travel and research grant, American Council of Learned Societies, 1966, for the Soviet Union and Bulgaria, and 1968, for the Soviet Union and the Near East.

WRITINGS:

Russian Interests in Palestine, 1882-1914: A Study in Religious and Educational Enterprise, Institute for Balkan Studies, 1963.

(Editor) *Russia under the Last Tsar,* University of Minnesota Press (Minneapolis), 1969.

(Editor) Alexander Solzhenitsyn, *A Lenten Letter to Patriarch Pimen,* Burgess Publishing (Minneapolis), 1972.

(With Wassilij Alexeev) *The Great Revival: The Russian Orthodox Church during the German Occupation,* Burgess Publishing, 1976.

(Editor with Robert L. Nichols) *Russian Orthodoxy under the Old Regime,* University of Minnesota Press, 1978.

(Editor) *Art and Culture in Nineteenth-Century Russia,* Indiana University Press (Bloomington), 1983.

(With Constantine A. Trypanis) *Kostis Palamas: A Portrait and an Appreciation,* Nostos Books (Minneapolis), 1985.

(With Peter R. Weisensel) *Russian Travelers to the Christian East from the Twelfth to the Twentieth Century,* Slavica (Columbus, OH), 1986.

(With Louis Coutelle and David R. Weinberg) *A Greek Diptych: Dionysios Solomos and Alexandros Papadiamantis,* Nostros Books, 1986.

(Editor with Dimitri Constas) *Greece Prepares for the Twenty-First Century,* Johns Hopkins University Press (Baltimore, MD), 1994.

Also contributor to *Religious and Ethical Encyclopedia,* [Greece]. Contributor to periodicals, including *Slavic Review, Balkan Studies, American Historical Review,* and *Middle East Journal.*

WORK IN PROGRESS: Russian Near Eastern Cultural Relations in the Nineteenth Century; translating *Travels to Russia,* by Nikos Kazantzakis; establishing an international study retreat center on Cyprus.

SIDELIGHTS: For more than a decade, Theofanis G. Stavrou traveled annually to the former Soviet Union, and he has made extensive trips through the Near East.*

*   *   *

STEPHENS, C(harles) Ralph   1943-

PERSONAL: Born January 14, 1943, in Nashville, TN; son of Charles Ralph and Eloise (Montgomery) Stephens; married Sandra Bell, January 15, 1960 (divorced, 1968); married Jennifer Burdick, March 4, 1972 (divorced, 1981); married Martha P. Schuberth (in management), May 17, 1986; children: (first marriage) Chuck; (second marriage) Matt, Kate. *Education:* David Lipscomb College, B.A., 1962; George Peabody College (now Vanderbilt University), M.A., 1963; University of Maryland at College Park, Ph.D., 1985.

ADDRESSES: Home—506 Woodlawn Rd., Baltimore, MD 21210. *Office*—Department of English, Essex Community College, 7201 Rossville Blvd., Baltimore, MD 21237.

CAREER: David Lipscomb College (now David Lipscomb University), Nashville, TN, instructor in English, 1962-65; Harding College (now University), Searcy, AR, assistant professor of English, 1965-67; Boston State College, Boston, MA, assistant professor of English, 1967-69; University of Maryland at College Park, part-time instructor in English, 1969-72; Essex Community College, Baltimore, MD, assistant professor, 1973-87, associate professor of English, 1987-91; professor of English and department head, 1991—.

MEMBER: Modern Language Association of America, National Council of Teachers of English, South Atlantic Modern Language Association, Society for the Study of Southern Literature, College English Association.

WRITINGS:

(Editor) *The Correspondence of Flannery O'Connor and the Brainard Cheneys,* University Press of Mississippi (Jackson, MS), 1986.

(Editor) *The Fiction of Anne Tyler* (essays), University Press of Mississippi, 1990.

(Editor with Lynda B. Salamon) *The Craft of Peter Taylor* (essays), University of Alabama (University, AL), in press.

SIDELIGHTS: C. Ralph Stephens told *CA:* "As a student at George Peabody College in Nashville, Tennessee, I became interested in the work and career of Brainard Cheney, and, later, in the role Cheney and his wife, the eminent librarian Frances Neel Cheney, played in the Southern literary community from the 1920s on. The friendship and correspondence between the Cheneys and Flannery O'Connor is but one example of the ways in which the Cheneys were involved with and influenced contemporary literary figures such as Robert Penn Warren, Allen Tate, Caroline Gordon, Donald Davidson, John Crowe Ransom, and Walter Percy."

*   *   *

STEWART, Harold Frederick 1916-
(Ern Malley, a joint pseudonym)

PERSONAL: Born December 14, 1916, in Sydney, Australia; son of Herbert (a public servant) and Muriel (Norris) Stewart. *Education:* Attended University of Sydney. *Politics:* "Anti-Politics." *Religion:* Shin Buddhist.

ADDRESSES: Home—501, Keifuku Dai-ni Manshon, Yamabana-icho Dacho 7-1, Shugakuin, Sakyo-ku, Kyoto 606, Japan.

CAREER: Poet, author, essayist, and translator. Broadcaster for Australian Broadcasting Commission, Sydney and Melbourne, Australia, during the 1940s; lecturer for Victorian Council of Adult Education, Victoria, Australia, during the 1940s and 1950s. *Military service:* Australian Army (non-combatant), 1942-46.

AWARDS, HONORS: Sydney Morning Herald prize for poetry, 1951; Australia Council grant, 1978; Senior Emeritus Writers fellow, Australia Council, 1982; Christopher Brennan Prize for Poetry, 1988.

WRITINGS:

POETRY

(With James McAuley under joint pseudonym Ern Malley) *The Darkening Ecliptic,* Reed & Harris (Adelaide, Australia), 1944, published as *Poems,* introduction by Max Harris, Lansdowne Press (Melbourne, Australia), 1961.

Phoenix Wings: Poems 1940-46, Angus & Robertson (Sydney, Australia), 1948.

Orpheus and Other Poems, Angus & Robertson, 1956.

The Exiled Immortal: A Song Cycle, Brindabella Press (Canberra, Australia), 1980.

By the Old Walls of Kyoto: A Year's Cycle of Landscape Poems with Prose Commentaries, Weatherhill (New York City), 1981.

(Under joint pseudonym Ern Malley) *Collected Poems,* Angus & Robertson (Pymble, Australia), 1993.

Also author of *New Phoenix Wings,* collected poems; *Over the Vermilion Bridge,* haiku in English; *Autumn Landscape Roll,* dramatic poem in thirty-two cantos. Contributor to periodicals, including *Hemisphere* and *Eastern Buddhist.*

TRANSLATOR

A Net of Fireflies: Japanese Haiku and Haiku Paintings, Tuttle (Rutland, VT), 1960.

A Chime of Windbells: A Year of Japanese Haiku, Tuttle, 1969.

(With Bando Shojun) *Tannisho: Passages Deploring Deviations of Faith,* Eastern Buddhist Press (Kyoto), 1980.

Also translator with Inagaki Hisao of *The Amida Sutra Mandala,* 1995.

WORK IN PROGRESS: "Prose verse that explains remote and esoteric references to the Western reader, designed to be readily understandable when read aloud to an audience without the text in front of them."

SIDELIGHTS: Harold Frederick Stewart, who also wrote under the joint pseudonym Ern Malley, has lived in Japan since the mid-1960s. Much of his work reflects his Shin Buddhist faith, and elements of Buddhist tenets permeate his poetry. *By the Old Walls of Kyoto* "is primarily an account of a journey," according to Carmen Blacker in the *Times Literary Supplement,* "but of a journey accomplished, as every pilgrimage must be, on two levels." Blacker comments that the twelve poems and companion prose exegeses follow two distinct paths: on the surface, a seasonal journey to and exploration of a dozen religious locations in Kyoto, and on a deeper level, an examination of Buddhist and Taoist metaphysics. Blacker writes: "Again and again he reminds us that the physical world is not the only reality, and, further, that this very physical world, cut off from its corresponding higher levels, becomes dead and meaningless. Our modern malady, with its loss of a spiritual centre, of purpose and meaning, recurs throughout the narrative." Blacker adds, "Only scant justice can be done in a short review to this large and remarkable book."

Ronald Dunlop notes in *Southerly* that "Stewart identifies several modes in which the poems work: narrative, descriptive, meditative, lyrical, dramatic, pastoral, elegiac, satirical." The critic adds that "the achievement of the sequence counters the view that the chief merit of his poetry is its technical refinement. However quixotic one may find Stewart's attitude to the workaday world from which the sequence steadily withdraws, there can be no doubt of his ability to probe the human condition in poetry in which his very disapproval is part of the texture." Dunlop concludes, "*By the Old Walls of Kyoto* offers rich fare both for those who repair to church for the music and for those who are drawn by the sermon."

Stewart wrote *CA:* "Last year I completed my final and culminating poetic work, entitled *Autumn Landscape-Roll,* an epic in thirty-two cantos, amounting to 5256 iambic pentameters, intricately rhymed. The initial conception of this poem dates back fifty years, which were devoted to study and research of the theme, the composition occupying twelve years of my seventh and eighth decades. The prologue presents a framing narrative, set in T'ang dynasty China during the reign of the Emperor Ming Huang. It retells the story of the rivalry between his two court painters, Wu and Li, and this returns briefly in the epilogue to give a surprise ending. The main narrative of twenty-eight cantos provides the reader with a guided tour through all the Taoist and Mahayana Buddhist purgatories and paradises, which the Chinese call a Divine Panorama, not a comedy, though it ends with the jovial laughter of the Buddha."

BIOGRAPHICAL/CRITICAL SOURCES:

Contemporary Poets, St. James Press (Detroit), 4th edition, 1985.

PERIODICALS

Eastern Buddhist (Kyoto), Volume 14, number 2, 1981, pp. 137-52.
Hemisphere (Canberra), December, 1973.
Quadrant (Sydney), August, 1977.
Southerly: A Review of Australian Literature, June, 1983, pp. 167-81.
Times Literary Supplement, October 30, 1981, p. 1272.
Westerly (Australia), December 1987, pp. 25-35.

*   *   *

STRATI, Saverio 1924-

PERSONAL: Born August 16, 1924, in Italy; son of Paolo (a mason) and Agatha (Romeo) Strati; married Hildegard Fleig, 1958; children: Giampaolo.

ADDRESSES: Home—Via Giotto, Scandicci, Firenze, Italy.

CAREER: Full-time writer.

MEMBER: Sindacato degli Serittori.

AWARDS, HONORS: Charles Veilon International Prize (Lausanne) for *Tibi e Tascia;* Sila Prize for *Gente in viag-*

gio; Napoli Prize for *Noi lazzaroni;* Campiello Prize for *Il Selvaggio di Santa Venere;* Pomarico Prize for *Il Diavolaro;* Prize Saverese cittao di Enna for *I Cari Parenti;* Prie Citta di Ciro Marina for *La Conca degli aranci;* Prie Citta di Cantanzaro et Citta di Caserta for *L'uomo in fondo al pozzo.*

WRITINGS:

La Marchesina, Mondadori (Milan), 1956.
La Teda, Mondadori, 1957, translation published as *Terrarossa,* Abelard, 1957.
Tibi e Tascia, Mondadori, 1959.
Mani vuote, Mondadori, 1960, translation by Peter Moule published as *Empty Hands,* Abelard, 1964.
Avventura in citta, Mondadori, 1962, translation by Angus Davidson published as *The Lights of Reggio,* J. Murray, 1962.
Il nodo, Mondadori, 1965.
Gente in viaggio, Mondadori, 1966.
Il codardo, Bietti (Milan), 1970.
Noi lazzaroni, Mondadori, 1972.
E' il nostro turno, Mondadori, 1975.
Il Selvaggio di Santa Venere, Mondadori, 1977.
I centro bambini, Lerici (Cosenza), 1977.
Il visionario e il ciabattino, Mondadori, 1978.
Terra di emigranti, Salani (Florence), 1979.
Il Diavolaro, Mondadori, 1980.
Piccolo grande Sud, Salani, 1981.
I Cari Parenti, Mondadori, 1982.
Ascolta, Stefano, Mursia, 1983.
La Conca degli aranci, Mondadori, 1987.
L'uomo in fondo al pozzo, Mondadori, 1989.
Il vecchio e l'orologio, Manni, 1994.

*   *   *

SWANDER, Mary 1950-

PERSONAL: Born November 5, 1950, in Carroll, IA; daughter of John Chester (an engineer) and Rita Marie (a teacher; maiden name, Lynch) Swander. *Education:* Attended Georgetown University, 1969-71; University of Iowa, B.A., 1973, M.F.A., 1976.

ADDRESSES: Home—Ames, IA. *Office*—203 Ross Hall, Iowa State University, Ames, IA 50011. *Agent*—Elizabeth Grossman, Sterling Lord Literistics, One Madison Ave., New York, NY 10010.

CAREER: Lake Forest College, Lake Forest, IL, assistant professor of English, 1976-79; freelance writer in Iowa City, IA, 1979-81; writer in residence at Interlochen Academy of the Arts, 1982; Iowa State University, Ames, assistant professor of English, 1986—. University of Iowa, visiting professor, 1990-91. Massage therapist, 1982—; hypnotherapist, 1986—.

MEMBER: American Massage Therapists Association, American Association of Professional Hypnotherapists, Associated Writing Programs.

AWARDS, HONORS: National-Discovery Award, 1976, for poetry; Carl Sandburg Award from Chicago Public Library, 1982, for poetry; awards from Ingram Merrill Foundation, 1981 and 1986, for poetry; award for poetry from National Endowment of the Arts, 1987; Quill and Travel Award from the Garden Writers Association of America for best magazine writing in 1993; Whiting Writer's Award, 1994.

WRITINGS:

POEMS

Needlepoint, Smokeroot Press, 1977.
Succession, University of Georgia Press (Athens), 1980.
Driving the Body Back, Knopf (New York City), 1986.
Lost Lake, Owl Creek Press, 1986.
Heaven-and-Earth House, Knopf, 1994.

OTHER

Driving the Body Back (play), first produced, 1987.
(With Jane Anne Staw) *Parsnips in the Snow: Talks with Midwestern Gardeners,* University of Iowa Press (Iowa City), 1990.
(With Christopher Frank) *Dear Iowa* (play), first produced in Iowa, 1991.
(With Cornelia Mutel) *Land of the Fragile Giants* (essays and artwork), University of Iowa Press, 1994.

Contributor of poems to magazines, including *Antioch Review, Iowa Review, Missouri Review, Ploughshares, Nation, Pequod, New Republic, New York Times Magazine, New Yorker, Natural Health, National Gardening,* and *Christian Science Monitor.*

SIDELIGHTS: Autobiographical and rooted in rural life and religious faith, the poems of Mary Swander speak of natural wonders, of learning from the land, and of those who live on the land and work it. Her book *Succession* has earned praise and sparked comparisons with the work of Georgia writer Flannery O'Connor. Like O'Connor, Swander uses country scenes and details to "deal with the interiors of characters and with the fact, and mystery, of death," writes Joyce Coyne Dyer in *Iowa Woman.* Swander writes with "precision and brilliance" about people and places she has known, creating "a poetic genealogy that is invested with emotion."

Swander's *Driving the Body Back* shows her skill in creating a narrative stitched together with authentic characters and idioms. Like a Midwest version of Faulkner's *As I Lay*

Dying or Chaucer's *Canterbury Tales,* Swander tells stories which Dyer, in *Poet and Critic,* calls "sometimes outrageous, often entertaining, and always emotional." Louise Erdrich, in the *New York Times Book Review,* notes how Swander's "novelistic form is direct and interesting" as she details, through the voices of nine eccentric and vivid family members, the driving of the poet's mother across Iowa to be buried in the town in which she was born, giving the reader "a unique perspective on the minutiae of everyday rural and small-town life." In *Heaven-and-Earth House,* Swander "steps up into the big leagues of her art," according to Pat Monaghan in *Booklist,* as "her poems attend to life's small joys: a muddy road, calm weather, spicy apples." The critic for *Publishers Weekly* finds that the poems create a "music of Midwest rural encounters" as the reader walks along "a pathway with 'common' language: the rhythms of weather, humor and talk."

Swander's interest in the natural world and the people of the Midwest is also reflected in the book *Parsnips in the Snow: Talks with Midwestern Gardeners,* which she wrote with Jane Anne Staw. Focusing on amateurs who raise vegetables for their own consumption, the book profiles twelve home gardeners from Kansas, Minnesota, Illinois and several other states. Comments from some fifty other gardeners are also offered to provide what David Rompf in the *Philadelphia Inquirer* calls "a small chorus of Midwestern voices." The authors "have chosen a society of peaceful zealots whose company we can only envy," notes the critic for *Publishers Weekly.* Rompf calls *Parsnips in the Snow* an "inviting and generous book" which may spur its readers to "go out and dig up the back yard." Allen Lacy, writing in the *New York Times Book Review,* claims that "after reading this charming book, I felt as if I had just spent some wonderful hours with remarkably decent and caring human beings."

BIOGRAPHICAL/CRITICAL SOURCES:

PERIODICALS

Antioch Review, winter, 1987, p. 84.
Bloomsbury Review, May, 1990, p. 18.
Booklist, May 15, 1994.
Christian Science Monitor, May 25, 1990, p. 13.
Iowa Woman, spring, 1984.
Los Angeles Times Book Review, November 23, 1986, p. 3.
New York Times Book Review, June 1, 1986, p. 36; June 10, 1990, p. 13.
Philadelphia Enquirer, March 25, 1990.
Poet and Critic, fall, 1986, pp. 55-60.
Poetry, May, 1986, p. 100.
Publishers Weekly, February 14, 1986, p. 61; January 26, 1990, p. 415; March 28, 1994, p. 88.

Small Press Review, February, 1987, p. 4.

*   *   *

SZAJKOWSKI, Zosa
  See FRYDMAN, Szajko

T

TAO MULIAN
  See TOTTEN, George Oakley III

*   *   *

TATE, Joan 1922-

PERSONAL: Born in 1922; married; three children.

ADDRESSES: Home—7 College Hill, Shrewsbury SY1 1LZ, England.

CAREER: Writer and translator.

MEMBER: PEN International, Society of Authors, Amnesty International.

WRITINGS:

JUVENILE/YOUNG ADULT

Sam and Me, Macmillan (London), 1968.
Whizz Kid, Macmillan, 1969, published as *An Unusual Kind of Girl,* 1969.
The Nest, Macmillan, 1969.
The Cheapjack Man, Macmillan, 1969.
The Gobbleydock, Macmillan, 1969.
The Tree House, Macmillan, 1969.
The Ball, Macmillan, 1969.
Your Town, David & Charles, 1972.
Ben and Annie, Doubleday, 1972.
Jack and the Rock Cakes, Brockhampton, 1972.
Grandpa and My Little Sister, Brockhampton, 1972.
Taxi!, Schoeningh, 1973.
How Do You Do?, Schoeningh, 1974.
The World of the River, Dent, 1974.
You Can't Explain Everything, Longman, 1976.
Billoggs, Pelham Books, 1976.
See You, Longman, 1977.
On Your Own I, Wheaton, 1977.

On Your Own II, Wheaton, 1978.
The House That Jack Built, Pelham Books, 1978.
See How They Run, Pelham Books, 1979.
Cat Country, Ram Publishing, 1979.
Turn Again, Whittington, Pelham Books, 1980.
Frankie Flies, Macmillan, 1980.
Jumping Jo, Macmillan, 1980.
Luke's Garden [and] *Gramp* (also see below), Harper, 1981.
Clee and Nibs, Puffin, 1990.

PUBLISHED BY HEINEMANN

Jenny, 1964.
The Crane, 1964.
The Rabbit Boy, 1964.
Coal Hoppy, 1964.
The Silver Grill, 1965.
The Next Doors, 1965.
Picture Charlie, 1965.
Lucy, 1965.
The Tree, 1966, published as *Tina and David,* Nelson, 1973.
The Holiday, 1966.
Tad, 1966.
Bill, 1966.
Mrs. Jenny, 1966.
Bits and Pieces, 1968.
The Circus and Other Stories, 1968.
Letters to Chris, 1968.
The Crow, 1968.
Luke's Garden, 1968, published with *Gramp,* Harper, 1981.
Jenny and Mrs. Jenny, 1968, published as *Out of the Sun,* 1968.
Clipper, 1969, published as *Ring on My Finger,* 1971.
The Long Road Home, 1971.
Wump Day, 1972.
Dad's Camel, 1972.

PUBLISHED BY ALMQVIST & WIKSELL

The Lollipop Man, 1967, Macmillan, 1969.

The Wild Boy, 1967, Harper, 1973, published as *Wild Martin,* Heinemann, 1968.

The Train, 1967.

The New House, 1968.

The Soap Box Car, 1968.

Polly, 1969.

The Great Birds, 1969.

The Old Car, 1969.

(With Sven Johansson and Bengt Astrom) *Going Up* (language text), with workbook, Volume 1, 1969, Volume 2, 1970, Volume 3, 1974.

The Letter and Other Stories, 1969.

Puddle's Tiger, 1969.

The Caravan, 1969.

Edward and the Uncles, 1969.

The Secret, 1969.

The Runners, 1969.

Night Out and Other Stories, 1970.

The Match and Other Stories, 1970.

Dinah, 1970.

The Man Who Rang the Bell, 1970.

Ginger Mick, 1970.

Journal for One, 1970.

Hullo Minibooks, 1980.

TRANSLATOR

John Einar Aberg, *Do You Believe in Angels,* Hutchinson, 1963.

Dagmar Edqvist, *Black Sister,* Doubleday, 1963.

Maertha Buren, *A Need to Love,* Dodd, 1964.

Berndt Olsson, *Noah,* Hutchinson, 1964.

Buren, *Camilla,* Dodd, 1965.

Per Wahloeoe, *The Assignment,* Knopf, 1965.

Ralph Herrmanns, *River Boy: Adventures on the Amazon,* Harcourt, 1965.

Mika Waltari, *The Roman,* Putnam, 1966.

Folke Henschen, *History of Diseases,* Longmans, Green, 1966, published as *The History and Geography of Diseases,* Dial, 1967.

Nan Inger, *Katrin,* Hamish Hamilton, 1966.

Maria Lang, *Wreath for the Bride,* Hodder & Stoughton, 1966.

Lang, *No More Murders,* Hodder & Stoughton, 1967.

Lang, *Death Awaits Thee,* Hodder & Stoughton, 1967.

Sven Gillsaeter, *From Island to Island,* Allen & Unwin, 1968.

Wahloeoe, *A Necessary Action,* Pantheon, 1968, published as *The Lorry,* M. Joseph.

Margit Fjellman, *Queen Louise of Sweden,* Allen & Unwin, 1968.

Wahloeoe and Maj Sjoewall, *The Man Who Went Up in Smoke,* Pantheon, 1969.

Carl Nylander, *The Deep Well,* Allen & Unwin, 1969.

Hans Heiberg, *Ibsen,* Allen & Unwin, 1969.

Wahloeoe, *The Steel Spring,* Knopf, 1970.

Goeran Bergman, *Why Does Your Dog Do That?,* Hutchinson, 1970.

Anders Bodelsen, *Freezing Point,* Knopf, 1970.

Wahloeoe and Sjoewall, *The Fire-Engine That Vanished,* Pantheon, 1970.

Gunnel Beckman, *Admission to the Feast,* Macmillan, 1971.

Doris Dahlin, *The Sit-In Game,* Viking, 1972.

Beckman, *A Room of His Own,* Viking, 1972.

Wahloeoe, *The Generals,* Pantheon, 1973.

Beckman, *Mia,* Bodley Head, 1974.

Astrid Lindgren, *That Emil,* Brockhampton, 1974.

Barbro Lindgren, *Alban,* A. & C. Black, 1974.

Olle Hoegstrand, *The Debt,* Pantheon, 1974.

A. Lindgren, *The Lionheart Brothers,* Brockhampton, 1974.

Lennart Frick, *The Threat,* Brockhampton, 1974.

Beckman, *The Loneliness of Mia,* Viking, 1975.

Bodelsen, *Operation Cobra,* Pelham Books, 1975.

Bjorn Borg, *The Bjorn Borg Story,* Pelham Books, 1975.

Thomas Dineson, *My Sister, Isak Dineson,* M. Joseph, 1975.

Ole Lund, *Otto Is a Rhino,* Pelham Books, 1975.

Merete Kruuse, *Scatty Ricky,* Pelham Books, 1975.

Lief Esper Anderson, *Witch Fever,* Pelham Books, 1976.

Kare Holt, *The Race,* M. Joseph, 1976.

A. Lindgren, *Emil and the Bad Tooth,* Hodder & Stoughton, 1976.

Max Lundgren, *Summer Girl,* Macmillan, 1976.

Irmelin Sandman Lilius, *Gold Crown Lane,* Oxford University Press, 1976.

Sjoewall and Wahloeoe, *The Terrorists,* Random House, 1976.

Gun Bjoerk and Ingvar Bjoerk, *Shrews,* Pelham Books, 1977.

G. Bjoerk and I. Bjoerk, *Bees,* Pelham Books, 1977.

Hans-Erik Hellberg, *Follow My Leader,* Macmillan, 1977.

Lundgren, *For the Love of Lisa,* Macmillan, 1977.

Svend Otto, *Jasper the Taxi Dog,* Pelham Books, 1977.

Otto, *Tim and Trisha,* Pelham Books, 1977.

Lilius, *The Goldmaker's House,* Oxford University Press, 1977, published with *Horses of the Night,* Delacorte.

Stig Weimar, *Denmark Is Like This,* Kaye & Ward, 1977.

Eva Bexell, *The Minister's Naughty Grandchildren,* Bodley Head, 1978.

G. Bjoerk and I. Bjoerk, *Ants,* Pelham Books, 1978.

G. Bjoerk and I. Bjoerk, *Frogs,* Pelham Books, 1978.

Anne Bulow-Olsen, *Plant Communities,* Penguin Books, 1978.

Gunnel Linde, *I Am a Werewolf Cub,* Dent, 1978.

Otto, *A Christmas Book,* Pelham Books, 1978.

Martha Sandwall-Bergstrom, *Anna Keeps Her Promise,* Blackie & Son, 1978.

Sandwall-Bergstrom, *Anna All Alone,* Blackie & Son, 1978.

Sandwall-Bergstrom, *Anna at Bloom Farm,* Blackie & Son, 1978.

Bexell, *Christmas with Grandfather,* Bodley Head, 1979.

K. Arne Blom, *The Limits of Pain,* Ram Publishing, 1979, Raven House, 1980.

Eva Eriksson, *Hocus Pocus,* Methuen, 1979.

Eriksson, *Sometimes Never,* Methuen, 1979.

Robert Fisker, *Sparrow Falls Out of the Nest,* Pelham Books, 1979.

Eigel Holm, *The Biology of Flowers,* Penguin Books, 1979.

Ulf Malmgren, *When the Leaves Begin to Fall,* Oxford University Press, 1979.

Jan Martensson, *Death Calls on the Witches,* Ram Publishing, 1979.

Otto, *Inuk and His Sledge-Dog,* Pelham Books, 1979.

Otto, *Karen and the Space Machine,* Pelham Books, 1979.

Sandwall-Bergstrom, *Anna Wins Through,* Blackie & Son, 1979.

Sandwall-Bergstrom, *Anna at the Manor House,* Blackie & Son, 1979.

Sandwall-Bergstrom, *Anna Solves the Mystery,* Blackie & Son, 1979.

Lilius, *Horses of the Night,* Oxford University Press, 1979, published with *The Goldmaker's House,* Delacorte.

Elisabeth Soderstrom, *In My Own Key,* Hamish Hamilton, 1979.

Inger Halsoer Hagerup, *Helter Skelter,* Pelham Books, 1979.

Sven Krister Swahn, *The Twilight Visitors,* Methuen, 1980.

Lilius, *King Tulle,* Pelham Books, 1980.

Allan Rune Pettersson, *Frankenstein's Aunt,* Hodder & Stoughton, 1980, Little, Brown, 1981.

G. Bjoerk, *Mountain Walk,* Pelham Books, 1980.

Maud Reuterswaerd, *Days with Woodie,* Pelham Books, 1980.

G. Bjoerk, *Snakes,* Pelham Books, 1980.

G. Bjoerk, *Spiders,* Pelham Books, 1980.

Fisker, *Sparrow Flies Away,* Pelham Books, 1980.

Asbjoernsen and Moe, *The Runaway Pancake,* Pelham Books, 1980.

Otto, *Jon's Big Day,* Pelham Books, 1980.

Hans Hansen, *Jenny Moves House,* Pelham House, 1981.

Maria Marcus, *A Taste for Pain,* Souvenir Press, 1981.

Otto, *The Giant Fish* (also see below), Pelham Books, 1981.

Otto, *Children of the Yangtze River,* Pelham Books, 1982.

Karin Lorentzen, *Lanky Longlegs,* Atheneum, 1982.

Jan Ekstroem, *Deadly Reunion,* Scribner, 1983.

Christer Kihlman, *Sweet Prince,* Peter Owen, 1983.

Otto, *The Giant Fish and Other Stories,* Larousse, 1983.

Ekstroem, *The Ancestral Precipice,* Macmillan, 1983.

Kihlman, *All My Sons,* Peter Owen, 1984.

Hakanson and others, *Course in Spanish,* Oxford University Press, 1984.

Otto, *Ling and the Little Devils,* Pelham Books, 1984.

Oscar Hedlund, *My Best Loved Sticks,* Arlington Press, 1984.

Norell and others, *Jukebox Hits,* Cambridge University Press, 1984.

Otto, *The Princess and the Sun, the Moon and the Stars,* Pelham Books, 1985.

Per Olov Enquist, *The March of the Musicians,* Collins, 1985.

Dea Trier Moerch, *Winter's Child,* University of Nebraska Press, 1986.

Otto, *Avalanche,* Pelham Books, 1986.

Otto, *The Donkey and the Dog,* 1986.

Per Waestberg, *Assignment in Africa,* Farrar, Strauss, 1986.

Tore Zetterholm, *Illustrated Companion to World Literature,* Orbis, 1986.

P. C. Jersild, *Children's Island,* University of Nebraska Press, 1987.

Sven Nordqvist, *Christmas and the House Gnome,* Corona, 1987.

Jersild, *House of Babel,* Nebraska University Press, 1988.

Ingmar Bergman, *The Magic Lantern,* Viking, 1988.

Ingrid Rosell, *Reflections of a World,* Viking, 1988.

Goeran Schildt, *Goodbye Daphne,* Books from Finland, 1988.

Moerch, *Evening Star,* University of Nebraska Press, 1988.

Elsa Beskow, *Around the Year,* Floris Books, 1988.

Lars Welinder, *The Christmas Present,* Corona, 1988.

Sara Lidman, *Naboth's Stone,* Norvik Press, 1988.

Kihlman, *The Downfall of Gerd Bladh,* Peter Owen, 1988.

(With Marlaine Delargy) Solveig von Schoultz, *Heartwork,* Forest, 1990.

Reuterswaerd, *A Way from Home,* Turton & Chambers, 1990.

Kihlman, *The Blue Mother,* Nebraska University Press, 1990.

Pettersson, *Frankenstein's Aunt Again,* Hodder & Stoughton, 1990.

Beskow, *The Flower Feast,* Floris Books, 1990.

Beskow, *Eddie, Freda and Little Pip,* Floris Books, 1990.

Reuterswaerd, *Noah Is My Name,* Turton & Chambers, 1990.

Bent Schoenberg, *Hans Brenaa,* Dance Books, 1990.

Oscar Parland, *The Year of the Bull,* Peter Owen, 1991.

Annika Idstroem, *My Brother Sebastian,* UNESCO/Forest Books, 1991.

Parland, *The Enchanted Way,* Peter Owen, 1991.

Beskow, *Peter's Old House,* Floris Books, 1991.
Sigrid Combuechen, *Byron: A Novel,* Heinemann, 1991.
Cecilia Lindqvist, *China—Empire of the Written Symbol,* CollinsHarvill, 1992.
Agneta Pleijel, *The Dog Star,* Peter Owen, 1992.
Selma Lagerloef, *The Wonderful Adventures of Nils,* Floris Books, 1992.
Beskow, *Christopher's Harvest Time,* Floris Books, 1992.
Kjell Epsmark, *Route Tournante,* Forest Books, 1993.
Bergman, *The Best Intentions,* Arcade, 1993.
Knud Faldbakken, *Twilight Country,* Peter Owen, 1993.
Bergman, *Sunday's Children,* Arcade, 1994.
Bergman, *Sunday's Child,* Harvill, 1994.
Britt Ekland, *Sweet Life,* Headline, 1994.
Faldbakken, *Sweetwater,* Peter Owen, 1994.

Also translator of *Five Questions on World Peace,* 1986; *Trelleborg,* 1988; *Teddy Bear,* Barrons, 1988; *Sweden in Fact,* 1990; *Swedish National Cultural Policies,* 1991; and *Man on the Hillside,* a musical drama by Katarina Frostenson, 1992.

OTHER

Also author of *Safari,* 1980, *Panda Car,* 1980, *Action Books,* 1981; *How to Go Shopping, How to Get Help, How to Eat Out,* and others in series, Hirschgraben, 1982-83; *Disco Books,* 8-volume series, 1975. Contributor of poems and stories to anthologies, including *A Third Poetry Book,* Oxford University Press, 1982; *Appropriate English,* Macmillan, 1984; *A Book of English,* Haum, 1987; *King of Nowhere,* Oxford University Press, 1989; *Project English,* Blackwell, 1991; and *Autobiography,* Oxford University Press, 1991. Contributor to periodicals, including *Scandinavian Review.*

Tate's books have been translated into French, German, Swedish, Danish, Norwegian, Afrikaans, and Japanese.

WORK IN PROGRESS: Books on the Shadow Theatre of Thailand, India, Malaysia, China, Indonesia, and the Middle East; two works of fiction, *Catspoon and Fiddle* and *Jimmy;* numerous translations.

SIDELIGHTS: Joan Tate told *CA,* "I am always writing or translating," and describes her working hours as "9-6 every day, more or less." Believing that "no one can teach you to write," she advises aspiring authors "just to write."

BIOGRAPHICAL/CRITICAL SOURCES:

PERIODICALS

Los Angeles Times Book Review, September 18, 1988, p. 1.
New York Times Book Review, December 14, 1980, p. 37; August 24, 1986, p. 18; December 21, 1986, p. 26; September 18, 1988, p. 1.
Times (London), April 18, 1991, p. 16.

Times Literary Supplement, November 21, 1980, p. 1324; July 29, 1983, p. 804; June 17, 1988, p. 670; May 10, 1991.
Washington Post Book World, December 12, 1982, p. 8; September 25, 1988, p. 3.

*   *   *

TATLOW, Antony 1935-

PERSONAL: Born June 25, 1935, in Dublin, Ireland; son of Katherine Faith Warren Evans and Anthony Fitzgerald Tatlow; married Anita Diergarten; children: Maureen, Dermot, Deirdre. *Education:* Trinity College, Dublin, B.A., 1957, M.A., 1964.

ADDRESSES: Home—3 Felix Villas, 61 Mount Davis Rd., Hong Kong. *Office*—Department of English Studies and Comparative Literature, University of Hong Kong, Hong Kong.

CAREER: University of Hong Kong, Hong Kong, assistant lecturer, 1965-66, lecturer, 1966-72, senior lecturer in comparative literature, 1972-81, reader in comparative literature, 1981-87, professor of comparative literature, 1987—, head of department of comparative literature, 1989. Adviser to Hong Kong Institute for the Promotion of Chinese Culture; consultant to Central Academy of Drama, Beijing, China. Member of advisory board of Literary Research, 1990—, and advisory board of Colloquia Germanica, 1993—, co-editor of *The Brecht Yearbook,* 1990—.

MEMBER: International Association of Germanic Studies, International Brecht Society (vice-president, 1979-82; president, 1982-90), International Comparative Literature Association, Hong Kong Comparative Literature Association (president, 1980-82).

WRITINGS:

(Editor) *Language Problems in Southeast Asian Universities,* Association of Southeast Asian Institutes of Higher Learning, 1968.
Brechts chinesische Gedichte (title means "Brecht's Chinese Poems"), Suhrkamp, 1973.
The Mask of Evil: Brecht's Response to the Poetry, Theatre, and Thought of China and Japan; A Comparative and Critical Evaluation, Peter Lang, 1977.
(Editor with T. W. Wong) *Brecht and East Asian Theatre,* Hong Kong University Press, 1982.
(Editor) *The Teaching of Literature in ASAIHL Universities,* Hong Kong University Press, 1983.
(Translator with Yvonne Kapp, Hugh Rorrison, and John Willett) *Bertolt Brecht: Short Stories, 1921-1946,* Methuen (New York City), 1983.

Repression and Figuration: From Totem to Utopia, Department of Comparative Literature of University of Hong Kong, 1990.

Textual Anthropology: A Practice of Reading, Peking University Press (Beijing), 1994.

Shakespeare in Comparison: A Politics of the Sign, Department of Comparative Literature of University of Hong Kong, 1994.

WORK IN PROGRESS: Comedy, an investigation of unconscious repression in a culture; *Brecht and the Unconscious.*

SIDELIGHTS: Antony Tatlow told *CA:* "I came to Hong Kong in 1965 to teach in the university's department of modern languages. Although I planned to stay for three years, I have remained for twenty-two. Nothing prepared me for Hong Kong, for the contradictions it brought into focus with its trading convenience, political absurdity, economic engine, social squalor, and cultural challenge. It was an enigma of stunning physical beauty. Perhaps as nowhere else, Hong Kong embodies the tensions of our world: First and Third, East and West, North and South. It expresses these so clearly because its political and social space are unique and protected by that uniqueness.

"At the university we were supposed to produce the 'leaders for the future.' For our students 'leadership' meant a career in the middle ranks of the bureaucracy, a prospect which they did not find greatly enspiriting. Hong Kong was not so much a cultural desert then as a cultural vacuum. It was both an inauspicious and a perfect place for basic research in cultural studies. However, teaching Western culture in this very different environment was a constantly, disturbingly, and suggestively defamilarizing experience. Under the circumstances, longterm projects in cultural studies seemed the only possible course. I ultimately focused my attention on the writings of German playwright and poet Bertolt Brecht due to the range of his encounters with East Asian culture. Assembling this information took ten years; drawing attention to its existence took a few more. Since then I have widened the scope of these intercultural studies both by deepening the theoretical questions and by extending the range of inquiry to a process I am calling 'dialectics of acculturation.'

"As global modernization threatens fundamental natural equilibrium, the exploration and development of traditional relationalist philosophical and cultural models and their global implementation has become vital to our survival. Likewise, comparative cultural studies of the actual and potential relationships between traditional and modern cultural models have a crucial role to play. With its political future now ascertained, Hong Kong has become a place where these global cultural issues—in all their un-

certainty and complexity—can be uniquely and visibly addressed."

* * *

TAYLOR, Harry
See GRANICK, Harry

* * *

TEC, Nechama 1931-

PERSONAL: Born May 15, 1931, in Lublin, Poland; came to the United States in 1952, naturalized in 1960; daughter of Roman (a businessman) and Esther (Hachamoff) Bawnik; married Leon Tec (a child psychiatrist), February 14, 1950; children: Leora, Roland. *Education:* Columbia University, B.S. (cum laude), 1954, M.A., 1955, Ph.D., 1963.

ADDRESSES: Home—11 Rockyfield Rd., Westport, CT 06880. *Office*—Department of Sociology, University of Connecticut, Scofieldtown Rd., Stamford, CT 06903.

CAREER: New York State Department of Mental Hygiene, New York City, research sociologist in biometrics, 1956-57; Columbia University, New York City, lecturer in School of General Studies, 1957-60; Rutgers University, Douglass College, New Brunswick, NJ, instructor in sociology, 1959-60; Columbia University, lecturer in sociology, 1968-71; Trinity College, Hartford, CT, visiting professor of sociology, 1971-72; University of Connecticut, Stamford, associate professor, 1974-87, professor of sociology, 1987—. Research director, Mid-Fairfield Child Guidance Center, Norwalk, CT, 1968-79. Guest lecturer, Elmhurst (IL) College, April, 1993; scholar at International Institute for Holocaust Research, Yad Vashem, Jerusalem, 1995. Member of advisory board, Braun Center for Holocaust Studies, and of international advisory board of directors of the Braun Center's Foundation to Sustain Righteous Christians, both of the Anti-Defamation League of B'nai B'rith. Lectures extensively in the United States and abroad; has appeared on numerous television and radio shows.

MEMBER: American Sociological Association, Authors Guild, Authors League of America, PEN, Phi Beta Kappa.

AWARDS, HONORS: Merit of Distinction Awards, Anti-Defamation League of B'nai B'rith, for *Dry Tears: The Story of a Lost Childhood* and *When Light Pierced the Darkness: Christian Rescue of Jews in Nazi-Occupied Poland;* Myrtle Wreath Award in the humanitarian/author category for the state of Connecticut, Hadassah, 1987; Pulitzer Prize nomination and Christopher Award, 1991, both for *In the Lion's Den: The Life of Oswald Rufeisen;* National Endowment for the Humanities fellowship, 1991-92; Littauer Foundation grant, 1992-93; Memorial Foundation for Jewish Culture grant, 1992-93; International Ann Frank Special Recognition Prize, 1994, for *Defiance: The Bielski Partisans.*

WRITINGS:

Gambling in Sweden, Bedminster (Totowa, NJ), 1964.

Grass Is Green in Suburbia: A Sociological Study of Adolescent Usage of Illicit Drugs, Libra Publishers (Long Island, NY), 1974.

Dry Tears: The Story of a Lost Childhood, Wildcat Publishing (Westport, CT), 1982, published with new epilogue, Oxford University Press (New York City), 1984.

When Light Pierced the Darkness: Christian Rescue of Jews in Nazi-Occupied Poland, Oxford University Press, 1986.

In the Lion's Den: The Life of Oswald Rufeisen, Oxford University Press, 1990.

Defiance: The Bielski Partisans, Oxford University Press, 1993.

Contributor to books, including *Lessons and Legacies: The Meaning of the Holocaust in a Changing World,* edited by Peter Hayes, Northwestern University Press (Evanston, IL), 1991; *Burning Memory: Times of Testing and Reckoning,* edited by Alice L. Eckardt, Pergamon (Elmsford, NY), 1993; and *The Hidden Child: The Secret Survivors of the Holocaust,* Ballantine (New York City), 1993. Contributor to *Proceedings* of the eighth and ninth World Congress of Jewish Studies, 1982 and 1986. Contributor to numerous periodicals, including *International Social Science Review, Adolescence, East European Quarterly, Contemporary Sociology, Journal of Marriage and Family, Journal of Social Science and Medicine,* and *Los Angeles Times Book Review.*

Some of Tec's work has been published in Hebrew and Dutch.

WORK IN PROGRESS: Ongoing research "about compassion, altruism, resistance to evil, and the rescue of Jews during World War II."

SIDELIGHTS: Based on interviews with both rescuers and survivors, Nechama Tec's *When Light Pierced the Darkness: Christian Rescue of Jews in Nazi-Occupied Poland* "celebrates one segment of Polish society—men and women from many backgrounds and social circumstances who risked their lives to help Jews escape," writes Michael R. Marrus in the *Washington Post Book World.* Yet, as Gene Lyons notes in *Newsweek,* "to read *When Light Pierced the Darkness* is to encounter the Holocaust anew

from a unique and bewildering angle." Jan Tomasz Gross in the *New York Times Book Review* elaborates, stating, "what is unusual about [the] book is that it both emphasizes Polish rescue efforts and reveals a ubiquitous hostility towards Jews." A reviewer in *Publishers Weekly* observes that "balancing a scientist's dispassion and her own clearly passionate attitudes toward both the Holocaust and Poland, Tec presents systematic sociological evidence about the characteristics of people apt to risk their lives to save others." While Timothy Garton Ash in the *New York Review of Books* comments that "Tec concludes . . . the only sociological generalization that can safely be made about people who helped Jews is that peasants were the class least likely to do so," Gross remarks that "most of the rescuers . . . had a strong sense of independence and individuality . . . ready to defy their own society." "It was the book, plus Tec's promise of anonymity," writes *Newsweek*'s Lyons, "that persuaded both survivors and protectors to grant her the extensive interviews that form the basis for [*When Light Pierced the Darkness*]."

BIOGRAPHICAL/CRITICAL SOURCES:

PERIODICALS

New York Review of Books, December 19, 1985.
New York Times Book Review, January 12, 1986.
Newsweek, January 27, 1986.
Publishers Weekly, November 15, 1985.
Washington Post Book World, March 30, 1986.

*   *   *

THOMAS, Joyce Carol 1938-

PERSONAL: Born May 25, 1938, in Ponca City, OK; daughter of Floyd David (a bricklayer) and Leona (a housekeeper and hair stylist; maiden name, Thompson) Haynes; married Gettis L. Withers (a chemist), May 31, 1959 (divorced, 1968); married Roy T. Thomas, Jr. (a professor), September 7, 1968 (divorced, 1979); children: Monica Pecot, Gregory Withers, Michael Withers, Roy T. Thomas III. *Education:* Attended San Francisco City College, 1957-58, and University of San Francisco, 1957-58; College of San Mateo, A.A., 1964; San Jose State College (now University), B.A., 1966; Stanford University, M.A., 1967.

ADDRESSES: Home—Berkeley, CA. *Agent*—Jack Z. Tantleff, 375 Greenwich St., Suite 700, New York, NY 10013.

CAREER: Worked as a telephone operator in San Francisco, CA, 1957-58; Ravenwood School District, East Palo Alto, CA, teacher of French and Spanish, 1968-70; San Jose State College (now University), San Jose, CA, assistant professor of black studies, 1969-72, reading program director, 1979-82, professor of English, 1982-83; Contra Costa College, San Pablo, CA, teacher of drama and English, 1973-75; St. Mary's College, Moranga, CA, professor of English, 1975-77; full-time writer, 1982—. Visiting associate professor of English at Purdue University, spring, 1983; full professor of English, University of Tennessee, 1989—.

MEMBER: Dramatists Guild, Authors Guild, Authors League of America.

AWARDS, HONORS: Danforth Graduate Fellow, University of California at Berkeley, 1973-75; Stanford University scholar, 1979-80, and Djerassi Fellow, 1982 and 1983; *New York Times* outstanding book of the year citation, American Library Association (ALA) best book citation, and Before Columbus American Book Award, Before Columbus Foundation (Berkeley, CA), all 1982, and National Book Award for children's fiction, 1983, all for *Marked by Fire;* Coretta Scott King Honor Book Award, ALA, 1984, for *Bright Shadow;* named Outstanding Woman of the Twentieth Century, Sigma Gamma Rho, 1986; *A Gathering of Flowers: Stories about Being Young in America* was a National Conference of Christians and Jews recommended title for children and young adults, 1991; Coretta Scott King Honor Book Award, ALA, and Notable Children's Trade Book in the field of social studies, National Council for Social Studies and Children's Book Council, both 1994, for *Brown Honey in Broomwheat Tea.*

WRITINGS:

YOUNG ADULT NOVELS

Marked by Fire, Avon (New York City), 1982.
Bright Shadow (sequel to *Marked by Fire*), Avon, 1983.
Water Girl, Avon, 1986.
The Golden Pasture, Scholastic (New York City), 1986.
Journey, Scholastic, 1990.
When the Nightingale Sings, HarperCollins (New York City), 1992.

POETRY

Bittersweet, Firesign Press, 1973.
Crystal Breezes, Firesign Press, 1974.
Blessing, Jocato Press, 1975.
Black Child, illustrated by Tom Feelings, Zamani Productions, 1981.
Inside the Rainbow, Zikawana Press, 1982.
Brown Honey in Broomwheat Tea, illustrated by Floyd Cooper, HarperCollins, 1993.
Gingerbread Days, illustrated by Cooper, HarperCollins, 1995.

PLAYS

(And producer) *A Song in the Sky* (two-act), produced in San Francisco at Montgomery Theater, 1976.
Look! What a Wonder! (two-act), produced in Berkeley at Berkeley Community Theatre, 1976.
(And producer) *Magnolia* (two-act), produced in San Francisco at Old San Francisco Opera House, 1977.
(And producer) *Ambrosia* (two-act), produced in San Francisco at Little Fox Theatre, 1978.
Gospel Roots (two-act), produced in Carson, CA, at California State University, 1981.
I Have Heard of a Land, produced in Oklahoma City, OK, at Claussen Theatre, 1989.
When the Nightingale Sings (musical; based on Thomas's novel of the same title), produced in Knoxville, TN, at Clarence Brown Theatre, 1991.

OTHER

(Editor) *A Gathering of Flowers: Stories about Being Young in America,* HarperCollins, 1990.

Contributor to periodicals, including *American Poetry Review, Black Scholar, Calafia, Drum Voices, Giant Talk,* and *Yardbird Reader.* Editor of *Ambrosia* (women's newsletter), 1980.

ADAPTATIONS: Marked by Fire was adapted by James Racheff and Ted Kociolek for the stage musical *Abyssinia,* first produced in New York City at the C.S.C. Repertory Theatre in 1987.

SIDELIGHTS: Joyce Carol Thomas's background as a migrant farm worker in rural Oklahoma and California supplies her with the prolific stock of characters and situations that fill her novels. The author admittedly fell in love with words and with the songs she heard in church, and has spent much of her time as a writer trying to recreate the sounds of singing with her written language. She is well known for her book of poems *Brown Honey in Broomwheat Tea;* her ground-breaking anthology, *A Gathering of Flowers: Stories about Being Young in America;* and her young adult novels *Marked by Fire* and *Bright Shadow,* which are set in Thomas's hometown and focus on the indomitable spirit of Abyssinia Jackson and her people.

Thomas grew up in Ponca City, Oklahoma, a small, dusty town where she lived across from the school. "Although now I live half a continent away from my hometown," Thomas related in *Something about the Author Autobiography Series (SAAS),* "when it comes to my writing I find that I am still there." She has set three of her novels in her hometown: *Marked by Fire, Bright Shadow,* and *The Golden Pasture.*

Thomas loved school as a child and became anxious whenever it appeared she might be late because she did not want to miss anything. However, she usually missed the first month of school in order to finish up her farm work. Times were lean for Thomas's family, but they always made do. This she attributes partly to her mother's genius at making healthy foods that were not expensive; she has memories of huge spreads being laid out for Sunday dinners. These scenes of food have stuck with Thomas, for she finds food is one of the focuses in her novels. "Because in such a home food was another language for love, my books are redolent of sugar and spice, kale and collards," Thomas commented in *SAAS.*

When Thomas was ten years old, the family moved to rural Tracy, California. There Thomas learned to milk cows, fish for minnows, and harvest tomatoes and grapes. She also became intimately acquainted with black widow spiders—there was a nest of them under her bed. She was later to use this experience in her novel *Journey.* Likewise, she had a similar experience with wasps when her brother locked her in a closet containing a wasp nest; *Marked by Fire* contains some scary scenes with these insects.

In Tracy, California, Thomas continued her long summers harvesting crops. She worked beside many Mexicans and began a love affair with their language. "When the Spanish speakers talked they seemed to sing," Thomas remarked in *SAAS.* When she went to college—which she managed to do by working full-time as a telephone operator as well as raising her children—she majored in Spanish and French. "From this base of languages I taught myself all I know about writing," she related in *SAAS.* She went on to earn a master's degree from Stanford University, and then taught foreign languages in public school.

From 1973 to 1978, Thomas wrote poetry and plays for adults and became a celebrated author. She traveled to conferences and festivals all over the world, including Lagos, Nigeria. In 1982, Thomas's career took a turn when she published *Marked by Fire,* a novel for a young adult audience. Steeped in the setting and traditions of her hometown, the novel focuses on Abyssinia Jackson, a girl who was born in a cotton field during harvest time. The title refers to the fact that she received a burn on her face from a brush fire during her birth. This leaves her "marked for unbearable pain and unspeakable joy," according to the local healer.

The pain begins when Abyssinia is raped by an elder in the church when she is ten. Abby becomes mute after the violent act and is nursed back to health through the strength of the local women and her family. Abby's mother is named Patience in honor of Thomas's mother, who was a very patient parent. Strong, the father, has left the family in their time of need, but returns to them later—ironically—because he is not strong enough to face a crisis in his life. When Abby eventually regains her voice, she is able to tell her friend Lily Norene that after the rape she "felt dirty. Dirtier than playing in mud. The kind of dirt you can't ever wash off. . . . But the worst part was I felt like I was being spit on by God." It is the seeming abandonment by God that strikes Abby to the core—she must work through the horror before she can recover completely. Mother Barker, the town's midwife and healer, has a special role in the rehabilitation of Abby. In a more macabre way, so does Trembling Sally, a frightening, crazy woman who assaults the young girl with strange trials of fire, water, and insects. Eventually, Abby recovers with Mother Barker's help.

Marked by Fire has been well received by critics. Wendell Wray wrote in *Best Sellers* that Thomas "captures the flavor of black folk life in Oklahoma. . . . [She] has set for herself a very challenging task. . . . [But] Thomas' book works." Critic Dorothy Randall-Tsuruta commented in *Black Scholar* that Thomas's "poetic tone gives this work what scents give the roses already so pleasing in color. In fact often as not the lyrical here carries the reader beyond concerns for fast action. There too Thomas's short lived interest in writing plays figures in her fine regard and control of dialog." Hazel Rochman, writing in *School Library Journal,* admitted that "the lack of a fast-paced narrative line and the mythical overtones may present obstacles to some readers," but said that "many will be moved" by Abby's story.

The book was placed on required reading lists at many high schools and universities. Commenting on her stormy novel, Thomas once stated that "as a writer I work to create books filled with conflict. . . . I address this quest in part by matching the pitiful absurdities and heady contradictions of life itself, in part by leading the heroine to twin fountains of magic and the macabre, and evoking the holy and the horrible in the same breath. Nor is it ever enough to match these. Through the character of Abyssinia, I strive for what is beyond these, seeking, as do many writers, to find newer worlds."

Bright Shadow, a sequel to *Marked by Fire,* was published in 1983. In this work, Abyssinia goes to college and ends up falling in love with Carl Lee Jefferson. Abby is a young woman now, searching for what she wants as she completes her pre-medical studies. For reasons she can't figure out, Abby's father disapproves of Carl Lee. She suspects, however, that it is because of Carl Lee's alcoholic father. At the same time, the psychically sensitive Abby begins to have forebodings about her aunt's new husband. These feelings are validated when Aunt Serena is found brutally murdered.

Carl Lee begins to show his true colors when he is there to support Abby through her grief. Soon he has a revelation of his own when he finds out that the mysterious

Cherokee woman that has been lurking around town is actually his mother. Despite these difficult hurdles, nothing is able to disrupt the young couple's love and support for one another. It is because of Carl Lee that Abby finds the light when all she can see are the dark shadows of her aunt's death. *Bright Shadow* concludes when Abby has a dream in which her aunt revisits her and gives her a lesson: "We are all taken from the same source: pain and beauty. One is the chrysalis that gives to the other some gift that even in death creates a new dimension in life."

Critical reaction to *Bright Shadow* was generally more mixed than for *Marked by Fire. School Library Journal* contributor Carolyn Caywood found the plot of *Bright Shadow* touched with melodrama and lacking in credibility, but admitted that Thomas's "story is readable and her sensuously descriptive passages celebrating the physical beauty of the black characters are a nice touch." In the *Bulletin of the Center for Children's Books,* Zena Sutherland said that *Bright Shadow* as "a love story . . . is appealing, and the characterization is strong." However, she felt that "the often-ornate phraseology" sometimes weakens the story.

Several of Thomas's later books also feature the popular characters she created in *Marked by Fire* and *Bright Shadow,* including *The Golden Pasture,* which journeys back to Carl Lee's earlier life on his grandfather's ranch, and *Water Girl,* which tells the story of Abyssinia's teenage daughter Amber.

In 1990 Thomas edited the well-received anthology, *A Gathering of Flowers: Stories about Being Young in America.* The characters in these pieces represent various ethnic groups, including Native Americans, Asians, Hispanics, African Americans, and Anglos, and the authors include Gerald Vizenor, Jeanne Wakatsuki Houston, and Gary Soto. A critic noted in the *Bulletin of the Center for Children's Books* that "The collection is indeed rich and colorful, containing strong individual voices." *Voice of Youth Advocates* reviewer Judith A. Sheriff declared, "These stories will provide young adults with authentic glimpses of ethnic worlds they may seldom encounter personally."

In 1992 Thomas published *When the Nightingale Sings,* a young adult novel about the orphaned Marigold. The fourteen-year-old girl—a talented gospel singer—is living with a foster mother whose verbal abuse and bad temper make her less than an ideal parent. Although she is forced to spend her time cleaning and giving singing lessons to Ruby's unlikable children, Marigold resists believing in her foster mother's insults and instead concentrates on her singing. When the members of the Rose of Sharon Baptist Church hear her voice in the distance, their search for a new lead gospel singer just might be over. Although *Bulletin of the Center for Children's Books* contributor Betsy

Hearne found the book's realistic plot to be at odds with its "fairy tale tone," Hazel S. Moore commented in *Voice of Youth Advocates,* "The element of suspense carries the story back to its roots—the African American family deeply involved with the African American Church."

Thomas's award-winning 1993 work, *Brown Honey in Broomwheat Tea,* is a collection of poetry illustrated by Floyd Cooper. *School Library Journal* reviewer Lyn Miller-Lachmann described it as "twelve short, interrelated poems about family, love, and African-American identity" which "are accessible, lyrical, and moving, with thought-provoking phrases and images." In the course of the book a family battles poverty and growing pains with love and pride. Cathy Collison, writing in the *Detroit Free Press,* commented on the recurring imagery that links the pieces: "The poems return often to tea, brewing the words into a blend as rich and seasoned as the warm Cooper portrait of a grandmother."

With her imagination and ability to bring authenticity to her novels, Thomas has been highly praised and often compared to other successful African-American women authors, like Maya Angelou, Toni Morrison, and Alice Walker. Thomas takes scenes and characters from her youth and crafts them into powerful fiction. "If I had to give advice to young people," Thomas commented in her *SAAS* essay, "it would be that whatever your career choice, prepare yourself to do it well. Quality takes talent and time. Believe in your dreams. Have faith in yourself. Keep working and enjoying today even as you reach for tomorrow. If you choose to write, value your experiences. And color them in the indelible ink of your own background."

BIOGRAPHICAL/CRITICAL SOURCES:

BOOKS

Authors and Artists for Young Adults, Volume 12, Gale (Detroit, MI), 1994.
Children's Literature Review, Volume 19, Gale, 1990.
Contemporary Literary Criticism, Volume 35, Gale, 1985.
Dictionary of Literary Biography, Volume 33: *Afro-American Fiction Writers after 1955,* Gale, 1984.
Pearlman, Mickey, and Katherine U. Henderson, editors, *Inter/view: Talks with America's Writing Women,* University Press of Kentucky, 1990.
Something about the Author Autobiography Series, Volume 7, Gale, 1989, pp. 299-311.
Thomas, Joyce Carol, *Bright Shadow,* Avon, 1983.
Thomas, Joyce Carol, *Marked by Fire,* Avon, 1982.
Yalom, Margaret, editor, *Women Writers of the West,* Capra Press, 1982.

PERIODICALS

Bakersfield Californian, February 9, 1983.

Berkeley Gazette, July 21, 1983.
Best Sellers, June, 1982, pp. 123-124.
Black Scholar, summer, 1982, p. 48.
Bulletin of the Center for Children's Books, February, 1984, p. 119; January, 1991; February, 1993, p. 194.
Detroit Free Press, December 22, 1993.
New Directions, January/February, 1984.
Publishers Weekly, October 11, 1993, p. 87.
San Francisco Chronicle, April 12, 1982.
School Library Journal, March, 1982, p. 162; January, 1984, pp. 89-90; November, 1993.
Voice of Youth Advocates, December, 1990; June, 1993, p. 96.

* * *

THOMPSON, Josiah 1935-

PERSONAL: Born January 17, 1935, in East Liverpool, OH; son of Josiah D. (in sales) and Marion (Postles) Thompson; married Nancy Willis, December 27, 1958; children: Lis, Everson. *Education:* Yale University, B.A., 1957, M.A., 1962, Ph.D., 1964.

ADDRESSES: Agent—Gerard McCauley, P.O. Box 456, Cranbury, NJ 08512.

CAREER: Yale University, New Haven, CT, instructor in philosophy, 1964-65; Haverford College, Haverford, PA, assistant professor, 1965-70, associate professor, 1970-76, professor of philosophy, 1976-77; since 1979, operator of a private detective agency in San Francisco, CA. Consultant to *Life* magazine on the assassination of President John F. Kennedy. *Military service:* U.S. Naval Reserve, 1957-59; became lieutenant junior grade.

MEMBER: American Association of University Professors.

AWARDS, HONORS: Guggenheim fellow, 1969-70.

WRITINGS:

The Lonely Labyrinth: Kierkegaard's Pseudonymous Works, Southern Illinois University Press, 1967.
Six Seconds in Dallas, Geis, 1967.
(Editor) *Kierkegaard: A Collection of Critical Essays,* Doubleday, 1972.
Kierkegaard, Knopf, 1973.
Gumshoe: Reflections in a Private Eye, Little, Brown, 1988.

SIDELIGHTS: Josiah Thompson's second book, *Six Seconds in Dallas,* is the result of his exhaustive research into the assassination of President John F. Kennedy. A. V. Krebs, Jr., writes in *Commonweal* that in *Six Seconds in Dallas* Thompson "chooses to concentrate solely on the

six important seconds in Dealy Plaza. Using sketches of the important Abraham Zapruder film . . . , twenty-one other known still and motion pictures taken in the plaza, and numerous drawings and charts . . . , Thompson carefully and systematically shows how . . . the same bullet which first hit Kennedy could not have also wounded Texas Gov. John Connally. . . . Thompson, after pointing out the [Warren] Commission's major errors in evaluating those six crucial seconds, shows how available evidence suggests that there were three riflemen firing at the Presidential motorcade."

Even though Thompson was prohibited by *Life* from reproducing frames of the famous Zapruder film, he did, as Fred J. Cook points out, have "one great advantage. He happened to be employed as an adviser by *Life,* and *Life* possessed the original of the Zapruder film, which few persons have seen. The film in the National Archives in Washington, the one used by the FBI and the Warren Commission, is a copy of a copy—and so not nearly so clear and sharp as the original [that] Thompson was privileged to study." *Life* later brought suit against Thompson and Bernard Geis Associates, his representatives, for publishing the sketches of the Zapruder film; the magazine alleged that the book infringed on its rights to the film.

In 1976, Thompson left his tenured position in the philosophy department at Haverford College on sabbatical. He relocated to the San Francisco Bay area to work on a book on Friedrich Nietzsche. "But his work hit a snag," write Tim Allis and Maria Wilhelm in *People* magazine. In fact, Thompson went through a sort of mid-life crisis. " 'When we look at the professor, here's what we see,' " he tells Allis and Wilhelm. " 'He's had a patrician education, he's published three books and had a Guggenheim Fellowship, he has a lovely, loving wife, two terrific children, a cat and a Volvo. My very success had become a velvet trap. I felt a kind of deadness.' " Thompson then turned away from philosophy and went to work for a detective agency. "The job absorbed him," declares Jeffrey A. Frank in the *Washington Post Book World,* "and he never turned back."

Thompson chronicles his career change in *Gumshoe: Reflections in a Private Eye.* "The book is part confession and part thriller," states Charles Bremner in the *Times,* "a return to words by a man who chose to shun them in search of what he calls clarity in a life of action." Dashiell Hammett's Sam Spade, Raymond Chandler's Philip Marlowe, and the novels of John le Carre replaced the works of Kierkegaard and Nietzsche as the models of Thompson's life. In fact, Frank quotes Thompson as saying that Hammett's *The Maltese Falcon* became " 'a kind of original text against which I kept comparing my own experience. . . . There's no truth anywhere in the story, only ambiguous half-truths, only a face seen darkly in a mirror, a figure disappearing around a corner. . . . And that . . .

is how it seems to be. That was why Hammett was taking up so much space in the back of my head.' " But *Gumshoe,* praises Thomas D'Evelyn in the *Christian Science Monitor,* "is more than an act of homage. It's a good and courageous book written as if Spade himself watched the proceedings as of old, 'with the polite detached air of a disinterested spectator.' "

BIOGRAPHICAL/CRITICAL SOURCES:

PERIODICALS

Chicago Tribune, September 7, 1988.
Christian Science Monitor, June 15, 1988, p. 19.
Commonweal, September 20, 1968, pp. 637-638.
Nation, February 26, 1968, pp. 277-281.
Newsweek, June 13, 1988, p. 75.
New Yorker, June 10, 1967.
New York Times, December 9, 1967; February 18, 1968; July 5, 1988.
New York Times Book Review, February 18, 1968.
People, September 19, 1988, pp. 142-144.
Times (London), November 2, 1988.
U.S. News and World Report, July 11, 1988, p. 51.
Washington Post Book World, July 24, 1988.*

*   *   *

TITCHENER, Louise 1941-
   (Josie March, Anne Silverlock, Jane Silverwood; Alyssa Howard, Alexis Hill Jordan, Clare Richards, and Claire Richmond, joint pseudonyms).

PERSONAL: Born December 27, 1941, in Detroit, MI; daughter of Edward (an electrician) and Maud (a nurse; maiden name, Wood) Fiorell; married John Titchener (a professor of philosophy), August 20, 1962; children: Clare, Johnny. *Education:* University of Michigan, B.A., 1961; Ohio State University, M.A., 1964. *Avocational interests:* Figure skating, sailing, reading, walking around Baltimore's Inner Harbor.

ADDRESSES: Home—250 S. President St., #602, Baltimore, MD 21202. *Agent*—Linda Hayes, 7902 Nottingham Way, Ellicott City, MD 21043.

CAREER: Instructor in English composition at Howard Community College, Columbia, MD, and at University of Maryland, Baltimore County, Catonsville, 1964-78; freelance writer, 1978—.

MEMBER: Romance Writers of America (member of board of directors), Sisters in Crime, Science Fiction Writers of America.

AWARDS, HONORS: Woodrow Wilson fellow, 1962.

WRITINGS:

(Under pseudonym Josie March) *The Perfect Figure* (young adult novel), Silhouette (New York City), 1982.
Dress Circle, Ballantine (New York City), 1988.
Handle with Care, Harlequin (New York City), 1989.
Greenfire (science fiction novel), TSR Inc. (Lake Geneva, WI), 1993.
Homebody (suspense novel), HarperCollins (New York City), 1993.
ManTrap (suspense novel), HarperCollins, 1994.

Also author of young adult novel *On Edge,* Crown.

ROMANCE NOVELS UNDER PSEUDONYM ANNE SILVERLOCK

Casanova's Master, Dell (New York City), 1984.
With Each Caress, Dell, 1985.
Invincible Love, Dell, 1985.
Fantasy Lover, Dell, 1986.
In the Heat of the Sun, Dell, 1986.

ROMANCE NOVELS UNDER PSEUDONYM JANE SILVERWOOD

Voyage of the Heart, Harlequin, 1985.
Aphrodite's Promise, Dell, 1985.
Slow Melt, Harlequin, 1986.
A Permanent Arrangement, Harlequin, 1986.
Eye of the Jaguar, Harlequin, 1993.
Silent Starlight, Harlequin, 1994.

ROMANCE NOVELS WITH CAROLYN MALES, EILEEN BUCKHOLTZ, AND RUTH GLICK, UNDER JOINT PSEUDONYM ALYSSA HOWARD

Love Is Elected, Silhouette, 1981.
Southern Persuasion, Silhouette, 1983.

ROMANCE NOVELS WITH RUTH GLICK, UNDER JOINT PSEUDONYM ALEXIS HILL JORDAN

The Arms of Love, Dell, 1983.
Brian's Captive, Dell, 1983.
Reluctant Merger, Dell, 1984.
Summer Wine, Dell, 1984.
Beginner's Luck, Dell, 1984.
Mistaken Image, Dell, 1985.
Hopelessly Devoted, Dell, 1985.
Summer Stars, Dell, 1985.
Stolen Passion, Dell, 1986.
Indiscreet, Silhouette, 1988.

ROMANCE NOVELS WITH CAROLYN MALES, UNDER JOINT PSEUDONYM CLARE RICHARDS

Renaissance Summer, Silhouette, 1985.

ROMANCE NOVELS WITH CAROLYN MALES, UNDER JOINT PSEUDONYM CLAIRE RICHMOND

Runaway Heart, Harlequin, 1986.

Bride's Inn, Harlequin, 1987.
Pirate's Legacy, Harlequin, 1989.
Hawaiian Heat, Harlequin, 1993.

OTHER

Contributor of articles and photographs to magazines and newspapers, including *Change, Country, Seventeen, Sailing, Child Life, Writer's Digest, Washington Post, Christian Science Monitor,* and *Baltimore Sun.*

WORK IN PROGRESS: "Currently, I'm working on a thriller with paranormal elements set in New Orleans and tentatively titled *Deja Vu.* I'm also working on two mystery novels, both set in Baltimore."

SIDELIGHTS: "My writing interests," Louise Titchener told *CA,* "have gone through many sea changes over the years. Right now, I'm interested in writing mystery and suspense with a strong female protagonist. I'm also interested in writing fantasy and mystery and suspense novels with a fantasy element to them."

*   *   *

TOTTEN, George Oakley III 1922-
(Tao Mulian)

PERSONAL: Born July 21, 1922, in Washington, DC; son of George Oakley, Jr. (an architect) and Vicken (a sculptor; maiden name, von Post) Totten; married Astrid Maria Anderson (a professor and researcher in social psychology), June 26, 1948 (died April 26, 1975); married Lilia Huiying Li (an author and lecturer), July 1, 1976; children: (first marriage) Vicken Yuriko, Linnea Catherine. *Education:* Columbia University, A.B., 1946, A.M., 1949; Yale University, M.A., 1950, Ph.D., 1954; Stockholm University, Docentur i Japanologi, 1978.

ADDRESSES: Home—5129 Village Green, Los Angeles, CA 90016. *Office*—Center for Multiethnic and Transnational Studies, University of Southern California, 743 West Adams Blvd., Los Angeles, CA 90007.

CAREER: Columbia University, East Asian Institute, New York City, lecturer in government, 1954-55; Tufts University, Fletcher School of Law and Diplomacy, Medford, MA, research associate in Far Eastern affairs, 1955-58; Massachusetts Institute of Technology, Cambridge, assistant professor of political science, 1958-59; Boston University, Boston, MA, assistant professor of history and political science, 1959-61; University of Rhode Island, Kingston, associate professor of political science, 1961-64; University of Southern California, Los Angeles, associate professor, 1965-68, professor of political science, 1968-92, professor emeritus, 1992—, director of East Asian Studies Center, 1974-77, chair of political science department, 1980-86.

Visiting professor at various universities, including Eastern Michigan University, 1965, Sophia University, Tokyo, 1967, Waseda University, Tokyo, 1971-73, University of Stockholm, 1977-79, and University of Hawaii at Manoa, 1993; affiliated scholar, Center for Multiethnic and Transnational Studies, University of Southern California; senior counselor, Center for Pacific Asia Studies, Stockholm University, Sweden. Chair of Columbia University Seminar on Japan, 1962-63; Visiting Asian Professors Program, University of Rhode Island, coordinator, 1962-64; California Private Universities and Colleges Year-in-Japan Program at Waseda University, director, 1968-72, resident director and professor, 1971-72; University of Southern California-University of Los Angeles Joint East Asia Language and Area Center, director; Center of Pacific Asia Studies, University of Stockholm, director, 1986-89. Producer of biweekly radio program, "The Open Shoji on Japan," for KPFK-FM, Los Angeles, 1968-69. *Military service:* U.S. Army, Military Intelligence, 1942-46; became first lieutenant.

MEMBER: World Association of World Federalists, World Federalists—USA (chapter vice-president, 1965, regional vice-president, 1985—), European Association for Japanese Studies, American Historical Association, American Political Science Association, Japanese Political Science Association, Association for Asian Studies (member of program committee, 1968-69), Society for Asian and Comparative Philosophy, Association for Korean Studies (member of executive board, 1976—), Deutsche Gesellschaft fuer Ostasienkunde, Foereningen foer Orientaliska Studier, National Committee on United States-China Relations, United States-China People's Friendship Association, International Studies Association, Japan American Student Conference (member of national advisory committee, 1984—), Association of Korean Political Studies in North America, American Civil Liberties Union (member of chapter executive board, 1963-65), American Association of University Professors, Committee of Concerned Asian Scholars, Japan America Society of Southern California (council member, 1982—), Southern California China Colloquium, Southern California Japan Seminar (chairman, 1970-82), Los Angeles-Guangzhou (Canton) Sister City Committee (member of board of directors, 1983—).

WRITINGS:

Studies on Japan's Social Democratic Parties, Yale University Press (New Haven, CT), Volume I: *The Social Democratic Movement in Prewar Japan,* 1966, Volume II: (with Alan B. Cole and Cecil H. Uyehara) *Socialist Parties in Postwar Japan,* 1966.
(With Robert L. Friedheim and others) *Japan and the New Ocean Regime,* Westview (San Francisco, CA), 1984.

EDITOR

(With Hattie Kwahar Colton and Kenneth E. Colton) *Japan since Recovery of Independence: The Annals,* American Academy of Political and Social Science, 1956.

Democracy in Prewar Japan: Groundwork or Facade?, D. C. Heath (Boston, MA), 1965.

(And contributor with Willard A. Beling) *Developing Nations: Quest for a Model,* Van Nostrand (New York City), 1970.

(And contributor and author of introduction) Nym Wells and Kim San, *Song of Ariran: A Korean Communist in the Chinese Revolution,* Ramparts (San Francisco, CA), 1973, revised edition published as *Arirang,* Tongnyok [Seoul], 1992.

(And contributor with Jon R. Schmidhauser) *The Whaling Issue in U.S.-Japan Relations,* Westview, 1978.

(And co-translator) Ch'ien Mu, *Traditional Government in Imperial China: Critical Analysis,* St. Martin's (New York City), 1982.

(With Zhou Shulian, and contributor) *China's Economic Reform: Administering the Introduction of the Market Mechanism,* Westview, 1992.

TRANSLATOR

(And contributor) Harry Wray and Hilary Conroy, editors, *Japan Examined: Perspectives on Modern Japanese History,* Praeger, University of Hawaii Press, 1983.

OTHER

Contributor to numerous books, including *Sources of Japanese Tradition,* compiled by Ryusaku Tsunoda and others, Columbia University Press, 1958; *The Dictionary of Political Science,* compiled by Joseph Dunner, Philosophical Library, 1964; *Postwar Japan 1945 to the Present,* Pantheon, 1973; *Beyond China's Independent Foreign Policy: Challenge for the U.S. and Its Allies,* edited by James C. Hsiung, Praeger, 1985; and *Transient Societies: Japanese and Korean Studies in a Transitional World,* University of Tampere [Finland], 1993. Contributor to encyclopedias and dictionaries; contributor of articles on Japan, China, and Korea, and of book reviews to professional journals, popular magazines, and newspapers. Member of editorial advisory board, *Journal of Asian Studies,* 1965-67, and *Studies in Comparative Communism,* 1970—; member of editorial board, *Bulletin of Concerned Asian Scholars,* 1974-78.

Some of Totten's work has been translated into Japanese and published under name Tao Mulian.

WORK IN PROGRESS: Research on Chinese political thought and its development in Korea and Japan, problems in the reunifications of such countries as China and Korea, and "how the Chinese interpret the 'Japanese miracle' in comparison with the Americans."

SIDELIGHTS: George Oakley Totten III told *CA:* "Throughout my life I have been very concerned with promoting world peace through friendship and mutual understanding. While I have spent most of my life in the United States (which is my fatherland, where my father's ancestors go back long before the American Revolution), as a child I had an opportunity to visit Sweden, where my mother came from, and which I consider my motherland. In addition to English, I learned Swedish, French, and German very early, and in college I studied Chinese. The Second World War took me to Asia after I learned Japanese in the Army's first intensive classes, and since then I have never lost my fascination with the Orient. I devoted myself to political science, since I came to believe that mankind's most fundamental challenge was to devise ways to allow for peaceful change, both within countries—between the dominant elements and the opposition—and among nations, large and small, industrialized and developing. I developed expertise in studying and teaching about the politics and history of political thought in China, Japan, and Korea. I have always tried to make some contribution to bring about understanding and friendship among those nations and with the United States and Sweden and to think out ways in which North and South Korea and the Chinese mainland and Taiwan might be peacefully reintegrated to their mutual benefit, and how Japan might regain its north islands from the Soviet Union through negotiation. While my interests have been far-flung, this interest in peace and friendship holds them together. I am fortunate to have found a wonderful wife, a Chinese writer and lecturer, who shares the same basic motivation." In addition to speaking Swedish, Japanese, Chinese, and German, Totten has added Korean to his linguistic repertoire. His writings have also been published in Chinese, Korean, French, Swedish, German, Spanish, and Italian.

BIOGRAPHICAL/CRITICAL SOURCES:

PERIODICALS

New Statesman, July 28, 1967.

*   *   *

TRIBE, Ivan M(athews) 1940-

PERSONAL: Born May 1, 1940, in Albany, OH; son of Henry M. (a house painter) and Dorothy (Reeves) Tribe; married Deanna Lynn Tripp (a home economist), December 23, 1966. *Education:* Ohio University, B.S.Ed., 1962, M.A., 1967; University of Toledo, Ph.D., 1976. *Politics:* Republican. *Religion:* Protestant.

ADDRESSES: Home—111 East High St., McArthur, OH 45651. *Office*—Department of General Studies and Liberal Arts, Rio Grande College, Rio Grande, OH 45674.

CAREER: Mayor of Albany, OH, 1962-65; high school history teacher at public schools in Vinton and Meigs Counties, OH, 1964-70; Rio Grande College, Rio Grande, OH, lecturer, 1976-77, assistant professor, 1977-84, associate professor, 1984-90, professor of history 1990—. Member of city council of Albany, 1961; member of Athens County Board of Elections, 1964-68.

MEMBER: Organization of American Historians, Ohio Academy of History, Phi Alpha Theta, York Rite Masonic Bodies, Shrine.

AWARDS, HONORS: Appalachian studies fellow at Berea College, 1980 and 1985; American Recorded Sound Collections Award, 1994, for *The Stonemans: An Appalachian Family and the Music That Shaped Their Lives.*

WRITINGS:

The First Fifty Years of a Midwestern Rural Community, Athens County Historical Society (Athens, OH), 1980.

Mountaineer Jamboree: Country Music in West Virginia, University Press of Kentucky (Lexington), 1984.

Little Cities of Black Diamonds: Urban Development in the Hocking Coal Region, 1870-1900, Athens County Historical Society, 1986.

Sprinkled with Coal Dust: Life and Work in the Hocking Coal Region, 1870-1900, Athens County Historical Society, 1989.

The Stonemans: An Appalachian Family and the Music That Shaped Their Lives, University of Illinois Press (Champaign), 1993.

Contributor to *Encyclopedia of East Tennessee* and *Definitive Country: The Encyclopedia of Country Music.* Contributor of articles and reviews to history and country music journals.

WORK IN PROGRESS: A book on country music in the Carolinas for the University Press of Kentucky; *Queen City Country: Cincinnati as a Country Music Center,* a book on country music in Cincinnati for the University of Illinois Press.

SIDELIGHTS: Ivan M. Tribe told *CA:* "I am much interested in the history and culture of the common man, especially at the regional and local level. Most of my research and publications have tended to fall into two areas: the development of local communities, particularly coal mining towns; and the historical evolution of country and western music. My hope as a scholar and a teacher is that I have made noteworthy contributions to these two significant, but often overlooked, segments of America's heritage."

TURNER, Stephen P. 1951-
(Steve Turner)

PERSONAL: Born March 1, 1951, in Chicago, IL; son of Lawrence L. Turner (a real estate manager) and Natalie Stephens (a physician); second marriage to Kimberly Anne Wills (a housewife), April 21, 1990; children: Evan Wills. *Education:* University of Missouri, Columbia, A.B., 1971, A.M. (sociology), 1971, A.M. (philosophy), 1972, Ph.D., 1975. *Religion:* "Slight residue of Calvinism."

ADDRESSES: Home—103 Second Ave., Pass-A-Grille, St. Petersburg Beach, FL 33706. *Office*—University of South Florida, Tampa, FL 33620.

CAREER: University of North Florida, Jacksonville, adjunct lecturer in sociology, 1975; University of South Florida, St. Petersburg, assistant professor, 1975-79, associate professor, 1979-84, professor, 1984-87, graduate research professor of sociology, 1987-89, graduate research professor of philosophy, 1989—, director of the Center for Interdisciplinary Studies in Culture and Society, 1984—. Visiting professor at Virginia Polytechnic Institute and State University, Blackburg, 1982, at University of Notre Dame, 1985, and at Boston University.

AWARDS, HONORS: National Endowment for the Humanities fellow, 1991-92.

MEMBER: American Philosophical Association, American Sociological Association, History of Science Society, International Sociological Association, Society for Social Studies of Science.

WRITINGS:

Sociological Explanation as Translation, Cambridge University Press (New York City), 1980.

(Under name Steve Turner, with Frank Weed) *Conflict in Organizations: Practical Guidelines Any Manager Can Use,* Spectrum Books (Englewood Cliffs, NJ), 1983.

(With Regis A. Factor) *Max Weber and the Dispute Over Reason and Values: A Study in Philosophy, Ethics, and Politics,* Routledge & Kegan Paul (London), 1984.

(Editor with Mark Wardell) *Sociological Theory in Transition,* Allen & Unwin (London), 1986.

The Search for a Methodology of Social Science, Reidel (Dordrecht, Holland), 1986.

(With Jonathan Turner) *The Impossible Science: An Institutional Analysis of American Sociology,* Sage Publications (Beverly Hills, CA), 1990.

(Editor with Dirk Kaesler) *Sociology Responds to Fascism,* Routledge & Kegan Paul, 1992.

(Editor) *Emile Durkheim: Sociologist and Moralist,* Routledge & Kegan Paul, 1992.

The Social Theory of Practices: Tradition, Tacit Knowledge, and Presuppositions, University of Chicago Press (Chicago, IL), 1994.

(With Factor) *Max Weber: The Lawyer as Social Thinker,* Routledge & Kegan Paul, 1994.

Contributor of articles and reviews to academic journals in philosophy, science studies, sociology, and politics.

WORK IN PROGRESS: A book on the political theory of science.

SIDELIGHTS: Stephen P. Turner told *CA:* "I began publishing very young, and it seemed to me then that I had plenty of time: to write things that interested me, or that I could learn something from doing, or that served some immediate demand of academic life (of which there were far too many). I resolved that I would get serious after I turned forty—quit writing things I didn't like very much, or was writing for the wrong reasons. This was a difficult resolution to keep. There are many reasons to write—and

especially to edit (an activity that I seem fated to, or cursed with)—that are compelling, even though the results may not be especially pleasing. Some topics are interesting, and writing is a chance to think about them in a disciplined way. One feels a responsibility to other topics, a need to speak for them. And writing is often done as a favor, or to return one. *The Social Theory of Practices: Tradition, Tacit Knowledge, and Presuppositions* and *Max Weber: the Lawyer as Social Thinker,* are my 'after-forty' books. I have tried to keep my resolution with these books, and think of them as a thing apart from my other writing."

BIOGRAPHICAL/CRITICAL SOURCES:

PERIODICALS

Times Higher Education Supplement, April 27, 1984.
Times Literary Supplement, March 27, 1981.

*   *   *

TURNER, Steve
   See TURNER, Stephen P.

U

URE, Jean 1943-
(Jean Gregory; Ann Colin, Sarah McCulloch, pseudonyms)

PERSONAL: Surname pronounced "Ewer"; born January 1, 1943, in Surrey, England; daughter of William (an insurance officer) and Vera (Belsen) Ure; married Leonard Gregory (an actor and writer), 1967. *Education:* Attended Webber-Douglas Academy of Dramatic Art, 1965-67. *Religion:* None. *Avocational interests:* Reading, writing letters, walking dogs, playing with cats, music, working for animal rights.

ADDRESSES: Home—88 Southbridge Rd., Croydon, Surrey CR0 1AF, England. *Agent*—Maggie Noach, 21 Redan St., London W14 0AB, England.

CAREER: Writer. Worked variously as a waitress, cook, washer-up, nursing assistant, newspaper seller, shop assistant, theater usherette, temporary shorthand-typist, translator, secretary with NATO and UNESCO, and television production assistant.

MEMBER: Society of Authors, Vegan Society, Animal Aid.

AWARDS, HONORS: American Library Association best book for young adults citation, 1983, for *See You Thursday.*

WRITINGS:

JUVENILE FICTION

Ballet Dance for Two, F. Watts, 1960, published in England as *Dance for Two,* illustrated by Richard Kennedy, Harrap, 1960.

Hi There, Supermouse!, illustrated by Martin White, Hutchinson, 1983, published in the United States as *Supermouse* (Junior Literary Guild selection), illustrated by Ellen Eagle, Morrow, 1984.

You Two, illustrated by Eagle, Morrow, 1984, published in England as *The You-Two,* illustrated by White, Hutchinson, 1984.

Nicola Mimosa, illustrated by White, Hutchinson, 1985, published in the United States as *The Most Important Thing,* illustrated by Eagle, Morrow, 1986.

Megastar, Blackie, 1985.

Swings and Roundabouts, Blackie, 1986.

A Bottled Cherry Angel, Hutchinson, 1986.

Brenda the Bold, illustrated by Glenys Ambrus, Heinemann, 1986.

Tea-Leaf on the Roof, illustrated by Val Sassoon, Blackie, 1987.

War with Old Mouldy!, illustrated by Alice Englander, Methuen, 1987.

Who's Talking?, Orchard, 1987.

Frankie's Dad, Hutchinson, 1988.

(With Michael Lewis) *A Muddy Kind of Magic,* Blackie, 1988.

(With Lewis) *Two Men in a Boat,* Blackie, 1988.

Cool Simon, Orchard, 1990.

Jo in the Middle, Hutchinson, 1990.

The Wizard in the Woods, Walker, 1990.

Fat Lollipop, Hutchinson, 1991.

William in Love, Blackie, 1991.

Wizard in Wonderland, Walker, 1991, Candlewick Press, 1993.

Spooky Cottage, Heinemann, 1992.

The Unknown Planet, Walker, 1992.

Wizard in the Woods, Walker, 1992.

The Ghost That Lives on the Hill, Methuen, 1992.

Bossyboots, Hutchinson, 1993.

Captain Cranko and the Crybaby, Walker, 1993.

Phantom Knicker Nicker, Blackie, 1993.

Star Turn, Hutchinson, 1994.

NOVELS

The Other Theater, Transworld, 1966.
The Test of Love, Corgi, 1968.
If You Speak Love, Corgi, 1972.
Had We but World Enough and Time, Corgi, 1972.
The Farther Off from England, White Lion, 1973.
Daybreak, Corgi, 1974.
All Thy Love, Corgi, 1975.
Marriage of True Minds, Corgi, 1975.
No Precious Time, Corgi, 1976.
Hear No Evil, Corgi, 1976.
Curtain Fall, Corgi, 1978.
Masquerade, Corgi, 1979.
A Girl Like That, Corgi, 1979.
(Under pseudonym Ann Colin) *A Different Class of Doctor,* Corgi, 1980.
(Under pseudonym Ann Colin) *Doctor Jamie,* Corgi, 1980.
(Under name Jean Gregory) *Love beyond Telling,* Corgi, 1986.

YOUNG ADULT FICTION

A Proper Little Nooryeff, Bodley Head, 1982, published in the United States as *What If They Saw Me Now?,* Delacorte, 1984.
If It Weren't for Sebastian, Bodley Head, 1982, Delacorte, 1985.
You Win Some, You Lose Some, Bodley Head, 1984, Delacorte, 1987.
The Other Side of the Fence, Bodley Head, 1986, Delacorte, 1988.
One Green Leaf, Bodley Head, 1987, Delacorte, 1989.
Play Nimrod for Him, Bodley Head, 1990.
Plague 99, Methuen, 1990, Harcourt, 1991.
Dreaming of Larry, Doubleday, 1991.
Come Lucky April, Methuen, 1992.
Always Sebastian, Bodley Head, 1993.
A Place to Scream, Doubleday, 1993.

"RIVERSIDE THEATER ROMANCE" SERIES

Early Stages, Corgi, 1977.
Dress Rehearsal, Corgi, 1977.
All in a Summer Season, Corgi, 1977.
Bid Time Return, Corgi, 1978.

"THURSDAY" TRILOGY

See You Thursday (Junior Literary Guild selection), Kestrel, 1981, Delacorte, 1983.
After Thursday, Kestrel, 1985, Delacorte, 1987.
Tomorrow Is Also a Day, Methuen, 1989.

"WOODSIDE SCHOOL" SERIES

The Fright, Orchard Books, 1987.
Loud Mouth, Orchard Books, 1988.

Soppy Birthday, Orchard Books, 1988.
King of Spuds, Orchard Books, 1989.
Who's for the Zoo?, Orchard Books, 1989.

"VANESSA" TRILOGY

Trouble with Vanessa, Transworld, 1988.
There's Always Danny, Transworld, 1989.
Say Goodbye, Transworld, 1989.

GEORGIAN ROMANCES; UNDER PSEUDONYM SARAH McCULLOCH

Not Quite a Lady, Corgi, 1980, Fawcett, 1981.
A Most Insistent Lady, Corgi, 1981.
A Lady for Ludovic, Corgi, 1981.
Merely a Gentleman, Corgi, 1982.
A Perfect Gentleman, Corgi, 1982.

TRANSLATOR

Henri Vernes, *City of a Thousand Drums,* Corgi, 1966.
Vernes, *The Dinosaur Hunters,* Corgi, 1966.
Vernes, *The Yellow Shadow,* Corgi, 1966.
Jean Bruce, *Cold Spell,* Corgi, 1967.
Bruce, *Top Secret,* Corgi, 1967.
Vernes, *Treasure of the Golcondas,* Corgi, 1967.
Vernes, *The White Gorilla,* Corgi, 1967.
Vernes, *Operation Parrot,* Corgi, 1968.
Bruce, *Strip Tease,* Corgi, 1968.
Noel Calef, *The Snare,* Souvenir Press, 1969.
Sven Hassel, *March Battalion,* Corgi, 1970.
Hassel, *Assignment Gestapo,* Corgi, 1971.
Laszlo Havas, *Hitler's Plot to Kill the Big Three,* Corgi, 1971.
Hassel, *SS General,* Corgi, 1972.
Hassel, *Reign of Hell,* Corgi, 1973.

OTHER

Contributor of articles to periodicals, including *Vegan, Writers' Monthly, Books for Keeps,* and *School Librarian.*

SIDELIGHTS: Jean Ure's young adult books combine her lively sense of humor with unique stories that often contain off-beat situations and characters. Ure is a vegetarian who is avid about animal rights, and while her books make references to these tendencies among her characters, they are never preachy. Class struggles, homosexuality, sexual awakenings, and feminism are also among her topics, all of which she delivers with freshness and currency.

Ure does not remember a time when she did not want to be a writer. In Surrey, England, as a young girl she would steal notebooks from her school in order to fill them with imaginative stories. "I was brought up in a tradition of writing, inasmuch as my father's family were inveterate ode writers, sending one another long screeds of poetry on every possible occasion," Ure recalled in an essay for the *Something about the Author Autobiography Series* (*SAAS*).

Being outside of the popular crowd at school caused Ure to fantasize about many things. Being a compulsive writer, she wrote down these fantasies and, at the age of sixteen, Ure became a published writer. "Writing *Dance for Two* was a very cathartic exercise and brought me great solace," she related in *SAAS*. "I almost managed to believe that . . . I really *did* have a sweetheart called Noel, that I really *was* a ballet dancer." For several years after this initial publication she concentrated her efforts on writing romantic novels and translating books.

The year 1980 was a turning point for Ure. She wrote in *SAAS*: "I really emerged as myself, with a book for young adults called *See You Thursday.*" It focuses on a blind pianist named Abe and a sixteen-year-old rebel named Marianne. Although Abe is eight years older, wiser, and from a different background than Marianne, the pair become attracted to each other, and the relationship blossoms as Marianne sheds her shyness and finds a new maturity. In *After Thursday,* the romance of Abe and Marianne is further tested by their differing perspectives on independence.

Ure was extremely happy to have found this fresh audience for her writing. "The reason I turned to writing for young adults was, basically, that it offered a freedom which 'genre' writing does not allow," she related in *SAAS*. Ure used her instinctive talent for writing to create these books. She commented, "When I created Abe, my blind pianist, I did the very minimum of research into blindness but was able to gain direct knowledge, albeit to a severely limited extent, of how it would be to be blind by tying a scarf about my eyes and blundering around the house." *See You Thursday* won the American Library Association's best book for young adults citation in 1983.

Ure returned to the themes of autonomy and awakening sexuality in the "Vanessa" trilogy—which includes *Trouble with Vanessa, There's Always Danny,* and *Say Goodbye*—as well as in *The Other Side of the Fence.* Describing the first two books of the "Vanessa" trilogy as more than a romantic tale, Stephanie Nettell in the *Times Literary Supplement* labelled Ure's novels "intelligent, spiky and imaginative." Similarly enthusiastic about *The Other Side of the Fence,* reviewers such as the *Bulletin of the Center for Children's Books* contributor Zena Sutherland praised the novel as "mature and sensitive. . . . [It is] told with both momentum and nuance." This romance is unusual, however, because it concerns a young homosexual, Richard, who meets and finds friendship with Bonny, a girl who is attracted to him but cannot understand—until the end—why her sexual advances are not returned. Although one critic, *School Library Journal* writer Karen K.

Radtke, questioned Bonny's "naivete" regarding Richard (when she is otherwise street-smart), Radtke admitted that the story may be satisfying to teenagers who "harbor secret fantasies about . . . flaunting parental authority."

Ure's sensitive treatment of relationships is often the focus of critical reviews. The special rivalry between sisters is explored in *Supermouse* when a shy but talented girl, Nicola, is offered a dancing role over her more favored younger sister, Rose. Mary M. Burns in *Horn Book* wrote that even though the story is told from the point of view of an eleven-year-old, "the author has managed to suggest subtle emotions which underlie the family's values and actions." The story is continued in *The Most Important Thing* when Nicola, now fourteen, must decide whether her future career will include ballet, or whether she should concentrate instead on science and maybe become a doctor. Cynthia K. Leibold concluded in the *School Library Journal* that "Ure is skillful at creating colorful characters . . . and her characters execute their roles perfectly."

Coping with illness is the theme of two of Ure's contemporary works, *If It Weren't for Sebastian* and *One Green Leaf*—the first focusing on mental illness and the latter on a fatal physical sickness. Sebastian is an intense but peace-loving young man whose "strangeness" is an object of scorn and misunderstanding to others in *If It Weren't for Sebastian.* Maggie becomes his friend and soon discovers that Sebastian is being treated as an out-patient at a mental health clinic. Ure "here explores the borderline psychotic and his relationships with great sensitivity and understanding," declared Sutherland in a *Bulletin of the Center for Children's Books* review. Fatal illness is similarly treated with sympathy and skill in *One Green Leaf.* After an unsuccessful surgery, it becomes obvious that David's cancer is terminal. Ure's emphasis, however, is on how David copes, and on the affection of his friends during his illness. According to Tess McKellen in the *School Library Journal,* the author "dramatizes successfully the effect of unexpected tragedy on young minds and emotions" in the novel.

Ure confessed in *SAAS* that in her writing she sets out "to make people think: to make them examine their motives and question their assumptions." She concluded by summing up her reasons for writing, explaining that "it will always be my characters who interest me the most; and my aim, if conscious aim I have . . . , will still be to stimulate and entertain."

BIOGRAPHICAL/CRITICAL SOURCES:

BOOKS

Chevalier, Tracy, editor, *Twentieth-Century Children's Writers,* 3rd edition, St. James Press, 1989.
Children's Literature Review, Volume 34, Gale, 1994.

Something about the Author Autobiography Series, Volume 14, Gale, 1992.

PERIODICALS

British Book News, March, 1985.
Bulletin of the Center for Children's Books, December, 1983, p. 79; May, 1984, p. 176; June, 1984, p. 195; October, 1984, p. 36; June, 1985, p. 197; April, 1986, p. 160; June, 1986, p. 198; May, 1987, p. 180; February, 1988, p. 127; May, 1989, p. 238; October, 1991, p. 52.
Horn Book, December, 1983, p. 720; June, 1984, p. 334; August, 1984, p. 479; March, 1988, p. 212.
Publishers Weekly, November 25, 1983, p. 64; April 13, 1984, p. 72; February 8, 1985, p. 77; May 30, 1986, p. 68; June 12, 1987, p. 86.
School Library Journal, August, 1984, p. 87; October, 1984, p. 163; August, 1985, p. 82; May, 1986, p. 110; August, 1986, p. 108; April, 1988, p. 114; May, 1989, p. 128; October, 1991, p. 150; October, 1992, pp. 122-123; July, 1993, p. 87.
Times Literary Supplement, July 16, 1985, p. 910; November 28, 1986, p. 1347; June 9, 1989, p. 648; September 1, 1989, p. 957.
Voice of Youth Advocates, August-October, 1986, p. 152; October, 1989, p. 218.

*   *   *

URRY, John 1946-

PERSONAL: Born June 1, 1946, in London, England; son of Richard James (an accountant) and Wilga (a secretary; maiden name, Smith) Urry; children: Thomas, Amy. *Education:* Christ's College, Cambridge, B.A. (with first class honors), 1967, M.A., 1970, Ph.D., 1972.

ADDRESSES: Home—Lancaster, England. *Office*—Department of Sociology, Lancaster University, Lancaster LA1 4YL, England.

CAREER: Lancaster University, Lancaster, England, lecturer, 1970-81, senior lecturer, 1981-84, professor of sociology, 1985—, dean of social sciences faculty, 1989-94.

MEMBER: British Sociological Association, Regional Studies Association.

WRITINGS:

Reference Groups and the Theory of Revolution, Routledge & Kegan Paul (London), 1973.
(Editor with John Wakeford) *Power in Britain,* Heinemann (London), 1973.
(With Russell Keat) *Social Theory as Science,* Routledge & Kegan Paul, 1975, 2nd edition, 1982.
The Anatomy of Capitalist Societies, Macmillan (London), 1981.
(With Nicholas Abercrombie) *Capital, Labour, and the Middle Classes,* Allen & Unwin (London), 1983.
(Editor with Derek Gregory) *Social Relations and Spatial Structures,* Macmillan, 1985.
(With Linda Murgatroyd, Michael Savage, Dan Shapiro, and others) *Localities, Class, and Gender,* Pion (London), 1985.
(With Scott Lash) *The End of Organized Capitalism,* Polity Press (Oxford, England), 1987.
(With Abercrombie, Alan Warde, and others) *Contemporary British Society,* Polity Press, 1987.
The Tourist Gaze, Sage, 1990.
(With Paul Bagguley and others) *Restructuring Place, Class, and Gender,* Sage, 1990.
(With Scott Lash) *Economies of Signs and Space,* Sage, 1990.
Consuming Places, Routledge & Kegan Paul, 1995.

WORK IN PROGRESS: Research on travel, leisure, and tourism, class, urban change, and social theory.

V

VANCE, (Robert) Norman (Colbert) 1950-

PERSONAL: Born February 8, 1950, in Belfast, Northern Ireland; son of William (a headmaster) and Myrtle (a teacher; maiden name, Colbert) Vance; married Brenda Richardson (a university teacher and researcher), March 28, 1981; children: Robert, Alison. *Education:* Wadham College, Oxford, B.A., 1971, M.A., 1975, D.Phil., 1975. *Religion:* Christian. *Avocational interests:* Music.

ADDRESSES: Home—98 Prince Edward's Rd., Lewes, East Sussex BN7 1BH, England. *Office*—Arts Building, University of Sussex, Falmer, Brighton BN1 9QN, England.

CAREER: Oxford University, Oxford, England, Harold Salveson junior research fellow at New College, 1974-76; University of Sussex, Brighton, England, lecturer, 1976-93, professor of English, 1993—. Exchange professor at State University of New York College at Plattsburgh, 1985. Volunteer assistant church organist.

AWARDS, HONORS: Nomination as a book of the year, *Spectator,* 1985, for *The Sinews of the Spirit: The Ideal of Christian Manliness in Victorian Literature and Religious Thought;* nomination for literary prize, *Irish Times/*Aer Lingus, 1991, for *Irish Literature, a Social History: Tradition, Identity and Difference.*

WRITINGS:

The Sinews of the Spirit: The Ideal of Christian Manliness in Victorian Literature and Religious Thought, Cambridge University Press (Cambridge, England), 1985.
Irish Literature, a Social History: Tradition, Identity and Difference, Basil Blackwell (Oxford, England), 1990.
The Victorians and Ancient Rome, Basil Blackwell, in press.

Contributor of articles and reviews to periodicals, including *Irish Historical Studies, Journal of American Studies, Theology, Fortnight,* and *Queen's Quarterly.*

WORK IN PROGRESS: Irish Writing since 1800, for Longman (Essex, England).

SIDELIGHTS: Norman Vance once told *CA:* "My interest in Victorian studies probably stemmed from early reading in the books of my Victorian grandmother and conversations with her about her childhood. My other professional interests in Irish studies and religious studies again derive from childhood experience, compounded by later horror at the resurgence of quasi-religious, sectarian violence in my native Ulster."

The Sinews of the Spirit: The Ideal of Christian Manliness in Victorian Literature and Religious Thought analyzes the writings of such Victorian authors as Thomas Hughes, Charles Kingsley, F. D. Maurice, Thomas Carlyle, and Rudyard Kipling. Vance argues that the moral teachings of writers like Samuel Coleridge and Matthew Arnold were transformed by the Victorians into a kind of "muscular Christianity" and a return to the practice of medieval chivalry. Later the increase of athleticism resulted in social change, as reflected in the creation of the Young Men's Christian Association (YMCA) late in the nineteenth century and the development of religious missions in England's toughest slums. *Times Literary Supplement* reviewer David Newsome labelled Vance's book "a shrewd, entertaining and scholarly analysis," in which the author "confirms the significance of manliness . . . as defining the particular dynamism of that [Victorian] age as well as providing a sort of dialectic reflective of the major religious and philosophical controversies of the time."

Vance further told *CA* that *Irish Literature, a Social History: Tradition, Identity and Difference* "is a revisionist essay in Irish literary history which draws attention to the long-standing plurality and interaction of cultural traditions and notes the distinctive northern contribution to Irish literary development."

BIOGRAPHICAL/CRITICAL SOURCES:

PERIODICALS

Irish Review, spring, 1991, pp. 137-39.
Review of English Studies, February, 1987.
Times Literary Supplement, August 8, 1986.
Victorian Studies, winter, 1987.

*   *   *

VAN CLEVE, John Walter   1950-

PERSONAL: Born September 17, 1950, in Minneapolis, MN; son of John Woodbridge (a chemist) and Ethel (a teacher; maiden name, Dannenmaier) Van Cleve; married Judith Arden (in business), August 28, 1982; children: Courtney Anne, Leslie Allen, Stewart John. *Education:* Carleton College, B.A. (magna cum laude), 1972; University of Wisconsin—Madison, M.A., 1974, Ph.D., 1978.

ADDRESSES: Office—Department of Foreign Languages, Mississippi State University, Mississippi State, MS 39762-5720.

CAREER: Mississippi State University, Mississippi State, assistant professor, 1979-82, associate professor, 1982-87, professor of German, 1987—.

MEMBER: Modern Language Association of America, American Association of Teachers of German, American Association of University Professors, Phi Beta Kappa.

AWARDS, HONORS: Fulbright scholar, 1972-73.

WRITINGS:

Harlequin Besieged: The Reception of Comedy in Germany during the Enlightenment, Lang, 1980.
The Merchant in German Literature of the Enlightenment, University of North Carolina Press (Chapel Hill), 1986.
The Problem of Wealth in the Literature of Luther's Germany, Camden House (Columbia, SC), 1991.
Remarks on the Needed Reform of German Studies in the United States, Camden House, 1993.
Sebastian Brant's "The Ship of Fools" in Critical Perspective, 1800-1991, Camden House, 1993.

Contributor to literature and German studies journals.

van ITALLIE, Jean-Claude   1936-

PERSONAL: Born May 25, 1936, in Brussels, Belgium; came to United States in 1940, naturalized in 1952; son of Hugo Ferdinand (an investment banker) and Marthe Mathilde Caroline (Levy) van Itallie. *Education:* Harvard University, B.A., 1958; graduate study, New York University, 1959. *Religion:* Buddhist (Vajrayana).

ADDRESSES: Davenport Rd., Rowe, MA 01367; and 61 Jane St., 16M, New York, NY 10014.

CAREER: Playwright. *Transatlantic Review,* New York City, associate editor, 1959-61; Columbia Broadcasting System (CBS), New York City, researcher, 1962; Open Theatre, New York City, playwright-in-residence, 1963-68; New School for Social Research, New York City, instructor in playwriting, 1968 and 1972; Yale University, School of Drama, New Haven, CT, instructor in playwriting, 1969, visiting critic in playwriting, 1984-85; Princeton University, Princeton, NJ, lecturer, 1972-88. Teacher of playwriting, Naropa Institute, Boulder, CO, 1974-78, 1987-88; visiting Mellon Professor, Amherst College, 1976; part-time lecturer in theatre, New York University, 1982-88; instructor in playwriting, University of Colorado, Boulder, 1985, 1989, 1991; instructor in playwriting, Columbia University, 1986, American Repertory Theatre, Cambridge, MA, 1990; visiting professor of theatre, Middlebury College, Middlebury, VT, 1990.

MEMBER: Theatre Advisory Panel, National Council of the Arts, 1971-73.

AWARDS, HONORS: Rockefeller Foundation grant, 1962-63; Guggenheim fellow, 1973-74, 1980-81; Vernon Rice Drama Desk Award, Outer Circle Critics Award, and Jersey Journal Award, all 1967, for *America Hurrah;* Obie Award, 1969, for *The Serpent: A Ceremony;* Creative Artists Public Service award, 1975; Ph.D. (honorary), Kent State University, 1977; Ford Foundation grant, 1979; Playwrights Award, NEA, 1986.

WRITINGS:

PLAYS

From an Odets Kitchen, first produced by the Open Theatre Off-Broadway at Sheridan Square Playhouse, 1963.
The Murdered Woman, first produced by the Open Theatre Off-Broadway at Martinique Theatre, 1964.
America Hurrah (three one-acts; contains *Interview* [previously performed as *Pavane* Off-Off-Broadway at Cafe La Mama, 1965], *TV,* and *Motel* [previously performed as *America Hurrah* Off-Off-Broadway at Cafe La Mama, 1965; also see below]); first produced Off-Broadway at Pocket Theatre, 1966; Coward, 1967 (British publication under same title also contains

War [also see below] and *Almost Like Being* [also see below], Penguin, 1967).

War and Four Other Plays (contains *War* [one-act; first performed by Barr-Wilder-Albee Playwrights Unit Off-Off-Broadway at Vandam Theatre, 1963; produced Off-Broadway at Martinique Theatre, 1966], *I'm Really Here* [one-act; first produced by Barr-Wilder-Albee Playwrights Unit Off-Off-Broadway at Vandam Theatre, 1965]; *Almost Like Being* [one-act; first produced by Barr-Wilder-Albee Playwrights Unit Off-Off-Broadway at Vandam Theatre, 1965; published in *Tulane Drama Review,* summer, 1965], *Where is de Queen?* [one-act; first produced under title *Dream* by the Open Theatre Off-Off-Broadway at Cafe La Mama, 1965; produced as *Where is de Queen?* in Minneapolis, MN, at Firehouse Theatre, 1966], and *The Hunter and the Bird* [one-act; first produced by the Open Theatre Off-Broadway at Sheridan Square Playhouse, 1965]), Dramatists Play Service, 1967.

(With Sharon Thie) *Thoughts on the Instant of Greeting a Friend on the Street* (one-act; also see below; first produced with other plays under title *Collision Course* Off-Broadway at Cafe au Go Go, 1968), published in *Collision Course,* edited by Edward Parone, Random House, 1968.

(In collaboration with players of the Open Theatre, under direction of Joseph Chaikin) *The Serpent: A Ceremony* (one-act; first produced by Open Theatre in Rome at Teatro degli Arte, 1968; produced in Cambridge, MA, at Loeb Drama Center, 1969; produced by Open Theatre Off-Broadway at Public Theatre, 1969), Atheneum, 1969.

(With Megan Terry and Sam Sheppard) *Nightwalk,* produced in New York City by the Open Theatre Company, 1973.

Mystery Play (two-act; produced Off-Broadway at Cherry Lane Theatre, 1973), Dramatists Play Service, 1973, revised version published and produced as *The King of the United States* (produced in Westbeth, NY, at Theatre for the New City, 1973), Dramatists Play Service, 1975.

Seven Short and Very Short Plays (contains *Eat Cake* [produced in Denver, CO, 1971], *Take a Deep Breath* [one-act; first produced in New York City by the D.M.Z. political cabaret, 1969; also see below], *Photographs: Mary and Howard* [produced in Los Angeles, 1969], *Harold, Thoughts on the Instant of Greeting a Friend in the Street, The Naked Nun,* and *The Girl and the Soldier* [produced in Los Angeles, 1967]), Dramatists Play Service, 1973.

(Adapter) Anton Chekhov, *The Seagull* (first produced in Princeton, NJ, at McCarter Theatre, 1973), Dramatists Play Service, 1974.

A Fable (produced in New York City at Lenox Arts Center, 1975), Dramatists Play Service, 1976.

(Adapter) Chekhov, *The Cherry Orchard* (produced in New York City at Lincoln Center for the Performing Arts, 1977), Grove, 1977.

(Adapter) Euripides, *Medea,* first produced in Kent, OH, by Kent State University student group, 1979.

(Adapter) Chekhov, *The Three Sisters,* first produced in New York City by River Arts Productions, 1979.

Bag Lady (first produced in New York City at Theatre for the New City, November, 1979), Dramatists Play Service, 1980.

Paradise Ghetto, Studio Duplicating Service, 1982.

(Adapter) Chekhov, *Uncle Vanya* (first produced in New York City at Cafe La Mama, 1982), Dramatists Play Service, 1980.

The Tibetan Book of the Dead, or, How Not to Do It Again (first produced in New York City at Cafe la Mama, 1983), Dramatists Play Service, 1983.

Early Warnings (three short plays, including *Sunset Freeway, Bag Lady,* and *Final Orders;* produced in New York City at Manhattan Theatre Club, 1983), Dramatists Play Service, 1983.

(Translator) Jean Genet, *The Balcony,* 1986.

Calcutta, Kent State University Libraries, 1987.

Ancient Boys, produced in New York City at La Mama Annex, 1989.

(With Chaikin) *Struck Dumb,* (first produced in Los Angeles, 1991), published in *Best Plays, 1991-92,* Applause Books, 1992.

(Adaptor) Mikhail Bulgakov, *Master i Margarita,* (first produced in New York City at Theatre for the New City, 1993), Dramatists Play Service, 1994.

Also author of plays *Children of the Shore,* 1959, *The First Fool,* 1964, *The Traveller,* 1987, *The Airplane, Picnic in Spring, Simple Simon, The Worlds of Rip Van Winkle,* and *Naropa;* author and co-lyricist of *The Odyssey* (musical), 1991. Plays are represented in various anthologies, including *Eight Plays from Off-Off-Broadway,* edited by Nick Orzel and Michael Smith, Bobbs-Merrill, 1966; *Playwrights for Tomorrow, Volume III,* edited by Arthur H. Ballet, University of Minnesota Press, 1967; *The Off-Off-Broadway Book: The Plays, People, Theatres,* edited by Albert Poland, Bobbs-Merrill, 1972. Several of van Itallie's plays have been produced on television, including *Pavane* and *Thoughts on the Instant of Greeting a Friend on the Street,* both NET, 1969, and *America Hurrah* and *Take a Deep Breath,* both New York Television Theater, 1969.

SCREENPLAYS

Three Lives for Mississippi (based on the novel by William Bradford Huie), Cinema Center Films, 1971.

(Author of first draft) *Follies* (based on the musical by William Goldman), Twentieth Century-Fox, 1973.

Also wrote and produced a 20-minute film, *The Box Is Empty,* screened with other experimental films at Cinematheque, New York, NY, 1965.

Author of television scripts for CBS series *Look Up and Live:* "The Stepinac Case," 1963; "New Church Architecture, I," 1964; "New Church Architecture, II," 1964, "The Sounds of Courage," 1965; "Hobbies, or Things Are All Right with the Forbushers," 1967; and "Take a Deep Breath," 1969; also writer of eleven adaptations for the series, 1964-66.

OTHER

Author of unpublished book, *To India: A Journal.* Contributor to *Stories from the Transatlantic Review,* edited by Joseph F. McCrindle, Holt, 1970; *Behind the Scenes: Theatre and Film Reviews from the Transatlantic Review* (and author of introduction), edited by McCrindle, Holt, 1971; and *The American Theatre, 1970-1971,* International Theatre Institute of the United States and Scribner, 1972. Contributor to *New York Times, Village Voice, Transatlantic Review, Drama Review,* and other publications.

Van Itallie's papers have been collected at Kent State University.

SIDELIGHTS: "The first of the Off-Off-Broadway playwrights to attract considerable attention was Jean-Claude van Itallie," writes Mardi Valgemae. Identified with the Open Theatre group which is directed by Joseph Chaikin, van Itallie's plays explore the sources and dimensions of unhappiness and violence in American life; the inability to cope with the disparity between remembered, mythical ideals and present realities, the sentimental longing for the old, personal alienation, self-repression, and fear are shown to culminate in either violent behavior or withdrawal from the world. Phyllis Wagner writes, however, that these themes are underlined by a belief that "it is possible for human beings to expand beyond the cultural and personal limits they have imposed on themselves." In an interview with Wagner, van Itallie discusses the difficulty in confronting an audience with these issues, given the ritualistic nature of the theatre: "You go, and you discuss certain things during intermission and you go away and you've had a certain amount of pleasure. The playwright who is working seriously very much needs to get to the audience more directly. . . . He's got to use seduction, he's got to use shock, he's got to use different forms of theater." In *A Book on the Open Theater,* Robert Pasolli assesses this objective, which van Itallie shares with the Open Theatre, as "an effort to make visible in acting and staging those untidy masses of emotional and psychic experience which the Absurdists, Pinter, and the new American writers have tapped, to mine aspects of human experi-

ence which naturalism, realism, and what has been called 'the narrative fix' obscure."

While noting that "you can't transgress the boundaries of reality. Reality is everything . . .," van Itallie states that "you can transgress what you think are reality's boundaries. . . . You can certainly push beyond what you thought was allowable, what you thought was the shape of things." The extension of reality to include the realm of dreams is based on the idea that "reality is disguised and revealed in our dreams as a metaphor. If the metaphor a playwright chooses comes from deep enough within him, then he must have faith that, with the application of some craft, it will induce recognition in the audience of its own dream, conveying and revealing a share of the public unconscious . . . a private dream reshaped and publicly revealed to be everyone's." Although non-verbal communication is a major device in van Itallie's exploration of inner reality, language, when juxtaposed with dramatic action, provides an otherwise unattainable focus and helps to elicit from the audience the desired shock of recognition—in the playwright's words, the "Ah, Yes!" experience. He feels it necessary, however, to move away from the conventional use of dialogue, to counteract the "understandable, but frightening mistrust of words everywhere, because they are used as the lying tools of the power forces. . . . One has to find a new way to use language . . . where each word is chosen with care for its importance in juxtaposition with the other words and in juxtaposition with the action that's going on on stage—so that the total play comes out being a new language."

Robert Brustein, in his book *The Third Theatre,* states that van Itallie "has discovered the truest poetic function of the theatre, which is to . . . invent metaphors which can poignantly suggest a nation's nightmares and afflictions. These metaphors solve nothing, change nothing, but they do manage to relax frustration and assuage loneliness by showing that it is still possible for men to share a common humanity." In *Bag Lady* van Itallie selects as metaphor one of those women seen in many urban areas who live on the street and carry all their belongings with them in shopping bags. "There is something primordial about the arrangement: life is reduced to necessities," comments Mel Gussow. "The play is less a search for psychological motivations, for literal behavior patterns, than it is an attempt to give the character a kind of mythic stature. . . . Even after the play ends, we are not sure who she is and where she is from. She may even be an avatar. . . . The play is not, as one might expect, a literal transcription from the street, but a poetic interpretation by a discerning playwright."

A later work, *Early Warnings,* "transmits radar messages from a theatrical DEW line," according to Mel Gussow in a *New York Times* review. Gussow describes the three one-act plays—*Sunset Freeway, Bag Lady,* and *Final Orders*—as "auguries of impending doom, as perceived through the author's vivid imagination." The first involves an actress caught in freeway traffic en route to an audition. The last concerns two future astronauts in a space capsule circling toward disaster. Those plays, Gussow comments, "become parallel adventures," and he finds the three as a whole are "an intense experience. The acting, direction and sound design . . . are united in their precision. Taken together, the plays offer three-course food for thought."

In *Ancient Boys,* van Itallie explores the life of a gifted artist, Ruben, who has just died after battling AIDS. Several of Ruben's friends have gathered in his studio to reminisce, and the play unfolds as a series of flashbacks. Gussow observed in his *New York Times* review of *Ancient Boys* that "on the most immediate level, the play is simply too brief to give an adequate impression of the reasons why Ruben is the center of his universe," though he added that "van Itallie is somewhat more effective in depicting the people in Ruben's orbit than he is with the central character." Gussow concluded that *Ancient Boys* fails to live up to van Itallie's high standards, "promising one thing (a probing study of the effects of AIDS) and delivering another (a sentimentalized dramatization of a death in the family)."

Van Itallie once told *CA:* "[I] speak French, hate cities especially New York City where I live half the time because it's stimulating, love New England where I live on a farm the other part of the time when I'm not traveling which I like to do, don't eat meat or drink coffee, prefer herb teas and fresh fruit, worry about air pollution, the insanity of governments generally and ours in specific, protest whenever possible against war, do a lot of yoga and exercise, practice Buddhism, [and] treasure my good friends."

BIOGRAPHICAL/CRITICAL SOURCES:

BOOKS

Brustein, Robert, *The Third Theatre,* Knopf, 1969.
Contemporary Literary Criticism, Volume 3, Gale, 1975.
Lahr, John, *Up Against the Fourth Wall: Essays on Modern Theatre,* Grove, 1970.
Pasolli, Robert, *A Book on the Open Theater,* Bobbs-Merrill, 1970.
Theatre 2: American Theatre, 1968-69, International Theatre Institute, 1970.

PERIODICALS

Newsday, November 23, 1966.
New York Times, November 27, 1966; December 11, 1966; November 7, 1967; November 27, 1979; January 19, 1983; May 9, 1983; September 15, 1983; May 24, 1990; February 24, 1991.

Serif (entire issue), winter, 1972.
Tulane Drama Review, summer, 1966.
Twentieth Century Literature, October, 1971.
Washington Post, October 22, 1984; April 10, 1986.

*   *   *

VENUTI, Lawrence (Michael) 1953-

PERSONAL: Born February 9, 1953, in Philadelphia, PA; son of Michael (an upholsterer) and Lucille (a seamstress; maiden name, Rutigliano) Venuti; married Lindsay Davies, 1988. *Education:* Temple University, B.A., 1974; Columbia University, Ph.D., 1980.

ADDRESSES: Home—262 West 107th St., Apt. 4B, New York, NY 10025. *Office*—Department of English, Temple University, Philadelphia, PA 19122.

CAREER: Temple University, Philadelphia, PA, assistant professor, 1980-87, associate professor, 1987-92, professor of English, 1992—, director of creative writing program, 1990-92, director of graduate studies, 1992—. Adjunct assistant professor of writing at College of New Rochelle, 1979; adjunct lecturer in English at Manhattan Community College, 1979-80; adjunct professor of humanities at Cooper Union, 1980; adjunct assistant professor of English at Iona College, 1980. Served on PEN judiciary committee for Renato Poggioli Award, 1984, and for PEN Book-of-the-Month-Club Translation Award, 1991; member of the judiciary committee for the translator's fellowship competition, National Endowment for the Arts, 1988-90, 1993; judge of the Ezra Pound Prize for Literary Translation, University of Pennsylvania, 1992. Gives readings and lectures at various universities, including University of California at Santa Barbara, Carnegie Mellon University, Columbia University, Kent State University, State University of New York at Binghampton, and Oberlin College.

MEMBER: International PEN (translation committee, 1983—), Modern Language Association of America (founding member of the Executive Committee for the Discussion Group on Translation, 1993), American Literary Translators Association.

AWARDS, HONORS: Renato Poggioli Award, International PEN (American Center), 1980, for translation of *Delirium* from the Italian; National Endowment for the Arts translator's fellowship and Columbia University Translation Center Award, both 1983, both for *Restless Nights: Selected Stories of Dino Buzzati;* Premio di cultura from the Italian government, 1983, for translations; National Endowment for the Humanities translation grant, 1988, for *Fantastic Tales.*

WRITINGS:

(Translator) Barbara Alberti, *Delirium,* Farrar, Straus (New York City), 1980.

(Translator) Aldo Rossi, *A Scientific Autobiography,* MIT Press (Cambridge, MA), 1981.

(Translator) Francesco Alberoni, *Falling in Love,* Random House (New York City), 1983.

(Editor and translator) Dino Buzzati, *Restless Nights: Selected Stories of Dino Buzzati,* North Point Press (Berkeley, CA), 1983.

(Editor and translator) Buzzati, *The Siren: A Selection From Dino Buzzati,* North Point Press, 1984.

Our Halycon Dayes: English Prerevolutionary Texts and Postmodern Culture, University of Wisconsin Press (Madison), 1989.

(Editor and translator) I. U. Tarchetti, *Fantastic Tales,* Mercury House (Columbia, MO), 1992.

(Editor and contributor) *Rethinking Translation: Discourse, Subjectivity, Ideology,* Routledge & Kegan Paul (Boston, MA), 1992.

(Editor and translator) Milo De Angelis, *Finite Intuition: Selected Poetry and Prose,* Sun and Moon (College Park, MD), 1994.

The Translator's Invisibility, Routledge & Kegan Paul, 1994.

(Translator) Tarchetti, *Passion,* Mercury House, 1994.

Contributor of articles and translations to numerous periodicals, including *Antaeus, Boundary Two, Conjunctions, Criticism, Harper's, Journal of Medieval and Renaissance Studies, New York Times Book Review, Philadelphia Inquirer, SubStance, Sulfur, Testo a fronte* (Milan), *Textual Practice, Traduction,* and *TriQuarterly.* Editorial board member, *Assays: Critical Approaches to Medieval and Renaissance Texts,* 1990—; general editor, *Border Lines: Works in Translation,* Temple University Press, 1987—.

WORK IN PROGRESS: A study of translation in relation to such categories and practices as authorship, copyright, and scholarship; a translation of the Italian writer J. Rodolfo Wilcock's *The Babel of Iconoclasts.*

SIDELIGHTS: Lawrence Venuti told *CA:* "The kind of translation I value most is foreignizing, not domesticating, with the understanding that all translation domesticates to a certain extent by assimilating foreign writing to domestic cultural values. The question is always how to direct the violence that translation enacts on linguistic and cultural differences. Because translation wields enormous power in the construction of cultural identities for foreign countries, it seems urgent to direct its violence against domestic values that might exclude foreign cultures for whatever reason, aesthetic, racial, political. I choose to translate Italian literary works that deviate from the canons of Anglo-American culture (particularly such canons

as realism in fiction and confessionalism in poetry), and increasingly I aim to translate these works with strategies that are not canonical, drawing on the wide range of English forms available to writers, using, for example, archaism and slang as well as the current standard dialect. Foreignizing translation can not only question domestic writing, but enrich it by inspiring the development of new literary forms. This kind of translation is also a way to reimagine the role of the translator at an unpropitious time, when the global hegemony of the English-speaking countries and of English has led to grossly unequal exchanges with foreign cultures, lowering the numbers of translations published in the United States and the United Kingdom and banishing the translator to the margins of Anglo-American culture. Translators can help to change this situation, but only by taking it into account when they develop their projects."

BIOGRAPHICAL/CRITICAL SOURCES:

PERIODICALS

New Yorker, November 2, 1992.
New York Times Book Review, October 28, 1984.
Washington Post Book World, August 28, 1983.*

*   *   *

VIOLA, Herman J(oseph) 1938-

PERSONAL: Born February 24, 1938, in Chicago, IL; son of Joseph (a carpenter) and Mary (Incollingo) Viola; married Susan Patricia Bennett (a librarian), June 13, 1964; children: Joseph, Paul, Peter. *Education:* Marquette University, B.A., 1960, M.A., 1964; Indiana University, Ph.D., 1970.

ADDRESSES: Home—7307 Pinewood St., Falls Church, VA 22046-2725. *Office*—Museum of Natural History, Smithsonian Institution, Washington, DC 20560.

CAREER: National Archives, Washington, DC, archivist, 1966-68; *Prologue: Journal of the National Archives,* Washington, DC, founding editor, 1968-72; Smithsonian Institution, Washington, DC, director of National Anthropological Archives, 1972-86, director of quincentenary programs at Museum of Natural History, 1986—. *Military service:* U.S. Navy, 1962-64.

MEMBER: Society of American Archivists (program chair, 1972), Organization of American Historians, American History Association, Western History Association.

WRITINGS:

Thomas L. McKenney: Architect of America's Early Indian Policy, 1816-1830, Swallow Press (Athens, OH), 1974.

The Indian Legacy of Charles Bird King, Smithsonian Institution Press (Washington, DC), 1976.

Diplomats in Buckskins: A History of Indian Delegations in Washington City, Smithsonian Institution Press, 1981.

The National Archives of the United States, Abrams (New York City), 1984.

Exploring the West: A Smithsonian Book, Smithsonian Institution Press, 1987.

After Columbus: The Smithsonian Chronicle of the North American Indians, Smithsonian Books (Washington, DC), 1990.

Ben Nighthorse Campbell: An American Warrior, Orion Books (New York City), 1993.

EDITOR

(With Robert Kvasnicka) *The Commissioners of Indian Affairs,* University of Nebraska Press (Lincoln), 1979.

(With Carolyn Margolis) *Magnificent Voyagers: The U.S. Exploring Expedition, 1938-1942,* Smithsonian Institution Press, 1985.

(With Margolis) *Seeds of Change: A Quincentennial Commemoration,* Smithsonian Institution Press, 1991.

(And author of introduction) *The Memoirs of Charles Henry Veil: A Soldier's Recollections of the Civil War and the Arizona Territory,* Orion Books, 1993.

FOR CHILDREN

(With wife, Susan P. Viola) *Giuseppe Garibaldi,* Chelsea House (New York City), 1988.

Sitting Bull, illustrations by Charles Shaw, Raintree Publishers (Milwaukee, WI), 1990.

After Columbus: The Horse's Return to America, illustrations by Deborah Howland, Soundprints (Norwalk, CT), 1992.

Osceola, illustrations by Yoshi Miyake, Raintree Steck-Vaughn (Austin, TX), 1993.

BIOGRAPHICAL/CRITICAL SOURCES:

PERIODICALS

Los Angeles Times Book Review, September 30, 1984.
Washington Post Book World, August 23, 1981.

W

WALKER, Robert H(arris) 1924-

PERSONAL: Born March 15, 1924, in Cincinnati, OH; married Grace V. Burtt, 1953; children: three. *Education:* Northwestern University, B.S., 1945; Columbia University, M.A., 1950; University of Pennsylvania, Ph.D., 1955.

ADDRESSES: Home—915 26th St. N.W., Washington, DC 20037.

CAREER: U.S. Military Government, Shizuoka, Japan, education specialist, 1946-47; Carnegie Institute of Technology (now Carnegie-Mellon University), Pittsburgh, PA, instructor, 1950-51; University of Pennsylvania, Philadelphia, instructor, 1953-54; Haverford College, Haverford, PA, instructor, 1954-55; University of Wyoming, Laramie, assistant professor of American studies, 1955-59, acting director of School of American Studies, 1956-59; George Washington University, Washington, D.C., associate professor of American literature, 1959-63, professor of American civilization, 1963-94, director of American Studies Program, 1959-66 and 1968-70.

Visiting instructor at Jamestown College, 1961, Kyoto-Doshisha, 1964 and 1994, Stetson University, 1965, and University of Hawaii, 1967 and 1994. Director, Rose Bibliographical Project, 1974—; Washington editor, Algonquin Books, 1983—. Director of Peace Corps training in American studies and other disciplines at several universities, 1962-65; director, Division of Education public programs, National Endowment for the Humanities, 1966-68. Commissioner, Japan-U.S. Friendship Commission, 1977-81. Consultant to U.S. Information Agency, 1959—, and to other government and private agencies. *Military service:* U.S. Naval Reserve, 1942-61; on active duty, 1943-46; became lieutenant junior grade.

MEMBER: American Studies Association (national president, 1970-71), Phi Beta Kappa, Cosmos Club.

AWARDS, HONORS: U.S. Department of State specialist grants to Japan, 1964 and 1975, Germany, 1965 and 1986, Sweden, 1965 and 1983, Thailand, Iran, and Greece, all 1975, Israel, 1980, Brazil, 1981, and Italy, 1986; research grants from Washington S.T.A.R., 1966-67, and National Endowment for the Humanities, 1966-69; Fulbright grants to Australia, New Zealand, and Philippines, all 1971, and Sweden, 1987; fellow, George Lieb Harrison, 1952-53 and 1954-55, Woodrow Wilson International Center, 1972-73, Rockefeller Research Center, 1979, and Huntington Library and Hoover Institution, both 1980.

WRITINGS:

American Studies in the United States, Louisiana State University Press (Baton Rouge), 1958.

The Poet and the Gilded Age: Social Themes in Late Nineteenth-Century American Verse, University of Pennsylvania Press (Philadelphia), 1963.

Everyday Life in the Age of Enterprise, Putnam (New York City), 1967, published as *Life in the Age of Enterprise,* Capricorn Books (Toms River, NJ), 1971.

(Author of introduction) Kenneth Lynn, editor, *Visions of America: Eleven Historical Essays,* Greenwood Press (Westport, CT), 1973.

(Author of introduction) Ralph H. Gabriel, editor, *American Values: Continuity and Change,* Greenwood Press, 1974.

(Editor and author of introduction) *American Studies Abroad,* Greenwood Press, 1976.

(Editor and author of introduction) *The Reform Spirit in America: A Documentation of the Patterns of Reform in the American Republic,* Putnam, 1976.

(Editor and author of introduction) *American Studies: Topics and Sources,* Greenwood Press, 1976.

(Author of introduction) Robert Ernest Spiller, editor, *Milestones in American Literary History,* Greenwood Press, 1977.

(Author of introduction) Leonard Doob, editor, *Ezra Pound Speaking: Radio Speeches of Ezra Pound,* Greenwood Press, 1978.

(Author of introduction) Joseph S. Tulchin, editor, *Hemispheric Perspectives on the United States,* Greenwood Press, 1978.

(Author of introduction) W. A. Linn, *Horace Greeley,* Chelsea, 1980.

(Editor and author of introduction with Jefferson Kellogg) *Sources for American Studies,* Greenwood Press, 1983.

(Author of introduction) Clifford Brown and Robert J. Walker, compilers, *A Campaign of Ideas: The 1980 Anderson/Lucey Platform,* Greenwood Press, 1984.

Reform in America: The Continuing Frontier, University Press of Kentucky (Lexington), 1985.

(With Gabriel) *The Course of American Democratic Thought,* 3rd edition, Greenwood Press, 1986.

Cincinnati and the Big Red Machine, Indiana University Press (Bloomington), 1988.

Also contributor to books, including *New Directions in Graduate Education,* Council of Graduate Schools in the U.S., 1968; *Growth in America,* edited by C. L. Cooper, Greenwood Press, 1976; and *Portrait of America,* Volume 2, edited by Stephen B. Oates, Houghton (Boston), 1983. Editor of "Contributions in American Studies" monograph series, Greenwood Press, 1970—. Contributor of articles and book reviews to literature and history journals, including *American Historical Review, American Literature, American Quarterly, American Studies International, Christian Science Monitor, Commonweal,* and *Shenandoah.* Editor, *American Quarterly,* 1953-54; senior editor, *American Studies International,* 1970-81.

WORK IN PROGRESS: The history of ideas as an organizing principle in cultural history; the eighteenth-century idea of equality.

* * *

WALKER, Robert W(ayne) 1948-
(Geoffrey Caine, Glenn Hale, Stephen Robertson)

PERSONAL: Born November 17, 1948, in Corinth, MS; son of Richard Herman and Janie (McEachern) Walker; married Cheryl Ann Ernst, September 8, 1967; children: Stephen. *Education:* Northwestern University, B.S., 1971, M.S., 1972. *Politics:* "Nonpartisan."

ADDRESSES: Home—705 Lone Oak Dr., Port Orange, FL 32127. *Agent*—Andrew H. Zack, Scovil, Chichak & Galen Literary Agency, 381 Park Ave. S., Suite 1020, New York, NY 10016.

CAREER: Forest Road Junior High School, LaGrange, IL, English teacher, 1971-72; Northwestern University, Evanston, IL, associate registrar, 1972-76; American Dietetic Association, Chicago, IL, assistant coordinator of records in education department, 1976-81; free-lance writer and substitute teacher, 1981-87; Bethune-Cookman College, Daytona Beach, FL, instructor in English and writing, 1987-94; Daytona Beach Community College, Daytona Beach, instructor in English and writing, 1994—.

MEMBER: Mystery Writers of America, Horror Writers Association, Southeast Mystery Writers of America, Florida College English Association.

WRITINGS:

Sub-Zero! (suspense novel), Leisure Books (Norwalk, CT), 1979.

Daniel Webster Jackson and the Wrongway Railway (young adult novel), Oak Tree (San Diego, CA), 1982.

Spotty the Goat (juvenile picture book), May Davenport (Los Altos Hills, CA), 1983.

(With Donald W. Kruse and others) *There's a Skunk in My Trunk* (juvenile), May Davenport, 1984.

Brain Watch, Leisure Books, 1985.

Search for the Nile (young adult novel), Bantam (New York City), 1985.

Salem's Child, Leisure Books, 1987.

Aftershock, St. Martin's (New York City), 1987.

Disembodied, St. Martin's, 1988.

(Under pseudonym Glenn Hale) *Dr. O,* Zebra Books (New York City), 1991.

"DEAN GRANT, CHICAGO M.E." SERIES

Dead Man's Float, Pinnacle Books (New York City), 1989.

Razor's Edge, Pinnacle Books, 1989.

Burning Obsession, Pinnacle Books, 1989.

Dying Breath, Pinnacle Books, 1989.

"JESSICA CORAN, FBI MEDICAL EXAMINER/INSTINCT" SERIES

Killer Instinct, Berkley Publishing (New York City), 1992.

Fatal Instinct (sequel to *Killer Instinct*), Berkley Publishing, 1993.

Primal Instinct (sequel to *Fatal Instinct*), Berkley Publishing, 1994.

Pure Instinct (sequel to *Primal Instinct*), Berkley Publishing, 1995.

"RYNE LANARK DECOY" SERIES; UNDER PSEUDONYM STEPHEN ROBERTSON

Decoy, Pinnacle Books, 1989.

Decoy: Blood Ties, Pinnacle Books, 1989.

Decoy: Blood Tells, Pinnacle Books, 1990.

The Handyman, Pinnacle Books, 1990.

"ABE STROUD" ARCHAEOLOGY/HORROR SERIES; UNDER PSEUDONYM GEOFFREY CAINE

Curse of the Vampire, Berkley Publishing, 1991.
Wake of the Werewolf, Berkley Publishing, 1991.
Legion of the Dead, Berkley Publishing, 1992.

OTHER

Contributor of articles, stories, and reviews to periodicals. Creator of "Battlestormer" (computer software), Home Computer Software, 1985.

WORK IN PROGRESS: Book #5 in the "Jessica Coran, FBI Medical Examiner/Instinct" series, tentatively entitled *Mirror Instinct* (sequel to *Pure Instinct*); a novel, *Helsinger's Pit.*

SIDELIGHTS: Robert W. Walker told *CA:* "Nowadays a mystery or suspense novel has to have some extra spin on it, something special to get an editor excited. I have carved out the area of scientific investigation and forensics as centerpiece for my novels, particularly the 'Instinct' series with FBI Medical Examiner Jessica Coran as heroine. I usually decide on an area of forensics which will be central to the plot or capture of the killer, say handwriting analysis as I'm currently working on, or asphyxiation deaths, or deaths by drowning, or the key to the identity of the victim and thus the killer may lie in the bones.

"Once I decide on the main thrust the science will take, I also decide on a setting, usually a major metropolitan setting, and I make the place as exciting and exotic as I can. *Primal Instinct* is set in Hawaii and its sequel in New Orleans. A strong sense of character for the lead(s) is also imperative. I write the first three to five chapters without an outline, to get into the story in such a way as to not know everything myself. I'm not the kind of writer who knows the ending before I begin. Instead I enjoy beginning a novel with an opening chapter which raises twenty questions to which even I don't know the answers. It's like working without a net, and you're very likely to paint yourself into a corner, but *there's* the excitement and thrill.

"Only after the initial opening chapters, after I've gained momentum (dynamism) and a sense of direction, do I begin to outline/plot the rest of the story. I don't stick slavishly to this outline but use it as a guide. The only thing I stick slavishly to is a schedule. The writing has to be another job (I teach college-level English and writing full-time as well).

"All of my books utilize facts, often medical or scientific and generally in the area of forensic medicine; each is cast with a male and female lead who may or may not fall in love along the way. Of course, I also have to cast a disgust-

ingly awful villain who rivals the monsters in my previous horror titles, of which I've authored quite a few. My plots are generally developed around a pretty foul character and his pretty foul 'what if.' That is to say, what if you have a killer who's just interested in taking the victim's hands (*The Handyman,* 1990, under the Stephen Robertson pen name)? What if you have a maniac on the lose who 1) thinks he's a vampire and acts on this belief (*Killer Instinct,* 1992); 2) is a dyed-in-the-wool cannibal (*Fatal Instinct,* 1993); or 3) leaves no trace of the bodies (*Primal Instinct,* 1994)? Or what if you've got a hero who is convinced that he's the offspring of Bram Stoker's hero in *Dracula*—Van Helsing—and is destined to combat vampires (*Curse of the Vampire,* 1991, under pen name of Geoffrey Caine)?

"My purpose in writing is to entertain first, inform second, and perhaps most of all enjoy life, because writing makes me feel like a contributor, and the act of creation fills a deep-seated need in me. My advice to new writers is that in order to learn to plot well and tightly and dynamically, you must practice on the mystery format. After you've learned plotting in mystery, then branch out.

"I've written in a number of categories from young adult to horror and suspense, and every book—even those that fail to get published—teaches the author the dynamics of character building, plotting, setting, etc. Nothing is wasted. You learn by doing, and through time and trial and error, you eventually turn a mental corner to realize that it is possible, that you can weave a compelling story from the air or from research. Learning to write is not theoretical classroom stuff. It's a professional activity. A class can teach elements of writing, but the author himself or herself must do the doing, learn the craft, write the book. You really begin to become a wordsmith by doing it daily, day in and day out, setting yourself a schedule and goals. It takes extreme discipline. You have to go hunting the words every day. It's not done as a leisure time activity or when the so-called muse strikes. Inspiration strikes best when you're in the midst of perspiration.

"Through writing and rewriting (writing is rewriting) you keep pace with your schedule or plan of three pages or ten pages a day, one hour or five hours a day—whatever plan you put into motion for yourself. The important thing: have a schedule and keep to it as closely as possible."

BIOGRAPHICAL/CRITICAL SOURCES:

PERIODICALS

Chicago Reader, May 25, 1979.
Chicago Sun-Times, May 15, 1979.
Courier & Freeman News, April 14, 1987.
Daytona Beach News-Journal, July 24, 1990; May 11, 1991; August 9, 1992; October 17, 1993.

Elgin Herald, July 2, 1979.

Esprit, July, 1979.

Mystery Scene, November, 1993.

Orlando Sentinel, December 27, 1987; March 19, 1992; November 4, 1993.

Publishers Weekly, May 28, 1979; June 4, 1982; June 10, 1992.

Syracuse Herald-American, February 3, 1985.

Watertown Daily Times, January 28, 1985; February 25, 1985; April 3, 1985.

*   *   *

WALTON, Luke
See HENDERSON, Bill

*   *   *

WALZER, Michael (Laban) 1935-

PERSONAL: Born March 3, 1935, in New York, NY; son of Joseph P. and Sally (Hochman) Walzer; married Judith Borodovko, June 17, 1956; children: Sarah, Rebecca. *Education:* Brandeis University, B.A., 1956; Harvard University, Ph.D., 1961. *Religion:* Jewish.

ADDRESSES: Home—103 Linwood Circle, Princeton, NJ 08520-3625. *Office*—School of Social Science, Institute for Advanced Study, Princeton, NJ 08540.

CAREER: Princeton University, Princeton, NJ, assistant professor of politics, 1962-66; Harvard University, Cambridge, MA, associate professor, 1966-68, professor of government, 1968-80; Institute for Advanced Study, Social Science, Princeton, NJ, professor of social science, 1980—. Member of board of governors, Hebrew University, Jerusalem, 1975—; member of faculty advisory cabinet, United Jewish Appeal, 1977-81; trustee, Brandeis University, 1983-88; member of international affairs committee, American Jewish Congress.

MEMBER: Society of Ethical and Legal Philosophy, Conference on the Study of Political Thought.

AWARDS, HONORS: Fulbright fellow, Cambridge University, 1956-57, Harbison Award, Danforth Foundation, 1971.

WRITINGS:

The Revolution of the Saints: A Study in the Origins of Radical Politics, Harvard University Press (Cambridge, MA), 1965.

(Editor with Philip Green) *The Political Imagination in Literature,* Free Press (New York City), 1968.

Obligations: Essays on Disobedience, War, and Citizenship, Harvard University Press, 1970.

Political Action: A Practical Guide to Movement Politics, Quadrangle, 1971.

(Editor and author of introduction) *Regicide and Revolution: Speeches at the Trial of Louis XVI* (translated by Marian Rothstein), Columbia University Press (New York City), 1974, reprint 1993.

Just and Unjust Wars: A Moral Argument with Historical Illustrations, 1977, Basic Books (New York City), reprint 1992.

Radical Principles: Reflections of an Unreconstructed Democrat, Basic Books, 1980.

Spheres of Justice: A Defense of Pluralism and Equality, Basic Books, 1983.

Exodus and Revolution, Basic Books, 1985.

Interpretation and Social Criticism, Harvard University Press, 1987.

The Company of Critics: Social Criticism and Political Commitment in the Twentieth Century, Basic Books, 1989.

What It Means to Be an American, Marsilio (New York City), 1992.

Thick and Thin: Moral Argument at Home and Abroad, University of Notre Dame Press (Notre Dame, IN), 1994.

Also contributor to *Political Theory and Political Education,* Princeton University Press, 1980; *Boundaries: National Autonomy and Its Limits,* Rowan & Littlefield, 1981. Editor, *Dissent,* 1976—; contributing editor, *New Republic,* 1976—; member of editorial board, *Philosophy and Public Affairs.* Also a contributor to philosophy and policy journals.

SIDELIGHTS: Michael Walzer "is a political scientist, a social scientist, a political philosopher or a social one, a gently polemical journalist, an ethical putterer," comments Richard Eder in the *Los Angeles Times.* Formerly a professor of government at Harvard University, Walzer now teaches social science at the Institute for Advanced Study in Princeton. In his numerous books and essays, he tackles such vexing moral issues as the ethics of warfare and the role of the welfare state, speaking always from a socialist perspective and frequently illuminating his theories with examples from history. *New York Times Book Review* contributor Werner J. Dannhauser believes that Walzer "qualifies as a champion of freedom" because he advocates "a greater amount of community political participation, human self-fulfillment and hence liberation." Nick Kotz of the *Washington Post Book World* identifies Walzer's "overriding theme" as "the search for a better society, a self-governing democracy of free men and women dedicated both to protecting their own individual freedoms and to pursuing a common purpose." Critics also applaud Walzer's ability to present complex arguments in a graceful, coherent style.

In *Spheres of Justice: A Defense of Pluralism and Equality,* Walzer outlines a pluralistic theory of social justice that allows that all people are not created equal—some are born with intelligence, wealth, and talent, while others may be lacking in one of these attributes or even all three. While egalitarians strive for a "simple" equality that aims to keep people as equal as possible in their overall situations, Walzer proposes a "complex" equality that acknowledges individual differences and advocates a different kind of justice.

Rather than restricting the amount of money a person can make, for example, Walzer would instead limit the "spheres" where it has power. "The key to [Walzer's] solution is to worry less about the distribution of money and more about limiting the things that money can buy," explains Michael J. Sandel in the *New York Times Book Review.* "This is the point of talking about *spheres* of justice. He maintains that different goods occupy different spheres, which are properly governed by different principles—welfare to the needy, honors to the deserving, political power to the persuasive, offices to the qualified, luxuries to those able and willing to pay for them." So long as goods are restricted to their appropriate spheres—or to continue with the example of money, so long as dollars are used to buy material goods rather than political favors or power—then justice prevails.

As a means of determining which goods fit which distributive principles—whether health care, for instance, should be distributed to all as an essential part of life or only to those with the money to pay for medical services—Walzer adopts the concept of community membership. This means that instead of being born with certain inalienable rights, people are born with only those rights considered inalienable by their particular society. For Walzer, "distributive justice must begin with [community] membership," Sandel explains, "because we are all members of political communities before we are bearers of rights. Whether we have a right to a particular good depends on the role that good plays in our communal life and on its importance to us as members."

Writing in the *New York Review of Books,* Ronald Dworkin praises Walzer's "concrete, political analysis. . . . His historical examples are often fascinating, and this, along with his clear prose, makes his book a pleasure to read. The examples are nicely judged to illustrate the characteristic features of each of his spheres of justice." Nonetheless, Dworkin concludes that Walzer's "central argument fails. The ideal of complex equality he defines is not attainable, or even coherent, and the book contains very little that could be helpful in thinking about actual issues of justice." The problem, according to Dworkin, stems from Walzer's assumption that societies such as ours are in agreement about which goods belong to which spheres.

Instead, he argues, such issues are constantly debated, analyzed and reevaluated. While acknowledging the contradictions inherent in Walzer's theory, Eder concludes that "Walzer is serious enough. His seriousness is that of Milovan Djilas, who emerged from his years as a social absolutist—and his subsequent years in prison—pale, gentle, and with a vision of utopia that he called, 'The Imperfect Society.'"

Walzer continues to expound his theories on social justice in *Exodus and Revolution,* in which he interprets the biblical story of the Israelites' escape from captivity in Egypt as a profound political document. *Los Angeles Times* writer Garry Abrams quotes Walzer's thesis: "The biblical account of the deliverance from Egypt is the crucial influence on and the crucial model for the idea of revolution as it has appeared in Western political thought." In support of his argument, Walzer cites St. Augustine, Thomas Aquinas, Machiavelii, John Knox, Georg Wilhelm Friedreich Hegel, Karl Marx, contemporary liberation theologists and others as thinkers who have used the book of Exodus to support their positions. Walzer, according to Abrams, divides "theorists of revolution" into two groups: those who believe liberation comes as a divine gift and those who believe the oppressed must take at least some responsibility for their own liberation. That Exodus contains such divergent ideas, explains Abrams, is among the reasons why Walzer focuses on it as a "supermarket of events and ideas that can and has been used to supply many modern political persuasions."

Herb Hain, reviewing *Exodus and Revolution* in the *Los Angeles Times,* discusses Walzer's comparison of Exodus with the ideas behind the American Revolution. In one passage, Walzer points out that Benjamin Franklin proposed an image of Moses lifting his rod and the Egyptians drowning for the Great Seal of the United States, while Jefferson preferred a column of Israelites marching through the wilderness. Hain also emphasizes Walzer's assertion that in Exodus men, women and children made a covenant with God, in contrast to Genesis, in which God spoke to Adam alone. "What's more," he continues, "the Covenant was made not only between God and Israel, but also by the people with one another, thus establishing the principle of social and communal responsibility." Hain notes further that the identical principle can be discerned in two of America's founding documents—the Mayflower Compact and the Declaration of Independence.

Thinking about Exodus also illuminates "some of the difficulties and dilemmas contained in the promise of liberation," comments *Newsweek*'s Jim Miller in a review of *Exodus and Revolution,* noting that the most difficult part comes when Moses descends from the mountain to find his people adoring the golden calf. Miller compares the passage in which Moses "asks for faithful volunteers to slay the idolaters" to modern political purges, and suggests that it raises questions about the right and wrong uses for the sword. Walzer himself, states Miller, "prefers to stress the traditional Jewish image of Moses as a patient teacher" leading his people through the wilderness whose hardships offer "harsh lessons about the unavoidable frustrations, failures and disappointments that are the genuine burden of freedom." In conclusion, Miller declares: "The book captures Walzer at his formidable best: learned, humane, lively."

In his *Interpretation and Social Criticism,* Walzer "wants to refute the claim that social criticism requires the radical detachment of critical distance" according to John Patrick Diggins in the *New York Times Book Review.* Diggins cites Walzer's statement that it is wrong to interpret society's standards on the basis of one's personal beliefs, which by definition cannot be extended to others. Among those figures to whom Walzer applies this censure are great philosophers and revolutionaries. "Mr. Walzer singles out Descartes's attempt to arrive at certainty solely by knowing the contents of mind," Diggins declares, adding that "Mr. Walzer reserves his strongest doubts for Sartre and Lenin, ideologues who translated social criticism into class warfare and judged their respective societies against their own, personal standards and prejudices."

Another of Walzer's arguments in *Interpretation and Social Criticism* is that the morality we experience on a daily basis is the route that should be followed for interpretation, a principle which he supports with examples from the ancient prophets of Israel. "The prophet does not claim to be creating a new morality but rather rediscovering a previously accepted and commonly understood one," notes Diggins. Walzer cites the prophet Amos as a perfect example of the social critic who challenges leaders, conventions and practices of a particular society based on values shared by all. Diggins opines that Walzer does not go far enough in explaining these shared values: "Mr. Walzer scarcely bothers to explain why equality is preferable to liberty." He also faults Walzer for not connecting his ideas to his own society: "It is curious that he does not connect his work with American history and culture." Overall, though, Diggins praises Walzer's *Interpretation and Social Criticism* as "learned, cogent and provocative. It avoids the pretensions of both scientific certainty and grand theory and treats social criticism as the 'educated cousin of common complaint.' It also succeeds brilliantly in making an ancient religion relevant to the contemporary political imagination."

In *The Company of Critics: Social Criticism and Political Commitment in the Twentieth Century,* Walzer continues to question the role of criticism in society. Reviewing the book in the *Times Literary Supplement,* Denis Donoghue quotes Walzer's definition of the three essential duties of social criticism: "The critic exposes the false appearances of his own society; he gives expression to his people's deepest sense of how they ought to live; and he insists that there are other forms of falseness and other, equally legitimate, hopes and aspirations." But then Donoghue quarrels with these guidelines: "Walzer assumes that 'all of us' have a moral sense, but he doesn't say what it is or how any of us came to have it." Donoghue also charges that *The Company of Critics,* which examines the work of eleven influential philosophers and critics, lacks any guiding theory or principle. "So his book is exactly the sum of its parts; a series of studies, each of them too brief to be entirely just to its occasion."

A comparison of eleven twentieth-century social critics is an interesting idea, says Peter Halban, in a *New Statesman* review of *Company of Critics,* but it does not follow through on its potential: "This is a coffee-table tally of alienated intellectuals and Walzer has an acute, interesting mind. But while the chapters on each thinker are almost unvaryingly sharp, Walzer's general discussion of the role of the social critic works less well. This may be something to do with his style, which is chatty, elliptical and allusive. It's too easy to read one of his sheeny paragraphs with pleasure only to realise at the end that you're not sure of quite what has been said."

New York Time Book Review's J. Peter Euben commends *The Company of Critics* as "richly textured, accessible and always respectful of its readers," further commenting that it "is an example of the sort of connected criticism it commends." According to Euben, Walzer, "a pluralist, a leftist Aristotelian who regards moral principles as embodied in the conventions, customs, beliefs, rituals and institutions of a particular people," when facing the basic questions of social criticism, comes down strongly on the side of those critics he finds most engaged, most a part of the society they analyze. "That is why Mr. Walzer admires the American writer Randolph Bourne's involvement in the life he criticized; the continuities between the Italian thinker Ignazio Silone's radicalism and his life and opinions before he became radical; George Orwell's love of England, which did nothing to inhibit his opposition to those who tyrannized the working class; Albert Camus's commitment to a morality of love and justice, and Martin Buber's insistence that he must tell the story of the Jewish experience while recognizing that no single correct account of nationalist aspirations is possible." Walzer, on the other hand, continues Euben, faults American political philosopher Herbert Marcuse, French philosopher Michel Paul Foucalt and Italian socialist theorist Antonio Gramsci for failing to carry out the true role of a critic: expressing the deepest sense of a people.

Euben cites some weaknesses in the book, including the lack of a clear audience for the subject, indistinct definitions of who "one's own people" really are, and a narrowly focused selection of social critics. "Mr. Walzer says he has chosen 'mainstream' critics; some feminists I know call them 'male-stream' critics," Euben quips. He goes on to suggest that "perhaps we need a third book on criticism from him . . . one that might include chapters on the black lesbian poet Audre Lorde, the American Indian writer Vine Deloria and the Chicano theologian Andres Guerero." Euben also faults Walzer for not sufficiently delineating his own political theories. "Mr. Walzer's ground is not so much absent as obscured, with unfortunate results." Despite these objections, Euben praises *The Company of Critics*: "This book proves again that Michael Walzer is a writer of rare elegance, intellectual range and moral seriousness."

Expanding on his theme of complex equality presented in *Spheres of Justice*, Walzer claims in *Thick and Thin: Moral Argument at Home and Abroad* that ethical thought operates within two important languages: One complex moral language that operates from a sphere of locally rooted events and conditions—the thick morality or argument—and one simple moral language that applies to everyone and operates from a sphere of universal standards—the thin morality or argument. Walzer argues that moral errors occur when we examine issues from the incorrect sphere of standards, such as when we apply a thin argument to a situation that should be judged by thick morality. Such is the case when we impose our cultural values on a different culture—we are applying our local standards universally onto a culture with different local standards.

Reviews for *Thick and Thin* were mixed. Hailing the book's poetic style, *Commonweal*'s Alan Wolfe asserts: "It is a moving, eloquent, and at times inspiring meditation on the problem of obligation." A *Kirkus Reviews* critic describes *Thick and Thin* as a "well-argued, if not always energetic, set of carefully wrought ideas on the state of public moral debate" but stresses that Walzer could expand his awareness of such issues as gender and race. *Library Journal*'s Leon H. Brody faults Walzer's writings for its "rambling, anecdotal quality more suitable to . . . [verbal] presentation . . . than to the more stringent requirements for publication" and adds that Walzer's arguments are not detailed enough for academics, but too technical for the general reader. Wolfe, on the other hand, although he reports a lack of consistency in part of Walzer's argument, finds much to commend in *Thick and Thin*. He summarizes: "*Thick and Thin* should be read, not only for its substantive argument, but also for the breadth of its examples and the beauty of its prose. Michael Walzer writes on some of the most explosive issues of the day in a voice that is always calm and thoughtful. Our culture is thicker because of his presence."

BIOGRAPHICAL/CRITICAL SOURCES:

PERIODICALS

Atlantic Monthly, February, 1978.
Commonweal, October 21, 1994, p. 24.
Kirkus Reviews, April 15, 1994, p 545.
Library Journal, May 15, 1994, p. 76.
Los Angeles Times, March 27, 1983; February 13, 1985; April 5, 1985.
Nation, September 28, 1970; March 25, 1978.
New Statesman, February 24, 1989, p. 40.
Newsweek, January 26, 1981; April 15, 1985, p. 92.
New York Review of Books, October 21, 1971; December 8, 1977; October 23, 1980; April 14, 1983.
New York Times, February 4, 1978, August 12, 1980; January 25, 1985.
New York Times Book Review, June 9, 1974; February 5, 1978; December 28, 1980; April 24, 1983; January 20, 1985; March 15, 1987, p. 11; January 18, 1989, p. 18.
Times Literary Supplement, July 26, 1974; October 23, 1981; March 3, 1989 p. 217.
Washington Post Book World, January 8, 1978; August 31, 1980.*

*   *   *

WATTS, Michael J(ohn) 1951-

PERSONAL: Born May 7, 1951, in Bristol, Gloucestershire, England; son of Ivan John (an engineer) and Barbara Joan (Pincott) Watts. *Education:* University College, London, B.S. (with first class honors), 1972; University of Michigan, M.A., 1974, Ph.D., 1979; attended University of Ibadan, Nigeria, 1977-78.

ADDRESSES: Home—771 Dolores St., San Francisco, CA 94110. *Office*—Institute of International Studies, University of California, Berkeley, CA 94720.

CAREER: University of Michigan, Center for Research on Economic Development, Ann Arbor, research associate, 1982-83; University of California, Berkeley, assistant professor, 1979-85, associate professor, 1985-88, professor of geography, 1988—, co-chairperson of the NDEA Berkeley-Stanford African Studies Center, 1980-84, director of Institute of International Studies, 1994—, senior scholar in residence at Townsend Humanities Center, 1994-95. Visiting professor, Pennsylvania State University, 1987, University of Warsaw (Poland), 1988, West Virginia University, 1988, University of Taipei, 1991, University of Hawaii, 1992, and Cornell University, 1992; distinguished visiting professor, University of Bergen (Norway), 1994; distinguished visiting lecturer, University College, London, 1994. Research associate, Centre for Social and Economic Research, Ahmadu Bello University

(Nigeria), 1978, University of Michigan, 1983-84, and Smithsonian Institution, 1990; visiting research fellow, University of Delhi, 1992.

Member of board of directors, Ethnographic Institute, 1984—, and Pacific Institute for Studies in Development, 1987—. Member of numerous selection panels and screening committees for project proposals, grant programs, and research fellowships. Organizer, convener, invited speaker/participant, or member of program committee of numerous workshops, conferences, and conventions, 1980—. Manuscript reviewer for more than thirty-five periodicals and publishers. Public speaker and lecturer. Consultant to many organizations, including Rockefeller Foundation, Ford Foundation, Field Museum of Natural History, and Northwest Immigrants Rights Project.

MEMBER: International African Institute, Association of American Anthropologists, American Council of Learned Societies, Association of African Studies, Association of Concerned African Scholars, Society for International Development.

AWARDS, HONORS: Research grants from Social Science Research Council/American Council of Learned Societies, 1980-81 and 1992-93, National Science Foundation, 1983-85, 1987-88, 1989-90, 1990-91, 1991-92, 1993-94, and 1994-95, Rockefeller Foundation, 1988-90, MacArthur Foundation, 1990-93, Norton Foundation, 1992-93, and University of California, 1994-96; National Endowment for the Humanities fellowship, 1984; runner-up for Herskovitz Prize, 1984, for *Silent Violence: Food, Famine, and Peasantry in Northern Nigeria;* distinguished teacher award, National Council for Geographic Education, 1984, and University of California, Berkeley, 1991; Gilbert White fellowship, 1985-86; Social Science Research Council/American Council of Learned Societies fellowship, 1990; MacArthur Foundation fellowship, 1992-94; Honors Award, Association of American Geographers, 1994.

WRITINGS:

Silent Violence: Food, Famine, and Peasantry in Northern Nigeria, University of California Press (Berkeley), 1983.

(Editor, author of introduction, and contributor) *State, Oil, and Agriculture in Nigeria,* Institute of International Studies Press (Berkeley), 1987.

(With Allan Pred) *Reworking Modernity: Capitalisms and Symbolic Discontent,* Rutgers University Press (New Brunswick, NJ), 1992.

(Editor with Peter Little, and contributor) *Peasants under Contract,* University of Wisconsin Press (Madison), 1993.

(Editor with Little) *Living under Contract: Contract Farming and Agrarian Transformation in Africa,* University of Wisconsin Press, 1994.

(Editor with P. Taylor and R. J. Johnston) *Geographies of Global Change: Remapping the World in the Late Twentieth Century,* Basil Blackwell (Oxford, England), 1994.

Manufacturing Discontent: Production Politics, Gender, and Households in African Agriculture, Heinemann (London), in press.

Also author of reports. Contributor to books, including *Political Economy of Nigeria,* edited by W. Zartman, Praeger (New York City), 1982; *Drought and Hunger in Africa,* edited by M. Glantz, Cambridge University Press (Cambridge, England), 1987; and *Money, Power, and Space,* edited by Nigel Thrift and others, Basil Blackwell, 1994. Contributor to *Encyclopaedia Britannica.* Contributor to *Proceedings* of conferences and annual meetings; member of editorial board, *Encyclopaedia of Sub-Saharan Africa,* Simon & Schuster (New York), 1991-94, and of *Annals of the Association of American Geographers,* 1993—. Contributor to numerous periodicals, including *Social Science Research Review, Journal of Peasant Studies, Review of International Political Economy, Ecologist, Transition, Cultural Anthropology,* and *Political Geography Quarterly.* Editor, *African Economic History,* 1989—; member of editorial board of numerous periodicals, including *African Studies Review,* 1982-89, *Development Studies Review,* 1987—, *Capitalism, Nature, Socialism,* 1988—, *ICARIA/Ecologia Politica,* 1989—, *Economic Geography,* 1991-94, *Society and Space,* 1992—, *Journal of Tropical Research,* 1993—, *Review of International Political Economy,* 1994—, and *Environmental History,* 1994—.

WORK IN PROGRESS: A follow-up book with Allan Pred to *Reworking Modernity,* entitled *Hypermodernity,* for Basil Blackwell; *Fathoming Famine: Rights, Entitlements, and Food for the Twenty-First Century,* with Hans-Georg Bohl; a project assessing the Kerala State, South India, land reform and agrarian strategy in the 1990s, initiated in 1992 through six months of field research.

*   *   *

WELLS, Rosemary   1943-

PERSONAL: Born January 29, 1943, in New York, NY; married Thomas Moore Wells (an architect), 1963; children: Victoria, Marguerite. *Education:* Attended Museum School, Boston, MA.

ADDRESSES: Home—738 Sleepy Hollow Rd., Briarcliff Manor, NY 10510.

CAREER: Freelance author and illustrator, 1968—. Worked for Allyn and Bacon, Boston, MA, and Macmillan Publishing Co., New York City.

AWARDS, HONORS: Honor Book citation, *Book World* Spring Children's Book Festival, 1972, for *The Fog Comes on Little Pig Feet;* Children's Book Showcase Award, Children's Book Council, 1974, for *Noisy Nora;* Citation of Merit, Society of Illustrators, 1974, for *Benjamin and Tulip;* Art Book for Children citation, Brooklyn Museum and Brooklyn Public Library, 1975, 1976, and 1977, all for *Benjamin and Tulip;* Irma Simonton Black Award, Bank Street College of Education, for *Morris's Disappearing Bag: A Christmas Story;* Edgar Allan Poe Special Award, Mystery Writers of America, 1981, for *When No One Was Looking; Hazel's Amazing Mother* was named one of the *New York Times* Best Illustrated Books, 1985; Washington Irving Children's Book Choice Award, Westchester Library Association, 1986, for *Peabody,* and 1988, for *Max's Christmas;* Boston Globe-Horn Book Award, 1989, for *Shy Charles;* Child Study Association Children's Books of the Year citations for *Morris's Disappearing Bag* and *Don't Spill It Again, James;* Booklist Children's Editor's Choice citations for *Max's Toys: A Counting Book, Timothy Goes to School,* and *Through the Hidden Door; Horn Book* Fanfare citation and West Australian Young Readers' Book Award, both for *When No One Was Looking;* International Reading Association/Children's Book Council Children's Choice citations for *Timothy Goes to School, A Lion for Lewis,* and *Peabody;* Virginia Young Readers Award, and New York Public Library Books for Teenagers citation, both for *The Man in the Woods;* Cooperative Children's Book Center citation for *Max's Bedtime;* runner-up for Edgar Allan Poe Award, Mystery Writers of America, and ALA Best Books for Young Adults citation for *Through the Hidden Door; Bulletin of the Center for Children's Books* Blue Ribbon for *The Little Lame Prince;* Parents' Choice Award, Parents' Choice Foundation, for *Shy Charles;* Golden Kite Award, Society of Children's Book Writers, and International Reading Association Teacher's Choices list, both for *Forest of Dreams;* International Reading Association Children's Choices citation for *Max's Chocolate Chicken;* many of Wells's books were named among the best books of the year by *School Library Journal* or received American Library Association (ALA) Notable Book citations or *American Bookseller* "Pick of the Lists" citations.

WRITINGS:

YOUNG ADULT FICTION

(And illustrator) *The Fog Comes on Little Pig Feet,* Dial (New York City), 1972.
None of the Above, Dial, 1974.
Leave Well Enough Alone, Dial, 1977.

When No One Was Looking, Dial, 1980.
The Man in the Woods, Dial, 1984.
(And illustrator) *Through the Hidden Door,* Dial, 1987.

JUVENILE

Forest of Dreams, illustrated by Susan Jeffers, Dial, 1988.
Lucy's Come to Stay, illustrated by Patricia Cullen-Clark, Dial, 1992. *Waiting for the Evening Star,* illustrated by Jeffers, Dial, 1993.

JUVENILE; SELF-ILLUSTRATED

John and Rarey, Funk (New York City), 1969.
Michael and the Mitten Test, Bradbury (Scarsdale, NY), 1969.
The First Child, Hawthorn (New York City), 1970.
Martha's Birthday, Bradbury, 1970.
Miranda's Pilgrims, Bradbury, 1970.
Unfortunately Harriet, Dial, 1972.
Benjamin and Tulip, Dial, 1973.
Noisy Nora, Dial, 1973.
Abdul, Dial, 1975.
Morris's Disappearing Bag: A Christmas Story, Dial, 1975.
Don't Spill It Again, James, Dial, 1977.
Stanley and Rhoda, Dial, 1978.
Good Night, Fred, Dial, 1981.
Timothy Goes to School, Dial, 1981.
A Lion for Lewis, Dial, 1982.
Peabody, Dial, 1983.
Hazel's Amazing Mother, Dial, 1985.
Shy Charles, Dial, 1988.
The Little Lame Prince (based on a story by Dinah Mulock Craik), Dial, 1990.
Fritz and the Mess Fairy, Dial, 1991.

"MAX" SERIES; SELF-ILLUSTRATED

Max's First Word, Dial, 1979.
Max's New Suit, Dial, 1979.
Max's Ride, Dial, 1979.
Max's Toys: A Counting Book, Dial, 1979.
Max's Bath, Dial, 1985.
Max's Bedtime, Dial, 1985.
Max's Breakfast, Dial, 1985.
Max's Birthday, Dial, 1985.
Max's Christmas, Dial, 1986.
Max's Chocolate Chicken, Dial, 1989.
Max's Dragon Shirt, Dial, 1991.
Max and Ruby's First Greek Myth: Pandora's Box, Dial, 1993.

"VOYAGE TO THE BUNNY PLANET" SERIES; SELF-ILLUSTRATED

First Tomato: A Voyage to the Bunny Planet, Dial, 1992.
The Island Light: A Voyage to the Bunny Planet, Dial, 1992.
Moss Pillows: A Voyage to the Bunny Planet, Dial, 1992.

ILLUSTRATOR

William S. Gilbert and Arthur Sullivan, *A Song to Sing, O!* (from *The Yeoman of the Guard*), Macmillan (New York City), 1968.

Gilbert and Sullivan, *W. S. Gilbert's "The Duke of Plaza Toro"* (from *The Gondoliers*), Macmillan, 1969.

Paula Fox, *Hungry Fred*, Bradbury, 1969.

Robert W. Service, *The Shooting of Dan McGrew [and] The Cremation of Sam McGee*, Young Scott Books, 1969.

(With Susan Jeffers) Charlotte Pomerantz, *Why You Look Like You When I Tend to Look Like Me*, Young Scott Books, 1969.

Rudyard Kipling, *The Cat That Walked by Himself*, Hawthorn, 1970.

Winifred Rosen Casey, *Marvin's Manhole*, Dial, 1970.

Marjorie Weinman Sharmat, *A Hot Thirsty Day*, Macmillan, 1971.

Ellen Conford, *Impossible, Possum*, Little, Brown (Boston, MA), 1971.

Beryl Williams and Dorrit Davis, *Two Sisters and Some Hornets*, Holiday House (New York City), 1972.

Virginia A. Tashjian, editor, *With a Deep-Sea Smile: Story Hour Stretches for Large or Small Groups*, Little, Brown, 1974.

Lore G. Segal, *Tell Me a Trudy*, Farrar, Straus (New York City), 1977.

OTHER

(With Johanna Hurley) *Cooking for Nitwits* (adult nonfiction), Dutton (New York City), 1989.

(Contributor) *Worlds of Childhood: The Art and Craft of Writing for Children* (adult nonfiction), edited by William Zinsser, Houghton Mifflin (Boston, MA), 1990.

(Contributor) *So I Shall Tell You a Story: The Magic World of Beatrix Potter*, Warne (New York City), 1993.

ADAPTATIONS: Max's Christmas and *Morris's Disappearing Bag* have been adapted as short films by Weston Woods.

SIDELIGHTS: "I do not feel that I get ideas. Books come on the [word processing] screen from outer space," writes Rosemary Wells, author and illustrator of picture books for toddlers and novels for teens, in an autobiographical *Horn Book* essay.

Seeming to diminish the theory that writing is hard work, Wells's words, offered as if in reply to the question always asked of writers, "Where do you get your ideas?," might shock aspiring writers looking for advice on how to perfect their own creative techniques. Elsewhere, however, Wells admits to more conventional sources of ideas including observing her own children for inspiration for many of her books for her youngest readers, or consulting memories from her own youth for her work for young adults. "I put into my books," she notes in her *Something About the Author Autobiography Series* (*SAAS*) sketch, "all of the things I remember. . . . Those remembrances are jumbled up and churned because fiction is always more palatable than truth. They become more true as they are honed and whittled into characters and stories."

Wells began her career as an art editor in the publishing industry in the early 1960s when she took what appeared to be a temporary position filling in for a vacationing art editor at Allyn and Bacon, textbook publishers. She was soon hired, however, to replace the absent employee on a permanent basis. In *SAAS* Wells calls this her "first lucky break and the only one I ever needed." Two years later, the couple moved to New York City so Tom could pursue his architectural studies at Columbia University. There, Wells found a job at the children's books division of Macmillan. She set her course for a career as an art director.

One day Wells happened to hear a song from the popular Gilbert and Sullivan opera, *The Yeoman of the Guard*, and quickly made some sketches using birds instead of people to illustrate the lyrics. She gave the sketches, placed together to resemble a finished book, to the editor in chief, Susan Hirshman, and waited to hear the reaction. In *Horn Book*, Wells recounts what happened next: "She looked at it. Then she put it down and sang the whole thing. Several other editors were invited into her office to join choruses from [two other Gilbert and Sullivan operas] *The Mikado* and *H.M.S. Pinafore*. Then, by the by, she said, 'Sit down, Rosemary, you're a Macmillan author now.'" Wells's first book, *A Song to Sing, O!*, was published in 1968. Encouraged by her success, Wells decided to illustrate another Gilbert and Sullivan song, this time "The Duke of Plaza Toro" from *The Gondoliers*. This book was published the following year.

Wells's reputation as an illustrator of books for children was secured when the book series for which she is most widely known—the books featuring Max and his sister Ruby—were born. After listening to the way her daughter Victoria bossed around her younger sister Marguerite (more commonly known as Beezoo), Wells seized upon the idea for what would become the first installment in the Max series, *Max's First Word*, in 1977. Working on pieces of illustration board that happened to be on her drawing table, Wells took only a few hours to produce a major innovation in children's literature. In "The Well-Tempered Children's Book," Wells's essay in *Worlds of Childhood: The Art and Craft of Writing for Children*, she recalls the experience: "I couldn't really understand what had happened. I had created what was clearly a picture book, but it was only sixteen pages long and wasn't for the usual nursery school and kindergarten crew. Picture books were thirty-two pages long, some even forty." Wells had succeeded in producing a funny, enjoyable story in only sixteen pages. Her editor loved it and asked her for three more and so *Max's Ride, Max's New Suit* and *Max's Toys: A Counting Book* followed. Continuing the story, Wells notes with pride: "Thus were born what came to be known in book circles as 'board books'—books that could survive a certain amount of infant vandalizing without coming apart and, even more important, could make mother and fathers and their babies laugh at themselves and each other and the world around them."

Interaction between siblings—especially in the form of sibling rivalry—is a theme that surfaces in several of Wells's young adult novels as well as in the "Max" books. But her novels for young people are so different from her picture books that some people—even librarians—are often startled to find they are written by the same person. Some readers might even question why such a successful illustrator would want to write lengthy books with, for the most part, no illustrations. Wells explains her motives in an essay she contributed to *Publishers Weekly* on whether story or pictures are the most important aspect of a children's book. "I am both an artist and a writer," claims the author. "But I am firmly convinced that the story comes first. . . . The child may be charmed, intrigued or even inspired by good illustration, but it is the sound of the words and the story that first holds the child's attention." Assessing her own talents in the same essay, Wells declares she is in fact "a better writer than . . . an illustrator."

As if easing into the world of writing for young adults, Wells first novel in the genre, *The Fog Comes on Little Pig Feet,* includes about a half a dozen full-page line drawings to illustrate the story. It is her only young adult novel that she illustrated throughout, although her 1987 mystery novel, *Through the Hidden Door,* does contain a few small drawings by the author. For inspiration for *The Fog Comes on Little Pig Feet* Wells searched her own memories. The novel tells the similar story of Rachel Saseekian who at thirteen is sent unwillingly to a boarding school. The novel is told in diary form through entries covering a two-week time period.

Wells's inclusion of many autobiographical details helped the main character come alive in the story, a point noticed by many critics. In *Publishers Weekly* Jean F. Mercier summarizes critical thought on the novel noting: "The book won raves, with most reviewers impressed by the real-life feel of the chief character." Some critics remarked on Wells's admirable transition from picture books to the novel genre. Mrs. John G. Gray claims in *Best Sellers* that *The Fog Comes On Little Pig Feet* proves that Wells's "writing abilities are an easy match for her already famous artistic talents." In her *School Library Journal* review of

the novel Alice Miller Bregman declares, "Young teens will devour this fast-paced, adequately written entertainment."

With *Leave Well Enough Alone,* Wells began writing mystery novels for young adults. The teenage protagonists of Wells's mysteries must make important ethical choices. Their decisions seem even more important because in these novels often the wrong choice could lead to physical danger. As to be expected, Wells once again delves into her past for a framework on which to set her narrative. Invoking her own memories of being a fourteen-year-old mother's helper in Pennsylvania, Wells weaves the story of Dorothy Coughlin, a fourteen-year-old girl from Newburgh, New York, who also spends one summer working as a mother's helper in Pennsylvania. As an added hint to the autobiographical nature of the novel, it is set in 1956, the year Wells herself became a teenager.

The reader is taken along for an exciting ride from clue to clue in this well-received mystery. Although several critics, like Zena Sutherland in *Bulletin of the Center for Children's Books,* find the plot a little "overcrowded," most reviewers admire Wells's sense of humor and the manner in which moral questions were developed in the narrative. In *Book World* Katherine Paterson writes, "I began this book laughing with delight at Rosemary Wells's marvelous re-creation of fourteenness."

In Wells's next young adult novel, *When No One Was Looking,* the author explores the world of tennis. This mystery features Kathy Bardy, a fourteen-year-old tennis star from Plymouth, Massachusetts, who loves tennis but harbors a secret ambition—just as Wells did, according to her *SAAS* entry—to be a baseball player. Kathy looks forward to the New England Championship competition where a win would guarantee her a spot in the Nationals. As Paul Heins notes in *Horn Book,* while *When No One Was Looking* begins "as a story of athletic prowess, the novel gradually develops as a series of moral issues that take on tragic overtones." When Ruth Gumm, the one tennis player skilled enough to beat Kathy, is found dead in the swimming pool at the Plymouth Bath and Tennis Club where Kathy practices with her coach, Marty, Kathy and her supporters are immediately under suspicion. One by one the suspects are cleared, but Kathy feels compelled to continue her sleuthing even after the real detectives consider the case closed. Her moral compulsion to find out all the facts related to the crime leads her to an unexpected conclusion. Realizing what consequences the truth will bring, Kathy cries bitterly to herself: "If only I hadn't bothered to go down to the police station, then at least I wouldn't know. I don't want to know. Why wasn't it enough for me to just know that I didn't do it?"

Although some critics point to either one or another character in the novel as being ill-defined, Wells is generally praised for this offering for the mystery-lover's book shelf. *School Library Journal* contributor Robert Unsworth observes: "There is a lot to this novel and most of it is excellent." Similarly, in the *New York Times Book Review* Anne Tyler notes that the book "has energy and style, and it ought to rivet the most restless young reader."

Wells continued her string of successful mysteries with the publication of *The Man in the Woods.* As in her earlier novels, this one features a teenage heroine who must struggle with a moral dilemma. In this case, fourteen-year-old Helen Curragh tries to figure out the identity of the Punk Rock Thrower after she accidentally witnesses him causing yet another car to crash after breaking its windshield with a tossed rock. Helen and fifteen-year-old Pinky Levy meet on the second day of school at New Bedford Regional High School, discover they are both on the staff of the school paper, the *Whaler,* and soon become embroiled in a frantic search through New Bedford documents dating back to the time of the Civil War. Together they gather clues, narrowly escape death, and uncover a secret one of New Bedford's oldest families has been covering up for over a hundred years. As the story ends, Helen must decide whether to write a story for the *Whaler* about their search and have a chance at being the first freshman ever to win the coveted gold medal for best story of the year or to keep what she knows to herself.

Critics praise the mystery-within-a-mystery plot developed in *The Man in the Woods.* They also applaud Wells' finely-drawn characters. In *School Library Journal,* for example, Drew Stevenson finds the historical details in the novel "a fascinating subplot," and in an additional comment writes, "the book . . . boasts an array of interesting characters, deftly brought to life." In *Horn Book,* Ethel L. Heins also calls attention to the novel's "wealth of vivid characters" and labels the work "a riveting contemporary tale of emotion, mystery, and suspense."

Although Pinky figured prominently in *The Man in the Woods, Through the Hidden Door* is her first young adult offering which depends almost entirely on male characters. Barney Pennimen is from Landry, Colorado, but attending Winchester Boys' Academy out East because his mother is dead and his father's antiques business takes him traveling a lot. Like parents in other Wells novels, Barney's father has ambitious goals for his son. "The Plan," according to Barney, includes the following: "Go to Winchester. Graduate with honors. Go on to Hotchkiss. Graduate with honors. Get into Harvard. Magma cum laude from there and on to Yale or Oxford (as he did)." Barney is an honor student who in order to fit in chooses to befriend a group of cruel but popular boys. As the friendships go sour and even the school headmaster

turns against him, Barney seeks the company of a bookish freshman loner named Snowy Cobb. The younger boy eventually leads Barney to a hidden cave where the two spend hours uncovering archaeological treasures. The cave becomes a safe-haven where Snowy and Barney can enjoy themselves and not be concerned about outside pressures of peers or parents.

Through the Hidden Door was a runner-up for the Edgar Allan Poe Award of the Mystery Writers of America and received citations recognizing it as both one of the American Library Association's Best Books for Young Adults and one of *Booklist*'s Children's Editor's Choices for the year. In her *Bulletin of the Center for Children's Books* review Sutherland gives the novel her highest recommendation, calling it "one of the best stories Rosemary Wells has written." *Kliatt Young Adult Paperback Book Guide* contributor Mary I. Purucker finds the book "fast paced, [and] well written." Other reviewers such as David Gale and Ilene Cooper praise Wells for her ability to develop both plot and characters with superb results. According to Gale's *School Library Journal* review, Snowy and Barney "are both fully realized characters" and the novel as a whole as "an absorbing school story with a twist." In her *Booklist* review Cooper describes *Through a Hidden Door* as "a riveting psychological thriller" and lauds the author's development of "her story in ways sure to get readers thinking."

"I believe," Wells writes in *Worlds of Childhood,* "that all stories and plays and paintings and songs and dances come from a palpable but unseen space in the cosmos. Ballets and symphonies written during our lifetime were there before we were born. According to how gifted we are, we are all given a large or small key to this treasury of wonders. I have been blessed with a small key to the world of the young."

BIOGRAPHICAL/CRITICAL SOURCES:

BOOKS

Sadker, Myra Pollack, and David Miller Sadker, *Now Upon a Time: A Contemporary View of Children's Literature,* Harper, 1977, pp. 66-67.

Something about the Author Autobiography Series, Volume 1, Gale, 1986, pp. 279-291.

Wells, Rosemary, *The Fog Comes on Little Pig Feet,* Dial, 1972.

Wells, *None of the Above,* Dial, 1974.

Wells, *Leave Well Enough Alone,* Dial, 1977.

Wells, *When No One Was Looking,* Dial, 1980.

Wells, *Through the Hidden Door,* Dial, 1987.

Zinsser, William, editor, *Worlds of Childhood: The Art and Craft of Writing for Children,* Houghton, 1990, pp. 121-143.

PERIODICALS

Best Sellers, July 15, 1972, p. 200; February 15, 1975, p. 519-520.

Booklist, April 15, 1987, p. 1296.

Bulletin of the Center for Children's Books, April, 1975, p. 139; October, 1977, p. 40; July-August, 1987, p. 220.

Christian Science Monitor, March 6, 1974, p. F2.

Growing Point, May, 1976, pp. 2891-92.

Horn Book, October, 1980, pp. 529-30; September-October, 1984, pp. 601-02; March/April, 1987, pp. 163-170; May/June, 1987, pp. 368-71; May/June, 1993, pp. 307-310.

Kliatt Young Adult Paperback Book Guide, April, 1989, p. 20.

New York Times Book Review, July 10, 1977, pp. 20-21; February 1, 1981, p. 28.

Publishers Weekly, August 5, 1974, p. 58; February 29, 1980, pp. 72-73; February 27, 1987, p. 146.

School Library Journal, May, 1972, p. 89; November, 1974, p. 69; May, 1977, p. 73; October, 1980, p. 159; May, 1984, p. 104; April, 1987, p. 114.

Times Literary Supplement, October 1, 1976, p. 1243.

Washington Post Book World, May 1, 1977, p. E4.*

*   *   *

WHIM-WHAM
See CURNOW, (Thomas) Allen (Monro)

*   *   *

WILHELM, Hans 1945-

PERSONAL: Born September 21, 1945, in Bremen, Germany; son of Heinrich (a bank executive) and Hanna (a homemaker; maiden name, Jurgens) Plate. *Education:* Attended business and art colleges in Bremen, Germany.

ADDRESSES: Home and office—7 Berkeley Rd., Westport, CT 06880.

CAREER: Marketing and advertising manager in Johannesburg, South Africa, 1965-77; writer, 1977—.

AWARDS, HONORS: Best Book of the Year award from *Eltern* magazine, 1983, for *The Trapp Family Book;* Best Children's Book of the Year award, *Time* 1983, for *Tales from the Land under My Table;* Best Illustration in Children's Books award, *Parent's Choice,* 1986, for *Blackberry Ink;* Children's Book Award, International Reading Association, 1986, for *A New Home, A New Friend;* Children's Book of the Year awards, Child Study Association of America, for *Blackberry Ink,* 1986, *The Funniest*

Knock-Knock Book Ever! and *Let's Be Friends Again!,* 1987; Gold Medallion Book Award, Christian Publishers Association, 1988, for *What Does God Do?*

WRITINGS:

(And illustrator) *Your Chinese Horoscope,* Avon (New York City), 1980.

(And illustrator) *Fun Signs,* Simon & Schuster (New York City), 1981.

CHILDREN'S BOOKS; ALL SELF-ILLUSTRATED

The Trapp Family Book, Heinemann (London), 1983, David & Charles, 1984.

Tales from the Land under My Table, Random House (New York City), 1983.

Our Christmas 1985, Grolier (Danbury, CT), 1985.

Bunny Trouble, Scholastic Inc. (New York City), 1985.

I'll Always Love You, Crown (New York City), 1985.

A New Home, A New Friend, Random House, 1985.

Don't Give Up, Josephine, Random House, 1985.

Totally Bored Boris, Random House, 1986.

Let's Be Friends Again!, Crown, 1986.

Waldo and the Desert Island Adventure, Random House, 1986.

Pirates Ahoy!, Parents Magazine Press (New York City), 1987.

What Does God Do?: God Speaks to Children about His Word, Sweet Publishing (Ft. Worth), 1987.

Oh, What A Mess, Crown, 1988.

Never Lonely Again, Grolier, 1988.

I Wouldn't Tell A Lie, Grolier, 1988.

Friends Are Forever, Grolier, 1988.

Tyrone, The Horrible, Scholastic Inc., 1988.

Waldo's Christmas Surprise, Random House, 1988.

Waldo, Tell Me about Guardian Angels, C. R. Gibson (Norwalk, CT), 1988.

Waldo, Tell Me about Me, C. R. Gibson, 1988.

Waldo, Tell Me about God, C. R. Gibson, 1988.

Waldo, Tell Me about Christ, C. R. Gibson, 1988.

Waldo, Tell Me about Christmas, C. R. Gibson, 1989.

More Bunny Trouble, Scholastic Inc., 1989.

Mother Goose on the Loose, Sterling Publishers (New York City), 1989.

Schnitzel's First Christmas, Simon & Schuster, 1989.

Waldo At The Zoo, C. R. Gibson, 1990.

Waldo, One, Two, Three, C. R. Gibson, 1990.

A Cool Kid like Me, Crown, 1990.

Tyrone, The Double Dirty Rotten Cheater, Scholastic Inc., 1991.

Schnitzel Is Lost, Simon & Schuster, 1991.

The Bremen Town Musicians, Scholastic Inc., 1992.

A Christmas Journey, C. R. Gibson, 1993.

Waldo, Tell Me about Dying, C. R. Gibson, 1993.

The Boy Who Wasn't There, Scholastic Inc., 1993.

Bad, Bad Bunny Trouble, Scholastic Inc., 1994.
I Hate My Bow, Scholastic Inc., 1995.
The Big Boasting Battle, Scholastic Inc., 1995.
Tyrone and the Swamp Gang, Scholastic Inc., 1995.
Razzle-Dazzle, Scholastic Inc., 1996.

ILLUSTRATOR

Pat Boone, *Favorite Bible Stories,* Random House 1984, Creation House (Wheaton, IL), 1990.

William Furstenberg, *Stone Soup,* Weekly Reader Family Books, 1984.

Eve Merriam, *Blackberry Ink,* Morrow (New York City), 1985.

Joseph Rosenbloom, *The Funniest Riddle Book Ever,* Sterling Publishing, 1985.

Rosenbloom, *The Funniest Joke Book Ever,* Sterling Publishing, 1986.

Rosenbloom, *The Funniest Knock-Knock Book Ever!,* Sterling Publishing, 1986.

David L. Harrison, *Wake Up, Sun,* Random House, 1986.

Emily Little, *David And The Giant,* Random House, 1987.

Rosenbloom, *The Funniest Dinosaur Book Ever,* Sterling Publishing, 1987.

Rosenbloom, *The Funniest Haunted House Book Ever,* Sterling Publishing, 1989.

Kathryn Cristaldi, *Little Squirrel's Christmas,* Random House, 1989.

Jane E. Gerver, *Piggy Wig,* Random House, 1989.

Wendy Cheyette Lewison, *Buzz—Said The Bee,* Scholastic Inc., 1992.

Jean Marzollo, *Halloween Cats,* Scholastic Inc., 1992.

Marzollo, *I'm Tyrannosaurus!,* Scholastic Inc., 1993.

Eve Merriam, *Higgle-Wiggle: Happy Rhymes,* Morrow, 1994.

Grace Maccarone, *Oink, Moo! How Do You Do?,* Scholastic Inc., 1994.

Nurit Karlin, *Ten Little Bunnies,* Simon & Schuster, 1994.

James Preller, *Hiccups for Elephant,* Scholastic Inc., 1995.

Marzollo, *Valentine cats,* Scholastic Inc., 1996.

SIDELIGHTS: Hans Wilhelm has earned a reputation as a creator of children's stories that both entertain and teach. For his willingness to treat topics that many authors of children's books shun as too sensitive for their young audiences, Wilhelm has received considerable critical praise. His best-known character is Waldo, a white, shaggy dog.

"When Waldo came into my life," Wilhelm told *CA,* "I soon realized that he was a very unusual dog with great strength, humor, and charm. In the beginning, I was his 'master' but now I'm not so sure anymore. . . . With several Waldo books, calendars, cards, puzzles, toys, cartoon strips, and a television series, he has taken over a large part of my time.

"But my true love belongs to the creation of children's books. In spite of all the frustrations and pain related to the writing and illustrating, it also gives me tremendous joy. And it is this joy I wish to communicate to others. Maybe that is the main reason why I make books."

Wilhelm has been praised for tackling subjects not often found in children's literature. *Los Angeles Times Book Review* contributor Kristiana Gregory was pleased to see the characters of *I'll Always Love You* "shown crying and feeling sad without embarrassment," and the book's reviewer for *Language Arts* observed, "In the best tradition of books that help children deal with the death of a pet, this one focuses on the good times, yet doesn't ignore the grief."

Wilhelm's talent as an illustrator has also attracted the attention of critics and won their approval. Sue Kreisman Siegel, writing in the *Fairfield Citizen-News,* called Wilhelm "an enchanter" who "casts his charming spells with words and pictures—on paper." And *New York Times Book Review* contributor Elaine Edelman praised Wilhelm's "way with his paintbrush" as "bright" and "full of sweetness." Critics have written admiringly of the compatibility of text and illustration in Wilhelm's work. "The warmth, humor, and real affection in the illustrations balance the somber topic," remarked the *Language Arts* reviewer of *I'll Always Love You.* Likewise, Gregory complimented that book's "tender, humorous watercolors" as "beautiful accompaniment" to the story.

BIOGRAPHICAL/CRITICAL SOURCES:

PERIODICALS

Books for Keeps, July, 1992, p. 9; September, 1992, p. 24.
Chicago Tribune Book World, January 4, 1987, p. 4.
Fairfield Citizen-News (Fairfield, CT), January 27, 1984.
Horn Book, September/October, 1988.
Junior Bookshelf, June, 1984.
Language Arts, January, 1986.
Library Talk, September, 1992, p. 41.
Los Angeles Times Book Review, July 27, 1980; December 15, 1985.
New York Times Book Review, December 11, 1983.
Publishers Weekly, May 13, 1988, p. 273; August 26, 1988, p. 88; December 9, 1988; June 8, 1990, p. 52; January 4, 1991, p. 71; October 25, 1991, p. 70; February 3, 1992, p. 80.
Time, December 19, 1983.
Trumbull Times (Trumbull, CT), July 24, 1986.
Westport News (Westport, CT), August 5, 1987; October 26, 1988.

WILLEFORD, Charles (Ray III)   1919-1988
(Will Charles)

PERSONAL: Born January 2, 1919, in Little Rock, AR; died of congestive heart failure, March 27, 1988, in Miami, FL; son of Charles Ray II and Aileen (Lowey) Willeford; married Mary Jo Norton (an English professor), July 1, 1951 (divorced, October, 1976); married third wife Betsy Poller (a newspaper columnist), May 30, 1981. *Education:* Palm Beach Junior College, A.A., 1960; University of Miami, A.B. (magna cum laude), 1962, M.A., 1964.

CAREER: U.S. Army, 1936-56, retiring as master sergeant; University of Miami, Coral Gables, FL, instructor in humanities, 1964-67; Miami-Dade Junior College, Miami, FL, assistant professor, 1967-68, chairman of departments of English and philosophy, 1968-70, associate professor of English, 1970-80. Script writer, New World Pictures, Hollywood, CA.

AWARDS, HONORS: Beacon Fiction Award, 1956, for *Pick-Up;* Mark Twain Award, Mark Twain Society of America, 1973, for *Cockfighter.* Received Silver Star, Bronze Star, Purple Heart, and Luxembourg Croix de Guerre.

WRITINGS:

Proletarian Laughter (poems), Alicat Bookshop Press (Yonkers, NY), 1948.
The Saga of Mary Miller (radio serial), broadcast by WLKH and AKAH, Armed Forces Radio Service, 1948.
High Priest of California (novel; also see below), Beacon Press (Boston), 1953.
Until I Am Dead (novel; later published as *Wild Wives;* also see below), Beacon Press, 1954.
Pick-Up (novel), Beacon Press, 1955.
Lust Is a Woman, Beacon Press, 1956.
The Basic Approach (television play), Canadian Broadcasting Corporation (CBC), 1956.
The Black Mass of Brother Springer (later published as *The Honey Gal*), Beacon Press, 1958.
The Director, Newsstand Library Publishers, 1960, published as *The Woman Chaser,* Carroll & Graf (New York City), 1990.
Understudy for Death, Newsstand Library Publishers, 1961, reprinted as *Understudy for Love,* Dennis McMillan (San Francisco), 1989.
No Experience Necessary, Newsstand Library Publishers, 1961.
The Machine in Ward Eleven (short stories), Belmont Books, 1963.
Poontang and Other Poems, New Athenean Press, 1967.
(Under pseudonym Will Charles) *The Hombre from Sonora,* Lenox Hill, 1971.

The Burnt Orange Heresy, Crown (New York City), 1971.
Cockfighter (originally published in 1962), Crown, 1972.
A Guide for the Undehemorrhoided (autobiography), Star Publishing (Belmont, CA), 1977.
Off the Wall (fictionalized biography of "Son of Sam" killer David Berkowitz), Pegasus Rex (Montclair, NJ), 1980.
Something about a Soldier (autobiography), Random House (New York City), 1986.
Kiss Your Ass Goodbye, Dennis McMillan, 1987.
New Forms of Ugly: The Immobilized Hero in Modern Fiction (literary criticism), Dennis McMillan, 1987.
Charles Willeford Trilogy: High Priest of California, Play, Wild Wives (*Wild Wives* was originally published as *Until I Am Dead*), Re/Search Publications (San Francisco), 1987.
I Was Looking for a Street (autobiography), Countryman Press (Woodstock, VT), 1988.
The Cockfighter Journal (diary from the filming of his 1962 novel), Maurice Neville (Santa Barbara, CA), 1989.
The Shark-Infested Custard (fiction; includes *Kiss Your Ass Goodbye* and a portion of *Everybody's Metamorphosis*), Underwood/Miller (Novato, CA), 1993.

"HOKE MOSELEY" DETECTIVE SERIES

Miami Blues, St. Martin's (New York City), 1984.
New Hope for the Dead, St. Martin's, 1985.
Sideswipe: A Novel (Mystery Guild selection), St. Martin's, 1987.
The Way We Die Now: A Novel, Random House, 1988.

OTHER

Also author of *Soldier's Wife,* 1958, *Born to Kill* (screenplay based on his novel *Cockfighter*), 1974, and *Everybody's Metamorphosis,* 1988. Past columnist for *Village Post* and *Miami Herald.* Contributor of fiction and nonfiction to periodicals, including *Books Abroad, Saturday Review, Playboy, Writer's Digest, Sports Illustrated,* and *Air Force.* Associate editor, *Alfred Hitchcock Mystery Magazine,* 1964.

The "Hoke Moseley" detective series novels have also been published in Denmark, England, France, Sweden, Germany, and Japan.

ADAPTATIONS: Cockfighter was made into a 1974 film released under several different titles (*Born to Kill, Wild Drifter,* and *Gamblin' Man*), directed by Roger Corman, produced by Monte Hellmann, and starring Warren Oates, with Willeford playing the character of Judge Ed Middleton; *Miami Blues* was made into a film of the same title, released by Orion Pictures Corporation in 1990, directed by George Armitage and produced by Jonathan Demme, starring Fred Ward as Sergeant Hoke Moseley,

Alec Baldwin as "Junior" Frenger, and Jennifer Jason Leigh as Susie Waggoner; Robert Redford has bought the film rights to *New Hope for the Dead, Sideswipe,* and *The Way We Die Now.*

SIDELIGHTS: Prior to his death in 1988, Charles Willeford had recently begun "attracting national attention," according to a *Los Angeles Times* obituary. The popularity of Willeford's "Hoke Moseley" series earned him numerous comparisons to giants in the detective thriller genre, yet his earlier work also collected many adherents. Sybil Steinberg noted in a *Publishers Weekly* interview with Willeford that while "his peers, notably Elmore Leonard, Joseph Hansen and Lawrence Block, have been hailing Willeford's mastery of his craft for years, Willeford's novels for a long time earned him only a cult following." Throughout his writing career, "Willeford continually experimented with genres and forms, and his canon runs the gamut from naturalistic melodramas to violent revenge scenarios, a hardboiled detective story, a western, war stories, and the genre-blasting police procedurals that would finally bring fame into his life," commented Richard Gehr in the *Village Voice Literary Supplement.* Gehr continued that Willeford's novels "provide nothing less than a non-bohemian (yet aesthetically charged) alternative history, a moral history, of America's past 40 years, from bust to boom and back again." In a London *Times* review, Marcel Berlins declared that Willeford's "extraordinary descriptions" of character and setting as well as his successful management of plot and timing "put him in the Elmore Leonard class."

Willeford's first three novels—*High Priest of California, Until I Am Dead* (later retitled *Wild Wives*), and *Pick-Up*—comprise "his San Francisco trilogy of bleak, *noir* novels," stated Steinberg in *Publishers Weekly.* Known by many critics as a pulp novelist because of his early work, Willeford told Steinberg how he wrote *High Priest of California:* " 'I was stationed at Hamilton Air Force Base, so I drove to San Francisco every weekend and holed up in a room at the Powell Hotel until I finished a book.' " Eventually, Willeford "segued into the police procedural format that seems finally to have made his name familiar to a wider audience," explained Steinberg.

With homicide Sergeant Hoke Moseley, protagonist of *Miami Blues, New Hope for the Dead, Sideswipe,* and *The Way We Die Now,* "Willeford is savvy enough to present his reader with a policeman dogged by a multiplicity of concerns and questions," wrote Paul Piazza in the *Washington Post Book World.* Janet Maslin described Hoke Moseley in the *New York Times* as "the antihero of Charles Willeford's crackerjack series of crime novels, written in the droll, unpredictable manner of Elmore Leonard but graced with a sharply evoked seediness all their own." She further characterized Moseley as "no or-

dinary detective. He's a broke, beleaguered veteran who loves shocking suspects by taking out his false teeth in their presence, and whose wiliness generates many other tricks for catching criminals off-guard." The *Village Voice Literary Supplement*'s Gehr wrote: "In the Hoke Moseley tetralogy, Willeford combined Elmore Leonard's flair for dialogue combined with James Ellroy's penchant for irrational violence. Hoke himself is a toothless, prematurely aged Vietnam vet in his early forties. . . . The divorced father of two teenaged daughters who eventually move in on him, Hoke eats, drinks, and smokes to an unhealthy degree. . . . He is thoroughly immobilized, thoroughly modern, save for his strict yet realistic police detective's morality." In the *Washington Post,* Rita Kempley suggested that actor Fred Ward, who portrays Sergeant Hoke Moseley in the film version of *Miami Blues,* "looks like a junkyard dog, a veteran of losing battles, toothless from chewing on bullets. . . . There's a distinctive down and out to this rumpled shamus."

The Hoke Moseley series explores the "minutiae of life in Florida's depression-belt," asserted Berlins of the London *Times.* A *Times Literary Supplement* reviewer noted that what interests the author "is character, and, above all, setting: the tacky, sleazy, junk-food side of American life." The *Washington Post Book World*'s Piazza added that Willeford's "technique ticks away like a time bomb: detail follows mundane detail—the minute particulars of a cop's life, the idiosyncracies of dress and fashion, the stifling humidity of a Miami summer—until unexpectedly the very ground we stand upon seems to be blown away."

About the setting in the film version of *Miami Blues,* Peter Rainer remarked in the *Los Angeles Times:* "The Miami of *Miami Blues* is an overheated griddle of shifty, sun-drenched psychopaths and hangdog lawmen. It's the modern equivalent of the Wild West—a wide open world of outlaws done up in bright pop colorations of flamingo pink and lime green." Kempley of the *Washington Post* observed, "It's the atmosphere, the faded pastels of Coral Gables, the Miami Nice just out of the villain's reach, that are so provocative."

Willeford's untimely death at age sixty-nine put a premature end to the Hoke Moseley series, and reviewers and critics have noted his passing. Berlins reflected in the London *Times* that the author's death "is a loss to crime writing." The *Washington Post Book World*'s Piazza maintained that Willeford "was a master craftsman to the end, and this last book [*The Way We Die Now*] only confirms what his readers already know: that Willeford is an exciting, original novelist."

Charles Willeford once told *CA:* "The turning point in my career occurred in October, 1959, when my long short story, 'The Machine in Ward Eleven,' was published in

Playboy. Prior to that time I had been advised by editors, writing teachers, and by other writers that it was impossible to have an insane person as a sympathetic hero. I did not believe them, because I had a hunch that madness was a predominant theme and a normal condition for Americans living in the second half of this century. The publication of 'The Machine in Ward Eleven' and its reception by readers confirmed what I had only heretofore suspected. Since then, of course, it has been reconfirmed for me many times, and by many contemporary writers and films and plays; but the acceptance of this condition does not mean that I am overjoyed by it. Happiness as a writer is still hard to come by in a nation where tranquilizers like valium outsell aspirin. At any rate, it was the understanding and the acceptance of the madness of our times that enabled me to write my best novel to date, *The Burnt Orange Heresy.*"

BIOGRAPHICAL/CRITICAL SOURCES:

BOOKS

Willeford, Charles, *A Guide for the Undehemorrhoided* (autobiography), Star Publishing, 1977.
Willeford, Charles, *Something about a Soldier* (autobiography), Random House, 1986.
Willeford, Charles, *I Was Looking for a Street* (autobiography), Countryman Press, 1988.

PERIODICALS

Harper's, October, 1971.
Los Angeles Times, April 20, 1990.
Los Angeles Times Book Review, April 10, 1988, p. 10.
New Yorker, April 23, 1984, p. 134.
New York Times, April 20, 1990.
New York Times Book Review, September 2, 1984, p. 12; April 19, 1987, p. 22.
Publishers Weekly, February 6, 1987, pp. 78-79.
Times (London), May 5, 1988; May 20, 1989.
Times Literary Supplement, July 1, 1988, p. 731; November 24, 1989, p. 1312.
Tribune Books (Chicago), February 22, 1987, p. 5; May 3, 1987, p. 5; July 17, 1988, p. 9.
Village Voice Literary Supplement, March, 1989, p. 30.
Washington Post, April 20, 1990.
Washington Post Book World, February 16, 1986, p. 7; May 17, 1987, p. 12; May 15, 1988, p. 8.

OBITUARIES:

PERIODICALS

Chicago Tribune, March 30, 1988.
Los Angeles Times, March 29, 1988.
New York Times, March 29, 1988.
Washington Post, March 29, 1988.*

—Sketch by Michaela Swart Wilson

WILLIAMS, David   1926-

PERSONAL: Born June 8, 1926, in Bridgend, Glamorganshire, Wales; son of Trevor K. (a journalist) and Rene (Morgan) Williams; married Brenda Holmes, August 18, 1951; children: Jonathan, Linda Benson. *Education:* St. John's College, Oxford, B.A., 1948, M.A., 1951. *Religion:* Episcopalian. *Avocational interests:* "I have a serious interest in and commitment to the prevention and alleviation of disability. I play golf and the piano, equally badly, and I enjoy unserious after-dinner speaking in the United Kingdom and the United States—more, probably, than the people who have to listen to me."

ADDRESSES: Home—Blandings, Pinewood Rd., Virginia Water, Surrey GU25 4PA, England. *Agent*—(American) Gelfman Schneider Literary Agency, 250 W. 57th St., New York, NY 10107. (British) John Farquharson Ltd. 28/29 Haymarket, London SW1Y 4SP, England.

CAREER: Gordon & Gotch Advertising Ltd., London, England, director, 1950-58; David Williams & Partners, London, managing director, 1958-68; David Williams & Ketchum Ltd., London, chairman, 1968-78; Ketchum Communications Ltd., Pittsburgh, director, 1968-83; Ketchum Group Holdings Ltd., London, vice-chairman, 1978-86. Governor of Pusey House, Oxford University, 1965—; vice-chairman of Royal Commonwealth Society for the Blind, 1966-85; chairman, National Stroke Campaign; council member of Advertising Standards Authority, 1976-80, and Impact Foundation. *Military service:* Royal Navy Offices, 1944-47.

MEMBER: Mystery Writers of America, Society of Authors, Crime Writers Association, Institute of Practitioners in Advertising (fellow), Detection Club, Archive at Mugar Memorial Library, Boston.

WRITINGS:

Last Seen Breathing ("Chief Inspector Merlin Parry" detective series), HarperCollins (England), 1994.
Death of a Prodigal ("Chief Inspector Merlin Parry" detective series), HarperCollins (England), in press.

"MARK TREASURE" DETECTIVE SERIES

Unholy Writ, Collins, 1976, St. Martin's, 1977.
Treasure by Degrees, St. Martin's, 1977.
Treasure Up in Smoke, St. Martin's, 1978.
Murder for Treasure, St. Martin's, 1980.
Copper, Gold, and Treasure, St. Martin's 1982.
Treasure Preserved, St. Martin's, 1983.
Advertise for Treasure, St. Martin's, 1984.
Wedding Treasure, St. Martin's, 1985.
Murder in Advent, St. Martin's, 1985.
Treasure in Roubles, Macmillan (London), 1986, St. Martin's, 1987.

Divided Treasure, Macmillan (London), 1987, St. Martin's, 1988.

Treasure in Oxford, Macmillan (London), 1988, St. Martin's, 1989.

Holy Treasure!, Macmillan (London), 1989, St. Martin's, 1990.

Prescription for Murder, Macmillan (London), 1990, St. Martin's, 1991.

Treasure by Post, Macmillan (London), 1991, St. Martin's, 1992.

Planning on Murder, HarperCollins (England), 1992.

Banking on Murder, HarperCollins (England), 1993.

OTHER

Author of short stories in magazines and anthologies, including *Ellery Queen Mystery Magazine* and *A Classic English Crime,* Pavilion, 1990. Author of the paper *Advertising and Social Conscience: Exploiting Products, Not People,* 1976.

WORK IN PROGRESS: The third mystery in the "Chief Inspector Merlin Parry" detective series.

SIDELIGHTS: David Williams turned to mystery writing after twenty-five years in advertising. In 1976 he published *Unholy Writ,* the first in his series of traditional British detective stories featuring the character Mark Treasure, a merchant banker and amateur sleuth. From the outset *Spectator* reviewer Patrick Cosgrave hailed Williams as a "remarkable" and "promising" new talent, ranking the author among renowned detective fiction writers such as Michael Innes, Agatha Christie, and Ngaio Marsh. Since writing *Unholy Writ,* Williams has added nearly a dozen titles to the "Mark Treasure" crime novel series and earned widespread critical acclaim in both England and the United States.

Critiquing Williams's second book, *Treasure by Degrees,* the *New York Times Book Review* cited "a good deal of humor and some sharp writing." Likewise, in its subsequent review of the 1982 book, *Copper, Gold, and Treasure,* the periodical noted Williams's "charm, authentic light touch," and sophisticated outlook on life. According to T. J. Binyon in the *Times Literary Supplement, Advertise for Treasure,* published in 1984, represents the best of Williams's detective series, offering "good plot, bright dialogue, sharp characters." Marcel Berlins, on the other hand, observed in the London Times that 1985's "exuberant [and] witty" *Murder in Advent* was his choice for all-time best "Mark Treasure" caper.

Williams told *CA:* "I began writing detective stories on Sunday afternoons as self-fulfillment around 1975. The advertising agency I had founded had by that time become so large that I found it difficult any more to identify as author with the end product. Three years later I had a long-ish illness; writing then became a remedial activity for a while and possibly saved my life. After I recovered, at fifty-two, it made more sense to be a full-time writer than to return to a hectic business life. The sense of this decision was amply confirmed by the especial success of *Murder for Treasure* in 1980.

"My books are unstructured in the sense that I do not work to a synopsis. I never know who the villain is going to be until toward the end of the story when one of the characters elects himself or herself! I start with a group of people, a locale, and usually a focus of interest like an old house, a valuable painting, or an important document—and then let the people interact.

"I value the humor in my own writing and other people's, along with prose that has melody. My mentors were Edmund Crispin, Michael Innes, and Emma Lathen, and I strive to fashion my work to be as rereadable as I find nearly all of theirs to be."

BIOGRAPHICAL/CRITICAL SOURCES:

PERIODICALS

Citizen, July 7, 1989.
Daily Mail, August 13, 1994.
Independent, July 15, 1989.
Mystery and Detective Monthly, October, 1989.
New York Times Book Review, January 1, 1978; September 12, 1982; September 9, 1989.
Spectator, June 25, 1977, December 3, 1977.
Sunday Telegraph, July 17, 1994.
Sunday Times, May 28, 1989.
Times (London), November 7, 1985.
Times Literary Supplement, July 20, 1984.
Tribune, June 6, 1989.

*   *   *

WILLIAMS, Joan   1928-

PERSONAL: Born September 26, 1928, in Memphis, TN.; daughter of Priestly H. and Maude (Moore) Williams; married Ezra Drinker Bowen, 1954 (divorced, 1970); married John Faragason, 1970; children: (first marriage) Ezra Drinker, Matthew Williams. *Education:* Bard College, B.A., 1950; Fairfield University, M.A., 1985. *Avocational interests:* Sailing and skiing.

ADDRESSES: Home—4714 Lorece Ave., Memphis, TN 38117. *Agent*—Harold Ober Associates, 40 East 49th St., New York, NY.

CAREER: Full-time writer. "I lived briefly in New Orleans where I worked in a Doubleday bookshop. In New York, for two years before I married, I answered letters-to-the-editor for *Look Magazine.*"

MEMBER: PEN, Authors Guild.

AWARDS, HONORS: National Institute of Arts and Letters, grant in literature, 1962; John P. Marquand First Novel Award, 1962, for *The Morning and the Evening;* Guggenheim fellow, 1986.

WRITINGS:

The Morning and the Evening, Atheneum (New York City), 1961.
Old Powder Man, Harcourt (New York City), 1966.
The Wintering, Harcourt, 1971.
County Woman, Little, Brown (Boston, MA), 1982.
Pariah and Other Stories, Little, Brown, 1983.
Pay the Piper, Dutton (New York City), 1988.

Co-author with William Faulkner of the teleplay *The Graduation Dress,* produced on General Electric Theatre for Columbia Broadcasting System, October 30, 1960. Also author of short stories published in various publications, including *Atlantic Monthly, Saturday Evening Post, Esquire, Virginia Quarterly Review,* and *Mademoiselle.*

SIDELIGHTS: Joan Williams' literary career began in 1949 when, following the publication of her first story entitled "Rain Later," she met and initiated a correspondence with William Faulkner. Williams soon became a protegee and close friend of Faulkner, even collaborating with him to write the script for the teleplay *The Graduation Dress.* In addition to frequent comparisons to Faulkner, Williams has become highly regarded by many critics for both her individual voice and her interpretations of the Southern genre. Reviewer David Boroff notes: "She is a gifted writer in superb control of her craft." In his review of *The Morning and the Evening,* critic Granville Hicks writes: "[Her] style is quiet but assured, and she tells her story in a calm, straightforward fashion. What gives it its depth is her insight, which has freed her from reliance on Southern cliches, or cliches of any kind. She speaks in her own voice, and it is worth listening to."

Despite Williams' early success and established reputation, her fourth novel entitled *County Woman* has received mixed reviews. Set in Mississippi in 1962, the book is, in the words of *Chicago Tribune* reviewer Polly Morrice, about a "middle-aged woman searching for true direction" during the turmoil of "the Old South giving way to the New." Allie McCall's conventional way of life is dramatically transformed when she decides to run for constable of Itna Homa, a small farming community near Oxford. Her decision alters her traditional lifestyle, which in-

cludes caring for both her elderly father and her husband. The Southern political climate of the 1960s becomes the backdrop and parallel to Allie's change. As one of the characters says when she hears the radio announcement about James Meredith's admission to the University of Mississippi, "Then it's the end. The end of living the way us Southern white people have." A reviewer for the *New Yorker* remarks, "Allie's new restlessness is not only mirrored in but magnified by the events in the news." However, Morrice concludes: "Whole lot of shakin' up goes on in the few months' span of *County Woman,* too much for us to read it as a plausible chronicle of social evolution." *Los Angeles Times* reviewer Elizabeth Wheeler calls it a "put-down-housewife-wakes-and-smells-the-coffee" plot, typical of a "new genre of fiction" emerging in the 1980s. While she praises Williams' writing, especially the "lively and authentic-sounding Southern voices," she finds the rest "a bit unsatisfactory" and Allie McCall's transformation overly dramatic.

Other critics disagree with such criticism, commending Williams for her authentic setting and knowledge of subject. *Detroit News* reviewer Anne Tyler believes the novel's "drawbacks don't amount to a hill of beans (as one of the Itna Homas might put it)." She goes on to praise Williams' "faultless ear and eye" for rural community settings and characters and believes *County Woman* to be a "wide, deep window upon a fascinating little world." *Washington Post Book World* critic Jonathan Yardley agrees, calling it "an intelligent and well-written novel, one with a secure grasp on time, place and character. . . . Williams remembers precisely what the rural South was like two decades ago, not merely the details but the attitudes, and she gets it down exactly right."

A *Washington Post Book World* critic calls Williams' *Pariah and Other Stories* a collection which "charts the territory of the rural and small-town South—the land where porches sag on tenant houses, where screen doors slap on summer days, where matrons while away hot afternoons over bridge games." The *New York Times Book Review*'s Edith Milton claims: "At [the stories'] deepest level, they have an apocalyptic resonance; the affection and warmth at their center is surrounded by a sense of universal and ever intensifying darkness." Anne Tyler in the *Detroit News* finds "endurance" to be "the thread running through this book. Most of the stories (whether the early ones or the later, generally more polished ones) explore the ways in which people manage to trudge along in spite of everything—poverty, loneliness, change, injustice, old age, or simple exhaustion." She calls the story "Jesse" "perhaps the best piece in the book" and believes it to be "not so much a story as a poem, and an absolutely beautiful one."

BIOGRAPHICAL/CRITICAL SOURCES:

BOOKS

Dictionary of Literary Biography, Gale (Detroit, MI), Volume 6, 1980.

PERIODICALS

Best Sellers, June 15, 1971, p. 138.
Booklist, May 15, 1961; September 1, 1971, p. 39; February 15, 1982, p. 746; August 1983, p. 1450; May 15, 1988, p. 1573.
Chicago Tribune, May 9, 1982, p. 2.
Christian Science Monitor, May 18, 1961.
Detroit News, February 7, 1982; September 4, 1983.
Hudson Review, spring 1972, p. 166.
Kirkus Review, February 1, 1971, p. 138; December 1, 1981, p. 1489; June 1, 1983, p. 638; March 15, 1988, p. 407.
Library Journal, March 15, 1971, p. 978; March 1, 1982, p. 564; June 15, 1983, p. 1276.
Los Angeles Times Book Review, September 15, 1985, p. 8.
National Review, February 5, 1982, p. 116.
New York Times Book Review, May 21, 1961; September 18, 1983, p. 14.
New Yorker, March 15, 1982, p. 143; October 10, 1983, p. 167.
Publishers Weekly, January 25, 1971, p. 260; December 18, 1981, p. 58; June 10, 1983, p. 56; March 25, 1988, p. 52.
San Francisco Chronicle, May 30, 1961.
Saturday Review, May 13, 1961.
Time, May 19, 1961.
Village Voice Literary Supplement, February 1982, p. 4.
Virginia Quarterly Review, summer 1971, p. R96.
Washington Post Book World, February 7, 1982, p. 3; August 7, 1983, p. 8; October 13, 1985, p. 16; May 29, 1988, p. 3.

*   *   *

WILLIAMS, Joy 1944-

PERSONAL: Born February 11, 1944, in Chelmsford, MA; daughter of William Lloyd (a minister) and Elisabeth (Thomas) Williams; married Rust Hills (a writer and editor); children: Caitlin. *Education:* Marietta College, M.A. (magna cum laude), 1963; University of Iowa, M.F.A., 1965. *Politics:* Democrat. *Religion:* Protestant.

ADDRESSES: Home—Florida. *Agent*—Amanda Urban, International Creative Management, 40 West 57th St., New York, NY 10019.

CAREER: Writer. U.S. Navy, Mate Marine Laboratory, Siesta Key, FL, researcher and data analyst, 1967-69; visiting instructor at University of Houston, 1982, University of Florida, 1983, University of California, Irvine, 1984, University of Iowa, 1984, and University of Arizona, 1987-92.

MEMBER: Phi Beta Kappa.

AWARDS, HONORS: National Endowment for the Arts grant, 1973; Guggenheim fellowship, 1974; National Magazine Award for fiction, 1980, for "The Farm"; literature citation, 1989, and Straus Living Award, 1993-97, both from American Academy of Arts.

WRITINGS:

State of Grace (novel), Doubleday (New York City), 1973.
The Changeling (novel), Doubleday, 1978.
Taking Care (short stories), Random House (New York City), 1982.
The Florida Keys: A History and Guide, Random House, 1986.
Breaking and Entering (novel), Random House, 1988.
Escapes (short stories), Random House, 1990.

CONTRIBUTOR OF SHORT STORIES TO ANTHOLOGIES

William Abrahams and Richard Poirier, editors, *O. Henry Prize Story Collection,* Doubleday, 1966.
Gordon Lish, editor, *Secret Lives of Our Time,* Doubleday, 1973.
Pat Rotter, editor, *Bitches and Sad Ladies,* Harper Magazine Press (New York City), 1974.
Lish, editor, *All Our Secrets Are the Same,* Norton (New York City), 1977.
Theodore Solotaroff, editor, *Best American Short Stories, 1978,* Houghton (Boston), 1978.
R. V. Cassell, editor, *The Norton Anthology of Short Fiction,* Norton, 1978.
Women on Woman Alone, Dell (New York City), 1978.
Tobias Wolff, editor, *Matters of Life and Death,* Ecco Press (New York City), 1982.
Great Esquire Fiction, Viking (New York City), 1983.
Litzinger and Oates, editors, *Story,* Health, 1985.
Gail Godwin and Shannon Ravenel, editors, *Best American Short Stories, 1985,* Houghton, 1985.
Raymond Carver and Ravenel, editors, *American Short Stories, 1986,* Houghton, 1986.
Best American Short Stories, 1987, Houghton, 1987.
Carver and Jenks, editors, *American Short Story Masterpieces,* Delacorte (New York City), 1987.

OTHER

Contributor of short stories and essays to various publications, including *Paris Review, Esquire, Tri-Quarterly, New Yorker, Grand Street,* and *Ms.*

SIDELIGHTS: "I think Joy Williams may be the most 'relevant' woman writing at this time," remarks Anatole

Broyard in his *New York Times* review of Williams's first novel, *State of Grace.* "I can't tell which moves me more: her historical inevitability or her talent." In her novels and short stories, Williams writes with a surrealistic intensity of how ordinary lives are vulnerable to horror and hopelessness. Although critics have responded somewhat unevenly to her fiction, they nonetheless recognize her unique talent and skill. Gail Godwin observes in the *Chicago Tribune Book World:* "Joy Williams 'writes like' nobody but Joy Williams, and that is distinctively sufficient. . . . She has her own sound. Her writing style is laconic, austere, yet numinously suggestive."

Williams first attracted popular and critical attention with *State of Grace,* an impressionistic novel in which "shards of experiences slowly assemble into a powerful portrayal of . . . a heroine cursed by total recall," says an *Antioch Review* contributor. The novel follows the heroine "from her pregnancy to the birth of her child," writes David Bromwich in *Commentary,* "with generous flashbacks to her religious childhood and her early free-living and free-loving adulthood." Godwin cautions in the *New York Times Book Review* that while the "fated heroine of this bleak but beautifully-crafted first novel may well be the final perfected archetype of all the 'sad ladies' . . . [she] is no simple 'slice-of-despair' character; her sad story becomes, through the author's skill and intention, transubstantiated into significant myth." Although the *Antioch Review* contributor believes the book's nonlinear structure causes problems with unity, the critic finds a "totally involving immediacy" in the novel and concludes: "All Joy Williams needs is the ability to better organize and control the visions of her extraordinary imagination. She is almost certain to write a novel that will be even finer than this one."

The Changeling, Williams's impressionistic and not easily categorized second novel, did not quite fulfill the expectations that several critics held for it. Broyard, for example, acknowledges in the *New York Times* that *State of Grace* is a "startlingly good novel, but it pains me to have to say that *The Changeling* is a startlingly bad one. . . . Harsh as it may sound, I find that nothing works." Broyard calls the story line "an arbitrary muddle about a young woman who is more or less kidnapped by a man who marries her and takes her to live on an island." Strange occurrences on this island prompt a *New Yorker* contributor to wonder, is this a "horror story or something more serious? The steady decay of [the heroine's] mental powers, skillfully rendered by Joy Williams, may persuade the reader that the title is a metaphor for a schizophrenic."

In the *Hudson Review,* Patricia Meyer Spacks assesses the novel as an "increasingly surrealistic account . . . , which retreats altogether from the public realm into a self-indulgent phantasmagoria of privacy"; Spacks also sus-

pects that the corresponding stylistic shift from "outer to inner events . . . reflects unsure novelistic purpose." Similarly, Godwin finds the stream-of-consciousness ending disappointing and seemingly evasive because of its unanswered questions. However, Godwin concludes in the *Chicago Tribune Book World* that Williams may be luring the reader to "[his or her] own solutions—and to await with anticipation her future fictions."

Discussing *The Changeling* in the *New York Times Book Review,* Alice Adams appreciates the inherent difficulty in writing about the "borderland between psychosis and reality, the land of private mythology of the 'grotesque.'" And while she believes Williams is a "talented, skillful writer . . . [who] evokes the feel and smell of certain moments with an eerie precision," Adams finds the novel "unconvincing and ultimately unsatisfactory . . . , instead of the very good one that I believe Joy Williams could write." Nevertheless, D. Keith Mano speaks favorably in the *National Review* of the multifarious elements in *The Changeling,* crediting Williams with a willingness "to stretch and reconnoiter her talent" on what he deems "a book of risks: primeval myth, enchantment, animal metamorphosis, strange island, symbolism, insanity: more Gothic architecture than Chartres has. Only a daredevil novelist would try to renovate this tenement genre."

Taking Care, Williams's first collection of short stories, has generated much favorable response from critics, many of whom consider the stories both individually and collectively successful. The "finely made and perfectly matched stories . . . hold love up to us like a dark, fractured bauble that we should see, reflected and to our astonishment, what moments in our familiar lives it dominates," writes Richard Ford in the *Chicago Tribune Book World.* David Quammen suggests that "social disfunction and the discontinuity of relationships" permeate the collection, and he adds in the *New York Times Book Review* that most of the stories are "focused on the imperfect efforts of husbands and wives trying marriage for the second or third time, and on the children surviving (in various degrees of disability) from earlier attempts." Ford finds that "most often and touchingly, Williams' characters live without love, and grow melancholy for wanting it," and he maintains that "Williams writes about such yearnings and their attendant pretensions with a rare, transforming intelligence." Joyce Kornblatt, who detects a similarity in spirit between these stories and those of Flannery O'Connor and Joyce Carol Oates, observes in the *Washington Post Book World* that "madness, murder, the surrender of hope become commonplace rather than extreme behaviors, and even those characters who sustain the ability to love seem perplexed, even encumbered, by their triumph."

Caroline Thompson writes in the *Los Angeles Times* that "gathered together, the stories project a cumulative impression that couldn't be communicated by any single of them." Brina Caplan commends Williams for the subtle yet devastating effect of her collection, and writes in the *Nation:* "*Taking Care,* story by story and incident by incident, withdraws meaning from the lives it represents. In each case, what remains is a gem of despair, worked into the shape of finality by skillful slights of hand." "Transcending religious and political systems of belief, Williams speaks to us from a plane of pure feeling," suggests Kornblatt. "Like fine music, these stories circumvent the intellect. Williams seems to make the works themselves transparent and we gaze directly into the souls of her characters."

BIOGRAPHICAL/CRITICAL SOURCES:

BOOKS

Contemporary Literary Criticism, Volume 31, Gale, 1985.

PERIODICALS

Antioch Review, November, 1973.
Carolina Quarterly, fall, 1973, pp. 106-108.
Chicago Tribune Book World, June 18, 1978; May 2, 1982.
Commentary, September, 1973, pp. 85-86.
Esquire, July, 1973, pp. 26, 28.
Hudson Review, winter, 1978-79, pp. 663-676.
Los Angeles Times, April 22, 1982.
Nation, April 24, 1982, pp. 500-502.
National Review, August 4, 1978.
New Yorker, September 25, 1978.
New York Times, November 7, 1973; June 3, 1978.
New York Times Book Review, April 22, 1973, pp. 2-3; July 2, 1978, pp. 6, 17; February 14, 1982, pp. 11, 34.
Saturday Review, February, 1982.
Virginia Quarterly Review, autumn, 1978, p. 134; winter, 1983.
Washington Post Book World, March 21, 1982, p. 4.

*   *   *

WINSTON, Kenneth I(rwin) 1940-

PERSONAL: Born June 17, 1940, in Boston, MA; son of Edward K. and Sylvia (Cline) Winston; married Mary Jo Bane (Commissioner of Social Services for the State of New York), May 31, 1975. *Education:* Harvard University, B.A., 1962; Columbia University, M.A., 1968, Ph.D., 1970. *Avocational interests:* Birding, hiking.

ADDRESSES: Home—207 Savin Hill Ave., Boston, MA 02125. *Office*—Department of Philosophy, Wheaton College, Norton, MA 02766.

CAREER: Columbia University, New York, NY, instructor in philosophy, 1968-69; Wheaton College, Norton,

MA, assistant professor, 1969-76, associate professor, 1976-82, professor of philosophy, 1982—. Research fellow at Center for the Study of Law and Society, Berkeley, CA, 1972-73; visiting assistant professor at Brown University, 1975; Harvard University, lecturer, 1978-79, visiting scholar at Harvard Law School, 1980-81; lecturer at Boston College, 1983, 1986; research fellow at Kennedy School of Government, Harvard University, 1984-85; visiting professor at Kennedy School of Government, 1986-91.

MEMBER: American Philosophical Association, Conference for the Study of Political Thought, Society of Philosophy and Public Affairs, American Society for Political and Legal Philosophy.

AWARDS, HONORS: Fellow of American Council of Learned Societies, 1972-73, and National Endowment for the Humanities, 1980-81; John Dewey senior fellow of the Center for Dewey Studies, 1984-85.

WRITINGS:

EDITOR

The Principles of Social Order: Selected Essays of Lon L. Fuller, Duke University Press (Durham, NC), 1981.
(With Mary Jo Bane) *Gender and Public Policy: Cases and Comments,* Westview (Boulder, CO), 1993.
(With John T. Noonan, Jr.) *The Responsible Judge: Readings in Judicial Ethics,* Praeger (New York City), 1993.

OTHER

Contributor of articles to law and philosophy journals, including *California Law Review* and *Civil Liberty Law Review.* Contributor to *Bird Observer of Eastern Massachusetts.*

WORK IN PROGRESS: A Theory of Legislation, completion expected in 1995.

*   *   *

WITCOVER, Jules (Joseph) 1927-

PERSONAL: Born July 16, 1927, in Union City, NJ; son of Samuel (a mechanic) and Sadie (Carpenter) Witcover; married Marian Laverty, June 14, 1952 (divorced, 1990); children: Paul, Amy, Julie. *Education:* Columbia College, A.B., 1949; Columbia Graduate School of Journalism, M.S.J., 1951. *Politics:* Independent. *Religion:* Roman Catholic.

ADDRESSES: Home—3042 Q St. N.W., Washington, DC 20007-3080. *Office*—*Baltimore Sun,* Washington Bureau, 1627 K St. N.W., Washington, DC 20006-1702.

CAREER: Journalist in Hackensack, NJ, 1949-50, Providence, RI, 1951-53, and Newark, NJ, 1953; *Syracuse Herald-Journal,* Syracuse, NY, Washington correspondent, 1954-62; Newhouse National News Service, Washington, DC, senior correspondent and chief political writer, 1962-68, Washington columnist, 1968-69; *Los Angeles Times,* Washington Bureau, Washington, DC, correspondent, 1970-72; *Washington Post,* Washington, DC, member of national staff, 1973-76; *Washington Star,* political columnist, 1977-81, political editor, 1979-81; *Tribune Media Services* syndicate, Chicago, syndicated columnist with Jack W. Germond, 1977-81; *Baltimore Evening Sun,* Washington, DC, columnist, 1981—. *Military service:* U.S. Navy, 1945-46.

MEMBER: White House Correspondents Association.

AWARDS, HONORS: Reid Foundation fellowship in Europe, 1958; Sigma Delta Chi Award for Washington correspondence, 1962; Alumni award, Columbia Graduate School of Journalism, 1974; Front Page Award, Washington-Baltimore Newspaper Guild, 1985, for criticism/commentary.

WRITINGS:

85 Days: The Last Campaign of Robert Kennedy, Putnam (New York City), 1969, Quill (New York City), 1988.

The Resurrection of Richard Nixon, Putnam, 1970.

White Knight: The Rise of Spiro Agnew, Random House (New York City), 1972.

(With Richard M. Cohen) *A Heartbeat Away: The Investigation and Resignation of Vice President Spiro T. Agnew,* Viking (New York City), 1974.

Marathon: The Pursuit of the Presidency, 1972-1976, Viking, 1977.

The Main Chance (novel), Viking, 1979.

(With Jack W. Germond) *Blue Smoke and Mirrors: How Reagan Won and Why Carter Lost the Election of 1980,* Viking, 1981.

(With Germond) *Wake Us When It's Over: Presidential Politics of 1984,* Macmillan (New York City), 1985.

(With Germond) *Whose Broad Stripes and Bright Stars?: The Trivial Pursuit of the Presidency, 1988,* Warner, 1989.

Sabotage at Black Tom: Imperial Germany's Secret War in America, 1914-1917, Algonquin, 1989.

Crapshoot; Rolling the Dice on the Vice Presidency: From Adams and Jefferson to Truman and Quayle, Crown (New York City), 1992.

(With Germond) *Mad As Hell: Revolt at the Ballot Box, 1992,* Warner, 1993.

Also contributor to national magazines, including *Esquire, Nation, New Republic,* and *Saturday Review.*

SIDELIGHTS: Jules Witcover's political reporting has earned him a solid reputation for in-depth coverage of presidential and vice-presidential politics. Christopher Lehmann-Haupt of the *New York Times* called Witcover "a savvy political reporter blessed with both an instinct for the jugular and a gift for knitting together a compelling narrative from a complex tangle of details." Godfrey Hodgson, writing in the *New York Times Book Review,* described Witcover as "one of the ablest and most expert political reporters in Washington."

Marathon: The Pursuit of the Presidency, 1972-1976 is, noted Hodgson, "Witcover's first attempt at the grand canvas, the full-dress, set-piece history of a whole Presidential campaign." Several critics noted that Witcover's journalistic approach highlights the behind-the-scenes maneuvering and personal anecdotes that characterize any election. What's more, Lehmann-Haupt pointed out, *Marathon* is so extraordinarily detailed that even close observers of the election will learn about the intricacies of presidential politics from reading it. "In short," wrote Lehmann-Haupt, "*Marathon* has just about everything, as they say. If you happened to miss the 1976 election—and don't be too sure you didn't—reading [*Marathon*] is the perfect way to catch up."

Many reviewers have favorably compared Witcover's books about presidential politics to Theodore H. White's *The Making of the President* series. Wrote Ken Bode in the *New Republic:* "If *Marathon* is Jules Witcover's bid to displace Teddy White as the instant historian of presidential campaigns, then it's a success and, I say, welcome. *Marathon* is just what it ought to be—straightforward, unadulterated politics, not cluttered with highblown personal reminiscences of time spent at the foot of the throne." David J. E. Scrivens of the Toronto *Globe and Mail* made a similar point about Witcover's and Germond's *Whose Broad Stripes and Bright Stars?: The Trivial Pursuit of the Presidency, 1988,* stating, "Jack W. Germond and Jules Witcover have improved upon White by writing more tightly and less impressionistically."

In *Crapshoot; Rolling the Dice on the Vice Presidency: From Adams and Jefferson to Truman and Quayle,* Witcover offers a brief overview of the careers of American vice presidents, in what the *New York Times Book Review*'s Michael Kazin described as "brisk, colloquial prose." "A special variety of gallows humor has always attended the men . . . whose only essential task has been to wait for their boss to quit or die," Kazin noted. However, Witcover's objective, according to Kazin, is more ambitious than simply preserving the one-liners that circulated about these men. "[Witcover] tries," wrote Kazin, "to persuade us to take the choice of candidate for the second spot more seriously." Kazin contends that Witcover's critique of the nominating process is overwhelmed by a wealth of information about the history of the position it-self. Nonetheless, Kazin concluded, "It is good to have all these stories collected in one volume."

BIOGRAPHICAL/CRITICAL SOURCES:

PERIODICALS

Atlantic Monthly, September, 1977.

Book World, February 2, 1969.

Commonweal, February 3, 1978.

Globe and Mail (Toronto), March 3, 1990.

Life, April 7, 1972.

New Republic, December 3, 1977, p. 38; December 17, 1977, p. 34.

Newsweek, July 18, 1977.

New York Review of Books, August 4, 1977, p. 3.

New York Times, June 7, 1969; July 29, 1970; April 17, 1972; August 8, 1977.

New York Times Book Review, February 2, 1969; August 9, 1970; August 14, 1977; May 14, 1978; August 6, 1989, p. 21; February 23, 1992, p. 6; May 31, 1992.

Saturday Review, February 8, 1969.

Village Voice, October 29, 1970.

Washington Post, July 29, 1970; July 16, 1989.

Washington Post Book World, July 10, 1977; December 4, 1977; June 24, 1979; May 8, 1988; June 9, 1989; September 1, 1989; January 26, 1992.